LABOUR AND INDUSTRIAL LAWS

LABOUR AND INDUSTRIAL LAWS

Fifth Edition

P.K. PADHI

Professor, XLRI Jamshedpur
and
Former Principal, University Law College
Utkal University, Bhubaneswar

PHI Learning Private Limited

Delhi-110092

2025

In fond memory of ***Shri Asoke K. Ghosh*** *(October 1942 – February 2024), Founder Chairman and Managing Director of PHI Learning, whose vision endlessly inspires.*

The Legacy Continues....

Published by Pushpita Ghosh, PHI Learning Private Limited, Rimjhim House, 111, Patparganj Industrial Estate, Delhi-110092 and Printed by Glorious Printer, Delhi-110092.

₹1195.00

LABOUR AND INDUSTRIAL LAWS, Fifth Edition
P.K. Padhi

ISBN-978-81-19364-81-7 (Print Book)
ISBN-978-81-19364-97-8 (e-Book)

The export rights of the book are vested solely with the publisher.

Contents

Preface

I received many calls and messages on 1st January 2024 from my students to whom I taught in XLRI Jamshedpur and HR fraternity of different central PSUs and private company enquiring about 5th edition **Labour and Industrial Laws** Book along with New Year Wish. I promised them as a return gift on 1st January 2024 that the 5th Edition Book shall come to the market before 1st July 2024.

There is no significant amendment made so far to any of the labour legislations. However, there are some important decisions of the Supreme Court which needs to be understood for better understanding and compliance. All important decisions of the Apex Court are incorporated with comment in this edition. There are few topics, like, Issues of 240 days, gratuity entitlement after 4 years 9 months, calculation of retrenchment compensation, meaning of sham and camouflage and many more are discussed in this edition.

I am sure that the readers will appreciate this edition like the earlier ones.

P.K. PADHI

Preface to the First Edition

The progress and prosperity of a country depends on industrialization. India has been experiencing fast industrial growth and is able to compete in the international market in all fields of production. Self-sustained growth, rapid industrialization, rapid rise in the standard of living of the people, maximization of employment, and equality of opportunity are the main objectives of the economic and social policies of our country.

Harmonious relations in every sphere of human activity are essential for the socio, economic and political progress. But increasing complexity of the modern industrial system has tended constantly to widen the gap between those who own and manage the industry and those who work for it. This gap gives rise to conflict in labour-management relations, resulting in the fall in production and hardship to the community.

The conflict of interest between the working class and management is always with us. Workers' effort to achieve higher wages and other economic benefits, security of employment, greater freedom and dignity at the workplace have always been viewed with suspicious attitude by the employers and have been resisted by them as encroachments upon their profitability, their freedom to 'hire and fire' and control the operation of their enterprises. That is what the labour is always about and that is what a great deal of politics is always about. It is essential that the scholars or professionals dealing with the subject should have a clear picture about what the labour law is or ought to be.

Being a teacher of labour law, I have made an attempt to explain the labour law through a commentary style with the help of decided case or cases of the Supreme Court of India. This book is primarily meant for LL.B., LL.M., IR, CS, LSW, ICWA and management students.

I must express my sincere thanks to my colleague and friend Dr. E.M. Rao, Professor of PM&IR, XLRI Jamshedpur, who inspired me to write this book. My thanks are due to my wife, Priti, who took care of my (late) father against all odds and allowed me to complete this book in time. My special thanks to Mr. B. Jagan Rao who helped me in preparing the table of cases, etc.

Finally, I am grateful to the Publisher, PHI Learning Private Limited, New Delhi, especially to Ms. Pushpita Ghosh, who persuaded me to write a book on labour law and be a member of PHI Learning family.

P.K. PADHI

Table of Cases

B

C

D

I

J

1 Introduction

A Constitution means a document having a special legal sanctity which sets out the frame-work and principles that define the nature and extent of government. Most of the Constitutions seek to regulate the relationship between institutions of the state, i.e. in a basic sense the relationship between the executive, the legislative and the judiciary. The Indian Constitution is the lengthiest and the most detailed of all the written Constitutions of the world.

The Constitution is the source of all legislations. So, it is necessary to have a close look at the Indian Constitution before taking up Indian labour legislations. This chapter deals with some of the important provisions of the Constitution with relevant judicial decisions, which are having a direct or indirect bearing on labour laws.

CONSTITUTION OF INDIA VIS-A-VIS LABOUR LEGISLATIONS

Matters related to labour laws are covered in List III (Concurrent List) of the Seventh Schedule to the Constitution of India. Entries relevant to labour laws in this list are as follows:

- Entry No. 22—Trade unions; industrial and labour disputes
- Entry No. 23—Social security and social insurance
- Entry No. 24—Welfare of labour including conditions of work, provident funds, employers' liability, workmen's compensation, invalidity and old age pensions and maternity benefits.
- Entry No. 36—Factories

The only exception is that industrial disputes concerning union employees are contained in List I, i.e. Union List and thus is a Union subject.

Thus the Central Government as well as the State Government can pass laws in respect of labour matters. However, most of the labour laws have been passed by the Parliament and are uniform all over India. Some of the Acts have been modified by States to suit their requirements. However, the main Acts, like the Payment of Gratuity Act, the Employees' Provident Funds Act, the Employees' State Insurance Act, the Factories Act, etc. are uniform all over India.

FUNDAMENTAL RIGHTS AND LABOUR LAWS

Part III of the Indian Constitution provides a long list of fundamental rights which run from Art. 12 to 35 of the Constitution. These fundamental rights represent the basic values cherished by the people of this country since the Vedic times and they are calculated to protect the dignity of the individual and create conditions in which every human being can develop his personality to the fullest extent. They weave a 'pattern of guarantees' on the basic structure of human rights and impose negative obligations on the State not to encroach upon individual liberty in its various dimensions.[1] These rights are regarded as fundamental because they are most essential for a man to live like a human being in a democratic society like ours. Therefore, the State cannot make any law by which it can take away any of the rights guaranteed in the Part III of owe Constitution. If it passes such a law, it may be declared void either by the Supreme Court or the High Court. Article 13 of the Constitution confers such power on the Supreme Court and the High Court, which is otherwise known as *judicial review*. Thus judicial review is the power of the Courts to declare any legislative action void if such action abridges or takes away any of the rights provided in Part III of the Constitution. Therefore, it can be said that any law, including labour law, enforced in this country is bound to give respect to the Part III of the Constitution, otherwise such law will be declared null and void.

The following Articles of the Constitution are having a direct relationship with labour laws.

ARTICLE 12: Definition

In this part, unless the context otherwise requires, "the State" includes the Government and Parliament of India and the Government and the Legislature of each of the States and all local or other authorities within the territory of India or under the control of the Government of India.

What is and what is not a 'State' has been the subject matter of rich case laws under Art. 12. Article 12 defines the term 'State' as used in different Articles of Part III and Part IV of the Constitution. It says that unless the context otherwise requires the term 'State' includes the following:

1. The Government and Parliament of India, i.e. Executive and Legislature of the Union/Union executive and Union legislature.
2. The Government and the Legislature of each State, i.e. Executive and Legislature of States/State executive and State legislature.
3. All local or other authorities within the territory of India.
4. All local or other authorities under the control of Government of India.

The term 'State' thus includes the executive as well as the legislative organ of the Union and States. So, action of these bodies can be challenged before the Court as violating fundamental rights and the writ petition can be entertained.

---

1. *Maneka Gandhi* v. *Union of India*, AIR 1978 SC 597.

The tests for determining as to when a corporation can be said to be an instrumentality or agency of Government may now be culled out from the judgment in the *International Airport Authority*'s case.[2] These tests are not conclusive or clinching, but they are merely indicative indicia which have to be used with care and caution because while stressing the necessity of a wide meaning to be placed on the expression 'other authorities', it must be realised that it should not be stretched so far as to bring in every autonomous body which has some nexus with the Government with the sweep of the expression. A wide enlargement of the meaning must be tempered by a wise limitation. We may summarise the relevant tests gathered from the decision in the *International Airport Authority*'s case as follows:

(1) "One thing is clear that if the entire share capital of the corporation is held by Government, it would go a long way towards indicating that the corporation is an instrumentality or agency of the Government."

(2) "Where the financial assistance of the State is so much as to meet almost entire expenditure of the corporation it would afford some indication of the corporation being impregnated with governmental character."

(3) "It may also be a relevant factor ... whether the corporation enjoys monopoly status conferred or protected by the State."

(4) "Existence of deep and pervasive State control may afford an indication that the corporation is a State agency or instrumentality."

(5) "If the functions of the corporation are of public importance and closely related to governmental functions, it would be a relevant factor in classifying the corporation as an instrumentality or agency of Government."

(6) "Specifically, if a department of the Government is transferred to a corporation it would be a strong factor supportive of the inference that the corporation is an instrumentality or agency of Government."

If on consideration of these above mentioned relevant factors, it is found that the corporation is an instrumentality or agency of the Government, it would, as pointed out in the *International Airport Authority*'s case, be an 'authority' and, therefore, a 'State' within the meaning of the expression in Art. 12.[3] The Court in *Ajay Hasia* case held as follows:

> "We may point out that it is immaterial for this purpose whether the corporation is created by a statute or under a statute. The test is whether it is an instrumentality or agency of the Government and not as to how it is created. The inquiry has to be not as to how the juristic person is born but why it has been brought into existence. The corporation may be a statutory corporation created by a statute or it may be a Government company or a company formed under the Companies Act, 1956 or it may be a society registered under the Societies Registration Act, 1860 or any other similar statute. Whatever be its genetical origin, it would be an 'authority' within the meaning of Article 12 if it is an instrumentality or agency of the Government and that would have to be decided on a proper assessment of the facts in the light of the relevant factors. The concept of instrumentality or agency of the Government is not limited to a corporation created by a statute but is equally applicable to a company or society and in a given case it would have to be decided, in consideration of the relevant factors, whether the company or society is an instrumentality or agency of the

2. *Ramana Dayaram Shetty* v. *The International Airport Authority of India*, AIR 1979 SC 1628.
3. *Ajay Hasia* v. *Khalid Mujib Sehravardi*, AIR 1981 SC 487.

Government so as to come within the meaning of the expression 'authority' as mentioned in Art. 12."[4]

It has been also observed that an instrumentality or agency of the State having operation outside India must comply with Indian labour legislation.[5]

The question came before the Supreme Court for consideration whether Balmer Lawrie and Co. Ltd. would be considered as a State within the meaning of Article 12 of the Constitution and hence would be amenable to writ jurisdiction? In *Balmer Lawrie and Co. Ltd.* v. *Partha Sarathi Sen Roy* [AIR 2013 SC (Supp) 926] the Supreme Court observed that every governmental function need not be sovereign. State activities are multifarious. Therefore, a scheme or a project, sponsoring trading activities may well be among the State's essential functions, which contribute towards its welfare activities aimed at the benefit of its subjects, and such activities can also be undertaken by private persons, corporate and companies. Thus, considering the wide ramifications, sovereign functions should be restricted to those functions, which are primarily inalienable, and which can be performed by the State alone. Such functions may include legislative functions, the administration of law, eminent domain, maintenance of law and order, internal and external security, grant of pardon etc. Therefore, mere dealing in a subject by the State, or the monopoly of the State in a particular field, would not render an enterprise sovereign in nature.

A public authority is a body which has public or statutory duties to perform, and which performs such duties and carries out its transaction for the benefit of the public, and not for private profit. Article 298 of the Constitution provides that the executive power of the Union and the State extends to the carrying on of any business or trade. A public authority is not restricted to the government and the legislature alone, and it includes within its ambit, various other instrumentalities of State action. The law may bestow upon such organization, the power of eminent domain. The State being an abstract entity, can only act through an instrumentality or an agency of natural or juridical persons. The concept of an instrumentality or agency of the government is not limited to a corporation created by a statute, but is equally applicable to a company, or to a society. In a given case, the Court must decide, whether such a company or society is an instrumentality or agency of the government, so as to determine whether the same falls within the meaning of expression 'authority', as mentioned in Article 12 of the Constitution, upon consideration of all relevant factors. It is thus evident that it is rather difficult to provide an exhaustive definition of the term 'authorities', which would fall within the ambit of Article 12 of the Constitution. This is precisely why, only an inclusive definition is possible. It is in order to keep pace with the broad approach adopted with respect to the doctrine of equality enshrined in Arts. 14 and 16 of the Constitution, that whenever possible Courts have tried to curb the arbitrary exercise of power against individuals by centers of power, and therefore, there has been a corresponding expansion of the judicial definition of the term State, as mentioned in Art. 12 of the Constitution. In light of the changing Socio-economic policies of country, and the variety of methods by which government functions are usually performed, the Court must examine, whether an inference can be drawn to the effect that such an authority is in fact an instrumentality of the State under Article 12 of

4. *Ibid.* at p. 496 per Bhagwati, J.
5. *Lena Khan* v. *Union of India,* AIR 1987 SC 1515.

the Constitution. It may not be easy for the Court, in such a case, to determine which duties form a part of private action, and which form a part of State action, for the reason that the conduct of the private authority, may have become so entwined with government policies, or so impregnated with governmental character, so as to become subject to the constitutional limitations that are placed upon State action. Therefore, the Court must determine whether the aggregate of all relevant factors once considered, would compel a conclusion as regards the body being bestowed with State responsibilities.

In order to determine whether an authority is amenable to writ jurisdiction except in the case of *habeas corpus* or *quo warranto*, it must be examined, whether the company/corporation is an instrumentality or an agency of the State, and if the same carries on business for the benefit of the public; whether the entire share capital of the company is held by the government; whether its administration is in the hands of a Board of Directors appointed by the government; and even if the Board of Directors has been appointed by the government, whether it is completely free from governmental control in the discharge of its functions; whether the company enjoys monopoly status; and whether there exists within the company, deep and pervasive State control. The other factors that may be considered are whether the functions carried out by the company/corporation are closely related to government or any department of Govt. has been transferred to the company/corporation, and the question in each case, would be whether in light of the cumulative facts as established, the company is financially, functionally and administratively under the control of the government. In the event that the Government provides financial support to a company, but does not retain any control/watch over how it is spent, then the same would not fall within the ambit of exercising deep and pervasive control. Such control must be particular to the body in question, and not general in nature. It must be deep and pervasive. The control should not therefore, be merely regulatory.

Balmer Lawrie and Co. Ltd. is considered as a State because the Company in question is a Govt. Company and its administrative control is with the Ministry of Petroleum and its directors are appointed mainly from Govt. service. Further its policy and issues of management are governed by Central Govt. and day to day business is dependent on instructions issued by ministry. The directors are appointed by President of India. Company receives Grant in aid from Govt. Decision as to salary of employees needs approval of Ministry. Salary structure is decided by Bureau of public enterprises of Govt. and reservation policy of Govt. is applicable to company. Facts clearly show that Govt. has dominating functional and administrative control over company. Company in question is therefore authority amenable to writ jurisdiction.

ARTICLE 13: Laws inconsistent with or in derogation of the fundamental rights

(1) All laws in force in the territory of India immediately before the commencement of this Constitution, in so far as they are inconsistent with the provisions of this Part, shall, to the extent of such inconsistency, be void.

(2) The State shall not make any law which takes away or abridges the rights conferred by this Part and any law made in contravention of this clause shall, to the extent of the contravention, be void.

(3) In this article, unless the context otherwise requires,—

(a) "law" includes any Ordinance, order, bye-law, rule, regulation, notification, custom or usages having in the territory of India the force of law;

(b) "laws in force" includes laws passed or made by a Legislature or other competent authority in the territory of India before the commencement of this Constitution and not previously repealed, notwithstanding that any such law or any part thereof may not be then in operation either at all or in particular areas.

(4) Nothing in this article shall apply to any amendment of this Constitution made under Article 368.

The main object of Art. 13 is to protect the fundamental rights provided in Part III of the Constitution. The first clause relates to the laws already existing or in force and declares that pre-Constitution laws are void to the extent to which they are inconsistent with the fundamental rights. The second clause relates to post-Constitution laws and prohibits the State from making a law which either takes away completely or abrogates in part a fundamental right. Article 13, in fact, provides for judicial review of all legislation in India, past as well as future. This power has been conferred on the High Courts and the Supreme Court of India (Art. 226 & Art. 32) which can declare a law unconstitutional if it is inconsistent with any of the provisions of Part III of the Constitution. Clause (3) of Art. 13 gives the term 'law' a very broad connotation which includes any ordinance, order, bye-law, rule, regulation, notification, custom or usages having the force of law. Clause (4) seeks to ensure that a constitutional amendment does not fall within the definition of law in Art. 13 and its validity cannot be challenged on the ground that it violates a fundamental right. However, Parliament cannot amend the basic structure of the Indian Constitution. In *Keshavananda Bharati* v. *State of Kerala,*[6] the Court, while upholding the validity of the Constitution (24th Amendment) by which Art. 13(4) was inserted, held that there were certain basic features which could not be amended under the amending power.

ARTICLE 14: Equality before law

The State shall not deny to any person equality before the law or the equal protection of the laws within the territory of India.

The word 'any person' in Art. 14 of the Constitution denotes that the guarantee of equal protection of laws is available to any person which includes any company or association. The protection of Art. 14 can be extended to both citizens and non citizens and natural person as well as legal person. The equal protection of laws guaranteed by Art. 14 does not mean that all laws must be general in character. It does not mean that the same laws should apply to all persons. It does not even mean that every law made must have a universal application, for all persons are not by nature, attainment or circumstances in the same position. The varying needs of different classes of person often require separate treatment. From the very nature of the society, there should be different laws in different places. In fact, an identical treatment in equal circumstances would amount to inequality. So, a reasonable classification is permitted as it is necessary for the society to progress.

6. AIR 1973 SC 1461.

What Art. 14 prohibits is class legislation and not reasonable classification for the purpose of legislation. The classification, however, must not be 'arbitrary, artificial, or evasive.' It must be based on some real and substantial distinction bearing a just and reasonable relation to the object sought to be achieved by the legislation. Article 14 applies where equals are treated differently without any reasonable basis. But where equal and unequal are treated differently, Art. 14 has no application. If the rule making authority takes care to reasonably classify persons for a particular purpose and if it deals equally with all persons belonging to a well-defined class, then it would not be open to the charge of discrimination. But to pass the test of permissible classification two conditions must be fulfilled:

(a) that the classification must be founded on an intelligible *differentia* which distinguishes persons or things which are grouped together from others left out of the group; and
(b) that the differentia must have a rational relation to the object sought to be achieved by the statute in question.

The classification may be founded on different basis and what is necessary is that there must be a nexus between the basis of classification and the object under consideration. Art. 14 of the Constitution does not insist that the classification should be scientifically perfect and a Court would not interfere unless the alleged classification results in apparent inequality. When a law is challenged to be discriminatory essentially on the ground that it denies equal treatment or protection, the question for determination by Court is not whether it has resulted in inequality but whether there is some difference which bears a just and reasonable relation to the object of legislation. Mere differentiation does not *per se* amount to discrimination within the inhibition of the equal protection clause. To attract the operation of the clause it is necessary to show that the selection or differentiation is unreasonable or arbitrary; that it does not rest on any rational basis having regard to the object which the legislature has in view. If a law deals with members of a well-defined class then it is not obnoxious and it is not open to the charge of denial of equal protection on the ground that it has no application to other persons. It is for the rule making authority to determine what categories of persons would embrace within the scope of the rule and merely because some categories which would stand on the same footing as those which are covered by the rule are left out would not render the Rule or the Law enacted in any manner discriminatory and violative of Art. 14. It is not possible to exhaust the circumstances or criteria which may afford a reasonable basis for classification in all cases. It depends on the object of the legislation and what it really seeks to achieve.[7]

The Supreme Court in re *The Special Courts Bill*[8] laid down some propositions for general information and suggested guidelines for the application and non application of Art. 14. They are as the follows:

1. The first part of Art. 14, which was adopted from the Irish Constitution, is a declaration of equality of the civil rights of all persons within the territory of India. It enshrines a basic principle of republicanism. The second part, which is a corollary of the first and is based on the last clause of the first section of the

7. *K. Thimmappa* v. *Chairman Central Board of Directors, SBI,* AIR 2001 SC 467.
8. AIR 1979 SC 478.

Fourteenth Amendment of the American Constitution, enjoins that equal protection shall be secured to all such persons in the enjoyment of their rights and liberties without discrimination or favouritism. It is a pledge to the protection of equal laws, i.e., laws that operate alike on all persons under like circumstances.

2. The State, in the exercise of its governmental power, has out of necessity to make laws operating differently on different groups or classes of persons within its territory to attain particular ends, in giving effect to its policies, and it must possess, for that purpose, large powers of distinguishing and classifying persons or things to be subjected to such laws.
3. The constitutional command to the State, to afford equal protection of its laws, sets a goal not attainable by the invention and application of a precise formula. Therefore, classification need not be constituted by an exact or scientific exclusion or inclusion of persons or things. The Courts should not insist on delusive exactness or apply doctrinaire tests for determining the validity of classification in any given case. Classification is justified if it is not palpably arbitrary.
4. The principle underlying the guarantee of Art. 14 is not that the same rules of law should be applicable to all persons within the Indian territory or that the same remedies should be made available to them irrespective of differences in circumstances. It only means that all persons similarly circumstanced shall be treated alike both in privileges conferred and liabilities imposed. Equal laws would have to be applied to all in the same situation and there should be no discrimination between one person and another if as regards the subject matter of the legislation their position is substantially the same.
5. By the process of classification, the State has the power to determine as to who should be regarded as a class for the purposes of legislation and in relation to a law enacted on a particular subject. This power, no doubt, in some degree is likely to produce some inequality; but if a law deals with the liberties of a number of well-defined classes, it is not open to the charge of denial of equal protection on the ground that it has no application to other persons. Classification thus means segregation in classes which have a systematic relation, usually found in common properties and characteristics. It postulates a rational basis and does not mean herding together of certain persons and classes arbitrarily.
6. The law can make and set apart the classes according to the needs and exigencies of the society and as suggested by experience. It can recognise even degree of evil but the classification should never be arbitrary, artificial or evasive.
7. The classification must not be arbitrary but be rational, that is to say, it must not only be based on some qualities or characteristics which are to be found in all the persons grouped together and not in others who are left out but those qualities or characteristics must have a reasonable relation to the object of the legislation. In order to pass the test two conditions must be fulfilled, namely (a) that the classification must be founded on an intelligible differentia which distinguishes those that are grouped together from others, and (b) that differentia must have a rational relation to the object sought to be achieved by the Act.

8. The differentia which is the basis of the classification and the object of the Act are distinct things and what is necessary is that there must be a nexus between them. In short, while Art. 14 forbids class discrimination by conferring privileges or imposing liabilities upon persons arbitrarily selected out of a large number of other persons similarly situated in relation to the privileges sought to be conferred or the liabilities proposed to be imposed, it does not forbid classification for the purpose of legislation, provided such classification is not arbitrary in the sense mentioned above.
9. If the legislative policy is clear and definite and as an effective method of carrying out that policy a discretion is vested by the statute upon a body of administrators or officers to make selective application of the law to certain classes or groups of persons, the statute itself cannot be condemned as a piece of discriminatory legislation. In such cases, the power given to the executive body would impose a duty on it to classify the subject-matter of legislation in accordance with the objective inducted in the statute. If the administrative body proceeds to classify persons or things on a basis which has no rational relation to the objective of the legislature, its action can be annulled as of denuding against the equal protection clause. On the other hand, if the statute itself does not disclose a definite policy or objective and it confers authority on another to make selection at its pleasure, the statute would be held on the face of it to be discriminatory, irrespective of the way in which it is applied.
10. Whether a law conferring discretionary powers on an administrative authority is constitutionally valid or not should not be determined on the assumption that such authority will act in an arbitrary manner in exercising the discretion committed to it. Abuse of power given by law does occur; but the validity of the law cannot be contested because of such an apprehension. Discretionary power is not necessarily a discriminatory power.
11. Classification necessarily implies the making of a distinction or discrimination between persons classified and those who are not members of that class. It is the essence of a classification that upon the class are cast duties and burdens different from those resting upon the general public. Indeed, the very idea of classification is that of inequality, so that it goes without saying that the mere fact of inequality in no manner determines the matter of constitutionality.
12. Whether an enactment providing for special procedure for the trial of certain offences is or is not discriminatory and violative of Art. 14 must be determined in each case as it arises, for no general rule applicable to all cases can safely be laid down. A practical assessment of the operation of the law in the particular circumstances is necessary.
13. A rule of procedure laid down by law comes as much within the purview of Art. 14 as any rule of substantive law and it is necessary that all litigants, who are similarly situated, are able to avail themselves of the same procedural rights for relief and for defence with like protection and without discrimination.

Equal Pay for Equal Work

It is true that the principle of 'equal pay for equal work' is not expressly declared by our Constitution to be a fundamental right. But it certainly is a constitutional goal. Article 39(d) of the Constitution proclaims 'equal pay for equal work for both men and women' as a Directive Principle of State Policy. Equal pay for equal work for both men and women means equal pay for equal work for everyone and as between the sexes. The Directive Principles, as has been pointed out in some of the judgments of the Court, have to be read into the fundamental rights as a matter of interpretation. Article 14 of the Constitution enjoins the State not to deny any person equality before the law or the equal protection of the laws and Art. 16 declares that there shall be equality of opportunity for all citizens in matters relating to employment or appointment to any office under the State. These equality clauses of the Constitution must mean something to everyone. To the vast majority of the people the equality clauses of the Constitution would mean nothing if they are unconcerned with the work they do and the pay they get. To them, the equality clauses will have some substance if equal work means equal pay. Accordingly, the Supreme Court in *Randhir Singh* v. *Union of India,*[9] while construing Arts. 14 and 16 in the light of the Preamble and Art. 39(d), held that the principle *equal pay for equal work* is deducible from those Articles and may be properly applied to cases of unequal scales of pay based on no classification or irrational classification, though those drawing the different scales of pay do identical work under the same employer.

The issue which arises before the Supreme Court in 2016 in *State of Punjab & Others* v. *Jagjit Singh & Others* for consideration is, whether temporarily engaged employees (daily-wage employees, ad-hoc appointees, employees appointed on casual basis, contractual employees and the like), are entitled to minimum of the regular pay-scale, along with dearness allowance (as revised from time to time) on account of their performing the same duties, which are discharged by those engaged on regular basis, against sanctioned posts. Therefore the Court prefers to examine the above issue in two stages. In the first stage the Court referred the situations where the principle of *'equal pay for equal work'* has been extended to employees engaged on regular basis and in second stage, the Court examined how the same has been applied with reference to different categories of temporary employees.

The Apex Court has laid down the parameters wherein the principle of 'equal pay for equal work' was invoked and considered. And they are as follows:

(1) The 'onus of proof', of parity in the duties and responsibilities of the subject post with the reference post, under the principle of 'equal pay for equal work', lies on the person who claims it. He who approaches the Court has to establish, that the subject post occupied by him, requires him to discharge equal work of equal value, as the reference post.

(2) The mere fact that the subject post occupied by the claimant, is in a "different department" vis-a-vis the reference post, does not have any bearing on the determination of a claim under the principle of 'equal pay for equal work'. Persons discharging identical duties cannot be treated differently in the matter of their pay, merely because they belong to different departments of Government.

9. AIR 1982 SC 879.

(3) The principle of 'equal pay for equal work', applies to cases of unequal scales of pay based on no classification or irrational classification.

(4) For equal pay, the concerned employees with whom equation is sought should be performing work, which besides being functionally equal, should be of the same quality and sensitivity.

(5) Persons holding the same rank or designation in different departments, but having dissimilar powers, duties and responsibilities, can be placed in different scales of pay, and cannot claim the benefit of the principle of 'equal pay for equal work'. Therefore, the principle would not be automatically invoked, merely because the subject and reference posts have the same nomenclature.

(6) In determining equality of functions and responsibilities, under the principle of 'equal pay for equal work', it is necessary to keep in mind that the duties of the two posts should be of equal sensitivity, and also, qualitatively similar. Differentiation of pay-scales for posts with difference in degree of responsibility, reliability and confidentiality would fall within the realm of valid classification, and therefore, pay differentiation would be legitimate one. The nature of work of the subject post should be the same and not less onerous than the reference post. The volume of work and the level of responsibility should be the same. If these parameters are not met, parity cannot be claimed under the principle of 'equal pay for equal work'.

(7) For placement in a regular pay-scale, the claimant has to be a regular appointee. The claimant should have been selected on the basis of a regular process of recruitment. An employee appointed on a temporary basis cannot claim to be placed in the regular pay.

(8) Persons performing the same or similar functions, duties and responsibilities can also be placed in different pay-scales in the same post, for example – 'selection grade'. But this difference must emerge out of a legitimate foundation, such as – merit or seniority or some other relevant criteria.

(9) If the qualifications for recruitment to the subject post vis-a-vis the reference post are different, it may be difficult to conclude that the duties and responsibilities of the posts are qualitatively similar or comparable. In such a cause, the principle of 'equal pay for equal work' cannot be invoked.

(10) The reference post with which parity is claimed under the principle of 'equal pay for equal work' has to be at the same hierarchy in the service. Pay-scales of posts may be different if the hierarchy of the posts in question and their channels of promotion are different. Even if the duties and responsibilities are same, parity would not be permissible, as against a superior post, such as a promotional post.

(11) A comparison between the subject post and the reference post under the principle of 'equal pay for equal work', cannot be made, where the subject post and the reference post are in different establishments, having a different management or even, where the establishments are in different geographical locations though owned by the same master. Persons engaged differently, and being paid out of different funds, would not be entitled to pay parity.

(12) Different pay-scales, in certain eventualities, would be permissible even for posts clubbed together at the same hierarchy in the cadre. As for instance, if the duties and

responsibilities of one of the posts are more onerous, or exposed to higher nature of operational work or risk, the principle of 'equal pay for equal work' would not be applicable. And also when, the reference post includes the responsibility to take crucial decisions, and that is not so for the subject post.

(13) The priority given to different types of posts under the prevailing policies of the Government can also be a relevant factor for placing different posts under different pay-scales. Herein also, the principle of 'equal pay for equal work' would not be applicable.

(14) The parity in pay under the principle of 'equal pay for equal work' cannot be claimed, merely on the ground, that at an earlier point of time, the subject post and the reference post were placed in the same pay-scale. The principle of 'equal pay for equal work' is applicable only when it is shown that the incumbents of the subject post and the reference post, discharge similar duties and responsibilities.

(15) For parity in pay-scales under the principle of 'equal pay for equal work', equation in the nature of duties is of paramount importance. If the principal nature of duties of one post is teaching, whereas that of the other is non-teaching, the principle would not be applicable. If the dominant nature of duties of one post is of control and management, whereas the subject post has no such duties, the principle would not be applicable. Likewise, if the central nature of duties of one post is of quality control, whereas the subject post has minimal duties of quality control, the principle would not be applicable.

(16) There can be a valid classification in the matter of pay-scales between employees even holding posts with the same nomenclature i.e., between those discharging duties at the headquarters, and others working at the institutional/sub-office level.

(17) The principle of 'equal pay for equal work' would not be applicable, where a differential higher pay-scale is extended to persons discharging the same duties and holding the same designation with the objective of ameliorating stagnation or on account of lack of promotional avenues.

(18) Where there is no comparison between one set of employees of one organization, and another set of employees of a different organization, there can be no question of equation of pay-scales, under the principle of 'equal pay for equal work', even if two organizations have a common employer. Likewise, if the management and control of two organizations is with different entities, which are independent of one another, the principle of 'equal pay for equal work' would not apply.

Article 15: Prohibition of discrimination on grounds of religion, race, caste, sex or place of birth

(1) The State shall not discriminate against any citizen on grounds only of religion, race, caste, sex, place of birth or any of them.

(2) No citizen shall, on grounds only of religion, race, caste, sex, place of birth or any of them, be subject to any disability, liability, restriction or condition with regard to—

(a) access to shops, public restaurants, hotels and places of public entertainment; or
(b) the use of wells, tanks, bathing ghats, roads and places of public resort maintained wholly or partly out of State funds or dedicated to the use of general public.

(3) Nothing in this article shall prevent the State from making any special provision for women and children.

(4) Nothing in this article or in Cl. (2) of Art. 29 shall prevent the State from making any special provision for the advancement of any socially and educationally backward classes of citizens or for the Scheduled Castes and the Scheduled Tribes.

(5) Nothing in this article or in sub-clause (g) of clause (1) of Article 19 shall prevent the State from making any special provision, by law, for the advancement of any socially and educationally backward classes of citizens or for the Scheduled Castes or the Scheduled Tribes in so far as such special provisions relate to their admission to educational institutions including private educational institutions, whether aided or unaided by the State, other than the minority educational institutions referred to in clause (1) of Article 30.

Article 16: Equality of opportunity in matters of public employment

(1) There shall be equality of opportunity for all citizens in matters relating to employment or appointment to any office under the State.

(2) No citizen shall, on grounds only of religion, race, caste, sex, descent, place of birth, residence or any of them, be ineligible for, or discriminated against in respect of any employment or office under the State.

(3) Nothing in this article shall prevent the Parliament from making any law prescribing, in regard to a class or classes of employment or appointment to an office under the Government of, or any local or other authority within, a State or Union territory, any requirement as to residence within that State or Union territory prior to such employment or appointment.

(4) Nothing in this article shall prevent the State from making any provision for the reservation of appointments or posts in favour of any backward class of citizens, which, in the opinion of the State, is not adequately represented in the services under the State.

(4A) Nothing in this article shall prevent the State from making any provision for reservation in the matter of promotion, with consequential seniority, to any class or classes of post in the services under the State in favour of the Scheduled Castes and the Scheduled Tribes which in the opinion of the State are not adequately represented in the services under the State.

(4B) Nothing in this article shall prevent the State from considering any unfilled vacancies of a year which are reserved for being filled up in that year in accordance with any provision for reservation made under Cl. (4) or Cl. (4A) as a separate class of vacancies to be filled up in any succeeding year or years and such class of vacancies shall not be considered together with the vacancies of the year in which they are being filled up for determining the ceiling of fifty percent reservation of total number of vacancies of that year.

(5) Nothing in this article shall affect the operation of any law which provides that the incumbent of an office in connection with the affairs of any religious or denominational institution or any member of the governing body thereof shall be a person professing a particular religion or belonging to a particular denomination.

The main object of Art. 16 is to create a constitutional right to equality of opportunity and employment in public offices. This article is confined to citizens as distinguished from other persons. Further, it is confined to employment or appointment to an office 'under the State'. This article can be looked from the angle of the reservation policy in respect to public offices.

Reservation Policy and Article 16

The scope and extent of Art. 16(4) has been examined thoroughly by nine judges of the Supreme Court in *Indra Sawhney* v. *Union of India*,[10] popularly known as the *Mandal* case. The majority opinion of the Supreme Court on the various aspects of reservations provided in Art. 16(4) may be summarized as follows:

1. Backward Class of citizen in Art. 16(4) can be identified on the basis of caste, not only on economic basis.
2. Backward Classes in Art. 16(4) are not similar to as socially and educationally backward in Art. 15(4).
3. Creamy layer can be and must be excluded.
4. Reservation shall not exceed 50 per cent.

A little clarification is essential: all reservations are not of the same nature. There are two types of reservations, which may, for the sake of convenience, be referred to as *vertical reservations* and *horizontal reservations*. The reservations in favour of Scheduled Castes, Scheduled Tribes, and other backward classes [under Article 16(4)] may be called 'vertical reservations' whereas reservations in favour of physically handicapped [under Art. 16(1)] can be referred to as 'horizontal reservations'. Horizontal reservations cut across the vertical reservations—what is called *inter-lock reservations*. To be more specific, suppose 3 per cent of the vacancies are reserved in favour of physically handicapped persons; this would be a reservation related to Art. 16(1). The persons selected against this quota will be placed in the appropriate category; if he belongs to Scheduled Caste category, he will be placed in that quota by making necessary adjustments; similarly, if he belongs to open competition (O.C.) category, he will be placed in that category by making necessary adjustments. Even after providing for these horizontal reservations, the percentage of reservations in favour of backward class of citizens remains—and should remain—the same. This is how these reservations are worked out in several States and there is no reason as to why this procedure should not be continued. It is, however, made clear that the rule of 50 per cent shall be applicable only to reservations proper; they shall not be—indeed cannot be applicable to exemptions, concessions, relaxations, if any, provided to 'Backward Class of Citizens' under Art. 16(4).

5. Reservation can be made by Executive Order.
6. No reservation in promotions.

10. AIR 1993 SC 477.

Effect of Constitutional Amendment in 1995 and 2001

The Supreme Court in *Indra Sawhney* case categorically held that there would not be any reservation in promotion but the Parliament in 1995 inserted Cl. 4A to Art. 16 (further amended in 2001) which provides that nothing in this Article shall prevent the State from making any provision for reservation in the matter of promotion, with consequential seniority, to any class or classes of post in the services under the State in favour of the Schedule Castes and the Scheduled Tribes which, in the opinion of the State, are not adequately represented in the service under the State. This means that reservation, in promotion in Government job, will be continued in favour of SC and ST even after *Mandal* case if the Government wants to do so. The Parliament therefore nullified the decision of the Supreme Court held in *Mandal* case.

Effect of Constitutional Amendment in 2000

Clause 4B was inserted into Art. 16 in 2000 by eighty-first amendment. This clause again nullifies the decision of *Mandal* case by permitting backlog vacancy to constitute a different unit altogether. That means the maximum limit as prescribed by the Supreme Court in *Mandal* case is no longer valid.

Article 19: Protection of certain rights regarding freedom of speech etc.

(1) All citizens shall have the right—
 (a) to freedom of speech and expression;
 (b) to assemble peaceably and without arms;
 (c) to form associations or unions or cooperative societies;
 (d) to move freely throughout the territory of India;
 (e) to reside and settle in any part of the territory of India; and
 (f) ***
 (g) to practise any profession, or to carry on any occupation, trade or business.

(2) Nothing in sub-clause (a) of Cl. (1) shall affect the operation of any existing law, or prevent the State from making any law, in so far as such law imposes reasonable restrictions on the exercise of the right conferred by the said sub-clause in the interests of the sovereignty and integrity of India, the security of the State, friendly relations with foreign States, public order, decency or morality or in relation to contempt of court, defamation or incitement to an offence.

(3) Nothing in sub-clause (b) of the said clause shall affect the operation of any existing law in so far as it imposes, or prevent the State from making any law imposing, in the interests of the sovereignty and integrity of India or public order, reasonable restrictions on the exercise of the right conferred by the said sub-clause.

(4) Nothing in sub-clause (c) of the said clause shall affect the operation of any existing law in so far as it imposes, or prevent the State from making any law imposing, in the interests of the sovereignty and integrity of India or public order or morality, reasonable restrictions on the exercise of the right conferred by the said sub-clause.

(5) Nothing in sub-clauses (d) and (e) of the said clause shall affect the operation of any existing law in so far as it imposes, or prevent the State from making any law imposing, reasonable restrictions on the exercise of any of the rights conferred by the said sub-clauses either in the interests of the general public or for the protection of the interests of any Scheduled Tribe.

(6) Nothing in sub-clause (g) of the said clause shall affect the operation of any existing law in so far as it imposes, or prevent the State from making any law imposing, in the interests of the general public, reasonable restrictions on the exercise of the right conferred by the said sub-clause, and, in particular, nothing in the said sub-clause shall affect the operation of any existing law in so far as it relates to, or prevent the State from making any law relating to,—

(i) the professional or technical qualifications necessary for practising any profession or carrying on any occupation, trade or business, or

(ii) the carrying on by the State, or by a corporation owned or controlled by the State, of any trade, business, industry or service, whether to the exclusion, complete or partial, of citizens or otherwise.

Article 19(1) provides six freedoms which are available only to the citizens. These freedoms are not absolute in nature. No modern State can afford to provide any unrestricted freedom to its citizen. If the citizens are given complete and absolute liberty without any social control, it will lead to frustration and it may be a cause of destruction of an orderly society. A perusal of Art. 19 makes it abundantly clear that none of the rights enumerated in Cl. (1) is an absolute right, for each of these rights is liable to be curtailed by laws made or to be made by the State to the extent mentioned in Cls. (2) to (6) of that article. Those clauses save the power of the State to make laws imposing certain specified restrictions on the several rights. The restriction which may be imposed under any of the clauses must be reasonable and not arbitrary. Hence a valid restriction must satisfy the following two tests:

1. The restriction must be for the purposes mentioned in Cls. 2 to 6 of Art. 19; and
2. The restriction must be a reasonable restriction.

Test of Reasonable Restriction

The phrase 'reasonable restriction' connotes that the limitation imposed on a person in the enjoyment of the right should not be arbitrary or excessive in nature, beyond what is required in the interests of the public. The word 'reasonable' implies intelligent care and deliberation, that is, the choice of a course which reason dictates. Legislation which arbitrarily or excessively invades the right cannot be said to contain the quality of reasonableness and unless it strikes a proper balance between the freedom guaranteed in Art. 19(1) and the social control permitted by Cl. (6) of Art. 19, it must be held to be wanting in that quality.[11] The determination by the legislature of what constitutes a reasonable restriction is not final or conclusive; it is subject to the supervision by the judiciary, i.e. High Court and the Supreme Court. In the matter of fundamental rights, the Supreme Court watches and guards the rights guaranteed by the Constitution, and in exercising its functions, it has the power to set aside an Act of the

11. *Chintaman Rao* v. *State of M.P.*, AIR 1951 SC 118.

Legislature if it is in violation of the freedoms guaranteed by the Constitution. However, there is no definite formula to judge the reasonableness of a restriction. Each case is to be judged on its own merits. The Supreme Court has laid down the following guidelines for determining the reasonableness of restriction.

1. In judging the reasonableness of the restrictions imposed by Cl. (5) of Art. 19, the court has to bear in mind the Directive Principles of State Policy.[12]
2. Restrictions must not be arbitrary or of an excessive nature so as to go beyond the requirement of the interest of the general public.[12]
3. In order to judge the quality of the reasonableness no abstract or general pattern or a fixed principle can be laid down so as to be of universal application and the same will vary from case to case.[13]
4. A just balance has to be struck between the restriction imposed and the social control envisaged by Cl. (6) of Art. 19.[14]
5. There must be a direct and proximate nexus or a reasonable connection between the restriction imposed and the object which is sought to be achieved. In other words, the Court has to see whether by virtue of the restriction imposed on the right of the citizen, the object of the statute is really fulfilled or frustrated. If there is a direct nexus between the restriction and the object of the Act, then a strong presumption in favour of the constitutionality of the Act will naturally arise.[15]
6. Another test of reasonableness of restrictions is the prevailing social values whose needs are satisfied by restrictions meant to protect social welfare.[16]
7. So far as the nature of reasonableness is concerned, it has to be viewed not only from the point of view of the citizen but also from the problem before the legislature and the object which is sought to be achieved by the statute. In other words, the Courts must see whether the social control envisaged in Cl. (6) of Art. 19 is being effectuated by the restrictions imposed on the fundamental right. It is obvious that if the Courts look at the restrictions only from the point of view of the citizen who is affected it will not be a correct or safe approach inasmuch as the restriction is bound to be irksome and painful to the citizen even though it may be for the public good. Therefore, a just balance must be struck in relation to the restriction and the public good that is done to the people at large. It is obvious that, however important the right of a citizen or an individual may be, it has to yield to the larger interests of the community.[17]

Article 19 and Demonstration

The first question that came before the Supreme Court in *Kameshwar Prasad* v. *State of Bihar*[18] was whether the right to make a 'demonstration' is covered by either or both of

12. *Pathumma* v. *State of Kerala,* AIR 1978 SC 771.
13. *State of Madras* v. *V.G. Row,* AIR 1952 SC 196.
14. *Narendra Kumar* v. *Union of India,* AIR 1960 SC 430.
15. *K.K. Kochuni* v. *State of Madras,* AIR 1960 SC 1080.
16. *State of Uttar Pradesh* v. *Kaushaliya,* AIR 1964 SC 416.
17. *Joti Pershad* v. *Administrator for the Union Territory of Delhi,* AIR 1961 SC 1602.
18. AIR 1962 SC 1166.

the two freedoms guaranteed by Art. 19(1)(a) and 19(1)(b). A demonstration is defined in the Concise Oxford Dictionary as 'an outward exhibition of feeling, as an exhibition of opinion on political or other question especially a public meeting or procession.' In Webster, it is defined as 'a public exhibition by a party, sect or society ... as by a parade or mass-meeting.' Without going into the niceties of language, it might be broadly stated that a demonstration is 'a visible manifestation of the feelings or sentiments of an individual or a group.' It is thus a communication of one's ideas to others to whom it is intended to be conveyed. It is in effect, therefore, a form of speech or of expression, because speech need not be vocal since signs made by a dumb person are also a form of speech. The Court accordingly held that a demonstration might take the form of an assembly and even then the intention is to convey to the person or authority to whom the communication is intended the feelings of the group which assembles. It necessarily follows that there are forms of demonstration which would fall within the freedoms guaranteed by Art. 19(1)(a) and 19(1)(b). It is needless to add that from the very nature of things, a demonstration may take various forms; it may be noisy and disorderly, for instance, stone-throwing by a crowd may be cited as an example of a violent and disorderly demonstration and this would not obviously be within Art. 19(1)(a) or (b). It can equally be peaceful and orderly, for instance when the members of the group merely wear some badge drawing attention to their grievances.

Article 19 and Right to Form Unions

Article 19(1)(c) of the Constitution of India guarantees to all its citizens the right to form associations and unions. However, such right can be restricted by making suitable legislation under Cl. (4) of Art. 19. The point for discussion could be formulated thus: When Art. 19(1)(c) guarantees the right to form associations, it is also implied that the fulfilment of every object of an association so formed is also a protected right, with the result that there is a constitutional guarantee that every association shall effectively achieve the purpose for which it was formed without interference by law except on grounds relevant to the preservation of public order or morality set out in Art. 19(4). The Supreme Court in *All India Bank Employees' Association* v. *National Industrial Tribunal (Bank Disputes), Bombay*[19] held that a right to form unions guaranteed by Art. 19(1)(c) thus does not carry with it a fundamental right in the union so formed to achieve every object for which it was formed. Even a very liberal interpretation of Art. 19(1)(c) cannot lead to the conclusion that the trade unions have a guaranteed right to an effective collective bargaining or to strike, either as part of collective bargaining or otherwise. The right to strike or the right to declare a lock-out may be controlled or restricted by appropriate industrial legislation, and the validity of such legislation would have to be tested not with reference to the criteria laid down in Art. 19(4) but by totally different considerations.

Article 19 and Closure

Article 19(1)(g) guarantees that all citizens shall have the right 'to practise any profession, or to carry on any occupation, trade or business.' The right to carry on a profession, trade or

19. AIR 1962 SC 171.

business is not absolute. It can be regulated or restricted by authority of law. Thus the State can make any law under Art. 19(6). Such restrictions may be:

1. Imposing reasonable restriction in the interest of the public.
2. Prescribing professional or technical qualifications necessary for practising any profession or carrying on any occupation, trade or business.
3. Enabling the State to carry on any trade, business, industry or service to the exclusion of citizens wholly or partially.

The right to close a business is an integral part of the fundamental right to carry on business. But as no right is absolute in its scope, so is the nature of this right. It can certainly be restricted, regulated or controlled by law in the interest of general public. If one does not start a business at all, then, perhaps, under no circumstances he can be compelled to do so. Such a negative aspect of a right to carry on a business may be equated with the negative aspects of the right embedded in the concept of the right to freedom of speech, to form an association or to acquire or hold property. Perhaps under no circumstances a person can be compelled to speak; to form an association or to acquire or hold a property. But by imposing reasonable restrictions, he can be compelled not to speak; not to form an association or not to acquire or hold property. Similarly, total prohibition of business is possible by putting reasonable restrictions within the meaning of Art. 19(6) on the right to carry on the business. But the greater the restriction, the more is the need for strict scrutiny by the Court. The right to close down a business is an integral part of right to carry it on. It is not correct to say that a right to close down a business can be equated or placed at par as high as the right not to start and carry on a business at all. Equally so, or rather, more emphatically, it cannot be accepted that the right to close down a business is not an integral part of the right to carry on a business, but it is a right appurtenant to the ownership of the property, or that it is not a fundamental right at all. It is wrong to say that an employer has no right to close down a business once he starts it. If he has such a right, as obviously he has, it cannot but be a fundamental right embedded in the right to carry on any business guaranteed under Art. 19(1)(g) of the Constitution.[20]

The concept of Socialism or a socialist State has undergone changes from time to time, from country to country and from thinkers to thinkers. But some basic concept still holds the ground. The difference pointed out by Supreme Court in *Akadasi Padhan* v. *State of Orissa*[21] between the doctrinaire approach to the problem of socialism and the pragmatic one is very apt and may enable the courts to lean more and more in favour of nationalisation and State ownership of an industry after the addition of the word 'Socialist' in the Preamble to the Constitution. But so long as the private ownership of an industry is recognised and governs an overwhelmingly large proportion of our economic structure, is it possible to say that the principles of socialism and social justice can be pushed to such an extreme so as to ignore completely or to a very large extent the interests of another section of the public, namely the private owners of the undertakings? Most of the industries are owned by limited companies in which a number of shareholders, both big and small, hold the shares. There are creditors and

20. *Excel Wear* v. *Union of India*, AIR 1979 SC 25.
21. AIR 1963 SC 1047.

depositors and various other persons connected with or having dealings with the undertakings. Does socialism go to the extent of not looking into the interests of all such persons? In a State-owned undertaking, the Government or the Government company is the owner. If they are compelled to close down, they probably may protect the labour by several other methods at their command, even, sometimes, at the cost of the public exchequer. It may not be always advisable to do so, but that is a different question. But in the private sector, obviously the two matters involved in running it are not on the same footing. One part is the management of the business done by the owner or their representatives, and the other is, running the business for return to the owner not only for the purpose of meeting his livelihood or expenses but also for the purpose of the growth of the national economy by formation of more and more capital. Does it stand to reason that by such rigorous provisions like those contained in Ss. 25-O and 25-R all these interests should be completely or substantially ignored?

The Supreme Court in *Excel Wear* case held that S. 25-O of the Act as a whole and S. 25-R in so far as it relates to the awarding of punishment for infraction of the provisions of S. 25-O are constitutionally bad and invalid for violation of Art. 19(1)(g) of the Constitution. Intrinsically, no provision of Chapter VB suggests that the object of carrying on the production can be achieved by the refusal to grant permission although in the Objects and Reasons of the Amendment Act such an object seems to be there, although remotely, and secondly, it is highly unreasonable to achieve the object by compelling the employer not to close down in public interest for maintaining production.

The reasonableness has got to be tested both from the procedural and substantive aspects of the law. Nobody has got a right to carry on the business if he cannot pay even the minimum wages to the labour. He must then retire from business. But to tell him to pay and not to retire even if he cannot pay is pushing the matter to an extreme.

In case of bona fide closures, though the reasons given by the employers are correct, adequate and sufficient, yet the permission to close may be refused on ground of public interest, because the interest of labour for the time being is bound to suffer as it makes a worker unemployed. Such a situation, as far as reasonably possible, should be prevented. Public interest and social justice do require the protection of the labour. But is it reasonable to give them protection against all unemployment after affecting the interests of so many persons interested and connected with the management apart from the employers? Is it possible to compel the employer to manage the undertaking even when they do not find it safe and practicable to manage the affairs? Can they be asked to go on facing tremendous difficulties of management even at the risk of their person and property? Can they be compelled to go on incurring losses year after year? In S. 25FFF, retrenchment compensation was allowed in cases of closure and if closure was occasioned on account of unavoidable circumstances beyond the control of the employer, a ceiling was put on the amount of compensation under the proviso. The explanation postulates the financial difficulties including financial losses or accumulation of undisposed stocks, etc. as the closing of an undertaking on account of unavoidable circumstances beyond the control of the employer, but by a deeming provision only the ceiling in the matter of compensation is not made applicable to the closure of an undertaking for such reasons. In 1972, by insertion of S. 25FFA in Chapter V-A of the Act, an employer was enjoined to give notice to the Government of an intended closure. But gradually the net was cast too wide and the freedom of the employer was tightened to such an extent by the introduction of Ss. 25-O and 25-R that it has reached a breaking point from the point of view of the employers. A situation may arise both from the point of view of law and order and the financial aspect that the employer may find it impossible to carry on the business any longer. He must not be allowed to be whimsical or capricious in the matter, ignoring the interests of the labour altogether. But that can probably be remedied by awarding different slabs of compensation in different situations. It is not quite correct to say that because compensation is not a substitute for the remedy of prevention of unemployment, the latter remedy must be the only one. If it were so, then in no case closure can be or should be allowed.

As S. 25-O was declared unconstitutional by the Supreme Court in *Excel Wear* case, S. 25-O was amended in 1982 and came into force in 1984. In *Orissa Textile and Steel Ltd., M/s.* v. *State of Orissa,*[22] the constitutional validity of amended S. 25-O was challenged on the ground that the right to do any trade and business within the meaning of Art. 19(1)(g) includes right to close down the place of business. The amended S. 25-O requires that one has to obtain the permission from the appropriate Government before closing down the place of business, infringing the freedom to close down the place of business. The Court observed that the reason why S. 25-O was struck down in *Excel Wear* case was that no time limit had been fixed while refusing permission to close down. This is now cured by sub-section (4) of the amended S. 25-O. This sub-section provides that the order of the appropriate Government shall remain in force for one year from the date of such order. Thus at the end of the year, it is always open to the employer to apply again for permission to close. There is no substance in the submission that the employer cannot apply again (at the end of the year) on the same grounds. If the reasons were genuine and adequate, the very fact that they have persisted for a year more is sufficient to necessitate a fresh look. Also, if the reasons have persisted for a year, it can hardly be said that they are the same. The difficulties faced during the year, provided they are genuine and adequate, would by themselves be additional grounds. Also, by the end of the year, the interest of the general public or the other relevant factors, which necessitated refusal of permission on the earlier occasion, may not prevail. The appropriate Government would necessarily have to make a fresh enquiry, give a reasonable opportunity of being heard to the employer, workmen and all concerned. Therefore, providing for a period of one year makes the restriction reasonable, and S. 25-O is constitutionally valid.

ARTICLE 20: Protection in respect of conviction for offences

1. No person shall be convicted of any offence except for violation of the law in force at the time of the commission of the act charged as an offence, nor be subjected to a penalty greater than that which might have been inflicted under the law in force at the time of the commission of the offence.
2. No person shall be prosecuted and punished for the same offence more than once.
3. No person accused of any offence shall be compelled to be a witness against himself.

The word '*person*' used in each clause of Article 20, must be regarded as applicable to a corporation also which is accused, prosecuted, convicted or punished for an offence.

22. AIR 2002 SC 708.

Article 20(1) is known as *'ex post facto law'* and Article 20(2) is nothing but a principle of 'double jeopardy' whereas Article 20(3) is popularly known as 'self incrimination'.

ARTICLE 21: Protection of life and personal liberty

No person shall be deprived of his life or personal liberty except according to the procedure established by law.

Article 21 is one of the most important and dangerous articles in our Constitution because, in the course of time, its application has been widened beyond what was originally thought of. It includes many aspects of human rights, such as right to live with human dignity, right to livelihood, right to privacy, right to shelter, right to health and medical assistance, right to die, right to get pollution free water and air, right to education, right to free legal aid, right to speedy trial, prevention of sexual harassment of working women, etc. This article can be used by every one as its boundary seems to be unlimited. That is why Art. 21 is known as *lawyers' paradise*. Most of the time, labour law also rotates within Art. 21 of the Constitution.

Article 21 requires that no one shall be deprived of his life or personal liberty except by the procedure established by law and this procedure must be reasonable, fair and just and not arbitrary, whimsical or fanciful. The right to life enshrined in Art. 21 cannot be restricted to mere animal existence. It means something much more than just physical survival. The right to life includes the right to live with human dignity and all that goes along with it, namely, the bare necessities of life such as adequate nutrition, clothing and shelter over the head and facilities for reading, writing and expressing oneself in diverse forms, freely moving about and mixing and commingling with fellow human beings.[23] In *Maneka Gandhi*[24] case, the Supreme Court gave a new dimension to Art. 21. The Court held that the right to 'live' is not merely confined to physical existence but it includes within its ambit the right to live with human dignity.

In *People's Union for Democratic Rights* v. *Union of India*[25] (popularly known as Asiad case), the Supreme Court, while dealing the issues like child labour, contract labour and bonded labour, held that the violations of labour laws should not be viewed with great indifference and unconcern as if they are trifling offences undeserving of judicial severity. Labour laws are enacted for improving the conditions of workers and the employers cannot be allowed to buy off immunity against violations of labour laws by paying a paltry fine which they would not mind paying, because by violating the labour laws they would be making profit which would far exceed the amount of fine. If violations of labour laws are going to be punished only by meagre fines, it would be impossible to ensure observance of the labour laws and the labour laws would be reduced to nullity. They would remain merely paper tigers without any teeth or claws. Violations of labour laws must be viewed with strictness and whenever any violations of labour laws are established, the errant employers should be punished by imposing adequate punishment.

---

23. *Francis Coralie Mullin* v. *Administrator, Union Territory of Delhi,* AIR 1981 SC 746.
24. *Maneka Gandhi* v. *Union of India,* AIR 1978 SC 597.
25. AIR 1982 SC 1473.

In *Olga Tellis* v. *Bombay Municipal Corporation*[26] (popularly known as Pavement dwellers case), a Constitution Bench of the Supreme Court held that right to life enshrined in Art. 21 includes *right to livelihood* also. Chandrachud, C.J., said as follows:

> "It does not mean merely that life cannot be extinguished or taken away as, for example, by the imposition and execution of the death sentence, except according to the procedure established by law. That is but one aspect of the right to life. An equally important facet of that right is the right to livelihood because, no person can live without the means of living, that is, the means of livelihood. If the right to livelihood is not treated as a part of the constitutional right to life, the easiest way of depriving a person of his right to life would be to deprive him of his means of livelihood to the point of abrogation. Such deprivation would not only denude the life of its effective content and meaningfulness but it would make life impossible to live. And yet, such deprivation would not have to be in accordance with the procedure established by law, if the right to livelihood is not regarded as a part of the right to life. That, which alone makes it possible to live, leave aside what makes life livable, must be deemed to be an integral component of the right to life. Deprive a person of his right to livelihood and you shall have deprived him of his life."[27]

In *Delhi Development Horticulture Employees*' *Union* v. *Delhi Administration, Delhi,*[28] the petitioner-workmen who were employed on daily wages had filed these petitions for their absorption as regular employees in the Development Department of the Delhi Administration and for injunction prohibiting the termination of their services and also for the difference in wages paid to them and those paid to the regular employees. The petitions are resisted on behalf of the respondents contending that there is no scope for the absorption of the petitioners as they were employed on daily wages with a clear understanding that the schemes under which they were employed had no provision for regularisation of any workman. The *Olga Tellis* case has been referred to where it has been said that as a necessary logical corollary, right to life would include the right to livelihood and, therefore, right to work. Accordingly, the workmen in question insisted that if the 'right to work' is included within Art. 21 in *Olga Tellis* case, then why they would not be absorbed? But the Court in this case held that this country has so far not found it feasible to incorporate the right to livelihood as a fundamental right in the Constitution. This is because the country has so far not attained the capacity to guarantee it, and not because it considers it any the less fundamental to life. Advisedly, therefore, it has been placed in the Chapter on Directive Principles, Art. 41 of which enjoins upon the State to make effective provision for securing the same '*within the limits of its economic capacity and development*'. Thus even while giving the direction to the State to ensure the right to work, the Constitution-makers thought it prudent not to do so without qualifying it. The Court further held that viewed in the context of the facts of the present case, it is apparent that the schemes under which the petitioners were given employment have been evolved to provide income for those who are below the poverty line and particularly during the periods when they are without any source of livelihood and, therefore, without any income whatsoever. The schemes were further meant for the rural poor, for the object of the schemes was to start tackling the problem of poverty from that end.

---

26. AIR 1986 SC 180.
27. *Ibid.* at pp. 193–194 per Chandrachud, C.J.
28. AIR 1992 SC 789.

In *D.K. Yadav* v. *J.M.A. Industries*,[29] the Supreme Court held that the right to life enshrined in Art. 21 includes right to livelihood and therefore before terminating the service of a workman, on the ground of fair play, it is necessary for the management to provide a reasonable opportunity to a workman to explain his case. The procedure prescribed for depriving a person of his livelihood must meet the requirements of Art. 14, that is, it must be right, just and fair and not arbitrary, fanciful or oppressive. In other words, it must be in conformity with the rules of natural justice. Accordingly, the Court set aside the order of the Labour Court and ordered reinstatement of an employee with 50 per cent back wages.

In *Parmanand Katara* v. *Union of India*,[30] the Supreme Court held that it is the duty of a doctor, whether working in the Government hospital or private, to extend medical aid to the injured immediately to preserve life without waiting for the legal formalities to be complied with by the police under Cr. P.C. The Court observed as follows:

> "There can be no second opinion that preservation of human life is of paramount importance. That is so on account of the fact that once life is lost, the status quo ante cannot be restored as resurrection is beyond the capacity of man. The patient whether he be an innocent person or be a criminal liable to punishment under the laws of the society, it is the obligation of those who are in charge of the health of the community to preserve life so that the innocent may be protected and the guilty may be punished. Social laws do not contemplate death by negligence to tantamount to legal punishment. Article 21 of the Constitution casts the obligation on the State to preserve life. The provision as explained by this Court in scores of decisions has emphasised and reiterated with gradually increasing emphasis on that position. A doctor at the Government hospital positioned to meet this State obligation is, therefore, duty-bound to extend medical assistance for preserving life. Every doctor whether at a Government hospital or otherwise has the professional obligation to extend his services with due expertise for protecting life. No law or State action can intervene to avoid/delay the discharge of the paramount obligation cast upon members of the medical profession. The obligation being total, absolute and paramount, laws of procedure whether in statutes or otherwise, which would interfere with the discharge of this obligation cannot be sustained and must, therefore, give way."[31]

In *Paschim Banga Khet Mazdoor Samity* v. *State of W.B.*,[32] the Court went further beyond *Parmanand Katara* case and held that the Constitution envisages the establishment of a welfare State at the federal level as well as at the State level. In a welfare State the primary duty of the Government is to secure the welfare of the people. Providing adequate medical facilities to the people is an essential part of the obligations undertaken by the Government in a welfare State. The Government discharges this obligation by running hospitals and health centers which provide medical care to the person seeking to avail those facilities. Article 21 imposes an obligation on the State to safeguard the right to life of every person. Preservation of human life is thus of paramount importance. The Government hospitals run by the State and the Medical Officers employed therein are duty-bound to extend medical assistance for preserving human life. Failure on the part of a Government hospital to provide timely medical treatment to a person in need of such treatment results in violation of his right to life guaranteed under Art. 21. In the present case there was breach of the said right, guaranteed

29. (1993) 3 SCC 258.
30. AIR 1989 SC 2039.
31. *Ibid.* at p. 2043 per Ranganath Misra, J.
32. AIR 1996 SC 2426.

under Art. 21, when Hakim Seikh was denied treatment at the various Government hospitals which were approached, even though his condition was very serious at that time and he was in need of immediate medical attention. Since the said denial of the right of Hakim Seikh guaranteed under Art. 21 was by officers of the State in hospitals run by the State, the State cannot avoid its responsibility for such denial of the constitutional right of Hakim Seikh. In respect of deprivation of the constitutional rights guaranteed under Part III of the Constitution, the position is well settled that adequate compensation can be awarded by the Court in case of such violation by way of redress in proceedings under Arts. 32 and 226 of the Constitution.

The Supreme Court in *Consumer Education and Research Centre* v. *Union of India*[33] has given much importance to the health of workers and observed that right to life includes right to health. It further observed that right to life of a worker is meaningless without his right to health. Thus right to life of a worker means not only meaningful existence but also robust health and vigour without which worker would lead a life of misery. Lack of health denudes his livelihood. Compelling economic necessity to work in an industry exposed to health hazards due to indigence to bread-winning for himself and his dependants should not be at the cost of the health and vigour of the workman. Facilities and opportunities, as enjoined in Art. 38, should be provided to protect the health of the workman. Provision for medical test and treatment invigorates the health of the worker for higher production or efficient service. Continued treatment, while in service or after retirement, is a moral, legal and constitutional concomitant duty of the employer and the State. Therefore, it must be held that the right to health and medical care is a fundamental right under Art. 21 read with Arts. 39(c), 41 and 43 of the Constitution and thereby making the life of the workman meaningful and purposeful with dignity of person. Right to life includes protection of the health and strength of the worker which is a minimum requirement to enable a person to live with human dignity. The State, be it Union or State Government, or an industry, public or private, is enjoined to take all such action which will promote health, strength and vigour of the workman during the period of employment and leisure and even after his retirement. The health and strength of the worker is an integral facet of right to life. Denial thereof denudes the workman of the finer facets of life, violating Art. 21. The right to human dignity, development of personality, social protection, right to rest and leisure are fundamental human rights of a workman assured by the Charter of Human Rights, in the Preamble and Arts. 38 and 39 of the Constitution. Facilities for medical care and health against sickness ensure stable manpower for economic development and would help the workers generate devotion to their duty and dedication to give their best, physically as well as mentally, in the production of goods or services. The health of the worker enables him to enjoy the fruits of his labour, keeping him physically fit and mentally alert for leading a successful life, economically, socially and culturally. Medical facilities to protect the health of the workers are therefore the fundamental and human rights to the workmen. The Court accordingly held as follows:

> "Therefore, we hold that right to health, medical aid to protect the health and vigour of a worker while in service or post retirement is a fundamental right under Article 21, read with Articles 39(e), 41, 43, 48A and all related to Articles and fundamental human rights to make the life of the workman meaningful and purposeful with dignity of person."[34]

33. AIR 1995 SC 922.
34. *Ibid.* at p. 940 per K. Ramaswamy, J.

The Court further laid down certain guidelines to be followed by all asbestos industries in the country and they are as follows:

1. To maintain and keep maintaining the health record of every worker up to a minimum period of 40 years from the beginning of the employment or 15 years after retirement or cessation of the employment whichever is later.
2. The Membrane Filter test, to detect asbestos fibre should be adopted by all the factories or establishments at par with the Metalliferrous Mines Regulations, 1961; and Vienna Convention and Rules issued thereunder.
3. All the factories whether covered by the Employees State Insurance Act or Workmen's Compensation Act or otherwise are directed to compulsorily insure health coverage to every worker.
4. The Union and the State Governments are directed to review the standards of permissible exposure limit value of fibre/cc in tune with the international standards.
5. The Union and all the State Governments are directed to consider inclusion of such of those small scale factory or factories or industries to protect health hazards of the worker engaged in the manufacture of asbestos or its ancillary products.
6. Every worker suffering from occupational health hazards would be entitled for compensation of ₹1 lakh.

In *Kirloskar Brothers Ltd.* v. *Employee's State Insurance Corpn.*,[35] the Supreme Court, following the *Consumer Education and Research Centre* case, held that in expanding economic activity in liberalised economy, Part IV of the Constitution enjoins not only the State and its instrumentalities but even private industries to ensure safety to the workman and to provide facilities and opportunities for health and vigour of the workman assured in relevant provisions in Part IV, which are integral part of right to equality under Art. 14 and right to invigorated life under Art. 21 which are fundamental rights of the workman.

Article 21A: Education for children[36]

The State shall provide free and compulsory education to all children of the age of 6 to 14 years in such manner as the State may, by law, determine.

The Supreme Court in a landmark judgment in *Unni Krishnan* v. *State of A.P.*[37] held that the 'right to education' upto the age of 14 years is a fundamental right within the meaning of Art. 21 of the Constitution. In response to it, the Government enacted Constitution (86th Amendment) Act, 2002 and accordingly Art. 21A is added to Part III of the Constitution.

Article 22: Protection against arrest and detention in certain cases

1. No person who is arrested shall be detained in custody without being informed, as soon as may be, of the grounds for such arrest nor shall he be denied the right to consult, and to be defended by, a legal practitioner of his choice.

35. AIR 1996 SC 3261.
36. Inserted by The Constitution (86th Amendment) Act, 2002.
37. (1993) 1 SCC 645.

2. Every person who is arrested and detained in custody shall be produced before the nearest magistrate within a period of twenty four hours of such arrest excluding the time necessary for the journey from the place of arrest to the court of the magistrate and no such person shall be detained in custody beyond the said period without the authority of a magistrate.
3. Nothing in clauses (1) and (2) shall apply (a) to any person who for the time being is an enemy alien; or (b) to any person who is arrested or detained under any law providing for preventive detention.
4. No law providing for preventive detention shall authorise the detention of a person for a longer period than three months unless (a) an Advisory Board consisting of persons who are, or have been, or are qualified to be appointed as, Judges of a High Court has reported before the expiration of the said period of three months that there is in its opinion sufficient cause for such detention.
5. When any person is detained in pursuance of an order made under any law providing for preventive detention, the authority making the order shall, as soon as may be, communicate to such person the grounds on which the order has been made and shall afford him the earliest opportunity of making a representation against the order.
6. Nothing in clause (5) shall require the authority making any such order as is referred to in that clause to disclose facts which such authority considers to be against the public interest to disclose.
7. Parliament may by law prescribe
   (a) the circumstances under which, and the class or classes of cases in which, a person may be detained for a period longer than three months under any law providing for preventive detention without obtaining the opinion of an Advisory Board in accordance with the provisions of sub clause (a) of clause (4);
   (b) the maximum period for which any person may in any class or classes of cases be detained under any law providing for preventive detention; and
   (c) the procedure to be followed by an Advisory Board in an inquiry under sub clause (a) of clause (4).

ARTICLE 23: Prohibition of traffic in human beings and forced labour

1. Traffic in human beings and begar and other similar forms of forced labour are prohibited and any contravention of this provision shall be an offence punishable in accordance with law.
2. Nothing in this article shall prevent the State from imposing compulsory service for public purpose, and in imposing such service the State shall not make any discrimination on grounds only of religion, race, caste or class or any of them.

Now many of the fundamental rights enacted in Part III operate as limitations on the power of the State and impose negative obligations on the State not to encroach on individual liberty and they are enforceable only against the State. But there are certain fundamental rights conferred by the Constitution which are enforceable against the whole world and they are to be found *inter alia* in Arts. 17, (abolition of untouchability) 23 and 24. Article 23 is clearly designed to protect the individual not only against the State but also against other private citizens. Article 23 is not limited in its application against the State but it prohibits *'traffic in human beings and begar and other similar forms of forced labour'* practised by anyone else. The sweep of Article 23 is wide and unlimited and it strikes at *'traffic in human beings and begar and other similar forms of forced labour'* wherever they are found. The reason for enacting this provision in the chapter on fundamental rights is to be found in the socio-economic condition of the people at the time when the Constitution was enacted. The Constitution makers, when they set out to frame the Constitution, found that they had an enormous task before them of changing the socio-economic structure of the country and bringing about socio-economic regeneration with a view to reaching social and economic justice to the common man. The political revolution was completed and it had succeeded in bringing freedom to the country, but freedom was not an end in itself, it was only a means to an end, the end being the raising of the people to higher levels of achievement and bringing about their total advancement and welfare. Political freedom had no meaning unless it was accompanied by social and economic freedom and it was therefore necessary to carry forward the social and economic revolution with a view to creating socio-economic conditions in which every one would be able to enjoy basic human rights and participate in the fruits of freedom and liberty in an egalitarian social and economic framework. It was with this end in view that the Constitution makers enacted the Directive Principles of State Policy in Part IV of the Constitution setting out the constitutional goal of a new socio-economic order.

There was one feature of our national life which was ugly and shameful and which cried for urgent attention—the existence of bonded or forced labour in large parts of the country. This evil was the relic of a feudal exploitative society, and it was totally incompatible with the new egalitarian socio-economic order which 'We the people of India' were determined to build and constituted a gross and most revolting denial of basic human dignity. It was therefore necessary to eradicate this pernicious practice and wipe it out altogether from the national scene and this had to be done immediately because with the advent of freedom, such practice could not be allowed to continue any longer. Obviously, it would not have been enough merely to include abolition of forced labour in the Directive Principles of State Policy, because then the outlawing of this practice would not have been legally enforceable and it would have continued to plague our national life in violation of the basic constitutional norms and values until some appropriate legislation could be brought by the legislature forbidding such practice. The Constitution makers, therefore, decided to give effect to their resolution to obliterate and wipe out this evil practice by enacting constitutional prohibition against it in the chapter on fundamental rights, so that the abolition of such practice may become enforceable and effective as soon as the Constitution came into force. This is the reason why the provision enacted in Art. 23 was included in the chapter on fundamental rights. The prohibition against *'traffic in human beings and begar and other similar forms of forced labour'* is clearly intended to be a general prohibition, total in its effect and all pervasive in its range and it is enforceable not only against the State but also against any other person indulging in any such practice.

Then the question is, what is the true scope and meaning of the expression 'traffic in human beings and begar and other similar forms of forced labour' in Art. 23? What are the forms of forced labour prohibited by that Article and what kind of labour provided by a person can be regarded as forced labour so as to fall within this prohibition?

When the Constitution makers enacted Art. 23 they had before them Art. 4 of the Universal Declaration of Human Rights, but they deliberately departed from its language and employed words which would make the reach and content of Art. 23 much wider than that of Art. 4 of the Universal Declaration of Human Rights. They banned traffic in human beings which is an expression of much larger amplitude than 'slave trade' and they also interdicted begar and other similar forms of forced labour. The question is, what is the scope and ambit of the expression 'begar and other similar forms of forced labour'? Is this expression wide enough to include every conceivable form of forced labour and what is the true scope and meaning of the words 'forced labour?' The word 'begar' in this Article is not a word of common use in English language. It is a word of Indian origin which, like many other words, has found its way in the English vocabulary. It is very difficult to formulate a precise definition of the word 'begar' but there can be no doubt that it is a form of forced labour under which a person is compelled to work without receiving any remuneration. Article 23 is intended to abolish every form of forced labour. The words 'other similar forms of forced labour' are used in Art. 23 not with a view to importing the particular characteristic of 'begar' that labour or service should be exacted without payment of any remuneration but with a view to bringing within the scope and ambit of that Article all other forms of forced labour, and since 'begar' is one form of forced labour, the Constitution makers used the words 'other similar forms of forced labour'. If the requirement that labour or work should be exacted without any remuneration were imported in other forms of forced labour, they would straightway come within the meaning of the word 'begar'. Every form of forced labour, 'begar' or otherwise, is within the inhibition of Art. 23 and it makes no difference whether the person who is forced to give his labour or service to another is remunerated or not. Even if remuneration is paid, labour supplied by a person would be hit by this Article if it is forced labour, that is, labour supplied not willingly but as a result of force or compulsion. It is therefore clear that even if a person has contracted with another to perform service, and there is consideration for such service in the shape of liquidation of debt or even remuneration, he cannot be forced, by compulsion of law or otherwise, to continue to perform such service, as that would be forced labour within the inhibition of Art. 23. This Article strikes at every form of forced labour even if it has its origin in a contract voluntarily entered into by the person obligated to provide labour or service. The reason is that it offends against human dignity to compel a person to provide labour or service to another against his wish, even though it be in breach of the contract entered into by him.

What Art. 23 prohibits is 'forced labour', that is, labour or service which a person is forced to provide. 'Force' which makes such labour or service 'forced labour' may arise in several ways. It may be physical force, which may compel a person to provide labour or service to another, or it may be force exerted through a legal provision such as a provision for imprisonment or fine in case the employee fails to provide labour or service, or it may even be compulsion arising from hunger and poverty, want and destitution. Any factor which deprives a person of a choice of alternatives and compels him to adopt one particular course of action may properly be regarded as 'force' and if labour or service is compelled as a result of such 'force', it would be 'forced labour'. The word 'force' must therefore be construed to include not only physical or legal force but also force arising from the compulsion of economic circumstances, which leave no choice of alternatives to a person in want and compels him to provide labour or service even though the remuneration received for it is less than the minimum wage.[38] The Supreme Court in *People's Union for Democratic Rights* case (popularly known as Asiad case), where ₹1 was deducted by the Jamadars from the wages to be paid to the workers employed by the contractor for Asiad Project in Delhi as a result of which the workers did not get the minimum wage of ₹9.75 per day, held to be violation of Art. 23 of the Constitution.

In *Bandhua Mukti Morcha* v. *Union of India*[39] (popularly known as Bonded Labour case), a petition by way of public interest litigation (PIL) was filed by an organisation, dedicated to the cause of release of bonded labourers, alleging that a large number of labourers from Maharashtra, M.P., U.P., and Rajasthan were working under 'inhuman and intolerable conditions' in stone quarries situated in Faridabad District of State of Haryana and some of them were bonded labourers. The Court held that Art. 21 assures the right to live with human dignity, free from exploitation. The State is under a constitutional obligation to see that there is no violation of the fundamental right of any person, particularly when he belongs to the weaker sections of the community and is unable to wage a legal battle against a strong and powerful opponent who is exploiting him. Both the Central Government and the State Government are therefore bound to ensure the observance of various social welfare and labour laws enacted by Parliament for the purpose of securing to the workmen a life of basic human dignity in compliance with the Directive Principles of State Policy. Whenever it is shown that a labourer is made to provide forced labour, the Court would raise a presumption that he is required to do so in consideration of an advance or other economic consideration received by him and he is therefore a bonded labourer. This presumption may be rebutted by the employer and also by the State Government if it so chooses, but unless and until satisfactory material is produced for rebutting this presumption, the Court must proceed on the basis that the labourer is a bonded labourer entitled to the benefits of the provisions of the Act. The State Government cannot be permitted to repudiate its obligation to identify, release and rehabilitate the bonded labourers on the plea that though the labourers concerned may be providing forced labour, the State Government does not owe any obligation to them unless and until they show in an appropriate legal proceeding conducted according to the rules of adversary system of justice that they are bonded labourers.

ARTICLE 24: Prohibition of employment of children in factories, etc.

No child below the age of fourteen years shall be employed to work in any factory or mine or engaged in any other hazardous employment.

Discussed in chapter relating to Child Labour (Prohibition & Regulation) Act, 1986.

---

38. *People's Union for Democratic Rights* v. *Union of India,* AIR 1982 SC 1473.
39. AIR 1984 SC 802.

RIGHT TO CONSTITUTIONAL REMEDIES

ARTICLE 32: Remedies for enforcement of rights conferred by this Part

1. The right to move the Supreme Court by appropriate proceedings for the enforcement of the rights conferred by this Part is guaranteed.
2. The Supreme Court shall have power to issue directions or orders or writs, including writs in the nature of habeas corpus, mandamus, prohibition, quo warranto and certiorari, whichever may be appropriate, for the enforcement of any of the rights conferred by this Part.
3. Without prejudice to the powers conferred on the Supreme Court by Cls. (1) and (2), Parliament may by law empower any other court to exercise within the local limits of its jurisdiction all or any of the powers exercisable by the Supreme Court under Cl. (2).
4. The right guaranteed by this article shall not be suspended except as otherwise provided for by this Constitution.

A right without a remedy is meaningless. It is the remedy which makes the right real. If there is no remedy, there is no right at all. Therefore, our Constitution, after providing the various rights under Part-III, ensures a guaranteed remedy under Art. 32. Commenting upon Art. 32, Dr. Ambedkar remarked in the Constituent Assembly in the following words:

> "If I was asked to name any particular Article of the Constitution as the most important—an Article without which this Constitution would be a nullity—I would not refer to any other Article except this one. It is the very soul of the Constitution and the very heart of it."[40]

Article 32(1) guarantees the right to move the Supreme Court by appropriate proceedings for the enforcement of the rights conferred by Part III of the Constitution. Article 32(2) provides that the Supreme Court shall have the power to issue directions or orders or writs in the nature of *habeas corpus, mandamus*, prohibition, *quo warranto* and *certiorari* for the enforcement of any of the rights conferred by Part III of the Constitution. Article 32(3) provides that the Parliament may by law empower any other Court to exercise within the local limits of its jurisdiction all or any of the powers exercisable by the Supreme Court under Cl. (2). Clause (4) says that the right guaranteed by Art. 32 shall not be suspended except as otherwise provided by the Constitution.

The Supreme Court's power to enforce Fundamental Rights is the widest under Art. 32(1). The petitioner only has to make out that there is an infringement of any of the Fundamental Rights claimed by him. The writs asked for under Art. 32 must be correlated to one or more of the Fundamental Rights and can only be made for the enforcement of such rights.[41] Granting of relief under Art. 32 is not discretionary. The citizens are ordinarily entitled to get appropriate relief under Art. 32, once it is shown that their fundamental rights have been illegally or unconstitutionally infringed. It is the duty of the Supreme Court to

---

40. Constituent Assembly Debates Vol. VII, p. 953.
41. *Santa Bai* v. *Bombay*, AIR 1958 SC 532. See also *Bhagwan Das* v. *Union of India*, AIR 1956 SC 175.

enforce the guaranteed fundamental rights. Accordingly Justice Gajendragadkar in *Daryao* v. *State of U.P.*,[42] aptly said:

> "There can be no doubt that the fundamental right guaranteed by Art. 32(1) is a very important safeguard for the protection of the fundamental rights of the citizens, and as a result of the said guarantee, this Court has been entrusted with the solemn task of upholding the fundamental rights of the citizens of this country. It is the privilege and duty of this Court to uphold those rights."[43]

So, one may draw the conclusion that it is not merely a right of the individual to move the Supreme Court but also a duty of the Supreme Court to enforce the fundamental rights. The Supreme Court is thus constituted as the protector and guarantor of the fundamental rights.[44] Article 32(1), being put in Part III, is itself a fundamental right and Art. 32(4) provides that this right shall not be suspended except as otherwise provided for by this Constitution. There is only one situation when this right can be suspended, i.e. under Art. 359. The President may suspend the right to move any Court for the enforcement of such rights as the Presidential Notification may specify. However, as Cl. (4) clearly indicates, the right under Art. 32(1) cannot be taken away by any other method.

While interpreting Art. 32, it must be borne in mind that our approach must be guided not by any verbal or formalistic canons of construction but by the paramount object and purpose for which Art. 32 has been enacted and placed in Part III of the Constitution, thereby making it a fundamental right in the Constitution. Its interpretation must receive illumination from the trinity of provisions of the Constitution, namely the Preamble, the fundamental rights and the Directive Principles of State Policy. Article 32(1) confers the right to move the Supreme Court for the enforcement of any of the fundamental rights, but it does not say as to who shall have the right to move the Supreme Court, nor does it say by what proceedings the Supreme Court may be so moved. Neither there is any limitation in the words of Art. 32(1) that the fundamental right which is sought to be enforced by moving the Supreme Court should be one belonging to the person who moves the Supreme Court, nor does it say that the Supreme Court should be moved only by a particular kind of proceeding. It is clear on the plain language of Art. 32(1) that whenever there is a violation of a fundamental right, any one can move the Supreme Court for its enforcement.

Then again Art. 32(1) says that the Supreme Court can be moved for the enforcement of a fundamental right by any *appropriate* proceeding. There is no limitation in regard to the kind of proceeding envisaged in Art. 32(1) except that the proceeding must be appropriate and this requirement of appropriateness must be judged in the light of the purpose for which the proceeding is to be taken, namely enforcement of a fundamental right. The Constitution makers deliberately did not lay down any particular form of proceeding for the enforcement of a fundamental right, nor did they stipulate that such proceeding should conform to any rigid pattern or straightjacket formula. They knew that in a country like India where there is so much of poverty, ignorance, illiteracy, deprivation and exploitation, any insistence on a rigid formula of proceeding for the enforcement of a fundamental right would become

---

42. AIR 1961 SC 1457.
43. *Ibid.* at p. 1461 per Gajendragadkar, J.
44. See *Ramesh Thappar* v. *State of Madras,* AIR 1950 SC 124.

self-defeating because it would place enforcement of such rights beyond the reach of the common man, and the entire remedy for the enforcement of fundamental rights, which the Constitution makers regarded as so precious and invaluable that they elevated it to the status of a fundamental right, would become a mere rope of sand so far as the large masses of the people in this country are concerned. The Constitution makers, therefore, advisedly provided Art. 32(1) that the Supreme Court may be moved by any appropriate proceeding, appropriate not in terms of any particular form but appropriate with reference to the purpose of the proceeding. That is the reason why it was held by the Supreme Court in the *Judges Appointment and Transfer* case[45] that where a member of the public acting bona fide moves the Court for the enforcement of a fundamental right on behalf of a person or class of persons, who on account of poverty or disability or socially or economically disadvantaged position cannot approach the Court for relief, such member of the public may move the Court even by just writing a letter, because it would not be right or fair to expect a person acting *pro bono publico* to incur expenses out of his own pocket for going to a lawyer and preparing a regular writ petition for being filed in Court for the enforcement of the fundamental right of the poor and deprived sections of the community, and in such a case, a letter addressed by him can legitimately be regarded as an *appropriate* proceeding.

But then the question arises as to what is the power which may be exercised by the Supreme Court when it is moved by an *appropriate* proceeding for the enforcement of a fundamental right. The only provision made by the Constitution makers in this behalf is to be found in Art. 32(2) which confers power on the Supreme Court to issue directions or orders or writs including writs in the nature of *habeas corpus, mandamus,* prohibition, *quo warranto* and *certiorari,* whichever may be appropriate, for the enforcement of any of the fundamental rights. It will be seen that the power conferred by Art. 32(2) is in the widest terms. It is not confined to issuing the high prerogative writs *of habeas corpus, mandamus*, prohibition, *certiorari* and *quo warranto*, which are hedged in by strict conditions differing from one writ to another. But it is much wider and includes within its matrix power to issue any directions, orders or writs which may be appropriate for the enforcement of the fundamental right in question and this is made amply clear by the inclusive clause which refers to *in the nature of habeas corpus, mandamus, prohibition, quo warranto and certiorari.* It is not only the high prerogative writs which can be issued by the Supreme Court but also writs in the nature of these high prerogative writs and, therefore, even if the conditions for the issue of any of these high prerogative writs are not fulfilled, the Supreme Court would not be constrained to fold its hands in despair and plead its inability to help the citizen who has come before it for judicial redress, but would have power to issue any direction, order or writ including a writ in the nature of any high prerogative writ. This provision conferring on the Supreme Court power to enforce the fundamental rights in the widest possible terms shows the anxiety of the Constitution makers not to allow any procedural technicalities to stand in the way of the enforcement of fundamental rights. The Constitution makers clearly intended that the Supreme Court should have ample power to issue whatever direction, order or writ may be appropriate in a given case for the enforcement of a fundamental right. But what procedure shall be followed by the Supreme Court in exercising the power to issue such direction, order or writ?

45. *S.P. Gupta* v. *President of India*, AIR 1982 SC 149.

That is a matter on which the Constitution is silent and advisedly so, because the Constitution makers never intended to fetter the discretion of the Supreme Court to evolve a procedure appropriate in the circumstances of a given case for the purpose of enabling it to exercise its power of enforcing a fundamental right. Neither Art. 32(2) nor any other provision of the Constitution requires that any particular procedure shall be followed by the Supreme Court in exercising its power to issue an appropriate direction, order or writ. The purpose for which the power to issue an appropriate direction, order or writ is conferred on the Supreme Court is to secure enforcement of a fundamental right and obviously, therefore, whatever procedure is necessary for the fulfilment of that purpose must be permissible to the Supreme Court.[46]

Article 32 prescribes five types of writs and they are as follows:

Habeas Corpus

Habeas Corpus is a Latin term which literally means *you may have the body*. The writ is issued in the form of an order calling upon a person by whom another person is detained to produce that person before the Court and to let the Court know by what authority he has detained that person. If it is found that the detained person has been detained illegally, the Court will order that he be released. Thus, the main object of the writ is to give quick and immediate remedy to a person who is unlawfully detained whether in prison or private custody.

Who can apply for the writ

The general rule is that an application can be made by a person who is illegally detained. But in certain cases, an application of *habeas corpus* can be made by any person on behalf of the detained person/or detenue/prisoner, i.e. a friend or a relation.

In case of an application for a writ of *habeas corpus*, the practice evolved by the Supreme Court is not to follow the strict rules of pleading nor place undue emphasis on the question as to on whom the burden of proof lies. Even a postcard written by a detenue from jail has been sufficient to stir the Court into examining the legality of detention. The Supreme Court has consistently shown great anxiety for personal liberty and refused to throw out a petition merely on the ground that it does not disclose a prima facie case invalidating the order of detention. Whenever a petition for a writ of *habeas corpus* has come up before the Supreme Court, it has almost invariably issued a rule calling upon the detaining authority to justify the detention. Once the rule is issued, it is the bounden duty of the Court to satisfy itself that all the safeguards by the law have been scrupulously observed and the citizen is not deprived of his personal liberty otherwise than in accordance with law. Where large masses of people are poor, illiterate and ignorant and access to the courts is not easy on account of lack of financial resources, it would be most unreasonable to insist that the petitioner should set out clearly and specifically the grounds on which he challenges the order of detention and make out a *prima facie* case in support of those grounds before a rule is issued, or to hold that the detaining authority should not be liable to do anything more than just meet the specific grounds of challenge put forward by the petitioner in the petition. The burden of showing that the detention is in accordance with the procedure established by law has always been

46. *Bandhua Mukti Morcha* v. *Union of India*, AIR 1984 SC 802.

placed by the Court on the detaining authority, because Art. 21 of the Constitution provides in clear and explicit terms that no one shall be deprived of his life or personal liberty except in accordance with the procedure established by law.[47]

Technicalities and legal necessities are no impediment to the Court entertaining even an informal communication as a proceeding for *habeas corpus* if the basic facts are found. The writ of *habeas corpus* cannot be used only for releasing a person illegally detained but also for protecting him from treatment inside jails. In *Sunil Batra* v. *Delhi Administration*[48] the Supreme Court held as follows:

> "The Court is always ready to correct injustice but it is no practical proposition to drive every victim to move the court for a writ, knowing the actual hurdles and the prison realities. True, technicalities and legal niceties are no impediment to the court entertaining even an informal communication as a proceeding for habeas corpus if the basic facts are found; still, the awe and distance of courts, the legalese and mystique, keep the institution unapproachable. More realistic is to devise a method of taking the healing law to the injured victim. That system is best where the remedy will rush to the injury on the slightest summons. So, within the existing, dated legislation, new meanings must be read. Of course, new legislation is the best solution, but when lawmakers take far too long for social patience to suffer, as in this very case of prison reform, courts have to make do with interpretation and carve on wood and sculpt on stone ready at hand and not wait for far away marble architecture. Counsel rivetted their attention on this pragmatic engineering and jointly helped the court to constitutionalise the Prisons Act prescriptions. By this legal energetics they desired the court to read into vintage provisions legal remedies."[49]

When it will lie

The writ of *habeas corpus* will lie if the power of detention vested in an authority was exercised *mala fide* and is made with collateral or ulterior purposes.[50] But if the detention is justified, the High Court will not grant the writ of *habeas corpus*. The detention is illegal if it is not made in accordance with the procedure established by law. The law must be a valid one and the procedure must be strictly followed [Art. 21]. The detention is lawful if the conditions laid down in Art. 22 are complied with. The detention becomes unlawful if a person who is arrested is not produced before the Magistrate within 24 hours of his arrest and he will be entitled to be released on the writ of *habeas corpus*. The legislature which deprives a person of his personal liberty by law must be competent to make that law. If the law is unlawful, the detention will be unlawful.

Mandamus

The word *mandamus* means "the order". The writ of *mandamus* is thus an order by a superior court commanding a person or a public authority (including the Government and public corporation) to do or forbear to do something in the nature of public duty or in certain cases of a statutory duty.[51] For instance, a licensing officer is under a duty to issue a licence to an

47. *Icchu Devi* v. *Union of India,* AIR 1980 SC 1984.
48. AIR 1980 SC 1579.
49. *Ibid.* at p. 1594 per Krishna Iyer, J.
50. *A.K. Gopalan* v. *State of Madras*, AIR 1950 SC 27.
51. *See* A.T. Markose, *Judicial Control of Administrative Action in India*, p. 364.

applicant who fulfils all the conditions laid down for the issue of such licence. But despite the fulfilment of such conditions if the officer or the authority concerned refuses or fails to issue the licence, the aggrieved person has a right to seek the remedy through a writ of *mandamus.*

When it will lie

The writ or order in the nature of *mandamus* would be issued when there is a failure to perform a mandatory duty. But even in cases of alleged breaches of mandatory duty, the party must show that he has made a distinct demand to enforce that duty and the demand was met with refusal.[52]

1. A writ of *mandamus* can only be granted when there is in the applicant a right to compel the performance of some duty cast upon the authority.[53] The duty sought to be enforced must be a public duty, that is, duty cast by law. A private right cannot be enforced by the writ of *mandamus.*
2. A writ of *mandamus* can be issued to public authority to restrain it from acting under a law which has been declared unconstitutional.

Thus a writ of *mandamus* can be granted only in cases where there is a statutory duty imposed upon the officer concerned, and there is a failure on the part of that officer to discharge the statutory obligation. The chief function of this writ is to compel the performance of public duties prescribed by the statute and to keep the subordinate tribunal and officers exercising public functions within the limits of their jurisdiction. It follows, therefore, that an order of *mandamus* may be issued to compel the authorities to do something which imposes a legal duty and the aggrieved party has a legal right under the statute to enforce its performance.

The High Courts have the power to issue a writ of *mandamus* where the Government or a public authority has failed to exercise or has wrongly exercised the discretion conferred upon it by a statute or a rule or a policy decision of the Government or has exercised such discretion *mala fide* or on irrelevant considerations or by ignoring the relevant considerations and materials or in such a manner as to frustrate the object of conferring such discretion of the policy for implementing such discretion.[54]

When it will not lie

A writ of *mandamus* will not be granted in the following circumstances:

1. When the duty is merely discretionary in nature, the writ of *mandamus* will not lie. In *State of M.P.* v. *Mandawara,*[55] the M.P. Government made a rule, making it discretionary to grant dearness allowance to its employees at a particular rate. The Supreme Court held that the writ of *mandamus* could not be issued to compel the Government to exercise its power.

52. *Saraswati Industrial Syndicate Ltd.* v. *Union of India,* AIR 1975 SC 46; Halsbury's *Laws of England,* 3rd ed., Vol. 13, p. 106.
53. *State of M.P.* v. *G.C. Mandawara,* AIR 1954 SC 493.
54. *Controller Land Auditor General of India* v. *K.S. Jagannathan,* (1986) 2 SCC 679.
55. AIR 1954 SC 493.

2. A writ of *mandamus* does not lie against a private individual or any private organization because they are not entrusted with a public duty.[56]
3. A writ of *mandamus* cannot be granted to enforce an obligation arising out of contract.[57]

Prohibition

A writ of prohibition is issued primarily to prevent an inferior court or tribunal from exceeding its jurisdiction or acting contrary to the principles of natural justice. It is issued by a superior Court to inferior courts for the purpose of preventing inferior courts from usurping a jurisdiction with which it was not legally vested, or, in other words, to compel inferior courts to keep within the limits of their jurisdiction.[58] Thus, the writ is issued in both cases—where there is excess of jurisdiction and where there is absence of jurisdiction.[59]

Prohibition and certiorari—Distinguished

Prohibition has much in common with *certiorari.* Both the writs are issued with the object of restraining the inferior courts from exceeding their jurisdiction. The difference between the two writs was explained by the Supreme Court in *Hari Vishnu Kamath* v. *Ahmad Ishaque.*[60] The Court observed that there is one fundamental distinction between the two writs, namely a writ of prohibition and a writ of *certiorari*. They are issued at different stages of the proceedings. When an inferior court takes up for hearing a matter over which it has no jurisdiction, the person against whom the proceedings are taken can move the superior Court for a writ of prohibition, and on that, an order will be issued forbidding the inferior Court from continuing the proceedings. On the other hand, if the Court hears that cause or matter and gives a decision, the party aggrieved would have to move the superior Court for a writ of *certiorari*, and on that, an order will be made quashing the decision on the ground of want of jurisdiction. Broadly speaking a writ of prohibition will lie when the proceedings are to any extent pending and a writ of *certiorari* for quashing after they have been terminated in a final decision.

Both writs of prohibition and *certiorari* have, as their object to restrain the inferior Courts from exceeding their jurisdiction, and they could be issued not merely to Courts but to all authorities exercising judicial or quasi-judicial functions. When the case is pending before the Court but has not finally been disposed of, the Supreme Court has to apply both prohibition and *certiorari*—prohibition to prevent the Court from proceeding further with the case and *certiorari* for quashing what has already been decided.[61] Thus, the object of the writ of prohibition is, in short, prevention rather than cure, while *certiorari* is used as a cure. Prohibition, like *certiorari,* lies only against judicial and quasi-judicial bodies. It does not lie against a public authority which acts purely in an executive or administrative capacity, nor to a legislative body.

56. *Barada Kania* v. *State of West Bengal*, AIR 1963 Cal. 161.
57. *Bihar E.G.F. Co-operative Society* v. *Sipahi Singh,* AIR 1977 SC 2149.
58. *East India Commercial Co.* v. *Collector of Customs,* AIR 1962 SC 1893.
59. *S. Govinda Menon* v. *Union of India,* AIR 1967 SC 1274.
60. AIR 1955 SC 233.

Certiorari

A writ of *certiorari* is issued by a superior Court (Supreme Court and High Courts) to an inferior court or body exercising judicial or quasi-judicial functions to remove a suit from such inferior court or body and adjudicate upon the validity of the proceedings or body exercising judicial or quasi-judicial functions. It may be used before the trial to prevent an excess or abuse of jurisdiction and remove the case for trial to higher court. It is invoked also after trial to quash an order which has been made without jurisdiction or in violation of the principles of natural justice. Commenting on the scope of the writ, the Supreme Court in the *Province of Bombay* v. *Khushaldas*[61] held that whenever any body of persons having legal authority to determine questions, affecting the rights of subject, and having the duty to act judicially, act in excess of their legal authority a writ of *certiorari* lies. It does not lie to remove merely ministerial act or to remove or cancel executive administrative acts.

Writ lies on judicial bodies

One of the fundamental principles in regard to the issuing of a writ of *certiorari* is that the writ can be availed of only to remove or to adjudicate upon the validity of judicial acts. The expression 'judicial acts' includes the exercise of *quasi-judicial* functions by administrative bodies or authorities or persons obliged to exercise such functions and is used in contrast which are purely ministerial acts.[62] Whether a body is to act in a judicial manner or not is a question to be decided in each case in the light of the circumstances of the case. The Supreme Court had occasion to consider the nature of the two kinds of acts, namely judicial which includes quasi-judicial and administrative a number of times. In *Province of Bombay* v. *Khusaldas S. Advani,*[63] it adopted the celebrated definition of a quasi-judicial body given by Atkin L.J. in *R.* v. *Electricity Commissioners,*[64] which is as follows:

> "Whenever any body of persons having legal authority to determine questions affecting rights of subjects, and having the duty to act judicially act in excess of their legal authority they are subject to the controlling jurisdiction of the King's Bench Division exercised in these writs."

This definition insists on three requisites, each of which must be fulfilled to make the act of the body a quasi-judicial act. The body of persons:

(i) must have legal authority,
(ii) to determine questions affecting the rights of subjects, and
(iii) must have the duty to act judicially.

After analysing the various cases, Das, J. laid down the following principles as deducible therefrom in *Khusaldas S. Advani*'s case:

(i) That if a statute empowers an authority, not being a Court in the ordinary sense, to decide disputes arising out of a claim made by any party under the statute which

61. AIR 1950 SC 22.
62. *T.C. Basappa* v. *T. Nagappa,* AIR 1954 SC 440.
63. AIR 1950 SC 222.
64. (1924) 1 K.B. 171.

claim is opposed by another party and to determine the respective rights of the contesting parties who are opposed to each other, there is a lis and prima facie and in the absence of anything in the statute to the contrary it is the duty of the authority to act judicially and the decision of the authority is a quasi-judicial act; and

(ii) that if a statutory authority has power to do any act which will prejudicially affect the subject, then although there are not two parties apart from the authority and the contest is between the authority proposing to do the act and the subject opposing it, the final determination of the authority will yet be a quasi-judicial act, provided the authority is required by the statute to act judicially.

Grounds on which writ can be issued

With regard to the character and scope of the writ of *certiorari* and the conditions under which it can be issued, the following propositions may be taken as already established:

1. *Certiorari* will be issued for correcting errors of jurisdiction, or when an inferior Court or Tribunal acts without jurisdiction or in excess of it, or fails to exercise it.
2. *Certiorari* will also be issued when the Court or Tribunal acts illegally in the exercise of its undoubted jurisdiction, or when it decides without giving an opportunity to the parties to be heard, or violates the principles of natural justice.
3. The Court issuing a writ of *certiorari* acts in exercise of a supervisory and not appellate jurisdiction.

One consequence of this is that the Court will not review findings of fact reached by the inferior Court or Tribunal, even if they be erroneous. This is on the principle that a Court which has jurisdiction over a subject matter has jurisdiction to decide wrong as well as right, and when the Legislature does not choose to confer a right of appeal against that decision, it would be defeating its purpose and policy, if a superior Court were to rehear the case on the evidence and substitute its own findings in *certiorari.*

Natural Justice and Certiorari

A writ of *certiorari* may be issued against a Court and Tribunal in case of the violation of the principles of natural justice and they are:

(a) free from bias and interest in the subject matter; and

(b) *audi alteram partem,* i.e. the parties must be given reasonable opportunity to be heard.

In the case of bias and interest in the subject matter, it can be further said that, no one shall be a judge of his own cause, and justice should not only be done but manifestly and undoubtedly seen to be done.

When it will not lie

The writ of *certiorari* cannot be issued against a private body.

Quo warranto

The words *quo warranto* means 'what is your authority'. By this writ the holder of an office is called upon to show to the court under what authority he holds the office. The object of the writ is to prevent a person from holding an office which he is not legally entitled to hold. If the inquiry leads to the finding that the holder of the office has no valid title to it, the Court may pass an order preventing the holder to continue in office and may also direct the person holding the office illegally to vacate the office immediately.

Who can apply

A writ of *quo warranto* can be claimed by a person if he satisfies the Court that:

(i) the office in question is a public office; and
(ii) it is held by a person without legal authority.

The writ of *quo warranto* is not issued in respect of an office of a private character. An application for the writ challenging the legality of an appointment to an office of a public nature may lie at the instance of any private person, although he is not personally aggrieved or interested in the matter. It is not necessary that the petitioner for *quo warranto* must have legal right in the office. Any member of public can challenge the right of a person to hold a public office. In *G.D. Karkare* v. *Shevde*,[65] the appointment of Advocate-General of M.P. was challenged by a private individual who had no legal interest in that office. The Court issued a writ of *quo warranto* against the Advocate-General.

DIRECTIVE PRINCIPLES OF STATE POLICY (Part IV)

Here, an attempt has been made to find out the actual position and value of the Directive Principles under the Constitution. Three problems generally existed while creating relationship between the Fundamental Rights and the Directive Principles. The first view is that the Fundamental Rights are superior to the Directive Principles. So, the Directive Principles must give way to the Fundamental Rights because Fundamental Rights are sacred and inalienable and are so basic for the human beings that they must prevail over any other part of the Constitution. Another reason for such supremacy of the Fundamental Rights over the Directive Principles may be due to literal interpretation of Art. 37 which declares that the Directive Principles are not justiciable. The second view is that the Fundamental Rights and Directive Principles are of equal importance. To give absolute primacy to one over the other is to disturb the harmony of the Constitution. In case of conflict, attempt must be made to harmonise them with each other. The third view is that Directive Principles are superior to Fundamental Rights.[66]

---

65. AIR 1952 Nag 330.
66. See H.M. Seervai, *Constitutional Law of India*, Bombay, N.M. Tripathi, (1984) p. 1570. Where the author discussed the relationship of Fundamental Rights and Directive Principles through three periods, i.e., the first period begins with *Madras* v. *Champakaam Dorairajan* (1951) SCR 525 and ends with *Chandra Bhavan* v. *Mysore* (1970) 2 SCR 600 and ends with *Minerva Mills Ltd.* v. *Union*, AIR 1980 SC 1789. Third period starts with *Minerva Mills* case and there after.

The Directive Principles of State Policy contained in Part IV of the Constitution set out the aims and objectives to be taken up by the State in the governance of the country. This novel feature of the Constitution is borrowed from the Constitution of Ireland which had copied it from the Spanish Constitution. Dr. Ambedkar, Chairman of the Drafting Committee, explained the underlying objects of the Directive Principles in the following words:

> "Every Government shall be on the evil, both in its daily affairs and also at the end of a certain period when the others and the electorate will be given an opportunity to assess the work done by the Government while we have established political democracy, it is also the desire that we should lay down as our ideal economic democracy. There are various ways in which people believe that economic democracy can be brought about; we have deliberately introduced in the language that we have used in the directive principles something which is fixed or rigid...."[67]

Thus it is clear that the main object in enacting the Directive Principles appears to have been to set standards of achievements before the Legislature and Executive, the local and other authorities by which their success or failure can be judged. It was also hoped that those failing to implement the directives might receive a rude awakening at the polls.[68]

However, according to Art. 37, these principles are not enforceable by any court of law. The reason behind the non-enforceability and non-justiciability of these principles is that they impose positive obligation on the State. While taking positive action, the government functions under several restraints, the most crucial of these being that of economic resources. The Constitution makers, therefore, taking a pragmatic view, refrained from giving teeth to these principles. Nevertheless, the Constitution declares these principles as 'fundamental' in the governance of the country, and the 'State' has been placed under an obligation to apply them in making laws. The courts, however, do not enforce any of the Directive Principles as it does not create any justiciable right in favour of an individual.[69] Even a Court will not issue an order or a writ of *Mandamus* to the Government to fulfill Directive Principles.[70]

Fundamental Rights occupy a unique place in the lives of civilized societies and have been variously described in judgments of the Supreme Court as 'transcendental', 'inalienable' and 'primordial'. They constitute the ark of the Constitution.[71] Speaking about the importance of fundamental rights, Justice Bhagwati observed in *Maneka Gandhi* v. *Union of India:*[72]

> "These fundamental rights represent the basic values cherished by the people of this country (India) since the Vedic times and they are calculated to protect the dignity of the individual and create conditions in which every human being can develop his personality to the fullest extent."[73]

Fundamental Rights create negative obligations on the State, i.e. the State is required to refrain from doing something. Article 13 declares that a law inconsistent with the Fundamental Rights is void. But there has never been such a provision in the Constitution

67. Constituent Assembly Debates, Vol. VII, pp. 494–95.
68. H.M. Seervai, *Constitutional Law of India*, Bombay, N.M. Tripathi (1984), p. 1577; See also Dr. J.N. Pandey, *The Constitutional Law of India*, Allahabad, Central Law-Agency (1989), p. 237.
69. *K. Rajendran* v. *Tamil Nadu*, AIR. 1982 SC 1107.
70. *Rajan Dwivedi* v. *Union of India,* AIR 1983 SC 624.
71. See, *Minerva Mills Ltd.* v. *Union of India*, AIR 1980 SC 1789.
72. AIR 1978 SC 597.
73. *Ibid.* at p. 619 per Bhagwati, J.

as regards the Directive Principles. Therefore a law inconsistent with the Directive Principles cannot be declared invalid.[74]

After the advent of the Constitution, the Supreme Court observed[75] that a Directive Principle could not override a Fundamental Right, and, in case of conflict between the two, the Fundamental Right would prevail over the Directive Principles. The Supreme Court, while dealing with a Government order regarding reservation of seats for admission into Medical Colleges on communal lines, observed:[76]

> "The directive principles—which by Art. 37 are expressly made un-enforceable by a Court, cannot override the provisions found in Part III. The chapter on Fundamental Rights is sacrosanct and not liable to be abridged by any Legislative or Executive or Executive Act".[77]

But a year later, when the Court dealt with Zamindari Abolition cases, its attitude was considerably modified. In the *State of Bihar* v. *Kameshwar Singh*,[78] the Court relied on Art. 39 in deciding that a certain Zamindari Abolition Act had been passed for a public purpose within the meaning of Art. 31. Finally, in Re *Kerala Education Bill* case,[79] the Supreme Court observed that though the Directive Principles cannot override the Fundamental Rights, nevertheless in determining the scope and ambit of Fundamental Rights, the Court may not entirely ignore the Directive Principles. Attempt should be made to give effect to both as much as possible.

Harmonious Construction of Parts III and IV

In course of time, the Court started giving a good deal of value to the Directive Principles from a legal point of view. The Court adopted the view that although Directive Principles were non-enforceable, nevertheless, while interpreting a statute, the Court could look for light to the 'lodestar' of Directive Principles. The Court began to implement the value underlying these principles to the extent possible. The Supreme Court in *Golaknath* v. *State of Punjab*[80] emphasized that the Fundamental Rights and Directive Principles formed an integrated scheme which was elastic enough to respond to the changing needs of the society. In *Minerva Mills Ltd.* v. *Union of India*,[81] the Supreme Court quoted Granville Austin's view and observed that Part III and Part IV are like two wheels of a chariot, no one is less important than the other. If one will be taken the other will lose its efficacy. They are like a twin formula for achieving social revolution. In other words, the Indian Constitution is founded on the bedrock of the balance between Part III and Part IV. To give absolute primacy to one over the other is to disturb the harmony of the Constitution. The Court further observed that merely because the Directive Principles are non-justiciable, it does not follow that they are in any way subservient or inferior to the Fundamental Rights. The Directive Principles impose

74. *Deep Chand* v. *State of U.P.*, AIR 1959 SC 648.
75. *State of Madras* v. *Champakam Dorairajan* (1951) SCR 525.
76. *Ibid.*
77. *Ibid.* at p. 531 per Das, J.
78. AIR 1952 SC 352.
79. AIR 1958 SC 956.
80. AIR 1967 SC 1653.
81. AIR 1980 SC 1789.

an obligation on the State to take positive action for creating socio-economic conditions in which there will be an egalitarian social order with social and economic justice to all, so that individual liberty will become a cherished value and the dignity of the individual a living reality, not only for a few privileged persons but for the entire people of the country. It will thus be seen that the Directive Principles enjoy a very high place in the constitutional scheme and it is only in the framework of the socio-economic structure envisaged in the Directive Principles that the Fundamental Rights are intended to operate, for it is only then that they can become meaningful and significant for the millions of our poor and deprived people who do not have even the bare necessities of life and who are living below the poverty line.

It is not correct to say that under our constitutional scheme, Fundamental Rights are superior to Directive Principles, or that the Directive Principles must yield to the Fundamental Rights. Both are in fact equally fundamental and the courts have therefore in recent times tried to harmonise them by importing the Directive Principles in the construction of the Fundamental Rights. If a law is enacted for the purpose of giving effect to a Directive Principle and it imposes a restriction on a Fundamental Right, it would be difficult to condemn such restriction as unreasonable or not in public interest. So also where a law is enacted for giving effect to a Directive Principle in furtherance of the constitutional goal of social and economic justice, it may have conflict with a formalistic and doctrinaire view of equality before the law, but it would almost always conform to the principle of equality before the law in its total magnitude and dimension, because the equality clause in the Constitution does not speak of mere formal equality before the law but embodies the concept of real and substantive equality which strikes at inequalities arising on account of vast social and economic differentials and is consequently an essential ingredient of social and economic justice. Recently, the Supreme Court observed that a real attempt should be made to harmonize and reconcile the Directive Principles and Fundamental Rights and any collision between the two should be avoided as far as possible.[82]

Part IV Superior to Part III

The importance of the Directive Principles has been considerably enhanced by the Constitution 25th Amendment, 1971 (Art. 31-C was added accordingly). The first part of Art. 31-C provides that no law which is intended to give effect to the Directive Principles contained in Arts. 39(b) and (c) shall be deemed to be void on the ground that it is inconsistent with or takes away or abridges any of the rights conferred by Arts. 14, 19 and 31. The second part of Art. 31-C provides that no law containing a declaration for giving effect to such policy can be called in question on the ground that it does in fact give effect to such policy. The validity of the first part of the Art. 31-C was upheld in *Kesavananda Bharati* v. *State of Kerala*.[83]

Article 31-C was again amended by the 42nd Amendment Act 1976 by which the scope of Art. 31-C was extended to all the directives contained in Part IV in place of Arts. 39(b) and (c) only. Thus in effect 25th Amendment gave primacy to Directive Principles contained

82. *Tamil Nadu* v. *Abu*, AIR 1964 SC 326.
83. AIR 1973 SC 1461.

in Arts. 39(b) and (c) over the Fundamental Rights in Arts. 14, 19 or 31, whereas the 42nd Amendment gave precedence to all the Directive Principles over the Fundamental Rights guaranteed in Arts. 14, 19 or 31 of the Constitution.[84] However, in *Minerva Mills* v. *Union of India*,[85] the Supreme Court declared the 42nd Amendment unconstitutional on the ground that it destroys the basic features of the Constitution and observed that the goals set out in Part IV have to be achieved without destroying the guarantees given in Part III. But in *Sanjeev Coke Mfg. Co* v. *Bharat Coking Coal Ltd.*,[86] the Supreme Court expressed its doubts on the validity of its decision in *Minerva Mills* case. A five-judge Bench held that the question regarding the validity of the 42nd Amendment was not directly at issue in *Minerva Mills* case and therefore the view of the Supreme Court was treated as obiter. Since the validity of Art. 31-C as originally introduced in the Constitution has been upheld in *Kesavananda Bharati* case, it should lead to the conclusion that Art. 31-C as amended by the 42nd Amendment is also valid. Nevertheless, it has been said:

> "... In building up a just social order it is something imperative that the Fundamental Rights should be subordinated to Directive Principles..."[87]

Justice Bhagawati, even in the year 1980, stressed the dominating nature of the Directive Principles over Government action in *M/s Kasturilal* v. *State of J.K.*[88] and observed:

> "... While an action which is inconsistent with or runs counter to a Directive Principle would *prima facie* incur the reproach of being unreasonable."[89]

From the above discussion, it is seen that the judiciary treated the Directive Principles as inferior to the Fundamental Rights in the early stage. But when the importance of the Directive Principles were recognized, the Court seems to have harmonised these principles with the Fundamental Rights and much importance has been given by saying that the directives should be interpreted in the light of the Fundamental Rights and even suggested supremacy of the Directive Principles over the Fundamental Rights. But the Court has never said that the Directive Principles are justiciable specifically. In recent cases even though the directives *per se* are not to be enforced by the Court, nor can the Court compel the State to undertake legislation to implement a directive, the Supreme Court has been issuing various directions to Government and the administrative authorities to take positive action to remove the grievances which have been caused by non-implementation of the Directives.[90] Thus, the Directive Principles are being enforced indirectly by the Court by issuing directions.[91] The trend of the judicial decisions is that the Directive Principles represent the common background of the Fundamental Rights, keeping pace with time.

---

84. Article 31 was omitted by the Constitution 44th Amendment Act, 1978.
85. AIR 1980 SC 1789.
86. AIR 1983 SC 239.
87. *Kesavananda* v. *State of Kerala*; AIR 1973 SC 1461 at p. 1951 per Mathew, J.
88. AIR 1980 SC 1992.
89. *Ibid.* at p. 2000 per Bhagwati, J.
90. *Comptroller* v. *Jagannathan*, AIR 1987 SC 537.
91. See *Centre of Legal Research* v. *State of Kerala*, AIR 1987 SC 2195. The Court issued suitable directions so that the Government may perform its duty to implement the Directives, e.g. to promote the legal aid programme. See also *Sheela* v. *Union of India*, AIR 1986 SC 1773; see also *Lakshmikant* v. *Union of India*, AIR 1987 SC 232.

Article 36: Definition

In this Part, unless the context otherwise requires, 'the State' has the same meaning as in Part III.

Article 37: Application of the principles contained in this Part

The provisions contained in this Part shall not be enforceable by any court, but the principles therein laid down are nevertheless fundamental in the governance of the country and it shall be the duty of the State to apply these principles in making laws.

Article 39: Certain principles of policy to be followed by the State

The State shall, in particular, direct its policy towards securing—

(a) that the citizens, men and women equally, have the right to an adequate means of livelihood;
(b) that the ownership and control of the material resources of the community are so distributed as best to subserve the common good;
(c) that the operation of the economic system does not result in the concentration of wealth and means of production to the common detriment;
(d) that there is equal pay for equal work for both men and women;
(e) that the health and strength of workers, men and women, and the tender age of children are not abused and that citizens are not forced by economic necessity to enter avocations unsuited to their age or strength;
(f) that children are given opportunities and facilities to develop in a healthy manner and in conditions of freedom and dignity and that childhood and youth are protected against exploitation and against moral and material abandonment.

Article 41: Right to work, to education and to public assistance in certain cases

The State shall, within the limits of its economic capacity and development, make effective provision for securing the right to work, to education and to public assistance in cases of unemployment, old age, sickness and disablement, and in other cases of undeserved want.

Article 42: Provision for just and humane conditions of work and maternity relief

The State shall make provision for securing just and humane conditions of work and for maternity relief.

Article 43: Living wage, etc., for workers

The State shall endeavour to secure, by suitable legislation or economic organisation or in any other way, to all workers, agricultural, industrial or otherwise, work, a living wage, conditions of work ensuring a decent standard of life and full enjoyment of leisure and social and cultural opportunities and, in particular, the State shall endeavour to promote cottage industries on an individual or co-operative basis in rural areas.

ARTICLE 43A: Participation of workers in management of industries

The State shall take steps, by suitable legislation or in any other way, to secure the participation of workers in the management of undertakings, establishments or other organisations engaged in any industry.

ARTICLE 45: Provision for free and compulsory education for children

The State shall endeavour to provide, early childhood care and education for all children until they complete the age of six years.

ARTICLE 51: Promotion of international peace and security

The State shall endeavour to—

(a) promote international peace and security;

(b) maintain just and honourable relations between nations;

(c) foster respect for international law and treaty obligations in the dealings of organised peoples with one another; and

(d) encourage settlement of international disputes by arbitration.

ARTICLE 123: Power of President to promulgate Ordinances during recess of Parliament

(1) If at any time, except when both Houses of Parliament are in session, the President is satisfied that circumstances exist which render it necessary for him to take immediate action, he may promulgate such Ordinances as the circumstances appear to him to require.

(2) An Ordinance promulgated under this article shall have the same force and effect as an Act of Parliament, but every such Ordinance—

(a) shall be laid before both Houses of Parliament and shall cease to operate at the expiration of six weeks from the reassembly of Parliament, or, of before the expiration of that period resolutions disapproving it are passed by both Houses, upon the passing of the second of those resolutions; and

(b) may be withdrawn at any time by the President.

Explanation: Where the Houses of Parliament are summoned to reassemble on different dates, the period of six weeks shall be reckoned from the later of those dates for the purposes of this clause.

(3) If and so far as an Ordinance under this article makes any provision which Parliament would not under this Constitution be competent to enact, it shall be void.

President can issue ordinance when one of the houses of the Parliament is not in session. The maximum validity of an ordinance is 6 months and 6 weeks. An ordinance will expire after 6 weeks once both houses of the Parliament are in session. A constitutional amendment cannot be made through ordinance route. Ordinance route is envisaged for immediate action; for example; if the President is satisfied that circumstances exist which render it necessary for him to take immediate action; he may promulgate such Ordinances as the circumstances appear to him to require. It should be noted that the ordinance making power with the President is a case of subordinate legislation, where the actual lawmaking authority – Parliament – delegates its power to the executive, when the Parliament is in recess.

ARTICLE 136: Special leave to appeal by the Supreme Court

(1) Notwithstanding anything in this Chapter, the Supreme Court may, in its discretion, grant special leave to appeal from any judgment, decree, determination, sentence or order in any cause or matter passed or made by any court or tribunal in the territory of India.

(2) Nothing in clause (1) shall apply to any judgment, determination, and sentence or order passed or made by any court or tribunal constituted by or under any law relating to the Armed Forces.

Article 136 empowers the Supreme Court to grant in its discretion special leave to appeal from:

(a) any judgment, decree, determination, sentence or order,

(b) in any case or matter,

(c) passed or made by any court or tribunal in the territory of India. The only exception to this power of the Supreme Court is with regard to any judgment, etc. of any court or tribunal constituted by or under any law relating to the Armed Forces.

Under Article 136, the Supreme Court is authorised to grant in its discretion special leave to appeal from (a) any judgment, decree, determination, sentence or order, (b) in any case or matter, (c) passed or made by any court or tribunal in the territory of India. The only exception to this power of the Supreme Court is with regard to any judgment, etc. of any court or tribunal constituted by or under any law relating to the Armed Forces.

Article 136 vests very wide powers in the Supreme Court. The power given under this Article is in the nature of a special residuary power which is exercisable outside the purview of ordinary law. Articles 132 to 135 deal with ordinary appeals to the Supreme Court in cases where the needs of justice demand interference by the highest Court of the land. This Article is worded in the widest possible terms. It vests in the Supreme Court a plenary jurisdiction in the matter of entertaining and hearing appeals by granting special leave against any kind of judgment or order made by any Court or Tribunal (except a Military Tribunal) in any proceedings and the exercise of this power is left entirely to the discretion of the court unfettered by any restrictions and this power cannot be curtailed by any legislation short of amending the Article itself.

Under Article 136, the power of the Supreme Court to grant special leave to appeal is not confined to orders or determination of a court of law, but includes tribunals also. Several tests have been laid down by the Supreme Court to determine whether a particular body or authority is a tribunal within the ambit of Art. 136. The tests are not exhaustive in all cases. It is not necessary that all the tests laid down may be present in a given case while some tests may be present, others may be lacking. It is, however, absolutely necessary that the authority in order to come within the ambit of Article 136(1) as tribunal must be constituted by the State and is vested with some function of judicial powers of the State. This particular test must be present while some of the other tests may or may not be present at the same time. Thus, a tribunal is a body of authority although not a court having all the' attributes of a court, which is vested with judicial power to adjudicate on question of law or fact affecting the rights of all citizens in a judicial manner. However, it does not include a tribunal which have purely administrative or executive functions or a Tribunal having only legislative functions without any quasi-judicial functions.

In *Clerks and Depot Cashiers of the Calcutta Tramways Co. Ltd.* v. *Calcutta Tramways Co. Ltd.* [AIR 1957 SC 78] it was held that Supreme Court may interfere with the decisions arrived at by Tribunals under the following grounds:

(i) where the Tribunal acts in excess of the jurisdiction conferred upon it under the statute or regulation creating it or where it ostensibly fails to exercise a patent jurisdiction;

(ii) where there is an apparent error on the face of the decision;

(iii) where the Tribunal has erroneously applied well accepted principles of juris-prudence; and

(iv) where awards are made in violation of natural justice.

Article 141: Law declared by Supreme Court to be binding on all Courts

The law declared by the Supreme Court shall be binding on all Courts within the territory of India.

The Supreme Court while interpreting "*all Court*" in *Bengal Immunity Co. Ltd.* v. *State of Bihar* [AIR 1955 SC 661] held that there is nothing in our Constitution which prevents the Supreme Court from departing from a previous decision if it is convinced of its error and its baneful effect on the general interests of the public.

Obiter Dicta

The Supreme Court has laid down that the following categories of decisions of the Apex Court have no binding force:

(a) *Obiter dicta*, i.e., statements which are not part of the *ratio decidendi.*

(b) A decision *per incurium*, i.e., a decision given in ignorance of the terms of a statute or rule having the force of a statute.

(c) A decision passed by *sub silentio*, i.e., without any argument or debate on the relevant question.

(d) An order made with the consent of the parties, and with a reservation that it should not be treated as precedent.

ARTICLE 142: Enforcement of decrees and orders of Supreme Court and orders as to discovery, etc.

(1) The Supreme Court in the exercise of its jurisdiction may pass such decree or make such order as is necessary for doing complete justice in any cause or matter pending before it, and any decree so passed or order so made shall be enforceable throughout the territory of India in such manner as may be prescribed by or under any law made by Parliament and, until provision in that behalf is so made, in such manner as the President may by order prescribe.

(2) Subject to the provisions of any law made in this behalf by Parliament, the Supreme Court shall, as respects the whole of the territory of India, have all and every power to make any order for the purpose of securing the attendance of any person, the discovery or production of any documents, or the investigation or punishment of any contempt of itself.

The Supreme Court in *Delhi Development Authority* v. *Skipper Construction Company (P) Ltd.* (AIR 1996 SC 2005) while considering the nature and ambit of Article 142 observed that it is advisable to leave the power under Art. 142 undefined and uncatalogued so that it remains elastic enough to be moulded to suit the situation. The very fact that this power is conferred only upon the Supreme Court, and on no one else, is itself an assurance that it will be used with due restraint and circumspection keeping in view the ultimate object of doing complete justice between the parties.

It is important to note that Article 142 reads as 'complete justice' rather than the term 'justice'. The reasons may be complete justice is much wider concept to that of justice. The main purpose of Article 142 and the endeavor to do complete justice has been explained by the Apex Court in *Manohar Lal Sharma* v. *Principal Secretary* (AIR 2014 SC 666) held that the Supreme Court has been conferred under Article 142 with very wide powers for proper and effective administration of justice. The power to do complete justice under Article 142 is in the nature of a corrective measure whereby equity is given preference over law to ensure that no injustice is caused. (*Supreme Court Bar Association v. Union of India,* AIR 1998 SC 189).

ARTICLE 226: Power of High Courts to issue certain writs

(1) Notwithstanding anything in Art. 32, every High Court shall have powers, throughout the territories in relation to which it exercises jurisdiction, to issue to any person or authority, including in appropriate cases, any Government, within those territories directions, orders or writs, including writs in the nature of *habeas corpus, mandamus*, prohibition, *quo warranto* and *certiorari*, or any of them, for the enforcement of any of the rights conferred by Part III and for any other purpose.

(2) The power conferred by Cl. (1) to issue directions, orders or writs to any Government, authority or person may also be exercised by any High Court exercising jurisdiction

in relation to the territories within which the cause of action, wholly or in part, arises for the exercise of such power, notwithstanding that the seat of such Government or authority or the residence of such person is not within those territories.

(3) Where any party against whom an interim order, whether by way of injunction or stay or in any other manner, is made on, or in any proceedings relating to, a petition under Cl. (1), without—

(a) furnishing to such party copies of such petition and all documents in support of the plea for such interim order; and

(b) giving such party an opportunity of being heard,

makes an application to the High Court for the vacation of such order and furnishes a copy of such application to the party in whose favour such order has been made or the counsel of such party, the High Court shall dispose of the application within a period of two weeks from the date on which it is received or from the date on which the copy of such application is so furnished, whichever is later, or where the High Court is closed on the last day of that period, before the expiry of the next day afterwards on which the High Court is open; and if the application is not so disposed of, the interim order shall, on the expiry of that period, or, as the case may be, the expiry of the said next day, stand vacated.

(4) The power conferred on a High Court by this article shall not be in derogation of the power conferred on the Supreme Court by Cl. (2) of Art. 32.

ARTICLE 227: Power of superintendence over all courts by the High Court

(1) Every High Court shall have superintendence over all courts and tribunals throughout the territories interrelation to which it exercises jurisdiction

(2) Without prejudice to the generality of the foregoing provisions, the High Court may

(a) call for returns from such courts;

(b) make and issue general rules and prescribe forms for regulating the practice and proceedings of such courts; and

(c) prescribe forms in which books, entries and accounts shall be kept by the officers of any such courts

(3) The High Court may also settle tables of fees to be allowed to the sheriff and all clerks and officers of such courts and to attorneys, advocates and pleaders practising therein:

Provided that any rules made, forms prescribed or tables settled under clause (2) or clause (3) shall not be inconsistent with the provision of any law for the time being in force, and shall require the previous approval of the Governor

(4) Nothing in this article shall be deemed to confer on a High Court power of superintendence over any court or tribunal constituted by or under any law relating to the Armed Forces

In *Radhey Shyam and Another* v. *Chhabi Nath and others*, (2015) 5 SCC 423 The Supreme Court discussed the scope of Article 227 and observed that under Article 227 of the

Constitution, the High Court has the power of superintendence over all Courts and Tribunals throughout the territory in relation to which it exercises jurisdiction. The power to issue writs is not the same as the power of superintendence. The power of superintendence conferred upon every High Court by Article 227 is a supervisory jurisdiction intended to ensure that subordinate Courts and Tribunals act within the limits of their authority and according to law. Under Article 227 what comes up before the High Court is the order or judgment of a subordinate court or tribunal for the purpose of ascertaining whether in giving such judgment or order that subordinate court or tribunal has acted within its authority and according to law. The power under Article 227 of the Constitution is intended to be used sparingly and only in appropriate cases in order to keep the subordinate Courts and Tribunals within the bounds of their authority and not for correcting mere errors. The power may be exercised in cases occasioning grave injustice or failure of justice such as when:

(i) The court or tribunal has assumed a jurisdiction which it does not have,

(ii) Has failed to exercise a jurisdiction which it does have, such failure occasioning a failure of justice, and

(iii) The jurisdiction though available is being exercised in a manner which tantamount to overstepping the limits of jurisdiction.

ARTICLE 254: Inconsistency between laws made by Parliament and laws made by the Legislatures of States

(1) If any provision of a law made by the Legislature of a State is repugnant to any provision of a law made by Parliament which Parliament is competent to enact, or to any provision of an existing law with respect to one of the matters enumerated in the Concurrent List, then, subject to the provisions of clause (2), the law made by Parliament, whether passed before or after the law made by the Legislature of such State, or, as the case may be, the existing law, shall prevail and the law made by the Legislature of the State shall, to the extent of the repugnancy, be void

(2) Where a law made by the Legislature of a State with respect to one of the matters enumerated in the concurrent List contains any provision repugnant to the provisions of an earlier law made by Parliament or an existing law with respect to that matter, then, the law so made by the Legislature of such State shall, if it has been reserved for the consideration of the President and has received his assent, prevail in that State:

Provided that nothing in this clause shall prevent Parliament from enacting at any time any law with respect to the same matter including a law adding to, amending, varying or repealing the law so made by the Legislature of the State.

It would be seen that so far as clause (1) of Article 254 is concerned it clearly lays down that where there is a direct collision between a provision of a law made by the State and that made by Parliament with respect to one of the matters enumerated in the Concurrent List, then, subject to the provisions of clause (2), the State law would be void to the extent of the repugnancy. This naturally means that where both the State and Parliament occupy the field contemplated by the Concurrent List then the Act passed by Parliament being prior in point of time will prevail and consequently the State Act will have to yield to the Central Act, In fact, the scheme of the Constitution is a scientific and equitable distribution of legislative powers between Parliament and the State Legislatures. *First,* regarding the matters contained in List I, i.e. the Union List to the Seventh Schedule, Parliament alone is empowered to legislate and the State Legislatures have no authority to make any law in respect of the Entries contained in List I, *Secondly,* so far as the Concurrent List is concerted, both Parliament and the State Legislatures are entitled to legislate in regard to any of the Entries appearing therein, but that is subject to the condition laid down by Article 254 (1). *Thirdly,* so far as the matters in List II, i.e. the State List are concerned, the State Legislatures alone are competent to legislate on them and only under certain conditions Parliament can do so. It is, therefore, obvious that in such matters repugnancy may result from the following circumstances:

1. Where the provisions of a Central Act and a State Act in the Concurrent List are fully inconsistent and are absolutely irreconcilable, the Central Act will prevail and the State Act will become void in view of the repugnancy.
2. Where however, a law passed by the State comes into collision with a law passed by Parliament on an Entry in the Concurrent List, the State Act shall prevail to the extent of the repugnancy and the provisions of the Central Act would become void provided the State Act has been passed in accordance with clause (2) of Article 254.
3. Where a law passed by the State Legislature while being substantially within the scope of the entries in the State List entrenches upon any of the Entries in the Central List the constitutionality of the law may be upheld by invoking the doctrine of pith and substance if on an analysis of the provisions of the Act it appears that by and large the law falls within the four corners of the State List and entrenchment, if any, is purely incidental or inconsequential.
4. Where, however, a law made by the state Legislature on a subject covered by the Concurrent List is inconsistent with and repugnant to a previous law made by Parliament, then such a law can be protected by obtaining the assent of the President under Article 254 (2) of the Constitution. The result of obtaining the assent of the president would be that so far as the State Act is concerned, it will prevail in the State and overrule the provisions of the Central Act in their applicability to the State only. Such a state of affairs will exist only until Parliament may at any time make a law adding to, or amending, varying or repealing the law made by the State Legislature under the proviso to Article 254.

The Supreme Court in *M. Karunanidhi* v. *Union of India* (AIR 1979 SC 898) in a Constitution Bench summarized the test of repugnancy as follows:

1. That in order to decide the question of repugnancy it must be shown that the two enactments contain inconsistent and irreconcilable provisions, so that they cannot stand together or operate in the same field.
2. That there can be no repeal by implication unless the inconsistency appears on the face of the two statutes.
3. That where the two statutes occupy a particular field, but there is room or possibility of both the statutes operating in the same field without coming into collision with each other, no repugnancy results.

4. That where there is no inconsistency but a statute occupying the same field seeks to create distinct and separate offences, no question of repugnancy arises and both the statutes continue to operate in the same field.

The above rule of repugnancy is, however, subject to the exception provided in clause (2) of this Article. According to clause (2) if a State Law with respect to any of the matters enumerated in the Concurrent List contains any provision repugnant to the provisions of an earlier law made by Parliament, or an existing law with respect of that matter, then the State Law if it has been reserved for the assent of the President and has received his assent, shall prevail notwithstanding such repugnancy. But it would still be possible for the Parliament under the provision to clause (2) to override such a law by subsequently making a law on the same matter. If it makes such a law the State Law would be void to the extent of repugnancy with the Union Law.

* * *

2 The Industrial Disputes Act, 1947

The conflict between the employers and the employees is inherent in the industrial society. One argues for more investment opportunity and the other argues for better standard of living. There cannot be any rule or regulation through which such conflicting interests can be eliminated permanently. However, the Industrial Disputes Act was enacted to provide machinery and forum for the settlement of such conflicting and seemingly irreconcilable interests without disturbing the peace and harmony in industry in assuring industrial growth, which is a prerequisite of a welfare state. It has been rightly said that the Industrial Disputes Act is a piece of legislation calculated to ensure social justice to both employers and employees and advance progress of industry by bringing about harmony and cordial relationship between the parties. In the words of Krishna Iyer, J.:

> "The Industrial Disputes Act is a benign measure which seeks to pre-empt industrial tensions, provide energies of partners in production may not be dissipated in counter-productive battles and assurances of industrial justice may create a climate of goodwill."[1]

The Act aims at settlement of all industrial disputes arising between the capital and labour by peaceful method and through the machinery of conciliation, arbitration and, if necessary, by approaching the adjudication under the Act. After examining the salient provisions of the Act, S.K. Das, J., in *Workmen of Dimakuchi Tea Estate* v. *Dimakuchi Tea Estate*,[2] summed up the principal objects of the Act as follows:

1. Promotion of measures for securing and preserving amity and good relations between the employer and workmen;
2. An investigation and settlement of industrial disputes, between employers and employers, employers and workmen or workmen and workmen;
3. Prevention of illegal strike and lock-out;
4. Relief to workmen in the matter of lay-off and retrenchment; and
5. Collective bargaining.

The focus and emphasis given to each object, stated above, differs from industry to industry, depending on the growth of unionism, attitude of management and workers, leadership qualities and the Government policy. If adjudication finds favour with some industries, collective bargaining is preferred by some. Yet others opt for either conciliation or arbitration, and so on.

---

1. *Life Insurance Corporation* v. *D.J. Bahadur*, (1980) Lab.I.C. 1218 at p. 1226 (SC).
2. AIR 1958 SC 353.

Industrial Disputes Act has provided an elaborate machinery comprising the following agencies for the settlement of disputes.

1. Works Committee
2. Conciliation Officer
3. Boards of Conciliation
4. Courts of Inquiry
5. Labour Courts
6. Tribunals
7. National Tribunal
8. Grievance Settlement Authority
9. Voluntary Arbitration

The long title of the Act provides the object of the Act as follows:

An Act to make provision for the investigation and settlement of industrial disputes, and for certain other purposes. Whereas it is expedient to make provision for the investigation and settlement of industrial disputes, and for certain other purposes hereinafter appearing.

CHAPTER I

PRELIMINARY

SECTION 1: Short title, extent and commencement

(1) This Act may be called the Industrial Disputes Act, 1947.

(2) It extends to the whole of India.

(3) It shall come into force on the first day of April, 1947.

SECTION 2: Definitions

In this Act, unless there is anything repugnant in the subject or context,—

(a) **"appropriate Government"** means—

(i) in relation to any industrial disputes concerning any industry carried on by or under the authority of the Central Government, or by a railway company or concerning any such controlled industry as may be specified in this behalf by the Central Government or in relation to an industrial dispute concerning a Dock Labour Board established under section 5A of the Dock Workers (Regulation of Employment) Act, 1948 (9 of 1948), or the Industrial Finance Corporation of India Ltd. formed and registered under the Companies Act, 1956 (1 of 1956) or the Employees' State Insurance Corporation established under section 3 of the Employees' State Insurance Act, 1948 (34 of 1948), or the Board of Trustees constituted under section 3A of the Coal Mines Provident Fund and Miscellaneous Provisions Act, 1948 (46 of 1948), or the Central Board of Trustees and the State Boards of Trustees constituted under section 5A and section 5B, respectively, of the Employees' Provident Fund and Miscellaneous Provisions Act, 1952 (19 of 1952), or the Life Insurance Corporation of India established under section 3 of the Life Insurance Corporation Act, 1956 (31 of 1956), or the Oil and Natural Gas Corporation Ltd. registered under the Companies Act, 1956 (1 of 1956) or the Deposit Insurance and Credit Guarantee Corporation established under section 3 of the Deposit Insurance and Credit Guarantee Corporation Act, 1961 (47 of 1961), or the Central Warehousing Corporation established under section 3 of the Warehousing Corporations Act, 1962 (58 of 1962), or the Unit Trust of India established under section 3 of the Unit Trust of India Act, 1963 (52 of 1963), or the Food Corporation of India established under section 3, or a Board of Management established for two or more contiguous States under section 16, of the Food Corporations Act, 1964 (37 of 1964), or the Airports Authority of India constituted under section 3 of the Airports Authority of India Act, 1994 (55 of 1994) or a Regional Rural Bank established under section 3 of the Regional Rural Banks Act, 1976 (21 of 1976), or the Export Credit and Guarantee Corporation Limited or the Industrial Reconstruction Bank of India Ltd., the National Housing Bank established under section 3 of the National Housing Bank Act, 1987 (53 of 1987) or the Banking Service Commission established under section 3 of the Banking Service Commission Act, 1975, or an air transport service, or a banking or an insurance company, a mine, an oil-field, a Cantonment Board, or a major port, any company in which not less than fifty-one per cent of the paid-up share capital is held by the Central Government, or any corporation, not being a corporation referred to in this clause, established by or under any law made by Parliament, or the Central public sector undertaking, subsidiary companies set up by the principal undertaking and autonomous bodies owned or controlled by the Central Government, the Central Government, and

(ii) in relation to any other industrial dispute, including the State public sector undertaking, subsidiary companies set up by the principal undertaking and autonomous bodies owned or controlled by the State Government, the State Government:

Provided that in case of a dispute between a contractor and the contract labour employed through the contractor in any industrial establishment where such dispute first arose, the appropriate Government shall be the Central Government or the State Government, as the case may be, which has control over such industrial establishment;

(aa) **arbitrator** includes an umpire;

(aaa) **average pay** means the average of the wages payable to a workman—

(i) in the case of monthly paid workman, in the three complete calendar months,

(ii) in the case of weekly paid workman, in the four complete weeks,

(iii) in the case of daily paid workman, in the twelve full working days, preceding the date on which the average pay becomes payable if the workman had worked for three complete calendar months or four complete weeks or twelve full working days, as the case may be, and where such calculation cannot be made, the average pay shall be calculated as the average of the wages payable to a workman during the period he actually worked;

(b) **award** means an interim or a final determination of any industrial dispute or of any question relating thereto by any Labour Court, Industrial Tribunal or National Industrial Tribunal and includes an arbitration award made under section 10A;

(bb) **banking company** means a banking company as defined in section 5 of the Banking Companies Act, 1949 (10 of 1949), having branches or other establishments in more than one State, and includes the Export-Import Bank of India, the Industrial Reconstruction Bank of India, the Small Industries Development Bank of India established under section 3 of the Small Industries Development Bank of India Act, 1989 (39 of 1989), the Reserve Bank of India, the State Bank of India, a corresponding new bank constituted under section 3 of the Banking Companies (Acquisition and Transfer of Undertakings) Act, 1970 (5 of 1970) a corresponding new bank constituted under section 3 of the Banking Companies (Acquisition and Transfer of Undertakings) Act, 1980 (40 of 1980) and any subsidiary bank as defined in the State Bank of India (Subsidiary Banks) Act, 1959 (38 of 1959);

(c) **Board** means a Board of Conciliation constituted under this Act;

(cc) **closure** means the permanent closing down of a place of employment or part thereof;

(d) **conciliation officer** means a conciliation officer appointed under this Act;

(e) **conciliation proceeding** means any proceeding held by a conciliation officer or Board under this Act;

(ee) **controlled industry** means any industry the control of which by the Union has been declared by any Central Act to be expedient in the public interest;

(f) **Court** means a Court of Inquiry constituted under this Act;

(g) **employer** means—

(i) in relation to an industry carried on by or under the authority of any department of the Central Government or a State Government, the authority prescribed in this behalf, or where no authority is prescribed, the head of the department;

(ii) in relation to an industry carried on by or on behalf of a local authority, the chief executive officer of that authority;

(gg) **executive**, in relation to a trade union, means the body by whatever name called, to which the management of the affairs of the trade union is entrusted;

(i) a person shall be deemed to be **independent** for the purpose of his appointment as the chairman or other member of a Board, Court or Tribunal, if he is unconnected with the industrial dispute referred to such Board, Court or Tribunal or with any industry directly affected by such dispute:

Provided that no person shall cease to be independent by reason only of the fact that he is a shareholder of an incorporated company which is connected with, or likely to be affected by, such industrial dispute; but in such a case, he shall disclose to the appropriate Government the nature and extent of the shares held by him in such company;

(j) **industry** means any business, trade, undertaking, manufacture or calling of employers and includes any calling, service, employment, handicraft, or industrial occupation or avocation of workmen;

The definition of industry may be divided in two parts, i.e. substantive part and inclusive part. The first part of the definition provides the meaning of industry whereas the second part is included to the first part of the definition. The first part of the definition can be looked from the employer's point of view as the last two words used in the first part are 'of employers', and accordingly the second part of the definition can be looked from the workman's point of view as the last two words incorporated in the second part are 'of workman'. The Supreme Court in *Secretary Madras Gymkhana Club Employees' Union* v. *Management of the Gymkhana Club*[3] categorically observed that the definition of 'industry' is in two parts. In its first part, it means any business, trade, undertaking, manufacture or calling of employers. This part of the definition determines an industry by reference to occupation of employers in respect of certain activities. These activities are specified by five words and they determine what an industry is and what the cognate expression 'industrial' is intended to convey. This is the denotation of the term, or what the word denotes.

The second part views the matter from the angle of employees and is designed to include something more in what the term primarily denotes. By the second part of the definition, any calling, service, employment, handicraft, or industrial occupation or avocation of workmen is included in the concept of industry. This part gives the extended connotation.

If the activity can be described as an industry with reference to the occupation of the employers, the ambit of the industry under the force of the second part takes in the different kinds of activity of the employees mentioned in the second part. But the second part standing alone cannot define 'industry'. By the inclusive part of the definition, the labour force employed in an industry is made an integral part of the industry for purposes of industrial disputes although industry is ordinarily something which employers create or undertake. The words used in an inclusive definition denote extension and cannot be treated as restricted in any sense. Where the Courts are dealing with an inclusive definition, it would be inappropriate to put a restrictive interpretation upon terms of wider denotation.[4] In 1970, just after *Gymkhana Club* case where the Supreme Court held that *the definition of ' industry' is in two parts,* the Supreme Court in *Management of Safdarjung Hospital, New Delhi* v. *Kuldip Singh Sethi*[5] held that the first and second part of the definition are not to be read in isolation. They are two counterparts of the same industry.

They are two sides of the same coin.[6] The Supreme Court after referring to the definition of 'industry' in S. 4 of the Commonwealth Conciliation and Arbitration Act (1909–1910) (Acts Nos. 13 of 1904 and 7 of 1910) of Australia, observed in *Safdarjung Hospital* case as follows:

> "It is not necessary to view our definition in two parts. The definition read as a whole denotes a collective enterprise in which employers and employees are associated. It does not exist either by employers alone or by employees alone. It exists only when there is a relationship between employers and employees, the former engaged in business, trade, undertaking, manufacture or calling of employers and the latter engaged in any calling, service, employment, handicraft or industrial occupation or avocation. There must, therefore, be an enterprise in which the employers follow their avocations as detailed in the definition and employ workmen who follow one of the avocations detailed for workmen. The definition no doubt seeks to define 'industry' with reference to employers' occupation but includes the employees, for without the two there can be no industry. An industry is only to be found

3. AIR 1968 SC 554.
4. *State of Bombay* v. *Hospital Mazdoor Sabha,* AIR 1960 SC 610.
5. AIR 1970 SC 1407.
6. See, O.P. Malhotra's, *The Law of Industrial Disputes*, 6th ed., Vol. I, p. 133.

when there are employers and employees, the former relying upon the services of the latter to fulfill their own occupations."[7]

Analysis of the Definition

The first part of the definition refers to five activities, namely 'business', 'trade', 'undertaking', 'manufacture' or 'calling'. The expression 'business' is wider than the term 'trade.' Business means an enterprise which is an occupation as distinguished from pleasure.[8] The word 'trade' in this context in its primary sense means exchange of goods for goods or goods for money; and the secondary meaning may be any business carried on with a view to make profit, whether manual, or mercantile, as distinguished from the liberal arts or learned professions and from agriculture.[9] The word 'undertaking' is the most elastic. According to Webster's dictionary 'undertaking' means 'anything undertaken', or 'any business, work or project which one engages in or attempts, as an enterprise.' The word undertaking in the context of the definition has been understood to mean any business or any work or project which one engages in or attempts as an enterprise analogous to business or trade.[10] Manufacture is a kind of productive in which the making of articles or material, often on a large-scale, is by physical labour or mechanical power.[8] The word 'calling' is again a very wide word and it means one's usual occupation, avocation, business or trade.[11] Calling denotes the following of a profession or trade.[8] The second part of the definition refers to 'calling', 'service', 'employment', 'handicraft', or 'industrial occupation' or 'avocation'. The word 'calling' has been used in both the parts of the definition. In the first part, it refers to the employers whereas in the second part it refers to the workmen. The word service used in the second part of the definition is of a very wide import. The word 'employment' brings in the contract of service between the employer and the employee. The word 'handicraft' means any manual labour exercised by way of trade or for purpose of gain in or incidental to the making of any article or a part of any article. The word 'avocation' is a word of wide signification, meaning the way in which a man passes his life or spends his time. The word 'occupation' is a word of a still wider signification. In other words, what does not amount to avocation, may amount to an occupation. The word 'occupation' or 'avocation' is, however, qualified by the word 'industrial', which indicates that the 'occupation or avocation' in which the workmen are employed should be of an 'industrial character'.[12]

Is Municipal Corporation an Industry?

In 1953, the question came before the Supreme Court in *D.N. Banerji* v. *P.R. Mukherjee*[13] for consideration that whether the activities of the municipal corporation would fall within

7. *Ibid.* at p. 1412 per Hidayatullah, C.J.
8. *Secretary Madras Gymkhana Club Employees' Union* v. *Management of the Gymkhana Club*, AIR 1968 SC 554.
9. Halsbury's *Laws of England*, 3rd ed., Vol. 38, p. 8.
10. *D.N. Banerji* v. *P.R. Mukherjee*, AIR 1953 SC 58.
11. *State of Bombay* v. *Hospital Mazdoor Sabha*, AIR 1960 SC 610.
12. *See*, O.P. Malhotra's, *The Law of Industrial Disputes*, 6th ed., Vol. I, pp. 133–134.
13. AIR 1953 SC 58.

the ambit of the definition of industry. The Court held that in true sense the activities of the municipal corporation could not be brought within the scope of the expression 'business' or 'trade', however it may fall within the scope of the expression 'undertaking'. The Court posed a question and observed that if the public utility service is carried on by a corporation like a Municipality which is the creature of a statute, and which functions under the limitations imposed by the statute, does it cease to be an industry for this reason? The only ground on which one could say that what would amount to the carrying on of an industry if it is done by a private person ceases to be so if the same work is carried on by a local body like a Municipality is that in the latter, there is nothing like the investment of any capital or the existence of a profit-earning motive as there generally is in a business. But neither the one nor the other seems a *'sine qua non'* or necessary element in the modern conception of industry. The observations made by the Supreme Court in this case are that to constitute an industry, it is not necessary that there should be some amount of investment of capital or there must be a profit motive. In 1957, the Supreme Court in *Baroda Borough Municipality* v. *Its Workman*[14] reiterated the view of *D.N. Banerji* case, but travelled further by introducing a proposition, i.e. 'analogous to trade or business' and accordingly observed as follows:

> "It is now finally settled by the decision of this Court in *D.N. Banerji* v. *P.R. Mukherjee* (A) (supra) that a municipal undertaking of the nature, we have under consideration here is an 'industry' within the meaning of the definition of that word in S. 2(j) of the Industrial Disputes Act 1947, and that the expression 'industrial dispute' in that Act includes disputes between municipalities and their employees in branches of work that can be regarded as analogous to the carrying on of a trade or business."[15]

In 1960, in an appeal before the Supreme Court in *Corporation of the City of Nagpur* v. *Its employees*,[16] the question was raised as to whether and to what extent the activities of the Corporation of the City of Nagpur came under the definition of 'industry' in S. 2(14) of the C.P. and Berar Industrial Disputes Settlement Act, 1947. The Court, while considering the function of a municipality corporation observed that a corporation may discharge a dual function. It may be statutorily entrusted with regal functions strictly so-called, such as making of laws, disposal of certain cases judicially, etc., and also with other welfare activities. The former, being delegated regal functions, must be excluded from the ambit of the definition of 'industry'. Barring the regal functions of a municipality, if such other activities of it, if undertaken by an individual, would be industry, then they would equally be industry in the hands of a municipality. Accordingly, the following departments of the municipal corporation of the city of Nagpur were declared as industry and they are as follows: (i) Tax Department; (ii) Public Conveyance Department; (iii) Fire Brigade Department; (iv) Lighting Department; (v) Water Works Department; (vi) City Engineers Department; (vii) Enforcement (encroachment) Department; (viii) Sewage Department; (ix) Health Department; (x) Market Department; (xi) Public Gardens Department; (xii) Public Works Department; (xiii) Assessment Department; (xiv) Estate Department; (xv) Education Department; (xvi) Printing Press Department; (xvii) Building Department; and (xviii) General Administration Department.

14. AIR 1957 SC 110.
15. *Ibid.* at p. 113 per S.K. Das, J.
16. AIR 1960 SC 675.

The result of the discussion may be summarized as follows:

(1) The definition of 'industry' in the Act is very comprehensive. It is in two parts: one part defines it from the standpoint of the employer, and the other from the standpoint of the employee. If an activity falls under either part of the definition, it will be an industry within the meaning of the Act.

(2) The history of industrial disputes and the legislation recognizes the basic concept that the activity shall be an organized one and not that which pertains to private or personal employment.

(3) The regal functions described as primary and inalienable functions of State though statutorily delegated to a corporation are necessarily excluded from the purview of the definition. Such regal functions shall be confined to legislative power, administration of law and judicial power.

(4) If a service rendered by an individual or a private person would be an industry, it would equally be an industry in the hands of a corporation.

(5) If a service rendered by a corporation is an industry, the employees in the departments connected with that service, whether financial, administrative or executive, would be entitled to the benefits of the Act.

(6) If a department of a municipality discharges many functions, some pertaining to industry as defined in the Act and other non-industrial activities, the predominant functions of the department shall be the criterion for the purposes of the Act.

The above mentioned three cases were referred in 1978 in *Bangalore Water Supply and Sewerage Board* v. *A. Rajappa*[17] where seven judges exhaustively discussed the scope of 'industry' as defined in S. 2(j) of the Industrial Disputes Act, 1947. In *Bangalore Water Supply* case, a formula has been evolved, which is known as *Triple Test*, to determine whether a particular activity would fall within the scope of the definition of industry or not.

Is Hospital an Industry?

Due to conflicting judicial dictum as to whether a hospital is an industry or not, it is thought proper to analyze some cases in order to get a clear picture on the issue which came before the Supreme Court in 1960 in *State of Bombay* v. *Hospital Mazdoor Sabha*[18] for the first time. In considering the question as to whether the group of hospitals run by the appellant undoubtedly for the purpose of giving medical relief to the citizens and for helping to impart medical education are an undertaking or not, it would be pertinent to enquire whether an activity of a like nature would be an undertaking if it is carried on by a private citizen or a group of private citizens. There is no doubt that if a hospital is run by private citizens for profit, it would be an undertaking very much like the trade or business in their conventional sense. It has already been stated that the presence of profit motive is not essential for bringing an undertaking within S. 2(j). If that be so, then in case a private citizen runs a hospital without charging any fees from the patients treated in it, it would nevertheless be an undertaking under S. 2(j). Thus, the character of the activity involved in running a hospital brings the

17. AIR 1978 SC 548.
18. AIR 1960 SC 610.

institution of the hospital within S. 2(j). Does it make a difference that the hospital is run by the Government in the interpretation of the word 'undertaking' in S. 2(j)? The Court, while rejecting the argument, held that it is the character of the activity which decides the question as to whether the activity in question attracts the provision of S. 2(j) or not. It is immaterial as to who conducts the activity and whether it is conducted for profit or not.

The next question raised before the Court was that is *quid pro quo* necessary for bringing an activity under S. 2(j)? It has been urged before the Court that though profit motive may not be essential, it is nevertheless necessary that the person who carries on the activity should receive some consideration in return, and it is only if the test of *quid pro quo* is satisfied that an activity should be treated as an undertaking. Though this argument is put in a slightly different form in substance, it is really based on the idea that profit motive is necessary to make any activity an 'undertaking' analogous to trade or business. If the absence of profit motive is immaterial, why should an activity be excluded from S. 2(j) merely on the ground that the person responsible for the conduct of the activity expects no consideration and does not want any *quid pro quo* and is actuated by philanthropic or charitable motive? The Court held that in deciding the question as to whether any activity in question is an undertaking under S. 2(j), the doctrine of *quid pro quo* can have no application. Therefore, the Court finally held that the conduct and running of the group of hospitals by the appellant in the instant case amounted to an undertaking under S. 2(j).

In 1970, in *Management of Safdarjung Hospital* v. *Kuldip Singh Sethi,*[19] the *Hospital Mazdoor Sabha* case was overruled. In *Safdar Jung Hospital* case, the Court showed its dissatisfaction on the findings of the Supreme Court in *Hospital Mazdoor Sabha* case and accordingly observed that if a hospital, nursing home or dispensary is run as a business in a commercial way, elements of an industry may be found there. In that case the hospital is more than a place where persons can get treated for their ailment. It becomes a business. Hospitals run by the Government and even by private associations, not on commercial lines but on charitable lines or as part of the functions of Government Department of Health, cannot be included in the definition of industry. The first and the second parts of the definition are not to be read in isolation as if they were different industries but only as aspects of the occupation of employers and employees in an industry. They are two counterparts in one industry. In 1975, in *Dhanrajgirji Hospital* v. *The Workmen,*[20] where Dhanrajgirji Hospital, Sholapur was not carrying on any economic activity in the nature of trade or business. It was not rendering any material services by bringing in any element of trade or business in its activity.

The main activity of the hospital began by imparting training in general nursing and midwifery. There were quite a good number of trainees and the beds in the hospital were meant for their practical training. Even in the deed of trust, it was said that the hospital was to be maintained for the public of Sholapur and the trustees may do any and all other acts which might be beneficial for maintaining and running the said hospital to the best advantage of the public of Sholapur. Thus the Dhanrajgirji Hospital, Sholapur was not considered as an industry within the meaning of the Industrial Disputes Act. The Court in this case relied on the decision of *Safdarjung Hospital* case. It is important to note that both the cases, namely *Safdarjung Hospital* and *Dhanrajgirji Hospital* were overruled in *Bangalore Water Supply* case

19. AIR 1970 SC 1407.
20. AIR 1975 SC 2032.

in 1978. Further, it is interesting to note that in 1971 in *Management of Hospitals, Orissa* v. *Class IV Employees,*[21] the Supreme Court held that a hospital run by the Government as a part of its function is not an industry and further held that the mere fact that payment is accepted in respect of some beds cannot lead to the inference that the hospitals are run as a business in a commercial way. Primarily, hospitals are meant as free service by the Government to the patients without any profit motive. The Court applied the principle enunciated in *Safdarjung Hospital* case and observed as follows:

> "All these are institutions run by the Government and they are no more than places where persons can get treated. They are being run as a part of the function of the Government of Orissa and were being run as departments of Government. Consequently, the principle laid down in the *Safdarjung Hospital* case (1970) 1 SCC 735 (AIR 1970 SC 1407) (supra) is fully applicable and negatives the contention of the workmen that these references were competent."[22]

All the above discussions can be summarized as follows.

(a) Hospitals run by the Government as part of its sovereign functions with the sole object to provide free service to the patients are not industry.
(b) All other hospitals, either managed by private or public or for charitable purpose or for commercial purpose, would be an industry provided that they satisfy the requirements of Triple Test laid down in *Bangalore Water Supply* case in 1978.

Is Educational Institution an Industry?

In 1963 in *University of Delhi* v. *Ram Nath*[23] two appeals by special leave arose out of two petitions filed against the University of Delhi and Principal, Miranda House University College for Women (appellants 1 and 2) by two of their employees Ram Nath and Asgar Masih (respondents 1 and 2 respectively) under S. 33C(2) of the Industrial Dispute Act, 1947. The claim made by the two employees was mainly against appellant No. 1. Appellant No. 2, which was the University College for women, was run by appellant No. 1, and so, in substance, the claim made by the two employees was mainly against appellant No. 1.

Ram Nath's case was that he had been employed as driver by appellant No. 2 on Oct. 1, 1949. He was served with a notice on 1st May 1961 that since his services were no longer required, he would be discharged from his employment on payment of one month's salary in lieu of notice. Inevitably, the services of Ram Nath had to be retrenched, and so, there was no dispute of the fact that the retrenchment was genuine and there was no element of mala fides or unfair labour practice involved in it. It was also a common ground that if the employee is a workman within the meaning of the Act, and the work carried on by the appellants is an industry under S. 2(j). Section 25F has not been complied with and retrenchment amount payable under it had not been paid to the respondent. The petitions made by the respondent was resisted by appellant No. 1 on the preliminary ground that appellant No. 1 was not an employer under S. 2(g), and that the work carried on by it was not an industry under S. 2(j), and so, the application made under S. 33C(2) was incompetent. The Tribunal had rejected

21. AIR 1971 SC 1259.
22. *Ibid.* at p. 1261 per Bhargava, J.
23. AIR 1963 SC 1873.

this preliminary objections and having considered the merits, had passed an order in favour of the respondent directing the appellants to pay ₹1050 to the respondent, Ram Nath, as retrenchment compensation. It is the validity of this award that was challenged before the Supreme Court by the appellants, and the only ground on which the challenge was made is that the work carried on by appellant No. 1 is not an industry under S. 2(j).

The Supreme Court while reading Ss. 2(g), (j) and (s) together held that it is clear that the work of imparting education conducted by educational institutions like the University of Delhi and the college run by it is not an industry within the meaning of S. 2(j). It would be unreasonable to hold that educational institutions are employers within the meaning of S. 2(g), or that the work of teaching carried on by them is an industry because essentially the creation of a well-educated, healthy young generation imbued with a rational progressive outlook on life which is the sole aim of education, can in no case be compared or assimilated with what may be described as an industrial process. The Court further observed that education seeks to build up the personality of the pupil by assisting his physical, intellectual, moral and emotional development. To speak of this educational process in terms of industry sounds so completely incongruous that one is not surprised that the Act has deliberately so defined workmen under S. 2(s) as to exclude teachers from its scope. Hence it is clear that any problems connected with teachers and their salaries are outside the purview of the Act, and since the teachers form the sole class of employees with whose cooperation education is imparted by educational institutions, their exclusion from the purview of the Act necessarily corroborates the conclusion that education itself is not within its scope. It is true that like all educational institutions, the University of Delhi employed subordinate staff such as peons, drivers employed for driving college buses run for the convenience of the students, etc., and this subordinate staff does the work assigned to it; but in the main scheme of imparting education, this subordinate staff play such a minor, subordinate and insignificant part that it would be unreasonable to allow this work to lend its industrial colour to the principal activity of the University which is imparting education. The work of promoting education is carried on by the University and its teachers and if the teachers are excluded from the purview of the Act, it would be unreasonable to regard the work of imparting education as industry only because its minor, subsidiary and incidental work may seem to partake of the character of service which may fall under S. 2(j). However, *University of Delhi* v. *Ram Nath*[24] case has been overruled in *Bangalore Water Supply* case in 1978. The Court in this case categorically held that:

> "Our conclusion is that the University of Delhi (AIR 1963 SC 1873) case was wrongly decided and that education can be and is, in its institutional form, an industry."[25]

However, in 1961 in *Ahmedabad Textile Industry's Research Association* v. *State of Bombay*,[26] the Supreme Court observed that though it is difficult to state definitely or exhaustively the attributes which would make an activity an undertaking under S. 2(j), on the ground that it is analogous to trade or business, it can be said, as a working principle, that the manner in which the activity in question is organised or arranged, the condition of the

24. AIR 1963 SC 1873.
25. *Ibid.* at p. 584 per Krishna Iyer, J.
26. AIR 1961 SC 484.

cooperation between the employer and the employee is necessary for its success and its object to render material service to the community can be regarded as some of the features which are distinctive of activities to which S. 2(j) applies. Applying the above tests the Court held that the Ahmedabad Textile Industry's Research Association carries on an activity which clearly comes within the definition of the word 'industry' in S. 2(j), and which cannot be assimilated to a purely educational institution and hence when a dispute arises between it and some of its employees, it is an industrial dispute which could be properly referred for adjudication under the Act.

Is Club an Industry?

In 1968, in *Secretary Madras Gymkhana Club Employees' Union* v. *Management of the Gymkhana Club*[27] the Supreme Court had to consider whether a club was an industry. This case came before the Supreme Court on appeal by way of special leave as the Industrial Tribunal, Madras by its award, September 2, 1964 had held that the management of the Gymkhana Club, Madras was not liable to pay bonus to its workmen for the year 1962, as the Club was not 'an industry'. The Madras Gymkhana Club, which was admittedly a member's club and not a proprietary club, had, at the time of dispute, a membership of 1200. The object of the club was to provide a venue for sports and games and facilities for recreation and entertainment. As part of its latter activities, it arranged dance, dinner and other parties and ran a catering department, which provided food and refreshments not only generally but also for dinners and parties on special occasions. The club employed six officers, twenty clerks and a large number of peons, stewards, butlers, gate attendants, etc., in all 194 employees. The Supreme Court, while deciding the issue whether Madras Gymkhana Club was an industry or not, observed as follows:

> "Every human activity in which enters the relationship of employers and employees, is not necessarily creative of an industry. Personal services rendered by domestic and other servants, administrative services of public officials, service in aid of occupations of professional men, such as doctors and lawyers, etc., employment of teachers and so on may result in relationship in which there are employers on the one side and employees on the other but they must be excluded because they do not come within the denotation of the term 'industry'."[28]

Primarily, therefore, industrial disputes occur when the operation undertaken rests upon the cooperation between employers and employees with a view to production and distribution of material goods, in other words, wealth, but they may arise also in cases where the cooperation is to produce material services. The normal cases are those in which the production or distribution is of material goods or wealth and they will fall within the expression trade, business and manufacture. Hidayatullah, J. concluded:

> "... where the activity is to be considered as an industry, it must not be casual but must be distinctly systematic. The work for which labour of workmen is required, must be productive and the workmen must be following an employment, calling or industrial avocation. The salient fact in this context is that the workmen are not their own masters but render service at the behest of masters. This follows from the second part of the definition of industry.

---

27. AIR 1968 SC 554.
28. *Ibid.* at p. 562 per Hidayatullah, J.

> They again when private individuals are the employers, the industry is run with capital and with a view to profits. These two circumstances may not exist when Government or a local authority enter upon business, trade, manufacture or an undertaking analogous to trade."[29]

Accordingly, the Court held that the Madras Gymkhana Club being a members' club is not an industry.

In 1969, in *Cricket Club of India* v. *Bombay Labour Union*,[30] the question was whether the Cricket Club of India, Bombay was an "industry" within the meaning of S. 2(j) of the Industrial Disputes Act. The club was a members' club and not a proprietary club, though it was incorporated as a company under the Companies Act. At the relevant time, the Club had a membership of about 4800 and was employing 397 employees. The principal objects of the Club were to encourage and promote various sports, particularly the game of cricket in India and elsewhere, to lay out grounds for the game of cricket, and also to finance and assist in financing cricket matches and tournaments. In addition, it provided a venue for sports and games as well as facilities for recreation and entertainment for the members. It maintained tennis courts. The indoor games included billiards, table tennis, badminton and squash. It also maintained a swimming pool. The club had also provision for residence of members, for which purpose it had constructed 48 residential flats and 40 residential rooms, some of which were air-conditioned. Members occupying these residential flats and rooms were charged. There was also a Catering Department which provided food and refreshments for the members coming to the club as well as those residing in the residential portion, and it also made arrangements for dinners and parties for outside agencies on special occasions at the request of members. But such occasions were very few and were not such as to amount to a regular feature. The affairs of the club were managed by an Executive Committee and various honorary office bearers. Apart from all these, there were a certain number of buildings just outside the stadium which were let out for use as shops and offices by business concerns. The income that the club earned was primarily from these last mentioned constructions. There were life members, ordinary members, temporary members, service members and honorary members. Guests, both local and from outstation, were admitted only when they were introduced by a member. The club owned immovable properties of the value of about ₹67 lakhs from which an income in the range of about ₹4 lakhs a year accrued to the club. The other regular source of income was the subscription paid by each member. Entrance fees paid by the members were treated as a contribution to the capital of the club. In the cricket ground, which had a stadium attached to it, matches and various tournaments were held, including Test Matches between the Indian teams and foreign teams visiting India. On these occasions, public were admitted on tickets sold by the club. In the Catering Department alone, the turnover of the club was around ₹10 lakhs a year. Out of 397 employees, only 14 attended the three immovable properties consisting of the Club Chambers, North Stand Building, and Stadium House. As regards the buildings let out as shops and offices, there would be no need at all for the Club to maintain an employee-staff in order to look after those buildings so that it was likely that all the 14 employees, who attended the immovable properties, must be doing so primarily in order to look after the club buildings and the residential accommodation. Apart from members, no one was allowed to stay in the residential rooms and in exceptional cases, where some

29. *Ibid.* at pp. 563–564 per Hidayatullah, J.
30. AIR 1969 SC 276.

important visitors came to the club or competitors taking part in tournaments visited this place, they were permitted to stay in these residential rooms but in such cases, they were all made honorary members of the Club.

Provision for stall twice a year at the time of open badminton and table tennis tournaments, for providing snacks and soft drinks to competitors and spectators at concessional rates was not for the purpose of carrying on an activity of selling snacks and soft drinks to outsiders, but was really intended to provide facility to persons participating in or coming to watch the tournament in order that the tournaments may run successfully. These stalls were thus brought into existence as a part of the activity of promotion of games and was not a systematic activity for the purpose of carrying on transactions of sale of snacks and soft drinks to outsiders. The opening of stalls on two such occasions in a year with this limited object could not be held to be an undertaking of the nature of business or trade. The fact that the Club catered for functions of outside agencies on certain occasions, did not make it an industry, inasmuch as, these functions were arranged at the request of the members of the club from whom it realised the dues and who were responsible for payment to it. The Club thus in catering for such functions, was in fact catering for its members and was not at all intending to carry on an activity of providing the facility of catering at the instance of outsiders. Moreover, such functions did not form a systematic arrangement.

One of the principal objects of the club being promotion of the game of cricket in India, selling tickets to spectators for entry in the stadium at the time of test matches and selling a block of seats to organisations at concessional rates did not make this activity of the club an undertaking in the nature of trade or business. It was, in fact, an activity in the course of promotion of the game of cricket and it was incidental that the club was able to make an income on these few occasions which was later utilised for the purpose of fulfilling its other objects as incorporated in the Memorandum of Association. The holding of the Test matches was primarily organised by the club for the purpose of promoting the game of cricket. This activity by the club could not by itself, lead to the inference that the club was carrying on an industry. The income which accrued to the club from renting out buildings outside the stadium for the use of shops and offices of business concerns, could not be considered in considering the question whether the club was an industry, as this income could not be held to be the income that accrued to it with the aid and cooperation of the employees.

The circumstances of incorporation of the club as a limited company was not of importance. It was true that for purposes of contract law and for purposes of suing or being sued, the fact of incorporation made the club a separate legal entity, but the decision whether the club was an industry or not could not be based on such legal technicalities. What had to be seen was the nature of the activity in fact and in substance. Though the club was incorporated as a company, it was not like an ordinary company constituted for the purpose of carrying on business. There were no shareholders. No dividends were ever declared and no distribution of profits took place. Admission to the club was by payment of admission fee and not by purchase of shares. Even this admission was subject to balloting. The membership was not transferable like the right of shareholders. There was the provision for expulsion of a member under certain circumstances which feature never exists in the case of a shareholder holding shares in a Limited Company. The membership was fluid. A person retained rights as long as he continued as a member and got nothing at all when he ceased to be a member, even though he might have paid a large amount as admission fee. He even lost his rights on expulsion. In these circumstances, it was clear that the club could not be treated as a separate legal entity of the nature of a limited company carrying on business. The club, in fact, continued to be a members' club without any shareholders and, consequently, all services provided in the club for members had to be treated as activities of a self-serving institution.

Basing on above stated reasoning and applying the principle of *Madras Gymkhana Club* case, the Supreme Court held that the club was not an 'industry'. It was a self-service club. It was wrong to equate the catering facilities provided by the club to its members or their guests (members paying for that) with a hotel. The catering facility also was in the nature of a self-service by the club to its members. It is important to note that both the cases, namely *Madras Gymkhana Club* and *Cricket Club of India* were overruled in *Bangalore Water Supply* Case in 1978. Hence the club would be an industry after 1978.

Is Solicitor's Firm an Industry?

In 1962, in *National Union of Commercial Employees* v. *M.R. Meher, Industrial Tribunal, Bombay*,[31] the question whether a solicitor's firm is an industry or not came before the Supreme Court for consideration. The Court evolved a test to determine whether any activity amounts to industry and accordingly observed that the concept of industry postulates partnership between capital and labour or between the employer and his employees. It is under this partnership that the employer contributes his capital and the employees their labour and the joint contribution of capital and labour leads directly to the production which the industry has in view. In other words, the cooperation between capital and labour or between the employer and his employees, which is treated as a working test in determining whether any activity amounts to an industry, is the cooperation which is directly involved in the production of goods or in the rendering of service. It cannot be suggested that every form or aspect of human activity in which capital and labour cooperate or employer and employees assist each other is an industry. The distinguishing feature of an industry is that for the production of goods or for the rendering of service, cooperation between capital and labour or between the employer and his employees must be direct and must be essential. The Court held that a solicitor's firm carrying on the work of an attorney does not satisfy the test mentioned above and is not an 'industry' within the meaning of S. 2(j). There are different categories of servants employed by a firm, each category being assigned separate duties and functions. But it must be remembered that the service rendered by a solicitor functioning either individually or working together with partners is service which is essentially individual; depending upon the professional equipment, knowledge and efficiency of the solicitor concerned. Subsidiary work which is purely of an incidental type and which is intended to assist the solicitor in doing his job has no direct relation to the professional service ultimately rendered by the solicitor. The work of the clerk who types correspondence or that of the accountant who keeps accounts has no direct or essential nexus or connection with the advice which is the duty of the solicitor to give his client. There is no doubt, a kind of co-operation existing between the solicitor and his employees, but that cooperation has no direct or immediate relation to the professional service which the solicitor renders to his client. Looking at this question in a broad and general way,

31. AIR 1962 SC 1080.

it is not easy to conceive that a liberal profession like that of an attorney could have been intended by the Legislature to fall within the definition of 'industry' under S. 2(j).

The very concept of the liberal professions has its own special and distinctive features which do not readily permit the inclusion of the liberal professions into the four corners of industrial law. The essential basis of an industrial dispute is that it is a dispute arising between capital and labour in enterprises where capital and labour combine to produce commodities or to render service. This essential basis would be absent in the case of liberal professions. A person following a liberal profession does not carry on his profession in any intelligible sense with the active cooperation of his employees and the principal, if not the sole, capital which he brings into his profession is his special or peculiar intellectual and educational equipment. That is why on broad and general considerations which cannot be ignored, a liberal profession like that of an attorney must be deemed to be outside the purview of the definition of 'industry' under S. 2(j). The work of a solicitor is, in a loose sense, of course, business and so if the solicitors entered into an agreement in restraint of trade, its validity would have to be judged on the basis that their work is in the nature of business. That, however, is not relevant in determining the question as to whether the said work is an 'industry' under S. 2(j).

This case has been overruled in *Bangalore Water Supply* Case in 1978. Hence thereafter a solicitor's firm would be an industry.

Bangalore Water Supply Case

The Supreme Court decision of Seven Judges in *Bangalore Water Supply and Sewerage Board* v. *A. Rajappa*[32] has exhaustively discussed the scope of 'industry' as defined in S. 2(j) of the Industrial Disputes Act, 1947. It has overruled the following decisions mainly on the ground that the result of the decisions was to cut down the scope of 'industry' and they are as follows:

The *Management of Safdarjung Hospital* v. *Kuldip Singh Sethi;*[33] *Dhanrajgirji Hospital* v. *The Workmen;*[34] *National Union of Commercial Employees* v. *M.R. Meher, Industrial Tribunal, Bombay;*[35] *The University of Delhi and another* v. *Ram Nath;*[36] *Madras Gymkhana Club Employees' Union* v. *Management;*[37] *Cricket Club of India* v. *Bombay Labour Union and another.*[38]

Triple Test

Where there is

(i) a systematic activity,

32. AIR 1978 SC 548.
33. AIR 1970 SC 1407.
34. AIR 1975 SC 2032.
35. AIR 1962 SC 1080.
36. AIR 1963 SC 1873.
37. AIR 1968 SC 554.
38. AIR 1969 SC 276.

(ii) organized by the cooperation between the employer and the employee,

(iii) for the production and/or distribution of goods and services calculated to satisfy human wants and wishes, not spiritual nor religious wants.

The triple test is an indicator or may be a guideline to determine whether a particular organization or activity would be considered as an industry. Once the triple test is satisfied, without going further, one can safely draw the conclusion that the activity or organization in question is an industry. However, the triple test laid down in *Bangalore Water Supply* case is not free from ambiguity. If an organization satisfies conditions (i) and (ii) of the triple test and also produces certain goods or provides services only to satisfy human wants, then only it would be an industry. In other words, if an organization satisfies conditions (i) and (ii) of the triple test and also, produces certain goods or provides services to satisfy spiritual or religious wants, then it would not be an industry. But the question lies as to where to draw the line.

The Supreme Court in *Bangalore Water Supply* case laid down the following basic principles for necessary guidance.

(a) Absence of profit motive or gainful objective is irrelevant, be the venture in the public, joint, private or other sector.

(b) The true focus is functional and the decisive test is the nature of the activity with special emphasis on the employer-employee relations.

(c) If the organization is a trade or business, it does not cease to be one because of philanthrophy animating the undertaking.

(d) If in a pious or altruistic mission many employ themselves, free or for small honoraria or like return, mainly drawn by sharing in the purpose or cause, such as lawyers volunteering to run a free legal services clinic, or doctors serving in their spare hours in a free medical center or ashramites working at the bidding of the holiness, divinity or like central personality, and the services are supplied free or at nominal cost and those who serve are not engaged for remuneration or on the basis of master and servant relationship, then, the institution is not an industry even if stray servants, manual or technical, are hired. Such eleemosynary or like undertakings alone are exempted—not other generosity, compassion, developmental passion or project.

The Dominant Nature Test

(i) Where a complex of activities, some of which qualify for exemption, others not, involve employees on the total undertaking, some of whom are not 'workmen' as in the *University of Delhi* case or some departments are not productive of goods and services if isolated, even then, the predominant nature of the services and the integrated nature of the departments as explained in the *Corporation of Nagpur* case will be the true test. The whole undertaking will be 'industry' although those who are not 'workmen' by definition may not be benefitted by the status.

(ii) Notwithstanding the previous clauses, sovereign functions, strictly understood, (alone) qualify for exemption, not the welfare activities or economic adventures undertaken by Government or statutory bodies.

(iii) Even in departments discharging sovereign functions, if there are units which are industries and they are substantially severable, then they can be considered to come within S. 2(j).

(iv) Constitutional and competently enacted legislative provisions may well remove from the scope of the Act categories which otherwise may be covered thereby.

Application of noscitur a sociis

If birds of a feather flock together and *noscitur a sociis* is a commonsense guide to construction, 'undertaking' must be read down to conform to the restrictive characteristic shared by the society of words before and after. Nobody will torture 'undertaking' in S. 2(j) to mean meditation or *musheira* which are spiritual and aesthetic undertakings. Wide meanings must fall in line and discordance must be excluded from a sound system.

1982 Amended definition

Substituted by The Industrial Disputes (Amendment) Act, 1982. But this amended definition has not yet been enforced.

Section 2(j): '*industry*' means any systematic activity carried on by cooperation between an employer and his workmen (whether such workmen are employed by such employer directly or by or through any agency, including a contractor) for the production, supply or distribution of goods or services with a view to satisfy human wants or wishes (not being wants or wishes which are merely spiritual or religious in nature), whether or not,—

(i) any capital has been invested for the purpose of carrying on such activity; or

(ii) such activity is carried on with a motive to make any gain or profit, and includes—

(a) any activity of the Dock Labour Board established under section 5A of the Dock Workers (Regulation of Employment) Act, 1948 (9 of 1948);

(b) any activity relating to the promotion of sales or business or both carried on by an establishment.

but does not include—

1. any agricultural operation except where such agricultural operation is carried on in an integrated manner with any other activity (being any such activity as is referred to in the foregoing provisions of this clause) and such other activity is the predominant one.

Explanation: For the purposes of this sub-clause, "agricultural operation" does not include any activity carried on in a plantation as defined in Cl. (f) of section 2 of the Plantations Labour Act, 1951 (69 of 1951); or

2. hospitals or dispensaries; or
3. educational, scientific, research or training institutions; or
4. institutions owned or managed by organisations wholly or substantially engaged in any charitable, social or philanthropic service; or
5. khadi or village industries; or

6. any activity of the Government relatable to the sovereign functions of the Government including all the activities carried on by the departments of the Central Government dealing with defence research, atomic energy and space; or
7. any domestic service; or
8. any activity, being a profession practised by an individual or body or individuals, if the number of persons employed by the individuals or body of individuals in relation to such profession is less than ten; or
9. any activity, being an activity carried on by a cooperative society or a club or any other like body of individuals, if the number of persons employed by the co-operative society, club or other like body of individuals in relation to such activity is less than ten.

The amended definition may be divided into three parts, i.e. (a) substantive part; (b) inclusive part; and (c) exclusive part.

Substantive Part

The substantive part is the first para of the definition which provides the meaning of industry, i.e. 'industry' means any systematic activity carried on by cooperation between an employer and his workmen (whether such workmen are employed by such employer directly or by or through any agency, including a contractor) for the production, supply or distribution of goods or services with a view to satisfy human wants or wishes (not being wants or wishes which are merely spiritual or religious in nature), whether or not,—

(i) any capital has been invested for the purpose of carrying on such activity; or
(ii) such activity is carried on with a motive to make any gain or profit.

After a careful perusal of the decision of the *Bangalore Water Supply* case, it is seen that the substantive part of the amended definition is just copied from the Triple Test laid down in *Bangalore Water Supply* case which was decided in 1978. The Parliament amended the definition of industry in 1982, but without applying its mind, because what has been said by His Lordship, Krishna Iyer, J. in *Bangalore Water Supply* case in 1978 is placed as such in the amended definition of industry.

Inclusive Part

Two activities are included in the amended definition in an inclusive manner and they are as follows:

(a) any activity of the Dock Labour Board established under section 5A of the Dock Workers (Regulation of Employment) Act, 1948 (9 of 1948);
(b) any activity relating to the promotion of sales or business or both carried on by an establishment.

Exclusive Part

Many activities are excluded from the ambit of the definition of industry in 1982 amendment. It is interesting to note that the activities which are declared to be industry, such as hospital, educational institution, club etc. in the *Bangalore Water Supply* case in 1978, have been placed outside the purview of the definition of industry. The intention of the Parliament seems to nullify the decision of the *Bangalore Water Supply* case or to show its dominant power over the Supreme Court.

The amended definition has not been enforced so far. So, the definition provided in the Act is the law at present and the *Bangalore Water Supply* case holds its position intact and the view given by the Supreme Court in *Bangalore Water Supply* case is the law for the country. It is pertinent to mention the view of the Supreme Court in 1998 in *Coir Board, Ernakulam, Cochin* v. *Indira Devi P.S.*,[39] where Mrs. Sujata V. Manohar, J. categorically observed looking to the uncertainty prevailing in this area and in the light of the experience of the last two decades in applying the test laid down in *Bangalore Water Supply* case. Therefore it is necessary that the decision be re-examined. The experience of the last two decades does not appear to be entirely happy. Instead of leading to industrial peace and welfare of the community (which was the avowed purpose of artificially extending the definition of industry), the application of the Industrial Disputes Act to organisations which were, quite possibly, not intended to be so covered by the machinery set up under the Industrial Disputes Act, might have done more damages than good, not merely to the organisations but also to the employees by the curtailment of employment opportunities. The sweeping test propounded in *Bangalore Water Supply* case that every organisation which does useful service and employs people can be labelled as industry is not contemplated by the Act. Matter was directed to be placed before the Hon'ble Chief Justice of India to consider whether a larger Bench should be constituted to re-consider the decision in *Bangalore Water Supply and Sewerage Board* case.

In 2002, in *Union of India* v. *Shree Gajanan Maharaja Sansthan,*[40] an important issue came before the Supreme Court for its consideration as to whether the writ of *mandamus* can be issued against the Government, compelling it to give effect to the Industrial Disputes (Amendment) Act, 1982. The Court held that there may be a practical difficulty on the part of the Government in the enforcement of laws and those difficulties cannot be foreseen when the law is passed. It is, therefore, necessary to leave the judgment to the executive as to when the law should be brought into force. When enforcement of a provision in a statute is left to the discretion of the Government without laying down any objective standards, no writ of mandamus could be issued directing the Government to consider the question whether the provision should be brought into force and when it can do so. Delay in implementing the will of the Parliament may, certainly draw adverse criticism, but it is the domain of the Government to decide when to enforce the Amendment Act.

Bangalore Water Supply Case and Thereafter

The Supreme Court has applied the Triple Test in the following cases to determine whether a particular organization or activity is an industry or not. However, it is not exhaustive, rather only illustrative. In 1979, in *Swaraj Ashram, M/s. Kanpur* v. *Industrial Tribunal (III) U.P.*,

39. AIR 1998 SC 2801.
40. 2002 (93) FLR 1200 (SC).

Kanpur,[41] it was held that Swaraj Ashram Servodaya Nagar, Kanpur is an 'industry' in the light of the decision of *Bangalore Water Supply* case. In the same year, in *Avon Services Production Agencies (P) Ltd., M/s.* v. *Industrial Tribunal, Haryana,*[42] the question came before the Supreme Court for consideration whether painting section of a factory would fall within the concept of 'undertaking' in order to constitute an industry as per S. 2(j) of the Act. The Court relied on *Bangalore Water Supply* case and observed that the expression, 'undertaking' is not defined in the Act. It finds its place in the definition of the expression 'industry' in S. 2(j). While ascertaining the amplitude of the expression 'undertaking' in the definition of 'industry', *noscitur a sociis* canon of construction is to be invoked and a restricted meaning has to be assigned to it. While thus reading down the expression, in the context of S. 25FFF it must mean a separate and distinct business or a commercial or trading or industrial activity. It cannot comprehend an infinitesimally small part of a manufacturing process. Accordingly, it was held that the painting section of a factory is not an 'undertaking' and therefore, in consequence, not an industry.

In 1986 in *Gopal* v. *Administrative Officer, Madhya Pradesh Khadi and Village Industries Board,*[43] the M.P. Khadi and Village Industries Board was held to be an 'industry' within the meaning of S. 2(19) of the M.P. Industrial Relations Act (1960), which reads as follows:

"Industry means—

(a) any business, trade, manufacture, undertaking or calling of employers;

(b) any calling, service, employment, handicraft or industrial occupation or avocation of employees; and includes—

(i) agriculture and agricultural operations;

(ii) any branch of any industry or group of industries which the State Government may, by notification, declare to be an industry for the purposes of this Act."

One of the functions of the Board was 'to support, encourage, assist and carry on Khadi and Village Industries and in the matters incidental to such trade or business'. What the Board did was to supply raw wool to Cooperative Societies, so that Societies could engage themselves in useful work. The Societies after weaving raw wool, converted it into spun blankets and supplied them to the Board. The blankets so spun were not the properties of the Societies. The Society could not sell the goods prepared out of the wool supplied by the Board to anybody else. They had to be given back to the Board. The blankets so supplied from various centres to the Board, had necessarily to be sold in the open market. This act of sale would clearly come within the definition of the word 'trade' or 'business' as contemplated in S. 2(19) of the M.P. Industrial Relations (1960) Act. In 1988 in *A. Sundarambal* v. *Govt. of Goa, Daman and Diu,*[44] the Supreme Court held that a teacher employed in a school does not fall within the definition of the expression 'workman', though the school is an industry in view of the definition of 'workman' as it now stands. Therefore, when the service of the teacher is terminated, it cannot be referred under S. 10 of the Act. The teachers employed by educational institutions, whether the said institutions are imparting primary, secondary,

41. AIR 1979 SC 1210.
42. AIR 1979 SC 170.
43. AIR 1986 SC 504.
44. AIR 1988 SC 1700.

graduate or postgraduate education, cannot be called 'workmen' within the meaning of S. 2(s) of the Act. Imparting of education which is the main function of teachers cannot be considered as skilled or unskilled manual work or supervisory work or technical work or clerical work. Imparting of education is in the nature of a mission or a noble vocation. A teacher educates children, moulds their character, builds up their personality and makes them fit to become responsible citizens. Children grow under the care of teachers. The clerical work done by them, if any, is only incidental to their principal work of teaching.

In 1988, the Supreme Court seemed to be critical and too much concerned about the enforcement of 1982 amendment, which provides *inter alia* the definition of 'industry'.

In *Des Raj* v. *State of Punjab,*[45] the Supreme Court relied on the dominant nature test evolved by Krishna Iyer, J., in *Bangalore Water Supply* case and held that the irrigation department of Government clearly come within the ambit of 'industry'. The Court seemed too much concerned about the non-implementation of the amended definition and showed its inclination for its immediate effect. The Court observed as follows:

> "We have not been able to gather as to why even six years after the amendment has been brought to the definition of industry in S. 2(j) of the Act, the same has not been brought into force. This Court on more than one occasion has indicated that the position should be clarified by an appropriate amendment and when keeping in view the opinion of this Court, the law was sought to be amended, it is appropriate that the same should be brought into force as such or with such further alterations as may be considered necessary, and the legislative view of the matter is made known and the confusion in the field is cleared up."[46]

In 1990 in *Karnani Properties Ltd.* v. *State of W.B.*,[47] a company engaged in the business of real estate had rented several flats in buildings owned by it. The company also rendered to the tenants services like arrangements for supply of water, free supply of electricity, washing and cleaning floors, lift services, electric repairs and replacements, sanitary repairs. For offering these services to the tenants, the company had employed a number of workmen and these services which undoubtedly conferred material benefits on the tenants and constituted material services, were rendered by the employees. Activity carried on by the company was undoubtedly not casual and was distinctly systematic and for profit earning. Therefore, the Supreme Court held that the activity carried on by the company fell within the ambit of the expression 'industry' defined in S. 2(j). In 1996 in *Chief Conservator of Forests* v. *Jagannath Maruti Kondhare,*[48] the question before the Supreme Court was whether the Forest Department of the State Government was an 'Industry' within the meaning of S. 2(j) of the Industrial Disputes Act, 1947 which definition has been adopted by the Maharashtra Recognition of Trade Unions and Prevention of Unfair Labour Practices Act, 1971. The Court held that Forest Dept. of State Government is an industry as the scheme (Panchgaon Parwati Scheme) framed by it intended to fulfill recreational and educational aspirations of the public and it also undertook social forestry work meant for preservation of forests and environment. The work undertaken, as stated above, by the Department cannot be regarded as a part of

45. AIR 1988 SC 1182.
46. *Ibid.* at p. 1193 per Ranganath Misra, J.
47. AIR 1990 SC 2047.
48. AIR 1996 SC 2898.

sovereign function of the State, hence the Forest Department falls within the ambit of S. 2(j) of the Act.

Again in *Sub-Divisional Inspector of Post. Vaikam* v. *Theyyam Joseph*,[49] the Supreme Court observed that the welfare measures partake of the character of sovereign functions and the traditional duty to maintain law and order is no longer the concept of the State. The Directive Principles of State policy enjoin on the State diverse duties under Part IV of the Constitution and the performance of the duties is a constitutional function. One of the duties of the State is to provide telecommunication service to the general public as an amenity, and so is one essential part of the sovereign functions of the State as a welfare State. Postal and Telecommunication Departments are not, therefore, industry. The same view has been taken by the Supreme Court in 1997 in *Bombay Telephone Canteen Employees' Association* v. *Union of India*[50] and reiterated the position by holding that Telephone Nigam is not an industry. It is important to note that both the cases have been overruled in 1998 in *General Manager, Telecom* v. *S. Srinivasa Rao*[51] where the Supreme Court observed that a two-Judge Bench of the Supreme Court in *Theyyam Joseph* case held that the functions of the Postal Department are part of the sovereign functions of the State and it is, therefore, not an 'industry' within the definition of S. 2(j) of the Industrial Disputes Act, 1947. Incidentally, this decision was rendered without any reference to the seven-Judge Bench decision in *Bangalore Water Supply* case. In a later two-Judge Bench decision in *Bombay Telephone Canteen Employees' Association* case, *Theyyam Joseph*'s decision was followed for taking the view that the Telephone Nigam is not an 'industry'. Reliance was placed in *Theyyam Joseph*'s case for that view. However, in *Bombay Telephone Canteen Employees' Association* case (i.e. the latter decision), a reference to the *Bangalore Water Supply* case is made. After referring to the decision in Bangalore Water Supply, it was observed that if the doctrine enunciated in Bangalore Water Supply is strictly applied, the consequences is 'catastrophic'. With due respect to the Honorable Court, the author is unable to accept this view due to simple reason that it is in direct conflict with the seven-Judge Bench decision in *Bangalore Water Supply* case. It is needless to say that it is not permissible for the Court having any Bench of lesser strength, to take a view contrary to that in Bangalore Water Supply which was decided by the seven-Judge Bench or to bypass that decision so long as it holds the field. Judicial discipline requires that smaller Bench has to respect and follow the decision of larger Bench. In the light of the above discussions, it is submitted that the decision in *Theyyam Joseph* case, and *Bombay Telephone Canteen Employees' Association* case cannot be treated as correct law. This being the position, both the cases have been overruled by the three-Judge Bench of the Supreme Court in *General Manager, Telecom* case as aforesaid.

The question raised in the appeal in *Agricultural Produce Market Committee* v. *Ashok Harikuni*[52] has been drawing the attention of the Supreme Court since the enactment of the Industrial Disputes Act, 1947 and even after the passage of more than 50 years, the issue remains as fertile as ever because of the wide, vaporous definition of the word 'industry' under the said Act. This wide definition has given an opportunity to both the employer and the

---

49. AIR 1996 SC 1271.
50. AIR 1997 SC 2817.
51. AIR 1998 SC 656.
52. AIR 2000 SC 3116.

employee for raising issues, one trying to pull out of this definition, to be out of the clutches of the said Act, the other bringing within it, to receive benefit under it. There is a tug of war repeatedly between the two, in spite of various decisions of the Apex Court. The question raised in this appeal was:

Whether the appellant, an Agricultural Produce Market Committee, established under the Karnataka Agricultural Produce Marketing (Regulation) Act, 1966, is an 'industry' as contemplated under the Industrial Disputes Act, 1947.

The total argument is confined within the concept of 'sovereign function' of the committee in question. Therefore, it is thought proper to discuss what constitutes a 'sovereign function' in today's scenario. The argument is based on 'sovereign function' because 'sovereign functions', as held in *Bangalore Water-Supply* case, could be exempted from the ambit of the definition of industry. The Court observed that sovereign function in the new sense may have very wide ramifications, but essentially sovereign functions are primary inalienable functions which only State could exercise. Thus, various functions of the State may be the ramifications of 'sovereignty', but they all cannot be construed as primary inalienable functions.

Broadly, it is taxation, eminent domain and police power which covers its field. It may cover its legislative functions, administration of law, eminent domain, maintenance of law and order, internal and external security, grant of pardon. So, the dichotomy between sovereign and non-sovereign function could be found by finding which of the functions of the State could be undertaken by any private person or body. The one which could be undertaken by a private person cannot be a sovereign function. In a given case, even in subject on which the State has the monopoly may also be non-sovereign in nature. Mere dealing in subject of monopoly of the State would not make any such enterprise sovereign in nature. Absence of profit-making or mere quid pro would also not make such enterprise to be outside the ambit of 'industry'. The question whether a function is sovereign or non-sovereign depends on the nature of power and the manner of its exercise. What is approved to be 'sovereign' is defence of the country, raising armed forces, making peace or war, foreign affairs, power to acquire and retain territory. These are not amenable to the jurisdiction of ordinary Civil Courts. The other functions of the State including welfare activity of State could not be construed as 'sovereign' exercise of power. Hence, every governmental function need not be 'sovereign'. State activities are multifarious. From the primal sovereign power, which exclusively inalienably could be exercised by the Sovereign alone, whereas all the welfare activities of the State can be undertaken by any private person. Even if a statute confers on any statutory body any function, which could be construed to be 'sovereign' in nature, would not mean every other function under the same statute to be also sovereign. The Court should examine the statute to distinguish one from the other by comprehensively examining the various provisions of that statute. In interpreting any statute to find if it is an 'industry' or not, the Court has to find its pith and substance. That is why Courts have been defining 'industry' in the widest permissible limits and 'sovereign' functioning within its limited orbit. The Court accordingly held that in view of the preamble, objects and reasons and the scheme of the Act, the predominant object clearly being regulation and control of trading of agricultural produce, the appellant-committee including its functionaries cannot be said to be performing functions which are sovereign in character. Most of its functions could be undertaken even by private persons. Thus, the appellant would fall within the definition of 'industry' under S. 2(j) of the Industrial Disputes Act.

In 2001, in *Bharat Bhawan Trust* v. *Bharat Bhawan Artists Association*,[53] the Supreme Court held that the Bharat Bhawan Trust is an institution engaged in the promotion of art and culture. Production of plays, which is the main activity of the institution, in fact, is not a systematic activity resulting in some kind of services or goods. Therefore, such institution cannot be classified as an 'industry'. Artists employed by the institution engaged in the production of drama or in theatre management do not indulge in any manual, unskilled or other kinds of work, mentioned in the definition of workman under S. 2(s) of the Act. Therefore, artists employed by such institution are not workmen. In 2002, in *MGT of Som Vihar A.O.H.M. Socy Ltd.* v. *Workmen C/o. I.E. and G. Mazdoor*,[54] the Supreme Court observed that the decision in *Bangalore Water Supply* case, if correctly understood, is not an authority for the proposition that domestic servants are also to be treated to be workmen even when they carry on work in respect of one or many masters. It is clear that when personal services are rendered to the members of a society and that society is constituted only for the purposes of those members to engage the services of such employees, such activity of that society should not be treated as an industry.

(k) **industrial dispute** means any dispute or difference between employers and employers or between employers and workmen, or between workmen and workmen, which is connected with the employment or non-employment or the terms of employment or with the conditions of labour, of any persons.

The definition of 'industrial dispute' in S. 2(k) requires three things:

(i) There should be a dispute or difference.

(ii) The dispute or difference should be between employers and employers, or between employers and workmen, or between workmen and workmen.

(iii) The dispute or difference must be connected with the employment or non-employment or the terms of employment or with the conditions of labour, of any person.

The first part thus refers to the factum of a real and substantial dispute, the second part to the parties to the dispute and the third to the subject matter of the dispute.[55] The Supreme Court had an occasion to interpret the expression *'any person'* used in S. 2(k) of the Act in *Workmen of Dimakuchi Tea Estate* v. *Management of Dimakuchi Tea Estate*.[56] It observed that having regard to the scheme and objects of the Act and its other provisions, the expression *'any person'* in S. 2(k) of the Act must be read subject to such limitations and qualifications as arise from the context; the two crucial limitations are: (i) the dispute must be a real dispute between the parties to the dispute (as indicated in the first two parts of the definition clause) so as to be capable of settlement or adjudication by one party to the dispute giving necessary relief to the other, and (ii) the person regarding whom the dispute is raised must be one in whose employment, non-employment, terms of employment, or conditions of labour (as the case may be) the parties to the dispute have a direct or substantial interest. In the absence of such interest, the dispute cannot be said to be a real dispute between the parties. Where the workmen raise a dispute as against their employer, the person regarding

53. AIR 2001 SC 3348.
54. AIR 2002 SC 2530.
55. *Standard-Vacuum Refining Co. of India Ltd.* v. *Their Workmen,* AIR 1960 SC 948.
56. AIR 1958 SC 353.

whose employment, non-employment, terms of employment or conditions of labour the dispute is raised need not be, strictly speaking, a 'workman' within the meaning of the Act, but must be one in whose employment, non-employment, terms of employment or conditions of labour, the workmen as a class have a direct or substantial interest. In the present case, the person was not a workman as he belonged to the medical or technical staff, which was altogether different from the category of workmen, and the workmen of the establishment had neither direct nor substantial interest in his employment or non-employment. Thus it cannot be said, even assuming that he was a member of the same Trade Union, that the dispute regarding his termination of service was an industrial dispute within the meaning of S. 2(k) of the Act.

(ka) **industrial establishment or undertaking** means an establishment or undertaking in which any industry is carried on:

Provided that where several activities are carried on in an establishment or undertaking and only one or some of such activities is or are an industry or industries, then,—

(a) if any unit of such establishment or undertaking carrying on any activity, being an industry, is severable from the other unit or units of such establishment or undertaking, such unit shall be deemed to be a separate industrial establishment or undertaking;

(b) if the predominant activity or each of the predominant activities carried on in such establishment or undertaking or any unit thereof is an industry and the other activity or each of the other activities carried on in such establishment or undertaking or unit thereof is not severable from and is, for the purpose of carrying on, or aiding the carrying on of, such predominant activity or activities, the entire establishment or undertaking or, as the case may be, unit thereof shall be deemed to be an industrial establishment or undertaking.

(kk) **insurance company** means an insurance company as defined in S. 2 of the Insurance Act, 1938 (4 of 1938), having branches or other establishments in more than one State.

(kka) **khadi** has the meaning assigned to it in Cl. (d) of S. 2 of the Khadi and Village Industries Commission Act, 1956 (61 of 1956).

(kkb) **Labour Court** means a Labour Court constituted under S. 7.

(kkk) **lay-off** (with its grammatical variations and cognate expressions) means the failure, refusal or inability of an employer on account of shortage of coal, power or raw materials or the accumulation of stocks or the breakdown of machinery or natural calamity or for any other connected reason to give employment to a workman whose name is borne on the muster-rolls of his industrial establishment and who has not been retrenched.

Explanation: Every workman whose name is borne on the muster-rolls of the industrial establishment and who presents himself for work at the establishment at the time appointed for the purpose during normal working hours on any day and is not given employment by the employer within two hours of his so presenting himself, shall be deemed to have been laid-off for that day within the meaning of this clause: Provided that if the workman, instead of being given employment at the commencement of any shift for any day, is asked to present himself for the purpose during the second half of the shift for the day and is given employment, then, he shall be deemed to have been laid-off only for one-half of that day.

Provided further that if he is not given any such employment even after so presenting himself, he shall not be deemed to have been laid-off for the second half of the shift for the day and shall be entitled to full basic wages and dearness allowance for that part of the day;

According to the dictionary meaning, lay-off means to discontinue work or activity, to dismiss or discharge temporarily. When workers are in employment and they are laid off, that immediately results in their unemployment, howsoever, temporary.

After reading the definition of 'lay-off' given in S. 2(kkk) carefully, it is clear that the unemployment of the workman, either for a whole day or part thereof, is not his own creation. It is independent of any action or reaction on the part of the workman himself. Section 2(kkk) defines a lay-off as meaning the failure, refusal or inability on the part of an employer on account of shortage of coal, power or raw materials or the accumulation of stocks or the breakdown of machinery or natural calamity or for any other connected reason to give employment to a workman whose name is borne on the muster-rolls of his industrial establishment and who has not been retrenched. It is clear that the lay-off takes place for one or more of the reasons specified in the definition. Lay-off may be due to shortage of coal or shortage of power or shortage of raw materials or accumulation of stocks or breakdown of machinery or any other reason. 'Any other reason' to which the definition refers must be a reason which is allied or analogous to the reasons already specified. It has been held in *Management of Kairbetta Estate* v. *Rajamanickam*[57] that *'any other reason'* must be similar to the preceding reasons specified in the definition. The Supreme Court interpreted the phrase *'any other reason'* by applying the principle of *ejusdem generis.*

The principle underlying *ejusdem generis* is applied when the statutory provision concerned contains an enumeration of specific words, the subject of the enumeration thereby constituting a class or category but which class or category is not exhausted at the same time by the enumeration and the general term follows the enumeration with no specific indication of any different legislative intention. This rule, which normally envisages words of general nature following specific and particular words to be construed as limited to things which are of the same nature as those specified, also requires to be applied with great caution and not pushed too far so as to unduly or unnecessarily limit general and comprehensive words to dwarf size. De hors the doctrine or maxim concerned useful in the matter of construction of a statute or its provisions, the intent of the legislature cannot altogether be ignored and a construction which really subserves the purpose of the enactment must only be adopted than one which will defeat it and thereby ensure in the process that no part of the provision is rendered surplus or otiose.[58]

Relevant Provisions Relating to Lay-off

It is advisable to read the definition of 'lay-off' along with the other relevant provisions provided in the Industrial Disputes Act for better clarity and understanding. Therefore, one

57. AIR 1960 SC 893.
58. *Municipal Corporation of Greater Bombay* v. *BPCL,* AIR 2002 SC 1638.

has to read Ss. 2(kkk), 25-C, 25-E, 25-M and 25-B in the first instance. Section 25-B is having no direct relevancy to the concept of 'lay-off'; however, it provides the meaning of 'continuous service' and therefore it helps the reader to know the meaning of 'continuous service' while reading S. 25-C of the Act. Furthermore, one has to refer to S. 25L to know the meaning of 'industrial establishment' because the very word can be found while reading S. 25M of the Act.

In *Workmen of M/s. Firestone Tyre and Rubber Co. of India (P) Ltd.* v. *Firestone Tyre and Rubber Co.* (AIR 1976 SC 1775) where Firestone Tyre and Rubber Co, the respondent in this appeal, has its Head Office at Bombay. It manufactures tyres at its Bombay factory and sells the tyres and other accessories in the markets throughout the country. There was a strike in the Bombay factory from 3rd March, 1967 to 16th May, 1967 and again from 4th October, 1967. As a result of the strike, there was a short supply of tyres. There were 30 employees at the relevant time. 17 workmen out of 30 were laid-off by the management as per their notice dated the 3rd February, 1968 which reads as follows:

> "Management is unable to give employment to the following workmen due to much reduced production in the company's factory resulting from strike in one of the factory departments. These workmen are, therefore, laid-off in accordance with law with effect from 5th February, 1968."

The lay-off of the 17 workmen whose names were mentioned in the notice was recalled by the management on the 22nd April, 1968. The workmen were not given their wages or compensation for the period of lay-off. An industrial dispute was raised and referred by the Delhi Administration on the 17th April, 1968 even when the lay-off was in operation. The reference was in the following terms:

> "Whether the action of the management to 'lay-off' 17 workmen with effect from 5th Feb. 1968 is illegal and/or unjustified, and if so, to what relief are these workmen entitled?"

The Presiding Officer of the Industrial Tribunal, Delhi has held that the workmen are not entitled to any lay-off compensation. Hence this is an appeal by their Union.

The question which falls for determination before the Supreme Court is whether the management had a right to lay-off their workmen and whether the workmen are entitled to claim wages or compensation.

The Supreme Court observed that chapter VA of the ID Act provides for lay-off and retrenchment compensation where as S. 25A of the ID Act excludes the Industrial Establishments in which less than 50 workmen on an average per working day had been employed in the preceding calendar month from the application of S. 25C to S. 25E. S. 25C of the ID Act provides for the right of laid-off workmen for compensation which would be 50% of the total of the basic wages and dearness allowance. It would be noticed that the relevant sections dealing with the matters of lay-off in Chapter VA are not applicable to certain types of Industrial Establishments. The respondent company is one such Establishment because it employed only 30 workmen at the relevant time. In such a situation the question beset with difficulty of solution is whether the laid-off workmen were entitled to any compensation, if so, what?

The Supreme Court has referred S. 25J of the ID Act which provides:

"(1) The provisions of this Chapter shall have effect notwithstanding anything inconsistent there with contained in any other law including standing orders made under the Industrial Employment (Standing Orders) Act, 1946:

Provided that where under the provisions of any other Act or Rules, orders or notifications issued there under or under any standing orders or under any award, contract of service or otherwise, a workman is entitled to benefits in respect of any matter which are more favourable to him than those to which he would be entitled under this Act, the workman shall continue to be entitled to the more favourable benefits in respect of that matter, notwithstanding that he receives benefits in respect of other matters under this Act.

(2) For the removal of doubts, it is hereby declared that nothing contained in this Chapter shall be deemed to affect the provisions of any other law for the time being in force in any State in so far as that law provides for the settlement of industrial disputes, but the rights and liabilities of employers and workmen in so far as they relate to lay-off and retrenchment shall be determined in accordance with the provisions of this Chapter."

The effect of S. 25J of the ID Act is that for the period of lay-off in an Industrial Establishment to which the said provisions apply, compensation will have to be paid in accordance with S. 25C. But if a workman is entitled to benefits which are more favourable to him than those provided in the ID Act, he shall continue to be entitled to the more favourable benefits. The rights and liabilities of employers and workmen in so far as it relate to lay-off and retrenchment, except as provided in S. 25J, have got to be determined in accordance with the provisions of Chapter VA.

The Supreme Court further referred to explanation (i) appended to sub-sec. (2) of S. 25-B of the ID Act which reads:

"he has been laid-off under an agreement or as permitted by standing orders made under the Industrial Employment (Standing Orders) Act, 1946, or under this Act or under any other law applicable to the industrial establishment."

The Supreme Court observed that in the instant case the number of workmen being only 30, there were no Standing Orders certified under the Industrial Employment (Standing Orders) Act, 1946 and there was no condition provides in the contract of service of the concerned workman regarding lay-off. In such a situation the conclusion seems to be inescapable that the workmen were laid-off without any authority of law or the power in the management under the contract of service. In Industrial Establishments where there is a power in the management to lay-off a workman and to which the provisions of Chapter VA apply, the question of payment of compensation will be governed and determined by the said provisions. Otherwise Chapter VA is not a complete Code as was argued on behalf of the respondent company in the matter of payment of lay-off compensation. This case, therefore, goes out of Chapter VA and hence the workmen would be entitled to their full wages.

The Supreme Court held that in a case of compensation for lay-off the position is quite distinct and different. If the term of contract of service or the statutory terms engrafted in the Standing Orders do not give the power of lay-off to the employer, the employer will be bound to pay compensation for the period of lay-off which ordinarily and generally would be equal to the full wages of the concerned workmen. If, however, the terms of employment confer a right of lay-off on the management, then, in the case of an industrial establishment which is governed by Chap. VA, compensation will be payable in accordance with the provisions contained therein. But compensation or no compensation will be payable in the case of an industrial establishment to which the provisions of Chapter VA do not apply, and it will be so as per the terms of the employment.

(l) **lock-out** means the temporary closing of a place of employment or the suspension of work, or the refusal by an employer to continue to employ any number of persons employed by him.

Distinction between Lay-off and Lock-out

The concept of lay-off and lock-out is quite different. The Supreme Court in *Management of Kairbetta Estate* v. *Rajamanickam*[57] tried to distinguish these two concepts as the question raised before the Court was whether the concept of lock-out can be brought within the ambit of the definition of lay-off provided in S. 2(kkk) of the Act. The Supreme Court, while answering in negative, observed:

1. Lay-off generally occurs in a continuing business, whereas a lock-out is the closure of the business temporarily or for the time being.
2. In the case of a lay-off, owing to the reasons specified in S. 2(kkk), the employer is unable to give employment to one or more workmen. In the case of a lock-out, the employer closes the business and locks out the whole body of workmen for reasons which have no relevance to the causes specified in S. 2(kkk).
3. The nature of the two concepts is entirely different and so are their consequences. In the case of a lay-off, the employer may be liable to pay compensation as provided by Ss. 25C, 25-D, and 25-E of the Act; but this liability cannot be invoked in the case of a lock-out. The liability of the employer in cases of lock-out would depend upon whether the lock out was justified and legal or not; but whatever be the liability, the provisions applicable to the payment of lay-off compensation cannot be applied to the cases of lock-out.
4. Lock-out, being an antithesis to strike, is declared by the employer as the weapon of the collective bargaining and available to the employer to persuade, by a coercive process, the employees to see his point of view and to accept his demands while lay-off is actuated by the exigencies of the business.

Similarities between Lay-off and Lock-out

1. Both lay-off and lock-out are of a temporary nature and they are warranted only in the case of emergency, however the nature of emergency in each case is different.
2. In both the cases, the relationship of employment is only suspended temporarily.
3. A lay-off resorted to in contravention of the provisions of S. 25M is illegal and punishable under S. 25Q of the Act and if the compensation is not paid, which is due on the part of the employer to pay as per S. 25C of the Act, the employer or the person who contravenes such provision, as the case may be, will be punished under S. 31(2) of the Act, whereas lock-out declared in contravention of the provisions of Ss. 10(3), 10A(4A), 22 or 23 is illegal and punishable under S. 26 of the Act.

(la) **major port** means a major port as defined in Cl. (8) of S. 3 of the Indian Ports Act, 1908 (15 of 1908).

(lb) **mine** means a mine as defined in Cl. (j) of sub-section (1) of S. 2 of the Mines Act, 1952 (35 of 1952).

(ll) **National Tribunal** means a National Industrial Tribunal constituted under S. 7B.

(lll) **office bearer**, in relation to a trade union, includes any member or the executive thereof, but does not include an auditor.

(m) **prescribed** means prescribed by rules made under this Act.

(n) **public utility service** means—

(i) any railway service or any transport service for the carriage of passengers or goods by air;

(ia) any service in, or in connection with the working of, any major port or dock;

(ii) any section of an industrial establishment, on the working of which the safety of the establishment or the workmen employed therein depends;

(iii) any postal, telegraph or telephone service;

(iv) any industry which supplies power, light or water to the public;

(v) any system of public conservancy or sanitation;

(vi) any industry specified in the First Schedule which the appropriate Government may, if satisfied that public emergency or public interest so requires, by notification in the Official Gazette, declare to be a public utility service for the purposes of this Act, for such period as may be specified in the notification:

Provided that the period so specified shall not, in the first instance, exceed six months but may, by a like notification, be extended from time to time, by any period not exceeding six months, at any one time, if in the opinion of the appropriate Government, public emergency or public interest requires such extension;

(o) **railway company** means a railway company as defined in S. 3 of the Indian Railways Act, 1890 (9 of 1890);

(oo) **retrenchment** means the termination by the employer of the service of a workman for any reason whatsoever, otherwise than as a punishment inflicted by way of disciplinary action, but does not include—

(a) voluntary retirement of the workman; or

(b) retirement of the workman on reaching the age of superannuation if the contract of employment between the employer and the workman concerned contains a stipulation in that behalf; or

(bb) termination of the service of the workman as a result of the non-renewal of the contract of employment between the employer and the workman concerned on its expiry or of such contract being terminated under a stipulation in that behalf contained therein; or

(c) termination of the service of a workman on the ground of continued ill-health.

'Retrenchment' means the termination by the employer of the service of a workman for any reason whatsoever, otherwise than as a punishment inflicted by way of disciplinary action, but does not include—

(i) voluntary retirement of the workman; or
(ii) retirement of the workman on reaching the age of superannuation; or
(iii) termination of the service of a workman as a result of the non-renewal of the contract of employment; or
(iv) termination of the service of a workman on the ground of continued ill-health.

The definition of retrenchment may be divided into two parts, i.e. substantive part and exclusive part. The substantive part provides the meaning of retrenchment, whereas the exclusive part provides the different reasons of termination of service of a workman.

(i) voluntary retirement of the workman; or
(ii) retirement of the workman on reaching the age of superannuation; or
(iii) termination of the service of a workman as a result of the non-renewal of the contract of employment; or
(iv) termination of the service of a workman on the ground of continued ill-health.

Further, it is to be noted that if the service of the workman is terminated due to punishment by way of disciplinary action, it is definitely not a case of retrenchment as the definition itself provides. In a nutshell, it can be said that five reasons of termination of service of a workman are excluded from the ambit of the definition of retrenchment.

Relevant Provisions Relating to Retrenchment

The definition of 'retrenchment' should be read along with the relevant provisions such as Ss. 2(oo), 25F, 25G, 25H, 25N and 25B of the Act. Section 25B is having no direct relevancy to the concept of 'retrenchment', however, it provides the meaning of 'continuous service' and therefore helps the reader to know the meaning of 'continuous service' while reading Ss. 25F and 25N of the Act. Furthermore one has to refer to S. 25L to know the meaning of 'industrial establishment' because the very word is found while reading S. 25N of the Act.

Analysis of the Definition

After reading the definition of retrenchment, one can very well say that the Legislature does not provide any ground of retrenchment, rather it provides the different grounds which are excluded from the ambit of the definition. The key words used by the Legislature in S. 2(oo) *for any reason whatsoever* provide no meaning. Therefore, the Supreme Court in *Barsi Light Railway Co. Ltd.* v. *K.N. Joglekar*[59] interpreted and held that retrenchment as defined in S. 2(oo) and as used in S. 25-F has no wider meaning than the ordinarily accepted connotation of the word. It means the discharge of surplus labour or staff by the employer for any reason whatsoever, otherwise than as a punishment inflicted by way of disciplinary action. In *Santosh Gupta* v. *State Bank of Patiala*,[60] the question came before the Supreme Court for consideration whether non-passing of the examination amounts to retrenchment. The fact of the case is as follows:

59. AIR 1957 SC 121.
60. AIR 1980 SC 1219.

Santosh Gupta, the appellant workman (a woman), was employed in the State Bank of Patiala, from July 13, 1973 till August 21, 1974, when her services were terminated. It was an admitted fact that the workman had worked for 240 days, in the year preceding August 21, 1974. According to the workman the termination of her services was 'retrenchment' within the meaning of that expression in S. 2(oo) of the Industrial Disputes Act, 1947, since it did not fall within any of the excepted cases mentioned in S. 2(oo). On the other hand, the contention of the management was that the termination of services was not due to discharge of surplus labour. It was due to the failure of the workman to pass the test which would have enabled her to be confirmed in the service. Therefore, it was not retrenchment within the meaning of S. 2(oo) of the Industrial Disputes Act.

The Court held that the expression *termination of service for any reason whatsoever* provided in S. 2(oo) covers every kind of termination of service except those expressly excluded from the purview of the definition. Thus, the discharge of the workman on the ground that she did not pass the test which would have enabled her to be confirmed was retrenchment within the meaning of S. 2(oo) and, therefore, the requirements of S. 25F had to be complied with. The Supreme Court in *Management of Karnataka State Road Transport Corporation, Bangalore* v. *M. Boraiah*[61] held that as retrenchment, as defined in S. 2(oo), covers every case of termination of services except those embodied in the definition, discharge from employment or termination of service of a probationer would also amount to retrenchment. In *Delhi Cloth and General Mills Co. Ltd.* v. *Shambhu Nath Mukherji*,[62] the Supreme Court held that striking off the name of the workman from the rolls by the management is termination of his service. Such termination of service is retrenchment within the meaning of S. 2(oo) of the Act. In *L. Robert D'Souza* v. *Executive Engineer, Southern Railway*,[63] the Supreme Court, while accepting the ratio of *Delhi Cloth and General Mills Co. Ltd.* v. *Shambhu Nath Mukherji*,[62] held that if the service of the workman is terminated by the employer due to unauthorized absence, it can be characterized as retrenchment.

In *Punjab Land Development and Reclamation Corporation Ltd.* v. *Presiding Officer, Labour Court*,[64] the question that came before the Supreme Court for consideration was whether the retrenchment under the Industrial Disputes Act means termination of the service of the workman as surplus labour, for any reason whatsoever, or it means termination by the employer of the service of the workman, for any reason whatsoever, otherwise than as punishment inflicted by way of disciplinary action and those expressly excluded from the ambit of the definition. After reviewing its earlier decision, the Court held that the second view is correct and observed that, had the Parliament envisaged the surplus of workman is the only ground for retrenchment, then the excluding grounds as mentioned in S. 2(oo) would not have been provided, nevertheless there would not have been a phrase like 'for any reason whatsoever' inserted in the definition. It seems that there may be many reasons for retrenchment.

In a recent case, the Supreme Court in *S.M. Nilajkar* v. *Telecom District Manager, Karnataka*[65] observed that 'retrenchment' in its ordinary connotation is discharge of labour

61. AIR 1983 SC 1320.
62. AIR 1978 SC 8.
63. AIR 1982 SC 854.
64. (1990) II LLJ 70 (SC).
65. AIR 2003 SC 3553.

as surplus though the business or work itself is continued. It is well settled by a catena of decisions that labour laws being beneficial pieces of legislation are to be interpreted in favour of the beneficiaries, in case of doubt, or where it is possible to take two views of a provision. It is also well settled that the Parliament has employed the expression 'the termination by the employer of the service of a workman for any reason whatsoever' while defining the term retrenchment, which is suggestive of the legislative intent to assign the term retrenchment a meaning wider than what it is understood to have in common parlance. There are four exceptions carved out of the artificially extended meaning of the term retrenchment, and, therefore, the termination of service of a workman so long as it is attributable to the act of the employer would fall within the meaning of retrenchment dehors the reason for termination. To be excepted from within the meaning of 'retrenchment', the termination of service must fall within one of the four excepted categories. A termination of service which does not fall within the categories (a), (b), (bb) and (c) would fall within the meaning of retrenchment.

From the judicial trends, the following points may be submitted.

1. All retrenchment is termination, but all termination is not retrenchment.
2. The question whether retrenchment includes termination of all kinds is a matter of fact depending on the nature of termination.
3. Termination of service due to retrenchment will be considered only in a running industry.
4. Retrenchment is not confined only to the permanent workman.
5. The active participation of the employer is necessary for terminating the service of a workman on the ground of retrenchment as the definition prescribes so.
6. If the service of the workman is terminated due to any of the five excluding grounds mentioned in S. 2(oo), then it will not be a case of retrenchment.

From the above discussion, it is seen that the ground of retrenchment is not confined only to the case of surplusage, even though the constitutional Bench in *Barsi Light* case specifically observed that retrenchment as defined in S. 2(oo) and as used in S. 25-F has no wider meaning than the ordinary accepted connotation of the word. It means the discharge of surplus labour or staff by the employer for any reason whatsoever, otherwise than as a punishment inflicted by way of disciplinary action. The meaning of retrenchment has been extended by the Supreme Court what even the Legislature might not have thought and that too without considering the decision of the constitutional Bench. But we should not forget the sense the word retrenchment actually means or conveys. In *Kamaleshkumar Rajanikant Mehta* v. *Presiding Officer, Central' Govt. Industrial Tribunal No. 1*,[66] the High Court of Bombay has given a note of caution against such wider interpretation of this term. The Court observed:

> "It was not, and could never have been, the intention of the Legislature to make retrenchment synonymous with termination on grounds like loss of confidence, insub-ordination or inefficiency. The criterion for retrenchment is superfluity or surplusage of labour or staff in a running business, caused by any reason whatsoever, such as economy, rationalisation in industry, installation of new labour-saving machinery, or devices, standardisation or

66. (1979) 39 FILR 329 (337, 341) (Bom).

improvement of plant or technique and the like. Surplusage or superfluity is the fulcrum round which the concept of retrenchment must turn."

(p) **settlement** means a settlement arrived at in the course of conciliation proceeding and includes a written agreement between the employer and workmen arrived at otherwise than in the course of conciliation proceeding where such agreement has been signed by the parties thereto in such manner as may be prescribed and a copy thereof has been sent to an officer authorised in this behalf by the appropriate Government and the conciliation officer;

In the Act, as originally passed, settlement was defined as follows:

"Settlement means a settlement arrived at in the course of conciliation proceedings."

Any private settlement or bipartite negotiation or agreement arrived at between the parties to the dispute was outside the scope of the definition. Accordingly, a settlement arrived at otherwise than in the course of conciliation proceeding was not given any legal status at all. The Industrial Disputes (Amendment) Act of 1956 removed this lacuna by redefining the word 'settlement'.

"Settlement means a settlement arrived at in the course of conciliation proceedings and includes a written agreement between the employer and workmen arrived at otherwise than in the course of conciliation proceeding where such agreement has been signed by the parties thereto in such manner as may be prescribed and a copy thereof has been sent to an officer authorised in this behalf by the appropriate Government and the Conciliation Officer".

The definition of settlement now envisages two categories of settlement—namely, those arrived at outside the conciliation proceedings and those arrived at in the course of conciliation proceedings. A settlement which belongs to the first category has limited application in that it merely binds the parties to the agreement, but the settlement belonging to the second category has extended application since it is binding on all the parties to the industrial disputes, to all others who were summoned to appear in the conciliation proceedings and to all persons employed in the establishment or part of the establishment, as the case may be, to which the dispute related on the date of the dispute and to all others who joined the establishment thereafter. A settlement arrived at in the course of conciliation proceedings with a recognized majority union will be binding on all workmen of the establishment, even when those who belong to the minority union had objected to the same. Recognized union having majority of members is expected to protect the legitimate interest of labour and enter into a settlement in the best interest of labour. This is with the object to uphold the sanctity of settlement reached with the active assistance of the Conciliation Officer and to discourage an individual employee or minority union from scuttling the settlement. When a settlement is arrived at during the conciliation proceedings, it is binding on the members of the Workers' Union as laid down by S. 18(3)(d) of the Act. It would *ipso facto* bind all the existing workmen who are all parties to the industrial dispute and who may not be members of unions that are signatories to such settlement under S. 12(3) of the Act.[67]

---

67. *National Engineering Industries Ltd.* v. *State of Rajasthan,* AIR 2000 SC 469.

Relevant Provisions in the Act

One should read Ss. 2(p), 18(1), 18(3), 19(1), 19(2), 19(7) and 29 sequence wise so that one can get a clear picture of the definition of settlement, binding effect, life of the settlement, the manner of repudiation of such settlement and punishment in case of breach.

Settlement Arrived at in the Course of Conciliation Proceedings

In *Bata Shoe Co., (P) Ltd.* v. *D.N. Ganguly*,[68] the question posed was as to what is meant by the words *in the course of conciliation proceedings* appearing in S. 18 of the Act. One thing is clear that these words refer to the duration when the conciliation proceedings are pending. But do these words mean that any agreement arrived at between the parties during this period would be binding under S. 18 of the Act? Or do they mean that a settlement arrived at in the course of conciliation proceedings postulates that that settlement should have been arrived at between the parties with the concurrence of the Conciliation Officer? As we read this provision, we feel that the legislature, when it made a settlement, reached during the course of conciliation proceedings, binding not only on the parties thereto but also on all present and future workmen, intended that such settlement was arrived at with the assistance of the conciliation officer and was considered by him to be reasonable and therefore had his concurrence. Section 12 of the Act prescribes duties of the conciliation officer and S. 12(2) provides that the conciliation officer shall for the purpose of bringing about settlement of the dispute without delay investigate the dispute and all matters affecting the merits and the right settlement thereof and may do all such things as he may think fit for the purpose of inducing the parties to come to a fair and amicable settlement of the dispute. Section 12(3) provides that if a settlement of the dispute or of any of the matters in dispute is arrived at in the course of the conciliation proceedings, the conciliation officer shall send a report thereof to the appropriate Government together with a memorandum of the settlement signed by the parties to the dispute. Reading these two provisions, i.e. Ss. 12(2) and 12(3) along with S. 18 of the Act, it seems clear and beyond doubt that a settlement which is made binding under S. 18 on the ground that it is arrived at in the course of conciliation proceedings is a settlement arrived at with the assistance and concurrence of the conciliation officer. It is only such a settlement which is arrived at while the conciliation proceedings are pending that can be binding under S. 18.

Settlement Arrived at Otherwise Than in the Course of Conciliation Proceedings

The first part of the definition, viz. a settlement in the course of conciliation proceedings is the denotation of the word 'settlement'. But 'a written agreement between an employer and a workman arrived at otherwise than in the course of conciliation proceedings' has been brought within the ambit of the definition in an inclusive manner. This extended meaning is the connotation of the definition. It is further required that such an agreement of settlement

68. AIR 1961 SC 1158.

should be signed by the parties thereto in the prescribed manner and a copy thereof should be sent to the 'appropriate Government' and the Conciliation Officer.

(q) **strike** means a cessation of work by a body of persons employed in any industry acting in combination, or a concerted refusal, or a refusal under a common understanding, of any number of persons who are or have been so employed to continue to work or to accept employment.

Strike as a weapon was evolved by the workers as a form of direct action during their long struggle with the employers. It is essentially a weapon of last resort, being an abnormal aspect of the employer-employee relationship and involves withdrawal of labourer, disrupting production, services and the running of the enterprise. It is a use by the labourer of their economic power to bring the employer to see and meet their viewpoint over the dispute between them. In addition to the total cessation of work, it takes various forms such as working to rule, go slow, refusal to work overtime when it is compulsory and a part of the contract of employment, 'irritation strike' or staying at work but deliberately doing everything wrong, 'running-sore strike', i.e. disobeying the lawful order, sit-down, stay-in and lie-down strike, etc. The cessation or stoppage of works whether by the employees or by the employer is detrimental to the production and economy and to the well-being of the society as a whole. It is for this reason that the industrial legislation, while not denying the right of workmen to strike, has tried to regulate it along with the right of the employer to lock-out and has also provided machinery for peaceful investigation, settlement, arbitration and adjudication of the disputes between them. Where such industrial legislation is not applicable, the contract of employment and the service rules and regulations many times provide for a suitable machinery for the resolution of the disputes. When the law or the contract of employment or the service rules provide for a machinery to resolve the dispute, in that case resorting to strike or lock-out as a direct action is prima facie unjustified. This is particularly so when the provisions of the law or of the contract or of the service rules in that behalf are breached. In such a case, the action is also illegal.

The question whether a strike or lock-out is legal or illegal does not present much difficulty for resolution, since all that is required to be examined to answer the question is whether there has been a breach of the relevant provisions. However, whether the action is justified or unjustified has to be examined by taking into consideration various factors. In almost all such cases, the prominent question that arises is whether the dispute was of such a nature that its solution could not brook delay and await resolution by the mechanism provided under the law or the contract or the service rules. The strike or lock-out is not to be resorted to because the party concerned has a superior bargaining power or the requisite economic muscle to compel the other party to accept its demand. Such indiscriminate use of power is nothing but assertion of the rule of 'might has the right'. Its consequences are lawlessness, anarchy and chaos in the economic activities, which are most vital and fundamental to the survival of the society. Such action, when the legal machinery is available to resolve the dispute, may be hard to justify. This will be particularly so when it is resorted to by the section of the society which can well await the resolution of the dispute by the machinery provided for the same. The strike or lock-out as a weapon has to be used sparingly for redressal of urgent and pressing grievances when no other means are available or when the available means have failed to resolve it. It has to be resorted to compel the other party to the dispute to see the justness of the demand. It is not to be utilised to cause hardship to the society at large so as to strengthen the bargaining power. It is for this reason that industrial legislation such as the Industrial Disputes Act, 1947 places additional restrictions on strikes and lock-outs in public utility services.

With the emergence of the organised labour, particularly in public undertakings and public utility services, the old balance of economic power between the management and the workmen has undergone a qualitative change in such undertakings. Today, the organised labour in these institutions has acquired even the power of holding the society at large to ransom, by withholding labour and thereby compelling the managements to give into their demands whether reasonable or unreasonable. What is forgotten many times, is that as against the employment and the service conditions available to the organised labour in these undertakings, there are millions who are either unemployed or underemployed or employed on less than statutorily minimum remuneration. The employment that workmen get and the profits that the employers earn are both generated by the utilisation of the resources of the society in one form or the other whether it is land, water, electricity or money which flows either as share capital, loans from financial institutions or subsidies and exemptions from the Governments. The resources are to be used for the well-being of all by generating more employment and production and ensuring equitable distribution. They are not meant to be used for providing employment, better service conditions and profits only for some. In this task, both the capital and labour are to act as the trustees of the said resources on behalf of the society and use them as such. They are not to be wasted or frittered away by strikes and lock-outs. Every dispute between the employer and the employee has, therefore, to take into consideration the third dimension, viz. the interests of the society as a whole, particularly the interest of those who are deprived of their legitimate basic economic rights and are more unfortunate than those in employment and management. The justness or otherwise of the action of the employer or the employee has, therefore, to be examined also on the anvil of the interests of the society which such action tends to affect. This is true of the action in both the public and private sectors, but more imperatively so in the public sector. The management in the public sector is not a capitalist and the labour an exploited lot. Both are paid employees and owe their existence to the direct investment of public funds. Both are expected to represent public interests directly and to promote them.[69]

The conflict between the two groups, management and employees, is always with us and it is inevitable as one of them argues for more investment and the other argues for better standard of living now. That is what the labour law is always about and that is what a good deal of politics is always about. There is no such legislation available either in India or anywhere else that can avoid the conflict between these two classes whose interests are diametrically opposite. However there are rules, regulations, legislations, ordinances, etc. which generally regulate both the parties and prevent or restrict the industrial conflict by providing suitable norms and machineries and one of such legislation is the Industrial Disputes Act, 1947.

---

69. *Syndicate Bank* v. *K. Umesh Nayak*, AIR 1995 SC 319.

Section 2(q), Industrial Disputes Act, 1947 defines 'strike' as:

> "a cessation of work by a body of persons employed in any industry acting in combination, or a concerted refusal, or a refusal under a common understanding, of any number of persons who are or have been so employed to continue to work or to accept employment."

Relevant Provisions Relating to Strike

In order to understand the concept of strike, one has to read all the provisions available under the Industrial Disputes Act, 1947 relating to strike. The provisions that are having a direct bearing on strike are Ss. 2(q), 10(3), 10A(4A), 22, 23, 24, 25, 26, 27 and 28. Section 2(q) provides the definition of strike. Sections 10(3) and 10A(4A) empower the appropriate Government to prohibit the continuance of any strike, if it deems fit, once such dispute has been referred to the Board, Labour Court, Tribunal or National Tribunal under S. 10 or to an Arbitrator under S. 10A, respectively. Sections 22 and 23 prohibit strike in public utility service and also refer to industrial establishment other than public utility service. Section 24 speaks about illegal strike whereas S. 25 prohibits financial aid to illegal strike. Sections 26, 27 and 28 prescribe punishment for illegal strike, penalty for instigation to take part in a strike and penalty for giving financial aid to illegal strike.

Is Strike a Fundamental Right?

The question came before the Supreme Court in *All India Bank Employees' Association* v. *National Industrial Tribunal*[70] for consideration that whether the right guaranteed to form a union provided in Art. 19(1)(c) of the Constitution carries within it a concomitant right that the achievement of the object for which the union is formed. In other words, it was submitted that when Art. 19(1)(c) guarantees the right to form associations, a guarantee is also implied that the fulfilment of every object of an association so formed is also a protected right, with the result that there is a constitutional guarantee that every association shall effectively achieve the purpose for which it was formed, without interference by law except on grounds relevant to the preservation of public order or morality set out in Art. 19(4) of the Constitution. However, the Court, while rejecting the contention, held that the right to form unions guaranteed by Art. 19(1)(c) thus does not carry with it a fundamental right in the union so formed to achieve every object for which it was formed. Even a very liberal interpretation of Art. 19(1)(c) cannot lead to the conclusion that the trade unions have a guaranteed right to an effective collective bargaining or to strike, either as part of collective bargaining or otherwise. The right to strike or the right to declare a lock-out may be controlled or restricted by appropriate industrial legislation, and the validity of such legislation would have to be tested not with reference to the criteria laid down in Cl. (4) of Art. 19 but by totally different considerations.

In *Kameshwar Prasad* v. *State of Bihar*,[71] the question came before the Constitutional Bench regarding constitutional validity of Rule 4A of the Bihar Government Servants' Conduct Rules, 1956 which prohibits any form of demonstration and resort to strike. The Court held that a demonstration is a visible manifestation of the feelings or sentiments of

70. AIR 1962 SC 171.
71. AIR 1962 SC 1166.

an individual, or a group. It is thus a communication of one's ideas to others to whom it is intended to be conveyed. It is in effect, therefore, a form of speech or of expression, because speech need not be vocal since signs made by a dumb person would also be a form of speech. There are forms of demonstration which would fall within the freedoms guaranteed by Art. 19(1)(a) and 19(1)(b). A violent and disorderly demonstration would not obviously be within Art. 19(1)(a) or (b). But a peaceful and orderly demonstration would fall within the freedoms guaranteed under these Clauses. So a peaceful demonstration is considered as a fundamental right which is nothing but a by-product of Arts. 19(1)(a) and 19(1)(b) of the Constitution. The Supreme Court, therefore, allowed the appeal in part and granted the appellants a declaration that R. 4-A in the form in which it stood prohibiting *any form of demonstration,* was violative of the appellants' rights under Art. 19(1)(a) and (b) and should therefore be struck down. It is only necessary to add that the rule, insofar as it prohibits a strike, cannot be struck down since there is no fundamental right to resort to strike.

In *B.R. Singh* v. *Union of India*,[72] the Supreme Court observed that the necessity to form unions is obviously for voicing the demands and grievances of labourers. Trade unionists act as mouthpieces of labourers. The strength of a trade union depends on its membership. Therefore, trade unions with sufficient membership strength are able to bargain more effectively with the managements. This bargaining power would be considerably reduced if it is not permitted to demonstrate. Strike in a given situation is only a form of demonstration. There are different modes of demonstrations, e.g. go slow, sit-in, work-to-rule, absentism, etc. and strike is one such mode of demonstration by workers for their rights. The right to demonstrate, and therefore the right to strike, is an important weapon in the armory of the workers. This right has been recognised by almost all democratic countries. Though not raised to the high pedestal of a fundamental right, it is recognised as a mode of redress for resolving the grievances of workers. But the right to strike is not absolute under our industrial jurisprudence and restrictions have been placed on it.

In *T.K. Rangarajan* v. *Govt. of T.N.*,[73] the unprecedented action taken by the Tamil Nadu Government terminating the services of all Government servants who resorted to strike was challenged before the High Court of Madras by filing writ petitions under Arts. 226/227 of the Constitution. Learned single Judge, by interim order, *inter alia* directed the State Government that suspension and dismissal of employees without conducting any enquiry shall be kept in abeyance until under further orders and such employees be directed to resume duty. That interim order was challenged by the State Government by filing writ appeals. On behalf of the Government employees, writ petitions were filed challenging the validity of the Tamil Nadu Essential Services Maintenance Act, 2002 and also the Tamil Nadu Ordinance No. 3 of 2003.

The Division Bench of the High Court set aside the interim order and arrived at the conclusion that without exhausting the alternative remedy of approaching the Administrative Tribunal, writ petitions were not maintainable. It was pointed out to the Court that the total detentions were 2211, out of which 74 were ladies and only 165 male and 7 female personnel have so far been enlarged on bail, which reveals the pathetic conditions of the arrestees. The arrestees were mainly clerks and subordinate staff. The Court, therefore, directed that those

72. AIR 1990 SC 1.
73. AIR 2003 SC 3032.

who were arrested and lodged in jails be released on bail. That order was challenged by filing a writ petition under Art. 32 before the Supreme Court. The Supreme Court at the outset held that under Art. 226 of the Constitution, the High Court is empowered to exercise its extraordinary jurisdiction to meet unprecedented extraordinary situation having no parallel. It is equally true that extraordinary powers are required to be sparingly used. The facts of the present case reveal that this was most extraordinary case, which called for interference by the High Court, as the State Government had dismissed about two lacs employees for going on strike.

However, the Court held that Government servant has neither fundamental nor statutory nor moral right to go on strike. Law on this subject is well settled and it has been repeatedly held by Supreme Court that the employees have no fundamental right to resort to strike. There is no statutory provision empowering the employees to go on strike. Further, there is a prohibition to go on strike under Rule 22 of Tamil Nadu Government Servants Conduct Rules, 1973. Rule 22 provides that "no Government servant shall engage himself in strike or in incitements thereto or in similar activities." Apart from the statutory rights, Government employees cannot claim that they can hold the society to ransom by going on strike. Even if there is injustice to some extent, as presumed by such employees, in a democratic welfare State, they have to resort to the machinery provided under different statutory provisions for redressal of their grievances. Strike as a weapon is mostly misused which results in chaos and total mal-administration. Strike affects the society as a whole. In a society where there is a large-scale unemployment and a number of qualified persons are eagerly waiting for employment in Government departments or in public sector undertakings, strikes cannot be justified on any equitable ground. For redressing their grievances, instead of going on strike, if employees do some more work honestly, diligently and efficiently, such gesture would not only be appreciated by the authority but also by people at large. The reason being, in a democracy even though they are Government employees, they are part and parcel of the governing body and owe duty to the society.

It is submitted therefore that neither the Constitution nor the Supreme Court of India has provided at any point of time by which the workmen, either governed by the Industrial Disputes Act or the Government employees governed by their respective Rules prescribed by their respective States concerned, are having a fundamental right to strike. However, the ratio of *T.K. Rangarajan* case is confined to the Government servants only. So, the author is of the opinion that it has nothing to do with the other employees or industrial workmen to whom Rule 22 of Tamil Nadu Government Servants Conduct Rules, 1973 does not apply, as Rule 22 specifically provides that "no Government servant shall engage himself in strike or in incitements thereto or in similar activities."

Further, the author is of the opinion that the right to strike may be a legal right and such right is available to such workmen who are governed under the Industrial Disputes Act. It is true that the Industrial Disputes Act nowhere uses the word legal strike, rather Ss. 24, 25, 26, 27 and 28 of the Act speak about illegal strikes. Section 24 prescribes that a strike shall be illegal if it is commenced or declared in contravention of S. 22 or 23 or 10(3) or 10A(4A). If the strikers declare the strike without contravening any of the provisions of S. 22 or 23, as the case may be, then such strike would definitely be construed as legal strike. Therefore, it can be said that the right to strike is not a fundamental right, rather it can be a legal right.

Whether Pen down Strike is a Strike within Section 2(q)?

The Supreme Court in *Punjab National Bank Ltd.* v. *All India Punjab National Bank Employees' Federation*[74] held that on a plain and grammatical construction of the definition in S. 2(q), it would be difficult to exclude a strike where workmen enter the premises of their employment and refuse to take their tools in hand and start their usual work. Refusal under common understanding to continue to work is a strike, and if in pursuance of such common understanding the employees entered the premises of the employer and refused to take their pens in their hands, that would no doubt be a strike under S. 2(q). So, per se a pen down strike cannot be treated as illegal; but if it is found to be illegal because it was commenced in contravention of S. 23(b), mere participation in such an illegal strike cannot necessarily involve the rejection of the striker's claim for reinstatement. The general hypothetical consideration that pen down strikes may in some cases lead to rowdy demonstrations, or result in disturbances or violence, or shake the credit of the employer would not justify the conclusion that even if the strikers are peaceful and non-violent and have done nothing more than occupying their seats during office hours, their participation in the strike would by itself disqualify them from claiming reinstatement.

Go-slow and Strike

'Go-slow', which is a picturesque description of deliberate delaying of production by workmen pretending to be engaged in the factory, is one of the most pernicious practices that discontented or disgruntled workmen some time resort to. It would not be wrong to call this dishonest. For, while thus delaying production and thereby reducing the output, the workmen claim to have remained employed and thus to be entitled to full wages. Apart from this, go-slow is likely to be much more harmful than total cessation of work by strike. For, while during a strike most of the machinery can be fully turned off, in go-slow the machinery is kept going on a reduced speed, which is often extremely damaging to machinery parts. For all these reasons, go-slow has always been considered a serious type of misconduct.

Some light on the mystery is however thrown by the fact that in Bihar, a Committee, to consider and report on the question of 'go-slow' in industries, was appointed by the Bihar Central Standing Labour Advisory Board and the report of the Committee was submitted in 1951. The Committee made several recommendations including one that 'go-slow', without at least 7 days' notice, should be treated at par with strike. It also recommended however that workers should not resort to 'go-slow' without at least 7 days notice, that the notice would remain in force for 4 weeks but that it would not be necessary to notify the exact date of starting the 'go-slow' during the pendency of conciliation proceeding but that the conciliation proceeding must be concluded within four weeks of the notice. The Committee went to the length of recommending that 'go-slow' due to malpractices by the management would be justified. By a resolution dated December 1, 1951, the Government of Bihar was pleased to accept the recommendations of the go-slow Committee.[75] In *SU Motors Ltd.* v. *Their*

74. AIR 1960 SC 160.
75. *Bharat Sugar Mills* v. *Jai Singh* (1961) II LLJ 644 (SC).

Workmen,[76] the Supreme Court, while dealing with the nature of go-slow and consequences thereof, observed that there cannot be two opinion that go-slow is a serious misconduct, being a covert and a more damaging breach of the contract of employment. It is an insidious method of undermining discipline and at the same time, a crude device to defy the norms of work. It has been roundly condemned as an industrial action and has not been recognized as a legitimate weapon of the workmen to redress their grievances. In fact, the Model Standing Orders as well as the Certified Standing Orders of most of the industrial establishments define it as a misconduct and provide for a disciplinary action for it. Hence, once it is proved, those guilty of it have to face the consequences, which may include a deduction from wages and even dismissal from service.

Strike—Legal and Illegal vis-a-vis Justified and Unjustified

Justice Krishna Iyer in *Crompton Greaves Ltd.* v. *The Workmen*[77] held that in order to entitle the workmen to wages for the period of strike, the strike should be legal as well as justified. A strike is legal if it does not violate any of the provisions of the statute. Again, a strike cannot be said to be unjustified unless the reasons for it are entirely perverse or unreasonable. Whether a particular strike was justified or not is a question of fact which has to be judged in the light of the facts and circumstances of each case. It is well settled that the use of force or violence or acts of sabotage resorted to by the workmen during a strike disentitles them to wages for the strike period.

The strike cannot be said to be illegal if it does not contravene any provision of the law. Section 24 of the Industrial Disputes Act prescribes the grounds where the strike would be declared illegal. In other words, if a strike is resorted to and it does not violate the norms prescribed in S. 24 of the Act, then it may be safely construed that the said strike would be a legal one. However, Justice Sinha, C.J. in *India General Navigation and Railway Co. Ltd.* v. *Their Workmen*[78] categorically observed that a strike in respect of a public utility service, which is clearly illegal, cannot at the same time be characterized as 'perfectly justified.' These two conclusions cannot co-exist in law. The law has made a distinction between a strike which is illegal and one which is not, but it has not made any distinction between an illegal strike which may be said to be justifiable and one which is not justifiable. This distinction is not warranted by the Act, and is wholly misconceived, specially in the case of employees in a public utility service. Every one participating in an illegal strike is liable to be dealt with departmentally, of course, subject to the action of the Department being questioned before an Industrial Tribunal, but it is not permissible to characterize an illegal strike as justifiable. The only question of practical importance which may arise in the case of an illegal strike, would be the kind or quantum of punishment, and that, of course, has to be modulated in accordance with the facts and circumstances of each case. Therefore, the tendency to condone what has been declared to be illegal by statute, must be deprecated, and it must be clearly understood by those who take part in an illegal strike that thereby they make themselves liable to be dealt with by their employers.

76. [1990] II LLJ 39 (SC).
77. AIR 1978 SC 1489.
78. AIR 1960 SC 219.

Assuming that it is open to the management to dismiss a workman who has taken part in an illegal strike, in determining the question of punishment, a clear distinction has to be made between those workmen who not only joined in such strike but also took part in obstructing the loyal workmen from carrying on their work, or took part in violent demonstrations, or acted in defiance of law and order, on the one hand, and on the other those workmen who were more or less silent participators in such a strike. It is not in the interest of the industry that there should be a wholesale dismissal of all the workmen who merely participated in such a strike. It is certainly not in the interest of the workmen themselves. An Industrial Tribunal, therefore, has to consider the question of punishment, keeping in view the overriding consideration of the full and efficient working of the industry as a whole. The punishment of dismissal or termination of services has, therefore, to be imposed on such workmen who had not only participated in the illegal strike, but also fomented it, and had been guilty of violence or doing acts detrimental to the maintenance of law and order in the locality where work had to be carried on.

Wages for Strike Period

The question came before the Supreme Court in *Syndicate Bank* v. *K. Umesh Nayak*[79] by way of an appeal which has been referred to the Constitution Bench in view of the apparent conflicting decision given by the Apex Court in three cases, i.e. a three-Judge Bench decision in *Management of Churakulam Tea Estate (P) Ltd.* v. *The Workmen,*[80] and a two-Judge Bench decision in *Crompton Greaves Ltd.* v. *Its Workmen,*[81] on the one hand, and a two-Judge Bench decision in *Bank of India* v. *T.S. Kelawala,*[82] on the other.

The question is whether workmen who go on strike, whether legal or illegal, are entitled to wages for the period of strike. In the first two cases, viz. *Churakulam Tea Estate* and *Crompton Greaves*, the view taken is that the strike must be both legal and justified to entitle the workmen to the wages for the period of strike, whereas the latter decision in *T.S. Kelawala* case the Apex Court has taken the view that whether the strike is legal or illegal, the employees are not entitled to wages for the period of strike. However, it is pertinent to mention that in *T.S. Kelawala* case the question whether the strike was justified or not was not raised at all and, therefore, its justification was neither discussed nor answered. Secondly, the first two decisions, viz. *Churakulam Tea Estate* and *Crompton Greaves* were not cited while deciding the said case and hence there was no occasion to consider the said decisions there. The decisions were not cited probably because the question of the justifiability or otherwise of the strike did not fall for consideration. It is, however, apparent from the earlier two decisions, viz. *Churakulam Tea Estate* and *Crompton Greaves* that the view taken there is not that the employees are entitled to wages for the strike period merely because the strike is legal. The view is that for such entitlement the strike has to be both legal and justified. In other words, if the strike is illegal but justified or if the strike is legal but unjustified, the employees would not be entitled to the wages for the strike period. Since the question whether the employees

79. AIR 1995 SC 319.
80. AIR 1969 SC 998.
81. AIR 1978 SC 1489.
82. (1990) 4 SCC 744.

are entitled to wages, if the strike is justified, did not fall for consideration in the latter case, viz. in *T.S. Kelawala*, there is, as stated in the beginning, only an apparent conflict of the decisions.

The Supreme Court accordingly, while endorsing the view taken in *T.S. Kelawala* case, held that the workers are not entitled to wages for the strike period even if the strike is legal. To be entitled to the wages for the strike period , the strike has to be both legal and justified. Whether the strike is legal or justified are questions of law and fact to be decided on the evidence on record. The legality or illegality of the strike can be looked from the Industrial Disputes Act whereas justifiability or unjustifiability of the strike can be looked from the charter of demands.

Strike vis-a-vis Section 10(3) and Section 10A(4A)

Section 10(3) empowers the appropriate Government to prohibit the continuance of a strike if it is in connection with a dispute referred to one of the fora created under the said statute. Section 10A(4A) confers similar power on the appropriate Government where the industrial dispute which is the cause of the strike is referred to Arbitration and a notification in that behalf is issued under S. 10(3A).

A very short question came before the Supreme Court in *Delhi Administration, Delhi* v. *Workmen of Edward Keventers*[83] for consideration regarding the scope of S. 10(3) of the Industrial Disputes Act, 1947. The appellant, Delhi Administration, was faced with the question of referring several disputes, 16 in number, for adjudication under S. 10(1) of the Act. The workmen had raised all these disputes although many of them were perhaps covered by an earlier settlement. The issue before the Court was, when the power to prohibit a strike with which the State/appropriate Government is armed under S. 10(3) of the Act can be put into operation. As it needs a reasonable construction of the provision itself, it is thought proper to quote S. 10(3) itself:

> "Where an industrial dispute has been referred to a Board, (Labour Court, Tribunal or National Tribunal) under this section, the appropriate Government may by order prohibit the continuance of any strike or lockout in connection with such dispute which may be in existence on the date of the reference."

A plain reading of the sub-section leaves no room for doubt in our mind that two conditions are necessary to make S. 10(3) applicable. There must be an industrial dispute existing and such existing dispute must have been referred to a Board, Labour Court, Tribunal or National Tribunal under this section, namely, S. 10(1). Section 10 stands as a self-contained Code as it were so far as this subject-matter is concerned. The prohibitory power springs into existence only when such dispute has been made the subject of reference under S. 10(1). What then is such dispute? The such ness of the dispute is abundantly brought out in the preceding portion of the sub-section. Clearly, there must be an industrial dispute in existence. Secondly, such dispute must have already been referred for adjudication. Then, and then alone, the power to prohibit in respect of such referred dispute can be exercised.

The Court asks a problem to itself that if twenty good grounds of dispute are being raised in a charter of demands by the workmen and the appropriate Government unilaterally

83. AIR 1978 SC 976.

and subjectively decides to refer only one ground out of twenty for adjudication, how can S. 10(3) be invoked and thereby the workmen would be deprived to go on strike in support of those nineteen demands which have not been referred. This would be productive not of industrial peace, which is the objective of the Industrial Disputes Act, but counter-productive of such a purpose.

The Court held that in regard to such disputes as are not referred under S. 10(1), S. 10(3) cannot operate. This stands to reason and justice and a demand which is suppressed by a prohibitory order and is not allowed to be ventilated for adjudication before a Tribunal will explode into industrial unrest and run contrary to the policy of industrial jurisprudence. Thus, on principle and the text of the law, it is submitted that S. 10(3) comes into play when the basis of the strike is covered by S. 10(1). Reference of a dispute and prohibition of a strike on other demands is impermissible.

But the above stated decision does not seem to be correct on a true construction of S. 10(3). The position of law is that when there is a strike in connection with number of demands some of which have been referred to adjudication under S. 10(1), the Government has the right to prohibit the continuance of the strike by invoking S. 10(3) of the Act. However, after prohibition of the continuance of the strike in existence at the time of reference, the workmen may commence a fresh strike in connection with the demands not referred to adjudication for consideration, after complying with the requirements of Ss. 22 or 23 as the case may be. The Delhi High Court has correctly observed in *Keventers Karmachari Sangh* v. *Lt. Governor of Delhi*[84] that even if one of the demands has been referred as industrial disputes, the strike will be in connection with such disputes and the power to prohibit the continuance of the strike can be exercised. Any other interpretation is likely to lead to absurd results. Take a case where the notice of strike contains demands, only some of which can be referred to as industrial disputes and others are not. It cannot be suggested that if the demands which cannot be referred to as industrial disputes are not referred, an order for prohibiting the continuance of the strike cannot be passed.

(qq) **trade union** means a trade union registered under the Trade Unions Act, 1926 (16 of 1926);

(r) **Tribunal** means an Industrial Tribunal constituted under section 7A and includes an Industrial Tribunal constituted before the 10th day of March, 1957, under this Act;

(ra) **unfair labour practice** means any of the practices specified in the Fifth Schedule;

(rb) **village industries** has the meaning assigned to it in Cl. (h) of S. 2 of the Khadi and Village Industries Commission Act, 1956 (61 of 1956).

(rr) **wages** means all remuneration capable of being expressed in terms of money, which would, if the terms of employment, expressed or implied, were fulfilled, be payable to a workman in respect of his employment or of work done in such employment, and includes—

(i) such allowances (including dearness allowance) as the workman is for the time being entitled to;

84. (1971) 2 Lab LJ 375 (Del).

(ii) the value of any house accommodation, or of supply of light, water, medical attendance or other amenity or of any service or of any concessional supply of food-grains or other articles;

(iii) any travelling concession;

(iv) any commission payable on the promotion of sales or business or both; but does not include—

(a) any bonus;

(b) any contribution paid or payable by the employer to any pension fund or provident fund or for the benefit of the workman under any law for the time being in force;

(c) any gratuity payable on the termination of his service.

(s) **workman** means any person (including an apprentice) employed in any industry to do any manual, unskilled, skilled, technical, operational, clerical or supervisory work for hire or reward, whether the terms of employment be express or implied, and for the purposes of any proceeding under this Act in relation to an industrial dispute, includes any such person who has been dismissed, discharged or retrenched in connection with, or as a consequence of, that dispute, or whose dismissal, discharge or retrenchment has led to that dispute, but does not include any such person—

(i) who is subject to the Air Force Act, 1950 (45 of 1950), or the Army Act, 1950 (46 of 1950), or the Navy Act, 1957 (62 of 1957); or

(ii) who is employed in the police service or as an officer or other employee of a prison; or

(iii) who is employed mainly in a managerial or administrative capacity; or

(iv) who, being employed in a supervisory capacity, draws wages exceeding ten thousand per mensem or exercises, either by the nature of the duties attached to the office or by reason of the powers vested in him, functions mainly of a managerial nature.

The definition of workman provided in S. 2(s) may be divided into three parts—substantive part, inclusive part and exclusive part. The substantive part provides the meaning of workman as 'workman' means any person (including an apprentice) employed in any industry to do any manual, unskilled, skilled, technical, operational, clerical or supervisory work for hire or reward, whether the terms of employment be express or implied. The inclusive part enumerates different categories of workman and brings within the ambit of the definition of workman such person who has been dismissed, discharged or retrenched in connection with the industrial disputes. However, they are considered to be workmen for the purpose of any proceeding under this Act in relation to such industrial dispute. The exclusive part specifically excludes the categories of person enumerated in Cl. (i) to (iv) of S. 2(s) of the Act. After reading the substantive part of the definition, it is seen that every person employed in the industry would be a workman irrespective of his status, that is, temporary, permanent or probationer.

On a fair reading of the provisions in S. 2(s) of the Act, it is clear that workman means any person employed in any industry to do any manual, unskilled, skilled, technical, operational, clerical or supervisory work for hire or reward including any such person who has been dismissed, discharged or retrenched.

The latter part of the section excludes four classes of employees including a person employed mainly in a managerial or administrative capacity, or a person employed in a supervisory capacity drawing wages exceeding ₹10,000 per month or exercises functions mainly of a managerial nature. It has to be taken as an accepted principle that in order to come within the meaning of the expression 'workman' in S. 2(s), the person has to be discharging any one of the types of the work enumerated in the first portion of the section. If the person does not come within the first portion of the section, then it is not necessary to consider the further question as to whether he comes within any of the classes of workmen excluded under the latter part of the section. The question whether the person concerned comes within the first part of the section depends upon the nature of duties assigned to him and/or discharged by him. The duties of the employee may be spelt out in the service rules or regulations or standing order or the appointment order or in any other material in which the duties assigned to him may be found. When the employee is assigned a particular type of duty and has been discharging the same till the date of the dispute, then there may not be any difficulty in coming to a conclusion whether he is a workman within the meaning of S. 2(s). If, on the other hand, the nature of duties discharged by the employee is multifarious, then the further question that may arise for consideration is, which of them is his principal duty and which are the ancillary duties performed by him. While deciding the question whether a particular person is a workman within the meaning of S. 2(s) of the Act, designation of the employee is not of much importance and certainly not conclusive in the matter as to whether or not he is a workman. Accordingly, the Supreme Court in *Arkal Govind Raj Rao* v. *Ciba Geigy of India Ltd., Bombay*[85] held that where an employee has multifarious duties and a question is raised whether he is a workman or someone other than a workman, the Court must find out what are the primary and basic duties of the person concerned and if he is incidentally asked to do some other work, may not necessarily be in tune with the basic duties, these additional duties cannot change the character and status of the person concerned. In other words, the dominant purpose of employment must be first taken into consideration and the gloss of some additional duties must be rejected while determining the status and character of the person.

The definition of workman provided in the Act spells out seven types of employment and they are as follows:

(i) Manual work
(ii) Unskilled work
(iii) Skilled work
(iv) Technical work
(v) Operational work
(vi) Clerical work
(vii) Supervisory work

An employee of any industry in question would be a workman provided that his nature of employment must fall within the seven categories of employment as mentioned above.

85. AIR 1985 SC 985.

In other words, a person cannot be assumed to be a workman on the ground that he does not come within the four exceptions in S. 2(s). The specification of the seven types of work in the definition in S. 2(s) obviously is intended to lay down that an employee is to become a workman only if he is employed to do work of one of those types, while there may be employees who, not doing any such work, would be out of the scope of the word 'workman' without having to resort to the exceptions. In practice, quite a large number of employees are employed in industries to do work of more than one of the kinds mentioned in the definition. In such cases, it would be necessary to determine under which classification he will fall for the purpose of finding out whether he does or does not go out of the definition of 'workman' under the exceptions. For this purpose, a workman must be held to be employed to do that work which is the main work he is required to do, even though he may be incidentally doing other type of work.[86]

The question as to whether an employee is a workman or not has to be determined with reference to his principal nature of duties and functions and therefore it needs to look into the fact of the case from where one can very well ascertain the nature of job generally the workman concerned usually performs or is expected to perform. So, it is not possible to lay down any straitjacket formula, which would be applied in all cases and all circumstances. Accordingly, the Supreme Court in *S.K. Maini* v. *M/s. Carona Sahu Company Limited*[87] held that whether or not an employee is a workman under S. 2(s) of the Industrial Disputes Act is required to be determined with reference to his principal nature of duties and functions. Such question is required to be determined with reference to the facts and circumstances of the case and materials on record and it is not possible to lay down any straitjacket formula which can decide the dispute as to the real nature of duties and functions being performed by an employee in all cases. When an employee is employed to do the types of work enumerated in the definition of workman under S. 2(s), there is hardly any difficulty in treating him as a workman under the appropriate classification but in the complexity of industrial or commercial organisations, quite a large number of employees are often required to do more than one kind of work. In such cases, it becomes necessary to determine under which classification the employee will fall for the purpose of deciding whether he comes within the definition of workman or goes out of it. The designation of an employee is not of much importance and what is important is the nature of duty he performs. The determinative factor is the main duties of the employee concerned and not some work incidentally done. In other words, what is, in substance, the work which the employee does, or what, in substance, he is employed to do. Viewed from this angle, if the employee is mainly doing supervisory work but incidentally or for a fraction of time also does some manual or clerical work, the employee should be held to be doing supervisory work. Conversely, if the main work is of manual, clerical or of technical nature, the mere fact that some supervisory or other work is also done by the employee incidentally, or only a small fraction of working time is devoted to some supervisory work, the employee will come within the purview of workman as defined in S. 2(s).

86. *Burmah Shell Oil Storage and Distributing Co. of India Ltd.* v. *Burmah Shell Management Staff Asscn.*, AIR 1971 SC 922.
87. AIR 1994 SC 1824.

In the instant case, an employee was working as the Shop Manager/In-charge of Carona Sahu Co. Ltd. By virtue of his being in-charge of the shop, he was the principal officer in charge of the management of the shop. His principal function was of administrative and managerial nature. It is true that he himself was also required to do some work of clerical nature, but, by and large, he being in charge of the management of the shop had been principally discharging the administrative and managerial work. A manager or an administrative officer is generally invested with the power of supervision in contradistinction to the stereotype work of a clerk. An employee discharging managerial duties and functions may not, as a matter of course, be invested with the power of appointment and discharge of other employees. It is not unlikely that in a big set-up, such power is not invested to a local manager but such power is given to some superior officers also in the management cadre at the divisional or regional level. The unit in a local shop may not be large but management of such small unit may fulfill the requirements and incidence of managerial functions. On a close scrutiny of the nature of duties and functions of the Shop Manager with reference to his admitted terms and conditions of service, it is evident that he was not a workman under S. 2(s) of the Industrial Disputes Act, 1947.

In *E.S.I.C. Medical Officer's Association* v *E.S.I.C. & Another* (MANU/SC/1199/2013). The question came before the Supreme Court for consideration whether medical doctors discharging functions of Medical Officers, i.e. treating patients in Employees' State Insurance Corporations' dispensaries/hospitals are "workmen" within meaning of Section 2(s) of the ID Act ? The Supreme Court considers the nature of the job that a doctor performs and the Court in this cases distinguishes profession vis-à-vis occupation and held that a medical professional treating patients and diagnosing diseases cannot be held to be a "workmen" within the meaning of S. 2(s) of the ID Act. Doctors' profession is a noble profession and is mainly dedicated to serve the society, which demands professionalism and accountability. Distinction between occupation and profession is of paramount importance. An occupation is a principal activity related to job, work or calling that earns regular wages for a person and a profession, on the other hand, requires extensive training, study and mastery of the subject, whether it is teaching students, providing legal advice or treating patients or diagnosing diseases. Persons performing such functions cannot be seen as a workman within the meaning of S. 2(s) of the ID Act.

Supervisor vis-a-vis Workman

The substantive part of the definition of workman provided in S. 2(s) of the Act specifically provides that any person employed in any industry to do any supervisory work will be a workman. Whereas the exclusive part of the definition excludes such a person from the ambit of the definition of workman if:

(a) he draws wages exceeding ₹10,000 per month, or
(b) exercises, either by nature of his duties attached to the office or by reason of powers vested in him, functions mainly of a managerial nature.

Thus, a person employed in any industry to do any supervisory work and not drawing wages exceeding ₹10,000 per month can be a workman as per S. 2(s) of the Act. Whereas a person employed in any industry drawing wages less than ₹10,000 per month may not be a workman if he is attached with duties or power vested in him some managerial function. But in determining the question as to whether a person is employed in an industry in a supervisory capacity or otherwise, the mere designation cannot be the deciding factor as to construe whether such a person is a workman or not.

The question whether a person is employed in a supervisory capacity or clerical work, depends upon whether the main and principal duties carried out by him are those of a supervisory character, or of a nature carried out by a clerk. If a person is mainly doing supervisory work, but, incidentally or for a fraction of time, also does some clerical work, it would have to be held that he is employed in supervisory capacity, and conversely, if the main work done is of clerical nature, the mere fact that some supervisory duties are also carried out incidentally or as a small fraction of the work done by him will not convert his employment as a clerical one in supervisory capacity. The Supreme Court, while considering the fact of a case in *Ananda Bazar Patrika* v. *The Workmen*,[88] observed that the principal work that the employee concerned was doing was that of maintaining and writing the case book and of preparing various returns. Being the seniormost clerk, he was put in charge of the Provident Fund Section and was given a small amount of control over the other clerks working in his section. The only power he could exercise over them was to allocate work between them, to permit them leave during office hours, and to recommend their leave applications. Accordingly, the Court held that these few minor duties of a supervisory nature cannot convert his office of senior clerk in-charge into that of a supervisor.

In deciding about the status of an employee, whether workman or supervisor, his designation alone cannot be said to be decisive and what really should go into consideration is the nature of his duties and the powers conferred upon as well as the functions assigned to him.[89] Therefore, it was also held that a person appointed and working at the relevant point of time as an Inspector, discharging duties, powers and obligations envisaged under S. 15, Maharashtra Act of 1969, is not a workman as defined in S. 2(s) of the Industrial Disputes Act, 1947.[90] In *H.R. Adyanthaya* v. *Sandoz (India) Ltd.*,[89] it was held that as the medical representatives do not perform duties of skilled and technical nature, they are not workmen. The connotation of the word "skilled" in the context in which it is used in the definition of workman in S. 2(s), will not include the work of a sales promotion employee such as the medical representative. That word has to be construed *ejusdem generis* and thus construed, would mean skilled work whether manual or non-manual, which is of a genre of the other types of work mentioned in the definition. The work of promotion of sales of the product or services of the establishment is distinct from and independent of the types of work covered by the said definition.

Ordinarily, a supervisor occupies a position of command and is authorized to take independent decisions or is authorized to act in certain matters within the limit of his authority without the sanction of his seniors. He is a person to supervise the work of someone, so it implies that some employees are supposed to be under his control and he is in a position to direct such employees what to do, how to do, and when to do.

88. (1970) 3 SCC 248.
89. AIR 1994 SC 2608.
90. *Hussan Mithu Mhasvadkar* v. *Bombay Iron and Steel Labour Board,* AIR 2001 SC 3290.

The Supreme Court in *Mukesh K. Tripathi* v. *Sr. Divisional Manager, L.I.C.*[91] considered the fact of the case where the appellant was appointed as Apprentice Development Officer in Life Insurance Corporation and could not adduce any evidence whatsoever as regards the nature of his duties so as to establish that he had performed any skilled, unskilled, manual, technical or operational duties. The Court therefore read the offer of appointment with scheme which clearly provided that he was appointed as apprentice and not to do any skilled, unskilled, manual, technical or operational job. The onus was on the appellant to prove that he was a workman. He failed to prove the same. Furthermore, the duties and obligation of a Development Officer of the Corporation by no stretch of imagination can be held to be performed by an apprentice. A *workman* within the meaning of S. 2(s) of the Industrial Disputes Act, 1947 must not only establish that he is not covered by the provisions of the Apprenticeship Act but must further establish that he is employed in the establishment for the purpose of doing any work contemplated in the definition. Even in a case where a period of apprenticeship is extended, a further written contract carrying out such intention need not be executed. But in a case where a person is allowed to continue without extending the period of apprenticeship either expressly or by necessary implication and regular work is taken from him, he may become a workman. A person who claims himself to be an apprentice has certain rights and obligations under the statute. In case any person raises a plea that his status has been changed from apprentice to a workman, he must plead and prove the requisite facts. In absence of any pleading or proof that either by novation of the contract or by reason of the conduct of the parties, such a change has been brought about, an apprentice cannot be held to be workman.

Is an Apprentice a Workman?

This question was elaborately discussed by the Supreme Court in 2004 in *U.P. State Electricity Board* v. *Shiv Mohan Singh*[92] and it held that the nature and character of the apprentice is nothing but that of a trainee and he is supposed to enter into a contract and by virtue of that contract he is to serve for a fixed period on a fixed stipend. Sub-section (4) of S. 4 of the Apprentices Act, 1961 only lays down that such contract should be registered with the Apprenticeship Adviser. But by non-registration of the contract, the position of the apprentice is not changed to that of a workman.

It is amply clear from the scheme of the Apprentices Act that the apprentice is recruited for the purpose of training as defined in S. 2(aa) of the Act, that an apprentice is a person who is undergoing apprenticeship training in pursuance of a contract of apprenticeship and the apprenticeship training has been defined under S. 2(aaa). That clearly speaks that an apprentice is to undergo apprenticeship training in any industry or establishment under the employer in pursuance of the contract and in terms of the conditions pertaining to that particular trade. Section 6 of the Apprentices Act fixes the period of training and S. 7 states that the contract of apprenticeship shall terminate on the expiry of the period of apprenticeship training. Therefore, it is clear that the nature and character of the apprentice is that of a trainee only, and on the expiry of the training, there is no corresponding obligation

91. AIR 2004 SC 4179.
92. AIR 2004 SC 5009.

on the part of the employer to employ him. The Apprentices Act further makes it clear by virtue of S. 18 that the apprentice trainees are not workers. It clearly lays down that if an apprentice trainee is undergoing apprenticeship training in a designated trade in an establishment, he shall be a trainee and not a worker. It further contemplates that the provisions of labour laws shall not apply in relation to such apprentice. In this connection, reference to the definition of workman given in S. 2(r) of the Apprentices Act, 1961 must be made as it says that it will not include apprentice. Section 20 also lays down as to how a dispute arising under this Apprentices Act, 1961 can be settled. The authority for resolving such a dispute has been given to the Apprenticeship Adviser. Therefore, for any dispute which arises between the apprentice and the employer, remedy has been provided under this Act and there is no need to go to the Labour Court. Therefore, throughout the Act the stress has been laid on the fact that apprentices are not workers. Non-registration of the contract with the Apprenticeship Adviser will not change the nature and character of the apprentices.

The expression 'shall' appearing in S. 4(4) of the Apprentices Act, 1961 is directory and non-registration of the contract will not change the character of the apprentice and they will not acquire the status of a workman. In order to interpret the word 'shall' appearing in any enactment, one has to see the context in which it appears and the effect thereof. The intention of the Apprentices Act is basically to recruit and train persons capable of being employed in the industries. Apart from the statement of objects and reasons, there are provisions in the Act which clearly contemplate that such trained persons shall not fall in the definition of workmen as it specifically excludes the apprentices as defined in S. 2(r). The definition makes it clear that they are apprentices for a purpose undergoing a training, and in S. 18, it has been clearly mentioned that they will be treated as trainees and not workmen and thus no labour laws will apply in relation to such apprentices. Viewing the expression 'shall' in this context, the word shall in S. 4(4) cannot be construed as being mandatory. Sub-section (4) of S. 4 of 1961 Act only says that the contract of apprenticeship should be forwarded to the Adviser that is purely a ministerial/administrative act so that a proper record is maintained by the Apprenticeship Advisor. Nothing turns beyond this. It is purely an administrative act and not forwarding the contract of apprenticeship to the Apprenticeship Adviser will not change the character of the incumbent and it will not render the contract of apprenticeship invalid or void. If the contract or apprenticeship is to be treated as mandatory and the contract is not sent, then the effect will be that the apprentice will not be entitled to any benefit flowing from the Act. In fact, treating the expression 'shall' as mandatory will be counter-productive to the interest of the trainees.

Even from social legislation point of view, the word 'shall' appearing in of S. 4(4) of the Apprentices Act should be construed as directory as it will benefit the apprentice trainee, otherwise it will be oppressive to the welfare of the apprentice. The definition of workman given in S. 2(s) of the Industrial Disputes Act, 1947 includes apprentice. But it is not applicable to the apprentices appointed under the Apprentices Act, 1961. The Apprentices Act is a Code in itself and it clearly stipulates in S. 2(aa) that apprentice means a person who is undergoing apprenticeship training in pursuance of a contract of apprenticeship and the workers are employed for wages for work done by them. Section 18 clearly mentions that the apprentices are not workmen and "the provisions of any law with respect to labour law shall not apply to or in relation to such apprentice." The application of both the Industrial Disputes Acts therefore stands excluded to the apprentice engaged under 1961 Act.

Justice S.B. Sinha, while delivering the concurrent judgment in the instant case, held that if a contract of apprenticeship is entered into the violation of the terms and conditions thereof although may lead to penal consequences, but the same would not render the contract of apprenticeship void or illegal. In the event, the Apprenticeship Adviser can obtain information about such violation and take suitable steps in that regard under the Act or the Rules, but he has not been conferred any power to declare such contract of apprenticeship to be *ipso facto* void *ab initio*. Section 20 also provides resolution of disputes between an apprentice and the employer arising out of the contract of apprenticeship by referring it to the Apprenticeship Advisor for decision. But even while resolving a conflict, he cannot bring the contract to an end. Once a contract of apprenticeship commences, the same cannot be brought to an end, except in accordance with law. By reason of non-registration of the contract of apprenticeship, the same does not become a nullity. If it is to be held that by reason of non-registration of such contract of apprenticeship the contract itself comes to an end, it would be detrimental to the interest of the apprentices, which would frustrate the object of the Act.

The definition of apprentice nowhere states that an apprentice, in order to obtain the benefits of the said Act, must also be registered. Section 18 of the Act says that an apprentice shall not be a worker. It does not say that an unregistered apprentice shall be a worker. Only because the word 'shall' has been employed in sub-s. (4) of S. 4, the same may not be held to be imperative in character having regard to the fact that not only a contract of apprenticeship commences but also in view of the fact that an application for registration of apprenticeship contract is required to be made within a period of three months in terms of Rule 4-B of the Apprenticeship Rules, 1962. The Act nowhere provides for the consequences of non-registration.

Sub-section (4) of S. 4 of the Act can also be held to be directory having regard to the rule laid down in *Heydon's case*. The rule directs that the Courts must adopt that construction which 'shall suppress the mischief and advance the remedy.' Prior to 1973, the provision for registration was mandatory in character. Having regard to the delay which occasioned for registration of contract of apprenticeship, the amendment of 1973 was brought about; pursuant whereto or in furtherance whereof the contract of apprenticeship commences. If the purpose of the amendment was to make the contract workable even without registration, there can be no reason as to why the provision should be construed as imperative in character so as to render a contract of apprenticeship a nullity. In absence of any such specific provision in the statute, it cannot be said that in the event of commission of a breach by the employer, the contract of apprenticeship shall become a contract of employment.

Is a Teacher a Workman?

Even though an educational institution has to be treated as an industry in view of the decision in the *Bangalore Water Supply and Sewerage Board* v. *A. Rajappa*,[93] the question whether teachers in an educational institution can be considered as workmen still remains to be decided.

In order to be a workman, a person should satisfy the following conditions: (i) he should be a person employed in an industry for hire or reward; (ii) he should be engaged in skilled or unskilled manual, supervisory, technical or clerical work; and (iii) he should not be a

93. AIR 1978 SC 548.

person falling under any of the four clauses, i.e. (i) to (iv) mentioned in the definition of 'workman' in S. 2(s) of the Act. The definition also provides that a workman employed in an industry to do any skilled or unskilled manual, supervisory, technical or clerical work for hire or reward includes any such person who has been dismissed, discharged or retrenched in connection with, or as a consequence of, an industrial dispute, or whose dismissal, discharge or retrenchment has led to that dispute.

In *A. Sundarambal* v. *Govt. of Goa, Daman and Diu*,[94] the Supreme Court was primarily concerned with the meaning of the words 'skilled or unskilled manual, supervisory, technical or clerical work'. If an employee in an industry is not a person engaged in doing work falling in any of these categories, he would not be a workman at all even though he is employed in an industry. The question for consideration before the Court was whether a teacher in a school falls under any of the four categories, namely a person doing any skilled or unskilled manual work, supervisory work, technical work or clerical work. If he does not satisfy any one of the above descriptions, he would not be a workman even though he is an employee of an industry.[95] The Court is of the view that the teachers employed by educational institutions whether the said institutions are imparting primary, secondary, graduate or postgraduate education cannot be called as 'workmen' within the meaning of S. 2(s) of the Act. Imparting of education, which is the main function of teachers cannot be considered as skilled or unskilled manual work or supervisory work or technical work or clerical work. Imparting of education is in the nature of a mission or a noble vocation. A teacher educates children, he moulds their character, builds up their personality and makes them fit to become responsible citizens. Children grow under the care of teachers. The clerical work, if any they may do, is only incidental to their principal work of teaching. The Court accordingly held that teachers cannot be treated as 'workmen' as defined under the Act. The Court further categorically said that it is not possible to accept the suggestion that having regard to the object of the Act, all employees in an industry except those falling under the four exceptions (i) to (iv) in S. 2(s) of the Act should be treated as workmen. The acceptance of this argument will render the words 'to do any skilled or unskilled manual, supervisory, technical or clerical work' meaningless.

Tests to Determine Whether an Employee is a Workman

1. It is the dominant purpose of the employment that is relevant and not some additional duties which may be performed by the employee.
2. It is not the designation of the post held by the employee which is relevant, but what is relevant is the nature of duties performed by the employee.
3. The Court has to find out whether the employee can bind the company in the matter of some decision taken on behalf of the company.
4. What is the nature of the supervisory duties performed by the employee? Do they include directing the subordinate to do their work and/or to oversee their performance?

94. AIR 1988 SC 1700.
95. *May and Baker (India) Ltd.* v. *Their Workmen,* AIR 1967 SC 678.

5. Does the employee have power either to recommend or sanction leave of the workman working under him?
6. Does he have the power to take any disciplinary action against the workman working under him?
7. Does he have the power to assign duties and distribute the work?
8. Does the employee have the authority to indent material and to distribute the same among the workmen?
9. Does the employee have power to supervise the work of men or does he supervise only machines and not the work of men?
10. Does the employee have any workmen working under him and does he write their confidential report?

Relatively better off section of employees categorized as workmen like Airlines pilots, etc. do not merely carry out instructions from superior authority but are also required and empowered to take various kinds of on-the-spot decisions in various situations and particularly in exigencies. Their functions, therefore, cannot merely be categorized as those of ordinary workmen. We, therefore, recommend that Government may lay down a list of such highly paid jobs who are presently deemed as workmen category as being outside the purview of the laws relating to workmen and included in the proposed law for the protection of non-workmen. Another alternative is that the Government fix a cut-off limit of remuneration, which is substantially high enough, in the present context, such as ₹25,000 p.m. beyond which employees will not be treated as ordinary 'workmen'. It would be logical to keep all the supervisory personnel, irrespective of their wage/salary, outside the rank of worker and keep them out of the purview of the labour laws meant for workers. All such supervisory category of employees should be clubbed along with the category of persons who discharge managerial and administrative functions. The Commission would also recommend that such a modified definition of worker could be adopted in all the labour laws. We expect managements to take care of the interests of supervisory staff as they will now be part of the managerial fraternity.[96]

SECTION 2A: Dismissal, etc., of an individual workman to be deemed to be an industrial dispute

(1) Where any employer discharges, dismisses, retrenches, or otherwise terminates the services of an individual workman, any dispute or difference between that workman and his employer connected with, or arising out of, such discharge, dismissal, retrenchment or termination shall be deemed to be an industrial dispute notwithstanding that no other workman nor any union of workmen is a party to the dispute.

(2) Notwithstanding anything contained in section 10, any such workman as is specified in sub-section (1) may, make an application direct to the Labour Court or Tribunal for adjudication of the dispute referred to therein after the expiry of forty-five days from the date he has made the application to the Conciliation Officer of the appropriate

96. Report of the Second National Commission on Labour, Conclusion and Recommendation, Chapter 13, para 6.19 & 6.20.

Government for conciliation of the dispute, and in receipt of such application the Labour Court or Tribunal shall have powers and jurisdiction to adjudicate upon the dispute, as if it were a dispute referred to it by the appropriate Government in accordance with the provisions of this Act and all the provisions of this Act shall apply in relation to such adjudication as they apply in relation to an industrial dispute referred to it by the appropriate Government.

(3) The application referred to in sub-section (2) shall be made to the Labour Court or Tribunal before the expiry of three years from the date of discharge, dismissal, retrenchment or otherwise termination of service as specified in sub-section (1).

CHAPTER II

AUTHORITIES UNDER THIS ACT

SECTION 3: Works Committee

(1) In the case of any industrial establishment in which one hundred or more workmen are employed or have been employed on any day in the preceding twelve months, the appropriate Government may by general or special order require the employer to constitute in the prescribed manner a Works Committee consisting of representatives of employers and workmen engaged in the establishment so however that the number of representatives of workmen on the Committee shall not be less than the number of representatives of the employer. The representatives of the workmen shall be chosen in the prescribed manner from among the workmen engaged in the establishment and in consultation with their trade union, if any, registered under the Indian Trade Unions Act, 1926 (16 of 1926).

(2) It shall be the duty of the Works Committee to promote measures for securing and preserving amity and good relations between the employer and workmen and, to that end, to comment upon matters of their common interest or concern and endeavour to compose any material difference of opinion in respect of such matters.

The Works Committee duly constituted under the Act does not represent the workmen for all purposes; but only for the purpose of the functions of the Works Committee. Section 3(2) of the Act sets out the functions of the Works Committee in these words:

> "It shall be the duty of the Works Committee to promote measures for securing and preserving amity and good relations between the employer and workmen and, to that end, to comment upon matters of their common interest or concern and endeavour to compose any material difference of opinion in respect of such matters."

The language used by the Legislature makes it clear that the Works Committee was not intended to supplant or supersede the Unions for the purpose of collective bargaining; they are not authorised to consider real or substantial changes in the conditions of service; their task is only to smooth away frictions that might arise between the workmen and the management in day-to-day work. By no stretch of imagination can it be said that the duties

CHAPTER IIA

NOTICE OF CHANGE

SECTION 9A: Notice of change

No employer, who proposes to effect any change in the conditions of service applicable to any workman in respect of any matter specified in the Fourth Schedule, shall effect such change,—

(a) without giving to the workmen likely to be affected by such change a notice in the prescribed manner of the nature of the change proposed to be effected; or

(b) within twenty-one days of giving such notice:

Provided that no notice shall be required for effecting any such change—

(a) where the change is effected in pursuance of any settlement or award; or

(b) where the workmen likely to be affected by the change are persons to whom the Fundamental and Supplementary Rules, Civil Services (Classification, Control and Appeal) Rules, Civil Services (Temporary Service) Rules, Revised Leave Rules, Civil Service Regulations, Civilians in Defence Services (Classification, Control and Appeal) Rules or the Indian Railway Establishment Code or any other rules or regulations that may be notified in this behalf by the appropriate Government in the Official Gazette, apply.

Section 9A makes it obligatory upon an employer who proposes to effect any change in the conditions of service applicable to any workman in respect of any matter specified in the Fourth Schedule to give a notice of desired or intended change. It cannot do so without giving to the workman likely to be affected by the change, a notice in the prescribed manner of the nature of the change proposed to be effected and within 21 days of giving such notice. There is a proviso to S. 9A which provides exceptions to the rule of giving 21 days' notice. The proviso clause categorically provides that 21 days' notice is not required for affecting any change in the condition of service in the following situations:

(a) where the change is effected in pursuance of any settlement or award; or

(b) workmen governed under Civil Services Rules, etc.

In order to attract S. 9A, the proposed change must be in the conditions of service applicable to the workman in respect of any matters specified in the Fourth Schedule. If the proposed change falls in any of the matters specified in the Fourth Schedule, the change can be effected after giving a notice in the prescribed manner and waiting for 21 days after giving such notice. When a workman is retrenched it cannot be said that change in his conditions of service is effected. The conditions of service are set out in the Fourth Schedule. No item in the Fourth Schedule covers the case of retrenchment. In fact, retrenchment is specifically covered by Item 10 of the Third Schedule. Now, if retrenchment, which connotes termination of service, cannot constitute change in conditions of service in respect of any item mentioned in the Fourth Schedule, S. 9A would not be attracted. If the proposed change does not cover any matter in the Fourth Schedule, S. 9A is not attracted and no notice is necessary.[99]

99. *L. Robert D'Souza* v. *Executive Engineer*, Southern Railway, AIR 1982 SC 854.

In *Harmohinder Singh* v. *Kharga Canteen, Ambala Cantt.*,[100] the basic question that arose before the Supreme Court for consideration was whether an employee's service can be terminated in accordance with the Standing Orders, introduced subsequent to his entering a service. The appellant was appointed as a salesman by the respondent canteen and subsequently as a cashier. The letter of appointment and the Standing Orders, *inter alia*, provided that the service of the appellant could be terminated by one month's notice by either party. The Standing Orders also provided that the "services of all canteen employees will be on temporary basis extendable on six monthly basis". In 1988, Para 3-A was introduced in the Standing Orders of the respondent. The amended Standing Order provided that maximum permissible service for an employee is of 15 years. On completion of 15 years of service with the canteen, the appellant was terminated. The appellant challenged the Standing Order as violative of S. 9A of the Industrial Disputes Act on grounds that changes in the conditions of service were made without any notice.

It was held that the conditions of service, for change of which notice is to be given under the 4th Schedule of the Industrial Dispute Act, do not, in terms, include the subject matter of the amended Standing Orders namely, the fixation of a period of service or date of retirement. No argument has been advanced as to which of the eleven items of Schedule 4 could, even by a process of interpretation, include the amended para of Standing Orders. There is nothing on record to show that prior to the introduction of the amended para of Standing Orders, the workmen of the canteen continued, as a matter of right, till they reached the age of superannuation applicable to Government servants. On the contrary, the Standing Orders expressly provide that the services of canteen workers were temporary and for a period of six months. It cannot be said that the introduction of a maximum period of service would operate to the detriment of the employee who was otherwise entitled to serve only for six months and was liable to be dismissed merely upon the service of a month's notice. It was not necessary, therefore, to give any notice to the workmen under S. 9A of the Act before introducing such change in the Standing Orders. Besides, the canteen's averment that the amended Standing Orders were duly intimated to all its employees who had also signed the same has not been disputed by the appellant.

It is clear from the very wordings of S. 9A read with item No. 10 of the Fourth Schedule that any management which seeks to introduce a new working pattern for its existing workforce by any future scheme of rationalisation, standardisation or improvement of plant or technique which has a tendency to lead to future retrenchment of workmen has to give prior notice of the proposed change. Notice under S. 9A must precede the introduction of rationalisation concerned; it cannot follow the introduction of such a rationalisation. In the present case, in the composing department of the appellant-newspaper where the respondent was working, composing work was earlier being done by hand, i.e. manually. The appellant installed a photo type machine on experimental basis. In a few months of successful working, the machine ceased to be on experimental basis and became a stark reality and this machine had necessarily a tendency to displace the workmen who were earlier working in the hand composing department. As per the scheme of S. 9A, a notice could have been sent before the machine was brought in the premises as an experimental measure, or at least before the

100. AIR 2001 SC 2681.

date when the same was continued to be installed as a confirmed necessary component of machinery for printing at the appellant's premises at Nagpur. If such a notice was given to the respondent-workman and other workmen similarly situated, they could have persuaded the appellant to resort to any other type of rationalisation, or to absorb them on suitable jobs in the same premises in any other department of the appellant at Nagpur. That opportunity was never made available to the respondent. Therefore, notice under S. 9A issued after installation of the machine and after bringing into force the rationalisation scheme was *ex facie* a stillborn and incompetent notice and was clearly violative of the provisions of S. 9A of the Act, which amounted to putting the cart before the horse. Such an incompetent and illegal notice under S. 9A could not legally enable the appellant to terminate the services of the respondent. If it is accepted that machine can be introduced on experimental basis first or even after it has already worked for some time and is required to be continued as a full-fledged machine, as and when the employer decides to terminate the services of the workmen as a direct consequence of such introduction of machine, he can give notice under S. 9A of the Act at any such time, then the very scheme of S. 9A read with Sch. IV, Item No. 10 of the Industrial Disputes Act could be rendered ineffective and inoperative.[101]

In *Tata Iron and Steel Co. Ltd., M/s.* v. *Workmen of M/s. Tata Iron and Steel Co. Ltd.*,[102] the question came before the Supreme Court whether notice is required under S. 9A if management proposes to change in weekly days of rest from Sunday to some other day. The Court referred entry no. 8 of Schedule 4 of the Act and held that indeed, entry no. 8 dealing with *"withdrawal of customary concession or privilege or change in usage"* is wide enough to take within its fold the change of weekly holidays from Sunday to some other day of the week, because it seems that fixation of Sundays as weekly rest days is founded on usage and/or is treated as a customary privilege and any change in such weekly holidays would fall within the expressions *'change in usage'* or '*customary privilege*'. Notice for effecting such change would be necessary under S. 9A. Change without notice would be ineffective. The real object and purpose of S. 9A is to afford an opportunity to the workmen to consider the effect of a proposed change and, if necessary, to represent their view on the proposal. Even assuming that the alteration of the date of the holiday for Diwali will amount to a change in the condition of service, but there is no question of a contravention of S. 9A, when the majority of the workmen themselves requested the employer to make the alteration.[103] The requirement of a notice to workmen would arise only if they are likely to be affected prejudicially. A change in the conditions of service contemplated by the S. 9A should be understood in that sense. It is not intended to cover a case where the proposal, for instance, is to hike the pay scale or to provide better employment condition by a unilateral decision of the employer. The whole object of the section is apparently to prevent a unilateral action on the part of the employer changing the conditions of service to the prejudice of the workman. Section 9A cannot be attracted to a situation where an option is given to the workmen concerned to accept the change or to continue under the existing terms.[104] Section 9A is also equally applicable to the minority education protected under Art. 30(1) of the Constitution of

101. *Lokmat Newspaper Pvt. Ltd., M/s.* v. *Shankarprasad,* AIR 1999 SC 2423.
102. AIR 1972 SC 1917.
103. *Assam Match Company Ltd.* v. *Bijoy Lal Sen,* AIR 1973 SC 2155.
104. *Tamil Elct. Workers Federation* v. *M.S. Electricity Board,* [1962] II LLJ 136 (Mad.).

India.[105] The Second National Commission on Labour recommended that there need not be a statutory obligation for the employer to give prior notice, in regard to item 11 of the Fourth Schedule for the purpose of increase in the workforce, as is the position now under S. 9A of the ID Act. Further, the Commission is of the view that notice of change, issued by an employer as per provisions of S. 9A, should not operate as a stay under S. 33, though such a decision of the management will be justiciable under S. 33A.[106]

SECTION 9B: Power of Government to exempt

Where the appropriate Government is of opinion that the application of the provisions of S. 9A to any class of industrial establishments or to any class of workmen employed in any industrial establishment affect the employers in relation thereto so prejudicially that such application may cause serious repercussion on the industry concerned and that public interest so requires, the appropriate Government may, by notification in the Official Gazette, direct that the provisions of the said section shall not apply or shall apply, subject to such conditions as may be specified in the notification, to that class of industrial establishments or to that class of workmen employed in any industrial establishment.

CHAPTER IIB[107]

GRIEVANCE REDRESSAL MACHINERY

SECTION 9C: Setting up of Grievance Redressal Machinery

(1) Every industrial establishment employing twenty or more workmen shall have one or more Grievance Redressal Committee for the resolution of disputes arising out of individual grievances.

(2) The Grievance Redressal Committee shall consist of equal number of members from the employer and the workmen.

(3) The chairperson of the Grievance Redressal Committee shall be selected from the employer and from among the workmen alternatively on rotation basis every year.

(4) The total number of members of the Grievance Redressal Committee shall not exceed more than six:

Provided that there shall be, as far as practicable one woman member if the Grievance Redressal Committee has two members and in case the number of members are more than two, the number of women members may be increased proportionately.

(5) Notwithstanding anything contained in this section, the setting up of Grievance Redressal Committee shall not affect the right of the workman to raise industrial dispute on the same matter under the provisions of this Act.

105. *Hospital Employees Union* v. *Christian Medical College,* (1987) 4 SCC 691.
106. Report of the Second National Commission on Labour, p. 43, para 6.82.
107. Substituted by the Industrial Dispute (Amendment) Act, 2010, w.e.f. 15-09-2010.

(6) The Grievance Redressal Committee may complete its proceedings within thirty days on receipt of a written application by or on behalf of the aggrieved party.

(7) The workman who is aggrieved of the decision of the Grievance Redressal Committee may prefer an appeal to the employer against the decision of Grievance Redressal Committee and the employer shall, within one month from the date of receipt of such appeal, dispose of the same and send a copy of his decision to the workman concerned.

(8) Nothing contained in this section shall apply to the workmen for whom there is an established Grievance Redressal Mechanism in the establishment concerned.

CHAPTER III

REFERENCE OF DISPUTES TO BOARDS, COURTS OR TRIBUNALS

SECTION 10: Reference of disputes to Boards, Courts or Tribunals

(1) Where the appropriate Government is of opinion that any industrial dispute exists or is apprehended, it may at any time, by order in writing,—

(a) refer the dispute to a Board for promoting a settlement thereof; or

(b) refer any matter appearing to be connected with or relevant to the dispute to a Court for inquiry; or

(c) refer the dispute or any matter appearing to be connected with, or relevant to, the dispute, if it relates to any matter specified in the Second Schedule, to a Labour Court for adjudication; or

(d) refer the dispute or any matter appearing to be connected with, or relevant to, the dispute, whether it relates to any matter specified, in the Second Schedule or the Third Schedule, to a Tribunal for adjudication:

Provided that where the dispute relates to any matter specified in the Third Schedule and is not likely to affect more than one hundred workmen, the appropriate Government may, if it so thinks fit, make the reference to a Labour Court under Cl. (c):

Provided further that where the dispute relates to a public utility service and a notice under S. 22 has been given, the appropriate Government shall, unless it considers that the notice has been frivolously or vexatiously given or that it would be inexpedient so to do, make a reference under this sub-section notwithstanding that any other proceedings under this Act in respect of the dispute may have commenced:

Provided also that where the dispute in relation to which the Central Government is the appropriate Government, it shall be competent for that Government to refer the dispute to a Labour Court or an Industrial Tribunal, as the case may be, constituted by the State Government.

(1A) Where the Central Government is of opinion that any industrial dispute exists or is apprehended and the dispute involves any question of national importance or is of such a nature that industrial establishments situated in more than one State are likely to be interested in, or affected by, such dispute and that the dispute should be adjudicated by a National Tribunal, then, the Central Government may, whether or not it is the appropriate Government in relation to that dispute, at any time, by order in writing, refer the dispute or any matter appearing to be connected with, or relevant to, the dispute, whether it relates to any matter specified in the Second Schedule or the Third Schedule, to a National Tribunal for adjudication.

(2) Where the parties to an industrial dispute apply in the prescribed manner, whether jointly or separately, for a reference of the dispute to a Board, Court, Labour Court, Tribunal or National Tribunal, the appropriate Government, if satisfied that the persons applying represent the majority of each party, shall make the reference accordingly.

(2A) An order referring an industrial dispute to a Labour Court, Tribunal or National Tribunal under this section shall specify the period within which such Labour Court, Tribunal or National Tribunal shall submit its award on such dispute to the appropriate Government:

Provided that where such industrial dispute is connected with an individual workman, no such period shall exceed three months:

Provided further that where the parties to an industrial dispute apply in the prescribed manner, whether jointly or separately, to the Labour Court, Tribunal or National Tribunal for extension of such period or for any other reason, and the presiding officer of such Labour Court, Tribunal or National Tribunal considers it necessary or expedient to extend such period, he may for reasons to be recorded in writing, extend such period by such further period as he may think fit:

Provided also that in computing any period specified in this sub-section, the period, if any, for which the proceedings before the Labour Court, Tribunal or National Tribunal had been stayed by any injunction or order of a Civil Court shall be excluded:

Provided also that no proceedings before a Labour Court, Tribunal or National Tribunal shall lapse merely on the ground that any period specified under this sub-section had expired without such proceedings being completed.

(3) Where an industrial dispute has been referred to a Board, Labour Court, Tribunal or National Tribunal under this section, the appropriate Government may by order prohibit the continuance of any strike or lock-out in connection with such dispute which may be in existence on the date of the reference.

(4) Where in an order referring an industrial dispute to a Labour Court, Tribunal or National Tribunal under this section or in a subsequent order, the appropriate Government has specified the points of dispute for adjudication, the Labour Court or the Tribunal or the National Tribunal, as the case may be shall confine its adjudication to those points and matters incidental thereto.

(5) Where a dispute concerning any establishment or establishments has been, or is to be, referred to a Labour Court, Tribunal or National Tribunal under this section and the appropriate Government is of opinion, whether on an application made to it in this behalf or otherwise, that the dispute is of such a nature that any other

establishment, group or class of establishments of a similar nature is likely to be interested in, or affected by, such dispute, the appropriate Government may, at the time of making the reference or at any time thereafter but before the submission of the award, include in that reference such establishment, group or class of establishments, whether or not at the time of such inclusion any dispute exists or is apprehended in that establishment, group or class of establishments.

(6) Where any reference has been made under sub-section (1A) to a National Tribunal, then notwithstanding anything contained in this Act, no Labour Court or Tribunal shall have jurisdiction to adjudicate upon any matter which is under adjudication before the National Tribunal, and accordingly,—

(a) if the matter under adjudication before the National Tribunal is pending in a proceeding before a Labour Court or Tribunal, the proceeding before the Labour Court or the Tribunal, as the case may be, in so far as it relates to such matter, shall be deemed to have been quashed on such reference to the National Tribunal; and

(b) it shall not be lawful for the appropriate Government to refer the matter under adjudication before the National Tribunal to any Labour Court or Tribunal for adjudication during the pendency of the proceeding in relation to such matter before the National Tribunal.

Explanation: In this sub-section, 'Labour Court' or 'Tribunal' includes any Court or Tribunal or other authority constituted under any law relating to investigation and settlement of industrial disputes in force in any State.

(7) Where any industrial dispute, in relation to which the Central Government is not the appropriate Government, is referred to a National Tribunal, then notwithstanding anything contained in this Act, any reference in section 15, section 17, section 19, section 33A, section 33B and section 36A to the appropriate Government in relation to such dispute shall be construed as a reference to the Central Government but, save as aforesaid and as otherwise expressly provided in this Act, any reference in any other provision of this Act to the appropriate Government in relation to that dispute shall mean a reference to the State Government.

(8) No proceedings pending before a Labour Court, Tribunal or National Tribunal in relation to an industrial dispute shall lapse merely by reason of the death of any of the parties to the dispute being a workman, and such Labour Court, Tribunal or National Tribunal shall complete such proceedings and submit its award to the appropriate Government.

The different authorities which are constituted under the Act are set up with different ends in view and are invested with powers and duties necessary for the achievement of the purposes for which they are set up. The appropriate Government is invested with a discretion to choose one or the other of the authorities for the purpose of investigation and settlement of industrial disputes, and whether it sets up one authority or the other for the achievement of the desired ends depends upon its appraisement of the situation as it obtains in a particular industry or establishment.

It is not necessary that all the steps which are contemplated in the manner indicated in S. 10 for reference of disputes to Boards, Courts or Tribunals should be taken seriatim one after the other. Whether one or the other of the steps should be taken by the appropriate Government must depend upon the exigencies of the situation, the imminence of industrial strife resulting in cessation or interruption of industrial production and breach of industrial peace endangering public tranquility and law and order. What step would be taken by the appropriate Government in the matter of the industrial dispute must, therefore, be determined by the surrounding circumstances, and the discretion vested in the appropriate Government for setting up one or the other of the authorities for the purpose of investigation and settlement of industrial disputes must be exercised by it having regard to the exigencies of the situation and the objects to be achieved. No hard and fast rule can be laid down as to the setting up of one or the other of the authorities for the purpose of bringing about the desired end which is the settlement of industrial disputes and promotion of industrial peace, and it is hardly legitimate to say that such discretion as is vested in the appropriate Government will be exercised 'with an evil eye and an unequal hand'.[108]

Section 10 provides wide power to the appropriate Government and the appropriate Government is the instrument to activate the adjudicatory authorities constituted in the Act. The legislature has, knowingly or purposefully, used some terminology in S. 10(1) which need clarification as they are not free from ambiguity and subject to interpretation. Section 10(1) starts with:

> "where the appropriate Government is of opinion that any industrial dispute exists or is apprehended, it may at any time, by order in writing refer..."

After reading the above provision, it seems that the appropriate Government is having absolute authority to take the decision whether in fact, any industrial dispute exists or is apprehended. Such decision is purely based on the opinion of the appropriate Government in the light of the words, *of opinion,* used in the provision and such opinion may be a subjective one. Even though the appropriate Government is of opinion that the industrial dispute exits or is apprehended, it is not bound by law to refer the matter in the light of the words, *it may*, used in the provision. If the appropriate Government, for example, is of opinion that any industrial dispute exists or is apprehended and it thinks it proper to refer the matter to the adjudicaotry authorities constituted in the Act for adjudication, the question that comes to our mind is when it is to be referred? There is no such time limit prescribed in S. 10 to refer. Such conclusion may be drawn in view of the words, *at any time* used in S. 10. The author thought it proper to solve these issues with the help of judicial decisions.

The first question to be posed is whether while exercising the power conferred by S. 10 to refer an industrial dispute to a Tribunal for adjudication, the appropriate Government is discharging an administrative function or a quasi-judicial function. In *State of Madras* v. *C.P. Sarathy,*[109] a Constitution Bench of the Supreme Court observed:

> "But, it must be remembered that in making a reference under S. 10(1) the Government is doing an administrative act and the fact that it has to form an opinion as to the factual existence of an industrial dispute as a preliminary step to the discharge of its function does

108. *Niemla Textile Finishing Mills Ltd.* v. *2nd Punjab Tribunal,* AIR 1957 SC 329.
109. AIR 1953 SC 53.

> not make it any the less administrative in character. The Court cannot, therefore, canvass the order of reference closely to see if there was any material before the Government to support its conclusion, as if it was a judicial or quasi-judicial determination."[110]

In *C.P. Sarathy* case, the Court held on construction of S. 10(1) of the Central Act that the function of the appropriate Government there under is an administrative function. It was so held presumably because the Government cannot go into the merits of the dispute, its function being only to refer such a dispute for adjudication so that the industrial relations between the employer and his employees may not continue to remain disturbed and the dispute may be resolved through a judicial process as speedily as possible.[111] In *Shambu Nath Goyal* v. *Bank of Baroda, Jullundur*,[112] it was held that in making a reference under S. 10(1), the appropriate Government is doing an administrative act and the fact that it has to form an opinion as to the factual existence of an industrial dispute as a preliminary step to the discharge of its function does not make it any less administrative, in character. Thus, while exercising power of making a reference under S. 10(1), the appropriate Government performs an administrative act and not a Judicial or quasi-judicial act.

The view that while exercising power under S. 10(1), the Government performs administrative function can be supported by all alternative line of reasoning. Assuming that making or refusing to make a reference under S. 10(1) is a quasi-judicial function, there is bound to be a conflict of jurisdiction if the reference is ultimately made. A quasi-judicial function is, to some extent, an adjudicatory function in a lis between two contending parties. The Government as an umpire, assuming that it is performing a quasi-judicial function when it proceeds to make a reference, would imply that the quasi-judicial determination of *lis prima facie* shows that one who raised the dispute has established merits of the dispute. The inference necessarily follows from the assumption that the function performed under S. 10(1) is a quasi-judicial function. Now by exercising power under S. 10, a reference is made to a Tribunal for adjudication and the Tribunal comes to the conclusion that there was no merit in the dispute prima facie a conflict of jurisdiction may emerge. Therefore, the view that while exercising power under S. 10(1), the function performed by the appropriate Government is administrative function and not a judicial or quasi-judicial function, is beyond the pale of controversy.

If the Government performs an administrative act while either making or refusing to make a reference under S. 10(1), it cannot delve into the merits of the dispute and take upon itself the determination of lis. That would certainly be in excess of the power conferred by S. 10. Section 10 requires the appropriate Government to be satisfied that an industrial dispute exists or is apprehended. This may permit the appropriate Government to determine prima facie whether an industrial dispute exists or the claim is frivolous or bogus or put forth for extraneous and irrelevant reasons, not for justice or industrial peace and harmony. Every administrative determination must be based on grounds relevant and germane to the exercise of power. If the administrative determination is based on grounds irrelevant, extraneous or not germane to the exercise of power, it is liable to be questioned in exercise of the power of judicial review. Therefore, the Court may not issue writ of mandamus, directing the

110. *Ibid.* at p. 57 per Patanjali Sastri, C.J.
111. *Western India Match Co. Ltd.* v. *Western India Match Co. Workers Union,* AIR 1970 SC 1205.
112. AIR 1978 SC 1088.

Government to make a reference, but it can, after examining the reasons given by the appropriate Government for refusing to make a reference, come to a conclusion that they are irrelevant, extraneous or not germane to the determination and then can direct the Government to reconsider the matter.[113] Section 10(1) confers a discretionary power and this discretionary power can be exercised on being satisfied that an industrial dispute exists or is apprehended. There must be some material before the Government on the basis of which it forms an opinion that an industrial dispute exists or is apprehended. The power conferred on the appropriate Government is an administrative power and the action of the Government in making the reference is an administrative act. The adequacy or sufficiency of the material on which the opinion was formed is beyond the pale of judicial scrutiny. If the action of the Government in making the reference is impugned by a party, it would be open to such a party to show that what was referred was not an industrial dispute and that the Tribunal had no jurisdiction to make the Award, but if the dispute was an industrial dispute, its factual existence and the expediency of making reference in the circumstances of a particular case are matters entirely for Government to decide upon, and it will not be competent for the Court to hold the reference bad and quash the proceedings for want of jurisdiction merely because there was, in its opinion, no material before the Government on which it could have come to an affirmative conclusion on those matters.

The Government does not lack the power to make the reference in respect of the same industrial dispute which it once declined to refer. Nor is it necessary that the Government must have some fresh material made available to it subsequent to its refusal to make a reference, for the formation of a fresh opinion, for making the reference.

The only requirement for taking action under S. 10(1) is that there must be some material before the Government which will enable it to form an opinion that an industrial dispute exists or is apprehended. This is an administrative function of the Government as the expression is understood in contradistinction to judicial or quasi-judicial function. Merely because the Government rejects a request for a reference or declines to make a reference, it cannot be said that the industrial dispute has ceased to exist, nor could it be said to be a review of any judicial or quasi-judicial order or determination. The industrial dispute may nonetheless continue to remain in existence, and if at a subsequent stage the appropriate Government is satisfied that in the interest of industrial peace and for promoting industrial harmony it is desirable to make a reference, the appropriate Government does not lack power to do so under S. 10(1), nor is it precluded from making the reference on the only ground that on an earlier occasion it had declined to make the reference. The expression *at any time* in S. 10(1) will clearly negative the contention that once the Government declines to make a reference, the power to make a reference under S. 10(1) in respect of the same dispute gets exhausted. A refusal on the part of the appropriate Government to make a reference is not indicative of an exercise of power under S. 10(1), the exercise of the power would be a positive act of making a reference. Therefore, when the Government declines to make a reference, the source of power is neither dried up nor exhausted. It only indicates that the Government for the time being refused to exercise the power but that does not denude the power. The power to make the reference remains intact and can be exercised if the material

---

113. *Ram Avtar Sharma* v. *State of Haryana,* AIR 1985 SC 915.

and relevant considerations for exercise of power are available; they being in the continued existence of the dispute and the wisdom of referring it, in the larger interest of industrial peace and harmony.[114]

In *Sultan Singh* v. *State of Haryana*,[115] the Supreme Court held that an order issued under S. 10 of the Act is an administrative order and the Government is entitled to go into the question whether an industrial dispute exists or is apprehended and it will be only a subjective satisfaction on the basis of material on record and being an administrative order no lis is involved. In 2004, in *Mukand Ltd.* v. *Mukand Staff and Officers' Association*,[116] an important issue of vital public importance came before the Supreme Court for consideration, namely whether the Industrial Tribunal is justified in adjudicating upon the service conditions of employees, who are not 'workmen' under the Industrial Disputes Act, 1947. The fact of the case reveals that the order of reference passed in the present case, states that dispute between M.S. Mukand Ltd., L.B.S. Marg, Kurla, Bombay-400070 and the workmen employed under them has been referred to the Tribunal. It is, therefore, clear that the Tribunal, being a creature of the reference, cannot adjudicate matters not within the purview of the dispute actually referred to it by the order of reference. In the facts and circumstances of the present case, the Tribunal could not have adjudicated the issues of the salaries of the employees who are not workmen under the Act, nor could it have covered such employees by its award. Even assuming that the reference covered the non-workmen, the Tribunal, acting within its jurisdiction under the Act, could not have adjudicated the dispute insofar as it related to the 'non-workmen'.

The contentions that Tribunal can adjudicate the dispute relating to non-workmen cannot be supported on grounds that, the workmen can, in appropriate case, espouse the cause of non-workmen because under the definition of 'industrial disputes' under S. 2(k), the dispute may not only be related to workmen but to any person including non-workmen, provided, however, that there is community of interest between the 'workmen' and the 'non-workmen', that the provisions of S. 18(3)(d) of the Act make the award not only binding on the workmen but also on the non-workmen, who may be in employment on the date of the dispute, or may have subsequently become employed in the establishment and that under S. 18(3)(b) the Tribunal has power to summon parties other than parties to the order or reference, to appear in the proceedings as parties to the dispute. This has a reference to proper and necessary parties, as such parties need not necessarily belong to the category of employer or workman. In the instant case, the Tribunal, after considering the material before it, has not arrived at a finding that the non-workmen are a necessary party to the reference or the requirement of issuing summons to the non-workmen under S. 18 of the Act in accordance with law has been complied with. Moreover, the reference covers as it does 'Mukund Ltd. and the workmen employed by them.' The award thus can be made effective and enforceable in respect of the workmen.

Disputes can be raised only by the workmen with the employer. The workmen, however, can in appropriate cases espouse the cause of non-workmen if there is community of interest between the workmen and the non-workmen. In the instant case, it is an admitted fact that

114. *Avon Services Production Agencies (P) Ltd., M/s.* v. *Industrial Tribunal, Haryana,* AIR 1979 SC 170.
115. AIR 1996 SC 1007.
116. AIR 2004 SC 3905.

the community of interest or estoppel has never been pleaded. If the non-workmen are given the status and protection available to the workmen, it would mean that the entire machinery and procedure of the Act would apply to the non-workmen with regard to their employment/non-employment, the terms of employment, the conditions of labour, etc. This would cast on the appellant-company the onerous burden of compliance with the provisions of the Act in respect of non-workmen. Such situation is not envisaged by the Act which is solely designed to protect the interests of the workmen as defined in S. 2(s) of the Act.

Sections 10(1) and 12(5)

When the appropriate Government considers the question as to whether a reference should be made under S. 12(5), it has to act under S. 10(1) of the Act, and S. 10(1) confers discretion on the appropriate Government either to refer the dispute or not to refer it for industrial adjudication accordingly as it is of the opinion that it is expedient to do so or not. In other words, in dealing with an industrial dispute in respect of which a failure report has been submitted under S. 12(4), the appropriate Government ultimately exercises its power under S. 10(1), subject to this that S. 12(5) imposes an obligation on it to record reasons for not making the reference when the dispute has gone through conciliation and a failure report has been made under S. 12(4). It is true that if the dispute in question raises questions of law, the appropriate Government should not purport to reach a final decision on the said questions of law, because that would normally lie within the jurisdiction of the Industrial Tribunal. Similarly, on disputed questions of fact, the appropriate Government cannot purport to reach final conclusions, for that again would be the province of the Industrial Tribunal. But it would not be possible to accept the plea that the appropriate Government is precluded from considering even prima facie the merits of the dispute when it decides the question as to whether its power to make a reference should be exercised under S. 10(1) read with S. 12(5) or not. If the claim made is patently frivolous, or is clearly belated, the appropriate Government may refuse to make a reference. Likewise, if the impact of the claim on the general relations between the employer and the employees in the region is likely to be adverse, the appropriate Government may take that into account in deciding whether a reference should be made or not. It must, therefore, be held that a prima facie examination of the merits cannot be said to be foreign to the enquiry which the appropriate Government is entitled to make in dealing with a dispute under S. 10(1).[117]

Reference vis-à-vis Writ of Mandamus

It is necessary to remember that in entertaining an application for a writ of mandamus against an order made by the appropriate Government under S. 10(1) read with S. 12(5), the Court is not sitting in appeal over the order and is not entitled to consider the propriety or the satisfactory character of the reasons given by the said Government. It would be idle to suggest that in giving reasons to a party for refusing to make a reference under S. 12(5), the appropriate Government has to write an elaborate order indicating exhaustively all the reasons that weighed in its mind in refusing to make a reference. It is no doubt desirable that the party

117. *Bombay Union of Journalists* v. *State of Bombay,* AIR 1964 SC 1617.

concerned should be told clearly and precisely the reasons why no reference is made, because the object of S. 12(5) appears to be to require the appropriate Government to state its reasons for refusing to make a reference, so that the reasons should stand public scrutiny. But that does not mean that a party challenging the validity of the Government's decision not to make a reference can require the Court in writ proceedings to examine the propriety or correctness of the said reasons. If it appears that the reasons given show that the appropriate Government took into account a consideration which was irrelevant or foreign, that no doubt, may justify the claim for a writ of mandamus.

It is submitted that if the appropriate Government does not refer the matter under S. 10 of the Act due to *malafide* intention, the Court may interfere and the writ of mandamus may lie against the appropriate Government, thereby it may be directed to refer the matter. In *Nirmal Singh* v. *State of Punjab*[118] where the Labour Commissioner, while exercising the powers of the State Government under S. 12 for making reference, declined to refer the dispute for adjudication on the ground that the delinquent, a bank employee, was not a 'workman' within the meaning of S. 2(s) but no reasons were given by him to justify that conclusion. All that he stated in his order was that the post held by the delinquent did not fall 'within the category of workman'. The Supreme Court declined to remand the matter to the Labour Commissioner asking him to state his reasons why the delinquent was not a workman as it would entail delay and, therefore, directed the Labour Commissioner to make a reference either to the Labour Court or to the Industrial Tribunal under S. 12(5), as he considers proper. In *V. Veerarajan* v. *Govt. of T.N.*[119] where in an appeal against rejection by the State Government to make a reference, the Supreme Court, after finding that the grounds as given by the State Government were not germane, instead of directing to make a reference, sent back the matter to the State Government to give an opportunity to it of giving other valid reasons in support of its order, and the State Government again supported its order of rejection of reference on grounds which were not germane or relevant for the purpose of such decision. Accordingly, the Supreme Court directed the State Government to refer the dispute for adjudication to the Labour Court.

The Supreme Court in 2000 in *Secretary, Indian Tea Association* v. *Ajit Kumar Barat*[120] observed that the appropriate Government would not be justified in making a reference under S. 10 of the Act without satisfying itself on the facts and circumstances brought to its notice that an industrial dispute exists or is apprehended, and if such a reference is made it is desirable, wherever possible, for the government to indicate the nature of dispute in the order of reference. The order of the appropriate Government making a reference under S. 10 of the Act is an administrative order and not a judicial or quasi-judicial one and the Court, therefore, cannot canvass the order of the reference closely to see if there was any material before the Government to support its conclusion, as if it was a judicial or quasi-judicial order. An order made by the appropriate Government under S. 10 of the Act being an administrative order no lis is involved, as such an order is made on the subjective satisfaction of the Government. If it appears from the reasons given that the appropriate Government took into account any consideration irrelevant or foreign material, the Court may in a given case consider the case

118. AIR 1984 SC 1619.
119. AIR 1987 SC 695.
120. AIR 2000 SC 915.

for a writ of mandamus. It would, however, be open to a party to show that what was referred by the Government was not an industrial dispute within the meaning of the Act.

Time Limit for Reference

The words *at any time* used in S. 10(1) provides no time limit for the reference of the matter by the appropriate Government to the authorities provided under the same provision. The Supreme Court in *Shalimar Works Limited, M/s.* v. *Their Workmen*[121] held that it is true that there is no limitation prescribed for reference of disputes to an Industrial Tribunal; even so it is only reasonable that disputes should be referred as soon as possible after they have arisen and after conciliation proceedings have failed.

There is no hard and fast rule regarding the time for making the order of reference. However, the appropriate Government should refer the dispute within a reasonable time. What is reasonable depends upon the facts and circumstances of each case. In *Ajaib Singh* v. *Sirhind Co-op. Mkg.-cum-Processing Service Society Ltd.*,[122] the Supreme Court held that the provisions of Art. 137 of the Schedule to the Limitation Act, 1963 are not applicable to the proceedings under the Act and that the relief under it cannot be denied to the workmen merely on the ground of delay. The plea of delay, if raised by the employer, is required to be proved as a matter of fact by showing the real prejudice and not as a merely hypothetical defence. No reference to the Labour Court can be generally questioned on the ground of delay alone. Even in a case where the delay is shown to be existing, the Tribunal, Labour Court or Board, dealing with the case, can appropriately mould the relief by declining to grant back wages to the workman till the date he raised the demand regarding his illegal retrenchment/termination or dismissal. The Court may also in appropriate cases direct the payment of part of the back wages instead of full back wages. In the instant case delay of 7 years was held to be reasonable. In *Management of M/s. Indian Iron and Steel Co. Ltd.* v. *Prahlad Singh*,[123] it was held that 13 years is too late to entertain the case and thereby the relief sought for was denied. In *Nedungadi Bank Ltd.* v. *K.P. Madhavankutty*,[124] the Supreme Court held:

> "Law does not prescribe any time limit for the appropriate Government to exercise its powers under S. 10 of the Act. It is not that this power can be exercised at any point of time and to revive matters which had since been settled. Power is to be exercised reasonably and in a rational manner. There appears to us to be no rational basis on which the Central Government has exercised powers in this case after lapse of about seven years of order dismissing the respondent from service. At the time reference was made no industrial dispute existed or could be even said to have been apprehended. A dispute which is stale could not be the subject-matter of reference under S. 10 of the Act. As to when a dispute can be said to be stale would depend on the facts and circumstances of each case. When the matter has become final, it appears to us to be rather incongruous that the reference be made under S. 10 of the Act in the circumstances like the present one. In fact it could be said that there was no dispute pending at the time when the reference in question was made. The only ground advanced by the respondent was that two other employees who were

121. AIR 1959 SC 1217.
122. AIR 1999 SC 1351.
123. AIR 2001 SC 69.
124. AIR 2000 SC 839.

dismissed from service were reinstated. Under what circumstances they were dismissed and subsequently reinstated is nowhere mentioned. Demand raised by the respondent for raising industrial dispute was ex facie bad and incompetent."[125]

Constitutional Validity of Section 10

Having regard to the provisions of the Act, it is clear that S. 10 is not discriminatory in its ambit and the appropriate Government is at liberty as and when the occasion arises to refer the industrial disputes arising or threatening to arise between the employers and the workmen to one or the other of the authorities according to the exigencies of the situation. No two cases are alike in nature and the industrial disputes which arise, or are apprehended to arise in particular establishments or undertakings, require to be treated having regard to the situation prevailing in the same. There cannot be any classification, and the reference to one or the other of the authorities has necessarily got to be determined in the exercise of its best discretion by the appropriate Government. Such discretion is neither an unfettered or an uncontrolled discretion nor an unguided one because the criteria for the exercise of such discretion are to be found within the terms of the Act itself.

It cannot also be urged that there is an unguided and unfettered discretion in the matter of changing the period of operation of the award. The appropriate Government cannot merely by its own volition change the period without having regard to the circumstance of a particular case. There is no warrant for the suggestion that such discretion will be exercised by the appropriate Government arbitrarily or capriciously, or so as to prejudice the interests of any of the parties concerned. Therefore, the relevant provisions of the Act and, in particular, S. 10 thereof cannot be held to be unconstitutional and void as infringing the fundamental rights guaranteed under Art. 14 and Art. 19(1)(f) and (g) of the Constitution of India.[126]

The law on the point may briefly be summarized as follows:

1. The appropriate Government would not be justified in making a reference under S. 10 of the Act without satisfying itself on the facts and circumstances brought to its notice that an industrial dispute exists or is apprehended, and if such a reference is made, it is desirable, wherever possible, for the Government to indicate the nature of the dispute in the order of reference.
2. The order of the appropriate Government making a reference under S. 10 of the Act is an administrative order and not a judicial or quasi-judicial one, and the Court, therefore, cannot canvass the order of the reference closely to see if there was any material before the Government to support its conclusion, as if it was a judicial or *quasi-judicial* order.
3. An order made by the appropriate Government under S. 10 of the Act being an administrative order no *lis* is involved, as such an order is made on the subjective satisfaction of the Government.
4. If it appears from the reasons given that the appropriate Government took into account any consideration irrelevant or foreign material, the Court may in a given case consider the case for a writ of mandamus.

---

125. *Ibid.* at p. 842 per D.P. Wadhwa, J.
126. *Niemla Textile Finishing Mills Ltd.* v. *2nd Punjab Tribunal,* AIR 1957 SC 329.

5. It would, however, be open to the party to show that what was referred by the Government was not an industrial dispute within the meaning of the Act.

SECTION 10A: Voluntary reference of disputes to arbitration

(1) Where any industrial dispute exists or is apprehended and the employer and the workmen agree to refer the dispute to arbitration, they may, at any time before the dispute has been referred under S. 10 to a Labour Court or Tribunal or National Tribunal, by a written agreement, refer the dispute to arbitration and the reference shall be to such person or persons (including the presiding officer of a Labour Court or Tribunal or National Tribunal) as an arbitrator or arbitrators as may be specified in the arbitration agreement.

(1A) Where an arbitration agreement provides for a reference of the dispute to an even number of arbitrators, the agreement shall provide for the appointment of another person as umpire who shall enter upon the reference, if the arbitrators are equally divided in their opinion, and the award of the umpire shall prevail and shall be deemed to be the arbitration award for the purposes of this Act.

(2) An arbitration agreement referred to in sub-section (1) shall be in such form and shall be signed by the parties thereto in such manner as may be prescribed.

(3) A copy of the arbitration agreement shall be forwarded to the appropriate Government and the conciliation officer and the appropriate Government shall, within one month from the date of the receipt of such copy, publish the same in the Official Gazette.

(3A) Where an industrial dispute has been referred to arbitration and the appropriate Government is satisfied that the persons making the reference represent the majority of each party, the appropriate Government may, within the time referred to in sub-section (3), issue a notification in such manner as may be prescribed; and when any such notification is issued, the employers and workmen who are not parties to the arbitration agreement but are concerned in the dispute, shall be given an opportunity of presenting their case before the arbitrator or arbitrators.

(4) The arbitrator or arbitrators shall investigate the dispute and submit to the appropriate Government the arbitration award signed by the arbitrator or all the arbitrators, as the case may be.

(4A) Where an industrial dispute has been referred to arbitration and a notification has been issued under sub-section (3A), the appropriate Government may, by order, prohibit the continuance of any strike or lock-out in connection with such dispute which may be in existence on the date of the reference.

(5) Nothing in the Arbitration Act, 1940 (10 of 1940), shall apply to arbitrations under this section.

It is necessary to examine the scheme of the relevant provisions of the Industrial Disputes Act which has a bearing on the voluntary reference to the arbitrator, the powers of the said arbitrator and the procedure which he is required to follow. Section 10A deals with voluntary reference of disputes to arbitration. This provision was inserted by the Industrial Disputes (Amendment and Miscellaneous Provisions) Act, 1956, and it came into force with effect from

10-03-1957. Consequent upon the addition of this provision, several changes were made in the other provisions of the Act. Section 2(b), which defines an award, was amended by the addition of the words "it includes an arbitration award made under S. 10A". In other words, as a result of the amendment of the definition of the word 'award', an arbitration award has now become an award for the purposes of the Act. The inclusion of the arbitration award, within the meaning of S. 2(b) has led to the application of Ss. 17, 17A, 18(2), 19(3), 21, 29, 30, 33C and 36A to the arbitration award. Under S. 17(2), an arbitration award, when published under S. 17(1), shall be final and shall not be called in question by any Court in any manner whatsoever. Section 17A provides that the arbitration agreement shall become enforceable on the expiry of thirty days from the date of its publication under S. 17, and under S. 18(2), it is binding on the parties to the agreement who referred the dispute to arbitration; under S. 19(3), it shall, subject to the provisions of S. 19, remain in operation for a period of one year provided that the appropriate Government may reduce the said period and fix such other period as it thinks fit; provided further that the said period may also be extended as prescribed under the said proviso. The other sub-sections of S. 19 would also apply to the arbitration award. Section 21 which requires certain matters to be kept confidential, is applicable and so S. 30 which provides for a penalty for the contravention of S. 21, also applies. Section 29, which provides for penalty for breach of an award, can be invoked in respect of an arbitration award. Section 33C which provides for a speedy remedy for the recovery of money from an employer is applicable; and S. 36A can also be invoked for the interpretation of any provision of the arbitration award. In other words, since an arbitration award has been included in the definition of the word 'award', these consequential changes have been made in the Act in order to make applicable to an arbitration award.

Section 20, which deals with the commencement and conclusion of proceeding, provides, *inter alia*, by sub-section (3) that proceedings before an arbitrator under S. 10A shall be deemed to have commenced on the date of the reference of the dispute for arbitration and such proceedings shall be deemed to have concluded on the date on which the award becomes enforceable under S. 17A. It would be noticed that just as in the case of proceedings before the Industrial Tribunal commencement of the proceedings is marked by the reference under S. 10, so the commencement of the proceedings before the arbitrator is marked by the reference made by the parties themselves, and that means the commencement of the proceedings takes place even before the appropriate Government has entered on the scene and has taken any action in pursuance of the provisions of S. 10A.

Rules have been framed by the Central Government and some of the State Governments under S. 38(2)(aa), and these rules make provisions for the form of arbitration agreement, the place and time of hearing, the power of the arbitrator to take evidence, the manner in which the summons should be served, the powers of the arbitrator to proceed *ex parte*, if necessary, and the power to correct mistakes in the award and such other matters. Some of these Rules (as for instance, Central Rules 7, 8, 13, 15, 16 and 18 to 28) seem to make a distinction between an arbitrator and the other authorities under the Act, whereas the Rules framed by some of the States (for instance the Rules framed by the Madras State 31, 37, 38, 39, 40, 41 and 42) seem to treat the arbitrator on the same basis as the other appropriate authorities under the Act. That, shortly stated, is the position of the relevant provisions of the Statute and the Rules framed there under. It is in the light of these provisions that we must now consider the character of the arbitrator who enters upon arbitration proceedings as a result of the reference made to him under S. 10A.

In *Engineering Mazdoor Sabha* v. *Hind Cycles Ltd.*[127] the learned Solicitor-General contended that such an arbitrator is no more and no better than a private arbitrator, to whom a reference can be made by the parties under an arbitration agreement as defined by the Arbitration Act, 1940. He argues that such an arbitrator has to act judicially, has to follow a fair procedure, take evidence, hear the parties and come to his conclusion in the light of the evidence adduced before him; and that is all that the arbitrator to whom reference is made under S. 10A does. It may be that the arbitration award is treated as an award for certain purposes under the Act; but the position, in law, still remains that it is an award made by an arbitrator appointed by the parties. Just as an award made by a private arbitrator becomes a decree subject to the provisions of Ss. 15, 16, 17 and 30 of the Arbitration Act, and thus binds the parties, so does an award of the arbitrator under S. 10A become binding on the parties by virtue of the relevant provisions of the Act.

On the other hand, Mr. Pai has urged that it would be unreasonable to treat the present arbitrator as a private arbitrator, because S. 10A gives statutory recognition to the appointment of the arbitrator and the consequential changes made in the Act and the statutory rules framed there under clearly show that he has been clothed with quasi-judicial powers and his proceedings are regulated by rules of procedure. Therefore, it would be appropriate to treat him as a statutory arbitrator and as such, a writ of certiorari would lie against his decision under Art. 226.

Having regard to the several provisions contained in the Industrial Disputes Act and the rules framed there under, the Supreme Court (Six Judge-Bench) in the instant case held that an arbitrator appointed under S. 10A cannot be treated to be exactly similar to a private arbitrator to whom a dispute has been referred under an arbitration agreement under the Arbitration Act. The arbitrator under S. 10A is clothed with certain powers, his procedure is regulated by certain rules and the award pronounced by him is given by statutory provisions a certain validity and a binding character for a specified period. Having regard to these provisions, it may perhaps be possible to describe such an arbitrator as, in a loose sense, a statutory arbitrator.

The decisions of the arbitrators to whom industrial disputes are voluntarily referred to under S. 10-A, Industrial Disputes Act, 1947, are, no doubt, quasi-judicial decisions and amount to a determination or order under Art. 136(1). But an arbitrator acting under S. 10A is not a 'Tribunal' under Art. 136, even though some of "the trappings of a Court" are present in his case. As one of the essential conditions for invoking Art. 136(1) is not satisfied, special leave to appeal to the Supreme Court, from the decision of an arbitrator acting under S. 10A, Industrial Disputes Act, cannot be granted.

The question whether an act is a judicial or a quasi-judicial one, or a purely executive act depends on the terms of the particular rules and the nature, scope and effect of the particular powers in exercise of which the act may be done and would, therefore, depend on the facts and circumstances of each case. The cases brought before the law Courts, which decide such cases accordingly, definitely would fall under the category of judicial decision, whereas

127. AIR 1963 SC 874.

issues decided by the administrative or executive bodies fall clearly under the category of administrative or executive orders. Even Judges, in certain matters, have to act administratively, while administrative or executive authorities may have to act quasi-judicially in dealing with some matters entrusted to their jurisdiction. Where an authority is required to act judicially either by an express provision of the statute under which it acts or by necessary implication of the said statute, the decisions of such an authority generally amount to quasi-judicial decisions.

But the fact that the arbitrator under S. 10A is not exactly in the same position as a probate arbitrator, does not mean that he is a Tribunal under Art. 136. Even if some of the trappings of a Court are present in his case, he lacks the basic, the essential and the fundamental requisite in that behalf because he is not invested with the State's inherent judicial power. He is appointed by the parties and the power to decide the dispute between the parties who appoint him is derived by him from the agreement of the parties and from no other source. The fact that his appointment once made by the parties is recognised by S. 10A and after his appointment, he is clothed with certain powers and has thus, no doubt, some of the trappings of a court, does not mean that the power of adjudication which he is exercising is derived from the State and the main test in determining the question about the character of an adjudicating body is not satisfied.

For invoking Art. 136(1), two conditions must be satisfied: (i) the act complained of must have the character of a judicial or a quasi-judicial act as distinguished from a mere executive or administrative act, and (ii) the authority whose act is complained against must be a Court or a Tribunal. Unless both the conditions are satisfied, Art. 136(1) cannot be invoked.

From the mere fact that a writ under Art. 226 may lie against the award pronounced by an arbitrator acting under S. l0A, it cannot be concluded that such an arbitrator is a 'tribunal' within Art. 136(1). It is so because Art. 226 is, in a sense, wider than Art. 136, the power conferred under Art. 226 not being conditioned or limited by the requirement that the writs can be issued only against an order of a court or a tribunal. The reference under S. 10A is not made by the Government but by the parties themselves. The act of reference, therefore, is not the act of the appropriate Government, but of the parties themselves. It cannot, therefore, be contended that an arbitrator acting under S. 10A cannot be distinguished from an Industrial Tribunal acting under S. 10 of the Act.

In *Rohtas Industries Ltd.* v. *Rohtas Industries Staff Union*,[128] the question came before the Supreme Court for consideration whether an arbitrator can compel the workers engaged in an illegal strike to compensate the loss of business. The Court while dealing the issue looked into the faction of the arbitrator constituted under S. 10A of the Act and held that arbitrator functioning under S. 10A of the Industrial Disputes Act is a statutory Tribunal. Further, it held that the award of the arbitrator can be set aside if an apparent error of law is found in it. Accordingly, Krishna Iyer, J., on behalf of the Court, observed:

> "The arbitrator under S. 10A of the Industrial Disputes Act, (as amended in 1964) has power to bind even those who are not parties to the reference or agreement and the whole exercise under S. 10A as well as the source of the force of the award on publication derives from the statute. It is legitimate to regard such an arbitrator as part of the methodology of the sovereign's dispensation of justice, thus falling within the rainbow of statutory tribunals amenable to judicial review. An award under S. 10A is not only not invulnerable but more

128. AIR 1976 SC 425.

sensitively susceptible to the writ lancet being a quasi-statutory body's decision. Admittedly, such an award can be upset if an apparent error of law stains its face. The distinction, in this area, between a private award and one under S. 10A is fine, but real."[129]

The Court further observed that in order to determine whether an award by the arbitrator under S. 10A of the Industrial Disputes Act suffers from errors of law apparent on the face of it, what is important is a question of law arising on the face of the facts found and its resolution ex facie or *sub silentio*. The arbitrator may not state the law as such. Even then, such cute silence confers no greater or subtler immunity on the award than plain speech. The need for a speaking order, where considerable numbers are affected in their substantial rights, may well be a facet of natural justice or fair procedure. If erroneous law is found as the necessary buckle between the facts found and the conclusions recorded, the award bears its condemnation on its bosom. A minimal judicialisation by statement laconic or lengthy, of the essential law that guides the decision is not only reasonable and desirable but has, over the ages, been observed by arbitrators and quasi-judicial tribunals as a norm of processual justice. The Court while dealing the main issue as aforesaid held that since the Industrial Disputes Act which creates rights and remedies has to be considered as one homogenous whole, it has to be regarded *uno flatu*, in one breath, as it were. On this doctrinal basis, the remedy for the illegal strike (a concept which is the creature not of the common law but of S. 24 of the Act) has to be sought exclusively in S. 26 of the Act. The claim for compensation and the award thereof in arbitral proceedings is invalid on its face. Such a compensation for loss of business is not a dispute or difference between employers and workmen '*which is connected with the employment or non-employment or the terms of employment or with the conditions of labour, of any person.*'

In *Karnal Leather Karamchari Sanghatan* v. *Liberty Footwear Company*,[130] an appeal by special leave that came before the Supreme Court from a decision of the single Judge of Punjab and Haryana High Court raises a very short but important question of law relating to the validity of an arbitral award made before publishing the arbitration agreement under the Industrial Disputes Act, 1947.

The fact of the case reveals the following factual propositions.

The respondent-1 is a registered partnership firm carrying on its trading activities in leather foot wears under the name and style of 'Liberty Footwear Company'. It has its head office at Karnal in the State of Haryana. It had a serious dispute with the workers. The workers' union complained that the management has illegally terminated more than 200 workers. This dispute, however, remained unsettled and the workers went on strike which took a violent turn. The management had to lay-off certain workers which added fuel to the fire. The agitation of the workers before the factory premises created law and order problem forcing the police to intervene. The Labour Commissioner and other top officials of the District arrived and they initiated conciliation proceedings. The then Labour Minister and the Public Health Minister of the State Government were also alerted. They also came and extended their good offices to bring about a settlement. They succeeded in their efforts. Both the parties entered into an agreement containing the terms of settlement of their

129. *Ibid.* at pp. 429–430 per Krishna Iyer, J.
130. AIR 1990 SC 247.

dispute. It was mutually agreed that a committee consisting of five persons, two from the management and two from the union with the Deputy Commissioner, Karnal as the President should be constituted. They would be the arbitrators to determine the said dispute. The committee of arbitrators was accordingly constituted. The Committee gave its award directing the management to reinstate in all the 159 workmen. This was the beginning of another dispute which led to frustrated litigation. The management did not reinstate the workers. It challenged the validity of the award by way of writ petition in the High Court. The award was challenged on the ground that the arbitration agreement was not published in the official Gazette as required under sub-section (3) of S. 10A of the Act and the award made without such publication would be invalid. The learned single Judge of the High Court accepted the writ petition. He expressed the view that the requirement of the sub-s. (3) of S. 10A is mandatory and its non-compliance would vitiate the award. With this conclusion he quashed the award and directed the State Government to publish the agreement in the Gazette. He also directed the Committee to determine the dispute afresh and pass an award after publication of the agreement.

The employees' union without preferring Letters Patent Appeal before the High Court against the judgment of learned single, Judge directly appealed to the Supreme Court by obtaining special leave. Ordinarily, the Supreme Court does not entertain a special leave petition if the party does not exhaust the remedy available to him by way of appeal. But in view of the importance of the question raised and the need to decide it promptly in the interest of industrial adjudication, the Court proceeded to consider the appeal on merits.

> The principal question that arises for consideration is whether non-publication of the arbitration agreement as required under sub-s. (3) of S. 10A, renders the arbitral award invalid and unenforceable.

The Court referred the view of different High Courts and they are as follows:

A Division Bench of the Madhya Pradesh High Court in *Modern Stores* v. *Krishnadas*[131] took the view that the publication of arbitration agreement in the *Gazette* is obligatory, that is, a *sine qua non*, but the requirement of time *within one month* is only directory and not imperative. A similar view was expressed by the Punjab and Haryana High Court in *Landara Engineering and Foundary Works, Phillaur* v. *the Punjab State*.[132] The Delhi High Court in *Mineral Industry Association* v. *Union of India*[133] has also accepted the same principle by simply following the decision of the M.P. High Court in *Modern Stores* Case. The Orissa High Court in *Rasbehary Mohanty* v. *Presiding Officer*, *Labour Court*[134] has held that if the arbitration agreement is not published as required under sub-section (3), it would be an infraction of the statutory provisions in the matter of reference to the arbitrator and in the making of an award. The Kerala High Court in *Kathyee Cotton Mills Ltd.* v. *District Labour Officer*[135] has expressed the view that the requirements of sub-section (3) are mandatory and a failure to comply with the provisions would vitiate the award.

131. AIR 1970 MP 16.
132. 1969 Lab IC 52.
133. AIR 1971 Delhi 160.
134. 1974 Lab IC 1085.
135. (1989) 1 LLJ 417.

Considering the above view, the Supreme Court held:

> "Now look at the provisions of sub-section (3). It is with respect to time for publication of the agreement. But publication appears to be not necessary for validity of the agreement. The agreement becomes binding and enforceable as soon as it is entered into by the parties. Publication is also not an indispensable foundation of jurisdiction of the arbitrator. The jurisdiction of the arbitrator stems from the agreement and not by its publication in the Official Gazette. Why then publication is necessary? Is it an idle formality. Far from it, it would be wrong to construe sub-section (3) in the manner suggested by counsel for the appellant. The Act seeks to achieve social justice on the basis of collective bargaining. Collective bargaining is a technique by which dispute as to conditions of employment is resolved amicably by agreement rather than coercion. The dispute is settled peacefully and voluntarily although reluctantly between labour and management. The voluntary arbitration is a part of infrastructure of dispensation of justice in the industrial adjudication. The arbitrator thus falls within the rainbow of statutory tribunals. When a dispute is referred to arbitration, it is therefore, necessary that the workers must be made aware of the dispute as well as the arbitrator whose award ultimately would bind them. They must know what is referred to arbitration, who is their arbitrator and what is in store for them. They must have an opportunity to share their views with each other and if necessary to place the same before the arbitrator. This is the need for collective bargaining and there cannot be collective bargaining without involving the workers. The Union only helps the workers in resolving their disputes with management but ultimately it would be for the workers to take decision and suggest remedies. It seems to us, therefore, that the arbitration agreement must be published before the arbitrator considers the merits of the dispute. Non-compliance of this requirement would be fatal to the arbitral award."[136]

Arbitrators' Power in the Case of Discharge and Dismissal

(Discussed, please refer S. 11A)

Section 10 vis-a-vis Section 10A

It must be recognised that in the modern welfare state, healthy industrial relations are a matter of paramount importance. In attempting to solve industrial disputes, industrial adjudication, therefore, should not be delayed. Voluntary arbitration appears to be the best method for settlement of industrial disputes. The disputes can be resolved speedily and in less than a year, typically in a few months. The Tribunal adjudication of reference under S. 10(1) often drags on for several years, thus defeating the very purpose of the industrial adjudication. Arbitration is also cheaper than litigation with less legal work and no motion practice. It has limited document discovery with quicker hearings and is less formal than trials. The greatest advantage of arbitration is that there is no right of appeal, review or writ petition. Besides, it may as well reduce the company's litigation costs and its potential exposure to ruinous liability apart from redeeming the workmen from frustration. Sections 10 and 10A of the Act are the alternative remedies to settle an industrial dispute. An industrial dispute can either be referred to an Industrial Tribunal for adjudication under S. 10, or the parties can enter into an arbitration agreement and refer it to an arbitrator under S. 10A. But once the parties have chosen their remedy under S. 10A, the Government cannot refer that dispute for adjudication under S. 10.

---

136. *Ibid.* at p. 254 per K. Jagannatha Shetty, J.

CHAPTER IV

PROCEDURE, POWERS AND DUTIES OF AUTHORITIES

SECTION 11: Procedure and powers of conciliation officers, Boards, Courts and Tribunals

(1) Subject to any rules that may be made in this behalf, an arbitrator, a Board, Court, Labour Court, Tribunal or National Tribunal shall follow such procedure as the arbitrator or other authority concerned may think fit.

(2) A conciliation officer or a member of a Board, or Court or the presiding officer of a Labour Court, Tribunal or National Tribunal may for the purpose of inquiry into any existing or apprehended industrial dispute, after giving reasonable notice, enter the premises occupied by any establishment to which the dispute relates.

(3) Every Board, Court, Labour Court, Tribunal and National Tribunal shall have the same powers as are vested in a Civil Court under the Code of Civil Procedure, 1908 (5 of 1908), when trying a suit, in respect of the following matters, namely—

(a) enforcing the attendance of any person and examining him on oath;
(b) compelling the production of documents and material objects;
(c) issuing commissions for the examination of witnesses;
(d) in respect of such other matters as may be prescribed;

and every inquiry or investigation by a Board, Court, Labour Court, Tribunal or National Tribunal, shall be deemed to be a judicial proceeding within the meaning of Ss. 193 and 228 of the Indian Penal Code (45 of 1860).

(4) A conciliation officer may enforce the attendance of any person for the purpose of examination of such person or call for and inspect any document which he has ground for considering to be relevant to the industrial dispute or to be necessary for the purpose of verifying the implementation of any award or carrying out any other duty imposed on him under this Act, and for the aforesaid purposes, the conciliation officer shall have the same powers as are vested in a Civil Court under the Code of Civil Procedure, 1908 (5 of 1908), in respect of enforcing the attendance of any person and examining him or of compelling the production of documents.

(5) A Court, Labour Court, Tribunal or National Tribunal may, if it so thinks fit, appoint one or more persons having special knowledge of the matter under consideration as assessor or assessors to advise it in the proceeding before it.

(6) All conciliation officers, members of a Board or Court and the presiding officers of a Labour Court, Tribunal or National Tribunal shall be deemed to be public servants within the meaning of S. 21 of the Indian Penal Code (45 of 1860).

(7) Subject to any rules made under this Act, the costs of, and incidental to, any proceeding before a Labour Court, Tribunal or National Tribunal shall be in the discretion of that Labour Court, Tribunal or National Tribunal and the Labour

Court, Tribunal or National Tribunal, as the case may be, shall have full power to determine by and to whom and to what extent and subject to what conditions, if any, such costs are to be paid, and to give all necessary directions for the purposes aforesaid and such costs may, on application made to the appropriate Government by the person entitled, be recovered by that Government in the same manner as an arrear of land revenue.

(8) Every Labour Court, Tribunal or National Tribunal shall be deemed to be a Civil Court for the purposes of sections 345, 346 and 348 of the Code of Criminal Procedure, 1973 (5 of 1898).

(9) Every award made, order issued or settlement arrived at by or before Labour Court or Tribunal or National Tribunal shall be executed in accordance with the procedure laid down for execution of orders and decree of a Civil Court under order 21 of the Code of Civil Procedure, 1908 (5 of 1908).

(10) The Labour Court or Tribunal or National Tribunal, as the case may be, shall transmit any award, order or settlement to a Civil Court having jurisdiction and such Civil Court shall execute the award, order or settlement as if it were a decree passed by it.

It is clear that the Tribunal, being a creature of the reference, cannot adjudicate matters not within the purview of the dispute actually referred to it by the order of reference. In the facts and circumstances of the present case, the Tribunal could not have adjudicated the issues of the salaries of the employees who are not workmen under the Act, nor could it have covered such employees by its award. Even assuming that the reference covered the non- workmen, the Tribunal, acting within its jurisdiction under the Act, could not have adjudicated the dispute insofar as it is related to the 'non-workmen'. The contentions that Tribunal can adjudicate the dispute relating to non-workmen cannot be supported on grounds that the workmen can, in appropriate case, espouse the cause of non-workmen because under the definition of 'industrial disputes' under Cl. (k) of S. 2, the dispute may not only be related to workmen but to any person including non-workmen, provided, however, that there is community of interest between the 'workmen' and the 'non-workmen', that the provisions of Cl. (d) of sub-section (3) of S. 18 of the Act make the award not only binding on the workmen but also on the non-workmen who may have been in the employment on the date of the dispute or may have subsequently become employed in the establishment and that under S. 18(3)(b) the Tribunal has power to summon parties other than parties to the order or reference, to appear in the proceedings as parties to the dispute. This has a reference to proper and necessary parties, as such parties need not necessarily belong to the category of employer or workman. In the instant case, the Tribunal, after considering the material before it, have not arrived at a finding that the non-workmen are a necessary party to the reference or the requirement of issuing summons to the non-workmen under S. 18 of the Act, in accordance with law has been complied with. Moreover, the reference covers as it does "Mukand Ltd. and the workmen employed by them." The award thus can be made effective and enforceable in respect of the workmen.[137]

Section 11(3) of the Act prescribes, *inter alia,* that the Tribunal shall have the same powers as are vested in a Civil Court under the Code of Civil Procedure, when trying a suit in

137. *Mukand Ltd.* v. *Mukand Staff and Officers' Association,* AIR 2004 SC 3905.

respect of the matters specified in Clauses (a) to (d); Cl. (a) refers to enforcing the attendance of any person and examining him on oath; Cl. (b) has reference to the power to compel the production of documents and material objects; Cl. (c) is in respect of issuing commissions for the examination of witnesses; and Cl. (d) is in respect of such other matters as may be prescribed. It is thus clear that the power to add a party to the proceedings pending before a Tribunal which may be exercised under the Code of Civil Procedure under Order 1 Rule 10 is not included in S. 11(3), and there is no other section which confers such a power on the tribunal. Therefore, if S. 18(b) contemplates that persons other than parties to the industrial dispute can be summoned, there is no specific provision conferring power on the Tribunal to summon them, and that inevitably suggests that the power must be read as being implicit in S. 18(b) itself.[138]

In *Punjab National Bank Ltd.* v. *Ram Kunwar, Industrial Tribunal, Delhi,*[139] the question that came for decision before the Supreme Court was a very short one. The respondents appearing before the Court had sought to support the impugned order on the strength of the provisions of S. 11(7) of the Industrial Disputes Act, 1947. Section 11(7) was added by Act 48 of 1950 and which reads, *inter alia,* that the costs of, and incidental to, any proceeding before a Tribunal shall be in the discretion of that Tribunal, and the Tribunal shall have full power to determine by and to whom and to what extent and subject to what conditions, if any, such costs are to be paid and to give all necessary directions for the purposes aforesaid. The question was whether the respondent no. 1 had power, in the exercise of his discretion under the provisions of S. 11(7) to direct the payment of costs in advance by one of the parties to the dispute to the other parties in a pending proceeding, irrespective of the final result of that proceeding.

Section 11(3) enumerates certain powers vested in a Civil Court under the Code of Civil Procedure, and says that every Board, Court and Tribunal under the Act shall have those powers; the last enumerated power is in general terms, being *in respect of such other matters as may be prescribed.* No rules made under the Act, bearing on the question of costs have been brought to the notice; therefore, all that can be said, with regard to the effect of S. 11(3), is that except the enumerated powers, other powers vested in a Civil Court under the Code of Civil Procedure have not been given to the Board, Court or Tribunal under the Act. The Act, however, contains a separate provision in the matter of costs and that is S. 11(7). A comparison of the sub-section with S. 35 of the Code of Civil Procedure shows that the sub-section is in terms similar to those of S. 35 of the Code of Civil Procedure except for the concluding portion of the sub-section which relates to the recovery of costs as arrears of land revenue. There is also another difference that sub-sections (2) and (3) of S. 35 of the Civil Procedure Code do not find place in the Act. The Court therefore held that on a plain reading of the sub-section, it is manifest that:

(1) the expression *costs of any proceeding* means costs of the entire proceeding as determined on its conclusion and not costs in a pending proceeding, nor costs to be incurred in future by a party; and

138. *Hochtief Gammon* v. *Industrial Tribunal, Bhubaneshwar, Orissa,* AIR 1964 SC 1746.
139. AIR 1957 SC 276.

(2) the expression *costs incidental to any proceeding* similarly means costs of interlocutory applications, etc.—such costs as have been determined thereon, at the conclusion of the hearing.

Neither of the two expressions has any reference to costs payable in advance or to be incurred in future by a party; far less do they refer to halting and travelling allowances to be incurred by a party while attending the Court on his own behalf. The Court further held:

> "It is not disputed that sub-s. (7) of S. 11 of the Act gives a discretion to the Tribunal, and it has full power to determine by and to whom and to what extent and subject to what conditions, if any, the costs are to be paid. It is clear, however, that the discretion is a judicial discretion and must be exercised according to the rules of reason and justice—not by chance or caprice or private opinion or some fanciful idea of benevolence or sympathy. It is a negation of justice and reason to direct the appellant to pay in advance the costs of the respondents irrespective of the final result of the proceeding. The general rule is that costs follow the event unless the Court, for good reasons, otherwise orders."[140]

SECTION 11A: Powers of Labour Courts, Tribunals and National Tribunals to give appropriate relief in case of discharge or dismissal of workmen

Where an industrial dispute relating to the discharge or dismissal of a workman has been referred to a Labour Court, Tribunal or National Tribunal for adjudication, and in the course of the adjudication proceedings, the Labour Court, Tribunal or National Tribunal, as the case may be, is satisfied that the order of discharge or dismissal was not justified, it may, by its award, set aside the order of discharge or dismissal and direct reinstatement of the workman on such terms and conditions, if any, as it thinks fit, or give such other relief to the workman including the award of any lesser punishment in lieu of discharge or dismissal as the circumstances of the case may require:

Provided that in any proceeding under this section the Labour Court, Tribunal or National Tribunal, as the case may be, shall rely only on the materials on record and shall not take any fresh evidence in relation to the matter.

Section 11A was incorporated in the Industrial Disputes Act, 1947 by S. 3 of the Industrial Disputes (Amendment) Act, 1971. The Amendment Act passed by the Parliament received the assent of the President on December 8, 1971. Sub-section (2) of S. 1 provided for its coming into force on such date as the Central Government by notification in the Official Gazette appoints. The Central Government by notification No. F.S. 110-18/-1/71-LR, I dated 14-12-1971 appointed the 15th day of December, 1971, as the date on which the said Act would come into force. Accordingly, the Amendment Act came into force with effect from December 15, 1971.

Regarding S. 11A, in the Statement of Objects and Reasons, it is stated as follows:

In *Indian Iron and Steel Co. Ltd.* v. *Their Workmen,*[141] the Supreme Court, while considering the Tribunal's power to interfere with the management's decision to dismiss, discharge or terminate the services of a workman, has observed that in case of dismissal on misconduct, the Tribunal does not act as a Court of appeal and substitute its own judgment for

---

140. *Ibid.* at p. 279 per S.K. Das, J.
141. AIR 1958 S.C. 130 at p. 138.

that of the management and that the Tribunal will interfere only when there is want of good faith, victimisation, unfair labour practice, etc. on the part of the management.

The International Labour Organisation, in its recommendation (No. 119) concerning termination of employment at the initiative of the employer, adopted in June 1963, has recommended that a worker aggrieved by the termination of his employment should be entitled to appeal against the termination among others, to a neutral body such as an arbitrator, a Court, an arbitration committee or a similar body and that the neutral body concerned should be empowered to examine the reasons given in the termination of employment and the other circumstances relating to the case and to render a decision on the justification of the termination. The International Labour Organization has further recommended that the neutral body should be empowered (if it finds that the termination of employment was unjustified) to order that the worker concerned unless reinstated with unpaid wages, should be paid adequate compensation or afforded some other relief.

In accordance with these recommendations, it is considered that the Tribunal's power in an adjudication proceeding relating to discharge or dismissal of a workman should not be limited and that the Tribunal should have the power in cases wherever necessary to set aside the order of discharge or dismissal and direct reinstatement of the workman on such terms and conditions, if any, as it thinks fit, or give such other reliefs to the workmen including the award of any lesser punishment in lieu of discharge or dismissal as the circumstances of the case may require. For this purpose, a new S. 11A is proposed to be inserted in the Industrial Disputes Act, 1947.

Legal Positions Before Section 11A

After a careful observation of the decisions of the Supreme Court in *Indian Iron and Steel Co.* case,[142] *Punjab National Bank* case,[143] *Bharat Sugar Mills* case,[144] *Ritz Theatre* case,[145] *Khardah Co.* case,[146] *Motipur Sugar Factory* case,[147] *R.K. Jain* case,[148] and *Delhi Cloth and General Mills* case,[149] following observations are made:

(1) The right to take disciplinary action and to decide upon the quantum of punishment are mainly managerial functions, but if a dispute is referred to a Tribunal, the latter has power to see if the action of the employer is justified.

(2) Before imposing the punishment, an employer is expected to conduct a proper enquiry in accordance with the provisions of the Standing Orders, if applicable, and the principles of natural justice. The enquiry should not be an empty formality.

(3) When a proper enquiry has been held by an employer, and the finding of misconduct is a plausible conclusion flowing from the evidence adduced at the said

142. *Indian Iron and Steel Co. Ltd.* v. *Their Workmen,* AIR 1958 SC 130.
143. *Punjab National Bank Ltd.* v. *Its Workmen,* AIR 1960 SC 160.
144. *M/s. Bharat Sugar Mills Ltd.* v. *Jai Singh* (1962) 3 SCR 684.
145. *Management of Ritz Theatre (P) Ltd.* v. *Its Workmen,* AIR 1963 SC 295.
146. *Khardah Co. Ltd.* v. *Their Workmen,* AIR 1964 SC 719.
147. *Workmen of Motipur Sugar Factory (P) Ltd.* v. *Motipur Sugar Factory,* AIR 1965 SC 1803.
148. *State Bank of India.* v. *R.K. Jain,* AIR 1972 SC 136.
149. *Delhi Cloth and General Mills Co. Ltd.* v. *Ludh Budh Singh,* (1972) 1 LLJ 180.

enquiry, the Tribunal has no jurisdiction to sit in judgment over the decision of the employer as an appellate body. The interference with the decision of the employer will be justified only when the findings arrived at in the enquiry are perverse, or the management is guilty of victimisation, unfair labour practice or *malafide*.

(4) Even if no enquiry has been held by an employer, or if the enquiry held by him is found to be defective, the Tribunal in order to satisfy itself about the legality and validity of the order, has to give an opportunity to the employer and the employee to adduce evidence before it. It is open to the employer to adduce evidence for the first time justifying his action, and it is open to the employee to adduce evidence contra.

(5) The effect of an employer not holding an enquiry is that the Tribunal would not have to consider only whether there was a prima facie case. On the other hand, the issue about the merits of the impugned order of dismissal or discharge is at large before the Tribunal and the latter, on the evidence adduced before it, has to decide for itself whether the misconduct alleged is proved. In such cases, the point about the exercise of managerial functions does not arise at all. A case of defective enquiry stands on the same footing as no enquiry.

(6) The Tribunal gets jurisdiction to consider the evidence placed before it for the first time in justification of the action taken only if no enquiry has been held, or after the enquiry conducted by an employer is found to be defective.

(7) It has never been recognised that the Tribunal should straightway, without anything more, direct reinstatement of a dismissed or discharged employee once it is found that no domestic enquiry has been held or the said enquiry is found to be defective.

(8) An employer, who wants to avail himself of the opportunity of adducing evidence for the first time before the Tribunal to justify his action, should ask for it at the appropriate stage. If such an opportunity is asked for, the Tribunal has no power to refuse. The giving of an opportunity to an employer to adduce evidence for the first time before the Tribunal is in the interest of both the management and the employee and to enable the Tribunal itself to be satisfied about the alleged misconduct.

(9) Once the misconduct is proved either in the enquiry conducted by an employer or by the evidence placed before a Tribunal for the first time, punishment imposed cannot be interfered with by the Tribunal except in cases where the punishment is so harsh as to suggest victimisation.

(10) In a particular case, after setting aside the order of dismissal, whether a workman should be reinstated or paid compensation is, as held by the Supreme Court in *The Management of Panitole Tea Estate* v. *The Workmen,*[150] within the judicial decision of a Labour Court or Tribunal.

Legal Position After Section 11A

Section 11A empowers only Labour Court, Tribunals and National Tribunals to entertain the case of discharge or dismissal. We find that the word 'discharge' is not intended by the

150. AIR 1971 SC 2171.

(2) A National Tribunal shall consist of one person only to be appointed by the Central Government.

(3) A person shall not be qualified for appointment as the presiding officer of a National Tribunal unless he is, or has been, a Judge of a High Court.

(4) The Central Government may, if it so thinks fit, appoint two persons as assessors to advise the National Tribunal in the proceeding before it.

Section 7C: Disqualifications for the presiding officers of Labour Courts, Tribunals and National Tribunals

No person shall be appointed to, or continue in, the office of the presiding officer of a Labour Court, Tribunal or National Tribunal, if—

(a) he is not an independent person; or

(b) he has attained the age of sixty-five years.

Section 8: Filling of vacancies

If, for any reason a vacancy (other than a temporary absence) occurs in the office of the presiding officer of a Labour Court, Tribunal or National Tribunal or in the office of the chairman or any other member of a Board or Court, then, in the case of a National Tribunal, the Central Government and in any other case, the appropriate Government, shall appoint another person in accordance with the provisions of this Act to fill the vacancy, and the proceeding may be continued before the Labour Court, Tribunal, National Tribunal, Board or Court, as the case may be, from the stage at which the vacancy is filled.

Section 9: Finality of orders constituting Boards, etc.

(1) No order of the appropriate Government or of the Central Government appointing any person as the chairman or any other member of a Board or Court or as the presiding officer of a Labour Court, Tribunal or National Tribunal shall be called in question in any manner; and no act or proceeding before any Board or Court shall be called in question in any manner on the ground merely of the existence of any vacancy in, or defect in the constitution of, such Board or Court.

(2) No settlement arrived at in the course of a conciliation proceeding shall be invalid by reason only of the fact that such settlement was arrived at after the expiry of the period referred to in sub-s. (6) of S. 12 or sub-s. (5) of S. 13, as the case may be.

(3) Where the report of any settlement arrived at in the course of conciliation proceeding before a Board is signed by the chairman and all the other members of the Board, no such settlement shall be invalid by reason only of the casual or unforeseen absence of any of the members including the chairman of the Board during any stage of the proceeding.

(f) he is or has been a Deputy Chief Labour Commissioner (Central) or Joint Commissioner of the State Labour Department, having a degree in law and at least seven years' experience in the labour department including three years of experience as Conciliation Officer:

Provided that no such Deputy Chief Labour Commissioner or Joint Labour Commissioner shall be appointed unless he resigns from the service of the Central Government or State Government, as the case may be, before being appointed as the presiding officer; or

(g) he is an officer of Indian Legal Service in Grade III with three years' experience in the grade.

Section 7A: Tribunals

(1) The appropriate Government may, by notification in the Official Gazette, constitute one or more Industrial Tribunals for the adjudication of industrial disputes relating to any matter, whether specified in the Second Schedule or the Third Schedule and for performing such other functions as may be assigned to them under this Act.

(2) A Tribunal shall consist of one person only to be appointed by the appropriate Government.

(3) A person shall not be qualified for appointment as the presiding officer of a Tribunal unless—

(a) he is, or has been, a Judge of a High Court; or

(aa) he has, for a period of not less than three years, been a District Judge or an Additional District Judge.

(b) he is or has been a Deputy Chief Labour Commissioner (Central) or Joint Commissioner of the State Labour Department, having a degree in law and at least seven years' experience in the labour department including three years of experience as Conciliation Officer:

Provided that no such Deputy Chief Labour Commissioner or Joint Labour Commissioner shall be appointed unless he resigns from the service of the Central Government or State Government, as the case may be, before being appointed as the presiding officer; or

(c) he is an officer of Indian Legal Service in Grade III with three years' experience in the grade."

(4) The appropriate Government may, if it so thinks fit, appoint two persons as assessors to advise the Tribunal in the proceeding before it.

Section 7B: National Tribunals

(1) The Central Government may, by notification in the Official Gazette, constitute one or more National Industrial Tribunals for the adjudication of industrial disputes which, in the opinion of the Central Government, involve questions of national importance or are of such a nature that industrial establishments situated in more than one State are likely to be interested in, or affected by, such disputes.

functions of the Works Committee included the decision on such an important matter he alteration in the conditions of service by rationalisation. "To promote measures for ring and preserving amity and good relations between the employer and workmen" is their function and to that end they are authorised to "comment upon matters of their common cern or interest and endeavour to compose any material difference of opinion in respect uch matters."

The question of introduction of rationalisation scheme may be said to be a matter of mon interest between the employers and workmen; but the duty and authority of the ks Committee could not extend to anything more than making comments thereupon and ndeavour to compose any material difference of opinion in respect of such matters. Neither nments' nor the 'endeavour' could be held to extend to decide the question on which erences have arisen or are likely to arise one way or the other. It was rightly pointed out he Labour Appellate Tribunal in *Kemp and Co. Ltd.* v. *Their Workmen*[97] that:

> "the Works Committee are normally concerned with problems arising in the day-to-day working of the concern and the functions of the Works Committee are to ascertain the grievances of the employees and when occasion arises to arrive at some agreement also. But the function and the responsibility of the works committee as their very nomenclature indicates cannot go beyond recommendation and as such they are more or less bodies who in the first instance endeavour to compose the differences and the final decision rests with the union as a whole."

The fact that the workmen's representatives on the Works Committee agreed to the oduction of the rationalisation scheme is therefore in no way binding on the workmen or r Union.[98]

CTION 4: Conciliation officers

(1) The appropriate Government may, by notification in the Official Gazette, appoint such number of persons as it thinks fit, to be conciliation officers, charged with the duty of mediating in and promoting the settlement of industrial disputes.

(2) A conciliation officer may be appointed for a specified area or for specified industries in a specified area or for one or more specified industries and either permanently or for a limited period.

CTION 5: Boards of Conciliation

(1) The appropriate Government may as occasion arises by notification in the Official Gazette constitute a Board of Conciliation for promoting the settlement of an industrial dispute.

(2) A Board shall consist of a chairman and two or four other members, as the appropriate Government thinks fit.

(3) The chairman shall be an independent person and the other members shall be persons appointed in equal numbers to represent the parties to the dispute and any person

(1955) 1 L LJ 48.

North Brook Jute Co., Ltd., M/s. v. *Their Workmen,* AIR 1960 SC 879.

appointed to represent a party shall be appointed on the recommendation of t party:

Provided that, if any party fails to make a recommendation as aforesaid within prescribed time, the appropriate Government shall appoint such persons as it thinks fit represent that party.

(4) A Board, having the prescribed quorum, may act notwithstanding the absence the chairman or any of its members or any vacancy in its number:

Provided that if the appropriate Government notifies the Board that the services of chairman or of any other member have ceased to be available, the Board shall not act unt new chairman or member, as the case may be, has been appointed.

SECTION 6: Courts of Inquiry

(1) The appropriate Government may as occasion arises by notification in the Offi Gazette constitute a Court of Inquiry for inquiring into any matter appearing to connected with or relevant to an industrial dispute.

(2) A Court may consist of one independent person or of such number of independ persons as the appropriate Government may think fit and where a Court consists two or more members, one of them shall be appointed as the chairman.

(3) A Court, having the prescribed quorum, may act notwithstanding the absence of chairman or any of its members or any vacancy in its number:

Provided that, if the appropriate Government notifies the Court that the services of chairman have ceased to be available, the Court shall not act until a new chairman has b appointed.

SECTION 7: Labour Courts

(1) The appropriate Government may, by notification in the Official Gazette, consti one or more Labour Courts for the adjudication of industrial disputes relating to matter specified in the Second Schedule and for performing such other functions may be assigned to them under this Act.

(2) A Labour Court shall consist of one person only to be appointed by the appropr Government.

(3) A person shall not be qualified for appointment as the presiding officer of a Lab Court, unless—

(a) he is, or has been, a Judge of a High Court; or

(b) he has, for a period of not less than three years, been a District Judge or Additional District Judge; or

(c) Repealed.

(d) he has held any judicial office in India for not less than seven years; or

(e) he has been the presiding officer of a Labour Court constituted under Provincial Act or State Act for not less than five years.

(2) the above evidence and, in addition, any further evidence laid before the Tribunal, or
(3) evidence placed before the Tribunal for the first time in support of the action taken by an employer as well as the evidence adduced by the workmen contra.

The above mentioned items, by and large, should be considered to be the *materials on record* as specified in the Proviso. The expression *material on record* should not be limited to only that material that has been placed in a domestic enquiry. The Proviso only confines the Tribunal to the materials on record before it as specified above, when considering the justification or otherwise of the order of discharge or dismissal. It is only on the basis of these materials that the Tribunal is obliged to consider whether the misconduct is proved and the further question whether the proved misconduct justifies the punishment of dismissal or discharge. It also prohibits the Tribunal from taking any fresh evidence either for satisfying itself regarding the misconduct or for altering the punishment. From the Proviso, it is not certainly possible to come to the conclusion that when once it is held that an enquiry has not been held or is found to be defective, an order reinstating the workman will have to be made by the Tribunal. Nor does it follow that the Proviso deprives an employer of his right to adduce evidence for the first time before the Tribunal. The expression 'fresh evidence' has to be read in the context in which it appears, namely as distinguished from the expression 'materials on record'. If so read, the Proviso does not present any difficulty at all.

The Legislature in S. 11A has provided for the first time to interfere with the punishment imposed by an employer. When such wide powers have been now conferred on Tribunals, the Legislature obviously felt that some restrictions have to be imposed regarding what matters could be taken into account. Such restrictions are found in the Proviso. The Proviso only emphasises that the Tribunal has to satisfy itself one way or the other regarding misconduct, the punishment and the relief to be granted to workmen only on the basis of the *materials on record* before it. What are those materials have already been mentioned above.

Section 11A empowers the Tribunal to interfere with the punishment imposed by the management, but it does not mean that the management is having no obligation to hold an enquiry before passing an order of discharge or dismissal. The Apex Court has consistently been holding in many cases that an employer is expected to hold a proper enquiry according to the Standing Orders and principles of natural justice. It is also to be remembered that such an enquiry should not be an empty formality. If a proper enquiry is conducted by an employer without violating the principles of natural justice and a correct finding arrived at regarding the misconduct, the Tribunal, even though it has now power under S. 11A to differ from the conclusions arrived at by the management, will have to give very cogent reasons for not accepting the view of the employer. Further, by holding a proper enquiry, the employer will also escape the charge of having acted arbitrarily or mala fide. It cannot be over-emphasised that conducting of a proper and valid enquiry by an employer will be conducive to harmonious and healthy relationship between him and the workmen and it will serve the cause of industrial peace.

Retrospective Effect of Section 11A

It has already been mentioned that S. 11A was incorporated in the Industrial Disputes Act, 1947 by S. 3 of the Industrial Disputes (Amendment) Act, 1971. Accordingly, the Amendment Act came into force with effect from December 15, 1971.

the decision in *Indian Iron and Steel Co. Ltd.* case can no longer be invoked by an employer. The Tribunal is now at liberty to consider not only whether the finding of misconduct recorded by an employer is correct but also to differ from the said finding if a proper case is made out. What was once largely in the realm of the satisfaction of the employer has ceased to be so; and now it is the satisfaction of the Tribunal that finally decides the matter.

If there has been no enquiry held by the employer, or if the enquiry is held to be defective, it is open to the employer to adduce evidence for the first time before the Tribunal justifying the order of discharge or dismissal. It is not correct to say that the right of the employer to adduce evidence before the Tribunal for the first time which was recognized by the Supreme Court in many occasions such as *Delhi Cloth and General Mills Co.* v. *Ludh Budh Singh*,[152] *Workmen of the Motipur Sugar Factory Private Ltd.* v. *Motipur Sugar Factory Private Ltd.*[153] etc. has been taken away by S. 11A. There is no indication in the section that the said right has been abrogated. If the intention of the Legislature had been to do away with such a right, the section would have been differently worded. Admittedly, there are no express words to that effect, and there is no indication that the section has impliedly changed the law in that respect. Therefore, the position is that the employer is entitled to adduce evidence for the first time before the Tribunal even if he had held no enquiry, or the enquiry held by him was found to be defective. Of course, an opportunity will have to be given to the workman to lead evidence contra.[154]

Another change that has been effected by S. 11A is the power conferred on a Tribunal to alter the punishment imposed by an employer, if the Tribunal comes to the conclusion that the misconduct is established, either by the domestic enquiry accepted by it or by the evidence adduced before it for the first time. The Tribunal originally had no power to interfere with the punishment imposed by the management. Once the misconduct is proved, the Tribunal had to sustain the order of punishment unless it was harsh indicating victimisation. Under S. 11A, though the Tribunal may hold that the misconduct is proved, nevertheless it may be of the opinion that the order of discharge or dismissal for the said misconduct is not justified. In other words, the Tribunal may hold that the proved misconduct does not merit punishment by way of discharge or dismissal. It can, under such circum-stances, award to the workman only lesser punishment instead. The power to interfere with the punishment and alter the same has been now conferred on the Tribunal by S. 11A.

Materials on Record

The expression *materials on record* occurring in the Proviso cannot be confined only to the materials which were available at the domestic enquiry. On the other hand, the *materials on record* in the Proviso must be held to refer to materials on record before the Tribunal.

They take in:

(1) the evidence taken by the management at the enquiry and the proceedings of the enquiry, or

152. AIR 1972 SC 1031.
153. AIR 1965 SC 1803.
154. *Workmen of M/s. Firestone Tyre and Rubber Co. of India P. Ltd.* v. *Management,* AIR 1973 SC 1227.

concerned, as his discharge or dismissal is illegal. Even in cases where a domestic enquiry has been held and finding of misconduct recorded, the Labour Tribunals have now full power and jurisdiction to re-appraise the evidence and to satisfy themselves whether the evidence justifies the finding of misconduct. Even if the enquiry proceedings are held to be proper and the finding of misconduct is also accepted, the Tribunal has now power to consider whether the punishment of dismissal or discharge was necessary for the type of misconduct of which the workman is found guilty. In such circumstances, the Tribunal can also give any other relief to the workman, including the imposition of a lesser punishment. In cases where an employer had not conducted any enquiry, or when the enquiry conducted by him is held to be defective, the employer will not be given any opportunity to adduce evidence before the Labour Tribunal for justifying his action. Various decisions of this Court have emphasised that there is an tion on the part of an employer to hold a proper enquiry before dismissing or discharging man. It has also been stated that the enquiry should conform to certain well-defined es and that it should not be an empty formality. If the management being fully aware position in law, does not conduct an enquiry or conducts a defective enquiry, the order d by it is illegal, and it cannot take advantage of such illegality or wrong committed by d seek a further opportunity before the Tribunal of adducing evidence for the first time. nerally, the Standing Orders also provide for the conduct of an enquiry before imposing a punishment. The Standing Orders have been held to be statutory terms of conditions of service. If an employer does not conform to the provisions of the Standing Orders, he commits an illegality and an order passed, which is illegal, has only to be straightway set aside by the Tribunal.

'Tribunal's Power to Interfere' with 'The Order of Dismissal'

Before S. 11A was inserted in the Industrial Disputes Act, 1947, the Tribunal had no power to interfere with its finding of misconduct recorded in the domestic enquiry unless one or other infirmities pointed out by the Tribunal as in the light of the decision of the Supreme Court in *Indian Iron and Steel Co. Ltd.* v. *Their Workmen.*[151] The conduct of disciplinary proceeding and the punishment to be imposed were all considered to be a managerial function which the Tribunal had no power to interfere unless the finding was perverse or the punishment was so harsh as to lead to an inference of victimisation or unfair labour practice. This position has now been changed by S. 11A.

Satisfaction of a Tribunal Regarding Discharge or Dismissal

The words *in the course of the adjudication proceeding, the Tribunal is satisfied that the order of discharge or dismissal was not justified* clearly indicate that the Tribunal is now clothed with the power to reappraise the evidence in the domestic enquiry and satisfy itself whether the said evidence relied on by an employer established the misconduct alleged against a workman. What was originally a plausible conclusion that could be drawn by an employer from the evidence, has now given place to a satisfaction being arrived at by the Tribunal that the finding of misconduct is correct. The limitations imposed on the powers of the Tribunal by

151. AIR 1958 SC 130.

Legislature to have the same or analogous meaning as the word 'dismiss'. The reason is obvious. The word 'dismiss' necessarily connotes an action of the employer who seeks to impose punishment on his misconducting employee. Such a punishment cannot be imposed without following the principles of natural justice and the relevant applicable rules of domestic enquiry. But the word 'discharge' is not necessarily confined to orders of termination by way of penalty only. The word 'discharge' has wider connotations. A misconducting employee facing charges in a domestic enquiry may be punished by way of an order of dismissal imposed on him which may make him ineligible for any other employment, but if it is found that the charges which are proved are not that serious but the employee does not deserve to be continued in service, then an order of discharge by way of lesser penalty can be imposed on him. Such an order would remain a punitive discharge. In other words, the employer wants to punish the employee for his misconduct but does not want h[illegible] become ineligible for employment elsewhere considering less serious nature of proved c[illegible] of misconduct against him in domestic inquiry. But the matter does not end there. In [illegible] jurisprudence, the term 'discharge' has assumed a wider connotation and may include [illegible] fold not only punitive discharge orders but also *simpliciter* discharge orders where the em[illegible] seeks to snap the relationship of employer and employee but without any intention to pe[illegible] the employee. He does so because of exigencies of service and employment conditions wh[illegible] may require him to say goodbye to the employee but without any intention to punish him. Such *simpliciter* discharge orders can be illustrated as follows:

An employee, on probation, may not be found to be suitable and may not earn sufficient merit so as to be confirmed in service. Consequently, his probation may be terminated and an order of *simpliciter* discharge can be passed against him. There may also be other cases of single discharge under the contract of employment for a fixed period where an employee on efflux of time may be terminated. There may also be cases where an employee may become surplus and would no longer be required by the employer. An order of retrenchment, therefore, may be passed against him subject, of course, to the statutory requirements of S. 25-F of the Industrial disputes Act if they are applicable. These illustrations are not exhaustive but they indicate such orders of discharge are passed by an employer who does not want to punish the employees but still is not in a position to continue them in service. Such *simpliciter* discharge orders are also a category of discharge orders. Therefore, the word 'discharge', as employed by the Legislature in item no. 1 of Schedule IV, cannot necessarily be confined only to punitive discharges as tried to be submitted by learned counsel for the appellant. Once we consider the words 'discharge' and 'dismissal' as employed in the opening part of item No. 1 by the Legislature in the light of various clauses representing different situations under which such discharge or dismissal orders are said to amount to 'unfair labour practice' on the part of the employers, it becomes at once clear that the Legislature was not contemplating only punitive discharge orders but non-punitive discharge orders as well.

Section 11A makes it obligatory for an employer to hold a proper domestic enquiry in which all material evidence will have to be adduced. When a dispute is referred for adjudication and it is found that the domestic enquiry conducted by the management is defective, or if it is found that no domestic enquiry at all had been conducted, the order of discharge or termination passed by the employer becomes, without anything more, unjustified and the Labour Tribunals have no option but to direct the reinstatement of the workman

to the conclusion on its own appraisal of evidence adduced before it that the dismissal was justified, its approval of the order of dismissal made by the employer in a defective inquiry would still relate back to the date when the order was made. The Court said:

> "...If the inquiry is defective for any reason, the Labour Court would also have to consider for itself on the evidence adduced before it whether the dismissal was justified. However, on coming to the conclusion on its own appraisal of evidence adduced before it that the dismissal was justified its approval of the order of dismissal made by the employer in a defective inquiry would still relate back to the date when the order was made.... In the present case an inquiry has been held which is said to be defective in one respect and dismissal has been ordered. The respondent had however to justify the order of dismissal before the Labour Court in view of the defect in the inquiry. It has succeeded in doing so and therefore the approval of the Labour Court will relate back to the date on which the respondent passed the order of dismissal. The contention of the appellant therefore that dismissal in this case should take effect from the date from which the Labour Court's award came into operation must fail."[160]

In *Gujarat Steel Tubes Ltd.* case, *Kalyani* case was cited to support the view of relation back of the award to the date of the employer's termination orders, but the Court did not agree with the ratio of *Kalyani* case and held that jurisprudentially, approval is not creative but confirmatory and therefore relates back. A void dismissal is just void and does not exist. If the Tribunal, for the first time, passes an order recording a finding of misconduct and thus breathes life into the dead shell of the management's order, pre-dating of the nativity does not arise. Further, the Court held that where the management discharges a workman by an order which is void for want of an enquiry or for blatant violation of rules of natural justice, the relation back doctrine cannot be invoked.

With great respect, we must say that the above quoted observations in *Gujarat Steel Tubes Ltd.* case are not in line with the decision of *Kalyani* case, even though it was decided by the Constitution Bench. Hence it is not binding and it is per *incuriam* too. Accordingly, the Court held that the order of punishment in the present case operated from November 18, 1981 when it was made by the employer and not from December 11, 1985, the date of Labour Court's award. In 2004, the Supreme Court in *Engg. Laghu Udyog Employees' Union* v. *Judge, Labour Court*[161] held that S. 11A of the Industrial Disputes Act, 1947 confers a wide power upon the Labour Court, Tribunal or the National Tribunal to give appropriate relief in case of discharge or dismissal of workmen. While adjudicating on a reference made to it, the Labour Court, Tribunal or the National Tribunal, as the case may be, if satisfied that the order of discharge or dismissal was not justified, it may, while setting aside the same, direct reinstatement of the workman on such terms and conditions, if any, as it thinks fit, or give such other relief to the workman including the award of any lesser punishment in lieu of discharge or dismissal as the circumstances of the case may require. Thus, only in a case where the satisfaction is reached by the Labour Court or the Tribunal, as the case may be, that an order of dismissal was not justified, the same can be set aside. So long as the same is not set aside, it remains valid. But once, whether on the basis of the evidences brought on record in the domestic enquiry or by reason of additional evidence, the employer makes out a case justifying the order of dismissal, such an order of dismissal cannot be given effect to

160. *P.H. Kalyani* v. *M/s. Air France, Calcutta*, AIR 1963 SC 1756 at p. 1759 per Wanchoo, J.
161. AIR 2004 SC 4951.

only from the date of the award but from the date of passing of the order of punishment. In the instant case, as the charges were proved before the Labour Court, the order of termination would relate back to the date of original order.

Loss of Confidence

Loss of confidence means a situation where due to certain circumstances, an employer loses confidence in a workman in such a way that the employer no longer considers it appropriate for the workmen to render their services in the relevant capacity within the organisation.

Tests for establishing 'Loss of Confidence'

The Supreme Court of India in *Kanhaiyalal Agrawal* v. *Factory Manager* ((2001) 9 SCC 609) listed three conditions or 'tests' to be satisfied for concluding that the employer has validly 'lost confidence' in his worker, and they are as follows;

1. Whether the worker holds a position of trust and confidence?
2. Whether the worker has abused his position of trust and committed an act that results in forfeiting his employment?
3. Whether it would be embarrassing and inconvenient to the employer or detrimental to the discipline or security of the establishment to continue the worker in service?

The Supreme Court has always been critical of violent behaviour by workers who show their protest at the workplace. This view has been reiterated in the case of *Indian Railway Construction Company Limited* v. *Ajay Kumar*.[162] The case involved the dismissal of an employee, without any inquiry, for allegedly assaulting a senior officer and ransacking his office. The management argued that as per the rules of the organisation, the inquiry could be dispensed with for special reasons in special circumstances. The employee being a trade union leader pleaded victimisation by the management. The Supreme Court observed that the misconduct attributed to the employee resulted in 'loss of confidence' and hence dismissal without inquiry was not illegal. The Court said that an employee had to act with a sense of discipline and decorum and exhibition of muscle power to secure a right is improper. At the same time, the employer has the duty of looking into and, as far as practicable, obviating the genuine grievances of the employees. Lack of cordial working environment will be destructive for the common interests of both the employer and the employee. While the Supreme Court upheld the dismissal of the employee, it also directed payment of compensation of ₹15 lakh to the employee to balance the grievances against the management.

In *Punjab Dairy Development Corporation Limited* v. *Kala Singh*,[163] the respondent, who was working as a dairy helper-cum-cleaner for collecting the milk from various centres, was charged for the misconduct that on April 28, 1990 and on other dates, he inflated the quantum of the milk supplies in milk centers to the Corporation and also inflated the quality of the fat contents, while there were less fat contents. After conducting the domestic enquiry, the disciplinary authority dismissed him from service. On reference, the Labour Court found that the domestic enquiry conducted by the appellant was defective. Consequently, an opportunity

162. (2003) 4 SCC 579.
163. AIR 1997 SC 2661.

was given to the management to adduce evidence afresh to justify the order of dismissal. Accordingly, evidence was adduced by the appellant as well as the delinquent-respondent. On consideration of the evidence, the Labour Court by its award dated Nov. 14, 1990 held that the charge had been proved against the respondent. On the quantum of punishment, it was held that the punishment was not disproportionate to the magnitude of the misconduct of the respondent.

The Supreme Court has used the phrase 'loss of confidence' which may not be for the first time while upholding the award of Labour Court, held that on the basis of the evidence adduced before it, no doubt, the Labour Court has not elaborately considered the entire evidence but agreed to the decision that the misconduct has been proved. In view of the proof of misconduct, the necessary consequence would be that the Management has lost the confidence that the appellant would truthfully and faithfully carry on his duties and consequently the Labour Court rightly declined to exercise the power under S. 11A to grant relief of reinstatement with minor penalty.

Where a man who had made false vouchers, duped the bank customer, misappropriated the whole amount and on the top of it, never botherd to return the money, it could not therefore be, by any stretch of imagination, called and brushed aside as 'temporary mis-appropriation'. The Madras High Court has rightly observed that the Tribunal had not taken into account the grave consequences of the fact on the part of the appellant and had merely dubbed the whole affairs as 'youth indiscretion'.

A mere continuation of the service itself does not add any credit to the employee and cannot be compared with the grave misconduct that the appellant had committed. The Court held that the Tribunal had gravely erred in awarding the service back along with the 50% of the back wages. The Court observed that the appellant was working as a bank clerk and was in reality holding the position of 'trust'. He not only abused that position but went on to drive nails to his coffin by making false representation one after the other.[164]

In 2004, the Supreme Court invoked the principle of 'loss of confidence' in *Divisional Controller, KSRTC (NWKRTC)* v. *A.T. Mane*[165] where the respondent was working as a conductor in the Chikodi depot of the appellant-Corporation. On May 31, 1999, when the bus in which he was on duty returned back to the depot after its trip from Haragiri to Chikodi, on a surprise check he was found to be in possession of unaccounted money of ₹93 over and above the amount equivalent to the tickets issued by him. Under Regulation applicable to the respondent, the respondent was not to carry more than ₹5 as his personal money while on duty so as to obviate the defence of the delinquent conductors that the excess money was their personal money. Basing on these facts, the appellant drew an inference that this excess amount of ₹93 was the amount collected by the respondent from the passengers without issuing any tickets or issuing tickets of lesser denomination than that was issued. On the said investigation report, the departmental enquiry was instituted against the respondent and having found him guilty of the said charge, the disciplinary authority awarded the punishment of dismissal.

Being aggrieved by the said order, the respondent preferred a claim before the Additional Labour Court, Hubli praying for setting aside the order of dismissal and for reinstatement with consequential benefits. The Labour Court after hearing the parties concerned came to the

164. *Francis Vincent Neelankovil* v. *Industrial Tribunal, Madras*, 2004 (2) LLN 363.
165. AIR 2004 SC 4761.

conclusion that the inquiry conducted by the management was fair and proper. However, it came to the conclusion that the only charge against the respondent was being in possession of ₹93 which was in excess of the sale of tickets, no presumption could be drawn that it was an amount received by non-issuance of tickets to passengers. It held that the Corporation ought to have examined the passengers from whom such amount was collected without issuing tickets or issuing tickets of lesser denomination. Since the same was not done, the Labour Court came to the conclusion that the order of dismissal was uncalled for and as also highly disproportionate compared with the smallness of the amount. Hence, it made the award directing the reinstatement of the respondent with full back-wages and continuity of service and other consequential benefits.

The aggrieved Corporation preferred a writ petition before the High Court of Karnataka. The learned single Judge who heard the writ petition agreed with the Labour Court that since the Corporation failed to examine the passengers from whom the said excess amount was collected, the charge of non-issuance of tickets or issuance of tickets of lesser denomination could not be upheld. The learned single Judge also agreed with the Labour Court that the punishment awarded was also excessive, however, it thought fit to reduce the back-wages to 75% as compared to the full back-wages awarded by the Labour Court.

The appeal filed against the said judgment before the Division Bench of the High Court of Karnataka was dismissed by the Division Bench on two grounds. Firstly it held that there was a delay of 16 days in preferring the appeal. However, the Court observed that it would have certainly condoned the said delay had there been any merit in the appeal. Having said so, the Division Bench held that they do not find any merit in the appeal and agreed with the single Judge that the order of reinstatement with reduced back-wages was a just order.

The Supreme Court observed that the only ground on which the finding of the domestic Tribunal has been set aside was that the passengers concerned were not examined or their statements were not recorded, in spite of there being other material to establish the misconduct of the respondent, and accordingly held that the Courts below have erred in allowing the claim of the respondent. The Court relied on the ratio laid down in *State of Haryana* v. *Rattan Singh*[166] as the fact of *Rattan Singh* case is very similar to that of *Divisional Controller, KSRTC (NWKRTC)* case.

The fact of *Rattan Singh* case reveals that the Inspector who conducted the checking established the misconduct of the respondent based on which a finding was given that the respondent was guilty of the misconduct alleged. Based on the said finding, the disciplinary authority had punished the respondent by an order of dismissal. But the Labour Court and the learned single Judge rejected the said finding and set aside the punishment imposed solely on the ground that the evidence of the passengers concerned was not adduced and their statements were not recorded by the Inspector which, as stated in the *Rattan Singh's* case, is not a condition precedent.

The Supreme Court, while dealing with the question of quantum of punishment, observed that one should bear in mind the fact that it is not the amount of money misappropriated that becomes a primary factor for awarding punishment, on the contrary, it is the 'loss of confidence' which is the primary factor to be taken into consideration. When a person is found guilty of misappropriating the corporation's fund, there is nothing wrong in the

166. AIR 1977 SC 1512.

Corporation 'losing confidence' or faith in such a person and awarding a punishment of dismissal. Therefore, the Supreme Court in this case held that the Courts below have erred in interfering with the finding of fact on an erroneous basis and concluded that the findings of the Labour Court and that of the learned single Judge are unsustainable in law. The finding of the Division Bench also is liable to be set aside.

In *Depot Manager, APSRTC* v. *Raghuda Siva Sankar Prasad* [AIR 2007 SC 152] where the respondent joined as cleaner in the APSRTC and while working as mechanic, he was involved in a serious case of theft. A charge sheet was issued to the respondent framing four charges and they are as follows:

1. For having stolen the Corporation property of fuel injection pump which was fitted to the engine which constitutes misconduct under APSRTC Employees Conduct, Regulation, 1963.
2. For having stolen the Corporation property of an alternator when it was fitted to the parked vehicle in the garage which constitutes misconduct under APSRTC Employees Conduct Regulations, 1963.
3. For having unauthorizedly entered into the tyres section and stolen the new tube of which constitutes misconduct under APSRTC Employees Conduct Regulations, 1963.
4. For having stolen the sponge sheets SR from the garage of Gajuwaka depot which constitutes misconduct under APSRTC Employees Conduct Regulations, 1963.

An Enquiry Officer was appointed to enquire into the charges and submitted the report. Full and fare opportunity was given to the respondent to defend himself. The Enquiry Officer, on completion of the domestic enquiry, had submitted a report holding the respondent guilty of all the charges that were levelled against him. A criminal case was also initiated against the respondent where the Criminal Court acquitted the respondent of the charges that were levelled against him. Basing on the Enquiry Officer's report, the Depot Manager, on independently examining the matter, came to a conclusion that orders of removal would be an appropriate punishment for the proved charges of theft. Accordingly, the Depot Manager issued proceedings for removing the respondent from the services of the Corporation.

Aggrieved by the order of his removal, the respondent raised an Industrial Dispute where the Labour Court upheld the decision of the Corporation and held that the punishment of removal was justified under the factual circumstances of the case. Aggrieved by the award of the Labour Court, the respondent preferred a writ petition before the High Court of Andhra Pradesh. The learned Single Judge of the High Court came to a conclusion that the charges of theft were correctly proved against the respondent. But, however, came to a conclusion that punishment of removal was not in consonance with the gravity of the charges proved against the respondent. Accordingly, the High Court held that the Labour Court ought to have exercised its power under S. 11-A of the Industrial Disputes Act. Accordingly, the Single Judge held that the respondent had put in 12 years of unblemished service and deserved a lenient view in the matter. Hence, the learned Single Judge passed a judgment by setting aside the order of removal and directed reinstatement of the respondent with continuity of service but without back wages. The Appellant-Corporation preferred a writ appeal before the Division Bench of the High Court but the Division Bench of the High Court dismissed the writ appeal filed by the appellant. Aggrieved against the order passed by the Division Bench, the Corporation approached the Supreme Court.

The Supreme Court observed that the High Court has failed to appreciate that the delinquent employee categorically admitted that he had stolen the property of the Corporation. The Labour Court rightly ordered removal of the respondent from service and categorically held that the delinquent employee does not deserve any sympathy. It seems that the learned Single Judge considered the past conduct of the delinquent employee as one of the ground in taking a lenient view. However, it is to be remembered that past conduct of workman is not relevant in departmental proceedings. Likewise, the learned Single Judge has erred in holding that the workman did not involve in any misconduct of theft during his past services and on that ground, granted reinstatement with continuity of service. The learned Judges of the High Court have also failed to appreciate that once an employee lost the confidence of employer, it would not be safe and in the interest of the Corporation to continue the employee in the service. The punishment, imposed by the management in the facts and circumstances of the case, is not disproportionate and that the punishment of removal from service is the just and reasonable and proportionate to the proved misconduct. On the basis of the above reasoning the Supreme Court held that the theft committed by the respondent amounts to misconduct and, therefore, the order passed by the single judge and Divisional Bench was set a side.

The Court further observed that the respondent has no legal right to continue in the Corporation. The loss of confidence occupies the primary factor. When the employee is found guilty of theft, there is nothing wrong in the Corporation losing confidence or faith in such an employee and awarding punishment of removal. In such cases, there is no place of generosity or place of sympathy on the part of the judicial forums and interfering with the quantum of the punishment. Accordingly, the order of removal passed by the Labour Court was confirmed.

The background facts in a nutshell are as follows:

Gujarat Ambuja Cement Pvt. Ltd.; hereafter, respondent, is a public utility services as per S. 2(n) read with Schedule I of the Industrial Disputes Act, 1947. In 1989–1990, there were certain disputes between the management and the employees. There was an extended strike in which a large number of employees employed by the respondent-company participated. This disrupted the working of the plant where the concerned workmen were employed. The respondent-company, therefore, initiated disciplinary action against the striking employees. The Charge sheet was against the workmen who had participated in the strike. Since the workmen did not participate in the departmental proceedings they were proceeded *ex parte*. Eventually, eight workmen were dismissed from the service by the respondent-company by order dated 01-03-1990. The concerned workmen, therefore, raised industrial disputes challenging their dismissal orders.

The question relating to legality of the departmental proceedings was examined by the Labour Court and held that the enquiry conducted was legal and proper, but the Labour Court found that some of the charges were not proved and therefore it was held that so far as the strike is concerned it was established that the workmen were not justified in going on strike. It was noted that undisputedly the concerned workmen had participated in a strike. Accordingly, the Labour Court had held that denial of back wages for a period of 14 to 15 years for which the concerned workmen remained out of employment would be sufficient punishment for the misconduct proved against them. However, the Labour Court also proceeded to consider the question of quantum of punishment and held that the order of dismissal cannot be sustained. The High Court held that once the charges have been proved, the Labour Court ought not to have interfered with the quantum of punishment. Accordingly, the employer's Special Civil Applications were allowed and those filed by the workmen were dismissed. Thereafter the workmen approached the Supreme Court and the Court held that when the Labour Court found that the workmen had proceeded on illegal strike and that they were leading participants in such a strike, the Labour Court ought not to have interfered with the quantum of punishment especially when it was established that the employer is a Public Utility Service and that the strike prolonged for a period of four to five months. Even in the absence of any further proof of involvement of the workmen for other misconduct of unruly behaviour, abusing superior officers, preventing officers from entering the premises, preventing co-workers from resuming duties and threatening the family members of the workmen and collecting union subscription illegally, it is doubtful whether the Labour Court could have reduced the punishment and substituted the order of dismissal of lesser punishment. The Supreme Court further observed that the power under said S. 11-A has to be exercised judiciously and the Industrial Tribunal or the Labour Court, as the case may be, is expected to interfere with the decision of a management under Section 11-A only when it is satisfied that punishment imposed by the management is wholly and shockingly disproportionate to the degree of guilt of the workman concerned. To support its conclusion, the Industrial Tribunal or the Labour Court, as the case may be, has to give reasons in support of its decision. The power has to be exercised judiciously and mere use of the words '*disproportionate*' or '*grossly disproportionate*' by itself will not be sufficient. The relief granted by the Labour Court or Industrial Tribunal, as the case may be, must be seen to be logical and tenable within the framework of the law and should not incur and justify the criticism that the jurisdiction of the Courts tends to degenerate into misplaced sympathy, generosity and private benevolence. It is essential to maintain the integrity of legal reasoning and the legitimacy of the conclusions. They must emanate logically from the legal findings and the judicial results must be seen to be principled and supportable on those findings. Expansive judicial mood of mistaken and misplaced compassion at the expense of the legitimacy of the process will eventually lead to mutually irreconcilable situations and denude the judicial process of its dignity, authority, predictability and respectability. [*U.B. Gadhe* v. *G.M., Gujarat Ambuja Cement Pvt. Ltd.,* AIR 2008 SC 99]

Abusing and Manhandling

In *Mahindra and Mahindra Ltd.* v. *N.B. Naravade* case,[167] a workman was dismissed for having used abusive and filthy language against his supervisor. The Labour Court, a Single Judge and a Division Bench of the High Court found the workman guilty of the alleged misconduct, but reduced the penalty of dismissal to reinstatement with continuity of service while reducing the extent of back-wages to be paid to him.

The Supreme Court construed S. 11A of the Industrial Disputes Act, 1947 as vesting a certain amount of discretion in the labour court/industrial tribunal in interfering with the quantum of punishment awarded by the management. Such discretion was, however, available

167. Civil Appeal No. 1508 of 2003, delivered on 22 February, 2005.

only on the existence of certain factors like punishment being disproportionate to the gravity of misconduct so as to disturb the conscience of the court, or the existence of any mitigating circumstances which require the reduction of the sentence, or the past conduct of the workman which may persuade the labour court to reduce the punishment.

In the case on hand, the Supreme Court held that the language used by the workman was such that it could not be tolerated in any civilised society. Use of such abusive language against a superior officer, not once but twice, in the presence of his subordinates cannot be termed to be an indiscipline calling for a lesser punishment.

His sole defence, having been that he did not remember abusing the engineer concerned, was not entertained by the Supreme Court. The fact of the case reveals that the workman had been charge-sheeted more than once earlier, and more lenient penalties visited on him then. Basing on the character of the workman concerned, the Supreme Court set aside all the concurrent findings of the three Courts below it.

The facts of *Management, W.B. Colliery of M/s. TISCO Ltd.* v. *Ram Pravesh Singh* [AIR 2008 SC1162] are as follows:

The respondent-workman was working as Senior Dumper Operator under the Management of the appellant. The workman was deputed at Open Caste Mine, West Bokaro on 2nd of March, 1994 during the first shift from 5.00 a.m. to 1.00 p.m. The respondent left the place of his duty before the end of his shift duty and went to Rajiv Nagar area where Shri Harbans Kumar, Senior Officer (Security), along with a number of security personnel and other workers, was discharging his duties in connection with prevention of unauthorized constructions on the company's land. The respondent-workman along with few others approached Shri Harbans Kumar and shouted at him using abusive language and threatened him with dire consequences in case the unauthorized construction was demolished. The respondent-workman, on being asked not to behave in the said manner, assaulted Shri Harbans Kumar with his hands and also resorted to brick-bating as a result of which Shri Harbans Kumar and Shri S.P. Yadav sustained injuries on the face and other parts of the body.

The management issued a charge sheet to the workman whereby he was served a show-cause notice as to why disciplinary action should not be taken against him under Clauses 22(18) and 22(5) of the Standing Orders of the Company for the following misconduct:

"*(a) leaving work without permission (b) indecent, riotous and disorderly behaviour with a superior as well as co-worker.*"

The concerned workman submitted his reply denying all charges brought against him. The Management decided to conduct an enquiry and accordingly appointed an Enquiry Officer. The Enquiry Officer after giving full opportunity to the concerned workman came to the conclusion that the charges levelled against him were established beyond reasonable doubt and submitted his report. The Punishing Authority after going through the Enquiry Report and related enquiry papers, satisfied himself that charges levelled against the respondent had been established and recommended for dismissal of the concerned workman from the Company with immediate effect. The workman was accordingly dismissed on 25th of April, 1994. The dismissed workman raised an industrial dispute and the Government of India, Ministry of

Labour, in exercise of its powers under S. 10(1)(d) of the Industrial Disputes Act, 1947, referred the following dispute to the Tribunal for adjudication:

> "Whether the action of the Management of West Bokaro Collieries of M/s. TISCO Ltd. PO-Ghatotand, Dist. Hazaribagh in dismissing Shri Ram Pravesh, Ex. Sr. Dumper Operator from the services of the Company w.e.f. 25-4-1994 is justified? If not, to what relief the workman is entitled?"

The Industrial Tribunal set aside the order of dismissal passed against the workman by holding that the Management had failed to substantiate the charges brought against the concerned workman beyond reasonable doubt. Accordingly, order of dismissal passed against the concerned workman was set aside and he was ordered to be reinstated with 50% back wages. Management, thereafter, filed the writ petition before the High Court which was dismissed by the Learned Single Judge, aggrieved against which Management filed Letters Patent Appeal which has also been dismissed. The management approached the Supreme Court where the Court observed that the Tribunal has interfered with the findings recorded by the domestic Tribunal as if it was the Appellate Tribunal. There was evidence present on record regarding indecent, riotous and disorderly behaviour of the workman towards his superiors. The Management witnesses who were present at the scene of occurrence have unequivocally deposed about the misbehaviour of the workman towards his superiors. Their evidence has been discarded by the Tribunal by observing that in the absence of independent evidence, the statements of the workmen who were present at the scene of occurrence could not be believed. Industrial Tribunal fell in error in discarding the evidence produced by the Management only because the independent witnesses were not produced. It is nobody's case that the independent witnesses were available at the scene of occurrence and the Management had failed to produce them. It is possible that at the time of occurrence, only the workers of the Management and the persons who were trying to put up the construction unauthorizedly were the persons present and no independent evidence was available. Statements of the fellow workmen had established the misconduct of the concerned workman. It was a legitimate conclusion which could be arrived at and it would not be open to the Industrial Tribunal to substitute the said opinion by its own opinion. The Court further observed that findings recorded by the Tribunal that the workman had left the place of duty at 12.25 p.m. and, therefore, he could not have reached the place of occurrence at 12.30 p.m. after collecting his other associates, is not based on any evidence. The case of the Management is that the respondent had left his place of duty at 12.05 p.m. and reached the place of occurrence at 12.30 p.m. after collecting his fellow workmen. There was sufficient time for the workman to reach the place of occurrence within half an hour as the distance between the place of duty and the place of occurrence was only 1 km. The duty of the respondent-workman was up to 1.00 o'clock. Even if, it is accepted that he left the place of duty at 12.25 p.m., then also, he left the place of duty during his duty hours.

> The Tribunal has set aside the report of the Enquiry Officer and the order of dismissal passed by the Punishing Authority by observing that the charges against the respondent were not proved beyond reasonable doubt.

It has repeatedly been held by the Supreme Court in many cases that the acquittal in a criminal case would not operate as a bar for drawing up of a disciplinary proceeding against a delinquent. It is a well settled principle of law that yardstick and standard of proof in a criminal case is different from the one in disciplinary proceedings. While the standard of proof in a criminal case is proof beyond all reasonable doubt, the standard of proof in a departmental proceeding is preponderance of probabilities. Therefore, the Supreme Court set aside the order passed by the High Court as well as the Tribunal and, the order passed by the domestic Tribunal and the Punishing Authority is restored.

In *Mahindra and Mahindra Ltd.* v. *N.B. Naravade* [AIR 2005 SC 1993] it is alleged that the respondent-workman used abusive and filthy language against his supervisor, an inquiry was instituted against the said workman and the Inquiry Officer after considering the material produced in the proceedings before him found him guilty of misconduct and recommended his dismissal and based on such recommendation service of the respondent was terminated by the disciplinary authority on 5-3-1991. However, in regard to punishment of dismissal imposed on the respondent-workman the Labour Court came to the conclusion that the same was harsh and improper hence, deserved to be set aside and substituted the said punishment by directing the respondent's reinstatement with continuity of service but with 2/3rd back-wages w.e.f. 5-3-1993. Being aggrieved by the order of Labour Court, the appellant preferred a writ petition before the learned single Judge of the High Court of Bombay. The learned single Judge in the said writ petition by a short order dismissed the writ petition. The said order of the learned single Judge reads as follows:

> "The Labour Court has exercised its jurisdiction under Section 11-A of the Industrial Disputes Act. It has given its own reasons and he is right in observing that denial of 1/3 back wages for the intervening period from 5-3-93 till 13-3-2001 would be a good punishment of the allegations proved before the Court. It would act as deterrent and reformative. He has learnt the cost of the abusive words used by him. He will not get 1/3 wages for the whole intervening period. In my opinion there is no illegality or infirmity in the exercise of the jurisdiction under Section 11-A of the Act to warrant any interference by this Court under Article 226 of the Constitution of India. There is no miscarriage of justice as the guilty workman has received proportionate punishment. There is no merits in the writ petition hence it is rejected."

Against the said order of the learned single Judge the appellant preferred writ appeal before the Division Bench of the High Court. The Division Bench of the High Court held as follows:

> "Since the misconduct has been proved and in view of the nature of the past service record, we are of the opinion that depriving the workman of 60% of his back wages would be a punishment commensurate with his past record and the misconduct proved against him. Dismissal from service will be too harsh considering the totality of service, gravity of misconduct and 15 years of service put in by him."

Hence the management prefers appeal before the Supreme Court. The Supreme Court observed that the language used by the workman was filthy and the language used by the workman cannot be tolerated by any civilized society. Use of such abusive language against a superior officer, that too not once but twice, in the presence of his subordinates cannot be termed to be an indiscipline calling for lesser punishment. Accordingly, the Court held that the order of the Division Bench, single Judge of the High Court and that of the Labour Court to the extent that it sets aside the order of dismissal and directs the reinstatement, is quashed and uphold the order of the disciplinary authority dismissing the respondent-workman from service.

Order for Reinstatement and Award of Back Wages

The manner, in which *back-wages* is viewed, has undergone a significant change in the last two decades. It is no longer considered to be an automatic or natural consequence of reinstatement. We may refer to the latest of a series of decisions on this question. In *U.P. State Brassware Corpn. Ltd.* v. *Udai Narain Pandey* [AIR 2006 SC 586], the Supreme Court following *Allahabad Jal Sansthan* v. *Daya Shankar Rai* [2005 (5) SCC 124], and *Kendriya Vidyalaya Sangathan* v. *S.C. Sharma* [2005 (2) SCC 363] held that although the direction to pay full back wages on a declaration that the order of termination was invalid used to be the usual result, but now, with the passage of time, a pragmatic view of the matter is being taken by the courts realizing that an industry may not be compelled to pay to the workman for the period during which he apparently contributed little or nothing at all to it and/or for a period that was spent unproductively as a result whereof the employer would be compelled to go back to a situation which prevailed many years ago, namely when the workman was retrenched or dismissed. The changes were brought about by the subsequent decisions of the Supreme Court, may be due to the changes in the policy decisions of the Government in the wake of prevailing market economy, globalization, privatization and outsourcing. No precise formula can be laid down as to under what circumstances payment of entire back wages should be allowed. Indisputably, it depends upon the facts and circumstances of each case. It would, however, not be correct to contend that it is automatic. It should not be granted mechanically only because on technical grounds or otherwise an order of termination is found to be in contravention of the provisions Industrial Disputes Act. While granting relief, application of mind on the part of the Industrial Court is imperative. Payment of full back wages cannot therefore be the natural consequence.

There is also a misconception that whenever reinstatement is directed, *continuity of service* and *consequential benefits* should follow, as a matter of course. The disastrous effect of granting several promotions as a *consequential benefit* to a person who has not worked for 10 to 15 years and who does not have the benefit of necessary experience for discharging the higher duties and functions of promotional posts, is seldom visualized while granting consequential benefits automatically. Whenever courts or Tribunals direct reinstatement, they should apply their judicial mind to the facts and circumstances to decide whether *continuity of service* and/or *consequential benefits* should also be directed. [*A.P.S.R.T.C.* v. *S. Narasa Goud* [2003 (2) SCC 212], *A.P.S.R.T.C.* v. *Abdul Kareem* [2005 (6) SCC 36] and *R.S.R.T.C.* v. *Shyam Bihari Lal Gupta* [2005 (7) SCC 406].

Coming back to back wages, even if the court finds it necessary to award back wages, the question will be whether back wages should be awarded fully or only partially (and if so the percentage). That depends upon the facts and circumstances of each case. Any income received by the employee during the relevant period on account of alternative employment or business is a relevant factor to be taken note of while awarding back wages, in addition to the several other factors which are deemed to be necessary.

In 2007 *J.K. Synthetics Ltd.* v. *K.P. Agrawal* [AIR 2007 SC (Supp) 637] the Supreme Court held as follows:

"Where the power under Article 226 or Section 11-A of the Industrial Disputes Act (or any other similar provision) is exercised by any court to interfere with the punishment on the ground that it is excessive and the employee deserves a lesser punishment, and a consequential direction is issued for reinstatement, the court is not holding that the employer was in the wrong or that the dismissal was illegal and invalid. The court is merely exercising its discretion to award a lesser punishment. Till such power is exercised, the dismissal is valid and in force. When the punishment is reduced by a court as being excessive, there can be either a direction for reinstatement or a direction for nominal lumpsum compensation. And if reinstatement is directed, it can be effective either prospectively from the date of such substitution of punishment (in which event, there is no continuity of service) or retrospectively, from the date on which the penalty of termination was imposed (in which event, there can be a consequential direction relating to continuity of service). What requires to be noted in cases where finding of misconduct is affirmed and only the punishment is interfered with (as contrasted from cases where termination is held to be illegal or void) is that there is no automatic reinstatement; and if reinstatement is directed, it is not automatically with retrospective effect from the date of termination. Therefore, where reinstatement is a consequence of imposition of a lesser punishment, neither back wages nor continuity of service nor consequential benefits follow as a natural or necessary consequence of such reinstatement. In cases where the misconduct is held to be proved, and reinstatement is itself a consequential benefit arising from imposition of a lesser punishment, award of back wages for the period when the employee has not worked, may amount to rewarding the delinquent employee and punishing the employer for taking action for the misconduct committed by the employee. That should be avoided. Similarly, in such cases, even where continuity of service is directed, it should only be for purposes of pensionary/retirement benefits, and not for other benefits like increments, promotions, etc. But there are two exceptions. The first is where the court sets aside the termination as a consequence of employee being exonerated or being found not guilty of the misconduct. Second is where the court reaches a conclusion that the inquiry was held in respect of a frivolous issue or petty misconduct, as a camouflage to get rid of the employee or victimize him, and the disproportionately excessive punishment is a result of such scheme or intention. In such cases, the principles relating to back wages, etc. will be the same as those applied in the cases of an illegal termination." [*J.K. Synthetics Ltd.* v. *K.P. Agrawal,* AIR 2007 SC (Supp) 637 at p. 645 *per* RAVEENDRAN, J.]

In *U.P.S.R.T.C.* v. *Mahendra Nath Tiwari* [AIR 2006 SC 405] where the respondent was appointed as a conductor of a bus by the Uttar Pradesh State Road Transport Corporation (hereinafter referred to as "U.P.S.R.T.C."). On the allegation that he was found to be driving the bus and that no ticket had been issued to a lone passenger found in the bus and he had in his possession used tickets, disciplinary proceedings were initiated against the respondent. A domestic enquiry was conducted through a retired judicial officer. He found that the respondent was unauthorizedly driving the bus and that no ticket had been issued to a lone passenger sitting in the bus when the checking party inspected the bus. He also found that the respondent had in his possession 12 used tickets. Based on the finding at the enquiry and after hearing the respondent, U.P.S.R.T.C. imposed a punishment of removal against the respondent.

At the instance of the respondent, the matter was sent to the labour court. The Presiding Officer found that the domestic enquiry relied on by the U.P.S.R.T.C. was not proper. The Presiding Officer directed the reinstatement of the respondent with continuity of service and all the remaining dues but directed the stoppage of his annual increment. He further directed that the respondent will receive his annual increment only when he satisfied his senior officers for three years without any charges or complaint against him. Apparently, what he meant was that the question of increment would depend upon the respondent satisfying his superiors over a period of three years. The U.P.S.R.T.C. filed a writ petition in the High Court of Allahabad and the High Court dismissed the writ petition. The learned judge also accepted the argument that the respondent was given a totally disproportionate and harsh punishment for his misconduct. The judgment of the High Court was challenged before the Supreme Court.

The Supreme Court held that the respondent did not deserve the award of back wages to him. In fact, he must consider himself lucky to have been reinstated. When a conductor drives a bus for which he is not authorized, he is endangering the public as well as the property of his employer. This by itself is a serious misconduct justifying dismissal of a conductor. Similarly, the fact that one passenger was found travelling and had not been issued a ticket for that journey, constitutes a grave charge against a conductor who is really in a position of trust as far as the employer-Corporation in concerned. He is duty bound to collect the fare from every passenger on behalf of his employer. The same is the position regarding the unexplained twelve used tickets, found in his possession. That prima facie suggests that there is room to doubt the honesty of the respondent. When a person like the conductor of a bus, who has the obligation to make proper collection of the charges from the passengers on issuing tickets to them, is found to have passengers in the bus, even if it be only one, to whom he had not issued a ticket, it clearly amounts to a clear violation of the duty imposed on him. It is really a breach of the duty cast on the conductor who is acting on behalf of the employer. Whether it is one passenger or ten passengers it would make no difference in principle in the absence of any explanation in that behalf. It was simply the case of a conductor who had violated the Regulations or the terms of his employment and had betrayed his employer, which in any event, is a grave misconduct justifying a dismissal. Therefore, the Court allowed the appeal in part and set aside the award of back wages. The respondent would be entitled to wages or salary only from the date of his being reinstated pursuant to the direction of the labour court. If anything has been paid to him in excess, U.P.S.R.T.C. would be entitled to adjust the same from his future salary in monthly instalments and/or recover it from his retiral benefits, if he is not still in service or by proceeding otherwise.

In a similar situation in *U.P. State Road Transport Corporation, Dehradun* v. *Suresh Pal* [AIR 2006 SC 3227] where a bus conductor was found guilty of not issuing tickets to twenty passengers and thereby he was charge sheeted and after holding a domestic enquiry, he was dismissed from service. After dismissal from service he raised an industrial dispute. A reference was made to the Labour Court and the Labour Court upheld the dismissal. Aggrieved against order of Labour Court, the respondent filed writ petition before the High Court of Uttaranchal at Nainital. The learned Single Judge though confirmed the findings of Labour Court against the delinquent but reduced the punishment from that of dismissal to that of punishment of one censure entry and stoppage of two increments with cumulative effect. It is, however, held that the respondent shall not be paid back wages but the continuity of the service shall be given to him with cumulative effect as aforesaid. Hence, the Corporation filed SLP. The Supreme Court observed:

> "If incumbent like the petitioner starts misappropriating the money by not issuing a ticket and pocketing the money thereby causing loss to the Corporation then this is a serious misconduct. It is unfortunate that the petitioner was appointed in 1988 and in the first year of service he started indulging in malpractice then what can be expected from him in the future. If this is the state of affairs in the first year of service and if such persons

are allowed to let off to the light punishment then this will be a wrong signal to the other persons similarly situated. Therefore, in such cases the incumbent should be weeded out as fast as possible and the same has been upheld by the Labour Court. We are firmly of the view that such instances should not be dealt with lightly so as to pollute the atmosphere in the Corporation and other co-workers. ... If such kind of misconduct is dealt with lightly and courts start substituting the lighter punishment in exercising the jurisdiction under Article 226 of the Constitution then it will give a wrong signal to the Society. All the State Road Transport Corporations in the country have gone in red because of the misconduct of such kind of incumbents; therefore, it is the time that misconduct should be dealt with iron hands and not leniently." [*U.P. State Road Transport Corporation, Dehradun* v. *Suresh Pal* [AIR 2006 SC 3227 at p. 3228 *per* A.K. Mathur, J.]

In view of the above discussion the Supreme Court set aside the order of the learned Single Judge and confirm the order of dismissal passed by the Corporation. The Supreme Court in the *Management of Regional Chief Engineer P.H.E.D. Ranchi v. Their Workmen Rep. by District Secretary* [2018 LLR 1167 (S.C.)] held that a workman has no right to claim back wages from his employer as of right only because the Court has set aside his dismissal order in his favour and directed his reinstatement in service. Further the Court held that it is necessary for the workman in such cases to plead and prove with the aid of evidence that after his dismissal from the service, he was not gainfully employed anywhere and had no earning to maintain himself or/and his family. The employer is also entitled to prove it otherwise against the employee, namely, that the employee was gainfully employed during the relevant period and hence not entitled to claim any back wages. However, Initial burden is on the employee.

SECTION 12: Duties of conciliation officers

(1) Where any industrial dispute exists or is apprehended, the conciliation officer may, or where the dispute relates to a public utility service and a notice under section 22 has been given, shall hold conciliation proceedings in the prescribed manner.

(2) The conciliation officer shall, for the purpose of bringing about a settlement of the dispute, without delay, investigate the dispute and all matters affecting the merits and the right settlement thereof and may do all such things as he thinks fit for the purpose of inducing the parties to come to a fair and amicable settlement of the dispute.

(3) If a settlement of the dispute or of any of the matters in dispute is arrived at in the course of the conciliation proceedings the conciliation officer shall send a report thereof to the appropriate Government or an officer authorised in this behalf by the appropriate Government together with a memorandum of the settlement signed by the parties to the dispute.

(4) If no such settlement is arrived at, the conciliation officer shall, as soon as practicable after the close of the investigation, send to the appropriate Government a full report setting forth the steps taken by him for ascertaining the facts and circumstances relating to the dispute and for bringing about a settlement thereof, together with a full statement of such facts and circumstances, and the reasons on account of which, in his opinion, a settlement could not be arrived at.

(5) If, on a consideration of the report referred to in sub-section (4), the appropriate Government is satisfied that there is a case for reference to a Board, Labour Court, Tribunal or National Tribunal, it may make such reference. Where the appropriate Government does not make such a reference it shall record and communicate to the parties concerned its reasons therefor.

(6) A report under this section shall be submitted within fourteen days of the commencement of the conciliation proceedings or within such shorter period as may be fixed by the appropriate Government:

Provided that, subject to the approval of the conciliation officer, the time for the submission of the report may be extended by such period as may be agreed upon in writing by all the parties to the dispute.

SECTION 13: Duties of Board

(1) Where a dispute has been referred to a Board under this Act, it shall be the duty of the Board to endeavour to bring about a settlement of the same and for this purpose the Board shall, in such manner as it thinks fit and without delay, investigate the dispute and all matters affecting the merits and the right settlement thereof and may do all such things as it thinks fit for the purpose of inducing the parties to come to a fair and amicable settlement of the dispute.

(2) If a settlement of the dispute or of any of the matters in dispute is arrived at in the course of the conciliation proceedings, the Board shall send a report thereof to the appropriate Government together with a memorandum of the settlement signed by the parties to the dispute.

(3) If no such settlement is arrived at, the Board shall, as soon as practicable after the close of the investigation, send to the appropriate Government a full report setting forth the proceedings and steps taken by the Board for ascertaining the facts and circumstances relating to the dispute and for bringing about a settlement thereof, together with a full statement of such facts and circumstances, its findings thereon, the reasons on account of which, in its opinion, a settlement could not be arrived at and its recommendations for the determination of the dispute.

(4) If, on the receipt of a report under sub-section (3) in respect of a dispute relating to a public utility service, the appropriate Government does not make a reference to a Labour Court, Tribunal or National Tribunal under section 10, it shall record and communicate to the parties concerned its reasons therefor.

(5) The Board shall submit its report under this section within two months of the date, on which the dispute was referred to it or within such shorter period as may be fixed by the appropriate Government:

Provided that the appropriate Government may from time to time extend the time for the submission of the report by such further periods not exceeding two months in the aggregate:

Provided further that the time for the submission of the report may be extended by such period as may be agreed on in writing by all the parties to the dispute.

SECTION 14: Duties of Courts

A Court shall inquire into the matters referred to it and report thereon to the appropriate Government ordinarily within a period of six months from the commencement of its inquiry.

SECTION 15: Duties of Labour Courts, Tribunals and National Tribunals

Where an industrial dispute has been referred to a Labour Court, Tribunal or National Tribunal for adjudication, it shall hold its proceedings expeditiously and shall, within the period specified in the order referring such industrial dispute or the further period extended under the second proviso to sub-section (2A) of section 10, submit its award to the appropriate Government.

SECTION 16: Form of report or award

(1) The report of a Board or Court shall be in writing and shall be signed by all the members of the Board or Court, as the case may be:

Provided that nothing in this section shall be deemed to prevent any member of the Board or Court from recording any minute of dissent from a report or from any recommendation made therein.

(2) The award of a Labour Court or Tribunal or National Tribunal shall be in writing and shall be signed by its presiding officer.

SECTION 17: Publication of reports and awards

(1) Every report of a Board or Court together with any minute of dissent recorded therewith, every arbitration award and every award of a Labour Court, Tribunal or National Tribunal shall, within a period of thirty days from the date of its receipt by the appropriate Government, be published in such manner as the appropriate Government thinks fit.

(2) Subject to the provisions of section 17A, the award published under sub-section (1) shall be final and shall not be called in question by any Court in any manner whatsoever.

SECTION 17A: Commencement of the award

(1) An award (including an arbitration award) shall become enforceable on the expiry of thirty days from the date of its publication under section 17:

Provided that—

(a) if the appropriate Government is of opinion, in any case where the award has been given by a Labour Court or Tribunal in relation to an industrial dispute to which it is a party; or

(b) if the Central Government is of opinion, in any case where the award has been given by a National Tribunal, that it will be inexpedient on public grounds affecting national economy or social justice to give effect to the whole or any part of the award, the appropriate Government, or as the case may be, the Central Government may, by notification in the Official Gazette, declare that the award shall not become enforceable on the expiry of the said period of thirty days.

(2) Where any declaration has been made in relation to an award under the proviso to sub-section (1), the appropriate Government or the Central Government may, within ninety days from the date of publication of the award under section 17, make an order rejecting or modifying the award, and shall, on the first available opportunity, lay the award together with a copy of the order before the Legislature of the State, if the order has been made by a State Government, or before Parliament, if the order has been made by the Central Government.

(3) Where any award as rejected or modified by an order made under sub-section (2) is laid before the Legislature of a State or before Parliament, such award shall become enforceable on the expiry of fifteen days from the date on which it is so laid; and where no order under sub-section (2) is made in pursuance of a declaration under the proviso to sub-section (1), the award shall become enforceable on the expiry of the period of ninety days referred to in sub-section (2).

(4) Subject to the provisions of sub-section (1) and sub-section (3) regarding the enforceability of an award, the award shall come into operation with effect from such date as may be specified therein, but where no date is so specified, it shall come into operation on the date when the award becomes enforceable under sub-section (1) or sub-section (3), as the case may be.

Section 17(1) lays down that every award shall, within a period of thirty days from the date of its receipt by the appropriate Government, be published in such manner as the appropriate Government thinks fit. The use of the word '*shall*' is a pointer to S. 17(1) being mandatory. Reading Ss. 17 and 17A together, there is no doubt that the intention behind S. 17(1) is that a duty is cast on the Government to publish the award within 30 days of its receipt and the provision for its publication is mandatory and not directory.

It seems that when the word '*shall*' was used in S. 17(1) the intention of the legislature is to give a mandate to Government to publish the award within the time fixed therein which can be found from S. 17(2) of the Act which provides that *"the award published under sub-section (1) shall be final and shall not be called in question by any court in any manner whatsoever"*. Obviously, when the Legislature intended the award on publication to be final, it could not have intended that the Government concerned had the power to withhold publication of the award.

Section 17A empowers the appropriate Government in certain circumstances to declare that the award shall not become enforceable on the expiry of thirty days from the date of its publication, which under S. 17A is the date of the enforceability of the award. Section 17A also envisages that the award must be published, though the Government may declare in certain contingencies that it may not be enforceable. Sub-section (2) of S. 17A also gives power to the Government to make an order rejecting or modifying the award within ninety days from the date of its publication. It is clear after reading Ss. 17 and 17A together that the intention behind S. 17(1) is that a duty is cast on the Government to publish the award within thirty days of its receipt and the provision for its publication is mandatory and not merely directory. In *Sirsilk Ltd.* v. *Govt. of A.P.*,[168] an order referring certain disputes between the appellant and its workmen was made to the Industrial Tribunal, Andhra Pradesh on June 6, 1956. The Tribunal sent its award to Government in September 1957. Under S. 17 of the Industrial Disputes Act, the award has to be published by the appropriate Government within a period of thirty days from the date of its receipt by the Government in such manner as the Government thinks fit. However, before the Government could publish the award under S. 17, the parties to the dispute, which had been referred for adjudication, came to a settlement and on October 1, 1957, a letter was written to Government signed jointly on behalf of the employer and the employees intimating that the dispute, which had been pending before the Tribunal, had been settled and a request was made to Government not to publish the award. The Government, however, expressed its inability to withhold the publication of the award, the view taken by the Government being that S. 17 of the Act was mandatory and the Government was bound to publish the award. Thereupon, the appellants filed writ petitions before the High Court under Art. 226 of the Constitution praying that the Government may be directed not to publish the award sent to it by the Industrial Tribunal. The High Court held that S. 17 was mandatory and it was not open to the Government to withhold publication of an award sent to it by an Industrial Tribunal. Therefore, it was not open to the High Court to direct the Government not to publish the award when the law enjoined upon it to publish it. The writ petitions were therefore dismissed. This case came before the Supreme Court on appeal for consideration.

The appellants submitted before the Court that the publication of an award under S. 17 of the Act is directory and not mandatory. In the alternative, it is also submitted that even if S. 17 is considered mandatory, some via media has to be found in view of the conflict that would arise between an award published under S. 17(1) and a settlement which is binding under S. 18(1), and therefore where there is a settlement arrived at by the parties and which is binding under S. 18(1), it would be appropriate for the Government not to publish the award.

The Court held that the publication of the award under S. 17(1) as directory cannot be accepted. Section 17(1) lays down that every award shall within a period of thirty days from the date of its receipt by the appropriate government be published in such manner as the appropriate Government thinks fit. The use of the word *'shall'* is a pointer to S. 17(1) being mandatory, though, undoubtedly, in certain circumstances, the word 'shall' used in a statute may be equal to the word 'may'. But in the present case, however, it seems that when the word 'shall' was used in S. 17(1), the intention was to give a mandate to Government to publish the award within the time fixed therein. The Court further held that even though this may be so, it is to be reconciled—the mandatory character of the provision contained in S. 17(1) for the publication of the award to the equally mandatory character of the binding nature of the settlement arrived at between the parties as provided in S. 18(1). The Court specifically said that there should be no difficulty, if a settlement has been arrived at between the parties while the dispute is pending before the Tribunal, the parties would file the settlement before the Tribunal and the Tribunal would make the award in accordance with the settlement. In the instant case, the Court referred to *State of Bihar* v. *D.N. Ganguly*,[169] where a settlement had been arrived at between the parties while an industrial dispute was pending

168. AIR 1964 SC 160.
169. AIR 1958 SC 1018.

before a tribunal, the only remedy for giving effect to such a settlement would be to cancel the reference. In *D.N. Ganguly* case, the Supreme Court observed that though the Industrial Disputes Act did not contain any provision specifically authorising the Industrial Tribunal, to record a compromise and pass an award in its terms corresponding to the provisions of Order XXIII, Rule 3 of the Code of Civil Procedure, it would be very unreasonable to assume that the Industrial Tribunal would insist upon dealing with the dispute on the merits even after it is informed that the dispute has been amicably settled between the parties, and there can be no doubt that if a dispute before a Tribunal is amicably settled, the Tribunal would immediately agree to make an award in terms of the settlement between the parties. In that case the Supreme Court dealt with what would happen if a settlement was arrived at while the matter was pending before the Tribunal. The difficulty arises in the present case because the proceedings before the Tribunal had come to an end, and the Tribunal had sent its award to Government before the settlement was arrived at on October 1, 1957. In the present case difficulty however arises when the matter has gone beyond the purview of the Tribunal.

The Court travelled further in the present case and in order to avoid a possible conflict between S. 18(1) which makes the settlement arrived at between the parties, otherwise than in the course of conciliation proceeding, binding on the parties and the terms of an award which are binding under S. 18(3) on publication and accordingly held that the only way to resolve the possible conflict which would arise between a settlement which is binding under S. 18(1) and an award which may become binding under S. 18(3) on publication is to withhold the publication of the award once the Government has been informed jointly by the parties that a settlement binding under S. 18(1) has been arrived at. It is true that S. 17(1) is mandatory and ordinarily the Government has to publish an award sent to it by the Tribunal; but where a situation like the one in the present case arises which may lead to a conflict between a settlement under S. 18(1) and an award binding under S. 18(3) on publication, the only solution is to withhold the award from publication.

The matter may be looked at in another way. The reference to the Tribunal is for the purpose of resolving the dispute that may have arisen between employers and their workmen. Where a settlement is arrived at between the parties to a dispute, before the Tribunal, after the award has been submitted to Government but before its publication, there is in fact no dispute left to be resolved by the publication of the award. In such a case, the award sent to Government may very well be considered to have become infructuous and so the Government should refrain from publishing such an award because no dispute remains to be resolved by it. Accordingly, Wanchoo, J. delivered the majority opinion observed:

> "We are, therefore, of opinion that though S. 17(1) is mandatory and the Government is bound to publish the award received by it from an industrial tribunal, the situation arising in a case like the present is of an exceptional nature and requires reconciliation between S. 18(1) and S. 18(3), and in such a situation the only way to reconcile the two provisions is to withhold the publication of the award, as a binding settlement has already come into force in order to avoid possible conflict between a binding settlement under S. 18(1) and a binding award under S. 18(3). In such a situation we are of opinion that the Government ought not to publish the award under S. 17(1) and in cases where Government is going to publish it, it can be directed not to publish the award in view of the binding settlement arrived at between the parties under S. 18(1) with respect to the very matters which were the subject-matter of adjudication under the award."[170]

170. *Ibid.*, f.n. 168 at p. 164 per Wanchoo, J.

In *Remington Rand of India Ltd.* v. *The Workmen*,[171] the Supreme Court referred to *State of Uttar Pradesh* v. *Babu Ram Upadhya*,[172] where there is an elaborate discussion as to whether the use of the word 'shall' in a statute made the provision mandatory. It was accordingly observed that for ascertaining the real intention of the Legislature the Court may consider, inter alia, the nature and the design of the statute, and the consequences which would follow from construing it one way or the other, the impact of other provisions, and, above all, whether the object of the legislation will be defeated or furthered. It is thought proper here to mention the decision of the Kerala High Court where the question directly arose as to whether non-publication of the award within the period mentioned in S. 17(1) invalidated the award and the learned Judge observed that he was not inclined to accept that contention, although it was highly desirable that the award should be published within the time mentioned. He said:

> "Excepting that a slight delay in publishing the award under S. 17(1) results in postponing its finality under S. 17(2) or its becoming enforceable under S. 17A, no other consequence flows from the delay and therefore, in my view, the provisions of sub-section (1) of S. 17 should be considered only to be "merely directory...".[173]

Keeping the above principles in mind, the Supreme Court held that a provision as to time in S. 17(1) is merely directory and not mandatory. Section 17(1) makes it obligatory on the Government to publish the award. The limit of time has been fixed as showing that the publication of the award ought not to be held up. But the fixation of the period of 30 days mentioned, therein does not mean that the publication beyond that time will render the award invalid. It is not difficult to think of circumstances when the publication of the award within thirty days may not be possible. For instance, there may be a strike in the press, or there may be any other good and sufficient cause by reason of which the publication could not be made within thirty days. Therefore, if the award is rendered invalid, it would be attaching undue importance to a provision not in the mind of the legislature. It is well known that it very often takes a long period of time for the reference to be concluded, and the award to be made. If the award becomes invalid on the ground of publication after thirty days, it might entail a fresh reference with needless harassment to the parties.

The Second National Commission on Labour recommended that instead of waiting for the publication of the awards in the Official Gazette, awards of the competent Court including the Labour Court and the Labour Relations Commissions should be deemed to have come into effect unless an appeal is preferred within the prescribed period. The Labour Court should be empowered to enforce their own awards as well as the awards of Labour Relations Commissions. They should also be empowered to grant interim relief in case of extreme hardship. Officials of Labour Department at the Center and the States who are of and above the rank of Deputy Labour Commissioners/Regional Labour Commissioners with ten years experience in the labour department and a degree in law, may be eligible for being appointed as presiding officers of Labour Courts. The Central and State Labour Relations Commissions should be declared as set-up under Art. 323-B of the Constitution. The National Commission should be empowered with powers of the Supreme Court of India.[174]

171. AIR 1968 SC 224.
172. AIR 1961 SC 751.
173. *Erumeli Estate* v. *Industrial Tribunal* (1962) 2 LLJ 144 (Ker).
174. Report of The Second National Commission on Labour, Chapter 13, pp. 45–46, para 6.95.

SECTION 17B: Payment of full wages to workman pending proceedings in higher courts

Where in any case, a Labour Court, Tribunal or National Tribunal by its award directs reinstatement of any workman and the employer prefers any proceedings against such award in a High Court or the Supreme Court, the employer shall be liable to pay such workman, during the period of pendency of such proceedings in the High Court or the Supreme Court, full wages last drawn by him, inclusive of any maintenance allowance admissible to him under any rule if the workman had not been employed in any establishment during such period and an affidavit by such workman had been filed to that effect in such Court:

Provided that where it is proved to the satisfaction of the High Court or the Supreme Court that such workman had been employed and had been receiving adequate remuneration during any such period or part thereof, the Court shall order that no wages shall be payable under this section for such period or part, as the case may be.

The objects and reasons for enacting S. 17B are as follows:

When Labour Courts pass award of reinstatement, these are often contested by an employer in the Supreme Court or High Courts. It is felt that the delay in the implementation of the award causes hardship to the workman concerned. It is, therefore, proposed to provide the payment of wages last drawn by the workman concerned, under certain conditions, from the date of the award till the case is finally decided in the Supreme Court or High Courts.

It thus appears that the object underlying the enacting of the provisions contained in S. 17B is to give relief to the workman in whose favour an award of reinstatement has been passed by the Labour Court and the said award is under challenge in the High Court or the Supreme Court. The said relief has been given with a view to relieve the hardship that would be caused to a workman on account of delay in implementation of the award as a result of the pendency of the proceedings in the High Court or the Supreme Court.

The objects and reasons do not indicate the extent of relief to be granted to a workman in case the employer prefers appeal either to the High Court or the Supreme Court against the order of reinstatement passed by the Labour Court. However, S. 17B provides that the workman is entitled to get full wages last drawn inclusive of any maintenance allowance admissible to him under any rule. The expression "full wages last drawn" in S. 17B has been construed by the various High Courts and the Supreme Court on many occasions and they are as follows:

A Division Bench of the Karnataka High Court in *Vishveswaraya Iron and Steel Ltd.* v. *M. Chandrappa*,[175] has held that the words "*full wages last drawn*" take into their fold the wages drawn on the date of termination of the services plus the yearly increment and the dearness allowance to be worked out till the date of the award. In taking this view, the learned Judges have pointed out that it is not uncommon that the proceedings before the Labour Court linger on for years, and in some cases, it takes a decade and that if after a decade the full wages last drawn are to be paid from the date of the award during the pendency of the proceedings before the Court at the same rate at which the wages were last drawn by the workman when he was removed, dismissed or terminated from the service, it would cause him great prejudice and injustice and will result in harassment of the workman and that during the

175. 1994 (84) FJR 46.

last period of 10 years, there would be escalations in the cost of living and there would also be increase in the wages paid to the workman doing the work of similar nature.

In *Carona Sahu Co. Ltd.* v. *A.K. Munakhan*,[176] a Division Bench of the Bombay High Court, after referring to the decision of the Karnataka High Court in *Vishveswaraya Iron and Steel Ltd.* case, has laid down that the expression "full wages last drawn" means the full wages which the workman was entitled to draw in pursuance of the award and the implementation of which is suspended during the pendency of the proceedings. The learned Judges have observed that though the word 'drawn' connotes past tense, it is obvious that the proper construction of the section is that the workman is entitled to the full wages which the workman would have been entitled to draw but for the pendency of the proceedings in the High Court or the Apex Court. According to the learned Judges, every component of wages payable on the date of the award must be taken into consideration while determining what were the wages payable to the workman on the date of the award. It has been held that this interpretation of the expression "full wages last drawn" subserves the object and intention of the Parliament in enacting S. 17B of the Act.

The High Court of Punjab and Haryana in *Daladdi Co-operative Agriculture Service Society Ltd.* v. *Gurcharan Singh*,[177] has, however, taken a different view. The learned Judges have held that the provision in S. 17-B implies that if the workman is not gainfully employed in any establishment, he is entitled to the payment of wages at the same rate at which he was being paid immediately before the termination of his services.

According to the learned Judges, the Legislature while introducing S. 17B intended that the workman who remains unemployed in spite of an award having been passed by the competent court or Tribunal, should be paid at least the wages at the rate last drawn by him so that he may be able to subsist. It has been held that the workman who has not been reinstated is entitled to payment of wages only at the rate last drawn by him and not at the same rate at which the wages are being paid to the workmen who are actually working.

As per the decisions of the High Courts discussed above, the expression "full wages last drawn" in S. 17B can mean as follows:

(i) Wages only at the rate last drawn and not at the same rate at which the wages are being paid to the workmen who are actually working.[178]

(ii) Wages drawn on the date of termination of the services plus the yearly increment and the dearness allowance to be worked out till the date of the award.[179]

(iii) Full wages which the workman was entitled to draw in pursuance of the award and the implementation of which is suspended during the pendency of the proceedings.[180]

The first construction gives to the words "full wages last drawn" their plain and material meaning. The second and the third constructions read something more than their plain and material meaning in those words. In substance, these constructions read the words as "full

176. 1995 (70) Fac LR 25.
177. 1993 (5) Serv LR 719.
178. *Ibid.*, f.n. 177.
179. *Vishveswaraya Iron and Steel Ltd.* v. *M. Chandrappa*, 1994 (84) FJR 46) (Kant).
180. *Carona Sahu Co. Ltd.* v. *A.K. Munakhan*, 1995 (70) Fac LR 25 (Bom).

wages which would have been drawn". Such an extended meaning to the words does not find support in the language of S. 17B. Nor can this extended meaning be based on the object underlying the enactment of S. 17B.

The Supreme Court in *Dena Bank* v. *Kiritikumar T. Patel*[181] overruled *Vishveswaraya Iron and Steel Ltd.* case and *Carona Sahu Co.* case and observed that the words *"full wages last drawn"* in S. 17B cannot be read as *"full wages which would have been drawn"*. Such an extended meaning to the words *"full wages last drawn"* does not find support in the language of S. 17B. Nor can this extended meaning be based on the object underlying the enactment of S. 17B. Section 17B has been enacted by Parliament with a view to give relief to a workman who has been ordered to be reinstated under the award of a Labour Court or the Industrial Tribunal during the pendency of proceedings in which the said award is under challenge before the High Court or the Supreme Court. The object underlying the provision is to relieve to a certain extent the hardship that is caused to the workman due to delay in the implementation of the award. The payment which is required to be made by the employer to the workman is in the nature of subsistence allowance which would not be refundable or recoverable from the workman even if the award is set aside by the High Court or Supreme Court. Since the payment is of such a character, Parliament thought it proper to limit it to the extent of the wages which were drawn by the workman when he was in service and when his services were terminated and therefore used the words *"full wages last drawn"*. To read these words to mean wages which would have been drawn by the workman if he had continued in service if the order terminating his services had not been passed since it has been set aside by the award of the Labour Court or Industrial Tribunal, would result in so enlarging the benefit as to comprehend the relief that has been granted under the award that is under challenge. Since the amount is not refundable or recoverable in the event of the award being set aside, it would result in the employer being required to give effect to the award during the pendency of the proceedings, challenging the award before the High Court or the Supreme Court without his being able to recover the said amount in the event of the award being set aside. The provisions contained in S. 17B cannot be construed as casting such a burden on the employer. The words "full wages last drawn" must be given their plain and material meaning and cannot be given the extended meaning.

The word *'full'* in the expression *"full wages last drawn"* only emphasizes that all the emoluments, which are included in *'wages'* as defined in Cl. (rr) of S. 2 of the Act so as to include the amounts referred to in sub-clauses (i) to (iv), are required to be paid. It does not imply that the wages last drawn must be the wages which the workman would have drawn under the award. The position is clear from the fact that in S. 17B Parliament has used the words *"inclusive of any maintenance allowance admissible to him under any rule"*. These words indicate that maintenance allowance that is admissible under any rule is required to be paid, irrespective of the amount which was actually being paid as maintenance allowance to the workmen. But with regard to wages, Parliament has used the words *"full wages last drawn"* indicating that the wages that were actually paid and not the amount that would be payable or are required to be paid. The Supreme Court has travelled further in *Regional Authority, Dena Bank v. Ghanshyam*,[182] where the Court held that the import of S. 17B

181. AIR 1998 SC 511.
182. AIR 2001 SC 2270.

admits of no doubt that Parliament intended that the workman should get the last drawn wages from the date of the award till the challenge to the award is finally decided which is in accord with the Statement of the Objects and Reasons of the Industrial Disputes (Amendment) Act, 1982 by which S. 17B was inserted in the Act. Section 17B does not preclude the High Courts or the Supreme Court from granting better benefits more just and equitable on the facts of a case—than contemplated by that provision to a workman. However, it must be pointed out that while passing an interlocutory order, the interests of the employer should not be lost sight of. Even though the amount paid by the employer under S. 17B to the workman cannot be directed to be refunded in the event he loses the case in the writ petition, any amount over and above the sum payable under the said provision has to be refunded by him. It will, therefore, be in the interests of justice to ensure, if the facts of the case so justify, that payment of any amounts over and above the amount payable under S. 17B to him, is ordered to be paid on such terms and conditions as would enable the employer to recover the same.

Pre-requirements for Invoking Section 17B

The three necessary ingredients for the application of S. 17B are

(i) The Labour Court should have directed reinstatement of the workman.

(ii) The employer should have preferred proceedings against such award in the High Court or in the Supreme Court.

(iii) That the workman should not have been employed in any establishment during such period.

Constitutional Validity

In *Elpro International Ltd.* v. *K.B. Joshi,*[183] the validity of the provisions in S. 17B was challenged on the ground that the same are vague and arbitrary inasmuch as no provision is made as to what would happen to the amount paid if ultimately the employer succeeds and the award is quashed and set aside and are, therefore, violative of Art. 14 of the Constitution. It was also urged that the said provisions encroach upon the powers of the High Court and the Supreme Court under Arts. 226 and 136 of the Constitution. The Division Bench of the Bombay High Court rejected both the contentions. It was held that the absence of a provision as to what would happen to the amount paid under S. 17B, if ultimately the employer succeeds in the litigation, does not make the section either vague or arbitrary because what is to be paid under S. 17B is in the nature of subsistence allowance that is payable under S. 10A of the Industrial Employment (Standing Orders) Act, 1946, which is neither refundable nor recoverable irrespective of the result of the enquiry. As regards challenge on the ground of encroachment upon the powers of the High Court under Art. 226 and the Apex Court under Art. 136 of the Constitution, the High Court was of the view that S. 17B only guarantees to the workman the payment of wages by the employer during the pendency of the proceedings before the High Court or the Supreme Court and that too subject to the conditions laid down by the said section and the proviso, irrespective of the result of the

183. 1987 Lab IC 1468.

proceedings. It also imposes an obligation upon the workman concerned to file an affidavit before the Court stating that he has not been employed in any establishment during the pendency of the proceedings. Further, it also absolves the employer of his obligation to pay such wages if he is able to prove to the satisfaction of the court that the workman had been otherwise employed and had been receiving adequate remuneration. The High Court observed that S. 17B nowhere lays down that in extreme cases it is demonstrated that the award passed is either without jurisdiction or is otherwise a nullity or grossly erroneous or perverse, the High Court or the Supreme Court is deterred from exercising its powers under Arts. 226 and 136 of the Constitution. On that view the High Court held that S. 17B does not in any way encroach upon or override the powers of the High Court under Art. 226 and the Supreme Court under Art. 136 of the Constitution.

Similarly, in *The Kapurthala Central Co-operative Bank Ltd.* v. *The Presiding Officer, Labour Court, Jalandhar,*[184] the High Court of Punjab and Haryana considered the validity of the challenge to S. 17B as violative of the provisions of Art. 226 of the Constitution. Rejecting the said challenge, it held that S. 17B does not in any way interfere or restrict the same and that the section only guarantees the workers the payment of wages by the employer during the course of proceedings in the High Court or the Supreme Court, of course subject to the safeguard provided for irrespective of the result of the proceedings.

In *Dena Bank* v. *Kiritikumar T. Patel,*[185] the Supreme Court held that S. 17B, by conferring a right on the workman to be paid the amount of full wages last drawn by him during the pendency of the proceedings involving challenge to the award of the Labour Court, Industrial Tribunal or National Tribunal in the High Court or the Supreme Court, which amount is not refundable or recoverable in the event of the award being set aside, does not in any way preclude the High Court or the Supreme Court to pass an order directing payment of a higher amount to the workman if such higher amount is considered necessary in the interest of justice. Such a direction would be de hors the provisions contained in S. 17B and while giving the direction, the Court may also give directions regarding refund or recovery of the excess amount in the event of the award being set aside. In exercise of the power under Arts. 226 and 136 of the Constitution, an order cannot be passed denying the workman the benefit granted under S. 17B. The right of workman under S. 17B cannot be regarded as a restriction on the powers of the High Court or the Supreme Court under Arts. 226 and 136 of the Constitution.

In 2018 The Supreme Court in *Rajeshwar Mahto* v. *Alok Kumar Gupta, G.M. M/s. Birla Corporation Ltd.* [2018 LLR 368 (S.C.)] held that any payment made by the employer under Section 17-B of the I. D. Act is in the nature of subsistence allowance hence it is neither refundable nor recoverable. Such payment will be considered as independent in nature and it will not merge with the final order.

SECTION 18: Persons on whom settlements and awards are binding

(1) A settlement arrived at by agreement between the employer and workman otherwise than in the course of conciliation proceeding shall be binding on the parties to the agreement.

---

184. 1985 (2) 88 Pun LR 74.
185. AIR 1998 SC 511.

(2) Subject to the provisions of sub-section (3), an arbitration award which has become enforceable shall be binding on the parties to the agreement who referred the dispute to arbitration.

(3) A settlement arrived at in the course of conciliation proceedings under this Act or an arbitration award in a case where a notification has been issued under sub-section (3A) of section 10A or an award of a Labour Court, Tribunal or National Tribunal which has become enforceable shall be binding on—

(a) all parties to the industrial dispute;

(b) all other parties summoned to appear in the proceedings as parties to the dispute, unless the Board, arbitrator, Labour Court, Tribunal or National Tribunal, as the case may be, records the opinion that they were so summoned without proper cause;

(c) where a party referred to in Cl. (a) or Cl. (b) is an employer, his heirs, successors or assigns in respect of the establishment to which the dispute relates;

(d) where a party referred to in Cl. (a) or Cl. (b) is composed of workmen, all persons who were employed in the establishment or part of the establishment, as the case may be, to which the dispute relates on the date of the dispute and all persons who subsequently become employed in that establishment or part.

Sections 18(1) and 18(3) deal with the binding effect of the settlement. It would be noticed that S. 18 divides settlements into two categories. The first category consists of settlements which are arrived at otherwise than in the course of conciliation proceedings, which may be called *private settlement*. This category is envisaged by S. 18(1) of the Act. The second category consists of settlements which are arrived at "in the course of conciliation proceedings." This category is envisaged by S. 18(3) of the Act.

A bare perusal of S. 18 would show that a settlement arrived at by agreement between the employer and the workmen otherwise than in the course of conciliation proceeding is binding only on the parties to the agreement, whereas a settlement arrived at in the course of conciliation proceeding under the Act is binding not only on the parties to the industrial dispute but also on other persons specified in Cls. (b), (c) and (d) of sub-section (3) of S. 18 of the Act. In *Ramnagar Cane and Sugar Co. Ltd.* v. *Jatin Chakravorty,*[186] it was held that when an industrial dispute is thus raised and is decided either by settlement or by an award, the scope and effect of its operation is prescribed by S. 18 of the Act. Section 18(1) provides that a settlement arrived at by agreement between the employer and the workman otherwise than in the course of conciliation proceeding shall be binding on the parties to the agreement, whereas S. 18(3) provides that a settlement arrived at in the course of conciliation proceedings which has become enforceable shall be binding on all the parties specified in Cls. (a), (b), (c) and (d) of sub-section (3). Section 18(3)(d) makes it clear that, where a party referred to in Cl. (a) or (b) is composed of workmen, all persons who are employed in the establishment or part of the establishment, as the case may be, to which the dispute relates on the date of the dispute and all persons who subsequently become employed in that establishment or part, would be bound by the settlement.... In order to bind the workman, it is not necessary

186. AIR 1960 SC 1012.

to show that the said workman belongs to the Union which was a party to the dispute before the conciliator. The whole policy of S. 18 appears to be to give an extended operation to the settlement arrived at in the course of conciliation proceedings. And that is the object with which the four categories of persons bound by such settlement are specified in S. 18(3).

A similar view seems to have been held by another Division Bench of the Supreme Court in *The Jhagrakhan Collieries (P.) Ltd.* v. *G.C. Agrawal.*[187] The Supreme Court went further in *Tata Chemicals Ltd., M/s.* v. *The Workmen employed under M/s. Tata Chemicals Ltd.*[188] and held that even if a settlement regarding certain demand is arrived at otherwise than during the conciliation proceeding between the employer and the Union representing majority workmen, the same is not binding on the other Union who represents minority workmen and who was not a party to that settlement. The other Union can, therefore, raise the dispute in respect of the demand covered by the settlement and the same can be validly referred for adjudication. The Court further held that if any settlement is arrived at outside the conciliation proceeding between the employer and the majority Union and the workmen thereby accepted some of the benefits flowing from the settlement, however they are not signatories to it, such acceptance of benefit does not operate as estoppel against minority union raising same demands. In this situation, the theory of implied agreement by acquiescence cannot be attracted. In *Tata Engineering and Locomotive Co. Ltd., M/s.* v. *Their Workmen,*[189] the Supreme Court, taking a different stand from *Jhagrakhan Collieries* case, and *Tata Chemicals Ltd.* case held that if the settlement had been arrived at between the company and the union of the workers by a vast majority of the workers concerned with their eyes open and was also accepted by them in its totality, it must be presumed to be just and fair and not liable to be ignored merely because a small number of workers were not parties to it or refused to accept it, or because the tribunal was of the opinion that the workers deserved marginally higher emolument than they thought they did. A settlement cannot be weighed in any golden scales and the question whether it is just and fair has to be answered on the basis of principles different from those which come into play when an industrial dispute is under adjudication. When the settlement is just and fair and is arrived at by a union representing majority workmen, the question of acquiescence to the settlement by the workmen does not arise.

In a landmark judgment in the case of *Herbertsons Ltd.* v. *Workmen,*[190] the facts were that a dispute was referred for adjudication to the Tribunal which, after hearing, gave an award. The company appealed to the Supreme Court against the award by special leave. While the matter was pending before the Supreme Court in appeal, the workmen changed their loyalties, and resigned from the union which was party to the dispute, and joined another union. The company granted recognition to the said union, to which the workmen had transferred their loyalty. A settlement was arrived at between this latter union and the management. Copies of this settlement were forwarded to the Government and various other authorities so as to make it statutorily binding on the parties. It was common ground before the Court that this was a settlement under S. 18(1) of the Industrial Disputes Act and not under S. 18(3) of the Act, that is to say, it was a settlement outside conciliation proceedings

187. AIR 1975 SC 171.
188. AIR 1978 SC 828.
189. AIR 1981 SC 2163.
190. AIR 1977 SC 322.

and binding only on the parties to the dispute. The company made an application to the Court to pass judgment in terms of the settlement. The factual position that emerged was that one of the unions which had 193 members on its roll had entered into the settlement, while another union, claimed to have 55 members on its rolls, did not accept the settlement. In the aforesaid circumstance, the Supreme Court framed an issue to find out whether the settlement was fair and reasonable and ought to be accepted and then remanded it to the Tribunal to return a finding on the issue. The Tribunal's finding was that the settlement was partly fair and partly unfair. On this finding, it was urged that the appeal should be decided on merits. But the Supreme Court refused to do so, holding that:

> "When a recognised union negotiates with an employer, the workers as individuals do not come into the picture. It is not necessary that each individual worker should know the implications of the settlement since a recognised union, which is expected to protect the legitimate interests of labour, enters into a settlement in the best interests of labour. This would be the normal rule. We cannot altogether rule out exceptional cases where there may be allegations of mala fides, fraud or even corruption or other inducements. Nothing of that kind has been suggested against the President of the 3rd respondent in this case. That being the position, prima facie, this is a settlement in the course of collective bargaining and, therefore, is entitled to due weight and consideration."[191]

The Supreme Court further observed that there may be several factors that may influence the parties to come to a settlement as a phased endeavour in the course of collective bargaining. Once cordiality is established between the employer and labour in arriving at a settlement which operates well for the period that it is in force, there is always a likelihood of further advances in the shape of improved emoluments by voluntary settlement avoiding friction and unhealthy litigation. This is the quintessence of settlement which courts and tribunals should endeavour to encourage. It is in that spirit the settlement has to be judged and not by the yardstick adopted in scrutinising an award in adjudication. It further held that it is not possible to scan the settlement in bits and pieces, and hold some parts good and acceptable and others bad. Unless it can be demonstrated that the objectionable portion is such that it completely outweighs all the other advantages gained therein, the Court cannot consider a settlement as unfair and unjust.[192]

Binding Effect of a Private Settlement or Bipartite Negotiation

This sub-section was introduced along with the definition of settlement provided under S. 2(p) by the Amending Act of 1956, with a view to provide binding effect of a private settlement, which is otherwise known as *bipartite negotiation*, in order to remove the defects that existed in the previous law. Prior to the amendment, there was no provision to make such settlements binding even on the parties thereto. By the same amending Act, the definition of 'settlement' was also amended so as to include written agreements, between the employer and workmen, arrived at otherwise than in the course of conciliation proceedings.

Settlement of labour disputes by direct negotiation or settlement through collective bargaining is always to be preferred, for it is the best guarantee of industrial peace which is the aim of all legislation for the settlement of labour disputes. In order to bring about such a

191. *Ibid.* at p. 326 per Goswami, J.
192. *Ibid.* at p. 328 per Goswami, J.

settlement more easily, and to make it more workable and effective, it is no longer necessary, under the law, that the settlement should be confined to that arrived at in the course of a conciliation proceeding, but now includes, by virtue of the definition in S. 2(p) of the Act, a written agreement between the employer and the workmen arrived at otherwise than in the course of a conciliation proceeding where such agreement has been signed by the parties in the prescribed manner and a copy thereof has been sent to the authorised officers. Rule 58(2) of the Industrial Disputes (Central) Rules, 1957, prescribes the manner of signing the settlement. Under S. 18(1) of the Act, a settlement arrived at by agreement between the employer and the workmen otherwise than in the course of conciliation proceedings is binding on the parties to the agreement.[193]

Normally, it is the union or the representatives of the employees who enter into an agreement with the employer. All the employees do not, as a matter of fact, become parties, to the agreement. But the settlement signed by such representatives binds all those whom they represent. Therefore, the terms of the settlement become a part of the contract of employment of each individual workman represented by such representatives. If such a settlement is arrived at between the employer and the union representing majority of workmen, it shall not be binding on the other unions which are not a party to the settlement. A settlement becomes binding at once as soon as the memorandum of settlement has been signed by the parties in the prescribed manner and a copy of it is sent to the Government and the Conciliation Officer and it comes into operation on the date it is signed or on the date which might be mentioned in it for its coming into operation.[194] The language of S. 18(1) clearly shows that the settlement will be binding only *on the parties to the agreement*. The definition of *settlement* in S. 2(p) of the Act also states that *settlement* means a settlement arrived at *between the employer and the workmen*. So, normally in order that a settlement between the employer and the workmen may be binding on them, it has to be arrived at by an agreement between the employer and the workmen. Where the workmen are represented by a recognized Union, the settlement may be arrived at between the employer and the Union. If there is a recognized Union of the workmen and the Constitution of the Union provides that any of its office-bearers can enter into a settlement with the management on behalf of the Union and its members, a settlement may be arrived at between the employer and such office-bearer or bearers. But where the Constitution does not so provide specifically, the office-bearer or bearers who wish to enter into a settlement with the employer should have the necessary authorization by the executive committee of the Union or by the workmen. A reading of Rule 62(2)(b) clearly shows that it presupposes the existence of a settlement already arrived at between the employer and the workmen, and it only prescribes the form in which the memorandum of settlement should be signed and also by whom it is to be signed. It does not deal with the entering into or arriving at a settlement. Therefore, where a settlement is alleged to have been arrived at between an employer and one or more office-bearers of the Union, and the authority of the office-bearers who signed the memorandum of settlement to enter into the settlement is challenged or disputed, the said authority or authorization of the office-bearers who signed the memorandum of settlement has to be established as a fact, and it is not enough if the employer merely points out and relies upon the fact that the memorandum of settlement was signed by one or more of the office-bearers of the Union.

---

193. *New Standard Engineering Co. Ltd.* v. *N.L. Abhyankar,* AIR 1978 SC 982.
194. *Sirsilk Ltd.* v. *Govt. of A.P.,* AIR 1964 SC 160.

In *Brooke Bond India Ltd.* v. *Workmen,*[195] the purported settlement was arrived at not in the course of conciliation proceedings as there was no provision in the constitution of the Union authorising any office-bearer of the Union to enter into a settlement with the management. The resolutions passed by the executive committee of the Union did not support the claim that the Negotiation Committee was empowered to enter into a settlement without seeking ratification from the executive committee. The office-bearers who signed the agreement were not competent to enter into a settlement with the company and as such it cannot be said that an agreement was reached between the employer and the workmen represented by the Union. Unless the office-bearers who signed the agreement were authorised by the executive committee of the Union to enter into a settlement, or the constitution of the Union contained a provision that one or more of its members would be competent to settle a dispute with the management, no agreement between any office-bearer of the Union and the management can be called as a settlement as defined in S. 2(p).

In *Jhagrakhan Collieries (P) Ltd.* v. *G.C. Agrawal Central Govt. Industrial Tribunal cum-Labour Court,*[196] the Supreme Court held that from the perusal of S. 18, it would be clear that a settlement arrived at in the course of conciliation proceedings is binding not only on the actual parties to the industrial dispute but also on the heirs, successors or assignees of the employer on the one hand, and all the workmen in the establishment, present or future, on the other. In extending the operation of such a settlement beyond the parties thereto, sub-section (3) of the Section departs from the ordinary law of contract and gives effect to the principle of collective bargaining. But sub-section (3) cannot be invoked where it is a finding of the High Court that a settlement arrived at between the employer and the workmen is not deemed to be a settlement arrived at in the conciliation proceedings. According to the scheme of S. 18 read with S. 2(p), an agreement, made otherwise than in the course of conciliation proceedings, to be a settlement within the meaning of the Act must be a written agreement signed in the manner prescribed by the rules framed under the Act. An implied agreement by acquiescence or conduct such as acceptance of a benefit under an agreement to which the worker acquiescing or accepting the benefit was not a party, being outside the purview of the Act, is not binding on such a worker either under S. 18(1) or (3).

In *Sirsilk Ltd.* v. *Government of Andhra Pradesh,*[197] the Supreme Court travelled further only to attach more importance to the bipartite negotiation than adjudication. The fact of the case reveals that certain disputes between the appellant and its workmen were referred to the Industrial Tribunal, Andhra Pradesh, invoking S. 10 of the Act, on June 6, 1956. The Tribunal sent its award to Government in September 1957. Under S. 17 of the Industrial Disputes Act, 1947, the award has to be published by the appropriate Government within a period of thirty days from the date of its receipt by the Government in such manner as the Government thinks fit. However, the parties to the dispute came to a settlement and a letter was written to the Government, signed jointly, intimating that the dispute which had been pending before the Tribunal had been settled and a request was made to Government not to publish the award. The Government however expressed its inability to withhold the publication of the award, the view taken by the Government being that S. 17 of the Act was mandatory and the Government was bound to publish the award. Thereupon the appellant

195. AIR 1981 SC 1660.
196. AIR 1975 SC 171.
197. AIR 1964 SC 160.

filed a writ petition before the High Court under Art. 226 of the Constitution praying that the Government may be directed not to publish the award sent to it by the Industrial Tribunal. The High Court held that S. 17 was mandatory and it was not open to Government to withhold publication of an award sent to it by an Industrial Tribunal. Therefore, it was not open to the High Court to direct the Government not to publish the award when the law enjoined upon it to do so. The writ petition was therefore dismissed. In an appeal by special leave, the Supreme Court held that though the requirement of S. 17(1) to publish the award is mandatory, in the special circumstances of the case and with a view to avoid conflict between a settlement binding under S. 18(1) and an award binding under S. 18(3) on publication, the only solution was to withhold the publication of the award and that would not in any way have affected the mandatory requirement of S. 17(1) of the Act. Speaking for the Court, Wanchoo, J. observed:

> "Therefore, as soon as an agreement is signed in the prescribed manner and a copy of it is sent to the Government and the conciliation officer, it becomes binding at once on the parties to it and comes into operation on the date it is signed.... In such a case there is no scope for any inquiry by Government as to be *bona fide* character...".[198]

After reading this decision, the author is of opinion that this decision attached more importance to a bipartite negation than to the award of the adjudicator even after the award had been submitted to the Government for publication. Later, in *Amalgamated Coffee Estates Ltd.* v. *Their Workmen*,[199] the dispute having been raised in 1952 was referred for adjudication in 1954. It resulted in an award in 1956. But that was not the end of the dispute. The matter reached the Supreme Court, which granted special leave to appeal. Thereafter, the employer moved the Court for disposing of the appeal in terms of the settlement, which was arrived at between the employer and his workmen during the pendency of the appeal. This motion was resisted by some of the workmen on the ground that they were not parties to the agreement and the agreement, therefore, was not binding on them. The Court, in the circumstances, remitted the case to the Tribunal calling for a finding on the facts as to whether actually a large number of the workmen employed by the employer had accepted payments consistent with the terms of the agreement set up by the employer or not. The Tribunal returned the finding that the payments were made in terms of the settlement, that such payments were voluntarily and knowingly accepted by the workmen and that the settlement was a fair settlement. In view of these findings, the Supreme Court observed that the settlement was a fair one; hence the objection by the dissenting workmen could not be sustained.

The Supreme Court has travelled, in this case, beyond the *Sirsilk* case preferring a private settlement between the parties even to an award which had, in fact, been published and become binding under S. 18(3) and was the subject-matter of appeal before the Supreme Court. The approach of the Supreme Court was very pragmatic and reflects a mature under-standing of the employer-employee relationship. As the workmen did not favour the settlement, the Court could very well have taken the view that once the award was made and the jurisdiction of the Supreme Court invoked against it, it would decide the industrial dispute on merits and proceed to deliver the judgment.

But in the year 1970, the Supreme Court in *Workmen of Delhi Cloth and General Mills Ltd.* v. *Delhi Cloth and General Mills Ltd.*[200] appears to have taken a diametrically opposite

198. *Ibid.* at pp. 163–164 per Wanchoo, J.
199. (1965) II LLJ 110 (SC).
200. AIR 1970 SC 1851.

view holding that during the conciliation proceedings or after the failure of the conciliation proceedings, the parties cannot arrive at a private settlement and clothe it with a binding effect even on the members of the union which entered the settlement. In this connection, the Court said:

> "We do not think the management and the union can, when a dispute is 'referred to the Conciliation Officer, claim absolute freedom of contract to arrive at a settlement in all respects binding on all workmen, to which no objection whatsoever can even be raised by the workmen feeling aggrieved.... In the light of these provisions we do not think that S. 18(1) vests in the management and the union unfettered freedom to settle the dispute as they please and clothe it with a binding effect on all workmen or even on all member workmen of the Union."[201]

The above stated observations made by the Supreme Court in *Workmen at Delhi Cloth and General Mills Ltd.* case do not seem to be correct in the light of the decisions given by the same court in *Sirsilk and Amalgamated Coffee Estate* cases to which the attention of the Court does not appear to have been drawn.[202] In *Sirsilk* case, the Supreme Court directed the Government concerned to withhold the publication and in *Amalgamated Coffee Estates Ltd.* case the disputed parties were allowed to settle their disputes even after publication of the award. Whereas in *Workmen at Delhi Cloth and General Mills Ltd.* case, the Court emphatically stated that "*we do not think that Section 18(1) vests in the management and the union unfettered freedom to settle the dispute as they please and clothe it with a binding effect on all workmen or even on all member workmen of the Union*". In the year 1973, the Supreme Court again in *Workmen of Government Silk Weaving Factory, Mysore* v. *The Presiding Officer, Industrial Tribunal, Bangalore and Others*[203] took the same pragmatic view as taken in *Amalgamated Coffee Estate* case. In this case, two rival sets of office-bearers were claiming to represent the union, which was a party to the dispute. While the matter was under adjudication by the Tribunal, one set of office-bearers came to a settlement regarding the dispute. This settlement was, however, opposed by the rival group of office-bearers. The Tribunal in these circumstances posed two substantial questions for consideration.

(a) Whether the workmen or a majority of them, through their accredited representatives, have entered into a settlement of compromise with the management; and

(b) Whether the terms of such settlement are to the manifest advantage of the workmen.

The Tribunal's conclusion was that the settlement was a genuine settlement. It recorded a finding that the terms of the settlement are very fair and just and the workmen had received considerable benefits under the settlement. The Tribunal, while emphasising that the main purpose of the industrial adjudication is to establish peaceful industrial relationship between the employers and the employees, accepted the settlement and passed an award in terms thereof. The High Court dismissed the petition filed by the rival group of office-bearers against the award. The Supreme Court upheld the judgment of the High Court against which

201. *Ibid.* at p. 1856 per Dua, J.
202. The decision of the Supreme Court in *Workmen of Delhi Cloth and General Mills Ltd.* v. *Delhi Cloth and General Mills Ltd.*, AIR 1970 SC 1851, has been criticised. See Mohammad Saeek Khan 'Fairness of Settlement under S. 18(1) of the Industrial Disputes Act, 1947–A Critique,' 14 *Lawyer* 37 (1982).
203. AIR 1973 SC 1423.

the special leave to appeal was obtained, in view of the fact that the settlement was beneficial to a substantial body of workmen of the factory. The Supreme Court refused to go into the question as to whether there was a compliance with S. 36 and Rule 59 of the Industrial Disputes (Mysore) Rules, 1957.

This judgment again shows, a very pragmatic understanding and approach to industrial relations, which does not go by technicalities but by the substance of the matter.

However, the Supreme Court in 1975 took a different approach in the case of *Jhagrakhan Collieries (P) Ltd.* v. *Central Government*[204] where there were three rival unions in the establishment. Controversy arose while implementing the award to the Central Wage Board for coal mines industry. The company having refused to accede to the demands of the unions, one of the unions made an application to the Central Labour Court under S. 33C(2) of the Industrial Disputes Act for the determination of the dispute relating to variable dearness allowance. The rival union gave a charter of demands backed up with a strike notice. Thereupon, conciliation proceedings were held and a settlement arrived at before the Assistant Labour Commissioner. A copy of the settlement was sent to the Government as required by S. 12(3) of the Act. The Labour Court framed an issue in the following terms:

> "Whether the claims stand settled by reason of the settlement dated 22-10-1969, if any?"

On behalf of the workers, it was urged that the settlement was not binding because the Assistant Labour Commissioner was not a duly appointed Conciliation Officer. The Labour Court held that the settlement before the Assistant Labour Commissioner did not put an end to the dispute for the reason that the Assistant Labour Commissioner was not a duly appointed Conciliation Officer on the date on which the settlement was arrived at. The Supreme Court, relying on its earlier judgment in the case of *Ramnagar Cane & Sugar Co. Ltd.* v. *Jatin Chakravorty*[205] and the scope of S. 18, held that inasmuch as the settlement was not in conciliation proceedings, it could bind only the members of the union which arrived at the settlement.

Binding Effect of Settlements Arrived at in the Course of Conciliation Proceedings

Under S. 18(3), a settlement arrived at in the course of conciliation proceedings will be binding on all parties to the industrial dispute referred to in clause (a) to (d) of S. 18(3) which in the case of the employer will include his heirs, successors or assignees in respect of the establishment to which the dispute relates and in the case of a workman it will include all the persons who are employed in the establishment on the date of the dispute and all persons who subsequently become employed in the establishment. Such a settlement is binding in the same manner as the award of the adjudicatory authority. Recently, the Supreme Court in *Barauni Refinery Pragatisheel Shramik Parishad* v. *Indian Oil Corporation Ltd.*[206] has aptly said:

---

204. AIR 1975 SC 171.
205. AIR 1960 SC 1012.
206. AIR 1990 SC 1801.

"... A settlement arrived at in the course of conciliation proceedings with a recognised majority union will be binding on all workmen of the establishment, even those who belong to the minority union which has objected to the same. To that extent, it departs from the ordinary law of contract. The object obviously is to uphold the sanctity of settlement reached with the active assistance of the Conciliation Officer and to discourage an individual employee or a minority union from scuttling the settlement. There is an underlying assumption that a settlement reached with the help of the Conciliation Officer must be fair and reasonable and can, therefore, safely be made binding not only on the workmen belonging to the union signing the settlement but also on other. That is why a settlement arrived at in the course of conciliation proceeding is 'put on par with an award made by an adjudicatory authority.'"[207]

It is assumed that the conciliation Officer will not pursuade any union to settle unless he is satisfied that the settlement is fair and reasonable and it is in the larger interest of the industrial peace and in the interest of the workmen as a whole. The legislature has given a statutory effect to such a settlement by preventing agitation of the same dispute by other workmen for the statutory period even if they do not happen to be a party to it and are found to have not been agreeable to the terms indicated therein.

The whole policy of S. 18(3) appears to be to give an extended operation to the settlements arrived at in the course of conciliation proceedings and that is the object with which the four categories of persons bound by such settlement are specified in S. 18(3) of the Act. In extending the operation of such a settlement beyond the parties thereto, sub-section (3) departs from the ordinary law of contract and gives effect to the principle of collective bargaining.

SECTION 19: Period of operation of settlements and awards

(1) A settlement shall come into operation on such date as is agreed upon by the parties to the dispute, and if no date is agreed upon, on the date on which the memorandum of the settlement is signed by the parties to the dispute.

(2) Such settlement shall be binding for such period as is agreed upon by the parties, and if no such period is agreed upon, for a period of six months from the date on which the memorandum of settlement is signed by the parties to the dispute, and shall continue to be binding on the parties after the expiry of the period aforesaid, until the expiry of two months from the date on which a notice in writing of an intention to terminate the settlement is given by one of the parties to the other party or parties to the settlement.

(3) An award shall, subject to the provisions of this section, remain in operation for a period of one year from the date on which the award becomes enforceable under section 17A:

Provided that the appropriate Government may reduce the said period and fix such period as it thinks fit:

Provided further that the appropriate Government may, before the expiry of the said period, extend the period of operation by any period not exceeding one year at a time as it thinks fit so, however, that the total period of operation of any award does not exceed three years from the date on which it came into operation.

---

207. *Ibid.* at pp. 1806–1807 per Ahmedi, J.

(4) Where the appropriate Government, whether of its own motion or on the application of any party bound by the award, considers that since the award was made, there has been a material change in the circumstances on which it was based, the appropriate Government may refer the award or a part of it to a Labour Court, if the award was that of a Labour Court or to a Tribunal, if the award was that of a Tribunal or of a National Tribunal for decision whether the period of operation should not, by reason of such change, be shortened and the decision of Labour Court or the Tribunal, as the case may be, on such reference shall be final.

(5) Nothing contained in sub-section (3) shall apply to any award which by its nature, terms or other circumstances does not impose, after it has been given effect to, any continuing obligation on the parties bound by the award.

(6) Notwithstanding the expiry of the period of operation under sub-section (3), the award shall continue to be binding on the parties until a period of two months has elapsed from the date on which notice is given by any party bound by the award to the other party or parties intimating its intention to terminate the award.

(7) No notice given under sub-section (2) or sub-section (6) shall have effect, unless it is given by a party representing the majority of persons bound by the settlement or award, as the case may be.

Under S. 19(1) of the Act, a settlement shall come into operation:

(a) on the date which has been agreed upon by the parties to the dispute; or

(b) in case where no date has been agreed upon, on the date on which the memorandum of the settlement is signed by the parties to the dispute. Such settlement shall be binding under S. 19(2) of the Act for a period as is agreed by the parties, or for six months from the date on which the memorandum of settlement is signed by the parties to the dispute.

A settlement once entered into between the parties shall be operative until the same is terminated as provided in S. 19 of the Act. The object of such a provision is to ensure that once a settlement is entered into then industrial peace prevails, according cordialities between the parties during the period agreed upon. The same position should continue by extension of the settlement by operation of law. There is an option given to either party to terminate the settlement and such option is provided only to a party representing the majority of persons bound by the settlement as per S. 19(7). But in an appropriate case, the Government may make a reference under the Act on the ground that since the time when settlement was entered into there has been material changes in the circumstances. Section 19 of the Act limits the variation of settlement but if there has been any material change in the circumstances available in the establishment of an employer, certainly such a situation cannot be ignored altogether to state that settlement alone should be adhered to whatever be the situation. If such a settlement cannot be worked out in a congenial atmosphere between the workmen and the employer, it will be difficult to maintain industrial peace and these aspects are to be borne in mind by the Labour Court. Such considerations would not be altogether irrelevant, in giving the relief as sought for by the employee and to deny the same on the short ground of reference not being maintainable.[208]

---

208. *N.T.C. (APKKM) Ltd., M/s.* v. *Sree Yellamma C.W. and S. Mills Staff Assocn.,* AIR 2001 SC 652.

Period of Operation of Settlements

The short but important question which came for decision before the Supreme Court in *Shukla Manseta Industries Pvt. Ltd.* v. *The Workmen*[209] by special leave turns on the inter-pretation of S. 19(2) of the Industrial Disputes Act, 1947. Does law require that the notice of termination under S. 19(2) has to be given only after the date of expiry of a settlement?

The fact of the case reveals that there was a settlement between the appellant, *M/s. Shukla Manseta Industries Private Limited* and their *workmen* on July 6, 1970. The settlement came into force from July 6, 1970 and was to remain in force for a period of three years, that is, till July 5, 1973. The workmen, through their union, gave notice to the employer on May 6, 1973, terminating the settlement after the expiry of the period of two months from the date of the notice. Thus under the terms of the notice, the settlement would also have stood terminated at the instance of the workmen on July 5, 1973, which was also the date of the expiry of the settlement under the agreed terms. The workmen, thereafter, raised certain demands on August 1, 1973, and the State Government, in due course referred the dispute under S. 10(1)(d) of the Act to the Industrial Tribunal. The employer took a preliminary objection before the Tribunal that the reference was incompetent and invalid in view of the fact that there was no legal and valid termination of the settlement in accordance with the provisions of S. 19(2) of the Act. The workmen resisted the claim. The Tribunal overruled the preliminary objection and held that the notice was valid and the reference was competent. It is against this order of the Tribunal that the employer has come to this Court by special leave.

The Court observed that under the provisions of S. 19(2), it is clear that a settlement shall be binding for such period as is agreed upon by the parties and if there is no period mentioned in the agreement, for a period of six months from the date on which the settlement is signed by the parties. With regard to the period of operation of the settlement, S. 19(2) confers a statutory continuity of the settlement even after the expiry of the period agreed upon until the expiry of two months from the date on which a written notice of the intention to terminate the settlement is given by one party to the other. It is, therefore, clear that when a period is fixed in a settlement, the settlement remains in operation for the entire period and also thereafter until one or the other party gives written intimation of the intention to terminate the settlement and until expiry of two months from the date of such intimation.

The object of the provision under S. 19(2) is to ensure that once a settlement is arrived at, there prevails peace, accord and cordiality between the parties during the period agreed upon and if the settlement does not require to be altered for some reason or the other, the same climate prevails by extension of the settlement by operation of law. Section 19 is not a dead end freezing all manner of aspirations of labour or even, may be, sometimes, hardship suffered by the employer on account of a settlement. There is an option given to either party to terminate the settlement by a written intimation from the date of such notice. This is in accord with the policy of settlement of industrial disputes which is the principal object underlying the provisions of the Act.

The policy of the Act is to ban agitation over the matters covered by a settlement or by an award during the period specified under S. 19(2) and S. 19(6), respectively. To avoid

209. AIR 1977 SC 2246.

uncertainty and speculation, S. 19 prescribes *terminus a quo* and *a terminus ad quem*. If in a settlement there is no time limit agreed upon between the parties, the period of operation is a space of six months from the date of signing of the settlement and will also last until the expiry of two months from the date of receipt of the notice of termination of the settlement. If the period is fixed, it commences from the date as specified in the settlement and will theoretically end as agreed upon, but shall continue to operate under the law until the expiry of the requisite period of two months by a clear written notice.

The Court accordingly held that there is no legal bar to give advance intimation about the intention to terminate the settlement on the expiry of the agreed period and to start negotiation for a more favourable settlement immediately thereafter. The only condition that has to be fulfilled by such a notice is that the period of two months from the date of notice must end on the expiry of the settlement and not before it. In a given case, it may be even advantageous to the parties who do not want to continue the settlement to strike a new bargain without loss of time as that unnecessary bickering and resultant industrial unrest do not take place. Thus, where a settlement came into force from 6-7-1970 and was to remain in force for a period of 3 years, i.e. till 5-7-1973, a notice issued by the workmen to the employer on 6-5-1973 terminating the settlement after the expiry of a period of 2 months from the date of notice is valid. Under the terms of the notice, the settlement would terminate at the instance of the workmen on July 5, 1973, which is also the date of the expiry of the settlement under the agreed terms.

Advance notice can be given to terminate a settlement or an award provided the requisite period of two months required under S. 19(2) expires on the date of expiry of the settlement or award or thereafter. It is only if a notice under S. 19(2) or 19(6), expires with the period of operation of the award or settlement, such a notice will be invalid under the law. In that event, the settlement or the award will continue to be in operation and any reference by Government of a dispute during the period of settlement or an award without the same being terminated under the law will be invalid. Thus, S. 19(2) does not entitle a party to a settlement to repudiate the settlement while the same is in operation.

Reading S. 19 with the definition of settlement provided in S. 2(p), it would appear that a settlement will ensure for the duration of the period for which it has been agreed to between the parties, and if no period is agreed upon for a period of six months from the date on which the memorandum of settlement of the dispute is signed by the parties and where it is put to an end by a notice in writing, it will continue to be operative until the expiry of two months from the date on which that notice is given. It would appear that even where an agreement is for a fixed period, it will not only continue to be binding for the duration of the period of settlement but thereafter also until it is terminated by a notice in writing and even then it will continue for a period of two months from the date of such notice. While, no doubt, it is true that a notice must be in writing, such a notice can be inferred from correspondence between the parties. In *Cochin State Power, Light Corporation Ltd.* v. *Its Workmen,*[210] the Court observed:

> "There is however no form prescribed for terminating settlements under S. 19(2) of the Act and all that has to be seen is whether the provisions of S. 19(2) are complied with and in substance a notice is given as required thereunder".[211]

210. (1964) 2 LLJ 100 (SC).
211. *Ibid.* at p. 101 per Wanchoo, J.

There are three stages or phases with different legal effects in the life of an award or settlement. There is a specific period contractually or statutory fixed as the period of operation. Thereafter, the award or settlement does not become *non est* but continues to be binding. This is the second phase of legal efficacy but qualitatively different. Then comes the last phase. If the notice of intention to terminate is given under S. 19(2) or 19(6), then the third stage opens where the award or the settlement does survive and remains in force between the parties as a contract which has superseded the earlier contract and subsists until a new award or negotiated settlement takes its place. Like nature, law abhors a vacuum and even on the notice of termination under S. 19(2) or (6) the sequence and consequence cannot be just void but a continuance of the earlier terms, but with liberty to both sides to raise disputes, negotiate settlements or seek a reference and award. Until such a new contract or award replaces the previous one, the former settlement or award will regulate the relations between the parties. To hold the contrary is to invite industrial chaos by an interpretation of the Industrial Disputes Act whose primary purpose is to provide for industrial peace. To argue otherwise is to frustrate the rule of law.

The new contract which is created by an award continues to govern the relations between the parties 'till it is displaced by another contract'. On termination notice or notice of change, the award or settlement does not perish but survives to bind the old settlement or award, as the case may be, till reincarnation, in any modified form, in a fresh regulation of conditions of service by a settlement or award. In other words, when a notice intimating termination of an award or settlement is issued, the legal import is merely that the stage is set for fresh negotiations or industrial adjudication and until either effort ripens into a fresh set of conditions of service, previous award or settlement does regulate the relations between the employer and the employees. Therefore, it can be said that the settlement under the Industrial Disputes Act does not suffer death merely because of the notice issued under S. 19(2) of the Act. The notice is given by the party to the other party only intimating its intention to terminate the award. On the expiry of the period prescribed in S. 19(2), the settlement comes to an end. The ban lifts. The parties are no longer bound to maintain the industrial status quo in respect of matters covered by the settlement. They are at liberty to seek an alteration of the contract. But until altered, the contract continues to govern the relations between the parties in respect of the terms and conditions of service.[212]

Section 20: Commencement and conclusion of proceedings

(1) A conciliation proceeding shall be deemed to have commenced on the date on which a notice of strike or lock-out under section 22 is received by the conciliation officer or on the date of the order referring the dispute to a Board, as the case may be.

(2) A conciliation proceeding shall be deemed to have concluded—

(a) where a settlement is arrived at, when a memorandum of the settlement is signed by the parties to the dispute;

(b) where no settlement is arrived at, when the report of the conciliation officer is received by the appropriate Government or when the report of the Board is published under section 17, as the case may be; or

212. *Life Insurance Corporation of India* v. *D.J. Bahadur*, AIR 1980 SC 2181.

(c) when a reference is made to a Court, Labour Court, Tribunal or National Tribunal under section 10 during the pendency of conciliation proceedings.

(3) Proceedings before an arbitrator under section 10A or before a Labour Court, Tribunal or National Tribunal shall be deemed to have commenced on the date of the reference of the dispute for arbitration or adjudication, as the case may be and such proceedings shall be deemed to have concluded on the date on which the award becomes enforceable under section 17A.

SECTION 21: Certain matters to be kept confidential

There shall not be included in any report or award under this Act any information obtained by a conciliation officer, Board, Court, Labour Court, Tribunal, National Tribunal or an arbitrator in the course of any investigation or inquiry as to a trade union or as to any individual business (whether carried on by a person, firm or company) which is not available otherwise than through the evidence given before such officer, Board, Court, Labour Court, Tribunal, National Tribunal or arbitrator, if the trade union, person, firm or company, in question has made a request in writing to the conciliation officer, Board, Court, Labour Court, Tribunal, National Tribunal or arbitrator, as the case may be, that such information shall be treated as confidential; nor shall such conciliation officer or any individual member of the Board, or Court or the presiding officer of the Labour Court, Tribunal or National Tribunal or the arbitrator or any person present at or concerned in the proceedings disclose any such information without the consent in writing of the secretary of the trade union or the person, firm or company in question, as the case may be:

Provided that nothing contained in this section shall apply to a disclosure of any such information for the purposes of a prosecution under section 193 of the Indian Penal Code (45 of 1860).

CHAPTER V

STRIKES AND LOCK-OUTS

SECTION 22: Prohibition of strikes and lock-outs

(1) No person employed in a public utility service shall go on strike in breach of contract—

(a) without giving to the employer notice of strike, as hereinafter provided, within six weeks before striking; or

(b) within fourteen days of giving such notice; or

(c) before the expiry of the date of strike specified in any such notice as aforesaid; or

(d) during the pendency of any conciliation proceedings before a conciliation officer and seven days after the conclusion of such proceedings.

(2) No employer carrying on any public utility service shall lock-out any of his workmen—

(a) without giving them notice of lock-out as hereinafter provided, within six weeks before locking out; or

(b) within fourteen days of giving such notice; or

(c) before the expiry of the date of lock-out specified in any such notice as aforesaid; or

(d) during the pendency of any conciliation proceedings before a conciliation officer and seven days after the conclusion of such proceedings.

(3) The notice of lock-out or strike under this section shall not be necessary where there is already in existence a strike or, as the case may be, lock-out in the public utility service, but the employer shall send intimation of such lock-out or strike on the day on which it is declared, to such authority as may be specified by the appropriate Government either generally or for a particular area or for a particular class of public utility services.

(4) The notice of strike referred to in sub-section (1) shall be given by such number of persons to such person or persons and in such manner as may be prescribed.

(5) The notice of lock-out referred to in sub-section (2) shall be given in such manner as may be prescribed.

(6) If on any day an employer receives from any persons employed by him any such notices as are referred to in sub-section (1) or gives to any persons employed by him any such notices as are referred to in sub-section (2), he shall within five days thereof report to the appropriate Government or to such authority as that Government may prescribe the number of such notices received or given on that day.

Section 23: General prohibition of strikes and lock-outs

No workman who is employed in any industrial establishment shall go on strike in breach of contract and no employer of any such workman shall declare a lock-out—

(a) during the pendency of conciliation proceedings before a Board and seven days after the conclusion of such proceedings;

(b) during the pendency of proceedings before a Labour Court, Tribunal or National Tribunal and two months after the conclusion of such proceedings;

(bb) during the pendency of arbitration proceedings before an arbitrator and two months after the conclusion of such proceedings, where a notification has been issued under sub-section (3A) of section 10A; or

(c) during any period in which a settlement or award is in operation, in respect of any of the matters covered by the settlement or award.

Section 24: Illegal strikes and lock-outs

(1) A strike or a lock-out shall be illegal if—

(i) it is commenced or declared in contravention of section 22 or section 23; or

(ii) it is continued in contravention of an order made under sub-section (3) of section 10 or sub-section (4A) of section 10A.

(2) Where a strike or lock-out in pursuance of an industrial dispute has already commenced and is in existence at the time of the reference of the dispute to a Board, an arbitrator, a Labour Court, Tribunal or National Tribunal, the continuance of such strike or lock-out shall not be deemed to be illegal, provided that such strike or lock-out was not at its commencement in contravention of the provisions of this Act or the continuance thereof was not prohibited under sub-section (3) of section 10 or sub-section (4A) of section 10A.

(3) A lock-out declared in consequence of an illegal strike or a strike declared in consequence of an illegal lock-out shall not be deemed to be illegal.

Section 25: Prohibition of financial aid to illegal strikes and lock-outs

No person shall knowingly expend or apply any money in direct furtherance of support of any illegal strike or lock-out.

Chapter V-A

LAY-OFF AND RETRENCHMENT

Section 25A: Application of Sections 25C to 25E

(1) Sections 25C to 25E inclusive shall not apply to industrial establishments to which Chapter V-B applies, or—

(a) to industrial establishments in which less than fifty workmen on an average per working day have been employed in the preceding calendar month; or

(b) to industrial establishments which are of seasonal character or in which work is performed only intermittently.

(2) If a question arises whether an industrial establishment is of a seasonal character or whether work is performed therein only intermittently, the decision of the appropriate Government thereon shall be final.

Explanation: In this section and in sections 25C, 25D and 25E, "industrial establishment" means—

(i) a factory as defined in clause (m) of section 2 of the Factories Act, 1948 (63 of 1948); or

(ii) a mine as defined in clause (j) of section 2 of the Mines Act, 1952 (35 of 1952); or

(iii) a plantation as defined in clause (f) of section 2 of the Plantations Labour Act, 1951 (69 of 1951).

Section 25B: Definition of continuous service

For the purposes of this Chapter,—

(1) a workman shall be said to be in continuous service for a period if he is, for that period, in uninterrupted service, including service which may be interrupted on account of sickness or authorised leave or an accident or a strike which is not illegal, or a lock-out or a cessation of work which is not due to any fault on the part of the workman;

(2) where a workman is not in continuous service within the meaning of clause (1) for a period of one year or six months, he shall be deemed to be in continuous service under an employer—

(a) for a period of one year, if the workman, during a period of twelve calendar months preceding the date with reference to which calculation is to be made, has actually worked under the employer for not less than—

(i) one hundred and ninety days in the case of a workman employed below ground in a mine; and

(ii) two hundred and forty days, in any other case;

(b) for a period of six months, if the workman, during a period of six calendar months preceding the date with reference to which calculation is to be made, has actually worked under the employer for not less than—

(i) ninety-five days, in the case of a workman employed below ground in a mine; and

(ii) one hundred and twenty days, in any other case.

Explanation: For the purposes of clause (2), the number of days on which a workman has actually worked under an employer shall include the days on which—

(i) he has been laid-off under an agreement or as permitted by standing orders made under the Industrial Employment (Standing Orders) Act, 1946 (20 of 1946), or under this Act or under any other law applicable to the industrial establishment;

(ii) he has been on leave with full wages, earned in the previous years;

(iii) he has been absent due to temporary disablement caused by accident arising out of and in the course of his employment; and

(iv) in the case of a female, she has been on maternity leave; so, however, that the total period of such maternity leave does not exceed twelve weeks.

Section 25B of the Industrial Disputes Act defines the expression *'continuous service'* and this definition is applicable only for the purpose of Chapter V-A as S. 25B starts with the words *'for the purpose of this chapter'*. The words *'continuous service'* provide certain rights and advantages to workmen who have been in 'continuous service' for a specific period of time. The words 'continuous service' occur in Ss. 25B (definition of continuous service), 25C (right of workmen laid-off for compensation), 25F (conditions precedent to retrenchment of workmen), 25FF (compensation to workmen in case of transfer of undertakings), 25FFF (compensation to workmen in case of closing down of undertakings).

Section 25B is having two sub-sections. Sub-section (1) defines 'continuous service' for a period as uninterrupted service for that period and by fiction includes also the service interrupted for the enumerated reasons provided in the same sub-clause, whereas sub-section (2) introduces further fiction in calculating the continuous service for one year or six months.

It has been observed in *Mohan Lal* v. *Management of M/s. Bharat Electronics, Ltd.*[213] that Cls. (1) and (2) of S. 25B provide for two different contingencies. Sub-section (1) provides for uninterrupted service and sub-section (2) comprehends a case where the workman is not in continuous service. The language employed in sub-sections (1) and (2) does not admit of this dichotomy. Sub-sections (1) and (2) introduce a deeming fiction as to in what circumstances a workman could be said to be in continuous service for the purposes of Chapter V-A. Sub-section (1) provides a deeming fiction in that where a workman is in service for a certain period, he shall be deemed to be in continuous service for that period even if service is interrupted on account of sickness or authorised leave or an accident or a strike which is not illegal, or a lock-out or a cessation of work which is not due to any fault on the part of the workman. Situations such as sickness, authorised leave, an accident, a strike not illegal, a lock-out or a cessation of work would *ipso facto* interrupt a service. These interruptions have to be ignored to treat the workman in uninterrupted service and such service interrupted on account of the aforementioned causes, which would be deemed to be uninterrupted, would be continuous service for the period for which the workman has been in service. In industrial employment or for that matter in any service, sickness, authorised leave, an accident, a strike which is not illegal, a lock-out, and a cessation of work not due to any fault on the part of the workman, are known hazards and there are bound to be interruptions on that account. Sub-section (1) mandates that interruptions therein indicated are to be ignored meaning thereby that on account of such cessation, an interrupted service shall be deemed to be uninterrupted and such uninterrupted service shall for the purposes of Chapter V-A be deemed to be continuous service. That is only one part of the fiction.

Sub-section (2) incorporates another deeming fiction for an entirely different situation. It comprehends a situation where a workman is not in continuous service within the meaning of sub-section (1) for a period of one year or six months, he shall be deemed to be in continuous service under an employer for a period of one year or six months, as the case may be, if the workman during the period of 12 calendar months, just preceding the date with reference to which calculation is to be made, has actually worked under that employer for not less than 240 days. Sub-section (2) specifically comprehends a situation where a workman is not in continuous service as per the deeming fiction indicated in sub-section (1) for a period of one year or six months. In such a case, he is deemed to be in continuous service for a period of one year if he satisfies the conditions in clause (a) of sub-section (2). The conditions are that commencing the date with reference to which calculation is to be made, in case of retrenchment, the date of retrenchment, if in a period of 12 calendar months just preceding such date the workman has rendered service for a period of 240 days, he shall be deemed to be in continuous service for a period of one year for the purposes of Chapter V-A. It is not necessary for the purposes of sub-section (2)(a) that the workman should be in service

213. AIR 1981 SC 1253.

for a period of one year. If he is in service for a period of one year and that if that service is continuous service within the meaning of sub-section (1), his case would be governed by sub-section (1) and his case need not be covered by sub-section (2). Sub-section (2) envisages a situation not governed by sub-section (1). And sub-section (2) provides for a fiction to treat a workman in continuous service for a period of one year despite the fact that he has not rendered uninterrupted service for a period of one year but he has rendered service for a period of 240 days during the period of 12 calendar months counted backwards and just preceding the relevant date being the date of retrenchment. In other words, in order to invoke the fiction enacted in sub-section (2)(a), it is necessary to determine first the relevant date, i.e. the date of termination of service which is complained of as retrenchment. After that date is ascertained, move backward to a period of 12 months just preceding the date of retrenchment and then ascertain whether within the period of 12 months, the workman has rendered service for a period of 240 days or not. If these three facts are affirmatively answered in favour of the workman pursuant to the deeming fiction enacted in sub-section (2)(a), it will have to be assumed that the workman is in continuous service for a period of one year and he will satisfy the eligibility qualification enacted in S. 25F.

A typical question that came before the Supreme Court in *Sur Enamel and Stamping Works Ltd.* v. *The Workmen*[214] for consideration was whether a workman who has completed 240 days within less than 11 months of his total employment can be deemed to have completed one year of continuous service as per S. 25B of the Act. The Court held that on the plain terms of the section only a workman who has been in continuous service for not less that one year under an employer is entitled to its benefit. 'Continuous service' is defined as uninterrupted service, and includes service which may be interrupted merely on account of sickness or authorised leave or an accident or a strike which is not illegal or a lock-out or a cessation of work which is not due to any fault on the part of the workman. What is meant by 'one year of continuous service' has been defined in S. 25-B. Under this section, a workman who during a period of twelve calendar months has actually worked in an industry for not less than 240 days shall be deemed to have completed one year of continuous service in the industry.

In the instant case, Nagen Bora and Monoharan were both reappointed on March 10, 1959. Their services were terminated on January 15, 1960. Thus, their total period of employment was less than 11 months. The position therefore is that during a period of employment for less than 11 calendar months, these two persons worked for more than 240 days and therefore it would not satisfy the requirement of S. 25B. Further, it is held that before a workman can be considered to have completed one year of continuous service in an industry, it must be shown first that he was employed for a period of not less than 12 calendar months, and secondly that during those 12 calendar months he had worked for not less than 240 days. Whereas in the present case, the workmen have not at all been employed for a period of 12 calendar months, it becomes unnecessary to examine whether the actual days of work numbered 240 days or more. For, in any case, the requirements of S. 25B would not be satisfied by the mere fact of the number of working days being not less than 240 days.

214. AIR 1963 SC 1914.

A contrary view was expressed by the Supreme Court in *Surendra Kumar Verma* v. *Central Government Industrial Tribunal-cum-Labour Court, New Delhi*.[215] The Court observed that there is no stipulation that a workman should have been in employment or service under the employer for a whole period of 12 months. In fact, the thrust of the revision is that he need not be. That appears to be the plain meaning without gloss from any source. A workman who has actually worked for not less than 240 days during a period of 12 months shall be deemed to have been in continuous service for a period of 1 year whether or not he has in fact been in such continuous service for a period of 1 year. It is enough that he has worked for 240 days in a period of 12 months, it is not necessary that he should have been in the service of the employer for one whole year.

A note to the reader

The reader should not be confused after reading the judgments of Supreme Court i.e., *Sur Enamel* case and *Surendra Kumar Verma* case. As both the cases provides a contrary view to each other. The *Sur Enamel* case was decided on the basis of the definition of Continuous Service provided under Section 2(eee) of the ID Act which has been amended in the year 1964, whereas the *Surendra Kumar Verma* case is decided on the basis of the definition of Continuous Service which is provided under Section 25B of the ID Act.

Hence, the decision of *Sur Enamel* case is no longer a valid in the eye of law. The current position of law according to the *Surendra Kumar Verma* case is that a workman who had actually worked under the employer for 240 days during a period of 12 months shall be deemed to have been in continuous service for a period of one year whether or not he has in fact been in such continuous service for a period of one year. It is enough that he has worked for 240 days in a period of 12 months.

Whether 240 days includes Sundays or other paid holidays?

In *Workmen of A.E.I.B. Corpn.* v. *Management A.E.I.B. Corpn.*,[216] the question raised before the Supreme Court was whether Sundays and other paid holidays would be taken into account for the calculation of 240 days? The facts are that the workman joined the service of the American Express International Banking Corporation on November 4, 1974 as a typist-clerk in a temporary capacity and was employed as such, with a number of short breaks, till October 31, 1975 when his services were terminated. According to the workman, excluding the breaks in service, he 'actually worked under the employer' for 275 days during the period of 12 months immediately preceding October 31, 1975, whereas according to the employer, he actually worked for 220 days only. The difference between the two computations is due to the circumstance that the workman has included and counted Sundays and other paid holidays as days on which he 'actually worked under the employer', while the employer has not done so. The question for consideration is whether Sundays and other holidays for which wages are paid under the law, by contract or statute, should be treated as days on which the employee, 'actually worked under the employer' for the purposes to constitute one year of continuous service.

In the present case, the provision which is of relevance is S. 25B(2)(a)(ii) which provides that a workman who is not in continuous service for a period of one year shall be deemed to

215. AIR 1981 SC 422.
216. AIR 1986 SC 458.

be in continuous service for a period of one year if the workman during a period of twelve calendar months preceding the date with reference to which the calculation is to be made, has actually worked under the employer for not less than 240 days. This expression, 'actually worked under the employer' is interpreted by the Court and held that 'actually worked under the employer' cannot mean those days only when the workman worked with hammer, sickle or pen, but must necessarily comprehend all those days during which he was in the employment of the employer and for which he had been paid wages either under express or implied contract of service or by compulsion of statute, standing orders, etc.

In *DGM Oil & Natural Gas Corpn. Ltd. & Anr.* v. *Ilias Abdulrehman*,[217] the respondent workman contended that his services were terminated without complying S. 25F of the Industrial Disputes Act, 1947. The Supreme Court said that the number of days of work put in by a workman in broken periods in different departments cannot be taken as continuous employment for the purpose of S. 25F of the Industrial Disputes Act, 1947. The Court reiterated that the law applicable on the point is governed by the principles laid down in *Indian Cable Co. Ltd.* v. *Its Workmen*.[218]

Issue on 240 days

The question which requires the discussion is whether completion of 240 days in a year confers any right on an employee or workman to claim regularization in service.

In *Madhyamik Shiksha Parishad* v. *Anil Kumar Mishra and Ors.* (2005) 5 SCC 122, it was held that the completion of 240 days' work does not confer the right to regularization under the Industrial Disputes Act. It merely imposes certain obligations on the employer at the time of termination of the services. Further in *M.P. Housing Board and Anr.* v. *Manoj Shrivastava* (2006) 2 SCC 702 (Paragraph 17) after referring to several earlier decisions it has been reiterated that it is well settled that only because a person had been working for more than 240 days, he does not derive any legal right to be regularized in service. This view has been reiterated further in *Gangadhar Pillai* v. *Siemens Ltd.* (2007) 1 SCC 533.

In a recent case in *Hindustan Aeronautics Ltd.* v. *Dan Bahadur Singh* [AIR 2007 SC 2733] where the High Court has issued a direction to absorb the members of the respondent-Union as regular employees or such of them as may be required to do the quantum of work which may be available on perennial basis and has issued a further direction that they will be paid the wages of regular employees. It has also been directed that such of the members of the respondent-Union who are not absorbed as regular employees shall not be disengaged and shall be allowed to continue and shall be regularized as and when the perennial work is available. The direction issued by the High Court in effect has two components, i.e., creation of posts and also payment of regular salary as in absence of a post being available a daily wager cannot be absorbed as a regular employee of the establishment. However, the Supreme Court observed that creation and abolition of posts and regularization are a purely executive function. Hence, the Court cannot create a post where none exists. Also, the Court cannot issue any direction to absorb the respondents or continue them in service, or pay them salaries of regular employees, as these are purely executive functions. The Court cannot arrogate to itself the powers of the executive or legislature. There is broad separation of powers under

217. Civil Appeal No. 7229 of 2002.
218. 1962 (1) LLJ 409.

the Constitution, and the judiciary, too, must know its limits. Accordingly, the Supreme Court held that the impugned judgment of the learned single Judge which was affirmed in appeal by the Division Bench cannot be sustained and has to be set aside. The respondents are not entitled to the relief claimed by them.

The Supreme Court in 2023 in *Ganesh Digamar & Others* v. *State of Maharashtra* [2023 Live Law (SC) 801] has held that working for a long period on a contractual basis doesn't give workers the legal right to seek regularisation of their services. While considering the appeal of persons appointed in Guru Gobind Singh Institute of Engineering and Technology on contractual basis since 2011, the Supreme Court observed that though the petitioners have spent a long time at the institute, which does not mean that they had acquired any vested legal right to be regularised.

Regularization of Daily Wager, Temporary/Contractual Employee

A constitutional Bench of the Apex Court in *Secretary, State of Karnataka* v. *Umadevi* [AIR 2006 SC 1806] has categorically dealt the issue and observed that if it is a contractual appointment, the appointment comes to an end at the end of the contract, if it were an engagement or appointment on daily wages or casual basis, the same would come to an end when it is discontinued. Similarly, a temporary employee could not claim to be made permanent on the expiry of his term of appointment. It has also to be clarified that merely because a temporary employee or a casual wage worker is continued for a time beyond the term of his appointment, he would not be entitled to be absorbed in regular service or made permanent, merely on the strength of such continuance, if the original appointment was not made by following a due process of selection as envisaged by the relevant rules. It is not open to the Court to prevent regular recruitment at the instance of temporary employees whose period of employment has come to an end or of ad hoc employees who by the very nature of their appointment do not acquire any right. The High Courts should not ordinarily issue directions for absorption, regularization, or permanent continuance under Article 226 of the Constitution of India unless the recruitment itself was made regularly and in terms of the constitutional scheme.

While directing that appointments, temporary or casual, be regularized or made permanent, the Courts are swayed by the fact that the concerned person has worked for some time and in some cases for a considerable length of time. It is not as if the person who accepts an engagement either temporary or casual in nature, is not aware of the nature of his employment. He accepts the employment with eyes open. It may be true that he is not in a position to bargain—not at arms length—since he might have been searching for some employment so as to eke out his livelihood and accepts whatever he gets. But on that ground alone, it would not be appropriate to jettison the constitutional scheme of appointment and to take the view that a person who has temporarily or casually got employed should be directed to be continued permanently.

The concept of *equal pay for equal work* is different from the concept of conferring permanency on those who have been appointed on ad hoc basis, temporary basis, or based on no process of selection as envisaged by the Rules. This Court has in various decisions applied the principle of equal pay for equal work and has laid down the parameters for the application of that principle. The decisions are rested on the concept of equality enshrined in the Constitution in the light of the Directive Principles in that behalf. But the acceptance of that principle cannot lead to a position where the Court could direct that appointments made without following the due procedure established by law, be deemed permanent or issue directions to treat them as permanent.

The doctrine of *legitimate expectation* can be invoked to make a contractual employee as permanent employee. The fact that in certain cases the Court had directed regularization of the employees involved in those cases cannot be made use of to found a claim based on legitimate expectation. When a person enters a temporary employment or gets engagement as a contractual or casual worker and the engagement is not based on a proper selection as recognized by the relevant rules or procedure, he is aware of the consequences of the appointment being temporary, casual or contractual in nature. Such a person cannot invoke the theory of legitimate expectation for being confirmed in the post when an appointment to the post could be made only by following a proper procedure for selection.

Employees were engaged on daily wages in the concerned department or organization on a wage that was made known to them. There is no case that the wage agreed upon was not being paid. Those who are working on daily wages formed a class by themselves; they cannot claim that they are discriminated as against those who have been regularly recruited on the basis of the relevant rules. No right can be founded on an employment on daily wages to claim that such employee should be treated on a par with a regularly recruited candidate, and made permanent in employment even assuming that the principle could be invoked for claiming equal wages for equal work. There is no fundamental right in those who have been employed on daily wages or temporarily or on contractual basis, to claim that they have a right to be absorbed in service. The right to be treated equal with the other employees employed on daily wages, cannot be extended to a claim for equally treatment with those who were regularly employed. That would be treating *unequal as equal*.

The argument that Article 23 of the Constitution is breached the employment on daily wages amounts to forced labour, cannot be accepted. After all, the employees accepted the employment at their own volition and with eyes open as to the nature of their employment. The Governments also have been revising the minimum wages payable to them from time to time in the light of all relevant circumstances.

The argument that the right to life protected by Art. 21 of the Constitution would include the right to employment cannot be accepted at this juncture. The law is dynamic and Constitution is a living document. Maybe at some future point of time, the right to employment can also be brought in under the concept of right to life or even included as a fundamental right. If it would be treated as a part of right to life, would stand denuded by the preferring of those who have got in casually or those who have come through the back door.

Normally, what is sought for by such temporary employees when they approach the Court, is the issue of a writ of mandamus directing the employer, the State or its instrumentalities, to absorb them in permanent service or to allow them to continue. In this context, the question arises whether a mandamus could be issued in favour of such persons. At this juncture, it will be proper to refer to the decision of the Constitution Bench of the Supreme Court in *Dr. Rai Shivendra Bahadur* v. *The Governing Body of the Nalanda College* [(1962) Supp 2 SCR 144]. That case arose out of a refusal to promote the writ petitioner therein as the Principal of a college. The Supreme Court held that, in order that a mandamus may be issued to compel the authorities to do something, it must be shown that the statute imposes a legal duty on the authority and the aggrieved party had a legal right under the statute or rule to enforce it. This classical position continues and a mandamus could not be issued in favour of the employees directing the Government to make them permanent since the employees cannot show that they have an enforceable legal right to be permanently absorbed or that the State has a legal duty to make them permanent.

Is a Part-time Employee would be Entitled to Benefit of Continuous Service Under Sec. 25-B and Protection of Sec. 25-F

The Supreme Court in *Divisional Manager, New India Assurance Co. Ltd.* v. *A. Sankaralingam* [AIR 2009 SC 309] analyzed the definition of workman provided in Sec. 2(s) of the Industrial Disputes Act and referred its earlier decisions in order to solve the issue that came before the Supreme Court for consideration whether a part-time employee would be entitled to the benefit of continuous service under Sec. 25-B and protection of Sec. 25-F of Industrial Disputes Act? The facts of the case are as follows:

An employee was appointed by New India Assurance Company Ltd., on a monthly wage of ₹150. He thereafter made a request that his services be regularized but was on the contrary, informed orally that he was not required to work with effect from 15th March, 1989. He thereupon sought the intervention of the appropriate Government praying for his reinstatement, but conciliation efforts having failed, the matter was referred to the Industrial Tribunal for decision. The Tribunal in its award dated 10th September, 1998 held that the claimant before it, was not a workman within the meaning of Section 2(s) of the Industrial Disputes Act, 1947 as he had worked only as a part-time employee and that too on an ad hoc basis. The Tribunal also observed that as the duty hours of the workman were only one or two hours a day for which he was paid a sum of ₹150 p.m., and as he was entitled to work elsewhere as well, revealed his status as such. The workman challenged the award of the Tribunal before the Madras High Court. The learned Single Judge held that the fact that the workman had worked from the years 1986 to 1989 and as per the oral evidence, he had worked in the office till 5 o'clock had been admitted and it thus appeared that the finding that he was working only 2 hours a day was factually wrong. The learned Single Judge further held that the point for decision was not the workman's plea for regularization but as to whether his services had been wrongly terminated ignoring the procedure for retrenchment envisaged under Section 25-F of the Act and as such, the retrenchment itself was bad in law. The Court relied on Section 2(s) and Section 25-B of the Act to hold that these two definitions were not restricted in applicability to only full-time employees only. Both the Sections would apply to even part-time employees. The learned Single Judge, accordingly, quashed the award of the Tribunal and ordered the reinstatement of the workman with full back wages and left the matter of regularization of service to be considered by the employer in accordance with the law. This judgment was confirmed in appeal by the Division Bench. Dissatisfied with the judgment of the High Court the employer is in appeal.

The Court relied on its earlier decision where the Court in *Uttaranchal Forest Hospital Trust* v. *Dinesh Kumar* [2008 AIR SCW 445] and held that a workman employed on a part-time basis but under the control and supervision of an employer is a workman in term of Section 2(s) of the Act, and is entitled to claim the protection of Section 25F of the Act.

Section 25C: Right of workmen laid-off for compensation

Whenever a workman (other than a *badli* workman or a casual workman), whose name is borne on the muster rolls of an industrial establishment and who has completed not less than one year of continuous service under an employer, is laid-off, whether continuously or intermittently, he shall be paid by the employer for all days during which he is so laid-off, except for such weekly holidays as may intervene, compensation which shall be equal to fifty per cent of the total of the basic wages and dearness allowance that would have been payable to him had he not been so laid-off:

Provided that if during any period of twelve months, a workman is so laid-off for more than forty-five days, no such compensation shall be payable in respect of any period of the lay-off after the expiry of the first forty-five days, if there is an agreement to that effect between the workman and the employer:

Provided further that it shall be lawful for the employer in any case falling within the foregoing proviso to retrench the workman in accordance with the provisions contained in section 25F at any time after the expiry of the first forty-five days of the lay-off and when he does so, any compensation paid to the workman for having been laid-off during the preceding twelve months may be set off against the compensation payable for retrenchment.

Explanation: "*Badli* workman" means a workman who is employed in an industrial establishment in the place of another workman whose name is borne on the muster rolls of the establishment, but shall cease to be regarded as such for the purposes of this section, if he has completed one year of continuous service in the establishment.

Section 25C gives the right to the workman to get the compensation once he is laid off provided that his case must fall within the purview of the first para of S. 25C, i.e. his name is borne in the muster rolls, and he has completed one year of continuous service. In order to get the meaning of one year of continuous service, one has to refer to S. 25B of the Act. The right of workmen to lay-off compensation is obviously designed to relieve the hardship caused by unemployment due to no fault of the employee; involuntary unemployment also causes dislocation of trade and may result in general economic insecurity. Therefore, the right is based on grounds of humane public policy and the statute which gives such right should be liberally construed, and when there are disqualifying provisions, the latter should be construed strictly with reference to the words used therein.

In *Workmen of Dewan Tea Estate* v. *Their Management*,[219] the Supreme Court refused to accept the contention that S. 25C of the Act recognizes a common law right of the industrial employer to lay-off his workman and observed that it would be legitimate to hold that lay-off, which primarily gives rise to a claim for compensation under S. 25C, must be a lay-off as defined by S. 2(kkk). If the relevant clauses in the Standing Orders of industrial employers make provisions for lay-off and also prescribe the manner in which compensation should be paid to them for such lay-off, perhaps the matter may be covered by the said relevant clauses; but if the relevant clause merely provides for circumstances under which lay-off may be declared by the employer and a question arises as to how compensation has to be paid to the workmen thus laid-off, S. 25C can be invoked by workman provided, of course, the lay-off permitted by the Standing Order also satisfies the requirements of S. 2(kkk). When the laying off of the workmen is referred to in S. 25C, it is the laying-off as

219. AIR 1964 SC 1458.

defined by S. 2(kkk), and so workmen who can claim the benefit of S. 25C must be workmen who are laid-off and laid-off for reasons contemplated by S. 2(kkk); that is all that S. 25C means. If any case is not covered by the Standing Orders, it will necessarily be governed by the provisions of the Act, and lay-off would be permissible only where one or the other of the factors mentioned by S. 2(kkk) is present, and for such lay-off compensation would be awarded under S. 25C. Therefore, it is not correct to say that S. 25C recognises the inherent right of the employer to declare lay-off for reasons while he may regard as sufficient or satisfactory in that behalf. No such common law right can be spelt out from the provisions of S. 25C.

According to the provisions of S. 25C, a workman, who has completed one year of continuous service as defined in S. 25B of the Act and whose name is borne on the muster roll has been laid-off, will be entitled to 50 per cent of the total of the basic wages and dearness allowance which would have been paid to him had he not been so laid-off. It is to be noted that if a workman is so laid-off for more than 45 days, no compensation will be payable in respect of any period of lay-off after the expiry of the first 45 days if there is an agreement to the effect between the workman and the employer. An employer shall have the right in such case to retrench the workman in accordance with the provisions of S. 25F of the Act, at any time after the expiry of the first 45 days of the lay-off, and when he does so, any compensation paid to the workman for having been laid-off during the preceding twelve months, may be set off against the compensation payable for retrenchment.

SECTION 25D: Duty of an employer to maintain muster rolls of workmen

Notwithstanding that workmen in any industrial establishment have been laid-off, it shall be the duty of every employer to maintain for the purposes of this Chapter a muster roll and to provide for the making of entries therein by workmen who may present themselves for work at the establishment at the appointed time during normal working hours.

SECTION 25E: Workmen not entitled to compensation in certain cases

No compensation shall be paid to a workman who has been laid-off—

(i) if he refuses to accept any alternative employment in the same establishment from which he has been laid-off, or in any other establishment belonging to the same employer situate in the same town or village or situate within a radius of five miles from the establishment to which he belongs, if, in the opinion of the employer, such alternative employment does not call for any special skill or previous experience and can be done by the workman, provided that the wages which would normally have been paid to the workman are offered for the alternative employment also;

(ii) if he does not present himself for work at the establishment at the appointed time during normal working hours at least once a day;

(iii) if such laying-off is due to a strike or slowing-down of production on the part of workmen in another part of the establishment.

There are three disqualifying clauses in S. 25E. They show that the basis of the right to unemployment compensation is that the unemployment should be involuntary; in other words, due to no fault of the employees themselves; that is why no unemployment compensation is payable when suitable alternative employment is offered and the workman refuses to accept it as in Cl. (i) of S. 25E; or the workman does not present himself for work at the establishment as in Cl. (ii); or when the laying-off is due to a strike or slowing down of production on the part of workmen in another part of the establishment as in Cl. (iii). Obviously, the last clause treats the workmen in one establishment as one class and a strike or slow-down by some resulting in the laying-off of other workmen disqualifies the workmen laid-off from claiming unem-ployment compensation, the reason being that the unemployment is not really involuntary.[220]

The Supreme Court in *Workmen of M/s. Firestone Tyre and Rubber Co. of India (P) Ltd.* v. *Firestone Tyre and Rubber Co.*,[221] while interpreting Cl. (ii) of S. 25E, held that by lay-off, there is neither a temporary discharge of the workman nor a temporary suspension of his contract of service. Under the general law of master and servant, an employer may discharge an employee either temporarily or permanently but that cannot be without adequate notice. Mere refusal or inability to give employment to the workman when he reports for duty on one or more grounds mentioned in Cl. (kkk) of S. 2 is not a temporary discharge of the workman. Such a power, therefore, must be found out from the terms of contract of service or the Standing Orders governing the establishment. In the instant case, the number of workmen being only 30, there were no Standing Orders certified under the Industrial Employment (Standing Orders) Act, 1946. Nor was there any term of contract of service conferring any such right of lay-off. In such a situation, the conclusion seems to be inescapable that the workmen were laid-off without any authority of law or the power in the management under the contract of service. In Industrial Establishments where there is a power in the management to lay-off a workman and to which the provisions of Chapter V-A apply, the question of payment of compensation will be governed and determined by the said provisions. Otherwise Chapter V-A is not a complete Code as was argued on behalf of the respondent company in the matter of payment of lay-off compensation. This case, therefore, goes out of Chapter V-A. Ordinarily and generally the workmen would be entitled to their full wages but in a reference made under S. 10(i) of the Act. It is open to the Tribunal or the Court to award a lesser sum finding the justifiability of the lay-off.

In a case of compensation for lay-off, the position is quite distinct and different. If the terms of contract of service or the statutory terms engrafted in the Standing Orders do not give the power of lay-off to the employer, the employer will be bound to pay compensation for the period of lay-off which ordinarily and generally would be equal to the full wages of the workmen concerned. If, however, the terms of employment confer a right of lay-off on the management, then, in the case of an industrial establishment which is governed by Chapter V-A, compensation will be payable in accordance with the provisions contained therein. But compensation or no compensation will be payable in the case of an industrial establishment to which the provisions of Chapter V-A do not apply, and it will be so as per the terms of the employment. In the absence of any terms in the contract of service or in the statute or in the statutory rules or standing orders, an employer has no right to lay-off a workman without paying his wages.

---

220. *Associated Cement Companies Ltd.*, v. *Their Workmen*, AIR 1960 SC 56.
221. AIR 1976 SC 1775.

SECTION 25F: Conditions precedent to retrenchment of workmen

No workman employed in any industry who has been in continuous service for not less than one year under an employer shall be retrenched by that employer until—

(a) the workman has been given one month's notice in writing indicating the reasons for retrenchment and the period of notice has expired, or the workman has been paid in lieu of such notice, wages for the period of the notice;

(b) the workman has been paid, at the time of retrenchment, compensation which shall be equivalent to fifteen days' average pay for every completed year of continuous service or any part thereof in excess of six months; and

(c) notice in the prescribed manner is served on the appropriate Government or such authority as may be specified by the appropriate Government by notification in the Official Gazette.

The Legislature has enacted S. 25F, which provides some conditions to be complied with before retrenching a workman with a double purpose, i.e. (a) to save the employer from carrying the economic deadweight of surplusage of labour on the one hand; and (b) to provide compensation for workmen being thrown out of employment and to soften the rigour of hardship due to unemployment caused by retrenchment which was not their own creation. The Legislature has thus attempted to strike a balance between the two conflicting interests.

However, the Supreme Court in 2003 in *Pramod Jha* v. *State of Bihar*[222] categorically observed that the underlying object of S. 25F is two-fold. Firstly, a retrenched employee must have one month's time available at his disposal to search for alternate employment, and so either he should be given one month's notice of the proposed termination or he should be paid wages for the notice period. Secondly, the workman must be paid retrenchment compensation at the time of retrenchment or before, so that once having been retrenched, there should be no need for him to go to his employer demanding retrenchment compensation and the compensation so paid is not only a reward earned for his previous services rendered to the employer but is also a sustenance to the worker for the period which may be spent in searching for another employment. Section 25F nowhere speaks of the retrenchment compensation being paid or tendered to the worker along with one month's notice; on the contrary Cl. (b) expressly provides for the payment of compensation being made at the time of retrenchment and, by implication, it would be permissible to pay the same before retrenchment. Payment of tender of compensation after the time when the retrenchment has taken effect would vitiate the retrenchment and non-compliance with the mandatory provision, which has a beneficial purpose and a public policy behind, would result in nullifying the retrenchment. The nature of retrenchment compensation has been explained in *Indian Hume Pipe Co. Ltd.* v. *The Workmen,*[223] as follows:

> "As the expression 'retrenchment compensation' indicates it is compensation paid to a workman on his retrenchment and it is intended to give him some relief and to soften the rigour of hardship which retrenchment inevitably causes. The retrenched workman is, suddenly and without his fault, thrown on the street and has to face the grim problem of unemployment. At the commencement of his employment a workman naturally expects and looks forward to security of service spread over a long period; but retrenchment destroys

222. AIR 2003 SC 1872.
223. AIR 1960 SC 251.

his hopes and expectations. The object of retrenchment compensation is to give partial protection to the retrenched employee and his family to enable them to tide over the hard period of unemployment".[224]

Section 25F of the Industrial Disputes Act prescribes conditions precedent to retrenchment of workmen employed in an industrial establishment. The conditions prescribed are:

(a) one month's notice to the workmen by the employer indicating the reasons for retrenchment or payment of wages for the period of notice in lieu of such notice;
(b) payment of compensation at the time of retrenchment at the rate equivalent to 15 days' average pay for every completed year of continuous service or any part thereof in excess of six months; and
(c) notice to the appropriate Government or such authority as may be specified by the appropriate Government, in the prescribed manner.

If the conditions precedent to retrenchment are not fulfilled, then the order of retrenchment will not be effective at all. And, such order will be declared void *ab initio,* with the result that the relationship of the employer and the employee is not affected by the purported order of retrenchment and continues as before. In *State of Bombay* v. *Hospital Mazdoor Sabha,*[225] Justice Gajendragadkar observed that on a plain reading of S. 25F(b), it is clear that the requirement prescribed by it is a condition precedent for the retrenchment of the workman, and non-compliance with the said condition renders the impugned retrenchment invalid and in-operative. Section 25F(b) provides that no workman employed in any industry who has been in continuous service for not less than one year under an employer shall be retrenched by that employer until he has been paid at the time of retrenchment compensation which shall be equivalent to fifteen days' average pay for every completed year of service or any part thereof in excess of six months. The section provides that no workman shall be retrenched until the condition in question has been satisfied. When the section imposes in mandatory terms a condition precedent, non-compliance with the said condition would not render the impugned retrenchment invalid ... failure to comply with the said provision renders the impugned orders invalid and inoperative. If the order is already invalid and in-operative in law, it cannot be made operative by awarding some compensation later on. Section 25F of the Industrial Disputes Act lays down the conditions precedent to retrenchment and if the conditions precedent are not complied with, the order of retrenchment becomes only a purported order, but not a valid order in the eye of law. In such a case, the retrenched workman shall be entitled to be reinstated forthwith with full back wages from the date of impugned retrenchment till reinstatement.

In 2004, the Supreme Court in *Krishna Bahadur* v. *M/s Purna Theatre*[226] where the appellant herein was appointed in the post of Messenger-cum-Bearer in the establishment of the respondent herein, a Cinema House. He was subsequently confirmed on the said post. A disciplinary proceeding was initiated against him wherein he was found guilty, whereupon he was dismissed from services. The said order of dismissal was the subject matter of an industrial dispute. The Industrial Tribunal by an award set aside the said order of dismissal with full back-wages and compensation. The appellant was permitted to join his duties but back-wages were not paid. He was, however, retrenched from services within one month from his joining. A sum of ₹9,030 was paid as retrenchment compensation which the appellant

224. *Ibid.* at p. 253 per Gajendragadkar, J.
225. AIR 1960 SC 610.
226. 2004 SOL Case No. 574.

is said to have received under protest. A trade union known as Bengal Motion Pictures Employees Union took up the cause of the appellant, *inter alia*, on the ground of contravention of the legal requirements as contained in S. 25G of the Industrial Disputes Act, 1947 as also insufficiency of the amount of compensation paid to the appellant in terms of S. 25F(b) thereof. An industrial dispute against his retrenchment was raised before the Assistant Labour Commissioner which failed; whereupon the Industrial Tribunal was approached by the appellant. In the meanwhile, the appellant had also initiated a proceeding under S. 33C(2) of the Industrial Disputes Act, 1947 which ended in an amicable settlement in terms whereof the appellant allegedly agreed to receive a sum of ₹39,000 as full and final settlement. He had accepted a cheque for the aforementioned sum of ₹9,030 issued by the management allegedly as part payment of his compensation of ₹39,000 which was deducted from the settled amount.

The Industrial Tribunal held that that the retrenchment of the workman concerned was illegal and as such he should be deemed to be in continuous service with all benefits. A writ petition was filed by the respondent before the Calcutta High Court which was dismissed by a learned Single Judge, holding that the impugned retrenchment was effected without complying with the mandatory requirements of S. 25F(b) of the Industrial Disputes Act and that the Tribunal was well within its jurisdiction in recording a finding to that effect. Such a retrenchment must, accordingly, be held to be *void ab initio* and consequently, the respondent must be deemed to be in service and entitled to all consequential benefits. The respondent preferred an appeal before a Division Bench of the Calcutta High Court. The Court relied on the decision of the Apex Court in *Workmen of Sudder Workshop of Jhorhat Tea Company* v. *The Management,*[227] and held that once the workman accepts the substantial amount of compensation, there after he lost the right to complain any more. The workman, thus, came before the Supreme Court on appeal. The Court held that it is neither in doubt nor in dispute that the provision of S. 25F(b) is imperative in character. The requirement to comply with the provision of S. 25F(b) has been held to be mandatory in many cases such as *L. Robert D'Souza* v. *Executive Engineer, S. Rly.*;[228] *Santosh Gupta* v. *State Bank of Patiala*;[229] *Karnatka S.R.T.C.* v. *Boraiah*[230] before retrenchment of a workman is given effect to. In the event of any contravention of the said mandatory requirement, the retrenchment would be rendered *void ab initio*.

A closer examination of S. 25F shows that Cl. (c) cannot receive the same construction as Cls. (a) and (b). Section 25F(a) requires that the workman has to be given one month's notice in writing, indicating the reasons for retrenchment, and the period of notice has to expire before the retrenchment takes place. It also provides that the workman can be paid, in lieu of such notice, wages for the said period. Reading the latter part of Cl. (a) and Cl. (c) of S. 25F together, it seems to follow that in cases falling under the latter part of Cl. (a), the notice prescribed by Cl. (c) has to be given not before retrenchment but after retrenchment; otherwise the option given to the employer to bring about immediate retrenchment of the workman on paying him wages in lieu of notice would be rendered nugatory. Therefore, Cl. (c) cannot be held to be a condition precedent even though it has been included under S. 25F along with Cls. (a) and (b) which prescribe conditions precedent.

---

227. 1980 (II) LLJ 124 (SC).
228. AIR 1982 SC 854.
229. (1980) II LLJ 72 (SC).
230. (1984) 1 SCC 244.

One can also argue based on the negative form in which the provision is enacted and the use of the word 'until' that no doubt are in favour of the contention that Cl. (c) of S. 25F is a condition precedent, but the context seems to require a different treatment to the provision contained in Cl. (c). Besides, the requirement introduced by the use of the word 'until' is complied with even on the view that the nature of the condition prescribed by Cl. (c), is not condition precedent because after the retrenchment is effected, the employer has to comply with the condition of giving notice about the said retrenchment to the appropriate Government, and that is where the provision in Cl. (c) that the notice has to be served in the prescribed manner assumes significance. Rules have been framed by the Central Government and the State Governments in respect of this notice and, stated broadly, it does appear that these Rules do not require a notice to be served in every case before retrenchment is effected. In regard to retrenchment effected on paying the workman his wages in lieu of notice, the Rules seem to provide that the notice in that behalf should be served within the specified period prescribed by them; that is to say, under the Rules notice in such a case has to be served not before the retrenchment, but after the retrenchment within the specified period.

The object which the Legislature had in mind in making the two conditions mentioned in Cls. (a) and (b) of S. 25F obligatory and in constituting them into conditions precedent is obvious. These provisions have to be satisfied before a workman can be retrenched. The hardship resulting from retrenchment has been partially redressed by these two clauses, and so, there is every justification for making them conditions precedent. The same cannot be said about the requirement as to Cl. (c). Clause (c) is not intended to protect the interests of the workman as such. It is only intended to give intimation to the appropriate Government about the retrenchment, and that only helps the Government keep itself informed about the conditions of employment in the different industries within its region. There does not appear to be present any compelling consideration which would justify the making of the provisions prescribed by Cl. (c) a condition precedent as in the case of Cls. (a) and (b). Therefore, having regard to the object which is intended to be achieved by Cls. (a) and (b) as distinguished from the object which Cl. (c) has in mind, it would not be unreasonable to hold that Cl. (c), unlike Cls. (a) and (b), is not a condition precedent.[231] The benefit of S. 25F can be extended only to such workman who has completed one year of continuous service during a period of twelve calendar months preceding the date with reference to which calculation is to be made, has actually worked under an employer for not less than 190 days in case the workman employed below ground in a mine and 240 days in any other case. In other words, the conditions prescribed in S. 25F will not be necessary at all if the workman does not fall within the ambit of S. 25B which provides the meaning of continuous service. Therefore, it can be said that the condition precedent provided in S. 25F will be applicable to such workman who falls within the four walls of definition of retrenchment provided in S. 2(oo) and he has to satisfy the requirement mentioned in the definition of continuous service provided in S. 25B of the Act.

In *Haryana Urban Development Authority* v. *Om Pal* [AIR 2008 SC 475], where a daily wager worked for a period of 145 days in Sub-division No. 2. He, however, subsequently worked in Sub-division No. 3 for a period of 90 days. His services were terminated. It has not been denied or disputed that the two Sub-divisions constituted two different establishments. Only because there is one Controlling Authority, the same by itself would not mean that the establishments were not separate. The workman was not shown to be appointed in both the establishments by the same authority. Thus, once the two establishments are held to be separate

231. *Bombay Union of Journalists* v. *State of Bombay,* AIR 1964 SC 1617.

and distinct having different cadre strength of the workmen, if any, the period during which the workman was working in one establishment would not ensure to his benefit when he was recruited separately in another establishment, particularly when he was not transferred from one Sub-division to the other. Therefore, the order directing the reinstatement of workman with full back wages and continuity of service would be liable to be set aside.

Whether noncompliance of Section 25F of the ID Act would amount to reinstatement?

The ID Act under S. 25F prescribes certain procedures to be followed by the employer before retrenching a workman who has completed one year of continuous year of service; that is 240 days. If in a case, where the employer terminates a workman without compiling S. 25F of the ID Act would he be directed to pay compensation with consequential benefit and reinstating the concerned workman in question.

The similar question arises for consideration before the Supreme Court in *Assistant Engineer, Rajasthan Development Corporation & ANR.* v. *Gitam Singh* (2013) 1 SCR 679; where the workman had worked for only eight months as daily wager and his termination has been held to be in contravention of S. 25F of the ID Act and therefore the Labour Court directed the employer for reinstatement with continuity of service and 25 per cent back wages.

Mr. Sushil Kumar Jain, learned counsel for the respondent (workman) argued that reinstatement must follow where termination of a workman has been found to be in breach of Section 25F of ID Act. He heavily relied upon three decisions of the Supreme Court and they are *L. Robert D'Souza* v. *Executive Engineer, Southern Railway and Another* (1982) 1 SCC 645; *Harjinder Singh* v. *Punjab State Warehousing Corporation* (2010) 3 SCC 192; and *Devinder Singh* v. *Municipal Council, Sanaur* (2011) 6 SCC 584.

On behalf of the appellant, Ms. Shobha, learned counsel, challenged the finding of the Labour Court that the respondent had worked for 240 days continuously in the year preceding the date of termination. Alternatively, she submitted that the award of reinstatement with continuity of service and 25 per cent back wages in the facts of the case was unjustified as the respondent was only a daily wager; he worked for a very short period from 01.03.1991 to 31.10.1991. Ms. Sobha relied in a plethora of judgements of the Supreme Court like *Haryana State Electronics Development Corporation Ltd.* v. *Mamni* (2006) 9 SCC 43, *Mahboob Deepak* v. *Nagar Panchayat, Gajraula and Another* (2008) 1 SCC 575, *Jagbir Singh* v. *Haryana State Agriculture Marketing Board and Another* (2009) 15 SCC 327, *Senior Superintendent Telegraph (Traffic), Bhopal* v. *Santosh Kumar Seal and Others* (2010) 6 SCC 773 and *In-charge Officer and Another* v. *Shankar Shetty* (2010) 9 SCC 126, and she submitted that respondent was at best entitled to some compensation for unlawful termination.

It is interesting to note that the Apex Court in *Nagar Mahapalika (Now Municipal Corpn.)* v. *State of U.P. and Others* (2006) 5 SCC 127, while dealing with the non-compliance with the provisions of S 6-N (which is *pari materia* to S. 25-F of ID Act) of U.P. Industrial Disputes Act held that the grant of relief of reinstatement with full back wages and continuity of service in favour of retrenched workmen would not automatically follow or as a matter of course and the Court modified the award of reinstatement with compensation of ₹30,000 per workman.

In *Municipal Council, Sujanpur* v. *Surinder Kumar* (2006) 5 SCC 17, the Supreme Court after having accepted the finding that there was violation of S. 25-F of the ID Act, set aside the award of reinstatement with back wages and directed the workman to be paid monetary compensation in the sum of ₹50,000.

In *Telecom District Manager and others* v. *Keshab Deb* (2008) 8 SCC 402, the Court said that even if the provisions of Section 25-F of the I.D. Act had not been complied with, the workman was only entitled to just compensation.

In 2012 the Supreme Court in *Bharat Sanchar Nigam Limited* v. *Man Singh* (2012) 1 SCC 55, that was a case where the workmen, who were daily wagers during the year 1984–85, were terminated without following Section 25-F. The industrial dispute was raised after five years and although the Labour Court had awarded reinstatement of the workmen which was not interfered by the High Court, however the Supreme Court set aside the award of reinstatement and ordered payment of compensation.

The Supreme Court accordingly observed that in a case of wrongful termination of a daily wager, who had worked for a short period, the award of reinstatement cannot be said to be proper relief and rather award of compensation in such cases would be in consonance with the demand of justice. Before exercising its judicial discretion, the Labour Court has to keep in view all relevant factors, including the mode and manner of appointment, nature of employment, length of service, the ground on which the termination has been set aside and the delay in raising the industrial dispute before grant of relief in an industrial dispute.

In the instant case, the Court held that the workman was engaged as daily wager and he worked hardly for eight months. The Labour Court failed to exercise its judicial discretion appropriately. The judicial discretion exercised by the Labour Court suffers from serious infirmity. The Single Judge as well as the Division Bench of the High Court also erred in not considering the above aspect at all. The award directing reinstatement of the respondent (workman) with continuity of service and 25% back wages in the facts and circumstances of the case cannot be sustained and has to be set aside. Compensation of ₹50,000 by the appellant to the respondent (workman) shall meet the ends of justice.

After discussing above decisions of the Apex Court it is submitted that non compliance of S. 25-F of the ID Act would not be always *ipso facto* lead to reinstatement.

Retrenchment Compensation: Month means 26 days or 30 days?

The question came before the Supreme Court in *Guru Jambheshwar University* v. *Dharam Pal*, (AIR 2007 SC 1040) by way of an appeal with regards to the calculation of retrenchment compensation, whether a month means 26 days or 30 days.

The Labour Court has basically relied upon a decision laid down in the case of *Jeevanlal Ltd.* v. *Appellate Authority* (AIR 1984 SC 1842) and held that in case of monthly rated employee the fifteen days' wages shall be calculated by dividing the monthly rate of wages by twenty-six and multiplying the quotient by fifteen by referring the *explanation* of Section 4(2) of the Payment of Gratuity Act, 1972.

The Guru Jambheshwar University approached the High Court invoking the writ petition and the petition was also rejected by the same court. Then the aggrieved University approached the Supreme Court through a special leave petition.

The Supreme Court observed that there is no warrant or justification for importing the principle of 26 working days mentioned in Payment of Gratuity Act for determining the compensation which needs to be paid under Section 25-F(b) of the ID Act. The Supreme Court further said:

> "But, no such amendment has been made in the Industrial Disputes Act. If the legislature wanted that for the purposes of Section 25F(b) also the average pay had to be determined by dividing the monthly wages by twenty-six, a similar amendment could have been made. But the legislature has chosen not to do so. This is an additional reason for holding that the principle of "twenty-six working days" is not to be applied for determining the retrenchment compensation under Section 25F(b) of the Act."

The Supreme Court held that the retrenchment compensation shall be equivalent of 15 days average pay of 30 days and not 26 days. Therefore, the formula for the calculation of the retrenchment compensation shall be:

$$\frac{\text{Monthly Average Pay} \times 15 \times \text{Total number of completed year of service}}{30}$$

Section 25FF: Compensation to workmen in case of transfer of undertakings

Where the ownership or management of an undertaking is transferred, whether by agreement or by operation of law, from the employer in relation to that undertaking to a new employer, every workman who has been in continuous service for not less than one year in that undertaking immediately before such transfer shall be entitled to notice and compensation in accordance with the provisions of S. 25F, as if the workman had been retrenched:

Provided that nothing in this section shall apply to a workman in any case where there has been a change of employers by reason of the transfer, if—

(a) the service of the workman has not been interrupted by such transfer;

(b) the terms and conditions of service applicable to the workman after such transfer are not in any way less favourable to the workman than those applicable to him immediately before the transfer; and

(c) the new employer is, under the terms of such transfer or otherwise, legally liable to pay to the workman, in the event of his retrenchment, compensation on the basis that his service has been continuous and has not been interrupted by the transfer.

The first and foremost condition for the application of S. 25FF is that the ownership or management of an undertaking is transferred from the employer in relation to that undertaking to a new employer. What the section contemplates is that either ownership or the management of an undertaking should be transferred; normally this would mean that the ownership or the management of the entire undertaking should be transferred before S. 25FF comes into operation. If an undertaking conducts one business, it would normally be difficult to imagine that its ownership or management can be partially transferred to invoke the application of S. 25FF. A business conducted by an industrial undertaking would ordinarily be an integrated business, and though it may consist of different branches or departments, they would generally be interrelated with each other so as to constitute one whole business. In such a case, S. 25FF would not apply if a transfer is made in regard to a department or branch of the business run by the undertaking and the workmen would be entitled to contend that such a partial transfer is outside the scope of S. 25FF.

It may be that one undertaking may run several industries or businesses which are distinct and separate. In such a case, the transfer of one distinct and separate business may involve the application of S. 25FF. The fact that one undertaking runs these businesses would not necessarily exclude the application of S. 25FF solely on the ground that all the businesses or industries run by the said undertaking have not been transferred. It would be clear that in all cases of this character the distinct and separate businesses would normally be run on the basis that they are distinct and separate, employees would be separately employed in respect of all the said businesses and their terms and conditions of service may vary according to the character of the business in question. In such a case, it would not be usual to have one muster roll for all the employees and the organisation of employment would indicate clearly the distinctive and separate character of the different businesses. If that be so, then the transfer by the undertaking of one of its businesses may attract the application of S. 25FF. But where the undertaking runs several allied businesses in the same place or places, different considerations would come into play.

The muster roll showing the list of employees was common in regard to all the departments of business run by the transferor firm. The terms and conditions of service were the same for all the employees and what was most significant was the fact that the employees could be transferred from one department run by the transferor firm to another department; though the transferor conducted several branches of business which were more or less allied, the services of the employees were not confined to any one business, but were liable to be transferred from one branch to another. In the payment of bonus, all the employees were treated as constituting one unit and there was thus both the unity of employment and the identity of the terms and conditions of service. In fact, it was purely a matter of accident that the 57 workmen who were transferred happened to be engaged in retail business which was the subject matter of the transfer between the transferor firm and the transferee company. It was held that under these circumstances, only because the retail business had an identity of its own, it should not be treated as an independent and distinct business run by the firm and the transfer could not be deemed to have constituted the company into a successor-in-interest of the transferor firm for the purpose of S. 25FF. As in other industrial matters, so on this question too, it would be difficult to lay down any categorical or general proposition. Whether or not the transfer in question attracts the provisions of S. 25FF must be determined in the light of the circumstances of each case. It is hardly necessary to emphasise that in dealing with the problem, what industrial adjudication should consider is the matter of substance and not of form.

The question as to whether a transfer has been effected so as to attract S. 25FF must ultimately depend upon the evaluation of all the relevant factors and it cannot be answered by treating any one of them as of overriding or conclusive significance. Having regard to the facts which were relevant in the present case, the transferee company could not claim to be a successor-in-interest of the transferor firm so as to attract the provisions of S. 25FF of the Act. The transfer which had been effected by the firm in favour of the transferee company did not amount to the transfer of the ownership or management of an undertaking and so, Section 25FF and the proviso to it did not apply to the present case.[232] Workmen whose services are terminated in consequence of a transfer of an undertaking, whether by agreement or by operation of law, have a statutory right under S. 25FF, Industrial Disputes Act to compensation unless such right is defeated under the proviso to that section. The same is the position in the case of closure under S. 25FFF. Such compensation would be 'wages' as defined by

232. *Management of R.S. Madho Ram and Sons (Agencies) Private Ltd.* v. *The Workmen*, AIR 1964 SC 645.

S. 2(iv)(d) of the Payment of Wages Act as amended by Act 68 of 1957, as it is a "sum which by reason of the termination of employment of the person employed, is payable under any law ... which provides for the payment of such sum whether with or without deductions but does not provide for the time within which the payment is to be made." Since Ss. 25FF and 25FFF do not contain any conditions precedent, as in the case of retrenchment under S. 25F, and transfer and closure can validly take place without notice or payment of a month's wages *in lieu* thereof or payment of compensation, S. 25F cannot be said to have provided any time within which such compensation is to be paid. The words "in accordance with the provisions of S. 25F" in Ss. 25FF and 25FFF are used only as a measure of compensation and are not used for laying down any time within which the employer must pay the compensation. It would, therefore, appear that compensation payable under Ss. 25FF and 25FFF read with S. 25FF would be 'wages' within the meaning of S. 2 (vi)(d) of the Act.[233]

The first part of S. 25FF postulates that on a transfer of the ownership or management of an undertaking, the employment of workmen engaged by the said undertaking comes to an end, and it provides for the payment of compensation to the said employees because of the said termination of their services, provided, of course, they satisfied the test of the length of service prescribed by the section. The said part further provides the manner in which and the extent to which the said compensation has to be paid. Workmen shall be entitled to notice and compensation in accordance with the provisions of S. 25F, as if they had been retrenched. The last clause clearly brings out the fact that the termination of the services of the employees does not in law amount to retrenchment. The Legislature, however, wanted to provide that though such termination may not be retrenchment technically so called, nevertheless the employees in question whose services are terminated by the transfer of the undertaking should be entitled to compensation, and so S. 25FF provides that on such termination compensation would be paid to them as if the said termination was retrenchment. The words *'as if'* bring out the legal distinction between retrenchment defined by S. 2(oo) as it was interpreted by the Supreme Court in *Barsi Light Railway Co.* case, and termination of services consequent upon transfer with which it deals. In other words, the section provides that though termination of services on transfer may not be retrenchment, the workmen concerned are entitled to compensation as if the said termination was retrenchment. This provision has been made for the purpose of calculating the amount of compensation payable to such workmen; rather than provide for the measure of compensation over again. Section 25FF makes a reference to S. 25F for that limited purpose, and, therefore, in all cases to which S. 25FF applies, the only claim which the employees of the transferred concern can legitimately make is a claim for compensation against their employers. No claim can be made against the transferee of the said concern.

Reading, therefore, S. 25FF as a whole, it does appear that unless the transfer falls under the proviso, the employees of the transferred concern are entitled to claim compensation against the transferor and they cannot make any claim for re-employment against the transferee of the undertaking. Thus, the effect of the enactment of S. 25FF is to restore the position which the Legislature had apparently in mind when S. 25FF was originally enacted on September 5, 1956. By amending S. 25FF, the Legislature has made it clear that if industrial

233. *Payment of Wages Inspector, Ujjain* v. *Barnagar Electric Supply and Industrial Co. Ltd.*, AIR 1969 SC 590.

undertakings are transferred, the employees of such transferred undertakings should be entitled to compensation, unless, of course, the continuity in their service or employment is not disturbed and that can happen if the transfer satisfied the three requirements of the proviso.

Section 25H does not apply to the case of a genuine transfer of an industrial concern. Nor can the general principle underlying the provisions of the said section be invoked in dealing with the claim that they should be re-employed made by the workmen of the transferor company against the transferee society. For as soon as the transfer is effected under S. 25FF, all employees are entitled to claim compensation, unless, of course, the case of transfer falls under the proviso; and if these workmen who have been paid compensation are immediately entitled to claim re-employment from the transferee, it will not be fair that the vendor should pay compensation to his employees on the ground that the transfer brings about the termination of their services, and the vendee should be asked to take them back on the ground that the principles of social justice require him to do so. This double benefit in the form of payment or compensation and immediate re-employment cannot be said to be based on any considerations of fair play or justice. Fair play and justice obviously mean fair play and social justice to both the parties.[234]

Section 25FFA: Sixty days' notice to be given of intention to close down any undertaking

(1) An employer who intends to close down an undertaking shall serve, at least sixty days before the date on which the intended closure is to become effective, a notice, in the prescribed manner, on the appropriate Government stating clearly the reasons for the intended closure of the undertaking:

Provided that nothing in this section shall apply to—

(a) an undertaking in which—

(i) less than fifty workmen are employed, or

(ii) less than fifty workmen were employed on an average per working day in the preceding twelve months,

(b) an undertaking set up for the construction of buildings, bridges, roads, canals, dams or for other construction work or project.

(2) Notwithstanding anything contained in sub-section (1), the appropriate Government may, if it is satisfied that owing to such exceptional circumstances as accident in the undertaking or death of the employer or the like it is necessary so to do, by order, direct that provisions of sub-section (1) shall not apply in relation to such undertaking for such period as may be specified in the order.

Section 25 FFA requires the employer to give 60 days' notice to the Government of his intention to close down his undertaking to prevent sudden closure and to give an opportunity to the Government to consider whether it should take any measure in respect of such intended closure in accordance with the provisions of the Act. This section does not intend to take away the right to close down the place of business which is very much implicit within Art. 19(1)(g) of the Constitution, i.e. right to do any trade or business includes the right to close the place of business. The section only requires that before the closure, the intending employer should intimate to the appropriate Government at least 60 days before such closure,

234. *Anakapalle Co-operative Agricultural and Industrial Society Ltd.* v. *Workmen,* AIR 1963 SC 1489.

stating the reasons for the closure of the undertaking. The failure of the employer to comply with this requirement entails stringent penalty of imprisonment up to a term of six months or fine up to five thousand rupees or both as per S. 30A of the Act.

Requirement of Notice

Section 25FFA requires that an employer who intends to close down an undertaking shall have to serve a notice on the appropriate Government. The notice should comply with the following requirements:

(i) It should be in the prescribed manner.
(ii) The notice should state clearly the reasons for the intended closure.
(iii) The notice should be served on the appropriate Government at least 60 days before the date on which the intended closure is to become effective.

The question arises whether the failure of the employer to comply with these requirements makes the closure *illegal* or *non est*. The answer seems to be negative because the provision does not state so. The Bombay High Court in *Maharastra General Kamagar Union* v. *Glass Containers Pvt. Ltd.*[235] held that the closure would be illegal and invalid due to non compliance of requirement of notice as prescribed under S. 25FFA of the Act.

The requirement of notice provided in S. 25FFA(1) is somewhat analogous to the provision in Cl. (c) of S. 25, which also prescribes the requirement of notice to be served in a prescribed manner on the appropriate Government or on such authority as may be specified by the appropriate Government by notification in the Official Gazette before retrenching any workman employed in any industry. In *Bombay Union of Journalists* v. *State of Bombay*,[236] the Supreme Court held that Cl. (c) of S. 25F is not a condition precedent to valid retrenchment, though the breach of such requirement is no doubt a serious matter. The Court accordingly held:

> "A closer examination of S. 25F shows that Cl. (c) of S. 25F cannot receive the same construction as Cls. (a) and (b) of S. 25F. Section 25F(a) requires that the workman has to be given one month's notice in writing, indicating the reasons for retrenchment, and the period of notice has to expire before the retrenchment takes place. It also provides that the workman can be paid in lieu of such notice wages for the said period. Reading the latter part of Cl. (a) and Cl. (c) together, it seems to follow that in cases falling under the latter part of Cl. (a) the notice prescribed by Cl. (c) has to be given not before retrenchment, but after retrenchment; otherwise the option given to the employer to bring about immediate retrenchment of the workman on paying him wages in lieu of notice would be rendered nugatory. Therefore, Cl. (c) cannot be held to be a condition precedent even though it has been included under S. 25F along with Cls. (a) and (b) which prescribes conditions precedent."[237]

The same line of reasoning can be given to the requirement of notice as prescribed in S. 25FFA of the Act. Non-compliance of the requirement may entail to penal consequence prescribed in S. 30A.

---

235. (1983) I LLJ (Bom).
236. AIR 1964 SC 1617.
237. *Ibid.* at p. 1623 per Gajendragadkar, J.

Section 25FFF: Compensation to workmen in case of closing down of undertakings

(1) Where an undertaking is closed down for any reason whatsoever, every workman who has been in continuous service for not less than one year in that undertaking immediately before such closure shall, subject to the provisions of sub-section (2), be entitled to notice and compensation in accordance with the provisions of section 25F, as if the workman had been retrenched:

Provided that where the undertaking is closed down on account of unavoidable circumstances beyond the control of the employer, the compensation to be paid to the workman under clause (b) of section 25F shall not exceed his average pay for three months.

Explanation: An undertaking which is closed down by reason merely of—

(i) financial difficulties (including financial losses); or

(ii) accumulation of undisposed of stocks; or

(iii) the expiry of the period of the lease or licence granted to it; or

(iv) in a case where the undertaking is engaged in mining operations, exhaustion of the minerals in the area in which such operations are carried on;

shall not be deemed to be closed down on account of unavoidable circumstances beyond the control of the employer within the meaning of the proviso to this sub-section.

(1A) Notwithstanding anything contained in sub-section (1), where an undertaking engaged in mining operations is closed down by reason merely of exhaustion of the minerals in the area in which such operations are carried on, no workman referred to in that sub-section shall be entitled to any notice or compensation in accordance with the provisions of section 25F, if—

(a) the employer provides the workman with alternative employment with effect from the date of closure at the same remuneration as he was entitled to receive, and on the same terms and conditions of service as were applicable to him, immediately before the closure;

(b) the service of the workman has not been interrupted by such alternative employment; and

(c) the employer is, under the terms of such alternative employment or otherwise, legally liable to pay to the workman, in the event of his retrenchment, compensation on the basis that his service has been continuous and has not been interrupted by such alternative employment.

(1B) For the purposes of sub-sections (1) and (1A), the expressions "minerals" and "mining operations" shall have the meanings respectively assigned to them in Cls. (a) and (d) of section 3 of the Mines and Minerals (Regulation and Development) Act, 1957 (67 of 1957).

(2) Where any undertaking set up for the construction of buildings, bridges, roads, canals, dams or other construction work is closed down on account of the completion of the work within two years from the date on which the undertaking had been set up, no workman employed therein shall be entitled to any compensation under clause (b) of section 25F, but if the construction work is not so completed within two years, he

shall be entitled to notice and compensation under that section for every completed year of continuous service or any part thereof in excess of six months.

The Parliament amended the Industrial Disputes Act, 1947 by Act 43 of 1953 and incorporated therein Chapter V-A which contained Ss. 25A to 25J. By this chapter, provisions were made for payment of compensation for lay-off and retrenchment, and certain incidental provisions enunciating and regulating liability for payment of compensation were enacted. The President of India on April 27, 1957, promulgated Ordinance No. IV of 1957 which amended Chapter V-A of the Industrial Disputes Act, 1947. By this Ordinance, provision was made for payment with retrospective effect from December 1, 1956, of compensation to workmen on termination of employment upon transfer or closure of an industrial undertaking. This Ordinance was later replaced, with certain modification, by Act 40 of 1957 which came into force on June 6, 1957, but with retrospective effect from November 28, 1956. Section 25FFF, which was incorporated by the Amending Act of 1957, confers upon every workman who has been in continuous service for not less than one year immediately before the closure, right to notice and compensation in accordance with the provisions of S. 25F, and by the proviso thereto the maximum amount of compensation payable to a workman is limited to average pay for three months when the undertaking is closed on account of circumstances beyond the control of the employer. The explanation attached to proviso of S. 25FFF(1) provides that an undertaking closed down on account merely of financial difficulties (including financial losses) or accumulation of undisposed of stocks or the expiry of the period of lease or licence granted to it, or in case where the undertaking is engaged in mining operations, exhaustion of minerals in the area in which such operations are carried on are not to be deemed to have been closed down on account of unavoidable circumstances beyond the control of the employer within the meaning of the proviso.

Constitutional Validity of Section 25FFF

Compensation provided under S. 25FFF to workmen in case of closing down of undertakings was challenged in *Hathising Manufacturing Co., Ltd., M/s. Ahmedabad* v. *Union of India*[238] on three grounds.

(i) that it imposes unreasonable restrictions on the freedom guaranteed to every citizen by Art. 19(1)(g) of the Constitution to carry on business which freedom includes the right to close his business,

(ii) that it discriminates between different employers belonging to the same group placed in similar circumstances and thereby contravenes Art. 14 of the Constitution, and

(iii) that contrary to Art. 20 of the Constitution, it penalises acts which when committed were not offences.

So far as the first ground is concerned, it is necessary to consider the constitutional mandate provided in Art. 19 read with Art. 19(6). Article 19(1)(g) of the Constitution provides that all citizens shall have the right to practise any profession, or to carry on any occupation, trade or business. Thus the Constitution guarantees to every citizen and provides a fundamental right to carry on any trade or business, but this right is not absolute. Such right can be restricted under Art. 19(6) of the Constitution. Article 19(6) of the Constitution reads as follows:

238. AIR 1960 SC 923.

Nothing in sub-clause (g) of the said clause shall affect the operation of any existing law in so far as it imposes, or prevent the State from making any law imposing, in the interests of the general public, reasonable restrictions on the exercise of the right conferred by the said sub-clause, and, in particular, nothing in the said sub-clause shall affect the operation of any existing law in so far as it relates to, or prevent the State from making any law relating to—

(i) the professional or technical qualifications necessary for practising any profession or carrying on any occupation, trade or business, or

(ii) the carrying on by the State, or by a corporation owned or controlled by the State, of any trade, business, industry or service, whether to the exclusion, complete or partial, of citizens or otherwise.

In the interest of the general public, the law may impose restrictions on the freedom of the citizens to start, carry on or close their undertakings. Whether an impugned provision imposing a fetter on the exercise of the fundamental right guaranteed by Art. 19(1)(g) amounts to a reasonable restriction imposed in the interest of the general public must be adjudged not in the background of any theoretical standards or predeterminate patterns, but in the light of the nature and incidents of the right, the interest of the general public sought to be secured by imposing the restriction and the reasonableness of the quality and extent of the fetter upon the right. The Supreme Court in the present case held that the restrictions imposed by the impugned provision including the proviso are not unreasonable restrictions on the exercise of fundamental right of the employers to conduct and close their undertakings. The provision requiring the employers to pay compensation to their employees though restrictive of the fundamental freedom guaranteed by Art. 19(1)(g) is evidently in the interest of the general public, and is therefore saved by Art. 19(6) of the Constitution from the challenge that it infringes the fundamental right of the employers.

So far as the second ground is concerned, Art. 14 of the Constitution is not violated by making by law a distinction between employers who closed their undertakings on or before November 28, 1956, and those who close their undertakings after that date. [Section 25FFF came into force with effect from November 28, 1956]. The State is undoubtedly prohibited from denying to any person equality before the law or the equal protection of the laws, but by enacting a law which applies generally to all persons who come within its ambit as from the date on which it becomes operative, no discrimination is practised. When Parliament enacts a law imposing a liability as flowing from certain transactions prospectively, it evidently makes a distinction between those transactions which are covered by the Act and those which are not, because they were completed before the date on which the Act was enacted. This differentiation, however, does not amount to discrimination which is liable to be struck down under Art. 14.

Regarding the third ground, it is essential to mention Art. 20 of the Constitution in order to justify whether S. 25FFF is contrary to Art. 20 of the Constitution. Article 20 of the Constitution reads as follows:

1. No person shall be convicted of any offence except for violation of a law in force at the time of the commission of the act charged as an offence, nor be subjected to a penalty greater than that which might have been inflicted under the law in force at the time of the commission of the offence.

2. No person shall be prosecuted and punished for the same offence more than once.
3. No person accused of any offence shall be compelled to be a witness against himself.

The payment of compensation and wages in lieu of notice under the impugned section are not made conditions precedent to effective termination of employment. This section only creates a right for the employees: it does not enjoin the employers to do anything before closure. Section 31(2) of the Industrial Disputes Act, which imposes penal liability for contravention of the provisions of the Act, can therefore have no application in case of failure to make payment of compensation and wages for the period of notice under S. 25FFF(1). If liability to pay compensation is not a condition precedent to closure, by failing to discharge the liability to pay compensation and wages in lieu of notice, the employer does not contravene S. 25FFF(1). A statute may prohibit or command an act and in either case, disobedience thereof will amount to contravention of the statute. If the statute fixes criminal liability for contravention of the prohibition or the command which is made applicable to transactions which have taken place before the date of its enactment, the protection of Art. 20(1) may be attracted. But S. 25FFF(1) imposes neither a prohibition nor a command. Under S. 25F, there is a distinct prohibition against an employer against retrenching employees without fulfilling certain conditions. If this prohibition is infringed, evidently, criminal liability may arise. But there being no prohibition against closure of business without payment of compensation, S. 31(2) does not apply. Invoking S. 33(c) of the Industrial Disputes Act, liability to pay compensation may be enforced by coercive process, but that again does not amount to an infringement of Art. 20(1) of the Constitution. Undoubtedly, for failure to discharge liability to pay compensation, a person may be imprisoned under the statute providing for recovery of the amount, but failure to discharge a civil liability is not, unless the statute expressly so provides, an offence. The protection of Art. 20(1) avails only against punishment for an act which is treated as an offence, which when done was not an offence.

Accordingly, the Court in *Hathisingh* Case held that the impugned S. 25FFF(1) including the proviso and the explanation thereto are not unconstitutional as infringing the freedom guaranteed by Art. 19(1)(g) of the Constitution or as infringing Art. 14 or 20 of the Constitution.

Under S. 25FFF, closure of an undertaking cannot be limited or restricted only to financial, economic or other considerations of a like nature. All that has been laid down is that in case of a closure, the employer does not merely close down the place of business but he closes the business itself finally and irrevocably. The closure has to be genuine and bona fide in the sense that there should be a closure in fact and not a mere pretence of closure. The motive behind the closure is immaterial and what has to be seen is whether it was an effective one.

The entire set of circumstances and facts have to be taken into account while endeavouring to find out if, in fact, there has been a closure and the Tribunal or the court is not confined to any particular fact or set of facts or circumstances. The essence of the matter is the factum of closure by whatever reasons motivated. It is not necessary that the under-taking must be wound up, or that there should have been a transfer of the machinery or the factory before it could be said that the undertaking had been closed down.

Where about 150 out of a large number of workers virtually staged a gherao in the administrative office building of the Company, during the several hours preceding the declaration of closure by the management, and on account of the gherao, the magnitude of which was not inconsequential and which was likely to result in deterioration of relations between the management and the workers as also the apprehension expressed by the staff of danger to personal safety; held that the Management was faced with a situation in which it could well take a decision to close down the undertaking.

Ordinarily, the Supreme Court does not interfere with the findings of fact of a Tribunal, but where the question whether the undertaking was closed down or not by means of the notice was not considered in a proper manner by the Tribunal and its approach was erroneous and suffered from a number of infirmities, the conclusion arrived at by it cannot be regarded as sacrosanct or final.

The explanation appearing in the proviso to S. 25FFF gives some indication of the anxiety of the Legislature to expressly rule out certain contingencies which ordinarily could have been pleaded by the employer as unavoidable circumstances beyond his control. In the normal working of business of a commercial undertaking, financial losses or accumulation of undisposed stocks and the expiry of the period of the lease or the licence can ordinarily go a long way in establishing that it has virtually become impossible to carry on the business. Notwithstanding all this, the Legislature provided that in spite of the aforesaid difficulties or impediments or obstacles, the conditions of the proviso would not be satisfied merely by the happening or existence of the circumstances embodied in the explanation. The reason for doing so seems to be that whenever such difficulties, as are mentioned in the explanation, arise, the employer is not expected to sit idle and not to make an all-out effort like a prudent man of business in the matter of tiding over these difficulties for saving his business. The Legislature was apparently being very stringent and strict about the nature of the circumstances which would bring them within the proviso. The laying down of two pre-conditions therein in the language in which they are couched is significant and must be given due effect.

Where a large number of workers virtually staged a gherao in the administrative office of the company during the several hours preceding the declaration of closure by the management, but there had been no incidents involving physical violence, nor a series of incidents of any kind for any length of period preceding the gherao and no speech had been delivered by any of the representatives of the workers threatening or inciting bodily injury, with the exception of the gherao, there was nothing to furnish justification for the management for thinking that the working of the factory would involve unusual exertion or expense. Moreover, when neither any director nor other principal officer of the company was produced by the management before the Tribunal to give any other facts and circumstances from which it could be inferred that it appeared to the management that it was not possible to carry on the business by acting in a business like way and without unusual exertion, it could not be said that the closure of the undertaking was due to unavoidable circumstances beyond the control of the management and hence compensation would be payable as if the undertaking was closed down *"for any reason whatsoever"* within S. 25FFF(1) of the Act.[239]

Payment of Compensation—Not a Condition Precedent

There is a significant difference in phraseology between the text of S. 25F and S. 25FFF(1). Section 25F prescribes certain conditions precedent to retrenchment of workmen, whereas S. 25FFF(1) merely imposes liability to give notice and to pay compensation on closure of an undertaking which results in termination of employment of the workmen. Under S. 25F,

239. *Kalinga Tubes Ltd.* v. *Workmen*, AIR 1969 SC 90.

no workman employed in an industrial undertaking can be retrenched by the employer until (a) the workman has been given one month's notice in writing indicating the reason for retrenchment and the period has expired or the workman has been paid salary in lieu of such notice, (b) the workman has been paid retrenchment compensation equivalent to 15 days' average salary for every completed year of service, and (c) notice in the prescribed manner is served on the appropriate Government. Section 25FFF(1) however enacts that the workman shall be entitled to notice and compensation in accordance with the provision of S. 25F if the undertaking is closed for any reason, as if the workman has been retrenched. By the plain intendment of S. 25FFF(1), the right to notice and compensation for termination of employment flows from closure of the undertaking; the clause does not seek to make closure effective upon payment of compensation and upon service of notice or payment of wages in lieu of notice. An employer proposing to close his undertaking may serve notice of termination of employment, and if he fails to do so, he becomes liable to pay wages for the period of notice. On closure of an undertaking, the workmen are undoubtedly entitled to notice and compensation in accordance with S. 25F as if they had been retrenched, i.e. the workmen are entitled beside compensation to a month's notice or wages in lieu of such notice, but by the use of the words *"as if the workman had been retrenched*", the Legislature has not sought to place closure of an undertaking on the same footing as retrenchment under S. 25F. By S. 25F, a prohibition against retrenchment, until the conditions prescribed by that section are fulfilled, is imposed. In other words, there can be no valid retrenchment unless notice has been given or the wages in lieu of such notice have been paid along with the compensation. Whereas S. 25FFF(1) does not prohibit the termination of employment on closure of the undertaking without payment of compensation and without either serving notice or paying wages in lieu of notice. Payment of compensation and payment of wages for the period of notice are not therefore conditions precedent to closure.[240] It is true that S. 25FFF does not stipulate payment of compensation to closure as condition precedent, but it does not mean that the employer can get away by not making the payment at all. The employer has to pay the compensation within the reasonable time.

SECTION 25G: Procedure for retrenchment

Where any workman in an industrial establishment, who is a citizen of India, is to be retrenched and he belongs to a particular category of workmen in that establishment, in the absence of any agreement between the employer and the workman in this behalf, the employer shall ordinarily retrench the workman who was the last person to be employed in that category, unless for reasons to be recorded the employer retrenches any other workman.

There is no general law laid down anywhere in the Act except that laid down in S. 25G which provides a normal principle or procedure for retrenchment. This section prescribes that an employer shall ordinarily retrench the workman who was the last person to be employed in that category, unless for reasons to be recorded in writing, the employer retrenches any other workman. The rule of 'last come first go' has been statutorily recognised by S. 25G. By this section, a statutory obligation is imposed on the employer to follow the rule, and if he wants to depart from it, to record his reasons for the said departure. If the departure from the said rule does not appear to the Industrial Tribunal as valid or satisfactory, then the action of the

240. *Hathising Manufacturing Co., Ltd., M/s. Ahmedabad* v. *Union of India*, AIR 1960 SC 923.

management in so departing from the rule can be treated by the Tribunal as being *mala fide* or as amounting to unfair labour practice. In other words, departure from the ordinary industrial rule of retrenchment without any justification may itself, in a proper case, lead to the inference that the impugned retrenchment is the result of ulterior considerations and as such it is *mala fide* and amounts to unfair labour practice and victimisation. However, the employer may take into account consideration of efficiency and trustworthy character of the employees, and if he is satisfied that a person with a long service is inefficient, unreliable or habitually irregular in the discharge of his duties, it would be open to him to retrench his services while retaining in his employment employees who are more efficient, reliable and regular though they may be junior in service to the retrenched workmen. Normally, where the rule 'last come first go' is thus departed from, there should be reliable evidence preferably in the recorded history of the workmen concerned showing their inefficiency, unreliability or habitual irregularity. Whenever it is proved that the rule in question has been departed from, the employer must satisfy the Industrial Tribunal that the departure was justified; and in that sense the onus would undoubtedly be on the employer.[241] Once it is found that retrenchment is unjustified and improper, it is for the Labour Tribunals to consider what relief the retrenched workmen are entitled to. Ordinarily, if a workman has been improperly and illegally retrenched, he is entitled to claim reinstatement. The fact that in the meanwhile the employer has engaged other workmen would not necessarily defeat the claim for reinstatement of the retrenched workmen; nor can the fact that protracted litigation in regard to the dispute has inevitably meant delay, defeat such a claim for reinstatement.[242]

In *M/s. Om Oil and Oilseeds Exchange Ltd., Delhi* v. *Their Workmen*,[243] the Supreme Court further observed that 'last come first go' is not a 'universal principle' which would not be departed from by the management that the last should go first. The management has a discretion provided it acts bona fide and on good grounds. Shah, J. in that very ruling, while agreeing that a breach of the rule could not be assumed as prompted by mala fides or induced by unfair labour practice merely because of a departure or deviation, further observed that the Tribunal had to determine in each case whether the management had acted fairly and not with ulterior motive. The crucial consideration next mentioned by the learned Judge is that the management's decision to depart from the rule must be for valid and justifiable reasons, in which case "the senior employee may be retrenched before his junior in employment." Surely, valid and justifiable reasons are for the management to make out, and if made out, S. 25G will be vindicated and not violated. Indeed, that very decision stresses the necessity for valid and good grounds for varying the ordinary rule of 'last come first go'. Absence of mala fides by itself is no absolution from the rule in S. 25G. Affirmatively, some valid and justifiable grounds must be proved by the management to be exonerated from the 'last come first go' principle.

It must be remembered that the provision insists on the rule being applied categorically. That is to say, those who fall in the same category shall suffer retrenchment only in accordance with the principle of 'last come first go'.

Section 25G insists on the rule of 'last come first go' being applied categorywise. That is to say, those who fall in the same category shall suffer retrenchment only in accordance

241. *Swadesamitran Limited Madras.* v. *Their Workmen*, AIR 1960 SC 762.
242. *Punjab National Bank Ltd.* v. *All India Punjab National Bank Employees' Federation,* AIR 1960 SC 160.
243. AIR 1966 SC 1657.

with the principle of last come first go. Where the seniority list of particular workmen is the same, there is a telling circumstance to show that they fell in the same category. Grading for the purposes of scales of pay and like considerations will not create new categorisation. It is a confusion or unwarranted circumvention to contend that within the same category if grades for scales of pay, based on length of service etc., are evolved, that process amounts to creation of separate categories.[244]

Section 25H: Re-employment of retrenched workmen

Where any workmen are retrenched, and the employer proposes to take into his employment any persons, he shall, in such manner as may be prescribed, give an opportunity to the retrenched workmen who are citizens of India to offer themselves for re-employment, and such retrenched workmen who offer themselves for re-employment shall have preference over other persons.

Section 25H was inserted in the Industrial Disputes Act by the Amendment Act of 1953. It prescribes that if the employer proposes to employ new hand, then he has to provide an opportunity to the retrenched workman and preference is to be given to such workman over other person. This provision provides the benefit only to the retrenched workman. If the service of a workman is terminated otherwise than on retrenchment, he would not be entitled to re-employment under this section. Section 25H is to be looked along with S. 25G which provides that the last employed person will be retrenched first and the principle, 'last come first go' enunciated therein, is having its application to a particular category of workman. Therefore, the retrenched workman would be re-appointed in the same category.

In 2019 *in Management of the Barara Cooperative Marketing cum Processing Society Ltd.* v. *Pratap Singh* (2019 Supreme Court) wherein the respondent, Pratap Singh, was working with the appellant, Cooperative Marketing Society, as a Peon from 01.07.1973. The Society terminated the services of Ptatap Singh on 01.07.1985. Pratap Singh approached the Labour Court to decide the legality and correctness of his termination order. The Labour Court held the respondent's termination as bad in law and accordingly awarded lump sum compensation of ₹12,500 to the respondent in lieu of reinstatement in service. The Society and Pratap Singh both were aggrieved by the award and filed writ petitions before the High Court to challenge the legality and correctness of the award passed by the Labour Court. The High Court, however, dismissed both the writ petitions. The respondent, Pratap Singh, then accepted the compensation, which was awarded by the Labour Court.

In the year 1993, the respondent, Pratap Singh, filed a representation to the Society praying therein that since the Society has recently regularized the services of two peons on 01.01.1992, therefore, he has become entitled to claim reemployment in the appellant's services in terms of Section 25-H of the ID Act, 1947. The Society, however, did not accept the prayer made by Pratap Singh, the respondent. The Labour Court, by way of reference, held that the respondent was not entitled to claim any benefit of Section 25-H of the ID Act to claim reemployment in the appellant's services on the facts stated by the respondent in his statement of claim. The respondent felt aggrieved and filed writ petition in the High Court. The Single Judge allowed the writ petition and set aside the award of the Labour Court. The High Court directed reemployment of the respondent on the post of Peon in the appellant's services. The

244. *Workmen of Sudder Workshop of Jorehaut Tea Co. Ltd.* v. *Management of Jorehaut Tea Co. Ltd.*, AIR 1980 SC 1454.

appellant employer felt aggrieved and filed appeal before the Division Bench. The Division Bench dismissed the appeal and upheld the order of the Single Judge, which has given rise to the Society for filing the present appeal by way of special leave in the Supreme Court.

The only question to be decided by the Supreme Court in this case was, whether, the respondent, Pratap singh, is entitled to claim reemployment in the appellant's services in terms of Section 25-H of the ID Act. The Supreme Court observed that Section 25-H of the ID Act applies to the cases where employer has proposed to take into their employment any persons to fill up the vacancies. If so, the employer is required to give an opportunity to the "retrenched workman" and offer him reemployment and if such retrenched workman offers himself for reemployment, he shall have preference over other persons, who have applied for employment against the vacancy advertised. So, in order to attract the provisions of Section 25-H of the ID Act, it must be proved by the workman that firstly, he was the "retrenched employee" and secondly, his employer has decided to fill up the vacancies in their set up and, therefore, he is entitled to claim preference over those persons, who have applied against such vacancies for a job while seeking reemployment in the services. The case at hand is a case where the respondent's termination was held illegal and, in consequence thereof, he was awarded lump sum compensation of ₹12,500 in full and final satisfaction. It is not in dispute that the respondent also accepted the compensation. This was, therefore, not a case of a retrenchment of the respondent from service as contemplated under Section 25-H of the ID Act.

The most important point here is to be noted that the respondent was not entitled to invoke the provisions of Section 25-H of the ID Act and seek reemployment by citing the case of another employee (Peon) who was already in employment and whose services were only regularized by the appellant on the basis of his service record in terms of the Rules. The Court further made a distinction between the expression '*employment*' and '*regularization of the service*'. The expression '*employment*' signifies a fresh employment to fill the vacancies whereas the expression '*regularization of the service*' signifies that the employee, who is already in service, his services are regularized as per service regulations. Hence the Court held that the respondent cannot get the benefit of Section 25-H of the ID Act.

SECTION 25I: Recovery of moneys due from employees under this Chapter

Omitted by the Industrial Disputes (Amendment and Miscellaneous Provisions) Act, 1956 (36 of 1956), S. 19 (w.e.f. 10-3-1957).

SECTION 25J: Effect of laws inconsistent with this Chapter

(1) The provisions of this Chapter shall have effect notwithstanding anything inconsistent therewith contained in any other law including standing orders made under the Industrial Employment (Standing Orders) Act, 1946 (20 of 1946):

Provided that where under the provisions of any other Act or rules, orders or notifications issued thereunder or under any standing orders or under any award, contract of service or otherwise, a workman is entitled to benefits in respect of any matter which are more favourable to him than those to which he would be entitled under this Act, the workman shall continue to be entitled to the more favourable benefits in respect of that matter, notwithstanding that he receives benefits in respect of other matters under this Act.

(2) For the removal of doubts, it is hereby declared that nothing contained in this Chapter shall be deemed to affect the provisions of any other law for the time being in force in any State in so far as that law provides for the settlement of industrial disputes, but the rights and liabilities of employers and workmen in so far as they relate to lay-off and retrenchment shall be determined in accordance with the provisions of this Chapter.

Sub-section (1) of S. 25J of the Central Act lays down that Chapter V-A shall have effect notwithstanding anything inconsistent therewith contained in any other law. The proviso to that sub-section however saves any higher benefit available to a workman under any law, agreement or settlement or award. Sub-section (2) of S. 25J however makes a distinction between any machinery provided by any State law for settlement of industrial disputes and the substantive rights and liabilities arising under Chapter V-A of the Central Act where a lay-off or retrenchment takes place. It provides that while S. 25J would not affect the provision in a State law relating to settlement of industrial disputes, the rights and liabilities of employers and workmen in so far as they relate to lay-off and retrenchment shall be determined in accordance with Chapter V-A of the Central Act. Section 41(1) and S. 41(3) of the State Act prescribe alternative authorities to settle a dispute arising out of a retrenchment. Those authorities may exercise their jurisdiction under the State Act but they have to decide such dispute in accordance with the provisions of Chapter V-A of the Central Act. The said rights can be enforced by a workman personally, by himself filing an appeal under S. 41(1) of the State Act.

It is true that the State Act is a later Act and it has received the assent of the President, but since there is no repugnancy between the two laws, the State law cannot prevail so as to make the provisions of the Central Act relating to retrenchment ineffective in the State of Andhra Pradesh. The State Act does not contain any express provision making the provisions relating to retrenchment in the Central Act ineffective in so far as Andhra Pradesh is concerned. Chapter V-A of the Central Act which is the earlier law deals with cases arising out of lay-off and retrenchment. Section 25J of the Central Act deals with the effect of the provisions of Chapter V-A on other laws inconsistent with that Chapter. Sub-section (2) of S. 25J is quite emphatic about the supremacy of the provisions relating to the rights and liabilities arising out of lay-off and retrenchment. These are special provisions and they do not apply to all kinds of termination of services. Section 40 of the State Act deals generally with termination of service which may be the result of misconduct, closure, transfer of establishment, etc. If there is a conflict between the special provisions contained in an earlier law dealing with retrenchment and the general provisions contained in a later law generally dealing with terminations of service, the existence of repugnancy between the two laws cannot be easily presumed. Therefore, there is not even any implied repugnancy between the Central law and the State law.[245] The Supreme Court in *Rohtak and Hissar Districts Electric Supply*

245. *Krishna Dist. Co-operative Marketing Society Ltd., Vijayawada* v. *N.V. Purnachandra Rao,* AIR 1987 SC 1960.

Co. Ltd. v. *State of U.P.*[246] held that proviso to S. 25J(1) is one of the provisions contained in Chapter V-A which clearly and unambiguously lays down, *inter alia*, that where under any Standing Orders, a workman is entitled to benefits in respect of any matter covered by Chapter V-A which are more favourable to him than those to which he would be entitled under this Act, he shall continue to be entitled to the more favourable benefits in respect of that matter, notwithstanding that he receives benefits in respect of other matters under this Act. The position, therefore, is that S. 25J(2) makes Chapter V-A of the Central Act applicable to disputes in relation to compensation for lay-off, notwithstanding Ss. 6K and 6R of the U.P. Act; and amongst the provisions thus made applicable by S. 25J(2) is the proviso to S. 25J(1) under which the Standing Orders, which give more favourable benefits to the employees in respect of compensation for lay-off, will prevail over the provisions of the Central Act. Similarly, it is also held that the proviso to S. 25J(1) clearly means that if by any award or contract a workman is entitled to something more as retrenchment compensation than is provided by S. 25F the workman will be entitled to get that and the provisions of S. 25F, will not derogate from that right of the workman, i.e. will not reduce the compensation provided under the award or contract to the level provided under S. 25F.[247]

As far as S. 25J is concerned, it provides that the provisions of Chapter V-A of the Industrial Disputes Act, 1947 would have overriding effect irrespective of any other law including Standing Orders made under the Industrial Employment (Standing Orders) Rules, 1956.[248] In *Krishna District Co-operative Marketing Society Ltd.* v. *N.V. Purnachandra Rao*,[247] it was pointed out that the purpose of S. 25J(2) in Chapter V was to give an overriding effect to the provisions of retrenchment and lay-off in Chapter V-A over cognate provisions of State laws dealing with retrenchment and lay-off. In the above case, Venkataramiah, J. observed that by enacting S. 25J(2), Parliament, perhaps, intended that the rights and liabilities arising out of lay-off and retrenchment should be uniform throughout India where the Central Act was in force and did not wish that the States should have their own laws inconsistent with the Central law. In *P. Virudhachalam* v. *Management of Lotus Mills*,[249] a short but an interesting question that arose before the Supreme Court for consideration was whether an individual workman governed by the Industrial Disputes Act, 1947 can claim lay-off compensation under S. 25C of the Act despite a settlement arrived at during conciliation proceedings under S. 12(3) of the Act by a union of which he is not a member and when such settlement seeks to restrict the right of lay-off compensation payable to such workman as per the first proviso to S. 25C of the Act.

The Supreme Court while deciding the above issue referred S. 25J whether *"any other law"* as provided in S. 25J(1) would include even the Industrial Disputes Act. The Court observed that sub-section (1) of S. 25C lays down that if there is a legal lay-off imposed by the employer, the permanent workman covered by sweep of sub-section (1) of S. 25C would be entitled to be paid by way of lay-off compensation 50% of the total wages and dearness allowance during the relevant period of lay-off. However, because of the first proviso to the said section, the right of the workman to be paid 50% lay-off compensation during the relevant period of lay-off would be curtailed and restricted to 45 days only if there is an agreement to that effect between the workman and the employer. An individual workman cannot claim

246. AIR 1966 SC 1471.
247. *Brahmachari Research Institute, M/s. Calcutta-4* v. *Their Workmen*, AIR 1960 SC 257.
248. *Harmohinder Singh* v. *Kharga Canteen, Ambala Cantt.*, AIR 2001 SC 2681.
249. AIR 1998 SC 554.

lay-off compensation under S. 25C of the Act despite settlement arrived at during conciliation proceedings under S. 12(3) of the Act by a union of which he is not a member even when such settlement seeks to restrict the right of lay-off compensation payable to such workman as per the first proviso to S. 25C of the Act.

An agreement restricting the claim of lay-off compensation beyond the available period of 45 days can be said to be arrived at between the workman on the one hand, and the employer on the other, as there is such an agreement embedded in a binding settlement which has a legal effect of binding all the workmen in the institution as per S. 18(3) of the Act. Such binding effect of the embedded agreement in the written settlement arrived at during the conciliation proceedings would get telescoped into the first proviso to S. 25C(1) and bind all workmen even though individually they might not have signed the agreement with the management or their union might not have signed such agreement with the management on behalf of its member-workmen. The first proviso to S. 25C(1) clearly lays down that if there is an agreement for not paying any more lay-off compensation beyond 45 days between the workman and the employer, such an agreement has binding effect both on the employer and the workman concerned. Further, S. 25J of the Act cannot be relied upon for isolating effect of S. 18(3). All that is stated is that anything inconsistent with the provisions of Chapter V-A found to have been laid down by any other law including Standing Orders, etc. will have no effect. Even sub-section (2) of S. 25J is to the same effect. Therefore, S. 25J overrides any inconsistent provision of any other law or otherwise binding rule of conduct and makes the provisions of Chapter V-A operative of their own. It cannot be agreed that "any other law" as provided in S. 25J(1) would include even the Industrial Disputes Act, specially the provisions contained in S. 18 thereof. Section 25J(1) nowhere provides that the provisions of Chapter V-A shall have effect notwithstanding anything inconsistent contained in any other chapter of the Industrial Disputes Act as well as in any other law. Such a provision is conspicuously absent in S. 25J(1).

CHAPTER V-B

SPECIAL PROVISIONS RELATING TO LAY-OFF, RETRENCHMENT AND CLOSURE IN CERTAIN ESTABLISHMENTS

SECTION 25K: Application of Chapter V-B

(1) The provisions of this Chapter shall apply to an industrial establishment (not being an establishment of a seasonal character or in which work is performed only intermittently) in which not less than one hundred workmen were employed on an average per working day for the preceding twelve months.

(2) If a question arises whether an industrial establishment is of a seasonal character or whether work is performed therein only intermittently, the decision of the appropriate Government thereon shall be final.

In 2018 the Supreme Court in *National Kamgar Union* v. *Kran Rader Pvt. Ltd. & Ors.* [*2018 LLR 159* (*S.C.*)] observed that for closure of an industrial establishment under Chapter

VB of I.D. Act, to decide the strength of workmen, employees working as supervisors or managers would be excluded while counting 100 numbers of workmen.

Section 25L: Definitions

For the purposes of this Chapter,—

(a) "industrial establishment" means—

(i) a factory as defined in clause (m) of section 2 of the Factories Act, 1948 (63 of 1948);

(ii) a mine as defined in clause (j) of sub-section (1) of section 2 of the Mines Act, 1952 (35 of 1952); or

(iii) a plantation as defined in clause (f) of section 2 of the Plantations Labour Act, 1951 (69 of 1951);

(b) notwithstanding anything contained in sub-clause (ii) of clause (a) of section 2,—

(i) in relation to any company in which not less than fifty-one per cent of the paid-up share capital is held by the Central Government, or

(ii) in relation to any corporation not being a corporation referred to in sub-clause (i) of clause (a) of section 2 established by or under any law made by Parliament,

the Central Government shall be the appropriate Government.

Section 25M: Prohibition of lay-off

(1) No workman (other than a *badli* workman or a casual workman) whose name is borne on the muster rolls of an industrial establishment to which this Chapter applies shall be laid-off by his employer except with the prior permission of the appropriate Government or such authority as may be specified by that Government by notification in the Official Gazette (hereinafter in this section referred to as the specified authority), obtained on an application made in this behalf, unless such lay-off is due to shortage of power or to natural calamity, and in the case of a mine, such lay-off is due also to fire, flood, excess of inflammable gas or explosion.

(2) An application for permission under sub-section (1) shall be made by the employer in the prescribed manner stating clearly the reasons for the intended lay-off and a copy of such application shall also be served simultaneously on the workmen concerned in the prescribed manner.

(3) Where the workman (other than *badli* workmen or casual workmen) of an industrial establishment, being a mine, have been laid-off under sub-section (1) for reasons of fire, flood or excess of inflammable gas or explosion, the employer, in relation to such establishment, shall, within a period of thirty days from the date of commencement of such lay-off, apply, in the prescribed manner, to the appropriate Government or the specified authority for permission to continue the lay-off.

(4) Where an application for permission under sub-section (1) or sub-section (3) has been made, the appropriate Government or the specified authority, after making such enquiry as it thinks fit and after giving a reasonable opportunity of being heard to the employer, the workmen concerned and the persons interested in such lay-off,

may, having regard to the genuineness and adequacy of the reasons for such lay-off, the interests of the workmen and all other relevant factors, by order and for reasons to be recorded in writing, grant or refuse to grant such permission and a copy of such order shall be communicated to the employer and the workmen.

(5) Where an application for permission under sub-section (1) or sub-section (3) has been made and the appropriate Government or the specified authority does not communicate the order granting or refusing to grant permission to the employer within a period of sixty days from the date on which such application is made, the permission applied for shall be deemed to have been granted on the expiration of the said period of sixty days.

(6) An order of the appropriate Government or the specified authority granting or refusing to grant permission shall, subject to the provisions of sub-section (7), be final and binding on all the parties concerned and shall remain in force for one year from the date of such order.

(7) The appropriate Government or the specified authority may, either on its own motion or on the application made by the employer or any workman, review its order granting or refusing to grant permission under sub-section (4) or refer the matter or, as the case may be, cause it to be referred, to a Tribunal for adjudication:

Provided that where a reference has been made to a Tribunal under this sub-section, it shall pass an award within a period of thirty days from the date of such reference.

(8) Where no application for permission under sub-section (1) is made, or where no application for permission under sub-section (3) is made within the period specified therein, or where the permission for any lay-off has been refused, such lay-off shall be deemed to be illegal from the date on which the workmen had been laid-off and the workmen shall be entitled to all the benefits under any law for the time being in force as if they had not been laid-off.

(9) Notwithstanding anything contained in the foregoing provisions of this section, the appropriate Government may, if it is satisfied that owing to such exceptional circumstances as accident in the establishment or death of the employer or the like, it is necessary so to do, by order, direct that the provisions of sub-section (1), or, as the case may be, sub-section (3) shall not apply in relation to such establishment for such period as may be specified in the order.

(10) The provisions of section 25C (other than the second proviso thereto) shall apply to cases of lay-off referred to in this section.

Explanation: For the purposes of this section, a workman shall not be deemed to be laid-off by an employer if such employer offers any alternative employment (which in the opinion of the employer does not call for any special skill or previous experience and can be done by the workman) in the same establishment from which he has been laid-off or in any other establishment belonging to the same employer, situate in the same town or village, or situate within such distance from the establishment to which he belongs that the transfer will not involve undue hardship to the workman having regard to the facts and circumstances of his case, provided that the wages which would normally have been paid to the workman are offered for the alternative appointment also.

The object underlying the requirement of prior permission for lay-off of workmen introduced by S. 25M as indicated in the Statement of Objects and Reasons for the Amending

Act of 1976, is to prevent avoidable hardship to the employees resulting from lay-off by protecting employment to those already employed and to maintain higher tempo of production and productivity by preserving industrial peace and harmony. The said consideration coupled with the basic idea underlying the provisions of the Act, namely, settlement of industrial disputes and promotion of industrial peace, gives a sufficient indication of the factors which have to be borne in mind by the appropriate Government or authority by exercising its power to grant or refuse permission for lay-off under sub-section (2) of S. 25M.

It is evident that the Legislature has taken care in exempting the need for prior permission for lay-off in S. 25M if such lay-off is necessitated on account of power failure or natural calamities because such reasons being grave, sudden and explicit, no further scrutiny is called for. There may be various other contingencies justifying an immediate action of lay-off but then the Legislature in its wisdom has thought it desirable in the greater public interest that decision to lay-off should not be taken by the employer on his own assessment with immediate effect, but the employer must seek approval from the authority concerned which is reasonably expected to be alive to the problems associated with the industry concerned and other relevant factors, so that on scrutiny of the reasons pleaded for permitting lay-off, such authority may arrive at a just and proper decision in the matter of according or refusing permission to lay-off. Such authority is under an obligation to dispose of the application to accord permission for a lay-off expeditiously and, in any event, within a period not exceeding two months from the date of seeking permission. It may not be unlikely that in some cases, an employer may suffer unmerited hardship upto a period of two months within which his application for lay-off is required to be disposed of by the authority concerned, but having undertaken a productive venture by establishing an industrial unit employing a large number of labour force, such employer has to face such consequence on some occasions and may have to suffer some hardship for some time but not exceeding two months within which his case for a lay-off is required to be considered by the authority concerned, otherwise it will be deemed that the permission has been accorded. In the greater public interest for maintaining industrial peace and harmony and to prevent unemployment without just cause, the restriction imposed under sub-section (2) of S. 25M cannot be held to be arbitrary, unreasonable or far in excess of the need for which such restriction has been sought to be imposed.[250]

Constitutional Validity

The Division Bench of the Madras High Court *inter alia* held that S. 25M, as it stood under the said amendment Act, 1976, was constitutionally invalid for the reasons given by this Court in invalidating S. 25-O of the Industrial Disputes Act in the decision rendered in *Excel Wear* v. *Union of India.*[251] The Court after taking into account the respective submissions of the learned counsel for the parties and considering various decisions of the Supreme Court in deciding the question of reasonableness of the restriction imposed by a statute on the fundamental rights guaranteed by Art. 19 of the Constitution of India, the Court considered the following principles and guidelines laid down by the Supreme Court on different occasions before resolving the issue of constitutionality of S. 25M, and they are follows:

250. *Papnasam Labour Union* v. *Madura Coats Ltd.*, AIR 1995 SC 2200.
251. AIR 1979 SC 25.

(a) The restriction sought to be imposed on the fundamental rights guaranteed by Art. 19 of the Constitution must not be arbitrary or of an excessive nature so as to go beyond the requirement of felt need of the society and object sought to be achieved.

(b) There must be a direct and proximate nexus or a reasonable connection between the restriction imposed and the object sought to be achieved.

(c) No abstract or fixed principle can be laid down which may have universal application in all cases. Such consideration on the question of quality of reasonableness, therefore, is expected to vary from case to case.

(d) In interpreting constitutional provisions, the court should be alive to the felt need of the society and complex issues facing the people, which the legislature intends to solve through effective legislation.

(e) In appreciating such problems and felt need of the society, the judicial approach must necessarily be dynamic, pragmatic and elastic.

(f) It is imperative that for consideration of reasonableness of restriction imposed by a statute, the Court should examine whether the social control as envisaged in Art. 19 is being effectuated by the restriction imposed on the fundamental right.

(g) Article 19 guarantees certain freedoms to the citizen. But they do not confer any absolute or unconditional right and are subject to reasonable restriction which the legislature may impose in public interest. It is, therefore, necessary to examine whether such restriction is meant to protect social welfare, satisfying the need of prevailing social values.

(h) The reasonableness has got to be tested both from the procedural and substantive aspects. It should not be bound by processual perniciousness or jurisprudence of remedies.

(i) Restriction imposed on the fundamental right guaranteed under Art. 19 of the Constitution must not be arbitrary, unbridled, uncanalised, excessive, unreasonable and discriminatory. Exhypothesi, therefore, a restriction to be reasonable must also be consistent with Art. 14 of the Constitution.

(j) In judging the reasonableness of the restriction imposed by Cl. (6) of Art. 19, the Court has to bear in mind the Directive Principles of State Policy.

(k) Ordinarily, any restriction so imposed which has the effect of promoting or effectuating a directive principle can be presumed to be a reasonable restriction in public interest.

The Court also relied on *Meenakshi Mills* case and held that S. 25M is constitutional.

Section 25N: Conditions precedent to retrenchment of workmen

(1) No workman employed in any industrial establishment to which this Chapter applies, who has been in continuous service for not less than one year under an employer shall be retrenched by that employer until,—

(a) the workman has been given three months' notice in writing indicating the reasons for retrenchment and the period of notice has expired, or the workman has been paid in lieu of such notice, wages for the period of the notice; and

(b) the prior permission of the appropriate Government or such authority as may be specified by that Government by notification in the Official Gazette (hereafter in this section referred to as the specified authority) has been obtained on an application made in this behalf.

(2) An application for permission under sub-section (1) shall be made by the employer in the prescribed manner stating clearly the reasons for the intended retrenchment and a copy of such application shall also be served simultaneously on the workmen concerned in the prescribed manner.

(3) Where an application for permission under sub-section (1) has been made, the appropriate Government or the specified authority, after making such enquiry as it thinks fit and after giving a reasonable opportunity of being heard to the employer, the workmen concerned and the persons interested in such retrenchment, may, having regard to the genuineness and adequacy of the reasons stated by the employer, the interests of the workmen and all other relevant factors, by order and for reasons to be recorded in writing, grant or refuse to grant such permission and a copy of such order shall be communicated to the employer and the workmen.

(4) Where an application for permission has been made under sub-section (1) and the appropriate Government or the specified authority does not communicate the order granting or refusing to grant permission to the employer within a period of sixty days from the date on which such application is made, the permission applied for shall be deemed to have been granted on the expiration of the said period of sixty days.

(5) An order of the appropriate Government or the specified authority granting or refusing to grant permission shall, subject to the provisions of sub-section (6), be final and binding on all the parties concerned and shall remain in force for one year from the date of such order.

(6) The appropriate Government or the specified authority may, either on its own motion or on the application made by the employer or any workman, review its order granting or refusing to grant permission under sub-section (3) or refer the matter or, as the case may be, cause it to be referred, to a Tribunal for adjudication:

Provided that where a reference has been made to a Tribunal under this sub-section, it shall pass an award within a period of thirty days from the date of such reference.

(7) Where no application for permission under sub-section (1) is made, or where the permission for any retrenchment has been refused, such retrenchment shall be deemed to be illegal from the date on which the notice of retrenchment was given to the workman and the workman shall be entitled to all the benefits under any law for the time being in force as if no notice had been given to him.

(8) Notwithstanding anything contained in the foregoing provisions of this section, the appropriate Government may, if it is satisfied that owing to such exceptional circumstances as accident in the establishment or death of the employer or the like, it is necessary so to do, by order, direct that the provisions of sub-section (1) shall not apply in relation to such establishment for such period as may be specified in the order.

(9) Where permission for retrenchment has been granted under sub-section (3) or where permission for retrenchment is deemed to be granted under sub-section (4), every workman who is employed in that establishment immediately before the date of application for permission under this section shall be entitled to receive, at the time of retrenchment, compensation which shall be equivalent to fifteen days' average pay for every completed year of continuous service or any part thereof in excess of six months.

The object underlying the enactment of S. 25N, by introducing prior scrutiny of the reasons for retrenchment, is to prevent avoidable hardship to the employees resulting from retrenchment by protecting existing employment and to check the growth of unemployment which would otherwise be the consequence of retrenchment in industrial establishments employing large number of workmen. It is also intended to maintain higher tempo of production and productivity by preserving industrial peace and harmony. In that sense S. 25N seeks to give effect to the mandate contained in the Directive Principles of the Constitution. The restrictions imposed by S. 25N on the right of the employer to retrench the workmen must, therefore, be regarded as having been imposed in the interests of the general public.

Constitutional Validity

The validity of S. 25N was challenged before the various High Courts and there is a conflict of opinion among the High Courts. A Division Bench of the Andhra Pradesh High Court in *I.D.L. Chemicals Ltd.* v. *T. Gattiah*[252] has upheld the validity of S. 25N, while a Division Bench of the Madras High Court, in *K.V. Rajendran* v. *Dy. Commr. of Labour, Madurai*,[253] has taken a contrary view and has held S. 25N to be violative of the right guaranteed under Art. 19(1)(g) of the Constitution imposing unreasonable restrictions on the said right of the employer. A Full Bench of the Rajasthan High Court, in *M/s. J.K. Synthetics* v. *Union of India*,[254] has agreed with the view of the Madras High Court in *K.V. Rajendran's* case and has held S. 25N to be invalid. The Madras High Court and the Rajasthan High Courts have placed reliance on the decision of this court in *Excel Wear* v. *Union of India*,[255] and have held that the reasons for which this Court has struck down S. 25-O are equally applicable for judging the validity of S. 25N.

The Madras High Court as well as the Rajasthan High Court has held the provisions of S. 25N to be unconstitutional on two grounds:

(1) No principles or guidelines have been laid down for the exercise of the power conferred by sub-section (2) of S. 25N of the Act; and

(2) There is no provision for appeal or review against the order passed under sub-section (2).

---

252. D.B. Writ Appeal 16 of 1981, decided on December 4, 1981.
253. 1981 Lab IC 799.
254. (1984) 48 Fac LR 125.
255. AIR 1979 SC 25.

Both these questions have been considered by a Constitution Bench in *Workmen of Meenakshi Mills Ltd.* v. *Meenakshi Mills Ltd.*[256]

> "... we are unable to uphold the decisions of the said High Courts striking down S. 25N as unconstitutional on the ground that it is violative of Art. 19(1)(g) and is not saved by Art. 19(6) of the Constitution."[257]

Accordingly the Court held that S. 25N does not suffer from the vice of unconstitutionality on the ground that it is violative of the fundamental right guaranteed under Art. 19(1)(g) of the Constitution and is not saved by Art. 19(6) of the Constitution.

Right of Employer to Terminate Employee's Service

Ordinarily, any restriction so imposed which has the effect of promoting or effectuating a directive principle can be presumed to be a reasonable restriction in public interest. A restriction imposed on the employer's right to terminate the service of an employee is not alien to the Constitutional scheme which indicates that the employer's right is not absolute.

Retrenchment Procedure

Sub-section (1) of S. 25N contains provisions similar to those contained in S. 25F with one modification that the period of notice which is required to be given for retrenchment of a workman in an industrial establishment covered by S. 25K and falling within Chapter V-B, is three months instead of one month. The need for a longer period of notice is indicated by sub-section (3) of S. 25N because within a period of three months from the date of service of the said notice, the appropriate Government or authority is required to communicate the permission or refusal to grant the permission for retrenchment to the employer after making such enquiry as it thinks fit under sub-section (2) of S. 25N. The consequence of failure to keep this time schedule is indicated in sub-section (3) of S. 25N wherein it is provided that in case the Government or authority does not communicate the permission or the refusal to grant the permission to the employer within three months of the date of service of the notice, the Government or the authority shall be deemed to have granted the permission for such retrenchment on the expiration of the said period of three months.

Power of Appropriate Government to Grant or Refuse Permission

It appears that the employer is required to furnish detailed information in respect of the working of the industrial undertaking so as to enable the appropriate Government or authority to make up its mind whether to grant or refuse permission for retrenchment. Before passing such order, the appropriate Government or authority will have to ascertain whether the said information furnished by the employer is correct and the proposed action involving retrenchment of workmen is necessary, and if so, to what extent. For that purpose, it would be necessary for the appropriate Government or authority to make an enquiry after affording an opportunity to the employer as well as the workmen to represent their case and make a

256. AIR 1994 SC 2696.
257. *Ibid.* at p. 2727 per S.C. Agrawal, J.

speaking order containing reasons. This necessarily envisages exercise of functions which are not purely administrative in character and are quasi-judicial in nature. Therefore, while exercising its powers under sub-section (2) of S. 25N in the matter of granting or refusing permission for retrenchment, the appropriate Government or the authority does not exercise powers which are purely administrative but exercises powers which are quasi-judicial in nature.[258]

Granting or Refusal of Permission Need Not be in Entirety

It was contended on behalf of the employers in *Meenakshi Mills* case that while passing an order under sub-section (2) of S. 25N, the appropriate Government or authority can either grant or refuse permission for the proposed retrenchment in its entirety and that it is not permissible for the appropriate Government or authority to grant permission for retrenchment of some of the workmen out of the workmen proposed to be retrenched and refuse such permission in respect of the rest. But the Court held:

> "We do not find any words of limitation in sub-section (2) which preclude the appropriate Government or authority or to grant partial permission in respect of some of the workmen out of the workmen proposed to be retrenched and refuse the same in respect of the rest keeping in view the particular facts in relation to a particular establishment. Nor is there anything in sub-section (2) which requires the appropriate Government or authority to either grant permission for retrenchment of the entire lot of the workmen proposed to be retrenched or refuse to grant permission in respect of the entire lot of workmen. It may be that the appropriate Government or authority may feel that the demand of the management for the proposed retrenchment is pitched too high and that in view of the facts and circumstances revealed as a result of an enquiry it is found that the industrial establishment can be efficiently run after retrenching a few of the workmen proposed to be retrenched. In that event, it would be permissible for the appropriate Government or authority to grant permission for retrenchment of only some of the workmen proposed to be retrenched and to refuse such permission for the rest of the workmen."[258]

Retrenchment Need Not be Restricted to Surplus Labour

Retrenchment, as defined in S. 2(oo), means termination by the employer of the service of a workman for any reason whatsoever otherwise than as a punishment inflicted by way of disciplinary action and those expressly excluded by Cls. (a), (b), (bb) and (c) of the definition. In view of this settled position, it cannot be said that retrenchment means termination by the employer of the service of a workman as surplus labour. Such a restricted meaning of retrenchment cannot be held to govern the exercise of the power by the appropriate Government or the authority under sub-section (2) of S. 25N. In enacting Chapter V-B, the intention of Parliament was to alter the existing law relating to lay-off, retrenchment and closure in relation to larger industrial establishments falling within the ambit of Chapter V-B, because it was felt that the existing law enabled large-scale lay-offs, retrenchment and closures by large companies and undertakings and this had resulted in all round demoralising effect on workmen. Therefore, it could not be said that in enacting S. 25N, Parliament did not intend to alter the existing industrial law governing retrenchment of workmen.

258. *Ibid.*, f.n. 258 at p. 2715 per S.C. Agrawal, J.

Section 25-O: Procedure for closing down an undertaking

(1) An employer who intends to close down an undertaking of an industrial establishment to which this Chapter applies shall, in the prescribed manner, apply, for prior permission at least ninety days before the date on which the intended closure is to become effective, to the appropriate Government, stating clearly the reasons for the intended closure of the undertaking and a copy of such application shall also be served simultaneously on the representatives of the workmen in the prescribed manner:

Provided that nothing in this sub-section shall apply to an undertaking set up for the construction of buildings, bridges, roads, canals, dams or for other construction work.

(2) Where an application for permission has been made under sub-section (1), the appropriate Government, after making such enquiry as it thinks fit and after giving a reasonable opportunity of being heard to the employer, the workmen and the persons interested in such closure may, having regard to the genuineness and adequacy of the reasons stated by the employer, the interests of the general public and all other relevant factors, by order and for reasons to be recorded in writing, grant or refuse to grant such permission and a copy of such order shall be communicated to the employer and the workman.

(3) Where an application has been made under sub-section (1) and the appropriate Government does not communicate the order granting or refusing to grant permission to the employer within a period of sixty days from the date on which such application is made, the permission applied for shall be deemed to have been granted on the expiration of the said period of sixty days.

(4) An order of the appropriate Government granting or refusing to grant permission shall, subject to the provisions of sub-section (5), be final and binding on all the parties and shall remain in force for one year from the date of such order.

(5) The appropriate Government may, either on its own motion or on the application made by the employer or any workman, review its order granting or refusing to grant permission under sub-section (2) or refer the matter to a Tribunal for adjudication:

Provided that where a reference has been made to a Tribunal under this sub-section, it shall pass an award within a period of thirty days from the date of such reference.

(6) Where no application for permission under sub-section (1) is made within the period specified therein, or where the permission for closure has been refused, the closure of the undertaking shall be deemed to be illegal from the date of closure and the workmen shall be entitled to all the benefits under any law for the time being in force as if the undertaking had not been closed down.

(7) Notwithstanding anything contained in the foregoing provisions of this section, the appropriate Government may, if it is satisfied that owing to such exceptional circumstances as accident in the undertaking or death of the employer or the like it is necessary so to do, by order, direct that the provisions of sub-section (1) shall not apply in relation to such undertaking for such period as may be specified in the order.

(8) Where an undertaking is permitted to be closed down under sub-section (2) or where permission for closure is deemed to be granted under sub-section (3), every workman who is employed in that undertaking immediately before the date of application for permission under this section, shall be entitled to receive compensation which shall be equivalent to fifteen days' average pay for every completed year of continuous service or any part thereof in excess of six months.

Section 25-O, as it now stands, was incorporated by the Amendment Act 46 of 1982 (for the sake of convenience, the said section will hereinafter be referred to as the amended S. 25-O). Under the unamended S. 25-O, the order was to be passed on a subjective satisfaction of the appropriate Government. Now in amended S. 25-O(2), the words used are "*the appropriate Government may, after making such enquiry as it thinks fit, and after giving a reasonable opportunity of being heard to the employer, the workmen and persons interested in such closure may, having regard to the genuineness and adequacy of the reasons stated by the employer, interest of the general public and all other relevant factors by order and for reasons to be recorded in writing, grant or refuse to grant such permission.*" Thus, now the appropriate Government before passing an order is bound to make an enquiry. Now, the order passed by the appropriate Government has to be in writing and contain reasons. As in the case of retrenchment so also in closure, the employer has to give notice by filling up a form in which he has to give precise details and information. The requirement to make an enquiry postulates an enquiry into the correctness of the facts stated by the employer in the notice served by him and also all other relevant facts and circumstances including the bona fide of the employer. Now an opportunity to be heard would have to be afforded to the employer, workmen and all persons interested. The detailed information which the employer gives would enable the appropriate Government to make up its mind and collect necessary facts for the purposes of granting or refusing permission. The appropriate Government would have to ascertain whether the information furnished is correct and whether the proposed action is necessary and, if so, to what extent. The making of an enquiry, the affording of an opportunity to the employer, the workmen and all interested persons and the necessity to pass a written order containing reasons envisages exercise of functions which are not purely administrative in character but quasi-judicial in nature. The words "*the appropriate Government, after making such enquiry, as it thinks fit*" do not mean that the Government may dispense with the enquiry at its discretion. These words only mean that the Government has discretion about the nature of the enquiry it is to make.

The reason why S. 25-O was struck down in *Excel Wear* case[259] was that no time limit had been fixed while refusing permission to close down. This is now cured by sub-section (4) of the amended S. 25-O. This sub-section provides that the order of the appropriate Government shall remain in force for one year from the date of such order. Thus at the end of the year it is always open to the employer to apply again for permission to close. There is no substance in the submission that the employer would not be able to apply again (at the end of the year) on the same grounds. If the reasons were genuine and adequate, the very fact that they have persisted for a year more is sufficient to necessitate a fresh look. Also, if the reasons have persisted for a year, it can hardly be said that they are the same. The difficulties

259. *Excel Wear* v. *Union of India*, AIR 1979 SC 25.

faced during the year, provided they are genuine and adequate, would by themselves be additional grounds. Also, by the end of the year the interest of the general public or the other relevant factors, which necessitated refusal of permission on the earlier occasion, may not prevail. The appropriate Government would necessarily have to make a fresh enquiry, give a reasonable opportunity of being heard to the employer, workmen and all concerned. Therefore, providing for a period of one year makes the restriction reasonable, and S. 25-O is constitutionally valid.

Sub-section (3) of the amended S. 25-O provides that if the appropriate Government does not communicate the order within a period of 60 days from the date on which the application is made, the permission applied for shall be deemed to have been granted. The defect that there is no deemed provision for according approval in the section, also stands cured.

A Constitution Bench in *Orissa Textile and Steel Ltd., M/s.* v. *State of Orissa*[260] interpreted sub-section (5) of the amended S. 25-O which provides that the appropriate Government may, either on its own motion or on an application made by the employer or any workman, review its order granting or refusing permission or refer the matter to a Tribunal for adjudication. The Court held that a proper reading of sub-section (5) of amended S. 25-O shows that in the context in which it is used, the word *may* necessarily means *shall*. Thus the appropriate Government *shall* review the order if an application in that behalf is made by the employer or the workmen. Similarly, if so required by the employer or the workman, it shall refer the matter to a Tribunal for adjudication. In a review the appropriate Government would have to make an enquiry into all necessary facts, particularly into the genuineness and adequacy of the reasons stated by the employer. An opportunity of being heard would have to be given to the employer, workmen and all interested persons. The order on review would have to be in writing, giving reasons. The Court further held that in exercising powers of review, the appropriate Government would be performing quasi-judicial functions. Sub-section (5) of amended S. 25-O provides that the award should be passed within a period of 30 days from the date of reference. Even though it does not provide any time-frame within which the review is to be disposed of, it is settled law that the same would have to be disposed of within a reasonable period of time. The Court is of opinion that a period of 30 days would be a reasonable period for disposing of a review also. This review and/or reference under amended S. 25-O would be in addition to a judicial review under Art. 226 or Art. 32. The exercise of power being quasi-judicial, the remedy of judicial review under Art. 226 or Art. 32 was an adequate protection against the arbitrary action in the matter of exercising of power by the appropriate Government.

Amended S. 25-O lays down guidelines which are to be followed by the appropriate Government in granting or refusing permission to close down. It has to have regard to the genuineness and adequacy of the reasons stated by the employer. However, merely because the reasons are genuine and adequate cannot mean that permission to close must necessarily be granted. There could be cases where the interest of general public may require that no closure should take place. Undoubtedly, where the reasons are genuine and adequate, the interest of the general public must be of a compelling or overriding nature. Thus, by way

260. AIR 2002 SC 708.

of examples, if an industry is engaged in manufacturing of items required for defence of the country, then even though the reasons may be genuine and adequate it may become necessary, in the interest of general public, not to allow closure for some time. Similarly, if the establishment is manufacturing vaccines or drugs for an epidemic which is prevalent at that particular point of time, interest of general public may require not to allow closure for a particular period of time. Sub-section (7) of amended S. 25-O, which provides that if there are exceptional circumstances or accident in the undertaking or death of the employer or the like, the appropriate Government could direct that provision of sub-section (1) would not apply to such an undertaking, makes it clear that amended S. 25-O recognises that if there are exceptional circumstances then there could be no compulsion to continue to run the business. It must, however, be clarified that the Supreme Court is not laying down that some difficulty or financial hardship in running the establishment would be sufficient. The employer must show that it has become impossible to continue to run the establishment. Looked at from this point of view, the restrictions imposed are reasonable and in the interest of general public.

Amended S. 25-O is the law which lays down the restriction. There is nothing vague or ambiguous in its provision. It is S. 25-O which gives the power to grant or refuse permission. It would be impossible to enumerate or set out in S. 25-O all different contingencies or situations which may arise in actual practice. Each case would have to be decided on its own facts and on the basis of circumstances prevailing at the relevant time. All that can be set out in the section are guidelines. These have been set out in amended S. 25-O. The amended S. 25-O is not *ultra vires* the Constitution and it is saved by Art. 19(6) of the Constitution.[262] It is evident from the Scheme of various sub-sections of S. 25-O of the Act that whenever an application for closure of an industrial unit is made by an employer, the State Government before whom such application is made, is required to dispose of such application within sixty days from the date of making the application and communicate its decision within the said period of sixty days so that an employer does not suffer any hardship on account of failure on the part of the State Government to dispose of such application for permission for closure expeditiously. In order to compel the State Government to dispose of such application expeditiously not exceeding sixty days, provision has been made that if the decision of the State Government on the application for permission to close an industrial unit is not communicated within the said period of sixty days, it will be deemed that such permission has been granted. Since the decision on the application for permission for closure is to be taken by the executive authority, namely the State Government and no provision for statutory review before other authority has been made, the legislature has incorporated the provision of review by the State Government of its decision on the application for closure either on its own motion or on the basis of the application to be made by the aggrieved party. As the decision made by the State Government on the question of closure of an industrial unit cannot but bring about serious consequence affecting productivity, employment opportunities etc., the decision taken on the application for closure has been made operative for one year only, so that after such period if an employer still desires that the industrial unit should be closed, it may make a fresh application for permission to close the said unit. Since the decision made on an application for permission for closure is to remain operative only for a year, it will be only proper that an order by way of review, either on the aggrieved party's application or on own motion of the State Government, must be made within the said period of one year.

Otherwise, the right to make fresh application for permission to close after the expiry of one year from the date of rejection of permission for closure will lose its relevance. Anomalous situation may arise if the application for review, when presented within the said time-frame of one year, is allowed to be decided even after the expiry of the said time-frame of one year when the order passed by the State Government has already ceased to be operative. Although it has not been expressly indicated within what period a review application validly made is to be disposed of, the provision that order, on an application for closure, would remain in force for one year and in the absence of one embargo to make fresh application for such permission after expiry of one year, even if a review application remains pending, makes it abundantly clear that in the scheme of S. 25-O, the review application is to be made before expiry of the said time-frame of one year and such application is to be disposed of within such time-frame, otherwise such review application will become infructuous. The argument that a party should not be made to suffer simply on account of failure on the part of a statutory authority to dispose of review application within a time-frame and thereby rendering it infructuous, is not tenable because after expiry of the said time-frame of one year, the aggrieved party has a right to make a fresh application by incorporating all the material factors germane for consideration of its application for permission to close, including the factors indicated in review application. Neither the general principle of retaining jurisdiction to dispose of review application validly made nor the principle that an authority, if clothed with the power of review, will not become functus officio after expiry of the time frame of one year but it will retain its authority to dispose of the pending review application, will arise in the context of the scheme of S. 25-O. In effect, it can be said that the State Government would cease to have jurisdiction to review its order on the application for closure of an industrial unit after the expiry of one year from the date of rejection of the application for permission to close.[261]

Section 25P: Special provision as to restarting of undertakings closed down before commencement of the Industrial Disputes (Amendment) Act, 1976

If the appropriate Government is of opinion in respect of any undertaking of an industrial establishment to which this Chapter applies and which closed down before the commencement of the Industrial Disputes (Amendment) Act, 1976 (32 of 1976),

(a) that such undertaking was closed down otherwise than on account of unavoidable circumstances beyond the control of the employer;

(b) that there are possibilities of restarting the undertaking;

(c) that it is necessary for the rehabilitation of the workmen employed in such undertaking before its closure or for the maintenance of supplies and services essential to the life of the community to restart the undertaking or both; and

(d) that the restarting of the undertaking will not result in hardship to the employer in relation to the undertaking,

261. *Vazir Glass Works Ltd.* v. *Maharashtra General Kamgar Union*, AIR 1996 SC 1282.

it may, after giving an opportunity to such employer and workmen, direct, by order published in the Official Gazette, that the undertaking shall be restarted within such time (not being less than one month from the date of the order) as may be specified in the order.

Section 25Q: Penalty for lay-off and retrenchment without previous permission

Any employer who contravenes the provisions of section 25M or of section 25N shall be punishable with imprisonment for a term which may extend to one month, or with fine which may extend to one thousand rupees, or with both.

Section 25R: Penalty for closure

(1) Any employer who closes down an undertaking without complying with the provisions of sub-section (1) of S. 25-O shall be punishable with imprisonment for a term which may extend to six months, or with fine which may extend to five thousand rupees, or with both.

(2) Any employer, who contravenes an order refusing to grant permission to close down an undertaking under sub-section (2) of S. 25-O or a direction given under S. 25P, shall be punishable with imprisonment for a term which may extend to one year, or with fine which may extend to five thousand rupees, or with both, and where the contravention is a continuing one, with a further fine which may extend to two thousand rupees for every day during which the contravention continues after the conviction.

Section 25S: Certain provisions of Chapter V-A to apply to an industrial establishment to which this Chapter applies

The provisions of sections 25B, 25D, 25FF, 25G, 25H, and 25J in Chapter V-A shall, so far as may be, apply also in relation to an industrial establishment to which the provisions of this Chapter apply.

Chapter V-C

UNFAIR LABOUR PRACTICES

Section 25T: Prohibition of unfair labour practice

No employer or workman or a trade union, whether registered under the Trade Unions Act, 1926 (16 of 1926), or not, shall commit any unfair labour practice.

Section 25U: Penalty for committing unfair labour practices

Any person who commits any unfair labour practice shall be punishable with imprisonment for a term which may extend to six months or with fine which may extend to one thousand rupees or with both.

Chapter VI

PENALTIES

Section 26: Penalty for illegal strikes and lock-outs

(1) Any workman who commences, continues or otherwise acts in furtherance of, a strike which is illegal under this Act, shall be punishable with imprisonment for a term which may extend to one month, or with fine which may extend to fifty rupees, or with both.

(2) Any employer who commences, continues, or otherwise acts in furtherance of a lock-out which is illegal under this Act, shall be punishable with imprisonment for a term which may extend to one month, or with fine which may extend to one thousand rupees, or with both.

Section 27: Penalty for instigation, etc.

Any person who instigates or incites others to take part in, or otherwise acts in furtherance of, a strike or lock-out which is illegal under this Act, shall be punishable with imprisonment for a term which may extend to six months, or with fine which may extend to one thousand rupees, or with both.

Section 28: Penalty for giving financial aid to illegal strikes and lock-outs

Any person who knowingly expends or applies any money in direct furtherance or support of any illegal strike or lock-out shall be punishable with imprisonment for a term which may extend to six months, or with fine which may extend to one thousand rupees, or with both.

Section 29: Penalty for breach of settlement or award

Any person who commits a breach of any term of any settlement or award, which is binding on him under this Act, shall be punishable with imprisonment for a term which may extend to six months, or with fine, or with both, and where the breach is a continuing one, with a further fine which may extend to two hundred rupees for every day during which the breach continues after the conviction for the first and the Court trying the offence, if it fines the offender, may direct that the whole or any part of the fine realised from him shall be paid, by way of compensation, to any person who, in its opinion, has been injured by such breach.

Section 29 imposes punishment in case of breach of settlement or award. Any person who commits a breach of any settlement which is binding on him shall be punishable with imprisonment or with fine or with both as per S. 29 of the Act.

In order to invoke S. 29, the following points must be satisfied.

(a) There must be a breach of award or settlement whose life is not extinguished.

(b) The accused was bound by such settlement or award.

(c) The accused has committed the breach.

Section 30: Penalty for disclosing confidential information

Any person who wilfully discloses any such information as is referred to in section 21 in contravention of the provisions of that section shall, on complaint made by or on behalf of the trade union or individual business affected, be punishable with imprisonment for a term which may extend to six months, or with fine which may extend to one thousand rupees, or with both.

Section 30A: Penalty for closure without notice

Any employer who closes down any undertaking without complying with the provisions of section 25FFA shall be punishable with imprisonment for a term which may extend to six months, or with fine which may extend to five thousand rupees, or with both.

Section 31: Penalty for other offences

(1) Any employer who contravenes the provisions of section 33 shall be punishable with imprisonment for a term which may extend to six months, or with fine which may extend to one thousand rupees, or with both.

(2) Whoever contravenes any of the provisions of this Act or any rule made thereunder shall, if no other penalty is elsewhere provided by or under this Act for such contravention, be punishable with fine which may extend to one hundred rupees.

Chapter VII

MISCELLANEOUS

Section 32: Offence by companies, etc.

Where a person committing an offence under this Act is a company, or other body corporate, or an association of persons (whether incorporated or not), every director, manager, secretary, agent or other officer or person concerned with the management thereof shall, unless he proves that the offence was committed without his knowledge or consent, be deemed to be guilty of such offence.

SECTION 33: Conditions of service, etc., to remain unchanged under certain circumstances during pendency of proceedings

(1) During the pendency of any conciliation proceeding before a conciliation officer or a Board or of any proceeding before an arbitrator or a Labour Court or Tribunal or National Tribunal in respect of an industrial dispute, no employer shall,—

(a) in regard to any matter connected with the dispute, alter, to the prejudice of the workmen concerned in such dispute, the conditions of service applicable to them immediately before the commencement of such proceeding; or

(b) for any misconduct connected with the dispute, discharge or punish, whether by dismissal or otherwise, any workmen concerned in such dispute,

save with the express permission in writing of the authority before which the proceeding is pending.

(2) During the pendency of any such proceeding in respect of an industrial dispute, the employer may, in accordance with the standing orders applicable to a workman concerned in such dispute or, where there are no such standing orders, in accordance with the terms of the contract, whether express or implied, between him and the workman,—

(a) alter, in regard to any matter not connected with the dispute, the conditions of service applicable to that workman immediately before the commencement of such proceeding; or

(b) for any misconduct not connected with the dispute, or discharge or punish, whether by dismissal or otherwise, that workman:

Provided that no such workman shall be discharged or dismissed, unless he has been paid wages for one month and an application has been made by the employer to the authority before which the proceeding is pending for approval of the action taken by the employer.

(3) Notwithstanding anything contained in sub-section (2), no employer shall, during the pendency of any such proceeding in respect of an industrial dispute, take any action against any protected workman concerned in such dispute,—

(a) by altering, to the prejudice of such protected workman, the conditions of service applicable to him immediately before the commencement of such proceedings; or

(b) by discharging or punishing, whether by dismissal or otherwise, such protected workman,

save with the express permission in writing of the authority before which the proceeding is pending.

Explanation: For the purposes of this sub-section, a "protected workman", in relation to an establishment, means a workman who, being a member of the executive or other office bearer of a registered trade union connected with the establishment, is recognised as such in accordance with rules made in this behalf.

(4) In every establishment, the number of workmen to be recognised as protected workmen for the purposes of sub-section (3) shall be one per cent of the total number of workmen employed therein subject to a minimum number of five protected workmen and a maximum number of one hundred protected workmen and for the aforesaid purpose, the appropriate Government may make rules providing for the distribution of such protected workmen among various trade unions, if any, connected with the establishment and the manner in which the workmen may be chosen and recognised as protected workmen.

(5) Where an employer makes an application to a conciliation officer, Board, an arbitrator, a labour Court, Tribunal or National Tribunal under the proviso to sub-section (2) for approval of the action taken by him, the authority concerned shall, without delay, hear such application and pass, within a period of three months from the date of receipt of such application, such order in relation thereto as it deems fit:

Provided that where any such authority considers it necessary or expedient so to do, it may, for reasons to be recorded in writing, extend such period by such further period as it may think fit:

Provided further that no proceedings before any such authority shall lapse merely on the ground that any period specified in this sub-section had expired without such proceedings being completed.

The object of S. 33 is to provide for the continuance and termination of the pending proceedings in a peaceful atmosphere, undisturbed by any causes of friction between the employer and his employees. In substance, it insists upon the maintenance of the status quo pending the disposal of the industrial dispute between the parties; nevertheless, it recognises that occasions may arise when the employer may be justified in discharging or punishing his employees by dismissal; and so it allows the employer to take such action subject to the condition that before doing so, he must obtain the express permission in writing of the Tribunal. The ban is imposed in terms which are mandatory and S. 31(1) makes the contravention of the provisions of S. 33 an offence punishable as prescribed therein. Where an application is made by the employer for the requisite permission under S. 33, the jurisdiction of the Tribunal in dealing with such an application is limited. It has to consider whether a prima facie case has been made out by the employer for the dismissal of the employee in question. If the employer has held a proper enquiry into the alleged misconduct of the employee, and it does not appear that the proposed dismissal of the employee amounts to victimization or an unfair labour practice, the Tribunal has to limit its enquiry only to the question as to whether a *prima facie* case has been made out or not. In these proceedings, it is not open to the Tribunal to consider whether the order proposed to be passed by the employer is proper or adequate, or whether it errs on the side of excessive severity; nor can the Tribunal grant permission, subject to certain conditions, which it may deem to be fair. But it is significant that even if the requisite permission is granted to the employer under S. 33, that would not be the end of the matter. It is not that the permission granted under S. 33 validates the order of dismissal. It merely removes the ban; and so the validity of the order of dismissal still can be, and often is, challenged by the union of the employees by raising an industrial dispute in that behalf. The effect of compliance with the provisions of S. 33 is thus substantially different from the effect of compliance with Art. 311(2) of the

Constitution. In the latter classes of cases, an order of dismissal passed after duly complying with the relevant statutory provisions is final and its validity or propriety is no longer open to dispute; but in the case of S. 33, the removal of the ban merely enables the employer to make an order of dismissal and thus avoid incurring the penalty imposed by S. 31(1).

Where the employer fails to establish his specific case against any of the employees dismissed by him in contravention of S. 33, there is no reason why the normal rule should not prevail and the employees should not get the relief of reinstatement. The mere fact that the employer may have employed some other persons in the meanwhile would not necessarily defeat such a claim for reinstatement. However, much the court may sympathise with the employer's difficulty, caused by the fact that after the wrongful dismissals in question he had engaged fresh hands, the court cannot overlook the claims of the employees who had been wrongly dismissed. In the case of such wrongful dismissal, the normal rule would be that the employees thus wrongfully dismissed must be reinstated.[262] From the provisions of S. 33 it is manifest that punitive action by the employer, in whatever from it may be passed, is permissible against an ordinary workman, as distinguished from a protected workman, even during the pendency of proceedings before the Tribunal provided that the employer pays one month's wages and also applies to the Tribunal concerned for approval of his action. Since the action is punitive, namely, dismissal or discharge for misconduct, the Tribunal has to oversee the action to guarantee that no unfair labour practice or victimisation has been practised thereby. If the procedure of fair hearing has been observed, the Tribunal has to find in an application under S. 33 that a *prima facie* case is made out for dismissal. If, on the other hand, there is violation of the principles of natural justice in the enquiry, the Tribunal can go into the whole question relating to the misconduct and come to its own conclusion whether the same is established. Termination simpliciter or automatic termination of service under the conditions of service or under the standing orders is outside the scope of S. 33 of the Act. This does not mean that the employer has the last word about the termination of service of an employee and can get away with it by describing it to be a simple termination in his letter of discharge addressed to the employee. It is also not a correct proposition of law that in case of a complaint under S. 33A, the Tribunal would be debarred from going into the question whether, notwithstanding the form of the order, in substance, it is an action of dismissal for misconduct and not termination simpliciter.[263]

After reading Ss. 33 and 33A jointly, it appears that both the provisions intend to protect the workmen concerned in the disputes which form the subject matter of pending conciliation proceedings or proceedings by way of reference under S. 10 of the Act, against victimization by the employer on account of raising or continuing such pending disputes and to ensure that those pending proceedings are brought to expeditious termination in a peaceful atmosphere, undisturbed by any subsequent cause tending to further exacerbate the already strained relations between the employer and the workmen. To achieve this objective, a ban, subject to certain conditions, has been imposed by S. 33 on the ordinary right of the employer to alter the terms of his employees' services to their prejudice or to terminate their services under the general law governing contract of employment and S. 33A

262. *Punjab National Bank Ltd.* v. *All India Punjab National Bank Employees' Federation,* AIR 1960 SC 160.
263. *Mahendra Singh Dhantwal* v. *Hindustan Motors Ltd.,* AIR 1976 SC 2062.

provides for relief against contravention of S. 33, by way of adjudication of the complaints by aggrieved workmen considering them to be disputes referred or pending in accordance with the provisions of the Act. This ban, however, is designed to restrict interference with the general rights and liabilities of the parties under the ordinary law within the limits truly necessary for accomplishing the above objective. The employer is accordingly left free to deal with the employees when the action concerned is not punitive or mala fide or does not amount to victimisation or unfair labour practice. The anxiety of the legislature to effectively achieve the object of duly protecting the workmen against victimisation or unfair labour practices consistently with the preservation of the employer's bona fide right to maintain discipline and efficiency in the industry for securing the maximum production in a peaceful harmonious atmosphere is obvious from the overall scheme of these sections. Turning first to S. 33(1), which deals with the case of a workman concerned in a pending dispute who has been prejudicially affected by an action in regard to a matter connected with such pending dispute and S. 33(2) similarly deals with workmen concerned in regard to matters unconnected with such pending disputes. Section 33(1) bans alteration to the prejudice of the workman concerned in the conditions of service applicable to him immediately before the commencement of the proceedings and discharge or punishment whether by dismissal or otherwise of the workman concerned for misconduct connected with the dispute without express permission in writing of the authority dealing with the pending proceeding. Section 33(2) places a similar ban in regard to matters not connected with the pending dispute but the employer is free to discharge or dismiss the workman by paying wages for one month provided he applies to the authority dealing with the pending proceeding for approval of the action taken. It is noteworthy that the ban is imposed only in regard to action taken for misconduct whether connected or unconnected with the dispute. The employer is, therefore, free to take action against his workmen if it is not based on any misconduct on their part. In this connection, reference by way of contrast may be made to S. 33(3) which imposes an unqualified ban on the employer in regard to action by discharging or punishing the workman by dismissal or otherwise. Section 33 (3) protects "protected workman" and the reason is obvious for the blanket protection of such a workman. The legislature appears to be anxious for the interest of healthy growth and development of trade union movement to ensure them a complete protection against every kind of order of discharge or punishment because of their special position as an officer of a registered trade union recognised as such in accordance with the rules made in that behalf.

Section 33 in a Nutshell

It is very much clear that even during the pendency of an industrial dispute, the employer's right to make an alteration in the conditions of service is now recognised so long as it does not relate to a matter connected with the pending dispute, and this right can be exercised by him in accordance with the relevant standing orders. In regard to such alteration, no application is required to be made and no approval required to be obtained. When an employer, however, wants to dismiss or discharge a workman for alleged misconduct not connected with the dispute, he can do so in accordance with the standing orders but a ban is imposed on the exercise of this power by the proviso. The proviso requires that no such workman shall be discharged or dismissed unless two conditions are satisfied; the *first* is that the employee concerned should have been paid wages for one month, and the *second* is that an application should have been made by the employer to the appropriate authority for approval of the action taken. It is plain that whereas in cases falling under S. 33(1) no action can be taken by the employer unless he has obtained previously the express permission of the appropriate authority in writing, in cases falling under sub-section (2) the employer is required to satisfy the specified conditions but he need not necessarily obtain the previous consent in writing before he takes any action. The requirement that he must obtain 'approval' as distinguished from the requirement that he must obtain 'previous permission' indicates that the ban imposed by S. 33(2) is not as rigid or rigorous as that imposed by S. 33(1). The jurisdiction to give or withhold permission is prima facie wider than the jurisdiction to give or withhold approval. In dealing with the cases falling under S. 33(2), the industrial authority will be entitled to enquire whether the proposed action is in accordance with the standing orders, whether the employee concerned has been paid wages for one month, and whether an application has been made for approval as prescribed by the said sub-section. It is obvious that in cases of alteration of conditions of service falling under S. 33(2)(a), no such approval is required and the right of the employer remains unaffected by any ban. Therefore, putting it negatively, the jurisdiction of the appropriate industrial authority in holding an enquiry under S. 33(2)(b) cannot be wider and is, if at all, more limited than that permitted under S. 33(1), and in exercising its powers under S. 33(2) the appropriate authority must bear in mind the departure deliberately made by the legislature in separating the two classes of cases falling under the two sub-sections, and in providing for express permission in one case and only approval in the other. It is true that it would be competent to the authority in a proper case to refuse to give approval, for S. 33(5) expressly empowers the authority to pass such order in relation to the application made before it under the proviso to S. 33(2)(b) as it may deem fit; it may either approve or refuse to approve; it can, however, impose no conditions and pass no conditional order.

Section 33(3) deals with cases of protected workmen and it assimilates cases of alterations of conditions of service or orders of discharge or dismissal proposed to be made or passed in respect of them to cases falling under S. 33(1); in other words, where an employer wants to alter conditions of service in regard to a protected workman, or to pass an order of discharge or dismissal against him, a ban is imposed on his rights to take such action in the same manner in which it has been imposed under S. 33(1). Sub-section (4) provides for the recognition of protected workmen, and limits their number as therein indicated; and sub-section (5) requires that where an employer has made an application under the proviso to sub-section (2), the authority concerned shall without delay hear such application and pass as expeditiously as possible such orders in relation thereto as it deems fit. This provision brings out the legislative intention that, though an express permission in writing is not required in cases falling under the proviso to S. 33(2)(b), it is desirable that there should not be any time lag between the action taken by the employer and the order passed by the appropriate authority in an enquiry under the said proviso.

In order to attract S. 33(1)(a), the following features must be present:

(1) There is a proceeding in respect of an industrial dispute pending before the Tribunal.

(2) Conditions of service of the workmen applicable immediately before the commencement of the Tribunal proceeding are altered.

(3) The alteration of the conditions of service is in regard to a matter connected with the pending industrial dispute.

(4) The workmen whose conditions of service are altered are concerned in the pending industrial dispute.

(5) The alteration of the conditions of service is to the prejudice of the workmen.

Workmen Concerned in Such Dispute

The expression *workmen concerned in such dispute* in S. 33(1)(a) is not limited to the workmen directly or actually concerned in such dispute, but includes all workmen on whose behalf the dispute has been raised as well as those who would be bound by the award which may be made in the said dispute. Where an industrial dispute regarding some workmen was pending, the workmen under whom these workmen were working, is *a workman concerned in such dispute*, and if he is dismissed without the written permission of the Tribunal before whom the dispute is pending, he can make a complaint under S. 33A.[264]

During The Pendency of Any Proceeding

Both sub-section (1) and sub-section (2) of S. 33 employ the language *during the pendency of any proceeding* which clearly convey that obligation on the part of the employer under the said Section of seeking *express permission* for the purpose of sub-section (1) or *approval* for the purpose of sub-section (2) arises only when there are proceedings pending on industrial dispute before the Tribunal or other specified statutory adjudicatory authorities under the Act.

A dispute cannot be said to be pending before an Industrial Tribunal for the purpose of proviso to S. 33(2)(b) during the period when operation of the order of reference of dispute itself remained stayed. The Tribunal gets jurisdiction only on the reference made by the Government. When the operation of the very order of reference is stayed, the question of dispute pending before the Tribunal does not arise inasmuch as the reference order itself stand suspended. So long as the stay order is operating, it cannot be said that the dispute is pending before the Tribunal. Once the operation of order of reference is stayed, there is no question of dispute pending before the Tribunal so long as the said order remains in operation because reference precedes dispute. The effect of grant of stay of operation of the order of industrial reference is that the Industrial Tribunal cannot take up the reference for adjudication. Consequently, no action based on such reference can be taken by the Tribunal including grant or refusal of approval to the disciplinary action under S. 33(2) of the Act. The employer cannot, therefore, approach the Tribunal for seeking approval to its disciplinary action so long as the order of reference remains stayed by the order of the High Court. The provisions of S. 33 of the Act are attracted only when an industrial dispute is pending for adjudication and not merely when an order of reference is made by the Government.[265]

264. *New India Motors (P.) Ltd., M/s. New Delhi* v. *K.T. Morris,* AIR 1960 SC 875.
265. *B.P.L. Ltd., M/s.* v. *R. Sudhakar,* AIR 2004 SC 3606.

Section 33 and Suspension

The question came before the Supreme Court in *Management Hotel Imperial, New Delhi* v. *Hotel Workers' Union*[266] whether any wages to be paid to the workmen who are suspended pending permission being sought under S. 33 of the Act for their dismissal?

The Supreme Court deals with a basic question in this case that whether an employer is empowered to suspend an employee under the ordinary law of master and servant. The Court observed that it is now well settled that the power to suspend, in the sense of a right to forbid a servant to work, is not an implied term in an ordinary contract between master and servant, and that such a power can only be the creature either of a statute governing the contract, or of an express term in the contract itself. Ordinarily, therefore, the absence of such power either as an express term in the contract or in the rules framed under some statute would mean that the master would have no power to suspend a workman and even if he does so in the sense that he forbids the employee to work, he will have to pay wages during the so-called period of suspension. Where, however, there is a power to suspend either in the contract of employment or in the statute or the rules framed thereunder, the suspension has the effect of temporarily suspending the relation of master and servant with the consequence that the servant is not bound to render service and the master is not bound to pay. The Court, while dealing the issue as aforesaid, is of opinion that the ordinary law of master and servant as to suspension can be and should be held to have been modified in view of the fundamental change introduced by S. 33 in that law, and a term should be implied by Industrial Tribunals in the contract of employment that if the master has held a proper enquiry and come to the conclusion that the servant should be dismissed and in consequence suspends him, pending the permission required under S. 33, he has the power to order such suspension, thus suspending the contract of employment temporarily, so that there is no obligation on him to pay wages and no obligation on the servant to work. In dealing with this point, the basic and decisive consideration introduced by S. 33 must be borne in mind. The undisputed common law right of the master to dismiss his servant for proper cause has been subjected by S. 33 to a ban; and that in fairness must mean that, pending the removal of the said statutory ban, the master can, after holding a proper enquiry, temporarily terminate the relationship of master and servant by suspending his employee pending proceedings under S. 33. It follows therefore that if the Tribunal grants permission, the suspended contract would come to an end and there will be no further obligation to pay any wages after the date of suspension. If, on the other hand, the permission is refused, the suspension would be wrong and the workman would be entitled to all his wages from the date of suspension.

In *Fakirbhai Fulabhai Solanki* v. *Presiding Officer,*[267] where during the pendency of a reference made under the Industrial Disputes Act, 1947 (hereinafter referred to as 'the Act') to the Industrial Tribunal, Gujarat, the management served a charge-sheet on the appellant who was one of the workmen working in the factory belonging to the management of the Alembic Chemical Works Co. Ltd., Baroda, asking him to show cause why disciplinary action should not be taken against him for an alleged act of misconduct said to have been committed by him. The act of misconduct attributed to the appellant was that he was

266. AIR 1959 SC 1342.
267. AIR 1986 SC 1168.

playing cards along with two other workmen during the working hours of the factory. It was alleged that the appellant had given a letter addressed to Manager, Industrial Relations, Alembic Chemical Works Co. Ltd. admitting his guilt and tendering apology. The disciplinary enquiry was held against all the three workmen including the appellant. At the conclusion of the enquiry, the appellant was found guilty of the act of misconduct alleged to have been committed by him by the Inquiry Officer and it was decided by the management to dismiss him, but because the appellant was a protected workman as defined in the Explanation to sub-section (3) of S. 33 of the Act, permission of the Tribunal had to be obtained before dismissing him. The management made an application before the Tribunal for such permission. The appellant was, however, suspended from service with effect pending disposal of the application before the Tribunal but without any wages or allowances. The appellant also filed an application before the Tribunal under S. 33A of the Act complaining violation of S. 33 of the Act by the management. The Tribunal granted permission to the management to dismiss the appellant and rejected the complaint filed by him. Aggrieved by the said decision of the Tribunal, the appellant approached the Supreme Court by special leave under Art. 136 of the Constitution. The Court observed that the denial of payment of subsistence allowance to a workman placed under suspension during the pendency of the proceeding under S. 33(3) amounts to violation of the principles of natural justice. Since it is difficult to anticipate the result of the application made before the Tribunal, it is reasonable to hold that the workman against whom the application is made should be paid some amount by way of subsistence allowance to enable him to maintain himself and members of his family and also to meet the expenses of the litigation before the Tribunal. And if no amount is paid during the pendency of such an application, it has to be held that the workman concerned has been denied a reasonable opportunity to defend himself in the proceedings before the Tribunal. Such denial leads to violation of the principles of natural justice and consequently vitiates the proceedings before the Tribunal under sub-section (3) of S. 33 of the Act and any decision given in those proceedings against the workman concerned. There was also no material in this case to show that the appellant had sufficient means to defend himself before the Tribunal.

As in the instant case the permission was granted nearly after 6 years of application, the Court showed its dissatisfaction and held that an unscrupulous management may by all possible means delay the proceedings so that the workman may be driven to accept its terms instead of defending himself in the proceedings under S. 33(3) of the Act. To expect an ordinary workman to wait for such a long time in these days is to expect something which is very unusual to happen. Denial of payment of at least a small amount by way of subsistence allowance would amount to gross unfairness.

It is likely that in some cases filed under S. 33(1) or S. 33(3) of the Act (which are 'permission' clauses and not 'approval' clauses) pending before any authority, the management may not be paying any subsistence allowance to the workman concerned. It may be clarified that in such cases it shall be open to the management to pay within a reasonable time, to be fixed by the authority, the subsistence allowance for the period during which the workman is kept under suspension without wages and to continue the proceedings. Such subsistence allowance shall be the amount fixed under the Standing Orders, if any, which the management is liable to pay to the workman if he is kept under suspension during the pendency of such application, or in the absence of any such Standing Order by the authority before which such application is pending. In a case where the proceedings are completed and the order of dismissal is successfully challenged on the ground of non-payment of subsistence allowance for the period of suspension during the pendency of the application under S. 33(1) or S. 33(3) of the Act, it shall be open to the management to ask for the permission of the authority again under S. 33(1) or S. 33(3) of the Act after paying or offering to pay to the workman concerned within a reasonable time to be fixed by the authority concerned the arrears of subsistence allowance at the specified rate. But in the instant case, however, having regard to the circumstances of the case, the Court did not grant any such opportunity to the management to apply for permission again under S. 33(3) of the Act. Accordingly, the Court set aside the order/award of the Tribunal and dismissed the application made by the management under S. 33(3) of the Act and directed the management to reinstate the appellant in its service and to pay him all the wages and allowances due to him as if there was no break in the continuity of his service.

The Supreme Court in *M. Paul Anthony, Capt.* v. *Bharat Gold Mines Ltd.*[268] has taken a critical note in the case of non-payment of subsistence allowance during the suspension period. This case, of course, does not fall within the ambit of S. 33 of the Industrial Disputes Act, nevertheless, it can throw some light on the issue of non-payment of subsistence allowance during the period of suspension. The Supreme Court observed that on joining Government service, a person does not mortgage or barter away his basic rights as a human being, including his fundamental rights, in favour of the Government. The Government does not become the master of the body and soul of the employee just because it has power to appoint. The fundamental rights, including the right to life under Art. 21 of the Constitution or the basic human rights, are not surrendered by the employee. The provision for payment of subsistence allowance made in the Service Rules only ensures non-violation of the right to life of the employee. The Government by providing job opportunities to its citizens only fulfils its obligations under the Constitution, including the Directive Principles of the State Policy. The employee, on taking up an employment, only agrees to subject himself to the regulatory measures concerning his service. His association with the Government or any other employer, like Instrumentalist of the Government or Statutory or Autonomous Corporations etc., is regulated by the terms of contract of service or Service Rules made by the Central or the State Government under the Proviso to Art. 309 of the Constitution or other Statutory Rules including Certified Standing Orders.

Where the employee was not provided any subsistence allowance during the period of suspension and the adjournment prayed for by him on account of his illness, duly supported by medical certificates, was refused resulting in *ex parte* proceedings against him, the appellant has been punished in total violation of the principles of natural justice and he was literally not afforded any opportunity of hearing. Moreover, on account of his penury occasioned by non-payment of subsistence allowance, during pendency of departmental proceedings he could not undertake a journey to attend the disciplinary proceedings from his home town, the findings recorded by the Inquiry Officer at such proceedings, which were held *ex parte*, stand vitiated.

Suspension notwithstanding, non-payment of subsistence allowance is an inhuman act which has an unpropitious effect on the life of an employee. When the employee is placed

268. AIR 1999 SC 1416.

under suspension, he is demobilised and the salary is also paid to him at a reduced rate under the nick name of 'subsistence allowance', so that the employee may sustain himself. The very object of paying the reduced salary to the employee during the period of suspension would be frustrated. If even subsistence allowance is not paid because 'subsistence' means supporting life, especially a minimum livelihood. The act of non-payment of subsistence allowance can act as slow-poison, as the employee, if not permitted to sustain himself on account of non-payment of subsistence allowance, would gradually starve himself to death.

In *Ram Lakhan* v. *Presiding Officer*[269] the Supreme Court held that if the management has held a departmental enquiry against an employee, it has the right to place that employee under suspension, if on the basis of the findings recorded at the departmental enquiry, the management is, prima facie, of the opinion that the employee, on account of the charges having been proved, was liable to be dismissed from service. But the final order of dismissal could not be passed on account of a reference raised under the Industrial Disputes Act, 1947, which was already pending before the Tribunal. In such a situation, if the management makes an application under S. 33(1) of the Industrial Disputes Act for permission of the Tribunal to dismiss such employee from service, the management can, pending disposal of his application under S. 33(1), place that employee under suspension. Once the employee is placed under suspension, the management cannot take any work from the suspended employee nor can the employee claim full salary from the management. But the management has to pay the subsistence allowance to the employee so that he may sustain himself till the application under S. 33(1) is finally disposed of.

Just as the employer has no control over the disposal of the application under S. 33(1) of the Industrial Disputes Act, so also the employee has no control over the disposal of that application. Whether the employee would be retained in service or removed would be dependent upon the fate of the application. While the management can afford to wait for the disposal of that application, it would be impossible for an employee to survive only on his salary and wait for the disposal of that application for an indefinite period. It would not be possible for him to sustain himself. It is in this light that the right to receive reduced salary (subsistence allowance) for the period of suspension has to be read along with the right of the management to place the employee under suspension pending disposal of the application under S. 33(1) of the Industrial Disputes Act. Thus, the right of management to suspend and the right of the employee to receive subsistence allowance are intertwined and both must survive together.

Section 33(2)

Section 33 of the Act makes provision for insuring that the conditions of service remain unchanged during pendency of certain proceedings. Section 33(1) lays down that if an employer proposes to discharge a workman in relation to a matter connected with the dispute which might be pending before a Tribunal, the employer must put such proposal before the Tribunal and obtain its express permission in writing before carrying out the proposal whether it be for alteration of any conditions of service or for punishment or discharge of a workman by dismissal or otherwise.

269. AIR 2000 SC 1946.

Sub-section (2)(a), on the other hand, gives power to the employer to alter any conditions of service not connected with the dispute and this the employer can do without approaching the Tribunal where the dispute may be pending. It further permits the employer to discharge or punish, whether by dismissal or otherwise, any workman where this may be on account of any matters unconnected with the dispute pending before the Tribunal; but such discharge or dismissal is subject to the proviso, which imposes certain conditions on it. In other words, sub-section (2) of S. 33 deals with alteration in the conditions of service or the discharge or punishment by dismissal or otherwise of the workman concerned in the pending dispute but in regard to any matter not connected with such pending dispute. Though this provision also places a ban in regard to matters not connected with the pending dispute, it leaves the employer free to discharge or dismiss a workman by paying wages for one month and making an application to the authority dealing with the pending proceedings for its *'approval'* of the action taken. The action taken under S. 33(2) will become effective only if *'approval'* is granted. If the *'approval'* is refused, the order of dismissal will be invalid and inoperative in law. In other words, the order of dismissal has to be treated as *non est* and the workman will be taken to have never been dismissed.

In *M.D., T.N. State Transport Corpn.* v. *Neethivilangan Kumbakonam*,[270] the core question that arose for determination was what is the right of a workman after the application filed by the employer for approval of the order of his dismissal/discharge from service is refused by the Tribunal and what remedy is available to the workman in such a situation.

The facts of the case may be shortly stated thus: the appellant, *Tamil Nadu State Transport Corporation Ltd.,* initiated a departmental inquiry against the respondent *Neethivilangan,* who was a Junior Superintendent in the Head Office. The charges having been established in the departmental inquiry, an order for dismissing the respondent from service was passed. Thereafter, an application was made by the appellant for accord of approval under S. 33(2)(b), before the Tribunal. The Tribunal rejected the prayer for approval on merit. The appellant filed a writ petition challenging the order passed by the Tribunal, which was dismissed by the High Court. The appellant filed special leave petition in the Supreme Court which was also dismissed. Even after it failed to obtain approval of the Tribunal for the order of removal of the respondent, the appellant neither reinstated him in service nor paid him wages. The resultant position was that the respondent remained without work and without wages, though he was ready and willing to render service in the establishment. Under the compelling circumstances as noted above, the respondent filed a writ petition for reinstatement in service, for payment of wages and other consequential benefits. A single Judge of the High Court by the judgment allowed the writ petition on the following terms:

> "In the result, all the points (A) to (D) are answered in favour of the petitioner and against the respondent. This Court further holds that the petitioner is deemed to have been in service continuously since 5-3-1984 (the date of dismissal order passed by the management) onwards and deemed to be discharging his functions as an employee of the respondent and he is entitled to all arrears of salary with annual increments and all attendant and concomitant benefit for the said period and till date of reinstatement. There will be a direction directing the respondent to work out the money value of the same and pay the arrears within 12 weeks from today…."

270. AIR 2001 SC 2309.

The writ appeal filed by the appellant against the said judgment was dismissed by the Division Bench. Hence this appeal by the employer by special leave. The Supreme Court while dismissing the appeal held that while the employer has the discretion to initiate a departmental inquiry and pass an order of dismissal or discharge against the workman, the order remains in an inchoate state till the employer obtains order of approval from the Tribunal. By passing the order of discharge or dismissal, *de facto* relationship of employer and employee may be ended but not the *de jure* relationship, for that could happen only when the Tribunal accords its approval. The relationship of the employer and employee is not legally terminated till approval of discharge or dismissal is given by the Tribunal. In a case where the Tribunal refuses to accord approval to the action taken by the employer and rejects the petition filed under S. 33(2)(b) of the Act on merit, the employer is bound to treat the employee as continuing in service and give him all the consequential benefits. If the employer refuses to grant the benefits to the employee, the latter is entitled to have his right enforced by filing a petition under Art. 226 of the Constitution. There is no rational basis for holding that even after the order of dismissal or discharge has been rendered invalid on the Tribunal's rejection of the prayer for approval, the workman should suffer the consequences of such invalid order of dismissal or discharge till the matter is decided by the Tribunal again in an industrial dispute. Accepting this contention would render the bar contained in S. 33(1) irrelevant.

Effect of Contravention of Section 33(2)(b)

The principal question which arose before the Supreme Court in *Punjab Beverages Pvt. Ltd., M/s. Chandigarh* v. *Suresh Chand*[271] for consideration was, what is the effect of contravention of S. 33(2)(b) on an order of dismissal passed by an employer in breach of it. Does it render the order of dismissal void and inoperative so that the aggrieved workman can say that he continues to be in service and is entitled to receive wages from the employer?

The Court while dealing with the aforesaid issue observed that the contravention of S. 33 does not render the order of discharge or dismissal void and inoperative. The only remedy available to the workman for challenging the order of discharge or dismissal is provided under S. 33A, apart, of course, from the remedy under S. 10, and he cannot maintain an application under S. 33C(2) for determination and payment of wages on the basis that he continues to be in service. The workman can proceed under S. 33C(2) only after the Tribunal has adjudicated on a complaint under S. 33A, or on a reference under S. 10, that the order of discharge or dismissal passed by the employer was not justified and has set aside that order and reinstated the workman.

The withdrawal of the application for approval stands on the same footing as if no application under S. 33(2)(b) has been made at all, and in such cases it cannot be said that the approval has been refused by the Tribunal. The Tribunal having had no occasion to consider the application on merits, there can be no question of the Tribunal refusing approval to the employer. It is a well-settled rule of construction that not a single section of a statute should be read in isolation, but it should be construed with reference to the context and other provisions of the statute, so as, as far as possible, to make a consistent enactment of the whole statute. Section 33(2)(b) should be read with S. 33A and if these two sections are read together, it is

271. AIR 1978 SC 995.

clear that the legislative intent was not to invalidate an order of discharge or dismissal passed in contravention of S. 33, despite the mandatory language employed in the section and the penal provision enacted in S. 31(1).

Basing on the above observation, the Court held that mere contravention of S. 33 by the employer will not entitle the workman to an order of reinstatement, because inquiry under S. 33A is not confined only to the determination of the question as to whether the employer has contravened S. 33, but even if such contravention is proved, the Tribunal has to go further and deal also with the merits of the order of discharge or dismissal. The very fact that even after the contravention of S. 33 is proved, the Tribunal is required to go into the further question whether the order of discharge or dismissal passed by the employer is justified on the merits clearly indicates that the order of discharge is not rendered void and inoperative by such contravention. It is also significant to note that if the contravention of S. 33 were construed as having an invalidating effect on the order of discharge or dismissal, S. 33A would be rendered meaningless and futile. Such a highly anomalous result would never have been intended by the legislature.

The Supreme Court in this case followed the decision of *Equitable Coal Co.* case[272] and *Punjab National Bank* case.[273] It is important to note that *Punjab Beverages Pvt. Ltd.* case has been overruled by a Constitution Bench in *Jaipur Z.S.B.V. Bank Ltd.* v. *Ram Gopal Sharma.*[274] The necessity of constituting a Constitution Bench seems to be due to conflicting views expressed by the Supreme Court on the same issue in different cases in different times. The two Benches consisting of three learned Judges in *Strawboard Manufacturing Co.* v. *Govind*[275] and *Tata Iron and Steel Co. Ltd.* v. *S.N. Modak*,[276] have taken the view that if the approval is not granted under S. 33(2)(b) of the Industrial Disputes Act, 1947, the order of dismissal becomes ineffective from the date it was passed and, therefore, the employee becomes entitled to wages from the date of dismissal to the date of disapproval of the application. Another Bench of three learned Judges in *Punjab Beverages Pvt. Ltd. Chandigarh* v. *Suresh Chand and another*,[277] has expressed the contrary view that non-approval of the order of dismissal or failure to make application under S. 33(1)(b) would not render the order of dismissal inoperative; failure to apply for approval under S. 33(2)(b) would only render the employer liable to punishment under S. 31 of the Act and the remedy of the employee is either by way of a complaint under S. 33A or by way of a reference under S. 10(1)(d) of the Act.

It is important to note that a Constitution Bench of the Apex Court in the case of *P.H. Kalyani* v. *M/s. Air France Calcutta*,[278] referring to *Strawboard* case, has observed thus:

> "The main point which was raised in this appeal is now concluded by the decision of this Court in the *Strawboard Manufacturing Co. Limited, Saharanpur* v. *Govind.*[277] This Court has held in that case that "the proviso to S. 33(2)(b) contemplates the three things mentioned therein, namely, (i) dismissal or discharge, (ii) payment of wages, and

272. *Equitable Coal Co. Ltd.* v. *Algu Singh*, AIR 1958 SC 761.
273. *Punjab National Bank Ltd.* v. *All India Punjab National Bank Employees' Federation*, AIR 1960 SC 160.
274. AIR 2002 SC 643.
275. AIR 1962 SC 1500.
276. AIR 1966 SC 380.
277. AIR 1978 SC 995.
278. AIR 1963 SC 1756.

(iii) making of an application for approval, to be simultaneous and to be part of the same transaction so that the employer when he takes the action under S. 33(2) by dismissing or discharging an employee, should immediately pay him or offer to pay him wages for one month and also make an application to the tribunal for approval at the same time. It was further held that "the employer's conduct should show that the three things contemplated under the proviso, are parts of the same transaction; and the question whether the application was made as part of the same transaction or at the same time when the action was taken would be a question of fact and will depend upon the circumstances of each case."[279]

The Supreme Court in the instant case held that it is clear from the Proviso to S. 33(2)(b) that the employer may pass an order of dismissal or discharge and at the same time make an application for approval of the action taken by him. If the approval is not granted under S. 33(2)(b) of Industrial Disputes Act, 1947, the order of dismissal becomes ineffective from the date it was passed and failure to make application under S. 33(2)(b) would render the order of dismissal inoperative. In view of the decision of the Constitution Bench, the Supreme Court overruled the *Punjab Beverages* case and approved *Strawboard Mfg.* case and *Tata Iron and Steel Co.* case.

The Court further held that where an application is made under S. 33(2)(b) Proviso, the authority, before which the proceeding is pending for approval of the action taken by the employer, has to examine whether the order of dismissal or discharge is bona fide; whether it was by way of victimisation or unfair labour practice; whether the conditions contained in the proviso were complied with or not, etc. If the authority refuses to grant approval, obviously it follows that the employee continues to be in service as if the order of discharge or dismissal had never been passed. The order of dismissal or discharge passed invoking S. 33(2)(b) dismissing or discharging an employee brings the relationship of the employer and the employee to an end from the date of his dismissal or discharge, but that order remains incomplete and inchoate as it is subject to approval of the authority under the said provision. In other words, this relationship comes to an end *de jure* only when the authority grants approval. If approval is not given, nothing more is required to be done by the employee, as it will have to be deemed that the order of discharge or dismissal had never been passed. Consequently, the employee is deemed to have continued in service being entitled to all the benefits available. This being the position, there is no need of a separate or specific order for his reinstatement. But on the other hand, if approval is given by the authority and if the employee is aggrieved by such an approval, he is entitled to make a complaint under S. 33A challenging the order granting approval on any of the grounds available to him. Section 33A is available only to an employee and is intended to save his time and trouble inasmuch as he can straightway make a complaint before the very authority where the industrial dispute is already pending between the parties, challenging the order of approval instead of making efforts to raise an industrial dispute, get a reference and thereafter adjudication.

In this view, it is not correct to say that even though where the order of discharge or dismissal is inoperative for contravention of the mandatory conditions contained in the proviso, or where the approval is refused, a workman should still make a complaint under S. 33A and that the order of dismissal or discharge becomes invalid or void only when it is set aside under S. 33A, and that till such time he should suffer misery of unemployment in

279. *Ibid.* at p. 1758 per Wanchoo, J.

spite of statutory protection given to him by proviso to S. 33(2)(b). It is not correct to say that where the order of discharge or dismissal becomes inoperative because of contravention of proviso to S. 33(2)(b), S. 33A would be meaningless and futile. The said section has a definite purpose to serve, enabling an employee to make a complaint, if aggrieved by the order of the approval granted. Not making an application under S. 33(2)(b) seeking approval or withdrawing an application once made before any order is made thereon, is a clear case of contravention of proviso to S. 33(2)(b). An employer who does not make an application under S. 33(2)(b) or withdraws the one made, cannot be rewarded by relieving him of the statutory obligation imposed on him to make such an application. If it is so done, he will be happier or more comfortable than an employer who obeys the command of law and makes an application inviting scrutiny of the authority in the matter of granting approval of the action taken by him. Adherence to and obedience of law should be obvious and necessary in a system governed by rule of law. An employer by design can avoid to make an application after dismissing or discharging an employee, or file it and withdraw before any order is passed on it, on its merits, to take a position that such order is not inoperative or void till it is set aside under S. 33A notwithstanding the contravention of S. 33(2)(b) Proviso, driving the employee to have recourse to one or more proceeding by making a complaint under S. 33A or to raise another industrial dispute or to make a complaint under S. 31(1). Such an approach destroys the protection specifically and expressly given to an employee under the said proviso as against possible victimisation, unfair labour practice or harassment because of pendency of industrial dispute so that an employee can be saved from hardship of unemployment.

Section 31 speaks of penalty in respect of the offences stated therein. This provision is not intended to give any remedy to an aggrieved employee. It is only to punish the offender. The argument that S. 31 provides a remedy by an employee for contravention of S. 33 is unacceptable. Merely because penal provision is available or a workman has a further remedy under S. 33A to challenge the approval granted, it cannot be said that the order of discharge or dismissal does not become inoperative or invalid unless set aside under S. 33A. There is nothing in Ss. 31, 33 and 33A to suggest otherwise even reading them together in the context. These sections are intended to serve different purposes.

In *Indian Telephone Industries Ltd.* v. *Prabhakar H. Manjare*,[280] the company moved an application seeking approval of the order of dismissal of the respondent workman under S. 32(2)(b). The Tribunal found the order of dismissal invalid for non-compliance of the provisions of S. 33(2)(b) in that wages for one month were not paid; the order of the Tribunal remained unchallenged and reached finality. The company, treating the non-compliance of S. 33(2)(b) as mere technical breach, passed order of dismissal for the second time without any further/fresh inquiry and without paying wages to the respondent for the period from the date of first dismissal order, to the date of second dismissal order. The company again moved applications seeking approval of the order of dismissal before the Industrial Tribunal.

Held, having not challenged the earlier order of Tribunal refusing approval, it was not open to the company to make a second application seeking approval for the order of dismissal of the respondent, that too without paying full wages. Allowing the second application, seeking approval by the Tribunal by ignoring the dismissal of the earlier application made by the

280. AIR 2003 SC 195.

management for non-compliance of the mandatory provisions of law on the ground that the earlier application was not decided on merits, was not proper.

Section 33A: Special provision for adjudication as to whether conditions of service, etc., changed during pendency of proceedings

Where an employer contravenes the provisions of section 33 during the pendency of proceedings before a conciliation officer, Board, an arbitrator, a Labour Court, Tribunal or National Tribunal, any employee aggrieved by such contravention, may make a complaint in writing, in the prescribed manner,—

(a) to such conciliation officer or Board, and the conciliation officer or Board shall take such complaint into account in mediating in, and promoting the settlement of, such industrial dispute; and

(b) to such arbitrator, Labour Court, Tribunal or National Tribunal and on receipt of such complaint, the arbitrator, Labour Court, Tribunal or National Tribunal, as the case may be, shall adjudicate upon the complaint as if it were a dispute referred to or pending before it, in accordance with the provisions of this Act and shall submit his or its award to the appropriate Government and the provisions of this Act shall apply accordingly.

By S. 33A an employee aggrieved by a wrongful order of dismissal passed against him in contravention of S. 33 is given a right to move the Tribunal in redress of his grievance without having to take recourse to S. 10. In an enquiry under S. 33A, the employee would not succeed in obtaining an order of reinstatement merely by proving contravention of S. 33 by the employer. After such contravention is proved, it would still be open to the employer to justify the impugned dismissal on the merits. That is a part of the dispute which the Tribunal has to consider because the complaint made by the employee is treated as an industrial dispute and all the relevant aspects of the said dispute fall to be considered under S. 33A. Therefore, the enquiry under S. 33A is not confined only to the determination of the question as to whether the alleged contravention by the employer of the provisions of S. 33 has been proved or not. There can be no doubt that if under a complaint filed under S. 33A, a Tribunal has to deal not only with the question of contravention but also with the merits of the order of dismissal, the position cannot be any different when a reference is made to the Tribunal under S. 10. What is true about the scope of enquiry under S. 33A is *a fortiori* true in the case of an enquiry under S. 10.

A complaint can be made to the Tribunal under S. 33A of the Act if there has been violation or contravention of the provisions of S. 33 of the Act and if it is found that there has, in fact, been such a contravention, the Tribunal can proceed to adjudicate the dispute contained in a complaint on its merits. Thus, violation or contravention of the provisions of S. 33 of the Act would be the basic question that arises for consideration and before giving any relief to an aggrieved employee under this section, the Tribunal has to find out whether the employer's action falls within one of the following prohibitions contained in S. 33 of the Act.

(i) If the dispute pending adjudication has nothing to do with the alteration in conditions of service of a workman in contravention of S. 33(1)(a) of the Act or alteration of conditions of service of a 'protected workman' within S. 33(1) of the Act;

(ii) Discharges or punishes a workman by dismissal or otherwise for a misconduct connected with the pending dispute, without obtaining prior express permission in writing of the appropriate authority as required by S. 33(1)(b) of the Act;

(iii) Discharges or punishes a 'protected workman' by dismissal or otherwise for a misconduct not connected with the pending dispute, without obtaining prior express permission in writing of the appropriate authority as required by S. 33(3)(b) of the Act read with S. 33(1)(b) of the Act; or

(iv) Discharges or punishes a workman by dismissal or otherwise for a misconduct not connected with the pending dispute, without complying with the provisions of proviso to S. 33(2)(b) of the Act.

Thus, the contravention of the provisions of S. 33 of the Act is the foundation for exercise of the power under S. 33A of the Act. If this issue is answered against the employee, nothing further survives for consideration or action by the Tribunal under S. 33 of the Act. In other words, an application under S. 33A of the Act without proof of contravention of S. 33 of the Act would be incompetent.[281]

SECTION 33B: Power to transfer certain proceedings

(1) The appropriate Government may, by order in writing and for reasons to be stated therein, withdraw any proceeding under this Act pending before a Labour Court, Tribunal or National Tribunal and transfer the same to another Labour Court, Tribunal or National Tribunal, as the case may be, for the disposal of the proceeding and the Labour Court, Tribunal or National Tribunal to which the proceeding is so transferred may, subject to special directions in the order of transfer, proceed either de novo or from the stage at which it was so transferred:

Provided that where a proceeding under section 33 or section 33A is pending before a Tribunal or National Tribunal, the proceeding may also be transferred to a Labour Court.

(2) Without prejudice to the provisions of sub-section (1), any Tribunal or National Tribunal, if so authorized by the appropriate Government, may transfer any proceeding under section 33 or section 33A pending before it to any one of the Labour Courts specified for the disposal of such proceedings by the appropriate Government by notification in the Official Gazette and the Labour Court to which the proceeding is so transferred shall dispose of the same.

SECTION 33C: Recovery of money due from an employer

(1) Where any money is due to a workman from an employer under a settlement or an award or under the provisions of Chapter V-A or Chapter V-B, the workman

281. *Blue Star Employees' Union* v. *Ex. Off. Principal Secy. to Government*, AIR 2000 SC 3110.

himself or any other person authorised by him in writing in this behalf, or, in the case of the death of the workman, his assignee or heirs may, without prejudice to any other mode of recovery, make an application to the appropriate Government for the recovery of the money due to him, and if the appropriate Government is satisfied that any money is so due, it shall issue a certificate for that amount to the Collector who shall proceed to recover the same in the same manner as an arrear of land revenue:

Provided that every such application shall be made within one year from the date on which the money became due to the workman from the employer:

Provided further that any such application may be entertained after the expiry of the said period of one year, if the appropriate Government is satisfied that the applicant had sufficient cause for not making the application within the said period.

(2) Where any workman is entitled to receive from the employer any money or any benefit which is capable of being computed in terms of money and if any question arises as to the amount of money due or as to the amount at which such benefit should be computed, then the question may, subject to any rules that may be made under this Act, be decided by such Labour Court as may be specified in this behalf by the appropriate Government; within a period not exceeding three months:

Provided that where the presiding officer of a Labour Court considers it necessary or expedient so to do, he may, for reasons to be recorded in writing, extend such period by such further period as he may think fit.

(3) For the purposes of computing the money value of a benefit, the Labour Court may, if it so thinks fit, appoint a Commissioner who shall, after taking such evidence as may be necessary, submit a report to the Labour Court and the Labour Court shall determine the amount after considering the report of the Commissioner and other circumstances of the case.

(4) The decision of the Labour Court shall be forwarded by it to the appropriate Government and any amount found due by the Labour Court may be recovered in the manner provided for in sub-section (1).

(5) Where workmen employed under the same employer are entitled to receive from him any money or any benefit capable of being computed in terms of money, then, subject to such rules as may be made in this behalf, a single application for the recovery of the amount due may be made on behalf of or in respect of any number of such workmen.

Explanation: In this section "Labour Court" includes any court constituted under any law relating to investigation and settlement of industrial disputes in force in any State.

Section 33C(1) provides for a kind of execution proceedings and it contemplates that if money is due to a workman under a settlement or an award, or under the provisions of Chapter V-A, the workman is not compelled to take resort to the ordinary course of execution in the Civil Court, but may adopt a summary procedure prescribed by this sub-section. This sub-section postulates that a specific amount is due to the workman and the same has not been paid to him. If the appropriate Government is satisfied that the money is so due, then it is required to issue a certificate for the said amount to the Collector and that leads to the recovery of the said amount in the same manner as an arrear of land revenue.

The word "*benefit*" used in S. 33C(2) is not confined merely to non-monetary benefit which could be converted in terms of money; it takes in all kinds of benefits which may be monetary as well as non-monetary if the workman is entitled to them, and in such a case, the workman is given the remedy of moving the appropriate Labour Court with a request that the said benefits be computed or calculated in terms of money. Once such computation or calculation is made under S. 33C(2), the amount so determined has to be recovered as provided for in sub-section (1). In other words, having provided for the determination of the amount due to the workman in cases falling under sub-section (2), the legislature has clearly prescribed that for recovering the said amount, the workman has to revert to his remedy under sub-section (1).

Sub-section (3) empowers the Labour Court to appoint a Commissioner for the purposes of computing the money value of the benefit, and it lays down that if so appointed, the Commissioner shall take such evidence as may be necessary and submit his report to the Labour Court. The Labour Court is then required to proceed to determine the amount in the light of the report submitted by the Commissioner and other circumstances of the case. This means that proceedings taken under sub-section (2) may be determined by the Labour Court itself or, in a suitable case, may be determined by it after receiving a report submitted by the Commissioner appointed in that behalf. It is clear that if for computing in terms of money the value of the benefit claimed by the workman, an enquiry is required to be held and evidence has to be taken, the Labour Court may do that itself or may delegate that work to a Commissioner appointed by it. This position must be taken to be well settled after the decision of the Supreme Court in the *Punjab National Bank Ltd.* v. *K.L. Kharbanda.*[282]

Claims made under S. 33C(1), by itself, can be only claims referable to the settlement, award or the relevant provisions of Chapter V-A. These words of limitations are not to be found in S. 33C(2) and, to that extent, the scope of S. 33C(2) is undoubtedly wider than that of S. 33C(1). The three categories of claims mentioned in S. 33C(1) fall under S. 33C(2) and in that sense, S. 33C(2) can itself be deemed to be a kind of execution proceeding; but it is possible that claims not based on settlements, awards or made under the provisions of Chapter V-A may also be competent under S. 33C(2) and that may illustrate its wider scope.

Some of the claims which would not fall under S. 33C(2) are as follows. If an employee is dismissed or demoted and it is his case that the dismissal or demotion is wrongful, it would not be open to him to make a claim for the recovery of his salary or wages under S. 33C(2). His demotion or dismissal may give rise to an industrial dispute which may be appropriately tried, but once it is shown that the employer has dismissed or demoted him, a claim that the dismissal or demotion is unlawful and therefore the employee continues to be the workman of the employer and is entitled to the benefits due to him under a pre-existing contract, cannot be made under S. 33C(2). If a settlement has been duly reached between the employer and his employees and it falls under S. 18(2) or (3) of the Act and is governed by S. 19(2), it would not be open to an employee, notwithstanding the said settlement, to claim the benefit as though the said settlement had come to an end. If the settlement exists and continues to be

282. AIR 1963 SC 487.

operative, no claim can be made under S. 33C(2) inconsistent with the said settlement. If the settlement is intended to be terminated, proper steps may have to be taken in that behalf and a dispute that may arise thereafter may have to be dealt with according to the other procedure prescribed by the Act.

No limitation is prescribed for an application under S. 33C(2). But it does not mean that any unduly belated claims would be entertained. Side by side, it cannot be said that the workmen would be refused to be given a reasonable opportunity to prove their case only on the ground that they approached the Labour Court after considerable delay.

Whenever a workman is entitled to receive from his employer any money or any benefit which is capable of being computed in terms of money and which he is entitled to receive from his employer and is denied, he can approach Labour Court under S. 33C(2) of the Act. The benefit sought to be enforced under S. 33C(2) is necessarily a pre-existing benefit or one flowing from a pre-existing right. The difference between a pre-existing right or benefit on the one hand and the right or benefit which is considered just and fair on the other is vital. The former falls within the jurisdiction of the Labour Court exercising powers under S. 33C(2) of the Act while the latter does not. When a question arises as to the adjudication of a claim for back wages, all relevant circumstances which will have to be gone into are to be considered in a judicious manner. Therefore, the appropriate forum wherein such question of back wages could be decided is only in a proceeding to whom a reference under S. 10 of the Act is made. To state that merely upon reinstatement, a workman would be entitled, under the terms of award, to all his arrears of pay and allowances would be incorrect because several factors will have to be considered to find out whether the workman is entitled to back wages at all and to what extent.[283]

Difference between Section 33C(1) and Section 33C(2)

An analysis of the scheme of Ss. 33C(1) and 33C(2) shows that the difference between the two sub-sections is quite obvious. While the former sub-section deals with cases where money is due to a workman from an employer under a settlement or an award or under the provisions of Chapter V-A or V-B, the latter deals with cases where a workman is entitled to receive from the employer any money or any benefit which is capable of being computed in terms of money. Thus, where the amount due to the workmen, flowing from the obligations under a settlement, is pre-determined and ascertained or can be arrived at by any arithmetical calculation or simpliciter verification and the only inquiry that is required to be made is whether it is due to the workman or not, recourse to the summary proceedings under S. 33(C)(1) of the Act is not only appropriate but also desirable to prevent harassment to the workmen. Sub-section (1) of S. 33C entitles the workmen to apply to the appropriate Government for issuance of a certificate of recovery for any money due to them under an award or a settlement or under the provisions of Chapter V-A and the Government, if satisfied that a specific sum is due to the workmen, is obliged to issue a certificate for the recovery of the amount due. After the requisite certificate is issued by the Government to the Collector, the Collector is under a statutory duty to recover the amount due under the certificate issued to him. The procedure is aimed at providing a speedy, cheap and summary manner of recovery of the amount due, which

283. *State Bank of India* v. *Ram Chandra Dubey*, AIR 2000 SC 3734.

the employer has wrongfully withheld. The appropriate Government does not have the power to determine the amount due to any workman under sub-section (1) and that determination can only be done by the Labour Court under sub-section (2) or in a reference under S. 10(1) of the Act. Even after the determination is made by the Labour Court under sub-section (2), the amount so determined by the Labour Court, can be recovered through the summary and speedy procedure provided by sub-section (1). Sub-section (1) does not control or affect the ambit and operation of sub-section (2) which is wider in scope than sub-section (1). Besides, the rights conferred under S. 33C(2) exist in addition to any other mode of recovery which the workman has under the law.

Application of Maxim *Actio personalis moritur cum persona* and Section 33C

The maxim *actio personalis moritur cum persona*, though part of English Common Law, has been subjected to criticism even in England. It has been dubbed as unjust maxim, obscure in its origin, inaccurate in its expression and uncertain in its application. It has often caused grave injustice. The maxim means a personal action dies with the person, has a limited application. It operates in a limited class of actions *ex delicto* such as actions for damages for defamation, assault or other personal injuries not causing the death of the party, and in other actions where after the death of the party the relief granted could not be enjoyed or granting it would be nugatory.

The question that came before the Supreme Court in *Rameshwar Manjhi* v. *Management of Sangramgarh Colliery*[284] for consideration was whether an industrial dispute survives when the workman concerned dies during its pendency. Can the proceedings before the Tribunal/Labour Court be continued by the legal heirs/representatives of the deceased workman?

Relying upon the judgment of the Patna High Court in *Bihar Working Journalists' Union* v. *H.K. Chaudhuri*,[285] the Tribunal by its award has answered the question in the negative. There is a sharp difference of opinion between the Assam, Patna, Delhi and Orissa High Courts on the one hand, and Kerala and Gujarat High Courts on the other. The first set of High Courts have held that on the death of a workman the industrial dispute cannot survive and the proceedings must come to an end, whereas the Kerala and Gujarat High Courts have held that the industrial dispute survives the deceased workman and the reference can be continued by the legal heirs/representatives of the deceased workman.

The Patna High Court in *Bihar Working Journalists' Union* v. *H.K. Chaudhuri*,[287] on the interpretation of Cls. (c) and (d) of S. 18(3) of the Act, came to the conclusion that it was not the intention of the legislature to permit continuance of an industrial dispute at the instance of the heirs or the legal representatives of the deceased workman.

In *Horamani Naik* v. *Management, Samaj*,[286] the question before the Orissa High Court was whether during the pendency of an application under S. 33C(2) of the Act, on the death of the workman, his legal representatives could be substituted. R.N. Misra. J., speaking for the Division Bench of the Court, came to the conclusion that the heirs and legal represen-tatives of the deceased workman were not entitled to continue the proceedings. The learned Judges of the Orissa High Court followed the judgment of the Delhi High Court in *Yad Ram* v.

284. AIR 1994 SC 1176.
285. AIR 1968 Pat 135.
286. 1978 Lab IC 1630.

Bir Singh.[287] It is useful here to quote the reasoning of the Delhi High Court in *Yad Ram's* case, where it has been observed that an application under S. 33C(2) of the Act can be made only by the workman himself and if the workman dies during the pendency of such application, his heirs, successors and legal representatives cannot continue it in the specified Labour Court, because the Court cannot recognise anybody other than a workman as the applicant before it. The Court further held that the heirs, successors and legal representatives can take appropriate proceedings by way of a suit in a civil Court. However, they cannot be a party before the Labour Court after his death or an application cannot be made by the heirs, successors and legal representatives on behalf of the deceased workman under S. 33C(2).

As regards S. 33C(2) of the Act, the Bombay High Court in *Sitabai* v. *M/s. Auto Engineers*,[288] has taken a different view. It has held that a widow has a right to apply for computation of gratuity amount which became payable to her late husband.

In *Gwalior Rayons, Mavoor* v. *Labour Court*,[289] Chandrasekhara Menon, J. of the Kerala High Court sitting singly, dealt with the question with utmost clarity and held that there is no reason why the Labour Court should cease to exercise jurisdiction in considering the question whether the termination of the services of the two employees was justified or not merely because they died during the course of the proceedings. A decision on that is certainly in the interest of the other employees. And the benefits that would be due to the deceased employees on the finding of the Labour Court can be realised on behalf of their estate by their legal heirs under S. 33C(2) of the Act. In *Bank of Baroda* v. *Workmen*,[290] a Division Bench of the Gujarat High Court, followed the reasoning of Chandrasekhara Menon, J. in *Gwalior Rayons'* case. B.J. Divan, C.J., speaking for the Bench, observed that so far as the granting of relief of reinstatement is concerned, it would be nugatory on the death of the workman concerned pending the reference before the Tribunal or the Labour Court, as the case may be. However, reinstatement involves the concept of backwages also and very often the Tribunal has to pass orders providing for the backwages from the date of wrongful termination of the services till the date of reinstatement. It is only under the Industrial Disputes Act that in the field of industrial relations, the Tribunal concerned can direct reinstatement of the workman. Under the ordinary civil law, it is not open to a Civil Court to direct reinstatement of a workman. The only thing that a Civil Court can do is to provide for damages for wrongful termination of service or wrongful dismissal. Again, the whole concept under the Industrial Disputes Act of the Tribunal ascertaining whether the termination of services was proper, legal and just is unknown to the civil Courts. So, in the case of a deceased workman where the reference is under S. 2A of the Industrial Disputes Act, the heirs and legal representatives can agitate the question, firstly, whether the termination of the deceased workman was just, legal and proper, and secondly, if it was wrongful and invalid, then what compensation in terms of money could have been given to the workman from a particular date fixed by the Tribunal till the date of reinstatement, and if reinstatement cannot be granted because of the death of the workman, till the date of his death. It is therefore in this context of S. 306 of the Succession Act that the right to prosecute these special proceedings before the Industrial Tribunal survives

287. 1974 Lab IC 970.
288. 1972 Lab IC 733.
289. (1978) 2 Lab LJ 188.
290. 1980 Lab IC 177.

to the administrators, executors, heirs and legal representatives of the deceased workman. It is only a cause of action for personal injury or in the case of defamation or assault or battery or malicious prosecution which cannot be said to survive after the death of the person concerned.

The Supreme Court in *Rameshwar Manjhi* case did not accept the views of the Patna, Delhi and Orissa High Courts and held that in the case of death of a workman, his heirs and legal representatives can continue the reference or apply to the Labour Court or Industrial Tribunal, as the case may be, under S. 33C(2) of the Act.

In *Namor Ali Choudhury* v. *Central Inland Water Transport Corporation Ltd.*,[291] the Supreme Court interpreted the expression *if any question arises as to the amount of money due* used in S. 33(2) and observed that on a plain reading of the wordings of the section, it would be found that where any workman is entitled to receive from the employer any money and if any question arises as to the amount of money due, then the question may be decided by the Labour Court. The expression *if any question arises as to the amount of money due* embraces within its ambit any one or more of the following kinds of disputes.

(1) Whether there is any settlement or award as alleged?
(2) Whether any workman is entitled to receive from the employer any money at all under any settlement or an award, etc.?
(3) If so, what will be the rate or quantum of such amount?
(4) Whether the amount claimed is due or not?

Broadly speaking, these will be the disputes which will be referable to the question as to the amount of money due. If the right to get the money on the basis of the settlement or the award is not established, no amount of money will be due. If it is established, then it has to be found out, albeit, it may be by mere calculation, as to what is the amount due. For finding it out, it is not necessary that there should be a dispute as to the amount of money due also. The fourth kind of dispute obviously and literally will be covered by the phrase "amount of money due". A dispute as to all such questions or any of them would attract the provisions of S. 33C(2) of the Act and make the remedy available to the workman concerned.

SECTION 34: Cognizance of offences

(1) No Court shall take cognizance of any offence punishable under this Act or of the abetment of any such offence, save on complaint made by or under the authority of the appropriate Government.
(2) No Court inferior to that of a Metropolitan Magistrate or a Judicial Magistrate of the first class, shall try any offence punishable under this Act.

In the case of *M/s. Tobu Enterprises Limited and others* v. *The Lt. Governor, Delhi, and others*,[292] the only question which arose for consideration was whether a private person could be authorised under S. 34 to file a complaint for an offence under S. 25U of the Industrial Disputes Act (Section 25U prescribes the penalty for committing an unfair labour practice). The Delhi High Court came to the conclusion that under the provisions of S. 34, the

291. AIR 1978 SC 275.
292. C.W.P. No. 1715 of 1991.

appropriate Government could file the complaint itself or the complaint could be filed under its authority, but there could not be two extremes, that is, either the appropriate Government itself filed the complaint or it could authorise any private party to do so. The complaint had to be filed either by the appropriate Government or its functionaries. If the authority to file a complaint was given to a private person, it was likely to be abused. There would be no check on the complainant to prosecute the complaint with due diligence. He would not be interested in a fair trial and might be actuated by personal vendetta against the accused, frustrating a fair and speedy trial. The appropriate Government had to have control over the whole of the prosecution. The Delhi High Court found itself unable to agree with the view taken to the contrary by a Full Bench of the Karnataka High Court in *S.N. Hada* v. *The Binny Ltd. Staff Association.*[293] An identical question had been raised before the Full Bench of the Karnataka High Court and the Full Bench held that if the view was taken that only the Government or its agent could file the complaint, then the provisions of S. 30, providing for the filing of the complaint by or on behalf of a trade union or a business which was affected, would become redundant. This could not have been the intention of the legislature. Viewed from any angle, the Full Bench found it difficult to hold that under S. 34, a private body or a person other than an agent of the Government could not be authorised by the Government to file a complaint.

In *Raj Kumar Gupta* v. *Lt. Governor, Delhi,*[294] the learned counsel submitted before the Supreme Court that only a delegate of the appropriate Government appointed under the provisions of S. 39 could be authorised by the appropriate Government to file a complaint under S. 34. There was, in any event, an implied limitation in S. 34, having regard to the nature of a criminal prosecution and the general policy that a prosecution could only be at the instance of the Government. Learned counsel cited the judgment of this Court in *Ishwar Singh Bagga* v. *State of Rajasthan,*[295] upon which the Delhi High Court had relied in the case of *M/s. Tobu Enterprises Ltd.* The Supreme Court in the instant case referred various penal provisions of the Industrial Disputes Act, such as penalties prescribed for the offences of illegal strikes and lock-outs (Ss. 26, 27 and 28), of breach of a settlement or award (S. 29), of disclosing confidential information (S. 30), of closure without notice (S. 30A), and of altering conditions of service pending proceedings (S. 31 read with S. 33) and observed that these offences most closely concern workmen, the representative trade unions and employers. In the light of the foregoing discussion, the Court held that the provisions of S. 34 require that no Court shall take cognizance of any offence punishable under the said Act or of the abetment of such offence save on a complaint made by the appropriate Government or under the authority of the appropriate Government. There is no limitation therein in regard to the party to whom the authorisation may be given. It is the workman, the trade union and the employer who are most concerned with offences under the said Act and neither the terms of S. 34 nor public policy require that they should be excluded from making such complaints. At the same time, the provisions of S. 34 are in the nature of a limitation on the entitlement of a workman or a trade union or an employer to complain of offences under the said Act. They should not, in public interest, be permitted to make frivolous, vexatious or otherwise

293. 1989 Lab IC 165.
294. AIR 1997 SC 2680.
295. AIR 1987 SC 628.

patently untenable complaints, and to this end, S. 34 requires that no complaint shall be taken cognizance of unless it is made with the authorisation of the appropriate Government.

The Court interpreted the words *or under the authority of* in S. 34(1) of the Act and held as follows:

> "The argument that the words *"or under the authority of"* in S. 34(1) are only clarificatory and an amplification of the provisions of S. 39 must be rejected. Section 39 empowers the appropriate Government to delegate the powers exercisable by it under the said Act. This is altogether different from the concept of authorisation to file a complaint under S. 34. If the powers under S. 34 have been delegated under S. 39, the delegate can file the complaint himself or authorise someone else to file it. Learned counsel's argument, if accepted, would render the words "or under the authority of" in S. 34 *otiose* and that is impermissible. These words necessarily must be given due meaning and the meaning is that the appropriate Government may authorise someone other than itself, even a non-Government servant, to file a complaint under S. 34."[296]

SECTION 35: Protection of persons

(1) No person refusing to take part or to continue to take part in any strike or lock-out which is illegal under this Act shall, by reason of such refusal or by reason of any action taken by him under this section, be subject to expulsion from any trade union or society, or to any fine or penalty, or to deprivation of any right or benefit to which he or his legal representatives would otherwise be entitled, or be liable to be placed in any respect, either directly or indirectly, under any disability or at any disadvantage as compared with other members of the union or society, anything to the contrary in the rules of a trade union or society notwithstanding.

(2) Nothing in the rules of a trade union or society requiring the settlement of disputes in any manner shall apply to any proceeding for enforcing any right or exemption secured by this section, and in any such proceeding the Civil Court may, in lieu of ordering a person who has been expelled from membership of a trade union or society to be restored to membership, order that he be paid out of the funds of the trade union or society such sum by way of compensation or damages as that Court thinks just.

SECTION 36: Representation of parties

(1) A workman who is a party to a dispute shall be entitled to be represented in any proceeding under this Act by—

(a) any member of the executive or other office bearer of a registered trade union of which he is a member;

(b) any member of the executive or other office bearer of a federation of trade unions to which the trade union referred to in clause (a) is affiliated;

(c) where the worker is not a member of any trade union, by any member of the executive or other office bearer of any trade union connected with, or by any

296. *Ibid.* at p. 2683 per Bharucha, J.

other workman employed in, the industry in which the worker is employed and authorized in such manner as may be prescribed.

(2) An employer who is a party to a dispute shall be entitled to be represented in any proceeding under this Act by—

(a) an officer of an association of employers of which he is a member;

(b) an officer of a federation of association of employers to which the association referred to in clause (a) is affiliated;

(c) where the employer is not a member of any association of employers, by an officer of any association of employers connected with, or by any other employer engaged in, the industry in which the employer is engaged and authorized in such manner as may be prescribed.

(3) No party to a dispute shall be entitled to be represented by a legal practitioner in any conciliation proceedings under this Act or in any proceedings before a Court.

(4) In any proceeding before a Labour Court, Tribunal or National Tribunal, a party to a dispute may be represented by a legal practitioner with the consent of the other parties to the proceeding and with the leave of the Labour Court, Tribunal or National Tribunal, as the case may be.

The Act envisages investigation and settlement of industrial disputes, and with that end in view has created various authorities at different levels, all independent of one another. The word adjudication occurs only with reference to labour courts, industrial tribunals and national tribunals. These bodies are manned by judicial officers. The conciliation proceedings held by a Board or a Conciliation Officer are mainly concerned with mediation for promoting settlement of industrial disputes. It is reasonable to suppose that the presence of legal practitioners in conciliation may divert attention to technical pleas and will detract from the informality of the proceedings, impeding a smooth and expeditious settlement. Legal practitioners entrusted with their briefs cannot be blamed if they bring forth their legal training and experience to the aid and benefit of their clients. But labour law operates in a field where there are two unequal contestants. The Act, therefore, takes care of the challenge of the situation in which the weaker party is pitted against the stronger before adjudicating authorities. That appears to be one of the reasons for introducing consent of the parties for representation by legal practitioners. Employers, with their purse, naturally, can always secure the services of eminent counsel.

Industrial law in India did not commence with a show of cold shoulder to lawyers as such. There was an unimpeded entrance of legal practitioners to adjudication halls before Tribunals when the Act first came into force on April 1, 1947. Three years later, when the Labour Appellate Tribunals were constituted under the Industrial Disputes (Appellate Tribunal) Act 1950, a restriction was imposed on the parties in engagement of legal practitioners before the Appellate Tribunal without the consent of the parties and leave of the Tribunal. When this was introduced in the appellate forum, the same restriction was imposed for the first time upon representations of parties by legal practitioners before the Industrial Tribunals as well [*see,* S. 34 of the Industrial Disputes (Appellate Tribunal) Act, 1950]. In view of the recent thinking in the matter of proffering legal aid to the poor and weaker sections of the people, it may even be possible that the conditional embargo under S. 36(4) may be lifted or its rigour considerably reduced by leaving the matter to the Tribunals' permission as has been the case under the English law.

Restriction on parties in respect of legal representation before Industrial Courts is not a new phenomenon. It was there in England in the Industrial Courts Act, 1919 (9 and 10 Geo 5 c 69) and does not appear to be altered even by the Industrial Relations Act, 1971. Section 9 of the English Act provides that except as provided by rules, "no person shall be entitled to appear on any such proceedings by counsel or solicitor." However, Rule 8 of the Industrial Court (Procedure) Rules 1920 allows persons to appear by counsel or solicitor with permission of the court.

Section 36 provides for representation of parties before the Tribunals and the Labour Court. Under S. 36(1), a workman who is a party to a dispute shall be entitled to be represented in any proceedings under the Act by three classes of officers mentioned in (a), (b) and (c) of that sub-section. Similarly, under S. 36(2), an employer who is a party to a dispute shall be entitled to be represented in any proceeding under the Act by three classes of officers mentioned in (a), (b) and (c) of that sub-section. By sub-section (3), a total ban is imposed on representation of a party to a dispute by a legal practitioner in any conciliation proceedings under this Act or in any proceedings before a Court of enquiry. Section 36(4) introduces the requirement of prior consent of the opposite party and leave of the Tribunals and of the Labour Court, as the case may be, for enabling a party to be represented by a legal practitioner.

The parties, however, will have to conform to the conditions laid down in S. 36(4) in the matter of representation by legal practitioners. Both the consent of the opposite party and the leave of the Tribunal will have to be secured to enable a party to seek representation before the Tribunal through a legal practitioner *qua* legal practitioner. This is the clear significance of S. 36(4) of the Act.

If, however, a legal practitioner is appointed as an officer of a company or corporation or is not a practising advocate, the fact that he was earlier a legal practitioner or has a legal degree will not stand in the way of the company or the corporation being represented by him. Similarly, if a legal practitioner is an officer of an association of employers or of a federation of such associations, there is nothing in S. 36(4) to prevent him from appearing before the Tribunal under the provisions of S. 36(2) of the Act. Again, an office bearer of a trade union or a member of its executive, even though he is a legal practitioner, will be entitled to represent the workmen before the Tribunal under S. 36(1) in the former capacity. The legal practitioner in the above two cases will appear in the capacity of an officer of the association in the case of an employer and in the capacity of an office bearer of the union in the case of workmen and not in the capacity of a legal practitioner. The fact that a person is a legal practitioner will not affect the position if the qualifications specified in S. 36(1) and S. 36(2) are fulfilled by him.

It must be made clear that there is no scope for enquiry by the Tribunal into the motive for appointment of such legal practitioners as office bearers of the trade unions or as officers of the employers' associations. When the law provides for a requisite qualification for exercising a right, fulfillment of the qualification in a given case will entitle the party to be represented before the Tribunal by such a person with that qualification. How and under what circumstances these qualifications have been obtained will not be relevant matters for consideration by the Tribunal in considering an application for representation under S. 36(1) and S. 36(2) of the Act. Once the qualifications under S. 36(1) and S. 36(2) are fulfilled prior to appearance before Tribunals, there is no need under the law to pursue the matter in order to find out whether the appointments are in circumvention of S. 36(4) of the Act. Motive of the appointment cannot be made an issue before the Tribunal.

The Supreme Court in *Paradip Port Trust, Paradip* v. *Their Workmen*[297] observed:

> "We have given anxious consideration to the above submission. It is true that "and" in a particular context and in view of the object and purpose of a particular legislation may be read as "or" to give effect to the intent of the legislature. However, having regard to the history of the present legislation, recognition by law of the unequal strength of the parties in adjudication proceedings before a Tribunal, intention of the law being to discourage representation by legal practitioners as such, and the need for expeditious disposal of cases, we are unable to hold that "and" in S. 36(4) can be read as "or".[298]

Consent of the opposite party is not an idle alternative but a ruling factor in S. 36(4). The question of hardship, pointed out by the Solicitor General in the instant case, is a matter for the legislature to deal with and it is not for the courts to invoke the theory of injustice and other consequences to choose a rather strained interpretation when the language of S. 36 is clear and unambiguous. Accordingly, the Court held that a lawyer, simpliciter, cannot appear before an Industrial tribunal without the consent of the opposite party and leave of the Tribunal merely by virtue of a power of attorney executed by a party. A lawyer can appear before the Tribunal in the capacity of an office bearer of a registered trade union or an officer of association of employers and no consent of the other side and leave of the Tribunal will, then, be necessary.[299] Section 36 of the Act provides for representation of the parties to a dispute. The workmen are entitled by virtue of sub-section (1) to be represented in a proceeding under the Act by a member of the executive or other office bearer of a registered trade union of which they are members, or of a federation of trade unions to which that trade union is affiliated, and where the workman is not a member of any trade union, he can be represented by a member of the executive or other office bearer of a trade union connected with, or by any other workman employed in, the industry in which the workman is employed. It is not obligatory, however, that a workman who is a party to a dispute must be represented by another. He may participate in the proceeding himself.[299] It has been also held that a workman has no right to be represented by the Union in an inquiry before the management.[300]

The basic principle is that an employee has no right to representation in the departmental proceedings by another person or a lawyer unless the Service Rules specifically provide for the same. The right to representation is available only to the extent specifically provided for in the Rule. In *Kalindi* v. *Tata Locomotive and Engineering Company Ltd.*,[301] it was held that a workman against whom a departmental enquiry is held by the management has no right to be represented at such enquiry by an outsider, not even by a representative of his Union though the management may, in its discretion, allow the employee to avail of such

297. AIR 1977 SC 36.
298. *Ibid.* at p. 44 Goswami, J.
299. *Ameteep Machine Tools, M/s.* v. *Labour Court, Haryana*, AIR 1980 SC 2135.
300. *Central Bank of India Ltd.* v. *Karunamoy Banerjee*, AIR 1968 SC 266.
301. AIR 1960 SC 914.

assistance. Similarly, in *Dunlop Rubber Company* v. *Workmen,*[302] it was laid down that an employee has no right to be represented in the disciplinary proceedings by another person unless the Service Rules specifically provided for the same. A Three-Judge Bench of the Supreme Court in *Crescent Dyes and Chemicals Ltd* v. *Ram Naresh Tripathi,*[303] laid down that the right to be represented in the departmental proceedings initiated against a delinquent employee can be regulated or restricted by the management or by the Service Rules. It was held that the right to be represented by an advocate in the departmental proceedings can be restricted and regulated by statutes or by the Service Rules including the Standing Orders, applicable to the employee concerned. The whole case law was reviewed by the Supreme Court in *Bharat Petroleum Corporation Ltd.* v. *Maharashtra Genl. Kamgar Union,*[304] and it was held that a delinquent employee has no right to be represented by an advocate in the departmental proceedings and that if a right to be represented by a co-workman is given to him, the departmental proceedings would not be bad only for the reason that the assistance of an advocate was not provided to him.

Model Standing Orders, no doubt, provided that a delinquent employee could be represented in the disciplinary proceedings through another employee who may not be the employee of the parent establishment to which the delinquent belongs and may be an employee elsewhere, though he may be a member of the Trade Union, but this rule of representation has not been disturbed by the Certified Standing Orders, inasmuch as it still provides that the delinquent employee can be represented in the disciplinary proceedings through an employee. The only embargo is that the representative should be an employee of the parent establishment. The choice of the delinquent in selecting his representative is affected only to the extent that the representative has to be a co-employee of the same establishment in which the delinquent is employed. There appears to be some logic behind this as a co-employee would be fully aware of the conditions prevailing in the parent establishment, its Service Rules, including the Standing Orders, and would be in a better position, than an outsider, to assist the delinquent in the domestic proceedings for a fair and early disposal. The basic features of the Model Standing Orders are thus retained and the right of representation in the disciplinary proceedings through another employee is not altered, affected or taken away.[306] A similar view has been taken by the Supreme Court in *CIPLA Ltd., M/s.* v. *Ripu Daman Bhanot,*[305] where the Service Rules provide for representation by a co-workman on behalf of the delinquent medical representative in the departmental enquiry. Therefore, it was held that he does not have a right to be represented by advocate in the departmental enquiry.

Section 36A: Power to remove difficulties

(1) If, in the opinion of the appropriate Government, any difficulty or doubt arises as to the interpretation of any provision of an award or settlement, it may refer the question to such Labour Court, Tribunal or National Tribunal, as it may think fit.

(2) The Labour Court, Tribunal or National Tribunal to which such question is referred shall, after giving the parties an opportunity of being heard, decide such question and its decision shall be final and binding on all such parties.

---

302. AIR 1965 SC 1392.
303. (1993) 2 SCC 115.
304. AIR 1999 SC 401.
305. AIR 1999 SC 1635.

Section 36A empowers the appropriate Government to refer any question to the Tribunal if the said Government is satisfied that any difficulty or doubt arises as to the interpretation of any provision of an award made by the said Tribunal. It further provides that when such a question is referred to it, the Tribunal shall, after giving the parties an opportunity of being heard, decide such question and its decision shall be final and binding on all such parties. It is thus clear that the scope of a enquiry under S. 36A is limited to the decision of the difficulties or doubts arising as to the interpretation of any provision in the award. If the words used in any provision of an award are ambiguous or obscure and it is not reasonably possible to interpret them, the difficulty arising from the use of such ambiguous or obscure words may be resolved by moving the appropriate Government to make a reference under S. 36A. It is obvious that any question about the propriety, correctness or validity of any provision of the award would be outside the purview of the enquiry contemplated by the section. If a party to the award is aggrieved by any of its provisions on the merits, the only remedy available to it is by making an appeal, say for instance, under Art. 136 of the Constitution to the Supreme Court. A grievance felt by a party against any provision of the award can be ventilated only in that way and not by adopting the procedure prescribed by S. 36A. Thus, the enquiry permissible under S. 36A is limited to the question of the interpretation of the provision of the award in question and no more. A proceeding, therefore, contemplated by S. 36A is not a proceeding intended to enable the Tribunal to review or modify its own order; it is intended to enable the Tribunal only to clarify the provisions of its award where a difficulty or doubt arises about the interpretation of the provisions.[306]

The legal effect of reference under S. 36A is to reopen the earlier reference proceedings which terminated in an award, though only for the limited purpose of the interpretation of the provisions of that award in respect of such difficulties or doubts as required removal. All parties to the original reference which resulted in the award must, as a matter of law, be deemed necessarily to be parties to the proceedings to the reference under S. 36A as well. A company, which is a party in an earlier reference terminating in an award, cannot in proceedings for reference under S. 36A for interpreting the terms of that award, by merely presenting a formal application to withdraw from the proceedings, cease to be a party to those proceedings so as to avoid the legal consequences which flow by reason of the pendency of those proceedings. Even non-participation of workmen in those proceeding will not change the legal position.[307]

Section 36A vis-a-vis Section 33C(2)

The scope of S. 36A is different from that of S. 33C(2), because S. 36A is not concerned with the implementation or execution of the award at all, which is the sole purpose of S. 33C(2). Section 33C(2) deals with cases of implementation of individual rights of workmen falling under its provisions, whereas S. 36A deals merely with a question of interpretation of the award where a dispute arises in that behalf between the workmen and the employer and the appropriate Government is satisfied that the dispute deserves to be resolved by reference under S. 36A.

306. *Kirloskar Oil Engines Ltd., Kirkee* v. *The Workmen*, AIR 1966 SC 1903.
307. *Ballarpur Collieries Co.* v. *Presiding Officer, C.G.I.T. Dhanbad*, AIR 1972 SC 1216.

SECTION 36B: Power to exempt

Where the appropriate Government is satisfied in relation to any industrial establishment or undertaking or any class of industrial establishments or undertakings carried on by a department of that Government that adequate provisions exist for the investigation and settlement of industrial disputes in respect of workmen employed in such establishment or undertaking or class of establishments or undertakings, it may, by notification in the Official Gazette, exempt, conditionally or unconditionally such establishment or undertaking or class of establishments or undertakings from all or any of the provisions of this Act.

SECTION 37: Protection of action taken under the Act

No suit, prosecution or other legal proceeding shall lie against any person for anything which is in good faith done or intended to be done in pursuance of this Act or any rules made thereunder.

SECTION 38: Power to make rules

(1) The appropriate Government may, subject to the condition of previous publication, make rules for the purpose of giving effect to the provisions of this Act.

(2) In particular and without prejudice to the generality of the foregoing power, such rules may provide for all or any of the following matters, namely:

(a) the power and procedure of conciliation officers, Boards, Courts, Labour Courts, Tribunals and National Tribunals including rules as to the summoning of witnesses, the production of documents relevant to the subject-matter of an inquiry or investigation, the number of members necessary to form a quorum and the manner of submission of reports and awards;

(aa) the form of arbitration agreement, the manner in which it may be signed by the parties, the manner in which a notification may be issued under sub-section (3A) of S. 10A, the powers of the arbitrator named in the arbitration agreement and the procedure to be followed by him;

(aaa) the appointment of assessors in proceedings under this Act;

(b) the constitution and functions of and the filling of vacancies in Works Committees, and the procedure to be followed by such Committees in the discharge of their duties;

(c) the salaries and allowances and the terms and conditions for appointment of the presiding officers of the Labour Court, Tribunal and the National Tribunal including the allowances admissible to members of Courts, Boards and to assessors and witnesses;

(d) the ministerial establishment which may be allotted to a Court, Board, Labour Court, Tribunal or National Tribunal and the salaries and allowances payable to members of such establishments;

(e) the manner in which and the persons by and to whom notice of strike or lock-out may be given and the manner in which such notices shall be communicated;

(f) the conditions subject to which parties may be represented by legal practitioners in proceedings under this Act before a Court, Labour Court, Tribunal or National Tribunal;

(g) any other matter which is to be or may be prescribed.

(3) Rules made under this section may provide that a contravention thereof shall be punishable with fine not exceeding fifty rupees.

(4) All rules made under this section shall, as soon as possible after they are made, be laid before the State Legislature or, where the appropriate Government is the Central Government, before both Houses of Parliament.

(5) Every rule made by the Central Government under this section shall be laid, as soon as may be after it is made, before each House of Parliament while it is in session for a total period of thirty days which may be comprised in one session or in two or more successive sessions, and if before the expiry of the session immediately following the session or the successive sessions aforesaid both Houses agree in making any modification in the rule, or both Houses agree that the rule should not be made, the rule shall thereafter have effect only in such modified form or be of no effect, as the case may be; so, however, that any such modification or annulment shall be without prejudice to the validity of anything previously done under that rule.

Section 39: Delegation of powers

The appropriate Government may, by notification in the Official Gazette, direct that any power exercisable by it under this Act or rules made thereunder shall, in relation to such matters and subject to such conditions, if any, as may be specified in the direction, be exercisable also,

(a) where the appropriate Government is the Central Government, by such officer or authority subordinate to the Central Government or by the State Government or by such officer or authority subordinate to the State Government, as may be specified in the notification; and

(b) where the appropriate Government is a State Government, by such officer or authority subordinate to the State Government as may be specified in the notification.

Section 40: Power to amend Schedules

(1) The appropriate Government may, if it is of opinion that it is expedient or necessary in the public interest so to do, by notification in the Official Gazette, add to the First Schedule any industry, and on any such notification being issued, the First Schedule shall be deemed to be amended accordingly.

(2) The Central Government may, by notification in the Official Gazette, add to or alter or amend the Second Schedule or the Third Schedule and on any such notification being issued, the Second Schedule or the Third Schedule, as the case may be, shall be deemed to be amended accordingly.

(3) Every such notification shall, as soon as possible after it is issued, be laid before the Legislature of the State, if the notification has been issued by a State Government, or before Parliament, if the notification has been issued by the Central Government.

FIRST SCHEDULE

INDUSTRIES WHICH MAY BE DECLARED TO BE PUBLIC UTILITY SERVICES UNDER SUB-CLAUSE (VI) OF CLAUSE (N) OF SECTION 2

See [Section 2(n)(vi)]

1. Transport (other than railways) for the carriage of passengers or goods, by land or water.
2. Banking.
3. Cement.
4. Coal.
5. Cotton textiles.
6. Foodstuffs.
7. Iron and Steel.
8. Defence establishments.
9. Service in hospitals and dispensaries.
10. Fire brigade service.
11. India Government Mints.
12. India Security Press.
13. Copper Mining.
14. Lead Mining.
15. Zinc Mining.
16. Iron Ore Mining.
17. Service in any oilfield.
18. [***]
19. Service in the uranium industry.
20. Pyrites Mining Industry.
21. Security Paper Mill, Hoshangabad.
22. Services in the Bank Note Press, Dewas.
23. Phosphorite Mining.
24. Magnesite Mining.
25. Currency Note Press.
26. Manufacture or production of mineral oil (crude oil), motor and aviation spirit, diesel oil, kerosene oil, fuel oil, diverse hydrocarbon oils and their blends including synthetic fuels, lubricating oils and the like.

27. Service in the International Airports Authority of India.
28. Industrial establishments, manufacturing or producing nuclear fuel and components, heavy water and allied chemicals, and atomic energy.

SECOND SCHEDULE

MATTERS WITHIN THE JURISDICTION OF LABOUR COURTS

See (Section 7)

1. The propriety or legality of an order passed by an employer under the standing orders;
2. The application and interpretation of standing orders;
3. Discharge or dismissal of workmen including reinstatement of, or grant of relief to, workmen wrongfully dismissed;
4. Withdrawal of any customary concession or privilege;
5. Illegality or otherwise of a strike or lock-out; and
6. All matters other than those specified in the Third Schedule.

THIRD SCHEDULE

MATTERS WITHIN THE JURISDICTION OF INDUSTRIAL TRIBUNALS

See (Section 7A)

1. Wages, including the period and mode of payment;
2. Compensatory and other allowances;
3. Hours of work and rest intervals;
4. Leave with wages and holidays;
5. Bonus, profit sharing, provident fund and gratuity;
6. Shift working otherwise than in accordance with standing orders;
7. Classification by grades;
8. Rules of discipline;
9. Rationalisation;
10. Retrenchment of workmen and closure of establishment; and
11. Any other matter that may be prescribed.

FOURTH SCHEDULE

CONDITIONS OF SERVICE FOR CHANGE OF WHICH NOTICE IS TO BE GIVEN

See (Section 9A)

1. Wages, including the period and mode of payment;
2. Contribution paid, or payable, by the employer to any provident fund or pension fund or for the benefit of the workmen under any law for the time being in force;
3. Compensatory and other allowances;
4. Hours of work and rest intervals;
5. Leave with wages and holidays;
6. Starting, alternating or discontinuance of shift working otherwise than in accordance with standing orders;
7. Classification by grades;
8. Withdrawal of any customary concession or privilege or change in usage;
9. Introduction of new rules of discipline, or alteration of existing rules, except insofar as they are provided in standing orders;
10. Rationalisation, standardization or improvement of plant or technique which is likely to lead to retrenchment of workmen;
11. Any increase or reduction (other than casual) in the number of persons employed or to be employed in any occupation or process or department or shift, not occasioned by circumstances over which the employer has no control.

FIFTH SCHEDULE

UNFAIR LABOUR PRACTICES

See [Section 2(ra)]

I. ON THE PART OF EMPLOYERS AND TRADE UNIONS OF EMPLOYERS

(1) To interfere with, restrain from, or coerce, workmen in the exercise of their right to organise, form, join or assist a trade union or to engage in concerted activities for the purposes of collective bargaining or other mutual aid or protection, that is to say:—

(a) threatening workmen with discharge or dismissal, if they join a trade union;

(b) threatening a lock-out or closure, if a trade union is organised; and

(c) granting wage increase to workmen at crucial periods of trade union organisation, with a view to undermining the efforts of the trade union at organisation.

(2) To dominate, interfere with or contribute support, financial or otherwise, to any trade union, that is to say—

   (a) an employer taking an active interest in organising a trade union of his workmen; and
   (b) an employer showing partiality or granting favour to one of several trade unions attempting to organise his workmen or to its members, where such a trade union is not a recognised trade union.

(3) To establish employer-sponsored trade unions of workmen.

(4) To encourage or discourage membership in any trade union by discriminating against any workman, that is to say—

   (a) discharging or punishing a workman, because he urged other workmen to join or organise a trade union;
   (b) discharging or dismissing a workman for taking part in any strike (not being a strike which is deemed to be an illegal strike under this Act);
   (c) changing seniority rating or workmen because of trade union activities;
   (d) refusing to promote workmen to higher posts on account of their trade union activities;
   (e) giving unmerited promotions to certain workmen with a view to creating discord amongst other workmen, or to undermine the strength of their trade union;
   (f) discharging office bearers or active members of the trade union on account of their trade union activities.

(5) To discharge or dismiss workmen—

   (a) by way of victimisation;
   (b) not in good faith, but in the colourable exercise of the employer's rights;
   (c) by falsely implicating a workman in a criminal case on false evidence or on concocted evidence;
   (d) for patently false reasons;
   (e) on untrue or trumpet up allegations of absence without leave;
   (f) in utter disregard of the principles of natural justice in the conduct of domestic enquiry or with undue haste;
   (g) for misconduct of a minor technical character, without having any regard to the nature of the particular misconduct or the past record or service of the workman, thereby leading to a disproportionate punishment.

(6) To abolish the work of a regular nature being done by workmen, and to give such work to contractors as a measure of breaking a strike.

(7) To transfer a workman mala fide from one place to another, under the guise of following management policy.

(8) To insist upon individual workmen, who are on a legal strike to sign a good conduct bond, as a pre-condition to allowing them to resume work.

(9) To show favouritism or partiality to one set of workers regardless of merit.

(10) To employ workmen as "*badlis*", casuals or temporaries and to continue them as such for years, with the object of depriving them of the status and privileges of permanent workmen.

(11) To discharge or discriminate against any workman for filing charges or testifying against an employer in any enquiry or proceeding relating to any industrial dispute.

(12) To recruit workmen during a strike which is not an illegal strike.

(13) Failure to implement award, settlement or agreement.

(14) To indulge in acts of force or violence.

(15) To refuse to bargain collectively, in good faith with the recognised trade unions.

(16) Proposing or continuing a lock-out deemed to be illegal under this Act.

II. ON THE PART OF WORKMEN AND TRADE UNIONS OF WORKMEN

(1) To advise or actively support or instigate any strike deemed to be illegal under this Act.

(2) To coerce workmen in the exercise of their right to self-organisation or to join a trade union or refrain from joining any trade union, that is to say—

(a) for a trade union or its members to picketing in such a manner that non-striking workmen are physically debarred from entering the work places;

(b) to indulge in acts of force or violence or to hold out threats of intimidation in connection with a strike against non-striking workmen or against managerial staff.

(3) For a recognised union to refuse to bargain collectively in good faith with the employer.

(4) To indulge in coercive activities against certification of a bargaining representative.

(5) To stage, encourage or instigate such forms of coercive actions as wilful, "go slow", squatting on the work premises after working hours or "gherao" of any of the members of the managerial or other staff.

(6) To stage demonstrations at the residence of the employers or the managerial staff members.

(7) To incite or indulge in wilful damage to employer's property connected with the industry.

(8) To indulge in acts of force or violence or to hold out threats of intimidation against any workman with a view to prevent him from attending work.

* * *

3 The Contract Labour (Regulation and Abolition) Act, 1970

The object of the Contract Labour (Regulation and Abolition) Act, 1970 is to prevent exploitation of contract labour and also to introduce better conditions of work. A workman is deemed to be employed as contract labour when he is hired in connection with the work of an establishment by or through a contractor. Contract workmen are indirect employees. Contract labour differs from direct labour in terms of employment relationship with the establishment and method of wage payment.

Contract labour, by and large, is not borne on pay-roll nor is paid directly. Contract workmen are hired, supervised and remunerated by the contractor, who, in turn, is remunerated by the establishment hiring the services of the contractor.

Statement of Objects and Reasons

The Government of India has been deeply concerned about the exploitation of workers under the contract labour system. With a view to remove the difficulties of contract labour and bearing in mind the recommendations of various commissions and committees and the decisions of the Supreme Court, particularly in the case of *Standard Vacuum Refining Company* in 1960, the Contract Labour (Regulation and Abolition) Act was enacted in 1970. This Act seeks to regulate the employment of contract labour in certain establishments and to provide for its abolition under certain circumstances. The Statement of Objects and Reasons of the Act are as follows:

The system of employment of contract labour lends itself to various abuses. The question of its abolition has been under the consideration of Government for a long time. In the second five-year plan, the Planning Commission made certain recommendations, namely, undertaking of studies to ascertain the extent of the problem of contract labour, progressive abolition of system and improvement of service, conditions of contract labour where the abolition was not possible. The matter was discussed at various meetings of Tripartite Committees at which the State Governments were also represented and general consensus of opinion was that the system should be abolished wherever possible or practicable and that in cases where this system could not be abolished altogether, the working conditions of contract labour should be regulated so as to ensure payment of wages and provisions of essential amenities.

"The proposed Bill aims at abolition of contract labour in respect of such categories as may be notified by appropriate Government in the light of certain criteria that have been laid down, and at regulating the service conditions of contract labour where abolition is not possible. The Bill provides for the setting up of Advisory Boards of a tripartite character, representing various interests, to advise Central and State Governments in administering the legislation and registration of establishments and contractors. Under the scheme of the Bill, the provision and maintenance of certain basic welfare amenities for contract labour, like drinking water and first-aid facilities, and in certain cases rest rooms and canteens, have been made obligatory. Provisions have also been made to guard against details in the matter of wage payment."[1]

Act in a Nutshell

The Contract Labour (Regulation and Abolition) Act contains 35 provisions and is divided into seven chapters. The Central Act, as its preamble shows, is to regulate the employment of contract labour in certain establishments and to provide for the abolition in certain circumstances and for matters connected therewith. Under sub-section (4) of S. 1, the Act applies to the establishments mentioned therein as well as to every contractor who employs the number of workers referred to in Cl. (b). There is no controversy that the Act applies to the appellant establishment. Section 2 defines the various expressions such as "appropriate Government", "contract labour", "contractor", "establishment" and "principal employer".

Chapter II deals with the Advisory Boards. Section 3(1) empowers the Central Government to constitute the Central Advisory Contract Labour Board to advise it with regard to matters arising out of the administration of the Act. Sub-section (2) provides for the composition of the said Board and from Cl. (c), it is seen that among other persons, the said Board is to consist of the representatives of the contractor, workmen and the industries concerned. Under the proviso to sub-section (3), the number of members nominated to represent the workmen shall not be less than the number of members nominated to represent the principal employers and the contractors. Section 4 deals with the constitution of a similar Advisory Board by the State Government. The said State Advisory Board is also to comprise, among other persons, the representatives of the industry, the contractor and the workmen. A proviso to sub-section (3) of S. 4, similar to the proviso to sub-section (3) of S. 3, has also been enacted.

Chapter III, containing Ss. 6 to 10, deals with the registration of establishments employing contract labour. Section 6 deals with the appointment of registering officers by the appropriate Government by notification in the Official Gazette. Section 7 makes it compulsory on the part of every principal employer of an establishment to which the Act applies to make an application to the registering officer within the time prescribed for registration of the establishment. Section 8 deals with revocation of registration in the circumstances mentioned therein. Section 9, dealing with the effect of non-registration, prohibits the principal employer of an establishment to which the Act applies from employing contract labour if the

1. *B.H.E.L. Workers Association, Hardwar* v. *Union of India,* AIR 1985 SC 409.

establishment has not been registered under S. 7 within the time prescribed, or in the case of an establishment in respect of which registration has been revoked under S. 8. Section 10, which prohibits the employment of contract labour and which is an important provision, is as follows:

(1) Notwithstanding anything contained in this Act, the appropriate Government may, after consultation with the Central Board or, as the case may be, a State Board, prohibit, by notification in the Official Gazette, employment in contract labour in any process, operation or other work in any establishment.

(2) Before issuing any notification under sub-s. (1) in relation to an establishment, the appropriate Government shall have regard to the conditions of work and benefits provided for the contract labour in that establishment and other relevant factors, such as—

(a) whether the process, operation or other work is incidental to, or necessary for the industry, trade, business, manufacture or occupation that is carried on in the establishment;

(b) whether it is of perennial nature, that is to say, it is of sufficient duration having regard to the nature of industry, trade, business, manufacture or occupation carried on in that establishment;

(c) whether it is done ordinarily through regular workmen in that establishment or an establishment similar thereto;

(d) whether it is sufficient to employ considerable number of whole-time workmen.

Explanation: If a question arises whether any process or operation or other work is of perennial nature, the decision of the appropriate Government thereon shall be final.

The following points emerge from S. 10(1). The appropriate Government has power to prohibit the employment of contract labour in any process, operation or other work in any establishment; (2) Before issuing a notification prohibiting contract labour, the appropriate Government has to consult the Central or State Board, as the case may be; (3) Before issuing any notification under sub-section (1), prohibiting the employment of contract labour, the appropriate Government is bound to have regard not only to the conditions of work and benefits provided or the contract labour in a particular establishment, but also other relevant factors enumerated in Cls. (a) to (d) of sub-section (2); and (4) under the Explanation, which really relates to Cl. (b), the decision of the appropriate Government on the question whether any process, operation or other work is of perennial nature, shall be final.

Chapter IV deals with licensing of contractors. Two sections in this chapter have to be noted, namely Ss. 11 and 12. Section 11 deals with the appointment of licensing officers by the appropriate Government for the purpose of Chapter IV. Sub-section (1) of S. 12 prohibits a contractor to whom the Act applies from undertaking or executing any work through contract labour except under and in accordance with the licence issued in that behalf by the licensing officers. Sub-section (2) of S. 12 provides for a license issued to a contractor containing conditions relating to hours of work, fixation of wages and other essential amenities in respect of contract labour, which the appropriate Government may deem fit to impose by the rules made under S. 35. Sections 13, 14 and 15 relate to the procedure for the grant of licence, revocation, suspension and amendment of licences and appeals by persons aggrieved by the orders made under Ss. 7, 8, 12 and 14.

Chapter V deals with the welfare and health of contract labour. There are provisions made for the establishment of canteens and rest houses and to provide other facilities to the contract labour by the contractor. Section 20 casts a liability on the principal employer to provide the amenities referred to under Ss. 16, 17, 18, and 19 for the benefit of contract labour employed in his establishment if the contractor fails to provide these amenities. That section also enables the principal employer, if he provides those amenities, to recover from the contractor expenses so incurred by him. Section 21 makes the contractor responsible for payment of wages to the contract labour. Sub-section (2) of S. 21 makes it obligatory on every principal employer to nominate a representative duly authorised by him to be present at the time of disbursement of wages by the contractor. The said sub-section also casts a duty on such representative to certify the amounts paid as wages as prescribed by the rules. Sub-section (4) makes the principal employer liable to pay wages in full or the unpaid balance due, as the case may be, in case the contractor fails to make the payment within the period prescribed. It also enables the principal employer to recover from the contractor the amount so paid to the labour.

Chapter VI provides for penalty for a person who contravenes any of the provisions of the Act or the Rules.

Chapter VII deals with miscellaneous matters. Section 29 makes it obligatory on a principal employer and contractor to maintain the registers and records as provided therein. Section 30 provides that the Central Act shall have effect notwithstanding anything inconsistent therewith contained in any other law or in the terms of any agreement of contract of service or in any standing orders applicable to the establishment whether made before or after the commencement of the Act. No doubt, the said section also saves any agreement or contract or standing order where under the contract labour gets more benefits than those conferred on them under the Act. Section 33 gives power to the appropriate Government to make rules for carrying out the purpose of the Act and also in respect of various other matters mentioned in Cls. (a) to (p) of sub-section (2).[2]

Constitutional Validity of the Act

The Supreme Court examined the validity of the Act in *Gammon India Ltd.* v. *Union of India*[3] and found that there is no unreasonableness in the measure. Repealing the contention that the application of the Act in respect of pending work amounted to unreasonable restriction on the contractors under Art. 19(1)(g), it was held that the pendency of contract is not a relevant consideration. The subject matter of the legislation is not contract. It is contract labour. The Supreme Court also rejected the contention that the provisions of the Act are unconstitutional and unreasonable because of impracticability of implementation. The canteens, rest rooms, supply of drinking water, latrines, urinals, first-aid facilities are amenities for the dignity

2. *Vegoils Pvt. Ltd* v. *Workmen*, AIR 1972 SC 1942.
3. AIR 1974 SC 960.

of human labour and are not in excess of the object of the Act. There is no violation of Art. 14. The classification is not arbitrary. The legislature has made uniform laws for all contractors.

Main Features of the Act

(1) The Act applies to every establishment in which twenty or more workmen are employed or were employed on any day of the preceding twelve months as contract labour and to every contractor who employs or who employed on any day of the preceding twelve months twenty or more workmen. The appropriate Government is further empowered to extend the provisions of the Act to every establishment or contractor employing such number of workmen being less than twenty to be specified in the notification.

(2) The Act does not apply to establishments where the work performed is of intermittent or casual nature. The Act applies to establishments of the Government and local authorities as well.

(3) The Central Government and the State Government are required to set up Central Advisory Board and State Advisory Boards which are authorised to constitute committees as deemed proper. The functions of the Boards would be advisory on matters arising out of the administration of the Act as may be referred to them. The Boards are also to carry out the functions assigned to them under the Act.

(4) Every establishment covered under the Act will have to be registered by the principal employer. In case of non-registration of an establishment, which should have been registered, the employment of contract labour is prohibited and in case of breach could be visited by penal consequences. Likewise, every contractor to whom the Act applies shall obtain a licence and shall not undertake or execute any work through contract labour except under and in accordance with the licence issued.

(5) The Act authorises the appropriate Government to make rules for the establishment of canteens. For the welfare and health of contract labour, provision is to be made for rest-rooms, first-aid, wholesome drinking water, latrines and urinals. In case of failure on the part of the contractor to provide the said facilities, the principal employer is made liable to provide the amenities.

(6) The contractor is required to pay wages and a duty is cast on him to ensure the disbursement of wages in the presence of the authorised representative of the principal employer. In case of failure on the part of the contractor to pay wages either in part or in full, the principal employer is liable to pay the same. The principal employer is authorised to recover the amount either by deductions from the amount due to the contractor or as debt payable by the contractor.

(7) The Act makes provision for the appointment of an inspecting staff, for maintenance of registers and records, for penalties for the contravention of provisions of the Act and rules thereunder, and for making rules for carrying out the purpose of the Act.

(8) Apart from the regulatory measures provided under the Act for the benefit of the contract labour, the appropriate government is authorised, after consultation with the Central Board or State Board, as the case may be, to prohibit, by notification in the Official Gazette, employment of contract labour in any establishment.

(9) In order to carry out the purposes of the Act, rules have to be framed both by the Central and the State Governments. If any government fails to frame rules, the provisions of the Act would be ineffective.

Non-observance of provisions of the Act violative of Article 21

Article 21 of the Constitution speaks about the protection of life and personal liberty of an individual and it reads:

No person shall be deprived of his life or personal liberty except according to the procedure established by law.

In the well-known public interest litigation case relating to workmen engaged in various Asiad projects.[4] The Supreme Court, while considering the preliminary objection that a writ petition under Art. 32 could not be maintainable unless it complained of a breach of some fundamental right and since writ petitions before the Supreme Court merely alleged violation of the labour laws, held that the same was not maintainable and was liable to be dismissed.

But the Court observed:

> "...there is the complaint of non-observance of the provisions of the Contract Labour (Regulation & Abolition) Act 1970 and the inter-State Migrant Workmen (Regulation of Employment and Conditions of Service) Act 1979 and this is also in our opinion a complaint relating to violation of Art. 21. This Article has acquired a new dimension as a result of the decision of this Court in *Maneka Gandhi* v. *Union of India* (1978) 2 SCR 621(663): (AIR 1978 SC 597) and it has received its most expansive interpretation in *Francis Coralie Mullin* v. *The Administrator, Union Territory of Delhi* (1981) 2 SCR 516: (AIR 1981 SC 746). Where it has been held by this Court that the right of life guaranteed under this Article is not confined merely to physical existence or to the use of any faculty or limb through which life is enjoyed or the soul communicates with outside world but it also includes within its scope and ambit the right to live with basic human dignity and the State cannot deprive any one of this precious and invaluable right because no procedure by which such deprivation may be effected can ever be regarded as reasonable, fair and just. Now the rights and benefits conferred on the workmen employed by a contractor under the provisions of the Contract Labour (Regulation and Abolition) Act 1970 and the Inter-State Migrant Workmen (Regulation of Employment and Conditions of Service) Act, 1979 are clearly intended to ensure basic human dignity to the workmen and if the workmen are deprived of any of these rights and benefits to which they are entitled under the provisions of these two pieces of social welfare legislation, that would clearly be a violation of Art.

4. *Peoples' Union for Democratic Rights* v. *Union of India*, AIR 1982 SC 1473.

21 by the Union of India, the Delhi Administration and the Delhi Development Authority which, as principal employers, are made statutorily responsible for securing such rights and benefits to the workmen."[5]

CHAPTER I

PRELIMINARY

SECTION 1: Short title, extent, commencement and application

(1) This Act may be called the Contract Labour (Regulation and Abolition) Act, 1970.

(2) It extends to the whole of India.

(3) It shall come into force on such date as the Central Government may, by notification in the Official Gazette, appoint and different dates may be appointed for different provisions of this Act.

(4) It applies—

(a) to every establishment in which twenty or more workmen are employed or were employed on any day of the preceding twelve months as contract labour;

(b) to every contractor who employs or who employed on any day of the preceding twelve months twenty or more workmen:

Provided that the appropriate government may, after giving not less than two months' notice of its intention so to do, by notification in the Official Gazette, apply the provisions of this Act to any establishment or contractor employing such number of workmen less than twenty as may be specified in the notification.

(5) (a) It shall not apply to establishments in which work only of an intermittent or casual nature is performed.

(b) If a question arises whether work performed in an establishment is of an intermittent or casual nature, the appropriate Government shall decide the question after consultation with the Central Board or, as the case may be, a State Board, and its decision shall be final.

Explanation: For the purpose of this sub-section, work performed in an establishment shall not be deemed to be of an intermittent nature—

(i) if it was performed for more than one hundred and twenty days in the preceding twelve months, or

(ii) if it is of a seasonal character and is performed for more than sixty days in a year.

5. *Ibid.* at p. 1485 per Bhagwati, J.

Long Title and Preamble to the Act

The long title and preamble to the Act prescribes that it is an Act to regulate the employment of contract labour in certain establishments and to provide for its abolition in certain circumstances and for matters connected therewith. The long title itself suggests that the Act does not provide or intend for the total abolition of contract labour, but only abolition of certain circumstances, and for the regulation of the employment of contract labour in certain circumstances. Such intention can be gathered after reading the total legislation as a whole. Section 10 of the Act is the only provision that prohibits employment of contract labour in any process, operation or other work in any establishment. The other provisions of the Act, either directly or indirectly, facilitate for regulating the condition of employment of the contract labour. The Supreme Court has rightly observed in *Deena Nath* v. *National Fertilizer Ltd.*[6] that the Act, as can be seen from the scheme of the Act, is merely to regulate the employment of contract labour in certain establishments and provides for its abolition in certain circumstances. The Act does not provide for total abolition of contract labour but it provides for abolition by the appropriate Government in appropriate cases under S. 10 of the Act. In other words, it can be said that the framers of the Act have allowed and recognised contract labour and they have never purported to abolish it in its entirety. The primary object appears to be that there should not be exploitation of the contract labourers by the contractor or the establishment.[7] The Act was passed to prevent the exploitation of contract labour and also to introduce better conditions of work. The Act provides for regulation and abolition of contract labour. The underlying policy of the Act is to abolish contract labour, wherever possible and practicable, and where it cannot be abolished altogether, the policy of the Act is that the working conditions of the contract labour should be so regulated as to ensure payment of wages and provision of essential amenities. That is why the Act provides for regulated conditions of work and contemplates progressive abolition to the extent contemplated by S. 10 of the Act. Section 10 of the Act deals with abolition while the rest of the Act deals mainly with regulation. The dominant idea of S. 10 of the Act is to find out whether contract labour is necessary for the industry, trade, business, manufacture or occupation which is carried on in the establishment.[8]

Applicability and Non-applicability of the Act

So far as applicability of the Act is concerned, S. 1(4) may be looked from two angles, one from the establishment point of view and the other from contractor point of view. The Act applies to all establishments in which 20 or more workmen are employed or were employed on any day of the preceding twelve months as contract labour and to every contractor who employs or who employed on any day of the preceding twelve months 20 or more workmen. Even if this number of contract labour or workmen is less than twenty, the Act would still be applicable if the said limit of twenty had reached for even a day during the preceding twelve months. The appropriate Government has also power under proviso to S. 1(4) to apply the Act

6. AIR 1992 SC 457.
7. *R.K. Panda* v. *SAIL,* (1994) 5 SCC 304.
8. *Gammon India Ltd.* v. *Union of India*, AIR 1974 SC 960.

to any establishment or contractor employing such lesser number of workmen than twenty as may be specified. This power can be exercised by issuing a notification in the Official Gazette after giving at least two months' notice of its intention to do so.

Section 1(5) makes the Act inapplicable to establishments in which work only of an intermittent or casual nature is performed and the appropriate Government has been empowered to decide all questions whether the work performed in an establishment is or is not of an intermittent or casual nature. It has been clarified that in case the work in any establishment was performed for more than one hundred and twenty days in the preceding twelve months, or in the case of establishments of seasonal character, for more than sixty days in a year, it will not be deemed to be of an intermittent nature.

Act Applicable to Government

According to S. 1(4), the Act shall apply to all establishments in which 20 or more workmen are employed or were employed on any day of the preceding 12 months as contract labour and to every contractor who employs or has employed on any day of the preceding 12 months, 20 or more workmen. The Act does not apply to establishments in which work of an intermittent or casual nature alone is performed. Section 2(e) defines an establishment as meaning: (i) any office or department of the government or a local authority; or (ii) any place where any industry, trade, business, manufacture or occupation is carried on. The definitions 'establishment' and 'principal employer' clearly do not exclude but, on the other hand, expressly include the government or any of its departments and the Act applies to them too. The Act is not applicable to private employers only.

Computation of Twenty or More Workmen

It is the aggregate of the contract labour employed in an establishment, either for different purposes or through different contractors, that has to be taken into account to determine the number of workmen for the purposes of applicability of the Act to an establishment.

Work of an Intermittent or Casual Nature

The Act does not define 'works of an intermittent or casual nature'. The explanation at the end of sub-section (5) clarifies that in case the work in any establishment was performed for more than one hundred and twenty days in the preceding twelve months, or, in the case of establishments of seasonal character, it is performed for more than sixty days in a year, it shall not be deemed to be of an intermittent nature. This only means that work which may otherwise be of an intermittent nature in the ordinary, popular and natural sense of the expression, shall not be deemed to be of an intermittent nature if it is performed for more than the prescribed number of days. This does not mean that work which is not otherwise of an intermittent nature shall be deemed to be of an intermittent nature if it is performed for less than the prescribed number of days. The number of days is obviously not intended to be the sole test to justify exemption under sub-section (5). If it were so, the sub-section would have been worded in a simpler language, with no necessity for removal of doubts by the appropriate government, or for the explanation.

Section 2: Definitions

(1) In this Act, unless the context otherwise requires,—

(a) **appropriate Government** means,—

(i) in relation to an establishment in respect of which the appropriate government under the Industrial Disputes Act, 1947 (14 of 1947), is the Central Government, the Central Government;

(ii) in relation to any other establishment, the Government of the State in which that other establishment is situated;

(b) a workman shall be deemed to be employed as **contract labour** in or in connection with the work of an establishment when he is hired in or in connection with such work by or through a contractor, with or without the knowledge of the principal employer;

(c) **contractor**, in relation to an establishment, means a person who undertakes to produce a given result for the establishment, other than a mere supply of goods or articles of manufacture to such establishment, through contract labour or who supplies contract labour for any work of the establishment and includes a sub-contractor;

(d) **controlled industry** means any industry the control of which by the Union has been declared by any Central Act to be expedient in the public interest;

(e) **establishment** means—

(i) any office or department of the Government or a local authority, or

(ii) any place where any industry, trade, business, manufacture or occupation is carried on;

(f) **prescribed** means prescribed by rules made under this Act;

(g) **principal employer** means—

(i) in relation to any office or department of the Government or a local authority, the head of that office or department or such other officer as the Government or the local authority; as the case may be, may specify in this behalf,

(ii) in a factory, the owner or occupier of the factory and where a person has been named as the manager of the factory under the Factories Act, 1948 (63 of 1948), the person so named.

(iii) in a mine, the owner or agent of the mine and where a person has been named as the manager of the mine, the person so named,

(iv) in any other establishment, any person responsible for the supervision and control of the establishment.

Explanation: For the purpose of sub-clause (iii) of this clause, the expressions "mine", "owner" and "agent" shall have the meanings respectively assigned to them in clause (j), clause (l) and clause (c) of sub-section (1) of section 2 of the Mines Act, 1952 (35 of 1952);

(h) **wages** shall have the meaning assigned to it in clause (vi) of section 2 of the Payment of Wages Act, 1936 (4 of 1936);

(i) **workman** means any person employed in or in connection with the work of any establishment to do any skilled, semi-skilled or unskilled manual, supervisory, technical or clerical work for hire or reward, whether the terms of employment be express or implied, but does not include any such person—

(A) who is employed mainly in a managerial or administrative capacity; or

(B) who, being employed in a supervisory capacity draws wages exceeding five hundred rupees per mensem or exercises, either by the nature of the duties attached to the office or by reason of the powers vested in him, functions mainly of a managerial nature; or

(C) who is an out-worker, that is to say, a person to whom any article and materials are given out by or on behalf of the principal employer to be made up, cleaned, washed, altered, ornamented, finished, repaired, adapted or otherwise processed for sale for the purposes of the trade or business of the principal employer and the process is to be carried out either in the home of the out-worker or in some other premises, not being premises under the control and management of the principal employer.

(2) Any reference in this Act to a law which is not in force in the State of Jammu and Kashmir shall, in relation to that State, be construed as a reference to the corresponding law, if any, in force in that State.

A definition is a statement that sets forth and delimits the meaning of a word, phrase and expression used in the Act. It performs two functions, namely (i) the avoidance of ambiguities; and (ii) the avoidance by means of abbreviation of tedious repetitions. Once an expression has been defined, that expression, whenever it occurs in the Act, rules and notification issued thereunder, should be taken in the same sense. The Courts are also not free to construe otherwise unless it is so warranted. The Supreme Court in *Barsi Light Railway Co. Ltd.* v. *K.N. Joglekar and others*[9] observed:

> "That there is no doubt that when the Act itself provides dictionary for the words used, we must look into that dictionary first for an interpretation of the word used in the statute. We are not concerned with any presumed intention of the legislature; our task is to get at the intention as expressed in the statute."[10]

Section 2(1)(b) Contract Labour

"A workman shall be deemed to be employed as "contract labour" in or in connection with the work of an establishment when he is hired in or in connection with such work by or through a contractor, with or without the knowledge of the principal employer."

The following propositions may be drawn after reading the definition of contract labour mentioned above:

---

9. AIR 1957 SC 121.
10. *Ibid.* at p. 126 per S.K. Das, J.

(i) he must be a workman as per S. 2(1)(i) of the Act;
(ii) he is hired by or through a contractor;
(iii) he is hired in connection with the work of an establishment defined under S. 2(1)(e) of the Act;
(iv) knowledge of his engagement to the principal employer is immaterial.

Work of an establishment

The phrase *work of an establishment* is categorically interpreted and described by the Supreme Court in *Gammon India Ltd.* v. *Union of India*[11] and the following observations are made.

The petitioners contend that they are not contractors within the definition of the Act. They advance two reasons. First, the work of the petitioners is not any part of the work of the principal employer nor is it the work "in connection with the work of the establishment", namely, principal employer. Second, the work of the petitioners is normally not done in the premises of the "establishment" of the principal employer. By way of illustration, it is said that if a banking company, which is an establishment and which carries on its business in Delhi, employs the petitioners to construct a building in Allahabad, the building to be constructed is not the work of the bank. It is said that the only work of the bank as an establishment is banking work and, therefore, the work of construction is not the banking work of the establishment. Therefore, the petitioners contended that the workmen employed by the petitioners are not workmen in connection with the work of the establishment.

The Court observed that the contention of the petitioners is unsound. When the banking company employs the petitioners to construct a building, the petitioners are in relation to the establishment contractors who undertake to produce a given result for the bank. The petitioners are also persons who undertake to produce the result through contract labour. The petitioners may appoint sub-contractors to do the work. To accede to the petitioners contention that the construction work which is away from the place where the industry, trade, business of the establishment is carried on is not the work of the establishment is to render the words *"work of any establishment"* devoid of ordinary meaning. The construction of the building is the work of the establishment. The building is the property of the establishment. Therefore, the construction work is the work of the establishment. That is why a workman is deemed to be employed as contract labour in connection with the work of an establishment.

The place where business or trade or industry or manufacture or occupations is carried on is not synonymous with "the work of the establishment" when a contractor employs contract labour in connection with the work of the establishment. The error of the petitioners lies in equating the work of the establishment with the actual place where the business, industry or trade is carried on and the actual work of the business, industry or trade.

The expression *"work of an establishment"* means the work site where the construction work of the establishment is carried on by the petitioners by employing contract labour. Every clause of a statute is to be construed with reference to the context and other provisions of the Act to make a consistent and harmonious meaning of the statutes relating to the subject

11. AIR 1974 SC 960.

matter. The interpretation of the words will be by looking at the context, the collocation of the words and the object of the words relating to the matters. The words are not to be viewed detached from the context of the statute. The words are to be viewed in relation to the whole context. The definitions of contractor, workmen, contract labour, establishment, principal employer all indicate that the work of an establishment means the work site of the establishment where a building is constructed for the establishment. The construction is the work of the establishment. The expression "employed in or in connection with the work of the establishment" does not mean that the operation assigned to the workmen must be a part or incidental to the work performed by the principal employer. The contractor is employed to produce the given result for the benefit of the principal employer in fulfilment of the undertaking given to him by the contractor. Therefore, the employment of the contract labour, namely the workmen by the contractor, is in connection with the work of the establishment. The petitioners are contractors within the meaning of the Act. The work which the petitioners undertake is the work of the establishment.

Now it is construed that if the work of the contractor is part and parcel of the work of the establishment and is not a separate activity carried on by the contractor for his own purpose, then such work would definitely be the work of an establishment. However, what is to be seen in each particular case is, what is the main purpose of the activity carried on by the person. If the main purpose of the activity is totally unrelated to the activity of the establishment, though incidentally it may be pertaining to the work undertaken by the establishment, then such an activity undertaken by the person would not be covered by the mischief of the provision. In each particular case, therefore, what is to be determined is, whether there is a direct nexus between the activity of the establishment and the activity of the person with whom the establishment has entered into some transaction.

The next thing to be determined is, whether there is any direct nexus established between the activity of the establishment and the end product of the activity of the person with whom the establishment has entered into the transaction.[12]

In connection with the work of an establishment

The work which is the prime factor is the work of the establishment. It follows that any person who is in some manner or other connected with the work of the establishment would come within the ambit of contract labour. The use of the word 'such' before 'work' is significant.

The work incidental or preliminary to the work of the establishment would be work in or in connection with the work of the establishment. Where the petitioner had undertaken to collect and manufacture, when necessary, quarry products to be supplied to the railway and the work of such collection and manufacture was done for and on behalf of the railway, it was held that the workmen employed by the petitioner for such work were to be deemed as 'contract labour' under the Act and that the petitioner was a contractor.[13]

---

12. *State of Gujarat* v. *Sarabhai Chimanlal Sheth & Co.* [1984] 2 LLJ 334.
13. *H.C. Bothra* v. *Union of India* [1976] Lab IC 1199 (Gau).

Section 2(1)(c)

"Contractor, in relation to an establishment, means a person who undertakes to produce a given result for the establishment, other than a mere supply of goods or articles of manufacture to such establishment, through contract labour or who supplies contract labour for any work of the establishment and includes a sub-contractor."

The above definition can be analysed as follows:

(i) A contractor is a person who undertakes to produce a given result for the establishment through contract labour;

(ii) A contractor is a person who supplies contract labour for any work of the establishment;

(iii) A contractor includes a sub-contractor;

(iv) A person whose only obligation towards the establishment is a mere supply of goods or articles of manufacture to such establishment cannot be a contractor for the purpose of the Act.

Furthermore, the definition may be divided into three parts, such as substantive part, exclusive part and inclusive part. The substantive part may be the first part of the definition, i.e. contractor, in relation to an establishment, means a person who undertakes to produce a given result for the establishment; exclusive part may be the second part of the definition, i.e. other than a mere supply of goods or articles of manufacture to such establishment; and inclusive part may be the last part of the definition which speaks contractor includes sub-contractor.

Thus, the basic requirement for a person to be 'contractor' in terms of the definition is that he must either execute his contract through 'contract labour' or supply 'contract labour'.

CHAPTER II

THE ADVISORY BOARDS

SECTION 3: Central Advisory Board

(1) The Central Government shall, as soon as may be, constitute a Board to be called the Central Advisory Contract Labour Board (hereinafter referred to as the Central Board) to advise the Central Government on such matters arising out of the administration of this Act as may be referred to it and to carry out other functions assigned to it under this Act.

(2) The Central Board shall consist of—

(a) a Chairman to be appointed by the Central Government;

(b) the Chief Labour Commissioner (Central), *ex officio*;

(c) such number of members, not exceeding seventeen but not less than eleven, as the Central Government may nominate to represent that government, the Railways, the coal industry, the mining industry, the contractors, the workmen and any other interests which, in the opinion of the Central Government, ought to be represented on the Central Board.

(3) The number of persons to be appointed as members from each of the categories specified in sub-section (2), the term of office and other conditions of service of, the procedure to be followed in the discharge of their functions by, and the manner of filling vacancies among, the members of the Central Board shall be such as may be prescribed:

Provided that the number of members nominated to represent the workmen shall not be less than the number of members nominated to represent the principal employers and the contractors.

In pursuance of S. 3 of the Act, the Central Government is authorised to constitute a Central Advisory Board as soon as possible and the direction is mandatory. The object of constituting such Central Board is two-fold:

(i) to advise the Central Government on such matters arising out of the administration of this Act as may be referred by the Central Government to the Central board, and
(ii) to carry out other functions assigned to it under this Act.

It is implied that the Central Government is having discretionary power either to refer or not to refer any matter for advice as well as the choice of the matter to be referred for advice rests with the Central Government.

If the Central Government is an appropriate Government, then the Central Government is bound to consult the Central Board before exercising its powers as appropriate Government under S. 1(5)(b) and S. 10(1) of the Act. Section 1(5)(b) provides that If a question arises whether work performed in an establishment is of an intermittent or casual nature, the appropriate government shall decide the question after consultation with the Central Board or, as the case may be, the State Board, and its decision shall be final. Section 10(1) empowers the appropriate Government to prohibit the employment of contract labour in any process, operation or other work in any establishment after consultation with the Central Board or, as the case may be, a State Board. When the Central Government is the appropriate Government, the Central Board has to be consulted under both these Sections and where a State Government is the appropriate Government, the State Board concerned has to be consulted.

Sub-section (2) provides for the composition of the Central Board and it is seen that the Board is constituted by the representatives of the contractor, workmen and the industries concerned. Sub-section (3) prescribes that the number of workmen represented in the Board shall not be less than the number of members nominated to represent the principal employers and contractors. The intention may be for effective participation with equal power to that of other group in order to protect their interest.

SECTION 4: State Advisory Board

(1) The State Government may constitute a Board to be called the State Advisory Contract Labour Board (hereinafter referred to as the State Board) to advise the State

Government on such matters arising out of the administration of this Act as may be referred to it and to carry out other functions assigned to it under this Act.

(2) The State Board shall consist of—

(a) a Chairman to be appointed by the State Government;

(b) the Labour Commissioner, *ex officio*, or in his absence any other officer nominated by the State Government in that behalf;

(c) such number of members, not exceeding eleven but not less than nine, as the State Government may nominate to represent that Government, the industry, the contractors, the workmen and any other interests which, in the opinion of the State Government, ought to be represented on the State Board.

(3) The number of persons to be appointed as members from each of the categories specified in sub-section (2), the term of office and other conditions of service of, the procedure to be followed in the discharge of their functions by, and the manner of filling vacancies, among, the members of the State Board shall be such as may be prescribed:

Provided that the number of members nominated to represent the workmen shall not be less than the number of members nominated to represent the principal employers and the contractors.

Like S. 3, S. 4 requires that the number of members nominated to represent workmen shall not be less than the members nominated to represent the principal employers and contractors on the State Advisory Board.

Section 5: Power to constitute committees

(1) The Central Board or the State Board, as the case may be, may constitute such committees and for such purpose or purposes as it may think fit.

(2) The committee constituted under sub-section (1) shall meet at such time and places and shall observe such rules of procedure in regard to the transaction of business at its meetings as may be prescribed.

(3) The members of a committee shall be paid such fees and allowances for attending its meetings as may be prescribed:

Provided that no fees shall be payable to a member who is an officer of Government or of any corporation established by any law for the time being in force.

The Supreme Court in *Food Corporation of India Workers' Union* v. *Food Corporation of India*[14] misread S. 5 of the Act as it issued the writ of mandamus and accordingly directed all the State Governments except the State of Madhya Pradesh for appointing a committee under S. 5 of the Act within three months.

It is submitted that S. 5 of the Act empowers only the Central Board or the State Board, as the case may be, to constitute the committees and it has nothing to do with the State Government. After reading Ss. 3, 4 and 5, the following points are noted.

14. AIR 1985 SC 488.

Section 3: The Central Government *shall, as soon as may be,* constitute a Board.

Section 4: The State Government *may* constitute a Board.

Section 5: The Central Board or the State Board, as the case may be, *may* constitute such committees.

Section 3 is a mandatory one whereas S. 4 is discretionary. If the State Government will not exercise its power under S. 4, it is presumed that the State Government cannot be directed to constitute a State Advisory Board, so writ of mandamus may not lie; whereas the Central Government can be directed to constitute a Central Board in case of non-compliance of mandatory provision of S. 3 of the Act. The Court can issue the writ of mandamus and direct the Central Government to constitute a Board as required under S. 3 of the Act.

Section 5 provides altogether a different connotation. Section 5 provides that the Central Board constituted under S. 3 and the State Board constituted under S. 4, as the case may be, may constitute such other committees as it may think fit. So it appears that S. 5 confers a discretionary power on the Central and State Boards to constitute such other committees.

CHAPTER III

REGISTRATION OF ESTABLISHMENTS EMPLOYING CONTRACT LABOUR

SECTION 6: Appointment of registering officers

The appropriate Government may, by an order notified in the Official Gazette—

(a) appoint such persons, being Gazetted Officers of Government, as it thinks fit to be registering officers for the purposes of this Chapter; and

(b) define the limits, within which a registering officer shall exercise the powers conferred on him by or under this Act.

This section makes it clear that only the Gazetted Officers of the Government can be appointed as registering officers under the Act and such appointment has to be made by an order notified in the Official Gazette. This section empowers the appropriate Government to define the limits within which a registering officer shall exercise the powers conferred on him by or under this Act.

SECTION 7: Registration of certain establishments

(1) Every principal employer of an establishment to which this Act applies shall, within such period as the appropriate Government may, by notification in the Official Gazette, fix in this behalf with respect to establishment generally or with respect to any class of them, make an application to the registering officer in the prescribed manner for registration of the establishment:

Provided that the registering officer may entertain any such application for registration after expiry of the period fixed in this behalf if the registering officer is satisfied that the applicant was prevented by sufficient cause from making the application in time.

(2) If the application for registration is complete in all respects, the registering officer shall register the establishment and issue to the principal employer of the establishment a certificate of registration containing such particulars as may be prescribed.

This section imposes an obligation on the principal employer to apply for registration in the prescribed manner. If the application for registration is complete in all respects, the registering officer shall register the establishment and issue to the principal employer of the establishment a certificate of registration containing such particulars as may be prescribed. If an establishment falls within the purview of the Act and the principal employer does not apply for registration of the establishment to the registering officer as required under S. 7 the Act, the principal employer will not be permitted to employ the contract labour as per S. 9 of the Act.

Section 8: Revocation of registration in certain cases

If the registering officer is satisfied, either on a reference made to him in this behalf or otherwise, that the registration of any establishment has been obtained by misrepresentation or suppression of any material fact, or that for any other reason the registration has become useless or ineffective and, therefore requires to be revoked, the registering officer may, after giving an opportunity to the principal employer of the establishment to be heard and with the previous approval of the appropriate Government, revoke the registration.

The registering officer may revoke the registration of any establishment on the following grounds:

1. that the registration of any establishment has been obtained by misrepresentation; or
2. that the registration of any establishment has been obtained by suppression of any material fact, or
3. that for any other reason the registration has become useless or ineffective.

The word misrepresentation has not been defined in the Contract Labour (Regulation & Abolition) Act, 1970. Hence it is worthwhile to refer S. 18 of the Indian Contract Act, 1872.

Section 18 of the Indian Contract Act, 1872 defines 'misrepresentation' as follows:

"Misrepresentation" means and includes—

(1) the positive assertion, in a manner not warranted by the information of the person making it, of that which is not true, though he believes it to be true;

(2) any breach of duty which, without an intent to deceive, gains an advantage to the person committing it, or anyone claiming under him; by misleading another to his prejudice, or to the prejudice of any one claiming under him;

(3) causing, however innocently, a party to an agreement, to make a mistake as to the substance of the thing which is subject of the agreement.

The registering officer has to provide reasonable opportunity to the principal employer of the establishment to be heard before revoking the registration of any establishment and to obtain the previous approval of the appropriate Government for such revocation.

SECTION 9: Effect of non-registration

No principal employer of an establishment, to which this Act applies, shall—

(a) in the case of an establishment required to be registered under section 7, but which has not been registered within the time fixed for the purpose under that section;

(b) in the case of an establishment the registration in respect of which has been revoked under section 8,

employ contract labour in the establishment after the expiry of the period referred to in clause (a) or after the revocation of registration referred to in clause (b), as the case may be.

If an establishment, to which this Act applies, has not been registered required to be registered under S. 7 within the stipulated time fixed for the purpose, or the registration of any establishment has been revoked under S. 8, the principal employer is not entitled to engage contract labour thereafter.

SECTION 10: Prohibition of employment of contract labour

(1) Notwithstanding anything contained in this Act, the appropriate Government may, after consultation with the Central Board or, as the case may be, a State Board, prohibit, by notification in the Official Gazette, employment of contract labour in any process, operation or other work in any establishment.

(2) Before issuing any notification under sub-section (1) in relation to an establishment, the appropriate Government shall have regard to the conditions of work and benefits provided for the contract labour in that establishment and other relevant factors, such as—

(a) whether the process, operation or other work is incidental to, or necessary for the industry, trade, business, manufacture or occupation that is carried on in the establishment;

(b) whether it is of perennial nature, that is to say, it is of sufficient duration having regard to the nature of industry, trade, business, manufacture or occupation carried on in that establishment;

(c) whether it is done ordinarily through regular workmen in that establishment or an establishment similar thereto;

(d) whether it is sufficient to employ considerable number of whole-time workmen.

Explanation: If a question arises whether any process or operation or other work is of perennial nature, the decision of the appropriate Government thereon shall be final.

The Act was passed to prevent the exploitation of contract labour and also to introduce better conditions of work. The Act provides for regulation and abolition of contract labour. The underlying policy of the Act is to abolish contract labour, wherever possible and practicable, and where it cannot be abolished altogether, the policy of the Act is that the working conditions of the contract labour should be so regulated as to ensure payment of wages and provision of essential amenities. That is why the Act provides for regulated conditions of work and contemplates progressive abolition to the extent contemplated by S. 10 of the Act. Section 10 of the Act deals with abolition while the rest of the Act deals mainly with regulation. The dominant idea of S. 10 of the Act is to find out whether contract labour is necessary for the industry, trade, business, manufacture or occupation which is carried on in the establishment.[15]

Notwithstanding Anything Contained in this Act

Section 10(1) opens with a *non-obstante* clause, which means notwithstanding any statute to the contrary. A *non-obstante* clause is usually used in a provision to indicate that that provision should prevail despite anything to the contrary in the provision mentioned in such *non-obstante* clause. In case there is any inconsistency or a departure between the *non-obstante* clause and another provision, one of the objects such clause is to indicate that it is the *non-obstante* clause which would prevail over the other clause, provided, of course, that there is no repugnancy between the two provisions. In view of this, and particularly in view of the aims and objective of the Act that it is passed for abolition of the contract labour where possible must prevail over the other provisions of the Act which merely relate to regulation of contract labour.

Consultation with the Board

The appropriate Government is duty bound under S. 10(1) to consult with the Central Board or the State Board, as the case may be, before prohibiting employment of contract labour in any process, operation or other work in any establishment. However, it does not mean that the appropriate Government is bound to accept the advice given by the Board. The role of the Central Board or the State Board is only advisory but the ultimate discretion to prohibit engagement of contract labour in any process, operation or other work in any establishment rests with the appropriate Government. What is expected that the appropriate Government should not bypass the Board constituted under the Act before issuing notification under S. 10(1). Consultation with the Central Board or the State Board, as the case may be, is mandatory and condition precedent to the issuance of prohibition notification under S. 10(1) of the Act.

Other Work in any Establishment

Section 10(1) empowers the Government to prohibit employment of contract labour in any process, operation or other work in any establishment. The meaning of the phrase 'other work in any establishment' came before the Supreme Court for consideration because similar words, namely, 'work of an establishment' and 'any work of the establishment' are found in the

15. *Gammon India Ltd.* v. *Union of India,* AIR 1974 SC 960.

definition of 'contract labour' provided under S. 2(1)(b) and the definition of 'contractor' provided under S. 2(1)(c) of the Act, respectively. The Supreme Court in *Gammon India Ltd.* v. *Union of India*[17] observed that the words "other work in any establishment" in S. 10 of the Act are important. The work in the establishment will be apparent from S. 10(2) of the Act as incidental or necessary to the industry, trade, business, manufacture or occupation that is carried on in the establishment. The Government, before notifying prohibition of contract labour for work which is carried on in the establishment, will consider where the work is of a perennial nature in that establishment or work is done ordinarily through regular workmen in that establishment. The words "work of an establishment" which are used in defining a workman as contract labour being employed in connection with the work of an establishment indicate that the work of the establishment is not the same as work in the establishment contemplated in S. 10 of the Act. The words "other work in any establishment" in S. 10 are to be construed as *ejusdem generis*. The expression "other work" in the collocation of words process, operation or other work in any establishment occurring in S. 10 has not the same meaning as the expression "in connection with the work of an establishment", spoken in relation to workmen or contractor.

Shall have Regard to

The phrase 'shall have regard to' only implies a guideline for the appropriate Government to consider the conditions of work and benefits provided for contract labour engaged in that establishment in question before prohibiting the employment of contract labour along with other relevant factors mentioned in Cls. (a) to (d) of S. 10(2) of the Act.

Other Relevant Factors, Such as

Section 10(2) of the Act prescribes guidelines for the appropriate Government to consider before issuing a notification prohibiting the employment of contract labour in any process, operation or other work in any establishment. They are:

(i) condition of work of the contract labour in the establishment in question;
(ii) benefits provided for the contract labour in that establishment;
(iii) other relevant factors mentioned in the sub-clauses (a) to (d) of S. 10(2) of the Act.

The use of the words *such as* makes it clear that the phrase *other relevant factors* mentioned in the sub-clauses (a) to (d) of S. 10(2) of the Act is not exhaustive, rather illustrative only. Hence, the appropriate Government may consider, if it so likes, other relevant factors also in addition to the above mentioned factors. The other relevant factors could be: financial condition of the principal employer or whether there would be sufficient work for all the workmen if contract labour would be absorbed or the practice in vogue in other industries, and the like.

Process, Operation or Other Work

A notification was issued by the Government of Karnataka under S. 10 of the Act on 11-4-1997 prohibiting with effect from the date of publication of the notification employment of contract labour in industrial canteens and factories employing 250 workers or above in the State of Karnataka. Writ petitions were filed before the High Court of Karnataka challenging the validity of the same on various grounds. However, the High Court upheld the validity of the said notifications and dismissed the writ petitions. Hence, these petitions came to the apex court under Art. 136 of the Constitution. The Supreme Court in *Barat Fritz Werner Ltd.* v. *State of Karnataka*[16] held that S. 10 of the Act provides for prohibition of employment of contract labour in any process, operation or other work in an establishment. The words *"process, operation or other work"* need not be interpreted to mean only the core activity and not peripheral activity as is sought to be suggested by learned counsel for petitioners. In sub-section (2) of S. 10 of the Act, certain guidelines have been provided for the Government before the issue of any notification to find out whether the "process, operation or other work" is incidental to or necessary for the industry, trade, business, manufacture or occupation that is carried on in the establishment. The expression used therein is wide in ambit to cover other activity arising in industry and not merely the actual manufacture. Otherwise to understand the expression *"process, operation or other work"* other than the meaning given in Cl. (a) of sub-section (2) of S. 10 would be to narrow down the meaning thereto. That does not seem to be the intention of the enactment at all.

The following points emerge from S. 10(1) of the Act:

(i) The appropriate Government has power to prohibit the employment of contract labour in any process, operation or other work in any establishment.

(ii) Before issuing a notification prohibiting contract labour, the appropriate Government has to consult the Central or State Board, as the case may be, comprising the representatives of the workmen, contractor and the industry.

(iii) Before issuing any notification under S. 10(1), prohibiting the employment of contract labour, the appropriate Government is bound to have regard not only to the conditions of work and benefits provided for the contract labour in a particular establishment, but also other relevant factors enumerated in Cls. (a) to (d) of S. 10(2) and any other conditions if in the opinion of the appropriate Government they are relevant for the purpose.

(iv) Under the Explanation which really relates to Cl. (b), the decision of the appropriate Government on the question whether any process, operation or other work is of perennial nature, shall be final.

In 2003, two important cases, i.e. *National Thermal Power Corporation Ltd.* v. *Karri Pothuraju*[17] and *Mishra Dhatu Nigam Ltd.* v. *M. Venkataiah*[18] were decided by the Supreme Court on 13-08-2003 where facts of both the cases were very much similar and both the cases were decided by the same judges, namely S. Rajendra Babu and Doraiswamy Raju, JJ. As both the cases deal with the same issue, it is not necessary to discuss both the cases in detail. Hence *National Thermal Power Corporation Ltd.* case is considered for discussion. In *National Thermal Power Corporation Ltd.* case, an appeal had been filed against the order

16. AIR 2001 SC 1257.
17. AIR 2003 SC 3647.
18. AIR 2003 SC 3124.

dated 27-11-1996 of a Division Bench of the Andhra Pradesh High Court in Writ Appeal No. 385 of 1996, whereunder the Division Bench, while setting aside the order of the learned Single Judge in Writ Petition No. 3793 of 1992, allowed the claims in the writ petition to the extent and subject to the conditions specified in the order. The appellant, National Thermal Power Corporation Ltd., Ramagundam Super Thermal Power Station, is a Public Sector Undertaking of the Government of India. It started a canteen in the year 1983 for the benefit of the employees of their unit through a contractor, and from that time onwards, it was being run through contractors engaged from time to time. The total number of employees, at the relevant point of time, were said to be 2300 and about 54 persons were said to have been working in the canteen in various capacities—cooks, servers, cleaners, etc. It is not in controversy that the appellant is a factory governed by the provisions of the Factories Act and S. 46 of the said Act, 1948 casts a mandatory duty and obligation on the appellant to provide and maintain a canteen for the benefit of all those serving in the unit. The respondents, at least many of them, were said to be working from the year 1983, though engaged by contractors. The Deputy Manager, Administration and his subordinates were said to supervise the working of the canteen in respect of preparation, service and maintenance, to ensure quality of service and make beneficial to the workers. It is also claimed that the said authority issued identity cards also to the workers for entering the factory premises. Apparently, taking advantage of certain decisions of courts, including the Supreme Court, the respondent-workers moved the High Court by means of the writ petition filed under Art. 226 of the Constitution, seeking for a direction to the appellant to regularize their services with attendant benefits.

The appellants disputed the claim, contending that the canteen was run as a beneficial measure, to cater to the needs of workers in the unit, that contractors used to be engaged periodically, at times different contractors for different period, depending upon the successful offer made pursuant to invitation of tenders, that they have nothing to do with the total strength of workers engaged by such contractors, that they are neither workers relating to the manufacturing activities of the appellant-undertaking nor they perform any work incidental thereto or by any means could claim to be workers of the appellant within the meaning of the Industrial Disputes Act, 1947. The control, if at all, was said to be to ensure that there is no industrial unrest on account of the manner of running the canteen and proper food articles are made available hygienically and at the rates stipulated without sacrificing the quality of the food stuffs, eatables and beverages and such supervision cannot make them workers under the control of the appellant and that the relationship of master and servant and disciplinary control over them was also with their employer-contractor, at all times.

The learned Senior Counsel appearing on behalf of the appellant placed strong reliance upon the decisions given in *Indian Petrochemicals Corporation Ltd. & Another* v. *Shramik Sena & Others*[19] and other related decisions to contend that the Division Bench went wrong in reversing the decision of the learned Single Judge and that the respondent-workers, who are indisputably the workers in the canteen, engaged by the contractor, cannot claim to be a part of the appellant's establishment and claim for regularisation in the service of the appellant-undertaking and consequently the order under challenge is liable to be set aside. Per contra, the learned Senior Counsel appearing for the respondent-workers placed reliance

---

19. (1996) 6 SCC 439.

upon the decisions reported in *Indian Overseas Bank* v. *I.O.B. Staff Canteen Workers' Union & Another*[20] as well as *Steel Authority of India Ltd. & Others* v. *National Union Waterfront Workers & Others*[21] and in *VST Industries Ltd.* v. *VST Industries Workers' Union & Another*[22] to contend that the decision of the Division Bench does not require any interference in this appeal. Reliance was also placed on an earlier decision of the Supreme Court in *The Saraspur Mills Co. Ltd.* v. *Ramanlal Chimanlal & Others*[23] for sustaining the decision of the High Court under challenge.

An analysis of the cases, discussed above, shows that they fall in three classes.

(i) Where contract labour is engaged in or in connection with the work of an establishment and employment of contract labour is prohibited either because the industrial adjudicator/court ordered abolition of contract labour, or because the appropriate Government issued notification under S. 10(1) of the Act, no automatic absorption of the contract labour working in the establishment was ordered.

(ii) Where the contract was found to be a sham and nominal, rather a camouflage, in which case the contract labour working in the establishment of the principal employer were held, in fact and in reality, the employees of the principal employer himself. Indeed, such cases do not relate to abolition of contract labour but present instances wherein the Court pierced the veil and declared the correct position as a fact at the stage after employment of contract labour stood prohibited.

(iii) Where in discharge of a statutory obligation of maintaining a canteen in an establishment the principal employer availed the services of a contractor, the Courts have held that the contract labour would indeed be the employees of the principal employer.

Basing on the above discussion, the Court held:

> "Consequently, we consider it to be too late in the day for the appellant, which had an obligation under the Factories Act, 1948 to run the canteen to contend to the contrary. So far as the case on hand is concerned, the Division Bench has chosen to leave liberty to the appellant to consider the claims of the workers as to whether they satisfy the requirements and whether they are otherwise unfit for confirmations. In the light of all these, we are unable to countenance the challenge to the decision of the High Court, as either legitimate or valid one. The appeal, therefore, fails and shall stand dismissed. No costs."[24]

Non-Compliance of Section 10 vis-à-vis Notification Issued by the Appropriate Government Prohibiting the Employment of Contract Labour

The impugned notification issued by the Central Government on December 9, 1976, reads as under:

---

20. (2000) 4 SCC 245.
21. (2001) 7 SCC 1.
22. (2001) 1 SCC 298.
23. (1974) 3 SCC 66.
24. *National Thermal Power Corporation Ltd.* v. *Karri Pothuraju,* AIR 2003 SC 3647 at p. 3649 per Rajendra Babu, J.

"S.O. No.779(E)8/9-12-76 in exercise of the power conferred by sub-section (1) of Section 10 of the Contract Labour (Regulation and Abolition) Act, 1970 (37 of 1970) the Central Government after consultation with the Central Advisory Contract Labour Board hereby prohibits employment of contract labour on and from the 1st March, 1977, for sweeping, cleaning, dusting and watching of buildings owned or occupied by the establishments in respect of which the appropriate Government under the said Act is the Central Government…".

Such notification was challenged on the ground of non-application of mind of the Central Government and non-compliance of the conditions mentioned in S. 10 of the Act. The Supreme Court in *Steel Authority of India Ltd.* v. *National Union Waterfront Workers*[25] observed that before issuing notification under sub-section (1) of S. 10 in respect of an establishment, the appropriate Government is enjoined to have regard to: (i) the conditions of work; (ii) the benefits provided for the contract labour; and (iii) other relevant factors like those specified in Cls. (a) to (d) of sub-section (2) of S. 10 of the Act. The list is not exhaustive. The appropriate Government may also take into consideration other relevant factors of the nature enumerated in sub-section (2) of S. 10 before issuing notification under S. 10(1) of the Act. Now reading the definition of "establishment" in S. 10, the position that emerges is that before issuing notification under sub-section (1), an appropriate Government is required to: (i) consult the Central Board/State Board; (ii) consider the conditions of work and benefits provided for the contract labour and (iii) take note of the factors such as mentioned in Cls. (a) to (d) of sub-section (2) of S. 10, referred to above, with reference to any office or department of the Government or local authority or any place where any industry, trade, business, manufacture or occupation is carried on. This clearly indicates that the Central Government had not adverted to any of the essentials, referred to above, except the requirement of consultation with the Central Advisory Board. Consideration of the factors mentioned above has to be in respect of each establishment, whether individually or collectively, in respect of which notification under sub-section (1) of S. 10 is proposed to be issued. The impugned noti-fication apart from being an omnibus notification does not reveal compliance of sub-section (2) of S. 10. This is ex-facie contrary to the postulates of S. 10 of the Act. Besides, it also exhibits non-application of mind by the Central Government. Therefore, the impugned notification cannot be sustained.

Writ Jurisdiction vis-à-vis Abolition of Contract Labour

In view of the provision in S. 10 of the Act, it is only the appropriate Government which has the authority to abolish the system of contract labour in accordance with the provisions of the said section. No court including the industrial adjudicator has jurisdiction to do so. The exclusive jurisdiction to abolish contract labour in any establishment lies with the appropriate Government and therefore the High Court can neither issue a writ to abolish the contract labour nor prevent a principal employer from engaging contract labour where no order under S. 10 of the Act, abolishing contract labour, is passed by the appropriate Government. The Supreme

25. AIR 2001 SC 3527.

Court has categorically dealt with the issue in *B.H.E.L. Workers Association, Hardwar* v. *Union of India*[26] and observed that it is not possible for this Court in an application under Art. 32 of the Constitution to embark into an enquiry whether these thousand and odd workmen working in various capacities and engaged in multifarious activities do work identical with work done by the workmen directly employed by the B.H.E.L. and whether for that reason they should be treated not as contract labour but as direct employees of the B.H.E.L.

The learned counsel appearing for the B.H.E.L. Workers Association advanced the extreme argument that the Court must declare a total ban on the employment of contract labour in public sector undertakings. It was argued that the employment of contract labour has been frowned upon by various committees appointed by the Government and the Parliament itself thought that the employment of contract labour was undesirable and, therefore, enacted the Contract Labour (Regulation and Abolition) Act, 1970. It was submitted that in order to give effect to the intention of Parliament as well as the Directive Principles of State Policy, the Court should declare illegal the employment of contract labour by the State or by any public sector undertaking as a public sector undertaking is a State for the purposes of Art. 12 of the Constitution of India. In other words, the counsel wants the Supreme Court by its writ to abolish the employment of contract labour by the State and by all public sector undertakings.

But their Lordships observed:

> "We are afraid that, that would be nothing but the exercise of activity with which function the Court is not entrusted by the Constitution.... It is not for the court to enquire into the question and to decide whether the employment of contract labour in any process, operation or other work in any establishment should be abolished or not. This is a matter for the decision of the Government after considering the matters required to be considered under S. 10 of the Act."[27]

In *Steel Authority of India Ltd.* v. *Union of India* (AIR 2006 SC 3229) which is popularly known as SAIL-II case wherein the Supreme Court held that the CLRA Act is a complete code by itself. It not only provides for regulation of contract labour but also abolition thereof. Relationship of employer and employee is essentially a question of fact. Determination of the said question would depend upon a large number of factors. Ordinarily, a writ court would not go into such a question. The Court further held that neither the Labour Court nor the writ court could determine the question as to whether the contract labour should be abolished or not, the same being within the exclusive domain of the Appropriate Government.

In *A.P.S.R.T.C.* v. *G. Srinivas Reddy* (AIR 2006 SC 1465) there was no notification under Section 10(1) of CLRA Act, prohibiting contract labour. There was also neither a contention nor a finding that the contract with the contractor was sham and nominal and the contract labour working in the establishment were, in fact, employees of the principal employer. In view of the principles laid down in *SAIL-I* case, the Supreme Court held that the High Court could not have directed absorption of respondents who were held to be contract labour, by assuming that the contract labour system was only a camouflage and that there was a direct relationship of employer and employee between the Corporation and the respondents. If respondents want the relief of absorption, they will have to approach the Industrial Tribunal/

26. *Ibid.*, f.n. 3. AIR 1985 SC 409.
27. *Ibid.* at pp. 411 & 413 per Chinnappa Reddy, J.

Court and establish that the contract labour system was only a ruse/camouflage to avoid labour law benefits to them. The High Court could not, in exercise of its jurisdiction under Article 226, direct absorption of respondents, on the ground that work for which respondents were engaged as contract labour, was perennial in nature.

Consequence after Abolition the Employment of Contract Labour

What would be the consequence that ensues from abolition is the question? It is true that we find no express provision in the Act declaring the contract labour working in the establishment of the principal employer in the particular service to be the direct employees of the principal employer. Does the Act intend to deny the workman to continue to work under the Act or does it intend to denude him of the benefit of permanent employment and, if so, what would be the remedy available to him? This question was discussed by the Supreme Court in *Air India Statutory Corporation* v. *United Labour Union*[28] and it held that the Act does not provide total abolition of the contract labour system under the Act. The Act regulates contract labour system to prevent exploitation of the contract labour. The Preamble to the Act furnishes the key to its scope and operation. The Act regulates not only employment of contract labour in the establishment covered under the Act and its abolition in certain circumstances covered under S. 10(2) but also "matters connected therewith". The phrase "matters connected therewith" gives clue to the intention of the Act. The enforcement of the provisions to establish canteen in every establishment under S. 16 is to supply food to the workmen at the subsidised rates as it is a right to food, a basic human right. Similarly, the provision in S. 17 to provide rest rooms to the workmen is a right to leisure enshrined in Art. 43 of the Constitution. Supply of wholesome drinking water, establishment of latrine and urinals as enjoined under S. 18 are part of the basic human right to health assured under Art. 39 and right to just and humane conditions of work assured under Art. 42. All of them are fundamental human rights to the workmen and are facets of right to life guaranteed under Art. 21.

When the principal employer is enjoined to ensure those rights and payment of wages while the contract labour system is under regulation, the question arises whether after abolition of the contract labour system those workmen should be left in a lurch, denuding them of the means of livelihood and the enjoyment of the basic fundamental rights provided while the contract labour system is regulated under the Act? The Advisory Committee constituted under S. 10(1) is required to consider whether the process, operation and other work is incidental to or necessary for the industry, trade, business, manufacture or occupation that is carried on in the establishment, whether it is of a perennial nature, that is to say, whether it is of substantive duration having regard to the nature of industry, trade, business, manufacture or occupation carried on in that establishment, whether it is done ordinarily through regular workmen in the establishment or an establishment similar thereto, whether it is sufficient to employ considerable number of wholetime workmen. Upon consideration of these facts, recommendation for abolition is made by the Advisory Board, and then the appropriate Government examines the question and takes a decision in that behalf. The

28. AIR 1997 SC 645.

explanation to S. 10(2) provides that when any process or operation or other work is of perennial nature, the decision of the appropriate Government thereon shall be final. It would thus give indication that on the abolition of the contract labour system by publication of the notification in the Official Gazette, the necessary concomitant is that the wholetime workmen are required for carrying on the process, operation or other work being done in the industry, trade, business, manufacture or occupation in that establishment. When the condition of the work which is of perennial nature, etc., as envisaged in sub-section (2) of S. 10, is satisfied, the continuance of contract labour stands prohibited and abolished. The concomitant result would be that the source of regular employment became open.

The plea that the contractor might have employed a number of workmen who may be in excess of the requirement and, therefore, the principal employer on abolition of the contract labour may be burdened with excess workmen is more imaginary than real. The principal employer as a worldly businessman in his practical commercial wisdom would not allow the contractor to do so. On the contrary, the principal employer would see to it that the contractor brings only those number of workmen who are required to discharge their duties to carry out the work of the principal employer on his establishment through, of course, the agency of the contractor. In fact, the scheme of the Act and regulations framed thereunder clearly indicate that even the number of the workmen required for the given contract work is to be specified in the licence given to the contractor. And all the more, even, apart from that, after the absorption of the erstwhile contract workmen by the principal employer on abolition of contract labour system under S. 10, it is always open for the employer as an entrepreneur, in an appropriate case, if the excess working staff is not found to be required by him, to retrench such excess staff in accordance with the provisions of the Industrial Disputes Act, 1947.

His Lordship S.B. Majumdar, J., in his concurring judgment, observed that S. 10 nowhere provides in express term that on abolition of contract labour the workmen would become direct employees of the principal employer. It is obvious that no such express provision was required to be made as the very concept of abolition of a contract labour system wherein the work of the contract labour is of perennial nature for the establishment and which otherwise would have been done by regular workmen, would posit improvement of the lot of such workmen and not its worsening. Implicit in the provision of S. 10 is the legislative intent that on abolition of contract labour system, the erstwhile contract-workmen would become direct employees of the employer on whose establishment they were earlier working and were enjoying all the regulatory facilities under Chapter V prior to the abolition of such contract labour system. Though the legislature has expressly not mentioned the conse-quences of such abolition, the very scheme and ambit of S. 10 of the Act clearly indicates the inherent legislative intent of making the erstwhile contract labourers direct employees of the employer on abolition of the intermediary contractor. If it is held that on abolition of contract labour system the erstwhile contract labourers are to be thrown out of the establishment lock, stock and barrel, it would amount to throwing the baby out with the bathwater.

Therefore, it is submitted that the Court took a pragmatic approach and cast a duty on the principal employer to absorb the contract labour once a notification for abolition of the contract labour is made under S. 10(1) of the Act. Otherwise, the true intention of the Act would be frustrated. The intention of the Act is to abolish the contract labour wherever and whenever there is possibility, but not throwing the workers out of job rather through absorption.

However, the *Air India* case was overruled prospectively in *Steel Authority of India Ltd.* v. *National Union Waterfront Workers*[27] and the Supreme Court took just a diametrically opposite view to that of *Air India* case. The Court in this case observed that neither S. 10 of the CLRA Act nor any other provision in the Act, whether expressly or by necessary implication, provides for automatic absorption of contract labour on issuing a notification by appropriate Government under sub-section (1) of S. 10, prohibiting employment of contract labour, in any process, operation or other work in any establishment. Consequently, the principal employer cannot be required to order absorption of the contract labour working in the establishment concerned.

The concept of automatic absorption of the contract labour on issuance of notification under S. 10 prohibiting employment of contract labour in an establishment is neither alluded to in the report of the Joint Committee of Parliament on the Contract Labour (Regulation and Abolition) Bill, 1967 nor in the statement of Objects and Reasons of the Act. The scheme of the Act is to regulate conditions of workers in contract labour system and to provide for its abolition by the appropriate Government as provided in S. 10 of the CLRA Act. The various regulatory and welfare measures provided under the various provisions of the Act clearly bespeak treatment of contract labour as employees of the contractor and not of the principal employer. It is, therefore, difficult to perceive in S. 10 any implicit requirement of automatic absorption of contract labour by the principal employer in the establishment concerned on issuance of notification by the appropriate Government under S. 10(1) prohibiting employment of contract labour in a given establishment.

It is important to mention here the view expressed by the Hon'ble Finance Minister while presenting 2001–02 Budget. He said that the rigidities inherent in the existing legislation regarding contract labour inhibit growth in the employment in many service activities. Section 10 of the existing Act envisages prohibition of contract labour in work/process/operation if the conditions set therein like perennial nature of job, etc. are fulfilled. Section 10 enables the contract labour engaged in prohibited jobs to become direct employees of the principal employer. To overcome this difficulty and at the same time to ensure the protection of labour, it is proposed to bring an amendment to facilitate outsourcing of activities without any restriction as well as to offer contract appointments. It would not differentiate between core and non-core activities, and provide protection to labour engaged in outsourced activities in terms of their health, safety, welfare, social security, etc. It would also provide for larger compensation based on last drawn wages as retrenchment compensation for every year of service.

The aforesaid measures, according to the Finance Minister, would promote industrial investment in labour-intensive and export-oriented activities, providing for renewed industrial growth, while, at the same time, would safeguard the interest of workers.

The aforesaid statement of the Finance Minister received mixed reaction from the employers' and workers' Federation. The Employers' Federation of Southern India (EFSI) welcomed Mr. Sinha's announcement as a 'major step'. They felt that the proposal would benefit the medium scale industries, which are the ones that need to adopt new technology and reduce the labour force. They also felt that if the amendments go through, the labour market will become more flexible, more workers can be hired legitimately.

On the other hand, the Trade Unions feel that with the proposed amendment of the Contract Labour (Regulation and Abolition) Act, employers would go in for more contractual appointments. Further, the proposed amendment would facilitate outsourcing of activities to contract labour and also ease the appointment of contract labour.

As per the recent press statement, the Government's Draft Bill to amend the Contract Labour (Regulation and Abolition) Act is ready and is proposed to be introduced in Parliament in its current session. The Amendment Bill will take away from the 1970 Act its power to abolish contract labour in various jobs, which are of perennial nature. The amendment Bill seeks to delete the provision under which any contract employment can be prohibited. It will provide complete freedom to an employer to decide the activities "which he will like to outsource".[29]

The Second National Commission on Labour recommended on this issue as follows:

The Commission is conscious of the fact that in the fast changing economic scenario and changes in technology and management, which are entailed in meeting current challenges, there cannot be a fixed number of posts in any organisations for all time to come. Organisations must have the flexibility to adjust the number of this workforce based on economic efficiency. It is essential to focus on core competencies if an enterprise wants to remain competitive. We would, therefore, recommend that contract labour shall not be engaged for core production/services activities. However, for sporadic seasonal demand, the employer may engage temporary labour for core production/service activity. We are aware that off-loading, perennial, non-core services like canteen, watch and ward, cleaning etc. to other employing agencies to take care of three aspects:

1. there have to be provisions that ensure that performed perennial core services are not transferred to other agencies or establishments;
2. where such services are being performed by employees on the payrolls of the enterprises, no transfer to other agencies should be done without consulting, bargaining(negotiating) agents; and
3. where the transfer of such services does not involve any employee who is currently in service of the enterprise, the management will be free to entrust the service to outside agencies. The contract labour will, however, be remunerated at the rate of a regular worker engaged in the same organisation doing work of a comparable nature or if such worker does not exist in the organisation, at the lowest salary of a worker in a comparable grade, i.e. unskilled, semi-skilled or skilled. The principal employer will also ensure that the prescribed social security and other benefits are extended to the contract worker. There is a reason that compels us to make this recommendation. At many of the centres we visited, we were told during evidence, that there were cases of contractors making deductions from the wages of contract workers as their contribution towards social security, and then absconding without depositing either the contribution realised from the workers or their own contributions into the appropriate social security fund.[30]

---

29. See S.C. Srivastava, *Impact of Repeal of Section 10 of the Contract Labour (Regulation and Abolition) Act, 1970,* Management of Contract Labour in India, Shri Ram Centre, New Delhi (2004), p. 119.
30. Government of India (2002), Report of the Second National Commission on Labour, Chapter 13, pp. 47–48, Para 6.109.

CHAPTER IV

LICENSING OF CONTRACTORS

SECTION 11: Appointment of licensing officers

The appropriate Government may, by an order notified in the Official Gazette,—

(a) appoint such person, being Gazetted Officers of Government, as it thinks fit to be licensing officers for the purposes of this Chapter; and

(b) define the limits, within which a licensing officer shall exercise the powers conferred on licensing officers by or under this Act.

This section makes it clear that only Gazetted Officers of the Government can be appointed as licensing officers under the Act and such appointment has to be made by an order notified in the Official Gazette. This section empowers the appropriate Government to define the limits within which a licensing officer shall exercise the powers conferred on him by or under this Act.

SECTION 12: Licensing of contractors

(1) With effect from such date as the appropriate Government may, by notification in the Official Gazette, appoint, no contractor to whom this Act applies, shall undertake or execute any work through contract labour except under and in accordance with a licence issued in that behalf by the licensing officer. .

(2) Subject to the provisions of this Act, a licence under sub-section (1) may contain such conditions including, in particular, conditions as to hours of work, fixation of wages and other essential amenities in respect of contract labour as the appropriate Government may deem fit to impose in accordance with the rules, if any, made under section 35 and shall be issued on payment of such fees and on the deposit of such sum, if any, as security for the due performance of the conditions as may be prescribed.

Section 12 provides two aspects, namely licensing of contractors from undertaking or executing any work through contract labour except under and in accordance with a licence. A licence may contain such conditions including conditions as to hours of work, fixation of wages and other essential amenities in respect of contract labour. Such licence is issued on payment of such fees and on the deposit of such sum, if any, as security for the due performance of the conditions as may be prescribed.

Effect of Non-compliance with S. 7 and/or S. 12 of the Act

The question involved is that if the principal employer does not get registration under S. 7 of the Act and/or the contractor does not get a licence under S. 12 of the Act whether the persons so appointed by the principal employer through the contract would be deemed to be the direct employees of the principal employer or not.

There is a direct conflict between the decisions of the High Courts of Punjab, Kerala on the one hand, and the decisions of Madras, Bombay, Gujarat and Karnataka High Courts, on the other. The view of the Punjab and Kerala High Courts is that the only consequence of non-compliance either by the principal employer under S. 7 of the Act or by the contractor in complying with S. 12 of the Act is that they are liable for prosecution under the Act; whereas the view of the High Courts of Madras, Bombay, Gujarat and Karnataka is that in such a situation, the contract labour becomes directly the employee of the principal employer.

The Division Bench of the Punjab and Haryana High Court in *Gian Singh* v. *F.C.I.*,[31] held that if the principal employer does not get registration as required under S. 7 of the Act and/or the contractor does not get the licence under S. 12 of the Act, the only consequence is the penal provisions contained in Ss. 23 and 24 of the Act and that the principal employer or contractor can be prosecuted under those sections, but the Act nowhere provides that employees employed through the contractor would become the employees of the principal employer. The High Court of Kerala in the case of *P. Karunakaran* v. *The Chief Commercial Superintendent*,[32] took the same view as taken by the Punjab and Haryana High Court. A similar view was expressed by the Delhi High Court in the case of *New Delhi General Mazdoor Union* v. *Standing Conference of Public Enterprises*.[33] The Bombay High Court in the case of *United Labour Union* v. *Union of India*[34] held that the combined effect of these provisions makes it clear that for a valid employment of contract labour, two conditions must be fulfilled, viz. (1) every principal employer of an establishment must be registered, and (2) the contractor must have a valid licence. In other words, the mere registration by the principal employer or the holding of licence by the contractor alone will not enable the management to treat the workmen as contract labour. Where either or both the conditions are not fulfilled, the necessary implication would be that the workmen remain workmen of the principal employer.

The Division Bench of the Gujarat High Court in the case of *Food Corporation of India Workers' Union* v. *Food Corporation of India*[35] observed that the Certificate of Registration is required to be obtained by the principal employer, issued by the appropriate Government under the provisions of S. 7 of the Act. The licence is to be obtained by the contractors under the provisions of S. 12 of the Act. The workmen can be employed as contract labour only through licensed contractors. Unless both these conditions are complied with, the provisions of the Contract Labour (Regulation and Abolition) Act, 1970 would not be attracted. Both these conditions are required to be fulfilled, if one wishes to avail of the provisions of the Act. Even if one of the conditions is not complied with, the provisions of the Contract Labour (Regulation and Abolition) Act, 1970 would not be attracted. Therefore, in a situation wherein either of these two conditions is not satisfied, the position would be that a workman employed by an intermediary would be deemed to have been employed by the principal employer. In the

31. (1991) 1 Pun LR 1.
32. (1988) Lab I.C. 1346.
33. (1991) 2 Delhi Lawyer 189.
34. (1990) (60) Fac. L.R. 686.
35. (1990) Lab I.C. 1968.

result, it is declared that during the period when the two conditions of obtaining registration under S. 7 by the principal employer and of holding licence by the contractor are not complied with and the workmen are employed by contractor, the workmen can claim to be the direct employees of the principal employer.

The Supreme Court in *Dena Nath* v. *National Fertilisers Ltd.*[36] observed that the only consequence provided in the Act where either the principal employer or the labour contractor violates the provision of Ss. 9 and 12 respectively is the penal provision, as envisaged under the Act for which reference may be made to Ss. 23 and 25 of the Act. The Supreme Court has also endorsed a similar view in *Labourers Working on Salal Hydro-Project* v. *State of J. and K.*[37] and categorically observed that if contractors undertake or execute any work through contract labour without obtaining a licence required under S. 12 of the Act, they would be guilty of a criminal offence punishable under S. 23 or S. 24 of the Act.

Section 13: Grant of licences

(1) Every application for the grant of a licence under sub-section (1) of section 12 shall be made in the prescribed form and shall contain the particulars regarding the location of the establishment, the nature of process, operation or work for which contract labour is to be employed and such other particulars as may be prescribed.

(2) The licensing officer may make such investigation in respect of the application received under sub-section (1) and in making any such investigation the licensing officer shall follow such procedure as may be prescribed.

(3) A licence granted under this Chapter shall be valid for the period specified therein and may be renewed from time to time for such period and on payment of such fees and on such conditions as may be prescribed.

This section provides for the grant and renewal of licence to contractors. After receiving the application for grant of licence, the licensing officer is required to make such investigation in order to satisfy himself about the eligibility of the applicant for a licence.

Section 14: Revocation, suspension and amendment of licences

(1) If the licensing officer is satisfied, either on a reference made to him in this behalf or otherwise, that—

(a) a licence granted under section 12 has been obtained by misrepresentation or suppression of any material fact, or

(b) the holder of a licence has, without reasonable cause, failed to comply with the conditions subject to which the licence has been granted or has contravened any of the provisions of this Act or the rules made thereunder,

then without prejudice to any other penalty to which the holder of the licence may be liable under this Act, the licensing officer may, after giving the holder of the licence an opportunity of showing cause, revoke or suspend the licence or forfeit the sum, if any, or any portion

36. AIR 1992 SC 457.
37. AIR 1984 SC 177.

thereof deposited as security for the due performance of the conditions subject to which the licence has been granted.

(2) Subject to any rules that may be made in this behalf, the licensing officer may vary or amend a licence granted under section 12.

Section 15: Appeal

(1) Any person aggrieved by an order made under section 7, section 8, section 12 or section 14 may, within thirty days from the date on which the order is communi-cated to him, prefer an appeal to an appellate officer who shall be a person nominated in this behalf by the appropriate Government:

Provided that the appellate officer may entertain the appeal after the expiry of the said period of thirty days, if he is satisfied that the appellant was prevented by sufficient cause from filing the appeal in time.

(2) On receipt of an appeal under sub-section (1), the appellate officer shall, after giving the appellant an opportunity of being heard dispose of the appeal as expeditiously as possible.

Chapter V

WELFARE AND HEALTH OF CONTRACT LABOUR

Section 16: Canteens

(1) The appropriate Government may make rules requiring that in every establishment—

(a) to which this Act applies,

(b) wherein work requiring employment of contract labour is likely to continue for such period as may be prescribed, and

(c) wherein contract labour numbering one hundred or more is ordinarily employed by a contractor,

one or more canteens shall be provided and maintained by the contractor for the use of such contract labour.

(2) Without prejudice to the generality of the foregoing power, such rules may provide for—

(a) the date by which the canteens shall be provided;

(b) the number of canteens that shall be provided, and the standards in respect of construction, accommodation, furniture and other equipment of the canteens; and

(c) the foodstuffs which may be served therein and the charges which may be made therefore.

SECTION 17: Rest-rooms

(1) In every place wherein contract labour is required to halt at night in connection with the work of an establishment—

(a) to which this Act applies, and

(b) in which work requiring employment of contract labour is likely to continue for such period as may be prescribed,

there shall be provided and maintained by the contractor for the use of the contract labour such number of rest-rooms or such other suitable alternative accommodation within such time as may be prescribed.

(2) The rest-rooms or the alternative accommodation to be provided under sub-section (1) shall be sufficiently lighted and ventilated and shall be maintained in clean and comfortable condition.

SECTION 18: Other facilities

It shall be the duty of every contractor employing contract labour in connection with the work of an establishment to which this Act applies, to provide and maintain—

(a) a sufficient supply of wholesome drinking water for the contract labour at convenient places;

(b) a sufficient number of latrines and urinals of the prescribed types so situated as to be convenient and accessible to the contract labour in the establishment; and

(c) washing facilities.

SECTION 19: First-aid facilities

There shall be provided and maintained by the contractor so as to be readily accessible during all working hours a first-aid box equipped with the prescribed contents at every place where contract labour is employed by him.

SECTION 20: Liability of principal employer in certain cases

(1) If any amenity required to be provided under section 16, section 17, section 18 or section 19 for the benefit of the contract labour employed in an establishment is not provided by the contractor within the time prescribed therefor, such amenity shall be provided by the principal employer within such time as may be prescribed.

(2) All expenses incurred by the principal employer in providing the amenity may be recovered by the principal employer from the contractor either by deduction from any amount payable to the contractor under any contract or as a debt by the contractor.

This section casts responsibility on the principal employer to provide amenities if any amenity required to be provided under Ss. 16, 17, 18 or 19 is not provided by the contractor.

The principal employer will be entitled to recover the expenses incurred by him in this respect. The provisions relating to canteen and rest-room provided under Ss. 16 and 17 of the Act read with Central Rules 40 to 56 and Rule 25(2)(vi) were challenged before the Supreme Court in *Gammon India Ltd.* v. *Union of India*[38] as being incapable of implementation and also expensive as to amount to unreasonable restrictions under Art. 19(1)(g) of the Constitution of India. The plea was rejected by the Supreme Court on the ground of that these measures are amenities for the dignity of human being and in the interest of the public.

Section 21: Responsibility for payment of wages

(1) A contractor shall be responsible for payment of wages to each worker employed by him as contract labour and such wages shall be paid before the expiry of such period as may be prescribed.
(2) Every principal employer shall nominate a representative duly authorised by him to be present at the time of disbursement of wages by the contractor and it shall be the duty of such representative to certify the amounts paid as wages in such manner as may be prescribed.
(3) It shall be the duty of the contractor to ensure the disbursement of wages in the presence of the authorised representative of the principal employer.
(4) In case the contractor fails to make payment of wages within the prescribed period or makes short payment, then the principal employer shall be liable to make payment of wages in full or the unpaid balance due, as the case may be, to the contract labour employed by the contractor and recover the amount so paid from the contractor either by deduction from any amount payable to the contractor under any contract or as a debt payable by the contractor.

The object and purpose of S. 21 is to ensure that wages are paid by the contractor. If the contractor fails to pay wages that he is legally bound to pay, then the principal employer is under an obligation to pay the said wages and get reimbursed or consider as a debt payable by the contractor, as the case may be, under S. 21 of the Act.

Senior Regional Manager, Food Corporation of India, Calcutta v. Tulsi Das Bauri[39]

This appeal by special leave arose from the judgment of the Division Bench of the High Court of Calcutta that respondents were engaged as contract labour by Bhagwat Prasad Choudhury, contractor, and while they were working, they were refused payment of the full wages. As a consequence, they laid claim for payment of the amount. Ultimately, the Division Bench directed, by the impugned judgment, that the appellant shall be liable to pay the arrears of the balance of the amount of the wages.

The learned counsel appearing for the appellant contended that the arrears of wages are not wages under S. 21 of the Contract Labour (Regulation and Abolition) Act, 1973 and that, therefore, the appellant is not liable to make the payment to the respondents. The Supreme

38. AIR 1974 SC 960.
39. AIR 1997 SC 2446.

Court rejected the contention and observed that S. 21 postulates the responsibility for payment of wages. Under S. 21(1), a contractor shall be responsible for the payment of wages to each worker employed by him as contract labour and such wages shall be paid before the expiry of such period as may be prescribed.

Whereas S. 21(4) prescribes that in case the contractor fails to make payment of wages within the prescribed period or makes short payment, then the principal employer shall be liable to make payment of wages in full or the unpaid balance due, as the case may be, to the contract labour employed by the contractor and recover the amount so paid from the contractor either by deducting from any amount payable to the contractor under any contract or as a debt payable by the contractor. That liability has been prescribed under sub-section (2) of S. 21 of the Act thereof which says that every principal employer shall nominate a representative duly authorised by him to be present at the time of disbursement of wages by the contractor and it shall be the duty of such representative to certify the amounts paid as wages in such manner as may be prescribed. Thus, it is clear that the principal employer is required to pay the wages. The term 'wages' includes the balance of wages or arrears thereof. Under these circumstances, the Supreme Court dismissed the appeal.

CHAPTER VI

PENALTIES AND PROCEDURE

SECTION 22: Obstructions

(1) Whoever obstructs an inspector in the discharge of his duties under this Act or refuses or wilfully neglects to afford the inspector any reasonable facility for making any inspection, examination, inquiry or investigation authorised by or under this Act in relation to an establishment to which, or a contractor to whom, this Act applies, shall be punishable with imprisonment for a term which may extend to three months, or with fine which may extend to five hundred rupees, or with both.

(2) Whoever wilfully refuses to produce on the demand of an inspector any register or other document kept in pursuance of this Act or prevents or attempts to prevent or does anything which he has reason to believe is likely to prevent any person from appearing before or being examined by an inspector acting in pursuance of his duties under this Act, shall be punishable with imprisonment for a term which may extend to three months, or with fine which may extend to five hundred rupees, or with both.

SECTION 23: Contravention of provisions regarding employment of contract labour

Whoever contravenes any provision of this Act or of any rules made thereunder prohibiting, restricting or regulating the employment of contract labour, or contravenes any condition of a licence granted under this Act, shall be punishable with imprisonment for a term which may extend to three months, or with fine which may extend to one thousand rupees, or with both, and in the case of a continuing contravention with an additional fine which may extend to one hundred rupees for every day during which such contravention continues after conviction for the first such contravention.

Section 24: Other offences

If any person contravenes any of the provisions of this Act or of any rules made thereunder for which no other penalty is elsewhere provided, he shall be punishable with imprisonment for a term which may extend to three months, or with fine which may extend to one thousand rupees, or with both.

Section 25: Offences by companies

(1) If the person committing an offence under this Act is a company, the company as well as every person in charge of, and responsible to, the company for the conduct of its business at the time of commission of the offence shall be deemed to be guilty of the offence and shall be liable to be proceeded against and punished accordingly:

Provided that nothing contained in this sub-section shall render any such person liable to any punishment if he proves that the offence was committed without his knowledge or that he exercised all due diligence to prevent the commission of such offence.

(2) Notwithstanding anything contained in sub-section (1), where an offence under this Act has been committed by a company and it is proved that the offence has been committed with the consent or connivance of, or that the commission of the offence is attributable to any neglect on the part of any director, manager, managing agent or any other officer of the company, such director, manager, managing agent or such other officer shall also be deemed to be guilty of that offence and shall be liable to be proceeded against and punished accordingly.

Explanation: For the purpose of this section—

(a) "company" means any body corporate and includes a firm or other association of individuals; and

(b) "director", in relation to a firm, means a partner in the firm.

Section 26: Cognizance of offences

No court shall take cognizance of any offence under this Act except on a complaint made by, or with the previous sanction in writing of, the inspector and no court inferior to that of a Presidency Magistrate or a Magistrate of the first class shall try any offence punishable under this Act.

Section 27: Limitation of prosecutions

No court shall take cognizance of an offence punishable under this Act unless the complaint thereof is made within three months from the date on which the alleged commission of the offence came to the knowledge of an inspector:

Provided that where the offence consists of disobeying a written order made by an inspector, complaint, thereof may be made within six months of the date on which the offence is alleged to have been committed.

CHAPTER VII

MISCELLANEOUS

SECTION 28: Inspecting staff

(1) The appropriate government may, by notification in the Official Gazette, appoint such persons as it thinks fit to be inspectors for the purposes of this Act, and define the local limits within which they shall exercise their powers under this Act.

(2) Subject to any rules made in this behalf, an inspector may, within the local limits for which he is appointed—

(a) enter, at all reasonable hours, with such assistance (if any), being persons in the service of the Government or any local or other public authority as he thinks fit, any premises or place where contract labour is employed, for the purpose of examining any register or record or notice required to be kept or exhibited by or under this Act or rules made thereunder, and require the production thereof for inspection;

(b) examine any person whom he finds in any such premises or place and who, he has reasonable cause to believe, is a workman employed therein;

(c) require any person giving out work and any workman, to give any information, which is in his power to give with respect to the names and addresses of the person to, for and from whom the work is given out or received, and with respect to the payments to be made for the work;

(d) seize or take copies of such register, record of wages or notices or portions thereof as he may consider relevant in respect of an offence under this Act which he has reason to believe has been committed by the principal employer or contractor; and

(e) exercise such other powers as may be prescribed.

(3) Any information required to produce any document or thing or to give any information required by an inspector under sub-section (2) shall be deemed to be legally bound to do so within the meaning of section 175 and section 176 of the Indian Penal Code, 1860 (45 of 1860).

(4) The provisions of the Code of Criminal Procedure, 1898 (5 of 1898), shall, so far as may be, apply to any search or seizure under sub-section (2) as they apply to any search or seizure made under the authority of a warrant issued under section 98 of the said Code.

Section 29: Registers and other records to be maintained

(1) Every principal employer and every contractor shall maintain such registers and records giving such particulars of contract labour employed, the nature of work performed by the contract labour, the rates of wages paid to the contract labour and such other particulars in such form as may be prescribed.

(2) Every principal employer and every contractor shall keep exhibited in such manner as may be prescribed within the premises of the establishment where the contract labour is employed, notices in the prescribed form containing particulars about the hours of work, nature of duty and such other information as may be prescribed.

Section 30: Effect of laws and agreements inconsistent with this Act

(1) The provisions of this Act shall have effect notwithstanding anything inconsistent therewith contained in any other law or in the terms of any agreement or contract of service, or in any standing orders applicable to the establishment whether made before or after the commencement of the Act:

Provided that where under any such agreement, contract of service or standing orders the contract labour employed in the establishment are entitled to benefits in respect of any matter which are more favourable to them than those to which they would be entitled under this Act, the contract labour shall continue to be entitled to the more favourable benefits in respect of that matter, notwithstanding that they received benefits in respect of other matters under this Act.

(2) Nothing contained in this Act shall be construed as precluding any such contract labour from entering into an agreement with the principal employer or the contractor, as the case may be, for granting them rights or privileges in respect of any matter which are more favourable to them than those to which they would be entitled under this Act.

Any clause which begins with the expression "notwithstanding anything contained in this Act or in any other law for the time being in force" provides an overriding effect over all the provisions of the Act as well as any other law for the time being in force in case of conflict. By virtue of these words used in S. 30, it becomes clear that S. 30 will have overriding effect over any provision of any other law, agreement or contract of service, or in any standing orders in case of inconsistency.

The proviso further clarifies that the contract labour will continue to be entitled to the more favourable benefits available to them under any agreement, contract of service or standing orders in respect of any matters notwithstanding that they received benefits in respect of other matters under this Act. Section 30(2) authorises the contract labour to enter into agreements with the principal employer or contractor, as the case may be, for more favourable terms than are provided under this Act.

Section 31: Power to exempt in special cases

The appropriate Government may, in the case of an emergency, direct, by notification in the Official Gazette, that subject to such conditions and restrictions, if any, and for such period or periods, as may be specified in the notification, all or any of the provisions of this Act or the rules made thereunder shall not apply to any establishment or class of establishments or any class of contractors.

Section 32: Protection of action taken under this Act

(1) No suit, prosecution or other legal proceedings shall lie against any registering officer, licensing officer or any other Government servant or against any member of the Central Board or the State Board, as the case may be, for anything which is in good faith done or intended to be done in pursuance of this Act or any rule or order made thereunder.

(2) No suit or other legal proceeding shall lie against the Government for any damage caused or likely to be caused by anything which is in good faith done or intended to be done in pursuance of this Act or any rule or order made thereunder.

Section 33: Power to give directions

The Central Government may give directions to the Government of any State as to the carrying into execution in the State of the provisions contained in this Act.

Section 34: Power to remove difficulties

If any difficulty arises in giving effect to the provisions of this Act, the Central Government may, by order published in the Official Gazette, make such provisions not inconsistent with the provisions of this Act, as appears to it to be necessary or expedient for removing the difficulty.

Section 34 of the Act was challenged before the Supreme Court as unconstitutional on the ground of excessive delegation of power to the executive by the legislature in *Gammon India Ltd.* v. *Union of India.*[38] Reliance was placed by the petitioners on the decision of the Supreme Court in *Jalan Trading Co.* v. *Mazdoor Union.*[40] Section 34 of the Act in that case authorised the Government to provide by order for removal of doubts or difficulties in giving effect to the provisions of the Act. The Court held that it is for the legislature to make provisions for removal of doubts or difficulties. The section in that case contained a provision that the order must not be inconsistent with the purposes of the Act. Another provision in the section made the order of the Government final. The Court held that in substance there was the vice of delegation of legislation to executive authority. Two reasons were given. First, the section authorised the Government to determine for itself what the purposes of the Act were and to make provisions for removal of doubts or difficulties. Secondly, the power to remove the doubts or difficulties by altering the provisions of the Act would, in substance, amount

40. AIR 1967 SC 691.

to exercise of legislative authority and that could not be delegated to an executive authority. In the present case, neither finality nor alteration is contemplated in any order under S. 34 of the Act. Section 34 is for giving effect to the provisions of the Act. This provision is an application of the internal functioning of the administrative machinery. Difficulties can only arise in the implementation of rules. Therefore, S. 34 of the Act does not amount to excessive delegation.

SECTION 35: Power to make rules

(1) The appropriate Government may, subject to the condition of previous publication, make rules for carrying out the purposes of this Act.

(2) In particular, and without prejudice to the generality of the foregoing power, such rules may provide for all or any of the following matters, namely—

(a) the number of persons to be appointed members representing various interests on the Central Board and the State Board, the term of their office and other conditions of service, the procedure to be followed in the discharge of their functions and the manner of filling vacancies;

(b) the times and places of the meetings of any committee constituted under this Act, the procedure to be followed at such meetings including the quorum necessary for the transaction of business, and the fees and allowances that may be paid to the members of a committee;

(c) the manner in which establishments may be registered under section 7, the levy of a fee therefor and the form of certificate of registration;

(d) the form of application for the grant or renewal of a licence under section 13 and the particulars it may contain;

(e) the manner in which an investigation is to be made in respect of an application for the grant of a licence and the matters to be taken into account in granting or refusing a licence;

(f) the form of a licence which may be granted or renewed under section 12 and the conditions subject to which the licence may be granted or renewed, the fees to be levied for the grant or renewal of a licence and the deposit of any sum as security for the performance of such conditions;

(g) the circumstances under which licences may be varied or amended under section 14;

(h) the form and manner in which appeals may be filed under section 15 and the procedure to be followed by appellate officers in disposing of the appeals;

(i) the time within which facilities required by this Act to be provided and maintained may be so provided by the contractor and in case of default on the part of the contractor, by the principal employer;

(j) the number and types of canteens, rest-rooms, latrines and urinals that should be provided and maintained;

(k) the type of equipment that should be provided in the first-aid boxes;

(l) the period within which wages payable to contract labour should be paid by the contractor under sub-section (1) of section 21;

(m) the form of registers and records to be maintained by principal employers and contractors;

(n) the submission of returns, forms in which, and the authorities to which, such returns may be submitted;

(o) the collection of any information or statistics in relation to contract labour; and

(p) any other matter which has to be, or may be, prescribed under this Act.

(3) Every rule made by the Central Government under this Act shall be laid as soon as may be after it is made, before each House of Parliament while it is in session for a total period of thirty days which may be comprised in one session or in two successive sessions, and if before the expiry of the session in which it is so laid or the session immediately following, both Houses agree in making any modification in the rule or both Houses agree that the rule should not be made, the rule shall thereafter have effect only in such modified form or be of no effect, as the case may be; so, however, that any such modification or annulment shall be without prejudice to the validity of anything previously done under that rule.

(4) Every rule made by the State Government under this Act shall be laid, as soon as may be after it is made, before the State Legislature.

Same or Similar Kind of Work

Rule 25 (Central) provides *inter alia* as follows:

> "In cases where the workmen employed by the contractor perform the same or similar kind of work as the workmen directly employed by the principal employer of the establishment, the wage rates, holidays, hours of work and other conditions of service of the workmen of the contractor shall be the same as applicable to the workmen directly employed by the principal employer of the establishment on the same or similar kind of work:
>
> Provided that in the case of any disagreement with regard to the type of work, the same shall be decided by the Chief Labour Commissioner (Central)."

In *State of Haryana* v. *Charanjit Singh* (AIR 2006 SC 161) the Supreme Court held that the doctrine of *'equal pay for equal work'* is not an abstract doctrine and is capable of being enforced in a Court of law. But equal pay must be for equal work of equal value. The principle of *'equal pay for equal work'* has no mechanical application in every case. If the educational qualifications are different, then also the doctrine may have no application. A mere nomenclature designating a person as say a carpenter or a craftsman is not enough to come to the conclusion that he is doing the same work as another carpenter or craftsman in regular service. The quality of work which is produced may be different and even the nature of work assigned may be different. It is not just a comparison of physical activity. The application of the principle of *'equal pay for equal work'* requires consideration of various dimensions of a given job. The accuracy required and the dexterity that the job may entail may differ from job to job. It cannot be judged by the mere volume of work. There may be qualitative difference as regards reliability and responsibility. Functions may be the same but the responsibilities made a difference. Thus normally the applicability of this principle must be left to be evaluated and determined by an expert body. These are not matters where a writ Court can lightly interfere. Normally a party claiming '*equal pay for equal* work' should be required to raise a dispute in this regard. In any event the party who claims '*equal pay for equal work' has* to make necessary averments and prove that all things are equal. Thus, before any direction can be issued by a Court, the Court must first see that there are necessary averments and there is a proof. If the High Court, is on basis of material placed before it, convinced that there was equal work of equal quality and all other relevant factors are fulfilled it may direct payment of equal pay from the date of the filing of the respective writ petition.

Rule 25 requires that the Commissioner is to analyse the pleadings, evidence and documents placed on record and to arrive at a conclusion as to whether the workmen are performing the same duties as have been performed by the regular employees.

In *Panki Thermal Station* v. *Vidyut Mazdoor Sangthan* (AIR 2009 SC 2373) the Supreme Court provides guidelines to the Labour Commissioner how to reach into conclusion that both contract labour and pay-roll employees are performing same and similar work so that Rule 25 could be applied. The Supreme Court held that in the Commissioner's order there is no discussion as to how the Commissioner arrived at the conclusion about similarity of work. The Commissioner ought to have considered on the basis of pleadings and materials placed by the parties. The Commissioner was required to arrive at a conclusion that the workmen had been performing the same duties as are being performed by regular employees.

In *U.P. Rajya Vidyut Utpadan Board* v. *U.P. Vidyut Mazdoor Sangh* [AIR 2010 SC (Supp) 300] the Supreme Court interpreted the concept of "same and similar" and provides some inputs what constitutes same and similar thereby Rule 25 would be attracted. The fact of the case is as follows:

Uttar Pradesh Vidyut Mazdoor Sangh (hereinafter referred to as 'Union'), made an application under Rule 25(2)(v)(a) of the Uttar Pradesh Contract Labour (Regulation and Abolition) Rules, 1975, ('Rules, 1975' for short) before the Labour Commissioner, Kanpur praying therein that order be passed for payment of the same wages and other facilities in favour of contract labour working in second filtration plant of Anpara Thermal Power Project as are being paid by the employer to its employees in the main filtration plant. The Union set up the case that there are two filtration plants in Anpara Thermal Power Project; out of these plants in one plant (for the sake of convenience, hereinafter referred to as 'main plant') regular employees are employed by the Electricity Board while in the other filtration plant, contract labour is being employed through contractors. In both filtration plants, the nature of work done by all these employees is same but the workers are paid their wages at different rates. Twenty six workers, who have been directly appointed by the Electricity Board, are being paid regular pay scale with permissible allowances etc. while twenty eight contract workers engaged through two contractors are paid at the rate of ₹61 per day for unskilled work and ₹71.50 per day for semi-skilled work. The Union asserted that work in both the filtration plants is of the same nature.

U.P. Rajya Vidyut Utpadan Board resisted the application made by the Union on diverse grounds. That there are two water filtration plants in Anpara Thermal Power Project was admitted. However, it was submitted that main filtration plant is permanent having the capacity of treating three million gallons water per day while the second one is temporary having the capacity of treating three lac gallons per day. It was further submitted that from permanent filtration plant, supply is given to the entire colony and ITI passed/trained operators are being appointed by the department to run it; these appointments are made by the selection committee through selection procedure on the basis of eligibility and advertisement by the Board. The permanent plant runs 24 hours; it has six pumps and each has the capacity of 170 H.P. The chemicals are mixed at this plant mechanically and for its operation eligible and responsible employees are required. In the other filtration plant which is of temporary nature, employees are engaged through contractor for its operation. The temporary filtration plant is operated by skilled and semi-skilled employees who are engaged by contractors. These workers are paid wages at the rate declared by the labour department. The Board submitted before the Labour Commissioner that the work of the employees in the two filtration plants cannot be compared and, therefore, the employees working in the temporary filtration plant are not entitled to the same wages and facilities as are being paid to the regular employees working in the main filtration plant.

The Labour Commissioner, however, did not considered the reply submitted by the Board and vide his order dated October 24, 1998 held that the contract labour in temporary filtration plant should be paid the wages at the rate admissible to the workers in the main plant.

The Board challenged the order of the Labour Commissioner by filing writ petition before the High Court of Allahabad. The Single Judge dismissed the writ petition on May 14, 1999 holding that the findings recorded by the Labour Commissioner required no interference. Same view was also endorsed by the Divisional Bench as well.

The Supreme Court observed that Rule 25(2)(v)(a) incorporates the principle of '*equal pay for equal work*'. By statutory provision, it is mandated that the employees engaged by the employer through contractor who perform the same or similar kind of work must be paid the same wages and facilities as being paid to the employees employed directly by the principal employer of the establishment. In case of any controversy as to whether the workmen employed by the contractor perform the same or similar kind of work as employed directly by the principal employer of the establishment, the Labour Commissioner has been empowered to resolve such dispute.

The Supreme Court further observed that (*which may be considered the most important observation from the management's perspective):*

> "Nature of work, duties and responsibilities attached thereto are relevant in comparing and evaluating as to whether the workmen employed through contractor perform the same or similar kind of work as the workmen directly employed by the principal employer. Degree of skill and various dimensions of a given job have to be gone into to reach a conclusion that nature of the duties of the staff in two categories are on par or otherwise. Often the difference may be of a degree. It is well settled that nature of work cannot be judged by mere volume of work; there may be qualitative difference as regards reliability and responsibility."

In the instant case, the Labour Commissioner has not evaluated the facts placed before it. The order of the Labour Commissioner passed on October 24, 1998 which reads as follows:

> "I have fully considered all the facts and perused the records and documents produced by the parties. On the basis of the facts submitted, there is no reason before me on the basis of which the contract labour engaged through contractors who is working the similar work, should be given wages at a lesser rate than the permanent employees. Only minimum qualification could be the basis for the worker of both the plants to some extent. Therefore, considering all the facts my opinion is that 28 contract labour in temporary plant through contractor M/s. Eastern Engineering Corporation and M/s. Kheroni Constructions Company should be paid the wages at the rate admissible to the workers/labours in permanent plant. This is my decision in respect of application...."

As a matter of fact, the present appellants specifically set out the details of works in two water filtration plants thus:

There are two water filtration plants in Anpara Project. One is permanent having the capacity of treating 3 million Gallon water per day (3 M.G.D.) or 30 lacs gallon per day and the second is temporary having capacity of treating 3 million Gallons per day i.e. 3 lacs gallons per day. From permanent treatment plant, water supply is given to the entire permanent colony. This plant is very important and permanent. Therefore, I.T.I. passed/ trained operators are being appointed by the department to run it. The appointments are being made by the Selection Committee through selection procedure on the basis of eligibility and advertisement by the Board. Therefore, the operators and employees appointed on this plant are permanent employees of the department and they are fully responsible for the work done by them. The equipments installed at this plant are of permanent nature and it is being run 24 hours (day and night). There are 6 pumps at this plant and each has the capacity of 170 H.P. and consumes 9302.40 watts electricity. The chemicals are mixed at this plaint mechanically and for its operation eligible and responsible employees are required. The salary of these employees comes in the payscale of permanent employees who have been appointed. There are 26 employees have been appointed and working in this plant.

The other filtration plant is of temporary nature and is being operated till the next phase of the project is completed and after the completions of next phase it will be closed. From this plant water is supplied to the temporary colony and project area. It is being operated through contractor. The Department makes the payment to the contractor on the basis of item wise as per the work executed and not labour wise. The contractor used to make payment to his employees on the basis of minimum wages declared by the Government from time to time and not less than that amount. The contractor gets this plant operated by his 3 unskilled and 3 semi-skilled employees.

It is submitted that the above facts show that it will not be justiciable to compare the work and facilities of the employees working in permanent filtration plant with the employees working in Temporary Filtration Plant. The Labour Commissioner did not apply its mind judiciously rather reached into conclusion which is unwarranted. The Labour Commissioner ought to have evaluated to the nature of duties of the staff in the two categories, degree of skill and dimensions of the job for reaching the conclusion that the work done by the contract labour in the second filtration plant is same or similar to the kind of work done by the employees employed by the principal employer directly in the main plant. There is no discussion at all by the Labour Commissioner as to how he arrived at the conclusion about similarity of work. The evidence let in by the parties and the materials placed by them seem to have not at all been considered by the Labour Commissioner.

Therefore the Supreme Court allowed the appeal and held as follows:

> "We are afraid, the consideration of the question as to whether the workmen employed by the contractors in the second filtration plant perform the same or similar kind of work as the employees directly employed by the principal employer in the main plant by the Labour Commissioner as well as High Court is highly unsatisfactory. In a situation such as this, we are constrained to set aside the impugned judgment of the High Court as well as the order dated October 24, 1998 passed by the Labour Commissioner, Uttar Pradesh. The application made by the Union under Rule 25(2)(v)(a) of the Rules, 1975 is restored to the file of Labour Commissioner, Kanpur, Uttar Pradesh for fresh consideration in accordance with law."

Sham and Camouflage

"Sham" and "camouflage" are terms that are often used in different contexts, but they both generally involve the idea of deception or concealment. There is no legal definition provided either by parliament or the judiciary.

Sham: Meaning

A sham refers to something that is fake, false, or not genuine. It can be an imitation, or a pretence designed to deceive or mislead.

In the contract labour management, it is a known fact that the engagement of contract labour is the outcome of a contract which is signed by the principal employer and contractor. It is an undisputed fact that the relationship of contractor and contract labour is employer and employee relationship. If, at any point of time, it is found that the contractor is not available, and the principal employer does everything what the contractor is supposed to do, then it can be termed as the contract is 'sham' or 'bogus'.

Camouflage: Meaning

Camouflage involves disguising something by making it appear to be part of its surroundings. This is commonly seen in nature, where animals use coloration or patterns to blend in with their environment and avoid detection.

The law casts some duties and responsibilities on the contractor (employer) which needs to be performed for the benefit of the contract labour (employee). For example the wage shall be paid by the contractor, leave shall be approved/sanctioned by the contractor, performance appraisal shall be recorded by the contractor, punishment, if any, shall be imposed by the contractor, appointment letter and experience certificate shall be signed and issued by the contractor and many more. If the principal employer does all the activities what the contractor is supposed to do, then, it may constitute camouflage because the principal employer changing the colour and behaving like an employer (contractor).

But where there is no abolition of contract labour under Section 10 of CLRA Act, but the contract labours contend that the contract between principal employer and contractor is sham and nominal, the remedy is purely under the Industrial Disputes Act. The principles in *Gujarat Electricity Board* case (*Gujarat Electricity Board, Thermal Power Station Ukai* v. *Hind Mazdoor Sabha,* AIR 1995 SC 1893) continue to govern the issue. The remedy of the workmen is to approach the industrial adjudicator for an adjudication of their dispute that they are the direct employees of the principal employer and the agreement is sham, nominal and merely a camouflage, even when there is no order under Section 10(1) of CLRA Act. The industrial adjudicator can grant the relief sought if it finds that contract between principal employer and the contractor is sham, nominal and merely a camouflage to deny employment benefits to the employees and that there is in fact a direct employment. The Supreme Court evolved the following tests like:

(i) who pays the salary;
(ii) who has the power to remove/dismiss from service or initiate disciplinary action;
(iii) who can tell the employee the way in which the work should be done, in short who has direction and control over the employee.

But where there is no notification under Section 10 of the CLRA Act and where it is not proved in the industrial adjudication that the contract was sham/nominal and camouflage, then the question of directing the principal employer to absorb or regularize the services of the contract labour does not arise. The tests that are applied to find out whether a person is an employee or an independent contractor may not automatically apply in finding out whether the contract labour agreement is a sham, nominal and is a mere camouflage. For example, if the contract is for supply of labour, necessarily, the labour supplied by the contractor will work under the directions, supervision and control of the principal employer but that would not make the worker a direct employee of the principal employer, if the salary is paid by the contractor, if the right to regulate employment is with the contractor, and the ultimate supervision and control lies with the contractor. The principal employer only controls and directs the work to be done by a contract labour, when such labour is assigned/allotted/sent to him. But it is the contractor as employer, who chooses whether the worker is to be assigned/allotted to the principal employer or used otherwise. In short, worker being the employee of the contractor, the ultimate supervision and control lies with the contractor as he decides where the employee will work and how long he will work and subject to what conditions. Only when the contractor assigns/sends the worker to work under the principal employer, the worker works under the supervision and control of the principal employer but that is secondary control. The primary control is with the contractor.

In *Secretary, Haryana State Electricity Board* v. *Suresh* (AIR 1999 SC 1160) the Supreme Court while considering the factual situations which are considered by the Labour Court observed that it was found by the Labour Court and as confirmed by the High Court that the so called contractor Kashmir Singh was a mere name lender and had procured labour for the Board from the open market. He was almost a broker or an agent of the Board for that purpose. The Labour Court also noted that the Management witness Shri A.K. Chaudhary also could not tell whether Shri Kashmir Singh was a licensed contractor or not. That workman had made a statement that Shri Kashmir Singh was not a licensed contractor. Under these circumstances, it has to be held that factually there was no genuine contract system prevailing at the relevant time wherein the Board could have acted as only the principal employer and Kashmir Singh as a licensed contractor employing labour on his own account. It is also pertinent to note that nothing was brought on record to indicate that even the Board at the relevant time, was registered as principal employer under the Contract Labour Regulation and Abolition Act. Once the Board was not a principal employer and the so called contractor Kashmir Singh was not a licensed contractor under the Act, the inevitable conclusion that had to be reached was to the effect that the so called contract system was a mere camouflage, smoke and a screen and disguised in almost a transparent veil which could easily be pierced and the real contractual relationship between the Board, on the one hand, and the employees, on the other, could be clearly visualized.

The Constitution Bench of the Supreme Court, in *SAIL* 2001(SAIL-I) case made it clear that neither Section 10 nor any other provision in CLRA Act provides for automatic absorption of contract labour on issuing a notification by the appropriate Government under Section 10(1) of the CLRA Act and consequently the principal employer cannot be required to absorb the contract labour working in the establishment. The Court further held that on a prohibition notification being issued under Section 10(1) of the CLRA Act, prohibiting employment of contract labour in any process, operation or other work, if an industrial dispute is raised by any contract labour in regard to conditions of service, the industrial adjudicator will have to consider whether the contractor has been interposed either on the ground of having undertaken to produce any given result for the establishment or for supply of contract labour for work of the establishment under a genuine contract, or as a mere ruse/ camouflage to evade compliance with various beneficial legislations so as to deprive the workers of statutory benefits. If the contract is found to be sham or nominal and merely a camouflage, then the so-called contract labours will have to be treated as direct employees of the principal employer and the industrial adjudicator should direct the principal employer to regularize their services in the establishment subject to such conditions as it may specify for that purpose. On the other hand, if the contract is found to be genuine and at the same time there is a prohibition notification under Section 10(1) of CLRA Act, in respect of the establishment, the principal employer intending to employ regular workmen for the process, operation or other work of the establishment in regard to which the prohibition notification has been issued, it shall give preference to the erstwhile contract labour if otherwise found suitable, if necessary by giving relaxation of age. The Supreme Court in *SAIL-I* (2001) case did not specifically deal with the legal position as to when a dispute is brought before the Industrial Adjudicator as to whether the contract labour agreement is sham, nominal and merely a camouflage, when there is no prohibition notification under Section 10(1) of CLRA Act.

Further, the Supreme Court in 2009 in *International Airport Authority of India* v. *International Air Cargo Workers' Union* (AIR 2009 SC 3063) held that where there is no abolition of contract labour under Section 10 of CLRA Act, but the contract labour contends that the contract between principal employer and contractor is sham and nominal, the remedy is purely under the Industrial Disputes Act. The industrial adjudicator can grant the relief sought if it finds that contract between principal employer and the contractor is sham, nominal and merely a camouflage to deny employment benefits to the employees and that there is in fact a direct employment, by applying tests like:

(i) who pays the salary;
(ii) who has the power to remove/dismiss from service or initiate disciplinary action;
(iii) who can tell the employees the way in which the work should be done, in short who has direction and control over the employees.

The facts of the *International Airport Authority of India* v. *International Air Cargo Workers' Union* (AIR 2009 SC 3063) are as follows:

The International Airport Authority of India (IAAI) established a cargo complex at Madras. Under an agreement it granted a licence to a private company to be its ground handling agent in respect of export, import and transshipment of cargo consignments. Under the said agreement, licensee (Airfreight) was to receive payment from the owners of the cargo for the work done, had to engage the services of required number of workers for handling the cargo and be responsible for payment of wages to the workers. It was also required to pay a licence fee to IAAI. Subsequently, IAAI decided to take over the ground handling work and entrust it to a new licensee by inviting competitive tenders. Therefore, IAAI informed its licensee that the ground handling agency operations should be handed over to its officers. In the circumstances, the workers employed by the licensee in connection with the ground handling work, who were likely to be retrenched/discharged, made an appeal to IAAI to provide them employment. They also filed a writ petition seeking a direction to IAAI to employ all those workers who had been employed by the licensee in connection with the ground handling work at the Madras Airport cargo complex. In view of the appeal made by the said workers, IAAI unilaterally came forward with a scheme to mitigate their hardship, and filed a memo before the High Court. Under the scheme IAAI offered to accommodate the workers, except by way of regular absorption, in services of IAAI till it makes its own arrangement by giving contract for handling of cargo to a Society to be formed by workers of erstwhile licensee. The High Court recorded the memo filed by IAAI and dismissed the writ petition in view of the agreement expressed by the counsel for Workers Union. Thereafter, a Society was formed and IAAI entered into a contract with the Society to provide workers for handling of cargo. When the term of contract was coming to an end, the workers raised an industrial dispute demanding direct employment in service of IAAI. On a reference being made the Industrial Tribunal directed absorption of workers in services of IAAI on ground that the memo filed by IAAI in writ petition was a ploy to defeat legitimate right of workers to permanent status. The memo was a settlement and the Workers Union was pressurized to enter into the settlement. The contract entered into with workers' Society was sham, nominal or camouflage.

The Supreme Court held that the memorandum filed by IAAI was not a settlement between the parties, but was only an unilateral proposal by IAAI in a pending writ petition, and in view of the fact that the Union was agreeable to such a course and did not press the relief of absorption or direct employment under IAAI, it is not possible to hold that the terms of the memorandum were terms of a settlement arrived at by IAAI from a dominant position, by applying pressure on the workers. This is not a case of the workers giving up any right or interest, but a case of a benefit or concession being voluntarily extended by IAAI as a responsible organization, to mitigate hardship.

The finding that the workers were entitled to continue as direct casual labour of IAAI but for change in their status as contract labour, affected by IAAI is incorrect. The workers were the employees of licensee. IAAI had no obligation to give them employment on termination of licence. It was only on humanitarian grounds and to mitigate the hardship of these workers, IAAI proposed to give the cargo handling work to the society of workers. It also agreed purely as an interim measure to employ them as casual labourers till contract with society gets entered. Therefore, the direct casual employment given to the workers was purely an interim or ad hoc measure as part of the package proposal made by IAAI in its memorandum. The workers worked for less than 240 days as casual labourers under IAAI and were not entitled to claim the benefit of neither Section 25F nor regularisation on the basis of such short casual service as daily rated employees.

The fact that IAAI was directly making payment to workers of society and also was taking penal action on workers is based on no evidence. As such the finding that the contract for supply of contract labour was paper contract is improper. Merely because the contract labours work is under the supervision of the officers of the principal employer, it cannot be taken as evidence of direct employment under the principal employer.

In *International Airport Authority of India* case, the following three questions arise for consideration of the Supreme Court:

(i) Whether the agreement between the contractor society and the IAAI in regard to cargo handling work was sham and nominal and consequently, the workers engaged as contract labour in regard to cargo handling work, were the direct employees of IAAI?

(ii) Whether the status of loaders-cum-packers engaged in cargo handling work was illegally changed from that of direct casual labour to contract labour in violation of Section 9A of the Industrial Disputes Act, 1947?

(iii) In the absence of a notification under Section 10 of CLRA Act prohibiting the employment of contract labour in the process/operation of cargo handling work, whether the workmen employed as contract labour are entitled to claim absorption?

Considering the facts of the case the Supreme Court held as follows:

(i) The contract labour agreement between IAAI and the society was not sham, nominal or as a camouflage and the contract labour were not the direct employees of IAAI.

(ii) There was no violation of Section 9A of the Industrial Disputes Act.

(iii) In the absence of a notification under Section 10 of CLRA Act prohibiting the employment of contract labour in the operation of cargo handling work, the workmen employed as contract labour are not entitled to claim absorption.

In *Bengal Nagpur Cotton Mills* v. *Bharat Lal,* (2011) 1 SCC 635 where the Supreme Court cited the decision of *International Airport Authority* v. *International Air Cargo Workers'* (AIR 2009 SC 3063) which reads as follows:

> "If the contract is for supply of labour, necessarily, the labour supplied by the contractor will work under the directions, supervision and control of the principal employer but that would not make the worker a direct employee of the principal employer, if the salary is paid by contractor, if the right to regulate employment is with the contractor, and the ultimate supervision and control lies with the contractor.
>
> The principal employer only controls and directs the work to be done by a contract labour, when such labour is assigned/allotted/sent to him. But it is the contractor as employer, who chooses whether the worker is to be assigned/allotted to the principal employer or used otherwise. In short, worker being the employee of the contractor, the ultimate supervision and control lies with the contractor as he decides where the employee will work and how long he will work and subject to what conditions. Only when the contractor assigns/sends the worker to work under the principal employer, the worker works under the supervision and control of the principal employer but that is secondary control. The primary control is with the contractor."

It is submitted that the Supreme Court has indirectly allowed the Principal Employer to have only secondary supervision and secondary control which would not be a ground for declaring the contract labour as the employee of Principal Employer and it may not fall within the realm of sham and camouflage.

In 2014 in *National Aluminium Co. Ltd* v. *Ananta Kishore Rout* [AIR 2014 SC (Supp) 1469] where NALCO had established two schools for the benefit of the wards of its employees. The Writ Petitions were filed by the employees of each school for a declaration that they be treated as the employees of NALCO on grounds of, *inter alia*, real control and supervision by NALCO. The Supreme Court while answering the issue observed that it is the duty of the Court to ascertain whether there is complete control and supervision by the NALCO. In this regard, reference was made to the case of *Workmen of Nilgiri Coop. Mkt. Society Ltd.* v. *State of T.N.* (2004) 3 SCC 514, wherein this Court had observed as follows:

> "The control test and the organization test, therefore, are not the only factors which can be said to be decisive. With a view to elicit the answer, the Court is required to consider several factors which would have a bearing on the result: (a) who is the appointing authority; (b) who is the paymaster; (c) who can dismiss; (d) how long alternative service lasts; (e) the extent of control and supervision; (f) the nature of the job e.g. whether it is professional or skilled work; (g) nature of establishment; (h) the right to reject."

Accordingly the Supreme Court held that there may have been some element of control with NALCO because its officials were nominated to the Managing Committee of the said schools. However, it was observed that the above-said fact was only to ensure that the schools run smoothly and properly. In this regard, the Court observed as follows:

> ". ... However, this kind of "remote control" would not make NALCO the employer of these workers. This only shows that since NALCO is shouldering and meeting financial deficits, it wants to ensure that the money is spent for the rightful purposes."

In 2014 in *Balwant Rai Saluja* v. *Air India Ltd.* (2014) 9 SCC 407 the Supreme Court while dealing with a statutory canteen issue held as follows:

> "The workers engaged by a contractor to work in the statutory canteen of a factory would be the workers of the said factory, but only for the purposes of the Act, 1948, and not for other purposes, and further for the said workers, to be called the employees of the factory for all purposes, they would need to satisfy the test of employer–employee relationship and it must be shown that the employer exercises absolute and effective control over the said workers."

In 2018 in *Chennai Port Trust* v. *The Chennai Port Trust Industrial Employees' Canteen Workers Welfare Association and Ors* [2018 LLR 612 (S.C.)] where the Chennai Port Trust engaged the contract labour through a Co-operative society called "Chennai Port Trust Industrial Employees Co-operative Canteen Limited" to run and manage the canteen. It has been running since 1964. The employees working in the canteen have formed an Association known as "Chennai Port Trust Industrial Employees Canteen Workers Welfare Association."(Here in after Association)

The Association filed a writ petition in the High Court at Madras against the Chennai Port Trust espousing the cause of their members (employees working in the Canteen) and sought a writ of mandamus against the Chennai Port Trust directing the Port Trust to treat the employees working in the Canteen to be the regular employees of the Chennai Port Trust and accordingly pay them all attendant and monetary benefits at par with the regular employees of the Chennai Port Trust.

The Chennai Port Trust mainly opposed the writ petition on two issues:

> First, the Chennai Port Trust has no control whatsoever over any of the activities of the Canteen in question including any control over its employees; and
>
> Second, the question as to whether the canteen employees are to be treated as employees of the Chennai Port Trust or not is a question of fact, and, therefore, the writ petition is not the effective remedy to decide this question. According to the Chennai Port Trust, such issues should be raised before the Industrial Tribunal for its adjudication.

The Writ Court (Single Judge) allowed the writ petition filed by the Association and accordingly issued a writ of mandamus against the Chennai Port Trust and granted the reliefs claimed by the Association. The Chennai Port Trust felt aggrieved and filed intra court appeal before the Division Bench in the High Court. The Division Bench dismissed the appeal and upheld the order of the Single Judge, which has given rise to filing of the present appeal before the Supreme Court by way of special leave by the Chennai Port Trust.

The Supreme Court relied upon its earlier judgement of *Indian Petrochemicals Corporation Ltd. and Anr.* v. *Shramik Sena & Ors.,* [(1999) 6 SCC 439] where the issues and facts of the *Petrochemical Corporation* case are similar to the case in hand. The fact of the case reveals that:

(a) The Rules framed by the Society for running the canteen shall be subject to the approval of the Chairman is not denied. This proves that the ultimate control of the administration of the canteen is with the Port Trust.

(b) It is only the workers belonging to the Port Trust who are eligible to become members of the Society and not others.

(c) It is only the nominee of the Port Trust who can act as the Chairman of the Co-operative Society.

(d) The Port Trust administration has the right to audit the accounts of the canteen.

(e) Contractors shall be nominated by the Registrar only in consultation with the Chairman of the Chennai Port Trust.

(f) The Executive Engineer (Mechanical) of the Port Trust has been nominated as the President of the canteen and the entire canteen affairs are handled and controlled by the Chief Mechanical Engineer of the Port Trust.

(g) The financial matters are controlled by the Financial Adviser and Chief Accounts Officer of the Port Trust.

Therefore the Supreme Court dismissed the appeal and held that all canteen workers would be declared as the employees of the Port Trust.

In 2018 in *Food Corporation of India* v. *Gen. Secy. FCI India Employees Union and Others* [2018 LLR 1057 (S.C.)] where the FCI in its Chennai Branch Office engaged 955 contract labour through a Contract Labourers' Society to carry out the business operation.

A dispute arose between FCI and around 955 employees working in the Branch office at Chennai as to whether these 955 employees are the employees of the FCI or they are employed by the Contract Labourers' Society to work in the FCI to carry out their business operation and secondly, whether these 955 employees are entitled to claim regularization of their services as FCI employees.

As the dispute could not be resolved amicably hence the matter was referred to Industrial Tribunal and the Tribunal held that 955 employees would be regularized by FCI. FCI filed the writ petition where the Single Judge of the High Court dismissed the writ petition and up held the award of Tribunal. FCI felt aggrieved and filed intra court appeal to the Division Bench where the Division Bench also dismissed the appeal and hence FCI approached the Supreme Court.

The Supreme Court observed that:

1. The agreement with the contract labourer for doing the work had come to an end in 1991 and thereafter it was not renewed;
2. All the 955 workers were being paid wages directly by the FCI;
3. The nature of work, which these workers were performing, was of a perennial nature in the setup of the FCI;
4. All 955 workmen were performing their duties as permanent workers; and
5. No evidence was adduced by the FCI in rebuttal to prove their case against the workers' Union.

Therefore the Court held that 955 employees would be regularized.

In this case, *Bharat Heavy Electricals Ltd.* v. *Mahendra Prasad Jakhmola & Others* [Civil Appeals 1799–1800 of 2019] on 20 February 2019, BHEL had engaged contract labour through a contractor in its factory at Haridwar. The Contract Labours were being issued gate passes at the request of the contractor by the BHEL, for the sake of safety and from administrative point of view. However, it was specifically mentioned that they are the Contract labour. CISF takes care of the safety of the organisation. It was a known fact that no worker will be allowed to enter in the workplace if such gate passes are not issued.

On their termination from service, the contract labour approached the Labour Court claiming for their reinstatement. The Labour Court, after due consideration about supervision, superintendence and administrative control exercised by the establishment, gave a verdict in favour of the contract labour. In response to an appeal made, the Uttarakhand High Court upheld the decision of the Labour Court. Subsequently, BHEL raised an appeal before the Supreme Court. The Supreme Court relied on judgement of *International Airport Authority of India* v. *International Air Cargo Workers' Union* (AIR 2009 SC 3063) where 'supervision and control' was well explained. The Supreme Court held that;

If the contract is for supply of labour, necessarily, the labour supplied by the contractor will work under the directions, supervision and control of the principal employer but that would not make the worker a direct employee of the principal employer, if: (i) the salary is paid by a contractor; (ii) the right to regulate the employment is with the contractor; and (iii) the ultimate supervision and control lies with the contractor.

On this basis, the Supreme Court decided that even though the contract labour worked under the directions, supervision, and control of the principal employer (here, BHEL), such labour would still not be considered its direct workers if the concerned contractor was paying their salary, regulating their employment, and exercising their ultimate control and supervision. The primary control was with the contractor who paid salaries to the contract labour. In contrast, the control and supervision exercised by the principal employer were secondary in nature.

In 2023 in *Kirloskar Brothers Limited* v. *Ramcharan & Others* (2023 LLR 1) two questions were raised before the Court for consideration and they are as follows:

(a) whether the concept of automatic absorption of contract labour in the establishment of the principal employer on issuance of the abolition notification, is implied in Section 10 of the CLRA Act; and
(b) whether on a contractor engaging contract labour in connection with the work entrusted to him by a principal employer, the relationship of master and servant between him (the principal employer) and the contract labour, emerges.

The Court relied on the decisions of *SAIL* Case (2001) and *International Airport Authority* Case (2009) and held that under the contract and even under the provisions of the CLRA, a duty was cast upon the Principal Employer to pay all statutory dues, including salary of the workmen, payment of PF contribution, and in case of non-payment of the same by the contractor, after making such payment, the same can be deducted from the contractor's bill. Therefore, merely because sometimes the payment of salary was made and/or PF contribution was paid by the Principal Employer, which was due to non-payment of the same by the contractor, the contract labour shall not be automatically become the employees of the Principal Employer.

A Concluding Remark

The contract labour shall be declared as the pay roll employees of principal employer if it is proved that there is 'sham and camouflage'. This is the only rule available at this moment in India for the contract labour to be declared as the pay roll employees of principal employer. What is 'sham and camouflage' is a question of fact. Hence, the Industrial Court, being a fact-finding body, is the appropriate authority to justify whether it is a case of 'sham and camouflage' or not. The burden of proof lies on the contract labour to prove that the allegation made by him is a case of 'sham and camouflage'.

* * *

4 The Payment of Bonus Act, 1965

HISTORICAL DEVELOPMENT OF CONCEPT OF BONUS

Bonus was originally regarded as a gratuitous payment by an employer to his employees. The practice of paying bonus as an *ex gratia* payment had its early roots in the textile industry in Bombay and Ahmedabad. In 1917 and 1918, an increase of 10 and 15 per cent of wages was granted as war bonus to the textile workers by the employers. In October 1920, a Committee appointed by the Bombay Mill owners recommended to the member mills for the payment of bonus equal to one month's pay. Similarly, bonus was declared in 1921 and 1922. But as the trading conditions in the industry deteriorated, the mill owners declared in 1923 that they would be unable to pay bonus for the year. Thereupon, a strike began which became general towards the end of January 1924. In February 1924, a bonus dispute Committee was appointed by the Government of Bombay to consider the nature of, the conditions and the basis of bonus which had been granted to the employees in the textile mills and to declare whether the employees had established any enforceable claim, customary, legal or equitable. The Committee held that they had not established any enforceable claim, customary, legal or equitable, to an annual payment of bonus which could be upheld in a Court. The years that followed were years of depression and no major dispute about bonus arose, although bonuses were given on ad hoc basis by a few industrial undertakings.

During the Second World War, managements of textile mills paid cash bonus equivalent to a fraction of the surplus profit but this was also a voluntary payment. Disputes for the payment of bonus for the years 1948 and 1949 arose in the Bombay textile industry. On the said dispute having been referred to the Industrial Court, that Court expressed the view that since both labour and capital contributed to the profits of the industry, both were entitled to a legitimate return out of the profits and evolved a formula for charging certain prior liabilities on the gross profit of the accounting year and awarded a percentage of the balance as bonus. The Industrial Court excluded the mills which had suffered loss from the liability to pay bonus. In appeals against the said awards, the Labour Appellate Tribunal approved broadly the method of computing bonus as a fraction of the surplus profit. According to this formula, which has since been referred to as the Full Bench formula, the surplus available for distribution is to be determined after debiting certain prior charges from gross profits, viz. (i) provision for depreciation, (ii) reservation for rehabilitation, (iii) return of 6 per cent on paid-up capital, and (iv) return on working capital at a rate lower than the one on the paid-up capital. In *Muir Mills Company* v. *Suti Mills Mazdoor Union, Kanpur,*[1] the Supreme Court laid down the following principles:

(1) that bonus was not a gratuitous payment nor a deferred wage, and

(2) that where wages fall short of the living standard and the industry makes profit, part of which is due to the contribution of labour, a claim for bonus may legitimately be made by the workmen.

The Court, however, did not examine the propriety nor the order of priorities as between the several charges and the irrelative importance. Also, it did not examine the desirability of making any alterations in the said formula. These questions came to be examined for the first time in *Associated Cement Companies Ltd.* v. *Its Workmen,*[2] where the said formula was generally approved. Since that decision, the Supreme Court has accepted in several cases the said formula. The principal features of the formula are that each year for which bonus is claimed is a self-contained unit, that bonus is to be computed on the profits of the establishment during that year, that the gross profits are to be determined after debiting the wages and dearness allowance paid to the employees and other items of expenditure against total receipts as disclosed by the profit and loss account, and that against such gross profits the aforesaid four items are to be deducted as prior charges. The formula was not based on any legal right or liability, its object being only to distribute profits after reasonable allocations for the aforesaid charges. Attempts were thereafter made from time to time to have the said formula revised but they were rejected first in *Associated Cement Companies* case, and again in *The Ahmedabad Miscellaneous Industrial Workers' Union* v. *The Ahmedabad Electricity Co. Ltd.,*[3] where it was observed that the plea for revision raised an issue which affected all industries and, therefore, before any change was made, all industries and their workmen had to be heard and their pleas considered. The Court, therefore, suggested that the question of revising the formula should be "comprehensively considered by a high powered Commission". Taking up the aforesaid suggestion, the Government of India appointed a Commission, by its resolution dated December 6, 196l, the terms of reference whereof were, *inter alia:*

1. to define the concept of bonus and to consider in relation to industrial employment the question of payment of bonus based on profits and recommend principles for computation of such bonus and methods of payment;
2. to determine what the prior charges should be in different circumstances and how they should be calculated;
3. to determine conditions under which bonus payment should be made unit wise, industry wise and industry-cum-region wise;
4. to consider whether there should be lower limits irrespective of loss in particular establishment and upper limits for distribution in one year and, if so, the manner to carry forward the profits and losses over a prescribed period; and
5. to suggest an appropriate machinery and method for the settlement of bonus disputes.

1. AIR 1955 SC 170. See also *Baro Borough Municipality* v. *Its Workmen*, AIR 1957 SC 110; *The Shree Meenakshi Mills Ltd.* v. *The Workmen*, AIR 1958 SC 153 and *State of Mysore* v. *The Workers of Gold Mines*, AIR 1958 SC 923.
2. AIR 1959 SC 967.
3. AIR 1962 SC 1255.

After an elaborate enquiry, the Commission made the following, among others, recommendations:

1. That bonus was paid to the workers as share in the prosperity of the establishment and that the basic scheme of the bonus formula should be adhered to, viz. determination of bonus as a percentage of gross profits reduced by the following prior charges, viz. normal depreciation allowable under the Indian Income Tax including multiple shifting allowance, income tax and super tax at the current standard rate applicable for the year for which tax is to be calculated but not super profits tax, return on paid-up capital raised through preference shares at the actual rate of dividend payable, on other paid-up capital at 7 per cent and on reserves used as capital at 4 per cent. The Commission did not recommend provision for rehabilitation.
2. That 60 per cent of the available surplus should be distributed as bonus and excess should be carried forward and taken into account in the next year; the balance of 40 per cent should remain with the establishment into which should merge the saving in tax on bonus and the aggregate balance thus left to the establishment should be used for payment of gratuity, other necessary reserves, rehabilitation in addition to the provision made by way of depreciation in the prior charges, annual provision required for redemption of debentures, etc.
3. That the distinction between the basic wages and dearness allowance for the purpose of arriving at the bonus quantum should be done away with and bonus should be related to wages and dearness allowance taken together.
4. That minimum bonus should be 4 per cent of the total basic wage and dearness allowance paid during the year or ₹40 to each employee, whichever is higher, and in the case of children the minimum should be equivalent to 4 per cent of their basic wage and dearness allowance, or ₹25 whichever is higher.
5. That the maximum bonus should be equivalent to 20 per cent of the total basic wage and dearness allowance paid during the year.
6. That the bonus formula proposed should be deemed to include bonus to employees drawing a total basic pay and dearness allowance up to ₹1600 p.m. regardless of whether they were workmen as defined in the Industrial Disputes Act, 1947 or other corresponding Act provided that quantum of bonus payable to employees drawing total basic pay and allowance over ₹750 p.m. should be limited to what it would be if their pay and dearness allowance were ₹750 p.m.
7. That the formula should not apply to new establishments until they recouped all early losses including arrears of normal depreciation subject to the time limit of 6 years.
8. That the scheme should be applied to all bonus matters relating to the accounting year ending on any day in the calendar year 1962 except in those matters in which settlements had been reached or decisions had been given.

The fact that the Government of India accepted the majority of the Commission's recommendations is clear from the Statement of Objects and Reasons attached to Bill No. 49 of 1965 which they sponsored in Parliament. The Statement, *inter alia*, states that a "tripartite

Commission was set up by the Government of India by resolution dated 6th December 1961 to consider in comprehensive manner the question of payment of bonus based on profits to employees employed in establishments and to make recommendations to the Government. The Commission's report, containing the recommendations, was received by the Government on 24th January, 1964. By resolution dated 2nd September, 1964, Government announced acceptance of the Commission's recommendations subject to a few modifications as were mentioned therein". To implement these recommendations, the Payment of Bonus Ordinance, 1965 was promulgated on May 29, 1965, which was later replaced by the present Act, i.e. the Payment of Bonus Act, 1965, published on September 25, 1965. Thus, bonus, which was originally a voluntary payment acquired, under the Full Bench formula, the character of a right to share in the surplus profits enforceable through the machinery of the Industrial Disputes Act, 1947 and other corresponding Acts. Under the Act, liability to pay bonus has now become a statutory obligation imposed on the employers. From the history of the legislation, it is clear that the Government set a Commission to consider comprehensively the entire question of bonus in all its aspects, and the Commission accordingly considered the concept of bonus, the method of computation, the machinery for enforcement and a statutory formula in place of the one evolved by industrial adjudication.

MEANING OF BONUS

The primary meaning of the word "bonus", according to the definition given in the *New English Dictionary*, is "a boon or gift over and above what is nominally due as remuneration to the receiver and which is therefore something wholly to the good". *Webster's International Dictionary* defines bonus as "something given in addition to what is ordinarily received by or strictly due to the recipient". The Oxford Concise Dictionary defines it as "something to the good, into the bargain (and as an example) gratuity to workmen beyond their wages". **Corpus Juris Secundum**, Vol. 11, at page 515 ascribes the following meanings to bonus:

"An allowance in addition to what is usual, current or stipulated; a sum given or paid beyond what is legally inquired to be paid to the recipient; something given in addition to what is ordinarily received by or strictly due to the recipient" and adds: "It has been said to carry the idea of something uncertain and indefinite, something which may or may not be paid depending on varying circumstances and under particular conditions has been said to imply a benefit accruing to him who offers it and an inducement to the offeree."

This imports the conception of a boon, a gift or a gratuity otherwise described as an '*ex gratia*' payment. The word 'bonus' has, however acquired a secondary meaning in the sphere of industrial relations. It is classified among the methods of wage payment. It has been used especially in the United States of America to designate an award in addition to the contractual wage. It is usually intended as a stimulus to extra effort but sometimes represents the desire of the employer to share with his workers the fruits of their common enterprise.[4] The word 'bonus' is commonly used to denote an increase in salary or wages in contracts of employment. The offer of a bonus is the means frequently adopted to secure continuous service from an employee in order to enhance his efficiency and to augment his loyalty to his

4. *Encyclopaedia Britannica*, Vol. 3, p. 856.

employer and the employee's acceptance of the offer by performing the things called for by the offer, binds the employer to pay the bonus so called.[5]

It also gives another meaning to the word 'bonus', viz. increased compensation for services already rendered gratuitously or for a prescribed compensation where there is neither express nor implied understanding that additional compensation may be granted. This imports the conception that even though the payment is not strictly due to the recipient nor legally enforceable by him, a claim to the same may be laid by the employee under certain conditions, and if such a claim is entertained either by an agreement with the employer or by adjudication before a properly constituted Tribunal as on an industrial dispute arising, the same would ripen into a legally enforceable claim. A bonus may be a mere gift or gratuity as a gesture of goodwill and not enforceable, or it may be something which an employee is entitled to on the happening of a condition precedent and is enforceable when the condition is fulfilled. But in both cases it is something in addition to or in excess of that which is ordinarily received.[6]

The *Textile Labour Inquiry Committee* defined 'bonus' as follows:

The term bonus is applied to a cash payment made in addition to wages. It generally represents the cash incentive given conditionally on certain standards of attendance and efficiency being attained.There are, however, two conditions which have to be satisfied before a demand for bonus can be justified.

(1) when wages fall short at the living standard, and
(2) the industry makes huge profits part of which are due to the contribution which the workmen make in increasing production. The demand for bonus becomes an industrial claim when either or both these conditions are satisfied.

The principles for the grant of bonus were discussed and a formula was evolved by the Full Bench of the Labour Appellate Tribunal in *Mill Owners' Association, Bombay* v. *Rashtreeya Mill Mazdoor Sangh, Bombay.*[7]

"As both labour and capital contribute to the earnings of the industrial concern, it is fair that labour should derive some benefit, if there is a surplus after meeting prior or necessary charges" and the following were prescribed as the first charges on gross profits, viz.

- Provision for deprecation
- Reserves for rehabilitation
- A return at 6 per cent on the paid-up capital
- A return on the working capital at a lesser rate than the return on paid-up capital.

The surplus that remained after meeting the aforesaid deductions would be available for distribution as bonus.

It is, therefore, clear that the claim for bonus can be made by the employees only if as a result of the joint contribution of capital and labour, the industrial concern has earned profits. If in any particular year, the working of the industrial concern has resulted in loss, there is neither any basis nor justification for a demand for bonus. Bonus is not a deferred

5. *Attorney-General* v. *City of Wobur*, 317 Mass. 465.
6. *Great Western Garment Co. Ltd.* v. *Minister of National Revenue'*, 1948—1 DLR 225.
7. 1950 (II) LLJ 1247.

wage, because if it were so, it would necessarily rank for precedence before dividends. The dividends can only be paid out of profits and unless and until profits are made no occasion or question can also arise for distribution of any sum as bonus among, the employees. If the industrial concern has incurred a trading loss, there would be no profits of the particular year available for distribution of dividends, much less could the employees claim the distribution of bonus during that year.

THE SCHEME OF THE ACT

The preamble to the Act states that it is to provide for payment of bonus to persons employed in certain establishments on the basis of profits or on the basis of production or productivity and for matters connected therewith. Section 1(3) provides that it shall apply "save as otherwise provided in the Act" to (a) every factory and (b) every other establishment in which 20 or more persons are employed on any day during the accounting year. It is to be noted that this sub-section is in consonance with one of the Commission's recommendations, viz. that its bonus formula should not be applied to small shops and establishments which are not factories and which employ less than 20 persons. Having made clear that the Act is to apply only to those establishments mentioned in sub-section (3), sub-section (4) provides that the Act shall have effect in respect of the accounting year 1964 and every subsequent year. "Allocable surplus" under S. 2(4) means 67 per cent in cases falling under clause (a) and 60 per cent in other cases of the available surplus. Section 2(6) defines 'available surplus' to mean available surplus as computed under S. 5. Section 2(15) defines "establishment in private sector" to mean any establishment other than an establishment in public sector. Section 2(16) defines "establishment in public sector" as meaning (a) a Government company as defined in S. 617 of the Companies Act, 1956, and (b) a Corporation in which not less than 40 per cent of its capital is held by Government or the Reserve Bank of India or a Corporation owned by Government or the Reserve Bank of India. "Gross profits" as defined by S. 2(18) means gross profits calculated under S. 4.

Sections 4 and 5 provide for computation of gross profits and available surplus after deducting therefrom the sums referred to in S. 6, viz. depreciation admissible under S. 32(1) of the Income-tax Act or the relevant Agricultural Income Tax Act, development rebate or development allowance admissible under the Income Tax Act and such other sums as are specified in the Third Schedule. Section 7 deals with the calculation of direct tax. Sections 8 and 9 deal with eligibility of and disqualification from receiving bonus. Sections 10 to 15 deal with minimum and maximum bonus and the provisions for 'set-off' and 'set-on'. Sections 18, 19, and 21 to 31 deal with certain procedural and allied matters. Section 20 deals with certain establishments in public sector to which the Act is made applicable in certain events. Section 32 excludes from the application of the Act certain categories of employees and certain establishments therein specified. Section 34 provides for the overriding effect of the Act notwithstanding anything inconsistent therewith contained in any other law for the time being in force or in terms of any award, agreement, settlement or contract of service made before May 29, 1965. Section 35 saves the provisions of the Coal Mines Provident Fund and Bonus Schemes Act, 1948 or any scheme made there under. Section 36 empowers an appropriate Government having regard to the financial position and other relevant circumstances of any establishment or class of establishments if it is of the opinion that it would not be in public interest to apply all or any of the provisions of the Act thereto, to exempt for such period as may be specified by it such establishment or class of establishments from all or any of the provisions of the Act.

The scheme of the Act, broadly stated, is four-dimensional.

(1) to impose statutory liability upon all employers of every establishment covered by the Act to pay bonus to employees in the establishment;

(2) to define the principle of payment of bonus according to the prescribed formula;

(3) to provide for payment of minimum and maximum bonus and linking the payment of bonus with the scheme of "set-off and set-on"; and

(4) to provide machinery for enforcement of the liability for payment of bonus.

Ordinarily, a scheme imposing fresh liability would, it is apprehended, be made prospective, leaving the pending disputes to be disposed of according to the law in force before the Act.[8]

CONSTITUTIONAL VALIDITY OF THE ACT AND PROVISIONS

Validity of The Act

The Payment of Bonus Act was challenged on the grounds that it amounts to fraud on the Constitution or otherwise is a colourable exercise of legislative power. This argument was based on the sole premise that Parliament, while enacting the Bonus Act, modified certain principles which were declared by the Supreme Court in *Express Newspapers (Private) Ltd.* v. *Union of India.*[9] But it was held that by enacting the Payment of Bonus Act, Parliament has not attempted to trespass upon the province of the State legislature. It is true that by the impugned legislation certain principles declared by the Apex Court, e.g. in *Express Newspapers (Private) Ltd.* case (supra) in respect of grant of bonus were modified, but on that account it cannot be said that the legislation operates as fraud on the Constitution or is a colourable exercise of legislative power. Parliament has normally power within the framework of the Constitution to enact legislation which modifies principles enunciated by the Supreme Court as applicable to the determination of any dispute, and by exercising that power Parliament does not perpetrate fraud on the Constitution. An enactment may be charged as colourable, and on that account be void, only if it be found that the legislature has by enacting it trespassed upon a field outside its competence.[8]

Validity of Sections 1(3) and 1(5)

Sections 1(3) and 1(5) of the Payment of Bonus Act, which define the scope and applicability of the Act to every factory and other establishment which employs 20 or more persons, do not offend Art. 14 of the Constitution and hence are valid.[10]

---

8. *Jalan Trading Co., Private Ltd., M/s.* v. *Mill Mazdoor Sabha,* AIR 1967 SC 691.
9. AIR 1958 SC 578.
10. *Malabar Tiles Works* v. *Union of India*, AIR 1968 Ker. 143.

Validity of Section 2(13)

The definition of employee provided in S. 2(13) of the Act is within the ambit of the entries 23 and 24 in list III of Schedule VII of the Constitution. Hence S. 2(13) of the Act is valid.[11]

Validity of Section 10

The attack is on the provision for minimum bonus in S. 10 which provides that the employer is bound to pay to every employee a minimum bonus irrespective of profits. It was contented that S. 10 offends Art. 14 of the Constitution inasmuch as it makes no difference between companies making profits and companies having losses, whether marginal or heavy. The Court in *Jalan Trading Co.* case observed that equal protection of the laws is denied if in achieving a certain object, persons, objects or transactions similarly circumstanced are differently treated by law and the principle underlying that different treatment has no rational relation to the object sought to be achieved by the law. It was not laid down by the Supreme Court in *Kunnathat Thathunni Moopil Nair* v. *State of Kerala*[12] that imposition of uniform liability upon persons, objects or transactions which are unequal must, of necessity, lead to discrimination. Ordinarily, it may be predicated of unproductive agricultural land that it is incapable of being put to profitable agricultural use at any time. But that cannot be so predicated of an industrial establishment which has suffered loss in the accounting year, or even over several years successively. Such an establishment may suffer loss in one year and make profit in another. Section 10 undoubtedly places in the same class establishments which have made inadequate profits not justifying payment of bonus, establishments which have suffered marginal loss, and establishments which have suffered heavy loss. The classification so made is not unintelligible: all establishments which are unable to pay bonus under the scheme of the Act, on the result of the working the establishment, are grouped together. The object of the Act is to make an equitable distribution of the surplus profits of the establishment with a view to maintain peace and harmony between the three agencies which contribute to the earning of profits. Distribution of profits which is not subject to great fluctuations year after year, would certainly conduce to maintenance of peace and harmony and would be regarded equitable, and provision for payment of bonus at the statutory minimum rate, even if the establishment has not earned profit, is clearly enacted to ensure the object of the Act.

Whether the scheme for payment of minimum bonus is the best in the circumstances, or a more equitable method could have been devised, so as to avoid, in certain cases, undue hardship is irrelevant to the enquiry in hand. If the classification is not patently arbitrary, the Court will not rule it discriminatory merely because it involves hardship or inequality of burden. With a view to secure particular objects a scheme may be selected by the legislature, wisdom whereof may be open to debate; it may not even be demonstrated that the scheme is not the best in the circumstances and the choice of the legislature may be shown to be erroneous, but unless the enactment fails to satisfy the dual test of intelligible classification

---

11. *Ibid.*
12. AIR 1961 SC 552.

and rationality of the relation with the object of the law, it will not be subject to judicial interference under Art. 14. Invalidity of legislation is not established by merely finding faults with the scheme adopted by the legislature to achieve the purpose it has in view. Equal treatment of unequal objects, transactions or persons, is not liable to be struck down as discriminatory unless there is simultaneously absence of a rational relation to the object intended to be achieved by the law. Accordingly, it was held that S. 10 is not unconstitutional.

Validity of Section 15

Section 15 of the Payment of Bonus Act which deals with the 'set-on and set-off' scheme does not violate the provisions of Art. 14 or 19(1) of the Constitution and hence is valid.[13]

Validity of Section 21

Section 21 of the Bonus Act which provides for the mode of recovery of bonus due from an employer is not invalid. It only makes a provision making available the machinery for recovery of bonus due under the Act as arrears of land revenue.[10]

Validity of Section 27(2)(b) and (c)

Clauses (b) and (c) of sub-section (2) of S. 27 of the Payment of Bonus Act is valid and does not infringe Art. 19(1)(g) of the Constitution of India.

Validity of Section 32

Under S. 32 of the Payment of Bonus Act, employees of certain establishments are excluded from the purview of the Payment of Bonus Act. The Supreme Court has not given its opinion as to the validity of this section as neither the employer nor the Government of India has placed any material on which the vires of the section could be determined. Each class of employees specified in S. 32 requires separate treatment having regard to special circumstances and conditions governing their employment. It was held that it is open to any class of employees or employers affected by this section to challenge the exclusion of certain categories of employees and establishments from the applicability of the Act.[8]

Validity of Section 36

Under S. 36, the appropriate Government is invested with the power to exempt an establishment or a class of establishments from the operation of the Act, provided the Government is of the opinion that having regard to the financial position and other relevant circumstances of the establishment, it would not be in the public interest to apply all or any of the provisions of the Act. The condition for the exercise of that power is that the Government holds the opinion that it is not in the public interest to apply all or any of the provisions of the Act to an establishment or class of establishments, and that opinion is founded on a consideration of the financial position and other relevant circumstances. Parliament has clearly laid down the

13. *Ankey Cloth and General Mills v. Their Workmen*, 1966 (12) FLR 408.

principles and has given adequate guidance to the appropriate Government in implementing the provisions of S. 36. The power so conferred does not amount to delegation of legislative authority. Section 36 amounts to conditional legislation, and is not void. Whether in a given case, the power has been properly exercised by the appropriate Government would have to be considered when that occasion arises. This section was held to be valid. See the discussion on the topic under the head Exemptions from the Act in the chapter.[14]

An Act to provide for the payment of bonus to persons employed in certain establishments on the basis of profits or on the basis of production or productivity and for matters connected therewith

Be it enacted by Parliament in the Sixteenth Year of the Republic of India as follows—

SECTION 1: Short title, extent and application

(1) This Act may be called the Payment of Bonus Act, 1965.

(2) It extends to the whole of India.

(3) Save as otherwise provided in this Act, it shall apply to—

(a) every factory; and

(b) every other establishment in which twenty or more persons are employed on any day during an accounting year.

Provided that the appropriate Government may, after giving not less than two months' notice of its intention so to do, by notification in the Official Gazette, apply the provisions of this Act with effect from such accounting year as may be specified in the notification, to any establishment or class of establishments [including an establishment being a factory within the meaning of sub-clause (ii) of clause (m) of section 2 of the Factories Act, 1948 (63 of 1948) employing such number of persons less than twenty as may be specified in the notification; so, however, that the number of persons so specified shall in no case be less than ten.]

(4) Save as otherwise provided in this Act, the provisions of this Act shall, in relation to a factory or other establishment to which this Act applies, have effect in respect of the accounting year commencing on any day in the year 1964 and in respect of every subsequent accounting year:

Provided that in relation to the State of Jammu and Kashmir, the reference to the accounting year commencing on any day in the year 1964 and every subsequent accounting year shall be construed as reference to the accounting year commencing on any day in the year 1968 and every subsequent accounting year:

Provided further that when the provisions of this Act have been made applicable to any establishment or class of establishments by the issue of a notification under the proviso to sub-section (3), the reference to the accounting year commencing on any day in the year 1964 and every subsequent accounting year or, as the case may be, the reference to the accounting year commencing on any day in the year 1968 and every subsequent accounting year, shall, in relation to such establishment or class of establishments, be construed as a reference to the accounting year specified in such notification and every subsequent accounting year.

14. *Jalan Trading Co., Private Ltd., M/s.*, v. *Mill Mazdoor Sabha*, AIR 1967 SC 691.

(5) An establishment to which this Act applies shall continue to be governed by this Act notwithstanding that the number of persons employed therein falls below twenty or, as the case may be, the number specified in the notification issued under the proviso to sub-section (3).

SECTION 2: Definitions

In this Act, unless the context otherwise requires,—

(1) **accounting year** means—

(i) in relation to a corporation, the year ending on the day on which the books and accounts of the corporation are to be closed and balanced;

(ii) in relation to a company, the period in respect of which any profit and loss account of the company laid before it in annual general meeting is made up, whether that period is a year or not;

(iii) in any other case—

(a) the year commencing on the lst day of April; or

(b) if the accounts of an establishment maintained by the employer thereof are closed and balanced on any day other than the 31st day of March, then, at the option of the employer, the year ending on the day on which its accounts are so closed and balanced:

Provided that an option once exercised by the employer under paragraph (b) of this sub-clause shall not again be exercised except with the previous permission in writing of the prescribed authority and upon such conditions as that authority may think fit;

(2) **agricultural income** shall have the same meaning as in the Income-tax Act.

(3) **agricultural income tax law** means any law for the time being in force relating to the levy of tax on agricultural income;

(4) **allocable surplus** means—

(a) in relation to an employer, being a company (other than a banking company) which has not made the arrangements prescribed under the Income-tax Act for the declaration and payment within India of the dividends payable out of its profits in accordance with the provisions of section 194 of that Act, sixty-seven per cent of the available surplus in an accounting year;

(b) in any other case, sixty per cent of such available surplus;

(5) **appropriate government** means—

(i) in relation to an establishment in respect of which the appropriate Government under the Industrial Disputes Act, 1947 (14 of 1947), is the Central Government, the Central Government;

(ii) in relation to any other establishment, the Government of the State in which that other establishment is situate;

(6) **available surplus** means the available surplus computed under section 5;

(7) **award** means an interim or a final determination of any industrial dispute or of any question relating thereto by any Labour Court, Industrial Tribunal or National Tribunal constituted under the Industrial Disputes Act, 1947 (14 of 1947), or by any other authority constituted under any corresponding law relating to investigation and settlement of industrial disputes in force in a State and includes an arbitration award made under section 10A of that Act or under that law;

(8) **banking company** means a banking company as defined in section 5 of the Banking Companies Act, 1949 (10 of 1949), and includes the State Bank of India, any subsidiary bank as defined in the State Bank of India (Subsidiary Banks) Act, 1959 (38 of 1959), any corresponding new bank specified in the First Schedule to the Banking Companies (Acquisition and Transfer of Undertakings) Act, 1970 (5 of 1970)], any corresponding new bank constituted under section 3 of the Banking Companies (Acquisition and Transfer of Undertakings) Act, 1980 (40 of 1980)], any co-operative bank as defined in clause (bii) of section 2 of the Reserve Bank of India Act, 1934 (2 of 1934), and any other banking institution which may be notified in this behalf by the Central Government.

(9) **company** means any company as defined in section 3 of the Companies Act, 1956 (1 of 1956), and includes a foreign company within the meaning of section 591 of that Act;

(10) **co-operative society** means a society registered or deemed to be registered under the Co-operative Societies Act, 1912 (2 of 1912), or any other law for the time being in force in any State relating to co-operative societies;

(11) **corporation** means any body corporate established by or under any Central, Provincial or State Act but does not include a company or a co-operative society;

(12) **direct tax** means,—

(a) any tax chargeable under,—

(i) the Income-tax Act;

(ii) the Super Profits Tax Act, 1963 (14 of 1963);

(iii) the Companies (Profits) Surtax Act, 1964 (7 of 1964);

(iv) the agricultural income-tax law; and

(b) any other tax which, having regard to its nature or incidence, may be declared by the Central Government, by notification in the Official Gazette, to be a direct tax for the purposes of this Act;

(13) **employee** means any person (other than apprentice) employed on a salary or wages not exceeding twenty-one thousand rupees per mensem in any industry to do any skilled or unskilled manual, supervisory, managerial, administrative, technical or clerical work for hire or reward, whether the terms of employment be express or implied;

(14) **employer** includes,—

(i) in relation to an establishment which is a factory, the owner or occupier of the factory, including the agent of such owner or occupier, the legal representative of a deceased owner or occupier and where a person has been named as a manager of the factory under clause (f) of sub-section (1) of section 7 of the Factories Act, 1948 (63 of 1948), the person so named; and

(ii) in relation to any other establishment, the person who, or the authority which, has the ultimate control over the affairs of the establishment and where the said affairs are entrusted to a manager, managing director or managing agent, such manager, managing director or managing agent;

(15) **establishment in private sector** means any establishment other than an establishment in public sector;

(16) **establishment in public sector** means an establishment owned, controlled or managed by—

(a) a Government company as defined in section 617 of the Companies Act, 1956 (1 of 1956);

(b) a corporation in which not less than forty per cent of its capital is held (whether singly or taken together) by—

(i) the Government; or

(ii) the Reserve Bank of India; or

(iii) a corporation owned by the Government or the Reserve Bank of India;

(17) **factory** shall have the same meaning as in clause (m) of section 2 of the Factories Act, 1948 (63 of 1948);

(18) **gross profits** means the gross profits calculated under section 4;

(19) **Income-tax Act** means the Income-tax Act, 1961 (43 of 1961);

(20) **prescribed** means prescribed by rules made under this Act;

(21) **salary or wages** means all remuneration (other than remuneration in respect of overtime work) capable of being expressed in terms of money, which would, if the terms of employment, express or implied, were fulfilled, be payable to an employee in respect of his employment or of work done in such employment and includes dearness allowance (that is to say, all cash payments, by whatever name called, paid to an employee on account of a rise in the cost of living), but does not include,—

(i) any other allowance which the employee is for the time being entitled to;

(ii) the value of any house accommodation or of supply of light, water, medical attendance or other amenity or of any service or of any concessional supply of foodgrains or other articles;

(iii) any travelling concession;

(iv) any bonus (including incentive, production and attendance bonus);

(v) any contribution paid or payable by the employer to any pension fund or provident fund or for the benefit of the employee under any law for the time being in force;

(vi) any retrenchment compensation or any gratuity or other retirement benefit payable to the employee or any *ex gratia* payment made to him;

(vii) any commission payable to the employee.

Explanation: Where an employee is given in lieu of the whole or part of the salary or wages payable to him, free food allowance or free food by his employer, such food allowance or the value of such food shall, for the purpose of this clause, be deemed to form part of the salary or wages of such employee;

(22) Words and expressions used but not defined in this Act and defined in the Industrial Disputes Act, 1947 (14 of 1947), shall have the meanings respectively assigned to them in that Act.

SECTION 3: Establishments to include departments, undertakings and branches

Where an establishment consists of different departments or undertakings or has branches, whether situated in the same place or in different places, all such departments or undertakings or branches shall be treated as parts of the same establishment for the purpose of computation of bonus under this Act:

Provided that where for any accounting year a separate balance-sheet and profit and loss account are prepared and maintained in respect of any such department or undertaking or branch, then, such department or undertaking or branch shall be treated as a separate establishment for the purpose of computation of bonus, under this Act for that year, unless such department or undertaking or branch was, immediately before the commencement of that accounting year treated as part of the establishment for the purpose of computation of bonus.

Section 3 is an enabling provision in favour of the employers. When an establishment consists of different departments, undertakings or branches, all such departments, under-takings or branches shall be treated as a part of the same establishment for the purpose of computation of bonus under the Act. This means that the employees will be entitled to bonus on the basis of the surplus available from all the units put together. The proviso speaks of separate balance-sheet and profit and loss account being prepared and maintained for any accounting year in respect of one of the units of the whole undertaking. In such cases, the computation of allocable surplus for the payment of bonus should be on the basis of such separate profit and loss account and balance-sheet thus prepared and the employees will be entitled to claim bonus on this basis.

In *K.C.P. Employees' Association, Madras* v. *Management of K.C.P. Ltd.*,[15] the question revolved round only on the applicability of the proviso to S. 3 of the Payment of Bonus Act, 1965. The fact of the case reveals the following situation: the K.C.P. Limited, a public limited company, carries on three business adventures, viz. manufacture of sugar, of cement and of heavy engineering machinery. The factories concerned are in three different places in South India and employ workmen on different terms in three different units. It is a case concerned with the engineering unit known as the Central Workshop run at Tiruvottiyur, Madras. When the Payment of Bonus Act, 1965 came into force, the workmen of this unit, which was financially faring ill unlike the other two sister units, demanded bonus on the footing that the three different undertakings must be treated as one composite establishment and on the basis of the overall profits, bonus must be reckoned as provided in the Act. The

15. AIR 1978 SC 474.

respondents demurred on the ground that the Central Workshop was a separate undertaking to which the proviso to S. 3 applied and consequently the claim for bonus on the basis of a single establishment was untenably over-ambitious. Although the unit concerned was perhaps a losing proposition for the relevant years, the Tribunal upheld the claim of the workmen for both the years, but the two awards were challenged, by Writ Petition, in the High Court. The award relating to 1964–65 was upheld by a Single Judge of the High Court who took the view that since all the three units, though divergent and located in different places, were owned by the same company and, therefore, without more, were covered by the main part of S. 3 and the proviso stood repelled. The management duly carried an appeal before a Division Bench of that Court which also called up and heard the writ petition against the award relating to the year 1965–66. Both the awards were set aside, the holdings on the substantial points being adverse to the workmen. The workmen then approached the Supreme Court which held that the Central Workshop has had no 'separate' viable balance-sheet and profit and loss accounts in respect of' that undertaking and therefore the proviso of S. 3 is attracted.

A situation similar to *K.C.P. Employees'* case arose in *Workmen of M/s. Binny Ltd.* v. *Management of Binny Ltd.*[16] This is an appeal, by special leave, filed by the Binny Employees Association, a registered trade union, against the award made by the Industrial Tribunal, Madras. The first respondent is a company which commenced its business in the name and style of Binny Limited. The petitioners were formerly employed by Binny and Co. Ltd., and are now employed in the Finance Trading and Agency Division of the respondent-company. *M/s. Binny and Co. Limited,* in which the petitioners were formerly employed, was a well-established British company of a standing of more than 170 years with branches all over India. The company had accumulated huge reserves and was able to acquire interest in various other companies, such companies are *M/s. Buckingham and Carnatic Co. Ltd.; The Bangalore Woollen, Cotton and Silk Mills Co. Ltd.; Binny Engineering Works Ltd.; Gange Transport and Trading Company Ltd.;* and *Madura Company Private Ltd.*

Pursuant to orders passed in company petitions in various High Courts and in accordance with the scheme of amalgamation sanctioned by the High Courts, the undertakings of all the six companies referred to above were amalgamated with the respondent-company. The scheme of amalgamation made provisions for various matters. Clause 12 of the scheme provided that "all the employees of the amalgamating companies will become employees of the new company without interruption in service and on terms no less favourable to them". Clause 13 provided that "a separate profit and loss account would be prepared for each of the amalgamating companies for the financial year of 1969." Till the year 1968, the employees of *Binny and Co. Limited* viz., the petitioners, had been getting the maximum bonus of 20 per cent of their gross salary every year in view of the huge profits earned by the said company. However, in the financial year 1969, the respondent-company declared and paid the minimum bonus to the petitioners. The petitioners objected to this and raised a claim that they were entitled to receive bonus at 20 per cent of their gross salary on the basis of the separate profit and loss account for the company formerly known as *Binny and Company Limited.* This claim was referred to the Industrial Tribunal directing the question of fixation of the quantum of bonus for the year 1969 for adjudication. The Tribunal considered the evidence before it

16. AIR 1986 SC 509.

and also referred to the relevant provisions of the law governing the question and came to the conclusion that no separate balance-sheet was prepared for this company and the quantification of the bonus payable had to be made on the consolidated surplus available taking into account the balance-sheet of the amalgamating companies. Hence this appeal.

The Supreme Court referred to S. 3 of the Act and observed that this section provides that different departments or undertakings or branches of an establishment should be treated as parts of the same establishment for the purpose of computation of bonus under the Act. The proviso deals with situations where in any accounting year, a separate balance-sheet and profit and loss account are prepared and maintained in respect of any such department of an establishment. It is not disputed that the profit and loss account for the Binny and Company Limited was, in fact, prepared. Nor is it disputed that a trial balance-sheet was also prepared for this unit. But the company takes refuge in the plea that a separate balance-sheet was not prepared for this unit, to opt out of the proviso to S. 3. Accordingly, the Court held that the employees will be entitled to bonus on the basis of the surplus available from all the units put together. The proviso speaks of separate balance-sheet and profit and loss account being prepared and maintained for any accounting year in respect of one of the units of the whole undertaking. In such cases, the computation of allocable surplus for the payment of bonus should be on the basis of such separate profit and loss account and balance-sheet thus prepared and the employees will be entitled to claim bonus on this basis. The claim of the employees on this basis can be defeated only if this separate unit was treated as a part of the establishment for the computation of bonus, immediately before commencement of the accounting year in question. In this case, the company has not put forward a plea that for the previous year, Binny and Company Ltd. was treated as a part of the respondent-company for the purpose of computation of bonus. The only plea put forward is that no separate balance-sheet was prepared for this unit. The mere omission to prepare a separate balance-sheet for one of the amalgamating units will not by itself help the company to deny bonus to the employees of such a unit. When profit and loss account and trial balance-sheet are prepared, one fails to understand the difficulty in preparing the regular balance-sheet. Neither it is disputed, nor can it be disputed on the materials available before us, that the employees of Binny and Company Ltd. could get 20 per cent bonus as claimed by them. They cannot be denied this bonus merely on the ground that separate balance-sheet was not prepared for their unit when all the materials were available for preparation of such a balance-sheet. Therefore, the second part of the proviso to S. 3 is not attracted and, therefore, the order of the Industrial Tribunal is set aside. The appeal is allowed and it upheld the claim of the petitioners for 20 per cent bonus.

It is to be noted that the principal part of S. 3 lays down that different departments or undertakings or branches of an establishment are to be treated as parts of the same establishment for the purpose of computation of bonus under the Act. From the main provision, an exception is carved out by the proviso and there is a further exception to the proviso itself. The sum and substance of S. 3 is that an establishment initially takes in all establishments, undertakings and branches for the purpose of computation of bonus. But if in respect of any department, undertaking or branch separate balance-sheet and profit and loss account are prepared and maintained for any accounting year, then for that particular year computation of bonus shall be by treating it as a separate establishment. But this will be subject to a further exception that immediately before the commencement of that accounting year, namely the accounting year in which a separate balance sheet and profit and loss account is prepared and maintained, such a department or undertaking or branch has not been treated as a part of the establishment for the purpose of computation of bonus.[17]

SECTION 4: Computation of gross profits

The gross profits derived by an employer from an establishment in respect of the accounting year shall,—

(a) in the case of a banking company, be calculated in the manner specified in the First Schedule;

(b) in any other case, be calculated in the manner specified in the Second Schedule.

SECTION 5: Computation of available surplus

The available surplus in respect of any accounting year shall be the gross profits for that year after deducting therefrom the sums referred to in section 6:

Provided that the available surplus in respect of the accounting year commencing on any day in the year 1968 and in respect of every subsequent accounting year shall be the aggregate of,—

(a) the gross profits for that accounting year after deducting therefrom the sums referred to in section 6; and

(b) an amount equal to the difference between,—

(i) the direct tax, calculated in accordance with the provisions of section 7, in respect of an amount equal to the gross profits of the employer for the immediately preceding accounting year; and

(ii) the direct tax, calculated in accordance with provisions of section 7, in respect of an amount equal to the gross profits of the employer for such preceding accounting year after deducting therefrom the amount of bonus which the employer has paid or is liable to pay to his employees in accordance with the provisions of this Act for that year.

The first Full Bench in the *Mill Owners Association, Bombay* v. *The Rashtriya Mazdoor Sangh, Bombay*,[18] had laid down a general formula applicable for determining the available surplus of an industrial undertaking for the purposes of awarding bonus to its workmen. The first step in this regard is the ascertainment of the gross profits of a concern, which are arrived at after payment of wages and dearness allowances to the employees and other item of expenditure. The next step is to ascertain what are the prior charges which have to be deducted from the gross profits in order to arrive at the available surplus. The Full Bench formula concerns the claim of capital to prior charges which have to be taken into account to give a fair return to the investor and also to keep the industry working efficiently, which, in the long run, will ensure to the benefit of labour. The items considered as prior charges are:

17. *Workmen of H.M.T.* v. *Presiding Officer, National Tribunal Calcutta,* AIR 1973 SC 2300.
18. 1950 LLJ 1247 (FB) (LATI-Bom).

(1) Fair return on (a) paid-up capital; (b) working capital; (c) reserves utilised as working capital which obviates the necessity to borrow at higher rates of interest.

(2) Amount of money required for replacements, rehabilitation and modernization of machinery.

(3) Depreciation allowed by the Income-tax authorities being only a percentage of the written down value, the fund set apart yearly for depreciation and designated under that head would not be sufficient for those purposes, so an extra amount would have to be annually set apart under the heading reserves to make up the deficit.

The question as to what is the ratio of the available surplus which could be awarded as a bonus was also considered. The Full Bench felt that the answer was not an easy one, but essentially the quantum of bonus must depend upon the relative prosperity of the concern during the year under review which is reflected in the amount of surplus; the need of labour at existing wages is also an important consideration.

The Supreme Court in *Muir Mills Co. Ltd.* v. *Suri Mills Mazdoor Union, Kanpur,*[19] generally accepted the view of the Full Bench, that since labour and capital both contribute to the earning, they should derive benefit if there is a surplus after meeting the prior or necessary charges specified in the formula. However, neither the priority as between the prior charges and their relative acceptance nor the condition upon which they were allowed was examined by the Supreme Court, but it was nevertheless held that bonus is neither a gratuity nor gift nor can it be regarded as deferred payment. The principles enunciated by the First Full Bench had been approved in *U.P. Electricity Supply Co. Ltd.* v. *Their Workmen*,[20] as being also applicable to electricity undertakings. This decision was approved by the Supreme Court in *Shree Meenakshi Mills Ltd.* v. *Their Workmen*,[21] but that was not a case dealing with an electricity undertaking. The case which dealt directly with an electricity undertaking was *Tinnevelly-Tuticorin Electric Supply Co. Ltd.* v. *Their Workmen.*[22] In this case also the Supreme Court held that the Full Bench formula was applicable to electrical undertakings. In *Ahmedabad Misc. Industrial Workers Union* v. *Ahmedabad Electricity Co. Ltd.*,[23] the Full Bench formula applying the Income-tax Act rules to ascertain depreciation as a prior charge was approved.

The formula of the Full Bench both in the Textile case and its application to the electricity undertakings as held in the *U.P. Electricity* case has now been accepted by the Supreme Court in several cases with further clarification and elucidation. We can, therefore, deduce the following principles for ascertainment of the available surplus in respect of an industrial undertaking and/or an Electricity Undertaking.

(1) First, gross profits have to be ascertained and for that purpose the balance-sheet and the profit and loss account as required under the Companies Act have to be looked into. If the entries are contested, then they have to be proved like any other contested fact.

19. AIR 1955 SC 170.
20. 1955-2 LLJ 431 (FB) (LATI-Bom).
21. AIR 1958 SC 153.
22. AIR 1960 SC 782.
23. AIR 1962 SC 1255.

(2) The relevant year for which bonus is claimed is a self-sufficient unit and the appropriate accounts have to be made on the notional basis in respect of the said year. 'Once the bonus year is taken as a Unit self-sufficient by itself, the decision of the Labour Tribunal in regard to the refund of excess profits tax and the adjustment of the previous years depreciation and losses against the bonus year's profit must be treated as logical and sound.'

(3) The ascertainment of depreciation is according to the Income-tax Act and what is allowed as a prior charge is the annual notional normal depreciation and not the actual depreciation which is in fact allowed. The formula of the Full Bench in the *U.P. Electricity* case as explained and clarified in *Surat Electricity Co. Ltd. Staff Union* v. *Surat Electricity Co. Ltd.,*[24] was approved in the *Ahmedabad Miscellaneous Industrial Workers Union* case and in *Hamdard Dawakhana Wakf* v. *Its Workmen,*[25] Apart from the notional normal depreciation, the depreciation allowable under Income-tax Act for multiple shift is also allowable.

(4) In calculating the Income-tax for deduction as prior charge, it is not the notional normal depreciation alone that has to be deducted but the statutory depreciation, namely the concessions given under the Income-tax Act to the employers which would include the depreciation for multiple shifts, if any, and thereafter the Income-tax will have to be calculated.

(5) Return on paid-up capital allowable for deduction from the gross profits is 6%. This is generally the formula, adopted by the Full Bench for Industrial Undertakings, though it has been known to have allowed a slightly higher percentage of return in risky undertakings such as plantations.

(6) Return on working capital. This amount is also allowed but at a lower rate. The formula as approved by this Court is that if it is shown that the reserves were available and were actually used as working capital, whether the reserves utilised were depreciation reserves or any other, a return from 2 per cent to 4 per cent is allowable according to the industry, taking into consideration any special circumstances which may justify a claim for a higher interest. The utilisation of the reserves obviates the necessity to borrow from outside sources and pay higher interest which will be to the detriment of labour as the available surplus is likely to be less on this account.[26]

(7) Rehabilitation reserve also has to be provided for in order to keep the original capital of the business intact because assets of an undertaking waste and or lost by the end of a particular period depending on the nature of the undertaking and its assets. The only value of such assets at the end of the period is the scrap value. It is, therefore, necessary in the interest of labour as well as capital to provide for depreciation of such assets yearly and also to take into account and provide for the rise in prices. The determination of this reserve poses problems, but it was suggested that a reasonable method would be first to divide the undertaking into blocks such

24. 1957 (II) LLJ 648 (LATI-Bom).
25. 1962 (II) LLJ 772 (SC).
26. *Workmen* v. *Hindustan Motors Ltd.,* AIR 1968 SC 963.

as "plant and machinery" on the one hand, and other assets like roads, buildings, railway sidings etc. on the other. Then the cost of these separate blocks has to be ascertained and their probable future life has to be estimated. Once this estimate is made, it becomes possible to anticipate approximately the year when the plant or machinery would need replacement; and it is the probable price of such replacement on a future date that ultimately decides the amount to which the employer is entitled by way of replacement cost. The claim for rehabilitation includes also the claim for replacements and modernisation. It is quite conceivable that certain parts of machines, which constitute a block, may need rehabilitation, though the block itself can carry on for a number of years. This process of rehabilitation is a continued process and unlike replacement, its date cannot always be fixed or anticipated. So, with modernisation all these three items are included in the claim for rehabilitation. It is, therefore, necessary for Tribunals to exercise their discretion in admitting all the available evidence to determine this difficult question.

The deductions specified in items (5), (6) and (7) like those in items (3) and (4) are prior charges.

(8) In *Mathura Prasad Srivastave* v. *Sagour Electric Supply Co.*,[27] the claim for contingency reserve and development reserve, which have to be provided under the Electricity (Supply) Act, was upheld. It was observed that though these do not constitute a prior charge, they have to be taken into consideration, to arrive at the figure of bonus after ascertaining the available surplus. The Tribunal cannot fix such a high figure of bonus as to leave insufficient funds in the hands of the Company and make it difficult to provide for these two statutory reserves. After taking these into consideration, the ratio of available surplus for distribution as bonus would depend on a number of factors and is not susceptible to any general formula.

In *Binny Ltd.* v. *Their Workmen,*[28] the Supreme Court has observed, while computing of available surplus for the calculation of working capital, that the working capital cannot include fixed assets nor the capital works in progress as it represents the funds required for day-to-day running of the company. Further, the Court, while deciding the issue of bonus, held that rehabilitation reserve is a substantial item which goes to reduce the available surplus and as a result affects the right of the employees to receive the bonus. Hence, the employer will have to place all relevant materials and the Tribunal will have to scrutinize them carefully and be satisfied that the claim is justified. If a company has no scheme for rehabilitation, then, of course, its claim on that head must be rejected. In determining the claim of the employer for rehabilitation, two factors are essential to be ascertained, namely the multiplier, and that has to be done by reference to the purchase price of the machinery and the price which has to be paid for rehabilitation or replacement; and the determination of the diviser and that has to be done by deciding the probable life of the machinery. Mere production of balance-sheet and profit and loss accounts by themselves will not entitle an employer to sustain its claim for rehabilitation.

27. 1966 (II) LLJ 307 (SC).
28. AIR 1973 SC 353.

SECTION 6: Sums deductible from gross profits

The following sums shall be deducted from the gross profits as prior charges, namely,—

(a) any amount by way of depreciation admissible in accordance with the provisions of the sub-section (1) of section 32 of the Income-tax Act or in accordance with the provisions of the Agricultural Income-tax Law, as the case may be:

Provided that where an employer has been paying bonus to his employees under a settlement or an award or agreement made before the 29th May, 1965, and subsisting on that date after deducting from the gross profits notional normal depreciation, then, the amount of depreciation to be deducted under this clause shall, at the option of such employer (such option to be exercised once and within one year from date) continue to be such notional normal depreciation;

(b) any amount by way of development rebate or investment allowance or development allowance which the employer is entitled to deduct from his income under the Income-tax Act;

(c) subject to the provisions of section 7, any direct tax which the employer is liable to pay for the accounting year in respect of his income, profits and gains during that year;

(d) such further sums as are specified in respect of the employer in the Third Schedule.

SECTION 7: Calculation of direct tax payable by the employer

Any direct tax payable by the employer for any accounting year shall, subject to the following provisions, be calculated at the rates applicable to the income of the employer for that year, namely,—

(a) in calculating such tax no account shall be taken of,—

(i) any loss incurred by the employer in respect of any previous accounting year and carried forward under any law for the time being in force relating to direct taxes;

(ii) any arrears of depreciation which the employer is entitled to add to the amount of the allowance for depreciation for any following accounting year or years under sub-section (2) of section 32 of the Income-tax Act;

(iii) any exemption conferred on the employer under section 84 of the Income-tax Act or of any deduction to which he is entitled under sub-section (1) of section 101 of that Act, as in force immediately before the commencement of the Finance Act, 1965 (10 of 1965);

(b) where the employer is a religious or a charitable institution to which the provisions of section 32 do not apply and the whole or any part of its income is exempt from tax under the Income-tax Act, then, with respect to the income so exempted, such institution shall be treated as if it were a company in which the public are substantially interested within the meaning of that Act;

(c) where the employer is an individual or a Hindu Undivided Family, the tax payable by such employer under the Income-tax Act shall be calculated on the basis that the income derived by him from the establishment is his only income;

(d) where the income of any employer includes any profits and gains derived from the export of any goods or merchandise out of India and any rebate on such income is allowed under any law for the time being in force relating to direct taxes, then, no account shall be taken of such rebate;

(e) no account shall be taken of any rebate other than development rebate or investment allowance or development allowance or credit or relief or deduction (not hereinbefore mentioned in this section) in the payment of any direct tax allowed under any law for the time being in force relating to direct taxes or under the relevant annual Finance Act, for the development of any industry.

SECTION 8: Eligibility for bonus

Every employee shall be entitled to be paid by his employer in an accounting year, bonus, in accordance with the provisions of this Act, provided he has worked in the establishment for not less than thirty working days in that year.

SECTION 9: Disqualification for bonus

Notwithstanding anything contained in this Act, an employee shall be disqualified from receiving bonus under this Act, if he is dismissed from service for,—

(a) fraud; or

(b) riotous or violent behaviour while on the premises of the establishment; or

(c) theft, misappropriation or sabotage of any property of the establishment.

SECTION 10: Payment of minimum bonus

Subject to the other provisions of this Act, every employer shall be bound to pay to every employee in respect of the accounting year commencing on any day in the year 1979 and in respect of every subsequent accounting year, a minimum bonus which shall be 8.33 per cent of the salary or wages earned by the employee during the accounting year or one hundred rupees, whichever is higher, whether or not the employer has any allocable surplus in the accounting year:

Provided that where an employee has not completed fifteen years of age at the beginning of the accounting year, the provisions of this section shall have effect in relation to such employee as if for the words "one hundred rupees" the words "sixty rupees" were substituted.

SECTION 11: Payment of maximum bonus

(1) Where in respect of any accounting year referred to in section 10, the allocable surplus exceeds the amount of minimum bonus payable to the employees under that

section, the employer shall, in lieu of such minimum bonus, be bound to pay to every employee in respect of that accounting year bonus which shall be an amount in proportion to the salary or wages earned by the employee during the accounting year subject to a maximum of twenty per cent of such salary or wage.

(2) In computing the allocable surplus under this section, the amount set on or the amount set off under the provisions of section 15 shall be taken into account in accordance with the provisions of that section.

Section 12: Calculation of bonus with respect to certain employees

Where the salary or wage of an employee exceeds seven thousand rupees or minimum wages for the scheduled employment, as fixed by the appropriate Government, which over is higher per mensem, the bonus payable to such employee under section 10 or, as the case may be, under section 11, shall be calculated as if his salary or wage were seven thousand rupees or minimum wages for the scheduled employment, as fixed by the appropriate Government, which over is higher per mensem.

Explanation: For the purpose of this section, the expression "scheduled employment" shall have the same meaning assigned to it in clause (g) of section 2 of the Minimum Wages Act, 1948.

Section 13: Proportionate deduction in bonus in certain cases

Where an employee has not worked for all the working days in an accounting year, the minimum bonus of one hundred rupees or, as the case may be, of sixty rupees, if such bonus is higher than 8.33 per cent of his salary or wage of the days he has worked in that accounting year, shall be proportionately reduced.

Section 14: Computation of number of working days

For the purposes of section 13, an employee shall be deemed to have worked in an establishment in any accounting year also on the days on which,—

(a) he has been laid off under an agreement or as permitted by standing orders under the Industrial Employment (Standing Orders) Act, 1946 (20 of 1946), or under the Industrial Disputes Act, 1947 (14 of 1947), or under any other law applicable to the establishment;

(b) he has been on leave with salary or wages;

(c) he has been absent due to temporary disablement caused by accident arising out of and in the course of his employment; and

(d) the employee has been on maternity leave with salary or wages, during the accounting year.

Section 15: Set on and set off of allocable surplus

(1) Where for any accounting year, the allocable surplus exceeds the amount of maximum bonus payable to the employees in the establishment under section 11, then, the

excess shall, subject to a limit of twenty per cent of the total salary or wages of the employees employed in the establishment in that accounting year, be carried forward for being set on in the succeeding accounting year and so on up to and inclusive of the fourth accounting year to be utilised for the purpose of payment of bonus in the manner illustrated in the Fourth Schedule.

(2) Where for any accounting year, there is no available surplus or the allocable surplus in respect of that year falls short of the amount of minimum bonus payable to the employees in the establishment under section 10, and there is no amount or sufficient amount carried forward and set on under sub-section (1) which could be utilised for the purpose of payment of the minimum bonus, then such minimum amount or the deficiency, as the case may be, shall be carried forward for being set off in the succeeding accounting year and so on up to and inclusive of the fourth accounting year in the manner illustrated in the Fourth Schedule.

(3) The principle of set on and set off as illustrated in the Fourth Schedule shall apply to all other cases not covered by sub-section (1) or sub-section (2) for the purpose of payment of bonus under this Act.

(4) Where in any accounting year any amount has been carried forward and set on or set off under this section, then, in calculating bonus for the succeeding accounting year, the amount of set on or set off carried forward from the earliest accounting year shall first be taken into account.

Section 16: Special provisions with respect to certain establishments

(1) Where an establishment is newly set up, whether before or after the commence-ment of this Act, the employees of such establishment shall be entitled to be paid bonus under this Act in accordance with the provisions of sub-sections (1A), (1B) and (1C).

(1A) In the first five accounting years following the accounting year in which the employer sells the goods produced or manufactured by him or renders services, as the case may be, from such establishment, bonus shall be payable only in respect of the accounting year in which the employer derives profit from such establishment and such bonus shall be calculated in accordance with the provisions of this Act in relation to that year, but without applying the provisions of section 15.

(1B) For the sixth and seventh accounting years following the accounting year in which the employer sells the goods produced or manufactured by him or renders services, as the case may be, from such establishment, the provisions of section 15 shall apply subject to the following modifications, namely,—

(i) for the sixth accounting year,—

set on or set off, as the case may be, shall be made in the manner illustrated in the Fourth Schedule taking into account the excess or deficiency, if any, as the case may be, of the allocable surplus set on or set off in respect of the fifth and sixth accounting years;

(ii) for the seventh accounting year,—

set on or set off, as the case may be, shall be made in the manner illustrated in the Fourth Schedule taking into account the excess or deficiency, if any, as the case may be, of the allocable surplus set on or set off in respect of the fifth, sixth and seventh accounting years.

(1C) From the eighth accounting year following the accounting year in which the employer sells the goods produced or manufactured by him or renders services, as the case may be, from such establishment, the provisions of section 15 shall apply in relation to such establishment as they apply in relation to any other establishment.

Explanation I: For the purpose of sub-section (1), an establishment shall not be deemed to be newly set up merely by reason of a change in its location, management, name or ownership.

Explanation II: For the purpose of sub-section (1A), an employer shall not be deemed to have derived profit in any accounting year unless,—

(a) he has made provision for that year's depreciation to which he is entitled under the Income-tax Act or, as the case may be, under the Agricultural Income-tax Law; and

(b) the arrears of such depreciation and losses incurred by him in respect of the establishment for the previous accounting years have been fully set off against his profits.

Explanation III: For the purposes of sub-section (1A), (1B) and (1C), sale of the goods produced or manufactured during the course of the trial running of any factory or of the prospecting stage of any mine or an oil-field shall not be taken into consideration and where any question arises with regard to such production or manufacture, the decision of the appropriate Government, made after giving the parties a reasonable opportunity of representing the case, shall be final and shall not be called in question by any court or other authority.

(2) The provisions of sub-sections (1), (1A), (1B) and (1C) shall, so far as may be, apply to new departments or undertakings or branches set up by existing establishments:

Provided that if an employer in relation to an existing establishment consisting of different departments or undertakings or branches (whether or not in the same industry) set up at different periods has, before the 29th May, 1965, been paying bonus to the employees of all such departments or undertakings or branches irrespective of the date on which such departments or undertakings or branches were set up, on the basis of the consolidated profits computed in respect of all such departments or undertakings or branches, then, such employer shall be liable to pay bonus in accordance with the provisions of this Act to the employees of all such departments or undertakings or branches (whether set up before or after that date) on the basis of the consolidated profits computed as aforesaid.

Section 17: Adjustment of customary or interim bonus against bonus payable under the Act

Where in any accounting year,—

(a) an employer has paid any puja bonus or other customary bonus to an employee; or

(b) an employer has paid a part of the bonus payable under this Act to an employee before the date on which such bonus becomes payable,

then, the employer shall be entitled to deduct the amount of bonus so paid from the amount of bonus payable by him to the employee under this Act in respect of that accounting year and the employee shall be entitled to receive only the balance.

SECTION 18: Deduction of certain amounts from bonus payable under the Act

Where in any accounting year, an employee is found guilty of misconduct causing financial loss to the employer, then, it shall be lawful for the employer to deduct the amount of loss from the amount of bonus payable by him to the employee under this Act in respect of that accounting year only and the employee shall be entitled to receive the balance, if any.

SECTION 19: Time-limit for payment of bonus

All amounts payable to an employee by way of bonus under this Act shall be paid in cash by his employer,—

(a) where there is a dispute regarding payment of bonus pending before any authority under section 22, within a month from the date on which the award becomes enforceable or the settlement comes into operation, in respect of such dispute;

(b) in any other case, within a period of eight months from the close of the accounting year.

Provided that the appropriate Government or such authority as the appropriate Government may specify in this behalf may, upon an application made to it by the employer and for sufficient reasons, by order, extend the said period of eight months to such further period or periods as it thinks fit, so, however, that the total period so extended shall not in any case exceed two years.

SECTION 20: Application of Act to establishments in public sector in certain cases

(1) If in any accounting year an establishment in public sector sells any goods produced or manufactured by it or renders any services, in competition with an establishment in private sector, and the income from such sale or services or both is not less than twenty per cent of the gross income of the establishment in public sector for that year, then, the provisions of this Act shall apply in relation to such establishment in public sector as they apply in relation to a like establishment in private sector.

(2) Save as otherwise provided in sub-section (1), nothing in this Act shall apply to the employees employed by any establishment in public sector.

Section 21: Recovery of bonus due from an employer

Where any money is due to an employee by way of bonus from his employer under a settlement or an award or agreement, the employee himself or any other person authorised by him in writing in this behalf, or in the case of the death of the employee, his assignee or heirs may, without prejudice to any other mode of recovery, make an application to the appropriate Government for the recovery of the money due to him, and if the appropriate Government or such authority as the appropriate Government may specify in this behalf is satisfied that any money is so due, it shall issue a certificate for that amount to the Collector who shall proceed to recover the same in the same manner as an arrear of land revenue:

Provided that every such application shall be made within one year from the date on which the money became due to the employee from the employer:

Provided further that any such application may be entertained after the expiry of the said period of one year, if the appropriate Government is satisfied that the applicant had sufficient cause for not making the application within the said period.

Explanation: In this section and in sections 22, 23, 24 and 25 "employee" includes a person who is entitled to the payment of bonus under this Act but who is no longer in employment.

Section 22: Reference of disputes under the Act

Where any dispute arises between an employer and his employees with respect to the bonus payable under this Act or with respect to the application of this Act to an establishment in public sector, then, such dispute shall be deemed to be an industrial dispute within the meaning of the Industrial Disputes Act, 1947 (14 of 1947), or of any corresponding law relating to investigation and settlement of industrial disputes in force in a State and the provisions of that Act or, as the case may be, such law, shall, save as otherwise expressly provided, apply accordingly.

Section 23: Presumption about accuracy of balance sheet and profit and loss account of corporations and companies

(1) Where, during the course of proceedings before any arbitrator or Tribunal under the Industrial Disputes Act, 1947 (14 of 1947), or under any corresponding law relating to investigation and settlement of industrial disputes in force in a State (hereinafter in this section and in sections 24 and 25 referred to as the "said authority") to which any dispute of the nature specified in section 22 has been referred, the balance sheet and the profit and loss account of an employer, being a corporation or a company (other than a banking company), duly audited by the Comptroller and Auditor General of India or by auditors duly qualified to act as auditors of companies under sub-section (1) of section 226 of the Companies Act, 1956 (1 of 1956), are produced before it, then, the said authority may presume the statements and particulars contained in such balance sheet and profit and loss account to be accurate and it shall not be necessary for the corporation or the company to prove

the accuracy of such statements and particulars by the filing of an affidavit or by any other mode:

Provided that where the said authority is satisfied that the statements and particulars contained in the balance sheet or the profit and loss account of the corporation or the company are not accurate, it may take such steps as it thinks necessary to find out the accuracy of such statements and particulars.

(2) When an application is made to the said authority by any trade union being a party to the dispute or where there is no trade union, by the employees being a party to the dispute, requiring any clarification relating to any item in the balance sheet or the profit and loss account, it may, after satisfying itself that such clarification is necessary, by order, direct the corporation or, as the case may be, the company, to furnish to the trade union or the employees such clarification within such time as may be specified in the direction and the corporation or, as the case may be, the company, shall comply with such direction.

SECTION 24: Audited accounts of banking companies not to be questioned

(1) Where any dispute of the nature specified in section 22 between an employer, being a banking company, and its employees has been referred to the said authority under that section and during the course of proceedings the accounts to the banking company duly audited are produced before it, the said authority shall not permit any trade union or employees to question the correctness of such accounts, but the trade union or the employees may be permitted to obtain from the banking company such information as is necessary for verifying the amount of bonus due under this Act.

(2) Nothing contained in sub-section (1) shall enable the trade union or the employees to obtain any information which the banking company is not compelled to furnish under the provisions of section 34A of the Banking Regulation Act, 1949 (10 of 1949).

SECTION 25: Audit of accounts of employers, not being corporations or companies

(1) Where any dispute of the nature specified in section 22 between an employer, not being a corporation or a company, and his employees has been referred to the said authority under that section and the accounts of such employer audited by any auditor duly qualified to act as auditor of companies under sub-section (1) of section 226 of the Companies Act, 1956 (1 of 1956), are produced before the said authority, the provisions of section 23 shall, so far as may be, apply to the accounts so audited.

(2) When the said authority finds that the accounts of such employer have not been audited by any such auditor and it is of opinion that an audit of the accounts of such employer is necessary for deciding the question referred to it, then, it may, by order, direct the employer to get his accounts audited within such time as may be specified

in the direction or within such further time as it may allow by such auditor or auditors as it thinks fit and thereupon the employer shall comply with such direction.

(3) Where an employer fails to get the accounts audited under sub-section (2) the said authority may, without prejudice to the provisions of section 28, get the accounts audited by such auditor or auditors as it thinks fit.

(4) When the accounts are audited under sub-section (2) or sub-section (3) the provisions of section 23 shall, so far as may be, apply to the accounts so audited.

(5) The expenses of, and incidental to, any audit under sub-section (3) (including the remuneration of the auditor or auditors) shall be determined by the said authority (which determination shall be final) and paid by the employer and in default of such payment shall be recoverable from the employer in the manner provided in section 21.

Section 26: Maintenance of registers, records, etc.

Every employer shall prepare and maintain such registers, records and other documents in such form and in such manner as may be prescribed.

Section 27: Inspectors

(1) The appropriate Government may, by notification in the Official Gazette, appoint such persons as it thinks fit to be Inspectors for the purposes of this Act and may define the limits within which they shall exercise jurisdiction.

(2) An Inspector appointed under sub-section (1) may, for the purpose of ascertaining whether any of the provisions of this Act has been complied with—

- (a) require an employer to furnish such information as he may consider necessary;
- (b) at any reasonable time and with such assistance, if any, as he thinks fit, enter any establishment or any premises connected therewith and require anyone found in charge thereof to produce before him for examination any accounts, books, registers and other documents relating to the employment of persons or the payment of salary or wages or bonus in the establishment;
- (c) examine with respect to any matter relevant to any of the purposes aforesaid, the employer, his agent or servant or any other person found in charge of the establishment or any premises connected therewith or any person whom the Inspector has reasonable cause to believe to be or to have been an employee in the establishment;
- (d) make copies of, or take extracts from, any book, register or other document maintained in relation to the establishment; and
- (e) exercise such other powers as may be prescribed.

(3) Every Inspector shall be deemed to be a public servant within the meaning of the Indian Penal Code (45 of 1860).

(4) Any person required to produce any accounts, books, register or other documents or to give information by an Inspector under sub-section (1) shall be legally bound to do so.

(5) Nothing contained in this section shall enable an Inspector to require a banking company to furnish or disclose any statement or information or to produce, or give inspection of any of its books of account or other documents, which a banking company cannot be compelled to furnish, disclose, produce or give inspection of, under the provisions of section 34A of the Banking Regulation Act, 1949 (10 of 1949).

SECTION 28: Penalty

If any person,—

(a) contravenes any of the provisions of this Act or any rule made thereunder, or

(b) to whom a direction is given or a requisition is made under this Act fails to comply with the direction or requisition,

he shall be punishable with imprisonment for a term which may extend to six months, or with fine which may extend to one thousand rupees, or with both.

SECTION 29: Offences by companies

(1) If the person committing an offence under this Act is a company, every person who, at the time the offence was committed was in charge of, and was responsible to, the company for the conduct of business of the company, as well as the company, shall be deemed to be guilty of the offence and shall be liable to be proceeded against and punished accordingly:

Provided that nothing contained in this sub-section shall render any such person liable to any punishment if he proves that the offence was committed without his knowledge or that he exercised all due diligence to prevent the commission of such offence.

(2) Notwithstanding anything contained in sub-section (1), where an offence under this Act has been committed by a company and it is proved that the offence has been committed with the consent or connivance of, or is attributable to any neglect on the part of, any director, manager, secretary or other officer of the company, such director, manager, secretary or other officer shall also be deemed to be guilty of that offence and shall be liable to be proceeded against and punished accordingly.

Explanation: For the purposes of this section,—

(a) "company" means any body corporate and includes a firm or other association of individuals; and

(b) "director", in relation to a firm, means a partner in the firm.

SECTION 30: Cognizance of offences

(1) No court shall take cognizance of any offence punishable under this Act, save on complaint made by or under the authority of appropriate Government or an officer of the Government (not below the rank of a Regional Labour Commissioner in the

case of an officer of the Central Government, and not below the rank of a Labour Commissioner in the case of an officer of the State Government) specially authorised in this behalf by that Government.

(2) No court inferior to that of a Presidency Magistrate or a Magistrate of the First Class shall try any offence punishable under this Act.

SECTION 31: Protection of action taken under the Act

No suit, prosecution or other legal proceeding shall lie against the Government or any officer of the Government for anything which is in good faith done or intended to be done in pursuance of this Act or any rule made thereunder.

SECTION 31A: Special provision with respect to payment of bonus linked with production or productivity

Notwithstanding anything contained in this Act,—

(i) where an agreement or a settlement has been entered into by the employees with their employer before the commencement of the Payment of Bonus (Amendment) Act, 1976, (23 of 1976), or

(ii) where the employees enter into any agreement or settlement with their employer after such commencement,

for payment of an annual bonus linked with production or productivity in lieu of bonus based on profits payable under this Act, then, such employees shall be entitled to receive bonus due to them under such agreement or settlement, as the case may be:

Provided that any such agreement or settlement whereby the employees relinquish their right to receive the minimum bonus under section 10 shall be null and void in so far as it purports to deprive them of such right:

Provided further that such employees shall not be entitled to be paid such bonus in excess of twenty per cent of the salary or wage earned by them during the relevant accounting year.

SECTION 32: Act not to apply to certain classes of employees

Nothing in this Act shall apply to,—

(i) employees employed by the Life Insurance Corporation of India;

(ii) seamen as defined in clause (42) of section 3 of the Merchant Shipping Act, 1958 (44 of 1958);

(iii) employees registered or listed under any scheme made under the Dock Workers (Regulation of Employment) Act, 1948, (9 of 1948), and employed by registered or listed employers;

(iv) employees employed by an establishment engaged in any industry carried on by or under the authority of any department of the Central Government or a State Government or a local authority;

(v) employees employed by,—

(a) the Indian Red Cross Society or any other institution of a like nature (including its branches);

(b) universities and other educational institutions;

(c) institutions (including hospitals, chambers of commerce and social welfare institutions) established not for purposes of profit;

(vi) [* * *]

(vii) [* * *]

(viii) employees employed by the Reserve Bank of India;

(ix) employees employed by,—

(a) the Industrial Finance Corporation of India;

(b) any Financial Corporation established under section 3, or any joint Financial Corporation established under Section 3A of the State Financial Corporations Act, 1951 (63 of 1951);

(c) the Deposit Insurance Corporation;

(d) The National Bank of Agriculture and Rural Development;

(e) the Unit Trust of India;

(f) the Industrial Development Bank of India;

(fa) the Small Industries Development Bank of India established under Section 3 of the Small Industries Development Bank of India Act, 1989;

(ff) the National Housing Bank;

(g) any other financial institution other than a banking company being an establishment in public sector, which the Central Government may, by notification in the Official Gazette, specify, having regard to,—

(i) its capital structure;

(ii) its objectives and the nature of its activities;

(iii) the nature and extent of financial assistance or any concession given to it by the Government; and

(iv) any other relevant factor;

(x) omitted;

(xi) employees employed by inland water transport establishments operating on routes passing through any other country.

Section 33: Act to apply to certain pending disputes regarding payment of bonus

Omitted by the Payment of Bonus (Amendment) Act, 1976, w.e.f. 25th September, 1975.

Section 34: Effect of laws and agreements inconsistent with the Act

Subject to the provisions of section 31A, the provisions of this Act shall have effect notwithstanding anything inconsistent therewith contained in any other law for the time being in force or in the terms of any award, agreement, settlement or contract of service.

SECTION 35: Saving

Nothing contained in this Act shall be deemed to affect the provisions of the Coal Mines Provident Fund and Bonus Schemes Act, 1948 (46 of 1948), or of any scheme made thereunder.

SECTION 36: Power of exemption

If the appropriate Government, having regard to the financial position and other relevant circumstances of any establishment or class of establishments, is of opinion that it will not be in public interest to apply all or any of the provisions of this Act thereto, it may, by notification in the Official Gazette, exempt, for such period as may be specified therein and subject to such conditions as it may think fit to impose, such establishment or class of establishments from all or any of the provisions of this Act.

Section 36 empowers the appropriate Government to exempt an establishment or a class of establishments from the operation of the Act, provided the Government is of the opinion that having regard to the financial position and other relevant circumstances of the establishment, it would not be in the public interest to apply all or any of the provisions of the Act. The condition for the exercise of that power is that the Government holds the opinion that it is not in the public interest to apply all or any of the provisions of the Act to an establishment or class of establishments, and that opinion is founded on a consideration of the financial position and other relevant circumstances. Parliament has clearly laid down the principles and has given adequate guidance to the appropriate Government in implementing the provisions of S. 36. The power so conferred does not amount to delegation of legislative authority. Section 36 amounts to conditional legislation, and is not void. Whether in a given case, the powers has been properly exercised by the appropriate Government would have to be considered when that occasion arises.[29]

A mere look at S. 36 shows that before an appropriate Government can form its opinion regarding grant of partial or full exemption to any establishment or class of establishments which are otherwise already covered by the sweep of the Act, the following factual conditions must be found to have existed at the relevant time to enable the delegate to exercise its powers under the Act.

(1) The financial position of the establishment or class of establishments, as the case may be, must be such that it would not be in a public interest to apply all or any of the provisions of the Act to such establishment or establishments.

(2) There may be other relevant circumstances pertaining to such establishment or establishments which would require exercise of such power of exemption.

(3) Such exercise must be in public interest as a whole and not confined to the personal or private interest of the establishment or establishments concerned.

In the setting of the section and the way it will work, implicit in the section is the direction to the appropriate Government by the legislature that it should form its opinion on

29. *Ibid.*, f.n. 8.

objective facts furnished not only by the establishment or a class of establishments claiming such exemption but also by the employees who are likely to be affected by the exercise of such power and who should necessarily get an opportunity to submit their material in rebuttal. If this requirement is not read in the section, the exercise of power of exemption qua the establishment or a class of establishments, which will have a direct pernicious adverse effect on the employees who would otherwise earn statutory benefit of the provisions of the Act, would always remain a truncated, inchoate, half-baked and a still-born exercise of power and only on remand by competent Court the exercise would become an informed one.[30]

The Payment of Bonus Act is a piece of welfare legislation enacted for the benefit of a large category of workmen seeking a living wage to make their lives more meaningful and for fructifying the benevolent guarantee of Art. 21 of the Constitution. Bonus is treated as deferred wage. When Parliament in its wisdom has enacted such a beneficial piece of social legislation which already guarantees minimum statutory bonus to employees governed by it, if their employers are to be allowed to earn exemption from the sweep of such a beneficial legislation which would ipso facto adversely affect entire class of their employees, the conditions for exercise of such power of exemption have to be strictly and objectively fulfilled by the repository of such a drastic power. The Payment of Bonus Act has prescribed objective standards and has permitted the delegate to grant exemption and to withdraw the benefit of the statute which is being enjoyed by the persons and in such a situation, the principles of fair play or consultation or natural justice cannot be totally excluded. The Supreme Court in *State of T.N.* v. *K. Sabanayagam*[30] laid down the following procedural steps to be followed by the appropriate Government before granting exemption under S. 36 of the Act.

1. When such applications are received by the appropriate Government, which necessarily have to be supported by relevant data by the claimants, the receipt of such applications has to be brought to the notice of the employees, likely to be affected by grant of such applications, and for that purpose notices can be suitably affixed by the appropriate Government on the notice boards of the concerns or factory premises of the establishments where the workmen are working, mentioning the dates on which such applications are received and the grounds on which such exemptions are claimed under such applications.
2. Suitable public notice in newspapers having circulation in the area of operation of such establishments can be published and for that purpose suitable expenses can be required to be reimbursed by the claimants to the appropriate Government.
3. The employees concerned through their representative unions may, under these circumstances, be permitted to file their written representations with relevant data for rebutting the material furnished by the claimants so that the rival version put forward by the employees also will become available to the appropriate Government before it forms its opinion. For that purpose, the public notice and the notice to be affixed on the notice boards of the concerns should indicate the time within which such representations may be furnished with relevant data by the representative unions of the employees concerned.

30. AIR 1998 SC 344.

4. Though it is not necessary for the appropriate Government, before forming its opinion under S. 36 of the Act on the basis of the data furnished by the rival parties, to give any personal hearing either to the claimant-establishment or to the representative union of the employees, it may be still open in appropriate cases for the Government, if so thought fit, to give opportunity of personal hearing to the representatives of the establishments as well as of the employees if any elucidation is required in this connection.
5. For making the aforesaid exercise effective, if the employees concerned through their representative unions seek an opportunity to look into the material supplied by the establishments in support of their claims for exemption, inspection of such material can be made available to the unions of employees to enable them to file their representations and to furnish the data in rebuttal for opposing such claims.
6. Strict time schedule can be fixed by the appropriate Government within which the entire exercise can get completed so that the proceedings may not drag on for an indefinite period.

Other Relevant Circumstances

In the instant case, i.e. *Sabanayagam* case as aforesaid, the learned counsel for the appellant submitted that S. 36 of the Act also entitles the appropriate Government to take into consideration other relevant circumstances for exempting any establishment or class of establishments from the provisions of the Act. This may involve a policy decision on the part of the Government to give impetus to a class of industries in an area where the industrial development may be less so that new industries in that area can be attracted and their operation costs may be reduced. The Supreme Court held that it is to be kept in view that the financial position and other relevant circumstances are not independent of their nexus with the existing claimant-establishment or class of establishments and they do not refer to any future establishments which have yet not seen the light of the day and which have not still employed any employees who could be said to have earned any statutory benefits under the Act. Therefore, the *other relevant circumstances,* as mentioned in S. 36, will have to be read with the financial position of the claimant-establishments themselves and their other circumstances have to be seen on the touchstone of public interest to enable the appropriate Government to form its opinion under S. 36 quà the claims of such existing establishments.

Section 37: Power to remove difficulties Section

Omitted by the Payment of Bonus (Amendment) Act, 1976, w.r.e.f. 25th September, 1975.

Section 38: Power to make rules

(1) The Central Government may, subject to the condition of previous publications, by notification in the Official Gazette, make rules to carry out the provisions of this Act.

(2) In particular, and without prejudice to the generality of the foregoing power, such rules may provide for,—

(a) the authority for granting permission under the proviso to sub-clause (iii) of clause (1) of section 2;

(b) the preparation of registers, records and other documents and the form and manner in which such registers, records and documents may be maintained under section 26;

(c) the powers which may be exercised by an Inspector under clause (e) of sub-section (2) of section 27;

(d) any other matter which is to be, or may be, prescribed.

(3) Every rule made under this section shall be laid as soon as may be after it is made, before each House of Parliament, while it is in session for a total period of thirty days, which may be comprised in one session or in two or more successive sessions, and if before the expiry of the session immediately following the session or the successive sessions aforesaid both Houses agree in making any modification in the rule or both Houses agree that the rule should not be made, the rule shall thereafter have effect only in such modified form or be of no effect, as the case may be; so, however, that any such modification or annulment shall be without prejudice to the validity of anything previously done under that rule.

Section 39: Application of certain laws not barred

Save as otherwise expressly provided, the provisions of this Act shall be in addition to and not in derogation of the Industrial Disputes Act, 1947 (14 of 1947), or any corresponding law relating to investigation and settlement of industrial disputes in force in a State.

Section 39 and Section 22

It will be noticed that S. 39 provides that where a dispute arises between an employer and his employees (i) with respect to the bonus payable under the Act, or (ii) with respect to the application of the Act, such a dispute shall be deemed to be industrial dispute within the meaning of the Industrial Disputes Act, 1947 or any corresponding law relating to investigation and settlement of industrial disputes in force in a State, and the provisions of that Act and such law, as the case may be, shall, save as otherwise expressly provided, apply accordingly. An industrial dispute under the Industrial Disputes Act would be between a workman, as defined in that Act, and his employer and the dispute can be an industrial dispute if it is one as defined therein. But the definition of an "employee" under S. 2(13) of this Act is wider than that of a "workman" under the Industrial Disputes Act. A dispute between an employer and an employee, therefore, may not fall under the Industrial Disputes Act and in such a case the Act would not apply and its machinery for investigation and settlement would not be available. That being so, and in order that such machinery for investigation and settlement may be available, S. 22 has been enacted to create a legal fiction whereunder such disputes are deemed to be industrial disputes under the Industrial Disputes Act or any other corresponding law. For the purposes of such disputes, the provisions of the Industrial Disputes Act or such other law are made applicable. The effect of S. 22 thus is (i) to make the disputes referred to therein industrial disputes within the meaning of the Industrial Disputes Act or other corresponding law, and (ii) having so done, to apply the provisions of that Act or other corresponding law for investigation and settlement of such disputes. But the application of S. 22 is limited only to the two types of disputes referred to therein and not to others. Section 39, on the other hand, provides that "save as otherwise expressly provided the provisions of the Act shall be in addition to and not in derogation of the Industrial Disputes Act or any corresponding law relating to investigation and settlement of industrial disputes in force in a State." Except for providing for recovery of bonus due under a settlement, award, or agreement as an arrear of land revenue as laid down in S. 21, the Act does not provide any machinery for the investigation and settlement of disputes between an employer and an employee. If a dispute, for instance, were to arise as regards the quantum of available surplus, such a dispute not being one falling under S. 22, Parliament had to make a provision for investigation and settlement thereof. Though such a dispute would not be an industrial dispute as defined by the Industrial Disputes Act or other corresponding Act in force in a State, S. 39 by providing that the provisions of this Act shall be in addition to and not in derogation of the Industrial Disputes Act or such corresponding law makes available the machinery in that Act or the corresponding act available for investigation and settlement of industrial disputes thereunder for deciding the disputes arising under this Act.

As already seen, S. 22 artificially makes two kinds of disputes therein referred to as industrial disputes and having done so applies the provisions of the Industrial Disputes Act and other corresponding act in force for their investigation and settlement. But what about the remaining disputes? As the Act does not provide any machinery for their investigation and settlement, Parliament by enacting S. 39 has sought to apply the provisions of those Acts for investigation and settlement of the remaining disputes, though such disputes are not industrial disputes as defined in those Acts. Though, the words "in force in a State" after the words "or any corresponding law relating to investigation and settlement of industrial disputes" appear to qualify the words "any corresponding law" and not the Industrial Disputes Act, the Industrial Disputes Act is primarily a law relating to investigation and settlement of industrial disputes and provides machinery thereof. Therefore, the distinction made therein between that Act and the other laws does not seem to be of much point. It is thus clear that by providing in S. 39 that the provisions of this Act shall be in addition to and not in derogation of those Acts, Parliament wanted to avail of those Acts for investigation and settlement of disputes which may arise under this Act. The distinction between S. 22 and S. 39, therefore, is that whereas S. 22 by fiction makes the disputes referred to therein industrial disputes and applies the provisions of the Industrial Disputes Act and other corresponding laws for the investigation and settlement thereof, S. 39 makes available for the rest of the disputes the machinery provided in that Act and other corresponding laws for adjudication of disputes arising under this Act. Therefore, there is no question of a right to bonus under the Industrial Disputes Act or other corresponding Acts having been retained or saved by S 39. Neither the Industrial Disputes Act nor any of the other corresponding laws provides for a right to bonus. Item 5 in Schedule 3 to the Industrial Disputes Act deals with jurisdiction of tribunals set up under Ss. 7, 7-A and 7-B of that Act, but does not provide for any right to bonus. Such a right is statutorily provided for the first time by this Act.[31]

Section 40: Repeal and saving

(1) The Payment of Bonus Ordinance, 1965 (3 of 1965), is hereby repealed.

(2) Notwithstanding such repeal, anything done or any action taken under the said ordinance shall be deemed to have been done or taken under this Act as if this Act had commenced on the 29th May, 1965.

THE FIRST SCHEDULE: COMPUTATION OF GROSS PROFITS

[*See* Section 4(a)]

Accounting year ending ...

Item No.	*Particulars*	*Amount of sub-items* ₹	*Amount of main-items* ₹	*Remarks*
*1.	Net Profit as shown in the Profit and Loss Account after making usual and necessary provisions.			
2.	Add back provision for: (a) Bonus to employees (b) Depreciation (c) Development Rebate Reserve (d) Any other reserves Total of Item No. 2..........	₹.........		** **
3.	Add back also: (a) Bonus paid to employees in respect of previous accounting year. (b) The amount debited in respect of gratuity paid or payable to employees in excess of the aggregate of— (i) the amount, if any, paid to, or provided for payment to, an approved gratuity fund; and (ii) the amount actually paid to employees on their retirement or on termination of their employment for any reason. (c) Donations in excess of the amount admissible for income-tax. (d) Capital expenditure (other than capital expenditure on scientific research which is allowed as a deduction under any law for the time being in force relating to direct taxes) and capital losses (other than losses on sale of capital assets on which depreciation has been allowed for income-tax).			** **

31. *Sanghvi Jeevraj Ghewar Chand, M/s.* v. *Madras Chillies, Grains and Kirana Merchants Workers Union*, AIR 1969 SC 530.

Item No.	*Particulars*	*Amount of sub-items* ₹	*Amount of main-items* ₹	*Remarks*
	(e) Any amount certified by the Reserve Bank of India in terms of sub-section (2) of section 34A of the Banking Regulation Act, 1949 (10 of 1949). (f) Losses of, or expenditure relating to, any business situated outside India. Total of Item No. 3 ………	₹ ………		
4.	Add also income, profits or gains (if any) credited directly to published or disclosed reserves, other than— (i) capital receipts and capital profits (including profits on the sale of capital assets on which depreciation has not been allowed for income-tax); (ii) profits of, and receipts relating to, any business situated outside India; (iii) income of foreign banking companies from investments outside India. Net total of Item No. 4……	₹………		
5.	Total of Item Nos. 1, 2, 3 and 4………	₹ ………		
6.	Deduct: (a) Capital receipts and capital profits (other than profits on the sale of assets on which depreciation has been allowed for income-tax). (b) Profits of, and receipts relating to, any business situated outside India. (c) Income of foreign banking companies from investments outside India. (d) Expenditure or losses (if any) debited directly to published or disclosed reserves, other than— (i) capital expenditure and capital losses (other than losses on sale of capital assets on which depreciation has not been allowed for income-tax); (ii) losses of any business situated outside India. (e) In the case of foreign banking companies proportionate administrative (overhead) expenses of Head-office allocable to Indian business. (f) Refund of any excess direct tax paid for previous accounting years and excess provision, if any, of previous accounting years relating to bonus, depreciation, or development rebate, if written back. (g) Cash subsidy, if any, given by the Government or by any body corporate established by any law for the time being in force or by any other agency through budgetary grants, whether given directly or through any agency for specified purposes and the proceeds of which are reserved for such purposes. Total of Item No. 6……….	₹ ………		*** *** **** **** ****

Item No.	Particulars	Amount of sub-items ₹	Amount of main-items ₹	Remarks
7.	Gross profits for purposes of bonus (Item No. 5 minus Item No. 6)		₹ ………	

Explanation: In sub-item (b) of Item 3, "approved gratuity fund" has the same meaning assigned to it in clause (5) of section 2 of the Income-tax Act.

* Where the profit subject to taxation is shown in the profit and loss account and the provision made for taxes on income is shown, the actual provision for taxes on income shall be deducted from the profit.

** If, and to the extent, charged to Profit and Loss Account.

*** If, and to the extent, credited to Profit and Loss Account.

**** In the proportion of Indian Gross Profit (Item No. 7) to Total World Gross Profit (as per consolidated profit and loss account, adjusted as in Item No. 2 above only).

THE SECOND SCHEDULE: COMPUTATION OF GROSS PROFITS

[*See* Section 4(b)]

Accounting year ending ...

Item No.	Particulars	Amount of sub-items ₹	Amount of main-items ₹	Remarks
1.	Net profit as per profit and loss account.			
2.	Add back provision for: (a) Bonus to employees (b) Depreciation (c) Direct taxes, including the provision (if any) for previous accounting years (d) Development rebate/investment allowance/development allowance reserve (e) Any other reserves Total of Item No. 2 ……..	₹………		 * *
3.	Add back also: (a) Bonus paid to employees in respect of previous accounting years. (aa) The amount debited in respect of gratuity paid or payable to employees in excess of the aggregate of— (i) the amount, if any, paid to, or provided for payment to, an approved gratuity fund; and (ii) the amount actually paid to employees on their retirement or on termination of their employment for any reason. (b) Donations in excess of the amount admissible for income-tax. (c) Any annuity due, or commuted value of any annuity paid, under the provisions of section 280D of the Income-tax Act during the accounting year.			*

Item No.	Particulars	Amount of sub-items ₹	Amount of main-items ₹	Remarks
	(d) Capital expenditure (other than capital expenditure on scientific research which is allowed as a deduction under any law for the time being in force relating to direct taxes) and capital losses (other than losses on sale of capital assets on which depreciation has been allowed for income-tax or agricultural income-tax.). (e) Losses of, or expenditure relating to, any business situated outside India. Total of Item No. 3	₹ ………		*
4.	Add also income, profits or gains (if any) credited directly to reserves, other than— (i) capital receipts and capital profits (including profits on the sale of capital assets on which depreciation has not been allowed for income-tax or agricultural income-tax); (ii) profits of, and receipts relating to, any business situated outside India; (iii) income of foreign concerns from investments outside India. Net total of Item No. 4	₹ ………		
5.	Total of Item Nos. 1, 2, 3 and 4	₹ ………		
6.	Deduct: (a) Capital receipts and capital profits (other than profits on the sale of assets on which depreciation has been allowed for income-tax or agricultural income-tax). (b) Profits of, and receipts relating to, any business situated outside India. (c) Income of foreign concerns from investment outside India. (d) Expenditure or losses (if any) debited directly to reserves, other than— (i) capital expenditure and capital losses (other than losses on sale of capital assets on which depreciation has not been allowed for income-tax or agricultural income-tax) (ii) losses of any business situated outside India. (e) In the case of foreign concerns proportionate administrative (overhead) expenses of head office allocable to Indian business. (f) Refund of any direct tax paid for previous accounting years and excess provision, if any, of previous accounting years relating to bonus, depreciation, taxation or development rebate or development allowance, if written back.	₹ ………		** ** ** *** ***

Item No.	Particulars	Amount of sub-items ₹	Amount of main-items ₹	Remarks
	(g) Cash subsidy, if any, given by the Government or by any body corporate established by any law for the time being in force or by any other agency through budgetary grants, whether given directly or through any agency for specified purposes and the proceeds of which are reserved for such purposes. Total of Item No. 6	₹........	₹........	
7.	Gross Profits for purposes of bonus (Item No. 5 minus Item No. 6).			

Explanation: In sub-item (aa) of Item 3, "approved gratuity fund" has the same meaning assigned to it in clause (5) of section 2 of the Income-tax Act.

* If, and to the extent, charged to Profit and Loss Account.

** If, and to the extent, credited to Profit and Loss Account.

*** In the proportion of Indian Gross Profit (Item No. 7) to Total World Gross Profit (as per consolidated profit and loss account, adjusted as in Item No. 2 above only).

THE THIRD SCHEDULE

[*See* Section 6(d)]

Item No.	Category of employer	Further sums to be deducted
1.	Company, other than a banking company	(i) The dividends payable on its preference share capital for the accounting year calculated at the actual rate at which such dividends are payable; (ii) 8.5 per cent of its paid-up equity share capital as at the commencement of the accounting year; (iii) 6 per cent of its reserves shown in its balance sheet as at the commencement of the accounting year, including any profits carried forward from the previous accounting year: Provided that where the employer is a foreign company within the meaning of section 591 of the Companies Act, 1956 (1 of 1956), the total amount to be deducted under this item shall be 8.5 per cent on the aggregate of the value of the net fixed assets and the current assets of the company in India after deducting the amount of its current liabilities (other than any amount shown as payable by the company to its Head Office whether towards any advance made by the Head Office or otherwise or any interest paid by the company to its Head Office) in India.
2.	Banking company	(i) The dividends payable on its preference share capital for the accounting year calculated at the rate at which such dividends are payable; (ii) 7.5 per cent of its paid-up equity share capital as at the commencement of the accounting year; (iii) 5 per cent of its reserves shown in its balance sheet as at the commencement of the accounting year, including any profits carried forward from the previous accounting year;

Item No.	*Category of employer*	*Further sums to be deducted*
		(iv) any sum which, in respect of the accounting year, is transferred by it— (a) to a reserve fund under sub-section (1) of section 17 of the Banking Regulation Act, 1949 (10 of 1949); or (b) to any reserves in India in pursuance of any direction or advice given by the Reserve Bank of India, whichever is higher: Provided that where the banking company is a foreign company within the meaning of section 591 of the Companies Act, 1956 (1 of 1956), the amount to be deducted under this item shall be the aggregate of— (i) the dividends payable to its preference shareholders for the accounting year at the rate at which such dividends are payable on such amount as bears the same proportion to its total preference share capital as its total working funds in India bear to its total world working funds; (ii) 7.5 per cent of such amount as bears the same proportion to its total paid-up equity share capital as its total working funds in India bear to its total working funds; (iii) 5 per cent of such amount as bears the same proportion to its total disclosed reserves as its total working funds in India bear to its total world working funds; (iv) any sum which, in respect of the accounting year, is deposited by it with the Reserve Bank of India under sub-clause (ii) of clause (b) of sub-section (2) of section 11 of the Banking Regulation Act, 1949 (10 of 1949), not exceeding the amount required under the aforesaid provision to be so deposited.
3.	Corporation	(i) 8.5 per cent of its paid-up capital as at the commencement of the accounting year; (ii) 6 per cent of its reserves, if any, shown in its balance sheet as at the commencement of the accounting year, including any profits carried forward from the previous accounting year.
4.	Co-operative society	(i) 8.5 per cent of the capital invested by such society in its establishment as evidenced from its books of accounts at the commencement of the accounting year; (ii) such sums as has been carried forward in respect of the accounting year to a reserve fund under any law relating to co-operative societies for the time being in force.
5.	Any other employer not falling under any of the aforesaid categories.	8.5 per cent of the capital invested by him in his establishment as evidenced from his books of accounts at the commencement of the accounting year: Provided that where such employer is a person to whom Chapter XXII-A of the Income-tax Act applies, the annuity deposit payable by him under the provisions of that Chapter during the accounting year shall also be deducted:

Item No.	Category of employer	Further sums to be deducted
		Provided further that where such employer is a firm, an amount equal to 25 per cent of the gross profits derived by it from the establishment in respect of the accounting year after deducting depreciation in accordance with the provisions of clause (a) of section 6 by way of remuneration to all the partners taking part in the conduct of business of the establishment shall also be deducted, but where the partnership agreement, whether oral or written, provides for the payment of remuneration to any such partner, and— (i) he total remuneration payable to all such partners is less than the said 25 per cent the amount payable, subject to a maximum of forty-eight thousand rupees to each such partner; or (ii) the total remuneration payable to all such partners is higher than the said 25 per cent, such percentage, or a sum calculated at the rate of forty-eight thousand rupees to each such partner, whichever is less, shall be deducted under this proviso: Provided also that where such employer is an individual or a Hindu Undivided Family— (i) an amount equal to 25 per cent of the gross profits derived by such employer from the establishment in respect of the accounting year after deducting depreciation in accordance with the provisions of clause (a) of section 6; or (ii) forty-eight thousand rupees, whichever is less, by way of remuneration to such employer, shall also be deducted.
6.	Any employer falling under Item No. 1 or Item No. 3 or Item No. 4 or Item No. 5 and being a licensee within the meaning of the Electricity (Supply) Act, 1948 (54 of 1948).	In addition to the sums deductible under any of the aforesaid items, such sums as are required to be appropriated by licensee in respect of the accounting year to a reserve under the Sixth Schedule to that Act shall also be deducted.

Explanation: The expression "reserves" occurring in column (3) against Item Nos. 1(iii), 2(iii) and 3(ii) shall not include any amount set apart for the purpose of,—

(i) payment of any direct tax which, according to the balance sheet, would be payable;
(ii) meeting any depreciation admissible in accordance with the provisions of clause (a) of section 6;
(iii) payment of dividends which have been declared,

but shall include,—

(a) any amount, over and above the amount referred to in clause-(i) of this Explanation, set apart as specific reserve for the purpose of payment of any direct tax; and
(b) any amount set apart for meeting any depreciation in excess of the amount admissible in accordance with the provisions of clause (a) of section 6.

THE FOURTH SCHEDULE

[Sections 15 and 16]

In this Schedule, the total amount of bonus equal to 8.33 per cent of the annual salary or wages payable to all the employees is assumed to be ₹1,04,167. Accordingly, the maximum bonus to which all the employees are entitled to be paid (twenty per cent of the annual salary or wages of all the employees) would be ₹2,50,000.

Year	*Amount equal to sixty per cent or sixty-seven per cent, as the case may be, of available surplus allocable as bonus* ₹	*Amount payable as bonus* ₹	*Set on or Set off of the year carried forward* ₹	*Total set on or set off carried forward* ₹	*Of (year)*
1.	1,04,167	1,04,167#	Nil	Nil	
2.	6,35,000	2,50,000*	Set on 2,50,000*	Set on 2,50,000*	(2)
3.	2,20,000	2,50,000* (inclusive of 30,000 from year-2)	Nil	Set on 2,20,000	(2)
4.	3,75,000	2,50,000*	Set on 1,25,000	Set on 2,20,000 1,25,000	(2) (4)
5.	1,40,000	2,50,000* (inclusive of 1,10,000 from year-2)	Nil	Set on 1,10,000 1,25,000	(2) (4)
6.	3,10,000	2,50,000*	Set on 60,000	Set on Nil ## 1,25,000 60,000	(2) (4) (6)
7.	1,00,000	2,50,000* (inclusive of 1,25,000 from year-4 and 25,000 from year-6)	Nil	Set on 35,000	(6)
8.	Nil (due to loss)	1,04,167# (inclusive of 35,000 from year-6)	Set off 69,167	Set off 69,167	(8)
9.	10,000	1,04,167#	Set off 94,167	Set off 69,167 94,167	(8) (9)
10.	2,15,000	1,04,167# (after setting off 69,167 from year-8 and 41,666 from year-9)	Nil	Set off 52,501	(9)

Notes:

* Maximum amount admissible

\# Minimum amount admissible

\## The balance of ₹1,10,000 set on from year-2 lapses.

* * *

5 The Payment of Gratuity Act, 1972

HISTORICAL BACKGROUND OF THE ACT

Gratuity is a lump sum payment as a retiral benefit after superannuation or on termination of service for recognised reasons. Gratuity was treated as payment gratuitously made by the employer at his pleasure, but as a result of a series of decisions by Industrial Tribunals, gratuity came to be regarded as a legitimate claim.

Workmen have in course of time acquired a right to gratuity on determination of employment provided the employer can afford, having regard to his financial condition, to pay it. Before 1972, there was no statutory direction for payment of gratuity as it was in respect of provident fund and retrenchment compensation. The conditions for the grant of gratuity were, as observed in *Bharatkhand Textile Mfg. Co. Ltd.* v. *Textile Labour Association*:[1]

(i) financial capacity of the employer
(ii) his profit making capacity
(iii) the profits earned by him in the past
(iv) the extent of his reserves
(v) the chances of his replenishing them
(vi) the claim for capital invested by him.

But these were not exhaustive and there could be other material considerations in determining the terms and conditions of the gratuity scheme. The existence of other retiring benefits such as provident fund and retrenchment compensation or other benefits does not destroy the claim to gratuity: its quantum may, however, have to be adjusted in the light of the other benefits.

The Supreme Court in 1970, just before passing the Payment of Gratuity Act, specifically observed in *Delhi Cloth and General Mills Co. Ltd.* v. *The Workmen*[2] that gratuity in its etymological sense means a gift especially for services rendered or return for favours received. For some time in the early stages in the adjudication of industrial disputes, gratuity was treated as a gift made by the employer at his pleasure and the workmen had no right to claim it. But since then, there has been a long line of precedents in which it has been ruled that a claim for gratuity is a legitimate one, which the workmen may make and which, in appropriate cases,

1. (1960) II LLJ 21 (SC).
2. AIR 1970 SC 919.

may give rise to an industrial dispute. Gratuity paid to workmen is intended to help them after retirement on superannuation, death, retirement, physical incapacity, disability or otherwise. The object of a gratuity scheme is to provide a retiring benefit to workmen who have rendered long and unblemished service to the employer and thereby contributed to the prosperity of the employer. It is one of the efficiency devices, and is considered necessary for an orderly and human elimination from industry of superannuated or disabled employees who, but for such retiring benefits, would continue in employment even though they function inefficiently. It is not paid to an employee gratuitously or merely as a matter of boon.

NECESSITY OF PAYMENT OF GRATUITY ACT

As the object of the Payment of Gratuity Act shows, it was enacted because there was no central Act to regulate the payment of gratuity to industrial workers except the Working Journalists (Conditions of Service) Miscellaneous Provisions Act, 1955, which had come up for consideration in *Express Newspaper* (*Private*) *Ltd.* v. *Union of India*.[3] The Governments of Kerala and West Bengal had enacted their own statutes for payment of gratuity to workers employed in establishments in their States. Since the enactment of the Kerala and West Bengal Acts, some other State Governments had also voiced their intention to enact similar legislations in their States. It had, therefore, become necessary to have a central law on the subject so as to ensure a uniform pattern on payment of gratuity to the employees throughout the country. The enactment of a central law was also necessary to avoid different treatment to the employees of establishments having branches in more than one State, particularly when under the conditions of their service, the employees were liable to be transferred from one State to another. The proposal for central legislation on gratuity was discussed in the Labour Ministers' Conference and also in the Indian Labour Conference. There was general agreement in these conferences that the legislation on payment of gratuity be enacted as early as possible. While enacting the statute for West Bengal in August 1971, care had been taken to design its provisions in such a way that they could serve, as far as possible, as norms for the central law. The Bill had, therefore, been drafted on the lines of the West Bengal statute on the subject with some modifications, which had been made in the light of the views expressed at the Indian Labour Conference.

WHETHER GRATUITY IS PAYABLE ON RETRENCHMENT

Retrenchment compensation is not a retirement benefit. As the expression 'retrenchment compensation' indicates, it is compensation paid to a workman on his retrenchment and it is intended to give him some relief and to soften the rigour of the hardship which retrenchment inevitably causes. The retrenched workman is suddenly thrown out and has to face the grim problem of unemployment. At the commencement of his employment, a workman naturally expects and looks forward to security of service spread over a long period; but retrenchment destroys his hopes and expectations. The object of retrenchment compensation is to give partial protection to the retrenched employee and his family to enable them to tide over the hard period

3. AIR 1958 SC 578.

of unemployment. Gratuity is payable as a reward for long and meritorious service. Thus, the concept on which grant of retrenchment compensation is based is essentially different from the concept on which gratuity is founded. It was contended before the Supreme Court in *State of Punjab* v. *Labour Court, Jullundur*[4] that the Payment of Gratuity Act,1972 does not apply to a person on retrenchment. It was held that retrenchment is a termination of service and any termination of service except of superannuation would amount to "retirement" for the purpose of the Act. It is immaterial whether the retrenchment is because of the need to discharge labour on account of surplus labour or some other reason. In other words, "retrenchment" of an employee is a "retirement" is defined as "termination of the service of an employee otherwise than on superannuation". Gratuity is therefore payable on retrenchment.

ACT IN A NUTSHELL

Coming to the provisions of the present Act, it will be seen that the Act extends to the whole of India except to plantations and ports in the State of Jammu and Kashmir. The provisions of the Act apply uniformly to "(a) every factory, mine, oilfield, plantation, port and railway company; (b) every shop or establishment within the meaning of any law for the time being in force in relation to shops and establishments in a State, in which ten or more persons are employed, or were employed, on any day of the preceding twelve months; and (c) such other establishments or class of establishments, in which, ten or more employees are employed, or were employed, on any day of the preceding twelve months, as the Central Government may, by notification, specify in this behalf" as provided in sub-section (3) of S. 1 of the Act. It defines "retirement" under S. 2(q) to mean "termination of the service of an employee otherwise than on superannuation". Section 2(s) defines "wages" to mean "all emoluments which are earned by an employee while on duty or on leave in accordance with the terms and conditions of his employment and which are paid or are payable to him in cash and includes dearness allowance but does not include any bonus, commission, house rent allowance, overtime wages and any other allowance". Section 3 enables the appropriate Government to appoint any officer to be a Controlling Authority who shall be responsible for the administration of the Act. (The relevant provisions of S. 4 under which an employee becomes entitled to gratuity.) Section 5 then makes provision for exemption of those establishments, factories etc. and those employees or class of employees employed in any establishment, factory etc., who in the opinion of the appropriate Government are in receipt of gratuity or pensionary benefits which are not less favourable than the benefits conferred under the Act. Section 9 provides for penalties for those who avoid payment of gratuity to their employees, or contravene or make default in compliance with any other provision of the Act. Section 7, which provides for determination of the amount of gratuity enables under sub-section (1) a person who is eligible for payment of gratuity under Act or any person authorised in writing to act on his behalf, to send a written application to the employer within such time and in such form as may be prescribed for payment of such gratuity. Sub-section (2) obliges the employer, whether an application referred to in sub-section (1) has been made or not, to determine the amount of gratuity, as soon as it becomes payable and give

4. AIR 1979 SC 1981.

notice in writing to the person to whom it is payable and also to the Controlling Authority specifying the amount of gratuity so determined. Under sub-section (3), the employer is bound to arrange to pay the amount of gratuity within such time, as may be prescribed to the person to whom it is payable. Sub-section (4) enables the Controlling Authority to determine the amount of gratuity payable to an employee, after the enquiry and after giving the parties to the dispute a reasonable opportunity of being heard in case there is any dispute about the amount of gratuity payable or to the admissibility of any claim of an employee for payment of gratuity. Sub-section (7) of S. 7 provides for an appeal by the party aggrieved by the order passed by the Controlling Authority. Sub-section (8) entitles the Appellate Authority to confirm, modify or reverse the decision of the Controlling Authority after giving the parties to the appeal a reasonable opportunity of being heard. Under S. 8, where an amount of gratuity payable under the Act is not paid by the employer within the prescribed time to the person entitled thereto, the Controlling Authority can get it recovered through the Collector as arrears of land revenue for payment to the person entitled. Section 13 protects the amount of gratuity payable to the employee from attachment in execution of any decree or order of any civil, revenue or criminal court. Section 14 states that the provisions of the Act or any rule made thereunder shall have effect notwithstanding anything inconsistent therewith contained in any other enactment or in any instrument or contract having effect by virtue of any other enactment. Section 14 then lays down that the provisions of the Act and the Rules made thereunder shall have effect, notwithstanding anything inconsistent therewith contained in any enactment, other than the Act or in any instrument or contract having effect by virtue of any enactment other than the Act. Under S. 15, an appropriate Government has been empowered to make rules for the purpose of carrying out the provision of the Act.

SALIENT FEATURES OF THE ACT

The salient features of the Payment of Gratuity Act, 1972 are as follows:

(1) The Act is a self-contained and an exhaustive Act and the provisions of this Act and rules made under it have an overriding effect on all other Acts or instruments or contracts so far as they are inconsistent with this Act.

(2) The Act is fairly sweeping in coverage, as it applies to all factories, mines, oil fields, plantations, ports and railways irrespective of the number of workmen employed by them. It also covers shops and establishments employing 10 or more persons.

(3) The Act gives a statutory right of gratuity to all the employees, who have rendered five years' continuous service and whose services stand terminated after coming into force of the Act on account of superannuation, or retirement, or resignation, or death, or disablement.

(4) The Act provides both executive and quasi-judicial machinery for matters pertaining to nomination, determination and recovery of gratuity.

(5) The executive machinery pertains to maintenance of records regarding opening, change, or closure of establishments, display of notices, and maintenance of records by the controlling authority. The quasi-judicial functions have been divided between the employers and the Controlling Authority inasmuch as for payment of gratuity,

the first forum provided is an application to the employer. When the employer has declined or avoided payment of gratuity, then an application is required to be made to the Controlling Authority.

(6) The machinery provided for recovery rests with the Controlling Authority.

(7) The orders of the controlling Authority for payment or determination of gratuity are applicable before the appropriate Government or the appellate authority.

APPLICABILITY OF SECTION 33-C(2) OF THE INDUSTRIAL DISPUTES ACT, 1947

The question that came before the Supreme Court for consideration in *State of Punjab* v. *Labour Court, Jullundur*[4] was whether the employee can invoke S. 33-C(2) of the Industrial Disputes Act, 1947 for the payment of gratuity. It is urged that the Payment of Gratuity Act is a self-contained code incorporating all the essential provisions relating to payment of gratuity, which can be claimed under that Act, and its provisions impliedly exclude recourse to any other statute for that purpose. A perusal of the relevant provisions of the Act shows that Parliament has enacted a closely knit scheme providing for payment of gratuity. A controlling authority is appointed by the appropriate Government under S. 3, and Parliament has made him responsible for the administration of the entire Act. In what event gratuity will become payable and how it will be quantified are detailed in S. 4. Section 7(1) entitles a person eligible for payment of gratuity to apply in that behalf to the employer. Under S. 7(2), the employer is obliged, as soon as gratuity becomes payable and whether an application has or has not been made for payment of gratuity, to determine the amount of gratuity and inform the person to whom the gratuity is payable specifying the amount of gratuity so determined. He is obliged, by virtue of the same provisions, to inform the controlling authority also, thus ensuring that the controlling authority is seized at all times of information in regard to gratuity as it becomes payable. If a dispute is raised in regard to the amount of gratuity payable, or as to the admissibility of any claim to gratuity, or as to the person entitled to receive the gratuity, S. 7(4)(a) requires the employer to deposit with the controlling authority such amount as he admits to be payable by him as gratuity.

The controlling authority is empowered, under S. 7(4)(b), to enter upon an adjudication of the dispute, and after due inquiry, and after giving the parties to the dispute a reasonable opportunity of being heard, to determine the amount of gratuity payable. In this regard, the controlling authority has all the powers as are vested in a court while trying a suit under the Code of Civil Procedure, 1908 in respect of obtaining evidentiary material and the recording of evidence. The amount deposited by the employer with the controlling authority as the admitted amount of gratuity will be paid over by the controlling authority to the employee or his nominee or heir. Section 7(7) provides an appeal against the order of the controlling authority under S. 7(4) to the appropriate Government or such other authority as may be specified by the appropriate Government in that behalf. The appropriate Government or the appellant authority is empowered under S. 7(8), after giving the parties to the appeal a reasonable opportunity of being heard, to confirm, modify or reverse the decision of the controlling authority. Where the amount of gratuity payable is not paid by the employer within the prescribed time, the controlling authority is required by S. 8, on application made to it by the aggrieved person, to issue a certificate for that amount to the Collector. The Collector, thereupon, is empowered to recover the amount of gratuity, together with compound interest thereon at the rate of nine per cent per annum from the date of expiry of the prescribed time, as arrears of land revenue, and pay the same to the person entitled thereto.

It is apparent that the Payment of Gratuity Act enacts a complete Code containing detailed provisions, covering all the essential features of a scheme for payment of gratuity. It creates the right to payment of gratuity, indicates when the right will accrue, and lays down the principles for quantification of the gratuity. It provides further for recovery of the amount, and contains an especial provision that compound interest will be payable on delayed payment. For the enforcement of its provisions, the Act provides for the appointment of a controlling authority, who is entrusted with the task of administering the Act. The fulfillment of the rights and obligation of the parties is made his responsibility, and he has been invested with an amplitude of power for the full discharge of that responsibility. Any error committed by him can be corrected in appeal by the appropriate Government or an appellate authority, particularly constituted under the Act.

Upon all these considerations, the conclusion is inescapable that Parliament intended that proceedings for payment of gratuity due under the Payment of Gratuity Act must be taken under that Act and not under any other Act. Therefore, the Court held that the employee cannot invoke S. 33-C (2) of the Industrial Disputes Act to recover the gratuity, and the Labour Court has no jurisdiction to entertain such application thereof.

So it is submitted that where a serious dispute exists in regard to the basis of a claim for payment of gratuity, no proceedings will lie under S. 33-C (2) of the Industrial Disputes Act.

CONSTITUTIONALITY OF THE PAYMENT OF GRATUITY ACT, 1972

The Supreme Court had an occasion to look into the submission put forward before it in two appeals—whether S. 4 of the Payment of Gratuity Act, 1972 could be declared as unconstitutional.

These two appeals—*Bakshish Singh* v. *M/s. Darshan Engineering Works* and *Union of India* v. *M/s. Darshan Engineering Works*,[5] one by the Union of India and the other by the aggrieved employee—are directed against the decision dated 24 March, 1983 of the Punjab and Haryana High Court whereby the High Court has struck down S. 4(l)(b) of the Payment of Gratuity Act, 1972 as being violative of Art. 19(l)(g) of the Constitution of India.

The admitted fact of the case is that, Bakshish Singh, the appellant-employee, joined the services of the respondent—M/s. Darshan Engineering Works as a fitter on 2 March, 1968 and resigned from service on 10 December, 1978 after a total period of continuous service of more than 10 years. It is not disputed that at the time he joined the employment on 2 March, 1968, his age was 54 years 3 months, his date of birth being 17 December, 1913. This was known to the respondent-employer.

5. AIR 1994 SC 251.

The Payment of Gratuity Act came into force w.e.f. 21 September, 1972. On the employee's resignation w.e.f. 10 December, 1978 which was accepted by the respondent-employer, he claimed gratuity under S. 4(1)(b) of the Act. His claim not having been accepted, he approached the controlling authority under S. 7 of the Act. The claim was resisted by the employer on the ground first, that the employee was entitled to gratuity only till the date he reached his superannuation age which was 58 years and since he had not completed 5 years of service by the time he attained 58 years of age, he was not entitled to gratuity under S. 4(1) of the Act. *Secondly,* it was contended that in any case the amount of gratuity payable to the employee was only for the period up to the superannuation age and since he was drawing wages of ₹230 per month on the day he attained the superannuation age, he was entitled to a sum of ₹460 only, being the gratuity calculated at the rate of 15 days' salary per year of service till the date of superannuation.

Both the contentions were negatived by the controlling authority by pointing out that S. 4(1) provided for payment of gratuity to the employee on the termination of his employment after he has rendered continuous service of not less than five years on the occurrence of any of the three events, viz. (a) on the employee reaching his superannuation age, or (b) on his retirement or resignation, or (c) on his death or disablement due to accident or disease. In case of the third event, the qualifying continuous service of five years is not necessary. 'Retirement' is defined by S. 2(g) of the Act as 'termination of the service of an employee otherwise than on superannuation.' The first two events are independent of each other. Since in the present case the employer had not chosen to superannuate the employee on his attaining 58 years of age and had continued him in service till the employee himself resigned on 10 December, 1978, by which date he had completed more than 10 years of service, the employee was entitled to gratuity for the period of his entire service up to the date of his resignation. The controlling authority, therefore, calculated the amount of gratuity due to the employee as ₹1782 at the rate of 15 days' wages per year of service for all the 10 years, taking the last drawn wages of ₹335 per month as the basis of the said calculation. This order was challenged by the employer before the appellate authority under the Act. The appellate authority confirmed the finding of the controlling authority and dismissed the appeal. In the writ petition filed before the High Court under Arts. 226 and 227 of the Constitution, the High Court confirmed the interpretation placed on S. 4(1) of the Act by the controlling as well as the appellate authority and also held that the age of superannuation is irrelevant when the gratuity is payable under Cl. (b) of S. 4(1) on retirement or resignation, the said clause being independent of Cl. (a) of that section which provided for payment of gratuity on attaining the age of superannuation. However, the Court held that the provision of S. 4(l)(b) of the Act, which entitles an employee to gratuity on his retirement or resignation after a continuous service of only 5 years, was an unreasonable restriction on the employer to carry on his business and, therefore, violative of Art. 19(l)(g) of the Constitution.

The Court not only went into the question of striking down the provisions of S. 4(l)(b) but, for reasons which are not apparent to us, also denied the gratuity awarded to the employee by the lower authorities even after accepting the finding of the lower authorities that the employee had put in more than 10 years of service. It is not clear from the judgment of the High Court whether, although it found that the five years' qualifying service was unreasonable, ten years' qualifying service would also be similarly unreasonable according to it. In fact, the High Court has not thought it necessary to indicate what, according to it, would be a reasonable qualifying period of service for entitlement to the gratuity in case of retirement or resignation by the employee.

Therefore, the Supreme Court had an occasion to look into the matter which came before it on appeal. The Court held that the Payment of Gratuity Act, 1972, is of the genre of the Minimum Wages Act, the Payment of Bonus Act, the Provident Funds Act, the Employees' State Insurance Act, and other like statutes. These statutes lay down the minimum relevant benefits which must be made available to the employees. We have solemnly resolved to constitute this country, among others, into a socialist republic and to secure to all its citizens, which, of course, include workmen, social and economic justice. Article 38 requires the State to strive to promote the welfare of the people by securing and protecting, as effectively as it may, a social order in which, among other things, social and economic justice shall inform all the institutions of the national life. Article 39 states that the State shall, in particular, direct its policy towards securing, among others, that the citizens have the right to an adequate means to livelihood and that the health and strength of workers are not abused. Article 41 of the Constitution directs the State to make effective provision, among others, for securing public assistance in old age and in other cases of undeserved want. Article 42 enjoins the State to make provision for securing just and humane conditions of work while Art. 43 requires the State to endeavour to secure by (sic) conditions of work ensuring a decent standard of life and full enjoyment of leisure and social and cultural opportunities. Article 47 requires that the State shall regard the raising of the level of nutrition and standard of living of its people and the improvement of public health as one of its primary duties.

Further, there is a restriction placed on the exercise of the fundamental right under Art. 19(1)(g) by Cl. (6) of the said Article. That clause states that "nothing in sub-clause (g) of clause (1) shall affect the operation of any existing law or prevent the State from making any law imposing in the interests of the general public reasonable restrictions on the exercise of the right conferred by that sub-clause." It cannot be disputed that the present Act is a welfare measure introduced in the interest of the general public to secure social and economic justice to workmen, to assist them in their old age, and to ensure them a decent standard of life on their retirement.

The Court concluded that the provisions for payment of gratuity contained in S. 4(l)(b) of the Payment of Gratuity Act, 1972, are one of the minimal service conditions which must be made available to the employees notwithstanding the financial capacity of the employer to bear its burden and that the said provisions are a reasonable restriction on the right of the employer to carry on his business within the meaning of Art. 19(6) of the Constitution, the said provisions are both sustainable and valid. In the result, S. 4(l)(b) of the Payment of Gratuity Act, 1972, is declared to be valid and constitutional.

OBJECT OF THE ACT

Gratuity, as the word itself suggests, is a gratuitous payment given to an employee on discharge or retirement. The Act is not intended to do away with other retiral benefits already existed and were available to the employees. In bringing the Act, the legislature clearly intends to provide extra benefits to the employees.

The Payment of Gratuity Act, 1972 is enacted to introduce a scheme for payment of gratuity for certain industrial and commercial establishments as a measure for social security. It has now been universally recognised that all persons in society need protection against loss of income due to unemployment arising out of incapacity to work due to invalidity, old age, etc. For wage-earning population, security of income, when the worker becomes old or infirm, is of consequential importance. The provisions of social security measures, retiral benefits like gratuity, provident fund and pension (known as the triple-benefits) are of special importance. In bringing the Act on the statute-book, the intention of the legislature was not only to achieve uniformity and reasonable degree of certainty but also to create and bring into force a self-contained, all-embracing, complete, and comprehensive code relating to gratuity. The significance of this legislation lies in the acceptance of the principle of gratuity as a compulsory statutory retiral benefit.[6] The Act accepts, in principle, compulsory payment of gratuity as a social security measure to wage-earning population in industries, factories and establishments. Thus, the main purpose and concept of gratuity is to help the workman after retirement, whether retirement is a result of the rules of superannuation, or physical disablement or impairment of vital part of the body. Thus, it is a sort of financial assistance to tide over post retiral hardships and inconveniences.[7]

An Act to provide for a scheme for the payment of gratuity to employees engaged in factories, mines, oilfields, plantations, ports, railway companies, shops or other establishments and for matters connected therewith or incidental thereto.

SECTION 1: Short title, extent, application and commencement

(1) This Act may be called the Payment of Gratuity Act, 1972.

(2) It extends to the whole of India:

Provided that in so far as it relates to plantations or ports, it shall not extend to the State of Jammu and Kashmir.

(3) It shall apply to—

(a) every factory, mine, oilfield, plantation, port and railway company;

(b) every shop or establishment within the meaning of any law for the time being in force in relation to shops and establishments in a State, in which ten or more persons are employed, or were employed, on any day of the preceding twelve months;

(c) such other establishments or class of establishments, in which ten or more employees are employed, or were employed, on any day of the preceding twelve months, as the Central Government may, by notification, specify in this behalf.

(3A) A shop or establishment to which this Act has become applicable shall continue to be governed by this Act notwithstanding that the number of persons employed therein at any time after it has become so applicable falls below ten.

6. *Jeewanlal Ltd.* v. *Appellate Authority,* AIR 1984 SC 1842.
7. *Ahmedabad Pvt. Primary Teachers Assocn.* v. *Administrative Officer,* AIR 2004 SC 1426.

(4) It shall come into force on such date as the Central Government may, by notification, appoint.

It is very much clear from the above provisions that the Act is wide enough to bring within its scope the entire organised sector of industry and commerce. The Act is made applicable to every shop or establishment within the meaning of any law for the time being in force in relation to shops and establishments in a State, in which ten or more employees are employed, or were employed, on any day of the preceding twelve months. The first question which may be asked is, whether the law referred to in S. 1(3)(b) is a central enactment or even a State law.

When S. 1(3)(b) of the Act refers to *any law for the time being in force,* there will be no justification to introduce any limitation to the above stated phrase to mean that the law should either be a Central law or a State law. A State enactment is as much as law for the time being in force at a given point or time as a Central enactment. Therefore, it is enough for the purpose of S. 1(3)(b) of the Act to construe that there is a law in force in the State in relation to shop and establishment and it is immaterial whether the law is a State law or Central law. If an employee is working in a shop or an establishment within the meaning of any law for the time being in force, whether it is a State law or Central law, the provisions of the Act will be applicable provided that such employee falls within the scope of the definition of employee provided in S. 2(e) of the Payment of Gratuity Act.

In *State of Punjab* v. *Labour Court, Jullundur*[8] the question came before the Supreme Court on appeal by special leave that whether the provisions of S. 1(3) of the Payment of Gratuity Act, 1972 can be made applicable to "Hydel Upper Bari Doab Construction Project" of the Government of Punjab. The learned Additional Solicitor-General contends on behalf of the appellant that the Payment of Gratuity Act, 1972 cannot be invoked by the respondents because the Project does not fall within the scope of S. 1(3) of that Act.

Section 1(3) of the Act provides that the Act will apply to:

"(a) every factory, mine, oilfield, plantation, port and railway company;

(b) every shop or establishment within the meaning of any law for the time being in force in relation to shops and establishments in a State, in which ten or more persons are employed, or were employed, on any day of the preceding twelve months;

(c) such other establishment or class of establishments, in which ten or more employees are employed, or were employed on any day of the preceding twelve months, as the Central Government may, by notification, specify in this behalf."

For the purpose, it is Cl. (b) alone which needs to be considered for deciding whether the Act applies to the Project. The Labour Court has held that the Project is an establishment within the meaning of the Payment of Wages Act, S. 2(ii)(g) of which defines an "industrial establishment" to mean any 'establishment in which any work relating to the construction, development or maintenance of buildings, roads, bridges or canals, or relating to operations connected with navigation, irrigation or the supply of water, or relating to the generation, transmission and distribution of electricity or any other form of power is being carried on.' It is urged for the appellant that the Payment of Wages Act is not an enactment contemplated

8. AIR 1979 SC 1981.

by S. 1(3)(b) of the Payment of Gratuity Act. The Payment of Wages Act, it is pointed out, is a Central enactment and S. 1(3)(b), it is said, refers to a law enacted by the State Legislature.

The Supreme Court observed that S. 1(3)(b) speaks of *any law for the time being in force in relation to shops and establishments in a State*. There can be no dispute that the Payment of Wages Act is in force in the State of Punjab. Then, it is submitted, the Payment of Wages Act is not a law in relation to "shop and establishments". As to that, the Payment of Wages Act is a statute which, while it may not relate to shops, relates to a class of establishments, that is to say, industrial establishments. But, it is contended, the law referred to under S. 1(3)(b) must be a law which relates to both shops and establishment, such as the Punjab Shops and Commercial Establishments Act, 1958. It is difficult to accept that contention because there is no warrant for so limiting the meaning of the expression 'law' in S. 1(3), a law in relation to non-commercial establishments. The Punjab Shops and Commercial Establishment Act does not relate to all kinds of establishments. Besides shops, it relates to commercial establishments alone. Had the intention of Parliament been, when enacting S. 1(3)(b), to refer to a law relating to commercial establishments, it would not have left the expression 'establishments' unqualified. The Court has carefully examined the various provisions of the Payment of Gratuity Act, and held that S. 1(3)(b) of the Payment of Gratuity Act applies to every establishment within the meaning of any law for the time being in force in relation to establishments in a State. Such an establishment would include an industrial establishment within the meaning of S. 2(ii)(g) of the Payment of Wages Act. Accordingly, the Court further held that the Payment of Gratuity Act applies to an establishment in which any work relating to the construction, development or maintenance of buildings, roads, bridges or canals, or relating to operation connected with navigation, irrigation or supply of water, or relating to generation, transmission and distribution of electricity or any other form of power is being carried on. Therefore, it is held that the Hydel Upper Bari Doab Construction Project is an establishment, and the Payment of Gratuity Act applies to it.

In *Jotindra Nath Roy* v. *Surendra Bikram Singh Agarwal*,[9] this appeal came before the Supreme Court by one of the retired employees of the Trust created by one late Babu Lal Agarwal. It has been directed against the order passed in appeal by the Division Bench of the Calcutta High Court setting aside the order passed by a learned Single Judge of that Court in whereby the learned Single Judge had held that the appellant was entitled for pension as well as gratuity from the said Trust. Among other mattes, the scheme prepared by the Trustees provided for grant of pension and other facilities to the employees of the Trust and the relevant provisions in the said scheme were as under:

(a) The Trustees at their discretion may grant to such of the employees of the Estate, who have satisfactorily served with the Estate for a period of not less than 30 years, pension either by monthly payments or by payment of a lump sum.

(b) The pension granted to an employee in case of monthly payments should not ordinarily be more than one third of his last pay and in case of lump sum payment should not be a sum more than four thousand rupees.

9. AIR 1996 SC 1736.

(c) The Trustees may at their discretion also pay gratuity to such members of the family to an employee dying during his service with the Estate as they think fit. The amount of such gratuity shall not ordinarily exceed one year's full pay last drawn by such deceased employee.

It was alleged that in spite of the demand having been made by the appellant, the Trustees failed to release the amount of pension and gratuity payable to him and, therefore, the appellant approached the High Court for a direction to the Trustees to pay pension and gratuity with interest. Learned Single Judge took the view that the retirement benefits are no longer bounty of employers but they constitute a right under the law and, therefore, the appellant was entitled for the pension. As regards the gratuity, the learned Single Judge, relying on the provisions of S. 14 of the Payment of Gratuity Act, 1972, took the view that the scheme being silent with regard to the payment of gratuity does not alter the situation in so far as entitlement of gratuity is concerned. On appeal being preferred by the respondent, one of the Trustees, the Division Bench of the High Court took a contrary view, set aside the order of the learned Single Judge and dismissed the appellant's claim for pension and gratuity. The Division Bench took the view that the Trust cannot be regarded as an establishment as defined in S. 2(5) of the West Bengal Shops and Establishments Act, 1963 and, therefore, the provisions of the Payment of Gratuity Act, 1972 could not be attracted in the case of the appellant as the appellant did not fall in any of the categories mentioned in sub-clauses (a), (b) and (c) of sub-section (3) of S. 1 of the Payment of Gratuity Act, 1972.

The Supreme Court relied on Government notification published by the Government of India, Ministry of Labour and Rehabilitation Department, published in Part 2, S. 3(II) of the *Gazette* of India whereby the Trust Estate in question was treated to be an establishment and the provisions of the Employees Provident Funds and Family Pension Fund Act, 1952 were applied to the said Trust Estate of Babu Lal Agarwal in relation to employees of the said Trust, treating it to be an Establishment under the said Act.

This position strengthens the fact that the Trust has been treated to be an establishment. Consequently, the Court held that the provisions of the Payment of Gratuity Act would be attracted and the appellant would be entitled for gratuity also.

Section 2: Definitions

In this Act, unless the context otherwise requires,

(a) **appropriate Government** means,

(i) in relation to an establishment—

(a) belonging to, or under the control of, the Central Government,

(b) having branches in more than one State,

(c) of a factory belonging to, or under the control of, the Central Government,

(d) of a major port, mine, oilfield or railway company, the Central Government,

(ii) in any other case, the State Government.

(b) **completed year of service** means continuous service for one year.

(c) **continuous service** means continuous service as defined in section 2A.

(d) **controlling authority** means an authority appointed by the appropriate Government under section 3.

(e) **employee** means any person (other than an apprentice) who is employed for wages, whether the terms of such employment are express or implied, in any kind of work, manual or otherwise, in or in connection with the work of a factory, mine, oilfield, plantation, port, railway company, shop or other establishment to which this Act applies, but does not include any such person who holds a post under the Central Government or a State Government and is governed by any other Act or by any rules providing for payment of gratuity.

(f) **employer** means, in relation to any establishment, factory, mine, oilfield, plantation, port, railway company or shop—

(i) belonging to, or under the control of, the Central Government or a State Government, a person or authority appointed by the appropriate Government for the supervision and control of employees, or where no person or authority has been so appointed, the head of the Ministry or the Department concerned,

(ii) belonging to, or under the control of, any local authority, the person appointed by such authority for the supervision and control of employees or where no person has been so appointed, the chief executive office of the local authority,

(iii) in any other case, the person, who, or the authority which, has the ultimate control over the affairs of the establishment, factory, mine, oilfield, plantation, port, railway company or shop, and where the said affairs are entrusted to any other person, whether called a manager, managing director or by any other name, such person.

(g) **factory** has the meaning assigned to it in clause (m) of section 2 of the Factories Act, 1948 (63 of 1948);

(h) **family**, in relation to an employee, shall be deemed to consist of—

(i) in the case of a male employee, himself, his wife, his children, whether married or unmarried, his dependent parents and the dependent parents of his wife and the widow and children of his predeceased son, if any,

(ii) in the case of a female employee, herself, her husband, her children, whether married or unmarried, her dependent parents and the dependent parents of her husband and the widow and children of her predeceased son, if any:

Explanation: Where the personal law of an employee permits the adoption by him of a child, any child lawfully adopted by him shall be deemed to be included in his family, and where a child of an employee has been adopted by another person and such adoption is, under the personal law of the person making such adoption, lawful, such child shall be deemed to be excluded from the family of the employee.

(i) **major port** has the meaning assigned to it in clause (8) of section 3 of the Indian Ports Act, 1908 (15 of 1908).

(j) **mine** has the meaning assigned to it in clause (j) of sub-section (1) of section 2 of the Mines Act, 1952 (35 of 1952).

(k) **notification** means a notification published in the Official Gazette and the expression "notified" shall be construed accordingly.

(l) **oilfield** has the meaning assigned to it in clause (e) of section 3 of the Oilfields (Regulation and Development) Act, 1948 (53 of 1948).

(m) **plantation** has the meaning assigned to it in clause (f) of section 2 of the Plantations Labour Act, 1951 (69 of 1951).

(n) **port** has the meaning assigned to it in clause (4) of section 3 of the Indian Ports Act, 1908 (15 of 1908).

(o) **prescribed** means prescribed by rules made under this Act.

(p) **railway company** has the meaning assigned to it in clause (5) of section 3 of the Indian Railways Act, 1890 (9 of 1890).

(q) **retirement** means termination of the service of an employee otherwise than on superannuation.

(r) **superannuation**, in relation to an employee, means the attainment by the employee of such age as is fixed in the contract or conditions of service at the age on the attainment of which the employee shall vacate the employment.

(s) **wages** means all emoluments which are earned by an employee while on duty or on leave in accordance with the terms and conditions of his employment and which are paid or are payable to him in cash and includes dearness allowance but does not include any bonus, commission, house rent allowance, overtime wages and any other allowance.

Teachers not covered by Payment of Gratuity Act

The Supreme Court in *Ahmedabad Pvt. Primary Teachers Association* v. *Administrative Officer*[7] has ruled that school teachers are not covered by the definition of 'employee' under the provisions of the Payment of Gratuity Act, 1972 and hence are not entitled to payment of gratuity at the end of their service.

A Bench, comprising Justice Shivaraj V. Patil and Justice D.M. Dharmadhikari, gave the ruling upholding a Full Bench verdict of the Gujarat High Court stating that the Act would not apply to teachers. Having compared the various definition clauses of the word 'employee' in different enactments, with due regard to the different aims and objects of the various labour legislations, the Court is of the view that even on plain construction of the words and expression used in the definition of 'employee' in S. 2(e) of the Act, 'teachers', who are mainly employed for imparting education, are not intended to be covered for extending gratuity benefits under the Act. The reasons are as follows.

Teachers do not answer the description of being employees who are 'skilled', 'semi-skilled' or 'unskilled'. These three words used in association with each other intend to convey that a person who is 'unskilled' is one who is not 'skilled', and a person who is 'semi-skilled' may be one who falls between two categories meaning he is neither fully skilled nor unskilled. Section 2(e) of the Act defines 'employee', words 'skilled', 'semi-skilled' or 'unskilled' occur in the definition. In construing the said three words which are used in association with each other, the rule of construction *noscitur a sociis* may be applied. The meaning of each of these words is to be understood by the company it keeps. It is a legitimate rule of construction to construe words in an Act of Parliament with reference to words found in immediate connection with them. The actual order of these three words in juxtaposition indicates that the meaning of one takes colour from the other. The rule is explained differently: 'that meaning of doubtful words may be ascertained by reference to the meaning of words associated with it'. The word 'unskilled' is opposite of the word 'skilled' and the word 'semi-skilled' seems to describe a person who falls between the two categories, i.e. he is not fully skilled and also is not completely unskilled but has some amount of skill for the work for which he is employed. The word 'unskilled' cannot, therefore, be understood dissociated from the word 'skilled' and 'semi-skilled' to read and construe it to include in it all categories of employees irrespective of the nature of employment. If the legislature intended to cover all categories of employees for extending benefit of gratuity under the Act, specific mention of categories of employment in the definition clause was not necessary at all.

Any construction of definition clause which renders it superfluous or otiose has to be avoided. The teachers might have been imparted training for teaching, or there may be cases where teachers who are employed in primary schools are untrained. A trained teacher is not described in industrial field or service jurisprudence as a 'skilled employee'. Such adjective generally is used for employees doing manual or technical work. Similarly, the words 'semi-skilled' and 'unskilled' are not understood in educational establishments as describing the nature of job of untrained teachers. Even if all the words are read disjunctively or in any other manner, trained or untrained teachers do not plainly answer any of the descriptions of the nature of various employments given in the definition clause. Trained or untrained teachers are not 'skilled', 'semi-skilled', 'unskilled', 'manual', 'supervisory', 'technical' or 'clerical' employees. They are also not employed in 'managerial' or 'administrative' capacity. Occasionally, even if they do some administrative work as a part of their duty with teaching since their main job is imparting education, they cannot be held employed in 'managerial' or 'administrative' capacity. The teachers are clearly not intended to be covered by the definition of 'employee'. Further, the teaching staff being not covered by the definition of 'employee' cannot get advantage merely because by notification dated 3 April, 1997, issued in exercise of powers under S. 1(3)(c) of the Act 'educational institutions' as establishments are covered by the provisions of the Act.

The Court, however, clarifies that the said conclusion should not be misunderstood that teachers, although engaged in very noble profession of educating our young generation, should not be given any gratuity benefit. There are already in several States separate statutes, rules and regulations granting gratuity benefits to teachers in educational institutions which are more or less beneficial than the gratuity benefits provided under the Act. It is for the legislature to take cognizance of situation of such teachers in various establishments where gratuity benefits are not available and think of a separate legislation for them in this regard. That is the subject matter solely of the Legislature to consider and decide. The author is of opinion that *Ahmedabad Pvt. Primary Teachers Association's* case lost its importance after new definition of 'employee' inserted in 2009.

In 2019 an interesting and controversial question came before the Supreme Court in *Birla Institute of Technology* v. *State of Jharkhand & Ors.* (Supreme Court) 7th January 2019 where the fact of the case reveals that respondent joined in BIT as an Assistant Professor on 16.09.1971 and superannuated on 30.11.2001 after attaining the age of superannuation. Respondent made a representation to BIT and prayed therein for payment of gratuity amount under the Payment of Gratuity Act, 1972. The appellant, however, declined to pay the amount of gratuity as demanded by the respondent. Respondent, therefore, filed an application before the controlling authority under the Payment of Gratuity Act, 1972. By order dated 07.09.2002, the controlling authority (respondent No. 3) allowed the application filed by respondent No. 4 and directed the BIT to pay a sum of ₹3,38,796 along with interest at the rate of 10% p.a. towards the gratuity to the respondent.

The BIT filed appeal before the appellate authority under the Payment of Gratuity Act and the appellate authority dismissed the appeal. BIT approached the High Court and the High Court (Single Judge) dismissed the writ petition and upheld the orders of the authorities passed under the Act. BIT filed appeal before the Division Bench against the order passed by the Single Judge which was dismissed. BIT approached the Supreme Court by way of special leave.

The two Judge Bench examined this question in detail. Justice D.M. Dharmadhikari speaking for the Bench held that a teacher is not an employee within the meaning of the expression "employee" as defined under Section 2(e) of the Act and hence he/she is not entitled to claim any gratuity amount from his employer under the Act. In other words, it was held that since a teacher is not an employee under Section 2(e) of the Act, he has no right to invoke the provisions of the Act for claiming gratuity under the Act from his/her employer. The Court has relied on *Ahmadabad Pvt. Primary Teachers Association* v. *Administrative Officer and Others (2004) 1 SCC 755.*

On 9th January 2019, the Supreme Court realised that Section 2(e) and Section 13A which were amended in 2009 has not been considered hence the decision of the Court falls squarely as *per incuriam* and the Court declared *suo moto* that the decision pronounced by the Court will not be enforced. However the Supreme Court on 7th march 2019 ruled that teachers are entitled to gratuity and, the court has now held that the effect of the amendment made in the Payment of Gratuity Act on 31.12.2009 was two-fold. First, the law laid down by this Court in the case of Ahmadabad Pvt. Primary Teachers Association was no longer applicable against the teachers, and second, the teachers were held entitled to claim the amount of gratuity under the Payment of Gratuity Act from their employer with effect from 03.04.1997. Recalling its earlier judgement in which the Court rejected teachers' claims to gratuity, the Court said that in the light of the amendment made in the definition of the word 'employee' by Parliament with retrospective effect from 03.04.1997, the benefit of the Payment of Gratuity Act was also extended to the teachers from 03.04.1997.

Section 2A: Continuous service

For the purposes of this Act,—

(1) an employee shall be said to be in continuous service for a period if he has, for that period, been in uninterrupted service, including service which may be interrupted on account of sickness, accident, leave, absence from duty without leave (not being absence in respect of which an order treating the absence as break in service has been passed in accordance with the standing order, rules or regulations governing the employees of the establishment), lay off, strike or a lock-out or cessation of work not due to any fault of the employee, whether such uninterrupted or interrupted service was rendered before or after the commencement of this Act.

(2) where an employee (not being an employee employed in a seasonal establishment) is not in continuous service within the meaning of clause (1), for any period of

one year or six months, he shall be deemed to be in continuous service under the employer—

(a) for the said period of one year, if the employee during the period of twelve calendar months preceding the date with reference to which calculation is to be made, has actually worked under the employer for not less than—(i) one hundred and ninety days, in the case of an employee employed below the ground in a mine or in an establishment which works for less than six days in a week; and (ii) two hundred and forty days, in any other case;

(b) for the said period of six months, if the employee during the period of six calendar months preceding the date with reference to which the calculation is to be made, has actually worked under the employer for not less than—(i) ninety-five days, in the case of an employee employed below the ground in a mine or in an establishment which works for less than six days in a week; and (ii) one hundred and twenty days, in any other case;

Explanation: For the purpose of clause (2), the number of days on which an employee has actually worked under an employer shall include the days on which—

(i) he has been laid-off under an agreement or as permitted by standing orders made under the Industrial Employment (Standing Orders) Act, 1946 (20 of 1946), or under the Industrial Disputes Act, 1947 (14 of 1947), or under any other law applicable to the establishment;

(ii) he has been on leave with full wages, earned in the previous year;

(iii) he has been absent due to temporary disablement caused by accident arising out of and in the course of his employment; and

(iv) in the case of a female, she has been on maternity leave; so, however, that the total period of such maternity leave does not exceed such period as may be notified by the Central Government from time to time.

(3) where an employee employed in a seasonal establishment, is not in continuous service within the meaning of clause (1), for any period of one year or six months, he shall be deemed to be in continuous service under the employer for such period if he has actually worked for not less than seventy-five per cent of the number of days on which the establishment was in operation during such period.

In *Aspinwall and Co., Kulshekar, Mangalore* v. *Lalitha Padugady*,[10] the Supreme Court interprets the phrase 'continuous year of service' and provides a guideline for computation of gratuity. The Supreme Court observed that S. 4 postulates determination of the computed year of service, meaning thereby one year's period of continuous service, rendered by an employee for the purposes of computation of gratuity and therein a method is provided for determining a completed year of service. The starting point of the said period is from the date an employee gets employment. Completed year of service would plainly mean continuous service for one

10. AIR 1996 SC 580

year reckonable from the date of joining employment. It cannot be confused with that of a calendar year.

SECTION 3: Controlling authority

The appropriate Government may, by notification, appoint any officer to be a controlling authority, who shall be responsible for the administration of this Act and different controlling authorities may be appointed for different areas.

SECTION 4: Payment of gratuity

(1) Gratuity shall be payable to an employee on the termination of his employment after he has rendered continuous service for not less than five years,

(a) on his superannuation, or

(b) on his retirement or resignation, or

(c) on his death or disablement due to accident or disease:

Provided that the completion of continuous service of five years shall not be necessary where the termination of the employment of any employee is due to death or disablement:

Provided further that in the case of death of the employee, gratuity payable to him shall be paid to his nominee or, if no nomination has been made, to his heirs, and where any such nominees or heirs is a minor, the share of such minor, shall be deposited with the controlling authority who shall invest the same for the benefit of such minor in such bank or other financial institution, as may be prescribed, until such minor attains majority.

Explanation: For the purposes of this section, disablement means such disablement as incapacitates an employee for the work which he was capable of performing before the accident or disease resulting in such disablement.

(2) For every completed year of service or part thereof in excess of six months, the employer shall pay gratuity to an employee at the rate of fifteen days' wages based on the rate of wages last drawn by the employee concerned:

Provided that in the case of a piece-rated employee, daily wages shall be computed on the average of the total wages received by him for a period of three months immediately preceding the termination of his employment, and, for this purpose, the wages paid for any overtime work shall not be taken into account:

Provided further that in the case of an employee who is employed in a seasonal establishment and who is not so employed throughout the year, the employer shall pay the gratuity at the rate of seven days' wages for each season.

Explanation: In the case of a monthly rated employee, the fifteen days' wages shall be calculated by dividing the monthly rate of wages last drawn by him by twenty-six and multiplying the quotient by fifteen.

(3) The amount of gratuity payable to an employee shall not exceed such amount as may be notified by the Central Government from time to time.

(4) For the purpose of computing the gratuity payable to an employee who is employed, after his disablement, on reduced wages, his wages for the period preceding his disablement shall be taken to be the wages received by him during that period, and his wages for the period subsequent to his disablement shall be taken to be the wages as so reduced.

(5) Nothing in this section shall affect the right of an employee to receive better terms of gratuity under any award or agreement or contract with the employer.

(6) Notwithstanding anything contained in sub-section (1),

(a) the gratuity of an employee, whose services have been terminated for any act, wilful omission or negligence causing any damage or loss to, or destruction of, property belonging to the employer, shall be forfeited to the extent of the damage or loss so caused.

(b) the gratuity payable to an employee may be wholly or partially forfeited—

(i) if the services of such employee have been terminated for his riotous or disorderly conduct or any other act of violence on his part, or

(ii) if the services of such employee have been terminated for any act which constitutes an offence involving moral turpitude, provided that such offence is committed by him in the course of his employment.

After reading the first line of S. 4, one can say that this is a charging provision as it starts with that *gratuity shall be payable to an employee*. Section 4 may be divided into three parts. The *first part* relates to condition for gratuity, *the second part* relates to quantum of gratuity, and *the third part* relates to forfeiture of gratuity.

Condition for Gratuity

Section 4 provides that gratuity shall be payable to an employee on the termination of his employment after he has rendered continuous service for not less than five years. Gratuity is generally payable on superannuation or on retirement or the death or disablement of employee due to accident or disease. The condition of completion of service of five years shall not be necessary where the termination of employment is due to death or the disablement of the employee. In the case of death of the employee, gratuity payable to the employee shall be paid to his nominee, or if no nomination has been made, to his heirs. Disablement has been explained in the explanation to sub-section (1) of S. 4 of the Act as such disablement which incapacitates an employee for the work which he was capable of performing before the accident or disease resulting in such disablement.

Sub-section (1) of S. 4 of the Act incorporates the concept of gratuity being a reward for long, continuous and meritorious service. The emphasis therein is not on 'continuity of employment', but on rendering of 'continuous service'. The legislature inserted the two Explanation in the definition to extend the benefit to employees who are not in uninterrupted service for one year subject to the fulfilment of the conditions laid down therein. By the use of a legal fiction in these Explanations, an employee is deemed to be in 'continuous service' for purposes of sub-section (1) of S. 4 of the Act. The legislature never intended that the expression 'actually employed' in Explanation I and the expression 'actually worked' in Explanation II should have two different meanings because it wanted to extend the benefit to an employee who 'works' for a particular number of days in a year in either case.

Permanent employees are not entitled to payment of gratuity under sub-section (1) of S. 4 for the years in which they remained absent without leave for a number of days in a year and had actually worked for less than 240 days, due to absence without leave. Similarly, the badli employees are not covered by the substantive part of the definition of 'continuous service' in S. 2(c), but come within Explanation I and, therefore, are not entitled to payment of gratuity for the badli period, i.e. in respect of the years in which there was no work allotted to them due to their failure to report to duty.[11]

Can 4 years 9 months be considered for eligibility of Gratuity?

The Madras High Court in *Mettur Beardshell Ltd. Madras* v. *RLC (Central) & Ors.* (1998 LLR 1072), said that an employee rendering continuous service for a period of 240 days in a year will be deemed to have continued in service for one year as stipulated by section 2A of the Act. Thus, an employee who has put in service for 10 months and 18 days for the fifth year after first 4 years should be deemed to have completed continuous service of five years.

The similar decision was delivered by the Kerela High Court in the year 2015 in *Sreeja B* v. *The Regional Labour Commissioner* [2015 (2) KHC 427]. The Central Administrative Tribunal in *K.K. Thomas* v. *Delhi Metro Rail Corporation* and *Tony K John* v. *Chairman & MD, BSNL New Delhi* (10th February, 2023), in the year 2018 and 2023 respectively, also endorsed the similar view.

Quantum of Gratuity

Section 4(2) of the Act provides quantum of gratuity to be paid to the employee. It enumerates three situations as follows:

A. **General Principle for Monthly Rated Employee:** For every completed year of service or part thereof in excess of six months, the employer shall pay gratuity to an employee at the rate of fifteen days wages based on the rate of wages last drawn by the employee concerned. A formula for calculation of gratuity, for monthly rated employee, has been provided in the explanation to S. 4(2) of the Act, that is,

$$\frac{\text{Last drawn wages}}{26} \times 15 \times \text{number of years of service completed}$$

11. *Lalappa Lingappa* v. *Laxmi Vishnu Textile Mills Ltd.*, AIR 1981 SC 852.

The question of twenty-six days, as mentioned before, came to the Act in the year 1987 by the Payment of Gratuity (Amendment) Act, 1987 w.e.f. 1-10-1987, it is now placed in the Act as an explanation to S. 4(2), which is nothing but an outcome of the Supreme Court decision in *Shri Digvijay Woollen Mills Ltd.* v. *Mahendra Prataprai Buch.*[12] The Supreme Court in this case observed that ordinarily, a month is understood to mean 30 days, but the manner of calculating gratuity payable under the Act to the employees who work for 26 days a month should be taken as what they got for 26 working days and their fifteen days' wages worked out accordingly and not by just taking half of their wages for a month of 30 days or fixing their wages by dividing their monthly wages by 30. In other words, for the purpose of computing the amount of gratuity in respect of monthly rated employees, his monthly wages should be taken as what he got for 26 working days, his daily wages should be ascertained on that basis and his fifteen days' wages worked out accordingly and not by just taking half of his wages for a month of 30 days or fixing his daily wages by dividing his monthly wages by 30. Treating monthly wages as wages for 26 working days is not any thing unique or unknown.

The Court has further observed that the decision of some High Courts taking one view or other on the question and also decision based on some provisions of the Minimum Wages Act and other statutes are not relevant on the question of computation of fifteen days' wages under S. 4(2) of the Payment of Gratuity Act, 1972.

B. In the case of a piece-rated employee: Daily wages shall be computed on the average of the total wages received by the employee for a period of three months immediately preceding the termination of his employment, and, for this purpose, the wages paid for any overtime work shall not be taken into account:

$$\frac{\text{Average wages}}{26} \times 15 \times \text{number of years of service completed}$$

For the purpose of calculation of wages in the case of piece rated employee, incentive wages/bonus paid cannot be treated as 'piece rate wages'.[13]

C. Seasonal Establishment: In the case of an employee who is employed in a seasonal establishment and who is not so employed throughout the year, the employer shall pay the gratuity at the rate of seven days wages for each season.

D. Maximum: Section 4(3) of the Act provides that the amount of gratuity payable to an employee shall not exceed twenty lakh rupees as per the notification of the Central Government and it will not be taxable. The amount of twenty lakh rupees may be subject to change from time to time. There are many instances where the employees receive the gratuity as per actual, and, sometime, the amount may be more than twenty lakhs. In those cases, the excess amount (more than twenty lakhs) will be taxable.

E. Gratuity on Reduced Wages due to Disablement: Section 4(4) provides the method of calculating the gratuity for an employee receiving reduced wages after his disablement. It provides that an employee who is employed, after his disablement,

12. AIR 1980 SC 1944.
13. *T.I. Cycles of India, Ambattur* v. *M.K. Gurumani,* AIR 2001 SC 3465.

on reduced wages, his wages for the period preceding his disablement shall be taken to be the wages received by him during that period, and his wages for the period subsequent to his disablement shall be taken to be the wages as so reduced. Therefore, it is advisable to calculate the gratuity by applying the following formula.

$$\frac{\text{Last drawn wages [before disablement]}}{26} \times 15 \times \text{number of years of service completed}$$

$$+ \frac{\text{Last drawn wages [reduced rate after disablement, i.e. just before termination of employment]}}{26} \times 15 \times \text{number of years of service completed}$$

Forfeiture of Gratuity

Section 4(6) of the Act deals with the grounds for partial and total forfeiture of gratuity that may become payable to an employee. The gratuity payable to an employee whose services have been terminated for any act, wilful omission or negligence causing any damage or loss to, or destruction of, property belonging to the employer, shall be forfeited to the extent of the damage or loss so caused. The gratuity payable to an employee may be wholly or partially forfeited if the services of such employee have been terminated for his riotous or disorderly conduct or any other act of violence on his part, or if the services of such employee have been terminated for any act which constitutes an offence involving moral turpitude, provided that such offence is committed by him in the course of his employment.

Therefore, it is submitted that if an employee commits such misconduct as causing financial loss to his employer, the employer would, under the general law, have a right to take action against the employee for the loss caused and to deduct the amount to the extent of the damage or loss caused to him from the gratuity of such employee. The Supreme Court in *Remington Rand of India Ltd.* v. *Workmen,*[14] has rightly observed that though the employer could not deprive the workman of the gratuity in all cases of misconduct, he could do so where it consisted of acts involving violence against the management or other employees or riotous or disorderly behaviour in or near the place of employment. The gratuity scheme could also give a right to the employer to deduct from gratuity such amount of loss as is occasioned by the workman's misconduct.

In *Management of Tournamulla Estate* v. *Workmen,*[15] the workman concerned was charge-sheeted in respect of riotous and disorderly behaviour for having assaulted a tea maker inside the factory. A departmental enquiry was held wherein, it is said, he was given every opportunity to fully participate. He was found guilty of misconduct by the domestic Tribunal and was accordingly dismissed. There was a scheme of gratuity in force, which was and is not challenged by the respondent. Clause 4 of that scheme, which is called "Terms of Agreement", provides that if a dispute arises regarding a claim for payment of gratuity of a workman who has been dismissed for misconduct, such a dispute shall be referred to the labour court having jurisdiction, for decision. As a dispute arose with regard to the payment

14. AIR 1970 SC 1421.
15. AIR 1973 SC 2344.

of gratuity, the matter was referred to the Labour Court. The Labour court, however, referred to the judgment of the Supreme Court in *State of Punjab* v. *Suraj Parkash Kapur*,[16] in which the general argument was not accepted that in all cases where services of an employee are terminated for misconduct, gratuity should not be paid to him. However, the Apex Court has had occasion to consider in detail the various circumstances in which gratuity would be liable to forfeiture for misconduct of a particular nature. It was laid down in *Delhi Cloth and General Mills Co., Ltd.* v. *Workmen*,[17] that the object of having a gratuity scheme is to provide a retiring benefit to workmen who have rendered long and unblemished service to the employer and thereby contributed to the prosperity of the employer, and it is, therefore, not correct to say that no misconduct, however grave, may not be visited with forfeiture of gratuity. Misconduct could be of three kinds, namely:

(1) technical misconduct which leaves no trail of indiscipline,
(2) misconduct resulting in damage to the employer's property which might be compensated by forfeiture of gratuity or part thereof, and
(3) serious misconduct such as acts of violence against the management or other employees or riotous or disorderly behaviour in or near the place of employment, which, though not directly causing damage, is conducive to grave indiscipline.

Of the above mentioned misconducts, the *first* should involve no forfeiture, the *second* may involve forfeiture of the amount equal to the loss directly suffered by the employer in consequence of the misconduct, and the *third* will entail forfeiture of gratuity due to the workman. In other words, according to this decision, if a workman is guilty of a serious misconduct of the third category, then his gratuity can be forfeited in its entirety. For the reasons given above, the appeal is allowed and the award of the Labour court is set aside. It is hereby declared that the workman concerned will not be entitled to the gratuity earned by him.

Section 4(5): Award or Agreement

The scheme envisaged by the Gratuity Act secures the minimum for the employees in that behalf and express provisions are found in the Act under which better terms of gratuity, if already existing, are not merely preserved but better terms could be conferred on the employee in future. The expression '*award*' occurring in sub-section (5) of S. 4 does not mean, and cannot be confined to, 'existing award' but includes any award that would be made by an adjudicator wherein better terms of gratuity could be granted to the employees if the facts and circumstances warrant such grant. There is nothing in S. 4(5) which limits the expression 'award'. *Secondly,* it cannot be and was not that under sub-section (5), a gratuity scheme obtaining under an existing agreement or contract could not be improved upon by a fresh agreement or fresh contract between the employer and the employee and if that be so there is no reason as to why the expression 'award'

16. AIR 1963 SC 507.
17. *Ibid.*, f.n. 2.

should be construed as referring to an 'existing award' and not to include a fresh award that may be made by an adjudicator or an Industrial Court improving in favour of the employees the scheme obtaining under the Act or the existing award. *Thirdly*, the very fact that under sub-section (5) better terms of gratuity could be obtained by an employee by an agreement or contract with the employer, notwithstanding the scheme of gratuity obtaining under the Act, clearly suggests that no standardisation of the gratuity scheme contemplated by the Act was intended by the Legislature. This also becomes amply clear from the provisions of S. 5.[18]

In *D.T.C. Retired Employees' Association* v. *Delhi Transport Corporation,*[19] where the appellants receiving gratuity subsequently opted for pension which had never been a part of their service conditions. It is a condition precedent that in order to get the benefit of the Pension Scheme, they have to refund the gratuity received by them. It is neither illegal nor unjust on grounds that as the provisions contained in the Payments of Gratuity Act itself contemplate better terms of gratuity or other payment than what is permissible under the Act, the present pension scheme could only be construed as an award or agreement for better terms as per S. 4(5) of the Gratuity Act. The reason being sub-clause (5) of S. 4 is an exception to the main section under which gratuity is payable to the employee. In all welfare legislations, the amount payable to the employees or labourers is fixed at the minimum rate and there will not be any prohibition for the employer to give better perquisites or amounts than what is fixed under law. The employer, who is more concerned with industrial peace and better employer–employee relations, can always give benefit to the employees irrespective of any statutory minimum prescribed under law in respect of such reliefs and therefore provisions of S. 4(5) is of no assistance. The liability to refund gratuity cannot also be challenged as illegal on the ground that gratuity is an amount earned by the employee after long service. The reason being the appellants were paid gratuity for their long service, but at the time of receipt of this amount, they were not entitled to get pension. Now the appellants have opted for pension, that is, a similar relief given to them for the longer service rendered by them, they cannot have the benefit of both pension and gratuity.

Whether the Employee Would be Compelled to Deposit the Gratuity

The question came before the Supreme Court in *Balbir Kaur* v. *Steel Authority of India Ltd.*[20] whether any scheme can be introduced by which the employee or his dependent, as the case may be, would be compelled to deposit the gratuity due to him?

The Supreme Court, while interpreting S. 4 of the Act, contended that the question of compulsory depositing of the gratuity amount does not and cannot arise. As regards the gratuity amount, there is a mandate of the statute that gratuity is to be paid to the employee on his retirement or to his dependants in the event of his early death. The introduction of

18. *Workmen of Metro Theatre Ltd., Bombay* v. *M/s. Metro Theatre Ltd., Bombay,* AIR 1981 SC 1685.
19. AIR 2001 SC 1997.
20. AIR 2000 SC 1596.

Family Pension Scheme by which the employee is compelled to deposit the gratuity amount, as a matter of fact, runs counter to this beneficial piece of legislation (Act of 1972). The Payment of Gratuity Act, 1972 (as amended from time to time) is no longer in the realm of charity but a statutory right provided in favour of the employee. The statutory mandate is unequivocal and unambiguous in nature and runs to the effect that the gratuity is payable to the heirs or the nominees of the employees concerned, but by the introduction of the Family Pension Scheme, this mandate stands violated and as such the same cannot but be termed to be illegal in nature. The Court further observed that a mandatory statutory obligation cannot be trifled with by adaptation of a method which runs counter to the statute and statutory obligation cannot be left high and dry on the whims of the employer, irrespective of the factum of the employer being an authority within the meaning of Art. 12 of the Constitution or not.

Forfeiture of Gratuity not Automatic on Dismissal from Service

The question came before the Supreme Court for consideration in *Union Bank of India* v. *CG Ajay Babu* (Supreme Court 2018) whether the gratuity can be forfeited automatically on dismissal from service of an employee.

The fact of the case reveals that Ajay Babu was employed by the Union Bank of India as a Branch manager. During the course of his service, disciplinary proceedings were initiated against him on the ground that he failed to take all steps to ensure and protect the interests of the Bank, failed to discharge his duties with utmost devotion, and conducted himself in a manner "unbecoming of an officer." However, Ajay Babu was dismissed from service in June 2004. A few months before his dismissal order, Ajay Babu was served a show-cause notice and was asked to furnish his response on why the gratuity due to him should not be forfeited on account of his "*acts involving moral turpitude*."

Ajay Babu submitted his response to this show-cause notice in February 2004. However, his response was rejected and the bank forfeited the gratuity due to Ajay Babu citing provisions of the Act and the Bank's Gratuity Rules. This forfeiture of gratuity was challenged before the High Court wherein the Single Judge, without interfering in the dismissal from service, held that since the misconduct did not lead to financial loss to the Bank, the Respondent-Ajay Babu, was entitled to gratuity.

It was also held that as per the bipartite settlement prevailing in the bank, forfeiture of gratuity is permissible only in case the misconduct leading to the dismissal has caused financial loss to the Bank and only to the extent of the loss. The Court referred the bipartite settlement of the bank which reads as follows:

> "12.2 There will be no forfeiture of gratuity for dismissal on account of misconduct except in cases where such misconduct causes financial loss to the bank and in that case to that extent only."

The Supreme Court further proceeded to analyse Section 4(5) and Section 4(6) of the Payment of Gratuity Act. Section 4(5) says that "*nothing will affect the right of a person to receive better terms of the gratuity*." Whereas Section 4(6) lays down that gratuity of an employee who has been terminated on the grounds that he has wilfully caused damage to the employer, can to the extent of that loss or damage be forfeited. Further, it also provides that gratuity payable to an employee may be wholly or partially forfeited—

(i) if the services of such employee have been terminated for his riotous or disorderly conduct or any other act of violence on his part, or

(ii) if the services of such employee have been terminated for any act which constitutes an offence involving moral turpitude, provided that such offence is committed by him in the course of his employment.

The Court observed that sub-section (5) of Section 4 of the Act has an overriding effect on all other sub-sections of Section 4 whereas sub-Section (6) is a non-obstante clause only in respect of sub-section (1). In other words, sub-Section (5) has an overriding effect on all other sub-Sections under Section 4 of the Act. Thus, notwithstanding anything contained under Section 4 of the Act, an employee is entitled to receive better terms of gratuity under any award or agreement or contract with the employer.

The Supreme Court noted that the fact that the bipartite settlement clause exists is not disputed and neither is it contended that the respondent employee caused any financial loss to the Bank. Therefore, Section 4(6) of the Act which allows forfeiture of gratuity to the extent of loss caused, cannot be resorted to.

The Court further observed that it is not the conduct of a person involving moral turpitude that is required for forfeiture of gratuity but the conduct or the act should constitute an offence involving moral turpitude. The Court held that:

> "To be an offence, the act should be made punishable under law. That is absolutely in the realm of criminal law. It is not for the Bank to decide whether an offence has been committed. It is for the court."

The Court noted that apart from the disciplinary proceedings initiated by the appellant Bank, the Bank has not set the criminal law in motion either by registering an FIR or by filing a criminal complaint so as to establish that the misconduct leading to dismissal is an offence involving moral turpitude. Under sub-section (6)(b)(ii) of the Act, forfeiture of gratuity is permissible only if the termination of an employee is for any misconduct which constitutes an offence involving moral turpitude, and convicted accordingly by a court of competent jurisdiction.

Hence, the Court turned down the contention of the Bank and held as follows:

> "Hence, there is no justification for the forfeiture of gratuity on the ground stated in the order dated 20.04.2004 that the "misconduct proved against you amounts to acts involving moral turpitude". At the risk of redundancy, we may state that the requirement of the statute is not the proof of misconduct of acts involving moral turpitude but the acts should constitute an offence involving moral turpitude and such offence should be duly established in the court of law"

SECTION 4A: Compulsory insurance[21]

(1) With effect from such date as may be notified by the appropriate Government in this behalf, every employer, other than an employer or an establishment belonging to, or under the control of, the Central Government or a State Government, shall, subject to the provisions of sub-section (2), obtain an insurance in the manner prescribed, for his liability for payment towards the gratuity under this Act, from the Life Insurance Corporation of India established under the Life Insurance Corporation of India Act, 1956 (31 of 1956) or any other prescribed insurer:

Provided that different dates may be appointed for different establishments or class of establishments or for different areas.

(2) The appropriate Government may, subject to such conditions as may be prescribed, exempt every employer who had already established an approved gratuity fund in respect of his employees and who desires to continue such arrangement, and every employer employing five hundred or more persons who establishes an approved gratuity fund in the manner prescribed from the provisions of sub-section (1).

(3) For the purpose of effectively implementing the provisions of this section, every employer shall within such time as may be prescribed get his establishment registered with the controlling authority in the prescribed manner and no employer shall be registered under the provisions of this section unless he has taken an insurance referred to in sub-section (1) or has established an approved gratuity fund referred to in sub-section (2).

(4) The appropriate Government may, by notification, make rules to give effect to the provisions of this section and such rules may provide for the composition of the Board of Trustees of the approved gratuity fund and for the recovery by the controlling authority of the amount of the gratuity payable to an employee from the Life Insurance Corporation of India or any other insurer with whom an insurance has been taken under sub-section (1), or as the case may be, the Board of Trustees of the approved gratuity fund.

(5) Where an employer fails to make any payment by way of premium to the insurance referred to in sub-section (1) or by way of contribution to an approved gratuity fund referred to in sub-section (2), he shall be liable to pay the amount of gratuity due under this Act (including interest, if any, for delayed payments) forthwith to the controlling authority.

(6) Whoever contravenes the provisions of sub-section (5) shall be punishable with fine which may extend to ten thousand rupees and in the case of a continuing offence with a further fine which may extend to one thousand rupees for each day during which the offence continues.

21. Inserted by the Payment of Gratuity (Amendment) Act, 1987, with effect from the date yet to be notified.

Explanation: In this section "approved gratuity fund" shall have the same meaning as in clause (5) of section 2 of the Income-tax Act, 1961 (43 of 1961).

This provision has been inserted by the Payment of Gratuity (Amendment) Act, 1987, and it will come into effect from the date of notification, but it is yet to be notified.

SECTION 5: Power to exempt

(1) The appropriate Government may, by notification, and subject to such conditions as may be specified in the notification, exempt any establishment, factory, mine, oilfield, plantation, port, railway company or shop to which this Act applies from the operation of the provisions of this Act if, in the opinion of the appropriate Government, the employees in such establishment, factory, mine, oilfield, plantation, port, railway company or shop are in receipt of gratuity or pensionary benefits not less favourable than the benefits conferred under this Act.

(2) The appropriate Government may, by notification and subject to such conditions as may be specified in the notification, exempt any employee or class of employees employed in any establishment, factory, mine, oilfield, plantation, port, railway company or shop to which this Act applies from the operation of the provisions of this Act, if, in the opinion of the appropriate Government, such employee or class of employees are in receipt of gratuity or pensionary benefits not less favourable than the benefits conferred under this Act.

(3) A notification issued under sub-section (1) or sub-section (2) may be issued retrospectively a date not earlier than the date of commencement of this Act, but no such notification shall be issued so as to prejudicially affect the interests of any person.

SECTION 6: Nomination

(1) Each employee, who has completed one year of service, shall make, within such time, in such form and in such manner, as may be prescribed, nomination for the purpose of the second proviso to sub-section (1) of section 4.

(2) An employee may in his nomination, distribute the amount of gratuity payable to him, under this Act amongst more than one nominee.

(3) If an employee has a family at the time of making a nomination, the nomination shall be made in favour of one or more members of his family, and any nomination made by such employee in favour of a person who is not a member of his family, shall be void.

(4) If at the time of making a nomination the employee has no family, the nomination may be made in favour of any person or persons but if the employee subsequently acquires a family, such nomination shall forthwith become invalid and the employee shall make, within such time as may be prescribed, a fresh nomination in favour of one or more members of his family.

(5) A nomination may, subject to the provisions of sub-sections (3) and (4), be modified by an employee at any time, after giving to his employer a written notice in such form and in such manner as may be prescribed, of his intention to do so.

(6) If a nominee predeceases the employee, the interest of the nominee shall revert to the employee who shall make a fresh nomination, in the prescribed form, in respect of such interest.

(7) Every nomination, fresh nomination or alteration of nomination, as the case may be, shall be sent by the employee to his employer, who shall keep the same in his safe custody.

SECTION 7: Determination of the amount of gratuity

(1) A person who is eligible for payment of gratuity under this Act or any person authorised, in writing, to act on his behalf shall send a written application to the employer, within such time and in such form, as may be prescribed, for payment of such gratuity.

(2) As soon as gratuity becomes payable, the employer shall, whether an application referred to in sub-section (1) has been made or not, determine the amount of gratuity and give notice in writing to the person to whom the gratuity is payable and also to the controlling authority specifying the amount of gratuity so determined.

(3) The employer shall arrange to pay the amount of gratuity within thirty days from the date it becomes payable to the person to whom the gratuity is payable.

(3A) If the amount of gratuity payable under sub-section (3) is not paid by the employer within the period specified in sub-section (3), the employer shall pay, from the date on which the gratuity becomes payable to the date on which it is paid, simple interest at such rate, not exceeding the rate notified by the Central Government from time to time for repayment of long-term deposits, as that Government may, by notification specify:

Provided that no such interest shall be payable if the delay in the payment is due to the fault of the employee and the employer has obtained permission in writing from the controlling authority for the delayed payment on this ground.

(4) (a) If there is any dispute as to the amount of gratuity payable to an employee under this Act or as to the admissibility of any claim of, or in relation to, an employee for payment of gratuity, or as to the person entitled to receive the gratuity, the employer shall deposit with the controlling authority such amount as he admits to be payable by him as gratuity.

(b) Where there is a dispute with regard to any matter or matters specified in clause (a), the employer or employee or any other person raising the dispute may make an application to the controlling authority for deciding the dispute.

(c) The controlling authority shall, after due inquiry and after giving the parties to the dispute a reasonable opportunity of being heard, determine the matter or matters in dispute and if, as a result of such inquiry any amount is found to be payable to the employee, the controlling authority shall direct the employer to pay such amount or, as the case may be, such amount as reduced by the amount already deposited by the employer.

(d) The controlling authority shall pay the amount deposited, including the excess amount, if any, deposited by the employer, to the person entitled thereto.

(e) As soon as may be after a deposit is made under clause (a), the controlling authority shall pay the amount of the deposit—

(i) to the applicant where he is the employee; or

(ii) where the applicant is not the employee, to the nominee or, as the case may be, the guardian of such nominee or heir of the employee if the controlling authority is satisfied that there is no dispute as to the right of the applicant to receive the amount of gratuity.

(5) For the purpose of conducting an inquiry under sub-section (4), the controlling authority shall have the same powers as are vested in a court, while trying a suit, under the Code of Civil Procedure, 1908 (5 of 1908), in respect of the following matters, namely:

(a) enforcing the attendance of any person or examining him on oath;

(b) requiring the discovery and production of documents;

(c) receiving evidence on affidavits;

(d) issuing commissions for the examination of witnesses.

(6) Any inquiry under this section shall be a judicial proceeding within the meaning of sections 193 and 228, and for the purpose of section 196, of the Indian Penal Code, 1860 (45 of 1860).

(7) Any person aggrieved by an order under sub-section (4) may, within sixty days from the date of the receipt of the order, prefer an appeal to the appropriate Government or such other authority as may be specified by the appropriate Government in this behalf:

Provided that the appropriate Government or the appellate authority, as the case may be, may, if it is satisfied that the appellant was prevented by sufficient cause from preferring the appeal within the said period of sixty days, extend the said period by a further period of sixty days.

Provided further that no appeal by an employer shall be admitted unless at the time of preferring the appeal, the appellant either produces a certificate of the controlling authority to the effect that the appellant has deposited with him an amount equal to the amount of gratuity required to be deposited under sub-section (4), or deposits with the appellate authority such amount.

(8) The appropriate Government or the appellate authority, as the case may be, may, after giving the parties to the appeal a reasonable opportunity of being heard, confirm, modify or reverse the decision of the controlling authority.

It is evident from S. 7(2) that as soon as gratuity becomes payable, the employer, whether any application has been made or not, is obliged to determine the amount of gratuity and give notice in writing to the person to whom the gratuity is payable and also to the Controlling Authority specifying the amount of gratuity. Under S. 7(3), the employer shall arrange to pay the amount of gratuity within 30 days from the date it becomes payable. Under sub-section (3A) of S. 7, if the amount of gratuity is not paid by the employer within the period specified in sub-section (3), he shall pay, from the date on which the gratuity becomes payable to the date on which it is paid, simple interest at such rate not exceeding the rate notified by the Central Government from time to time for repayment of long-term deposits; provided that no such interest shall be payable if the delay in the payment is due to the fault of the employee and the employer has obtained permission in writing from the controlling authority for the delayed payment on that ground. From the provisions made in S. 7, a clear command can be seen mandating the employer to pay the gratuity within the specified time and to pay interest on the delayed payment of gratuity. No discretion is available to exempt or relieve the employer from payment of gratuity with or without interest, as the case may be. However, under the proviso to S. 7(3A), no interest shall be payable if delay in payment of gratuity is due to the fault of the employee and further condition that the employer has obtained permission in writing from the Controlling Authority for the delayed payment on that ground.

Under S. 8, provision is made for recovery of gratuity payable under the Act, if not paid by the employer within the prescribed time. The Collector shall recover the amount of gratuity with compound interest thereon as arrears of land revenue and pay the same to the person entitled. A penal provision is also made in S. 9 for non-payment of gratuity. The payment of gratuity with or without interest, as the case may be, does not lie in the domain of discretion, but it is a statutory compulsion. Specific benefits expressly given in a social beneficial legislation cannot be ordinarily denied. Employees on retirement have valuable rights to get gratuity and any culpable delay in payment of gratuity must be visited with the penalty of payment of interest was the view taken in *State of Kerala and Ors. v. M. Padmanabhan Nayyar.*[22] Earlier, there was no provision for payment of interest on the delayed payment of gratuity. Sub-section (3A) was added to S. 7 by an amendment, which came into force with effect from 1 October, 1987. In the case of *Charan Singh* v. *M/s. Birla Textiles and Another,*[23] this aspect was noticed in the following words:

> "There was no provision in the Act for payment of interest when the same was quantified by the Controlling Authority and before the Collector was approached for its realization. In fact, it is on the acceptance of the position that there was a lacuna in the law that Act 22 of 1987 brought about the incorporation of sub-section (3A) in Section 7. That provision has prospective application."[24]

---

22. 1985 (50) FLR 145.
23. AIR 1988 SC 2022.
24. *Ibid.* at p. 2023 per Ranganath Misra, J.

In the background of this legal position, now we turn to the facts of the present case *H. Gangahanume Gowda* v. *Karnataka Agro Industries Corpn. Ltd.*,[25] where the appellant was under suspension from 15-3-1999 to 21-5-1999. On attaining the age of superannuation, he retired from services of the respondent-Corporation on 1-1-2000. The learned single Judge, after considering the rival contentions, disposed of the writ petition issuing directions to the respondent-Corporation to settle the full salary and allowances for the period of suspension, gratuity, cash equivalent to leave salary, deferred leave, concession amount, etc. As regards the claim of interest on gratuity, the learned single Judge held:

> "since there was a doubt as to whether the petitioner is entitled to the gratuity, cash equivalent of leave salary etc., in view of the divergent opinion of the Courts during the pendency of an enquiry proceeding of a retired employee, in my view, the petitioner is not entitled to the relief of interest for the belated payment of gratuity and other amounts."

It is clear from what is extracted above from the order of learned single Judge that interest on delayed payment of gratuity was denied only on the ground that there was doubt whether the appellant was entitled to gratuity, cash equivalent to leave etc., in view of divergent opinion of the Courts during the pendency of the enquiry. The learned single Judge having held that the appellant was entitled for payment of gratuity and it was not right in denying the interest on the delayed payment of gratuity having due regard to S. 7(3A) of the Act. It was not the case of the respondent that the delay in the payment of gratuity was due to the fault of the employee and that it had obtained permission in writing from the Controlling Authority for the delayed payment on that ground. As noticed above, there is a clear mandate in the provisions of S. 7 to the employer for payment of gratuity within time and to pay interest on the delayed payment of gratuity. There is also a provision to recover the amount of gratuity with compound interest in case the amount of gratuity payable was not paid by the employer in terms of S. 8 of the Act. Since the employer did not satisfy the mandatory requirements of the proviso to S. 7(3A), no discretion was left to deny the interest to the appellant on belated payment of gratuity. Unfortunately, the Division Bench of the High Court, having found that the appellant was entitled for interest, declined to interfere with the order of the learned single Judge as regards the claim of interest on delayed payment of gratuity only on the ground that the discretion exercised by the learned single Judge could not be said to be arbitrary. In the first place, in the light of what is stated above, the learned single Judge could not refuse the grant of interest exercising discretion as against the mandatory provisions contained in S. 7 of the Act. The Supreme Court held that the Division Bench has committed an error in assuming that the learned single Judge could exercise the discretion in the matter of awarding interest and that such a discretion exercised was not arbitrary.

In the light of the facts stated and for the reasons aforementioned, the impugned order is set aside. The respondent is directed to pay interest at the rate of 10 per cent on the amount of gratuity to which the appellant is entitled from the date it became payable till the date of payment of the gratuity amount.

25. AIR 2003 SC 1526.

The question came before the Supreme Court for consideration that whether children born to a deceased Hindu employee from the second wife taken during subsistence of first marriage are entitled to share in family pension and gratuity? The Supreme Court in *Rameshwari Devi* v. *State of Bihar*[26] held that the second wife taken by a deceased Government employee during subsistence cannot be described as a widow of the deceased employee, as their marriage is void. Sons born out of the wedlock between the deceased employee and the second wife being the legitimate sons of the deceased would be entitled to the property of the deceased employee in equal shares along with that of the first wife and the sons born out of first wedlock. That being the legal position, when a Hindu male dies intestate, the children of the deceased employee born out of the second wedlock would be entitled to a share in the family pension and death-cum-retirement gratuity. The second wife was not entitled to anything and family pension would be admissible to minor children only till they attained majority.

Section 7A: Inspectors

(1) The appropriate Government may, by notification, appoint as many Inspectors, as it deems fit, for the purposes of this Act.

(2) The appropriate Government may, by general or special order, define the area to which the authority of an Inspector so appointed shall extend and where two or more Inspectors are appointed for the same area, also provide, by such order, for the distribution or allocation of work to be performed by them under this Act.

(3) Every Inspector shall be deemed to be a public servant within the meaning of section 21 of the Indian Penal Code, 1860 (45 of 1860).

Section 7B: Powers of Inspectors

(1) Subject to any rules made by the appropriate Government in this behalf, an Inspector may, for the purpose of ascertaining whether any of the provisions of this Act or the conditions, if any, of any exemption granted thereunder, have been complied with, exercise all or any of the following powers, namely:

(a) require an employer to furnish such information as he may consider necessary;

(b) enter and inspect, at all reasonable hours, with such assistants (if any), being persons in the service of the Government or local or any public authority, as he thinks fit, any premises of or place in any factory, mine, oilfield, plantation, port, railway company, shop or other establishment to which this Act applies, for the purpose of examining any register, record or notice or other document required to be kept or exhibited under this Act or the rules made thereunder, or otherwise kept or exhibited in relation to the employment of any person or the payment of gratuity to the employees, and require the production thereof for inspection;

26. AIR 2000 SC 735.

(c) examine with respect to any matter relevant to any of the purposes aforesaid, the employer or any person whom he finds in such premises or place and who, he has reasonable cause to believe, is an employee employed therein;

(d) make copies of, or take extracts from, any register, record, notice or other document, as he may consider relevant, and where he has reason to believe that any offence under this Act has been committed by an employer, search and seize with such assistance as he may think fit, such register, record, notice or other document as he may consider relevant in respect of that offence;

(e) exercise such other powers as may be prescribed.

(2) Any person required to produce any register, record, notice or other document or to give any information by an Inspector under sub-section (1) shall be deemed to be legally bound to do so within the meaning of sections 175 and 176 of the Indian Penal Code 1860 (45 of 1860).

(3) The provisions of the Code of Criminal Procedure, 1973 (2 of 1974) shall so far as may be, apply to any search or seizure under this section as they apply to any search or seizure made under the authority of a warrant issued under section 94 of that Code.

Section 8: Recovery of gratuity

If the amount of gratuity payable under this Act is not paid by the employer, within the prescribed time, to the person entitled thereto, the controlling authority shall, on an application made to it in this behalf by the aggrieved person, issue a certificate for that amount to the Collector, who shall recover the same, together with compound interest thereon at such rate as the Central Government may, by notification, specify, from the date of expiry of the prescribed time, as arrears of land revenue and pay the same to the person entitled thereto:

Provided that the controlling authority shall, before issuing a certificate under this section, give the employer a reasonable opportunity of showing cause against the issue of such certificate:

Provided further that the amount of interest payable under this section shall, in no case exceed the amount of gratuity payable under this Act.

According to S. 8, gratuity payable under the Act, if not paid by the employer within the prescribed limit to the person entitled thereto, is made recoverable as arrears of land revenue on certificate being issued by the Controlling Authority when the application is made in this regard. Section 9 makes it an offence if false statement or false representation is made by any person for the purpose of avoiding any payment to be made under this Act. The employer who contravenes any of the provisions of the Act or any Rules made thereunder is also made liable to suffer punishment, in both cases for a term exceeding one year.[27]

The Full Bench of the Patna High Court in *Champaran Sugar Co. Ltd.* v. *Jt. Labour Commissioner*[28] categorically held that it is manifest from the provisions of Ss. 4 and 8 of

27. *Mohal Lal* v. *Appellant Authority*, 1991 FLR (63) 543 (MP).
28. AIR 1987 Patna (FB).

the Act that it envisages the payment of gratuity either when it becomes payable or within the time prescribed. The very opening part of S. 8 would leave no manner of doubt that the mandatory statutory duty to pay gratuity is in terms laid on the employer. It is not made contingent on an application or a claim by the employee. Of course, a procedure is prescribed if the employer defaults in his duty to pay. What, however, deserves reiteration is that the Act in terms repeatedly lays the burden on the employer of tendering or paying the gratuity whenever it becomes payable to the employee within the time prescribed. Having thus laid the duty at the door of the employer to pay gratuity within the prescribed time, S. 8 also provides the sanction for such payment and the methodology for its recovery with interest for the delay in payment caused by the default of the employer. The Act is itself specific that the Controlling Authority in such cases would recover the gratuity with compound interest by the coercive process of the issuance of a certificate recoverable as arrears of land revenue by the Collector. Not only that, the terminus for calculating the same is fixed at the date of the expiry of the prescribed time.

It would seem somewhat plain from the above that the payment of interest is the mandate of the law itself and not dependent on an express claim by the employee thereof. Herein the employee's right to interest accrues from the failure of the employer to perform his statutory duty to tender and pay gratuity and not from any formal demand thereof by the employee. The Court in the instant case referred S. 7(2), (3) and (4)(a) and observed that it seems that irrespective of the fact whether an application is made by the employee to the employer or to the Controlling Authority, the employer is duty bound under the mandate of the law to determine the amount of gratuity due, to arrange to pay the same to the employee and in the event of a dispute, to deposit the admitted amount with the Controlling Authority. Therefore, if the basic claim of gratuity accrues irrespective of any application or express claim on behalf of the employee, it is somewhat elementary that the consequential claim of interest for delayed payment would equally accrue without any express claim therefor. To reiterate at the risk of repetition, it is the Act itself which mandates the payment of gratuity and the consequential payment of interest in the event of its failure within the prescribed time. These statutory rights stem from the statute and not from any application or claim therefor.

Section 9: Penalties

(1) Whoever, for the purpose of avoiding any payment to be made by himself under this Act or of enabling any other person to avoid such payment, knowingly makes or causes to be made any false statement or false representation shall be punishable with imprisonment for a term which may extend to six months, or with fine which may extend to ten thousand rupees or with both.

(2) An employer who contravenes, or makes default in complying with, any of the provisions of this Act or any rule or order made thereunder shall be punishable with imprisonment for a term which shall not be less than three months but which may extend to one year, or with fine which shall not be less than ten thousand rupees but which may extend to twenty thousand rupees, or with both:

Provided that where the offence relates to non-payment of any gratuity payable under this Act, the employer shall be punishable with imprisonment for a term which shall not be less than six months but which may extend to two years unless the court trying the offence, for reasons to be recorded by it in writing, is of opinion that a lesser term of imprisonment or the imposition of a fine would meet the ends of justice.

Section 10: Exemption of employer from liability in certain cases

Where an employer is charged with an offence punishable under this Act, he shall be entitled, upon complaint duly made by him and on giving to the complainant not less than three clear days' notice in writing of his intention to do so, to have any other person whom he charges as the actual offender brought before the court at the time appointed for hearing the charge; and if, after the commission of the offence has been proved, the employer proves to the satisfaction of the court—

(a) that he has used due diligence to enforce the execution of this Act, and

(b) that the said other person committed the offence in question without his knowledge, consent or connivance, that other person shall be convicted of the offence and shall be liable to the like punishment as if he were the employer and the employer shall be discharged from any liability under this Act in respect of such offence:

Provided that in seeking to prove as aforesaid, the employer may be examined on oath and his evidence and that of any witness whom he calls in his support shall be subject to cross-examination on behalf of the person he charges as the actual offender and by the prosecutor:

Provided further that, if the person charged as the actual offender by the employer cannot be brought before the court at the time appointed for hearing the charge, the court shall adjourn the hearing from time to time for a period not exceeding three months and if by the end of the said period the person charged as the actual offender cannot still be brought before the court, the court shall proceed to hear the charge against the employer and shall, if the offence be proved, convict the employer.

Section 11: Cognizance of offences

(1) No court shall take cognizance of any offence punishable under this Act save on a complaint made by or under the authority of the appropriate Government:

Provided that where the amount of gratuity has not been paid, or recovered, within six months from the expiry of the prescribed time, the appropriate Government shall authorise the controlling authority to make a complaint against the employer, whereupon the controlling authority shall, within fifteen days from the date of such authorisation, make such complaint to a Magistrate having jurisdiction to try the offence.

(2) No court inferior to that of a Metropolitan Magistrate or a Judicial Magistrate of the first class shall try any offence punishable under this Act.

Section 12: Protection of action taken in good faith

No suit or other legal proceeding shall lie against the controlling authority or any other person in respect of anything which is in good faith done or intended to be done under this Act or any rule or order made thereunder.

Section 13: Protection of gratuity

No gratuity payable under this Act and no gratuity payable to an employee employed in any establishment, factory, mine, oilfield, plantation, port, railway company or shop exempted under section 5 shall be liable to attachment in execution of any decree or order of any civil, revenue or criminal court.

Section 13 protects gratuity from being attached in execution of any decree or order of any civil, revenue or criminal court. Section 60 of the Code of Civil Procedure, 1908 provides a list of properties which are liable to attachment and sale in execution of decree. In *Calcutta Dock Labour Board* v. *Sandhya Mitra,*[29] the question which came before the Supreme Court for decision was whether gratuity payable to a workman employed under the Calcutta Dock Labour Board is attachable for satisfaction of a decree of the Court.

The Court held that S. 13 gives total immunity to gratuity from attachment. The Preamble to the Act clearly indicates the legislative intention that the Act sought to provide a scheme for payment of gratuity to all employees engaged in, *inter alia,* ports, and under this Act, gratuity was payable to workers. The gratuity which was payable to him squarely came within the purview of the Act and, therefore, became entitled to immunity under S. 13 thereof.

Section 13A: Validation of payment of gratuity

Notwithstanding anything contained in any judgment, decree or order of any court, for the period commencing on and from the 3rd day of April, 1997 and ending on the day on which the Payment of Gratuity (Amendment) Act, 2009, receives the assent of the President, the gratuity shall be payable to an employee in pursuance of the notification of the Government of India in the Ministry of Labour and Employment *vide* number S.O. 1080, dated the 3rd day of April, 1997 and the said notification shall be valid and shall be deemed always to have been valid as if the Payment of Gratuity (Amendment) Act, 2009 had been in force at all material times and the gratuity shall be payable accordingly:

Provided that nothing contained in this section shall extend, or be construed to extend, to affect any person with any punishment or penalty whatsoever by reason of the non-payment by him of the gratuity during the period specified in this section which shall become due in pursuance of the said notification.

Section 14: Act to Override Other Enactments, etc.

The provisions of this Act or any rule made thereunder shall have effect notwithstanding anything inconsistent therewith contained in any enactment other than this Act or in

29. AIR 1985 SC 996.

any instrument or contract having effect by virtue of any enactment other than this Act.

Section 14 of the Act is a *non-obstante* provision and is couched in a very wide language. It provides that if any of the provisions of any other Acts are inconsistent with the provisions of the Act, then the provisions of this Act will have overriding effect. However, in *Sarwan Singh* v. *Kasturi Lal*,[30] the Supreme Court held that when two or more laws operate in the same field and each contains a *non-obstante* clause stating that its provisions will override those of any other law, then such conflict has to be decided by reference to the object and purpose of the laws under consideration. Further, the Court held that for resolving inter se conflicts, another test is that the latter enactment must prevail over the earlier one.

In *Municipal Corporation of Delhi* v. *Dharam Prakash Sharma*,[31] one question that arose for consideration before the Supreme Court was whether an employee of the Municipal Corporation of Delhi would be entitled to payment of gratuity under the Payment of Gratuity Act when the Municipal Corporation of Delhi itself has adopted the provisions of the CCS (Pension) Rules, 1972 (hereinafter referred to as the "Pension Rules"), where under there is a provision both for payment of pension and gratuity. The contention of the learned counsel appearing for the appellant in this Court was that the payment of pension and gratuity under the Pension Rules is a package by itself and once that package is made applicable to the employees of the MCD, the provisions of payment of gratuity under the Payment of Gratuity Act cannot be held applicable. The Court has examined carefully the provisions of the Pension Rules as well as the provisions of the Payment of Gratuity Act and held that the Payment of Gratuity Act being a special provision for payment of gratuity, unless there is any provision therein which excludes its applicability to an employee who is otherwise governed by the provisions of the Pension Rules. The only provision which was pointed out is the definition of 'employee' in S. 2(e), which excludes the employees of the Central Government and State Governments receiving pension and gratuity under the Pension Rules but not an employee of the MCD. The MCD employee, therefore, would be entitled to the payment of gratuity under the Payment of Gratuity Act. The mere fact that gratuity is provided for under the Pension Rules will not disentitle him to get the payment of gratuity under the Payment of Gratuity Act. In view of the overriding provisions contained in S. 14 of the Payment of Gratuity Act, the provision for gratuity under Pension Rules will have no effect. Possibly for this reason, S. 5 of the Payment of Gratuity Act has conferred authority on the appropriate Government to exempt any establishment from the operation of the provisions of the Act if in its opinion the employees of such establishment are in receipt of gratuity or pensionary benefits not less favourable than the benefits conferred under this Act. Admittedly, MCD has not taken any steps to invoke the power of the Central Government under S. 5 of the Payment of Gratuity Act. In the aforesaid premises the Court held that the employees of the MCD would be entitled to the payment of gratuity under the Payment of Gratuity Act notwithstanding the fact that the provisions of the Pension Rules have been made applicable

30. AIR 1977 SC 265.
31. AIR 1999 SC 293.

to them for the purpose of determining the pension. Needless to mention that the employees cannot claim gratuity available under the Pension Rules.

In *E.I.D. Party (I) Ltd.* v. *G. Omkar Murthy and Others*,[32] the question that the employees getting wages more than ₹1600 per mensem at the time of voluntary retirement cannot claim gratuity under the Central Act came before the Court.

In these cases, the respondents-employees were in the employment of the appellant between the years 1958 and 1984. On October 1, 1984 voluntary retirement scheme was introduced and the respondents availed of that benefit and left the services after obtaining the terminal benefits as provided under the Payment of Gratuity Act, 1972 (hereinafter referred to as "the Central Act"). Thereafter, petitions were filed under S. 44 of the Andhra Pradesh Shops and Establishments Act, 1966 (hereinafter referred to as 'the State Act') claiming the difference between the gratuity received by them and the gratuity payable under S. 40 of the State Act. Before the Authority under the State Act, three objections were raised that (i) there has been inordinate delay in preferring the claim; (ii) for payment of gratuity the Central Act prevails over the State Act, and (iii) the question whether the gratuity, payable under the Central Act is more favourable than the State Act could not be examined by the trial Court concerned. The trial Court, however, gave relief to the workmen. The appellate authority dismissed all the three appeals. Revision petitions filed before the High Court also stood dismissed. Hence these appeals by special leave.

Four contentions were put forth before the Supreme Court, namely, that:

(i) The Central Act prevails over the State Act by virtue of Art. 254 of the Constitution and S. 40(3) is invalid and the claims are unsustainable;
(ii) Section 40(3) of the State Act stood repealed on the coming into force of the Andhra Pradesh Shops and Establishments Act, 1988 and gratuity became payable under S. 47(5) of the State Act where payment of gratuity is not payable under the Central Act;
(iii) Section 14 of the Central Act overrides other enactments in relation to gratuity; and
(iv) The respondents have been paid gratuity under the Central Act for the period covered and for the balance period of service gratuity is paid under the prevailing trust scheme.

At the relevant time when the respondents voluntarily retired from service, the definition of *'employee'* under S. 2(e) of the Central Act read as not to include employee whose wages exceeded ₹1,000 per mensem while the respondents-employees were all getting wages more than ₹1,600 per mensem and, therefore, the Central Act could not be applied. If that is so, it is certainly permissible for the respondents to have made an application for payment of gratuity under S. 40(3) of the State Act. Further, the scheme of the Central Act would indicate that it would not be applicable in cases where the State Act is more beneficial than the Central Act. In this case, the finding is that the State Act is more beneficial than the Central Act. Therefore, the contentions sought to be advanced on behalf of the appellant as to repugnancy or otherwise of the State Act would not arise at all. If both the enactments can

32. AIR 2001 SC 1407.

co-exist and can operate where one Act or the other is not available then we find no difficulty in making the State Act applicable on the fact situation available, as has been done in the present case. Therefore, the Court held that the contentions raised on behalf of the appellant are unsustainable.

SECTION 15: Power to make rules

(1) The appropriate Government may, by notification make rules for the purpose of carrying out the provisions of this Act.

(2) Every rule made by the Central Government under this Act shall be laid, as soon as may be after it is made, before each House of Parliament while it is in session, for a total period of thirty days which may be comprised in one session or in two or more successive sessions, and if, before the expiry of the session immediately following the session or the successive sessions aforesaid, both Houses agree in making any modification in the rule or both Houses agree that the rule should not be made, the rule shall, thereafter, have effect only in such modified form or be of no effect as the case may be; so, however, that any such modification or annulment shall be without prejudice to the validity of anything previously done under that rule.

* * *

6 The Industrial Employment (Standing Orders) Act, 1946

Prior to the enactment of these laws, the situation, as it prevailed in many industrial establishments, was that even terms and conditions of services were often not reduced to writing nor were they uniform in nature, though applicable to a set of similar employees. This position was wholly incompatible to the notions of social justice, inasmuch as there being no statutory protection available to the workmen, the contract of service was often so unilateral in character that it could be described as mere manifestation of subdued wish of the workmen to sustain their living at any cost. An agreement of this nature was an agreement between two unequals, namely those who invested their labour and toil, flesh and blood, as against those who brought in capital. The necessary corollary of such an agreement was the generation of conflicts at various levels, disturbing industrial peace and resulting necessarily in loss of production and sometimes even closure or lockout of the industrial establishment. In order to overcome this difficulty and achieve industrial harmony and peace, and Industrial Employment (Standing Orders) Act, 1946 was enacted, requiring the management to define, with sufficient precision and clarity, the conditions of employment under which the workmen were working in their establishments. The underlying object of the Act was to introduce uniformity in conditions of employment of workmen discharging similar functions in the same industrial establishment under the same management and to make those terms and conditions widely known to all the workmen before they could be asked to express their willingness to accept the employment.

The Industrial Employment (Standing Orders) Act was passed in 1946 because the legislature thought that it was expedient to require employers in individual establishments to define with sufficient precision the conditions of employment under them and to make the said conditions known to workmen employed by them. Prior to the passing of the Act, conditions of employment obtaining in several industrial establishments were governed by contracts between the employer and their employees. Sometimes the said conditions were reduced to writing and in many cases they were not reduced to writing but were governed by oral agreements. Inevitably, in many cases the conditions of service were not well defined and there was ambiguity or doubt in regard to their nature and scope. That is why the legislature took the view that in regard to industrial establishments to which the Act applied, the conditions of employment subject to which industrial labour was employed, should be well defined and should be precisely known to both the parties. With that object, the Act has made relevant provisions for making Standing Orders which, after they are certified, constitute the statutory terms of employment between the industrial establishments in question and their employees. That is the principal object of the Act.

The Industrial Employment (Standing Orders) Act, 1946 came into force on 23-4-1946. The matters which are to be provided in the standing orders are enumerated under 11 items in the Schedule to the Act. The expression "Standing Orders", as used in the Act, means rules relating to matters set out in the Schedule. When the draft standing orders are submitted to the certifying officer, the said officer has to satisfy himself that they make provision for every matter set out in the Schedule and that they are otherwise in conformity with the provisions of the Act. It is significant that originally under S. 4, it was not competent to the certifying officer to adjudicate upon the fairness or reasonableness of the provisions of any standing orders. The same disability was imposed on the appellate authority. This section has, however, been subsequently amended by Act 36 of 1956, and the effect of the amendment is that it has now been made the function of the certifying officer or the appellate authority to adjudicate upon the fairness or the reasonableness of the provisions of the standing orders. Prior to this amendment, however, all that the certifying officer had to do before certifying the said standing orders was to see that all the matters in the schedule are covered and that they are not otherwise inconsistent with the provisions of the Act. Under S. 7, standing orders, when certified, come into operation subject to its other provisions. Section 10 lays down that standing orders finally certified shall not, except on agreement between the employer and the workmen, or a trade union or other representative body of the workmen, be liable to modification until the expiry of six months from the date on which the standing orders or the last modifications thereof came into operation. Sub-section (2) of S. 10, prior to its amendment in 1956, authorised only the employer to apply for the modification of the standing orders. Subsequent to the said amendment, workmen also have been given the right to apply for such modification. It is thus clear that the scope of enquiry before the certifying officer and the appellate authority under the original Act was extremely limited, and the right to claim a modification of the standing orders was not given to the employees prior to the amendment of S. 10(2). Nevertheless, the standing orders when they are certified, become operative and bind the employer and all his employees. Subsequent to the amendment of the Act, the employees can raise the same dispute before the certifying officer or before the Appellate Tribunal and may in a proper case apply for its modification under S. 10(2) of the Act.

The Act was passed because the legislature thought that in many industrial establishments, the conditions of service were not uniform and sometimes were not even reduced to writing. This led to conflicts resulting in unnecessary industrial disputes. The object of passing the Act was thus to require employers to define with certainty the conditions of service in their establishments and to require them to reduce them to writing and to get them compulsorily certified. The matters in respect of which the conditions of employment had to be certified were specified in the Schedule to the Act.[1] The object of the Act is to have uniform standing orders providing for the matters enumerated in the Schedule to the Act and it is not intended that there should be different conditions of service for those who are employed before and those employed after the standing orders came into force. Once

1. *Shahdara (Delhi) Saharanpur Light Railway Co. Ltd.* v. *S.S. Railway Workers Union*, AIR 1969 SC 513.

the Standing Orders come into force, they bind all those presently in the employment of the establishment concerned as well those who are appointed thereafter.[2]

SCHEME OF THE ACT

The Act applies to every industrial establishment wherein one hundred or more workmen are employed or were employed on any day of the preceding twelve months. It can be extended even to establishments whose labour force is less than one hundred and it does not apply to any industry to which Chapter VII of the Bombay Industrial Relations Act, 1946, applies or to any industrial establishment to which the provisions of the Madhya Pradesh Industrial Employment (Standing Orders) Act, 1961, apply. The Certifying Officer under the Act means a Labour Commissioner or a Regional Labour Commissioner and includes any officer appointed by the appropriate government by notification in the Official Gazette to perform all or any of the functions of a Certifying Officer under the Act . The Act provides for an appeal against the order passed by the Certifying Officer and the "appellate authority" means an Industrial Court, wherever it exists or in its absence, an authority appointed by the appropriate Government by notification in the Official Gazette to exercise in such area as may be specified in the notification the functions of an appellate authority under the Act. "Standing Orders" are defined to mean rules relating to matters set out in the Schedule. Thus, the matters which have to be covered by the Standing Orders and in respect of which the employer has to make a draft for submission to the Certifying Officer are matters specified in the Schedule. Section 3 requires the submission of the draft of Standing Orders within six months from the date on which the Act becomes applicable to an industrial establishment. Under S. 4, the Standing Orders become certifiable if provisions are made therein for every matter set out in the Schedule and they are found to be otherwise in conformity with the provisions of the Act. After the amendment of this section made in 1956, the legislature has imposed upon the Certifying Officer and the appellate authority the duty to adjudicate upon the fairness or reasonableness of the provisions of any standing order. Prior to the amendment, it was not open to the said authorities to examine the fairness of the Standing Orders submitted by the employer. The result of S. 4, therefore, is that the Standing Orders have to provide for all the topics specified in the Schedule and they have to be in conformity with the Act. Their reasonableness can be examined by the appropriate authorities and suitable modifications can be made by them in accordance with their decision.

Section 5 provides for the procedure which has to be followed by the Certifying Officer before certifying the Standing Orders. The procedure is intended to give an opportunity to both the parties to be heard before the final order is passed. Section 6 provides for an appeal and S. 7 lays down that the Standing Orders shall come into operation on the expiry of 30 days from the date on which authenticated copies thereof are sent as required by S. 5(3), or where an appeal is preferred, on the expiry of seven days from the date on which the copies of the appellate order are sent under S. 6(2). Section 8 requires the Certifying Officer to keep a register of standing orders and under S. 9, the said Standing Orders have to be prominently posted by the employer in English and in the language understood by the majority of the

2. *Agra Electric Supply Co. Ltd.* v. *Alladin,* AIR 1970 SC 512.

workmen on special boards. Section 10 deals with the duration and modification of standing orders. It provides that except by agreement, the standing orders, after they are certified, shall not be liable to modification until the expiry of six months from the date on which they came into operation. Section 10(2) empowers both the employer and the workman to apply for a modification in the said standing orders. It would thus be clear that after they are certified, the standing orders have to remain in force for six months unless, of course, they are modified in the meanwhile by consent. After six months are over, an application for modification in the standing orders can be made either by the employer or the employees and the request would be considered after following the procedure prescribed by the Act for certifying the original standing orders. Section 10A prescribes for payment of subsistence allowance where a workman is suspended by the employer pending investigation or inquiry into complaints or charges of misconduct against him.

Section 11 confers the necessary powers of a Civil Court on the Certifying Officer and the appellate authority and S. 12 prohibits the admission of oral evidence which has the effect of adding or otherwise varying or contradicting standing orders as finally certified under the Act, in any Court. Section 13 provides for penalties and the procedure to enforce them. Section 13A deals with the problem of interpretation of the standing orders and S. 13B provides for exemption of industrial establishments therein specified. Section 14 confers on the appropriate Government power to exempt, conditionally or unconditionally, any industrial establishment, and S. 14A provides for delegation of powers. Section 15 confers on the appropriate Government the power to make rules to carry out the purposes of the Act, and, in particular, to provide for the matters covered by Cls. (a) to (e) of sub-Cl. (2). Section 15(3) contains the salutary provision that every rule made by the Central Government under S. 15 has to be placed before the House in the manner prescribed by it. The Schedule to the Act contains 11 clauses. Clauses 1 to 10 deal with the several topics in respect of which standing orders have to make a provision and Cl. 11 refers to any other matter which may be prescribed. This last clause lays down that an addition may be made by the appropriate Government if it is thought necessary to do so.

An Act to require employers in industrial establishments formally to define conditions of employment under them.

Whereas it is expedient to require employers in industrial establishments to define with sufficient precision the conditions of employment under them and to make the said conditions known to workmen employed by them;

It is hereby enacted as follows:

Section 1: Short title, extent and application

(1) This Act may be called the Industrial Employment (Standing Orders) Act, 1946.

(2) It extends to the whole of India.

(3) It applies to every industrial establishment wherein one hundred or more workmen are employed, or were employed on any day of the preceding twelve months:

Provided that the appropriate Government may, after giving not less than two months' notice of its intention so to do, by notification in the Official Gazette, apply the provisions of this Act to any industrial establishment employing such number of persons less than one hundred as may be specified in the notification:

(4) Nothing in this Act shall apply to—

(i) any industry to which the provisions of Chapter VII of the Bombay Industrial Relations Act, 1946 (11 of 1947), apply; or

(ii) any industrial establishment to which the provisions of the Madhya Pradesh Industrial Employment (Standing Orders) Act, 1961 (26 of 1961) apply:

Provided that notwithstanding anything contained in the Madhya Pradesh Industrial Employment (Standing Orders) Act, 1961 (26 of 1961), the provisions of this Act shall apply to all industrial establishments under the control of the Central Government.

Section 2: Interpretation

In this Act, unless there is anything repugnant in the subject or context,—

(a) **appellate authority** means an authority appointed by the appropriate Government by notification in the Official Gazette to exercise in such area as may be specified in the notification the functions of an appellate authority under this Act:

Provided that in relation to an appeal pending before an Industrial Court or other authority immediately before the commencement of the Industrial Employment (Standing Orders) Amendment Act, 1963 (39 of 1963), that Court or authority shall be deemed to be the appellate authority.

(b) **appropriate Government** means in respect of industrial establishments under the control of the Central Government or a Railway administration or in a major port, mine or oilfield, the Central Government, and in all other cases, the State Government:

Provided that where any question arises as to whether any industrial establishment is under the control of the Central Government, that Government may, either on a reference made to it by the employer or the workman or a trade union or other representative body of the workmen, or on its own motion and after giving the parties an opportunity of being heard, decide the question and such decision shall be final and binding on the parties.

(c) **Certifying Officer** means a Labour Commissioner or a Regional Labour Commissioner, and includes any other officer appointed by the appropriate Government, by notification in the Official Gazette, to perform all or any of the functions of a Certifying Officer under this Act.

(d) **employer** means the owner of an industrial establishment to which this Act for the time being applies, and includes—

(i) in a factory, any person named under clause (f) of sub-section (1) of section 7 of the Factories Act, 1948 (63 of 1948), as manager of the factory;

(ii) in any industrial establishment under the control of any department of any Government in India, the authority appointed by such Government in this behalf, or where no authority is so appointed, the head of the department;

(iii) in any other industrial establishment, any person responsible to the owner for the supervision and control of the industrial establishment.

(e) **industrial establishment** means—

(i) an industrial establishment as defined in clause (ii) of section 2 of the Payment of Wages Act, 1936 (4 of 1936), or

(ii) a factory as defined in clause (m) of section 2 of the Factories Act, 1948 (63 of 1948), or

(iii) a railway as defined in clause (4) of section 2 of the Indian Railways Act, 1890 (9 of 1890), or

(iv) the establishment of a person who, for the purpose of fulfilling a contract with the owner of any industrial establishment, employs workmen;

(f) **prescribed** means prescribed by rules made by the appropriate Government under this Act.

(g) **Standing orders** means rules relating to matters set out in the Schedule.

(h) **trade union** means a trade union for the time being registered under the Indian Trade Unions Act, 1926 (16 of 1926).

(i) **wages** and **workman** have the meanings respectively assigned to them in clauses (rr) and (s) of section 2 of the Industrial Disputes Act, 1947 (14 of 1947).

Section 3: Submission of draft standing orders

(1) Within six months from the date on which this Act becomes applicable to an industrial establishment, the employer shall submit to the Certifying Officer five copies of the draft standing orders proposed by him for adoption in his industrial establishment.

(2) Provision shall be made in such draft for every matter set out in the Schedule which may be applicable to the industrial establishment, and where model standing orders have been prescribed, shall be, so far as is practicable, in conformity with such model.

(3) The draft standing orders submitted under this section shall be accompanied by a statement giving prescribed particulars of the workmen employed in the industrial establishment including the name of the trade union, if any, to which they belong.

(4) Subject to such conditions as may be prescribed, a group of employers in similar industrial establishments may submit a joint draft of standing orders under this section.

Section 3 of the Act requires the employer to submit draft standing orders. Section 3(2) provides that in the draft thus submitted provision shall be made for every matter set out in the Schedule which may be applicable to the industrial establishment, and where model standing orders have been prescribed, shall be, so far as is practicable, in conformity with such model. It is common ground that model standing orders have been prescribed in the present case, and so it follows that under S. 3(2), the draft submitted by the appellants has to be in conformity with the model standing orders so far as is practicable. In other words, the effect of S. 3(2) is that, unless it is shown that it is impracticable to do so, the appellants' draft had to conform to the model. This position cannot be disputed. Then, the next relevant provision of the Act is contained in S. 4 which provides that standing orders shall be certifiable under this Act if (a) provision is made therein for every matter set out in the Schedule which is applicable to the industrial establishment, and (b) the standing orders are otherwise in conformity with the provisions of this Act. Section 5 provides for the procedure of the proceedings which are taken before the certifying officer. Section 5(2) lays down that after notice is given to the parties concerned, the certifying officer shall decide whether or not any modification of, or addition to, the draft submitted by the employer is necessary to render the draft standing orders certifiable under the Act, and shall make an order in writing accordingly. Sub-section (3) of S. 5 then provides for certifying the draft after making modifications, if any, under sub-section (2). Section 15(2)(b) provides that the rules which the appropriate government may make under the Act may set out model standing orders for the purpose of this Act. The cumulative effect of these provisions is that the certifying officer has to be satisfied that the draft standing orders deal with every matter set out in the Schedule and are otherwise in conformity with the provisions of the Act. This latter requirement necessarily imports the consideration specified in S. 3, sub-section (2), that is to say, the draft standing order must be in conformity with the model standing order which is provided under S. 15(2)(b) for the purposes of the Act, and, as we have already seen, unless it is shown that it would be impracticable to do so, the draft standing order must be in conformity with the model standing order. It is quite true that this requirement does not mean that the draft standing order must be in identical words, but it does mean that in substance it must conform to the model prescribed by the appropriate government.[3] A similar view has been endorsed by the Supreme Court in *Rohtak and Hissar Districts Electric Supply Co. Ltd.* v. *State of U.P.*[4] It held that under S. 3(2) of the Act the employers have to frame draft Standing Orders and they must normally cover the items given in the Schedule to the Act. If, however, it appears to the appropriate authorities that having regard to the relevant facts and circumstances, it would not be unfair and unreasonable to make a provision for a particular item, it would be competent for them to do so; but the employer cannot insist upon adding a condition to the Standing Order which relates to a matter which is not included in the Schedule. Section 3(2) of the Act specifically requires that the Standing Orders shall be, as far as practicable, in conformity with the model. These words indicate that the appropriate authority may permit departure from the Model Standing Orders if it is satisfied that insistence upon such conformity may be impracticable. This fact also shows that in a given case, the appropriate authority may permit departure from the Model Standing Orders and may come to the conclusion that one or the other of the conditions included in the Model standing Orders may not, for the time being, be included in the Standing Orders of any particular establishment.

SECTION 4: Conditions for certification of standing orders

Standing orders shall be certifiable under this Act if—

3. *Associated Cement Co. Ltd.* v. *P.D. Vyas,* AIR 1960 SC 665.
4. AIR 1966 SC 1471.

(a) provision is made therein for every matter set out in the Schedule which is applicable to the industrial establishment, and

(b) the standing orders are otherwise in conformity with the provisions of this Act;

and it shall be the function of the Certifying Officer or appellate authority to adjudicate upon the fairness or reasonableness of the provisions of any standing orders.

In the sunny days of the market economy theory, people believed that the economic law of demand and supply in the labour market would settle a mutually beneficial bargain between the employer and the workman. They took it for granted that such a bargain would secure fair terms and conditions of employment to the workman. This law they venerated as natural law. They had an abiding faith in the unity of this law. But the experience of the working of this law over a long period has belied their faith. Later generations discovered that the workman did not possess adequate bargaining strength to secure fair terms and conditions of service. When the workmen also made this discovery, they organised themselves in trade unions and insisted on collective bargaining with the employer. The advent of trade unions and collective bargaining created new problems of maintaining industrial peace and production for the society. It was therefore considered that the society has also an interest in the settlement of the terms of employment of industrial labour. While formerly there were two parties at the negotiating table, the employer and the workman, it is now thought that there should also be a third-party, the State, to represent the interest of the society. The Act gives effect to this new thinking. By S. 4, the Officer certifying the Standing Order is directed to adjudicate upon *the fairness or reasonableness* of the provisions of the Standing Order. The Certifying Officer is the statutory representative of the society. He should consider and weigh the social interest in the claims of the employer as well as in the demands of the workman. In 1956, Parliament effected radical changes in the Act, widening its scope and altering its very complexion. Section 4, as amended by Act 36 of 1956, entrusted the authorities under the Act with the duty to adjudicate upon fairness and reasonableness of the standing orders. The enquiry, when such standing orders are submitted for certification, is now two-fold.

(1) whether the standing orders are in consonance with the model standing orders, and

(2) whether they are fair and reasonable. The workmen, therefore, can raise an objection as to the reasonableness or fairness of the draft standing orders submitted for certification.[1]

In *Western India Match Co. Ltd.* v. *Workmen*,[5] the question that came before the Supreme Court for consideration was whether an agreement made between the employer and workman, which is inconsistent with the Standing Order, will prevail over the Standing Order. According to the Standing Order, a workman shall not be kept on probation for more than two months. If he has worked during these two months to the satisfaction of the Company, he becomes permanent. But as a result of special agreement, even though he has worked during these two months to the satisfaction of the Company, he will not be a permanent workman. While the Standing Order says, "Confirm him on the expiry of two months," the special agreement says, "No, wait till the expiry of six months." There is thus a conflict between them. They

5. AIR 1973 SC 2650.

cannot co-exist. The Court is of the opinion that the special agreement is inconsistent with the Standing Order to the extent of the additional four months' probation. The terms of employment specified in the Standing Order would prevail over the corresponding terms in the contract of service in existence on the enforcement of the Standing Order.

In *Bagalkot Cement Co. Ltd.,* v. *R.K. Pathan,*[6] it was held that under S. 4, the Standing Orders become certifiable if provisions are made therein for every matter set out in the Schedule and they are found to be otherwise in conformity with the provisions of the Act. After the amendment of this section made in 1956, the legislature has imposed upon the Certifying Officer and the appellate authority the duty to adjudicate upon the fairness or reasonableness of the provisions of any standing orders. Prior to the amendment, it was not open to the said authorities to examine the fairness of the Standing Orders submitted by the employer. The result of S. 4, therefore, is that the Standing Orders have to provide for all the topics specified in the Schedule and they have to be in conformity with the Act. Their reasonableness can be examined by the appropriate authorities and suitable modifications can be made by them in accordance with their decision.

In *Rohtak and Hissar Districts Electric Supply Co. Ltd.* v. *State of U.P.*,[4] it was held that the consent of the employees is, no doubt, a relevant factor which the certifying authorities may bear in mind in dealing with the question as to the fairness or reasonableness of the said Orders. If both the parties agree that certain Standing Orders submitted for certification are fair and reasonable, that, no doubt, is a consideration which the appropriate authority must take into account: but clearly, the appropriate authority cannot be denied the jurisdiction to deal with the matter according to its own judgment. It is for the appropriate authority to decide whether a particular Standing Order is fair or reasonable, or not. Sometimes, the employees may not be organised enough to resist the pressure of the employer or may not be articulate; and where the employees are not organised or strong enough to put forward their point of view vigorously, the fact that the employer has persuaded his employees to agree to the draft Standing Orders, will not preclude the appropriate authority from discharging its obligation by considering the fairness or reasonableness of the draft. The present case itself is an illustration in point. When the Standing Orders were drafted by the appellant and submitted for certification, it was found that the employees of the appellant had no union of their own: and so, three representatives were elected by the employees at the instance of the Labour Department. The fact that the employees' representatives have not appeared before the Court also shows that they are either not organised enough, or have not the financial capacity to take steps to engage lawyers to appear before the Court. In such a case, the consent of the employees can have no decisive significance in certification proceedings.

Section 5: Certification of standing orders

(1) On receipt of the draft under section 3, the Certifying Officer shall forward a copy thereof to the trade union, if any, of the workmen, or where there is no such trade union, to the workmen in such manner as may be prescribed, together with a notice in the prescribed form requiring objections, if any, which the workmen may desire

6. AIR 1963 SC 439.

to make to the draft standing orders to be submitted to him within fifteen days from the receipt of the notice.

(2) After giving the employer and the trade union or such other representatives of the workmen as may be prescribed an opportunity of being heard, the Certifying Officer shall decide whether or not any modification of or addition to the draft submitted by the employer is necessary to render the draft Standing Orders certifiable under this Act, and shall make an order in writing accordingly.

(3) The Certifying Officer shall thereupon certify the draft standing orders, after making any modifications therein which his order under sub-section (2) may require, and shall within seven days thereafter send copies of the certified standing orders authenticated in the prescribed manner and of his order under sub-section (2) to the employer and to the trade union or other prescribed representatives of the workmen.

The obligation imposed on the employer to have standing order certified, the duty of the certifying authority to adjudicate upon their fairness and reasonableness, the notice to be given to the union and in its absence to the representatives of the workmen, the right conferred on them to raise objections, the opportunity given to them of being heard before they are certified, the right of appeal and the right to apply for modifications given to workmen individually, the obligation on the employer to have them published in such a manner that they become easily known to the workmen—all these provisions abundantly show that once the standing orders are certified and come into operation, they become binding on the employer and all the workmen presently employed as also those employed thereafter in the establishment conducted by that employer. It cannot possibly be that such standing orders would bind only those who are employed after they come into force and not those who were employed previously but are still in employment when they come into force.

The right of being heard given to the union or, where there is no union, to the representatives of the workmen, the right of appeal and the right to apply for modification given to workmen individually clearly indicate that they were provided for because the standing orders, as they emerge after certification, are intended to be binding on all workmen in the employment of the establishment at the date when they come into force and those employed thereafter. Surely, the union or, in its absence, the representatives of workmen, who are given the right to raise objections either to the draft standing orders proposed by the employer or to the fairness and reasonableness of their provisions, could not have been intended to speak for workmen to be employed thereafter and not those whom they presently represent. Besides, if the standing orders were to bind only those who are subsequently employed, the result would be that there would be different conditions of employment for different classes of workmen, one set of conditions for those who are previously employed and another for those employed subsequently, and where they are modified, even several sets of conditions of service depending upon whether a workman was employed before the standing orders are certified or after, whether he was employed before or after a modification is made to any one of them and would bind only a few who are recruited after and not the bulk of them, who though in employment were recruited previously. Such a result could never have been intended by the legislature, for that would render the conditions of service of workmen as indefinite and diversified, as before the enactment of the Act. Why does

S. 3(3) of the Act require the employer to give particulars of the workmen employed by him at the date of his submission of the draft standing orders unless the object of making him furnish the particulars was to have uniformity of conditions of service and to make the standing orders binding on all those presently employed? That is why the Act also insists, among other things, that after they are certified, they must be made known to all workmen by posting them at or near the entrance through which they pass and in the language known to the majority of them.[2]

If before the actual date of certification of the draft standing orders the Officer before whom they were submitted as the Certifying Officer under the Central Standing Orders Act had acquired jurisdiction, the certification by him cannot be held to be void merely because on the date when the standing orders were submitted before him he had no jurisdiction. The position in law is that the application for certification of the standing orders, though invalid at the time it was made because the officer had no jurisdiction to deal with them, became a valid application when he did acquire jurisdiction. To put the matter in another way, the application should be deemed to have been renewed immediately after the officer acquired jurisdiction in the matter and so, that jurisdiction having continued up to the date of the certification, the certification also would be with jurisdiction and binding.[7]

Right of Representation of a Workman

In *Bharat Petroleum Corporation Ltd.* v. *Maharashtra General Kamgar Union*[8] the question arose before the Supreme Court for consideration relating to the representation of an employee in the disciplinary proceedings through another employee who, though not an employee of the appellant-Corporation was, nevertheless, a member of the Trade Union. The facts of the case are given below.

Para 14(4)(ba) of the Model Standing Orders, as framed by the Central Government under the Act for Industrial Establishments, not being Industrial Establishments in coalmines, provides as under:

"In the enquiry, the workman shall be entitled to appear in person or to be represented by an office bearer of a trade union of which he is a member."

Clause 29(4) of the Draft Standing Orders, as certified by the Appellate Authority, provides as under:

"29.4 (para-3): If it is decided to hold an enquiry the workman concerned will be given an opportunity to answer the charge/charges and permitted to be defended by a fellow workman of his choice, who must be an employee of the Corporation. The workman defending shall be given necessary time off for the conduct of the enquiry."

The vital difference between the model standing orders, as set out above, and the draft standing orders, as certified by the appellate authority, is that while under the model standing orders, a workman can be represented in the departmental proceedings by an office bearer of a Trade Union of which he is a member, he does not have this right under the draft standing

7. *General Manager, Bhilai Steel Project, Bhilai (M.P.)* v. *Steel Works' Union Bhopal*, AIR 1964 SC 1333.
8. AIR 1999 SC 401.

orders, as certified by the Appellate Authority, which restrict his right of representation by a fellow workman of his choice from among the employees of the appellant-Corporation. The contention of the learned counsel for the appellant is that the model standing orders, framed by the Central Government under the Industrial Employment (Standing Orders) Central Rules, 1946, can operate only during the period of time when the standing orders are not made by the Establishment itself. If and when those standing orders are made which, in any case, have to be compulsorily made in terms of the Act, they have to be submitted to the Certifying Officer and if they are certified, they take effect from the date on which they are notified and effectively replace the model standing orders. The order of the certifying officer is appealable before the Appellate Authority and the Appellate Authority can legally interfere with the order passed by the certifying officer and set it aside or uphold it. There is no restriction under the Act that the management or the establishment, or, for that matter, the employer would, adopt the model Standing Orders. It is contended that the standing orders have only to be in consonance with the model standing orders, besides being fair and reasonable.

The submission of the learned counsel for the respondent No. 1, on the contrary, is that the standing orders, as framed by the management, have to be on the lines indicated in the model standing orders and there cannot be a departure either in principle or policy from the model standing orders. It is contended that once it was provided by the model standing orders that an employee of the corporation can be represented by an employee of another establishment with the only restriction that he should be an office-bearer of a trade union, it was not open to the appellant to have made a provision in their standing orders that an employee of the Corporation would be represented in the disciplinary proceedings only by another employee of the Corporation. It is contended that this departure is impermissible in law and, therefore, the High Court was justified in setting aside the order of the appellate authority which had certified the draft standing orders submitted by the appellant.

The Supreme Court held that the Model Standing Orders, no doubt, provided that a delinquent employee could be represented in the disciplinary proceedings through another employee who may not be the employee of the parent establishment to which the delinquent belongs and may be an employee elsewhere, though he may be a member of the trade union, but this rule of representation has not been disturbed by the certified standing orders inasmuch as it still provides that the delinquent employee can be represented in the disciplinary proceedings through an employee. The only embargo is that the representative should be an employee of the parent establishment. The choice of the delinquent in selecting his representative is affected only to the extent that the representative has to be a co-employee of the same establishment in which the delinquent is employed. There appears to be some logic behind this as a co-employee would be fully aware of the conditions prevailing in the parent establishment, its service rules, including the standing orders, and would be in a better position, than an outsider, to assist the delinquent in the domestic proceedings for a fair and early disposal. The basic features of the model standing orders are thus retained and the right of representation in the disciplinary proceedings through another employee is not altered, affected or taken away. The standing orders conform to all standards of reasonableness and fairness and, therefore, the Appellate Authority was fully justified in certifying the Draft Standing Orders as submitted by the appellant.

Validity of Amended Standing Orders

The basic question which arose in *Harmohinder Singh* v. *Kharga Canteen, Ambala Cantt.*[9] was whether an employee's service can be terminated in accordance with the standing orders introduced subsequent to his entering a service. The fact of the case is as follows.

The appellant was appointed first as a salesman by the respondent canteen and subsequently as a cashier. The letter of appointment and the Standing Orders, *inter alia,* provided that the service of the appellant could be terminated by one month's notice by either party. The Standing Orders also provided that the "services of all canteen employees will be on temporary basis extendable on six monthly basis". In 1988, Para 3-A was introduced in the Standing Orders of the respondent. Amended Standing Order provided that maximum permissible service for an employee is 15 years. On completion of 15 years of service with the canteen, the appellant was terminated. The appellant challenged Standing Order as violative of S. 9A of the Industrial Disputes Act on grounds that changes in the conditions of service were made without any notice.

The Supreme Court held that the conditions of service for change of which notice is to be given under the Fourth Schedule of the Industrial Disputes Act does not, in terms, include the subject matter of amended Standing Orders, namely, the fixation of a period of service or date of retirement. No argument has been advanced as to which of the eleven items of Schedule 4 of the Industrial Disputes Act could, even by a process of interpretation, include the amended para of Standing Orders. There is nothing on record to show that prior to the introduction of amended para of Standing Orders, the workmen of the canteen continued as a matter of right till they reached the age of superannuation applicable to Government servants. On the contrary, the Standing Orders expressly provide that the services of canteen workers were temporary and for a period of six months. It cannot be said that the introduction of a maximum period of service would operate to the detriment of the employee who was otherwise entitled to serve only for six months and was liable to be dismissed merely upon service of a month's notice. Although the latter stipulation has been held to be unconstitutional as far as Government employees are concerned, but it would not be in case of the appellant who was not serving in or under the Government or any Governmental or Government controlled institution. It was not necessary, therefore, to give any notice to the workmen under S. 9A of the Act before introducing such change in the standing orders. Besides, the canteen's averment that the amended Standing Orders were duly intimated to all its employees, who had also signed the same, has not been controverted by the appellant.

Section 6: Appeals

(1) Any employer, workman, trade union or other prescribed representatives of the workmen aggrieved by the order of the Certifying Officer under sub-section (2) of section 5 may, within thirty days from the date on which copies are sent under sub-section (3) of that section, appeal to the appellate authority, and the appellate authority, whose decision shall be final, shall by order in writing confirm the standing

9. AIR 2001 SC 2681.

orders either in the form certified by the Certifying Officer or after amending the said standing orders by making such modifications thereof or additions thereto as it thinks necessary to render the standing orders certifiable under this Act.

(2) The appellate authority shall, within seven days of its order under sub-section (1), send copies thereof of the Certifying Officer, to the employer and to the trade union or other prescribed representatives of the workmen, accompanied, unless it has confirmed without amendment the standing orders as certified by the Certifying Officer, by copies of the standing orders as certified by it and authenticated in the prescribed manner.

Section 7: Date of operation of standing orders

Standing orders shall, unless an appeal is preferred under section 6, come into operation on the expiry of thirty days from the date on which authenticated copies thereof are sent under sub-section (3) of section 5, or where an appeal as aforesaid is preferred, on the expiry of seven days from the date on which copies of the order of the appellate authority are sent under sub-section (2) of section 6.

Section 8: Register of standing orders

A copy of all standing orders as finally certified under this Act shall be filed by the Certifying Officer in a register in the prescribed form maintained for the purpose, and the Certifying Officer shall furnish a copy thereof to any person applying therefor on payment of the prescribed fee.

Section 9: Posting of standing orders

The text of the standing orders as finally certified under this Act shall be prominently posted by the employer in English and in the language understood by the majority of his workmen on special boards to be maintained for the purpose at or near the entrance through which the majority of the workmen enter the industrial establishment and in all departments thereof where the workmen are employed.

Section 10: Duration and modification of standing orders

(1) Standing orders finally certified under this Act shall not, except on agreement between the employer and the workmen, or a trade union or other representative body of the workmen, be liable to modification until the expiry of six months from the date on which the standing orders or the last modifications thereof came into operation.

(2) Subject to the provisions of sub-section (1), an employer or workman or a trade union or other representative body of the workmen may apply to the Certifying Officer to have the standing orders modified, and such application shall be accompanied by five copies of the modifications proposed to be made, and where such modifications

are proposed to be made, by agreement between the employer and the workman or a trade union or other representative body of the workmen, a certified copy of that agreement shall be filed along with the application.

(3) The foregoing provisions of this Act shall apply in respect of an application under sub-section (2) as they apply to the certification of the first standing orders.

(4) Nothing contained in sub-section (2) shall apply to an industrial establishment in respect of which the appropriate Government is the Government of the State of Gujarat or the Government of the State of Maharashtra.

By amending S. 10(2) by the Amendment Act of 1956, both the workmen and the employer are given the right to apply for modification and due to the change made in S. 4, a modification has also now to be tested by the yardstick of fairness and reasonableness. The Act provides a speedy and cheap remedy available to the individual workman to have his conditions of service determined and also for their modification. By amending Ss. 4 and 10, Parliament not only broadened the scope of the Act but also gave a clear expression to the change in its legislative policy. Parliament knew that the workmen, even as the unamended Act stood, had the right to raise an industrial dispute, yet, not satisfied with such a remedy, it conferred by amending Ss. 4 and 10 the right to individual workmen to contest the draft standing orders submitted by the employer for certification on the ground that they are either not fair or reasonable, and more important still, the right to apply for their modification despite the finality of the order of the appellate authority under S. 6. Parliament thus deliberately gave a dual remedy to the workmen both under this Act and under the Industrial Disputes Act.

Section 10 does not state that once a standing order is modified and the modification is certified, no further modification is permissible except upon proof that new circumstances have arisen since the last modification. As a matter of fact, the legislature has not incorporated any words in the sub-section restricting the right to apply for modification, except of course the time limit of six months in sub-section (1).

Section 6 no doubt lays down that the order of the appellate authority in an appeal against the order of the certifying officer under S. 5 is final but that finality is itself subject to the right to apply for modification under S. 10(2). Therefore, it cannot be urged that the finality of the order under S. 6 was indicative of a condition precedent to the jurisdiction under S. 10(2) to entertain an application for modification on a new set of circumstances having arisen in the meantime. Section 6, when read with S. 12, indicates that the finality given to the certification by the appellate authority is against a challenge thereof in a Civil Court. But the finality given to the appellate authority's order is subject to the modification of those very standing orders certified by him. Section 10 itself does not lay down any restriction to the right to apply for modification. Apart from the right to apply for modification under the Act, the workmen can raise an industrial dispute with regard to standing orders. There is nothing in the Industrial Disputes Act restricting the right to raise such a dispute only when a new set of circumstances has arisen. If that right is unrestricted, it is not possible that the very legislature which passed both the Acts could have, while conferring the right on the workmen individually, restricted that right.[10]

10. *Shahdara (Delhi) Saharanpur Light Railway Co. Ltd.* v. *S.S. Railway Workers Union*, AIR 1969 SC 513.

The Act is a beneficent piece of legislation, and therefore unless compelled by any words in it, the Court would not be justified in importing in S. 10, through inference, only a restriction to the right conferred by it on account of supposed danger of multiplicity of applications. The policy of S. 10 is clear that a modification should not be allowed within six months from the date when the standing orders or the last modifications thereof came into operation. The object of providing the time limit was that the standing orders or their modification should be allowed to work for sufficiently long time to see whether they work properly or not. Even that time limit is not rigid because a modification even before six months is permissible if there is an agreement between the parties.

An application for modification would ordinarily be made where:

(1) a change of circumstances has occurred, or
(2) where experience of the working of the standing orders last certified results in inconvenience, hardship, anomaly, etc., or
(3) where some fact was lost sight of at the time of certification, or
(4) where the applicant feels that a modification will be more beneficial.

In category (1), there would be no difficulty as a change of circumstances has taken place. But in cases falling under the remaining three categories, there will be no change of circumstances. But that does not mean that though the implementation of the standing orders has resulted in hardship, inconvenience or anomaly, no modification can be asked for because there is no change of circumstances. In an application for modification, the issue before the authority would be not as to the reasonableness or fairness of the standing orders or their last modification, but whether the modification now applied for is fair and reasonable. Therefore, the contention that a change of circumstances is a condition precedent to the maintainability of an application under S. 10(2), or that an application for modification without proof of such a change amounts to review by the same authority of its previous order, is not correct.[11]

It has been urged in *Workmen of Dewan Tea Estate* v. *Their Management*[12] that the standing orders, which were duly certified under the Standing Orders Act, came into force in 1950, whereas S. 2(kkk), which defines a lay off under the Industrial Disputes Act, was added to the Act by the Amending Act 43 of 1953 on October 24, 1953. His argument is that the Standing Orders having been certified before the definition of the lay off was introduced in the Act, the management, the respondent in the instant case, is entitled to rely upon the said definition in support of the plea that the impugned lay off was justified. The Court observed that Standing Orders of the Dewan Tea Estate which were duly certified under the Industrial Employment (Standing Orders) Act (1946) and which came into force in 1950 became part of the statutory terms and conditions of service between the industrial employer and his employees. If the Standing Orders thus became part of the statutory terms and conditions of service, they would govern the relations between the parties unless, of course, it can be shown that any provision of the Industrial Disputes Act is inconsistent with the said Standing Orders. In that case, it may be permissible to urge that the statutory provision contained in the Act should override the Standing Order which had been certified before the said statutory provision was enacted.

11. *Ibid.*
12. AIR 1964 SC 1458.

In *Ghaziabad Engineering Co. Pvt. Ltd., M/s.* v. *Certifying Officer*[13] the question raised before the Supreme Court was whether the modification of the Standing Orders under the Industrial Employment (Standing Orders) Act, 1946 and the rules framed there under was illegally made by the Certifying Officer. The Court held that the modification itself related to grant of six days' casual leave (on a paid basis) to the workers in the appellant's factory in Ghaziabad. The certifying officer has considered this grant of casual leave as fair and reasonable having regard to the prevalent practice in the neighbouring industries of this industrial belt and also paying attention to the financial position of the appellant's undertaking. For this purpose, he has relied upon the fact that 20% bonus was paid under the Payment of Bonus Act, 1965 and has further stated that certain other factories have been giving paid casual leave for their workers. These facts persuaded him to grant the modification, although reducing the number of days to six as against twelve which the workers originally claimed. The Appellate Authority concurred by a separate discussion in the same conclusion. These are pure questions of fact and the Supreme Court's jurisdiction under Art. 136 cannot be exploited for canvassing points such as these. It is clear that the modifications was within the jurisdiction of the Certifying Officer and he has not contravened any provision of the Act, or any statute.

SECTION 10A: Payment of subsistence allowance

(1) Where any workman is suspended by the employer pending investigation or inquiry into complaints or charges of misconduct against him, the employer shall pay to such workman subsistence allowance—

(a) at the rate of fifty per cent of the wages which the workman was entitled to immediately preceding the date of such suspension, for the first ninety days of suspension; and

(b) at the rate of seventy-five per cent of such wages for the remaining period of suspension if the delay in the completion of disciplinary proceedings against such workman is not directly attributable to the conduct of such workman.

(2) If any dispute arises regarding the subsistence allowance payable to a workman under sub-section (1), the workman or the employer concerned may refer the dispute to the Labour Court, constituted under the Industrial Disputes Act, 1947 (14 of 1947), within the local limits of whose jurisdiction the industrial establishment wherein such workman is employed is situate and the Labour Court to which the dispute is so referred shall, after giving the parties an opportunity of being heard, decide the dispute and such decision shall be final and binding on the parties.

(3) Notwithstanding anything contained in the foregoing provisions of this section, where provisions relating to payment of subsistence allowance under any other law for the time being in force in any State are more beneficial than the provisions of this section, the provisions of such other law shall be applicable to the payment of subsistence allowance in that State.

13. AIR 1978 SC 769.

It is clear from S. 10A that the employer is required to pay subsistence allowance to a workman suspended pending inquiry at the rate of 50 per cent of wages for the first 90 days and at the rate of 75 per cent of wages for the remaining period of suspension, if delay in completion of disciplinary proceedings is not directly attributable to the conduct of the workman concerned. If under S. 10A(1)(b) of the Act only the words '*attributable to*' were used, the position would have been different but prefixing the word '*directly*' to the words '*attributable to*' makes a big difference to emphasise that in order to deny a workman subsistence allowance at the rate of 75 per cent, the delay should be directly attributable to the conduct of such workman in completion of disciplinary proceedings and not that every kind of delay is covered by the said provision. If that was the intention of the legislature, there was no need for emphasis by adding the word *'directly'* and instead they would have simply used the words *'attributable to'*. In the field of interpretation of statutes the Courts always presume that the legislature inserted every part thereof with a purpose and the legislative intention is that every part of the statute should have effect. Further, it cannot be said that a word or words used in a statute are either unnecessary or superfluous unless there are compelling reasons to say so, looking at the scheme of the statute having regard to the object and purpose sought to be achieved by it. In this view, the use of the word *'directly'* in the provision has to be given meaning and effect in the context of the said provision under the scheme of the Act. A plain reading and clear understanding of S. 10-A(1)(b) excludes the delay in completion of disciplinary proceedings caused on account of order granted by a competent court from the mischief of the said provision. It is only the delay that is directly attributable to the workman is covered by the said provision.

Where a workman is suspended by the employer, pending investigation or inquiry into a complaint or charges of misconduct against such workman, a statutory obligation is cast on the employer under the said provision to pay subsistence allowance at the rate mentioned and such a workman has a statutory right to get subsistence allowance. However, as an exception, a workman can be denied payment of subsistence allowance at the rate of 75 per cent after expiry of 90 days of suspension if the delay in the completion of disciplinary proceedings is directly attributable to the conduct of such workman.[14]

The word *"attribute"* means *"to ascribe to as belonging or pertaining"*, as stated in 'Words and Phrases' Permanent Edition. According to P. Ramanatha Aiyar's *Law Lexicon*, "attributable is a plain English word involving some casual connection between the loss of employment and that to which the loss is said to be attributable". This connection need not be that of a sole, dominant, direct or proximate cause and effect. A contributory casual connection is quite sufficient.

When a workman approaches a competent Court *bona fidely* to protect himself from the prejudice likely to be caused by continuing proceedings simultaneously in domestic inquiry, as also in the criminal case grounded on the same set of facts and succeeds in getting order from a competent judicial authority staying further proceedings in the disciplinary proceedings till the disposal of the criminal case, it cannot be said that delay on that account in completion of disciplinary proceedings is directly attributable to the conduct of such workman. It cannot be denied that a workman is also entitled to a free and fair trial in the criminal case. Hence, if a workman, in order to protect himself from the prejudice that may be caused by simultaneous

14. *B.D. Shetty* v. *M/s. Ceat Ltd.*, AIR 2001 SC 2953.

proceedings, approaches a competent judicial authority and that authority, on being satisfied, taking into consideration the facts and circumstances of the case, stays further proceedings in a domestic inquiry pending a criminal trial, the delay caused on that account in completion of domestic inquiry cannot be directly attributable to the conduct of such workman, because granting stay of further proceedings in a domestic inquiry does not depend on the pleasure or mere wish of a workman himself.[15]

After a careful reading of S. 10A of the Standing Orders Act, it appears that the delay which is directly attributable to the conduct of the workman in the said provision is obviously to the one where the workman unjustifiably, deliberately or designedly drags on or prolongs the domestic inquiry. To put it in other way, a workman cannot be permitted to take advantage of delay caused by himself in the absence of any order passed by a Court. If such a delay is also to be taken as covered by S. 10-A(1)(b), it may amount to, in a way, putting restraint or clog on the exercise of legal right of a workman to approach a court of law out of fear of losing subsistence allowance at the rate of 75 per cent. It is one thing to say that in a given case there should be no stay of disciplinary proceedings. It is another thing to say that in case stay is granted, there will be delay in completion of disciplinary proceedings, which is directly attributable to the conduct of a workman. Merely because legal proceedings will be pending in a court or before other authority and they take sometime for disposal, maybe inevitably, that itself cannot be the ground to deny subsistence allowance to a workman against a statutory obligation created on the employer under S. 10-A(1)(b). One must not lose sight of the fact that the Act is a beneficial piece of legislation and the provision of subsistence allowance made is intended to serve a definite purpose of sustaining the workman and his family members during the bad time when he is under suspension pending inquiry.

Section 11: Certifying officers and appellate authorities to have powers of Civil Court

(1) Every Certifying Officer and appellate authority shall have all the powers of a Civil Court for the purposes of receiving evidence, administering oaths, enforcing the attendance of witnesses, and compelling the discovery and production of documents, and shall be deemed to be a Civil Court within the meaning of sections 345 and 346 of the Code of Criminal Procedure, 1973 (2 of 1974).

(2) Clerical or arithmetical mistakes in any order passed by a Certifying Officer or appellate authority, or errors arising therein from any accidental slip or omission may, at any time, be corrected by that Officer or authority or the successor in office of such Officer or authority, as the case may be.

Section 12: Oral evidence in contradiction of standing orders not admissible

No oral evidence having the effect of adding to or otherwise varying or contradicting standing orders as finally certified under this Act shall be admitted in any Court.

---

15. *Ibid.*

SECTION 12A: Temporary application of model standing orders

(1) Notwithstanding anything contained in sections 3 to 12, for the period commencing on the date on which this Act becomes applicable to an industrial establishment and ending with the date on which the standing orders as finally certified under this Act come into operation under section 7 in that establishment, the prescribed model standing orders shall be deemed to be adopted in that establishment, and the provisions of section 9, sub-section (2) of section 13 and section 13A shall apply to such model standing orders as they apply to the standing orders so certified.

(2) Nothing contained in sub-section (1) shall apply to an industrial establishment in respect of which the appropriate Government is the Government of the State of Gujarat or the Government of the State of Maharashtra.

SECTION 13: Penalties and procedure

(1) An employer who fails to submit draft standing orders as required by section 3, or who modifies his standing orders otherwise than in accordance with section 10, shall be punishable with fine which may extend to five thousand rupees, and in the case of a continuing offence with a further fine which may extend to two hundred rupees for every day after the first during which the offence continues.

(2) An employer who does any act in contravention of the standing orders finally certified under this Act or his industrial establishment shall be punishable with fine which may extend to one hundred rupees, and in the case of a continuing offence with a further fine which may extend to twenty-five rupees for every day after the first during which the offence continues.

(3) No prosecution for an offence punishable under this section shall be instituted except with the previous sanction of the appropriate Government.

(4) No Court inferior to that of a Metropolitan Magistrate or Judicial Magistrate of the second class shall try any offence under this section.

SECTION 13A: Interpretation, etc., of standing orders

If any question arises as to the application or interpretation of a standing order certified under this Act, any employer or workman or a trade union or other representative body of the workmen may refer the question to any one of the Labour Courts constituted under the Industrial Disputes Act, 1947 (14 of 1947), and specified for the disposal of such proceeding by the appropriate Government by notification in the Official Gazette, and the Labour Court to which the question is so referred shall, after giving the parties an opportunity of being heard, decide the question and such decision shall be final and binding on the parties.

A bare reading of S. 13A would show that whenever the question arises relating to the interpretation of a Certified Standing Order, any of the parties, namely, either the employer or the employee, may refer the question of necessary decision on such dispute in relation to interpretation to any of the Labour Court constituted under the Industrial Disputes Act, 1947. When such dispute is referred, the Labour Court is enjoined to decide the same after hearing the parties and such decision is to be final and binding upon the parties. Undoubtedly, therefore, the Standing Orders Act makes a specific provision regarding the disputes pertaining to the interpretation of the Standing Orders and also the authority who should decide the same. It is , however, to be noted that the Standing Orders Act, either in S. 13-A or under any other provision of the Act, nowhere excludes the jurisdiction of the Industrial Court to deal with the issue pertaining to the interpretation of the clauses of the Standing Orders when such issue arises as an incidental issue in any proceedings pending before the Court. Neither S. 13-A on the face of it provides for exclusive jurisdiction to the Labour Court under the said provision as the sole authority to deal with the issue pertaining to the interpretation of the Standing Orders or the clauses thereof, nor it provides that when any such issue arises in any of the proceedings pending before any other Court, the same should refer to the Labour Court in terms of S. 13-A of the Standing Orders Act.[16]

Section 13-A of the Standing Orders Act enables an employer or a workman or a trade union or other representative body of the workmen to refer to the Labour Court any question relating to the application or interpretation of a standing order. The question that came before the Supreme Court in *Management of the Bangalore Woollen, Cotton and Silk Mills Co. Ltd.* v. *Workmen*[17] was whether the Industrial Tribunal will have the jurisdiction under the Industrial Disputes Act to adjudicate upon any disputes in relation to matters covered by the Standing Orders under the Standing Orders Act. The Court observed that the Standing Orders Act, which has for its object, the defining, with sufficient precision, the conditions of employment, under the industrial establishments and to make the said conditions known to the workmen employed by them, has provided more or less a speedy remedy to the workman, for the purpose of having a standing order modified, or for having any question relating to the application, or interpretation of a standing order, referred to a Labour Court. Accordingly, the Court held:

> "in our opinion, for holding that merely because the Standing Orders Act is a self-contained statute, with regard to the matters mentioned therein, the jurisdiction of the Industrial Tribunal, under the Act, to adjudicate upon the matters, covered by the standing orders, has been, in any manner, abridged or taken away. It will always be open, in a proper case, for the Union to raise an 'industrial dispute', as that expression is defined in S. 2(k) of the Act, and, if such a dispute is referred by the Government concerned, for adjudication, the Industrial Tribunal or Labour Court, as the case may be, will have jurisdiction to adjudicate, upon the same. But, it must also be borne in mind that an "industrial dispute, has to be raised by the Union, before it can be referred and it is not unlikely that a Union must be persuaded to raise the dispute, though the grievance of a particular workman, or a member of the Union, be otherwise well founded. Even if the Union takes up the dispute, the State Government may, or may not, refer it to the Industrial Tribunal. The discretion of the State Government, under S. 10 of the Act, is very wide. It may be that the workmen, affected by the standing orders, may not always, and in every case, succeed in obtaining a reference to the Industrial Tribunal, on a relevant point. These are some of the circumstances for giving a right and a remedy, to the workman, under the Standing Orders Act itself, but there is no indication, in the scheme of the Standing Orders Act, that the jurisdiction of the industrial Tribunal, to entertain an Industrial dispute, bearing upon the standing orders of an industrial establishment, and to adjudicate upon the same, has in any manner been abridged, or taken away, by the Standing Orders Act."[18]

16. *Welcom Group Searock Land's End* v. *Trayambak KarbhariWagh and Another*, 2003 (4) LLN 558.
17. AIR 1968 SC 585.
18. *Ibid.* f.n. 17 at p. 594 Vaidialingam, J.

Natural Justice vis-à-vis Section 13A

In *Lakshmi Precision Screws Ltd., M/s.* v. *Ram Bahagat*[19] the question that arose before the Supreme Court in 2002 was whether the principle of natural justice would be considered while interpreting any of the provision of the Standing Orders. Before dealing the issue in the instant case, it is necessary to have a look at the facts of the case and they are as follows.

The petitioner company engaged Ram Bahagat, the respondent-workman, on 8-12-1980. He continued to work till 12-10-1990 and thereafter absented himself without any prior information with effect from 13-10-1990. The Management waited for some days and eventually addressed a communication dated 17-10-1990 to the workman informing him that he had been absenting himself from duty with effect from 13-10-1990, without authorised leave or notice, he was advised to report back on duty within 48 hours of the receipt of the aforesaid letter and also to tender his explanation for his absence. In the letter dated 17-10-1990, he was warned that in case he failed to report for duty within the specified time, it would be presumed that he was no longer interested in serving the management and his name would be struck off from the rolls of the company under the Certified Standing Orders of the Company. The respondent workman did not comply with the condition stipulated in the letter dated 17-10-1990. He was informed through registered post, vide letter dated 25-10-1990, that his name had been removed from the muster rolls of the company. A perusal of the aforesaid letter shows that the aforesaid action had been taken under Cl. 9(f)(ii) of the Certified Standing Orders of the Company, in view of the fact that the respondent-workman had remained absent from duty for a period of 10 days continuously. Clause 9(f)(ii) of the Certified Standing Orders of the Company is being reproduced hereunder:

"9(f) Any workman who,

*** *** ***

(ii) absents himself for ten consecutive working days without leave shall be deemed to have left the firm's service without notice, thereby terminating his service."

The respondent-workman addressed a letter dated 30-1-1991, requesting the management to take him back on duty. In the aforesaid letter, he informed the management that he had been unwell during the period of his absence. In this behalf, he also enclosed his medical certificate as also a fitness certificate. In the letter dated 30-1-1991, he made a reference of the earlier letter dated 24-10-1990 sent by him to the management, requesting for leave on medical grounds. On the same date, i.e., 30-1-1991, he was informed that he had remained absent from duty without getting sanctioned leave and without any notice to the management, and that his name had been struck off from the rolls of the company under the Certified Standing Orders of the Company, vide letter dated 25-10-1990. Accordingly, the request of the respondent-workman for being taken back on duty was declined.

Having failed to persuade the management to take him back into service, the respondent-workman served a demand notice dated 29-3-1991. On failure of conciliation proceedings, the State Government made a reference of the dispute raised by the respondent-workman to the Presiding Officer, Labour Court, Rohtak.

On the basis of the evidence produced by the respondent-workman, the Labour Court concluded that almost the whole period of alleged absence of the respondent-workman was

19. AIR 2002 SC 2914.

proved to be on account of his illness and the respondent-workman's absence from duty was not intentional. Having arrived at the aforesaid conclusion, the Labour Court considered the validity of the order of the management on the basis of Cl. 9(f)(ii) of the Certified Standing Orders of the Company and held that the action of the management in terminating the services of the respondent-workman was not justified and thus ordered his reinstatement with continuity in service along with 67 per cent back wages. Aggrieved by the award of the Labour Court dated 1-2-1999, the management approached the High Court through a writ petition under Art. 226 of the Constitution. Significantly, the High Court did not, however, any misreading or misappreciation of evidence resulting into perversity as regards the order of the Tribunal and thus concurred upon the conclusion of the Tribunal. The petitioner-company invoked Art. 136 of the Constitution and approached the Supreme Court.

The Court, while considering the fact of the case observed that the rejection of the claim of the respondent-workman is absolutely arbitrary and without consideration of the material placed on record by the respondent-workman. The Labour Court examined in detail the factual position and returned a finding that the respondent-workman had not absented himself from service deliberately or intentionally and also that he had not abandoned his service. It was further concluded that his absence was based on account of his illness which could be affirmed from the medical certificates produced by him. In the aforesaid view of the matter, in our considered view, the action of the petitioner-management in rejecting the representation of the respondent-workman dated 30-1-1991 was clearly arbitrary and as such it is not sustainable in law. The Court further held that arbitrariness is an antithesis to rule of law: equity: fair play and justice—contract of employment there may be but it cannot be devoid of the basic principles of the concept of justice. Justice-oriented approach, as is the present trend in Indian jurisprudence, shall have to read as an in-built requirement of the basic of concept of justice, to wit, the doctrine of natural justice, fairness, equality and rule of law. The letter dated 17 October cannot by any stretch be treated to be an opportunity since it is only on the fourth day that such a letter was sent—the action of the appellant herein stands out to be devoid of any justification, neither it depicts acceptability of the doctrine of natural justice or the concept of fairness.

In *Managing Director, ECIL, Hyderabad* v. *B. Karunakar*,[20] the Constitution Bench of the Supreme Court held that when the Inquiry Officer is not the disciplinary authority, the delinquent employee has a right to receive a copy of the Inquiry Officer's report before the disciplinary authority arrives at its conclusions with regard to the guilt or innocence of the employee with regard to the charges levelled against him. That right is a part of the employee's right to defend himself against the charges levelled against him. A denial of the Inquiry Officer's report, before the disciplinary authority takes its decision on the charges, is a denial of reasonable opportunity to the employee to prove his innocence and is a breach of the principles of natural justice. Since the denial of the report of the Inquiry Officer is a denial of reasonable opportunity and a breach of the principles of natural justice, it follows that the statutory rules, if any, which deny the report to the employee are against the principles of natural justice and, therefore, invalid. The delinquent employee will, therefore, be entitled to a copy of the report even if the statutory rules do not permit the furnishing of the report

20. AIR 1994 SC 1074.

or are silent on the subject. Since it is the right of the employee to have the report to defend himself effectively, and he would not know in advance whether the report is in his favour or against him, it will not be proper to construe his failure to ask for the report, as the waiver of his right. Whether, therefore, the employee asks for the report or not, the report has to be furnished to him.

Although on account of the 42nd Amendment of the Constitution, it was no longer necessary to issue a notice to the delinquent employee to show cause against the punishment proposed and, therefore, to furnish a copy of the Inquiry Officer's report along with the notice to make representation against the penalty. Whenever the Inquiry Officer is other than the disciplinary authority and the report of the Inquiry Officer holds the employee guilty of all or any of the charges with proposal for any punishment or not, the delinquent employee is entitled to a copy of the report to enable him to make a representation to the disciplinary authority against it and the non-furnishing of the report amounts to a violation of the rules of natural justice. This was the law laid down in *Mohd. Ramzan Khan's* case[21] and it is appropriate that the said law should apply to employees in all establishments whether Government or non-Government, public or private. This will be the case whether there are rules governing the disciplinary proceeding or not and whether they expressly prohibit the furnishing of the copy of the report or are silent on the subject. Whatever be the nature of punishment, or whenever the rules require an inquiry to be held, for inflicting the punishment in question, the delinquent employee should have the benefit of the report of the Inquiry Officer before the disciplinary authority records its findings on the charges levelled against him.

When the employee is dismissed or removed from service and the inquiry is set aside because the report is not furnished to him, in some cases the non-furnishing of the report may have prejudiced him gravely, while in other cases it may have made no difference to the ultimate punishment awarded to him. Hence, to direct reinstatement of the employee with back-wages in all cases is to reduce the rules of justice to a mechanical ritual. The theory of reasonable opportunity and the principles of natural justice have been evolved to uphold the rule of law and to assist the individual to vindicate his just rights. They are not incantations to be invoked nor rites to be performed on all and sundry occasions. Whether, in fact, prejudice has been caused to the employee or not on account of the denial to him of the report has to be considered on the facts and circumstances of each case. Where, therefore, even after the furnishing of the report, no different consequence would have followed, it would be a perversion of justice to permit the employee to resume duty and to get all the consequential benefits. It amounts to rewarding the dishonest and the guilty and thus to stretching the concept of justice to illogical and exasperating limits. It amounts to an "unnatural expansion of natural justice", which in itself is antithetical to justice.

Hence, in all cases where the Inquiry Officer's report is not furnished to the delinquent employee in the disciplinary proceedings, the Courts and Tribunals should cause the copy of the report to be furnished to the aggrieved employee if he has not already secured it before coming to the Court/Tribunal, and give the employee an opportunity to show how his or her case was prejudiced because of the non-supply of the report. If after hearing the parties, the

21. *Union of India* v. *Mohd. Ramzan Khan*, AIR 1991 SC 471.

Court/Tribunal comes to the conclusion that the non-supply of the report would have made no difference to the ultimate findings and the punishment given, the Court/Tribunal should not interfere with the order of punishment. The Court/Tribunal should not mechanically set aside the order of punishment on the ground that the report was not furnished. The courts should avoid resorting to short-cuts. Since it is the Court/Tribunal which will apply their judicial mind to the question and give their reasons for setting aside or not setting aside the order of punishment, (and not any internal appellate or revisional authority), there would neither be a breach of the principles of natural justice nor a denial of the reasonable opportunity. It is only if the Court/Tribunal finds that the furnishing of the report would have made a difference to the result in the case that it should set aside the order of punishment. Where, after following the above procedure, the Court/Tribunal sets aside the order of punishment, the proper relief that should be granted is to direct reinstatement of the employee with liberty to the authority/management to proceed with the inquiry, by placing the employee under suspension and continuing the inquiry from the stage of furnishing him with the report. The question whether the employee would be entitled to the back-wages and other benefits from the date of his dismissal to the date of his reinstatement, if ultimately ordered, should invariably be left to be decided by the authority concerned according to law, after the culmination of the proceedings and depending on the final outcome. If the employee succeeds in the fresh inquiry and is directed to be reinstated, the authority should be at liberty to decide according to law how it will treat the period from the date of dismissal till the reinstatement and to what benefits, if any, and the extent of the benefits, he will be entitled. The reinstatement made as a result of the setting aside of the inquiry for failure to furnish the report should be treated as a reinstatement for the purpose of holding the fresh inquiry from the stage of furnishing the report and no more, where such fresh inquiry is held. That will also be the correct position in law. A similar view has been taken by the Supreme Court in 2004 in *N.T.C. (WBAB and O) Ltd.* v. *Anjan K. Saha.*[22]

Section 13B: Act not to apply to certain industrial establishments

Nothing in this Act shall apply to an industrial establishment in so far as the workmen employed therein are persons to whom the Fundamental and Supplementary Rules, Civil Services (Classification, Control and Appeal) Rules, Civil Services (Temporary Services) Rules, Revised Leave Rules, Civil Service Regulations, Civilians in Defence Service (Classification, Control and Appeal) Rules or the Indian Railway Establishment Code or any other rules or regulations that may be notified in this behalf by the appropriate Government in the Official Gazette, apply.

In the case of *U.P. State Electricity Board* v. *Hari Shanker Jain,*[23] three questions were raised before the Full Bench of Allahabad High Court for consideration and they are as follows.

(1) Whether the Industrial Employment (Standing Orders) Act, 1946 applies to the industrial establishments of the State Electricity Board?

22. AIR 2004 SC 4255.
23. AIR 1979 SC 65.

(2) Whether the Standing Orders framed for an industrial establishment of an electrical undertaking case to be operative on the purchase of the undertaking by the Board or on the framing of regulations under Section 79(c) of the Electricity (Supply) Act, 1948?

(3) Whether Section 13-B of the Industrial Employment (Standing Orders) Act, 1946, applies only to industrial establishments of the Government or also to other industrial establishments?

The Full Bench answered the question as follows:

1. The Industrial Employment (Standing Orders) Act, 1946 applies to the industrial establishment of the State Electricity Board.
2. The Standing Orders framed in an industrial establishment by an electrical undertaking do not cease to be operative on the purchase of the undertaking by the Board or on framing of the regulations under S. 79(c) of the Electricity (Supply) Act, 1948.
3. Section 13-B of the Industrial Employment (Standing Orders) Act, 1946, applies only to the industrial establishments of the government and to no other establishments.

Therefore, the U.P. State Electricity Board, having obtained a certificate from the High Court under Art. 133(1) of the Constitution, has moved the Supreme Court on appeal.

Shri P.K. Garg, advocate for the workmen, contended that the Industrial Employment (Standing Orders) Act was an Act specially designed to define and secure reasonable conditions of service for workmen in industrial establishments employing one hundred or more workmen, and to that end to compel employers to make Standing Orders and to get them certified by a quasi-judicial authority. It was, therefore, a special Act with reference to its subject matter. The Electricity (Supply) Act, on the other hand, was intended "to provide for the rationalisation of the production and supply of electricity, and generally for taking measures conducive to electrical development". It was not specially designed to define the conditions of service of employees of Electricity Boards or to displace the Standing Orders Act. The power given to an Electricity Board under S. 79(c) to make regulations providing for "the duties of officers and servants of the Board and their salaries, allowances and other conditions of service" was not more than the usual, general power possessed by every employer. Shri Grag argued that the Industrial Employment (Standing Orders) Act was a Special Act which dealt with the special subject of conditions of employment of workmen in industrial establishments and, therefore, in the matter of conditions of employment of workmen in industrial establishments, it prevailed over the provisions of the Electricity (Supply) Act. He urged that under S. 13-B of the Standing Orders Act, Government undertakings which had a comprehensive set of rules alone could be excluded from the applicability of the Act. He submitted that to permit a single rule or regulation made for a limited purpose to be notified under S. 13-B would have the disastrous effect of excluding the applicability of the whole of the Standing Orders Act.

The Court, while considering the object of the Directive Principles of State Policy enshrined in the Constitution of India in general and Arts. 42 and 43 in particular, held that the Industrial Employment (Standing Orders) Act is a special Act dealing with a specific subject, namely the conditions of service, enumerated in the Schedule, of workmen in industrial establishments. It is impossible to conceive that Parliament sought to abrogate the provisions of the Industrial Employment (Standing Orders) Act embodying as they do hard-won and precious right of workmen and prescribing as they do an elaborate procedure, including a quasi-judicial determination, by a general, incidental provision like S. 79(c) of the Electricity (Supply) Act. It is obvious that Parliament did not have before it the Standing Orders Act when it passed the Electricity (Supply) Act and Parliament never meant that the Standing Orders Act should stand *pro tanto* repealed by S. 79(c) of the Electricity (Supply) Act. Therefore, the provision of the Standing Orders Act must prevail over S. 79(c) of the Electricity (Supply) Act in regard to matters to which the Standing Orders Act applies.

The High Court in the instant case interpreted the expression *"any other rules or regulations"* contained in S. 13-B of the Standing Orders Act and held that these words should be read *ejusdem generis* with the expressions *"Fundamental and Supplementary Rules, Civil Services (Classification, Control and Appeal) Rules"* etc. and accordingly the High Court said that the provisions of S. 13-B could only be applied to industrial establishments in which the workmen employed could properly be described as Government servants. However, the Supreme Court is unable to agree that the application of the *ejusdem generis* rule leads to any such result. The true scope of the rule of *"ejusdem generis"* is that words of a general nature following specific and particular words should be construed as limited to things which are of the same nature as those specified. But the rule is one which has to be "applied with caution and not pushed too far". It is a rule which must be confined to narrow bounds so as not to unduly or unnecessarily limit general and comprehensive words. Therefore, the Supreme Court held that if a broad-based genus could consistently be discovered, there is no warrant to cut down general words to dwarf size. If giant it cannot be, dwarf it need not be. It is true that in S. 13-B the species specifically mentioned happens to be Government servants. But they also possess this common characteristic that they are all public servants enjoying a statutory status, and governed by statutory rules and regulations.

The Court further read different expressions, like *'rules and regulations'* and *"workmen ... to whom ... any other rules or regulations that may be notified in this behalf"* of S. 13-B and held that the words 'rules and regulations' have come to acquire a special meaning when used in statutes. They are used to describe subordinate legislation made by the authorities to whom the statute delegates that function. The words can have no other meaning in S. 13-B. Therefore, the expression "workmen ... to whom ... any other rules or regulations that may be notified in this behalf" means, in the context of S. 13-B, workmen enjoying a statutory status, in respect of whose conditions of service the relevant statute authorises the making of rules or regulations. The expression cannot be construed so narrowly as to mean Government servants only; nor can it be construed so broadly as to mean workmen employed by whomsoever, including private employers, so long as their conditions of service are notified by the Government under S. 13-B.

After considering the above stated argument, the Supreme Court, finally, held that the Industrial Employment (Standing Orders) Act is a special law in regard to the matters enumerated in the schedule and the regulations made by the Electricity Board, with respect to any of those matters, are of no effect unless such regulations are either notified by the Government under S. 13-B or certified by the Certifying Officer under S. 5 of the Industrial

Employment (Standing Orders) Act. In regard to matters in respect of which regulations made by the Electricity Board have not been notified by the Governor, or in respect of which no regulations have been made by the Board, the Industrial Employment (Standing Orders) Act shall continue to apply. In the present case, the regulation made by the Board with regard to age of superannuation having been duly notified by the Government, the regulation shall have effect notwithstanding the fact that it is a matter which could be the subject matter of Standing Orders under the Industrial Employment (Standing Orders) Act. A similar issue came before the Supreme Court in 1984 in *U.P. State Electricity Board* v. *Labour Court (I) U.P. Kanpur*[24] where Regulations of the Electricity Board were notified under S. 13-B of the Industrial Employment (Standing orders) Act, 1946. Therefore, the Court held that the regulation made by the Board with regard to the age of superannuation had been duly notified by the Government and it has been held that the regulation had effect notwithstanding the fact that it was a matter which could be the subject matter of standing orders under the Industrial Employment (Standing orders) Act, 1946.

SECTION 14: Power to exempt

The appropriate Government may by notification in the Official Gazette exempt, conditionally or unconditionally, any industrial establishment or class of industrial establishments from all or any of the provisions of this Act.

SECTION 14A: Delegation of powers

The appropriate Government may, by notification in the Official Gazette, direct that any power exercisable by it under this Act or any rules made thereunder shall, in relation to such matters and subject to such conditions, if any, as may be specified in the direction, be exercisable also—

(a) where the appropriate Government is the Central Government, by such officer or authority subordinate to the Central Government or by the State Government or by such officer or authority subordinate to the State Government, as may be specified in the notification;

(b) where the appropriate Government is a State Government, by such officer or authority subordinate to the State Government as may be specified in the notification.

SECTION 15: Power to make rules

(1) The appropriate Government may, after previous publication, by notification in the Official Gazette, make rules to carry out the purposes of this Act.

(2) In particular and without prejudice to the generality of the foregoing power, such rules may—

24. AIR 1984 SC 1450.

(a) prescribe additional matters to be included in the Schedule, and the procedure to be followed in modifying standing orders certified under this Act in accordance with any such addition;

(b) set out model standing orders for the purposes of this Act;

(c) prescribe the procedure of Certifying Officers and appellate authorities;

(d) prescribe the fee which may be charged for copies of standing order entered in the register of standing orders;

(e) provide for any other matter which is to be or may be prescribed:

Provided that before any rules are made under clause (a) representatives of both employers and workmen shall be consulted by the appropriate Government.

(3) Every rule made by the Central Government under this section shall be laid as soon as may be after it is made, before each House of Parliament while it is in session for a total period of thirty days which may be comprised in one session or in two or more successive sessions, and if, before the expiry of the session immediately following the session or the successive sessions aforesaid both Houses agree in making any modification in the rule or both Houses agree that the rule should not be made, the rule shall thereafter have effect only in such modified form or be of no effect, as the case may be; so however that any such modification or annulment shall be without prejudice to the validity of anything previously done under that rule.

The appropriate Government is having absolute power under S. 15 of the Act to include any matter in the Schedule. When the appropriate Government adds any item to the Schedule, the relevant question to ask would be whether it refers to the conditions of employment or not. If it does, it would be within the competence of the appropriate Government to add such an item. Section 15(1) confers wide powers on the appropriate Government to make rules to carry out the purposes of the Act; and S. 15(2) specifies some of the matters enumerated by Cls. (a) to (e), in respect of which rules may be framed. It is well settled that the enumeration of the particular matters by sub-section (2) will not control or limit the width of the powers conferred on the appropriate Government by sub-section (1) of S. 15; and so, if it appears that the item added by the appropriate Government has relation to conditions of employment, its addition cannot be challenged as being invalid in law. Whether or not such addition should be made, is a matter for the appropriate Government to decide in its discretion. The reasonableness of such addition cannot be questioned, because the power to decide which additions should be made has been left by the legislature to the appropriate Government. Having regard to the development of industrial law in this country during recent years, it cannot be said that gratuity or provident fund is not a term of conditions of employment in industrial establishments.[25]

---

25. *Rohtak and Hissar Districts Electric Supply Co. Ltd.* v. *State of U.P.*, AIR 1966 SC 1471.

THE SCHEDULE

[*See* Sections 2(g) and 3(2)]

MATTERS TO BE PROVIDED IN STANDING ORDERS UNDER THIS ACT

1. Classification of workmen, e.g., whether permanent, temporary, apprentices, probationers, badlies or fixed term employment.
2. Manner of intimating to workmen periods and hours of work, holidays, paydays and wage rates.
3. Shift working.
4. Attendance and late coming.
5. Conditions of procedure in applying for, and the authority which may grant leave and holidays.
6. Requirement to enter premises by certain gates, and liability to search.
7. Closing and reopening of sections of the industrial establishment, and temporary stoppages of work and the rights and liabilities of the employer and workmen arising therefrom.
8. Termination of employment, and the notice thereof to be given by employer and workmen.
9. Suspension or dismissal for misconduct, and acts or omissions which constitute misconduct.
10. Means of redress for workmen against unfair treatment or wrongful exactions by the employer or his agents or servants.
11. Any other matter which may be prescribed.

The nature and scope of the several clauses in the Schedule is discussed categorically in *Bagalkot Cement Co. Ltd.* v. *R.K. Pathan.*[26] In this case Cl. 5 was interpreted which reads as follows:

"Conditions of procedure in applying for, and the authority which may grant leave and holidays."

The contention raised before the Court that how many holidays the employee will have and how much leave, either casual or on medical grounds, he would be entitled to get, are matters outside the scope of the Schedule; they would be governed by the relevant provisions of any other law or by contract between the parties; they cannot be the subject matter of standing orders. The standing orders would provide for the conditions subject to which leave and holidays can be applied for, for the procedure in applying for the same, and for the authority which may grant the same.

In support of this contention, reliance has been placed on Cl. 3 in the Schedule which refers to shift working. It is urged that since the clause refers to shift working, the substantive

26. AIR 1963 SC 439.

provision in respect of shift working as well as the conditions subject to which it should be allowed would legitimately fall within its purview. If the legislature had intended that the substantive provision as to leave and holidays should be the subject matter of standing orders, it may well have referred to leave and holidays only in Cl. 5 without any further addition. The additional words introduced in Cl. 5 are words of limitation and they show that the substantive provision as to leave and holidays is outside the purview of that clause. It may be conceded that there is some force in this contention. The Court, however, observed that other considerations have to be borne in mind in construing Cl. 5. The Court, while referring the object of the Act, held that the Act was to require the employers to make the conditions of employment precise and definite and the Act ultimately intended to prescribe these conditions in the form of standing orders so that what used to be governed by a contract hereto before would now be governed by the statutory standing orders and it would not be reasonable to hold that conditions of employment to which the Preamble to the Act specifically refers would not include a provision for the quantum of leave and the quantum of holidays to which the employee would be entitled. Therefore, the word 'conditions' in Cl. 5 of the Schedule has to be reasonably construed in a broad and liberal sense. The dictionary meaning of the word 'condition' is a provision or a stipulation. Now a provision or a stipulation as to leave and holidays would necessarily include a provision for the quantum of holidays and leave and this construction would be consistent with the meaning of the word 'condition' as employed in the preamble to the Act. Mr. Ramamurthi who appeared *amicus curiae for the respondents at the request of the Court contended that to adopt the narrow construction of the word 'conditions' in Cl. 5 would defeat the very purpose of Cl. 5. He argued that merely providing for the procedure of application and for the authority who would grant leave and holidays without stipulating as to the quantum of leave and holidays would be almost meaningless. Hence, the Court held that the broad and liberal construction of the word 'condition' in Cl. 5 should be adopted. Further, it will not be inconsistent with the scheme of the Schedule to hold that the substantive provision for the granting of leave and holidays along with the conditions in respect of them have to be made by the Standing Orders under Cl. 5 of the Schedule. It is, therefore, appropriate to construe Cl. 5 as including a provision for the quantum and extent of leave and holidays.*

* * *

7 The Apprentices Act, 1961

The material resources of our country are limited. This is true for other countries as well. The resource crunch is, however, acute for us; and so whenever and wherever public money is invested, it has to be seen that there is a proper utilisation of the same in the sense that the public ultimately gets benefit of the same. This prelude is to highlight the idea of introducing some amount of investment in apprentice trainees to make them useful to the society. After Independence, a wave to have its own strong industrial base swept the country. Backed by Government policies, industrial growth had a quantum leap. With the industrial growth, a need was felt to have trained manpower and for that steps were taken to arrange for training of apprentices in the industry. After some years, it necessitated that the training being imparted to the apprentices should be regulated by legislation. Accordingly, the Apprentices Bill, 1961 was introduced in Parliament to provide for the regulation and control of training of apprentices.

STATEMENT OF OBJECTS AND REASONS

The long title of the Act provides: An Act to provide for the regulation and control of training of apprentices and for matters connected therewith. The idea of undertaking legislation for regulating the training of apprentices in industry had been under the consideration of the Government for a long time. Expert committees, which went into the question, recommended such legislation. Although certain establishments in the public and private sectors have been carrying out programmes of training of skilled workers on a systematic basis, industry in general has not as yet fully organised such programmes. In the context of the Five-Year Plan and the large-scale industrial development of the country, there is an increasing demand for skilled craftsmen. The Government considers that it is necessary fully to utilize the facilities available for the training of apprentices and to ensure their training in accordance with the programmes, standards and syllabi, drawn up by expert bodies. The Bill is intended to give effect to these objectives.

The Apprentices Act, 1961 was promulgated primarily for the purpose of recruiting the apprentices. The idea behind it was a strong industrial base across the country. For the industrial growth, it is necessary to have trained manpower and for that purpose the apprentices are recruited. The Act was amended in 1973 by which training of graduate engineers and diploma holders was introduced for "improving their employment potential" and to solve the immediate unemployment problem. Further amendment was made in 1986 aimed to provide "on the job training" to the products of vocational streams so that adequate competence and skill required for various occupations are acquired leading to "suitable." This Act is further amended in 2014 which provides definition of appropriate government to include an establishment operating in four or more states to be regulated by the central government. It also amends the definitions of: (i) designated trade, (ii) graduate or technician apprentice, (iii) trade apprentice, (iv) industry; and (v) worker. This Act adds two definitions: (i) optional trade, and (ii) portal-site. The 2014 Amendment Act adds that the minimum age for apprenticeship in designated trades related to hazardous industries shall be 18 years.

CHAPTER I

PRELIMINARY

SECTION 1: Short title, extent, commencement and application

(1) This Act may be called the Apprentices Act, 1961.

(2) It extends to the whole of India.

(3) It shall come into force on such date as the Central Government may, by notification in the Official Gazette, appoint; and different dates may be appointed for different States.

(4) The provisions of this Act shall not apply to—

(a) any area or to any industry in any area unless the Central Government by notification in the Official Gazette specifies that area or industry as an area or industry to which the said provisions shall apply with effect from such date as may be mentioned in the notification;

(b) [***] repealed;

(c) any such special apprenticeship scheme for imparting training to apprentices as may be notified by the Central Government in the Official Gazette.

SECTION 2: Definitions

In this Act, unless the context otherwise requires,—

(a) **All India Council** means the All India Council of Technical Education established by the resolution of the Government of India in the former Ministry of Education No. F. 16-10/44-E-III, dt. 30-11-1945.

(aa) **apprentice** means a person who is undergoing apprenticeship training in pursuance of a contract of apprenticeship.

The word 'apprentice' is not defined in the Act, nor is it specifically referred to in the definition of 'employee' by either inclusion or exclusion. We are unable to hold that in ordinary acceptation of the term 'apprentice', a relationship of master and servant is established under the law. According to *Chamber's Dictionary*, to serve apprenticeship means to undergo the training of an apprentice. According to the *Shorter Oxford English Dictionary*, apprentice is a learner of a craft; one who is bound by legal agreement to serve an employer for a period of years, with a view to learn some handicraft, trade, etc. in which the employer is reciprocally bound to instruct him. *Stroud's Judicial Dictionary* puts it thus:

> "In legal acceptation, an apprentice is a person bound to another for the purpose of learning his trade, or calling; the contract being of that nature that the master teaches and the other serves the master with the intention of learning."

While dealing with the nature of the relationship of master and servant in comparison with other relationships, it has been stated as follows:

> "By a contract of apprenticeship a person is bound to another for the purpose of learning a trade or calling, the apprentice undertaking to serve the master for the purpose of being taught, and the master undertaking to teach the apprentice. Where teaching on the part of the master or learning on the part of the other person is not the primary but only an incidental object, the contract is one of service rather than of apprenticeship; but, if the right of receiving instruction exists, a contract does not become one of service because, to some extent, the person to whom it refers does the kind of work, that is done by a servant, or because he receives pecuniary remuneration for his work."[1]

It is, therefore, inherent in the word 'apprentice' that there is no element of employment as such in a trade or industry but only on adequate well-guarded provision for training to enable the trainee after completion of his course to be suitably absorbed in earning employment as a regular worker. The fact that a trainee may have been absorbed in the company where he is undergoing the training is not relevant for the purpose of comprehending the content of the term.[2] The heart of the matter in apprenticeship is, therefore, the dominant object and intent to impart on the part of the employer and to accept on the part of the other person learning under certain agreed terms. That certain payment is made during the apprenticeship, by whatever name called, and that the apprentice has to be under certain rules of discipline do not convert the apprentice to a regular employee under the employer. Such a person remains a learner and is not an employee.[3]

Let us look at the definition of an apprentice provided in the Act and the definition of workman given in the Industrial Disputes Act, 1947.

Section 2(s) of the Industrial Disputes Act, 1947 defines workman as follows.

"'Workman' means any person (including an apprentice) employed in any industry to do any skilled or unskilled, manual, supervisory, technical or clerical work for hire or reward, whether the terms of employment be express or implied, and for the purposes of any proceeding under this Act in relation to an industrial dispute, includes any such person who has been dismissed, discharged or retrenched in connection with, or as a consequence of, that dispute, or whose dismissal, discharge or retrenchment has led to that dispute, but does not include any such person—

(i) who is subject to the Army Act, 1950 or the Air Force Act, 1950, or the Navy (Discipline) Act, 1934; or

(ii) who is employed in the police service or as an officer or other employee of a prison; or

1. Halsbury's *Laws of England*, 3rd ed., Vol. 25, para. 877, pp. 451–452.
2. *Employee's State Insurance Corpn.* v. *Tata Engineering and Co., Locomotive Co. Ltd.*, AIR 1976 SC 66.
3. *Ibid.*

(iii) who is employed mainly in a managerial or administrative capacity; or

(iv) who, being employed in a supervisory capacity, draws wages exceeding five hundred rupees per mensem or exercises, either by the nature of the duties attached to the office or by reason of the powers vested in him, functions mainly of a managerial nature."

Thus, it can be seen that The Industrial Disputes Act includes apprentice within the ambit of the definition of workman. But the expression appearing in S. 2(s) of the Industrial Disputes Act is not applicable to the apprentices appointed under the Apprentices Act, 1961. The Apprentices Act is a code in itself and it clearly stipulates in S. 2(aa) that apprentice means a person who is undergoing apprenticeship training in pursuance of contract of training and the workers are employed for wages for work done by them. Section 18 of the Apprentices Act clearly mentions that the apprentices are not workmen and *"the provisions of any law with respect to labour law shall not apply or in relation to such apprentices"*. Therefore, reading of the definition of apprentice in Ss. 2(aa) and 2(r) read with S. 18 of the Apprentices Act leaves no doubt whatsoever that this Act, which is a special Act, does not cover the apprentices and it precludes the application of any other labour laws including the Industrial Disputes Act, 1947.

In this connection, reference may be made to a decision of the Rajasthan High Court in the case of *Hanuman Prasad Choudhary and Etc.* v. *Rajasthan State Electricity Board, Jaipur*,[4] wherein Justice S.C. Agrawal observed:

> "An apprentice governed by the Apprentices Act is not a workman for the purpose of the Industrial Disputes Act and the provisions of the Industrial Disputes Act would not be applicable to him. There is apparent conflict between the provisions of S. 2(s), Industrial Disputes Act and S. 18 of the Apprentices Act inasmuch as S. 2(s) postulates that an apprentice is a workman to whom the provisions of Industrial Disputes Act would be applicable whereas S. 18 of the Apprentices Act declares that an apprentice governed by the Apprentices Act is not to be treated as a workman and the provisions of the Industrial Disputes Act would not be applicable to him. The conflict between the two laws can be resolved by applying the principle of harmonious construction. Apprentices Act is not an exhaustive Act to cover all types of apprentices because in view of the definition of term "apprentice" as contained in S. 2(aa) of the Apprentices Act, it is applicable only to persons who are undergoing apprenticeship training in pursuance of the contract of Apprentices executed under S. 4 of the said Act. It is possible to visualise persons who may be engaged as apprentices but who are not covered by the Apprentices Act. In that view of the matter, it can be said that for the purpose of S. 2(s) of the Industrial Disputes Act a person who is designated as Apprentice but is not governed by the Apprentices Act would be a workman governed by the provisions of the Industrial Disputes Act. But an apprentice who is governed by the provisions of the Apprentices Act would not be a workman under S. 2(s) of the Industrial Disputes Act and would not be governed by the provisions of the Industrial Disputes Act. Apart from the principle of harmonious construction, the Apprentices Act 1961 being a subsequent particular law as compared to I.D. Act, 1947 which is prior and general, the provisions of Apprentices Act, 1961 would prevail over those of I.D. Act."[5]

(aaa) **apprenticeship training** means a course of training in any industry or establishment undergone in pursuance of a contract of apprenticeship and under prescribed terms and conditions which may be different for different categories of apprentices.

4. 1986 Lab I C 1014.
5. *Ibid.* at p. 1019 per S.C. Agrawal, J.

(b) **Apprenticeship Adviser** means the Central Apprenticeship Adviser appointed under sub-section (1) of section 26 or the State Apprenticeship Adviser appointed under sub-section (2) of that section.

(c) **Apprenticeship Council** means the Central Apprenticeship Council or the State Apprenticeship Council established under sub-section (1) of section 24.

(d) **appropriate Government** means,—

(1) in relation to—

(a) the Central Apprenticeship Council, or

(aa) the Regional Boards, or

(aaa) the practical training of graduate or technician apprentices or of technician (vocational) apprentices, or;

(b) any establishment of any railway, major port, mine or oilfield, or

(bb) any establishment which is operating business or trade from different locations situated in four or more States, or

(c) any establishment owned, controlled or managed by—

(i) the Central Government or a department of the Central Government;

(ii) a company in which not less than fifty-one per cent of the share capital is held by the Central Government or partly by that government and partly by one or more State Governments;

(iii) a corporation (including a co-operative society) established by or under a Central Act which is owned, controlled or managed by the Central Government, the Central Government;

(2) in relation to—

(a) a State Apprenticeship Council, or

(b) any establishment other than an establishment specified in sub-clause (1) of this clause, the State Government;

(dd) **Board or State Council of Technical Education** means the Board or State Council of Technical Education established by the State Government.

(e) **designated trade** means any trade or occupation or any subject field in engineering or non-engineering or technology or any vocational course which the Central Government, after consultation with the Central Apprenticeship Council, may, by notification in the Official Gazette, specify as a designated trade for the purposes of this Act.

(f) **employer** means any person who employs one or more other persons to do any work in an establishment for remuneration and includes any person entrusted with the supervision and control of employees in such establishment.

(g) **establishment** includes any place where any industry is carried on and where an establishment consists of different departments or has branches, whether situated in the same place or at different places, all such departments or branches shall be treated as part of that establishment.

(h) **establishment in private sector** means an establishment which is not an establishment in public sector.

(i) **establishment in public sector** means an establishment owned, controlled or managed by—

(1) the Government or a department of the Government;

(2) a Government company as defined in section 617 of the Companies Act, 1956 (1 of 1956);

(3) a corporation (including a co-operative society) established by or under a Central, Provincial or State Act, which is owned, controlled or managed by the Government;

(4) a local authority.

(j) **graduate or technician apprentice** means an apprentice who holds, or is undergoing training in order that he may hold a degree or diploma in engineering or non-engineering or technology or equivalent qualification granted by any institution recognized by the Government and undergoes apprenticeship training in any designated trade;

(k) **industry** means any industry or business in which any trade, occupation or subject field in engineering or non-engineering or technology or any vocational course may be specified as a designated trade or optional trade or both

(l) **National Council** means the National Council for Training in Vocational Trades established by the resolution of the Government of India in the Ministry of Labour (Directorate General of Resettlement and Employment) No. TR/E.P.-24/56, dated 21-8-1956 and re-named as the National Council for Vocational Training by the resolution of the Government of India in the Ministry of Labour (Directorate General of Employment and Training) No. DGET/12/21/80-TC, dated 30-9-1981.

(ll) **Optional trade** means any trade or occupation or any subject field in engineering or non-engineering or technology or any vocational course as may be determined by the employer for the purposes of this Act;

(lll) **portal-site means** a website of the Central Government for exchange of information under this Act;

(m) **prescribed** means prescribed by the rules made under this Act.

(mm) **Regional Board** means any Board of Apprenticeship Training registered under the Societies Registration Act, 1860 (21 of 1860), at Bombay, Calcutta, Madras or Kanpur.

(n) **State** includes a Union Territory.

(o) **State Council** means a State Council for Training in Vocational Trades established by the State Government.

(p) **State Government** in relation to a Union Territory means the Administrator thereof;

(pp) **technician (vocational) apprentice** means an apprentice who holds or is undergoing training in order that he may hold a certificate in vocational course involving two years of study after the completion of the secondary stage of school education recognized by the All-India Council and undergoes apprenticeship training in any designated trade.

(q) **trade apprentice** means an apprentice who undergoes apprenticeship training in any designated trade.

(r) **worker** means any person working in the premises of the employer, who is employed for wages in any kind of work either directly or through any agency including a contractor and who gets his wages directly or indirectly from the employer but shall not include an apprentice referred to in clause (aa).

CHAPTER II

APPRENTICES AND THEIR TRAINING

SECTION 3: Qualifications for being engaged as an apprentice

The following qualifications are prescribed for a person to be engaged as an apprentice to undergo apprenticeship training in any designated trade, unless he—

(a) is not less than fourteen years of age, and for designated trades related to hazardous industries, not less than eighteen years of age; and

(b) satisfies such standards of education and physical fitness as may be prescribed:

Provided that different standards may be prescribed in relation to apprenticeship training in different designated trades and for different categories of apprentices.

SECTION 3A: Reservation of training places for the Scheduled Castes and the Scheduled Tribes in designated trades

(1) In every designated trade, training places shall be reserved by the employer for the Scheduled Castes and the Scheduled Tribes and where there is more than one designated trade in an establishment, such training places shall be reserved also on the basis of the total number of apprentices in all the designated trades in such establishment.

(2) The number of training places to be reserved for the Scheduled Castes and the Scheduled Tribes under sub-section (1) shall be such as may be prescribed, having regard to the population of the Scheduled Castes and the Scheduled Tribes in the State concerned.

Explanation: In this section, the expression "Scheduled Castes" and "Scheduled Tribes" shall have the meanings as in clauses (24) and (25) of Article 366 of the Constitution.

Article 366(24) of the Constitution of India defines the term Scheduled Caste as follows: "Scheduled Caste" means such castes, races or tribes or parts of or groups within such castes, races or tribes as are deemed under Article 341 to be Scheduled Castes for the purpose of this Constitution.

Article 366(25) of the Constitution of India defines the term Scheduled Tribes as follows:

"Scheduled Tribes" means such tribes or tribal communities or parts of or groups within such tribes or tribal communities as are deemed under Article 342 to be Scheduled Tribes for the purpose of this Constitution.

SECTION 3B: Reservation of training places for other Backward Classes in designated trades

(1) In every designated trade, training places shall be reserved by the employer for the Scheduled Castes and the Scheduled Tribes and where there is more than one designated trade in an establishment, such training places shall be reserved also on the basis of the total number of apprentices in all the designated trades in such establishment.

(2) The number of training places to be reserved for the Other Backward Classes under sub-section (1) shall be such as may be prescribed, having regard to the population of the Other Backward Classes in the State concerned.

SECTION 4: Contract of Apprenticeship

(1) No person shall be engaged as an apprentice to undergo apprenticeship training in a designated trade unless such person or, if he is a minor, his guardian has entered into a contract of apprenticeship with the employer.

(2) The apprenticeship training shall be deemed to have commenced on the date on which the contract of apprenticeship has been entered into under sub-section (1).

(3) Every contract of apprenticeship may contain such terms and conditions as may be agreed to by the parties to the contract:

Provided that no such term or condition shall be inconsistent with any provision of this Act or any rule made thereunder.

(4) Every contract of apprenticeship entered into under sub-section (1) shall be sent by the employer within thirty days to the Apprenticeship Adviser until a portal-site is developed by the Central Government, and thereafter the details of contract of apprenticeship shall be entered on the portal-site within seven days, for verification and registration

(4A) In the case of objection in the contract of apprenticeship, the Apprenticeship Adviser shall convey the objection to the employer within fifteen days from the date of receipt.

(4B) The Apprenticeship Adviser shall register the contract of apprenticeship within thirty days from the date of its receipt.

(5) [***]

(6) Where the Central Government, after consulting the Central Apprenticeship Counsel, makes any rule varying the terms and conditions of apprenticeship training, of any category of apprentices undergoing such training, then, the terms and conditions of every contract of apprenticeship relating to that category of apprentices and subsisting immediately before the making of such rule shall be deemed to have been modified accordingly.

The question which arose before the Supreme Court in *U.P. State Electricity Board* v. *Shiv Mohan Singh*[6] for interpretation was what is the effect of non-registration of the contract because sub-section (4) of S. 4 read with Rule 6 requires that every contract of apprentice shall be sent by the employer to the Apprenticeship Adviser for registration within three months. Therefore, in case the contract of apprenticeship is not sent to the apprenticeship adviser for registration, what will be the effect thereof?

The main question which has been agitated by the learned counsel for the appellant is that if an incumbent is appointed as an apprentice/trainee and even if a contract of such apprenticeship has not been registered, then also he does not cease to be an apprentice and his position does not become that of a workman. As against this, the learned counsel for the respondents has strenuously urged before the Court that non-registration of the contract of apprenticeship under sub-section (4) of S. 4 of the Apprentices Act, 1961, with the Apprenticeship Adviser would result in the breach of the contract and the status of an incumbent is changed from the apprentice to that of a workman. Therefore, the question arose that whether registration of the contract under sub-section (4) of S. 4 is mandatory or directory, and in case it is mandatory, then what is the effect; if it is directory, then what is the effect thereof. In this connection, it is further submitted by the learned counsel appearing for the respondent that the word 'shall' appearing in sub-section (4) of S. 4 means the registration of the contract is mandatory and if it is not registered, then the contract ceases and the incumbent becomes workman.

The Supreme Court observed that from the scheme of the Act it is more than apparent that the Apprentices Act, 1961 is a complete Code in itself and it lays down the conditions of the apprentices, what shall be their tenure, what shall be their terms and conditions, and what are their obligations and what are the obligations of the employer.

It also lays down that the apprentices are trainees and not workmen and if any dispute arises, then the settlement has to be done by the Apprenticeship Adviser as per S. 20 of the Apprentices Act, 1961 and his decision thereof is final. Under the scheme of the Act, it is further clear that the nature and character of the apprentice is nothing but that of a trainee and he is supposed to enter into a contract, and by virtue of that contract, he is to serve for a fixed period on a fixed stipend. This will not change the character of the apprentice to that of a workman under the employer where he is undergoing the apprentice training. Sub-section (4) of S. 4 only lays down that such contract should be registered with the Apprenticeship Adviser. But by non-registration of the contract, the position of the apprentice is not changed to that of a workman. It is more than clear from the scheme of the Act, the apprentice is recruited for the purpose of training as defined in S. 2(aa) of the Apprentices Act, 1961, that an apprentice is a person who is undergoing apprenticeship training in pursuance of a contract of apprenticeship and the apprenticeship training has been defined under S. 2(aaa). That clearly speaks that an apprentice is to undergo apprenticeship training in any industry or establishment under the employer in pursuance of the contract and in terms of the conditions pertaining to that particular trade. Section 6 lays down that what shall be the period of training and S. 7 very clearly shows that the contract of apprenticeship shall terminate on the expiry of the period of apprenticeship training.

Therefore, it is more than clear that the nature and character of the apprentice is that of a trainee only and on the expiry of the training, there is no corresponding obligation on

6. AIR 2004 SC 5009.

the part of the employer to employ him, which is also very clear from the provisions of S. 7 that the apprenticeship training shall terminate on the expiry of the period of training. It further makes clear, by virtue of S. 18, that the apprentice trainees are not workers. It clearly lays down that if an apprentice trainee is undergoing apprenticeship training in a designated trade in an establishment, he shall be a trainee and not a worker. It further contemplates that the provisions of labour laws shall not apply in relation to such apprentice. The definition of workman given in S. 2(r) also emphasises that it will not include apprentice. Section 20 also lays down that how a dispute arising under this Apprentices Act, 1961 can be settled. The authority for resolving such a dispute has been given to the Apprenticeship Adviser. Therefore, if any dispute arises between the apprentice and the employer, then remedy has been provided under this Act and not by way of resorting to the Labour Court. Therefore, throughout the Act, the stress has been laid that the apprentices are not to be treated as workers. Simply because the contract has not been registered with the Apprenticeship Adviser, that will not change the nature and character of the apprentices. It is true that sub-section (4) of S. 4 lays down that the contract of apprenticeship should be registered with the Apprenticeship Adviser so that the Apprenticeship Adviser can monitor and keep a record thereof. Just because the contract of apprenticeship is not registered, that will not render the contract as invalid, resulting in change of status of an apprentice to that of a workman. Section 21 further lays down that after the completion of the training of the apprentice, an incumbent will have to appear for a test to be conducted by the National Council to determine his proficiency in the designated trade in which he has undergone his apprenticeship training. Therefore, had there been an intention of the legislature to confer on them the status of a workman, all the provisions would not have been warranted at all.

Now, come to the question that the expression 'shall' appearing in sub-section (4) of S. 4, should be interpreted as mandatory. It depends upon the context in which such expression appears. In order to interpret the word "*shall*" appearing in any enactment, one has to see the context in which it appears and the effect thereof. Viewing the expression "*shall*" in the context it is used, the Court held that it cannot be construed as a mandatory. Sub-section (4) of S. 4 only says that the contract of apprenticeship should be forwarded to the Adviser, that is purely a ministerial/administrative act, so that a proper record is maintained by the Apprenticeship Adviser. Nothing turns beyond this. It is purely an administrative act and not forwarding the contract of the apprenticeship to the Apprenticeship Adviser will not change the character of the incumbent and it will not render the contract of apprenticeship invalid or void. If the contract of apprenticeship is to be treated as a mandatory and contract is not sent, then the effect will be that the apprentice will not be entitled to any benefit flowing from the Act. In fact, by treating the expression "*shall*" here as a mandatory, it will be more counter-productive to the interest of the trainees rather than for their benefit. Accordingly, the Court held:

> "Therefore, we hold that the expression "shall" appearing in sub-section (4) of Section 4 of the Apprentices Act, 1961 is directory and non-registration of the contract will not change the character of the apprentice and they will not acquire the status of a workman. Once an incumbent is appointed as an apprentice he will continue to be apprentice unless a formal order of appointment is followed."[7]

---

7. *Ibid.* at pp. 5022–5023 per A.K. Mathur, J.

A Division Bench of the Gujarat High Court in *Ballkhan Doskhan Joya* v. *Gujarat Electricity Board*[8] observed that the Central Legislations i.e. the Industrial Disputes Act and the Apprentice Act are fully aware to deal the situation that an apprentice, undergoing an apprenticeship training under an apprenticeship contract duly registered, would be only a 'trainee' and not a 'workman', to which other laws in respect of labour shall not apply. Therefore, in including apprentice in the definition of workman the legislative intention appears to be obvious that such apprentices, who are not undergoing apprenticeship training under a duly registered apprenticeship contract, envisaged by the Apprentices Act, and to whom provisions of S. 18 of the said Act are not applicable, would, nonetheless, be included in the definition of 'workman' under the Industrial Disputes Act and would get all the protection of labour laws. The Court further held that even after non-registration of the contract of apprenticeship, the appellant would only be a 'trainee', or an 'apprentice', as intended by the parties and he would not be an 'employee' or a 'workman', within the meaning of the Apprentices Act.

Section 5: Novation of contracts of apprenticeship

Where an employer with whom a contract of apprenticeship has been entered into, is for any reason unable to fulfil his obligation under the contract and with the approval of the Apprenticeship Adviser it is agreed between the employer, the apprentice or his guardian and any other employer that the apprentice shall be engaged as an apprentice under the other employer for the unexpired portion of the period of apprenticeship training, the agreement, on registration with the Apprenticeship Adviser, shall be deemed to be the contract of apprenticeship between the apprentice or his guardian and other employer, and on and from the date of such registration, the contract of apprenticeship with the first employer shall terminate and no obligation under that contract shall be enforceable at the instance of any party to the contract against the other party thereto.

When parties to a contract agree to substitute the existing contract with a new contract, it is called novation. Section 62 of the Indian Contract Act provides the effect of novation as under:

> "If the parties to a contract agree to substitute a new contract for it, or to rescind or alter it, the original contract need not be performed."

One of the essential requirements of 'novation', as contemplated by S. 62, is that there should be complete substitution of a new contract in place of the old. It is in that situation that the original contract need not be performed. Substitution of a new contract in place of the old contract which would have the effect of rescinding or completely altering the terms of the original contract, has to be by agreement between the parties. A substituted contract should rescind or alter or extinguish the previous contract. But if the terms of the two contracts are inconsistent and they cannot stand together, the subsequent contract cannot be said to be in substitution of the earlier contract.[9]

---

8. 2002 (92) FLR 914.
9. *Lata Construction* v. *Dr. Rameshchandra Ramniklal Shah*, AIR 2000 SC 380.

Section 5A: Regulation of optional trade

The qualification, period of apprenticeship training, holding of test, grant of certificate and other conditions relating to the apprentices in optional trade shall be such as may be prescribed.

Section 5B: Engagement of apprentices from other States

The employer may engage apprentices from other States for the purpose of providing apprenticeship training to the apprentices.

Section 6: Period of apprenticeship training

The period of apprenticeship training, which shall be specified in the contract of apprenticeship, shall be as follows:

(a) in the case of trade apprentices who, having undergone institutional training in a school or other institution recognised by the National Council, have passed the trade tests or examinations conducted by that Council or by an institution recognised by that Council, the period of apprenticeship training shall be such as may be prescribed or by an institution recognised by that Council;

(aa) in the case of trade apprentices who, having undergone institutional training in a school or other institution affiliated to or recognised by a Board or State Council of Technical Education or any other authority or courses approved under any scheme which the Central Government may, by notification which the Central Government may, by notification in the Official Gazette specify in this behalf, have passed the trade tests or examinations conducted by that Board or State Council or authority or by any other agency authorized by the Central Government, the period of apprenticeship training shall be such as may be prescribed;

(b) in the case of other trade apprentices, the period of apprenticeship training shall be such as may be prescribed;

(c) in the case of graduate or technician apprentices, technician (vocational) apprentices the period of apprenticeship training shall be such as may be prescribed.

Section 7: Termination of apprenticeship contract

(1) The contract of apprenticeship shall terminate on the expiry of the period of apprenticeship training.

(2) Either party to a contract of apprenticeship may make an application to the Apprenticeship Adviser for the termination of the contract, and when such application is made, shall send by post a copy thereof to the other party to the contract.

(3) After considering the contents of the application and the objections, if any, filed by the other party, the Apprenticeship Adviser may, by order in writing, terminate the contract, if he is satisfied that the parties to the contract or any of them have or has failed to carry out the terms and conditions of the contract and it is desirable in the interests of the parties or any of them to terminate the same:

Provided that where a contract is terminated—

(a) for failure on the part of the employer to carry out the terms and conditions of the contract, the employer shall pay to the apprentice such compensation as may be prescribed;

(b) for such failure on the part of the apprentice, the apprentice or his guardian shall refund to the employer as cost of training such amount as may be determined by the Apprenticeship Advisor.

(4) Notwithstanding anything contained in any other provision of this Act, where a contract of apprenticeship has been terminated by the Apprenticeship Adviser before the expiry of the period of apprenticeship training and a new contract of apprenticeship is being entered into with a new employer, the Apprenticeship Adviser may, if he is satisfied that the contract of apprenticeship with the previous employer could not be completed because of any lapse on the part of the previous employer, permit the period of apprenticeship training already undergone by the apprentice with his previous employer to be included in the period of apprenticeship training to be undertaken with the new employer.

Section 8: Number of apprentices for a designated trade and optional trade

(1) The Central Government shall prescribe the number of apprentices to be engaged by the employer for designated trade and optional trade.

(2) Several employers may join together either themselves or through an agency, approved by the Apprenticeship Adviser, according to the guidelines issued from time to time by the Central Government in this behalf, for the purpose of providing apprenticeship training to the apprentices under them.

Section 9: Practical and basic training of apprentices

(1) Every employer shall make suitable arrangement in his workshop for imparting a course of practical training to every apprentice engaged by him.

(2) The Central Apprenticeship Adviser or any other person not below the rank of an Assistant Apprenticeship Adviser authorised by the Central Apprenticeship Adviser in writing in this behalf shall be given all reasonable facilities for access to each such apprentice with a view to test his work and to ensure that the practical training is being imparted in accordance with the approved programme:

Provided that the State Apprenticeship Adviser or any other person not below the rank of an Assistant Apprenticeship Adviser authorised by the State Apprenticeship Adviser in writing in this behalf shall also be given such facility in respect of apprentices undergoing training in establishments in relation to which the appropriate Government is the State Government.

(3) Such of the trade apprentices who have not undergone institutional training in a school or other institution recognised by the National Council or any other institution affiliated to or recognised by the Board or State Council of Technical Education

or any other authority which the Central Government may, by notification in the Official Gazette, specify in this behalf, shall, before admission in the workshop for practical training, undergo a course of basic training and the course of basic training shall be given to the trade apprentices in any institute having adequate facilities.

(4) Where an employer employs in his establishment five hundred or more workers, the basic training shall be imparted to the trade apprentices either in separate parts of the workshop building or in a separate building which shall be set up by the employer himself, by the appropriate Government may grant loans to the employer on easy terms and repayable by easy installments to meet the cost of the land, construction and equipment for such separate building.

(4A) [***]

(4B) [***]

(5) [***]

(6) [***]

(7) In the case of an apprentice other than graduate or technician apprentice or technician (vocational) apprentice, the syllabus of and the equipment to be utilised for, practical training including basic training in any designated trade shall be such as may be approved by the Central Government in consultation with the Central Apprenticeship Council.

(7A) In the case of graduate or technician apprentices technician (vocational) apprentices, the programme of apprenticeship training and the facilities required for such training in any designated trade shall be such as may be approved by the Central Government in consultation with the Central Apprenticeship Council.

(8)(a) Recurring costs (including the cost of stipends) incurred by an employer in connection with basic training, imparted to trade apprentices other than those referred to in clauses (a) and (aa) of section 6 shall be borne—

(i) if such employer employs two hundred and fifty workers or more, by the employer;

(ii) if such employer employs less than two hundred and fifty workers, by the employer and the Government in equal shares up to such limit as may be laid down by the Central Government and beyond that limit, by the employer alone and

(b) Recurring costs (including the costs of stipends), if any, incurred by an employer in connection with practical training, including basic training, imparted to trade apprentices referred to in clauses (a) and (aa) of section 6 shall, in every case, be borne by the employer;

(c) Recurring costs (excluding the cost of stipends) incurred by an employer in connection with the practical training imparted to graduate or technician apprentices technician (vocational) apprentices shall be borne by the employer and the cost of stipends shall be borne by the Central Government and the employer in equal shares up to such limit as may be laid down by the Central Government and beyond that limit, by the employer alone except apprentices who holds degree or diploma in non engineering.

SECTION 10: Related instruction of apprentices

(1) A trade apprentice who is undergoing practical training in an establishment shall, during the period of practical training, be given a course of related instruction (which shall be appropriate to the trade) approved by the Central Government in consultation with the Central Apprenticeship Council, with a view to giving the trade apprentice such theoretical knowledge as he needs in order to become fully qualified as a skilled craftsman.

(2) Related instruction shall be imparted at the cost of appropriate government but the employer shall, when so required, afford all facilities for imparting such instruction.

(3) Any time spent by a trade apprentice in attending classes on related instruction shall be treated as part of his paid period of work.

(4) In the case of trade apprentices who, after having undergone a course of institutional training, have passed the trade tests conducted by the National Council or have passed the trade tests and examinations conducted by a Board or State Council of Technical Education or any other authority which the Central Government may, by notification in the Official Gazette, specify in this behalf, the related instruction may be given on such reduced or modified scale as may be prescribed.

(5) Where any person has, during his course in a technical institution, become a graduate or technician apprentice, technician (vocational) apprentice and during his apprenticeship training he has to receive related instruction, then, the employer shall release such person from practical training to receive the related instruction in such institution, for such period as may be specified by the Central Apprenticeship Adviser or by any other person not below the rank of an Assistant Apprenticeship Adviser authorised by the Central Apprenticeship Adviser in writing in this behalf.

SECTION 11: Obligations of employers

Without prejudice to the other provisions of this Act, every employer shall have the following obligations in relation to an apprentice, namely—

(a) to provide the apprentice with the training in his trade in accordance with the provisions of this Act, and the rules made thereunder;

(b) if the employer is not himself qualified in the trade, to ensure that a person who possesses the prescribed qualifications is placed in charge of the training of the apprentice;

(ab) to provide adequate instructional staff, possessing such qualifications as may be prescribed, for imparting practical and theoretical training and facilities for trade test of apprentices; and

(c) to carry out his obligations under the contract of apprenticeship.

SECTION 12: Obligations of apprentices

(1) Every trade apprentice undergoing apprenticeship training shall have the following obligations, namely,—

(a) to learn his trade conscientiously and diligently and endeavour to qualify himself as a skilled craftsman before the expiry of the period of training;

(b) to attend practical and instructional classes regularly;

(c) to carry out all lawful orders of his employer and superiors in the establishments; and

(d) to carry out his obligations under the contract of apprenticeship.

(2) Every graduate or technical apprentice technician (vocational) apprentice undergoing apprenticeship training shall have the following obligations, namely,—

(a) to learn his subject field in engineering or technology or vocational course conscientiously and diligently at his place of training;

(b) to attend the practical and instructional classes regularly;

(c) to carry out all lawful orders of his employer and superiors in the establishment;

(d) to carry out his obligations under the contract of apprenticeship which shall include the maintenance of such records of his work as may be prescribed.

SECTION 13: Payment to apprentices

(1) The employer shall pay to every apprentice during the period of apprenticeship training such stipend at a rate not less than the prescribed minimum rate, or the rate which was being paid by the employer on lst January, 1970 to the category of apprentices under which such apprentice falls, whichever is higher as may be specified in the contract of apprenticeship and the stipend so specified shall be paid at such intervals and subject to such conditions as may be prescribed.

(2) An apprentice shall not be paid by his employer on the basis of piece work nor shall be required to take part in any output bonus or other incentive scheme.

SECTION 14: Health, safety and welfare of apprentices

Where any apprentices are undergoing training in a factory, the provisions of Chapters III IV and V of the Factories Act, 1948, shall apply in relation to the health, safety and welfare of the apprentices as if they were workers within the meaning of that Act and when any apprentices are undergoing training in a mine, the provisions of Chapter V of the Mines Act 1952, shall apply in relation to the health and safety of the apprentices as if they were persons employed in the mine.

SECTION 15: Hours of work, overtime, leave and holidays

(1) The weekly and daily hours of work of an apprentice while undergoing practical training in a workplace shall be as determined by the employer subject to the compliance with the training duration, if prescribed.

(2) No apprentice shall be required or allowed to work overtime except with the approval of the Apprenticeship Adviser who shall not grant such approval unless he is satisfied that such overtime is in the interest of the training of the apprentice or in the public interest.

(3) An apprentice shall be entitled to such leave and holidays as are observed in the establishment in which he is undergoing training.

SECTION 16: Employer's liability for compensation for injury

If personal injury is caused to an apprentice, by accident arising out of and in the course of his training as an apprentice, his employer shall be liable to pay compensation which shall be determined and paid, so far as may be, in accordance with the provisions of the Workmen's Compensation Act, 1923, subject to the modifications specified in the Schedule.

SECTION 17: Conduct and discipline

In all matters of conduct and discipline, the apprentices shall be governed by the rules and regulations applicable to employees of the corresponding category in the establishment in which the apprentice is undergoing training.

SECTION 18: Apprentices are trainees and not workers

Save as otherwise provided in this Act,—

(a) every apprentice undergoing apprenticeship training in a designated trade in an establishment shall be a trainee and not a worker; and

(b) the provisions of any law with respect to labour shall not apply to or in relation to such apprentice.

SECTION 19: Records and returns

(1) Every employer shall maintain records of the progress of training of each apprentice undergoing apprenticeship training in his establishment in such form as may be prescribed.

(2) Until a portal-site is developed by the Central Government, every employer shall furnish such information and return in such form as may be prescribed, to such authorities at such intervals as may be prescribed.

(3) Every employer shall also give trade-wise requirement and engagement of apprentices in respect of apprenticeship training on portal-site developed by the Central Government in this regard.

SECTION 20: Settlement of disputes

(1) Any disagreement or dispute between an employer and an apprentice arising out of the contract to apprenticeship shall be referred to the Apprenticeship Adviser for decision.

(2) Any person aggrieved by the decision of the Apprenticeship Adviser under sub-section (1) may, within thirty days from the date of communication to him of such decision, prefer an appeal against the decision to the Apprenticeship Council and

such appeal shall be heard and determined by a Committee of that Council appointed for the purpose.

(3) The decision of the Committee under sub-section (2) and subject only to such decision, the decision of the Apprenticeship Adviser under sub-section (1) shall be final.

SECTION 21: Holding of test and grant of certificate and conclusion of training

(1) Every trade apprentice who has completed the period of training may appear for a test to be conducted by the National Council or any other agency authorized by the central government to determine his proficiency in the designated trade in which he has undergone his apprenticeship training.

(2) Every trade apprentice who passes the test referred to in sub-section (1) shall be granted a certificate of proficiency in the trade by the National Council or by other agency authorized by the Central Government.

(3) The progress in apprenticeship training of every graduate or technician apprentice technician (vocational) apprentice shall be assessed by the employer from time to time.

(4) Every graduate or technician apprentice or technician (vocational) apprentice who completes his apprenticeship training to the satisfaction of the concerned Regional Board, shall be granted a certificate of proficiency by that Board.

SECTION 22: Offer and Acceptance of Employment

(1) Every employer shall formulate its own policy for recruiting any apprentice who has completed the period of apprenticeship training in his establishment.

(2) Notwithstanding anything in sub-section (1), where there is a condition in a contract of apprenticeship that the apprentice shall, after the successful completion of the apprenticeship training, serve the employer, the employer shall, on such completion, be bound to offer suitable employment to the apprentice, and the apprentice shall be bound to serve the employer in that capacity for such period and on such remuneration as may be specified in the contract.

Provided that where such period or remuneration is not, in the opinion of the Apprenticeship Adviser, reasonable, he may revise such period or remuneration so as to make it reasonable, and the period and remuneration so revised shall be deemed to be the period or remuneration agreed to between the apprentice and the employer.

This provision contains a "*non obstante*" clause in sub-section (2) of Section 22 which reads as follows:

Notwithstanding anything in sub-section (1), where there is a condition in a contract of apprenticeship that the apprentice shall, after the successful completion of the apprenticeship training, serve the employer, the employer shall, on such completion, be bound to offer suitable employment to the apprentice, and the apprentice shall be bound to serve the employer in that capacity for such period and on such remuneration as may be specified in the contract.

Section 22 leaves no doubt that the employer is under an obligation to suitable employment to the apprentice if the contract of apprenticeship contains a condition that the apprentice shall serve the employer after the successful completion of the training. Indeed, when such an offer is made, the apprentice on his part is bound to serve the employer in the capacity in which he was working as an apprentice.

The question before the Supreme Court in *Narinder Kumar* v. *State of Punjab*[10] for consideration was whether there is a condition in the contract of apprenticeship of the appellants that they shall serve the employer after the successful completion of their apprenticeships training. In this behalf, paragraph 2 of the letters of appointment under which the appellants were appointed as apprentices is important. It reads thus:

> "It should be clearly understood that you shall be on stipendiary training for a period of one year and on successful completion of this training, you shall be absorbed in the department if there are vacancies, without any commitment subject to the stipulation that during the waiting period after one year's apprenticeship, you will not be paid any remuneration".

It was urged on behalf of the respondents that this particular term in the contract of apprenticeship cannot be construed as a condition that the apprentices shall, after the successful completion of their apprenticeship training, serve the employer. However, the Court observed:

> "It is not proper in such cases to indulge in a hair-splitting approach and find an escape for defeating the rights of employees. When paragraph 2 says that the apprentice, "shall be absorbed in the department", the only reasonable interpretation to put upon that expression is that it creates reciprocal rights and obligations on the parties to the contract of apprenticeship, namely, the employee and the employer. "You shall be absorbed" is a double edged term of the contract. It binds the employer to offer employment to the apprentice (if there is a vacancy) and, equally, it binds the apprentice to accept the offer."[11]

Another defence was taken by the State of Punjab that the words *"without any commitment"* which occur in paragraph 2 of the letters of appointment as stated above, show that there is no obligation on the part of the employer to employ the apprentices after their period of training is over. The Court refused to accept the submission made by the State of Punjab and held that there is no substance in that contention because, in the context in which the expression *"without any commitment"* occurs it only means that the obligation of the employer to offer employment to the apprentice and the corresponding obligation of the apprentice to serve the employer arises only if and when there is a vacancy in which the apprentice can be appointed. This is made clear by the clause, "*you shall be absorbed in the department if there are vacancies*", which precedes the expression "*without any commitment*". This is plain commonsense because, if there is no vacancy in which an apprentice can be appointed, there can be no obligation to appoint him and there can, evidently, be no obligation upon the apprentice to serve the employer. These reciprocal rights and obligations, namely, to serve and offer employment, arise on the occurrence of a vacancy in which an apprentice can be appointed. Accordingly the Court held:

> "We are also of the opinion that, apart from the implications arising out of Section 22(2) of the Apprentices Act, paragraph 2 of the letters of appointment creates a binding obligation upon the employer to absorb the apprentices in the department on the successful completion

10. AIR 1985 SC 2.
11. *Ibid.* at p. 277 per Chandrachud, C.J.

of the training period, provided there is a vacancy in which the apprentices can be appointed. It would be contrary both to the letter and spirit of paragraph 2 of the letters of appointment to hold that, even if there is a vacancy in which an apprentice can be appointed after the successful completion of his training, the employer is free not to appoint the apprentice and fill that vacancy by appointing an outsider. Such a reading of the assurance contained in paragraph 2 will also frustrate the very object of the provision made by the legislature in Section 22(2) of the Act. The object of that provision is to guarantee, to the extent of the existence of vacancies, that the apprentices will not be rendered jobless after they complete their training."[12]

The legislature did desire and made adequate provisions to see that the competent person receive due training to cater to the need of increasing demand for skilled craftsman on one hand, and to improve the employment potential of the trainees, on the other.

Good amount of money, which would be public money in case of public bodies like the Corporation, is also spent on training the apprentices. Further, during the period of training, the apprentices are put under a discipline akin to that of regular employee inasmuch as S. 17 states that in all matters of conduct and discipline, the apprentice shall be governed by the rules and regulations applicable to employees of the corresponding category in the establishment in which the apprentice is undergoing training. Section 16 requires payment to the apprentice in case of injury due to accident arising out of and in the course of training, in accordance with the provision of the Workmen's Compensation Act, 1924, as modified by the Act. The Rules have dealt with the hours of work (Rule 12) and grant of leave (Rule 13) also.

The aforesaid provisions are sufficiently indicative of the fact that the training imparted is desired to be result-oriented; and the trainees are treated as akin to employees. Even so, S. 22 of the Act states, and it is this provision which has been pressed into service by the appellants, that it shall not be obligatory on the part of the employer to offer any employment to any apprentice who has completed the period of his apprenticeship training in his establishment unless there be a condition in the contract to the contrary.[13] Considering the above stated view, the Supreme Court in *U.P. State Road Transport Corporation* v. *U.P. Parivahan Nigam Shishukhs Berozgar Sangh*[14] laid down certain guidelines for recruitment of the apprentice and they are as follows:

(1) Other things being equal, a trained apprentice should be given preference over direct recruits.
(2) A trainee would not be required to get his name sponsored by any employment exchange.
(3) If age bar would come in the way of the trainee, the same would be relaxed in accordance with what is stated in this regard, if any, in this service rule concerned. If the service rule be silent on this aspect, relaxation to the extent of the period for which the apprentice had undergone training would be given.
(4) The concerned training institute would maintain a list of the persons trained year-wise. The persons trained earlier would be treated as senior to the persons trained

12. *Ibid.* at p. 278 per Chandrachud, C.J.
13. *U.P. State Road Transport Corporation* v. *U.P. Parivahan Nigam Shishukhs Berozgar Sangh*, AIR 1995 SC 1115.
14. *Ibid.*

later. In between the trained apprentices, preference shall be given to those who are senior.

However, the Supreme Court in 2000 in *U.P. Rajya Vidyut Parishad Apprentice Welfare Association* v. *State of U.P.*[15] held that the apprentices have to go through the procedure of examination/interview and that they are entitled to the benefits of entries (i) to (iv) laid down in *U.P. State Road Transport Corporation* case.

CHAPTER III

AUTHORITIES

SECTION 23: Authorities

(1) In addition to the Government, there shall be the following authorities under this Act, namely—

(a) The National Council,
(b) The Central Apprenticeship Council,
(c) The State Council,
(d) The State Apprenticeship Council,
(e) The All India Council,
(f) The Regional Boards,
(g) The Boards or State Councils of Technical Education,
(h) The Central Apprenticeship Adviser, and
(i) The State Apprenticeship Adviser.

(2) Every State Council shall be affiliated to the National Council and every State Apprenticeship Council shall be affiliated to the Central Apprenticeship Council.

(2A) Every Board or State Council of Technical Education and every Regional Board shall be affiliated to the Central Apprenticeship Council.

(3) Each of the authorities specified in sub-section (1) shall, in relation to apprenticeship training under this Act, perform such functions as are assigned to it by or under this Act or by the Government:

Provided that the State Council also perform such functions as are assigned to it by the National Council and the State Apprenticeship Council and the Board or State Council of Technical Education shall also perform such functions as are assigned to it by the Central Apprenticeship Council.

SECTION 24: Constitution of Councils

(1) The Central Government shall, by notification in the Official Gazette, establish the

15. AIR 2000 SC 2621.

Central Apprenticeship Council and the State Government shall, by notification in the Official Gazette, establish the State Apprenticeship Council.

(2) The Central Apprenticeship Council shall consist of a Chairman and a Vice Chairman and such number of other members as the Central Government may think expedient, to be appointed by that Government by notification in the Official Gazette, from among the following categories of persons, namely—

(a) representatives of employees in establishments in the public and private sectors;

(b) representatives of the Central Government and of the State Governments;

(c) persons having special knowledge and experience on matters relating to industry, labour and technical education, and

(d) representatives of the All India Council and of the Regional Boards.

(3) The number of persons to be appointed as members of the Central Apprenticeship Council from each of the categories specified in sub-section (2), the term of office of, the procedure to be followed in the discharge of their functions by, and the manner of filling vacancies among, the members of the Council shall be such as may be prescribed.

(4) The State Apprenticeship Council shall consist of a Chairman and a Vice Chairman and such number of other members as the State Government may think expedient, to be appointed by that Government by notification in the Official Gazette, from among the following categories of persons, namely—

(a) representatives of employers in establishments in the public and private sectors;

(b) representatives of the Central Government and of the State Government;

(c) persons having special knowledge and experience on matters relating to industry, labour and technical education; and

(d) representatives of the Board or of the State Council of Technical Education.

(5) The number of persons to be appointed as members of the State Apprenticeship Council from each of the categories specified in sub-section (4), the term of office of, the procedure to be followed in the discharge of their functions by, and the manner of filling vacancies among, the members of the Council shall be such as the State Government may, by notification in the Official Gazette, determine.

(6) The fees and allowances, if any, to be paid to the Chairman and the Vice Chairman and the other members of the Central Apprenticeship Council, shall be such as may be determined by the Central Government and the fees and allowances if any, to be paid to the Chairman and the Vice-Chairman and the other members of the State Apprenticeship Council shall be such as may be determined by the State Government.

Section 25: Vacancies not to invalidate acts and proceedings

No act done or proceeding taken by the National Council, the Central Apprenticeship Council, the State Council or the State Apprenticeship Council under this Act shall be questioned on the ground merely of the existence of any vacancy in, or defect in the constitution of, such Council.

SECTION 26: Apprenticeship Advisers

(1) The Central Government shall, by notification in the Official Gazette, appoint a suitable person as the Central Apprenticeship Adviser.

(2) The State Government shall, by notification in the Official Gazette, appoint a suitable person as the State Apprenticeship Adviser.

(3) The Central Apprenticeship Adviser shall be the Secretary to the Central Apprenticeship Council and the State Apprenticeship Adviser shall be the Secretary to the State Apprenticeship Council.

SECTION 27: Deputy and Assistant Apprenticeship Advisers

(1) The Government may appoint suitable persons as Additional, Joint, Regional, Deputy and Assistant Apprenticeship Advisers to assist the Apprenticeship Adviser, in the performance of his functions.

(2) Every Additional, Joint, Regional, Deputy or Assistant Apprenticeship Adviser shall, subject to control of the Apprenticeship Advisor, perform such functions as may be assigned to him by the Apprenticeship Adviser.

SECTION 28: Apprenticeship Advisers to be public servants

Every Apprenticeship Adviser and every Additional, Joint, Regional, Deputy or Assistant Apprenticeship Adviser appointed under this Act, shall be deemed to be a public servant within the meaning of section 21 of the Indian Penal Code (45 of 1860).

SECTION 29: Powers of entry, inspection, etc.

(1) Subject to any rules made in this behalf the Central Apprenticeship Adviser, or such other person, not below the rank of an Assistant Apprenticeship Adviser, as may be authorised by the Central Apprenticeship Adviser in writing in this behalf may—

(a) with such assistants, if any, as he thinks fit, enter, inspect and examine any establishment or part thereof at any reasonable time;

(b) examine any apprentice employed therein or require the production of any register, record or other documents maintained in pursuance of this Act and take on the spot or otherwise statements of any person which he may consider necessary for carrying out the purposes of this Act;

(c) make such examination and inquiry as he thinks fit in order to ascertain whether the provisions of this Act and the rules made thereunder are being observed in the establishment;

(d) exercise such other powers as may be prescribed:

Provided that a State Apprenticeship Adviser or such other person, not below the rank of an Assistant Apprenticeship Adviser, as may be authorised by the State Apprenticeship Adviser in writing in this behalf may also exercise any of the powers specified in clauses (a), (b), (c), (d) of this sub-section in relation to establishments for which the appropriate Government is the State Government.

(2) Notwithstanding anything in sub-section (1), no person shall be compelled under this section to answer any question or make any statement which may tend directly or indirectly to incriminate him.

Section 30: Offences and penalties

(1) If any employer contravenes the provisions of this Act relating to the number of apprentices which he is required to engage under those provisions, he shall be given a month's notices in writing, by an officer duly authorized in this behalf by the appropriate Government, for explaining the reasons for such contravention.

(1A) In case the employer fails to reply the notice within the period specified under sub-section (1), or the authorized officer, after giving him an opportunity of being heard, is not satisfied with the reasons given by the employer, he shall be punishable with fine of five hundred rupees per shortfall of apprenticeship month for first three months and thereafter one thousand rupees per month till such number of seats are filled up.

(2) If any employer or any other person—

(a) required to furnish any information or return—

(i) refuses or neglects to furnish such information or return, or

(ii) furnishes or causes to be furnished any information or return which is false and which he either knows or believes to be false or does not believe to be true, or

(iii) refuses to answer, or gives a false answer to any question necessary for obtaining any information required to be furnished by him, or

(b) refuses or wilfully neglects to afford the Central or the State Apprenticeship Adviser, as may be authorised by the Central or the State Apprenticeship Adviser in writing in this behalf any reasonable facility for making any entry, inspection, examination or inquiry authorised by or under this Act, or

(c) requires an apprentice to work overtime without the approval of the Apprenticeship Adviser, or

(d) employs an apprentice on any work which is not connected with his training, or

(e) makes payment to an apprentice on the basis of piecework, or

(f) requires an apprentice to take part in any output bonus or incentive scheme,

(g) engages as an apprentice a person who is not qualified for being so engaged, or

(h) fails to carry out the terms and conditions of a contract of apprenticeship,

he shall be punishable with fine of one thousand rupees for every occurrence.

2(A) The provisions of this sections shall not apply to any establishment or industry which is under the Board for Industrial and Financial Reconstruction established under the Sick Industrial Companies (Special Provisions) Act, 1985 (1 of 1986).

Section 31: Penalty where no specific penalty is provided

If any employer or any other person contravenes any provision of this Act for which no punishment is provided in section 30, he shall be punishable with fine which shall not be less than one thousand rupees but may extend to three thousand rupees.

Section 32: Offences by companies

(1) If the person committing an offence under this Act is a company, every person who, at the time the offence was committed was in charge of, and was responsible to, the company for the conduct of business of the company, as well as the company, shall be deemed to be guilty of the offence and shall be liable to be proceeded against and punished accordingly:

Provided that nothing contained in this sub-section shall render any such person liable to such punishment provided in this Act if he proves that the offence was committed without his knowledge or that he exercised all due diligence to prevent the commission of such offence.

(2) Notwithstanding anything contained in sub-section (1), where an offence under this Act has been committed by a company and it is proved that the offence has been committed with the consent or connivance of, or is attributable to any negligence on the part of, any director, manager, secretary, or other officer of the company, such director, manager, secretary, or other officer shall also be deemed to be guilty of that offence and shall be liable to be proceeded against and punished accordingly.

Explanation: For the purposes of this section,—

(a) "company" means a body corporate and includes a firm or other association of individuals; and

(b) "director" in relation to a firm means a partner in the firm.

Section 33: Cognizance of offences

No court shall take cognizance of any offence under this Act or the rules made thereunder except on a complaint thereof in writing made by the Apprenticeship Adviser or the officer of the rank of Deputy Apprenticeship Adviser and above within six months from the date on which the offence is alleged to have been committed.

Section 34: Delegation of powers

The appropriate Government may, by notification in the Official Gazette, direct that any power exercisable by it under this Act or the rules made thereunder shall, in relation to such matters and subject to such conditions, if any, as may be specified in the direction, be exercisable also—

(a) where the appropriate Government is the Central Government by such officer or authority subordinate to the Central Government or by the State Government or by such officer or authority subordinate to the State Government, as may be specified in the notification; and

(b) where the appropriate Government is the State Government, by such officer or authority subordinate to the State Government, as may be specified in the notification.

SECTION 35: Construction of references

(1) Any reference in this Act or in the rules made thereunder to the Apprenticeship Council shall, unless the context otherwise requires, mean in relation to apprenticeship training in a designated trade in an establishment in relation to which the Central Government is the appropriate Government, the Central Apprenticeship Council and in relation to apprenticeship training in a designated trade in an establishment in relation to which the State Government is the appropriate Government, the State Apprenticeship Council.

(2) Any reference in this Act or in the rules made thereunder to the Apprenticeship Adviser shall, unless the context otherwise requires,—

(a) mean in relation to apprenticeship training in a designated trade in an establishment in relation to which the Central Government is the appropriate government, the Central Apprenticeship Adviser and in relation to apprenticeship training in a designated trade in an establishment in relation to which the State Government is the appropriate Government, the State Apprenticeship Adviser;

(b) be deemed to include an Additional, a Joint, a Regional, a Deputy or an Assistant Apprenticeship Adviser performing the functions of the Apprenticeship Adviser assigned to him under sub-section (2) of section 27.

SECTION 36: Protection of action taken in good faith

No suit, prosecution or other legal proceeding shall lie against any person for anything which is in good faith done or intended to be done under this Act.

SECTION 37: Power to make rules

(1) The Central Government may, after consulting the Central Apprenticeship Council, by notification in the Official Gazette, make rules for carrying out the purposes of this Act.

(1A) The powers to make rules under this section shall include the power to make such rules or any of them retrospectively from a date not earlier than the date on which this Act received the assent of the President, but no such retrospective effect shall be given to any such rule so as to prejudicially affect the interests of any such person to whom such rule may be applicable.

(2) Rules made under this Act may provide that a contravention of any such rule shall be punishable with fine which may extend to fifty rupees.

(3) Every rule made under this section shall be laid as soon as may be after it is made before each House of Parliament while it is in session for a total period of thirty

days which may be comprised in one session or in two or more successive sessions, and if before the expiry of the session immediately following the session or the successive sessions aforesaid both Houses agree in making any modification in the rules or both Houses agree that the rule should not be made, the rule shall thereafter have effect only in such modified form or be of no effect, as the case may be; so however that any such modification or annulment shall be without prejudice to the validity of anything previously done under that rule.

THE SCHEDULE

MODIFICATIONS IN THE WORKMEN'S COMPENSATION ACT, 1923 IN ITS APPLICATION TO APPRENTICES UNDER THE APPRENTICES ACT, 1961

[*See* Sections 16]

In the Workmen's Compensation Act, 1923,—

(1) in Section 2,—

(a) for clause (e), substitute—

(e) "employer" means an employer as defined in the Apprentices Act, 1961, who has engaged one or more apprentices;

(b) omit clause (k);

(c) for clause (m), substitute—

(m) "wages" means the stipend payable to an apprentice under section 13(1) of the Apprentices Act, 1961;

(d) for clause (n), substitute—

(n) "workman" means any person who is engaged as an apprentice as defined in the Apprentices Act, 1961, and who in the course of his apprenticeship training is employed in any such capacity as is specified in Schedule II;

(2) omit section 12;

(3) omit section 15;

(4) omit the proviso to section 21(1);

(5) omit the words "or a registered Trade Union" in section 24;

(6) omit clause (d) in section 30 (1);

(7) omit clause (vi), (xi), (xiii), (xvii), (xviii), (xx), (xxii), (xxiv), (xxv), (xxvi) and (xxxii) in Schedule II.

* * *

8 The Minimum Wages Act, 1948

With the emergence of the concept of a welfare state, collective bargaining between trade unions and capital has come into its own and has received statutory recognition; the state is no longer content to play the part of a passive onlooker in an industrial dispute. The old principle of the absolute freedom of contract and the doctrine of *laissez faire* have yielded place to new principles of social welfare and common good. Labour naturally looks upon the constitution of wage structures as affording a bulwark against the dangers of a depression, safeguard against unfair methods of competition between employers and a guarantee of wages necessary for the minimum requirements of employees. There can be no doubt that in fixing wage structures in different industries, industrial adjudication attempts, gradually and by stages though it may be to attain the principal objective of a welfare state, to secure "*to all citizens justice social and economic.*" To the attainment of this ideal, the Indian Constitution has given a pride of place and that is the basis of the new guiding principles of social welfare and common good.

Though social and economic justice is the ultimate ideal of industrial adjudication, its immediate objective in an industrial dispute, as to the wage structure, is to settle the dispute by constituting such a wage structure as would do justice to the interests of both labour and capital, establishing harmony between them and leading to their genuine and wholehearted cooperation in the task of production. It is obvious that cooperation between capital and labour would lead to more production and progress. In achieving this immediate objective, industrial adjudication takes into account several principles such as, the principle of comparable wages, productivity of the trade or industry, cost of living and ability of the industry to pay. The application of these and other relevant principles lead to the constitution of different categories of wage structures. These categories are sometimes described as living wage, fair wage and minimum wage. These terms, or their variants, the comfort or decency level, the subsistence level and the poverty or the floor level, cannot and do not mean the same thing in all countries nor even in different industries in the same country. It is very difficult to define or even to describe accurately the content of these different concepts. In the case of an expanding national economy, the contents of these expressions are also apt to expand and vary. What may be a fair wage in a particular industry in one country may be a living wage in the same industry in another country. Similarly, what may be a fair wage in a given industry today may cease to be fair and may border on the minimum wage in future. Industrial adjudication has naturally to apply carefully the relevant principles of wage structure and decide every industrial dispute so as to do justice to both labour and capital.

In deciding industrial disputes in regard to wage structure, one of the primary objectives is, and has to be, the restoration of peace and goodwill in the industry itself on a fair and just basis, to be determined in the light of all relevant considerations. There is, however, one principle which admits of no exceptions. No industry has a right to exist unless it is able to pay its workmen at least a bare minimum wage. It is quite likely that in underdeveloped countries, where unemployment prevails on a very large-scale, unorganised labour may be available on starvation wages: but the employment of labour on starvation wages cannot be encouraged or favoured in a modern democratic welfare state. If an employer cannot maintain his enterprise without cutting down the wages of his employees below even a bare subsistence or minimum wage, he would have no right to conduct his enterprise on such terms. In considering the pros and cons of the question, this position must be borne in mind.

It would not be correct to say that in no conceivable circumstances can the wage structure be revised to the prejudice of workmen. But even theoretically, no wage structure can or should be revised to the prejudice of workmen if the structure in question falls in the category of the bare subsistence or the minimum wage. If the wage structure in question falls in a higher category, then it would be open to the employer to claim its revision even to the prejudice of the workmen provided a case for such revision is made out on the merits to the satisfaction of the Tribunal. In dealing with a claim for such revision, the Tribunal may have to consider whether the employer's financial difficulties could not be adequately met by retrenchment in personnel already effected by the employer and sanctioned by the Tribunal. The Tribunal may also enquire whether the financial difficulties facing the employer are likely to be of a short duration or a fairly long time. It would indeed be very difficult to state exhaustively all considerations which may be relevant in a given case. After considering all the relevant facts, if the Tribunal is satisfied that a case for reduction in the wage structure has been established, then it would be open to the Tribunal to accede to the request of the employer to make appropriate reduction in the wage structure subject to such conditions as to time or otherwise that the Tribunal may deem fit or expedient to impose. The Tribunal must also keep in mind some important practical considerations. A substantial reduction in the wage structure is likely to lead to discontent among workmen and may result in disharmony between the employer and his employees; and that would never be for the benefit of the industry as a whole. On the other hand, in assessing the value or importance of possible discontent amongst workmen resulting from the reduction of wages, Industrial Tribunals will also have to take into account the fact that if any industry is burdened with a wage structure beyond its financial capacity, its very existence may be in jeopardy and that would ultimately lead to unemployment. All relevant considerations have to be carefully weighed and an attempt has to be made in each case to reach a conclusion which would be reasonable on the merits and would be fair and just to both the parties.

If in reaching its final conclusions that the wages paid are the irreducible minimum, the Appellate Tribunal has relied not only upon the alleged convention but also upon the other circumstances just mentioned, it would not be fair to say that its conclusion is vitiated in law or is otherwise unsound. Normally, the Supreme Court would be slow to entertain an objection that some of the considerations which have weighed with the Appellate Tribunal in reaching its final decision are either invalid or are not borne out by sufficient evidence on record. The fact that the concessional (special bonus, facility bonus, food concessions. etc.) payments have been made for some years also is a relevant factor to consider in dealing with the true character of these payments. If the Labour Appellate Tribunal took into account all these facts and held that the payments in question are not matters of bounty but that, in essence and in substance, they form part of the basic wage and dearness allowance payable to the workmen, there is no reason to interfere with its conclusion.[1]

CONCEPT OF WAGES

Broadly speaking, there are three categories of wages, viz.,

(1) the living wage,
(2) the minimum wage, and
(3) the fair wage.

The concept of living wage

The concept of the living wage, which has influenced the fixation of wages, statutorily or otherwise, in all economically advanced countries, is an old and well-established one, but most of the current definitions are of recent origin. The most expressive definition of the living wage is that of Justice Higgins of the Australian Commonwealth Court of Conciliation in the *Harvester* case. He defined the living wage as one appropriate for *"the normal needs of the average employee, regarded as a human being living in a civilized community"*. Justice Higgins has, at other places, explained what he meant by this cryptic pronouncement. The living wage must provide not merely for absolute essentials such as food, shelter and clothing but for *"a condition of frugal comfort estimated by current human standards."* He explained himself further by saying that it was a wage *"sufficient to insure the workmen food, shelter, clothing, frugal comfort, provision for evil days, etc., as well as regard for the special skill of an artisan if he is one"*. In a subsequent case, he observed that *"treating marriage as the usual fate of adult men, a wage which does not allow of the matrimonial condition and the maintenance of about five persons in a home would not be treated as a living wage"*.

According to the South Australian Act of 1912, the living wage means *"a sum sufficient for the normal and reasonable needs of the average employee living in a locality where work under consideration is done or is to be done."* The Queensland Industrial Conciliation and Arbitration Act provides that the basic wage paid to an adult male employee shall not be less than is *"sufficient to maintain a well-conducted employee of average health, strength and competence and his wife and a family of three children in a fair and average standard of comfort, having regard to the conditions of living prevailing among employees in the calling in respect of which such basic wage is fixed, and provided that in fixing such basic wage the earnings of the children or wife of such employee shall not be taken into account"*.

In a Tentative Budget Inquiry conducted in the United States of America in 1919, the Commissioner of the Bureau of Labour Statistics analysed the budgets with reference to three concepts, viz.,

1. *Crown Aluminium Works, Messrs.* v. *Their Workmen*, AIR 1958 SC 30.

(i) the pauper and poverty level,
(ii) the minimum of subsistence level, and
(iii) the minimum of health and comfort level,

It adopted the last for the determination of the living wage. The Royal Commission of the Basic Wage for the Commonwealth of Australia approved of this course and proceeded through norms and budget enquiries to ascertain what the minimum of health and comfort level should be. The commission quoted with approval the description of the minimum of health and comfort level in the following terms:

> "This represents a slightly higher level than that of subsistence, providing not only for the material needs of food, shelter, and body covering, but also for certain comforts, such as clothing sufficient for bodily comfort, and to maintain the wearer's instinct of self-respect and decency, some insurance against the more important misfortunes—death, disability and fire—good education for the children, some amusement, and some expenditure for self-development."[2]

Writing practically in the same language, the United Provinces Labour Enquiry Committee classified levels of living standard in four categories, viz.,

(i) the poverty level,
(ii) the minimum subsistence level,
(iii) the subsistence plus level, and
(iv) the comfort level.

It chose the subsistence plus level as the basis of what it called the "minimum living wage".

The Bombay Textile Labour Inquiry Committee 1937, considered the living wage standard at considerable length and, while accepting the concept of the living wage as described above, observed as follows:

> "... What we have to attempt is not an exact measurement of a well-defined concept. Any definition of a standard of living is necessarily descriptive rather than logical. Any minimum, after all, is arbitrary and relative. No completely objective and absolute meaning can be attached to a term like the "living wage standard" and it has necessarily to be judged in the light of the circumstances of the particular time and country."[3]

The Committee then proceeded through the use of norms and standard budgets to lay down what the basic wage should be, so that it might approximate to the living wage standard "in the light of the circumstances of the particular time and country."

The minimum Wage-Fixing Machinery published by the ILO has summarised these views as follows.

"In different countries estimates have been made of the amount of a living wage, but the estimates vary according to the point of view of the investigator. Estimates may be classified into at least three groups:

(1) the amount necessary for mere subsistence,

---

2. Cited in *Express Newspaper (Private) Ltd.* v. *Union of India*, AIR 1958 SC 578.
3. *Ibid.*

(2) the amount necessary for health and decency, and

(3) the amount necessary to provide a standard of comfort."[4]

It will be seen from this summary of the concepts of the living wage held in various parts of the world that there is general agreement that the living wage should enable the male earner to provide for himself and his family not merely the bare essentials of food, clothing and shelter but a measure of frugal comfort including education for the children, protection against ill-health, requirements of essential social needs, and a measure of insurance against the more important misfortunes including old age.[5]

Article 43 of our Constitution has also adopted as one of the Directive Principles of State Policy that:

"The State shall endeavour to secure, by suitable legislation or economic organisation or in any other way, to all workers, agricultural, industrial or otherwise, work, a living wage, conditions of work ensuring a decent standard of life and full enjoyment of leisure and social and cultural opportunities...."

This is the ideal to which our social welfare State has to approximate in an attempt to ameliorate the living conditions of the workers.

The concept of minimum wage

The International Convention of 1928 prescribes the setting up of minimum wage-fixing machinery in industries in which "no arrangements exist for the effective regulation of wages by collective agreement or otherwise and wages are exceptionally low...."

As a rule, though the living wage is the target, it has to be tempered, even in advanced countries, by other considerations, particularly the general level of wages in other industries and the capacity of industry to pay. This view has been accepted by the Bombay Textile Labour Inquiry Committee which says that the living wage basis affords an absolute external standard for the determination of the minimum and that where a living wage criterion has been used in the giving of an award or the fixing of a wage, the decision has always been tempered by other considerations of a practical character.

In India, however, the level of the national income is so low at present that it is generally accepted, that the country cannot afford to prescribe by law a minimum wage which would correspond to the concept of the living wage as described in the preceding paragraphs. What then should be the level of minimum wage which can be sustained by the present stage of the country's economy? Most employers and some Provincial Governments consider that the minimum wage can at present be only a bare subsistence wage. In fact, even one important All India organisation of employees had suggested that "a minimum wage is that wage which is sufficient to cover the bare physical needs of a worker and his family." Many others, however, consider that a minimum wage should also provide for some other essential requirements such as a minimum of education, medical facilities and other amenities. It has been also observed that a minimum wage must provide not merely for the bare sustenance of life but for the preservation of the efficiency of the worker. For this purpose, the minimum wage must also provide for some measure of education, medical requirements, and amenities".[6]

4. *Ibid.*
5. Report of the committee on Fair Wages (1947 to 1949), pp. 5–7, paras 6 and 7.
6. Report of the Committee on Fair Wages, pp. 7–9, paras 8–10.

There is also a distinction between a bare subsistence or minimum wage and a statutory minimum wage. The former is a wage which would be sufficient to cover the bare physical needs of a worker and his family, that is, a rate which has got to be paid to the workers irrespective of the capacity of the industry to pay. If an industry is unable to pay to its workmen at least a bare minimum wage, it has no right to exist.[7] The Supreme Court in *Hydro (Engineers) Pvt. Ltd., M/s.* v. *The Workmen*[8] has attached a progressive look to the concept of minimum wage and accordingly observed that the Act contemplates that minimum wage rates must ensure not merely the mere physical need of the worker which would keep him just above starvation but must ensure for him not only his subsistence and that of his family but also preserve his efficiency as a workman. It should, therefore, provide, as the Fair Wages Committee appointed by the Government recommended, not merely for the bare subsistence of his life but for the preservation of the worker and so must provide for some measure of education, medical requirements and amenities.

The concept of fair wage

The payment of fair wages to labour is one of the cardinal recommendations of the Industrial Truce Resolution. The Indian National Trade Union Congress is of the opinion that the wage fixed by collective agreements, arbitrators, and adjudicators could at least be treated, like the minimum wage, as the starting point and that wherever the capacity of an industry to pay a higher wage is established, such a higher wage should be deemed to be the fair wage. The minimum wage should have no regard to the capacity of an industry to pay and should be based solely on the requirements of the worker and his family. "A fair wages is", in the opinion of the Indian National Trade Union Congress, "a step towards the progressive realization of a living wage." Several employers, while they are inclined to the view that fair wages would, in the initial stages, be closely related to current wages, are prepared to agree that the prevailing rates could suitably be enhanced according to the capacity of an Industry to pay and that the fair wage would in time progressively approach the living wage. It is necessary to quote one other opinion, viz., that of the Government of Bombay, which has had considerable experience in the matter of wage regulation. The opinion of that Government is as follows:

> "Nothing short of a living wage can be a fair wage if under competitive conditions an industry can be shown to be capable of paying a full living wage. The minimum wage standards set up the irreducible level, the lowest limit or the floor below which no workers shall be paid.... A fair wage is settled above the minimum wage and goes through the process of approximating towards a living wage."

While the lower limit of the fair wage must obviously be the minimum wage, the upper limit is equally set by what may broadly be called the capacity of industry to pay. This will depend not only on the present economic position of the industry but on its future prospects. Between these two limits the actual wages will depend on a consideration of the following factors and in the light of the comments given below:

7. *Ibid.*, f.n. 2.
8. AIR 1969 SC 182.

(i) the productivity of labour;

(ii) the prevailing rates of wages in the same or similar occupations in the same or neighbouring localities;

(iii) the level of the national income and its distribution; and

(iv) the place of the industry in the economy of the country.[9]

It will be noticed that the "fair wage" is thus a means between the living wage and the minimum wage and even the minimum wage contemplated above is something more than the bare minimum or subsistence wage which would be sufficient to cover the bare physical needs of the worker and his family, a wage which would provide also for the preservation of the efficiency of the worker and for some measure of education, medical requirements and amenities.

This concept of minimum wage is in harmony with the advance of thought in all civilised countries and approximates to the statutory minimum wage which the State should strive to achieve having regard to the Directive Principles of State Policy mentioned above.

The enactment of the Minimum Wages Act, 1948 (XI of 1948) affords an illustration of an attempt to provide a statutory minimum wage. It is an Act to provide for fixing minimum rates of wages in certain employments and the appropriate Government is thereby empowered to fix different minimum rates of wages for:

(i) different scheduled employments;

(ii) different classes of work in the same scheduled employment;

(iii) adults, adolescents, children and apprentices, and

(iv) different localities; and

(v) such minimum rates of wages could be fixed by the hour, by the day or by any larger period as may be prescribed.

It will also be noticed that the content of the expressions "minimum wage", "fair wage" and "living wage" is not fixed and static. It varies and is bound to vary from time to time. With the growth and development of national economy, living standards would improve and so our notions about the respective categories of wages would expand and be more progressive.

It must, however, be remembered that whereas the bare minimum or subsistence wage would have to be fixed irrespective of the capacity of the industry to pay, the minimum wage thus contemplated postulates the capacity of the industry to pay and no fixation of wages which ignores this essential factor of the capacity of the industry to pay could ever be supported.

FIXATION OF WAGE

The fixation of a wage-structure is always a delicate task because a balance has to be struck between the demands of social justice, which requires that the workmen should receive their proper share of the national income, which they help to produce, with a view to improving

9. Report of the Committee on Fair Wages, pp. 4, 9–11, paras 11–15.

their standard of living, and the depletion, which every increase in wages makes in the profits as this tends to divert capital from industry into other channels thought to be more profitable. The task is not rendered any easier because conditions vary from region to region, industry to industry and establishment to establishment. To cope up with these differences, certain principles on which wages are fixed have been stated from time to time by the Apex Court. Broadly speaking, the *first* principle is that there is a minimum wage which, in any event, must be paid, irrespective of the extent of profits, the financial condition of the establishment or the availability of workmen on lower wages. This minimum wage is independent of the kind of industry and applies to all alike big or small. It sets the lowest limit below which wages cannot be allowed to sink in all humanity. The *second* principle is that wages must be fair, that is to say, sufficiently high to provide a standard family with food, shelter, clothing, medical care and education of children appropriate to the workman but not at a rate exceeding his wage earning capacity in the class of establishment to which he belongs. A fair wage is thus related to the earning capacity and the workload. It must, however, be realised that fair wage is not 'living wage' by which is meant a wage which is sufficient to provide not only the essentials above mentioned but a fair measure of frugal comfort with an ability to provide for old age and rainy days. Fair wage lies between the minimum wage, which must be paid in any event, and the living wage, which is the goal. As time passes and prices rise, even the fair wage fixed for the time being tends to sag downwards and then a revision is necessary. To a certain extent, the disparity is made up by the additional payment of dearness allowance. This allowance is given to compensate for the rise in the cost of living. But as it is not advisable to have a 100 per cent neutralisation lest it should lead to inflation, the dearness allowance is often a little less than 100 per cent neutralisation. In course of time even the addition of the dearness allowance does not sufficiently make up the gap between wages and cost of living and a revision of wages and/or dearness allowance then becomes necessary. This revision is done on certain principles.[10]

OBJECT

The object of the Act is to prevent exploitation of the workers, and for that purpose it aims at fixation of minimum wages which the employers must pay. The legislature undoubtedly intended to apply the Act to those industries or localities in which by reason of causes such as unorganised labour or absence of machinery for regulation of wages, the wages paid to workers were, in the light of the general level of wages and subsistence level, inadequate. Conditions of labour vary in different industries and from locality to locality, and the expediency of fixing minimum wages, and the rates thereof depends largely upon diverse factors which in their very nature are variable and can properly be ascertained by the Government which is in charge of the administration of the State. It is to carry out effectively the purpose of this enactment that power has been given to the appropriate Government to decide with reference to local conditions, whether it is desirable that minimum wages should be fixed in regard to any scheduled trade or industry, in any locality, and if it be deemed expedient to do so, the

10. *Kamani Metals and Alloys Ltd.* v. *The Workmen*, AIR 1967 SC 1175.

rates at which the wages should be fixed in respect of that industry in the locality.[11] The provisions of the Minimum Wages Act are intended to achieve the object of providing social justice to workmen employed in the scheduled employments by prescribing minimum rates of wages for them, and so in construing the said provisions the court should adopt what is sometimes described as a 'beneficent rule of construction.' If the relevant words are capable of two constructions preference may be given to that construction which helps to sustain the validity of the impugned notification; but it is obvious that an occasion for showing preference for one construction rather than the other can legitimately arise only when two constructions are reasonably possible, not otherwise.[12]

CONSTITUTIONAL VALIDITY OF THE ACT

In the case of *Edward Mills Co. Ltd. Beawar* v. *State of Ajmer*,[13] the validity of S. 27 of the Minimum Wages Act was challenged on the ground of excessive delegation. It was urged that the Act prescribed no principles and laid down no standard which could furnish an intelligent guidance to the administrative authority in making selection while acting under S. 27 and so the matter was left entirely to the discretion of the appropriate Government, which can amend the schedule in any way it liked and such delegation virtually amounted to a surrender by the legislature of its essential legislative function. This contention was rejected by Mukherjea, J., as he then was, who spoke for the Court. The learned judge observed that the legislature undoubtedly intended to apply the Act to those industries only where by reason of unorganised labour or want of proper arrangement for effective regulation of wages or for other causes the wages of labourers in a particular industry were very low. He also pointed out that conditions of labour vary under different circumstances and from State to State and the expediency of including a particular trade or industry within the schedule depends upon a variety of facts, which are by no means uniform and which can best be ascertained by a person who is placed in charge of the administration of a particular State. That is why the Court concluded that on enacting S. 27, it could not be said that the Legislature had in any way stripped itself of its essential powers or assigned to the administrative authority anything but an accessory or subordinate power, which was deemed necessary to carry out the purpose and the policy of the Act.

In the same year another attempt was made to challenge the validity of the Act in *Bijay Cotton Mills Ltd.* v. *State of Ajmer*.[14] This time the crucial sections of the Act, namely, Ss. 3, 4 and 5 were attacked, and the challenge was based on the ground that the restrictions imposed by them upon the freedom of contract violated the fundamental right guaranteed under Art. 19(1)(g) of the Constitution. It is contended by the learned counsel in the instant case that the Minimum Wages Act puts unreasonable restrictions upon the rights of the employer in the sense that he is prevented from carrying on trade or business unless he is prepared to pay minimum wages. The rights of the employees are also restricted, inasmuch as they are

11. *Bhikusa Yamasa Kshatriya, M/s* v. *Sangamner Akola Taluka Bidi Kamgar Union*, AIR 1963 SC 806.
12. *M.P. Mineral Industry Association, Nagpur* v. *Regional Labour Commissioner (Central), Jabalpur*, AIR 1960 SC 1068.
13. AIR 1955 SC 25.
14. AIR 1955 SC 33.

disabled from working in any trade or industry on the terms agreed to between them and their employers. It is pointed out that the provisions relating to the fixation of minimum wages are unreasonable and arbitrary. The whole thing has been left to the unfettered discretion of the "appropriate Government" and even when a committee is appointed, the report or advice of such committee is not binding on the Government. The decision of the committee is final and is not open to further review or challenge in any court of law.

The learned counsel further says that the restrictions put by the Act are altogether unreasonable and even oppressive with regard to one class of employers, who, for purely economic reasons, are not able to pay the minimum wages but who have no intention to exploit labour at all. In such cases the provisions of the Act have no reasonable relation to the object which it has in view. Therefore, the provisions of the Minimum Wages Act are illegal and *'ultra vires'* by reason of their conflict with the fundamental rights of the employers and the employee guaranteed under Art. 19(l)(g) of the Constitution and that they are not protected by Cl. (6) of Art. 19(1) of the Constitution of India.

The Court held that it can scarcely be disputed that securing of living wages to labourers which ensure not only bare physical subsistence but also the maintenance of health and decency, is conducive to the general interest of the public. This is one of the Directive Principles of State Policy embodied in Art. 43 of our Constitution. It is well known that in 1928, a Minimum Wages Fixing Machinery Convention was held at Geneva and the resolutions passed in that convention were embodied in the International Labour Code. The Minimum Wages Act is said to have been passed with a view to give effect to these resolutions. The Court cited the view of the Madras High Court[15] where the Madras High Court held that if the labourers are to be secured in the enjoyment of minimum wages and they are to be protected against exploitation by their employers, it is absolutely necessary that restraints should be imposed upon their freedom of contract and such restrictions cannot, in any sense, be said to be unreasonable. On the other hand, the employers cannot be heard to complain if they are compelled to pay minimum wages to their labourers even though the labourers, on account of their poverty and helplessness, are willing to work on lesser wages.

The Apex Court in the instant case could not really appreciate the argument of the learned counsel that the provisions of the Act are bound to affect harshly and even oppressively a particular class of employers, who, for purely economic reasons, are unable to pay the minimum wages fixed by the authorities but have absolutely no dishonest intention of exploiting their labourers. The Court, accordingly, held that if it is in the interest of the general public that the labourers should be secured adequate living wages, the intentions of the employers whether good or bad are really irrelevant. Individual employers might find it difficult to carry on the business on the basis of the minimum wages fixed under the Act, but this must be entirely due to the economic conditions of these particular employers. That cannot be a reason for striking down the law itself as unreasonable.

As regards the procedure for the fixing of minimum wages, the "appropriate Government" has undoubtedly been given very large powers. But it has to take into consideration, before fixing wages, the advice of the committee, if one is appointed, or the representations on its proposals made by persons who are likely to be affected thereby. Consultation with advisory

---

15. *South India Estate Labour Relations organisation* v. *State of Madras*, AIR 1955 Mad 45.

bodies has been made obligatory on all occasions of revision of minimum wages, and S. 8 of the Act provides for the appointment of a Central Advisory Board for the purpose of advising the Central as well as the State Government both in the matter of fixing and revision of minimum wages.

Such Central Advisory body is to act also as a coordinating agent for coordinating the work of the different advisory bodies. In the committees or the advisory bodies, the employers and the employees have an equal number of representatives and there are certain independent members besides them, who are expected to take a fair and impartial view of the matter. These provisions constitute an adequate safeguard against any hasty or capricious decision by the "appropriate Government".

Another contention of the learned counsel is that in suitable cases the "appropriate Government" has also been given the power of granting exemptions from the operation of the provisions of this Act. There is no provisions for a further review of the decision of the "appropriate Government". Mukherjea, J., as he then was, who again spoke for the Court, held that the restrictions were imposed in the interest of the general public and with a view to carry out one of the Directive Principles of State policy as embodied in Art. 43 and so the impugned sections were protected by the norms of Cl. (6) of Art. 19. In repelling the argument of the employers inability to meet the burden of the minimum wage rates, it was observed that the employers cannot be heard to complain if they are compelled to pay minimum wages to their labourers, even though the labourers, on account of their poverty and helplessness, are willing to work on lesser wages and that if individual employers might find it difficult to carry on business on the basis of minimum wages fixed under the Act, that cannot be the reason for striking down the law itself as unreasonable. The inability of the employers may in many cases be due entirely to the economic conditions of those employers.

It would thus be seen that these two decisions have firmly established the validity of the Act, and there can no longer be any doubt that in fixing the minimum wage rates as contemplated by the Act the hardship caused to individual employers or their inability to meet the burden has no relevance.[16]

Preamble to the Act

An Act to provide for fixing minimum rates of wages in certain employments. Whereas it is expedient to provide for fixing minimum rates of wages in certain employments;

It is hereby enacted as follows:

Section 1: Short title and extent

(1) This Act may be called the Minimum Wages Act, 1948.

(2) It extends to the whole of India.

The question raised before the Supreme Court in *Sanjit Roy* v. *State of Rajasthan*[17] was regarding the applicability of the Minimum Wages Act to the worker working under

16. *U. Unichoyi* v. *State of Kerala*, AIR 1962 SC 12.
17. AIR 1983 SC 328.

the famine relief work programme of the State of Rajasthan. Such famine relief work was done by the Government in accordance with the provisions of the Rajasthan Famine Relief Works Employees (Exemption from Labour Laws) Act, 1964 (hereinafter referred to as the Exemption Act), where the workers were paid the remuneration less than the minimum wages prescribed by the Government. When the writ petition reached for hearing before the Supreme Court, the State Government contended that since the construction work was a famine relief work, the Minimum Wages Act, 1948 was not applicable to the employees engaged on this construction work by reason of S. 3 of the Rajasthan Famine Relief Works Employees (Exemption from Labour Laws) Act, 1964. The principal grounds on which the constitutionality of the Exemption Act was challenged were based on Arts. 14 and 23 of the Constitution.

Justice Bhagwati confined his judgment only to a consideration of the attack based on Art. 23 and he categorically said that when the issue raised before the Court is well founded and it falls within the four walls of Art. 23 of the Constitution, there is no need of further investigation of the facts relating to the violation of Art. 14. Justice Bhagwati relied on the ratio of *Peoples Union for Democratic Rights* v. *Union of India,*[18] popularly known as *Asiad* Case, where the Supreme Court had occasion to consider the true meaning and effect of Art. 23. The Court pointed out in *Asiad* Case that the constitution makers, when they set out to frame the Constitution, found that the practice of 'forced labour' constituted an ugly and shameful feature of our national life, which cried for urgent attention. With a view to obliterating and wiping out of existence this revolting practice, which was a relic of a feudal exploitative society, totally incompatible with the new egalitarian, socio-economic order which "We the people of India" were determined to build, they enacted Art. 23 in the Chapter on Fundamental Rights. This Article, said the Court, is intended to eradicate the pernicious practice of 'forced labour' and to wipe it out altogether from the national scene and it is therefore not limited in its application against the State but it is also enforceable against any other person indulging in such practice. It is designed to protect the individual not only against the State but also against other private citizens. The Court observed that the expression *"other similar forms of forced labour"* in Art. 23 is of the widest amplitude and on its true interpretation, it covers every possible form of forced labour, begar or otherwise, and it makes no difference whether the person forced to give his labour or service to another is remunerated or not. Even if remuneration is paid, labour supplied by a person would be hit by this Article if it is forced labour, that is, labour supplied not willingly but as a result of force or compulsion and the same would be the position even if forced labour supplied by a person has its origin in a contract of service. The Court then considered whether there would be any breach of Art. 23 when a person provides labour or service to the State or to any other person and is paid less than the minimum wage for it and observed:

> "It is obvious that ordinarily no one would willingly supply labour or service to another for less than the minimum wage, when he knows that under the law he is entitled to get minimum for the labour or service provided by him. It may therefore be legitimately presumed that when a person provides labour or service to another against receipt of remuneration which is less than the minimum wage, he is acting under the force of some compulsion which drives him to work though he is paid less than what he is entitled under

18. AIR 1982 SC 1473.

> the law to receive. What Article 23 prohibits is 'forced labour' that is labour or service which a person is forced to provide and 'force' which would make such labour or service 'forced labour' may arise in several ways. It may be physical force which may compel a person to provide labour or service to another or it may be force exerted through a legal provision such as a provision for imprisonment or fine in case the employee fails to provide labour or service or it may even be compulsion arising from hunger and poverty, want and destitution. Any factor which deprives a person of a choice of alternatives and compels him to adopt one particular course of action may properly be regarded as force and if labour or service is compelled as a result of such 'force', it would be 'forced labour'. Where a person is suffering from hunger or starvation, when he has no resources at all to fight disease or to feed his wife and children or even to hide their nakedness, where utter grinding poverty has broken his back, and reduced him to a state of helplessness and despair and where no other employment is available to alleviate the rigour of his poverty, he would have no choice but to accept any work that comes his way, even if the remuneration offered to him is less than the minimum wage. He would be in no position to bargain with the employer; he would have to accept what is offered to him. And in doing so he would be acting not as a free agent with a choice between alternatives but under the compulsion of economic circumstances and the labour or service provided by him would be clearly 'forced labour'. There is no reason why the word 'forced' should be read in a narrow and restricted manner so as to be confined only to physical or legal 'force' particularly when the national charter, its fundamental document has promised to build a new socialist republic where there will be socio-economic justice for all and everyone shall have the right to work, to education and to adequate means of livelihood. The constitution makers have given us one of the most remarkable documents in history for ushering in a new socioeconomic order and the Constitution which they have forged for us has a social purpose and an economic mission and therefore every word or phrase in the Constitution must be interpreted in a manner which would advance the socioeconomic objective of the Constitution. It is not unoften that in a capitalist society economic circumstances exert much greater pressure on an individual in driving him to a particular course of action than physical compulsion or force of legislative provision. The word 'force' must therefore be construed to include not only physical or legal force but also force arising from the compulsion of economic circumstances which leaves no choice of alternatives to a person in want and compels him to provide labour or service even though the remuneration received for, it is less than the minimum wage. Of course, if a person provides labour or service to another against receipt of the minimum wage, it would not be possible to say that the labour or service provided by him is 'forced labour' because he gets what he is entitled under law to receive. No inference can reasonably be drawn in such a case that he is forced to provide labour or service for the simple reason that he would be providing labour or service against receipt of what is lawfully payable to him just like any other person who is not under the force of any compulsion. We are therefore of the view that where a person provides labour or service to another for remuneration which is less than the minimum wage, the labour or service provided by him clearly falls within the scope and ambit of the words 'forced labour' under Article 23. Such a person would be entitled to come to the Court for enforcement of his fundamental right under Article 23 by asking the Court to direct payment, of the minimum wage to him so that the labour or service provided by him ceases to be 'forced labour' and the breach of Article 23 is remedied."[19]

Therefore, the Supreme Court in *Sanjit Roy* case observed that where a person provides labour or service to another for remuneration which is less than the minimum wage, the labour or service provided by him clearly falls within the meaning of the words 'forced

---

19. *Ibid.* at pp. 1488–1489 per Bhagwati, J.

labour' and attracts the condemnation of Art. 23. Every person who provides labour or service to another is entitled at the least to the minimum wage, and if anything less than the minimum wage is paid to him, he can complain of violation of his fundamental right under Art. 23 and ask the Court to direct payment of the minimum wage to him so that the breach of Art. 23 may be abated. The Court further held:

> "If this be the correct position in law, it is difficult to see how the constitutional validity of the Exemption Act in so far as it excludes the applicability of the Minimum Wages Act, 1948 to the workmen employed in famine relief works can be sustained. Article 23, as pointed out above, mandates that no person shall be required or permitted to provide labour or service to another on payment of anything less than the minimum wage and if the Exemption Act, by excluding the applicability of the Minimum Wages Act 1948, provides that minimum wage may not be paid to a workman employed in any famine relief work, it would be clearly violative of Article 23. The respondent however contended that when the State undertakes famine relief work with a view to providing help to the persons affected by drought and scarcity conditions, it would be difficult for the State to comply with the labour laws, because if the State were required to observe the labour laws, the potential of the State to provide employment to the affected persons would be crippled and the State would not be able to render help to the maximum number of affected persons and it was for this reason that the applicability of the Minimum Wages Act, 1948 was excluded, in relation to workmen employed in famine relief work. This contention, plausible though it may seem is, in my opinion, unsustainable and cannot be accepted. When the State undertakes famine relief work, it is no doubt true that it does so in order to provide relief to persons affected by drought and scarcity conditions but nonetheless, it is work which ensures for the benefit of the State representing the society and if labour or service is provided by the affected persons for carrying out such work, there is no reason why the State should pay anything less than the minimum wage to the affected persons. It is not as if a dole or bounty is given by the State to the affected persons in order to provide relief to them against drought and scarcity conditions nor is the work to be carried out by the affected persons worthless or useless to the society so that under the guise of providing work what the State in effect and substance seeks to do is to give a dole or bounty to the affected persons. The Court cannot proceed on the basis that the State would undertake by way of famine relief, work which is worthless and without utility for the society and indeed no democratic State which is administered by a sane and sensible Government would do so because it would be sheer waste of human labour and resource which can usefully be diverted into fruitful and productive channels leading to the welfare of the community and creation of national asset or wealth. It is difficult to appreciate why the State should require the affected persons to provide labour or service on work which is of no use to the society, instead of simply distributing dole or bounty amongst the affected persons. There is no reason why the State should resort to such a camouflage. The presumption therefore must be that the work undertaken by the State by way of famine relief is useful to the society and, productive in terms of creation of some asset or wealth and when the State exacts labour or service from the affected persons for carrying out such work, for example, a bridge or a road, which has utility for the society and which is going to augment the wealth of the State, there can be no justification for the State not to pay the minimum wage to the affected persons. The State cannot be permitted to take advantage of the helpless condition of the affected persons and exact labour or service from them on payment of less than the minimum wage. No work of utility and value can be allowed to be constructed on the blood and sweat of persons who are reduced to a state of helplessness on account of drought and scarcity conditions. The State cannot under the guise of helping these affected persons exact work of utility and value from them without paying them the minimum wage. Whenever any labour or service is taken by the State from any person, whether he be affected by drought and scarcity

conditions or not, the State must pay, at the least minimum wage to such person on pain of violation of Article 23 and the Exemption Act in so far as it excludes the applicability of the Minimum Wages Act, 1948 to workmen employed on famine relief work and permits payment of less than the minimum wage to such workmen, must be held to be invalid as offending the provisions of Article 23."[20]

Section 2: Interpretation

In this Act, unless there is anything repugnant in the subject or context,—

(a) **adolescent** means a person who has completed his fourteenth years of age but has not completed his eighteenth year.

(aa) **adult** means a person who has completed his eighteenth years of age.

(b) **appropriate Government** means—

  (i) in relation to any scheduled employment carried on by or under the authority of the Central Government or a railway administration, or in relation to a mine, oilfield or major port, or any corporation established by a Central Act, the Central Government, and

  (ii) in relation to any other scheduled employment, the State Government.

(bb) **child** means a person who has not completed his fourteenth year of age.

(c) **competent authority** means the authority appointed by the appropriate Government by notification in its Official Gazette to ascertain from time to time the cost of living index number applicable to the employees employed in the scheduled employments specified in such notification.

(d) **cost of living index number**, in relation to employees in any scheduled employment in respect of which minimum rates of wages have been fixed, means the index number ascertained and declared by the competent authority by notification in the Official Gazette to be the cost of living index number applicable to employees in such employment.

(e) **employer** means any person who employs, whether directly or through another person, or whether on behalf of himself or any other person, one or more employees in any scheduled employment in respect of which minimum rates of wages have been fixed under this Act, and includes, except in sub-section (3) of section 26,—

  (i) in a factory where there is carried on any scheduled employment in respect of which minimum rates of wages have been fixed under this Act, any person named under clause (f) of sub-section (1) of section 7 of the Factories Act, 1948 (63 of 1948), as manager of the factory;

  (ii) in any scheduled employment under the control of any Government in India in respect of which minimum rates of wages have been fixed under this Act, the person or authority appointed by such Government for the supervision and control of employees or where no person or authority is so appointed the head of the department;

20. *Ibid.*, f.n. 17, at pp. 333–334 per Bhagwati, J.

(iii) in any scheduled employment under any local authority in respect of which minimum rates of wages have been fixed under this Act, the person appointed by such authority for the supervision and control of employees or where no person is so appointed, the chief executive officer of the local authority;

(iv) in any other case where there is carried on any scheduled employment in respect of which minimum rates of wages have been fixed under this Act, any person responsible to the owner for the supervision and control of the employees or for the payment of wages.

(f) **prescribed** means prescribed by rules made under this Act.

(g) **scheduled employment** means an employment specified in the Schedule, or any process or branch of work forming part of such employment.

(h) **wages** means all remuneration, capable of being expressed in terms of money, which would, if the terms of the contract of employment, express or implied, were fulfilled, be payable to a person employed in respect of his employment or of work done in such employment and includes house rent allowance, but does not include—

(i) the value of—

(a) any house, accommodation, supply of light, water, medical attendance, or

(b) any other amenity or any service excluded by general or special order of the appropriate government;

(ii) any contribution paid by the employer to any pension fund or provident fund or under any scheme of social insurance;

(iii) any travelling allowance or the value of any travelling concession;

(iv) any sum paid to the person employed to defray special expenses entailed on him by the nature of his employment; or

(v) any gratuity payable on discharge.

The Supreme Court in *Manganese Ore (India) Ltd.* v. *Chandi Lal Saha*[21] had to consider whether the attendance-bonus and the supply of grain at a concessional rate are the concessions which are capable of being expressed in terms of money and as such are remunerations within the definition of wages under S. 2(h) of the Act. The Court observed that the scheme of the Act recognises *"wages"* as defined under S. 2(h) and also *"wages in kind"* under S. 11 of the Act. Reading both the provisions together *"wages in kind"* can only become part of the *"wages"* if the conditions provided under sub-sections. (2), (3) and (4) of S. 11 of the Act are complied with. Admittedly, there was no notification by the Central Government under S. 11(3) of the Act and as such the supply of grain at a concessional rate cannot be considered *"wages"* under S. 2(h) of the Act. The Court examined the question from another angle. The supply of grain at concessional rate to the workers is in the nature of an amenity or an additional facility/service. The managements, specially of public undertakings, are bound by the Directive Principles of the State policy enshrined under Part IV of the Constitution of India. The workers must be ensured a living wage, just and humane conditions of work and a decent standard of life. The management must endeavour to secure for the workmen apart from *"wages"* other amenities like supply of essential commodities

21. AIR 1991 SC 520.

at concessional rates, medical aid, housing facility, education for children, old age benefits and opportunities for social, cultural and sports activities. All these amenities may be capable of being expressed in terms of money, but it is clear from the scheme of the Act that these concessions do not come within the definition given under S. 2(h). Therefore, the Court held that the supply of grain at a concessional rate to the workmen is an amenity and cannot be included in the rates of wages prescribed by the notification.

As regards the attendance-bonus, it was an additional payment made to the workmen as a means of procuring their regular attendance with the ultimate object of increasing production. The bonus was in the nature of extra remuneration for regular attendance. The said bonus was not payable to all the workmen at the time of joining the employment. It was payable to a workman who had put in continuous service for a specified period and who was loyal to the management. The attendance bonus was only an incentive and it was not a wage. There is a basic difference between the incentive bonus and the minimum wage. Every workman is entitled to the minimum wage from the very first day of his joining the employment whereas the bonus has to be earned and it becomes payable *"after the event"*. In the present case, the attendance bonus was payable after regular attendance for a specified period and remaining loyal to the management. The scheme of payment of attendance bonus was thus an incentive to secure regular attendance of the workmen. It was an additional payment made to the workmen as a means of increasing production. The Court relied on *M/s. Titaghur Paper Mills Co. Ltd.* v. *Its Workmen*[22] where the Supreme Court held that the payment of production bonus is in the nature of an incentive and is in addition to the wages, therefore, it cannot be treated as part of the minimum wages fixed under the Act.

(i) **employee** means any person who is employed for hire or reward to do any work, skilled or unskilled, manual or clerical, in a scheduled employment in respect of which minimum rates of wages have been fixed; and includes an out-worker to whom any articles or materials are given out by another person to be made up, cleaned, washed, altered, ornamented, finished, repaired, adapted or otherwise processed for sale for the purposes of the trade or business of that other person where the process is to be carried out either in the home of the out-worker or in some other premises not being premises under the control and management of that other person; and also includes an employee declared to be an employee by the appropriate government; but does not include any member of the Armed Forces of the Union.

The question that arose for consideration before the Supreme Court in *Haryana Unrecognised Schools Association* v. *State of Haryana*[23] was whether teachers of an educational institution can be held to be employee under S. 2(i) of the Minimum Wages Act to enable the Government to fix their minimum wages?

The fact of the case reveals that the Government of Haryana in exercise of power conferred under S. 27 of the Minimum Wages Act added in Part 1 of the Schedule Item No. 40 describing *"Employment in private coaching classes, schools including Nursery Schools and technical institutions"*, for the purpose of fixing minimum rate of wages for

22. AIR 1959 SC 1095.
23. AIR 1996 SC 2108.

the employees therein. By notification, the State Government in exercise of power conferred under sub-s. (2) of S. 5 of the Act fixed the minimum rate of wages in respect of the different categories of employees serving in such schools. Challenging these notifications, the writ petitions were filed essentially on the ground that the teachers of educational institution cannot come within the purview of the Act since they are not workmen within the meaning of the Industrial Disputes Act nor would they be employee under S. 2(i) of the Act. The High Court, however, dismissed the writ petition on the ground that the power of the State Government to add any employment to the Schedule under S. 27 of the Act is without any fetter and further that the appropriate Government has tried to mitigate the sufferings and exploitation of the educated trained/untrained teachers at the hands of the managements/ employers of the private educational institutions and S. 5 of the Act gives large powers to the appropriate Government. Hence, it is an appeal by special leave brought before the Supreme Court for consideration.

The learned counsel for the appellant contended before the Supreme Court that the object of the Act being to prevent exploitation of the workers, it aims at fixation of minimum wages which the employers must pay, the teachers of an educational institution cannot be brought within the purview of the Act. The learned counsel also contended that the definition of employee under S. 2(i) of the Act, even if given a liberal interpretation, will not bring within its sweep a teacher of an educational institution since the duty discharged by a teacher can neither be termed as manual or clerical nor can it be held to be skilled or unskilled. Accordingly, it is contended that the State Government has no power to fix the minimum wage of a teacher of an educational institution in exercise of power under S. 5(2) read with S. 27 of the Act. The learned counsel appearing for the respondent, on the other hand, contended that it was open for the State Government to add a particular category of employment to the Schedule in exercise of power under S. 27 of the Act and since the Management of the schools is exploiting the teachers, the State Government, to mitigate the grievance of the teachers, has fixed minimum wage under S. 5(2) of the Act and therefore the same should not be interfered with. It may be noted that the counsel, appearing for the appellant, in course of his argument, has submitted that the association which filed the writ petition and which is appellant before the Supreme Court consist of teachers and if teachers themselves do not urge to be brought within the purview of the Act, there was no need for the Government to bring them within the purview of the Act.

In view of the rival submissions at the Bar, the only question that crops up for consideration is whether the teachers of an educational institution can be brought within the purview of the Act and the appropriate Government can fix the minimum wage of such teachers by issuing notification under the Act.

The Apex Court held that a combined reading of S. 2(i) and S. 27 of the Act as well as the object of the legislation, it is explicitly clear that the State Government can add to either part of the Schedule any employment where persons are employed for hire or reward to do any work skilled or unskilled, manual or clerical. If the persons employed do not do the work of any skilled or unskilled or of a manual or clerical nature, then it would not be possible for the State Government to include such an employment in the Schedule in exercise of power under S. 27 of the Act. Since the teachers of an educational institution are not employed to do any skilled or unskilled or manual or clerical work and therefore could not be held to be an employee under S. 2(i) of the Act, it is beyond the competence of the State Government to bring them under the purview of the Act by adding the employment in educational institution in the Schedule in exercise of power under S. 27 of the Act. The Supreme Court, in the instant case, relied on the ratio of *Miss A. Sundarambal* v. *Govt. of Gao, Daman and Diu,*[24] where the Court held:

> "We are of the view that the teachers employed by educational institutions whether the said institutions are imparting primary, secondary, graduate or post graduate education cannot be called as workmen' within the meaning of S. 2(s) of the Act. Imparting of education which is the main function of teachers cannot be construed as skilled or unskilled manual work or clerical work. Imparting of education is in the nature of a mission or a noble vocation. A teacher educates children, he moulds their character, builds up their personality and makes them fit to become responsible citizens. Children grow under care of teachers. The clerical work, if any they may do, is only incidental to their work, if any they may do is only incidental to their principal work of teaching".[25]

Applying the aforesaid dictum to the definition of employee under S. 2(i) of the Act, it may be held that a teacher would not come within the said definition. Accordingly, the impugned notification so far as the teachers of the educational institution concerned are quashed.

In *Patel Ishwerbhai Prahladbhai* v. *Taluka Development Officer,*[26] the question raised before the Supreme Court was whether tube-well operators working in district and Taluka panchayats, being the Government servant, would be considered as employee under the Minimum Wages Act, or, in other words, whether the benefit provided under the Minimum Wages Act can be extended to the tube-well operators working in district and Taluka Panchayats, being the Government servant. The Court held that where certain tube-well operators were working in the district and Taluka panchayats, they would be in the scheduled employment as contemplated by S. 2(g), *"employment under any local authority"* being Item 6 in the Schedule to the Act, and as such, would be entitled to minimum wages and other benefits under the Act, such as payment for overtime work, when minimum wages had been fixed by the State Government in respect of tube-well operators generally even though they were government servants and that benefit was not extended to the operators concerned.

In *Labour Inspector (Central) Hyderabad* v. *Chittapur Stone Quarrying Co. (Pvt.) Ltd.,*[27] the Court held that stone breaking and stone crushing in relation to limestone is that activity in which non-stratified limestone, recognised as rock, is broken or crushed into irregular fragments or sizes and then marketed or otherwise used. The more valuable and rarer stratified limestone with Shahabad stone, which is suitable for use as dimension stone, is not the stone commercially exploited for breaking and crushing. Hence the employment of quarrying 'Shahabad stone' is not the same as the scheduled employment of stone breaking or stone crushing referred to in item 8 of the Schedule to the Minimum Wages Act. Consequently, the minimum wages fixed for the employment of stone breaking and stone crushing will not apply to the operation of quarrying Shahabad stone.

24. AIR 1988 SC 1700.
25. *Ibid.* at p. 1704 per Venkataramiah, J.
26. AIR 1983 SC 336.
27. AIR 1972 SC 1177.

SECTION 3: Fixing of minimum rates of wages

(1) The appropriate Government shall, in the manner hereinafter provided,—

(a) fix the minimum rates of wages payable to employees employed in an employment specified in Part I or Part II of the Schedule and in an employment added to either Part by notification under section 27:

Provided that the appropriate Government may, in respect of employees employed in an employment specified in Part II of the Schedule, instead of fixing minimum rates of wages under this clause for the whole State, fix such rates for a part of the State or for any specified class or classes of such employment in the whole State or part thereof;

(b) review at such intervals as it may think fit, such intervals not exceeding five years, the minimum rates of wages so fixed and revise the minimum rates, if necessary:

Provided that where for any reason the appropriate Government has not reviewed the minimum rates of wages fixed by it in respect of any scheduled employment within any interval of five years, nothing contained in this clause shall be deemed to prevent it from reviewing the minimum rates after the expiry of the said period of five years and revising them, if necessary, and until they are so revised the minimum rates in force immediately before the expiry of the said period of five years shall continue in force.

(1A) Notwithstanding anything contained in sub-section (1), the appropriate Government may refrain from fixing minimum rates of wages in respect of any scheduled employment in which there are in the whole State less than one thousand employees engaged in such employment, but if at any time, the appropriate Government comes to a finding after such inquiry as it may make or cause to be made in this behalf that the number of employees in any scheduled employment in respect of which it has refrained from fixing minimum rates of wages has risen to one thousand or more, it shall fix minimum rates of wages payable to employees in such employment as soon as may be after such finding.

(2) The appropriate Government may fix—

(a) a minimum rate of wages for time work (hereinafter referred to as "a minimum time rate");

(b) a minimum rate of wages for piece work (hereinafter referred to as "a minimum piece rate");

(c) a minimum rate of remuneration to apply in the case of employees employed on piece work for the purpose of securing to such employees a minimum rate of wages on a time work basis (hereinafter referred to as "a guaranteed time rate");

(d) a minimum rate (whether a time rate or a piece rate) to apply in substitution for the minimum rate which would otherwise be applicable, in respect of overtime work done by employees (hereinafter referred to as "overtime rate").

(2A) Where in respect of an industrial dispute relating to the rates of wages payable to any of the employees employed in a scheduled employment, any proceeding is pending before a Tribunal or National Tribunal under the Industrial Disputes Act, 1947 (14 of 1947) or before any like authority under any other law for the time being in force, or an award made by any Tribunal, National Tribunal or such authority is in operation, and a notification fixing or revising the minimum rates of wages in respect of the scheduled employment is issued during the pendency of such proceeding or the operation of the award, then, notwithstanding anything contained in this Act, the minimum rates of wages so fixed or so revised shall not apply to those employees during the period in which the proceeding is pending and the award made therein is in operation or, as the case may be, where the notification is issued during the period of operation of an award, during that period; and where such proceeding or award relates to the rates of wages payable to all the employees in the scheduled employment, no minimum rates of wages shall be fixed or revised in respect of that employment during the said period.

(3) In fixing or revising minimum rates of wages under this section,—

(a) different minimum rates of wages may be fixed for—

(i) different scheduled employments;

(ii) different classes of work in the same scheduled employment;

(iii) adults, adolescents, children and apprentices;

(iv) different localities;

(b) minimum rates of wages may be fixed by any one or more of the following wage periods, namely:

(i) by the hour,

(ii) by the day,

(iii) by the month, or

(iv) by such other larger wage-period as may be prescribed;

and where such rates are fixed by the day or by the month, the manner of calculating wages for a month or for a day, as the case may be, may be indicated:

Provided that where any wage-periods have been fixed under section 4 of the Payment of Wages Act, 1936 (4 of 1936), minimum wages shall be fixed in accordance therewith.

The short question raised before the Supreme Court for consideration in *Jaydip Paper Industries, M/s.* v. *Workmen,*[28] was whether the Tribunal was right in fixing wages at rates higher than the rates fixed by the Government under S. 3 of the Act.

It may be noted that it was during the pendency of the proceedings before the Tribunal that the notification by the Maharashtra Government fixing minimum rates of wages came into operation. S. 3(2A) would make it clear that even after the fixation of minimum rates of wages by the appropriate Government under S. 3 of the Act, it is open to an Industrial Tribunal adjudicating an industrial dispute relating to wages payable to the employees in a scheduled employment to fix minimum wages at higher or lower rates, if the dispute was pending at the time of fixation of minimum wages under S. 3 of the Act. So, it was open to the Tribunal to fix rates of minimum wages at rates higher than the rates fixed by the Government under S. 3 of the Act. In other words, the Tribunal was not bound by the fixation

28. AIR 1972 SC 605.

of the minimum rates of wages by the Government under the provisions of S. 3 of the Act and could fix higher rates as minimum wages in its award. The Court accordingly held that in the light of the provisions of S. 3(2A) of the Act, the Tribunal was not bound by the rates of minimum wages fixed by the Government under S. 3 of the Act and that it was open to the Tribunal to fix rates of minimum wages to be paid to the workmen concerned in the dispute at figures higher than those fixed by the Government.

The Minimum Wages Act, 1948 provides for fixation of minimum rates of wages in certain employments. Section 3(1)(a) provides that the appropriate Government shall fix the minimum rates of wages payable to employees employed in an employment specified in Part I or Part II of the Schedule. Sub-section (1A) of S. 3 enacts that "notwithstanding anything contained in sub-section (1), the appropriate Government may refrain from fixing minimum rates of wages in respect of any scheduled employment in which there are in the whole State less than 1,000 employees engaged in such employment." It is obvious that sub-section (1A) of S. 3 does not preclude the appropriate Government from fixing minimum rates of wages in respect of any scheduled employment even if there are in the whole State less than 1,000 employees engaged in such employment. It merely empowers the appropriate Government to refrain from fixing minimum rates of wages in respect of such employment, leaving it open to the appropriate Government to fix minimum rates of wages in respect of such employment, if it so thinks fit.[29]

SECTION 4: Minimum rate of wages

(1) Any minimum rate of wages fixed or revised by the appropriate government in respect of scheduled employments under section 3 may consist of—

(i) a basic rate of wages and a special allowance at a rate to be adjusted, at such intervals and in such manner as the appropriate Government may direct, to accord as nearly as practicable with the variation in the cost of living index number applicable to such workers (hereinafter referred to as the "cost of living allowance"); or

(ii) a basic rate of wages with or without the cost of living allowance, and the cash value of the concessions in respect of supplies of essential commodities at concessional rates, where so authorised; or

(iii) an all-inclusive rate allowing for the basic rate, the cost of living allowance and the cash value of the concessions, if any.

(2) The cost of living allowance and the cash value of the concessions in respect of supplies of essential commodities at concessional rate shall be computed by the competent authority at such intervals and in accordance with such directions as may be specified or given by the appropriate Government.

The Minimum Wages Act, 1948 does not define 'minimum wages' presumably because it would not be possible to lay down a uniform minimum wage for all industries throughout the country on account of different and varying conditions prevailing in industry to industry

29. *Ram Kumar Misra* v. *State of Bihar*, AIR 1984 SC 537.

and in one part of the country to another. The legislature also thought in inexpedient to apply the Act to all industries at a time and, therefore, it applied the Act to certain employments only specified in the Schedule thereto, leaving it to the appropriate government to add by notification to that effect industries in the said Schedule at suitable time and in appropriate conditions. But S. 4 of the Act provides that the minimum rates of wages may consist of a basic rate of wages and a special allowance at a rate to be adjusted or a basic rate of wages with or without the cost of living allowance and cash value of concessions in respect of supplies of essential commodities at concessional rates where so authorised or an all-inclusive rate allowing for the basic rate, the cost of living allowance and the cash value of the concessions, if any. Sub-section (2) of S. 4 provides that the cost of living allowances and the value of the concessions in respect of supplies of essential commodities at concessional rates shall be computed by the competent authority at such intervals and in accordance with such directions as may be given by the appropriate Government. It is thus clear that the concept of minimum wage does take in the factor of the prevailing cost of essential commodities whenever such minimum wage is to be fixed. The idea of fixing such wage in the light of cost of living at a particular juncture of time and of neutralising the rising prices of essential commodities by taking up scales of minimum wages with the cost of living index cannot, therefore, be said to be alien to the concept of a minimum wage. Furthermore, in the light of spiralling of prices in recent years, if the wage scales are to be realistic, it may become necessary to fix them so as to neutralise, at least partly, the price rise in essential commodities.[30]

The minimum wage must provide not merely for the bare subsistence of life but for the preservation of the efficiency of the worker and so it must also provide for some measure of education, medical requirements and amenities of himself and his family. While fixing the minimum wages, the capacity of the employer to pay is treated as irrelevant and the Act contemplates that rates of minimum wages should be fixed in schedule industries with a dual object of providing sustenance and maintenance of the worker and his family and preserving his efficiency as a worker. So it is required to take into consideration cost of bare subsistence of life and preservation of efficiency of the worker and for some measure of education, medical requirements and amenities. This cost is likely to vary depending upon the cost prevailing in the market of various items. If there are inflationary conditions prevailing in the country, then minimum wages fixed at a particular point of time would not serve the purpose. Therefore, S. 4 contemplates that minimum wages fixed at a particular point of time should be revised from time to time. Section 4 postulates that minimum wages fixed or revised by the appropriate Government under S. 3 may consist of basic rates of wages and special allowance at a rate to be adjusted at such intervals in such manner as the appropriate Government may direct to accord as nearly as practicable with a variation in the cost of living index number applicable to such workers; alternatively, it permits the fixation of basic rate of wages with or without cost of living allowance and the cash value of the concessions in respect of supplies of essential commodities at concessional rates where so authorised; or in the alternative, it permits an all-inclusive rate allowing for the basic rate, the cost of living allowance and the cash value of concessions, if any.

The purpose of S. 4 is to see that minimum wages can be linked with increase in cost of living so that increase in cost of living can be neutralised or all-inclusive rates of minimum

30. *Hydro (Engineers) Pvt. Ltd., M/s.* v. *The Workmen*, AIR 1969 SC 182.

wages can be fixed. But, from the aforesaid Ss. 3 and 4, it is apparent that what is fixed is total remuneration which should be paid to the employees covered by the schedule and not for payment of costs of different components which are taken into consideration for fixation of minimum rates of wages. It is thus clear that the concept of minimum wages does take in the factor of prevailing cost of essential commodities whenever such minimum wage is to be fixed. The idea of fixing such wage in the light of cost of living at a particular juncture of time and of neutralising the prices of essential commodities by linking up scales of minimum wages with the cost of living index is provided for in S. 4, but V.D.A. is part and parcel of wages. Once rates of minimum wages are prescribed under the Act, whether as all-inclusive under S. 4(1)(iii) or by combining basic plus dearness allowance under S. 4(1)(i) are not amenable to split up. It is one pay package. Neither the scheme nor any provision of the Act provides that the rates of minimum wages are to be split up on the basis of the cost of each necessities taken into consideration for fixing the same. Hence, in cases where the employer is paying total sum which is higher than minimum rates of wages fixed under the Act including the cost of living index (VDA), he is not required to pay VDA separately. However, higher wages should be calculated as defined in S. 2(h) of the Act. Section 2(h) specifically provides that value of the following items is not required to be computed for finding out whether employer pays minimum wages as prescribed under the Act:

(i) the value of any house, accommodation, supply of light, water, medical care, or any other amenity or any service excluded by general or special order of the appropriate Government

(ii) any pension fund or provident fund or under any scheme of social insurance

(iii) any travelling allowance or the value of any travelling concession

(iv) any sum paid to any person employed to defray special expenses curtailed on him by the nature of his employment or

(v) any gratuities payable on discharge.

But while deciding the question of payment of minimum wages, the competent authority is not required to bifurcate each component of the costs of each item taken into consideration for fixing minimum wages, as lump sum amount is determined for providing adequate remuneration to the workman so that he can sustain and maintain himself and his family and also preserve his efficiency as a worker. Dearness allowance is part and parcel or cost of necessities. In cases where the minimum rate of wages is linked up with V.D.A., it would not mean that it is a separate component which is required to be paid separately where the employer pays a total pay package which is more than the prescribed minimum rate of wages.[31]

SECTION 5: Procedure for fixing and revising minimum wages

(1) In fixing minimum rates of wages in respect of any scheduled employment for the first time under this Act or in revising minimum rates of wages so fixed, the appropriate Government shall either—

31. *Airfreight Ltd.* v. *State of Karnataka*, AIR 1999 SC 2459.

(a) appoint as many committees and sub-committees as it considers necessary to hold enquiries and advise it in respect of such fixation or revision, as the case may be, or

(b) by notification in the Official Gazette, publish its proposals for the information of persons likely to be affected thereby and specify a date, not less than two months from the date of the notification, on which the proposals will be taken into consideration.

(2) After considering the advice of the committee or committees appointed under clause (a) of sub-section (1), or as the case may be, all representations received by it before the date specified in the notification under clause (b) of that sub-section, the appropriate Government shall, by notification in the Official Gazette fix, or, as the case may be, revise the minimum rates of wages in respect of each scheduled employment, and unless such notification otherwise provides, it shall come into force on the expiry of three months from the date of its issue:

Provided that where the appropriate Government proposes to revise the minimum rates of wages by the mode specified in Cl. (b) of sub-section (1), the appropriate Government shall consult the Advisory Board also.

In *Chandra Bhawan Boarding and Lodging, Bangalore* v. *State of Mysore*,[32] it was contended that S. 5(1) of the Act is violative of Art. 14 of the Constitution as it confers unguided and uncontrolled discretion to the Government to follow either of the two alternative procedures prescribed in that section in the matter of fixing minimum wages. It was urged that under Cl. (a) of S. 5(1) the appropriate Government is required to appoint a committee representing all interests to hold a detailed enquiry regarding the employment concerned before advising the Government in the matter of fixing minimum wages, but under Cl. (b) of S. 5(1) all that the appropriate Government needs to do is to publish by notification in the Official Gazette its proposals for the information of the persons likely to be affected by those proposals and specify a date not less than two months from the date of the notification on which the proposals will be taken into consideration. It was urged that if the procedure prescribed in S. 5(1)(a) is adopted, it would be advantageous to the employers because in the committee to be appointed, there will be the representatives of the employers who know the difficulties of the employers and hence are in a position to acquaint their colleagues about the same, but if the procedure prescribed in S. 5(1)(b) is followed, the affected parties can only submit their written representations followed by some nominal oral representation in a crowded meeting. While dealing with the issue, the Court held:

> "It is true that this Court has firmly ruled that the procedural inequality, if read and substantial, is also within the vice of Article 14. But then, before a power can be held to be bad the same should be an unguided and unregulated one. But if a power is given to an authority to have recourse to different procedures under different circumstances, that power cannot be considered as an arbitrary power. It must also be remembered that power under Section 5(1) is given to the State Government and not to any petty official. The State Government can be trusted to exercise that power to further the purposes of the Act. It is not the law that the guidance for the exercise of a power should be gatherable from one of the provisions in the Act. It can be gathered from the circumstances that led to

32. AIR 1970 SC 2042.

the enactment of the law in question i.e., the mischief that was intended to be remedied, the preamble to the Act or even from the scheme of the Act."[33]

The concept of minimum wage is likely to undergo a change with the growth of our economy and with the change in the standard of living. It is not a static concept. Its concomitants must necessarily increase with the progress of the society. It is likely to differ from place to place and from industry to industry. That is clear from the provisions of the Act itself and is inherent in the very concept. That being the case, it is absolutely impossible for the legislature to undertake the task of fixing minimum wages in respect of any industry, much less in respect of an employment. That process must necessarily be left to the Government. Before minimum wages in any employment can be fixed, it will be necessary to collect considerable data. That cannot be done by the legislature. It can be best done by the Government. The legislature has determined the legislative policy and formulated the same as a binding rule of conduct. The legislative policy is enumerated with sufficient clearness. The Government is merely charged with the duty of implementing that policy. There is no basis for saying that the legislature had abdicated any of its legislative functions. The legislature has prescribed two different procedures for collecting the necessary data, one contained in S. 5(1)(a) and the other in S. 5(1)(b). In either case, it is merely a procedure for gathering the necessary information. The Government is not bound by the advice given by the committee appointed under S. 5(1)(a). Discretion to select one of the two procedures prescribed for collecting the data is advisedly left to the Government.

SECTION 6: Advisory committees and sub-committees

[Repealed by the Minimum Wages (Amendment) Act, 1957 (30 of 1957)]

SECTION 7: Advisory Board

For the purpose of coordinating work of committees and sub-committees appointed under section 5 and advising the appropriate Government generally in the matter of fixing and revising minimum rates of wages, the appropriate Government shall appoint an Advisory Board.

SECTION 8: Central Advisory Board

(1) For the purpose of advising the Central and State Governments in the matters of the fixation and revision of minimum rates of wages and other matters under this Act and for co-ordinating the work of the Advisory Boards, the Central Government shall appoint a Central Advisory Board.

(2) The Central Advisory Board shall consist of persons to be nominated by the Central Government representing employers and employees in the scheduled employments, who shall be equal in number, and independent persons not exceeding one-third of its total number of members; one of such independent persons shall be appointed the Chairman of the Board by the Central Government.

33. *Ibid.* at p. 2048 per Hegde, J.

SECTION 9: Composition of committees, etc.

Each of the committees, sub-committees and the Advisory Board shall consist of persons to be nominated by the appropriate Government representing employers and employees in the scheduled employments, who shall be equal in number, and independent persons not exceeding one-third of its total number of members; one of such independent persons shall be appointed the Chairman by the appropriate Government.

The sole question that arose before the Supreme Court in *State of A.P.* v. *Narayana Velur Beedi Manufacturing Factory*[34] related to the meaning of the word "independent" in S. 9 of the Minimum Wages Act, 1948. The Government Order, which was related to challenged, related to the revision of minimum wages in the Bidi industry. It was based on the recommendation of a committee consisting of six members, two of whom were Chief Inspector of Factories, Hyderabad, and Deputy Chief Inspector of Factories, Hyderabad; the former being the Chairman. These two officers were to be on the committee from among the category of independent persons mentioned in S. 9. The whole controversy centred on the question whether the aforesaid two officers could be regarded as independent persons.

There are a number of decisions of the High Courts. In majority of them, namely, *Jaswant Rai Beri* v. *State of Punjab*,[35] *D.M.S. Rao* v. *State of Kerala*,[36] *Bengal Motion Pictures Employees Union, Calcutta* v. *Kohinoor Pictures Private Ltd.*,[37] *Ramkrishna Ramnath Nagpur* v. *State of Maharashtra*,[38] *Chandrabhavan Boarding and Lodging* v. *State of Mysore*,[39] and *P. Gangadharan Pillai* v. *State of Kerala*,[40] it has been held that the mere fact that a person happens to be a Government servant or that he is an officer, he does not cease to be an independent person within the meaning of S. 9. The only two decisions in which a contrary view has been taken are *Narottamdas Harjivandas* v. *P.V. Gowarikar*,[41] and *Kohinoor Pictures (Private) Ltd.* v. *State of West Bengal.*[42]

In *Jaswant Rai Beri* case, the judge considered that in the context of S. 9, an independent person means a person who is neither an employer nor an employee in the employment for which minimum wages are to be fixed. The presence of independent persons is necessary to safeguard the interests of those whose requirements are met by the trade concerned. In a welfare State, according to it, it is the business of the Government to create conditions wherein private employers can carry on their trade profitably as long as the workmen are not exploited. In such circumstances, the appointment of a labour Commissioner, who is conversant with the employment conditions, cannot be objected to on the ground that he was not an independent person.

In *D.M.S. Rao* case, the Kerala High Court gave some additional reasons for supporting the view of *Jaswant Rai Beri* case. The Court referred to S. 2(i) of the Industrial Disputes

34. AIR 1973 SC 1307.
35. AIR 1958 Punj 425.
36. AIR 1963 Ker 115.
37. AIR 1964 Cal 519.
38. AIR 1964 Bom 51.
39. AIR 1968 Mys 156.
40. AIR 1968 Ker 218.
41. AIR 1961 M.P. 182.
42. (1961) 2 LLJ 741 (Cal).

Act 1947 for illustrating that a person shall be deemed to be independent for the purpose of his appointment as Chairman or other member of a Board, Court or Tribunal if he was unconnected with the industrial dispute referred to such Board, Court or Tribunal or with any industry directly affected by such dispute. This is what the learned Judge of Kerala High Court observed with reference to the provisions of S. 9.

A Division Bench of the Calcutta High Court in *Bengal Motion Pictures Employees Union* case referred to the legislative policy underlying the enactment of the Act. What is aimed at is the statutory fixation of minimum wages with a view to obviating the chances of exploitation of labour. Such being the main object, it was natural to expect that the Government would seek the assistance of persons who were well conversant with the conditions of labour, industrial competition, profits from the industry and various other relevant factors which are to be considered in fixing the minimum wages. It could hardly be doubted that persons like the Labour Commissioner or the Deputy Labour Commissioner are most suitable persons to be consulted for the purpose.

In *Narottamdas* case, the Madhya Pradesh High Court held that the expression "independent persons" did not mean persons who were independent only of employers and employees in the scheduled employment and included officials. The ordinary connotation of the word "independent person", it was pointed out, is of a person who is not dependent on any body, authority or organisation and who is able to form his own opinion without any control or guidance of any outside agency. It appears that in this case the learned Judges were influenced by the consideration that the State is actively interested in the wage earners and in the matter of fixation of minimum wages. That precluded Government officials from falling within the class of independent persons provided for by S. 9.

The respondents, in the instant case, have relied a great deal on the dictionary meanings of the word "independent" as given in Shorter Oxford English Dictionary. One of the principal meanings given is "not depending upon the authority of another; not in position of subordination; not subject to external control or rule." According to him, a Government official cannot be regarded as independent because he is to depend upon the authority of the government and is in position of subordination and is subject to external control. It has been strenuously urged that the whole object of having an advisory committee is to get an impartial opinion or advice in the matter of fixing of minimum wages. The committee has to consist of representatives of employers and the employees in the scheduled employment who have to be equal in number. The presence of independent persons not exceeding one-third of the total number of members is necessary to ensure that a proper balance is maintained between the view of the representatives of the employers and the employees respectively. If a government official and, in particular, one associated either with labour or factories in his official capacity is brought into the committee, he is likely to be biased in his views for various reasons. He may know the policy of the government or he may himself have participated in the formulation of that policy. He may have certain predilection because of special knowledge obtained by him while serving in a department which is connected with labour or industry. All these matters would divest him of the character of an independent person.

The Supreme Court, in the instant case, considered the views expressed by the majority of High Courts and held:

"In our judgment the view which has prevailed with the majority of the High Courts must be sustained. The committee or the advisory board can only tender advise which is not binding on the government while fixing the minimum wages or revising the same as the case may be. Of course the government is expected, particularly in the present democratic set up, to take that advise seriously into consideration and act on it but it is not bound to do so. The language of Section 9 does not contain any indication whatsoever that persons in the employment of the government would be excluded from the category of independent persons. These words have essentially been employed in contradistinction to representatives of employers and employees. In other words, apart from the representatives of employers and employees there should be persons who should be independent of them. It does not follow that persons in the service or employment of the government were meant to be excluded and they cannot be regarded as independent persons vis-a-vis the representatives of the employers and employees. Apart from this the presence of high government officials who may have actual working knowledge about the problems of employers and employees can afford a good deal of guidance and assistance in formulating the advice which is to be tendered under Section 9 to the appropriate government. It may be that in certain circumstances such persons who are in the service of the government may cease to have an independent character if the question arises of fixation of minimum wages in a scheduled employment in which the appropriate government is directly interested. It would, therefore, depend upon the facts of each particular case whether the persons who have been appointed from out of the class of independent persons can be regarded as independent or not. But the mere fact that they happen to be government officials or government servants will not divest them of the character of independent persons. We are not impressed with the reasoning adopted that a government official will have a bias or that he may favour the policy which the appropriate government may be inclined to adopt because when he is a member of an advisory committee or board he is expected to give an impartial and independent advice and not merely carry out what the government may be inclined to do. Government officials are responsible persons and it cannot be said that they are not capable of taking a detached and impartial view."[43]

SECTION 10: Correction of errors

(1) The appropriate Government may, at any time, by notification in the Official Gazette, correct clerical or arithmetical mistakes in any order fixing or revising minimum rates of wages under this Act, or errors arising therein from any accidental slip or omission.

(2) Every such notification shall, as soon as may be after it is issued, be placed before the Advisory Board for information.

SECTION 11: Wages in kind

(1) Minimum wages payable under this Act shall be paid in cash.

(2) Where it has been the custom to pay wages wholly or partly in kind, the appropriate Government being of the opinion that it is necessary in the circumstances of the case may, by notification in the Official Gazette, authorise the payment of minimum wages either wholly or partly in kind.

43. *Ibid.*, f.n. 34, at p. 1311 per Grover, J.

(3) If appropriate Government is of the opinion that provision should be made for the supply of essential commodities at concessional rates, the appropriate Government may, by notification in the Official Gazette, authorise the provision of such supplies at concessional rates.

(4) The cash value of wages in kind and of concessions in respect of supplies of essential commodities at concessional rates authorised under sub-sections (2) and (3) shall be estimated in the prescribed manner.

An interesting question raised before the Supreme Court in *Managanese Ore (India) Ltd.* v. *Chandi Lal Saha*[44] was whether the monetary value of the grain supplied at con-cessional rates and the amount paid as attendance-bonus can be included and counted into the minimum wages payable to the employees under the notification.

The Government of India by a notification issued under the Minimum Wages Act, 1948 fixed the minimum rates of wages payable to different categories of employees employed in Manganese mines. The minimum rate of wage in respect of the unskilled workers was fixed at ₹2.40 per day. The management, under an agreement, was paying to the employees attendance bonus and was supplying grain to them at concessional rates. The workmen employed with *Manganese Ore (India) Ltd.*, Nagger filed two applications under S. 33-C(2) of the Industrial Disputes Act, 1947 before the Central Government Labour Court at Nagger for recovery of the deficit amount of wages due to them from the management. According to them, unskilled and semi-skilled workers were entitled to ₹2.40 and ₹3.20 per day as minimum wages, but the management was illegally deducting out of their wages the cash value of various benefits and amenities such as attendance-bonus and concessional supply of foodgrains to them. The management opposed the applications before the Labour Court on the ground that the minimum wage was an all-inclusive wage which included the cash value of all benefits such as foodgrains supplied at concessional rates, bonus and various other amenities extended to the workmen. According to the management, the workmen were being paid wages in cash as well as in kind and the money value of those benefits was to be taken into consideration while computing the minimum wage. The Labour Court rejected the contention of the management and allowed the applications of the workmen. The Labour Court came to the conclusion that the monetary value of the grain supplied at concessional rate or the amount paid as attendance-bonus could not be counted towards the minimum rates of wages payable to the workmen under the notification.

The management challenged the above said orders of the Labour Court by way of writ petitions under Art. 226/227 of the Constitution of India before the Nagger Bench of the Bombay High Court. The High Court dismissed the writ petitions. The management challenged the decision of the High Court by way of Civil Appeal before the Apex Court.

Mr. G.L. Sanghi, learned Senior Advocate appearing for the appellant, raised the following points for consideration:

(1) The notification fixing the minimum wage specifically mentions that the minimum rates of wages are all-inclusive rates. According to Mr. Sanghi, the wages so fixed would include the amount paid by the management towards the attendance-bonus as well as the monetary benefit of the grain concession.

44. AIR 1991 SC 520.

(2) The grain concession and the attendance-bonus are the benefits which can be computed in money and as such are part of the minimum wage under the Act.

(3) The procedure to recover wages fixed under the Act has been provided under the said Act. Since S. 20 of the Act provides for elaborate machinery to get the grievances redressed under the Act, the Labour Court has no jurisdiction under S. 33-C(2) of the Industrial Disputes Act to entertain the application.

We may now consider the first argument of Mr. Sanghi. Section 11(1) provides that the minimum wages payable under the Act shall be paid in cash. Sub-sections (2) and (3) of S. 11 are exceptions to the mandate contained in S. 11(1). It is clear from the scheme of the section that the minimum wages payable under the Act are to be paid in cash unless there is a notification in the Official Gazette to the contrary under S. 11(2) or 11(3) of the Act. Admittedly, no such notification has been issued by the appropriate Government in the present case. The supply of essential commodities at concessional rates can only form part of the minimum wage, if it is authorised by the appropriate Government by a notification in the Official Gazette under S. 11(3) of the Act. Mr. Sanghi, however, contended that in view of para 2 of the notification issued under the Act, the compliance of sub-sections (3) and (4) of S. 11 was not required. The said para is as under:

"The minimum rates of wages are all-inclusive rates, and include also the wages for weekly day of rest".

According to Mr. Sanghi, reading para 2 of the notification along with S. 4(1)(iii) of the Act, the minimum rates of wages being all-inclusive, the management was entitled to deduct from the minimum wages the cash value of the grain concession. The Court rejected the contention raised by Mr. Sanghi and observed that S. 4(1)(iii) and S. 4(2) have to be read with S. 11 of the Act. There cannot be a wage in kind under the scheme of the Act unless there is a notification by the appropriate Government under S. 11(3) of the Act. Section 4(1)(iii) mentions only such *"cash value of the concession"* as has been authorised *"wage in kind"* under sub-section (3) of S. 11 of the Act. It is only the appropriate Government which can authorise the payment of minimum wages partly in kind. In the absence of any notification by the appropriate Government for the supply of essential commodities at concessional rates, the cash value of such concessions cannot be treated as wage in kind and cannot be deducted from the minimum wages which have to be paid in cash under S. 11(1) of the Act. There being no notification by the appropriate Government under S. 11(3) of the Act, the appellant cannot take any advantage from para 2 of the notification or from the provisions of S. 4(1)(iii) of the Act.

The second argument of Mr. Sanghi is based on the definition of wages under S. 2(h) of the Act. Please refer S. 2(h) of the Minimum Wages Act, where the issue is elaborately discussed.

The third argument of Mr. Sanghi is based on the procedure to recover wages fixed under the Act. Please refer S. 20 of the Minimum Wages Act, where the issue is elaborately discussed.

Section 12: Payment of minimum rates of wages

(1) Where in respect of any scheduled employment a notification under section 5 is in force, the employer shall pay to every employee engaged in a scheduled employment

under him wages at a rate not less than the minimum rate of wages fixed by such notification for that class of employees in that employment without any deductions except as may be authorised within such time and subject to such conditions as may be prescribed.

(2) Nothing contained in this section shall affect the provisions of the Payment of Wages Act, 1936 (4 of 1936).

Where a person provides labour or service to another for remuneration which is less than the minimum wage, the labour or service provided by him clearly falls within the scope and ambit of the words "forced labour" under Art. 23 of the Constitution. Such a person would be entitled to come to the Court for the enforcement of his fundamental right under Art. 23 by asking the Court to direct payment of the minimum wage to him so that the labour or service provided by him ceases to be "forced labour" and the breach of Art. 23 is remedied.

What Art. 23 prohibits is "forced labour", that is, labour or service which a person is forced to provide and 'force' which would make such labour or service "forced labour" may arise in several ways. It may be physical force which may compel a person to provide labour or service to another, or it may be force exerted through a legal provision such as a provision for imprisonment or fine in case the employee fails to provide labour or service, or it may even be compulsion arising from hunger and poverty, want and destitution. Any factor which deprives a person of a choice of alternatives and compels him to adopt one particular course of action may properly be regarded as "force", and if labour or service is compelled as a result of such "force", it would be "forced labour". There is no reason why the word "forced" should be read in a narrow and restricted manner so as to be confined only to physical or legal "force". The word "force" must, therefore, be construed to include not only physical or legal force but also force arising from the compulsion of economic circumstances which leaves no choice of alternatives to a person in want and compels him to provide labour or service, even though the remuneration received for it is less than the minimum wage.

In *People's Union for Democratic Rights* v. *Union of India*,[45] ₹1 per worker per day was deducted by the *jamadars* from the wages payable to the workers employed by contractors for the Asiad Projects with the result that the workers did not get the minimum wage of Rupees 9.25 per day. The Court held that the same amounted to infringement of Art. 23.

Section 13: Fixing hours for a normal working day, etc.

(1) In regard to any scheduled employment minimum rates of wages in respect of which have been fixed under this Act, the appropriate Government may—

(a) fix the number of hours of work which shall constitute a normal working day, inclusive of one or more specified intervals;

(b) provide for a day of rest in every period of seven days which shall be allowed to all employees or to any specified class of employees and for the payment of remuneration in respect of such days of rest;

45. AIR 1982 SC 1473.

(c) provide for payment for work on a day of rest at a rate not less than the overtime rate.

(2) The provisions of sub-section (1) shall, in relation to the following classes of employees, apply only to such extent and subject to such conditions as may be prescribed—

(a) employees engaged on urgent work, or in any emergency which could not have been foreseen or prevented;

(b) employees engaged in work in the nature of preparatory or complementary work which must necessarily be carried on outside the limits laid down for the general working in the employment concerned;

(c) employees whose employment is essentially intermittent;

(d) employees engaged in any work which for technical reasons has to be completed before the duty is over;

(e) employees engaged in a work which could not be carried on except at times dependent on the irregular action of natural forces.

(3) For the purposes of clause (c) of sub-section (2), employment of an employee is essentially intermittent when it is declared to be so by the appropriate Government on the ground that the daily hours of duty of the employee, or if there be no daily hours of duty as such for the employee, the hours of duty, normally include periods of inaction during which the employee may be on duty but is not called upon to display either physical activity or sustained attention.

Section 14: Overtime

(1) Where an employee, whose minimum rate of wages is fixed under this Act by the hour, by the day or by such a longer wage-period as may be prescribed, works on any day in excess of the number of hours constituting a normal working day, the employer shall pay him for every hour or for part of an hour so worked in excess at the overtime rate fixed under this Act or under any law of the appropriate Government for the time being in force, whichever is higher.

(2) Nothing in this Act shall prejudice the operation of the provisions of section 59 of the Factories Act, 1948 (63 of 1948) in any case where those provisions are applicable.

The Minimum Wages Act was enacted to enable Government to fix minimum rates of wages in certain employments. Since fixation of minimum wages must take into account the work-load also, provision must not only be made for prescribing the minimum wage but to correlate it to a specified amount of work. Any extra work beyond the specified work-load must be paid for at a higher or what is known as 'overtime' rate. Similarly, intervals of rest must punctuate suitably the hours of work and they must also be provided for in a scheme of the workday of workman. The Minimum Wages Act makes provision for all these matters either by itself or through Rules. The Central Government has framed the Minimum Wages (Central) Rules, 1950. The Act and the Rules between them provide not only for fixation of minimum wages but also for the work-load in relation to which the minimum wages are to be prescribed. They provide, on the one hand for, minimum wages, lay down the procedure for fixing or revising them and prescribe the rules in accordance with which the wages must be paid. On the other hand, the Act and the Rules fix the number of hours of work, payment of overtime and for hours of rest in the workday of the workman. The provisions of the Act and of the Rules are applicable to some employments only and they are shown in a Schedule appended to the Act. In *Workmen of the Bombay Port Trust* v. *Trustees of the Port of Bombay,*[46] it is an admitted fact that the workmen of the Bombay Port Trust come under the Schedule. The hours of work and the payment of overtime are, therefore, governed by the provisions of the Minimum Wages Act and the Minimum Wages (Central) Rules, 1950 and the controversy in this case must be appreciated and resolved in accordance with them.

In order to resolve the disputes, we have to refer Ss. 13 and 14 of the Minimum Wages Act and Rules Nos. 24 and 25.

Rule 24. "Number of hours of work which shall constitute a normal working day—

(1) The number of hours which shall constitute a normal working day shall be—

(a) in the case of an adult, 9 hours,

(b) in the case of a child, 4½ hours.

(2) The working day of an adult worker shall be so arranged that inclusive of the intervals for rest, if any, it shall not spread over more than twelve hours on any day.

(3) The number of hours of work in the case of an adolescent shall be the same as that of an adult or a child according as he is certified to work as an adult or a child by a competent medical practitioner approved by the Central Government.

(4) * * *

(4-A) No child shall be employed or permitted to work for more than 4½ hours on any day.

(5) Nothing in this rule shall be deemed to affect the provisions of the Factories Act, 1948".

Rule 25. Extra wages for overtime—

(1) When a worker works in an employment for more than nine hours on any day or for more than forty-eight hours in any week, he shall, in respect of overtime work be entitled to wages,

(a) in the case of employment in Agriculture, at one and a half time the ordinary rate of wages;

(b) in the case of any other scheduled employment, at double the ordinary rate of wages.

Explanation: The expression "ordinary rate of wages" means the basic wage plus such allowances including the cash equivalent of the advantages accruing through the concessional sale to the person employed of food grains and other articles as the person employed is for the time being entitled to but does not include a bonus.

(2) A register showing overtime payment shall be kept in form IV.

46. AIR 1966 SC 1201.

(3) Nothing in this rule shall be deemed to affect the provisions of the Factories Act, 1948."

The controversy in the present case is a narrow one. It is: whether the fixing of a two hours rest and two hours' overtime involves a breach of the two sections of the Act and the two rules quoted here? The workmen claim that under a scheme of 12-hours shifts with 8 hours work, overtime should be at least 3 hours, if not 4, and by fixing only two hours overtime, the Trustees are guilty of the breach of the Act and the Rules.

Unfortunately, the provisions of the Minimum Wages Act and Minimum Wages (Central) Rules, 1950 are not as clear as the corresponding provisions of the Factories Act, 1948 and they have led to long arguments before the Supreme Court.

Section 13 of the Act does not itself fix the hours of work of rest or overtime. That is done by the Rules. Section 13 only authorises Government to fix the number of hours which shall constitute a normal working day, inclusive of one or more specified intervals. The normal working day thus includes (a) hours of actual duty, and (b) one or more specified intervals. There may be one interval of rest, or there may be more intervals but whatever their number, they must be specified. Interval under S. 13 is obviously meant interval of rest and this is clear from Rule 24(2). There is no definition of interval either in the Act or the Rules, but the provisions of S. 13(2)(c) read with S. 13(3) give us an indication of what is meant by an interval of rest. It means a break in the work during which a workman, though present on duty, is not called upon to display either physical activity or sustained attention. But, it is not a period of mere inaction because there is no work for him. If it is the latter, it is counted as actual work period; if the former, it is counted as a period of rest, provided the period is specified beforehand, and the workmen is neither called upon to work nor expected to work.

Having thus distinguished between period of work and interval of rest, we have to look into Rule 24 which prescribed the number of hours of work, which is to constitute a normal working day. Sub-rule (1)(a) provides that the number of hours constituting a normal working day for an adult shall be 9. As the heading of the Rule shows, these are the hours of work. Sub-rule (2) then lays down that the working day of an adult shall be so arranged that inclusive of intervals for rest it shall not spread over more than twelve hours on any day. The distinction between intervals of rest and hours of work is thus made clear. From this it follows that on any single day the number of hours of work must not exceed 9 and together with the hours of rest, the total period of work and rest should not go beyond 12 hours. It is wrong to contend that the period of 9 hours must always include intervals of rest. It may or it may not. There is no provision in the Act and the Rules corresponding to S. 55 of the Factories Act to which reference will be made thereafter. In a 12-hour shift, the nine hours of work on any day can be spread over 12 hours and the extra hours will necessarily be hours of rest.

The contention of the workmen is that S. 13 fixes the number of hours in normal working day and this number is inclusive of one or more specified intervals. They read Rule 24, which prescribes a normal working day of 9 hours, as including within the 9 hours one or more intervals of rest. The Court rejected such contention and held that this is not a correct reading either of S. 13 or of Rule 24. There is clear antinomy between hours of work and intervals of rest in sub-rules (1) and (2) of Rule 24 and the phrase *'inclusive of one or more specified intervals'* governs the normal working day and not the number of hours of work.

The Court further observed that under sub-rule (2) of Rule 24, the working day of an adult can be so arranged that inclusive of intervals of rest, it does not exceed 12 hours on any day. A working day may extend to 12 hours but the number of hours of work cannot exceed 9. A working day of 12 hours is thus made up of hours of work and hours of rest and the number of hours of work (which cannot exceed 9) is part of the normal working day which may also include one or more specified intervals of rest. This determines what is a normal working day and what is meant by an interval of rest.

So far as the question of overtime is concerned, we have to refer S. 14 of the Act. Section 14 would be applied, if work on any day is taken which goes beyond 9 hours. Section 14 speaks of overtime. Overtime is payable for work in excess of the number of hours constituting a normal working day. From S. 13 read with Rule 24, we know that the number of hours constituting a normal working day is 9. We shall now read into S. 14, which lays down—

> *"Where an employee,... works on any day in excess of 9 hours, the employer, shall pay him for every hour or for part of an hour so worked in excess at the overtime rate...."*

Under Rule 25(1)(b), this overtime rate is double the ordinary rate of wages. Therefore, an employer can take actual work on any day up to 9 hours in a 12-hour shift, but he must pay a double rate for any hour or part of an hour of actual work in excess of 9 hours. He need not, however, pay for any interval of rest provided it is specified beforehand. These provisions are subject to one more check which we may now mention. The check is found in the later part of Rule 25(1) which says that the maximum number of hours of work in a week shall not exceed 48 and for any work in excess of 48 hours a week, overtime shall be payable. As there is a prescribed day of rest in a week, we get a working week of six days with a maximum of 48 hours' work. Average duration of actual work payable at ordinary rate of wages per day thus comes to 8 hours. Thus, if an employer takes actual work for 8 hours per day on 6 days in a week, he complies with all the provisions and need not pay overtime. He may go up to 9 hours on any day without paying any overtime provided he does not exceed 48 hours in the week. He can specify the intervals of rest and spread the 8 hours or 9 hours, as the case may be, together with intervals of rest over 12 hours in a twelve-hour shift. These periods of rest must not be periods during which the workman is on duty and inaction is due to want of work for him, but they must be predetermined periods of inaction during which the workman is neither called upon nor expected to display physical activity or sustained attention.

It is found that an employer having a 12-hour shift can fix 48 hours of work per week of six days at 8 hours per day. He is not compelled to give overtime for the remaining four hours unless he takes work during those hours, provided he has specified those hours as intervals of rest. If he takes work during the extra 4 hours or fails to specify the hours of rest, he must pay overtime. He can spread 8 hours with intervals of rest to 9, 10, 11 or 12 hours as he likes. For the hours of rest he is not required to pay overtime, but he must specify those hours. Overtime under S. 14 is only payable when the workman works in excess of the number of hours constituting a normal working day. That number is 9 hours for any day and work up to 9 hours on any day can be taken without paying overtime if the total number of hours in the week does not exceed 48. As in the present case, the total number of hours of work in a week is 48 (hours per day for 6 days), overtime is payable for that hour or part of an hour beyond which the workman is either made to work or the interval is not specified. The Port Trust can say that it will not take more than two hours extra work on any day and specify the remaining two hours as the intervals for rest. It is not compelled to fix only one interval or to make the interval of one hour only. It can fix two or three or even four without in any way going against the provisions of S. 13 or Rule 24.

The Supreme Court referred Ss. 54, 55 and 56 of the Factories Act dealing with the daily hours of work, intervals for rest and spread-over of the working time. It will be noticed that the arrangement of these sections is almost the same as the cognate provisions of the Minimum Wages Act. Here too, the hours of work cannot be more than 9 in a day and taken with the intervals for rest these 9 hours may be spread over 10½ hours. The only difference is that a worker must not be made to work for more than 5 hours at a stretch before he has had an interval for rest of half an hour at the least. The Supreme Court, after referring Ss. 54, 55 and 56 of the Factories Act, held:

> "There is no provision in the Minimum Wages Act which breaks up the hours of work by interposing a compulsory period of rest as is done by the latter part of S. 55 of the Factories Act. The reason perhaps, is that in some employments time for work depends on some extraneous factors and hours of rest cannot always be fixed to break up those hours. It is proverbial that time and tide do not wait for any man. Workers at a tidal dock must work when the tide is in and take their rest when the tide is out. It is for this reason that a variable recess is in force at the Prince's and Victoria Docks and due notice of the interval is given by specifying a day in advance the hours of rest. We do not think that the Trustees are guilty of infraction of the Minimum Wages Act by keeping the recess variable so long as they specify in advance the recess on any particular day."[47]

The Trustees cannot be compelled to break up the hours of work by interposing intervals for rest, if owing to the nature of the work there is difficulty in giving the intervals for rest in that manner on any particular day. According to their resolution, the recess is fixed as near the middle of the work as possible, depending on the tides. Accordingly, the Court held that the Flotilla crew has to remain on duty for full 12 hours and they work as and when they are required. Although their hours of duty are only 8, they are entitled, if present for work, for overtime up to 4 hours. The crew at the Alexandra Docks get a specified interval of one hour for rest and this makes up their 9 hours which is 8 hours' work and one hour interval for rest. They are, therefore, entitled to 3 hours' overtime if required to work beyond 9 hours on any day.

In *Municipal Council, Hatta* v. *Bhagat Singh*,[48] where the respondents are Moharrirs/ peons working with the appellant, Municipal Council, Hatta, filed an application under S. 22 of the Minimum Wages Act, 1948, before the Competent Authority (Labour Court) under the Minimum Wages Act, 1948 for payment of overtime on the ground that they were working for 4 additional hours every day. Their application has been allowed and the writ petition which was filed by the appellant before the High Court has been dismissed. So the appellant approached the Supreme Court.

---

47. *Ibid.* at p. 1206 per Hidayatullah, J.
48. AIR 1998 SC 1201.

The respondents who are employees of the appellant-Municipal Council are governed by the provisions of the Madhya Pradesh Municipalities Act, 1961. The respondents contended that they would be entitled to overtime under the Minimum Wages Act, 1948 by virtue of S. 14 of the said Act. According to them, service with Local Authority is one of the employments covered by the Minimum Wages Act, 1948. Now, the minimum wages, which are prescribed under the Minimum Wages Act, 1948 and which would be applicable to the respondents, are ₹50 per month. Admittedly, the respondents are getting wages above the minimum wages prescribed under the Minimum Wages Act, 1948. The question is whether S. 14 of the Minimum Wages Act, 1948 would apply to such persons.

The Court held that overtime under S. 14 is payable to those employees who are getting a minimum rate of wage as prescribed under the Minimum Wages Act, 1948. These are the only employees to whom overtime under S. 14 would become payable. In the present case, the respondents cannot be described as employees who are getting a minimum rate of wages fixed under the Minimum Wages Act, 1948. They are getting much more and that too under the Madhya Pradesh Municipal Service (Scales of Pay and Allowances) Rules, 1967. Therefore, S. 14 has no application to them. The respondents seem to have proceeded on the basis that because employment under any Local Authority is listed as Item 6 in the Schedule to the Minimum Wages Act, 1948, they would automatically get overtime under the said Act. Section 14, however, clearly provides for payment of overtime only to those employees who are getting minimum rate of wage under the Minimum Wages Act, 1948. It does not apply to those getting better wages under other statutory Rules.

Where employees had by implication agreed to work on weekly holidays and had agreed by implication to avail of two alternative additional holidays, it cannot be said that the employees are entitled to get overtime wages under the provisions of the Minimum Wages Act.[49]

SECTION 15: Wages of worker who works for less than normal working day

If an employee whose minimum rate of wages has been fixed under this Act by the day works on any day on which he was employed for a period less than the requisite number of hours constituting a normal working day, he shall, save as otherwise hereinafter provided, be entitled to receive wages in respect of work done by him on that day as if he had worked for a full normal working day:

Provided, however, that he shall not be entitled to receive wages for a full normal working day—

(i) in any case where his failure to work is caused by his unwillingness to work and not by the omission of the employer to provide him with work, and

(ii) in such other cases and circumstances as may be prescribed.

SECTION 16: Wages for two or more classes of work

Where an employee does two or more classes of work to each of which a different minimum

49. *Pune Municipal Corporation* v. *Suryakant Pandurang Dharward*, 2002 (95) FLR 559 (Bom).

rate of wages is applicable, the employer shall pay to such employee in respect of the time respectively occupied in each such class of work, wages at not less than the minimum rate in force in respect of each such class.

Section 17: Minimum time rate wages for piece work

Where an employee is employed on piece work for which minimum time rate and not a minimum piece rate has been fixed under this Act, the employer shall pay to such employee wages at not less than the minimum time rate.

Section 18: Maintenance of registers and records

(1) Every employer shall maintain such registers and records giving such particulars of employees employed by him, the work performed by them, the wages paid to them, the receipts given by them and such other particulars and in such form as may be prescribed.

(2) Every employer shall keep exhibited, in such manner as may be prescribed, in the factory, workshop or place where the employees in the scheduled employment may be employed, or in the case of out-workers, in such factory, workshop or place as may be used for giving out work to them, notices in the prescribed form containing prescribed particulars.

(3) The appropriate Government may, by rules made under this Act, provide for the issue of wage books or wage slips to employees employed in any scheduled employment in respect of which minimum rates of wages have been fixed and prescribed in the manner in which entries shall be made and authenticated in such wage books or wage slips by the employer or his agent.

Section 19: Inspectors

(1) The appropriate Government may, by notification in the Official Gazette, appoint such persons as it thinks fit to be Inspectors for the purposes of this Act and define the local limits within which they shall exercise their functions.

(2) Subject to any rules made in this behalf, an Inspector may, within the local limits for which he is appointed—

(a) enter, at all reasonable hours, with such assistants (if any), being persons in the service of the Government or any local or other public authority, as he thinks fit, any premises or place where employees are employed or work is given out to out-workers in any scheduled employment in respect of which minimum rates of wages have been fixed under this Act for the purpose of examining any register, record of wages or notices required to be kept or exhibited by or under this Act or rules made thereunder, and require the production thereof for inspection;

(b) examine any person whom he finds in any such premises or place and who, he has reasonable cause to believe, is an employee employed therein or an employee to whom work is given out therein;

(c) require any person giving out-work and any out-workers, to give any information, which is in his power to give, with respect to the names and addresses of the persons to, for and from whom the work is given out or received, and with respect to the payments to be made for the work;

(d) seize or take copies of such register, record or wages or notices or portions thereof as he may consider relevant in respect of an offence under this Act which he has reason to believe has been committed by an employer; and

(e) exercise such other powers as may be prescribed.

(3) Every Inspector shall be deemed to be a public servant within the meaning of the Indian Penal Code (45 of 1860).

(4) Any person required to produce any document or thing or to give any information by an Inspector under sub-section (2) shall be deemed to be legally bound to do so within the meaning of section 175 and section 176 of the Indian Penal Code (45 of 1860).

Section 20: Claims

(1) The appropriate Government may, by notification in the Official Gazette, appoint any Commissioner for Workmen's Compensation or any officer of the Central Government exercising functions as a Labour Commissioner for any region, or any officer of the State Government not below the rank of Labour Commissioner or any other officer with experience as a judge of a civil court or as a stipendiary Magistrate to be the Authority to hear and decide for any specified area all claims arising out of payment of less than the minimum rates of wages or in respect of the payment of remuneration for days of rest or for work done on such days under clause (b) or clause (c) of sub-section (1) of section 13 or of wages at the overtime rate under section 14, to employees employed or paid in that area.

(2) Where an employee has any claim of the nature referred to in sub-section (1), the employee himself, or any legal practitioner or any official of a registered trade union authorised in writing to act on his behalf, or any Inspector, or any person acting with the permission of the Authority appointed under sub-section (1) may apply to such Authority for a direction under sub-section (3):

Provided that every such application shall be presented within six months from the date on which the minimum wages or other amount became payable:

Provided further that any application may be admitted after the said period of six months when the applicant satisfies the Authority that he had sufficient cause for not making the application within such period.

(3) When any application under sub-section (2) is entertained, the Authority shall hear the applicant and the employer, or give them an opportunity of being heard, and after such further inquiry, if any, as it may consider necessary, may, without prejudice to any other penalty to which the employer may be liable under this Act, direct—

(i) in the case of a claim arising out of payment of less than the minimum rates of wages, the payment to the employee of the amount by which the minimum wages payable to him exceed the amount actually paid, together with the payment of such compensation as the Authority may think fit, not exceeding ten times the amount of such excess;

(ii) in any other case, the payment of the amount due to the employee, together with the payment of such compensation as the Authority may think fit, not exceeding ten rupees;

and the Authority may direct payment of such compensation in cases where the excess or the amount due is paid by the employer to the employee before the disposal of the application.

(4) If the Authority hearing any application under this section is satisfied that it was either malicious or vexatious, it may direct that a penalty not exceeding fifty rupees be paid to the employer by the person presenting the application.

(5) Any amount directed to be paid under this section may be recovered—

(a) if the Authority is a Magistrate, by the authority as if it were a fine imposed by the Authority as a Magistrate, or

(b) if the Authority is not a Magistrate, by any Magistrate to whom the Authority makes application in this behalf, as if it were a fine imposed by such Magistrate.

(6) Every direction of the Authority under this section shall be final.

(7) Every Authority appointed under sub-section (1) shall have all the powers of a civil court under the Code of Civil Procedure, 1908 (5 of 1908), for the purpose of taking evidence and of enforcing the attendance of witnesses and compelling the production of documents, and every such Authority shall be deemed to be a civil court for all the purposes of section 195 and Chapter XXXV of the Code of Criminal Procedure, 1898 (5 of 1898).

Any employee who feels himself aggrieved by the refusal of the employer to pay the minimum wages fixed under the Act has the right to make a complaint either by himself or through the prescribed agents to the Authority mentioned in the Act. Under sub-section (3) of S. 20, the Authority has to hear the applicant and the employer or give them an opportunity of being heard and could straightway give a direction to pay as regards the alleged non-payment of the minimum rates of wages and such compensation as he thinks fit, not exceeding ten times the amount of the excess of the minimum wages over that which was paid. It is true that the sub-section provides for a further inquiry but such inquiry is to be at the discretion of the authority. The nature and scope of the inquiry would depend on the exact controversy raised in the case. If it is of a trivial nature, the Tribunal can probably deal with it in a summary manner, but where it is alleged that the notification under the Act is not applicable to a certain class of workers, it is the duty of the authority to give a proper hearing to the parties, allowing them to tender such evidence as they think proper before making an order which may have far-reaching consequences.

There is no provision for appeal or revision against the direction of the Authority, although he may levy a penalty to the extent of ten times the amount by which the minimum wages overtop the payment actually made. Whatever he says is the final word on the subject. All this can but lead to the conclusion that S. 20 is not aimed at putting a seal on the adjudication if any under it. It is to be of a nature which suited the discretion of the officer concerned, although he is given the powers of a Civil Court in certain respects. In such a situation it is impossible to hold that the legislature meant to exclude the jurisdiction of Civil Courts to go into the question of non-payment of minimum wages claimed as final. It can be construed that sub-section (6) of S. 20 merely shows that the discretion of the Authority cannot be questioned under any provision of the Act. It does not exclude the jurisdiction of the Civil Court when the challenge is as to the applicability of the Act to a certain class of workers.[50]

A question raised before the Supreme Court in *Pali Devi* v. *Chairman, Managing Committee*[51] was, whether an ex-employee can invoke S. 20 of the Minimum Wages Act. The fact of the case reveals that the High Court of Punjab and Haryana allowed the writ petition of the respondent-Managing Committee of the Army School, Jallandhar, upsetting the orders of the Authority under the Minimum Wages Act, 1948, on the premise that the appellants seeking relief were its ex-employees and not existing ones, and hence disentitled to move a petition under S. 20(2) of the Act for appropriate relief. The High Court, relying on an earlier Division Bench decision of the Punjab High Court in *Municipal Commitee, Rajkot* v. *Sham Lal Kaura*,[52] took the view that the word employee, defined in S. 2(i) of the Act, did not include an ex-employee. It was held in the said case that a person who is not in the actual employment of the employer at the time of making an application under S. 20(2) of the Act was not entitled to seek relief. Therefore, the appellant approached the Supreme Court on Special Leave Petition.

Section 30 of the Act confers on the appropriate Government power to make rules. The Minimum Wages (Central) Rules, 1950, framed by the Central Government, prescribe Forms wherein particulars to be mentioned in the application for seeking relief are provided. Form VI, for the purpose of S. 20(2) so far relevant, provides:

"The applicant above-named states as follows:

(1) The applicant was/has been employed from .... to .... as ....., (category) in .... (establishment) of Shri/Messrs .... engaged in .... (nature of work) which is a scheduled employment within the meaning of Section 2(g) of the Minimum Wages Act.

(2) The opponent(s) is/are the employer(s) within the meaning of Section 2(a) of Minimum Wages Act.

(3) (a) The applicant has been paid wages at less than the minimum rate of wages fixed for his category of employment under the Act by ₹ .... per day for the period from .... to ....;

(b) The applicant has not been paid wages at ₹ .... per day for weekly days of rest from .... to ....;

(c) The applicant has not been paid wages at the overtime rate for the period from .... to ....;"

It is plain that paragraph one of the Form equates the past and the present as an alternative. It obviously establishes the right of an ex-employee to move a petition under S. 20(2) of the Act. The statutory language employed in the Form is a good hint to discern

50. *Pabbojan Tea Co., Ltd.* v. *Deputy Commissioner, Lakhimpur*, AIR 1968 SC 271.
51. AIR 1996 SC 1589.
52. (1965–66) 28 FJR 472.

the true scope of S. 20(2) to determine whether a past employee can invoke the provisions of the Act or not.

In *Wakefield Estate* v. *P.L. Perumal*,[53] a learned single judge of the Madras High Court took the view that since S. 20 the Act speaks only of employees and does not speak of past employees and since the word 'employee' is defined as a person who is employed, it must be held that the summary remedy provided by S. 20 is not available to past employees. This was the literal construction of S. 20(2) of the Act. Another learned single judge of the same High Court in *Murugan Transports* v. *P. Rathakrishnan*,[54] differed from the earlier view and held that in order to give full effect to the intendment of the Act, it would be necessary to bring within its fold, not merely the present, but also the past employee, who at one time being employee had earned the minimum wages.

In *Rajkot's* case, the Punjab High Court opted for the literal construction. Had the existence of the Rules and Form VI been brought to the notice of the Division Bench, perhaps the interpretation would have been different. Therefore, it cannot be said that the instant case was decided wrongly by the Punjab and Haryana High Court.

The Supreme Court held that on account of the preponderance of Authority, S. 20(2) and 2(i) has to be read along with the Rules and Form VI to lean in favour of the view that both past and present employees were entitled to move in the matter. Such would be a purposive approach, which would carry out the necessary intendment of the statute, for which the Rules and the Form lend a hand to carry out the objectives of the Act. The language employed therein, even though executive voiced, is more often than not, demonstrative of the legislative purpose. So viewed, the intendment of the statute is furthered if an ex-employee too is held entitled to seek relief under S. 20(2) of the Act.

The issue raised before the Supreme Court in *Managanese Ore (India) Ltd.* v. *Chandi Lal Saha*[55] for consideration was, whether S. 20 of the Minimum Wages Act is to be invoked or S. 33-C(2) of the Industrial Disputes Act is to be invoked in order to recover wages fixed under the Minimum Wages Act.

The Advocate appearing for the appellant is of opinion that since S. 20 of the Act provides for elaborate machinery to get the grievances redressed under the Act, the Labour Court has no jurisdiction under S. 33-C(2) of the Industrial Disputes Act to entertain the application. In order to resolve the above issue, the Court relied on *Town Municipal Council, Athani* v. *Presiding Officer, Labour Court, Hubli*[56] where it has been held that the Minimum Wages Act is concerned with the fixing of rates—rates of minimum wages, overtime rates, rate for payment of work on a day of rest and is not intended for enforcement of payment of wages. Under S. 20(1) of the Minimum Wages Act, in which provision is made for seeking remedy in respect of claims arising out of payment of less than minimum rates, or in respect of remuneration for days of rest, or for work on such days, or of wages at the overtime rates, the authority is to exercise jurisdiction for deciding claims which relates to rates of wages, rates for payment for work done on days of rest and overtime rates. The power under S. 20(3) of the Minimum Wages Act given to the Authority dealing with an application under

53. (1959–60) 16 FJR 1.
54. AIR 1961 Mad 310.
55. AIR 1991 SC 520.
56. AIR 1969 SC 1335.

S. 20(1) to direct payment of the actual amount found due, is only an incidental power for working out effectively the directions under S. 20(1) fixing various rates under the Act. That is, if there is no dispute as to rates between the employer and the employee and the only question is whether a particular payment at the agreed rate is due or not, then S. 20(1) of the Minimum Wages Act would not be attracted at all, and the appropriate remedy would only be either under S. 15(1) of the Payment of Wages Act, 1936, or under S. 33-C(2) of the Industrial Disputes Act.

In the present case, that is, *Managanese Ore Ltd.* case, there was no dispute regarding the rates of wages and it is admitted by the parties that the minimum rates of wages were fixed by the Government of India under the Act. The workmen demanded the minimum wages so fixed and the appellant denied the same to the workmen on extraneous considerations. Under the circumstances the remedy under S. 20 of the Act was not available to the workmen and the only remedy available is to invoke the jurisdiction of the Labour Court under S. 33-C(2) of the Industrial Disputes Act, 1947.

An application for a direction on the employer to pay minimum wages and other amounts payable under the Minimum Wages Act may be made under S. 20(2) of the Act to the Authority appointed under S. 20(1). The first proviso to S. 20(2) requires that

> *"every such application shall be presented within six months from the date on which the minimum wages or other amount became payable."*

The second proviso to S. 20(2) is as follows:

> *"Provided further that any application may be admitted after the said period of six months when the applicant satisfies the Authority that he had sufficient cause for not making the application within such period."*

The Supreme Court in *Sarpanch, Lonand Grampanchayat* v. *Ramgiri Gosavi*[57] held that the Authority has a discretion to condone the delay under second proviso to S. 20(2) in presenting the application provided sufficient cause for the entire delay is shown to its satisfaction. This discretion like other judicial discretion must be exercised with vigilance and circumspection according to justice, common sense, and sound judgment. The discretion is to know through law what is just. The words *"sufficient cause"* should receive a liberal construction so as to advance substantial justice when no negligence nor inaction nor want of bona fides is imputable to the applicant.

It must be remembered that in every case of delay, there can be some lapse on the part of the litigant concerned. That alone is not enough to turn down his plea and to shut the door against him. If the explanation does not smack of *mala fides* or it is not put forth as part of the dilatory strategy, the Court must show utmost consideration to the suitor. There is no illegality in the first respondent passing a composite order while exercising its discretion to entertain an application and also deciding the application for direction on the merits. Sufficient cause has been shown by the workmen, which sufficient cause has been accepted by the first respondent, though not in so many sentences, but stating that it has examined the cause shown and it is satisfied. This being a discretion exercised by the first respondent

57. AIR 1968 SC 222.

and being a sound discretion, which advanced the cause of justice and case of the workmen, who have been denied of the minimum wages, the Court declines to interfere with the orders passed by the first respondent.[58]

SECTION 21: Single application in respect of a number of employees

(1) Subject to such rules as may be prescribed, a single application may be presented under section 20 on behalf or in respect of any number of employees employed in the scheduled employment in respect of which minimum rates of wages have been fixed and in such cases the maximum compensation which may be awarded under sub-section (3) of section 20 shall not exceed ten times the aggregate amount of such excess or ten rupees per head, as the case may be.

(2) The Authority may deal with any number of separate pending applications presented, under section 20 in respect of employees in the scheduled employments in respect of which minimum rates of wages have been fixed, as a single application presented under sub-section (1) of this section and the provisions of that sub-section shall apply accordingly.

SECTION 22: Penalties for certain offences

Any employer who:

(a) pays to any employee less than the minimum rates of wages fixed for that employee's class of work, or less than the amount due to him under the provisions of this Act, or

(b) contravenes any rule or order made under section 13;

shall be punishable with imprisonment for a term which may extend to six months, or with fine which may extend to five hundred rupees, or with both:

Provided that in imposing any fine for an offence under this section, the Court shall take into consideration the amount of any compensation already awarded against the accused in any proceedings taken under section 20.

SECTION 22A: General provision for punishment of other offences

Any employer who contravenes any provision of this Act or of any rule or order made thereunder shall, if no other penalty is provided for such contravention by this Act, be punishable with fine which may extend to five hundred rupees.

SECTION 22B: Cognizance of offences

(1) No court shall take cognizance of a complaint against any person for an offence—

58. *Special Officer, Thanjavur Central Cooperative Bank Employees Cooperative Thrift and Credit Society Ltd.* v. *Deputy Commissioner of Labour and others,* 2003 (96) FLR 1180 (Mad).

(a) under clause (a) of section 22 unless an application in respect of the facts constituting such offence has been presented under section 20 and has been granted wholly or in part, and the appropriate Government or an officer authorised by it in this behalf has sanctioned the making of the complaint;

(b) under clause (b) of section 22 or under section 22A, except on a complaint made by or with the sanction of, an Inspector.

(2) No court shall take cognizance of an offence—

(a) under clause (a) or clause (b) of section 22, unless complaint thereof is made within one month of the grant of sanction under this section;

(b) under section 22A, unless complaint thereof is made within six months of the date on which the offence is alleged to have been committed.

SECTION 22C: Offences by companies

(1) If the person committing any offence under this Act is a company, every person who at the time the offence was committed, was in charge of, and was responsible to, the company for the conduct of the business of the company as well as the company shall be deemed to be guilty of the offence and shall be liable to be proceeded against and punished accordingly:

Provided that nothing contained in this sub-section shall render any such person liable to any punishment provided in this Act if he proves that the offence was committed without his knowledge or that he exercised all due diligence to prevent the commission of such offence.

(2) Notwithstanding anything contained in sub-section (1), where any offence under this Act has been committed by a company and it is proved that the offence has been committed with the consent or connivance of, or is attributable to any neglect on the part of, any director, manager, secretary, or other officer of the company, such director, manager, secretary or other officer of the company shall also be deemed to be guilty of that offence and shall be liable to be proceeded against and punished accordingly.

Explanation: For the purposes of this section—

(a) "company" means any body corporate and includes a firm or other association of individuals, and

(b) "director" in relation to a firm means a partner in the firm.

SECTION 22D: Payment of undisbursed amounts due to employees

All amounts payable by an employer to an employee as the amount of minimum wages of the employee under this Act or otherwise due to the employee under this Act or any rule or order made thereunder shall, if such amounts could not or cannot be paid to the employee on account of his death before payment or on account of his whereabouts not being known, be deposited with the prescribed authority who shall deal with the money so deposited in such manner as may be prescribed.

Section 22E: Protection against attachment of assets of employer with Government

Any amount deposited with the appropriate Government by an employer to secure the due performance of a contract with that Government and any other amount due to such employer from that Government in respect of such contract shall not be liable to attachment under any decree or order of any Court in respect of any debt or liability incurred by the employer other than any debt or liability incurred by the employer towards any employee employed in connection with the contract aforesaid.

Section 22F: Application of Payment of Wages Act, 1936 to scheduled employments

(1) Notwithstanding anything contained in the Payment of Wages Act, 1936 (4 of 1936), the appropriate Government may, by notification in the Official Gazette, direct that, subject to the provisions of sub-section (2), all or any of the provisions of the said Act shall, with such modifications, if any, as may be specified in the notification, apply to wages payable to employees in such scheduled employments as may be specified in the notification.

(2) Where all or any of the provisions of the said Act are applied to wages payable to employees in any scheduled employment under sub-section (1), the Inspector appointed under this Act shall be deemed to be the Inspector for the purpose of enforcement of the provisions so applied within the local limits of his jurisdiction.

Section 23: Exemption of employer from liability in certain cases

Where an employer is charged with an offence against this Act, he shall be entitled, upon complaint duly made by him, to have any other person whom he charges as the actual offender, brought before the Court at the time appointed for hearing the charge; and if, after the commission of the offence has been proved, the employer proves to the satisfaction of the Court—

(a) that he has used due diligence to enforce the execution of this Act, and

(b) that the said other person committed the offence in question without his knowledge, consent or connivance,

that other person shall be convicted of the offence and shall be liable to the like punishment as if he were the employer and the employer shall be discharged:

Provided that in seeking to prove, as aforesaid, the employer may be examined on oath, and the evidence of the employer or his witness, if any, shall be subject to cross-examination by or on behalf of the person whom the employer charges as the actual offender and by the prosecution.

Section 24: Bar of suits

No Court shall entertain any suit for the recovery of wages in so far as the sum so claimed—

(a) forms the subject of an application under section 20 which has been presented by or on behalf of the plaintiff, or

(b) has formed the subject of a direction under that section in favour of the plaintiff, or

(c) has been adjudged in any proceeding under that section not to be due to the plaintiff, or

(d) could have been recovered by an application under that section.

It is pertinent to note that S. 24 of the Act creates an express bar in respect of a particular kind of suits, namely, suits for recovery of wages in certain eventualities. The obvious intention is that a poor employee is not to be driven to file a suit for the payment of the deficit of his wages but that he can avail himself of the machinery provided by the Act to get quick relief. It does not in terms bar the employer from instituting a suit when his claim is that he has been called upon to pay wages and compensation to persons to whom are not governed by the notification under the Minimum Wages Act.[59]

Section 25: Contracting out

Any contract or agreement, whether made before or after the commencement of this Act, whereby an employee either relinquishes or reduces his right to a minimum rate of wages or any privilege or concession accruing to him under this Act shall be null and void in so far as it purports to reduce the minimum rate of wages fixed under this Act.

Section 26: Exemptions and exceptions

(1) The appropriate Government may, subject to such conditions, if any as it may think fit to impose, direct that the provisions of this Act shall not apply in relation to the wages payable to disabled employees.

(2) The appropriate Government, if for special reasons it thinks so fit, by notification in the Official Gazette, direct that subject to such conditions and for such period as it may specify the provisions of this Act or any of them shall not apply to all or any class of employees employed in any scheduled employment or to any locality where there is carried on a scheduled employment.

(2A) The appropriate Government may, if it is of opinion that having regard to the terms and conditions of service applicable to any class of employees in a scheduled employment generally or in a scheduled employment in a local area, or to any establishment or a part of any establishment in a scheduled employment, it is not necessary to fix minimum wages in respect of such employees of that class or in respect of employees in such establishment or such part of any establishment as are in receipt of wages exceeding such limit as may be prescribed in this behalf, direct, by notification in the Official Gazette, and subject to such conditions, if any as it may think fit to impose, that the provisions of this Act or any of them shall not apply in relation to such employees.

(3) Nothing in this Act shall apply to the wages payable by an employer to a member of his family who is living with him and is dependent on him.

59. *Pabbojan Tea Co. Ltd.* v. *Deputy Commissioner, Lakhimpur*, AIR 1968 SC 271.

Explanation: In this sub-section, a member of the employer's family shall be deemed to include his or her spouse or child or parent or brother or sister.

SECTION 27: Power of State Government to add to Schedule

The appropriate Government, after giving by notification in the Official Gazette not less than three months' notice of its intention so to do, may, by like notification, add to either Part of the Schedule any employment in respect of which it is of opinion that minimum rates of wages should be fixed under this Act, and thereupon the Schedule shall in its application to the State be deemed to be amended accordingly.

Section 5(2) empowers the appropriate Government to fix or revise minimum wages in regard to any of the employments in the Schedule to which the Act applies. This power can be exercised only if the employment in question is specified in the Schedule and the Act is therefore applicable to it. Whereas S. 27 confers a wider power on the appropriate Government, and in exercise of the said power the appropriate Government may add an employment to the Schedule. The nature and extent of the said two powers are thus quite separate and distinct and there can be no doubt that what can be done by the appropriate Government in exercise of its power under S. 27 cannot be done by it in exercise of its powers under S. 5(2). Section 27 empowers the appropriate Government to add items to the Schedule and it would be open to the appropriate government to adopt such a course if it is intended to achieve the object with which the impugned notification has been issued.[60] In *Lingegowd D. and S. Chamber Pvt. Ltd.* v. *Mysore Kirloskar Ltd.* (AIR 2006 SC 1967) where the appellant-Lingegowd Detective and Security Chamber (P) Limited filed a writ petition praying for setting aside the orders passed by the Authority under The Minimum Wages Act, 1948 that establishment of providing security personnel to various organisation was not a scheduled employment hence MW Act is not applicable to them. The learned Single Judge categorically held that MW Act is not applicable to the Security Service Providers Organisation as it is not a Scheduled Employment. The Division Bench of the High Court has held that since the principal employer's activities were included in the list of Scheduled employments, under the Schedule to the Act, there was no necessity of issuance of a separate Notification with reference to the employment of security staff procured through Lingegowd.

The Supreme Court held that the appellant Lingegowd has no liability to pay the minimum wages. The detective services or security do not form part of the scheduled employment as detailed in the Schedule. It was also justified in holding that there was no employee–employer relationship so far as the Mysore Kirloskar and the concerned workmen are concerned.

SECTION 28: Power of Central Government to give directions

The Central Government may give directions to State Government as to the carrying into execution of this Act in the State.

60. *M.P. Mineral Industry Association, Nagpur* v. *Regional Labour Commissioner (Central), Jabalpur*, AIR 1960 SC 1068.

SECTION 29: Power of Central Government to make rules

The Central Government may, subject to the condition of previous publication, by notification in the Official Gazette, make rules prescribing the term of office of the members, the procedure to be followed in the conduct of business, the method of voting, the manner of filling up casual vacancies in membership and the quorum necessary for the transaction of business of the Central Advisory Board.

SECTION 30: Power of appropriate Government to make rules

(1) The appropriate Government may, subject to the condition of previous publication, by notification in the Official Gazette, make rules for carrying out the purposes of this Act.

(2) Without prejudice to the generality of the foregoing power, such rules may—

(a) prescribe the term of office of the members, the procedure to be followed in the conduct of business, the method of voting, the manner of filling up casual vacancies in membership and the quorum necessary for the transaction of business of the committees, sub-committees, and the Advisory Board;

(b) prescribe the method of summoning witnesses, production of documents relevant to the subject-matter of the enquiry before the committees, sub-committees, and the Advisory Board;

(c) prescribe the mode of computation of the cash value of wages in kind and of concessions in respect of supplies of essential commodities at concessional rates;

(d) prescribe the time and conditions of payment of, and the deductions permissible from, wages;

(e) provide for giving adequate publicity to the minimum rates of wages fixed under this Act;

(f) provide for a day of rest in every period of seven days and for the payment of remuneration in respect of such day;

(g) prescribe the number of hours of work which shall constitute a normal working day;

(h) prescribe the cases and circumstance in which an employee employed for a period of less than the requisite number of hours constituting a normal working day shall not be entitled to receive wages for a full normal working day;

(i) prescribe the form of registers and records to be maintained and the particulars to be entered in such registers and records;

(j) provide for the issue of wage books and wage slips and prescribe the manner of making and authenticating entries in wage books and wage slips;

(k) prescribe the powers of Inspectors for purposes of this Act;

(l) regulate the scale of costs that may be allowed in proceedings under section 20;

(m) prescribe the amount of court-fees payable in respect of proceedings under section 20; and

(n) provide for any other matter which is to be or may be prescribed.

SECTION 30A: Rules made by Central Government to be laid before Parliament

(1) Every rule made by the Central Government under this Act shall be laid as soon as may be after it is made before each House of Parliament while it is in session for a total period of thirty days which may be comprised in one session or in two successive sessions, and if, before the expiry of the session in which it is so laid or the session immediately following, both Houses agree in making any modification in the rule or both Houses agree that the rule should not be made, the rule shall thereafter have effect only in such modified form or be of no effect, as the case may be, so, however, that any such modification or annulment shall be without prejudice to the validity of anything previously done under that rule.

(2) Every rule made by the State Government under this Act shall be laid, as soon as may be after it is made, before the State Legislature.

SECTION 31: Validation of fixation of certain minimum rates of wages

Where during the period—

(a) commencing on the 1st day of April, 1952, and ending with the date of the commencement of the Minimum Wages (Amendment) Act, 1954 (26 of 1954); or

(b) commencing on the 31st day of December, 1954, and ending with the date of the commencement of the Minimum Wages (Amendment) Act, 1957 (30 of 1957); or

(c) commencing on the 31st day of December, 1959, and ending with the date of the commencement of the Minimum Wages (Amendment) Act, 1961,

minimum rates of wages have been fixed by an appropriate Government as being payable to employees employed in any employment specified in the Schedule in the belief or purported belief that such rates were being fixed under clause (a) of sub-section (1) of section 3, as in force immediately before the commencement of the Minimum Wages (Amendment) Act, 1954 (26 of 1954), or the Minimum Wages (Amendment) Act, 1957 (30 of 1957), or the Minimum Wages (Amendment) Act, 1961 (31 of 1961), as the case may be, such rates shall be deemed to have been fixed in accordance with law and shall not be called in question in any court on the ground merely that the relevant date specified for the purpose in that clause had expired at the time the rates were fixed:

Provided that nothing contained in this section shall extend, or be construed to extend to affect any person with any punishment or penalty whatsoever by reason of the payment by him by way of wages to any of his employees during any period specified in this section of an amount which is less than the minimum rates of wages referred to in this section or by reason of non-compliance during the period aforesaid with any order or the rule issued under section 13.

THE SCHEDULE

[See Section 2(g) and 27]

PART I

(1) Employment in any woollen carpet making or shawl weaving establishment.
(2) Employment in any rice mill, flour mill or dal mill.
(3) Employment in any tobacco (including bidi making) manufactory.
(4) Employment in any plantation, that is to say, any estate which is maintained for the purpose of growing cinchona, rubber, tea or coffee.
(5) Employment in any oil mill.
(6) Employment under any local authority.
(7) Employment on the construction or maintenance of roads or in building operations.
(8) Employment in stone breaking or stone crushing.
(9) Employment in any lac manufactory.
(10) Employment in any mica works.
(11) Employment in public motor transport.
(12) Employment in tanneries and leather manufactory.
Employment in gypsum mines.
Employment in barytes mines.
Employment in bauxite mines.
Employment in manganese mines.
Employment in the maintenance of buildings and employment in the construction and maintenance of runways
Employment in china clay mines.
Employment in kyanite mines.
Employment in copper mines.
Employment in clay mines.
Employment in magnesite mines covered under the Mines Act, 1952
Employment in white clay mines.
Employment in stone mines.
Employment in steatite (including mines producing soapstone & talc).
Employment in ochre mines.
Employment in asbestos mines.
Employment in fire clay mines.
Employment in chromite mines.
Employment in quartizite mines.
Employment in quartz mines.
Employment in silica mines.
Employment in graphite mines.
Employment in felspar mines.

Employment in laterite mines.
Employment in dolomite mines.
Employment in red oxide mines.
Employment in wolfram mines.
Employment in iron-ore mines.
Employment in granite mines.
Employment in rock phosphate mines.
Employment in haemetite mines.
Employment in loading and unloading in railways, goods sheds.
Employment in docks and ports.
Employment in ashpit cleaning on railways.
Employment in marble and calcite mines.
Employment in uranium mines.
Employment in mica mines.
Employment in lignite mines.
Employment in gravel mines.
Employment in state mines.
Employment in laying of underground cables, electric lines, water supply lines and sewerage pipe lines.

PART II

(1) Employment in agriculture, that is to say, in any form of farming, including the cultivation and tillage of the soil, dairy farming, the production, cultivation, growing and harvesting of any agricultural or horticultural commodity, the raising of live-stock, bees or poultry, and any practice performed by a farmer or on a farm as incidental to or in conjunction with farm operations (including any forestry or timbering operations and the preparation for market and delivery to storage or to market or to carriage for transportation to market of farm produce).

* * *

9 The Payment of Wages Act, 1936

It is an Act "to regulate the payment of wages of certain classes of employed persons."

SECTION 1: Short title, extent, commencement and application

(1) This Act may be called the Payment of Wages Act, 1936.

(2) It extends to the whole of India.

(3) It shall come into force on such date as the Central Government may, by notification in the Official Gazette, appoint.

(4) It applies in the first instance to the payment of wages to persons employed in any factory, to persons employed (otherwise than in a factory) upon any railway by a railway administration or, either directly or through a sub-contractor, by a person fulfilling a contract with a railway administration, and to persons employed in an industrial or other establishment specified in sub-clauses (a) to (g) of clause (ii) of section 2.

(5) Appropriate Government may, after giving three months' notice of its intention of so doing, by notification in the Official Gazette, extend the provisions of this Act or any of them to the payment of wages to any class of persons employed in any establishment or class of establishments specified by the appropriate Government under sub-clause (h) of clause (ii) of section 2:

Provided that in relation to any such establishment owned by the Central Government, no such notification shall be issued except with the concurrence of that Government.

(6) This Act applies to wages payable to an employed person in respect of a wage period if such wages for that wage period do not exceed 24,000 rupees per month or such other higher sum which, on the basis of figures of the Consumer Expenditure Survey published by the National Sample Survey Organisation, the Central Government may, after every five years, by notification, in the Official Gazette, specify.

SECTION 2: Definitions

In this Act, unless there is anything repugnant in the subject or context,—

(i) appropriate Government means, in relation to railways, air transport services, mines and oil fields, the Central Government and, in relation to all other cases, the state Government.

(ia) **employed person** includes the legal representative of a deceased employed person;

(ib) **employer** includes the legal representative of a deceased employer.

(ic) **factory** means a factory as defined in clause (m) of section 2 of the Factories Act, 1948 (63 of 1948) and includes any place to which the provisions of that Act have been applied under sub-section (1) of section 85 thereof.

(ii) **industrial or other establishment** means any—

(a) tramway service, or motor transport service engaged in carrying passengers or goods or both by road for hire or reward;

(aa) air transport service other than such service belonging to, or exclusively employed in the military, naval or air forces of the Union or the Civil Aviation Department of the Government of India;

(b) dock, wharf or jetty;

(c) inland vessel, mechanically propelled;

(d) mine, quarry or oil-field;

(e) plantation;

(f) workshop or other establishment in which articles are produced, adapted or manufactured, with a view to their use, transport or sale;

(g) establishment in which any work relating to the construction, development or maintenance of buildings, roads, bridges or canals, or relating to operations connected with navigation, irrigation, or to the supply of water or relating to the generation, transmission and distribution of electricity or any other form of power is being carried on;

(h) any other establishment or class of establishments which the appropriate Government may, having regard to the nature thereof, the need for protection of persons employed therein and other relevant circumstances, specify, by notification in the Official Gazette.

(iia) **mine** has the meaning assigned to it in clause (j) of sub-section (1) of section 2 of the Mines Act, 1952 (35 of 1952).

(iii) **plantation** has the meaning assigned to it in clause (f) of section 2 of the Plantations Labour Act, 1951 (69 of 1951).

(iv) **prescribed** means prescribed by rules made under this Act.

(v) **railway administration** has the meaning assigned to it in clause 32 of section 2 of the Railways Act, 1989 (24 of 1989); and

(vi) **wages** means all remuneration (whether by way of salary, allowances, or otherwise) expressed in terms of money or capable of being so expressed which would, if the terms of employment, express or implied, were fulfilled, be payable to a person employed in respect of his employment or of work done in such employment, and includes—

(a) any remuneration payable under any award or settlement between the parties or order of a court;

(b) any remuneration to which the person employed is entitled in respect of overtime work or holidays or any leave period;

(c) any additional remuneration payable under the terms of employment (whether called a bonus or by any other name);

(d) any sum which by reason of the termination of employment of the person employed is payable under any law, contract or instrument which provides for the payment of such sum, whether with or without deductions, but does not provide for the time within which the payment is to be made;

(e) any sum to which the person employed is entitled under any scheme framed under any law for the time being in force;

but does not include—

(1) any bonus (whether under a scheme of profit sharing or otherwise) which does not form part of the remuneration payable under the terms of employment or which is not payable under any award or settlement between the parties or order of a court;

(2) the value of any house-accommodation, or of the supply of light, water, medical attendance or other amenity or of any service excluded from the computation of wages by a general or special order of the appropriate Government;

(3) any contribution paid by the employer to any pension or provident fund, and the interest which may have accrued thereon;

(4) any travelling allowance or the value of any travelling concession;

(5) any sum paid to the employed person to defray special expenses entailed on him by the nature of his employment; or

(6) any gratuity payable on the termination of employment in cases other than those specified in sub-clause (d).

The section itself is explicit that any sum payable under an award or any remuneration with respect to holidays or leave period is covered by it. The only exception made is that bonus under a scheme of profit sharing is excluded but bonus forming part of the remuneration has not been excluded. The award has not been filed by the petitioner. The petitioner has also not averred either before this Court or before the authorities below that claim included under the head of bonus did not form a part of the remuneration payable to the employees of the petitioner bank. It is settled that the workmen are entitled for grant of bonus as regular remuneration under the Payment of Bonus Act, 1965.[1]

Workmen whose services are terminated in consequence of a transfer of an undertaking, whether by agreement or by operation of law, have a statutory right under S. 25 FF of the Industrial Disputes Act to compensation unless such right is defeated under the proviso to that Section. The same is the position in the case of closure under S. 25FFF. Such compensation would be "wages" as defined by S. 2(iv)(d) of the Payment of Wages Act as amended by Act 68 of 1957 as it is a "*sum which by reason of the termination of employment of the person*

1. *District Co-operative Bank Ltd.* v. *Vth Additional District Judge, Azamgarh and others,* 2003 (97) FLR 66 (Alld).

employed, is payable under any law ... which provides for the payment of such sum whether with or without deductions but does not provide for the time within which the payment is to be made."

Since Ss. 25FF and 25FFF do not contain any conditions precedent, as in the case of retrenchment under S. 25F, and transfer and closure can validly take place without notice or payment of a month's wages in lieu thereof or payment of compensation, S. 25F can be said not to have provided any time within which such compensation is to be paid. The words "in accordance with the provisions of S. 25F" in Ss. 25FF and 25FFF are used only as a measure of compensation and are not used for laying down any time within which the employer must pay the compensation. It would, therefore, appear that compensation payable under Ss. 25FF and 25FFF read with S. 25FF would be "wages" within the meaning of S. 2(vi)(d) of the Act.[2]

Section 3: Responsibility for payment of wages

(1) Every employer shall be responsible for the payment of all wages required to be paid under this Act to persons employed by him and in the case of persons employed—

- (a) in factories, if a person has been named as the manager of the factory under clause (f) of sub-section (1) of section 7 of the Factories Act, 1948 (63 of 1948);
- (b) in industrial or other establishments, if there is a person responsible to the employer for the supervision and control of the industrial or other establishment;
- (c) upon railways (other than in factories), if the employer is the railway administration and the railway administration has nominated a person in this behalf for the local area concerned;
- (d) in the case of contractor, a person designated by such contractor who is directly under his charge; and
- (e) in any other case, a person designated by the employer as a person responsible for complying with the provisions of the Act;

the person so named, the person so responsible to the employer, the person so nominated, or the person so designated as the case may be, shall be responsible for such payment.

(2) Notwithstanding anything contained in sub-section (1) it shall be the responsibility of the employer to make payment of all wages required to be made under this Act in case the contractor or the person designated by the employer fails to make such payment.

Section 4: Fixation of wage-periods

(1) Every person responsible for the payment of wages under section 3 shall fix periods (in this Act referred to as wage-period) in respect of which such wages shall be payable.

(2) No wage-period shall exceed one month.

---

2. *Payment of Wages Inspector, Ujjain* v. *Barnagar Electric Supply and Industrial Co. Ltd.*, AIR 1969 SC 590.

SECTION 5: Time of payment of wages

(1) The wages of every person employed upon or in—

(a) any railway, factory or industrial or other establishment upon or in which less than one thousand persons are employed, shall be paid before the expiry of the seventh day,

(b) any other railway, factory or industrial or other establishment, shall be paid before the expiry of the tenth day,

after the last day of the wage-period in respect of which the wages are payable:

Provided that in the case of persons employed on a dock, wharf or jetty or in a mine, the balance of wages found due on completion of the final tonnage account of the ship or wagons loaded or unloaded, as the case may be, shall be paid before the expiry of the seventh day from the day of such completion.

(2) Where the employment of any person is terminated by or on behalf of the employer, the wages, earned by him shall be paid before the expiry of the second working day from the day on which his employment is terminated:

Provided that where the employment of any person in an establishment is terminated due to the closure of the establishment for any reason other than a weekly or other recognised holiday, the wages earned by him shall be paid before the expiry of the second day from the day on which his employment is so terminated.

(3) The appropriate Government may, by general or special order, exempt, to such extent and subject to such conditions as may be specified in the order, the person responsible for the payment of wages to persons employed upon any railway (otherwise than in a factory) or to persons employed as daily-rated workers in the Public Works Department of the appropriate Government from the operation of this section in respect of wages of any such persons or class of such persons:

Provided that in the case of persons employed as daily-rated workers as aforesaid, no such order shall be made except in consultation with the Central Government.

(4) Save as otherwise provided in sub-section (2), all payments of wages shall be made on a working day.

SECTION 6: Wages to be paid in current coin or currency notes or by cheque or crediting in bank account (2017 Amendment)

All wages shall be paid in current coin or currency notes or by cheque or by crediting the wages in the bank account of the employee.

Provided that the appropriate Government may, by notification in the Official Gazette, specify the industrial or other establishment, the employer of which shall pay to every person employed in such industrial or other establishment, the wages only by cheque or by crediting the wages in his bank account.

Section 7: Deductions which may be made from wages

(1) Notwithstanding the provisions of the Railways Act, 1989 (24 of 1989), the wages of an employed person shall be paid to him without deductions of any kind except those authorised by or under this Act.

Explanation I: Every payment made by the employed person to the employer or his agent shall, for the purposes of this Act, be deemed to be a deduction from wages.

Explanation II: Any loss of wages resulting from the imposition, for good and sufficient cause, upon a person employed of any of the following penalties, namely:

(i) the withholding of increment or promotion (including the stoppage of increment at an efficiency bar);

(ii) the reduction to a lower post or time-scale or to a lower stage in a time-scale; or

(iii) suspension;

shall not be deemed to be a deduction from wages in any case where the rules framed by the employer for the imposition of any such penalty are in conformity with the requirements, if any, which may be specified in this behalf by the appropriate Government by notification in the Official Gazette.

(2) Deductions from the wages of an employed person shall be made only in accordance with the provisions of this Act, and may be of the following kinds only, namely:

(a) fines;

(b) deductions for absence from duty;

(c) deductions for damage to or loss of goods expressly entrusted to the employed person for custody, or for loss of money for which he is required to account, where such damage or loss is directly attributable to his neglect or default;

(d) deductions for house-accommodation supplied by the employer or by Government or any housing board set up under any law for the time being in force (whether the Government or the board is the employer or not) or any other authority engaged in the business of subsidising house-accommodation which may be specified in this behalf by the appropriate Government by notification in the Official Gazette;

(e) deductions for such amenities and services supplied by the employer as the appropriate Government or any officer specified by it in this behalf may, by general or special order, authorise.

Explanation: The word "services" in this clause does not include the supply of tools and raw materials required for the purposes of employment;

(f) deductions for recovery of advances of whatever nature (including advances for travelling allowance or conveyance allowance), and the interest due in respect thereof, or for adjustment of over-payments of wages;

(ff) deductions for recovery of loans made from any fund constituted for the welfare of labour in accordance with the rules approved by the appropriate Government, and the interest due in respect thereof;

(fff) deductions for recovery of loans granted for house-building or other purposes approved by the appropriate Government, and the interest due in respect thereof;

(g) deductions of income-tax payable by the employed person;

(h) deductions required to be made by order of a court or other authority competent to make such order;

(i) deductions for subscriptions to, and for repayment of advances from any provident fund to which the Provident Funds Act, 1925 (19 of 1925), applies or any recognised provident fund as defined in clause (38) of section 2 of the Income Tax Act 1961 (43 of 1961) or any provident fund approved in this behalf by the appropriate Government, during the continuance of such approval;

(j) deductions for payments to co-operative societies approved by the appropriate Government or any officer specified by it in this behalf or to a scheme of insurance maintained by the Indian Post Office;

(k) deductions, made with the written authorisation of the person employed for payment of any premium on his life insurance policy to the Life Insurance Corporation Act of India established under the Life Insurance Corporation Act, 1956 (31 of 1956), or for the purchase of securities of the Government of India or of any State Government or for being deposited in any Post Office Savings Bank in furtherance of any savings scheme of any such Government.

(kk) deductions, made with the written authorisation of the employed person, for the payment of his contribution to any fund constituted by the employer or a trade union registered under the Trade Unions Act, 1926 (16 of 1926), for the welfare of the employed persons or the members of their families, or both, and approved by the appropriate Government or any officer specified by it in this behalf, during the continuance of such approval;

(kkk) deductions made with the written authorisation of the employed person, for payment of the fees payable by him for the membership of any trade union registered under the Trade Unions Act, 1926 (16 of 1926);

(l) deductions for payment of insurance premia on Fidelity Guarantee Bonds;

(m) deductions for recovery of losses sustained by a railway administration on account of acceptance by the employed person of counterfeit or base coins or mutilated or forged currency notes;

(n) deductions for recovery of losses sustained by a railway administration on account of the failure of the employed person to invoice, to bill, to collect or to account for the appropriate charges due to that administration whether in respect of fares, freight, demurrage, wharfage and cranage or in respect of sale of food in catering establishments or in respect of sale of commodities in grain shops or otherwise;

(o) deductions for recovery of losses sustained by a railway administration on account of any rebates or refunds incorrectly granted by the employed person where such loss is directly attributable to his neglect or default;

(p) deductions, made with the written authorisation of the employed person, for contribution to the Prime Minister's National Relief Fund or to such other Fund as the Central Government may, by notification in the Official Gazette, specify;

(q) deductions for contributions to any insurance scheme framed by the Central Government for the benefit of its employees.

(3) Notwithstanding anything contained in this Act, the total amount of deductions which may be made under sub-section (2) in any wage-period from the wages of any employed person shall not exceed—

(i) in cases where such deductions are wholly or partly made for payments to co-operative societies under clause (j) of sub-section (2), seventy-five per cent of such wages, and

(ii) in any other case, fifty per cent of such wages:

Provided that where the total deductions authorised under sub-section (2) exceed seventy five per cent or, as the case may be, fifty per cent of the wages, the excess may be recovered in such manner as may be prescribed.

(4) Nothing contained in this section shall be construed as precluding the employer from recovering from the wages of the employed person or otherwise any amount payable by such person under any law for the time being in force other than the Railways Act, 1989 (24 of 1989).

Deduction of Wages for Go-slow/Strike

There cannot be two opinions that go-slow is a serious misconduct being a covert and a more damaging breach of the contract of employment. It is an insidious method of undermining discipline and, at the same time, a crude device to defy the norms of work. It has been roundly condemned as an industrial action and has not been recognised as a legitimate weapon of the workmen to redress their grievances. In fact, the model standing orders as well as the certified standing orders of most of the Industrial establishments define it as a misconduct and provide for a disciplinary action for it. Hence, once it is proved, those guilty of it have to face the consequences which may include deduction of wages and even dismissal from service. The simplistic method of deducting uniform percentage of wages from the wages of all workmen, calculated on the basis of the percentage fall in production compared to the normal or average production, may not always be equitable. It is, therefore, necessary that in all cases where the factum of go-slow and/or the extent of the loss of production on account of it, is disputed, there should be a proper inquiry on charges which furnish particulars of the go-slow and the loss of production on that account. The rules of natural justice require it, and whether they have been followed or not will depend on the facts of each case.[3] Even in a case where action is resorted to on a mass-scale, some employees may not be a party to the action and may have genuinely desired to discharge their duties but could not do so for failure of the management to give the necessary assistance or protection or on account of other circumstances. The management will not be justified in deducting wages of such employees without holding an inquiry.

3. *Bank of India* v. *T.S. Kelawala,* 1990 (60) FLR 898.

Where the contract, Standing Orders or the service Rules/Regulations are silent on the subject, the management has the power to deduct wages for absence from duty when the absence is a concerted action on the part of the employees and the absence is not disputed. Whether the deduction from wages will be *pro rata* for the period of absence only or will be for a longer period will depend upon the facts of each case such as whether there was any work to be done in the said period, whether the work was in fact done and whether it was accepted and acquiesced in, etc. It is not enough that the employees attend the place of work. What is essential is that they must put in the work allotted to them. It is for the work and not for their mere attendance that the wages/salaries are paid. For the same reason, if the employees put in the allotted work but do not, for some reason, may be even as a protest, comply with the formalities such as signing the attendance register, no deduction can be effected from their wages. When the contract, Standing Orders, or the service Rules/Regulations are silent, but enactment such as the Payment of Wages Act providing for wage-cuts, for the absence from duty, is applicable to the establishment concerned, the wages can be deducted even under the provisions of such enactment.[4]

Section 8: Fines

(1) No fine shall be imposed on any employed person save in respect of such acts and omissions on his part as the employer, with the previous approval of the appropriate Government or of the prescribed authority, may have specified by notice under sub-section (2).

(2) A notice specifying such acts and omissions shall be exhibited in the prescribed manner on the premises in which the employment is carried on or in the case of persons employed upon a railway (otherwise than in a factory), at the prescribed place or places.

(3) No fine shall be imposed on any employed person until he has been given an opportunity of showing cause against the fine, or otherwise than in accordance with such procedure as may be prescribed for the imposition of fines.

(4) The total amount of fine which may be imposed in any one wage-period on any employed person shall not exceed an amount equal to three per cent of the wages payable to him in respect of that wage-period.

(5) No fine shall be imposed on any employed person who is under the age of fifteen years.

(6) No fine imposed on any employed person shall be recovered from him by instalments or after the expiry of ninety days from the day on which it was imposed.

(7) Every fine shall be deemed to have been imposed on the day of the act or omission in respect of which it was imposed.

(8) All fines and all realisations thereof shall be recorded in a register to be kept by the person responsible for the payment of wages under section 3 in such form as may be prescribed; and all such realisations shall be applied only to such purposes beneficial to the persons employed in the factory or establishment as are approved by the prescribed authority.

---

4. *Ibid.*

Explanation: When the persons employed upon or in any railway, factory or industrial or other establishment are part only of staff employed under the same management, all such realisations may be credited to a common fund maintained for the staff as a whole, provided that the fund shall be applied only to such purposes as are approved by the prescribed authority.

SECTION 9: Deductions for absence from duty

(1) Deductions may be made under clause (b) of sub-section (2) of section 7 only on account of the absence of an employed person from the place or places where, by the terms of his employment, he is required to work, such absence being for the whole or any part of the period during which he is so required to work.

(2) The amount of such deduction shall in no case bear to the wages payable to the employed person in respect of the wage-period for which the deduction is made in a larger proportion than the period for which he was absent bears to the total period, within such wage-period, during which by the terms of his employment, he was required to work:

Provided that, subject to any rules made in this behalf by the appropriate Government, if ten or more employed persons acting in concert absent themselves without due notice (that is to say without giving the notice which is required under the terms of their contracts of employment) and without reasonable cause, such deduction from any such person may include such amount not exceeding his wages for eight days as may by any such terms be due to the employer in lieu of due notice.

Explanation: For the purposes of this section, an employed person shall be deemed to be absent from the place where he is required to work if, although present in such place, he refuses, in pursuance of a stay-in strike or for any other cause which is not reasonable in the circumstances, to carry out his work.

SECTION 10: Deductions for damage or loss

(1) A deduction under clause (c) or clause (o) of sub-section (2) of section 7 shall not exceed the amount of the damage or loss caused to the employer by the neglect or default of the employed person.

(1A) A deduction shall not be made under clause (c) or clause (m) or clause (n) or clause (o) of sub-section (2) of section 7 until the employed person has been given an opportunity of showing cause against the deduction or otherwise than in accordance with such procedure as may be prescribed for the making of such deduction.

(2) All such deduction and all realisations thereof shall be recorded in a register to be kept by the person responsible for the payment of wages under section 3 in such form as may be prescribed.

SECTION 11: Deductions for services rendered

A deduction under clause (d) or clause (e) of sub-section (2) of section 7 shall not be made from the wages of an employed person, unless the house-accommodation amenity or service has been accepted by him, as a term of employment or otherwise, and such deduction shall not exceed an amount equivalent to the value of the house-accommodation amenity or service supplied and, in the case of deduction under the said clause (e), shall be subject to such conditions as the appropriate Government may impose.

SECTION 12: Deductions for recovery of advances

Deductions under clause (f) of sub-section (2) of section 7 shall be subject to the following conditions, namely:

(a) recovery of an advance of money given before employment began shall be made from the first payment of wages in respect of a complete wage-period, but no recovery shall be made of such advances given for travelling-expenses;

(aa) recovery of an advance of money given after employment began shall be subject to such conditions as the appropriate Government may impose;

(b) recovery of advances of wages not already earned shall be subject to any rules made by the appropriate Government regulating the extent to which such advances may be given and the instalments by which they may be recovered.

SECTION 12A: Deductions for recovery of loans

Deductions for recovery of loans granted under clause (fff) of sub-section (2) of section 7 shall be subject to any rules made by the appropriate Government regulating the extent to which such loans may be granted and the rate of interest payable thereon.

SECTION 13: Deductions for payments to cooperative societies and insurance schemes

Deductions under clause (j) and clause (k) of sub-section (2) of section 7 shall be subject to such conditions as the appropriate Government may impose.

SECTION 13A: Maintenance of registers and records

(1) Every employer shall maintain such registers and records giving such particulars of persons employed by him, the work performed by them, the wages paid to them, the deductions made from their wages, the receipts given by them and such other particulars and in such form as may be prescribed.

(2) Every register and record required to be maintained under this section shall, for the purposes of this Act, be preserved for a period of three years after the date of the last entry made therein.

SECTION 14: Inspectors

(1) An Inspector of Factories appointed under sub-section (1) of section 8 of the Factories Act, 1948 (63 of 1948), shall be an Inspector for the purposes of this Act in respect of all factories within the local limits assigned to him.

(2) The appropriate Government may appoint Inspectors for the purposes of this Act in respect of all persons employed upon a railway (otherwise than in a factory) to whom this Act applies.

(3) The appropriate Government may, by notification in the Official Gazette, appoint such other persons as it thinks fit to be Inspectors for the purposes of this Act, and may define the local limits within which and the class of factories and industrial or other establishments in respect of which they shall exercise their functions.

(4) An Inspector may,

(a) make such examination and inquiry as he thinks fit in order to ascertain whether the provisions of this Act or rules made thereunder are being observed;

(b) with such assistance, if any, as he thinks fit, enter, inspect and search any premises of any railway, factory or industrial or other establishment at any reasonable time for the purpose of carrying out the objects of this Act;

(c) supervise the payment of wages to persons employed upon any railway or in any factory or industrial or other establishment;

(d) require by a written order the production at such place, as may be prescribed, of any register maintained in pursuance of this Act and take on the spot or otherwise statements of any persons which he may consider necessary for carrying out the purposes of this Act;

(e) seize or take copies of such registers or documents or portions thereof as he may consider relevant in respect of an offence under this Act which he has reason to believe has been committed by an employer;

(f) exercise such other powers as may be prescribed:

Provided that no person shall be compelled under this sub-section to answer any question or make any statement tending to incriminate himself.

(4A) The provisions of the Code of Criminal Procedure, 1973 (2 of 1974) shall, so far as may be, apply to any search or seizure under this sub-section as they apply to any search or seizure made under the authority of a warrant issued under section 94 of the said Code.

(5) Every Inspector shall be deemed to be a public servant within the meaning of the Indian Penal Code, 1860 (45 of 1860).

Section 14A: Facilities to be afforded to Inspectors

Every employer shall afford an Inspector all reasonable facilities for making any entry, inspection, supervision, examination or inquiry under this Act.

Section 15: Claims arising out of deductions from wages or delay in payment of wages and penalty for malicious or vexatious claims

(1) The appropriate Government may, by notification in the Official Gazette, appoint—

(a) any Commissioner for workmen's compensation; or

(b) any officer of the Central Government exercising functions as,—

(i) Regional Labour Commissioner; or

(ii) Assistant Labour Commissioner with atleast two years' experience; or

(c) any officer of the State Government not below the rank of Assistant Labour Commissioner with at least two years' experience; or

(d) a presiding officer of any Labour Court or Industrial Tribunal, constituted under the Industrial Disputes Act 1947 (14 of 1947) or under any corresponding law relating to the investigation and settlement of industrial disputes in force in the State; or

(e) any other officer with experience as a Judge of a Civil Court or a Judicial Magistrate

as the authority to hear and decide for any specified area all claims arising out of deductions from the wages, or delay in payment of the wages, of persons employed or paid in that area, including all matters, incidental to such claims:

Provided that where the appropriate Government considers it necessary so to do, it may appoint more than one authority for any specified area and may, by general or special order, provide for the distribution or allocation of work to be performed by them under this Act.

(2) Where contrary to the provisions of this Act any deduction has been made from the wages of an employed person, or any payment of wages has been delayed, such person himself, or any legal practitioner or any official of a registered trade union authorised in writing to act on his behalf, or any Inspector under this Act, or any other person acting with the permission of the authority appointed under sub-section (1), may apply to such authority for a direction under sub-section (3):

Provided that every such application shall be presented within twelve months from the date on which the deduction from the wages was made, or from the date on which the payment of the wages was due to be made, as the case may be:

Provided further that any application may be admitted after the said period of twelve months when the applicant satisfies the authority that he had sufficient cause for not making the application within such period.

(3) When any application under sub-section (2) is entertained, the authority shall hear the applicant and the employer or other person responsible for the payment of wages under section 3, or give them an opportunity of being heard, and, after such further inquiry (if any) as may be necessary, may, without prejudice to any other penalty to which such employer or other person is liable under this Act, direct the refund to the employed person of the amount deducted, or the payment of the delayed wages, together with the payment of such compensation as the authority may think fit, not exceeding ten times the amount deducted in the former case and not exceeding three thousand rupees but not less than one thousand and five hundred rupees in the latter, and even if the amount deducted or the delayed wages are paid before the disposal of the application, direct the payment of such compensation, as the authority may think fit, not exceeding two thousand rupees:

Provided that a claim under this Act shall be disposed of as far as practicable within a period of three months from the date of registration of the claim by the authority:

Provided further that the period of three months may be extended if both parties to the dispute agree for any bonafide reason to be recorded by the authority that the said period of three months may be extended to such period as may be necessary to dispose of the application in a just manner:

Provided also that no direction for the payment of compensation shall be made in the case of delayed wages if the authority is satisfied that the delay was due to—

(a) a *bona fide* error or *bona fide* dispute as to the amount payable to the employed person, or

(b) the occurrence of an emergency, or the existence of exceptional circumstances, the person responsible for the payment of the wages was unable, inspite of exercising reasonable diligence; or

(c) the failure of the employed person to apply for or accept payment.

(4) If the authority hearing an application under this section is satisfied—

(a) that the application was either malicious or vexatious, the authority may direct that a penalty not exceeding three hundred seventy five rupees be paid to the employer or other person responsible for the payment of wages by the person presenting the application; or

(b) that in any case in which compensation is directed to be paid under sub-section (3), the applicant ought not to have been compelled to seek redress under this section, the authority may direct that a penalty not exceeding three hundred seventy five rupees be paid to the appropriate Government by the employer or other person responsible for the payment of wages.

(4A) Where there is any dispute as to the person or persons being the legal representative or representatives of the employer or of the employed person, the decision of the authority on such dispute shall be final.

(4B) Any inquiry under this section shall be deemed to be a judicial proceeding within the meaning of sections 193, 219 and 228 of the Indian Penal Code (45 of 1860).

(5) Any amount directed to be paid under this section may be recovered—

(a) if the authority is a Magistrate, by the authority as if it were a fine imposed by him as Magistrate, and

(b) if the authority is not a Magistrate, by any Magistrate to whom the authority makes application in this behalf, as if it were a fine imposed by such Magistrate.

The authority set up under S. 15 is undisputably a Tribunal of limited jurisdiction. Its power to hear and determine disputes must necessarily be found in the provisions of the Act. Such a Tribunal, it is undoubted, cannot determine any controversy which is not within the ambit of those provisions. In *A.V. D'Costa, Divisional Engineer, G.I.P. Railway* v. *B.C. Patel,*[5] the Supreme Court held that where the parties enter into the contract of service, say by correspondence and the contract is to be determined with reference to the letters that passed

5. AIR 1955 SC 412.

between them, it may be open to the authority set up under S. 15 to decide the controversy and find out what the terms of the contract, with reference to those letters, were. But if an employee were to say that his wages were ₹100 per month which he actually received as and when they fell due, but that he would be entitled to higher wages if his claims to be placed on the higher wages scheme had been recognized and given effect to, that would not be a matter within the ambit of his jurisdiction. The authority has the jurisdiction to decide what actually the terms of the contract between the parties were, that is to say, to determine the actual wages; but the authority has no jurisdiction to determine the question of potential wages. Where on the case, as made on behalf of the employee, orders of the superior officers are necessary to upgrade him from a daily wage earner to a higher cadre, the authority under the Act has not been empowered under S. 15 to make any such direction to those superior officers.

The employer is responsible to pay the employee only such wages as are shown in the relevant register of wages presumably maintained by the department under the provisions of the Act, but he cannot be directed to pay the employee higher wages on the determination by the authority that he should have been placed on the monthly wages scheme. The sole question raised before the Supreme Court in *Ambica Mills Co. Ltd.* v. *S.B. Bhatt*[6] related to the jurisdiction of authority under S. 15 of the Act. The Court specifically held that the only claims which can be entertained by the authority under S. 15 are claims arising out of deductions or delay made in payment of wages. The jurisdiction thus conferred on the authority to deal with these two categories of claims is exclusive. In dealing with claims arising out of deductions or delay made in payment of wages, the authority inevitably would have to consider questions incidental to the said matters. In determining the scope of these incidental questions, care must be taken to see that under the guise of deciding incidental matter the limited jurisdiction is not unreasonably or unduly extended. Care must also be taken to see that the scope of these incidental questions is not unduly limited so as to affect or impair the limited jurisdiction conferred on the authority. It would be inexpedient to lay down any hard and fast or general rule which would afford a determining test to demarcate the field of incidental facts which can be legitimately considered by the authority and those which cannot be so considered. The authority under S. 15 has jurisdiction to determine what the terms of the contract between the parties are, and if the terms of the contract are admitted and the only dispute is whether or not a particular employee falls within one category or another, that would be incidental to the decision of the main question as to what the terms of the contract are. Where the terms of a contract are admitted and the only point in dispute is which of the two subsisting contracts applies to the particular employee in question the authority has jurisdiction to decide the same.

It is explicit from the terms of S. 15(2) that the authority appointed under sub-section (1) has jurisdiction to entertain applications only in two classes of cases, namely, of deductions and fines not authorised under Ss. 7 to 13 and of delay in payment of wages beyond the wage periods fixed under S. 4 and the time of payment laid down in S. 5. The only applications which the authority can entertain are those where deductions unauthorised under the Act are made from wages, or there has been delay in payment beyond the wage

6. AIR 1961 SC 970.

period and the time of payment of wages fixed or prescribed under Ss. 4 and 5 of the Act. Section 15(2) postulates that the wages payable by the person responsible for payment under S. 3 are certain and such that they cannot be disputed. It is true that the authority has the jurisdiction to try matters which are incidental to the claim in question. It is also true that while deciding whether a particular matter is incidental to the claim or not, care should be taken neither to unduly expand nor curtail the jurisdiction of the authority. But it has, at the same time, to be kept in mind that the jurisdiction under S. 15 is a special jurisdiction. The authority is conferred with the power to award compensation over and above the liability for penalty of fine which an employer is liable to incur under S. 20.[7]

First proviso to S. 15(2) *ex facie* indicates two alternative *terminii a quo* for limitation, namely (i) the date on which deduction from wages was made, or (ii) the date on which the payment of the wages was due to be made. Terminus a quo (i) in the proviso expressly relates to the deduction of wages, while (ii) is referable to the delayed wages. It cannot be said that the two expressions "wages deducted" and "wages delayed", though used in the alternative, carry the same meaning, and in the proviso are always referable to one and the same time. The very fact, that two distinct starting points of limitation referable to two distinct concepts have been stated in the proviso, shows that the legislature had visualised that the date of deduction of wages and the due date of delayed wages, may not always coincide. The legislature is not supposed to indulge in tautology; and when it uses analogous words or phrases in the alternative, each may be presumed to convey a separate and distinct meaning, the choice of either of which may involve the rejection of the other.[8]

The second proviso to S. 15(2) is in substance similar to the provision in S. 5 of the Limitation Act. It cannot be disputed that in dealing with the question of condoning delay under S. 5 of the Limitation Act, the party has to satisfy the court that he had sufficient cause for not preferring the appeal or making the application within the prescribed time, and this has always been understood to mean that the explanation has to cover the whole of the period of delay. Therefore, the contention that if sufficient cause has been shown for not making the application within the period of six months, now at present twelve months, vide the Payment of Wages (Amendment) Act, 1964, w.e.f. 1965, prescribed by S. 15(2), then the application can be made any time thereafter, is not correct.[9]

SECTION 16: Single application in respect of claims from unpaid group

(1) Employed persons are said to belong to the same unpaid group if they are borne on the same establishment and if deductions have been made from their wages in contravention of this Act for the same cause and during the same wage-period or periods or if their wages for the same wage-period or periods have remained unpaid after the day fixed by section 5.

7. *Payment of Wages Inspector, Ujjain* v. *Barnagar Electric Supply and Industrial Co. Ltd.*, AIR 1969 SC 590.
8. *Dilbagh Rai Jerry* v. *Union of India,* AIR 1974 SC 130.
9. *Sitaram Ramcharan* v. *M.N. Nagrashana*, AIR 1960 SC 260.

(2) A single application may be presented under section 15 on behalf or in respect of any number of employed persons belonging to the same unpaid group, and in such case every person on whose behalf such application is presented may be awarded maximum compensation to the extent specified in sub-section (3) of section 15.

(3) The authority may deal with any number of separate pending applications, presented under section 15 in respect of persons belonging to the same unpaid group, as a single application presented under sub-section (2) of this section, and the provisions of that sub-section shall apply accordingly.

SECTION 17: Appeal

(1) An appeal against an order dismissing either wholly or in part an application made under sub-section (2) of section 15, or against a direction made under sub-section (3) or sub-section (4) of that section may be preferred, within thirty days of the date on which the order or direction was made, in a Presidency-town before the Court of Small Causes and elsewhere before the District Court—

(a) by the employer or other person, responsible for the payment of wages under section 3, if the total sum directed to be paid by way of wages and compensation exceeds three hundred rupees or such direction has the effect of imposing on the employer or the other person a financial liability exceeding one thousand rupees, or

(b) by an employed person, or any legal practitioner or any official of a registered trade union authorised in writing to act on his behalf or any Inspector under this Act, or any other person permitted by the authority to make an application under sub-section (2) of section 15, if the total amount of wages claimed to have been withheld from the employed person exceeds twenty rupees or from the unpaid group to which the employed person belongs or belonged exceeds fifty rupees, or

(c) by any person directed to pay a penalty under sub-section (4) of section 15.

(1A) No appeal under clause (a) of sub-section (1) shall lie unless the memorandum of appeal is accompanied by a certificate by the authority to the effect that the appellant has deposited the amount payable under the direction appealed against.

(2) Save as provided in sub-section (1) any order dismissing either wholly or in part an application made under sub-section (2) of section 15, or a direction made under sub-section (3) or sub-section (4) of that section shall be final.

(3) Where an employer prefers an appeal under this section the authority against whose decision the appeal has been preferred may, and if so directed by the court referred to in sub-section (1) shall, pending the decision of the appeal, withhold payment of any sum in deposit with it.

(4) The court referred to in sub-section (1) may, if it thinks fit, submit any question of law for the decision of the High Court and, if it so does, shall decide the question in conformity with such decision.

From a bare perusal of S. 17(1) of the Payment of Wages Act, it crystallises that there is no specific exclusion as to applicability of S. 5 of the Indian Limitation Act by virtue of the Payment of Wages Act, 1936 being a Special Law.

So far as S. 17 is concerned, the expressions employed are "may be preferred within 30 days." In the light of the discussion made above, it necessarily follows that intention of the legislature while enacting S. 17 of the Payment of Wages Act was not to exclude the Indian Limitation Act from applicability expressly to the proceeding under the Payment of Wages Act. In view of what has been discussed above, the first question is answered in affirmative that the provisions of the Payment of Wages Act is not a complete code in itself so far as the Limitation Act is concerned and it is necessarily to be supplemented by S. 29(2) of the Indian Limitation Act. The second question whether S. 5 of the Indian Limitation Act can be called in to apply to proceedings under S. 17 of the Payment of Wages Act by virtue of S. 29 of the Indian Limitation Act, 1963 is also decided in affirmative and it has been held that S. 5 of the Indian Limitation Act is fully applicable in the matter of appeal to be preferred under the Payment of Wages Act.[10] The Payment of Wages Act being a special law, which prescribes the mode and manner in which an appeal under S. 17(1A) of the Act has to be filed and the same has not been complied with, therefore, in view of the prohibitive language of S. 17(1A) of the Act, no appeal can be entertained as the same does not lie. Since the appeal has not been filed after following the procedure prescribed and beyond the limitation prescribed, the question of the application or otherwise of S. 29(2) of the Limitation Act will not arise.[11]

SECTION 17A: Conditional attachment of property of employer or other person responsible for payment of wages

(1) Where at any time after an application has been made under sub-section (2) of section 15 the authority, or where at any time after an appeal has been filed under section 17 by an employed person or any legal practitioner or any official of a registered trade union authorised in writing to act on his behalf or any Inspector under this Act or any other person permitted by the authority to make an application under sub-section (2) of section 15 the Court referred to in that section, is satisfied that the employer or other person responsible for the payment of wages under section 3 is likely to evade payment of any amount that may be directed to be paid under section 15 or section 17, the authority or the court, as the case may be, except in cases where the authority or court is of opinion that the ends of justice would be defeated by the delay, after giving the employer or other person an opportunity of being heard, may direct the attachment of so much of the property of the employer or other person responsible for the payment of wages as is, in the opinion of the authority or court, sufficient to satisfy the amount which may be payable under the direction.

(2) The provisions of the Code of Civil Procedure, 1908 (5 of 1908), relating to attachment before judgement under that Code shall, so far as may be, apply to any order for attachment under sub-section (1).

10. *U.P. State Electricity Board, Lucknow and others* v. *District Judge, Gorakhpur and others,* 2002 (95) FLR 583 (Alld).
11. *Executive Engineer, U.P.S.E.B.* v. *Prescribed Authority and others,* 2002 (2) CLR 759.

Section 18: Powers of authorities appointed under section 15

Every authority appointed under sub-section (1) of section 15 shall have all the powers of a civil court under the Code of Civil Procedure, 1908 (5 of 1908), for the purpose of taking evidence and of enforcing the attendance of witnesses and compelling the production of documents, and every such authority shall be deemed to be a civil court for all the purposes of section 195 and of Chapter XXVI of the Code of Criminal Procedure, 1973 (2 of 1974).

Section 19: Power to recover from employer in certain cases

[Repealed by the Payment of Wages (Amendment) Act, 1964 (53 of 1964), w.e.f. 1st, February, 1965.]

Section 20: Penalty for offences under the Act

(1) Whoever being responsible for the payment of wages to an employed person contravenes any of the provisions of any of the following sections, namely, section 5 except sub-section (4) thereof, section 7, section 8 except sub-section (8) thereof, section 9, section 10 except sub-section (2) thereof, and sections 11 to 13, both inclusive, shall be punishable with fine which shall not be less than one thousand five hundred rupees but which may extend to seven thousand five hundred rupees.

(2) Whoever contravenes the provisions of section 4, sub-section (4) of section 5, section 6, sub-section (8) of section 8, sub-section (2) of section 10 or section 25 shall be punishable with fine which may extend to three thousand seven hundred fifty rupees.

(2A) Whoever being required to nominate or designate a person under section 3 fails to do so, such person shall be punishable with fine which may extend to three thousand rupees.

(3) Whoever being required under this Act to maintain any records or registers or to furnish any information or return—

(a) fails to maintain such register or record; or

(b) wilfully refuses or without lawful excuse neglects to furnish such information or return; or

(c) wilfully furnishes or causes to be furnished any information or return which he knows to be false; or

(d) refuses to answer or wilfully gives a false answer to any question necessary for obtaining any information required to be furnished under this Act;

shall, for each such offence, be punishable with fine which shall not be less than one thousand five hundred rupees, but which may extend to seven thousand five hundred rupees.

(4) Whoever—

(a) wilfully obstructs an Inspector in the discharge of his duties under this Act; or

(b) refuses or wilfully neglects to afford an Inspector any reasonable facility for making any entry, inspection, examination, supervision, or inquiry authorised by or under this Act in relation to any railway, factory or industrial or other establishment; or

(c) wilfully refuses to produce on the demand of an Inspector any register or other document kept in pursuance of this Act; or

(d) prevents or attempts to prevent or does anything which he has any reason to believe is likely to prevent any person from appearing before or being examined by an Inspector acting in pursuance of his duties under this Act;

shall be punishable with fine which shall not be less than one thousand five hundred rupees but which may extend to seven thousand five hundred rupees.

(5) If any person who has been convicted of any offence punishable under this Act is again guilty of an offence involving contravention of the same provision, he shall be punishable on a subsequent conviction with imprisonment for a term which shall not be less than one month but which may extend to six months and with fine which shall not be less than three thousand seven hundred fifty rupees but which may extend to twenty two thousand five hundred rupees:

Provided that for the purpose of this sub-section no cognizance shall be taken of any conviction made more than two years before the date on which the commission of the offence which is being punished came to the knowledge of the Inspector.

(6) If any person fails or wilfully neglects to pay the wages of any employed person by the date fixed by the authority in this behalf, he shall, without prejudice to any other action that may be taken against him, be punishable with an additional fine which may extend to seven hundred fifty rupees for each day for which such failure or neglect continues.

Section 21: Procedure in trial of offences

(1) No court shall take cognizance of a complaint against any person for an offence under sub-section (1) of section 20 unless an application in respect of the facts constituting the offence has been presented under section 15 and has been granted wholly or in part and the authority empowered under the latter section or the Appellate Court granting such application has sanctioned the making of the complaint.

(2) Before sanctioning the making of a complaint against any person for an offence under sub-section (1) of section 20, the authority empowered under section 15 or the Appellate Court, as the case may be, shall give such person an opportunity of showing cause against the granting of such sanction, and the sanction shall not be granted if such person satisfies the authority or Court that his default was due to—

(a) a *bona fide* error or *bona fide* dispute as to the amount payable to the employed person, or

(b) the occurrence of an emergency or the existence of exceptional circumstances, such that the person responsible for the payment of the wages was unable, though exercising reasonable diligence, to make prompt payment, or

(c) the failure of the employed person to apply for or accept payment.

(3) No Court shall take cognizance of a contravention of section 4 or of section 6 or of a contravention of any rule made under section 26 except on a complaint made by or with the sanction of an Inspector under this Act.

(3A) No Court shall take cognizance of any offence punishable under sub-section (3) or sub-section (4) of section 20 except on a complaint made by or with the sanction of an Inspector under this Act.

(4) In imposing any fine for an offence under sub-section (1) of section 20 the court shall take into consideration the amount of any compensation already awarded against the accused in any proceedings taken under section 15.

Section 22: Bar of suits

No Court shall entertain any suit for the recovery of wages or of any deduction from wages insofar as the sum so claimed—

(a) forms the subject of an application under section 15 which has been presented by the plaintiff and which is pending before the authority appointed under that section or of an appeal under section 17; or

(b) has formed the subject of a direction under section 15 in favour of the plaintiff; or

(c) has been adjudged, in any proceeding under section 15, not to be owed to the plaintiff; or

(d) could have been recovered by an application under section 15.

Section 22A: Protection of action taken in good faith

No suit, prosecution or other legal proceeding shall lie against the Government or any officer of the Government for anything which is in good faith done or intended to be done under this Act.

Section 23: Contracting out

Any contract or agreement, whether made before or after the commencement of this Act, whereby an employed person relinquishes any right conferred by this Act shall be null and void insofar as it purports to deprive him of such right.

Section 24: Delegation of powers

The appropriate Government may, by notification in the Official Gazette, direct that any power exercisable by it under this Act shall, in relation to such matters and subject to such conditions, if any, as may be specified in the direction, be also exercisable—

(a) where the appropriate Government is the Central Government, by such officer or authority subordinate to the Central Government or by the State Government or by such officer or authority subordinate to the State Government, as may be specified in the notification;

(b) where the appropriate Government is a State Government, by such officer or authority subordinate to the State Government as may be specified in the notification.

Section 25: Display by notice of abstracts of the Act

The person responsible for the payment of wages to persons employed in a factory or an industrial or other establishment shall cause to be displayed in such factory or industrial or other establishment a notice containing such abstracts of this Act and of the rules made thereunder in English and in the language of the majority of the persons employed in the factory, or industrial or other establishment, as may be prescribed.

Section 25A: Payment of undisbursed wages in case of death of employed person

(1) Subject to the other provisions of the Act, all amounts payable to an employed person as wages shall, if such amounts could not or cannot be paid on account of his death before payment or on account of his whereabouts not being known,—

(a) be paid to the person nominated by him in this behalf in accordance with the rules made under this Act; or

(b) where no such nomination has been made or where for any reasons such amounts cannot be paid to the person so nominated, be deposited with the prescribed authority who shall deal with the amounts so deposited in such manner as may be prescribed.

(2) Where, in accordance with the provisions of sub-section (1), all amounts payable to an employed person as wages—

(a) are paid by the employer to the person nominated by the employed person; or

(b) are deposited by the employer with the prescribed authority,

the employer shall be discharged of his liability to pay those wages.

Section 26: Rule-making power

(1) The appropriate Government may make rules to regulate the procedure to be followed by the authorities and courts referred to in sections 15 and 17.

(2) Appropriate Government may, by notification in the Official Gazette, make rules for the purpose of carrying into effect the provisions of this Act.

(3) In particular and without prejudice to the generality of the foregoing power, rules made under sub-section (2) may—

(a) require the maintenance of such records, registers, returns and notices as are necessary for the enforcement of the Act, prescribe the form thereof and the particulars to be entered in such registers or records;

(b) require the display in a conspicuous place on premises where employment is carried on of notices specifying rates of wages payable to persons employed on such premises;

(c) Provide for the regular inspection of the weights, measures and weighing machines used by employers in checking or ascertaining the wages of persons employed by them;

(d) prescribe the manner of giving notice of the days on which wages will be paid;

(e) prescribe the authority competent to approve under sub-section (1) of section 8 acts and omissions in respect of which fines may be imposed;

(f) prescribe the procedure for the imposition of fines under section 8 and for the making of the deductions referred to in section 10;

(g) prescribe the conditions subject to which deductions may be made under the proviso to sub-section (2) of section 9;

(h) prescribe the authority competent to approve the purposes on which the proceeds of fines shall be expended;

(i) prescribe the extent to which advances may be made and the instalments by which they may be recovered with reference to clause (b) of section 12;

(ia) prescribe the extent to which loans may be granted and the rate of interest payable thereon with reference to section 12A;

(ib) prescribe the powers of Inspectors for the purposes of this Act;

(j) regulate the scale of costs which may be allowed in proceedings under this Act;

(k) prescribe the amount of court-fees payable in respect of any proceedings under this Act;

(l) prescribe the abstracts to be contained in the notices required by section 25;

(la) prescribe the form and manner in which nominations may be made for the purposes of sub-section (1) of section 25A, the cancellation or variation of any such nomination, or the making of any fresh nomination in the event of the nominee predeceasing the person making nomination, and other matters connected with such nominations;

(lb) specify the authority with whom amounts required to be deposited under clause (b) of sub-section (1) of section 25A shall be deposited, and the manner in which such authority shall deal with the amounts deposited with it under that clause;

(m) provide for any other matter which is to be or may be prescribed.

(4) In making any rule under this section appropriate Government may provide that a contravention of the rule shall be punishable with fine which shall not be less than ₹750 but which may extend to ₹1500.

(5) All rules made under this section shall be subject to the condition of previous publication, and the date to be specified under clause (3) of section 23 of the General Clauses Act, 1897 (10 of 1897), shall not be less than three months from the date on which the draft of the proposed rules was published.

(6) Every rule made by the Central Government under this section shall be laid, as soon as may be after it is made, before each House of Parliament while it is in session for a total period of thirty days which may be comprised in one session or in two or more successive sessions, and if, before the expiry of the session immediately following the session or the successive sessions aforesaid, both Houses agree in making any modification in the rule, or both Houses agree that the rule should not be made, the rule shall thereafter have effect only in such modified form or be of no effect, as the case may be; so however, that any such modification or annulment shall be without prejudice to the validity of anything previously done under that rule.

(7) All rules made under this section by the State Government shall, as soon as possible after they are made, be laid before the State Legislature.

* * *

10 The Trade Unions Act, 1926

MEANING OF TRADE UNION

The concept of trade union is analogous to the concept of man and the concept of democracy and therefore cannot be easily defined. Professor Coke in this context rightly observed that the trade unionism is shaped in each country not only by the form and stage of economic development, but also by the political conditions and by the general structure of the society in which it has to work. Sidney and Webb define the trade union as "a continuous association of wage earner for the purpose of maintaining and improving the conditions of their working lives."

The Trade Unions Act, 1926, under S. 2(h) provides the definition of trade union as follows:

"Trade Union" means any combination, whether temporary or permanent, formed primarily for the purpose of regulating the relations between workmen and employers or between workmen and workmen, or between employers and employers, or for imposing restrictive conditions on the conduct of any trade or business, and includes any federation of two or more Trade Unions.

THE ROLE OF TRADE UNION

Trade unions are unique organisations whose role is variously interpreted and understood by different interest groups in the society. Traditionally, trade unions' role has been to protect jobs and real earnings, secure better conditions of work and life and fight against exploitation and arbitrariness to ensure fairness and equity in employment contexts. In the wake of a long history of union movement and accumulated benefits under collective agreements, a plethora of legislations and industrial jurisprudence, growing literacy and awareness among the employees, and the spread of a variety of social institutions including consumer and public interest groups, the protective role must have undergone a qualitative change. It can be said that the protective role of trade unions remains in form but varies in substance.

There is a considerable debate on the purposes and role of trade unions. The predominant view, however, is that the concerns of trade unions extend beyond 'bread and butter' issues. Trade unions through industrial action (such as protests and strikes) and political action (influencing Government policy) establish minimum economic and legal conditions and restrain abuse of labour wherever the labour is organised. Trade unions are also seen as moral institutions, which will uplift the weak and downtrodden and render them the place, the dignity and justice they deserve.

Public opinion is hostile to trade unions in most countries. The public is not against unionism in principle. It is against the way unions and union leaders function. The public image of union leaders is that they are autocratic, corrupt and indifferent to the public interest. 'Too much power, too little morality' sums up the publics' assessment of unions.

TRADE UNIONS IN INDIA

The World Labour Report summarises the trade union situation in India in the following words: "Indian unions are too very fragmented. In many workplaces several trade unions compete for the loyalty of the same body of workers and their rivalry is usually bitter and sometimes violent. It is difficult to say how many trade unions operate at the national level since many are not affiliated to any all-India federation. The early splits in Indian trade unionism tended to be on ideological grounds each linked to a particular political party. Much of the recent fragmentation, however, has centred on personalities and occasionally on caste or regional considerations."

Unfortunately trade unionism in India suffers from a variety of problems such as politicisation of the unions, multiplicity of unions, inter-union rivalry, uneconomic size, financial debility and dependence on outside leadership.

GROWTH OF TRADE UNION MOVEMENT IN INDIA

The First Strike

The origin of the movement can be traced to sporadic labour unrest dating back to 1877 when the workers at the Empress mills at Nagpur struck following a wage cut. In 1884, 5000 Bombay Textile Workers submitted a petition demanding regular payment of wages, a weekly holiday, and a mid-day recess of thirty minutes. It is estimated that there were 25 strikes between 1882 and 1890. These strikes were poorly organised and short lived and inevitably ended in failure. The oppression by employers was so severe that workers preferred to quit their jobs rather than go on strike. Ironically, it was to promote the interests of British industry that the conditions of workers were improved. Concerned about low labour costs, which gave an unfair advantage to Indian factory-made goods, the Lancashire and Manchester Chambers of Commerce agitated for an inquiry into the conditions of Indian workers.

The First Factories Act

In 1875, the first Committee appointed to inquire into the conditions of factory work favoured legal restriction in the form of factory laws. The first Factories Act was adopted in 1881. The Factory Commission was appointed in 1885. The researcher takes only one instance, the statement of a witness to the same commission on the ginning and processing factories of Khandesh: "The same set of hands, men and women, worked continuously day and night for eight consecutive days. Those who went away for the night returned at three in the morning to make sure of being in time when the doors opened at 4 a.m., and for 18 hours' work, from 4 a.m. to 10 p.m., three or four annas was the wage. When the hands are absolutely tired out new hands are entertained. Those working these excessive hours frequently died." There was another Factories Act in 1891, and a Royal Commission on Labour was appointed in 1892. Restrictions on hours of work and on the employment of women were the chief gains of these investigations and legislation.

The First Workers' Organisation in India

Quite a large amount of pioneering work was done with remarkable perseverance by some eminent individuals notably by Narayan Lokhande who can be regarded as the father of India's modern trade union movement. The Bombay Millhands' Association formed in 1890 under the leadership of Narayan Lokhande was the first workers' organisation in India. Essentially a welfare organisation to advance workers' interests, the Association had no members, rules and regulations or funds. Soon, a number of other organisations of a similar nature came up, the chief among them being the Kamgar Hitvardhak Sabha and Social Service League. Organisations, which may more properly be called trade unions, came into existence at the turn of the century, notable among them being the Amalgamated Society of Railway Servants of India and Burma, Unions of Printers in Calcutta. The first systematic attempt to form a trade union on permanent basis was done in 1906 in the Postal Offices at Bombay and Calcutta. By the early years of the 20th century, strikes had become quite common in all major industries. Even at this time, there were visible links between nationalist politics and labour movement. In 1908, mill workers in Bombay went on strike for a week to protest against the conviction of the nationalist leader Bal Gangadhar Tilak on charges of sedition. There was also an outcry against the indenture system by which labour was recruited for the plantations, leading to the abolition of the system in 1922.

Madras Labour Union

The Madras Labour Union was founded in 1918. Although it was primarily an association of textile workers in the European owned Buckingham and Carnatic Mills, it also included workers in many other trades. Thiru Vi. Ka. and B.P. Wadia, the nationalist leaders, founded the Union. The monthly membership fee of the union was one anna. The major grievances of workers at this time were the harsh treatment meted out to Indian labour by the British supervisors, and the unduly short mid-day recess. The union managed to obtain an extension of the recess from thirty to forty minutes. It also opened a cheap grain shop and library for its members and started some welfare activities.

There was a major confrontation between the union and the management over the demand for a wage increase, which eventually led to a strike and lockout. The management filed a civil suit in the Madras High Court claiming that Wadia pay damages for inciting workers to breach their contract. As there was no legislation at this time to protect the trade union, the court ruled that the Madras Labour Union was an illegal conspiracy to hurt trading interests. An injunction was granted restraining the activities of the union. The suit was ultimately withdrawn as a result of a compromise whereby all victimised workers, with the exception of thirteen strike leaders, were reinstated and Wadia and other outside leaders severed their link with the union. Against this background, N.M. Joshi introduced a Bill for the rights of a Trade Union. But the then member for Industries, Commerce and Labour himself promised to bring legislation in the matter and the Trade Unions Act of 1926 was enacted.

By this time many active trade union leaders notably N.M. Joshi, Zabwalla, Solicitor Jinwalla, S.C. Joshi, V.G. Dalvi and Dr. Baptista, came on the scene and strong unions were organised specially in Port Trust, Dock staff, Bank employees (especially Imperial Bank and currency office), Customs, Income-Tax, Ministerial staff, etc.

Textile Labour Association

About the same time as the Madras Labour Union was being organised, Anusuyaben Sarabhai had begun doing social work among mill workers in Ahmedabad, an activity which was eventually to lead to the founding of the famous Mazdoor Mahajan-Textile Labour Association, in 1920. Mahatma Gandhi declared that the Textile Labour Association, Ahmedabad, was his laboratory for experimenting with his ideas on industrial relations and a model labour union. He was duly satisfied with the success of the experiment and advised other trade unions to emulate it.

There were a number of reasons for the spurt in unions in the 1920s. Prices had soared following World War I, and wages had not kept pace with inflation. The other major factor was the growth of the nationalist Home Rule Movement following the war, which nurtured the labour movement as part of its nationalist effort. At this time the workers had no conception of a trade union and needed the guidance of outside leaders. The outsiders were of many kinds. Some were philanthropists and social workers (who were politicians). They saw in labour a potential base for their political organisation. The politicians were of many persuasions including socialists communists and, Gandhians who emphasized social work and the voluntary settlement of disputes.

Formation of AITUC

The year 1920 also witnessed the formation of the All India Trade Union Congress (AITUC). The main body of labour legislation and paradoxically enough, even the formation of the AITUC owes virtually to the activities of the International Labour Organization (ILO). It was considered that the origin of the First World War was in the disparities between the developed and undeveloped countries. As a result, the treaty of Versailles established two bodies to cure this ill, viz., the League of Nations and the ILO. India was recognised as a founder member of the latter. This is a tripartite body on which each member state nominates its representatives. For the foundational conference of ILO held in 1919, the Government of India nominated N.M. Joshi as the labour member in consultation with the Social Service League, which was then making the greatest contribution for the cause of workers. The ILO has a very exercising machinery to see that various Governments take some actions on its conventions and recommendations. All labour legislations in India owe a debt to these conventions and recommendations of ILO. The formation of India's first Central Labour

Organisation was also wholly with the view to satisfy the credentials committee of ILO. It required that the labour member nominated by Government be in consultation with the most representative organisation of the country's labour. The AITUC came into existence in 1920 with the principal reason to decide the labour representative for lLO's first annual conference. Thus, the real fillip to the Trade union movement in India, both in matters of legislation and formation of Central Labour Organisation, came from an international body, viz., ILO and the Government's commitment to that body. Dependence on international political institution has thus been a birth malady of the Indian trade union movement and unfortunately it is not yet free from these defects.

The AITUC claimed 64 affiliated unions with a membership of 1,40,854 in 1920. Lala Lajpat Rai, the president of the Indian National Congress, became the first President of AITUC.

In 1924, there were 167 Trade unions with a quarter million members in India. The Indian factories Act of 1922 enforced a ten-hour day.

Trade Unions Act

The Indian Trade Unions Act 1926 made it legal for any seven workers to combine in a Trade Union. It also removed the pursuit of legitimate trade union activity from the purview of civil and criminal proceedings. This is still the basic law governing trade unions in the country.

Ideological Dissension

Ideological dissension in the labour movement began within few years of the AITUC coming into being. There were three distinct ideological groups in the trade union organisation: communists led by M.N. Roy and Shripad Amrut Dange, nationalists led by Gandhiji and Pandit Nehru, and moderates led by N.M. Joshi and V.V. Giri. There were serious differences between these three groups on such major issues as affiliation to international bodies, the attitude to be adopted towards the British rule and the nature of the relationship between trade unions and the broader political movement. The communists wanted to affiliate the AITUC to such leftist international organisations as the League against Imperialism and the Pan-Pacific Trade Union Secretariat.

The moderates wanted affiliation with the BLO and the International Federation of Trade Unions based in Amsterdam. The nationalists argued that affiliation with the latter organisations would amount to the acceptance of perpetual dominion status for the country under British hegemony. Similarly, the three groups saw the purpose of the labour movement from entirely different points of view. The party ideology was supreme to the communists, who saw the unions only as instruments for furthering this ideology. For the nationalists, independence was the ultimate goal and they expected the trade unions to make this their priority as well. The moderates, unlike the first two, were trade unionists at heart. They wanted to pursue trade unionism in its own right and not subjugate it completely to broader political aims and interests.

Formation of National Trade Union Federation

From the mid-1920s, the communists launched a major offensive to capture the AITUC. A part of their strategy was to start rival unions in opposition to those dominated by the nationalists. By 1928, they had become powerful enough to sponsor their own candidate for election to the office of the President of the AITUC in opposition to the nationalist candidate Nehru. Nehru managed to win the election by a narrow margin. In the 1929 session of the AITUC chaired by Nehru, the communists mustered enough support to carry a resolution affiliating the federation to international communist forum. This resolution sparked the first split in the labour movement. The moderates, who were deeply opposed to the affiliation of the AITUC with the League against Imperialism and the Pan-Pacific Secretariat, walked out of the federation and eventually formed the National Trade Union Federation (NTUF). Within two years of this event, the movement suffered a further split. On finding themselves a minority in the AITUC, the communists walked out of it in 1931 to form the Red Trade Union Congress. The dissociation of the communists from the AITUC was, however, short-lived. They returned to the AITUC the moment the British banned the Red Trade Union Congress. The British were most favourably disposed towards the moderate NTUF. N.M. Joshi, the moderate leader, was appointed a member of the Royal Commission.

The splintering away of the NTUF had cost the AITUC thirty affiliated unions with close on a hundred thousand members. However, the departure of the communists had not made much difference. In any case, the Red Trade Union Congress quickly fell apart, and the communists returned to the AITUC. During the next few years, there was reconciliation between the AITUC and NTUF as well. The realisation dawned that the split had occurred on issues such as affiliation with international organisations, which were of no concern to the ordinary worker. By 1940, the NTUF had dissolved itself completely and merged with the AITUC. It was agreed that the AITUC would not affiliate itself with any international organisation, and further that political questions would be decided only on the basis of a two-third majority.

On the whole, the1930s was a depressing period for Indian labour. There were wide-spread attempts to introduce rationalisation schemes and to effect wage cuts. The wartime inflation also took its toll. While the militant elements on the labour movement fought for the redressal of workers grievances, the movement itself was steeped in political dissent. The popular governments, voted to power in the 1937 elections, did not measure up to the workers' expectations although prominent labour leaders such as Nanda and Giri had taken over as labour ministers. They did pass some useful legislations; however a major piece of legislation was the Bombay Industrial Disputes Act of 1938, which attempted to eliminate inter union rivalries by introducing a system recognising the dominant union.

Formation of Indian Federation of Labour

In 1939, when the British unilaterally involved India in World War II, there was another wave of schisms in the labour movement. Congress governments voted to power in the 1937 elections resigned in protest against the country's involvement in an alien war, and the nationalists in the AITUC were naturally opposed to the war effort. But Roy and his supporters stood by the British. They founded a rival labour movement in 1941 called the Indian Federation of Labour (IFL). Initially the communists opposed the war effort and the British had in fact jailed most of their leaders. But there was a dramatic volt face in their position in 1942 when Soviet Russia joined the Allies.

In the same year, the nationalists launched the Quit India Movement under Gandhi's leadership. The British reacted to these developments by emptying the jails of communists and filling them up with nationalists. With the nationalists in jail, the AITUC was ripe for capture by the communists, and they made the most of the opportunity. By the end of the war, there were four distinct groups of trade unionists, two in jail and two out of it. Among the nationalists who were in jail, there had existed for some time a pressure group called the 'Congress Socialists'. The two groups outside jail were the Roy faction and communists who had in common their support for the British war effort, but had maintained their separate identities. The stage was set for a formal division of the labour movement, which would reflect the ideological differences.

At this juncture, the Government of India became quite active on the labour front and Dr. B.R. Ambedkar, the then Labour Member of the Executive Council to Viceroy, with the assistance of S.C. Joshi, was engaged and exercised to take action on all the recommendations of the Royal Commission on Labour. At their instance, a fact-finding committee was appointed to study the then existing situation. During the period 1945–47, most of the present labour legislations were drafted and the conciliation and other machinery were also well conceived. In 1947, when the National Government was formed S.C. Joshi, the then Chief Labour Commissioner, was entrusted with the work of implementing the various provisions of labour law. The whole of the present set-up owes a debt to the work that was done by him and V.V. Giri, the former President of India.

Formation of INTUC, HMS and UTUC

With the formation of National Government, Sardar Vallbhbhai Patel advocated very strongly the cause of forming a new central organisation of labour. It was his view that the National Government must have the support of organised labour and for this purpose the AITUC cannot be relied upon, since it was thriving on foreign support and used to change its colours according to the will of its foreign masters.

So, on May 1947, the Indian National Trade Union Congress (INTUC) was formed. The number of unions represented in the inaugural meet was around 200 with a total membership of over 5,75,000. There was now no doubt that the AITUC was the labour organisation of the communists, and the INTUC the labour organisation of the Congress. This was further confirmed when the Congress Socialists, who had stayed behind in the AITUC, decided to walk out in 1948 and form the Hind Mazdoor Panchayat (HMP). The socialists hoped to draw into their fold all non-congress and non-communist trade unionists. This hope was partly realised when the Roy faction IFL merged with the HMP to form the Hind Mazdoor Sabha (HMS). However, the inaugural session of the HMS witnessed yet another split in the labour movement. Revolutionary socialists and other non-communist Marxist groups from West Bengal under the leadership of Shri Mrinal Kanti Bose alleged that the HMS was dominated by socialists and decided to form the United Trade Union Congress (UTUC). The UTUC is formally committed to the pursuit of a classless society and non-political unionism. In practice, however, many of its members are supporters of the Revolutionary Socialist Party.

By the 1950s, the fragmentation of the labour movement on political lines had become a permanent fact. Disunity was costing the labour movement dearly. There were periodic attempts at unity, but nothing much came of them. The INTUC was firmly opposed to any alliance with the communists. The HMS was willing to consider a broad-based unity that would include all groups, but not for any arrangement with the AITUC alone. The major stumbling block to unity was the bitter experience other groups had with the communists in the 1930s. Even in specific industries such as railways where a merger between rival groups did take place, unity was short-lived. All that could be achieved between rival trade unions were purely local ad hoc arrangements.

Formation of Bhartiya Mazdoor Sangh

Before the rise of the Bharatiya Mazdoor Sangh (BMS), the labour field was dominated by political unionism. The recognised Central Labour Organisations were the wings of different political parties or groups. This often made workers the pawns in the power-game of different parties. The conscientious workers were awaiting the advent of a national cadre, based upon genuine trade unionism, i.e. an organisation of the workers for the workers and by the workers. They were equally opposed to political unionism as well as sheer economism, i.e. "bread butter unionism". They were votaries of *Rashtraneetee* or *Lokaneetee*. They sought protection and promotion of workers' interests within the framework of national interests, since they were convinced that there was no incompatibility between the two. They considered society as the third and more important party to all industrial relations, and the consumers' interest as the nearest economic equivalent to national interest. Some of them met at Bhopal on 23 July 1955 (the Tilak Jayanti Day) and announced the formation of a new National Trade Union Centre, Bharatiya Mazdoor Sangh.

During the All India Conference at Dhanbad in 1994, BMS gave the clarion call to all its workers to be prepared to face the *Third World War and Second War of Economic Independence* unleashed by the developed countries against the developing countries. The emissaries of the developed countries are the multinational companies who look up to India as an ideal market to sell their outdated consumer products and technologies with a view to siphon out the profits to their respective countries. In fact, there is a concerted effort to even change the tastes and outlook of the average Indian through satellite and junk food channels to suit them. One might recall that the Indians were addicted to tea and coffee by the then British rulers by distributing them free of cost during the 1940s. Today, not surprisingly, India is the largest consumers of both the beverages. Now in this decade, the soft drinks and potato chips rule the roost. BMS made it adequately clear that every country that has to develop has to adopt and adapt methods, which suits it, both culturally and economically. Today India needs *Modernisation and Not Blind Westernisation*. BMS Publications *Hindu Economics* by Shri M.G. Bokare and *Third Way* by Mananeeya Dattopant Thengdi are eye-openers to the planners of the nation in this direction. Practising Swadeshi is the only remedy to counter this onslaught.

In 1996, in its 41st year, BMS rededicated itself in organising the unorganised labour in the country (around 93% of the total workforce) with a view to raise their standard of living and protect them against exploitation. Every member of the BMS has donated at least ₹100 in the 40th year towards the cause.

BMS, encourages its workers to undertake social and constructive work along with day-to-day union work. During the Pakistan war, BMS unions suspended their demands and engaged themselves in repairing runways and donating blood for army men.

Formation of CITU and UTUC (LS)

By 1965, a splinter group of socialists headed by George Fernandes formed a second Hind Mazdoor Panchayat. The split in the communist movement inevitably divided the AITUC, leading to the emergence of the Centre of Indian Trade Unions (CITU) in 1970. The UTUC was also split into two along the ideological lines, the splinter group calling itself UTUC (Lenin Sarani), i.e. UTUC (LS). Regional Trade Union Organisations affiliated to regional political parties such as the DMK, AIADMK and MDMK in Tamil Nadu, and the Shiv Sena in Maharashtra have also emerged.

Central Trade Union Organisations (CTUOs) in India

At present, there are twelve CTUOs in India.

1. Bharatiya Mazdoor Sangh (BMS)
2. All India Trade Union Congress (AITUC)
3. Centre of Indian Trade Unions (CITU)
4. Hind Mazdoor Kisan Panchayat (HMKP)
5. Hind Mazdoor Sabha (HMS)
6. Indian Federation of Free Trade Unions (IFFTU)
7. Indian National Trade Union Congress (INTUC)
8. National Front of Indian Trade Unions (NFITU)
9. National Labour Organisation (NLO)
10. Trade Unions Coordination Centre (TUCC)
11. United Trade Union Congress (UTUC) and
12. United Trade Union Congress–Lenin Sarani (UTUC–LS)

In a significant development, two CTUOs, the AITUC and HMS decided to merge in a time-bound manner in a joint meeting of the working committees of the trade union organisations held on March 24, 1996.

TRADE UNIONS AND COLLECTIVE BARGAINING

Collective bargaining is the principal raison *d'etre* of the trade unions. However, to see that the trade union, which takes up the matter concerning service conditions of the workmen, truly represents the workmen employed in the establishment, it is essential that the trade union has got itself registered under the provisions of the Trade Unions Act, 1926. This gives a stamp of due formation of the trade union and assures the mind of the employer that the trade union is an authenticated body; the names and occupation of whose office-bearers also become known. But when in an establishment, be it an industry or an undertaking, there are more than one registered trade unions, the question as to with whom the employer should negotiate or enter into bargaining, assumes importance, because if the trade union claiming this right be one which has as its members minority of the workmen/employees, the settlement, even if any, arrived at between the employers and such a union, may not be acceptable to the majority and may not result in industrial peace. In such a situation, with whom the employer should bargain, or, to put it differently, who should be the sole bargaining agent, has been a matter of discussion and some dispute. The 'check off system' which once prevailed in this domain has lost its appeals; and so, efforts are on to find out which other system can foot the bill. The method of secret ballot is being gradually accepted. All concerned would, however, like to see that this method is so adapted and adjusted that it reflects the correct position as regards membership of the different trade unions operating in one and the same industry, establishment or undertaking.

Accordingly, the Supreme Court in *Food Corporation of India Staff Union* v. *Food Corporation of India*[1] directed that the following norms and procedure shall be followed for assessing the representative character of trade unions by the "secret ballot system" and they are as follows.

(i) As agreed to by the parties the relative strength of all the eligible unions by way of secret ballot be determined under the overall supervision of the Chief Labour Commissioner (Central) (CLC) as the appropriate Government is the Central Government in this case.

(ii) The CLC will notify the Returning Officer who shall conduct the election with the assistance of the management. The Returning Officer shall be an officer of the Government of India, Ministry of Labour.

(iii) The CLC shall fix the month of election while the actual date/dates of election shall be fixed by the Returning Officer. The Returning Officer shall require to furnish sufficient number of copies of the lists of all the employees/workers. The said list shall constitute the voters list.

(iv) The management shall display the voters list on the notice boards and other conspicuous places and shall also supply copies thereof to each of the unions for raising objections, if any. The unions will file the objections to the Returning Officer within the stipulated period and the decision of the Returning Officer shall be final.

(v) The management shall make necessary arrangement to:

(a) give wide publicity to the date/dates of election by informing the unions and by affixing notices on the notice board and also at other conspicuous places for the information of all the workers;

(b) print requisite number of ballot papers in the pro forma prescribed by the CLC incorporating therein the names of all the participating unions in an alphabetical order after ascertaining different symbols of respective unions;

(c) the ballot papers would be prepared in the pro forma prescribed by the CLC in Hindi/English and the concerned regional language;

(d) set up requisite number of polling stations and booths near the premises where the workers normally work; and

(e) provide ballot boxes with requisite stationery, boards, sealing wax, etc.

(vi) The Returning Officer shall nominate Presiding Officer for each of the polling station/booth with requisite number of polling assistants to conduct the election in an

1. AIR 1995 SC 1344.

impartial manner. The Presiding Officers and the polling assistants may be selected by the Returning Officer from amongst the officers of the management.

(vii) The election schedule indicating the dates for filing of nominations, scrutiny of nominations papers, withdrawal of nominations, polling, counting of votes and the declaration of results, shall be prepared and notified by the Returning Officer in consultation with the management. The election schedule shall be notified by the Returning Officer well in advance and at least one month's time shall be allowed to the contesting unions for canvassing before the date of filing the nominations.

(viii) To be eligible for participating in the election, the unions must have valid registration under the Trade Unions Act, 1926 for one year with an existing valid registration or the first day of filing of nomination.

(ix) The Presiding Officer shall allow only one representative to be present at each polling station/booth as observer.

(x) At the time of polling, the polling assistant will first score out the name of the employee/workman who comes for voting, from the master copy of the voters' list.

(xi) The Presiding Officer will hand over the ballot paper to the workman/employee concerned after affixing his signatures thereon. The signatures of the workman/ employee casting the vote shall also be obtained on the counterfoil of the ballot paper. He will ensure that the ballot paper is put inside the box in his presence after the voter is allowed to mark on the symbol of the candidate with the inked rubber stamp in camera. No employee/workman shall be allowed to cast his vote unless he produces his valid identity card before the Presiding Officer concerned. In the event of non production of identity card due to any reason, the voter may bring in an authorisation letter from his controlling officer certifying that the voter is the bona fide employee of the industry.

(xii) After the close of the polling, the Presiding Officer shall furnish detailed ballot paper account in the pro forma prescribed by the CLC indicating total ballot papers received, ballot papers used, unused ballot papers available etc. to the Returning Officer.

(xiii) After the close of the polling, the ballot boxes will be opened and counted by the Returning Officer or his representative in the presence of the representative of each of the unions. All votes which are marked more than once, spoiled, cancelled or damaged etc. will not be taken into account as valid votes but a separate account will be kept thereof.

(xiv) The contesting unions through their representatives present at the counting place may be allowed to file applications for re-counting of votes to the Returning Officer. The request would be considered by the Returning Officer and in a given case if he is satisfied that there is reason to do so he may permit recounting. However, no application for recounting shall be entertained after the results of the votes are declared.

(xv) The result of voting shall be compiled on the basis of valid votes polled in favour of each union in the pro forma prescribed by the CLC and signatures obtained thereon from the representatives of all the unions concerned as a proof of counting having been done in their presence.

(xvi) After declaring the results on the basis of the votes polled in favour of each union by the Returning Officer, he will send a report of his findings to the CLC.

(xvii) The union/unions obtaining the highest number of votes in the process of election shall be given recognition by the FCI for a period of five years from the date of the conferment of the recognition.

(xviii) It would be open to the contesting unions to object to the result of the election or any illegality or material irregularity which might have been committed during the election. Before the Returning Officer such objection can only be raised after the election is over. The objection shall be heard by the CLC and dispose of within 30 days of the filing of the same. The decision of the CLC shall be final subject to challenge before a competent court, if permitted under law, and advise him thereafter to procure the secret ballot paper from the Presiding Officer.

CHAPTER I

PRELIMINARY

SECTION 1: Short title, extent and commencement

(1) This Act may be called the Trade Unions Act, 1926.

(2) It extends to the whole of India.

(3) It shall come into force on such date as the Central Government may, by notification in the Official Gazette, appoint.

SECTION 2: Definitions

In this Act 'the appropriate Government' means, in relation to Trade Unions whose objects are not confined to one State, the Central Government, and in relation to other Trade Unions, the State Government, and, unless there is anything repugnant in the subject or context,—

(a) **executive** means the body, by whatever name called, to which the management of the affairs of a Trade Union is entrusted.

(b) **office-bearer**, in the case of a Trade Union, includes any member of the executive thereof, but does not include an auditor.

(c) **prescribed** means prescribed by regulations made under this Act.

(d) **registered office** means that office of a Trade Union which is registered under this Act as the head office thereof.

(e) **registered Trade Union** means a Trade Union registered under this Act.

(f) **Registrar** means—

(i) a Registrar of Trade Unions appointed by the appropriate Government under section 3, and includes any Additional or Deputy Registrar of Trade Unions; and

(ii) in relation to any Trade Union, the Registrar appointed for the State in which the head or registered office, as the case may be, of the Trade Union is situated.

(g) **trade dispute** means any dispute between employers and workmen or between workmen and workmen, or between employers and employers which is connected with the employment or non-employment, or the terms of employment or the conditions of labour, of any person, and "workmen" means all persons employed in trade or industry whether or not in the employment of the employer with whom the trade dispute arises.

(h) **Trade Union** means any combination, whether temporary or permanent, formed primarily for the purpose of regulating the relations between workmen and employers or between workmen and workmen, or between employers and employers, or for imposing restrictive conditions on the conduct of any trade or business, and includes any federation of two or more Trade Unions:

Provided that this Act shall not affect—

(i) any agreement between partners as to their own business;

(ii) any agreement between an employer and those employed by him as to such employment; or

(iii) any agreement in consideration of the sale of the goodwill of a business or of instruction in any profession, trade or handicraft.

CHAPTER II

REGISTRATION OF TRADE UNIONS

SECTION 3: Appointment of Registrars

(1) The appropriate Government shall appoint a person to be the Registrar of Trade Unions for each State.

(2) The appropriate Government may appoint as many Additional and Deputy Registrars of Trade Unions as it thinks fit for the purpose of exercising and discharging, under the superintendence and direction of the Registrar, such powers and functions of the Registrar under this Act as it may, by order, specify and define the local limits within which any such Additional or Deputy Registrar shall exercise and discharge the powers and functions so specified.

(3) Subject to the provisions of any order under sub-section (2), where an Additional or Deputy Registrar exercises and discharges the powers and functions of a Registrar in an area within which the registered office of a Trade Union is situated, the Additional or Deputy Registrar shall be deemed to be the Registrar in relation to the Trade Union for the purposes of this Act.

SECTION 4: Mode of registration

(1) Any seven or more members of a Trade Union may, by subscribing their names to the rules of the Trade Union and by otherwise complying with the provisions of

this Act with respect to registration, apply for registration of the Trade Union under this Act.

Provided that no trade union of workmen shall be registered unless at least ten per cent or one hundred of the workmen, whichever is less, engaged or employed in the establishment or industry with which it is connected are the members of such Trade Union on the date of making of application for registration:

Provided further that no trade union of workmen shall be registered unless it has on the date of making application not less than seven persons as its members, who are workmen engaged or employed in the establishment or industry with which it is connected.

(2) Where an application has been made under sub-section (1) for the registration of a Trade Union, such application shall not be deemed to have become invalid merely by reason of the fact that, at any time after the date of the application, but before the registration of the Trade Union, some of the applicants, but not exceeding half of the total number of persons who made the application, have ceased to be members of the Trade Union or have given notice in writing to the Registrar dissociating themselves from the application.

Section 5: Application for registration

(1) Every application for registration of a Trade Union shall be made to the Registrar, and shall be accompanied by a copy of the rules of the Trade Union and a statement of the following particulars, namely:

(a) the names, occupations and addresses of the members making the application;

(aa) in the case of a trade union of workmen, the names, occupations and address of the place of work of the members of the trade Union making the application;

(b) the name of the Trade Union and the address of its head office; and

(c) the titles, names, ages, addresses and occupations of the office-bearers of the Trade Union.

(2) Where a Trade Union has been in existence for more than one year before the making of an application for its registration, there shall be delivered to the Registrar, together with the application, a general statement of the assets and liabilities of the Trade Union prepared in such form and containing such particulars as may be prescribed.

Section 6: Provisions to be contained in the rules of a Trade Union

A Trade Union shall not be entitled to registration under this Act, unless the executive thereof is constituted in accordance with the provisions of this Act, and the rules thereof provide for the following matters, namely:

(a) the name of the Trade Union;

(b) the whole of the objects for which the Trade Union has been established;

(c) the whole of the purposes for which the general funds of the Trade Union shall be applicable, all of which purposes shall be purposes to which such funds are lawfully applicable under this Act;

(d) the maintenance of a list of the members of the Trade Union and adequate facilities for the inspection thereof by the office-bearers and members of the Trade Union;

(e) the admission of ordinary members who shall be persons actually engaged or employed in an industry with which the Trade Union is connected, and also the admission of the number of honorary or temporary members as office-bearers required under section 22 to form the executive of the Trade Union;

(ee) the payment of a minimum subscription by members of the Trade Union which shall be not less than—

  (i) one rupee per annum for rural workers;

  (ii) three rupee per annum for workers in other unorganised sector; and

  (iii) twelve rupees per annum for workers in any other case;

(f) the conditions under which any member shall be entitled to any benefit assured by the rules and under which any fine or forfeiture may be imposed on the members;

(g) the manner in which the rules shall be amended, varied or rescinded;

(h) the manner in which the members of the executive and the other office-bearers of the Trade Union shall be elected and removed;

(hh) the duration of period being not more than three years, for which the members of the executive and other office-bearers of the Trade Union shall be elected;

(i) the safe custody of the funds of the Trade Union, an annual audit, in such manner as may be prescribed, of the accounts thereof, and adequate facilities for the inspection of the account books by the office-bearers and members of the Trade Union; and

(j) the manner in which the Trade Union may be dissolved.

The dispute raised before the Supreme Court in *M.T. Chandersenan* v. *N. Sukumaran*[2] was that whether subscriptions not having been paid as required by the bye-laws, the members who have defaulted payment of their subscription can be members of the union. There is no doubt that if subscriptions are not paid in accordance with the bye-laws, persons who have failed to pay cannot be considered as members of the union. The Court directed that the subscriptions have to be paid and he is bound to accept the arrears as well as the current subscription and enroll them as members.

Section 7: Power to call for further particulars and to require alteration of name

(1) The Registrar may call for further information for the purpose of satisfying himself that any application complies with the provisions of section 5, or that the Trade Union is entitled to registration under section 6, and may refuse to register the Trade Union until such information is supplied.

(2) If the name under which a Trade Union is proposed to be registered is identical with that by which any other existing Trade Union has been registered or, in the

2. AIR 1974 SC 1789.

opinion of the Registrar, so nearly resembles such name as to be likely to deceive the public or the members of either Trade Union, the Registrar shall require the persons applying for registration to alter the name of the Trade Union stated in the application, and shall refuse to register the Union until such alteration has been made.

Section 8: Registration

The Registrar, on being satisfied that the Trade Union has complied with all the requirements of this Act in regard to registration, shall register the Trade Union by entering in a register, to be maintained in such form as may be prescribed, the particulars relating to the Trade Union contained in the statement accompanying the application for registration.

Section 9: Certificate of registration

The Registrar, on registering a Trade Union under section 8, shall issue a certificate of registration in the prescribed form which shall be conclusive evidence that the Trade Union has been duly registered under this Act.

Section 9A: Minimum requirement about membership of a Trade Union

A registered Trade Union of workmen shall at all times continue to have not less than ten per cent or one hundred of the workmen, whichever is less, subject to a minimum seven, engaged or employed in an establishment or industry with which it is connected, as its members.

Section 10: Cancellation of registration

A certificate of registration of a Trade Union may be withdrawn or cancelled by the Registrar—

(a) on the application of the Trade Union to be verified in such manner as may be prescribed, or

(b) if the Registrar is satisfied that the certificate has been obtained by fraud or mistake, or that the Trade Union has ceased to exist or has wilfully and after notice from the Registrar contravened any provision of this Act or allowed any rule to continue in force which is inconsistent with any such provision, or has rescinded any rule providing for any matter provision for which is required by section 6;

(c) if the Registrar is satisfied that a registered Trade Union of workmen ceases to have the requisite number of members:

Provided that not less than two months' previous notice in writing specifying the ground on which it is proposed to withdraw or cancel the certificate shall be given by the Registrar to the Trade Union before the certificate is withdrawn or cancelled otherwise than on the application of the Trade Union.

Section 11: Appeal

(1) Any person aggrieved by any refusal of the Registrar to register a Trade Union or by the withdrawal or cancellation of a certificate of registration may, within such period as may be prescribed, appeal,—

(a) where the head office of the Trade Union is situated within the limits of a Presidency-town, to the High Court, or

(aa) where the head office is situated in an area, falling within the jurisdiction of a Labour Court or an Industrial Tribunal, to that Court or Tribunal, as the case may be;

(b) where the head office is situated in any other area, to such Court, not inferior to the Court of an additional or assistant Judge of a principal Civil Court of original jurisdiction, as the appropriate Government may appoint in this behalf for that area.

(2) The appellate Court may dismiss the appeal, or pass an order directing the Registrar to register the Union and to issue a certificate of registration under the provisions of section 9 or setting aside the order for withdrawal or cancellation of the certificate, as the case may be, and the Registrar shall comply with such order.

(3) For the purpose of an appeal under sub-section (1) an appellate Court shall, so far as may be, follow the same procedure and have the same powers as it follows and has when trying a suit under the Code of Civil Procedure, 1908 (5 of 1908), and may direct by whom the whole or any part of the costs of the appeal shall be paid, and such costs shall be recovered as if they had been awarded in a suit under the said Code.

(4) In the event of the dismissal of an appeal by any Court appointed under clause (b) of sub-section (1), the person aggrieved shall have a right of appeal to the High Court, and the High Court shall, for the purpose of such appeal, have all the powers of an appellate Court under sub-sections (2) and (3), and the provisions of those sub-sections shall apply accordingly.

Section 12: Registered office

All communications and notices to a registered Trade Union may be addressed to its registered office. Notice of any change in the address of the head office shall be given within fourteen days of such change to the Registrar in writing, and the changed address shall be recorded in the register referred to in section 8.

Section 13: Incorporation of registered Trade Unions

Every registered Trade Union shall be a body corporate by the name under which it is registered, and shall have perpetual succession and a common seal with power to acquire and hold both movable and immovable property and to contract, and shall by the said name sue and be sued.

SECTION 14: Certain Acts not to apply to registered Trade Unions

The following Acts, namely:

(a) The Societies Registration Act, 1860 (21 of 1860),

(b) The Cooperative Societies Act, 1912 (2 of 1912),

(c) The Companies Act, 1956 (1 of 1956);

shall not apply to any registered Trade Union, and the registration of any such Trade Union under any such Act shall be void.

CHAPTER III

RIGHTS AND LIABILITIES OF REGISTERED TRADE UNIONS

SECTION 15: Objects on which general funds may be spent

The general funds of a registered Trade Union shall not be spent on any other objects than the following, namely:

(a) the payment of salaries, allowances and expenses to office-bearers of the Trade Union;

(b) the payment of expenses for the administration of the Trade Union, including audit of the accounts of the general funds of the Trade Union;

(c) the prosecution or defence of any legal proceeding to which the Trade Union or any member thereof is a party, when such prosecution or defence is undertaken for the purpose of securing or protecting any rights of the Trade Union as such or any rights arising out of the relations of any member with his employer or with a person whom the member employs;

(d) the conduct of trade disputes on behalf of the Trade Union or any member thereof;

(e) the compensation of members for loss arising out of trade disputes;

(f) allowances to members or their dependants on account of death, old age, sickness, accidents or unemployment of such members;

(g) the issue of, or the undertaking of liability under policies of assurance on the lives of members, or under policies insuring members against sickness, accident or unemployment;

(h) the provision of educational, social or religious benefits for members (including the payment of the expenses of funeral or religious ceremonies for deceased members) or for the dependants of members;

(i) the upkeep of a periodical published mainly for the purpose of discussing questions affecting employers or workmen as such;

(j) the payment, in furtherance of any of the objects on which the general funds of the Trade Union may be spent, of contributions to any cause intended to benefit workmen in general, provided that the expenditure in respect of such contributions in any financial year shall not at any time during that year be in excess of one-fourth of the combined total of the gross income which has up to that time accrued to the general funds of the Trade Union during that year and of the balance at the credit of those funds at the commencement of that year; and

(k) subject to any conditions contained in the notification, any other object notified by the appropriate Government in the Official Gazette.

SECTION 16: Constitution of a separate fund for political purposes

(1) A registered Trade Union may constitute a separate fund, from contributions separately levied for or made to that fund, from which payments may be made, for the promotion of the civic and political interests of its members, in furtherance of any of the objects specified in sub-section (2).

(2) The objects referred to in sub-section (1) are:

(a) the payment of any expenses incurred, either directly or indirectly, by a candidate or prospective candidate for election as a member of any legislative body constituted under the Constitution or of any local authority, before, during, or after the election in connection with his candidature or election; or

(b) the holding of any meeting or the distribution of any literature or documents in support of any such candidate or prospective candidate; or

(c) the maintenance of any person who is a member of any legislative body constituted under the Constitution or of any local authority; or

(d) the registration of electors or the election of a candidate for any legislative body constituted under the Constitution or for any local authority; or

(e) the holding of political meetings of any kind, or the distribution of political literature or political documents of any kind.

(2A) In its application to the State of Jammu and Kashmir, references in sub-section (2) to any legislative body constituted under the Constitution shall be construed as including references to the Legislature of that State.

(3) No member shall be compelled to contribute to the fund constituted under sub-section (1); and a member who does not contribute to the said fund shall not be excluded from any benefits of the Trade Union, or placed in any respect either directly or indirectly under any disability or at any disadvantage as compared with other members of the Trade Union (except in relation to the control or management of the said fund) by reason of his not contributing to the said fund; and contribution to the said fund shall not be made a condition for admission to the Trade Union.

This provision empowers a registered union to constitute a separate fund for the promotion of civil and political interest of its members. Section 16(2) enumerates the heads on which the fund can be utilised. Clause (c) of S. 16(2) is very wide which speaks about maintenance of a member of a legislative body would include all expenses by way of salary, allowance of office car, housing, clothing, telephone, etc. Section 16(3) specifically prescribes that the contribution to the fund is purely voluntary and non contribution to this fund will in no way affect the right of the members to get the benefit from the trade union. Contribution to the said fund shall not be made a condition for admission to the Trade Union.

SECTION 17: Criminal conspiracy in trade disputes

No office-bearer or member of a registered Trade Union shall be liable to punishment under sub-section (2) of S. 120-B of the Indian Penal Code (45 of 1860), in respect of any agreement made between the members for the purpose of furthering any such object of the Trade Union as is specified in S. 15, unless the agreement is an agreement to commit an offence.

This section grants immunity to the office-bearers or members of a registered trade union from punishment under sub-section (2) of S. 120-B of the Indian Penal Code dealing with criminal conspiracy. Such immunity is provided to the office bearers or members of the registered trade unions provided that an offence arises out of any agreement made between the members whose purpose is to further the objects of the Trade Union as is specified in S. 15 of the Trade Unions Act. However, such immunity is not available if any agreement is made to commit an offence.

It is important to mention that S. 15 of the Act deals with the object on which the general funds of the Union could be spent but all the items mentioned in the S. 15 relates to the object of the trade union.

Section 120-A of the Indian Penal Code, 1860 provides the meaning of criminal conspiracy as follows:

When two or more persons agree to do, or cause to be done,—

(1) an illegal act, or

(2) an act which is not illegal by illegal means, such an agreement is designated a criminal conspiracy:

Provided that no agreement except an agreement to commit an offence shall amount to a criminal conspiracy unless some act besides the agreement is done by one or more parties to such agreement in pursuance thereof.

Explanation: It is immaterial whether the illegal act is the ultimate object of such agreement, or is merely incidental to that object.

Section 120B of the Indian Penal Code prescribes the punishment of criminal conspiracy as follows:

(1) Whoever is a party to a criminal conspiracy to commit an offence punishable with death, imprisonment for life or rigorous imprisonment for a term of two years or upwards, shall, where no express provision is made in this Code for the punishment of such a conspiracy, be punished in the same manner as if he had abetted such offence.

(2) Whoever is a party to a criminal conspiracy other than a criminal conspiracy to commit an offence punishable as aforesaid shall be punished with imprisonment of either description for a term not exceeding six months, or with fine or with both.

Section 17 of the Trade Unions Act, 1926 is based on S. 3 of the English Conspiracy and Protection of Property Act, 1875, as amended by S. 5(3) of the Trade Disputes Act, 1906.

Therefore, it is thought that the scope of S. 17 can be looked from the decision of *Rookes* v. *Barnard,*[3] where his Lordship categorically said that if there be threats of violence this section gives no protection.

Trade unions have right to declare strikes and to do certain acts in furtherance of trade disputes. They are not liable criminally for conspiracy in the furtherance of such acts as the Trade Unions Act permits, but there is nothing in the Act which apart from immunity from criminal conspiracy allows immunity from any criminal offence. In fact any agreement to commit an offence would make them liable and S. 17 of the Trade Unions cannot be applied.

Section 17 extends immunity only to specified offence punishable under sub-section (2) of S. 120–B of the Indian Penal Code and that even is circumscribed by the last phrase in that section "*unless the agreement is to commit an offence*". It means that any criminal conspiracy punishable under sub-section (1) of S. 120-B of the Indian Penal Code is not covered by the immunity nor is any criminal conspiracy by any agreement to commit any offence.

Section 18: Immunity from civil suit in certain cases

(1) No suit or other legal proceeding shall be maintainable in any Civil Court against any registered Trade Union or any office-bearer or member thereof in respect of any act done in contemplation or furtherance of a trade dispute to which a member of the Trade Union is a party on the ground only that such act induces some other person to break a contract of employment, or that it is in interference with the trade, business or employment of some other person or with the right of some other person to dispose of his capital or of his labour as he wills.

(2) A registered Trade Union shall not be liable in any suit or other legal proceeding in any Civil Court in respect of any tortious act done in contemplation or furtherance of a trade dispute by an agent of the Trade Union if it is proved that such person acted without the knowledge of, or contrary to express instructions given by, the executive of the Trade Union.

Section 19: Enforceability of agreements

Notwithstanding anything contained in any other law for the time being in force, an agreement between the members of a registered Trade Union shall not be void or voidable merely by reason of the fact that any of the objects of the agreement are in restraint of trade:

Provided that nothing in this section shall enable any Civil Court to entertain any legal proceeding instituted for the express purpose of enforcing or recovering damages for the breach of any agreement concerning the conditions on which any members of a Trade Union shall or shall not sell their goods, transact business, work, employ or be employed.

Section 20: Right to inspect books of Trade Union

The account books of a registered Trade Union and the list of members thereof shall be open

3. 1964 AC 1129.

to inspection by an office-bearer or member of the Trade Union at such times as may be provided for in the rules of the Trade Union.

Section 21: Rights of minors to membership of Trade Unions

Any person who has attained the age of fifteen years may be a member of a registered Trade Union subject to any rules of the Trade Union to the contrary, and may, subject as aforesaid, enjoy all the rights of a member and execute all instruments and give all acquittances necessary to be executed or given under the rules.

Section 21A: Disqualifications of office-bearers of Trade Unions

(1) A person shall be disqualified for being chosen as, and for being a member of the executive or any other office-bearer of a registered Trade Union if—

(i) he has not attained the age of eighteen years;

(ii) he has been convicted by a Court in India of any offence involving moral turpitude and sentenced to imprisonment, unless a period of five years has elapsed since his release.

(2) Any member of the executive or other office-bearer of a registered Trade Union who, before the commencement of the Indian Trade Unions (Amendment) Act, 1964 (38 of 1964), has been convicted of any offence involving moral turpitude and sentenced to imprisonment, shall on the date of such commencement cease to be such member or office-bearer unless a period of five years has elapsed since his release before that date.

(3) In its application to the State of Jammu and Kashmir, reference in sub-section (2) to the commencement of the Indian Trade Unions (Amendment) Act, 1964 (38 of 1964), shall be construed as reference to the commencement of this Act in the said State.

Section 21-A prescribes the disqualifications which disentitle members of a registered trade union from being elected as: (a) member of the executive, or (b) an office-bearer of the union. The disqualifications are:

(a) he has not attained the age of eighteen years,

(b) he has been convicted of an offence involving moral turpitude for imprisonment.

However, a member of the registered union may be elected either to be a member of the executive or as an office-bearer, even though he has been convicted on the ground of moral turpitude once the period of five year is elapsed from the date of the release of such conviction.

Meaning of Moral Turpitude

'Moral turpitude' is a phrase which can hardly be accurately defined. It can have various shades of meaning in the various sets of circumstances. Normally as this phrase is understood, it is used in law with reference to crimes which refer to conduct that is inherently base, vile or depraved and contrary to the accepted rules of morality whether it is or is not punishable as a crime. They do not refer to the conduct which before it was made punishable as a crime was generally not regarded as wrong or corrupt.

In *Baleshwar Singh* v. *Distt. Magistrate and Collector of Banaras*,[4] a question arose as to whether conviction under S. 182, IPC, for making a false report was in respect of an offence involving moral turpitude and in answering this question in the affirmative, Mr. Justice Tandon observed that the expression '*moral turpitude*' is not defined anywhere but it means anything done contrary to justice, honesty, modesty or good morals. It implies depravity and weakness of character and disposition of the person charged with the particular conduct. Every false statement made by a person may not be 'moral turpitude', but it would be so if it discloses vileness or depravity in the doing of any private and social duty, which a person owes to his fellow-men or to his society in general.

SECTION 22: Proportion of office-bearers to be connected with the industry

(1) Not less than one-half of the total number of the office-bearers of every registered Trade Union in an unorganised sector shall be persons actually engaged or employed in an industry with which the Trade Union is connected:

Provided that the appropriate Government may, by special or general order, declare that the provisions of this section shall not apply to any Trade Union or class of Trade Unions specified in the order.

Explanation: For the purposes of this section, "unorganised sector" means any sector which the appropriate Government may, by notification in the Official Gazette, specify.

(2) Save as otherwise provided in sub-section (1), all office-bearers of a registered Trade Union, except not more than one-third of the total number of the office-bearers or five, whichever is less, shall be persons actually engaged or employed in the establishment or industry with which the Trade Union is connected.

Explanation: For the purposes of this sub-section, an employee who has retired or has been retrenched shall not be construed as outsider for the purpose of holding an office in a Trade Union.

(3) No member of the Council of Ministers or a person holding an office of profit (not being an engagement or employment in an establishment or industry with which the Trade Union is connected), in the Union or a State, shall be a member of the executive or other office-bearer of a registered Trade Union.

SECTION 23: Change of name

Any registered Trade Union may, with the consent of not less than two-thirds of the total number of its members and subject to the provisions of section 25, change its name.

4. AIR 1959 All 710.

Section 24: Amalgamation of Trade Unions

Any two or more registered Trade Unions may become amalgamated together as one Trade Union with or without dissolution or division of the funds of such Trade Unions or either or any of them, provided that the votes of at least one-half of the members of each or every such trade Union entitled to vote are recorded, and that at least sixty per cent of the votes recorded are in favour of the proposal.

Section 25: Notice of change of name or amalgamation

(1) Notice in writing of every change of name of every amalgamation, signed, in the case of a change of name, by the Secretary and by seven members of the Trade Union changing its name, and, in the case of an amalgamation, by the Secretary and by seven members of each and every Trade Union which is a party thereto, shall be sent to the Registrar, and where the head office of the amalgamated Trade Union is situated in a different State, to the Registrar of such State.

(2) If the proposed name is identical with that by which any other existing Trade Union has been registered or, in the opinion of the Registrar, so nearly resembles such name as to be likely to deceive the public or the members of either Trade Union, the Registrar shall refuse to register the change of name.

(3) Save as provided in sub-section (2), the Registrar shall, if he is satisfied that the provisions of this Act in respect of change of name have been complied with, register the change of name in the register referred to in section 8, and the change of name shall have effect from the date of such registration.

(4) The Registrar of the State in which the head office of the amalgamated Trade Union is situated shall, if he is satisfied that the provisions of this Act in respect of amalgamation have been complied with and that the Trade Union formed thereby is entitled to registration under section 6, register the Trade Union in the manner provided in section 8, and the amalgamation shall have effect from the date of such registration.

Section 26: Effects of change of name and of amalgamation

(1) The change in the name of a registered Trade Union shall not affect any rights or obligations of the Trade Union or render defective any legal proceeding by or against the Trade Union, and any legal proceeding which might have been continued or commenced by or against it by its former name may be continued or commenced by or against it by its new name.

(2) An amalgamation of two or more registered Trade Unions shall not prejudice any right of any of such Trade Unions or any right of a creditor or any of them.

Section 27: Dissolution

(1) When a registered Trade Union is dissolved, notice of the dissolution signed by seven members and by the Secretary of the Trade Union shall, within fourteen days

of the dissolution, be sent to the Registrar, and shall be registered by him if he is satisfied that the dissolution has been effected in accordance with the rules of the Trade Union, and the dissolution shall have effect from the date of such registration.

(2) Where the dissolution of a registered Trade Union has been registered and the rules of the Trade Union do not provide for the distribution of funds of the Trade Union on dissolution, the Registrar shall divide the funds amongst the members in such manner as may be prescribed.

Section 28: Returns

(1) There shall be sent annually to the Registrar, on or before such date as may be prescribed, a general statement, audited in the prescribed manner, of all receipts and expenditure of every registered Trade Union during the year ending on the 31st day of December next preceding such prescribed date, and of the assets and liabilities of the Trade Union existing on such 31st day of December. The statement shall be prepared in such form and shall comprise such particulars as may be prescribed.

(2) Together with the general statement there shall be sent to the Registrar a statement showing all changes of office-bearers made by the Trade Union during the year to which the general statement refers, together also with a copy of the rules of the Trade Union corrected up to the date of the despatch thereof to the Registrar.

(3) A copy of every alteration made in the rules of a registered Trade Union shall be sent to the Registrar within fifteen days of the making of the alteration.

(4) For the purpose of examining the documents referred to in sub-sections (1), (2) and (3), the Registrar, or any officer authorized by him, by general or special order, may at all reasonable times inspect the certificate of registration, account books, registers, and other documents, relating to a Trade Union, at its registered office or may require their production at such place as he may specify in this behalf, but no such place shall be at a distance of more than ten miles from the registered office of a Trade Union.

CHAPTER IV

REGULATIONS

Section 29: Power to make regulations

(1) The appropriate Government may make regulations for the purpose of carrying into effect the provisions of this Act.

(2) In particular and without prejudice to the generality of the foregoing power, such regulations may provide for all or any of the following matters, namely:

(a) the manner in which Trade Unions and the rules of Trade Unions shall be registered and the fees payable on registration;

(b) the transfer of registration in the case of any registered Trade Union which has changed its head office from one State to another;

(c) the manner in which, and the qualifications of persons by whom, the accounts of registered Trade Unions or of any class of such Unions shall be audited;

(d) the conditions subject to which inspection of documents kept by Registrars shall be allowed and the fees which shall be chargeable in respect of such inspections; and

(e) any matter which is to be or may be prescribed.

(3) Every notification made by the Central Government under sub-section (1) of Section 22, and every regulation made by it under sub-section (1), shall be laid, as soon as may be after it is made, before each House of Parliament, while it is in session, for a total period of thirty days which may be comprised in one session or in two or more successive sessions, and, if, before the expiry of the session immediately following the session or the successive sessions aforesaid both House agree in making any modification in the notification or regulation, or both Houses agree that the notification or regulation should not be made, the notification or regulation shall thereafter have effect only in such modified form or be of no effect, as the case may be; so, however, that any such modification or annulment shall be without prejudice to the validity of anything previously done under that notification or regulation.

(4) Every notification made by the State Government under sub-section (1) of Section 22, and every regulation made by it under sub-section (1), shall be laid, as soon as may be after it is made, before the State Legislature.

Section 30: Publication of regulations

(1) The power to make regulations conferred by section 29 is subject to the condition of the regulations being made after previous publication.

(2) The date to be specified in accordance with clause (3) of section 23 of the General Clauses Act, 1897 (10 of 1897), as that after which a draft of regulations proposed to be made will be taken into consideration shall not be less than three months from the date on which the draft of the proposed regulations was published for general information.

(3) Regulations so made shall be published in the Official Gazette, and on such publication shall have effect as if enacted in this Act.

The Supreme Court had occasion to discuss the procedure to be followed to amend the Union's Constitution in *Indian Oxygen Ltd.* v. *Their Workmen*.[5] The appellant company is an all India complex having establishments in different parts of the country. In Bihar alone,

5. AIR 1969 SC 306.

it has two factories, one at Jamshedpur and the other at Ranchi, and has depots at Patna and other towns. The factory at Jamshedpur is an establishment under the Bihar Shops and Establishments Act.

It appears, however, that the union at its general meeting held on January 6, 1963, purported to amend its constitution by a resolution passed thereat by changing the name of the union to Indian Oxygen Workers Union and making the workmen of all the establishments of the appellant company in Bihar eligible for its membership. The question which comes next is, whether the union's constitution was duly amended on January 6, 1963 as claimed by the union and held by the Tribunal. The constitution of the union prior to its purported amendment contained amongst other Articles, Art. 1 and Art. 3. These Articles read as follows:

"Article No. 1. Name and Address:

1. This Union is a Trade Union Organization of wage earners of the Indian Oxygen and Acetylene Co. Ltd., Jamshedpur and shall be called Indoxco Labour Union ....
3. The situation of the Registered Office shall not be changed except by resolution of the General Body Meeting specially held for the purpose. Any change of the address of the Registered Office of the Union will be communicated to the Registrar of the Trade Unions within 14 days of such change."

Article XII of the said constitution deals with alteration of rules and Cl. (c) thereof provides that copies of all new rules and amendments or revisions of rules shall be submitted to the Registrar within the prescribed period as required by S. 28(3) of the Trade Unions Act, 1926. This rule had to be incorporated in the constitution in view of the express terms of that section.

Section 6 of the Trade Unions Act provides that a trade union would not be entitled to registration under the Act unless the executive thereof is constituted in accordance with the provisions of this Act, and the rules thereof provide amongst other things for its name and the manner in which the rules shall be amended, varied or rescinded. Section 28(3) provides that a copy of every alteration made in the rules of a registered trade union shall be sent to the Registrar within fifteen days of the making of the alteration. Section 29 contains the power of the appropriate government to make regulations and sub-section 2(a) provides that without prejudice to the generality of the power in sub-section (1), such regulations may provide inter alia for the manner in which trade unions and their rules shall be registered. Section 30(3) lays down that regulations so made shall be published in the Official Gazette and on such publication shall have effect as if enacted in this Act. In pursuance of the power to make regulations, the Central Government framed Central Trade Unions Regulations, 1938, Regulation 9 whereof provided that on receiving a copy of an alteration made in the rules of a trade union under S. 28(3), the Registrar shall register the alteration in the register maintained for this purpose and shall notify the fact that he has done so to the secretary of the trade union.

The combined effect of Ss. 6(g), 28(3), 29 and 30(3) and Regulation 9 is that a registered union can alter its rules only in the manner provided in these provisions, that is, it has to send the amended rules to the Registrar within 15 days from the amendment and until the Registrar is satisfied that the amendments are in accordance with the rules of the union and on such satisfaction registers them in a register kept for that purpose and notifies that fact to the union's secretary, the amendments do not become effective. The union did not produce any evidence to show that the amendments purported to have been carried out by the said resolution dated January 6, 1963 were sent to the Registrar as provided in the aforesaid provisions nor did it produce any communication of the Registrar notifying the fact of his having registered the said amendments. Therefore, it was held that the Union's Constitution was not duly amended as no evidence was produced to show that the amendments purported to have been carried out by the resolution of the union at its meeting were not sent as provided in the aforesaid provisions, nor did it produce any communication of the Registrar notifying the fact of his having registered the said amendments.

CHAPTER V

PENALTIES AND PROCEDURE

SECTION 31: Failure to submit returns

(1) If default is made on the part of any registered Trade Union in giving any notice or sending any statement or other document as required by or under any provision of this Act, every office-bearer or other person bound by the rules of the Trade Union to give or send the same, or, if there is no such office-bearer or person every member of the executive of the Trade Union, shall be punishable, with fine which may extend to five rupees and, in the case of a continuing default, with an additional fine which may extend to five rupees for each week after the first during which the default continues:

Provided that the aggregate fine shall not exceed fifty rupees.

(2) Any person who wilfully makes, or causes to be made, any false entry in, or any omission from, the general statement required by section 28, or in or from any copy of rules or of alterations of rules sent to the Registrar under that section, shall be punishable with fine which may extend to five hundred rupees.

SECTION 32: Supplying false information regarding Trade Unions

Any person who, with intent to deceive, gives to any member of a registered Trade Union or to any person intending or applying to become a member of such Trade Union any document purporting to be a copy of the rules of the Trade Union or of any alterations to the same which he knows, or has reason to believe, is not a correct copy of such rules or alterations as are for the time being in force, or any person who, with the like intent, gives a copy of any rules of an unregistered Trade Union to any person on the pretence that such rules are the rules of a registered Trade Union, shall be punishable with fine which may extend to two hundred rupees.

SECTION 33: Cognizance of offences

(1) No Court inferior to that of a Presidency Magistrate or a Magistrate of the first class shall try any offence under this Act.

(2) No Court shall take cognizance of any offence under this Act, unless complaint thereof has been made by, or with the previous sanction of, the Registrar or, in the case of an offence under section 32, by the person to whom the copy was given, within six months of the date on which the offence is alleged to have been committed.

* * *

11 The Employees' Compensation Act, 1923

An Act to provide for the payment by certain classes of employers to their employees of compensation for injury by accident.

WHEREAS it is expedient to provide for the payment by certain classes of employers to their employees of compensation for injury by accident; it is hereby enacted as follows:

CHAPTER I

PRELIMINARY

SECTION 1: Short title, extent and commencement

(1) This Act may be called the Employees' Compensation Act, 1923.
(2) It extends to the whole of India.
(3) It shall come into force on the first day of July, 1924.

SECTION 2: Definitions

(1) In this Act, unless there is anything repugnant in the subject or context,—
   (a) **Omitted**
   (b) **Commissioner** means a Commissioner for Employees' Compensation appointed under Section 20.
   (c) **compensation** means compensation as provided for by this Act.
   (d) **dependent** means any of the following relatives of a deceased employee, namely:
      (i) a widow, a minor legitimate or adopted son, and unmarried legitimate or adopted daughter, or a widowed mother; and
      (ii) if wholly dependent on the earnings of the employee at the time of his death, a son or a daughter who has attained the age of 18 years and who is infirm;
      (iii) if wholly or in part dependent on the earnings of the employee at the time of his death,

(a) a widower,

(b) a parent other than a widowed mother,

(c) a minor illegitimate son, an unmarried illegitimate daughter or a daughter legitimate or illegitimate or adopted if married and a minor or if widowed and a minor,

(d) a minor brother or an unmarried sister or a widowed sister if a minor,

(e) a widowed daughter-in-law,

(f) a minor child of a pre-deceased son,

(g) a minor child of a pre-deceased daughter where no parent of the child is alive, or

(h) a paternal grandparent if no parent of the employee is alive.

Explanation: For the purposes of sub-clause (ii) and items (f) and (g) of sub-clause (iii), references to a son, daughter or child include an adopted son, daughter or child respectively.

(dd) **employee** means any person who is—

(i) a railway servant as defined in clause (34) of section 2 of the Railways Act, 1989 (24 of 1989), not permanently employed in any administrative, district or sub-divisional office of a railway and not employed in any such capacity as is specified in Schedule II, or

(ii) (a) a master, seaman or other member of the crew of a ship,

(b) a captain or other member of the crew of an aircraft,

(c) a person recruited as driver, helper, mechanic, cleaner or in any other capacity in connection with a motor vehicle,

(d) a person recruited for work abroad by a company,

and who is employed outside India in any such capacity as is specified in Schedule II and the ship, aircraft or motor vehicle, or company, as the case may be, is registered in India, or

(iii) employed in any such capacity as is specified in Schedule II, whether the contract of employment was made before or after the passing of this Act and whether such contract is expressed or implied, oral or in writing; but does not include any person working in the capacity of a member of the Armed Forces of the Union; and any reference to any employee who has been injured shall, where the employee is dead, include a reference to his dependants or any of them.

(e) **employer** includes any body of persons whether incorporated or not and any managing agent of an employer and the legal representative of a deceased employer, and, when the services of an employee are temporarily lent or let on hire to another person by the person with whom the employee has entered into a contract of service or apprenticeship, means such other person while the employee is working for him.

(f) **managing agent** means any person appointed or acting as the representative of another person for the purpose of carrying on such other person's trade or business, but does not include an individual manager subordinate to an employer.

(ff) **minor** means a person who has not attained the age of 18 years.

(g) **partial disablement** means, where the disablement is of a temporary nature, such disablement as reduces the earning capacity of an employee in any employment in which he was engaged at the time of the accident resulting in the disablement, and, where the disablement is of a permanent nature, such disablement as reduces his earning capacity in every employment which he was capable of undertaking at that time:

Provided that every injury specified in Part II of Schedule I shall be deemed to result in permanent partial disablement.

(h) **prescribed** means prescribed by rules made under this Act.

(i) **qualified medical practitioner** means any person registered under any Central Act, Provincial Act, or an Act of the Legislature of a State providing for the maintenance of a register of medical practitioners, or, in any area where no such last-mentioned Act is in force, any person declared by the State Government, by notification in the Official Gazette, to be a qualified medical practitioner for the purposes of this Act.

(k) **seaman** means any person forming part of the crew of any ship, but does not include the master of the ship.

(l) **total disablement** means such disablement, whether of a temporary or permanent nature, as incapacitates an employee for all work which he was capable of performing at the time of the accident resulting in such disablement:

Provided that permanent total disablement shall be deemed to result from every injury specified in Part I of Schedule I or from any combination of injuries specified in Part II thereof where the aggregate percentage of the loss of earning capacity, as specified in the said Part II against those injuries, amounts to one hundred per cent or more.

(m) **wages** includes any privilege or benefit which is capable of being estimated in money, other than a travelling allowance or the value of any travelling concession or a contribution paid by the employer an employee towards any pension or provident fund or a sum paid to an employee to cover any special expenses entailed on him by the nature of his employment.

(n) Omitted by the Workmen's Compensation (Amendment) Act, 2009, w.e.f. **18-01-2010**.

(2) The exercise and performance of the powers and duties of a local authority or of any department acting on behalf of the Government shall, for the purposes of this Act, unless a contrary intention appears, be deemed to be the trade or business of such authority or department.

(3) The Central Government or the State Government, by notification in the Official Gazette, after giving not less than three months' notice of its intention so to do, may, by a like notification, add to Schedule II any class of persons employed in any occupation which it is satisfied is a hazardous occupation, and the provisions of this Act shall thereupon apply, in case of a notification by the Central Government,

within the territories to which the Act extends, or, in the case of a notification by the State Government, within the State, to such classes of persons:

Provided that in making addition, the Central Government or the State Government, as the case may be, may direct that the provisions of this Act shall apply to such classes of persons in respect of specified injuries only.

In *Sunil Industries, M/s.* v. *Ram Chander Pradhan,*[1] the petitioner is a sole proprietary concern. It runs its workshop of shaping steel sheets into various shapes and forms. The respondent was, at the relevant time, working as a press operator with the appellant. The respondent sustained injuries to his right index finger and thumb while working on a press. The injuries necessitated amputation of 2.5 × 0.5 cm of the index finger. The respondent filed a claim under the Workmen's Compensation Act, 1923 claiming compensation of ₹25,000 with interest thereon at a rate of 16 per cent per annum. The appellant in his reply, *inter alia*, claimed that the provisions of the Workmen's Compensation Act would not apply to his establishment. However, the Commissioner held that the Workmen's Compensation Act applied and that the appellant was liable to pay compensation in a sum of ₹29,814 together with ₹5,000 as penalty and interest at 12 per cent per annum. The appellant preferred an appeal under S. 30 of the Workmen's Compensation Act before the High Court of Punjab and Haryana. That appeal came to be dismissed *in limine.*

The learned counsel for the appellant submitted before the Supreme Court that the Workmen's Compensation Act did not apply to the appellant's establishment. He submitted that S. 2(n)(ii) of the Act provides that 'a workman is a person employed in a capacity specified in Schedule II'. He then referred to Schedule II of the Act and pointed out that under Item 2 of Schedule II, a person would be a workman provided he is employed in any premises where a manufacturing process as defined in Cl. (k) of S. 2 of the Factories Act, 1948 was being carried on. He submitted that this showed that the provisions of the Factories Act were being incorporated into the Workmen's Compensation Act. He submitted that this is also clear from the fact that over the years, there have been a number of amendments to the Workmen's Compensation Act incorporating therein provisions of the Factories Act or provisions similar thereto. He then referred to Ss. 2(k) and 2(m) of the Factories Act and submitted that under the Factories Act, the manufacturing process must be in a factory where ten or more workers are working (if the manufacturing process is being carried on with the aid of power) or twenty or more persons are working (if the manufacturing process is being carried on without the aid of power). He submitted that a joint reading of all these provisions makes it clear that even for the purposes of the Workmen's Compensation Act only those persons who are employed in a factory within the meaning of the Factories Act, 1948 would be entitled to make a claim under the Workmen's Compensation Act.

The Supreme Court did not accept the submissions of the learned counsel and held that it is true that the Workmen's Compensation Act, 1923 has been amended on a number of occasions; however in spite of numerous amendments the legislature has purposely omitted to specifically provide that only a workman who is employed in a factory, as defined in the Factories Act, could make a claim. All that has been done is that in Schedule II of the Workmen's Compensation Act, it is *inter alia* clarified that persons employed, otherwise than in a clerical capacity, in any premises wherein a manufacturing process as defined in Cl. (k)

1. AIR 2001 SC 220.

of S. 2 of the Factories Act, 1948, are workmen. Significantly, the definition of the word "Factory" as appearing in Cl. (m) of S. 2 of the Factories Act, 1948 has not been incorporated in the Workmen's Compensation Act. Thus, it is clear that for the Workmen's Compensation Act to apply, it is not necessary that the workman should be working in a factory as defined in the Factories Act, 1948. It has not been denied that the workshop of the appellant would fall under Cl. (k) of S. 2 of the Factories Act. Therefore, the respondent would be a workman within the meaning of the words as defined in the Workmen's Compensation Act.

CHAPTER II

EMPLOYEES' COMPENSATION

SECTION 3: Employer's liability for compensation

(1) If personal injury is caused to an employee by accident arising out of and in the course of his employment, his employer shall be liable to pay compensation in accordance with the provisions of this Chapter:

Provided that the employer shall not be so liable—

(a) in respect of any injury which does not result in the total or partial disablement of the employee for a period exceeding three days;

(b) in respect of any injury, not resulting in death or permanent total disablement, caused by an accident which is directly attributable to—

(i) the employee having been at the time thereof under the influence of drink or drugs, or

(ii) the wilful disobedience of the employee to an order expressly given, or to a rule expressly framed, for the purpose of securing the safety of employees, or

(iii) the wilful removal or disregard by the employee of any safety guard or other device which he knew to have been provided for the purpose of securing the safety of employees,

(2) If an employee employed in any employment specified in Part A of Schedule III contracts any disease specified therein as an occupational disease peculiar to that employment, or if an employee, whilst in the service of an employer in whose service he has been employed for a continuous period of not less than six months (which period shall not include a period of service under any other employer in the same kind of employment) in any employment specified in Part B of Schedule III, contracts any disease specified therein as an occupational disease peculiar to that employment, or if an employee whilst in the service of one or more employers in any employment specified in Part C of Schedule III, for such continuous period as the Central Government may specify in respect of each such employment, contracts any disease specified therein as an occupational disease peculiar to that employment, the contracting of the disease shall be deemed to be an injury by accident

within the meaning of this section and, unless the contrary is proved, the accident shall be deemed to have arisen out of, and in the course of, the employment:

Provided that if it is proved,—

(a) that an employee whilst in the service of one or more employers in any employment specified in Part C of Schedule III has contracted a disease specified therein as an occupational disease peculiar to that employment during a continuous period which is less than the period specified under this sub-section for that employment, and

(b) that the disease has arisen out of and in the course of the employment;

the contracting of such disease shall be deemed to be an injury by accident within the meaning of this section:

Provided further that if it is proved that an employee who having served under any employer in any employment specified in Part B of Schedule III or who having served under one or more employers in any employment specified in Part C of that Schedule, for a continuous period specified under this sub-section for that employment and he has after the cessation of such service contracted any disease specified in the said Part B or the said Part C, as the case may be, as an occupational disease peculiar to the employment and that such disease arose out of the employment, the contracting of the disease shall be deemed to be an injury by accident within the meaning of this section.

(2A) If an employee employed in any employment specified in Part C of Schedule III contracts any occupational disease peculiar to that employment, the contracting whereof is deemed to be an injury by accident within the meaning of this section, and such employment was under more than one employer, all such employers shall be liable for the payment of the compensation in such proportion as the Commissioner may, in the circumstances, deem just.

(3) The Central Government or the State Government, after giving, by notification in the Official Gazette, not less than three months' notice of its intention so to do, may, by a like notification, add any description of employment to the employments specified in Schedule III, and shall specify in the case of employments so added the diseases which shall be deemed for the purposes of this section to be occupational diseases peculiar to those employments respectively, and thereupon the provisions of sub-section (2) shall apply in the case of a notification by the Central Government, within the territories to which this Act extends or, in case of a notification by the State Government, within the State as if such diseases had been declared by this Act to be occupational diseases peculiar to those employments.

(4) Save as provided by Sub-sections (2), (2A) and (3), no compensation shall be payable to an employee in respect of any disease unless the disease is directly attributable to a specific injury by accident arising out of and in the course of his employment.

(5) Nothing herein contained shall be deemed to confer any right to compensation on an employee in respect of any injury if he has instituted in a Civil Court a suit for damages in respect of the injury against the employer or any other person; and no suit for damages shall be maintainable by an employee in any Court of law in respect of any injury—

(a) if he has instituted a claim to compensation in respect of the injury before a Commissioner; or

(b) if an agreement has been come to between the employee and his employer providing for the payment of compensation in respect of the injury in accordance with the provisions of this Act.

Employer's Liability for Compensation (Accidents)

The employer of any establishment covered under this Act is required to compensate an employee:

(a) who has suffered an accident arising out of and in the course of his employment, resulting into (i) death, (ii) permanent total disablement, (iii) permanent partial disablement, or (iv) temporary disablement whether total or partial, or

(b) who has contracted an occupational disease.

Cases where Employer is Not Liable

(a) In respect of any injury which does not result in the total or partial disablement of the employee for a period exceeding **three days**;

(b) In respect of any injury not resulting in death or permanent total disablement caused by an accident which is directly attributable to—

(i) the employee having been at the time thereof under the influence of drink or drugs, or

(ii) the wilful disobedience of the employee to an order expressly given, or to a rule expressly framed, for the purpose of securing the safety of workmen, or

(iii) the wilful removal or disregard by the employee of any safety guard or other device which he knew to have been provided for the purpose of securing the safety of employee.

The burden of proving intentional disobedience on the part of the employee shall lie upon the employer.

(iv) when the employee has contracted a disease which is not directly attributable to a specific injury caused by the accident or to the occupation; and

(v) when the employee has filed a suit for damages against the employer or any other person, in a Civil Court.

In *Saurashtra Salt Manufacturing Co.* v. *Bai Valu Raja,*[2] the Supreme Court had an opportunity to provide the meaning and scope of the phrase "*arising out of and in the course of*" provided in S. 3(1) of the Workmen's Compensation Act. The appellant, in the instant case, is the Saurashtra Salt Manufacturing Co. It employs workmen both temporary and permanent. The salt works of the appellant is situated near a creek opposite to the town of Porbandar. There are at least two ways to go to the salt works from the said town, one an over

2. AIR 1958 SC 881.

land route nearly 6 to 7 miles long and the other via the creek which has to be crossed by a boat. At the Porbandar end of the creek is the Asmavati Ghat and the creek can be crossed from there at point A to the other side at point B, which is on a sandy piece of land. Those crossing the creek from point A alight from the boat at point B. From point B, after traversing the sandy area, one can reach the salt jetty of the salt works and the salt works itself. On the sandy area near point B, there is also a public footpath which goes to the salt works at point D, the distance being 1¼ mile.

A boat carrying certain workmen, who had been employed by the appellant, capsized due to bad weather and over-loading while crossing the creek from point B to point A. As the result of the accident, some of the workmen were drowned resulting in 7 cases for compensation being filed under the Workmen's Compensation Act. The Commissioner for Workmen's Compensation found that the accident arose out of and in the course of the employment of the workmen. Accordingly, he awarded compensation. The appellant appealed to the High Court of Saurashtra (now the High Court of Bombay). The High Court, after an elaborate discussion of the law, came to the same conclusion and dismissed the appeal with costs. In the appeal before the Supreme Court, it was urged on behalf of the appellant that although the compensation had been paid to the dependants of the drowned workmen and the appellant did not seek a refund of the same and the appellant must pay the costs of the respondents even in the event of success, it was essential for the appellant to have a decision whether in the circumstances disclosed in this case, in law, the appellant was liable to pay any compensation.

The Supreme Court has applied the theory of 'notional extension' and held:

> "As a rule, the employment of a workman does not commence until he has reached the place of employment and does not continue when he has left the place of employment, the journey to and from the place of employment being excluded. It is now well settled, however, that this is subject to the theory of notional extension of the employer's premises so as to include an area which the workman passes and repasses in going to and in leaving the actual place of work. There may be some reasonable extension in both time and place and a workman may be regarded as in the course of his employment even though he had not reached or had left his employer's premises. The facts and circumstances of each case will have to be examined very carefully in order to determine whether the accident arose out of and in the course of the employment of a workman, keeping in view at all times this theory of notional extension."[3]

The Supreme Court perused the evidence so recorded and observed that it is quite clear that there was no arrangement between the appellant and the Kharvas (the ferry man) to ferry to and from the salt works, across the creek, any workman of the appellant. According to the evidence, workmen of the salt works are charged by the Kharvas when they cross the creek in their boats. The only concession made by them on their own account is not to make such a charge in the case of any person who is a Kharva—a fellow caste man. It is also clear from the evidence on the record, both before and after remand, that the boats ferried across the creek are used by the public, every one of whom has to pay the charge for being ferried across the creek with the exception of a person of the Kharva caste. To reach point A on the map, a workman has to proceed in the town of Porbander via a public road. A workman

3. *Ibid.* at p. 882 per Jafer Imam, J.

then uses at point A, a boat, which is also used by the public, for which he has to pay the boatman's dues, to go to point B. From point B to the salt works, there is an open sandy area 450 to 500 feet long and 200 to 250 feet wide. This sandy area is also open to the public. From this sandy area, there is a footpath going to the salt jetty, point C and a foot-track going to the salt works, point D. There is no question that the foot-track going to the salt works is a public way. The footpath from the sandy area to the salt jetty, point C, may or may not be used by the public. For the purpose of this case, it may be assumed that a workman must necessarily use that footpath if he has to go to the salt jetty and from there to the various salt pans and salt reservoirs within the area of the salt works. The Court while considering the fact of the case held that it is well settled that when a workman is on a public road or a public place or on a public transport, he is there as any other member of the public and is not there in the course of his employment unless the very nature of his employment makes it necessary for him to be there. A workman is not in the course of his employment from the moment he leaves his home and is on his way to his work. He certainly is in the course of his employment if he reaches the place of work or a point or an area which comes within the theory of notional extension, outside of which the employer is not liable to pay compensation for any accident happening to him. In the present case, even if it be assumed that the theory of notional extension extends upon point D, the theory cannot be extended beyond it. The moment a workman left point B in a boat or left point A but had not yet reached point B, he could not be said to be in the course of his employment and any accident happening to him on the journey between these two points could not be said to have arisen out of and in the course of his employment. Both the Commissioner for Workmen's Compensation and the High Court were in error in supposing that the deceased workmen in this case were still in the course of their employment when they were crossing the creek between points A and B. The accident which took place when the boat was almost at point A resulting in the death of so many workmen was unfortunate, but for that accident the appellant cannot be made liable.

A short but difficult question as to the true construction of S. 3(1) of the Workmen's Compensation Act and its application was raised before the Supreme Court in *General Manager, BEST Undertaking, Bombay* v. *Agnes.*[4]

Before discussing the *BEST Undertaking* case, it is important to note that the words *"arising out of and in the course of his employment"* are *pari materia* with the corresponding section of English statute. Therefore, the said words have been authoritatively construed by the House of Lords in many cases. Here we discuss some of the cases because these cases are referred by the Supreme Court while disposing the *BEST Undertaking* case.

In *Cremins* v. *Guest, Keen and Nettlefolds Ltd.,*[5] the Court of Appeal had to deal with a problem similar to *BEST Undertaking* case, where *Cremins* was a collier in the employment of the company. He, along with other employees, lived at Dowlais, six miles from the colliery. A train composed of carriages belonging to the appellants, but driven by the Great Western Railway Company's men, daily conveyed Cremins and many other colliers from Dowlais to a platform at Bedlinog erected by the appellants, on land belonging to the said Railway Company. The platform was repaired and lighted by the appellants, and was under their

4. AIR 1964 SC 193.
5. (1908) 1 KB 469.

control. The colliers were the only persons allowed to use the platform, but there was a station open to the public at a short distance. The colliers walked from the platform by a high road to the colliery, which was about a quarter of a mile from the platform. A similar train conveyed the colliers from the platform to Dowlais. The colliers were conveyed free of charge. Cremins was waiting on the platform to get into the return train, when he was knocked down and was killed by the train. His widow applied for compensation under the Workmen's Compensation Act, 1906. Under S. 1 of the Act of 1906, she would be entitled to compensation if the accident arose "out of and in the course of his employment". The Court of Appeal held that the widow was entitled for compensation. Cozens-Hardy M.R. gave his reason for so holding that it was an implied term of the contract of service that these trains should be provided by the employers, and that the colliers should have the right, if not the obligation, to travel to and fro without charge.

Though the accident took place on the platform, this decision accepted the principle that it was an implied term of the contract of service that the colliers had to travel to and from the colliery by the trains provided by the employers. In that case, there was certainly a right in the colliers to use the train, but it is doubtful whether there was a legal duty on them to do so. But the Court was prepared to give a popular meaning to the word "duty" to take in the "expectation" of user in the particular circumstances of the case.

The House of Lords in *St. Helens Colliery Co. Ltd.* v. *Hewitson*[6] had taken a stricter and legalistic view of the concept of "duty". There, a workman employed at the colliery was injured in a railway accident while travelling in a special colliers' train from his work to his home at Maryport. By an agreement between the colliery company and the railway company, the latter agreed to provide special trains for the conveyance of the colliery company's workmen to and from the colliery and Maryport, and the colliery company agreed to indemnify the railway company against claims by the workmen in respect of accident, injury or loss while using the trains. Any workman who desired to travel by these trains signed an agreement with the railway company releasing them from all claims in case of accident, and the colliery company then provided him with a pass and charged him a sum representing less than the full amount of the agreed fare and this sum was deducted week by week from his wages. The House of Lords by a majority held that there being no obligation on the workmen to use the train, the injury did not arise in the course of the employment within the meaning of the Workmen's Compensation Act, 1906. Lord Atkinson made the following observation:

> "It must, however, be borne in mind that if the physical features of the locality be such that the means of transit offered by the employer are the only means of transit available to transport the workman to his work, there may, in the workman's contract of service, be implied a term that there was an obligation on the employer to provide such means and a reciprocal obligation on the workman to avail himself of them".[7]

The learned Lord had conceded that a term of obligation on the part of the employee to avail himself of a particular means of transit could be implied having regard to the peculiar circumstances of a case. This decision accepts the principle that there should be a duty or obligation on the part of the employee to avail himself of the means of transit offered by the employer; the said duty may be expressed or implied in the contract of service.

6. 1924 AC 59.
7. *Ibid.* at p. 70 per Atkinson, Lord.

In *Weaver* v. *Tredegar Iron and Coal Co. Ltd.*,[8] the House of Lords reviewed the entire law and gave a wider meaning to the concept of "duty". It was also a case of a collier. He was caught up in a press of fellow-workmen trying to board a train and was pushed off the railway platform and injured. The platform and train were both owned, managed and controlled by a railway company, but the platform was situated by the side of a railway line which ran through the colliery premises owned by the workmen's employers, and was accessible from the colliery premises only. It was not open to the public, and its name did not appear in the company's time table. Employees of the colliery used it under an arrangement between their employers and the company whereby special trains were stopped at the platform to take the men to and from their homes at a reduced fare, which was deducted by the employers from the workmen's wages. The injured workman claimed compensation. The House of Lords by a majority held that the accident arose in the course of and out of the employment and the injured workman was entitled to compensation. Lord Atkinson posed the question thus: Is he doing something in discharge of a duty of his employer directly or indirectly imposed upon him by his contract of service? Lord Atkinson observed that when all the cases have been looked at and considered, one is finally brought back to the words of the Act, *"the course of the employment*". The course of the employment begins when the workman enters the employment, and it ceases when he leaves the employment, it being his duty to do both.

Lord Wright puts the same idea differently and observed:

> "In a case like the preset, however, where a man was simply using the usual and proper way provided for leaving the colliery; I do not see the relevance of the idea of duty, except in the artificial sense that a man owes his employers a duty to come to his work and to go away when his work is ended. I think that it is in some such sense that duty has been referred to in certain of the cases of this nature".[9]

Lord Romer applied the following tests to the facts of the case:

> "In all cases, therefore, where a workman, on going to, or on leaving his work, suffers an accident on the way, the first question to be determined is whether the workman was at the place where the accident occurred in virtue of his status as a workman or in virtue of his status as a member of the public".[10]

He came to the conclusion that the employee in that case, when the accident happened, was there only by virtue of his status as an employee of the colliery.

The Court of Appeal in *Jenkins* v. *Elder Dempster Lines Ltd.*[11] once again construed the expression *"arising out of and in the course of employment"*. There, the ship in which the deceased was employed moored against the harbour mole of Las Palmas. At the landward end of the mole was a gateway where police were stationed for the purpose, ostensibly, of keeping unauthorized persons off the mole, but all kinds of people were allowed there and entry to it was practically unrestricted. Shortly after the ship moored, the deceased and other members of the crew went ashore for a short while. When they were returning to the ship, the policemen at the gate of the mole asked them which was their ship and allowed them to enter the mole.

8. (1940) 3 All ER 157.
9. *Ibid.* at p. 172 per Wright, Lord.
10. *Ibid.* at p. 175 per Romer, Lord.
11. (1953) 2 All ER 1133.

In the darkness, the deceased fell over the side of the mole and was drowned. In a claim by the widow against the employers for compensation under the Workmen's Compensation Act, her claim was not allowed. Sir Raymond Evershed, M.R., posed the question thus: "Was the workman at the relevant time acting in the scope of his employment?" He explained that one has to see whether the workman's presence at the point where he met with the accident is so related to his employment as to lead to the conclusion that he was acting within its scope.

This decision lays down a wider test, namely that there should be a nexus between the accident and the employment. The Supreme Court of India has considered the scope of the S. 3 of Workmen's Compensation Act in *Saurashtra Salt Manufacturing Co.* v. *Bai Valu Raja*[2] and accepted the doctrine of *"notional extension"* of the employer's premises in the context of an accident to an employee. Imam, J., delivering the judgment of the Court after considering the facts of that case held that the accident did not take place in the course of the employment.

The Supreme Court, after considering the above stated cases and other English cases, observed in *BEST Undertaking* case:

> "Under S. 3(1) of the Act the injury must be caused to the workman by an accident arising out of and in the course of his employment. The question, when does an employment begin and when does it cease, depends upon the facts of each case. But the Courts have agreed that the employment does not necessarily end when the "down tool" signal is given or when the workman leaves the actual workshop where he is working. There is a notional extension at both the entry and exit by time and space. The scope of such extension must necessarily depend on the circumstances of a given case. As employment may end or may begin not only when the employee begins to work or leaves his tools but also when he used the means of access and egress to and from the place of employment. A contractual duty or obligation on the part of an employee to use only a particular means of transport extends the area of the field of employment to the course of the said transport. Though at the beginning the word "duty" has been strictly construed, the later decisions have liberalized this concept. A theoretical option to take an alternative route may not detract from such a duty if the accepted one is of proved necessity or of practical compulsion. But none of the decisions cited at the Bar deals with a transport service operating over a large area like Bombay. They are therefore, of little assistance, except in so far as they laid down the principles of general application. Indeed, some of the laws Lords expressly excluded from the scope of their discussion cases where the exigencies of work compel an employee to traverse public streets and other public places. The problem that now arises before us is a novel one and is not covered by authority."[12]

The facts of the instant case reveal that a bus driver is recruited to the service of the BEST Undertaking. Before appointment, the rules and regulations of the Undertaking are explained to him and he enters into an agreement with the Undertaking on the basis of those terms. He is allotted to one depot, but he may be transferred to another depot. The working hours are fixed at 8 hours a day and he is under a duty to appear punctually at the depot at the calling time. If he is late by more than one hour, he will be marked absent. If he does not appear at the calling time or "misses his car", he will not be given any work for the day unless there is actually work available for him. If he "misses his car" more than three times in a month, he will be reverted to the extra list, i.e., the list of employees other than permanent. He is given a uniform. He is permitted to travel free of charge in a bus in the said uniform.

12. *General Manager, BEST Undertaking, Bombay* v. *Agnes*, AIR 1964 SC 193 at p. 199 per Subba Rao, J.

So long as he is in the uniform, he can only travel in the bus standing and he cannot occupy a seat even on payment of the prescribed fare, indicating thereby that he is travelling in that bus only in his capacity as bus driver of the Undertaking. He can also be transferred to different depots. It is manifest from the aforesaid rules that the timings are of paramount importance in the day's work of bus driver. The Court observed, after considering the above facts, that if he misses his car, he will be punished. If he is late by more than one hour, he will be marked absent for the day; and if he is absent for 3 days in a month, he will be taken out of the permanent list. Presumably to enable him to keep up punctuality and to discharge his onerous obligations, he is given the facility in his capacity as a driver to travel in any bus belonging to the Undertaking. Therefore, the Court held that the right to travel in the bus in order to discharge his duties punctually and efficiently is a condition of his service.

The Court has passed the remark that Bombay is a City of distances. The transport service practically covers the entire area of Greater Bombay. Without the said right, it would be very difficult for a driver to sign on and sign off at the depots at the schedule timings, for he has to traverse a long distance. But for this right, not only punctuality and timings is difficult to maintain, but his efficiency will also suffer. The Court further held that having regard to the class of employees it would be futile to suggest that they could as well go by local suburban trains or by walking. The former, they could not afford, and the latter, having regard to the long distances involved, would not be practicable. As the free transport is provided in the interest of service, having regard to the long distance a driver has to traverse to go to the depot from his house and vice versa, the use of the said buses is a proved necessity giving rise to an implied obligation on his part to travel in the said buses as a part of his duty. He is not exercising the right as a member of the public, but only as one belonging to a service. The entire Greater Bombay is the field or area of the service and every bus is an integrated part of the service. The decisions relating to accidents occurring to an employee in a factory or in premises belonging to the employer providing ingress or egress to the factory are not of much relevance to a case where an employee has to operate over a larger area in a bus, which is in itself an integrated part of a fleet of buses operating in the entire area. Though the doctrine of reasonable or notional extension of employment developed in the context of specific workshop factories or harbours, equally applies to such a bus service, the doctrine necessarily will have to be adopted to meet its peculiar requirements. While in a case of a factory, the premises of the employer which gives ingress or egress to the factory is a limited one, in the case of a city transport service, by analogy, the entire fleet of buses forming the service would be the "premises". An example may make our point clear.

Suppose, in view of the long distances to be covered by the employees, the Corporation, as a condition of service, provides a bus for collecting all the drivers from their houses so that they may reach their depots in time, and to take them back after the day's work, so that after the heavy work till about 7 p.m. they may reach their home without further strain on their health. Can it be said that the said facility is not the one given in the course of employment? It can even be said that it is the duty of the employees in the interest of the service to utilize the said bus both for coming to the depot and going back to their home. If that be so, what difference would it make if the employer, instead of providing a separate bus, throws open his entire fleet of buses for giving the employees the said facility? They are given that facility not as members of the public but as employees; not as a grace but as of right because efficiency of the service demands it. Accordingly, the Court held that when a driver going home from the depot or coming to the depot uses the bus, any accident that happens to him is an accident in the course of his employment and therefore his wife (Nanu Raman-bus driver) is entitled to compensation because the accident occurred to Nanu Raman during the course of his employment.

In *Mackinnon Mackenzie and Co. Private Ltd.* v. *Ibrahim Mahommad Issak,*[13] Shaikh Hassan Ibrahim was employed as a deck-hand, a seaman of category II on the ship. The medical log book of the ship showed that on December 13, 1961 Shaikh Hassan complained of pain in the chest and was, therefore, examined, but nothing abnormal was detected clinically. The Medical Officer on board the ship prescribed some tablets for Shaikh Hassan and he reported fit for work on the next day. On the 15th, however, he complained of insomnia and pain in the chest for which the Medical Officer prescribed sedative tablets. The official log book of the ship shows that on the 16th when the ship was in the Persian Gulf, Shaikh Hassan was seen near the bridge of the ship at about 2.20 a.m. He was sent back but at 3 a.m. he was seen on the Tween Deck when he told a seaman on duty that he was going to bed. At 6.15 a.m., he was found missing and a search was undertaken. The dead body, however, was not found either on that day or later on. The evidence does not show that it was a stormy night. The Commissioner made a local inspection of the ship and saw the position of the bridge and deck and found that there was a bulwark more than 3½ feet. Nobody saw the missing seaman at the so-called place of accident. The Additional Commissioner held that there was no material for holding that the death of the seaman took place on account of an accident which arose out of his employment. But in view of the serious and important nature of the issues, the High Court proceeded to decide the questions of law arising in the appeal. Chandrachud J., allowed the appeal and reversed the judgment of the Additional Commissioner.

The principal question that arises in this appeal before the Supreme Court is whether the accident arose in the course of employment and whether it arose out of employment within the meaning of S. 3 of the Act. The Supreme Court observed that to come within the Act, the injury by accident must arise both out of and in the course of employment. The words *"in the course of the employment"* mean *"in the course of the work which the workman is employed to do and which is incidental to it"*. The words *"arising out of employment"* are understood to mean that *"during the course of the employment, injury has resulted from some risk incidental to the duties of the service, which, unless engaged in the duty owing to the master, it is reasonable to believe the workman would not otherwise have suffered"*. In other words, there must be a causal relationship between the accident and the employment. The expression *"arising out of employment"* is again not confined to the mere nature of the employment. The expression applies to employment as such—to its nature, its conditions, its obligations and its incidents. If by reason of any of those factors the workman is brought within the zone of special danger, the injury would be one which arises 'out of employment'. To put it differently, if the accident had occurred on account of a risk which is an incident of the employment, the claim for compensation must succeed, unless of course the workman has exposed himself to an added peril by his own imprudent act.

13. AIR 1970 SC 1906.

In *Lancashire and Yorkshire Rly. Co.* v. *Highley,*[14] Lord Summer laid down the following test for determining whether an accident "*arose out of the employment*":

> "There is, however, in my opinion, one test which is always at any rate applicable, because it arises upon the very words of the Statute, and it is generally of some real assistance. It is this: Was it part of the injured person's employment to hazard, to suffer, or to do that which caused his injury? If yea, the accident arose out of his employment. If nay, it did not, because, what it was not part of the employment to hazard, to suffer, or to do, cannot well be the cause of an accident arising out of the employment...."

The Supreme Court further held that in the case of death caused by accident, the burden of proof rests upon the workman to prove that the accident arose out of employment as well as in the course of employment. But this does not mean that a workman who comes to court for relief must necessarily prove it by direct evidence. Although the onus of proving that the injury by accident arose both out of and in the course of employment rests upon the applicant, these essentials may be inferred when the facts proved justify the inference. On the one hand, the Commissioner must not surmise, conjecture or guess; on the other hand, he may draw an inference from the proved facts so long as it is a legitimate inference. It is of course impossible to lay down any rule as to the degree of proof which is sufficient to justify an inference being drawn, but the evidence must be such as would induce a reasonable man to draw it. The Court in this case set aside the decision of the High Court and allowed the appeal and held that the Additional Commissioner did not commit any error of law in reaching his finding and the High Court was not justified in reversing it.

In a recent case where the deceased who was a driver drove the vehicle on the direction of the insured and he had gone to Gurugunta from Siraguppa. There he had gone to a temple and was sitting on the steps of the pond in the temple and he slipped and fell into the water and died due to drowning. The question arose before the Supreme Court in *Mallikarjuna G. Hiremath* v. *Branch Manager, Oriental Insurance Co. Ltd.* [AIR 2009 SC 2019] whether the driver would be entitled to get the compensation under the Workmen's Compensation Act?

The Supreme Court held that an accident may lead to death but that an accident had taken place must be proved. Only because death has taken place in course of employment will not amount to accident. In other words, death must arise out of accident. There is no presumption that an accident had occurred. The Court further held that under Section 3(1) of the Workmen's Compensation Act it has to be established that there was some causal connection between the death of the workman and his employment. If the workman dies a natural death because of the disease which he was suffering or while suffering from a particular disease, he dies of that disease as a result of wear and tear of the employment, no liability would be fixed upon the employer. But if the employment is a contributory cause or has accelerated the death, or if the death was due not only to the disease but also the disease coupled with the employment, then it can be said that the death arose out of the employment and the employer would be liable. The Court accordingly held that the death of truck driver is due to drowning and accident took place when deceased after reaching destination and while he was sitting on the steps of temple pond. There is no causal connection between death of the driver and his employment so neither the employer nor insurer of vehicle liable to pay compensation.

---

14. 1917 AC 352.

Stress and Strain

In *Shakuntala Chandrakant Shreshti* v. *Prabhakar Maruti Garvali* [AIR 2007 SC 248] where Prakash Chandrakant Shreshti (hereinafter called 'the deceased') was working as a cleaner in a vehicle. He was travelling in the said vehicle in the night of 27-9-2002. He suddenly developed chest pain. He was admitted to Government Hospital, Mangaon where the doctor declared him dead. Indisputably, the incident had occurred while deceased was performing his duties. The mother of deceased filed a Claim Petition under the Workmen's Compensation Act, 1923 before the Commissioner for Workmen's Compensation which was registered as WCA/SR/19/2003. The vehicle being insured with the United India Insurance Company, it was also impleaded as a party.

The fact that at the time of his death, the deceased was discharging his duties is not disputed. The autopsy was conducted wherein the cause of death was opined as cardiac arrest due to Rupture Aortic Aneurysm. No injury on his body was found.

It was alleged:

"...My son died while working in the vehicle and due to the strain of work...."

The issue with which the Court is concerned is: Whether the accident occurred during the course of employment and out of employment?

There are a large number of English and American decisions, some of which have been taken note of in *Regional Director, E.S.I. Corporation* v. *Francis De Costa* [AIR 1997 SC 432] in regard to essential ingredients for such finding and the tests attracting the provisions of Section 3 of the Act.

The principles are:

(1) There must be a causal connection between the injury and the accident and the accident and the work done in the course of employment.

(2) The onus is upon the applicant to show that it was the work and the resulting strain which contributed to or aggravated the injury.

(3) If the evidence brought on records establishes a greater probability which satisfies a reasonable man that the work contributed to the causing of the personal injury, it would be enough for the workman to succeed, but the same would depend upon the fact of each case.

Injury suffered should be a physiological injury. Accident, ordinarily, would have to be understood as unforeseen or uncomprehended or could not be foreseen or comprehended. A finding of fact, thus, has to be arrived at, *inter alia*, having regard to the nature of the work and the situation in which the deceased was placed. There is a crucial link between the causal connections of employment with death. Such a link with evidence cannot be a matter of surmise or conjecture. If a finding is arrived at without pleading or legal evidence the statutory authority will commit a jurisdictional error while exercising jurisdiction.

The Court observed in the instant case that:

1. Stress and strain arising during the course of employment,
2. Nature of employment,
3. Injury aggravated due to stress and strain.

The deceased was travelling in a vehicle. The same by itself cannot give rise to an inference that the job was strenuous. Only because a person dies of heart attack, the same does not give rise to automatic presumption that the same was by way of accident. A person may be suffering from a heart disease, although he may not be aware of the same. Medical opinion will be of relevance providing guidance to court in this behalf. Circumstances must exist to establish that death was caused by reason of failure of heart was because of stress and strain of work. Stress and strain resulting in a sudden heart failure in a case of the present nature would not be presumed. No legal fiction therefore can be raised. As a person suffering from a heart disease may not be aware thereof, medical opinion therefore would be of relevance. Each case, therefore, has to be considered on its own fact and no hard and fast rule can be laid down therefore.

Similarly, in a case where it has been brought on record that the deceased was suffering from chest disease and was previously being treated for such disease. It is also noted that the job of the deceased was only to switch on or off and, therefore, the doctor had clearly opined that there was no scope for any stress or strain in his duties. [*Jyothi Ademma* v. *Plant Engineer, Nellore,* AIR 2006 SC 2830]

Accident Arising Out of and in The Course of Employment

An accident arising out of employment implies a casual connection between the injury and the accident and the work done in the course of employment. Employment should be the distinctive and the proximate cause of the injury. The three tests for determining whether an accident arose out of employment are:

1. At the time of injury the employee must have been engaged in the business of the employer and must not be doing something for his personal benefit;
2. That accident occurred at the place where he is performing his duties; and
3. Injury must have resulted from some risk incidental to the duties of the service, or inherent in the nature of the condition of employment.

The general principles that evolve are:

- There must be a casual connection between the injury and the accident and the work done in the course of employment;
- The onus is upon the applicant to show that it was the work and the resulting strain which contributed to or aggravated the injury;
- It is not necessary that the workman must be actually working at the time of his death or that death must occur while he was working or had just ceased to work; and
- Where the evidence is balanced, if the evidence shows a greater probability which satisfies a reasonable man that the work contributed to the causing of the personal injury, it would be enough for the workman to succeed. But where the accident involved a risk common to all humanity and did not involve any peculiar or exceptional danger resulting from the nature of the employment or where the accident was the result of an added peril to which the workman by his own conduct exposed himself, which peril was not involved in the normal performance of the duties of his employment, then the employer will not be liable.

Compensation in Case of Occupational Diseases

Employees employed in certain types of occupations are exposed to the risk of contracting certain diseases, which are peculiar and inherent to those occupations. An employee contracting an occupational disease is deemed to have suffered an accident out of and in the course of employment and the employer is liable to pay compensation for the same.

Occupational diseases have been categorised in Parts A, B and C of Schedule III. The employer is liable to pay compensation:

(a) When a employee contracts any disease specified in Part B, while in service for a continuous period of 6 months under one employer. (Period of service under any other employer in the same kind of employment shall not be included.)

(b) When a employee contracts any disease specified in Part C, while he has been in continuous service for a specified period, whether under one or more employers. (Proportionate compensation is payable by all the employers, if the employee had been in service under more than one employer.)

If an employee has after the cessation of that service contracted any disease specified in the said Part B or Part C as an occupational disease peculiar to the employment and that such disease arose out of the employment, the contracting of the disease shall be deemed to be an injury by accident within the meaning of the Act.

In *Rita Devi* v. *New India Assurance Co. Ltd.*,[15] the question raised before the Supreme Court is, can a murder be an accident in any given case? The Supreme Court, after considering the fact of the instant case, observed that there is no doubt that 'murder', as it is understood, in the common parlance is a felonious act where death is caused with intent and the perpetrators of that act normally have a motive against the victim for such killing. But there are also instances where murder can be by accident on a given set of facts. The difference between a 'murder' which is not an accident and a 'murder' which is an accident, depends on the proximity of the cause of such murder. The Court further observed that if the dominant intention of the act of felony is to kill any particular person, then such killing is not an accidental murder but is a murder simplicitor, while if the cause of murder or act of murder was originally not intended and the same was caused in furtherance of any other felonious act, then such murder is an accidental murder.

Applying the above stated principle in the instant case, the Supreme Court held that a driver of the auto rickshaw was duty bound to have accepted the demand of fare paying passengers to transport them to the place of their destination. During the course of this duty, if the passengers had decided to commit an act of felony of stealing the auto rickshaw and in the course of achieving the said object of stealing the auto rickshaw, they had to eliminate the driver of the auto rickshaw, then it cannot but be said that the death so caused to the driver of the auto rickshaw was an accidental murder. The stealing of the auto rickshaw was the object of the felony and the murder that was caused in the said process of stealing the auto rickshaw is only incidental to the act of stealing of the auto rickshaw. Therefore, it has to be said that on the facts and circumstances of this case the death of the deceased (Dasarath Singh) was caused accidentally in the process of committing the theft of the auto rickshaw.

15. AIR 2000 SC 1930.

The learned counsel for the respondents contended before the Court that since the Motor Vehicles Act has not defined the word 'death' and the legal interpretations relied upon by the Court is with reference to the definition of the word 'death' in the Workmen's Compensation Act and the same will not be applicable while interpreting the word 'death' in the Motor Vehicles Act because, according to the learned counsel, for the respondent the objects of the two Acts are entirely different. The learned counsel also contends on the facts of this case that no proximity could be presumed between the murder of the driver and the stealing of the auto rickshaw. The Supreme Court, while rejecting the contentions of the learned counsel for the respondent, held that the object of the two Acts, namely the Motor Vehicles Act and the Workmen's Compensation Act are no way different and the relevant object of both the Acts is to provide compensation to the victims of accidents. The only difference between the two enactments is that so far as the Workmen's Compensation Act is concerned, it is confined to workmen as defined under that Act, while the relief provided under Chapters X to XII of the Motor Vehicles Act is available to all the victims of accidents involving a motor vehicle. The Court referred to S. 167 of the Motor Vehicles Act and held that it is open to the claimants either to proceed to claim compensation under the Workmen's Compensation Act or under the Motor Vehicles Act. A perusal of the objects of the two enactments clearly establishes that both the enactments are beneficial enactments operating in the same field, hence judicially accepted interpretation of the word 'death' in Workmen's Compensation Act is applicable to the interpretation of the word death in the Motor Vehicles Act also.

SECTION 4: Amount of compensation

(1) Subject to the provisions of this Act, the amount of compensation shall be as follows, namely:

(a) where death results from the injury an amount equal to fifty per cent of the monthly wages of the deceased employee multiplied by the relevant factor; or an amount of one lakh and twenty thousand rupees, whichever is more;

(b) where permanent total disablement results from the injury an amount equal to sixty per cent of the monthly wages of the injured employee multiplied by the relevant factor, or an amount of one lakh and forty thousand rupees, whichever is more.

Explanation I: For the purposes of clause (a) and clause (b), "relevant factor", in relation to an employee means the factor specified in the second column of Schedule IV against the entry in the first column of that Schedule specifying the number of years which are the same as the completed years of the age of the employee on his last birthday immediately preceding the date on which the compensation fell due.

Explanation II: Omitted by the Workmen's Compensation (Amendment) Act, 2009, w.e.f. **18-01-2010**. Provided that the Central Government may, by notification in the Official Gazette, from time to time, enhance the amount of compensation mentioned in clauses (a) and (b);

(c) where permanent partial disablement results from the injury

(i) in the case of an injury specified in Part II of Schedule I, such percentage of the compensation which would have been payable in the case of permanent total disablement as is specified therein as being the percentage of the loss of earning capacity caused by that injury, and

(ii) in the case of an injury not specified in Schedule I, such percentage of the compensation payable in the case of permanent total disablement as is proportionate to the loss of earning capacity (as assessed by the qualified medical practitioner) permanently caused by the injury.

Explanation I: Where more injuries than one are caused by the same accident, the amount of compensation payable under this head shall be aggregated but not so in any case as to exceed the amount which would have been payable if permanent total disablement had resulted from the injuries;

Explanation II: In assessing the loss of earning capacity for the purposes of sub-clause (ii) the qualified medical practitioner shall have due regard to the percentages of loss of earning capacity in relation to different injuries specified in Schedule I;

(d) Where temporary disablement, whether total or partial, results from the injury a half-monthly payment of the sum equivalent to twenty-five per cent of monthly wages of the employee, to be paid in accordance with the provisions of sub-section (2).

(1A) Notwithstanding anything contained in sub-section (1), while fixing the amount of compensation payable to an employee in respect of an accident occurred outside India, the Commissioner shall take into account the amount of compensation, if any, awarded to such employee in accordance with the law of the country in which the accident occurred and shall reduce the amount fixed by him by the amount of compensation awarded to the employee in accordance with the law of that country.

(1B) The Central Government may, by notification* in the Official Gazette, specify, for the purpose of sub-section (1), such monthly wages in relation to an employee as it may consider necessary.

(2) The half-monthly payment referred to in clause (d) of sub-section (1) shall be payable on the sixteenth day—

(i) from the date of disablement where such disablement lasts for a period of twenty-eight days or more; or

(ii) after the expiry of a waiting period of three days from the date of disablement where such disablement lasts for a period of less than twenty-eight days; and thereafter half-monthly during the disablement or during a period of five years, whichever period is shorter:

Provided that—

(a) there shall be deducted from any lump sum or half-monthly payments to which the employee is entitled the amount of any payment or allowance which the employee has received from the employer by way of compensation during the period of disablement prior to the receipt of such lump sum or of the first half-monthly payment, as the case may be; and

(b) no half-monthly payment shall in any case exceed the amount, if any, by which half the amount of the monthly wages of the employee before the accident exceeds half the amount of such wages which he is earning after the accident.

Explanation: Any payment or allowance which the employee has received from the employer towards his medical treatment shall not be deemed to be a payment or allowance received by him by way of compensation within the meaning of clause (a) of the proviso.

(2A) The employee shall be reimbursed the actual medical expenditure incurred by him for treatment of injuries caused during the course of employment.

(3) On the ceasing of the disablement before the date on which any half-monthly payment falls due, there shall be payable in respect of that half-month a sum proportionate to the duration of the disablement in that half-month.

(4) If the injury of the employee results in his death, the employer shall, in addition to the compensation under sub-section (1), deposit with the Commissioner a sum of not less than five thousand rupees for payment of the same to the eldest surviving dependant of the employee towards the expenditure of the funeral of such employee or where the employee did not have a dependant or was not living with his dependant at the time of his death to the person who actually incurred such expenditure.

Provided that the Central Government may, by notification in the Official Gazette, from time to time, enhance the amount specified in this sub-section.

Calculation of Compensation

The amount of compensation payable by the employer shall be calculated as follows:

(a) **Death:** In case of death, 50% of the monthly wages × relevant factor or ₹1,20,000, whichever is more, and ₹5,000 for funeral expenses.

(b) **PTD:** In case of permanent total disablement specified under Schedule I, 60% of the monthly wages × relevant factor or ₹1,40,000, whichever is more.

(c) **PPD:** In case of partial permanent disablement specified under Schedule I, 60% of the monthly wages × relevant factor × the percentage of the loss in earning capacity (specified in Part II of Schedule I).

(d) **PPD not specified:** In case of partial permanent disablement not specified under Schedule I, 60% of the monthly wages × relevant factor × the percentage of the loss in earning capacity (as assessed by a qualified medical practitioner).

(e) **Temporary disablement:** In case of temporary disablement (whether total or partial), a half-monthly installment equal to 25% of the monthly wages, for the period of disablement or 5 years, whichever is shorter.

Section 4A: Compensation to be paid when due and penalty for default

(1) Compensation under section 4 shall be paid as soon as it falls due.

(2) In cases where the employer does not accept the liability for compensation to

the extent claimed, he shall be bound to make provisional payment based on the extent of liability which he accepts, and, such payment shall be deposited with the Commissioner or made to the employee, as the case may be, without prejudice to the right of the employee to make any further claim.

(3) Where any employer is in default in paying the compensation due under this Act within one month from the date it fell due, the Commissioner shall—

(a) direct that the employer shall, in addition to the amount of the arrears, pay simple interest thereon at the rate of twelve per cent per annum or at such higher rate not exceeding the maximum of the lending rates of any scheduled bank as may be specified by the Central Government, by notification in the Official Gazette, on the amount due; and

(b) if, in his opinion, there is no justification for the delay, direct that the employer shall, in addition to the amount of the arrears and interest thereon, pay a further sum not exceeding fifty per cent of such amount by way of penalty:

Provided that an order for the payment of penalty shall not be passed under clause (b) without giving a reasonable opportunity to the employer to show cause why it should not be passed.

Explanation: For the purposes of this sub-section, "scheduled bank" means a bank for the time being included in the Second Schedule to the Reserve Bank of India Act, 1934 (2 of 1934).

(3A) The interest and the penalty payable under sub-section (3) shall be paid to the employee or his dependant, as the case may be.

The neat question involved in *Kerala State Electricity Board* v. *Valsala K.*[16] is whether the amendment of Ss. 4 and 4A of the Workmen's Compensation Act, 1923, made by Act No. 30 of 1995 with effect from 15-9-1995, enhancing the amount of compensation and rate of interest, would be attracted to cases where the claims in respect of death or permanent disablement resulting from an accident caused during the course of employment, took place prior to 15-9-1995.

A four Judge Bench of the Supreme Court in *Pratap Narain Singh Deo* v. *Srinivas Sabata,*[17] speaking through Singhal, J., has held that an employer becomes liable to pay compensation as soon as the personal injury is caused to the workmen by the accident which arose out of and in the course of employment. Thus, the relevant date for determination of the rate of compensation is the date of the accident and not the date of adjudication of the claim. However, a two Judge Bench of the Supreme Court in *The New India Assurance Company Limited* v. *V.K. Neelakandan,*[18] took the view that the Workmen's Compensation Act, being a special legislation for the benefit of the workmen, the benefit as available on the date of adjudication should be extended to the workmen and not the compensation which was payable on the date of the accident. The two Judge Bench in *Neelakandan*'s case (supra), however,

16. AIR 1999 SC 3502.
17. AIR 1976 SC 222.
18. Civil Appeal Nos. 16904-16906 of 1996, decided on 6-11-1996.

did not take notice of the judgment of the larger Bench in *Pratap Narain Singh Deo's* case[17] as it presumably was not brought to the notice of their Lordships. Be that as it may, in view of the categorical law laid down by the larger Bench in *Pratap Narain Singh Deo's* case, the view expressed by the two Judge Bench in *Neelakandan*'s case[18] is not correct.

The Supreme Court, in the instant case, considered the view of the Full Bench of the Kerala High Court in *United India Insurance Co. Ltd.* v. *Alavi,*[19] wherein the Full Bench precisely considered the same question and examined both the above noted judgments. It took the view that the injured workman becomes entitled to get compensation the moment he suffers personal injuries of the types contemplated by the provisions of the Workmen's Compensation Act and it is the amount of compensation payable on the date of the accident and not the amount of compensation payable on account of the amendment made in 1995, which is relevant. The decision of the Full Bench of the Kerala High Court, to the extent it is in accord with the judgment of the larger Bench of the Supreme Court in *Pratap Narain Singh Deo* case. Therefore, the Supreme Court approves it.

SECTION 5: Method of calculating wages

In this Act and for the purposes thereof the expression "monthly wages" means the amount of wages deemed to be payable for a month's service (whether the wages are payable by the month or by whatever other period or at piece rates), and calculated as follows, namely:

(a) where the employee has, during a continuous period of not less than twelve months immediately preceding the accident, been in the service of the employer who is liable to pay compensation, the monthly wages of the employee shall be one-twelfth of the total wages which have fallen due for payment to him by the employer in the last twelve months of that period;

(b) where the whole of the continuous period of service immediately preceding the accident during which the employee was in the service of the employer who is liable to pay the compensation was less than one month, the monthly wages of the employee shall be the average monthly amount which, during the twelve months immediately preceding the accident, was being earned by an employee employed on the same work by the same employer, or, if there was no employee so employed, by an employee employed on similar work in the same locality;

(c) in other cases, including cases in which it is not possible for want of necessary information to calculate the monthly wages under clause (b), the monthly wages shall be thirty times the total wages earned in respect of the last continuous period of service immediately preceding the accident from the employer who is liable to pay compensation, divided by the number of days comprising such period.

Explanation: A period of service shall, for the purposes of this section be deemed to be continuous which has not been interrupted by a period of absence from work exceeding fourteen days.

---

19. 1998 (1) Ker LT 951 (FB).

SECTION 6: Review

(1) Any half-monthly payment payable under this Act, either under an agreement between the parties or under the order of a Commissioner, may be reviewed by the Commissioner, on the application either of the employer or of the employee accompanied by the certificate of a qualified medical practitioner that there has been a change in the condition of the employee or, subject to rules made under this Act, on application made without such certificate.

(2) Any half-monthly payment may, on review under this section, subject to the provisions of this Act, be continued, increased, decreased or ended, or if the accident is found to have resulted in permanent disablement, be converted to the lump sum to which the employee is entitled less any amount which he has already received by way of half-monthly payments.

SECTION 7: Commutation of half-monthly payments

Any right to receive half-monthly payments may, by agreement between the parties or, if the parties cannot agree and the payments have been continued for not less than six months, on the application of either party to the Commissioner be redeemed by the payment of a lump sum of such amount as may be agreed to by the parties or determined by the Commissioner, as the case may be.

SECTION 8: Distribution of compensation

(1) No payment of compensation in respect of an employee whose injury has resulted in death, and no payment of a lump sum as compensation to a woman or a person under a legal disability, shall be made otherwise than by deposit with the Commissioner, and no such payment made directly by an employer shall be deemed to be a payment of compensation:

Provided that, in the case of a deceased employee, an employer may make to any dependant advances on account of compensation of an amount equal to three months' wages of such employee and so much of such amount as does not exceed the compensation payable to that dependant shall be deducted by the Commissioner from such compensation and repaid to the employer.

(2) Any other sum amounting to not less than ten rupees which is payable as compensation may be deposited with the Commissioner on behalf of the person entitled thereto.

(3) The receipt of the Commissioner shall be a sufficient discharge in respect of any compensation deposited with him.

(4) On the deposit of any money under sub-section (1), as compensation in respect of a deceased employee the Commissioner shall, if he thinks necessary, cause notice to be published or to be served on each dependant in such manner as he thinks fit, calling upon the dependants to appear before him on such date as he may

fix for determining the distribution of the compensation. If the Commissioner is satisfied after any inquiry which he may deem necessary, that no dependant exists, he shall repay the balance of the money to the employer by whom it was paid. The Commissioner shall, on application by the employer, furnish a statement showing in detail all disbursements made.

(5) Compensation deposited in respect of a deceased employee shall, subject to any deduction made under sub-section (4), be apportioned among the dependants of the deceased employee or any of them in such proportion as the Commissioner thinks fit, or may, in the discretion of the Commissioner, be allotted to any one dependant.

(6) Where any compensation deposited with the Commissioner is payable to any person, the Commissioner shall, if the person to whom the compensation is payable is not a woman or a person under a legal disability, and may, in other cases, pay the money to the person entitled thereto.

(7) Where any lump sum deposited with the Commissioner is payable to a woman or a person under a legal disability, such sum may be invested, applied or otherwise dealt with for the benefit of the woman, or of such person during his disability, in such manner as the Commissioner may direct; and where a half-monthly payment is payable to any person under a legal disability, the Commissioner may, of his own motion or on an application made to him in this behalf, order that the payment be made during the disability to any dependant of the employee or to any other person, whom the Commissioner thinks best fitted to provide for the welfare of the employee.

(8) Where, on application made to him in this behalf or otherwise, the Commissioner is satisfied that, on account of neglect of children on the part of a parent or on account of the variation of the circumstances of any dependant or for any other sufficient cause, an order of the Commissioner as to the distribution of any sum paid as compensation or as to the manner in which any sum payable to any such dependant is to be invested, applied or otherwise dealt with, ought to be varied, the Commissioner may make such orders for the variation of the former order as he thinks just in the circumstances of the case:

Provided that no such order prejudicial to any person shall be made unless such person has been given an opportunity of showing cause why the order should not be made, or shall be made in any case in which it would involve the repayment by a dependant of any sum already paid to him.

(9) Where the Commissioner varies any order under sub-section (8) by reason of the fact that payment of compensation to any person has been obtained by fraud, impersonation or other improper means, any amount so paid to or on behalf of such person may be recovered in the manner hereinafter provided in section 31.

Section 9: Compensation not to be assigned, attached or charged

Save as provided by this Act, no lump sum or half-monthly payment payable under this Act shall in any way be capable of being assigned or charged or be liable to attachment or pass to any person other than the employee by operation of law, nor shall any claim be set off against the same.

Section 10: Notice and claim

(1) No claim for compensation shall be entertained by a Commissioner unless notice of the accident has been given in the manner hereinafter provided as soon as practicable after the happening thereof and unless the claim is preferred before him within two years of the occurrence of the accident or, in case of death, within two years from the date of death:

Provided that, where the accident is the contracting of a disease in respect of which the provisions of sub-section (2) of section 3 are applicable, the accident shall be deemed to have occurred on the first of the days during which the employee was continuously absent from work in consequence of the disablement caused by the disease:

Provided further that in case of partial disablement due to the contracting of any such disease and which does not force the employee to absent himself from work, the period of two years shall be counted from the day the employee gives notice of the disablement to his employer:

Provided further that if an employee who, having been employed in an employment for a continuous period, specified under sub-section (2) of section 3 in respect of that employment, ceases to be so employed and develops symptoms of an occupational disease peculiar to that employment within two years of the cessation of employment, the accident shall be deemed to have occurred on the day on which the symptoms were first detected.

Provided further that the want of or any defect or irregularity in a notice shall not be a bar to the entertainment of a claim—

(a) if the claim is preferred in respect of the death of an employee resulting from an accident which occurred on the premises of the employer, or at any place where the employee at the time of the accident was working under the control of the employer or of any person employed by him, and the employee died on such premises or at such place, or on any premises belonging to the employer, or died without having left the vicinity of the premises or place where the accident occurred, or

(b) if the employer or any one of several employers or any person responsible to the employer for the management of any branch of the trade or business in which the injured employee was employed had knowledge of the accident from any other source at or about the time when it occurred:

Provided further that the Commissioner may entertain and decide any claim to compensation in any case notwithstanding that the notice has not been given, or the claim has not been preferred in due time as provided in this sub-section, if he is satisfied that the failure so to give the notice or prefer the claim, as the case may be, was due to sufficient cause.

(2) Every such notice shall give the name and address of the person injured and shall state in ordinary language the cause of the injury and the date on which the accident happened, and shall be served on the employer or upon any one of several employers,

or upon any person responsible to the employer for the management of any branch of the trade or business in which the injured employee was employed.

(3) The State Government may require that any prescribed class of employers shall maintain at their premises at which employees are employed a notice-book, in the prescribed form, which shall be readily accessible at all reasonable times to any injured employee employed on the premises and to any person acting bona fide on his behalf.

(4) A notice under this section may be served by delivering it at, or sending it by registered post addressed to, the residence or any office or place of business of the person on whom it is to be served, or, where a notice-book is maintained, by entry in the notice book.

Section 10A: Power to require from employers statements regarding fatal accidents

(1) Where a Commissioner receives information from any source that an employee has died as a result of an accident arising out of and in the course of his employment, he may send by registered post a notice to the employee's employer requiring him to submit within thirty days of the service of the notice, a statement, in the prescribed form, giving the circumstances attending the death of the employee, and indicating whether, in the opinion of the employer, he is or is not liable to deposit compensation on account of the death.

(2) If the employer is of opinion that he is liable to deposit compensation, he shall make the deposit within thirty days of the service of the notice.

(3) If the employer is of opinion that he is not liable to deposit compensation, he shall in his statement indicate the grounds on which he disclaims liability.

(4) Where the employer has so disclaimed liability, the Commissioner, after such enquiry as he may think fit, may inform any of the dependants of the deceased employee that it is open to the dependants to prefer a claim for compensation, and may give them such other further information as he may think fit.

Section 10B: Reports of fatal accidents and serious bodily injuries

(1) Where, by any law for the time being in force, notice is required to be given to any authority, by or on behalf of an employer, of any accident occurring on his premises which results in death, or serious bodily injury, the person required to give the notice shall, within seven days of the death or serious bodily injury, send a report to the Commissioner giving the circumstances attending the death or serious bodily injury:

Provided that where the State Government has so prescribed the person required to give the notice may instead of sending such report to the Commissioner send it to the authority to whom he is required to give the notice.

Explanation: "Serious bodily injury" means an injury which involves, or in all probability will involve, the permanent loss of the use of, or permanent injury to, any limb, or the permanent loss of or injury to the sight or hearing, or the fracture of any limb, or the enforced absence of the injured person from work for a period exceeding twenty days.

(2) The State Government may, by notification in the Official Gazette, extend the provisions of sub-section (1) to any class of premises other than those coming within the scope of that sub-section, and may, by such notification, specify the persons who shall send the report to the Commissioner.

(3) Nothing in this section shall apply to factories to which the Employees' State Insurance Act, 1948 (34 of 1948), applies.

Section 11: Medical examination

(1) Where an employee has given notice of an accident, he shall, if the employer, before the expiry of three days from the time at which service of the notice has been effected, offers to have him examined free of charge by a qualified medical practitioner, submit himself for such examination, and any employee who is in receipt of a half-monthly payment under this Act shall, if so required, submit himself for such examination from time to time:

Provided that an employee shall not be required to submit himself for examination by a medical practitioner otherwise than in accordance with rules made under this Act, or at more frequent intervals than may be prescribed.

(2) If an employee, on being required to do so by the employer under sub-section (1) or by the Commissioner at any time, refuses to submit himself for examination by a qualified medical practitioner or in any way obstructs the same, his right to compensation shall be suspended during the continuance of such refusal or obstruction unless, in the case of refusal, he was prevented by any sufficient cause from so submitting himself.

(3) If an employee, before the expiry of the period within which he is liable under sub-section (1) to be required to submit himself for medical examination, voluntarily leaves without having been so examined the vicinity of the place in which he was employed, his right to compensation shall be suspended until he returns and offers himself for such examination.

(4) Where an employee, whose right to compensation has been suspended under sub-section (2) or sub-section (3), dies without having submitted himself for medical examination as required by either of those sub-sections, the Commissioner may, if he thinks fit, direct the payment of compensation to the dependants of the deceased employee.

(5) Where under sub-section (2) or sub-section (3) a right to compensation is suspended, no compensation shall be payable in respect of the period of suspension, and, if the period of suspension commences before the expiry of the waiting period referred to in clause (d) of sub-section (1) of section 4, the waiting period shall be increased by the period during which the suspension continues.

(6) Where an injured employee has refused to be attended by a qualified medical practitioner whose services have been offered to him by the employer free of charge or having accepted such offer has deliberately disregarded the instructions of such medical practitioner, then if it is proved that the employee has not thereafter been regularly attended by a qualified medical practitioner or having been so attended has deliberately failed to follow his instructions and that such refusal, disregard or failure was unreasonable in the circumstances of the case and that the injury has been aggravated thereby, the injury and resulting disablement shall be deemed to be of the same nature and duration as they might reasonably have been expected to be if the employee had been regularly attended by a qualified medical practitioner, whose instructions he had followed, and compensation, if any, shall be payable accordingly.

Section 12: Contracting

(1) Where any person (hereinafter in this section referred to as the principal) in the course of or for the purposes of his trade or business contracts with any other person (hereinafter in this section referred to as the contractor) for the execution by or under the contractor of the whole or any part of any work which is ordinarily part of the trade or business of the principal, the principal shall be liable to pay to any employee employed in the execution of the work any compensation which he would have been liable to pay if that employee had been immediately employed by him; and where compensation is claimed from the principal, this Act shall apply as if references to the principal were substituted for references to the employer except that the amount of compensation shall be calculated with reference to the wages of the employee under the employer by whom he is immediately employed.

(2) Where the principal is liable to pay compensation under this section, he shall be entitled to be indemnified by the contractor, or any other person from whom the employee could have recovered compensation and where a contractor who is himself a principal is liable to pay compensation or to indemnify a principal under this section he shall be entitled to be indemnified by any person standing to him in the relation of a contractor from whom the employee could have recovered compensation, and all questions as to the right to and the amount of any such indemnity shall, in default of agreement, be settled by the Commissioner.

(3) Nothing in this section shall be construed as preventing an employee from recovering compensation from the contractor instead of the principal.

(4) This section shall not apply in any case where the accident occurred elsewhere than on, in or about the premises on which the principal has undertaken or usually undertakes, as the case may be, to execute the work or which are otherwise under his control or management.

Section 13: Remedies of employer against stranger

Where an employee has recovered compensation in respect of any injury caused under circumstances creating a legal liability of some person other than the person by whom the compensation was paid to pay damages in respect thereof, the person by whom the compensation was paid and any person who has been called on to pay an indemnity under section 12 shall be entitled to be indemnified by the person so liable to pay damages as aforesaid.

Section 14: Insolvency of employer

(1) Where any employer has entered into a contract with any insurers in respect of any liability under this Act to any employee, then in the event of the employer becoming insolvent or making a composition or scheme of arrangement with his creditors or, if the employer is a company, in the event of the company having commenced to be wound up, the rights of the employer against the insurers as respects that liability shall, notwithstanding anything in any law for the time being in force relating to insolvency or the winding up of companies, be transferred to and vest in the employee, and upon any such transfer the insurers shall have the same rights and remedies and be subject to the same liabilities as if they were the employer, so, however, that the insurers shall not be under any greater liability to the employee than they would have been under to the employer.

(2) If the liability of the insurers to the employee is less than the liability of the employer to the employee, the employee may prove for the balance in the insolvency proceedings or liquidation.

(3) Where in any case such as is referred to in sub-section (1) the contract of the employer with the insurers is void or voidable by reason of non-compliance on the part of the employer with any terms or conditions of the contract (other than a stipulation for the payment of premia), the provisions of that sub-section shall apply as if the contract were not void or voidable, and the insurers shall be entitled to prove in the insolvency proceedings or liquidation for the amount paid to the employee:

Provided that the provisions of this sub-section shall not apply in any case in which the employee fails to give notice to the insurers of the happening of the accident and of any resulting disablement as soon as practicable after he becomes aware of the institution of the insolvency or liquidation proceedings.

(4) There shall be deemed to be included among the debts which under section 49 of the Presidency-towns Insolvency Act, 1909 (3 of 1909), or under section 61 of the Provincial Insolvency Act, 1920 (5 of 1920), or under section 530 of the Companies Act, 1956 (1 of 1956), are in the distribution of the property of an insolvent or in the distribution of the assets of a company being wound up to be paid in priority to all other debts, the amount due in respect of any compensation the liability wherefore accrued before the date of the order of adjudication of the insolvent or the date of the commencement of the winding up, as the case may be, and those Acts shall have effect accordingly.

(5) Where the compensation is a half-monthly payment, the amount due in respect thereof shall, for the purposes of this section, be taken to be the amount of the

lump sum for which the half-monthly payment could, if redeemable, be redeemed if application were made for that purpose under section 7, and a certificate of the Commissioner as to the amount of such sum shall be conclusive proof thereof.

(6) The provisions of sub-section (4) shall apply in the case of any amount for which an insurer is entitled to prove under sub-section (3), but otherwise those provisions shall not apply where the insolvent or the company being wound up has entered into such a contract with insurers as is referred to in sub-section (1).

(7) This section shall not apply where a company is wound up voluntarily merely for purposes of reconstruction or of amalgamation with another company.

SECTION 14A: Compensation to be first charge on assets transferred by employer

Where an employer transfers his assets before any amount due in respect of any compensation, the liability whereof accrued before the date of the transfer has been paid, such amount shall, notwithstanding anything contained in any other law for the time being in force, be a first charge on that part of the assets so transferred as consists of immovable property.

SECTION 15: Special provisions relating to masters and seamen

This Act shall apply in the case of employees who are masters of ships or seamen subject to the following modifications, namely:

(1) The notice of the accident and the claim for compensation may, except where the person injured is the master of the ship, be served on the master of the ship as if he were the employer, but where the accident happened and the disablement commenced on board the ship, it shall not be necessary for any seaman to give any notice of the accident.

(2) In the case of the death of a master or seaman, the claim for compensation shall be made within one year after the news of the death has been received by the claimant or, where the ship has been or is deemed to have been lost with all hands, within eighteen months of the date on which the ship was, or is deemed to have been, so lost.

Provided that the Commissioner may entertain any claim to compensation in any case notwithstanding that the claim has not been preferred in due time as provided in this sub-section, if he is satisfied that the failure so to prefer the claim was due to sufficient cause.

(3) Where an injured master or seaman is discharged or left behind in any part of India or in any foreign country any depositions taken by any Judge or Magistrate in that part or by any Consular Officer in the foreign country and transmitted by the person by whom they are taken to the Central Government or any State Government shall, in any proceedings for enforcing the claim, be admissible in evidence:

(a) if the deposition is authenticated by the signature of the Judge, Magistrate or Consular Officer before whom it is made;

(b) if the defendant or the person accused, as the case may be, had an opportunity by himself or his agent to cross-examine the witness; and

(c) if the deposition was made in the course of a criminal proceeding, on proof that the deposition was made in the presence of the person accused;

and it shall not be necessary in any case to prove the signature or official character of the person appearing to have signed any such deposition and a certificate by such person that the defendant or the person accused had an opportunity of cross-examining the witness and that the deposition if made in a criminal proceeding was made in the presence of the person accused shall, unless the contrary is proved, be sufficient evidence that he had that opportunity and that it was so made.

(4) No half-monthly payment shall be payable in respect of the period during which the owner of the ship is, under any law in force for the time being relating to merchant shipping, liable to defray the expenses of maintenance of the injured master or seaman.

(5) No compensation shall be payable under this Act in respect of any injury in respect of which provision is made for payment of a gratuity, allowance or pension under the War Pensions and Detention Allowances (Mercantile Marine, etc.) Scheme, 1939, or the War Pensions and Detention Allowances (Indian Seamen, etc.) Scheme, 1941, made under the Pensions (Navy, Army, Air Force and Mercantile Marine) Act, 1939, or under War Pensions and Detention Allowances (Indian Seaman) Scheme, 1942, made by the Central Government.

(6) Failure to give a notice or make a claim or commence proceedings within the time required by this Act shall not be a bar to the maintenance of proceedings under this Act in respect of any personal injury, if—

(a) an application has been made for payment in respect of the injury under any of the schemes referred to in the preceding clause, and

(b) the State Government certifies that the said application was made in the reasonable belief that the injury was one in respect of which the scheme under which the application was made makes provision for payments, and that the application was rejected or that payments made in pursuance of the application were discontinued on the ground that the injury was not such an injury, and

(c) the proceedings under this Act are commenced within one month from the date on which the said certificate of the State Government was furnished to the person commencing the proceedings.

Section 15A: Special provisions relating to captains and other members of crew of aircraft

This Act shall apply in the case of employees who are captains or other members of the crew of aircraft subject to the following modifications, namely:

(1) The notice of the accident and the claim for compensation may, except where the person injured is the captain of the aircraft, be served on the captain of the aircraft

as if he were the employer, but where the accident happened and the disablement commenced on board the aircraft it shall not be necessary for any member of the crew to give notice of the accident.

(2) In the case of the death of the captain or other member of the crew, the claim for compensation shall be made within one year after the news of the death has been received by the claimant or, where the aircraft has been or is deemed to have been lost with all hands, within eighteen months of the date on which the aircraft was, or is deemed to have been, so lost:

Provided that the Commissioner may entertain any claim for compensation in any case notwithstanding that the claim has not been preferred in due time as provided in this sub-section, if he is satisfied that the failure so to prefer the claim was due to sufficient cause.

(3) Where an injured captain or other member of the crew of the aircraft is discharged or left behind in any part of India or in any other country, any depositions taken by any Judge or Magistrate in that part or by any Consular Officer in the foreign country and transmitted by the person by whom they are taken to the Central Government or any State Government shall, in any proceedings for enforcing the claims, be admissible in evidence—

(a) if the deposition is authenticated by the signature of the Judge, Magistrate or Consular Officer before whom it is made;

(b) if the defendant or the person accused, as the case may be, had an opportunity by himself or his agent to cross-examine the witness;

(c) if the deposition was made in the course of a criminal proceeding, on proof that the deposition was made in the presence of the person accused,

and it shall not be necessary in any case to prove the signature or official character of the person appearing to have signed any such deposition and a certificate by such person that the defendant or the person accused had an opportunity of cross-examining the witness and that the deposition if made in a criminal proceeding was made in the presence of the person accused shall, unless the contrary is proved, be sufficient evidence that he had that opportunity and that it was so made.

Section 15B: Special provisions relating to employees abroad of companies and motor vehicles

This Act shall apply—

(i) in the case of employees who are persons recruited by companies registered in India and working as such abroad, and

(ii) persons sent for work abroad along with motor vehicles registered under the Motor Vehicles Act, 1988 (59 of 1988) as drivers, helpers, mechanics, cleaners or other employees, subject to the following modifications, namely:

(1) The notice of the accident and the claim for compensation may be served on the local agent of the company, or the local agent of the owner of the motor vehicle, in the country of accident, as the case may be,

(2) In the case of death of the employee in respect of whom the provisions of this section shall apply, the claim for compensation shall be made within one year after the news of the death has been received by the claimant:

Provided that the Commissioner may entertain any claim for compensation in any case notwithstanding that the claim has not been preferred in due time as provided in this sub-section, if he is satisfied that the failure so to prefer the claim was due to sufficient cause.

(3) Where an injured employee is discharged or left behind in any part of India or in any other country any depositions taken by any Judge or Magistrate in that part or by any Consular Officer in the foreign country and transmitted by the person by whom they are taken to the Central Government or any State Government shall, in any proceedings for enforcing the claims, be admissible in evidence—

(a) if the deposition is authenticated by the signature of the Judge, Magistrate or Consular Officer before whom it is made;

(b) if the defendant or the person accused, as the case may be, had an opportunity by himself or his agent to cross-examine the witness;

(c) if the deposition was made in the course of a criminal proceeding, on proof that the deposition was made in the presence of the person accused,

and it shall not be necessary in any case to prove the signature or official character of the person appearing to have signed any such deposition and a certificate by such person that the defendant or the person accused had an opportunity of cross-examining the witness and that the deposition if made in a criminal proceeding was made in the presence of the person accused shall, unless the contrary is proved, be sufficient evidence that he had that opportunity and that it was so made.

Section 16: Returns as to compensation

The State Government may, by notification in the Official Gazette, direct that every person employing employees, or that any specified class of such persons, shall send at such time and in such form and to such authority, as may be specified in the notification, a correct return specifying the number of injuries in respect of which compensation has been paid by the employer during the previous year and the amount of such compensation together with such other particulars as to the compensation as the State Government may direct.

Section 17: Contracting out

Any contract or agreement whether made before or after the commencement of this Act, whereby an employee relinquishes any right of compensation from the employer for personal injury arising out of or in the course of the employment, shall be null and void in so far as it purports to remove or reduce the liability of any person to pay compensation under this Act.

SECTION 18: Proof of age

Omitted by the Workmen's Compensation (Amendment Act, 1959, w.e.f. 1-6-1959.)

SECTION 18A: Penalties

(1) Whoever—

(a) fails to maintain a notice-book which he is required to maintain under sub-section (3) of section 10, or

(b) fails to send to the Commissioner a statement which he is required to send under sub-section (1) of section 10A, or

(c) fails to send a report which he is required to send under section 10B, or

(d) fails to make a return which he is required to make under section 16,

shall be punishable with fine which may extend to five thousand rupees.

(2) No prosecution under this section shall be instituted except by or with the previous sanction of a Commissioner, and no Court shall take cognizance of any offence under this section, unless complaint thereof is made within six months of the date on which the alleged commission of the offence came to the knowledge of the Commissioner.

CHAPTER III

COMMISSIONERS

SECTION 19: Reference to commissioners

(1) If any question arises in any proceedings under this Act as to the liability of any person to pay compensation including any question as to whether a person injured is or is not an employee or as to the amount or duration of compensation including any question as to the nature or extent of disablement, the question shall, in default of agreement, be settled by a Commissioner.

(2) No Civil Court shall have jurisdiction to settle, decide or deal with any question which is by or under this Act required to be settled, decided or dealt with by a Commissioner or to enforce any liability incurred under this Act.

SECTION 20: Appointment of commissioner

(1) The State Government may, by notification in the Official Gazette, appoint any person who is or has been a member of a State Judicial Service for a period of not less than five years or is or has been not less than five years an advocate or a pleader or is or has been a Gazetted Officer for not less than five years having educational qualifications and experience in personnel management, human resource development

and industrial relations to be a Commissioner for Employees' Compensation for such area as may be specified in the notification.

(2) Where more than one Commissioner has been appointed for any area, the State Government may, by general or special order, regulate the distribution of business between them.

(3) Any Commissioner may, for the purpose of deciding any matter referred to him for decision under this Act, choose one or more persons possessing special knowledge of any matter relevant to the matter under inquiry to assist him in holding the inquiry.

(4) Every Commissioner shall be deemed to be a public servant within the meaning of the Indian Penal Code (45 of 1860).

SECTION 21: Venue of proceedings and transfer

(1) Where any matter under this Act is to be done by or before a Commissioner, the same shall, subject to the provisions of this Act and to any rules made hereunder, be done by or before the Commissioner for the area in which—

(a) the accident took place which resulted in the injury; or

(b) the employee or in case of his death, the dependant claiming the compensation ordinarily resides; or

(c) the employer has his registered office:

Provided that no matter shall be processed before or by a Commissioner, other than the Commissioner having jurisdiction over the area in which the accident took place, without his giving notice in the manner prescribed by the Central Government to the Commissioner having jurisdiction over the area and the State Government concerned:

Provided further that, where the employee, being the master of a ship or a seaman or the captain or a member of the crew of an aircraft or an employee in a motor vehicle or a company, meets with the accident outside India any such matter may be done by or before a Commissioner for the area in which the owner or agent of the ship, aircraft or motor vehicle resides or carries on business or the registered office of the company is situate, as the case may be.

(1A) If a Commissioner, other than the Commissioner with whom any money has been deposited under section 8, proceeds with a matter under this Act, the former may for the proper disposal of the matter call for transfer of any records or money remaining with the latter and on receipt of such a request, he shall comply with the same.

(2) If a Commissioner is satisfied that any matter arising out of any proceedings pending before him can be more conveniently dealt with by any other Commissioner, whether in the same State or not, he may, subject to rules made under this Act, order such matter to be transferred to such other Commissioner either for report or for disposal, and, if he does so, shall forthwith transmit to such other Commissioner all documents relevant for the decision of such matter and, where the matter is transferred for disposal, shall also transmit in the prescribed manner any money remaining in his hands or invested by him for the benefit of any party to the proceedings:

Provided that the Commissioner shall not, where any party to the proceedings has appeared before him, make any order of transfer relating to the distribution among dependants of a lump sum without giving such party an opportunity of being heard.

(3) The Commissioner to whom any matter is so transferred shall, subject to rules made under this Act, inquire there into and, if the matter was transferred for report, return his report thereon or, if the matter was transferred for disposal, continue the proceedings as if they had originally commenced before him.

(4) On receipt of a report from a Commissioner to whom any matter has been transferred for report under sub-section (2), the Commissioner by whom it was referred shall decide the matter referred in conformity with such report.

(5) The State Government may transfer any matter from any Commissioner appointed by it to any other Commissioner appointed by it.

SECTION 22: Form of application

(1) Where an accident occurs in respect of which liability to pay compensation under this Act arises, a claim for such compensation may, subject to the provisions of this Act, be made before the Commissioner.

(1A) Subject to the provisions of sub-section (1), no application for the settlement of any matter by a Commissioner, other than an application by a dependant or dependants for compensation shall be made unless and until some question has arisen between the parties in connection therewith which they have been unable to settle by agreement.

(2) An application to a Commissioner may be made in such form and shall be accompanied by such fee, if any, as may be prescribed, and shall contain, in addition to any particulars which may be prescribed, the following particulars, namely:

(a) a concise statement of the circumstances in which the application is made and the relief or order which the applicant claims;

(b) in the case of a claim for compensation against an employer, the date of service of notice of the accident on the employer and, if such notice has not been served or has not been served in due time, the reason for such omission;

(c) the names and addresses of the parties; and

(d) except in the case of an application by dependants for compensation a concise statement of the matters on which agreement has and of those on which agreement has not been come to.

(3) If the applicant is illiterate or for any other reason is unable to furnish the required information in writing, the application shall, if the applicant so desires, be prepared under the direction of the Commissioner.

SECTION 22A: Power of commissioner to require further deposit in cases of fatal accident

(1) Where any sum has been deposited by an employer as compensation payable in respect of an employee whose injury has resulted in death, and in the opinion of the

Commissioner such sum is insufficient, the Commissioner may, by notice in writing stating his reasons, call upon the employer to show cause why he should not make a further deposit within such time as may be stated in the notice.

(2) If the employer fails to show cause to the satisfaction of the Commissioner, the Commissioner may make an award determining the total amount payable, and requiring the employer, to deposit the deficiency.

SECTION 23: Powers and procedure of commissioners

The Commissioner shall have all the powers of a Civil Court under the Code of Civil Procedure, 1908 (5 of 1908) for the purpose of taking evidence on oath (which such Commissioner is hereby empowered to impose) and of enforcing the attendance of witnesses and compelling the production of documents and material objects and the Commissioner shall be deemed to be a Civil Court for all the purposes of section 195 and of Chapter XXVI of the Code of Criminal Procedure, 1973 (2 of 1974).

SECTION 24: Appearance of parties

Any appearance, application or act, required to be made or done by any person before or to a Commissioner (other than an appearance of a party which is required for the purpose of his examination as a witness) may be made or done on behalf of such person by a legal practitioner or by an official of an Insurance Company or registered trade union or by an Inspector appointed under sub-section (1) of section 8 of the Factories Act, 1948 (63 of 1948), or under sub-section (1) of section 5 of the Mines Act, 1952, (35 of 1952), or by any other officer specified by the State Government in this behalf, authorised in writing by such person, or, with the permission of the Commissioner, by any other person so authorised.

SECTION 25: Method of recording evidence

The Commissioner shall make a brief memorandum of the substance of the evidence of every witness as the examination of the witness proceeds, and such memorandum shall be written and signed by the Commissioner with his own hand and shall form part of the record:

Provided that, if the Commissioner is prevented from making such memorandum, he shall record the reason of his inability to do so and shall cause such memorandum to be made in writing from his dictation and shall sign the same, and such memorandum shall form a part of the record:

Provided further that the evidence of any medical witness shall be taken down as nearby as may be word for word.

SECTION 25A: Time limit for disposal of cases relating to compensation

The Commissioner shall dispose of the matter relating to compensation under this Act within a period of three months from the date of reference and intimate the decision in respect thereof within the said period to the employee.

SECTION 26: Costs

All costs, incidental to any proceedings before a Commissioner, shall, subject to rules made under this Act, be in the discretion of the Commissioner.

SECTION 27: Power to submit cases

A Commissioner may, if he thinks fit, submit any question of law for the decision of the High Court and, if he does so, shall decide the question in conformity with such decision.

SECTION 28: Registration of agreements

(1) Where the amount of any lump sum payable as compensation has been settled by agreement, whether by way of redemption of a half-monthly payment or otherwise, or where any compensation has been so settled as being payable to a woman or a person under a legal disability a memorandum thereof shall be sent by the employer to the Commissioner, who shall, on being satisfied as to its genuineness, record the memorandum in a register in the prescribed manner:

Provided that—

(a) no such memorandum shall be recorded before seven days after communication by the Commissioner of notice to the parties concerned;
(b) omitted by Act 5 of 1929;
(c) the Commissioner may at any time rectify the register;
(d) where it appears to the Commissioner that an agreement as to the payment of a lump sum whether by way of redemption of a half-monthly payment or otherwise, or an agreement as to the amount of compensation payable to a woman or a person under a legal disability ought not to be registered by reason of the inadequacy of the sum or amount, or by reason of the agreement having been obtained by fraud or undue influence or other improper means, he may refuse to record the memorandum of the agreement and may make such order including an order as to any sum already paid under the agreement, as he thinks just in the circumstances.

(2) An agreement for the payment of compensation which has been registered under sub-section (1) shall be enforceable under this Act notwithstanding anything contained in the Indian Contract Act, 1872 (9 of 1872), or in any other law for the time being in force.

In *Roshan Deen* v. *Preeti Lal,*[20] Roshan Deen, a young man of 25, made a claim on the respondent (who was running a Flour Mill-cum-Sugarcane Factory) for a sum of ₹7 lakhs on the following factual averments: The claimant was a workman of the respondent's industrial establishment. On an ill-fated day in his life, he was operating a machine of the Mill, but in a sudden tweak he got himself snapped in the shaft of a column and was crushed by the fast rotating machine and was ruinously injured. His neck, hands, legs, etc. suffered

20. AIR 2002 SC 33.

multiple injuries including fractures. He was rushed to a private hospital and from there, to the Postgraduate Institute, Chandigarh. An emergency tracheotomy was performed to save his life as the endoscope revealed that his right vocal cord has been paralysed, the trachea and other vessels of the neck were impaired. One of his legs and one of his hands were amputated besides many other impairment suffered by him. Enough it is to say that he did not die of the injuries.

He filed a petition before the Commissioner for Workmen's Compensation, claiming compensation of ₹5 lakhs plus medical expenses of ₹2 lakhs, in accordance with the provisions of the Workmen's Compensation Act, 1923. While the claim petition was pending before the Commissioner for Workmen's Compensation, an application was filed in which it was stated, *inter alia*, that appellant and respondent had entered into an agreement with each other and, hence, the appellant did not want to pursue any claim against the respondent and, on the strength of the said agreement, requested the Commissioner to record the agreement. The application was purportedly signed by the respondent which signature was authenticated by an advocate. But there was no signature of the appellant on the application, instead a thumb impression was seen affixed which was identified by advocate R. Singh. The Commissioner accepted the agreement as genuine and disposed the claim accordingly.

The appellant filed a petition before the Commissioner praying for recalling the above order. He stated in the said petition that his advocate obtained his thumb impression on a certain document the contents of which were not disclosed to him and after paying him ₹9,500, the advocate told him that it was given pursuant to a decision rendered by the Commissioner; and he was asked to go to the office of the advocate again after 15 days. The appellant further stated in the said petition that when he went to the office of the advocate after 15 days, as required by him, the advocate refused to go with the appellant to the Commissioner. When he made enquiries about his case, he came to know of the order passed by the Commissioner. Immediately, he felt that a fraud had been played on him. The Commissioner thereupon passed an order after referring to S. 17 of the Act which declares any agreement (by which a workman relinquishes any right to get compensation from the employer for personal injury) as null and void. The respondent challenged the said order of the Commissioner before the High Court under Art. 227 of the Constitution. Learned single Judge of the High Court, despite his attention being drawn to S. 17 of the Act, went to the extent of observing that no fraud was played on the appellant. The appellant, therefore, approached the Supreme Court by way of special leave petition.

In this context, it is necessary to point out that S. 28 of the Act contains a provision for registration of agreements. Even the said provision shows that an agreement should be for disbursement of the amount "payable as compensation" and if any such agreement is arrived at, the section requires that a memorandum thereof shall be sent by the employer to the Commissioner who shall record the memorandum in a register in the prescribed manner. One of the clauses in the proviso indicates that if it appears to the Commissioner that an agreement ought not to be registered *"by reason of the inadequacy of the sum or amount, or by reason of the agreement having been obtained by fraud or undue influence or other improper means"*, the Commissioner has the power to refuse to record the memorandum of the agreement. Section 29 contains a mandate that if the memorandum of any agreement is not sent to the Commissioner, as required by the preceding section, *"the employer shall be liable to pay the full amount of compensation which he is liable to pay under the provisions of this Act."*

The Supreme Court held that when the appellant requested for recalling the said order that no such agreement had been arrived at, the Commissioner without difficulty noticed that the respondent also submitted to the Commissioner that he did not make any such statement before the Commissioner, the whole deliberations before the Commissioner smack of a fraud of a superlative degree played on the Commissioner. Accordingly, the Court held that the first order of the Commissioner will not be allowed to remain alive even for a moment. It is the byproduct of fraud and cheating. Therefore, it is bound to be set aside and restore the second order passed by the Commissioner. The Court further held:

> "Before disposing of this appeal we deem it necessary to make one more direction which, in our opinion, is required for completion of the even course of justice. The Bar Council of the State of Haryana should hold an inquiry into the allegations made by the petitioner against the Advocate Rajpal Panwar of Jagadhari as to whether he had played a chicanery to defraud the petitioner by obtaining his thumb impression and paying ₹9,500. We restrain ourselves from making any observation on the merits of the allegations made against the aforesaid Advocate. We direct the Registry of this Court to forward a copy of this judgment to the Secretary of the Bar Council of Haryana. This is to enable the said Bar Council to adopt such steps as they deem fit and necessary for disposal of the disciplinary proceedings as against the said Rajpal Panwar, Advocate Jagadhari."[21]

SECTION 29: Effect of failure to register agreement

Where a memorandum of any agreement, the registration of which is required by section 28, is not sent to the Commissioner as required by that section, the employer shall be liable to pay the full amount of compensation which he is liable to pay under the provisions of this Act, and notwithstanding anything contained in the proviso to sub-section (1) of section 4, shall not, unless the Commissioner otherwise directs, be entitled to deduct more than half of any amount paid to the employees by way of compensation whether under the agreement or otherwise.

SECTION 30: Appeals

(1) An appeal shall lie to the High Court from the following orders of a Commissioner, namely:

(a) an order awarding as compensation a lump sum whether by way of redemption of a half-monthly payment or otherwise or disallowing a claim in full or in part for a lump sum;

(aa) an order awarding interest or penalty under section 4A;

(b) an order refusing to allow redemption of a half-monthly payment;

(c) an order providing for the distribution of compensation among the dependants of a deceased employee, or disallowing any claim of a person alleging himself to be such dependant;

21. *Ibid.*, at p. 38 per Thomas, J.

(d) an order allowing or disallowing any claim for the amount of an indemnity under the provisions of sub-section (2) of section 12; or

(e) an order refusing to register a memorandum of agreement or registering the same or providing for the registration of the same subject to conditions:

Provided that no appeal shall lie against any order unless a substantial question of law is involved in the appeal and, in the case of an order other than an order such as is referred to in clause (b) unless the amount in dispute in the appeal is not less than three hundred rupees:

Provided further that no appeal shall lie in any case in which the parties have agreed to abide by the decision of the Commissioner, or in which the order of the Commissioner gives effect to an agreement come to by the parties.

Provided further that no appeal by an employer under clause (a) shall lie unless the memorandum of appeal is accompanied by a certificate by the Commissioner to the effect that the appellant has deposited with him the amount payable under the order appealed against.

(2) The period of limitation for an appeal under this section shall be sixty days.

(3) The provision of section 5 of the Limitation Act, 1963 (36 of 1963) shall be applicable to appeals under this section.

Section 30A: Withholding of certain payments pending decision of appeal

Where an employer makes an appeal under clause (a) of sub-section (1) of section 30, the Commissioner may, and if so directed by the High Court shall, pending the decision of the appeal withhold payment of any sum in deposit with him.

Section 31: Recovery

The Commissioner may recover as an arrear of land revenue any amount payable by any person under this Act, whether under an agreement for the payment of compensation or otherwise, and the Commissioner shall be deemed to be a public officer within the meaning of section 5 of the Revenue Recovery Act, 1890 (1 of 1890).

Chapter IV

RULES

Section 32: Power of the state government to make rules

(1) The State Government may make rules to carry out the purposes of this Act.

(2) In particular and without prejudice to the generality of the foregoing power, such rules may provide for all or any of the following matters, namely:

(a) for prescribing the intervals at which and the conditions subject to which an application for review may be made under section 6 when not accompanied by a medical certificate;

(b) for prescribing the intervals at which and the conditions subject to which an employee may be required to submit himself for medical examination under sub-section (1) of section 11;

(c) for prescribing the procedure to be followed by Commissioners in the disposal of cases under this Act and by the parties in such cases;

(d) for regulating the transfer of matters and cases from one Commissioner to another and the transfer of money in such cases;

(e) for prescribing the manner in which money in the hands of a Commissioner may be invested for the benefit of dependants of a deceased employee and for the transfer of money so invested from one Commissioner to another;

(f) for the representation in proceedings before Commissioners of parties who are minors or are unable to make an appearance;

(g) for prescribing the form and manner in which memoranda of agreements shall be presented and registered;

(h) for the withholding by Commissioners, whether in whole or in part of half-monthly payments pending decision on applications for review of the same;

(i) for regulating the scales of costs which may be allowed in proceedings under this Act;

(j) for prescribing and determining the amount of the fees payable in respect of any proceedings before a Commissioner under this Act;

(k) for the maintenance by Commissioners of registers and records of proceedings before them;

(l) for prescribing the classes of employers who shall maintain notice-books under sub-section (3) of section 10, and the form of such notice-books;

(m) for prescribing the form of statement to be submitted by employers under section 10A;

(n) for prescribing the cases in which the report referred to in section 10B may be sent to an authority other than the Commissioner;

(o) for prescribing abstracts of this Act and requiring the employers to display notices containing such abstracts;

(p) for prescribing the manner in which diseases specified as occupational diseases may be diagnosed;

(q) for prescribing the manner in which diseases may be certified for any of the purposes of this Act;

(r) for prescribing the manner in which, and the standards by which, incapacity may be assessed.

(3) Every rule made under this section shall be laid, as soon as may be after it is made, before the State Legislature.

SECTION 33: Power of local government to make rules

Omitted by the A.O. 1937.

SECTION 34: Publication of rules

(1) The power to make rules conferred by section 32 shall be subject to the condition of the rules being made after previous publication.

(2) The date to be specified in accordance with clause (3) of section 23 of the General Clauses Act, 1897 (10 of 1897), as that after which a draft of rules proposed to be made under section 32 will be taken into consideration, shall not be less than three months from the date on which the draft of the proposed rules was published for general information.

(3) Rules so made shall be published in the Official Gazette and, on such publication, shall have effect as if enacted in this Act.

SECTION 35: Rules to give effect to arrangements with other countries for the transfer of money paid as compensation

(1) The Central Government may, by notification in the Official Gazette, make rules for the transfer to any foreign country of money deposited with a Commissioner under this Act which has been awarded to or may be due to, any person residing or about to reside in such foreign country and for the receipt, distribution and administration in any State of any money deposited under the law relating to employees' compensation in any foreign country, which has been awarded to, or may be due to any person residing or about to reside in any State:

Provided that no sum deposited under this Act in respect of fatal accidents shall be so transferred without the consent of the employer concerned until the Commissioner receiving the sum has passed orders determining its distribution and apportionment under the provisions of sub-sections (4) and (5) of section 8.

(2) Where money deposited with a Commissioner has been so transferred in accordance with the rules made under this section, the provisions elsewhere contained in this Act regarding distribution by the Commissioner of compensation deposited with him shall cease to apply in respect of any such money.

SECTION 36: Rules made by Central Government to be laid before Parliament

Every rule made under this Act by the Central Government shall be laid as soon as may be after it is made before each House of Parliament while it is in session for a total period of thirty days which may be comprised in one session or in two or more successive sessions, and if, before the expiry of the session immediately following the session or the successive sessions aforesaid, both Houses agree in making any modification in the rule or both Houses agree that the rule should not be made, the rule shall thereafter have effect only in such modified form or be of no effect, as the case may be; so however that any such modification or annulment shall be without prejudice to the validity of anything previously done under that rule.

SCHEDULE I

[*See* Sections 2(1) and (4)]

PART I

List of Injuries Deemed to Result in Permanent Total Disablement

Sl. No.	*Description of injury*	*Percentage of loss of earning capacity*
1	Loss of both hands or amputation at higher sites	100
2	Loss of a hand and foot	100
3	Double amputation through leg or thigh, or amputation through leg or thigh on one side and loss of other foot	100
4	Loss of sight to such an extent as to render the claimant unable to perform any work for which eyesight is essential	100
5	Very severe facial disfigurement	100
6	Absolute deafness	100
	PART II **List of Injuries Deemed to Result in Permanent Partial Disablement** **Amputation cases – Upper limbs – Either arm**	
1	Amputation through shoulder joint	90
2	Amputation below shoulder with stump less than 20.32 cm from tip of acromion	80
3	Amputation from 20.32 cm from tip of acromion to less than 4" below tip of olecranon	70
4	Loss of a hand or of the thumb and four fingers of one hand or amputation from 11.43 cm below tip of olecranon	60
5	Loss of thumb	30
6	Loss of thumb and its metacarpal bone	40
7	Loss of four fingers of one hand	50
8	Loss of three fingers of one hand	30
9	Loss of two fingers of one hand	20
10	Loss of terminal phalanx of thumb	20
10A	Guillotine amputation of tip of thumb without loss of bone	10
	Amputation cases – Lower limbs	
11	Amputation of both feet resulting in end bearing stumps	90
12	Amputation through both feet proximal to the metatarso-phalangeal joint	80
13	Loss of all toes of both feet through the metatarso-phalangeal joint	40

Sl. No.	*Description of injury*	*Percentage of loss of earning capacity*
14	Loss of all toes of both feet proximal to the proximal inter-phalangeal joint	30
15	Loss of all toes of both feet distal to the proximal inter-phalangeal joint	20
16	Amputation at hip	90
17	Amputation below hip with stump not exceeding 12.70 cm in length measured from tip of great trenchanter but not beyond middle thigh	80
18	Amputation below hip with stump exceeding 12.70 cm in length measured from tip of great trenchanter but not beyond middle thigh	70
19	Amputation below middle thigh to 8.89 cm below knee	60
20	Amputation below knee with stump exceeding 8.89 cm but not exceeding 12.70 cm	50
21	Amputation below knee with stump exceeding 12.70 cm	50
22	Amputation of one foot resulting in end bearing	50
23	Amputation through on foot proximal to the metatarso-phalangeal joint	50
24	Loss of all toes of one foot through the metatarso-phalangeal joint	20
	Other injuries	
25	Loss of one eye, without complications, the other being normal	40
26	Loss of vision of one eye, without complications or disfigurement of eyeball, the other being normal	30
26A	Loss of partial vision of one eye	10
	Loss of – A – Fingers of right or left hand Index finger	
27	Whole	14
28	Two phalanges	11
29	One phalanx	9
30	Guillotine amputation of tip without loss of bone	5
	Middle finger	
31	Whole	12
32	Two phalanges	9
33	One phalanx	7
34	Guillotine amputation of tip without loss of bone	4
	Ring or little finger	
35	Whole	7
36	Two phalanges	6
37	One phalanx	5

Sl. No.	*Description of injury*	*Percentage of loss of earning capacity*
38	Guillotine amputation of tip without loss of bone	2
	B – Toes of right or left foot great toe	
39	Through metatarso-phalangeal joint	14
40	Part, with some loss of bone	3
	Any other toe	
41	Through metatarso-phalangeal joint	3
42	Part, with some loss of bone	1
	Two toes of one foot, excluding great toe	
43	Through metatarso-phalangeal joint	5
44	Part, with some loss of bone	2
	Three toes of one foot, excluding great toe	
45	Through metatarso-phalangeal joint	6
46	Part, with some loss of bone	6
	Four toes of one foot, excluding great toe	
47	Through metatarso-phalangeal joint	9
48	Part, with some loss of bone	3

Note: Complete and permanent loss of the use of any limb or member referred to in this Schedule shall be deemed to be equivalent to the loss of that limb or member.

SCHEDULE II

[*See* Section 2(1)(dd)]

List of Persons Who, Subject to the Provisions of Section 2(1)(dd), are Included in the Definition of Employees

The following persons are employees within the meaning of section 2(1)(dd) and subject to the provisions of that section, that is to say, any person who is—

(i) employed in railways, in connection with the operation, repair or maintenance of a lift or a vehicle propelled by steam or other mechanical power or by electricity or in connection with the loading or unloading of any such vehicle; or

(ii) employed in any premises wherein or within the precincts whereof a manufacturing process as defined in clause (k) of section 2 of the Factories Act, 1948 (63 of 1948), is being carried on, or in any kind of work whatsoever incidental to or connected with any such manufacturing process or with the article made, whether or not employment in any such work is within such premises or precincts and steam, water or other mechanical power or electrical power is used; or

(iii) employed for the purpose of making, altering, repairing, ornamenting, finishing or otherwise adapting for use, transport or sale of any article or part of an article in any premises.

Explanation: For the purposes of this clause, persons employed outside such premises or precincts but in any work incidental to, or connected with, the work relating to making, altering, repairing, ornamenting, finishing or otherwise adapting for use, transport or sale of any articles or part of an article shall be deemed to be employed within such premises or precincts; or

(iv) employed in the manufacture or handling of explosives in connection with the employer's trade or business; or

(v) employed in any mine as defined in clause (j) of section 2 of the Mines Act, 1952 (35 of 1952), in any mining operation or in any kind of work, incidental to or connected with any mining operation or with the mineral obtained, or in any kind of work whatsoever below ground; or

(vi) employed as the master or as a seaman of—

(a) any ship which is propelled wholly or in part by steam or other mechanical power or by electricity or which is towed or intended to be towed by a ship so propelled; or

(b) omitted;

(c) any sea-going ship not included in sub-clause (a) provided with sufficient area for navigation under sails alone; or

(vii) employed for the purpose of—

(a) loading, unloading, fuelling, constructing, repairing, demolishing, cleaning or painting any ship of which he is not the master or a member of the crew, or handling or transport within the limits of any port subject to the Ports Act, 1908 (15 of 1908) or the Major Port Trusts Act, 1963 (38 of 1963), of goods which have been discharged from or are to be loaded into any vessel; or

(b) warping a ship through the dock; or

(c) mooring and unmooring ships at harbour wall, berths or in pier; or

(d) removing or replacing dry dock caissons when vessels are entering or leaving dry docks; or

(e) the docking or undocking of any vessel during an emergency; or

(f) preparing splicing coir springs and check wires, painting depth marks on lock-sides, removing or replacing fenders whenever necessary, landing of gangways, maintaining life-buoys up to standard or any other maintenance work of a like nature; or

(g) any work on jolly-boats for bringing a ship's line to the wharf; or

(viii) employed in the construction, maintenance, repair or demolition of—

(a) any building which is designed to be or is or has been more than one storey in height above the ground or twelve feet or more from the ground level to the apex of the roof; or

(b) any dam or embankment which is twelve feet or more in height from its lowest to its highest point; or

(c) any road, bridge, tunnel or canal; or

(d) any wharf, quay, sea-wall or other marine work including any moorings of ships; or

(ix) employed in setting up, maintaining, repairing or taking down any telegraph or telephone line or post or any overhead electric line or cable or post or standard or fittings and fixtures for the same; or

(x) employed in the construction, working, repair or demolition of any aerial ropeway, canal, pipeline, or sewer; or

(xi) employed in the service of any fire brigade; or

(xii) employed upon a railway as defined in clause (31) of section 2 and sub-section (1) of section 197 of the Railways Act, 1989 (24 of 1989), either directly or through a sub-contractor, by a person fulfilling a contract with the railway administration; or

(xiii) employed as an inspector, mail guard, sorter or van peon in the Railway Mail Service, or as a telegraphist or as a postal or railway signaller or employed in any occupation ordinarily involving outdoor work in the Indian Posts and Telegraphs Department; or

(xiv) employed in connection with operations for winning natural petroleum or natural gas; or

(xv) employed in any occupation involving blasting operations; or

(xvi) employed in the making of any excavation or explosives have been used, or whose depth from its highest to its lowest point exceeds twelve feet; or

(xvii) employed in the operation of any ferry boat capable of carrying more than ten persons; or

(xviii) employed on any estate which is maintained for the purpose of growing cardamom, cinchona, coffee, rubber or tea; or

(xix) employed in the generating, transforming, transmitting or distribution of electrical energy or in generation or supply of gas; or

(xx) employed in a lighthouse as defined in clause (d) of section 2 of the Indian Lighthouse Act, 1927 (17 of 1927); or

(xxi) employed in producing cinematograph pictures intended for public exhibition or in exhibiting such pictures; or

(xxii) employed in the training, keeping or working of elephants or wild animals; or

(xxiii) employed in the tapping of palm-trees or the felling or logging of trees, or the transport of timber by inland waters, or the control or extinguishing of forest fires; or

(xxiv) employed in operations for the catching or hunting of elephants or other wild animals; or

(xxv) employed as a driver; or

(xxvi) employed in the handling or transport of goods in, or within the precincts of,—

(a) any warehouse or other place in which goods are stored, or

(b) any market; or

(xxvii) employed in any occupation involving the handling and manipulation of radium or X-rays apparatus, or contact with radio-active substances; or

(xxviii) employed in or in connection with the construction, erection, dismantling, operation or maintenance of an aircraft as defined in section 2 of the Indian Aircraft Act, 1934 (22 of 1934); or

(xxix) employed in horticultural operations, forestry, bee-keeping or farming by tractors or other contrivances driven by steam or other mechanical power or by electricity; or

(xxx) employed in the construction, working, repair or maintenance of a tube-well; or

(xxxi) employed in the maintenance, repair or renewal of electric fittings in any building; or

(xxxii) employed in a circus;

(xxxiii) employed as watchman in any factory or establishment; or

(xxxiv) employed in any operation in the sea for catching fish; or

(xxxv) employed in any employment which requires handling of snakes for the purpose of extraction of venom or for the purpose of looking after snakes or handling any other poisonous animal or insect; or

(xxxvi) employed in handling animals like horses, mules and bulls; or

(xxxvii) employed for the purpose of loading or unloading any mechanically propelled vehicle or in the handling or transport of goods which have been loaded in such vehicles; or

(xxxviii) employed in cleaning of sewer lines or septic tanks within the limits of a local authority; or

(xxxix) employed on surveys and investigation, exploration or gauge or discharge observation of rivers including drilling operations, hydrological observations and flood forecasting activities, ground water surveys and exploration; or

(xl) employed in cleaning of jungles or reclaiming land or ponds; or

(xli) employed in cultivation of land or rearing and maintenance of livestock or forest operations or fishing; or

(xlii) employed in installation, maintenance or repair of pumping equipment used for lifting of water from wells, tube wells, ponds, lakes, streams and the like; or

(xliii) employed in the construction, boring or deepening of an open well or dug well, bore well, bore-cum-dug well, filter-point and the like; or

(xliv) employed in spraying and dusting of insecticides or pesticides in agricultural operations or plantations; or

(xlv) employed in mechanised harvesting and threshing operations; or

(xlvi) employed in working or repair or maintenance of bulldozers, tractors, power tillers and the like; or

(xlvii) employed as artist for drawing pictures on advertisement boards at a height of 3.66 metre or more from the ground level; or

(xlviii) employed in any newspaper establishment as defined in the Working Journalists and Other Newspaper Employees (Conditions of Service) and Miscellaneous Provisions Act, 1955 (45 of 1955) and engaged in outdoor work.

(xlvix) employed as divers for work under water.

Explanation: Omitted 2009 Amendment Act w.e.f. 18-01-2010.

Schedule III

(*See* Section 3)

LIST OF OCCUPATIONAL DISEASES

Sl. No. 1	*Occupational disease* 2	*Employment* 3
	PART A	
1.	Infectious and parasitic diseases contracted in an occupation where there is a particular risk of contamination	(a) All work involving exposure to contracted in an occupation health or laboratory work; (b) All work involving exposure to veterinary work; (c) Work relating to handling animals, animal carcasses, part of such carcasses, or merchandise which may have been contaminated by animals or animal carcasses; (d) Other work carrying a particular risk of contamination.
2.	Diseases caused by work in compressed air	All work involving exposure to the risk concerned.
3.	Diseases caused by lead or its toxic compounds	All work involving exposure to the risk concerned.
4.	Poisoning by nitrous fumes	All work involving exposure to the risk concerned.
5.	Poisoning by organo phosphorus compounds	All work involving exposure to the risk concerned.
	PART B	
1.	Diseases caused by phosphorus or its toxic compounds	All work involving exposure to the risk concerned.
2.	Diseases caused by mercury or its toxic compounds	All work involving exposure to the risk concerned.
3.	Diseases caused by benzene or its toxic homologues	All work involving exposure to the risk concerned.
4.	Diseases caused by nitro and amido toxic derivatives of benzine or its homologues	All work involving exposure to the risk concerned.
5.	Diseases caused by chromium, or its toxic compounds	All work involving exposure to the risk concerned.
6.	Diseases caused by arsenic or its toxic compounds	All work involving exposure to the risk concerned.

Sl. No. 1	Occupational disease 2	Employment 3
7.	Diseases caused by radioactive substances or radiations	All work involving exposure to the substances and ionising action of radioactive ionising radiations.
8.	Primary epitheliomatous cancer of the skin caused by tar, pitch, bitumen, mineral oil, anthracene, or the compounds, products or residues of these substances	All work involving exposure to the risk concerned.
9.	Disease caused by the toxic halogen derivatives of hydrocarbons (of the aliphatic and aromatic series)	All work involving exposure to the risk concerned.
10.	Diseases caused by carbon disulphide	All work involving exposure to the risk concerned.
11.	Occupational cataract due to infra-red radiations	All work involving exposure to the risk concerned.
12.	Diseases caused by manganese or its toxic compounds	All work involving exposure to the risk concerned.
13.	Skin diseases caused by physical, chemical or biological agents not included in other items	All work involving exposure to the risk concerned.
14.	Hearing impairment caused by noise	All work involving exposure to the risk concerned.
15.	Poisoning by dinitrophenol or a homologue or by substituted dinitrophenol or by the salts of such substances	All work involving exposure to the risk concerned.
16.	Diseases caused by beryllium or its toxic compounds	All work involving exposure to the risk concerned.
17.	Diseases caused by cadmium or its toxic compounds	All work involving exposure to the risk concerned.
18.	Occupational asthma caused by recognised sensitising agents inherent to the work process	All work involving exposure to the risk concerned.
19.	Diseases caused by fluorine or its toxic compounds	All work involving exposure to the risk concerned.
20.	Diseases caused by nitroglycerine or other nitroacid esters	All work involving exposure to the risk concerned.
21.	Diseases caused by alcohols and ketones	All work involving exposure to the risk concerned.
22.	Diseases caused by asphyxiants: carbon monoxide, and its toxic derivatives, hydrogen sulphide	All work involving exposure to the risk concerned.
23.	Lung cancer and mesotheliomas caused by asbestos	All work involving exposure to the risk concerned.

Sl. No. 1	*Occupational disease* 2	*Employment* 3
24.	Primary neoplasm of the epithelial lining of the urinary bladder or the kidney or the ureter	All work involving exposure to the risk concerned.
25.	Snow blindness in snow bound areas	All work involving exposure to the risk concerned.
26.	Disease due to effect of heat in extreme cold climate	All work involving exposure to the risk concerned.
27.	Disease due to effect of cold in extreme cold climate	All work involving exposure to the risk concerned.
	PART B	
1.	Pneumoconioses caused by sclerogenic mineral dust (silicosis, anthraoosilicosis, asbestosis) and silico-tuberculosis provided that silicosis is an essential factor in causing the resultant incapacity or death.	All work involving exposure to the risk concerned.
2.	Baggassosis	All work involving exposure to the risk concerned.
3.	Bronchopulmonary diseases caused by cotton, flax hemp and sisal dust (Byssinosis)	All work involving exposure to the risk concerned.
4.	Extrinsic allergic alveelitis caused by the inhalation of organic dusts	All work involving exposure to the risk concerned.
5.	Bronchopulmonary diseases caused by hard metals	All work involving exposure to the risk concerned.
6.	Acute Pulmonary Oedema of High Altitude	All work involving exposure to the risk concerned.

SCHEDULE IV

(*See* Section 4)

Factors for Working Out Lump Sum Equivalent of Compensation Amount in Case of Permanent Disablement and Death.

	Completed years of age on the last birthday of the employee immediately preceding the date on which the compensation fell due									*Factors*
Not more than										
16	.	.	.	.	.	.	.	.	.	228.54
17	.	.	.	.	.	.	.	.	.	227.49
18	.	.	.	.	.	.	.	.	.	226.38
19	.	.	.	.	.	.	.	.	.	225.22

	Completed years of age on the last birthday of the employee immediately preceding the date on which the compensation fell due	***Factors***
Not more than		
20		224.00
21		222.71
22		221.37
23		219.95
24		218.47
25		216.91
26		215.28
27		213.57
28		211.79
29		209.92
30		207.98
31		205.95
32		203.85
33		201.66
34		199.40
35		197.06
36		194.64
37		192.14
38		189.56
39		186.90
40		184.17
41		181.37
42		178.49
43		175.54
44		172.52
45		169.44
46		166.29
47		163.07
48		159.80
49		156.47
50		153.09
51		149.67
52		146.20

	Completed years of age on the last birthday of the employee immediately preceding the date on which the compensation fell due									***Factors***
53	.	.	.	.	.	.	.	.	.	142.68
54	.	.	.	.	.	.	.	.	.	139.13
55	.	.	.	.	.	.	.	.	.	135.56
56	.	.	.	.	.	.	.	.	.	131.95
57	.	.	.	.	.	.	.	.	.	128.33
58	.	.	.	.	.	.	.	.	.	124.70
59	.	.	.	.	.	.	.	.	.	121.05
60	.	.	.	.	.	.	.	.	.	117.41
61	.	.	.	.	.	.	.	.	.	113.77
62	.	.	.	.	.	.	.	.	.	110.14
63	.	.	.	.	.	.	.	.	.	106.52
64	.	.	.	.	.	.	.	.	.	102.93
65 or more	.	.	.	.	.	.	.	.	.	99.37

*   *   *

12 The Employees' State Insurance Act, 1948

OBJECT OF THE ACT

The Employees' State Insurance Act (ESI Act) was enacted with the object of introducing a scheme of health insurance for industrial workers. The scheme envisaged by it is one of compulsory State Insurance providing for certain benefits in the event of sickness, maternity and employment injury to workmen employed in or in connection with the work in factories other than seasonal factories. The ESI Act, which has replaced the Workmen's Compensation Act, 1923 in the fields where it is made applicable, is far more wider than the Workmen's Compensation Act and enlarges the scope of compensation. Section 38 provides that all employees in factories or, establishment to which the ESI Act applies shall be insured in the manner provided in it. Under S. 39, the employer is also made liable to pay contribution. Section 42 provides for circumstances under which the employee need not pay his contribution. Section 46 provides for the benefits which the insured persons, their dependants and the persons mentioned therein, shall be entitled to get on happening of the events mentioned therein. Sections 51A to 51D create certain fictions in favour of the employee so as to have wider coverage for him. In case of an employment injury, S. 46 provides periodical payments to him or to his dependants in case of his death. Employment injury is defined by S. 2(8) to mean a personal injury to an employee caused by accident or an occupational disease arising out of and in the course of his employment, being an insurable employment, whether the accident occurs or the occupational disease is contracted within or outside the territorial limits of India. Section 2(9) defines 'employee' to mean any person employed for wages in or in connection with the work of a factory or establishment to which the ESI Act applies. It includes other persons but it is not necessary to refer to that part of the definition. 'Insured person' is defined by S. 2(14) to mean a person who is or was an employee in respect of whom contributions are or were payable under the Act and who is by reason thereof, entitled to any of the benefits provided by the ESI Act. The Second Schedule to the ESI Act specifies the injuries deemed to result in permanent total disablement or permanent partial disablement. Rule 54 of the Employees' State Instance (Central) Rules, 1950 provides the daily rate of benefit which the employee would get if an employment injury is suffered by him. Rule 57 provides for disablement benefits. Rule 58 provides for dependant's benefits in case the injured person dies as a result of an employment injury. Rule 60 provides for the medical benefits to insured person who ceases to be in an insured employment on account of permanent disablement. Other benefits are also conferred by the ESI Act and the Rules made thereunder.[1]

CONSTITUTIONAL VALIDITY OF THE ACT

In *Hindu Jea Band, M/s. Jaipur* v. *Regional Director, Employees' State Insurance Corporation, Jaipur,*[2] S. 1(5) is challenged as unconstitutional because it authorises the State Government to extend all or any of the provisions of the Act to other establishments in the State and thus suffers from the vice of excessive delegation of essential legislative powers. It is also contended that the application of the Act to business, like the one which is being carried on by the petitioner during certain seasons only of the year, is violative of Art. 14, Art. 19(1)(g) and Art. 21 of the Constitution. Having carefully considered the submission made by the learned counsel for the petitioner, the Supreme Court found no merit in any of the contentions urged in the writ petition. The writ petition is, therefore, dismissed.

CHAPTER I

PRELIMINARY

An Act to provide for certain benefits to employees in case of sickness, maternity and "employment injury" and to make provision for certain other matters in relation thereto.

WHEREAS it is expedient to provide for certain benefits to employees in case of sickness, maternity and employment injury and to make provision for certain other matters in relation thereto:

It is hereby enacted as follows:

SECTION 1: Short title, extent, commencement and application

(1) This Act may be called the Employees' State Insurance Act, 1948.

(2) It extends to the whole of India.

(3) It shall come into force on such date or dates as the Central Government may, by notification in the Official Gazette, appoint, and different dates may be appointed for different provisions of this Act and for different States or for different parts thereof.

(4) It shall apply, in the first instance, to all factories including factories belonging to the Government other than seasonal factories:

Provided that nothing contained in this sub-section shall apply to a factory or establishment belonging to or under the control of the Government whose employees are otherwise in receipt of benefits substantially similar or superior to the benefits provided under this Act.

(5) The appropriate Government may, in consultation with the Corporation and where the appropriate Government is a State Government, with the approval of the

1. *A. Trehan* v. *M/s. Associated Electrical Agencies*, AIR 1996 SC 1990.
2. AIR 1987 SC 1166.

Central Government, after giving one month's notice of its intention of so doing by notification in the Official Gazette, extend the provision of this Act or any of them, to any other establishment or class of establishments, industrial, commercial, agriculture or otherwise:

Provided that where the provisions of this Act have been brought into force in any part of a State, the said provisions shall stand extended to any such establishment or class of establishments within that part if the provisions have already been extended to similar establishment or class of establishments in another part of that State.

(6) A factory or an establishment to which this Act applies shall continue to be governed by this Act notwithstanding that the number of persons employed therein at any time falls below the limit specified by or under this Act or the manufacturing process therein ceases to be carried on with the aid of power.

The question raised before the Supreme Court in *Hindu Jea Band, M/s. Jaipur* v. *Regional Director, Employees' State Insurance Corporation, Jaipur*[3] was, whether a firm carrying on the business of playing music on occasions, such as, marriages and other social functions, can be asked to pay the contribution under the provisions of the Employees' State Insurance Act, 1948. A petitioner submitted his views before the Employees' State Insurance Court, Jaipur principally on two grounds: (i) that the place where it was carrying on business was not a shop, and (ii) that its business being one of intermittent or seasonal character, the Act could not be extended to its business.

The Employees' State Insurance Court rejected the petition filed by the petitioner and directed it to pay the amount which had been computed as the arrears by the Regional Director of the Employees' State Insurance Corporation, Jaipur. An appeal filed against the decision of the Employees' State Insurance Court, Jaipur by the petitioner, was dismissed by the High Court of Rajasthan. This petition under Art. 136 of the Constitution is filed against the judgment of the High Court.

It is not disputed that the Act did not apply to shops and such other establishments straightway on the Act coming into force in the State of Rajasthan. But by the notification dt. September 20, 1975 issued under sub-section (5) of S. 1 of the Act, the Government of Rajasthan extended all the provisions of the Act to certain classes of establishments and areas in the State notification. Item 3(iii) in the Schedule to the said notification brought within the purview of the Act shops in which 20 or more persons had been employed for wages on any day of the preceding 12 months and appointed on October 26, 1975, as the date from which the said notification would come into force. The petitioner, as held by the Employees' State Insurance Court, had employed 23 persons on wages during the relevant period. Since the petitioner did not comply with the provisions of the Act the authorities of the Employees' State Insurance Corporation, Jaipur called upon the petitioner to make contributions as required by the Act with effect from October 26, 1975. The petition before the Employees' State Insurance Court was filed by the petitioner on such a demand, being made on it, questioning the validity of the said demand.

The first contention urged in support of the petition is that since the petitioner was not selling any goods in the place of its business but was only engaged in arranging for musical

3. *Ibid.*, f.n. 2.

performances, on occasions such as marriages, etc., its business premises cannot be called a 'shop'. The Supreme Court did not agree with the narrow construction placed by the petitioner on the expression 'shop' which appears in the notification issued under S. 1(5) of the Act, which is a beneficent legislation.

The word 'shop' has not been defined in the Act. A shop is no doubt an establishment (other than a factory) to which the Act can be extended under S. 1(5) of the Act provided other requirements are satisfied. In Collins English Dictionary, the meaning of the word 'shop' is given thus: "(i) a place esp. a small building for the retail sale of goods and services and (ii) a place for the performance of a specified type of work; workshop". It is obvious from the above meaning that a place where services are sold on retail basis is also a shop. It is not disputed that the petitioner has been making available, on payment of the stipulated price, the services of the members of the group of musicians employed by it on wages. Therefore, the Supreme Court held that the place where the petitioner has been carrying on business is a shop to which the Act is applicable by virtue of the notification referred to above. The first contention, therefore, fails.

So far as the second contention is concerned, it was submitted before the Supreme Court that because the services are rendered by the employees engaged by the petitioner intermittently or during marriages, the Act would not be applied. The Court held that the petitioner cannot claim any exemption from the operation of the Act and the petitioner cannot rely on sub-section (4) of S. 1 of the Act which refers to factories only in support of its case. The Court observed that the Court is only concerned in this case with a shop and not a factory as defined under S. 2(12) of the Act. Moreover, the services of the employees of the petitioner are not confined only to marriages. It cannot also be said that marriages take place only during a specified part of the year. Nowadays marriages take place throughout the year. The petitioner provides music at several other social functions also which may take place during all seasons. The definition of an 'employee' under the Act has a wider meaning. The employees who worked outside the business premises but those whose duties are connected with the business are also 'employees' within the meaning of S. 2(9)(i) of the Act.[4] Even those employees who are paid daily wages or those who are part-time employees are employees for the purposes of the Act. Hence the Court did not find any merit in this Special Leave Petition. The petition, therefore, fails and it is dismissed.

In *E.S.I. Corpn.* v. *Hyderabad Race Club*,[5] the question raised before the Supreme Court for consideration was regarding the applicability of the Act in respect to the Hyderabad Race Club. The appellant—Hyderabad Race Club (the Club)—is aggrieved by the finding of the High Court that the club in question was held to be an establishment for the purpose of the Act, whereas its contention before the authorities below including the High Court was that it was not an establishment covered by the Act.

The grievance of the appellant—Employees State Insurance Corporation (the Corporation)—is that the High Court having come to the conclusion that the Hyderabad Race Club is an establishment under the Act erred in reducing its liability and holding that the demand made on the said club for contribution for the period between 1975 and 1986 was

4. See *Nagpur Electric Light and Power Co. Ltd.* v. *Regional Director Employees' State Insurance Corporation*, AIR 1967 SC 1364.
5. AIR 2004 SC 3972.

unreasonable because the law at that time on this point was uncertain. In this appeal, the appellant contends that the same cannot be a ground for exempting an establishment of its statutory liability once it is held that the establishment comes under the purview of the Act.

The Supreme Court, first, considered the case of the club whether it comes within the definition of 'establishment' under the provisions of the Act. It was the contention of the Club that the Club is not an establishment nor a shop within the meaning of Andhra Pradesh Shops and Establishment Act, 1988, hence the notification by which the Act was made applicable to the club was beyond the scope of the Act.

The Supreme Court relied on *M/s. Cochin Shipping Company* v. *E.S.I. Corporation*[6] and *Employees' State Insurance Corporation* v. *R.K. Swamy and others*,[7] and held that the institution like the appellant Club comes within the purview of the Act. So far as the contention of the corporation in their appeal is concerned, the same is confined to the question of limiting the liability of the Club for the period after 1985. It is argued that once the applicability of a statute is declared by a Court of law, the same applies from the date of the said law being brought into force. Hence, in the instant case, by the notification of 1975 the Club was brought within the purview of the Act and therefore, the liability of the Club started from the said date. Therefore, in this background, the High Court erred in exonerating the Club from its liability between the periods 1975 and 1985.

The Supreme Court observed that it is true, as contended by the learned counsel on behalf of the Corporation, that once a Court of law declared the applicability of a statute, the said declaration in the ordinary course should apply from the date the law in question was brought into force, but there could be exception to this principle depending upon the facts of the case. The Supreme Court further observed that it is undisputed that till the judgment of the case of *M/s. Hindu Jea Band, Jaipur* v. *Regional Director, Employees' State Insurance Corporation, Jaipur*,[2] the law in regard to the institutions like a Club coming within the purview of the definition of establishment for the purpose of the Act was nebulous. It was so understood even by the Corporation itself, which is evident from the fact that the action against the appellant for non-compliance of its liability was not taken for nearly 15 years until the visit of the Inspector of the Corporation on 17-6-1990. In that background, even the Corporation was not very certain whether the word establishment used in the notification concerned of 26-3-1975 included a club. Therefore, the Court held that the High Court was justified in coming to the conclusion to call upon the Club to make contribution for a period between 1975 and 1986 would be somewhat unreasonable. Thus, in the peculiar facts of this case, the Apex Court agreed with the finding of the High Court that the demand under the Act as against this Club can be enforced only from the year 1987 onwards.

In *K.R. Anitha* v. *Regional Director, E.S.I. Corpn.*,[8] the question raised before the Supreme Court was, whether the ESI Act would be applied to toddy shops established under the Kerala Abkari Act. The EI Court, after considering facts, respective contentions and referring to the provisions of the Act and the Abkari Act and Rules, concluded that toddy shops were the establishments that belonged to or were under the control of the Department of the Government and that the employees working in those shops were enjoying the benefits

6. (1992) 4 SCC 245.
7. (1994) 1 SCC 445.
8. AIR 2003 SC 3393.

substantially similar to those provided in the cases covered by the ESI Scheme. In this view, the EI Court held that the provisions of the ESI Scheme were not applicable to the employees working in toddy shops of the appellant during the relevant period. The Court also made it clear that since the proviso to S. 1(4) of the Act was added to the statute book only with effect from 20-10-1989, any demand for contribution for the prior period had to be viewed differently. In this view, the EI Court allowed the applications filed by the appellant and granted relief to them. The respondents challenged the validity and correctness of the orders passed by the EI Court by filing miscellaneous first appeals before the High Court. The High Court, after hearing the learned counsel for the parties and considering the respective contentions raised by them, allowed the appeals and set aside the judgment of the EI Court. The appellant moved to the Supreme Court questioning the validity and correctness of the impugned judgment.

The learned senior counsel for the appellants urged that (1) the toddy shops established under the Kerala Abkari Act are not covered by the Act since in a notification issued under S. 1(5) of the Act, they are not specifically included; though Government specifically included hotels and restaurants it intentionally excluded toddy shops while issuing notification in 1974; this exclusion was because the employees attached to a toddy shop are enjoying substantially similar or even superior benefits under the Abkari Welfare Fund Act; hence the High Court was wrong in holding that toddy shops are covered by the Act. (2) Toddy shops were owned and controlled by the State Government and employees of these shops were otherwise receiving benefits substantially similar or superior to the benefits provided under the Act; because of the same, the toddy shops were exempted from the purview of the Act by virtue of proviso to S. 1(4) of the Act; the State is the sole authority to do the business of any intoxicating substance and no citizen has any right to do such business; the appellants being only licensees (known as Abkari contractors) to run Abkari business of the Government, were only immediate employers under the State Government or its Excise Department, who is the principal employer; from various provisions of the Abkari Act, Rules and the licence conditions, it is clear that the authority to run the business is only limited and the main powers are vested with the Government itself. (3) The finding of the High Court that the establishments of the appellants, i.e. toddy shops having been covered by the Act, they shall continue to be governed by virtue of S. 1(6) of the Act even though sub-section (6) of S. 1 of the Act came into force with effect from 20-10-1989 by an amendment is not correct; even assuming that the Act was made applicable as on 20-10-1989 to the then contractors, that itself will not automatically make the Act applicable to the appellants since they contracted to run toddy shops in question for the first time in the year 1991–92.

In deposition, the learned senior counsel for the respondents made submissions supporting the reasons recorded by the High Court to arrive at the conclusions in accepting the plea of the respondents negativing the contentions raised on behalf of the appellants. He specifically pointed out that before the EI Court, as observed by the High Court in the impugned judgment, the appellants did not specifically contend that the toddy shops were not covered by the Act previously; the appellants only contended that the toddy shops functioning in the State are not covered by the Act; it was also not their case that the strength of the employees in toddy shops was less for being covered by the Act.

After careful consideration of the submissions made on either side and looking to the discussion made and reasons recorded by the High Court in the impugned judgment in the light of the facts and circumstances found in these cases, the Apex Court is unable to find fault with the impugned judgment. The Apex Court observed that in order to take shelter under the proviso to sub-section (4) of S. 1 of the Act, the appellants have to satisfy that (1) their establishments belonged to or were under the control of the Government; and (2) the employees in their establishments were otherwise receiving benefits substantially similar or superior to the benefits provided under the Act. The High Court rightly took the view that the toddy shops of the appellants neither belonged to the Government nor were they under the control of the Government. If the first requirement of the proviso itself is not satisfied, it becomes unnecessary to examine as to the satisfaction of second requirement of the proviso. No doubt, the State has the monopoly in liquor trade but it is open to the State to part with that right for a consideration so as to grant privilege of carrying on trade in liquor to the licensees. Under the Abkari Act, the right to run toddy shops is auctioned annually and licences are granted to carry on business in liquor subject to the provisions of the Abkari Act, Rules and conditions of licence. The provisions contained in the Abkari Act and Rules and conditions of licence having regard to the nature of business, namely, dealing with liquor, are regulatory. None of these provisions of the Act, Rules and conditions of licence interfere with a right to carry on business by licensee subject to the regulatory measures contained therein. In the matter of carrying on business and trade of liquor under licences granted to the appellants, it is proved that as to how financially, functionally and administratively the State either dominated or controlled. Looking into the facts of the case and keeping in view the provisions of the Abkari Act and Rules and conditions of licence, the control of the State Government in regard to trade in liquor by the licensees was merely regulatory. The Supreme Court, in the instant case, relied on the tests laid down in judgment of the Constitution Bench of the Apex Court in *Pradeep Kumar Biswas* v. *Indian Institute of Chemical Biology and others*[9] in the context of establishment of belonging to or under the control of the Government found in the proviso to sub-section (4) of S. 1 of the Act. Therefore, the Supreme Court held that the High Court was right in its conclusion that the said proviso did not cover the toddy shops of the appellants and that neither the State Government nor the Excise Department came in the picture of management of the business of the appellants. It is clear from the facts that the State had no participation in terms of finance and there was no Government participation in carrying on the business of liquor by the appellants either functionally or administratively. Thus, the appeals are dismissed.

The question raised before the Supreme Court in *Christian Medical College* v. *Employees' State Insurance Corpn.*[10] for consideration was, whether the equipment maintenance Deptt. of a hospital, which is part of a medical college, maintaining and repairing the equipment in the hospital such as X-ray, ECG and radiation equipment, kidney dialysis, heart and lung machine, operating table equipment, etc. being a 'factory' within the meaning of S. 2(12), would be covered by the ESI Act. The fact of the case reveals that the respondent, ESI Corporation, issued a notice to the appellant, Christian Medical College, stating that the Equipment Maintenance Department fell within the purview of S. 2(12) of the Employees' State Insurance Act, 1948 and that the appellant should comply with the provisions of the Act with retrospective effect. The appellant represented that the ESI Act

9. (2002) 5 SCC 111.
10. AIR 2001 SC 373.

would not apply to the Equipment Maintenance Department, *inter alia,* on the ground that this department was part and parcel of the appellant College. The respondent did not accept this explanation and threatened the appellant with legal action. The appellant filed a petition under S. 75 of the ESI Act before the District Court, Vellore. The District Judge held that the Equipment Maintenance Department was not separate and distinct from the appellant-hospital and that it was just a limb of the hospital. It was held that the Equipment Maintenance Department was not amenable to the provisions of the ESI Act and that the respondent was not entitled to apply the provisions of the ESI Act or to demand any contribution.

Being aggrieved by the decision of the District Judge, the respondent filed an appeal before the High Court. That appeal came to be dismissed. The learned single Judge held that the Equipment Maintenance Department was just a limb of the Medical College and it could not be separated from the main Institution. It was held that the primary and paramount character of the appellant-institution was to teach medicines to the students. It was held that this department was merely maintained for proper functioning of the main institution and it, therefore, could not be considered to be a factory, even assuming that manufacturing process was carried on there. The respondent approached the Supreme Court challenging the decision of the High Court.

The Supreme Court relied on *Andhra University* v. *R.P.F. Commissioner of A.P.*[11] and *Osmania University* v. *Regional Director, E.S.I.C.*,[12] cases where it was held that the ESI Act also applied to the Department of Publication and Press of the Osmania University. Therefore, the Supreme Court in the instant case held that a plain reading of these judgments shows that they are based on the principle that if the Departments are covered by the provisions of the Act, then they cannot be excluded. Thus, the provisions of the ESI Act are applicable to the Equipment Maintenance Department of the appellant.

In 2000, in *Transport Corporation of India* v. *E.S.I.C.*,[13] an important question raised before the Apex Court was, whether the ESI Act would be extended where an establishment having registered head office in one State and branch office in another State.

The establishment in issue in the instant case was the Transport Corporation of India which is a public limited company. Its head office, being a registered office, situated at Secunderabad in the State of Andhra Pradesh, was covered by the provisions of the Employees' State Insurance Act, 1948 by virtue of notification issued by the State of A.P. It was contended that the notification issued by the State of Andhra Pradesh cannot, by itself, cover the branch at Bombay during the relevant time when the State of Maharashtra had not issued any such notification covering road motor transport establishments in the earmarked areas situated in that State. From the factual data on record, it was clear that the branches of the appellant, though spread over different parts of the country, are part and parcel of the main establishment of the company which remains the 'employer' and the employees in different branches remain its 'employees'. There is a complete integrality of working of the employees in different branches and those working in the head office vis-a-vis the single and solitary management being the appellant-Corporation. In view of this admitted position on record, there is no escape from the conclusion that once the appellant Corporation having

11. AIR 1986 SC 463.
12. AIR 1986 SC 466.
13. AIR 2000 SC 238.

its registered head office at Andhra Pradesh is governed by the Act, its branch offices would also automatically get covered by the sweep of the Act by the very same notification.

The plea that if the notification issued by A.P. Government is held to cover branches of the appellant corporation situated in other States then such a notification would have extra territorial operation, which will be beyond the ambit, scope and authority of the Andhra Pradesh Government is more imaginary than real. It is easy to visualise that the Act applies to all factories wherever situated in India. That is the legislative intention. But so far as the other establishments are concerned, the 'appropriate Government' within whose territorial jurisdiction the main establishment is situated, meaning thereby, its head office being registered office is located, will get covered by the sweep of the notification issued by such 'appropriate Government' acting as delegate of the legislative power entrusted by Parliament to it. Once the appropriate Government exercises that power, all the establishments situated within the territories of that State will get covered by such a notification. Their branches within the State, admittedly, will be covered by the sweep of the notification read with the proviso of S. 1(5) of the Act.

So far as the branches situated outside the State are concerned, if the establishment is covered by the notification being situated within the territories of the State and if on facts it is found that such outside branches have functional integrality with the activities of the main establishment and are directly under the control and supervision of the main establishment, it could not be said that such notification issued by the State has any extra territorial operation. It has only territorial operation, meaning thereby, it covers within its sweep all establishments situated within the State and covered by the notification and also automatically covers all the branches situated outside the State which are factually found to be mere appendages and limbs and part and parcel of the very same establishment. The Act seeks to bring in its sweep by notifications issued from time to time by appropriate State Governments all the relevant establishments which are required to be covered by the sweep of the Central Act having all India operation. The contention that such a notification would have extra-territorial operation cannot, therefore, be countenanced. Once the factual data clearly points out that the Bombay branch of the appellant concern was a limb of the appellant concern covered by the Act and all its activities were appertaining to the main objects and purposes of the appellant-Corporation and through this branch the appellant was carrying on its activities on an integrated basis, it must be held that once the appellant was governed by the Act on account of the notification issued by the appropriate Government, namely, the State of Andhra Pradesh under S. 1(5) of the Act, and on which there cannot be any dispute, automatically the said notification took in its sweep all such branches of the appellant situated even outside the State of Andhra Pradesh which were having complete functional integrality with the main activities of the establishment, namely, the appellant concern. In fact, but for the branches and their activities, the appellant cannot effectively discharge its objects and purposes for which it is incorporated.

Furthermore, the Act is a beneficial piece of legislation intended to provide benefits to employees in case of sickness, maternity, employment injury and for certain other matters in relation thereto. It is enacted with a view to ensuring social welfare and for providing safe insurance cover to employees who were likely to suffer from various physical illnesses during the course of their employment. Such a beneficial piece of legislation has to be construed in its correct perspective so as to fructify the legislative intention underlying its enactment. When two views are possible on its applicability to a given set of employees, that view which furthers the legislative intention should be preferred to the one which would frustrate it. The express phraseology of S. 2(9) of the Act defining as 'employee' read with S. 38 of the Act clearly projects the legislative intention of spreading the beneficial network of the Act sufficiently wide for covering all employees working for the main establishment covered by the Act, even though actually stationed at different branches outside the State wherein the head office of the establishment is located. In any case, the said construction can reasonably flow from the aforesaid statutory provisions. If that is so, any other technical or narrower construction, even if permissible, cannot be countenanced, as that would frustrate the legislative intent underlying the enactment of such a beneficial social security scheme. Accordingly, it was held that ESI Act would be extended to the branch office as well, even though its registered head office is situated in one State and branch office in another State.

As the ESI Act may be applied to a shop by way of notification provided in S. 1(5) of the Act, hence the question raised before the Supreme Court in *Southern Agencies, M/s.* v. *A.P. Employees State Insurance Corpn.*[14] was about the meaning of shop and the criteria to constitute an establishment as shop. The Court held that the scope of the expression 'shop' used in the notification issued under the Act acquired an expanded meaning. Where in a premises any economic activity is carried on leading to sale or purchase, that premises will have to be held as a 'shop' for the purpose of the Act, even though there is no actual giving or taking of goods in such premises. If the business carried on in a premises results in having some nexus with the purchase or sale of goods, it is sufficient to be 'shop' for the purpose of the Act.

In the present case, the appellant supervises and controls the sales in all its branch offices and takes share of their income and, therefore, the nature of the activities carried on by the appellant is commercial or economical and would amount to parting with such services for a price through its different outlets. Further, the administrative office and different branches constitute a single entity. The evidence tendered by the General Manager indicated that the branches are responsible and answerable to the appellant; that the head office keeps track of the efficiency of each branch and its profitability; that the head office has control over the branch offices and gets information periodically as to stocks received and goods sold from each branch from time to time; that the business in respect of all branches is carried on with the same funds and there are transfers of employees as well from one branch to another; that a single audit is made by preparing a single statement of accounts including sales in all the branches which are put together. These factors clearly indicate that the administrative office at Rajamundry is nothing but a controlling office to supervise the sales taking place in different branches and thus falls within the definition of expression 'shop'. Accordingly, a consultancy firm engaged in consultancy services to its customers in respect of industrial, technical, marketing and management activities and preparation of project reports by engaging the services of architects engineers and other experts is held to be a shop for the purposes of applicability of the E.S.I. Act.[15]

---

14. AIR 2000 SC 3718.
15. *Kirloskar Consultants Ltd., M/s.* v. *Employees' State Insurance Corporation*, AIR 2000 SC 3720.

In *Employees State Insurance Corporation* v. *R.K. Swamy,*[16] the question raised before the Supreme Court for consideration related to the applicability of the ESI Act to an advertising agency, where a notification was issued under S. 1(5) of the Act by the Government of Maharashtra to extend the provisions of the Act, in consultation with the appellants (the Employees' State Insurance Corporation) and with the approval of the Central Government, after giving 6 months' notice of its intention so to do by a notification in the Official Gazette, to any establishment or classes of establishments, industrial, commercial, agricultural or otherwise. By the said notification, the Act was applied to, *inter alia,* shops. The relevant portion of the notification read thus:

"The following establishments wherein twenty or more employees are employed or were employed for wages on any day of the preceding twelve months, namely:

(i) hotels;
(ii) restaurants;
(iii) shops;
(iv) cinemas, including preview theatres; and
(v) newspapers establishments as defined in section 2(d) of the Working Journalists (Conditions of Service) and Miscellaneous Provisions Act, 1955 (43 of 1955)."

The Supreme Court observed, in the instant case, that clients call on an advertising agency to initiate campaigns for promotion of their products. Advertising campaigns can be conducted in the different media and otherwise. The advertising agency gives advice in this behalf and as to possible expenses. The advertising agency prepares and presents alternative campaigns for the client to choose from. For such purpose it must prepare the necessary art work and the appropriate words to go with it. It employs specialists in these fields. The advertising agency is paid for the service it renders as aforesaid by the client. It also receives commission from the media through whom advertising is done. Anyone who has products to sell may approach an advertising agency. The advertising agency will prepare an advertising campaign for him utilising the services of the experts it employs in this behalf. It sells the campaign to the client and receives the price thereof. Indubitably, the price will depend upon the nature of the campaign, but that does not make any great difference. Essentially, the advertising agency sells its expert services to a client to enable the client to launch an effective advertising campaign of his products. Without straining language, the premises of an advertising agency can, therefore, reasonably be said to be a 'shop', as now understood.

In *Regional Director, Employees' State Insurance Corporation* v. *Ram Chander,*[17] where the respondent, Ram Chander, was the proprietor of M/s. Commercial Tailors, Sojati Gate, Jodhpur. At all material times, he used to run a tailoring shop, where clothes were stitched. The shop employed at the relevant time about 10 or 12 persons as tailors. The number of employees, however, never exceeded 20. The clothes were supplied by the customers and these were stitched according to the different sizes of the customers. Such stitchings were done at the shop of the respondent herein manually by electric iron which was also used in the process of stitching. Finished clothes were also ironed. The Employees State Insurance Court, Rajasthan came to the conclusion as follows:

---

16. AIR 1994 SC 1154.
17. AIR 1988 SC 113.

> *"The applicant is a tailoring shop which has employed more than 20 persons on one occasion and less on other days and makes use of power in the shape of electric press which is used for ironing of stitched clothes for customers. The electric iron is also used during the process of stitching in addition to the ironing of finished clothes."*

The question before the Rajasthan High Court was whether such establishment was covered by the notification dated 20th September, 1975 and came within the mischief of the Act. The answer to that question would depend on the relevant notification being the notification dated 20th of September, 1975 issued under S. 1(5) of the Act. The notification reads as follows:

> *"for wages on any day of the preceding twelve months, and in any part of which a manufacturing process is being carried on with the aid of power or...."*

In order to answer the question whether the establishment of the respondent comes within the mischief of the Act, it is necessary, in view of the facts found as noted before, to determine only whether manufacturing process was carried on with the aid of power. It is manifest that there is use of electric power in the process of stitching. This is a finding of fact that the establishment or the shop employed more than 10 but less than 20 persons. It cannot also be disputed that by stitching commercially different goods are brought into existence. These are known differently, stitched shirt is undoubtedly a different commodity than unstitched cloth. It is so commercially known and treated. If by a process a different entity comes into existence, then it can be said that this was manufactured. The Supreme Court in the instant case relied on the judgment of *Empire Industries Ltd.* v. *Union of India*[18] where the court observed that the manufacture is complete as soon as by the application of one or more processes, the raw material undergoes some change. If a new substance is brought into existence or if a new or different article having a distinctive name, character or use result from particular processes, such process or processes would amount to manufacture. Whether manufacture has resulted by a process or not would depend on the facts and circumstances of the particular case. There is no doubt that the process must bring into existence a new item or a new commodity known differently in the market as such by people who use or deal with that goods. In that process, the ironing of clothes, as has been found, is an essential part and for that power is used. These are facts found and are not disputed. If that is the position, then it comes clearly within the purview of the Act in view of the other facts noted before and the employees are covered by the Act.

SECTION 2: Definitions

In this Act, unless there is anything repugnant in the subject or context,—

(1) **appropriate Government** means, in respect of establishment under the control of the Central Government or a railway administration or a major port or a mine oilfield, the Central Government, and in all other cases, the State Government.

18. AIR 1986 SC 662.

(3) **confinement** means labour resulting in the issue of a living child, or labour after twenty six weeks of pregnancy resulting in the issue of a child whether alive or dead.

(4) **contribution** means the sum of money payable to the Corporation by the principal employer in respect of an employee and includes any amount payable by or on behalf of the employee in accordance with the provisions of this Act.

(6) **Corporation** means the Employees State Insurance Corporation set up under this Act.

(6A) **dependant** means any of the following relatives of a deceased insured person, namely:

(i) a widow, a minor legitimate or adopted son, who has not attained age of 25 years, an unmarried legitimate or adopted daughter;

(ia) a widowed mother;

(ii) if wholly dependent on the earnings of the insured person at the time of his death, a legitimate or adopted son or daughter who has attained the age of twenty five years and is infirm;

(iii) if wholly or in part dependent on the earnings of the insured person at the time of his death,—

(a) a parent other than a widowed mother,

(b) a minor illegitimate son, an unmarried illegitimate daughter or a daughter legitimate or adopted or illegitimate if married and a minor or if widowed and a minor,

(c) a minor brother or an unmarried sister or a widowed sister if a minor,

(d) a widowed daughter-in-law,

(e) a minor child of a pre-deceased son,

(f) a minor child of a pre-deceased daughter where no parent of the child is alive, or

(g) a paternal grand-parent if no parent of the insured person is alive.

(7) **duly appointed** means appointed in accordance with the provisions of this Act or with the rules or regulations made thereunder.

(8) **employment injury** means a personal injury to an employee caused by accident or an occupational disease arising out of and in the course of his employment, being an insurable employment, whether the accident occurs or the occupational disease is contracted within or outside the territorial limits of India;

The definition given to "employment injury" in sub-section (8) of S. 2 envisages a personal injury to an employee caused by an accident or an occupational disease *"arising out of and in the course of his employment."* Therefore, the employee, in order to succeed, will have to prove that the injury that he had suffered arose out of and was in the course of his employment. Both the conditions will have to be fulfilled before he could claim any benefit under the Act. In *Regional Director, E.S.I. Corporation* v. *Francis De Costa,*[19] the accident

19. AIR 1997 SC 432.

took place one kilometre away from the place of employment. Unless it can be said that his employment began as soon as he sets out for the factory from his home, it cannot be said that the injury was caused by an accident *"arising out of ... his employment"*. A road accident may happen anywhere at any time. But such accident cannot be said to have arisen out of employment, unless it can be shown that the employee was doing something incidental to his employment.

By using the words *"arising out of ... his employment"*, the Legislature gave a restrictive meaning to "employment injury". The injury must be of such an extent as can be attributed to an accident or an occupational disease arising out of his employment. "Out of", in this context, must mean 'caused by the employment.' Of course, the phrase "out of" has an exclusive meaning also. If a man is described to be out of his employment, it means he is without a job. The other meaning of the phrase "out of" is "influenced, inspired, or caused by; out of pity; out of respect for him".[20] In the context of S. 2(8), the words *"out of"* indicate that the injury must be caused by an accident which had its origin in the employment. A mere road accident, while an employee is on his way to his place of employment, cannot be said to have its origin in his employment in the factory. The phrase *"out of the employment"* was construed in the case of *South Maitland Railways Pty. Ltd.* v. *James*,[21] where construing the phrase "out of the employment", Starke, J., held "the words *out of* require that the injury had its origin in the employment". Unless an employee can establish that the injury was caused or had its origin in the employment, he cannot succeed in a claim based on S. 2(8) of the Act.

The other words of limitation in sub-section (8) of S. 2 is *"in the course of his employment"*. The dictionary meaning of *"in the course of"* is "during (in the course of time, as time goes by), while doing."[22] The dictionary meaning indicates that the accident must take place within or during the period of employment. If the employee's work shift begins at 4.30 p.m., any accident before that time will not be *"in the course of his employment"*. The journey to the factory may have been undertaken for working at the factory at 4.30 p.m. But this journey was certainly not in course of employment. If "employment" begins from the moment the employee sets out from his house for the factory, then even if the employee stumbles and falls down at the doorstep of his house, the accident will have to be treated as to have taken place in the course of his employment. This interpretation leads to absurdity and has to be avoided.

Construing the meaning of the phrase *"in the course of his employment"*, it was noted by Lord Denning that the meaning of the phrase had gradually been widened over the last 30 years to include doing something which was reasonably incidental to the employee's employment. The test of "reasonably incidental" was applied in a large number of English decisions. But Lord Denning pointed out that in all those cases the workman was at the premises where he or she worked and was injured while on a visit to the canteen or other place for a break. Lord Denning, however, cautioned that the words "reasonably incidental" should be read in that context and should be limited to the cases of that kind. He observed:

> "Take a case where a man is going to or from his place of work on his own bicycle, or in his own car. He might be said to be doing something "reasonably incidental" to

20. *Webster Comprehensive Dictionary*, International Edition, 1984.
21. 67 CLR 496.
22. *The Concise Oxford Dictionary*, New Seventh Edition.

his employment. But if he has an accident on the way, it is well settled that it does not "arise out of and in the course of his employment". Even if his employer provides the transport, so that he is going to work as a passenger in his employer's vehicle (which is surely "reasonably incidental" to his employment), nevertheless, if he is injured in an accident, it does not arise out of and in the course of his employment. It needed a special "deeming" provision in a statute to make it "deemed" to arise out of and in the course of his employment."[23]

The Supreme Court referred the above observation of Lord Denning because the fact of the instant case is seemingly falling within it. In the instant case, a person was going from his home to his place of work. But he suffered injury in an accident on the way. It could not be said that the accident arose out of and in the course of his employment. It was faintly suggested by Mr. Chacko, appearing on behalf of the respondent, that the bicycle was bought by taking a loan from the employer. That, however, is of no relevance. He might have borrowed money from his company or from somewhere else for purchasing the bicycle. But the fact remains that the bicycle belonged to him and not employer. If he meets with an accident while riding his own bicycle on the way to his place of work, it cannot be said that the accident was reasonably incidental to the employment and was in the course of his employment. The deeming provision of S. 51-C, which came into force by way of an amendment effected by Employees' Life Insurance (Amendment) Act of 1966 (Act No. 44 of 1966), enlarged the scope of the phrase *"in the course of employment"* to include travelling as a passenger by the employer's vehicle to or from the place of work. The legal fiction contained in S. 51-C, however, does not come into play in this case because the employee was not travelling as a passenger in any vehicle owned or operated by or on behalf of the employer or by some other person in pursuance of an arrangement made by the employer.

The Court relied on *Saurashtra Salt Manufacturing Co.* v. *Bai Valu Raja,*[24] where the meaning of the words *"in the course of his employment"* appearing in S. 3(1) of the Workmen's Compensation Act, 1923, was examined by the Supreme Court. There, the appellant, a salt manufacturing company, employed workmen both temporary and permanent. The salt works was situated near a creek opposite to the town of Porbandar. The salt works could be reached by at least two ways from the town, one an over-land route nearly 6 to 7 miles long and other via a creek which had to be crossed by a boat. In the evening of 12-6-1952, a boat carrying some of the workmen capsized due to bad weather and overloading. As a result of this, some of the workmen were drowned. One of the questions that came up for consideration was whether the accident had taken place in the course of the employment of the workers. S. Jafer Imam, J., speaking for the Court, held: "As a rule, the employment of a workman does not commence until he has reached the place of employment and does not continue when he has left the place of employment, the journey to and from the place of employment being excluded." After laying down the principle broadly, S. Jafer Imam, J., went on to observe that there might be some reasonable extension in both time and place to this principle. A workman might be regarded as in the course of his employment even though he had not reached or had left his employer's premises in some special cases. The facts and circumstances of each case would have to be examined very carefully in order to determine

23. Quoted in *Regional Director, E.S.I. Corporation* v. *Francis De Costa,* AIR 1997 SC 432 at p. 435.
24. AIR 1958 SC 881.

whether the accident arose out of and in the course of the employment of a workman, keeping in view at all times this theory of notional extension. But, examining the facts of the case, in particular, after noticing the fact that the workman used a boat, which was also used as public ferry for which they had to pay the boatman's dues, the Supreme Court observed:

> "It is well settled that when a workman is on a public road or a public place or on a public transport he is there as any other member of the public and is not there in the course of his employment unless the very nature of his employment makes it necessary for him to be there. A workman is not in the course of his employment from the moment he leaves his home and is on his way to his work. He certainly is in the course of his employment if he reaches the place of work or a point or an area which comes within the theory of notional extension, outside of which the employer is not liable to pay compensation for any accident happening to him."[25]

Basing on the above discussions, the Court observed that in order to succeed, it has to be proved by the employee that (1) there was an accident, (2) the accident had a causal connection with the employment, and (3) the accident must have been occurred in course of employment. Considering the fact of the instant case, the Court held that as the employee was unable to prove that the accident had any causal connection with the work he was doing at the factory and in any event, it was not suffered in the course of employment, hence the appeal was allowed.

(9) **employee** means any person employed for wages in or in connection with the work of a factory or establishment to which this Act applies and—

- (i) who is directly employed by the principal employer on any work of, or incidental or preliminary to or connected with the work of, the factory or establishment, whether such work is done by the employee in the factory or establishment or elsewhere; or
- (ii) who is employed by or through an immediate employer on the premises of the factory or establishment or under the supervision of the principal employer or his agent on work which is ordinarily part of the work of the factory or establishment or which is preliminary to the work carried on in or incidental to the purpose of the factory or establishment; or
- (iii) whose services are temporarily lent or let on hire to the principal employer by the person with whom the person whose services are so lent or let on hire has entered into a contract of service;

and includes any person employed for wages on any work connected with the administration of the factory or establishment or any part, department or branch thereof or with the purchase of raw materials for, or the distribution or sale of the products of, the factory or establishment or any person engaged as an apprentice, not being an apprentice engaged under the Apprentices Act, 1961 (52 of 1961), and include such person engaged as apprentice whose training period is extended to any length of time but does not include—

- (a) any member of the Indian naval, military or air forces; or
- (b) any person so employed whose wages (excluding remuneration for overtime work) exceed such wages as may be prescribed by the Central Government:

25. *Ibid.,* at p. 883 per Jafer Imam, J.

Provided that an employee whose wages (excluding remuneration for overtime work) exceed such wages as may be prescribed by the Central Government at any time after (and not before) the beginning of the contribution period, shall continue to be an employee until the end of that period.

The sole question which falls for determination in *C.E.S.C. Limited* v. *Subhas Chandra Bose*[26] is, whether the right of the principal employer to reject or accept work on completion, on scrutinizing compliance with job requirements, as accomplished by a contractor, the immediate employer, through his employees, is in itself an effective and meaningful "supervision" as envisaged under S. 2(9) of the Employees' State Insurance Act, 1948.

The Supreme Court, after considering the fact of the instant case and *P.M. Patel's* case,[27] held that in whatever manner the word 'employee' under S. 2(9) be construed, liberally or restrictedly, the construction cannot go to the extent of ruling out the function and role of the immediate employer or obliterating the distance between the principal employer and the immediate employer. In some situations he is the cut-off. He is the one who stumbles in the way of direct nexus being established, unless statutorily functioned, between the employee and the principal employer. He is the one who in a given situation is the principal employer to the employee, directly employed under him. If the work by the employee is conducted under the immediate gaze or overseeing of the principal employer, or his agent, subject to other conditions as envisaged being fulfilled, he would be an employee for the purpose of S. 2(9). In the textual sense 'supervision' of the principal employer or his agent is on 'work' at the places envisaged and the word 'work' can neither be construed so broadly to be the final act of acceptance or rejection of work, nor so narrowly so as to be supervision at all times and at each and every step of the work. A harmonious construction alone would help carry out the purpose of the Act, which would mean moderating the two extremes. When the employee is put to work under the eye and gaze of the principal employer, or his agent, where he can be watched secretly, accidentally, or occasionally, while the work is in progress, so as to scrutinise the quality thereof and to detect faults therein, as also put to timely remedial measures by directions given, finally leading to the satisfactory completion and acceptance of the work, that would be supervision for the purposes of S. 2(9). It is the consistency of vigil, the proverbial 'a stitch in time saves nine'. The standards of vigil would of course depend on the facts of each case. Now this function, the principal employer, no doubt, can delegate to his agent who in the eye of law is his second-self, i.e. a substitute of the principal employer.

(10) **exempted employee** means an employee who is not liable under this Act to pay the employees' contribution.

(11) **family** means all or any of the following relatives of an insured person, namely:

(i) a spouse;

(ii) a minor legitimate or adopted child dependent upon the insured person;

(iii) a child who is wholly dependent on the earnings of the insured person and who is

(a) receiving education, till he or she attains the age of twenty-one years,

(b) an unmarried daughter;

---

26. AIR 1992 SC 573.
27. *P.M. Patel and Sons, M/s.* v. *Union of India*, AIR 1987 SC 447.

(iv) a child who is infirm by reason of any physical or mental abnormality or injury and is wholly dependent on the earnings of the insured person, so long as the infirmity continues;

(v) dependant parents, whose income from all sources does not exceed such income as may be prescribed by the Central Government;

(vi) in case the insured person is unmarried and his or her parents are not alive, a minor brother or sister wholly dependant upon the earnings of the insured person;

(12) **factory** means any premises including the precincts thereof—

(a) whereon ten or more persons are employed or were employed for wages on any day of the preceding twelve months, and in any part of which a manufacturing process is being carried on with the aid of power or is ordinarily so carried on, or

(b) whereon twenty or more persons are employed or were employed for wages on any day of the preceding twelve months, and in any part of which a manufacturing process is being carried on without the aid of power or is ordinarily so carried on,

but does not include a mine subject to the operation of the Mines Act, 1952 (35 of 1952) or a railway running shed.

(13) **immediate employer** in relation to employees employed by or through him, means a person who has undertaken the execution, on the premises of factory or an establishment to which this Act applies or under the supervision of the principal employer or his agent, of the whole or any part of any work which is ordinarily part of the work of the factory or establishment of the principal employer or is preliminary to the work carried on in, or incidental to the purpose of, any such factory or establishment, and includes a person by whom the services of an employee who has entered into a contract of service with him are temporarily lent or let on hire to the principal employer and includes a contractor.

(13A) **insurable employment** means an employment in a factory or establishment to which this Act applies.

(14) **insured person** means a person who is or was an employee in respect of whom contributions are or were payable under this Act and who is, by reason thereof, entitled to any of the benefits provided by this Act.

(14A) **managing agent** means any person appointed or acting as the representative of another person for the purpose of carrying on such other person's trade or business, but does not include an individual manager subordinate to an employer.

(14AA) **manufacturing process** shall have the meaning assigned to it in the Factories Act, 1948 (63 of 1948).

(14B) **mis-carriage** means expulsion of the contents of a pregnant uterus at any period prior to or during the twenty-sixth week of pregnancy but does not include any miscarriage, the causing of which is punishable under the Indian Penal Code (45 of 1860).

(15) **occupier** of the factory shall have the meaning assigned to it in the Factories Act, 1948 (63 of 1948).

(15A) **permanent partial disablement** means such disablement of a permanent nature, as reduces the earning capacity of an employee in every employment which he was capable of undertaking at the time of the accident resulting in the disablement:

Provided that every injury specified in Part II of the Second Schedule shall be deemed to result in permanent partial disablement.

(15B) **permanent total disablement** means such disablement of a permanent nature as incapacitates an employee for all work which he was capable of performing at the time of the accident resulting in such disablement:

Provided that permanent total disablement shall be deemed to result from every injury specified in Part I of the Second Schedule or from any combination of injuries specified in Part II thereof where the aggregate percentage of the loss of earning capacity, as specified in the said Part II against those injuries, amounts to one hundred per cent or more.

(15C) **power** shall have the meaning assigned to it in the Factories Act, 1948 (63 of 1948).

(16) **prescribed** means prescribed by rules made under this Act.

(17) **principal employer** means—

(i) in a factory, the owner or occupier of the factory and includes the managing agent of such owner or occupier, the legal representative of a deceased owner or occupier, and where a person has been named as the manager of the factory under the Factories Act, 1948 (63 of 1948), the person so named;

(ii) in any establishment under the control of any department of any Government in India, the authority appointed by such Government in this behalf or where no authority is so appointed, the head of the department;

(iii) in any other establishment, any person responsible for the supervision and control of the establishment.

It would thus be seen, after reading S. 2(17) of the ESI Act, that the principal employer is the exclusive owner or occupier of the factory and includes the managing agent or the owner or occupier, or whereas a person has been named as the manager of the factory under the Factories Act, the person so named or any other person responsible for the supervision and control of the establishment etc., is the principal employer. Having established the regional offices at the respective places, the person who keeps control or is responsible for the supervision of the establishment at the respective regional officers in connection with factory whose finished products are distributed or sold, would be the 'principal employer' for the purpose of the Act.[28]

(18) **regulation** means a regulation made by the Corporation.

(19) **Schedule** means a Schedule to this Act.

(19A) **seasonal factory** means a factory which is exclusively engaged in one or more of the following manufacturing processes, namely, cotton ginning, cotton or jute

28. *Kirloskar Brothers Ltd.* v. *Employee's State Insurance Corpn.*, AIR 1996 SC 3261.

pressing, decortications of ground-nuts, the manufacture of coffee, indigo, lac, rubber, sugar (including gur) or tea or any manufacturing process which is incidental to or connected with any of the aforesaid processes and includes a factory which is engaged for a period not exceeding seven months in a year—

(a) in any process of blending, packing or repacking of tea or coffee; or

(b) in such other manufacturing process as the Central Government may, by notification in the Official Gazette, specify.

In *Regl. Director, ESIC* v. *High Land Coffee Works of PFX Saldanha and Sons,*[29] the factories of the respondents were excluded from the operation of the Act since they were declared to be the seasonal factories. In the light of S. 1(4), seasonal factories are excluded from the purview of the Act. By Amending Act 44 of 1966, which came into force with effect from 28th January 1968, the definition of "seasonal factory" has been amended. After the said amendment, the Employees' State Insurance Corporation called upon the respondents to pay the contributions payable under the Act and threatened to take coercive steps to recover the arrears under the Revenue Recovery Act and prosecute them. Challenging the validity of the demand made, the respondents approached the Employees Insurance Court, *inter alia*, contending that the amendment to the definition of the expression *"seasonal factory"* brought out by the Amending Act 44 of 1966 has not altered the position of the seasonal factory as obtained prior to the amendment and S. 1(4) of the Act would still continue to exclude such factory from the operation of the Act. The Employees' Insurance Court accepted the respondent's plea. The Karnataka High Court has also agreed with the view taken by the Employees' Insurance Court. The Corporation has now approached the Supreme Court.

The sole question for consideration is whether the respondents' factories in view of the amendment to the definition of 'seasonal factory' have lost the benefit of exclusion from the Act. The High Court on this aspect has observed that the purpose of the amendment was to enlarge and not to restrict the statutory concept of 'seasonal factory' and the position of respondents establishments as seasonal factories under and for the purpose of the Act remained unaltered even after the amendment. The view taken by the High Court seems to be justified. The Statement of Objects and Reasons of the Bill which later became the Act 44 of 1966 indicates that the proposed amendment was to bring within the scope of the definition of 'seasonal factory' a factory which works for a period not exceeding seven months in a year (a) in any process of blending, packing or repacking of tea or coffee; or (b) in such other manufacturing process as the Central Government may, by notification in the Official Gazette, specify. The amendment, therefore, was clearly in favour of the widening the definition of 'seasonal factory'. The amendment is in the nature of expansion of the original definition as it is clear from the use of the words *'include a factory'*. The amendment does not restrict the original definition of "seasonal factory" but makes addition thereto by inclusion. The Court relied on its earlier decisions in order to give proper meaning to the word "include" and accordingly held that the word *'include'* in the statutory definition is generally used to enlarge the meaning of the preceding words and it is by way of extension, and not with restriction. The word *'include'* is very generally used in interpretation clauses in order to

29. AIR 1992 SC 129.

enlarge the meaning of words or phrases occurring in the body of the statute; and when it is so used, these words or phrases must be construed as comprehending, not only such things as they signify according to their natural import but also those things which the interpretation clause declares that they shall include.[30] Therefore, the Apex Court held that in view of these well-accepted statutory constructions, the decision of the High Court does not call for interference.

(20) **sickness** means a condition which requires medical treatment and attendance and necessitates abstention from work on medical grounds.

(21) **temporary disablement** means a condition resulting from an employment injury which requires medical treatment and renders an employee, as a result of such injury, temporarily incapable of doing the work which he was doing prior to or at the time of the injury.

(22) **wages** means all remuneration paid or payable, in cash to an employee, if the terms of the contract of employment, express or implied, were fulfilled and includes any payment to an employee in respect of any period of authorised leave, lock out, strike which is not illegal or lay-off and other additional remuneration, if any, paid at intervals not exceeding two months, but does not include—

(a) any contribution paid by the employer to any pension fund or provident fund, or under this Act;

(b) any travelling allowance or the value of any travelling concession;

(c) any sum paid to the person employed to defray special expenses entailed on him by the nature of his employment; or

(d) any gratuity payable on discharge.

The main body of the definition encompasses within its fold three kinds of payments made to the employees. The first is, all remuneration paid or payable in cash on fulfilment of the terms of employment. The second is, any payment made to an employee in respect of any period of authorised leave, etc. The third is other additional remuneration paid at intervals "not exceeding two months." The word 'other' appearing at the commencement of the third part of the definition of wages under S. 2(22) indicates that it must be remuneration or additional remuneration other than the remuneration which is referred to in the earlier part of the definition, viz., all remuneration paid or payable, in cash to an employee, if the terms of the contract of employment, express or implied, were fulfilled. It must be emphasised at this stage that under the third part of the definition of "wages" it is actual factum of payment which counts because the word used is 'paid' as distinguished from 'paid' or payable. The moment you get any additional remuneration other than the remuneration payable under the contract of employment and if this additional remuneration is paid at intervals not exceeding two months, it becomes "wages" by virtue of the third part of the definition of "wages."[31]

The definition of 'wages' under S. 2(22) is a more comprehensive definition which takes in its sweep, in the first part, all remuneration paid or payable to the employee. Therefore,

30. See: *C.I.T. Andhra Pradesh* v. *M/s. Taj Mahal Hotel, Secunderabad*, AIR 1972 SC 168; *State of Bombay* v. *The Hospital Mazdoor Sabha*, AIR 1960 SC 610.

31. *Handloom House, Ernakulam* v. *Regional Director, ESI*, AIR 1999 SC 1697.

the amount payable to an employee or actually paid to an employee if the terms of the contract of employment were fulfilled would constitute wage. A regular employee who is willing to work and whose services are taken by the employer gets the remuneration for the work actually done by him under the contract of employment. But in case of a suspended employee, he gets lesser amount by way of subsistence allowance but that is also as a remuneration for being continued on the roll of employment as an employee, and so far as he is concerned, he cannot be said to have not fulfilled his part of the terms of contract of employment as he is willing to offer his services, but it is the employer who prohibits him from actually giving his services under the contract of employment. The situation almost resembles to grant of half pay leave or leave on even more than half pay as the case may be. Therefore, it cannot be said that the suspended employee does not fulfill his part of the contract of employment or commits breach of any of the terms of the contract of employment. The prohibition, if any, is imposed by the employer against him and that prohibition in the absence of any rules and regulations governing the payment of remuneration during suspension to the employee concerned would have entitled the suspended employee to get the full remuneration because he was ready and willing to perform his part of the contract of employment, but it was the employer who prohibited him from performing his duties. But if there is a valid service regulation which reduces the scale of remuneration, during suspension, the employee gets that reduced permissible scale of remuneration by way of subsistence allowance. All the same, it cannot be said that it is not the remuneration paid to him though at a reduced rate. Subsistence allowance paid to a suspended employee, therefore, forms part of wages as per sub-section (22) of S. 2 of the Act and consequently, on the said amount the employee will be liable to contribute under S. 39 by way of employee's contribution and equally the employer would be liable to contribute his share by way of employer's contribution.[32]

The question for decision that came for consideration before the Supreme Court in *Whirlpool of India Ltd., M/s.* v. *Employees' State Insurance Corporation,*[33] is whether payments towards production incentive made by the appellant to its workers under the 'Production Incentive Scheme' falls within the scope and ambit of 'wages' as defined in S. 2(22) of the Act and also the effect of payments being made quarterly, i.e. at intervals exceeding two months.

Under the first part of the definition of 'wages' provided in S. 2(22), all the remune-ration paid or payable in cash to an employee, if the terms of the contract of employment, express or implied, were fulfilled would be 'wages'. Under this part, neither the actual payment not when the payment is made is of any relevance. The last part of S. 2(22) relates to payment of additional remuneration. The additional remuneration, if any, paid at intervals not exceeding two months and not falling in Cls. (a) to (d) would also be wages within the meaning of the term as defined. Under this part of the definition, there has to be payment and not only payability and the payment has to be at intervals not exceeding two months.

The High Court, while coming to the conclusion that the payment of production incentive to its workers by the appellant is 'wages' within the meaning of the Act, has relied

32. *Regional Director, Employees' State Insurance Corporation* v. *M/s. Popular Automobiles,* AIR 1997 SC 3956.
33. AIR 2000 SC 1190.

upon the decision of this Court in *Wellman (India) Pvt. Ltd.* v. *Employees' State Insurance Corporation,*[34] and *Modella Woollens Ltd.* v. *Employees' State Insurance Corporation.*[35] *Wellman's* case deals with the attendance bonus payable to the employees under the terms of settlement which became part of contract of employment and was thus held to be remuneration payable under the contract of employment that fell under the first part of the definition. In this case, it was held that the expression 'if any paid' after the words 'other additional remuneration' will be inconsistent if the remuneration is payable under the contract of employment, since such payment is not dependent on the will of the employer but on the fulfillment of the terms of the contract. Every remuneration payable under the contract would fall under the first part of the definition. The payment in *Wellman's* case fell within the first part of the definition of 'wages'. In *Modella Woollens'* case also, the payment of production bonus to the employees, though made at the end of each quarter, was held to be wages as the amount was payable under the agreement. Thus this case too was concerned with the first part of the definition of wages.

The Supreme Court, in the instant case, held that none of the aforesaid decisions has any applicability to the facts of the present case. The Supreme Court observed that the additional remuneration to become wages has to be 'paid' at intervals not exceeding two months as distinguished from 'being payable'. Thus, under the last part, there has to be actual payment. The High Court has found that the payment was made quarterly. The Apex Court has realized that there may be a possibility of misuse by employers by making the payment at a period exceeding two months and thus circumventing the provisions of the Act. However, the Court held when the word used in the last part of the S. 2(22) is 'paid', no further word can be used like 'payable' or other similar expression thereto. Therefore, the Court held that the payment of production incentive, on the facts of the present case, does not fall either under the first part or last part of the definition of the term 'wages' as defined in S. 2(22) of the Act.

The Employees' State Insurance Act is a welfare legislation and the definition of 'wages' is designedly wide. Any ambiguous expression is, of course, bound to receive a beneficent construction at our hands too. Now, under the definition, first, whatever remuneration is paid or payable to an employee under the terms of the contract of the employment, express or implied is wages; thus if remuneration is paid in terms of the original contract of employment or in terms of a settlement arrived at between the employer and the employees which by necessary implication becomes part of the contract of employment, it is wages; second, whatever payment is made to an employee in respect of any period of authorised leave, lock-out, strike which is not illegal or lay-off is wages; and third, other additional remuneration, if any, paid at intervals not exceeding two months is also wages. This is unqualified by any requirement that it should be pursuant to any term of the contract of employment, express or implied. However, 'wages' does not include any contribution paid by the employer to any pension fund or provident fund under the Act, any travelling allowance or the value of any travelling concession, any sum paid to the person employed to defray special expenses entailed on him by the nature of his employment and any gratuity payable on discharge. In *Harihar Polyfibers, M/s.* v. *Regional Director, E.S.I. Corporation,*[36]

34. AIR 1994 SC 1037.
35. 1994 Supp (3) SCC 580.
36. AIR 1984 SC 1680.

the Supreme Court held that wages as defined include remuneration paid or payable under the terms of the contract of employment, express or implied but further extends to other additional remuneration, if any, paid at intervals not exceeding two months, though outside the terms of employment. Thus, remuneration paid under the terms of the contract of the employment (express or implied) or otherwise if paid at intervals not exceeding two months is wages. The interposition of the clause 'and includes any payment to an employee in respect of any period of authorised leave, lock-out, strike which is not illegal or layoff' between the first clause, 'all remuneration paid or payable in cash to an employee, if the terms of the contract of employment, express or implied, was fulfilled' and the third clause, 'other additional remuneration, if any, paid at intervals not exceeding two months', makes it abundantly clear that while 'remuneration' under the first clause has to be under a contract of employment, express, or implied, 'remuneration' under the third clause need not be under the contract of employment, but may be any 'additional remuneration' outside the contract of employment. So, the Supreme Court observed that there is no reason to exclude 'house rent allowance', 'night shift allowance', incentive allowance and 'heat, gas and dust allowance' from the definition of 'wages'.

(23) **wage period** in relation to an employee means the period in respect of which wages are ordinarily payable to him whether in terms of the contract of employment, express or implied or otherwise;

(24) all other words and expressions used but not defined in this Act and defined in the Industrial Disputes Act, 1947 (14 of 1947), shall have the meanings respectively assigned to them in that Act.

Section 2A: Registration of factories and establishments

Every factory or establishment to which this Act applies shall be registered within such time and in such manner as may be specified in the regulations made in this behalf.

Chapter II

CORPORATION, STANDING COMMITTEE AND MEDICAL BENEFIT COUNCIL

Section 3: Establishment of Employees' State Insurance Corporation

(1) With effect from such date as the Central Government may, by notification in the Official Gazette, appoint in this behalf, there shall be established for the administration of the scheme of Employees' State Insurance in accordance with the provisions of this Act a Corporation to be known as the Employees' State Insurance Corporation.

(2) The Corporation shall be a body corporate by the name of Employees' State Insurance Corporation having perpetual succession and a common seal and shall by the said name sue and be sued.

SECTION 4: Constitution of Corporation

The Corporation shall consist of the following members, namely:

(a) a Chairman to be appointed by the Central Government;

(b) a Vice-Chairman to be appointed by the Central Government;

(c) not more than five persons to be appointed by the Central Government;

(d) one person each representing each of the States in which this Act is in force to be appointed by the State Government concerned;

(e) one person to be appointed by the Central Government to represent the Union territories;

(f) ten persons representing employers to be appointed by the Central Government in consultation with such organisations of employers as may be recognised for the purpose by the Central Government;

(g) ten persons representing employees to be appointed by the Central Government in consultation with such organisations of employees as may be recognised for the purpose by the Central Government;

(h) two persons representing the medical profession to be appointed by the Central Government in consultation with such organisations of medical practitioners as may be recognised for the purpose by the Central Government;

(i) three members of Parliament of whom two shall be members of the House of the People (Lok Sabha) and one shall be a member of the Council of States (Rajya Sabha) elected respectively by the members of the House of the people and the members of the Council of States; and

(j) the Director General of the Corporation, *ex officio*.

SECTION 5: Term of office of members of the Corporation

(1) Save as otherwise expressly provided in this Act, the term of office of members of the Corporation, other than the members referred to in clauses (a), (b), (c), (d) and (e) of section 4 and the *ex officio* member, shall be four years commencing from the date on which their appointment or election is notified:

Provided that a member of the corporation shall, notwithstanding the expiry of the said period of four years, continue to hold office until the appointment or election of his successor is notified.

(2) The members of the Corporation referred to in clauses (a), (b), (c), (d) and (e) of section 4 shall hold office during the pleasure of the Government appointing them.

Section 6: Eligibility for re-nomination or re-election

An outgoing member of the Corporation, the Standing Committee, or the Medical Benefit Council shall be eligible for reappointment or re-election as the cases may be.

Section 7: Authentication of orders, decisions, etc.

All orders and decisions of the Corporation shall be authenticated by the signature of the Director General of the Corporation and all other instruments issued by the Corporation shall be authenticated by the signature of the Director General or such other officer of the Corporation as may be authorised by him.

Section 8: Constitution of Standing Committee

A Standing Committee of the Corporation shall be constituted from among its members, consisting of—

(a) a Chairman, nominated by the Central Government;

(b) three members of the Corporation, appointed by the Central Government;

(bb) three members of the Corporation representing such three State Governments thereon as the Central Government may, by notification in the Official Gazette, specify from time to time;

(c) eight members elected by the Corporation as follows:

(i) Omitted

(ii) three members from among the members of the Corporation representing employers;

(iii) three members from among the members of the Corporation representing employees;

(iv) one member from among the members of the Corporation representing the medical profession; and

(v) one member from among the members of the Corporation elected by Parliament;

(d) the Director General of the Corporation, *ex officio*.

Section 9: Term of office of members of Standing Committee

(1) Save as otherwise expressly provided in this Act, the term of office of a member of the Standing Committee, other than a member referred to in clause (a) or clause (b) or clause (bb) of section 8, shall be two years from the date on which his election is notified:

Provided that a member of the Standing Committee, shall, notwithstanding the expiry of the said period of two years, continue to hold office until the election of his successor is notified:

Provided further that a member of the Standing Committee shall cease to hold office when he ceases to be a member of the Corporation.

(2) A member of the Standing Committee referred to in clause (a) or clause (b) or clause (bb) of section 8 shall hold office during the pleasure of the Central Government.

Section 10: Medical Benefit Council

(1) The Central Government shall constitute a Medical Benefit Council consisting of—

(a) the Director General, Employee's State Insurance Corporation, ex officio as chairman;

(b) the Director-General, Health Services, ex officio as Co-chairman;

(c) the Medical Commissioner of the Corporation, *ex officio*;

(d) one member each representing each of the States (other than Union territories) in which this Act is in force to be appointed by the State Government concerned;

(e) three members representing employers to be appointed by the Central Government in consultation with such organisations of employers as may be recognised for the purpose by the Central Government;

(f) three members representing employees to be appointed by the Central Government in consultation with such organisations of employees as may be recognised for the purpose by the Central Government; and

(g) three members, of whom not less than one shall be a woman, representing the medical profession, to be appointed by the Central Government in consultation with such organisations of medical practitioners as may be recognised for the purpose by the Central Government.

(2) Save as otherwise expressly provided in this Act, the term of office of a member of the Medical Benefit Council, other than a member referred to in any of the clause (a) to (d) of sub-section (1), shall be four years from the date on which his appointment is notified:

Provided that a member of the Medical Benefit Council shall, notwithstanding the expiry of the said period of four years continue to hold office until the appointment of his successor is notified.

(3) A member of the Medical Benefit Council referred to in clauses (b) and (d) of sub-section (1) shall hold office during the pleasure of the Government appointing him.

Section 11: Resignation of membership

A member of the Corporation, the Standing Committee or the Medical Benefit Council may resign his office by notice in writing to the Central Government and his seat shall fall vacant on the acceptance of the resignation by that Government.

Section 12: Cessation of membership

(1) A member of the Corporation, the Standing Committee or the Medical Benefit Council shall cease to be a member of that body if he fails to attend three consecutive meetings thereof:

Provided that the Corporation, the Standing Committee or the Medical Benefit Council, as the case may be, may, subject to rules made by the Central Government in this behalf, restore him to membership.

(2) Where in the opinion of the Central Government any person appointed or elected to represent employers, employees or the medical profession on the Corporation, the Standing Committee or the Medical Benefit Council, as the case may be, has ceased to represent such employers, employees or the medical profession, the Central Government may, by notification in the Official Gazette, declare that with effect from such date as may be specified therein such person shall cease to be a member of the Corporation, the Standing Committee or the Medical Benefit Council, as the case may be.

(3) A person referred to in clause (i) of section 4 shall cease to be a member on becoming a Minister or Speaker or Deputy Speaker of the House of the people or the Deputy Chairman of the Council of States or when he ceases to be a member of Parliament.

SECTION 13: Disqualification

A person shall be disqualified for being chosen as or for being a member of the Corporation, the Standing Committee or the Medical Benefit Council—

(a) if he is declared to be of unsound mind by a competent Court; or

(b) if he is an undischarged insolvent; or

(c) if he has directly or indirectly by himself or by his partner any interest in a subsisting contract with, or any work being done for, the Corporation except as a medical practitioner or as a shareholder (not being a Director) of a company; or

(d) if before or after the commencement of this Act, he has been convicted of an offence involving moral turpitude.

SECTION 14: Filling of vacancies

(1) Vacancies in the office of appointed or elected members of the Corporation, the Standing Committee and the Medical Benefit Council shall be filled by appointment or election, as the case may be.

(2) A member of the Corporation, the Standing Committee or the Medical Benefit Council appointed or elected to fill a casual vacancy shall hold office only so long as the member in whose place he is appointed or elected would have been entitled to hold office if the vacancy had not occurred.

SECTION 15: Fees and allowances

Members of the Corporation, the Standing Committee and the Medical Benefit Council shall receive such fees and allowances as may from time to time be prescribed by the Central Government.

SECTION 16: Principal officers

(1) The Central Government may, in consultation with the Corporation, appoint a Director General and a Financial Commissioner.

(2) The Director General shall be the Chief Executive Officer of the Corporation.

(3) The Director General and the Financial Commissioner shall be whole time officers of the Corporation and shall not undertake any work unconnected with their office without the sanction of the Central Government and of the Corporation.

(4) The Director General or the Financial Commissioner shall hold office for such period, not exceeding five years, as may be specified in the order appointing him. An outgoing Director General or the Financial Commissioner shall be eligible for reappointment if he is otherwise qualified.

(5) The Director General or the Financial Commissioner shall receive such salary and allowances as may be prescribed by the Central Government.

(6) A person shall be disqualified from being appointed as or for being the Director General or the Financial Commissioner if he is subject to any of the disqualification specified in section 13.

(7) The Central Government may at any time remove the Director General or the Financial Commissioner from office and shall do so if such removal is recommended by a resolution of the Corporation passed at a special meeting called for the purpose and supported by the votes of not less than two-thirds of the total strength of the Corporation.

SECTION 17: Staff

(1) The Corporation may employ such other staff of officers and servants as may be necessary for the efficient transaction of its business, provided that the sanction of the Central Government shall be obtained for the creation of any post the maximum monthly salary of which exceeds such salary as may be prescribed by the Central Government.

(2) (a) The method of recruitment, salary and allowances, discipline and other conditions of service of the members of the staff of the Corporation shall be such as may be specified in the regulations made by the Corporation in accordance with the rules and orders applicable to the officers and employees of the Central Government drawing corresponding scales of pay:

Provided that where the Corporation is of the opinion that it is necessary to make a departure from the said rules or orders in respect of any of the matters aforesaid, it shall obtain the prior approval of the Central Government.

Provided further that this sub-section shall not apply to appointment of consultants and specialists in various fields appointed on contract basis.

(b) In determining the corresponding scales of pay of the members of the staff under clause (a), the Corporation shall have regard to the educational qualifications, method of recruitment, duties and responsibilities of such officers and employees under the Central Government and in case of any doubt, the Corporation shall refer the matter to the Central Government whose decision thereon shall be final.

(3) Every appointment to posts (other than medical posts) corresponding to Group A and Group B posts under the Central Government shall be made in consultation with the Union Public Service Commission:

Provided that this sub-section shall not apply to an officiating or temporary appointment for a period not exceeding one year:

Provided further that any such officiating or temporary appointment shall not confer any claim for regular appointment and the services rendered in that capacity shall not count towards seniority or minimum qualifying service specified in the regulations for promotion to next higher grade.

(4) If any question arises whether a post corresponds to Group A and Group B post under the Central Government, the question shall be referred to that Government whose decision thereon shall be final.

Section 18: Powers of the Standing Committee

(1) Subject to the general superintendence and control of the Corporation, the Standing Committee shall administer the affairs of the Corporation and may exercise any of the powers and perform any of the functions of the Corporation.

(2) The Standing Committee shall submit for the consideration and decision of the Corporation all such cases and matters as may be specified in the regulations made in this behalf.

(3) The Standing Committee may, in its discretion, submit any other case or matter for the decision of the Corporation.

Section 19: Corporation's power to promote measures for health, etc., of insured persons

The Corporation may, in addition to the scheme of benefits specified in this Act, promote measures for the improvement of the health and welfare of insured persons and for the rehabilitation and re-employment of insured persons who have been disabled or injured and may incur in respect of such measures expenditure from the funds of the Corporation within such limits as may be prescribed by the Central Government.

Section 20: Meetings of Corporation, Standing Committee and Medical Benefit Council

Subject to any rules made under this Act, the Corporation, the Standing Committee and the Medical Benefit Council shall meet at such times and places and shall observe such rules or procedure in regard to transaction of business at their meetings as may be specified in the regulations made in this behalf.

SECTION 21: Supersession of the Corporation and Standing Committee

(1) If in the opinion of the Central Government, the Corporation or the Standing Committee persistently makes default in performing the duties imposed on it by or under this Act or abuses its powers, that Government may, by notification in the Official Gazette, supersede the Corporation, or in the case of the Standing Committee, supersede, in consultation with the Corporation, the Standing Committee:

Provided that before issuing a notification under this sub-section the Central Government shall give a reasonable opportunity to the Corporation or the Standing Committee, as the case may be, to show cause why it should not be superseded and shall consider the explanations and objections, if any, of the Corporation or the Standing Committee, as the case may be.

(2) Upon the publication of a notification under sub-section (1) superseding the Corporation or the Standing Committee, all the members of the Corporation or the Standing Committee, as the case may be, shall, as from the date of such publication, be deemed to have vacated their offices.

(3) When the Standing Committee has been superseded, a new Standing Committee shall be immediately constituted in accordance with section 8.

(4) When the Corporation has been superseded, the Central Government may—

(a) immediately appoint or cause to be appointed or elected new members to the Corporation in accordance with section 4 and may constitute a new Standing Committee under section 8;

(b) in its discretion, appoint such agency, for such period as it may think fit, to exercise the powers and perform the functions of the corporation and such agency shall be competent to exercise all the powers and perform all the functions of the Corporation.

(5) The Central Government shall cause a full report of any action taken under this section and the circumstances leading to such action to be laid before Parliament at the earliest opportunity and in any case not later than three months from the date of the notification superseding the Corporation or the Standing Committee, as the case may be.

SECTION 22: Duties of Medical Benefits Council

The Medical Benefit Council shall—

(a) advise the Corporation and the Standing Committee on matters relating to the administration of medical benefit, the certification for purposes of the grant of benefits and other connected matters;

(b) have such powers and duties of investigation as may be prescribed in relation to complaints against medical practitioners in connection with medical treatment and attendance; and

(c) perform such other duties in connection with medical treatment and attendance as may be specified in the regulations.

SECTION 23: Duties of Director General and the Financial Commissioner

The Director General and the Financial Commissioner shall exercise such powers and discharge such duties as may be prescribed. They shall also perform such other functions as may be specified in the regulations.

SECTION 24: Acts of Corporation, etc., not invalid by reason of defect in Constitution, etc.

No act of the Corporation, the Standing Committee or the Medical Benefit Council shall be deemed to be invalid by reason of any defect in the constitution of the Corporation, the Standing Committee or the Medical Benefit Council, or on the ground that any member thereof was not entitled to hold or continue in office by reason of any disqualification or of any irregularity in his appointment or election, or by reason of such act having been done during the period of any vacancy in the office of any member of the Corporation, the Standing Committee or the Medical Benefit Council.

SECTION 25: Regional Boards, Local Committees, Regional and Local Medical Benefit Councils

The Corporation may appoint Regional Boards, Local Committees and Regional and Local Medical Benefit Councils in such areas and in such manner, and delegate to them such powers and functions, as may be provided by the regulations.

CHAPTER III

FINANCE AND AUDIT

SECTION 26: Employees' State Insurance Fund

(1) All contributions paid under this Act and all other moneys received on behalf of the Corporation shall be paid into a fund called the Employees' State Insurance Fund which shall be held and administered by the Corporation for the purposes of this Act.

(2) The Corporation may accept grants, donations and gifts from the Central or any State Government, local authority, or any individual or body whether incorporated or not, for all or any of the purposes of this Act.

(3) Subject to the other provisions contained in this Act and to any rules or regulations made in this behalf, all moneys accruing or payable to the said Fund shall be

paid into the Reserve Bank of India or such other bank as may be approved by the Central Government to the credit of an account styled the Account of the Employees' State Insurance Fund.

(4) Such account shall be operated on by such officer as may be authorised by the Standing Committee with the approval of the Corporation.

Section 27: Grant by the Central Government

Omitted by amendment in 1966.

Section 28: Purposes for which the fund may be expended

Subject to the provisions of this Act and of any rules made by the Central Government in that behalf, the Employees' State Insurance Fund shall be expended only for the following purposes, namely:

(i) payment of benefits and provision of medical treatment and attendance to insured persons and, where the medical benefit is extended to their families, the provision of such medical benefit to their families, in accordance with the provisions of this Act and defraying the charges and costs in connection therewith;

(ii) payment of fees and allowances to members of the Corporation, the Standing Committee and the Medical Benefit Council, the Regional Boards, Local Committees and Regional and Local Medical Benefit Councils;

(iii) payment of salaries, leave and joining time allowances, travelling and compensatory allowances, gratuities and compassionate allowances, pensions, contributions to provident or other benefit fund of officers and servants of the Corporation and meeting the expenditure in respect of offices and other services set up for the purpose of giving effect to the provisions of this Act;

(iv) establishment and maintenance of hospitals, dispensaries and other institutions and the provisions of medical and other ancillary services for the benefit of insured persons and where the medical benefit is extended to their families, their families;

(v) payment of contributions to any State Government, local authority or any private body or individual, towards the cost of medical treatment and attendance provided to insured persons and, where the medical benefit is extended to their families, their families, including the cost of any building and equipment, in accordance with any agreement entered into by the Corporation;

(vi) defraying the cost (including all expenses) of auditing the accounts of the Corporation and of the valuation of its assets and liabilities;

(vii) defraying the cost (including all expenses) of the Employees' Insurance Courts set up under this Act;

(viii) payment of any sums under any contract entered into for the purposes of this Act by the Corporation or the Standing Committee or by any officer duly authorised by the Corporation or the Standing Committee in that behalf;

(ix) payment of sums under any decree, order or award of any Court or Tribunal against the Corporation or any of its officers or servants for any act done in the execution of his duty or under a compromise or settlement of any suit or other legal proceeding or claim instituted or made against the Corporation;

(x) defraying the cost and other charges of instituting or defending any civil or criminal proceedings arising out of any action taken under this Act;

(xi) defraying expenditure, within the limits prescribed, on measures for the improvement of the health and welfare of insured persons and for the rehabilitation and re-employment of insured persons who have been disabled or injured; and

(xii) such other purposes as may be authorised by the Corporation with the previous approval of the Central Government.

SECTION 28A: Administrative expenses

The types of expenses which may be termed as administrative expenses and the percentage of the income of the Corporation which may be spent for such expenses shall be such as may be prescribed by the Central Government and the Corporation shall keep its administrative expenses within the limit so prescribed by the Central Government.

SECTION 29: Holding of property, etc.

(1) The Corporation may, subject to such conditions as may be prescribed by the Central Government, acquire and hold property both movable and immovable, sell or otherwise transfer any movable or immovable property which may have become vested in or have been acquired by it and do all things necessary for the purposes for which the Corporation is established.

(2) Subject to such conditions as may be prescribed by the Central Government, the Corporation may from time to time, invest any moneys which are not immediately required for expenses properly defrayable under this Act and may, subject as aforesaid, from time to time re-invest or realise such investments.

(3) The Corporation may, with the previous sanction of the Central Government and on such terms as may be prescribed by it, raise loans and take measures for discharging such loans.

(4) The Corporation may constitute for the benefit of its staff or any class of them, such provident or other benefit fund as it may think fit.

SECTION 30: Vesting of the property in the Corporation

All property acquired before the establishment of the Corporation shall vest in the Corporation and all income derived and expenditure incurred in this behalf shall be brought into the books of the Corporation.

SECTION 31: Expenditure by Central Government to be treated as a loan

Omitted by the ESI (Amendment) Act, 1966.

SECTION 32: Budget estimates

The Corporation shall in each year frame a budget showing the probable receipts and the expenditure which it proposes to incur during the following year and shall submit a copy of the budget for the approval of the Central Government before such date as may be fixed by it in that behalf. The budget shall contain provisions adequate in the opinion of the Central Government for the discharge of the liabilities incurred by the Corporation and for the maintenance of a working balance.

SECTION 33: Accounts

The Corporation shall maintain correct accounts of its income and expenditure in such form and in such manner as may be prescribed by the Central Government.

SECTION 34: Audit

(1) The accounts of the Corporation shall be audited annually by the Comptroller and Auditor-General of India and any expenditure incurred by him in connection with such audit shall be payable by the Corporation to the Comptroller and Auditor-General of India.

(2) The Comptroller and Auditor-General of India and any person appointed by him in connection with the audit of the accounts of the Corporation shall have the same rights and privileges and authority in connection with such audit as the Comptroller and Auditor-General has, in connection with the audit of Government accounts and, in particular, shall have the right to demand the production of books, accounts, connected vouchers and other documents and papers and to inspect any of the offices of the Corporation.

(3) The accounts of the Corporation as certified by the Comptroller and Auditor-General of India or any other person appointed by him in this behalf together with the audit report thereon shall be forwarded to the Corporation which shall forward the same to the Central Government along with its comments on the report of the Comptroller and Auditor-General.

SECTION 35: Annual report

The Corporation shall submit to the Central Government an annual report of its work and activities.

SECTION 36: Budget, audited accounts and the annual report to be placed before Parliament

The annual report, the audited accounts of the Corporation, together with the report of the Comptroller and Auditor-General of India thereon and the comments of the Corporation on such report under section 34, and the budget as finally adopted by the Corporation shall be placed before the Parliament.

SECTION 37: Valuation of assets and liabilities

The Corporation shall, at intervals of three years, have a valuation of its assets and liabilities made by a valuer appointed with the approval of the Central Government:

Provided that it shall be open to the Central Government to direct a valuation to be made at such other times as it may consider necessary.

CHAPTER IV

CONTRIBUTIONS

SECTION 38: All employees to be insured

Subject to the provisions of the Act, all employees in factories, or establishments to which this Act applies shall be insured in the manner provided by this Act.

SECTION 39: Contributions

(1) The contribution payable under this Act in respect of an employee shall comprise contribution payable by the employer (hereinafter referred to as the employer's contribution) and contribution payable by the employee (hereinafter referred to as the employee's contribution) and shall be paid to the Corporation.

(2) The contributions shall be paid at such rates as may be prescribed by the Central Government:

Provided that the rates so prescribed shall not be more than the rates which were in force immediately before the commencement of the Employees' State Insurance (Amendment) Act, 1989.

(3) The wage period in relation to an employee shall be the unit in respect of which all contributions shall be payable under this Act.

(4) The contributions payable in respect of each wage period shall ordinarily fall due on the last day of the wage period, and where an employee is employed for part of the wage period, or is employed under two or more employers during the same wage period, the contributions shall fall due on such days as may be specified in the regulations.

(5) (a) If any contribution payable under this Act is not paid by the principal employer on the date on which such contribution has become due, he shall be liable to pay simple interest at the rate of twelve per cent per annum or at such higher rate as may be specified in the regulations till the date of its actual payment:

Provided that higher interest specified in the regulations shall not exceed the lending rate of interest charged by any scheduled bank.

(b) Any interest recoverable under clause (a) may be recovered as an arrear of land revenue or under section 45C to section 45-I.

Explanation: In this sub-section, "scheduled bank" means a bank for the time being included in the Second Schedule to the Reserve Bank of India Act, 1934 (2 of 1934).

SECTION 40: Principal employer to pay contributions in the first instance

(1) The principal employer shall pay in respect of every employee, whether directly employed by him or by or through an immediate employer, both the employer's contribution and the employee's contribution.

(2) Notwithstanding anything contained in any other enactment but subject to the provisions of this Act and the regulations, if any, made thereunder, the principal employer shall, in the case of an employee directly employed by him (not being an exempted employee), be entitled to recover from the employee the employee's contribution by deduction from his wages and not otherwise:

Provided that no such deduction shall be made from any wages other than such as relate to the period or part of the period in respect of which the contribution is payable, or in excess of the sum representing the employee's contributing for the period.

(3) Notwithstanding any contract to the contrary, neither the principal employer nor the immediate employer shall be entitled to deduct the employer's contribution from any wages payable to an employee or otherwise to recover it from him.

(4) Any sum deducted by the principal employer from wages under this Act shall be deemed to have been entrusted to him by the employee for the purpose of paying the contribution in respect of which it was deducted.

(5) The principal employer shall bear the expenses of remitting the contributions to the Corporation.

Under S. 40, the primary liability is of the employer to pay not only the employer's contribution but also the employee's contribution. Therefore, the employer cannot be heard to contend that since he had not deducted the employee's contribution on the wages of the employees, he could not be made liable for the same. The object of making a deeming entrustment under sub-section (4) of S. 40 will be altogether rendered nugatory if the employer is not made liable. After all, when he makes employee's contribution, he is entitled to deduct from the wages.

The Employees' State Insurance Act is a beneficial piece of social security legislation. Where the liability to pay contribution is related to the period when the business was running and till the date of its closure, it could not be said that the demand for payment of contribution could not stand or that the demand could not be enforced against a closed business. If that is accepted it would not promote the scheme and would avoid the mischief. On the contrary, it would perpetrate the mischief. Any employer can easily avoid his statutory liability and deny the beneficial piece of social security legislation to the employees, by closing down the business before recovery. That certainly is not the intendment of the Act. It could not also be said that since the business is closed and the employees had gone away, there is no liability to contribute. The liability to contribute arises from the date of commencement of the establishment and is a continuing liability till the closure. Furthermore, it is held that liability to pay contribution relating to period when business was running and notice of demand issued after closure of business is immaterial. Notice is only a reminder to the employer to discharge his statutory obligation to pay contribution which arose prior to closure.[37]

The question raised in *Employees' State Insurance Corporation* v. *M/s. Harrison Malayalam Pvt. Ltd.*[38] is that the employees of the contractor engaged by the respondent-Company to execute certain contract are covered by the Employees' State Insurance Act, 1948 and whether contribution in respect of them is payable although the contract was com-pleted much prior to the demand for such contribution made by the appellant-Corporation.

Both the Insurance Court and the High Court have held against the Corporation on the ground that workers in respect of which the contribution is demanded were casual employees of the contractor and since the contract was over long ago, they are not identifiable.

But the Supreme Court held that the ground given by both the Courts is not justifiable. The Supreme Court observed that under the Act, it was the duty of the respondent-Company to get the necessary details of the workmen employed by the contractor at the commencement of the contract since the primary responsibility of payment of the contribution is on the principal employer. On the admitted fact that the respondent-Company had engaged the contractor to execute the work, it was also the duty of the respondent-Company to get the temporary identity certificates issued to the workmen as per the provisions of Regulations 12, 14 and 15 of the Employees' State Insurance [General] Regulations, 1950 and to pay the contribution as required by S. 40 of the Act. Since the respondent-Company failed in its obligation, it cannot be heard to say that the workers are unidentifiable. It was within the exclusive knowledge of the respondent-Company as to how many workers were employed by its contractor. If the respondent-Company failed to get the details of the workmen employed by the contractor, it has only itself to think for its default. Since the workmen in fact were engaged by the contractor to execute the work in question and the respondent-Company had failed to pay the contribution, the appellant-Corporation was entitled to demand the contribution although both the contribution period and the corresponding benefit period had expired.

The scheme under the Act for insuring the workmen for conferring on them benefits in case of accident, disablement, sickness maternity etc. is distinct from the contract of insurance in general. Under the Act, the scheme is more akin to group insurance. The contribution paid entitles the workman insured to the benefit under the Act. However, he does not get any part of the contribution back if during the benefit period, he does not qualify for any of the benefits. The contribution made by him and by his employer is credited to the insurance fund created under the Act and it becomes available for others or for himself, during other benefit periods, if he continues in employment. What is more, there is no relation between the contribution made and the benefit availed of. The contribution is uniform for all workmen and is a percentage of the wages earned by them. It has no relation to the risks against which the workman stands statutorily insured. It is for this reason that the Act envisages automatic obligation to pay the contribution once the factory or the establishment is covered by the Act, and the obligation to pay the contribution commences from the date of the application

37. *Employees State Insurance Corporation* v. *M/s. Hotel Kalpaka International*, AIR 1993 SC 1530.
38. AIR 1993 SC 2655.

of the Act to such factory or establishment. The obligation ceases only when the Act ceases to apply to the factory/establishment. The obligation to make contribution does not depend upon whether the particular employee or employees cease to be employee/employees after the contribution period and the benefit period expire. Accordingly, the appeal was allowed and the decision of the Insurance Court as well as of the High Court was set aside.

The question raised before the Supreme Court in *Employees' State Insurance Corporation* v. *S.K. Agawam*[39] for consideration was whether the expression employer includes directors of a company, either singly or collectively, in view of Explanation 2 to S. 405 of IPC.

Section 405, Explanation 2 is as follows:

"405. Criminal breach of trust: Whoever, being in any manner entrusted with property, or with any dominion over property, dishonestly misappropriates or converts to his own use that property, or dishonestly uses or disposes of that property in violation of any direction of law prescribing the mode in which such trust is to be discharged, or of any legal contract, express or implied, which he has made touching the discharge of such trust, or wilfully suffers any other person so to do, commits "criminal breach of trust".

Explanation 1: . . .

Explanation 2: A person, being an employer, who deducts the employees' contribution from the wages payable to the employee for credit to the Employees' State Insurance Fund held and administered by the Employees' State Insurance Act, 1948, shall be deemed to have been entrusted with the amount of the contribution so deducted by him and if he makes default in the payment of such contribution to the said Fund in violation of the said Act, shall be deemed to have dishonestly used the amount of the said contribution in violation of a direction of law as aforesaid."

Explanation 2 was inserted by the Employees' State Insurance Amendment Act 38 of 1975. Explanation 2 makes "a person being an employer" who deducts the employee's contribution from the wages payable to the employee liable for criminal breach of trust if he commits a default in the payment of such contribution to the Employees' State Insurance Fund. Under S. 11 of the Indian Penal Code, the word "person" includes any company or association or body of persons whether incorporated or not. The Court has held that the term "a person being an employer" in Explanation 2 to S. 405 of the Indian Penal Code can refer only to the company who had employed the employees in question. The directors of that company could not be considered as employers under Explanation 2 to S. 405 of the Indian Penal Code. The Court further observed that even if one would read the definition of "principal employer" under the Employees' State Insurance Act, 1948 in Explanation 2 to S. 405 of the Indian Penal Code, the directors of the company would not be covered by the definition of "principal employer" when the company itself owns the factory and is also the employer of its employees at the head office.

In any event, in the absence of any express provision in the Indian Penal Code incorporating the definition of "principal employer" in Explanation 2 to S. 405, this definition cannot be held to apply to the term "employer" in Explanation 2. The term "employer" in

39. AIR 1998 SC 2676.

Explanation 2 must be understood as in ordinary parlance. In ordinary parlance, it is the company which is the employer and not its directors either singly or collectively.

SECTION 41: Recovery of contributions from immediate employer

(1) A principal employer, who has paid contribution in respect of an employee employed by or through an immediate employer, shall be entitled to recover the amount of the contribution so paid (that is to say the employer's contribution as well as the employee's contribution, if any) from the immediate employer, either by deduction from any amount payable to him by the principal employer under any contract, or as a debt payable by the immediate employer.

(1A) The immediate employer shall maintain a register of employees employed by or through him as provided in the regulations and submit the same to the principal employer before the settlement of any amount payable under sub-section (1).

(2) In the case referred to in sub-section (1), the immediate employer shall be entitled to recover the employee's contribution from the employee employed by or through him by deduction from wages and not otherwise, subject to the conditions specified in the proviso to sub-section (2) of section 40.

The short question involved in *Assistant Regional Director, Nagpur* v. *Model Mills Nagpur Ltd.*[40] is, whether the amount paid to its employees by the employer towards the authorised leave which they enjoy under the provisions of Ss. 79 and 80 of the Factories Act, 1948, is or is not to be included in the total wage bill of the employer for the purposes of computing its share of special contribution under S. 73(a) of the Employees' State Insurance Act, 1948. The dispute relates to a period prior to the amendment of the definition of the term "Wages" under S. 2(22) of the Act by Act No. 44/66. There is no dispute that the amount paid towards the authorised leave as aforesaid was not included in the definition of the term "Wages" as it then stood. The submission which was made on behalf of the appellant before the High Court and has been reiterated before the Supreme Court is that even though the definition of the term "Wages" did not include the amount paid towards the authorised leave, it became wages in view of the Explanation to S. 41 of the Act. This submission, however, did not find favour with the High Court. It has been pointed out by the High Court that the purpose of Ss. 40 and 41 of the Act was to enable the employer to recover the employee's contribution from the employee by deduction from his wages and not otherwise. It has further been pointed out by the High Court that the legal fiction created by the Explanation to S. 41 was for the aforesaid purpose of Ss. 40 and 41 and it could not be extended either to the definition of the term "Wages" or to the method of computation of the contribution as contemplated by Schedule 1 of the Act. Reference has also been made by the High Court to Explanation III of Para 2 of Schedule 1 which stated that except as provided by regulations, wages paid, salaries or allowances paid in respect of any period of leave or holidays other than the weekly holidays shall not be taken into account in calculating wages.

Having heard the learned counsel for the appellant, the Apex Court is of the opinion that the view taken by the High Court with regard to the interpretation of the definition of

40. AIR 1991 SC 314.

the term "Wages" as it then stood as also of Ss. 40 and 41 of the Act and the provisions contained in the 1st Schedule cannot be said to be in any manner erroneous. The Apex Court, accordingly, agrees with the view expressed by the High Court in the judgment under appeal with regard to the interpretation of the aforesaid provisions of the Act and finds no merit, and hence accordingly dismissed.

Section 42: General provisions as to payment of contributions

(1) No employee's contribution shall be payable by or on behalf of an employee whose average daily wages during a wage period are below such wages as may be prescribed by the Central Government.

Explanation: The average daily wages of an employee shall be calculated in such manner as may be prescribed by the Central Government.

(2) Contribution (both the employer's contribution and the employee's contribution) shall be payable by the principal employer for each wage period, in respect of the whole or part of which wages are payable to the employee and not otherwise.

Section 43: Method of payment of contribution

Subject to the provisions of this Act, the Corporation may make regulations for any matter relating or incidental to the payment and collection of contributions payable under this Act and without prejudice to the generality of the foregoing power such regulations may provide for—

(a) the manner and time of payment of contributions;

(b) the payment of contributions by means of adhesive or other stamps affixed to or impressed upon books, cards or otherwise and regulating the manner, times and conditions in, at and under which, such stamps are to be affixed or impressed;

(bb) the date by which evidence of contributions having been paid is to be received by the Corporation;

(c) the entry in or upon books or cards of particulars of contributions paid and benefits distributed in the case of the insured persons to whom such books or cards relate; and

(d) the issue, sale, custody, production, inspection and delivery of books or cards and the replacement of books or cards which have been lost, destroyed or defaced.

Section 44: Employers to furnish returns and maintain registers in certain cases

(1) Every principal and immediate employer shall submit to the Corporation or to such officer of the Corporation as it may direct such returns in such form and containing such particulars relating to persons employed by him or to any factory or establishment in respect of which he is the principal or immediate employer as may be specified in regulations made in this behalf.

(2) Where in respect of any factory or establishment the Corporation has reason to believe that a return should have been submitted under sub-section (1) but has not been so submitted, the Corporation may require any person in charge of the factory or establishment to furnish such particulars as it may consider necessary for the purpose of enabling the Corporation to decide whether the factory or establishment is a factory or establishment to which this Act applies.

(3) Every principal and immediate employer shall maintain such registers or records in respect of his factory or establishment as may be required by regulations made in this behalf.

Section 45: Social Security Officers, their functions and duties

(1) The Corporation may appoint such persons as Social Security Officers, as it thinks fit, for the purposes of this Act, within such local limits as it may assign to them.

(2) Any Social Security Officer appointed by the Corporation under sub-section (1) (hereinafter referred to as Social Security Officer), or other official of the Corporation authorised in this behalf by it may, for the purposes of enquiring into the correctness of any of the particulars stated in any return referred to in section 44 or for the purpose of ascertaining whether any of the provisions of this Act has been complied with—

(a) require any principal or immediate employer to furnish to him such information as he may consider necessary for the purposes of this Act; or

(b) at any reasonable time enter any office, establishment, factory or other premises occupied by such principal or immediate employer and require any person found in charge thereof to produce to such Social Security Officer or other official and allow him to examine such accounts, books and other documents relating to the employment of persons and payment of wages or to furnish to him such information as he may consider necessary; or

(c) examine, with respect to any matter relevant to the purposes aforesaid, the principal or immediate employer, his agent or servant, or any person found in such factory, establishment, office or other premises, or any person whom the said Social Security Officer or other official has reasonable cause to believe to be or to have been an employee;

(d) make copies of, or take extracts from, any register, account book or other document maintained in such factory, establishment, office or, other premises;

(e) exercise such other powers as may be prescribed.

(3) A Social Security Officer shall exercise such functions and perform such duties as may be authorised by the Corporation or as may be specified in the regulations.

(4) Any officer of the Corporation authorised in this behalf by it may, carry out re-inspection or test inspection of the records and returns submitted under section 44 for the purpose of verifying the correctness and quality of the inspection carried out by a Social Security Officer.

Section 45A: Determination of contributions in certain cases

(1) Where in respect of a factory or establishment no returns, particulars, registers or records are submitted, furnished or maintained in accordance with the provisions of section 44 or any Social Security Officer or other official of the Corporation referred to in sub-section (2) of section 45 is prevented in any manner by the principal or immediate employer or any other person, in exercising his functions or discharging his duties under section 45, the Corporation may, on the basis of information available to it, by order, determine the amount of contributions payable in respect of the employees of that factory or establishment:

Provided that no such order shall be passed by the Corporation unless the principal or immediate employer or the person in charge of the factory or establishment has been given a reasonable opportunity of being heard;

Provided further that no such order shall be passed by the Corporation in respect of the period beyond five years from the date on which the contribution shall become payable;

(2) An order made by the Corporation under sub-section (1) shall be sufficient proof of the claim of the Corporation under section 75 or for recovery of the amount determined by such order as an arrears of land revenue under section 45B or the recovery under section 45C to section 45-I.

Section 45AA: Appellate authority

If an employer is not satisfied with the order referred to in section 45A, he may prefer an appeal to an appellate authority as may be provided by regulation, within sixty days of the date of such order after depositing twenty-five per cent of the contribution so ordered or the contribution as per his own calculation, whichever is higher, with the Corporation:

Provided that if the employer finally succeeds in the appeal, the Corporation shall refund such deposit to the employer together with such interest as may be specified in the regulation.

Section 45B: Recovery of contributions

Any contribution payable under this Act may be recovered as an arrears of land revenue.

In *Employees' State Insurance Corporation* v. *Dwarka Nath Bhargwa,*[41] the Employees' State Insurance Corporation has challenged the order passed by the Allahabad High Court. The High Court has taken the view that the provisions of S. 45-B of the Employees' State Insurance Act, 1948 enabling recovery of contribution payable under the Act as arrears of land revenue cannot be pressed into service by the appellant-Corporation in the present case. Reason given by the High Court for the said conclusion is to the effect that the recoveries pertain to the period prior to the date on which S. 45-B was inserted in the statute book. The said section was brought into force on 28-1-1968, while the amount sought to be recovered became payable on 27-1-1967 and 24-1-1968. It is of course true that these amounts were

41. AIR 1997 SC 3518.

to be paid by the respondent-employer on these relevant dates, but these contributions were not made by the respondent in time. Therefore, they remained in arrears. After S. 45-B was brought on the statute book, notices were issued to the respondent on 24-4-1970 and 9-9-1970 for effecting recoveries of these unpaid amounts of contributions by resort to S. 45-B. The question, therefore, is as to whether for the aforesaid contributions which remained unpaid, resort to S. 45-B could be effected on any day after the said section came on the statute book. Now, a mere look at the said section shows that it is of procedural nature. It provides that *'any contributions payable under this Act may be recovered as arrears of land revenue'*. Consequently, on the date on which the recovery by way of arrears of land revenue is to be effected, the contribution in question should have remained unpaid.

It is not in dispute and cannot be disputed that the contributions in question had remained payable all throughout and were not paid by the respondent. The day on which recovery by way of land revenue was sought to be made, the section had already come into force. As it was a procedural provision, it could obviously apply retrospectively to cover all contributions which had remained unpaid even prior to the date on which the section came into force.

The Apex Court, therefore, held that S. 45-B can be pressed into service to effect recovery of unpaid contributions when the contributions have remained unpaid since prior to the coming into force of S. 45-B and have throughout also remained unpaid. Consequently, notices issued in the present case against the respondent could not be said to be unauthorised or incompetent. The appeal was accordingly allowed. The judgment and order of the High Court as well as that of the Employees' Insurance Court, Allahabad were set aside.

Section 45C: Issue of certificate to the recovery officer

(1) Where any amount is in arrear under this Act, the authorised officer may issue, to the Recovery Officer, a certificate under his signature specifying the amount of arrears and the Recovery Officer, on receipt of such certificate, shall proceed to recover the amount specified therein from the factory or establishment or, as the case may be, the principal or immediate employer by one or more of the modes mentioned below:

(a) attachment and sale of the movable or immovable property of the factory or establishment or, as the case may be, the principal or immediate employer;

(b) arrest of the employer and his detention in prison;

(c) appointing a receiver for the management of the movable or immovable properties of the factory or establishment or, as the case may be, the employer:

Provided that the attachment and sale of any property under this sections shall first be effected against the properties of the factory or establishment and where such attachment and sale is insufficient for recovering the whole of the amount of arrears specified in the certificate, the Recovery Officer may take such proceedings against the property of the employer for recovery of the whole or any part of such arrears.

(2) The authorised officer may issue a certificate under sub-section (1) notwithstanding that proceedings for recovery of the arrears by any other mode have been taken.

Section 45D: Recovery officer to whom certificate is to be forwarded

(1) The authorised officer may forward the certificate referred to in section 45C to the Recovery Officer within whose jurisdiction the employer—

(a) carries on his business or profession or within whose jurisdiction the principal place of his factory or establishment is situate; or

(b) resides or any movable or immovable property of the factory or establishment or the principal or immediate employer is situate.

(2) Where a factory or an establishment or the principal or immediate employer has property within the jurisdiction of more than one Recovery Officer and the Recovery Officer to whom a certificate is sent by the authorised officer—

(a) is not able to recover the entire amount by the sale of the property, movable or immovable, within his jurisdiction; or

(b) is of the opinion that, for the purpose of expediting or securing the recovery of the whole or any part of the amount, it is necessary so to do,

he may send the certificate or, where only a part of the amount is to be recovered, a copy of the certificate certified in the manner prescribed by the Central Government and specifying the amount to be recovered to the Recovery Officer within whose jurisdiction the factory or establishment or the principal or immediate employer has property or the employer resides, and thereupon that Recovery Officer shall also proceed to recover the amount due under this section as if the certificate or the copy thereof had been the certificate sent to him by the authorised officer.

Section 45E: Validity of certificate and amendment thereof

(1) When the authorised officer issues a certificate to a Recovery Officer under section 45C, it shall not be open to the factory or establishment or the principal or immediate employer to dispute before the Recovery Officer the correctness of the amount, and no objection to the certificate on any other ground shall also be entertained by the Recovery Officer.

(2) Notwithstanding the issue of a certificate to a Recovery Officer, the authorised officer shall have power to withdraw the certificate or correct any clerical or arithmetical mistake in the certificate by sending an intimation to the Recovery Officer.

(3) The authorised officer shall intimate to the Recovery Officer any orders withdrawing or canceling a certificate or any correction made by him under sub-section (2) or any amendment made under sub-section (4) of section 45F.

Section 45F: Stay of proceedings under certificate and amendment or withdrawal thereof

(1) Notwithstanding that a certificate has been issued to the Recovery Officer for the Recovery of any amount, the authorised officer may grant time for the payment of

the amount, and thereupon the Recovery Officer shall stay the proceedings until the expiry of the time so granted.

(2) Where a certificate for the recovery of amount has been issued, the authorised officer shall keep the Recovery Officer informed of any amount paid or time granted for payment, subsequent to the issue of such certificate.

(3) Where the order giving rise to a demand of amount for which a certificate for recovery has been issued has been modified in appeal or other proceedings under this Act, and, as a consequence thereof, the demand is reduced but the order is the subject-matter of a further proceeding under this Act, the authorised officer shall stay the recovery of such part of the amount of the certificate as pertains to the said reduction for the period for which the appeals or other proceeding remains pending.

(4) Where a certificate for the recovery of amount has been issued and subsequently the amount of the outstanding demand is reduced as a result of an appeal or other proceeding under this Act, the authorised officer shall, when the order which was the subject-matter of such appeal or other proceeding has become final and conclusive, amend the certificate or withdraw it, as the case may be.

Section 45G: Other modes of recovery

(1) Notwithstanding the issue of a certificate to the Recovery Officer under section 45C, the Director General or any other officer authorised by the Corporation may recover the amount by any one or more of the modes provided in this section.

(2) If any amount is due from any person to any factory or establishment or, as the case may be, the principal or immediate employer who is in arrears, the Director General or any other officer authorised by the Corporation in this behalf may require such person to deduct from the said amount the arrears due from such factory or establishment or, as the case may be, the principal or immediate employer under this Act and such person shall comply with any such requisition and shall pay the sum so deducted to the credit of the Corporation:

Provided that nothing in this sub-section shall apply to any part of the amount exempt from attachment in execution of a decree of a civil court under section 60 of the Code of Civil Procedure, 1908 (5 of 1908).

(3) (i) The Director General or any other officer authorised by the Corporation in this behalf may, at any time or from time to time, by notice in writing, require any person from whom money is due or may become due to the factory or establishment or, as the case may be, the principal or immediate employer or any person who holds or may subsequently hold money for or on account of the factory or establishment or, as the case may be, the principal or immediate employer, to pay to the Director General either forthwith upon the money becoming due or being held or at or within the time specified in the notice (not being before the money becomes due or is held) so much of the money as if sufficient to pay the amount due from the factory or establishment or, as the case may be, the principal or immediate employer in respect of arrears or the whole of the money when it is equal to or less than that amount.

(ii) A notice under this sub-section may be issued to any person who holds or may subsequently hold any money for or on account of the principal or immediate employer jointly with any other person and for the purposes of this sub-section, the shares of the joint-holders in such account shall be presumed, until the contrary is proved, to be equal.

(iii) A copy of the notice shall be forwarded to the principal or immediate employer at his last address known to the Director General or, as the case may be, the officer so authorised and in the case of a joint account to all the joint-holders at their last addresses known to the Director General or the officer so authorised.

(iv) Save as otherwise provided in this sub-section, every person to whom a notice is issued under this sub-section shall be bound to comply with such notice, and, in particular, where any such notice is issued to a post office, bank or an insurer, it shall not be necessary for any pass book, deposit receipt, policy or any other document to be produced for the purpose of any entry, endorsement or the like being made before payment is made notwithstanding any rule, practice or requirement to the contrary.

(v) Any claim respecting any property in relation to which a notice under this sub-section has been issued arising after the date of the notice shall be void as against any demand contained in the notice.

(vi) Where a person to whom a notice under this sub-section is sent objects to it by a statement on oath that the sum demanded or any part thereof is not due to the principal or immediate employer or that he does not hold any money for or on account of the principal or immediate employer, then, nothing contained in this sub-section shall be deemed to require such person to pay any such sum or part thereof, as the case may be, but if it is discovered that such statement was false in any material particular, such person shall be personally liable to the Director General or the Officer so authorised to the extent of his own liability to the principal or immediate employer on the date of the notice, or to the extent of the principal or immediate employer's liability for any sum due under this Act, whichever is less.

(vii) The Director General or the officer so authorised may, at any time or from time to time, amend or revoke any notice issued under this sub-section or extend the time for making any payment in pursuance of such notice.

(viii) The Director General or the officer so authorised shall grant a receipt for any amount paid in compliance with a notice issued under this sub-section and the person so paying shall be fully discharged from his liability to the principal or immediate employer to the extent of the amount so paid.

(ix) any person discharging any liability to the principal or immediate employer after the receipt of a notice under this sub-section shall be personally liable to the Director General or the officer so authorised to the extent of his own liability to the principal or immediate employer so discharge or to the extent of the principal or immediate employer's liability for any sum due under this Act, whichever is less.

(x) If the person to whom a notice under this sub-section is sent fails to make payment in pursuance thereof to the Director General or the officer so authorised, he shall be deemed to be a principal or immediate employer in default in respect of the amount specified in the notice and further proceedings may be taken against him for the realization of the amount as if it were an arrear due from him, in the manner provided in sections 45C to 45F and the notice shall have the same effect as an attachment of a debt by the Recovery Officer in exercise of his powers under section 45C.

(4) The Director General or the officer authorised by the Corporation in this behalf may apply to the court in whose custody there is money belonging to the principal or immediate employer for payment to him of the entire amount of such money, or if it is more than the amount due, an amount sufficient to discharge the amount due.

(5) The Director General or any officer of the Corporation may, if so authorised by the Central Government by general or special order, recover any arrears of amount due from a factory or an establishment or, as the case may be, from the principal or immediate employer by distraint and sale of its or his movable property in the manner laid down in the Third Schedule to the Income-tax Act, 1961 (43 of 1961).

Section 45H: Application of certain provisions of the Income-tax Act

The provisions of the Second and Third Schedules to the Income-tax Act, 1961 (43 of 1961) and the Income-tax (Certificate Proceedings) Rules, 1962, as in force from time to time, shall apply with necessary modifications as if the said provisions and the rules referred to the arrears of the amount of contributions, interests or damages under this Act instead of to the income-tax:

Provided that any reference in the said provisions and the rules to the "assessee" shall be construed as a reference to a factory or an establishment or the principal or immediate employer under this Act.

Section 45I: Definitions

For the purposes of sections 45C to 45H,—

(a) "authorised officer" means the Director General, Insurance Commissioner, Joint Insurance Commissioner, Regional Director or such other officer as may be authorised by the Central Government, by notification in the Official Gazette;

(b) "Recovery Officer" means any officer of the Central Government, State Government or the Corporation, who may be authorised by the Central Government, by notification in the Official Gazette, to exercise the powers of a Recovery Officer under this Act.

CHAPTER V

BENEFITS

SECTION 46: Benefits

(1) Subject to the provisions of this Act, the insured persons, their dependents or the persons hereinafter mentioned, as the case may be, shall be entitled to the following benefits, namely—

(a) periodical payments to any insured person in case of his sickness certified by a duly appointed medical practitioner or by any other person possessing such qualifications and experience as the Corporation may, by regulations, specify in this behalf (hereinafter referred to sickness benefit);

(b) periodical payments to an insured woman in case of confinement or mis-carriage or sickness arising out of pregnancy, confinement, premature birth of child or mis-carriage, such woman being certified to be eligible for such payments by an authority specified in this behalf by the regulations (hereinafter referred to as maternity benefit);

(c) periodical payments to an insured person suffering from disablement as a result of an employment injury sustained as an employee under this Act and certified to be eligible for such payments by an authority specified in this behalf by the regulations (hereinafter referred to as disablement benefit);

(d) periodical payments to such dependants of an insured person who dies as a result of an employment injury sustained as an employee under this Act, as are entitled to compensation under this Act (hereinafter referred to as dependents' benefit);

(e) medical treatment for and attendance on insured persons (hereinafter referred to as medical benefit); and

(f) payment to the eldest surviving member of the family of an insured person who has died, towards the expenditure on the funeral of the deceased insured person, or, where the insured person did not have a family or was not living with his family at the time of his death, to the person who actually incurs the expenditure on the funeral of the deceased insured person (to be known as funeral expenses):

Provided that the amount of such payment shall not exceed such amount as may be prescribed by the Central Government and the claim for such payment shall be made within three months of the death of the insured person or within such extended period as the Corporation or any officer or authority authorised by it in this behalf may allow.

(2) The Corporation may, at the request of the appropriate Government, and subject to such conditions as may be laid down in the regulations, extend the medical benefits to the family of an insured person.

Section 47: When person eligible for sickness benefit

Omitted by ESI (Amendment) Act, 1989, w.e.f. 1-2-1991.

Section 48: When person deemed available for employment

Omitted by ESI (Amendment) Act, 1966.

Section 49: Sickness benefit

The qualification of a person to claim sickness benefit, the conditions subject to which such benefit may be given, the rates and period thereof shall be such as may be prescribed by the Central Government.

Section 50: Maternity benefit

The qualification of an insured woman to claim maternity benefit, the conditions subject to which such benefit may be given, the rates and period thereof shall be such as may be prescribed by the Central Government.

Section 51: Disablement benefit

Subject to the provisions of this Act—

(a) a person who sustains temporary disablement for not less than three days (excluding the day of accident), shall be entitled to periodical payment at such rates and for such period and subject to such conditions as may be prescribed by the Central Government;

(b) a person who sustains permanent disablement, whether total or partial, shall be entitled to periodical payment at such rates and for such period and subject to such conditions as may be prescribed by the Central Government.

Section 51A: Presumption as to accident arising in course of employment

For the purposes of this Act, an accident arising in the course of an employee's employment shall be presumed, in the absence of evidence to the contrary, also to have arisen out of that employment.

Section 51B: Accidents happening while acting in breach of regulations, etc.

An accident shall be deemed to arise out of and in the course of an employee's employment notwithstanding that he is at the time of the accident acting in contravention of the provisions of any law applicable to him, or of any orders given by or on behalf of his employer or that he is acting without instructions from his employer, if—

(a) the accident would have been deemed so to have arisen had the act not been done in contravention as aforesaid or on without instructions from his employer, as the case may be; and

(b) the act is done for the purpose of and in connection with the employer's trade or business.

SECTION 51C: Accidents happening while travelling in employer's transport

(1) An accident happening while an employee is, with the express or implied permission of his employer, travelling as a passenger by any vehicle to or from his place of work shall, notwithstanding that he is under no obligation to his employer to travel by that vehicle, be deemed to arise out of and in the course of his employment, if—

(a) the accident would have been deemed so to have arisen had he been under such obligation; and

(b) at the time of the accident, the vehicle—

(i) is being operated by or on behalf of his employer or some other person by whom it is provided in pursuance of arrangements made with his employer, and

(ii) is not being operated in the ordinary course of public transport service.

(2) In this section "vehicle" includes a vessel and an aircraft.

SECTION 51D: Accidents happening while meeting emergency

An accident happening to an employee in or about any premises at which he is for the time being employed for the purpose of his employer's trade or business shall be deemed to arise out of and in the course of his employment, if it happens while he is taking steps, on an actual or supposed emergency at those premises, to rescue, succor or protect persons who are, or are thought to be or possibly to be, injured or imperiled, or to avert or minimize serious damage to property.

SECTION 51E: Accidents happening while commuting to the place of work and vice versa

An accident occurring to an employee while commuting from his residence to place of employment for duty or from the place of employment to his residence performing duty, shall be deemed to have arisen out of and in the course of employment if nexus between the circumstances, time and place in which the accident and the employment is established.

SECTION 52: Dependant's benefits

(1) If an insured person dies as a result of an employment injury sustained as an employee under this Act (whether or not he was in receipt of any periodical payment

for temporary disablement in respect of the injury) dependants' benefit shall be payable at such rates and for such period and subject to such conditions as may be prescribed by the Central Government to his dependants specified in sub-clause (i), sub-clause (ia) and sub-clause (ii) of clause (6A) of section 2.

(2) In case the insured person dies without leaving behind him the dependants as aforesaid, the dependants' benefit shall be paid to the other dependants of the deceased at such rates and for such period and subject to such conditions as may be prescribed by the Central Government.

SECTION 52A: Occupational disease

(1) If an employee employed in any employment specified in Part A of the Third Schedule contracts any disease specified therein as an occupational disease peculiar to that employment, or if an employee employed in the employment specified in Part B of that Schedule for a continuous period of not less than six months contracts any disease specified therein as an occupational disease peculiar to that employment or if an employee employed in any employment specified in Part C of that Schedule for such continuous period as the Corporation may specify in respect of each such employment, contracts any disease specified therein as an occupational disease peculiar to that employment, the contracting of the disease shall, unless the contrary is proved, be deemed to be an "employment injury" arising out of and in the course of employment.

(2) (i) Where the Central Government or a State Government, as the case may be, adds any description of employment to the employments specified in Schedule III to the Workmen's Compensation Act, 1923 (8 of 1923), by virtue of the powers vested in it under sub-section (3) of section 3 of the said Act, the said description of employment and the occupational diseases specified under that sub-section as peculiar to that description of employment shall be deemed to form part of the Third Schedule.

(ii) Without prejudice to the provisions of clause (i), the Corporation after giving, by notification in the Official Gazette, not less than three months' notice of its intention so to do, may, by a like notification, add any description of employment to the employments specified in the Third Schedule and shall specify in the case of employments so added the diseases which shall be deemed for the purposes of this section to be occupational diseases peculiar to those employments respectively and thereupon the provisions of this Act shall apply, as if such diseases had been declared by this Act to be occupational diseases peculiar to those employments.

(3) Save as provided by sub-sections (1) and (2), no benefit shall be payable to an employee in respect of any disease unless the disease is directly attributable to a specific injury by accident arising out of and in the course of his employment.

(4) The provisions of section 51A shall not apply to the cases to which this section applies.

SECTION 53: Bar against receiving or recovery of compensation or damages under any other law

An insured person or his dependants shall not be entitled to receive or recover, whether from the employer of the insured person or from any other person, any compensation or damages under the Workmen's Compensation Act, 1923 (8 of 1923), or any other law for the time being in force or otherwise, in respect of an employment injury sustained by the insured person as an employee under this Act.

A comparison of the relevant provisions of the Workmen's Compensation Act, 1923 and the ESI Act makes it clear that both the Acts provide for compensation to a workman/employee for personal injury caused to him by accident arising out of and in the course of his employment. The ESI is a latter Act and has a wider coverage. It is more comprehensive. It also provides for more compensation than what a workmen would get under the Workmen's Compensation Act. The benefits which an employee can get under the ESI Act are more substantial than the benefits which he can get under the Workmen's Compensation Act. The only disadvantage, if at all it can be called a disadvantage, is that he will get compensation under the ESI Act by way of periodical payments and not in a lump sum as under the Workmen's Compensation Act. If the legislature in its wisdom thought it better to provide for periodical payments rather than lump sum compensation, its wisdom cannot be doubted. Even if it is assumed that the workmen had a better right under the Workmen's Compensation Act in this behalf, it was open to the legislature to take away or modify that right. While enacting the ESI Act, the intention of the legislature could not have been to create another remedy and a forum for claiming compensation for an injury received by the employee by accident arising out of and in the course of his employment.

In this background and context, one has to consider the effect of the bar created by S. 53 of the ESI Act. The bar is against receiving or recovering any compensation or damages under the Workmen's Compensation Act or any other law for the time being in force or otherwise in respect of an employment injury. The bar is absolute as can be seen from the use of the words 'shall not be entailed to receive or recover, whether from the employer of the insured person or from any other person, any compensation or damages under the Workmen's Compensation Act, 1923 (8 of 1923), or any other law for the time being in force or otherwise." The words "employed by the legislature" are clear and unequivocal. When such a bar is created in clear and express terms, it would neither be permissible nor proper to infer a different intention by referring to the previous history of the legislation. That would amount to bypassing the bar and defeating the object of the provision. In view of the clear language of the section, there is no justification in interpreting or construing it as not taking away the right of the workman, who is an insured person and an employee under the ESI Act to claim compensation under the Workmen's Compensation Act. Therefore, the Supreme Court in *A. Trehan* v. *M/s. Associated Electrical Agencies*[42] is of the opinion that the High Court was right in holding that in view of the bar created by S. 53, the application for compensation filed by the appellant under the Workmen's Compensation Act was not maintainable.

Section 53 disentitles an employee who has suffered an employment injury from receiving compensation or damages under the Workmen's Compensation Act or any other

42. AIR 1996 SC 1990.

law for the time being in force or otherwise. The use of the expression *"or otherwise"* would clearly indicate that this section is not limited to ousting the relief claimed only under any statute but the wordings of the section are such that an insured person would not be entitled to make a claim in Torts which has the force of law under the ESI Act. Even though the ESI Act is a beneficial legislation, the legislature had thought it fit to prohibit an insured person from receiving or recovering compensation or damages under any other law, including Torts, in cases where the injury sustained by him is an employment injury.[43]

SECTION 54: Determination of question of disablement

Any question—

(a) whether the relevant accident has resulted in permanent disablement; or

(b) whether the extent of loss of earning capacity can be assessed provisionally or finally; or

(c) whether the assessment of the proportion of the loss of earning capacity is provisional or final; or

(d) in the case of provisional assessment, as to the period for which such assessment shall hold good,

shall be determined by a medical board constituted in accordance with the provisions of the regulations and any such question shall hereafter be referred to as the "disablement question".

SECTION 54A: References to medical boards and appeals to medical appeal tribunals and Employees' Insurance Courts

(1) The case of any insured person for permanent disablement benefit shall be referred by the corporation to a medical board for determination of the disablement question and if, on that or any subsequent reference, the extent of loss of earning capacity of the insured person is provisionally assessed, it shall again be so referred to the medical board not later than the end of the period taken into account by the provisional assessment.

(2) If the insured person or the Corporation is not satisfied with the decision of the medical board, the insured person or the Corporation may appeal in the prescribed manner and within the prescribed time to—

(i) the medical appeal tribunal constituted in accordance with the provisions of the regulations with a further right of appeal in the prescribed manner and within the prescribed time to the Employees' Insurance Court, or

(ii) the Employees' Insurance Court directly:

Provided that no appeal by an insured person shall lie under this sub-section if such person has applied for commutation of disablement benefit on the basis of the decision of the medical board and received the commuted value of such benefit:

43. *Western India Plywood Limited* v. *P. Ashokan*, AIR 1997 SC 3883.

Provided further that no appeal by the Corporation shall lie under this sub-section if the Corporation paid the commuted value of the disablement benefit on the basis of the decision of the medical board.

Section 55: Review of decisions by medical board or medical appeal Tribunal

(1) Any decision under this Act of a medical board or a medical appeal tribunal may be reviewed at any time by the medical board or the medical appeal tribunal, as the case may be, if it is satisfied by fresh evidence that the decision was given in consequence of the non-disclosure or misrepresentation by the employee or any other person of a material fact (whether the non-disclosure or misrepresentation was or was not fraudulent).

(2) Any assessment of the extent of the disablement resulting from the relevant employment injury may also be reviewed by a medical board, if it is satisfied that since the making of the assessment there has been a sub-spatial and unforeseen aggravation of the results of the relevant injury:

Provided that an assessment shall not be reviewed under this sub-section unless the medical board is of opinion that having regard to the period taken into account by the assessment and the probable duration of the aggravation aforesaid, substantial injustice will be done by not reviewing it.

(3) Except with the leave of a medical appeal tribunal, an assessment shall not be reviewed under sub-section (2) on any application made less than five years, or in the case of a provisional assessment, six months, from the date thereof and on such a review the period to be taken into account by any revised assessment shall not include any period before the date of the application.

(4) Subject to the foregoing provisions of this section, a medical board may deal with a case of review in any manner in which it could deal with it on an original reference to it, and in particular may make a provisional assessment notwithstanding that the assessment under review was final; and the provisions of section 54A shall apply to an application for review under this section and to a decision of a medical board in connection with such application as they apply to a case for disablement benefit under that section and to a decision of the medical board in connection with such case.

Section 55A: Review of dependants' benefit

(1) Any decision awarding dependants' benefit under this Act may be reviewed at any time by the Corporation if it is satisfied by fresh evidence that the decision was given in consequence of non-disclosure or misrepresentation by the claimant or any other person of a material fact (whether the non-disclosure, or misrepresentation was or was not fraudulent) or that the decision is no longer in accordance with this Act due to any birth or death or due to the marriage, re-marriage or cesser of infirmity of, or attainment of the age of eighteen years by, a claimant.

(2) Subject to the provisions of this Act, the Corporation may, on such review as aforesaid, direct that the dependent's benefit be continued, increased, reduced or discontinued.

Section 56: Medical benefit

(1) An insured person or (where such medical benefit is extended to his family) a member of his family whose condition requires medical treatment and attendance shall be entitled to receive medical benefit.

(2) Such medical benefit may be given either in the form of out patient treatment and attendance in a hospital or dispensary, clinic or other institution or by visits to the home of the insured person or treatment as inpatient in a hospital or other institution.

(3) A person shall be entitled to medical benefit during any period for which contributions are payable in respect of him or in which he is qualified to claim sickness benefit or maternity benefit or is in receipt of such disablement benefit as does not disentitle him to medical benefit under the regulations:

Provided that a person in respect of whom contribution ceases to be payable under this Act may be allowed medical benefit for such period and of such nature as may be provided under the regulations:

Provided further that an insured person who ceases to be in insurable employment on account of permanent disablement shall continue, subject to payment of contribution and such other conditions as may be prescribed by the Central Government, to receive medical benefit till the date on which he would have vacated the employment on attaining the age of superannuating had he not sustained such permanent disablement:

Provided also that an insured person who has attained the age of superannuation, a person who retires under a Voluntary Retirement Scheme or takes premature retirement, and his spouse shall be eligible to receive medical benefits subject to payment of contribution and such other conditions as may be prescribed by the Central Government.

Explanation: In this section, "superannuating", in relation to an insured person, means the attainment by that person of such age as is fixed in the contract or conditions of service as the age on the attainment of which he shall vacate the insurable employment or the age of sixty years where no such age is fixed and the person is no more in the insurable employment.

Section 57: Scale of medical benefit

(1) An insured person and (where such medical benefit is extended to his family) his family shall be entitled to receive medical benefit only of such kind and on such scale as may be provided by the State Government or by the Corporation, and an insured person or, where such medical benefit is extended to his family, his family shall not have a right to claim any medical treatment except such as is provided by the dispensary, hospital, clinic or other institution to which he or his family is allotted, or as may be provided by the regulations.

(2) Nothing in this Act shall entitle an insured person and (where such medical benefit is extended to his family) his family to claim reimbursement from the Corporation of any expenses incurred in respect of any medical treatment, except as may be provided by the regulations.

SECTION 58: Provision of medical treatment by State Government

(1) The State Government shall provide for insured persons and (where such benefit is extended to their families) their families in the State reasonable medical, surgical and obstetric treatment:

Provided that the State Government may, with the approval of the Corporation, arrange for medical treatment at clinics of medical practitioners on such scale and subject to such terms and conditions as may be agreed upon.

(2) Where the incidence of sickness benefit payment to insured persons in any State is found to exceed the all-India average, the amount of such excess shall be shared between the Corporation and the (Substituted for "Provincial" and "Province" by the A.O. 1950) State Government in such proportion as may be fixed by agreement between them:

Provided that the Corporation may in any case waive the recovery of the whole or any part of the share which is to be borne by the State Government.

(3) The corporation may enter into an agreement with a State Government in regard to the nature and scale of the medical treatment that should be provided to insured persons and (where such medical benefit is extended to the families) their families (including provision of buildings, equipment, medicines, and staff) and for the sharing of the cost thereof and of any excess in the incidence of sickness benefit to insured persons between the Corporation and the State Government.

(4) In default of agreement between the Corporation and any State Government as aforesaid the nature and extent of the medical treatment to be provided by the State Government and the proportion in which the cost thereof and of the excess in the incidence of sickness benefit shall be shared between the Corporation and that Government, shall be determined by an arbitrator who shall be or shall have been a Judge of the High Court of a State appointed by the Chief Justice of India and the award of the arbitrator shall be binding on the Corporation and the State Government.

(5) The State Government may, in addition to the Corporation under this Act, with the previous approval of the Central Government, establish such organisation (by whatever name called) to provide for certain benefits to employees in case of sickness, maternity and employment injury:

Provided that any reference to the State Government in the Act shall also include reference to the organisation as and when such organisation is established by the State Government.

(6) The organisation referred to in sub-section (5) shall have such structure and discharge functions, exercise powers and undertake such activities as may be prescribed.

Section 59: Establishment and maintenance of hospitals, etc., by Corporation

(1) The Corporation may, with the approval of the State Government establish and maintain in a State such hospitals, dispensaries and other medical and surgical services as it may think fit for the benefit of insured persons and (where such medical benefit is extended to their families) their families.

(2) The Corporation may enter into agreement with any local authority, private body or individual in regard to the provision of medical treatment and attendance for insured persons and (where such medical benefit is extended to their families) their families, in any area and sharing the cost thereof.

(3) The Corporation may also enter into agreement with any local authority, local body or private body for commissioning and running Employees' State Insurance hospitals through third party participation for providing medical treatment and attendance to insured persons and where such medical benefit has been extended to their families, to their families.

Section 59A: Provision of medical benefit by the Corporation in lieu of State Government

(1) Notwithstanding anything contained in any other provisions of this Act, the Corporation may, in consultation with the State Government, undertake the responsibility for providing medical benefit to insured persons and where such medical benefit is extended to their families, to the families of such insured persons in the State subject to the condition that the State Government shall share the cost of such medical benefit in such proportion as may be agreed upon between the State Government and the Corporation.

(2) In the event of the Corporation exercising its power under sub-section (1), the provisions relating to medical benefit under this Act shall apply, so far as may be, as if a reference therein to the State Government were a reference to the Corporation.

Section 59B: Medical and paramedical education

The corporation may establish medical colleges, nursing colleges and training institutes for its paramedical staff and other employees with a view to improve the quality of services provided under the Employee's State Insurance Scheme.

GENERAL

SECTION 60: Benefit not assignable or attachable

(1) The right to receive any payment of any benefit under this Act shall not be transferable or assignable.

(2) No cash benefit payable under this Act shall be liable to attachment or sale in execution of any decree or order of any Court.

SECTION 61: Bar of benefits under other enactments

When a person is entitled to any of the benefits provided by this Act, he shall not be entitled to receive any similar benefit admissible under the provisions of any other enactment.

SECTION 62: Persons not to commute cash benefits

Save as may be provided in the regulations no person shall be entitled to commute for a lump sum any disablement benefit admissible under this Act.

SECTION 63: Persons not entitled to receive benefit in certain cases

Save as may be provided in the regulations, no person shall be entitled to sickness benefit or disablement benefit for temporary disablement on any day on which he works or remains on leave or on a holiday in respect of which he receives wages or on any day on which he remains on strike.

SECTION 64: Recipients of sickness or disablement benefit to observe conditions

A person who is in receipt of sickness benefit or disablement benefit (other than benefit granted on permanent disablement)—

(a) shall remain under medical treatment at a dispensary, hospital, clinic or other institution provided under this act and shall carry out the instructions given by the medical officer or medical attendant in charge thereof;

(b) shall not while under treatment do anything which might retard or prejudice his chances of recovery;

(c) shall not leave the area in which medical treatment provided by this Act is being given, without the permission of the medical officer, medical attendant or such other authority as may be specified in this behalf by the regulations; and

(d) shall allow himself to be examined by any duly appointed medical officer or other person authorised by the Corporation in this behalf.

SECTION 65: Benefits not to be combined

(1) An insured person shall not be entitled to receive for the same period—

(a) both sickness benefit and maternity benefit; or

(b) both sickness benefit and disablement benefit for temporary disablement; or

(c) both maternity benefit and disablement benefit for temporary disablement.

(2) Where a person is entitled to more than one of the benefits mentioned in sub-section (1), he shall be entitled to choose which benefit he shall receive.

SECTION 66: Corporation's right to recover damages from employer in certain cases

Omitted by the ESI (Amendment) Act, 1966.

SECTION 67: Corporations right to be indemnified in certain cases

Omitted, *ibid.*

SECTION 68: Corporation's rights where a principal employer fails or neglects to pay any contribution

(1) If any principal employer fails or neglects to pay any contribution which under this Act he is liable to pay in respect of any employee and by reason thereof such person becomes disentitle to any benefit or entitled to a benefit on a lower scale, the Corporation may, on being satisfied that the contribution should have been paid by the principal employer, pay to the person the benefit at the rate to which he would have been entitled if the failure or neglect had not occurred and the Corporation shall be entitled to recover from the principal employer either—

(i) the difference between the amount of benefit which is paid by the Corporation to the said person and the amount of the benefit which would have been payable on the basis of the contributions were in fact paid by the employer; or

(ii) twice the amount of the contribution which the employer failed or neglected to pay, whichever is greater.

(2) The amount recoverable under this section may be recovered as if it were an arrear of land-revenue or under section 45C to section 45-I.

SECTION 69: Liability of owner or occupier of factories, etc., for excessive sickness benefit

(1) Where the Corporation considers that the incidence of sickness among insured persons is excessive by reason of—

(i) insanitary working conditions in a factory or establishment or the neglect of the owner or occupier of the factory or establishment to observe any health regulations enjoined on him by or under any enactment, or

(ii) insanitary conditions of any tenements or lodgings occupied by insured persons and such unsanitary conditions are attributable to the neglect of the owner of the tenements or lodgings to observe any health regulations enjoined on him by or under any enactment,

the Corporation may send to the owner or occupier of the factory or establishment or to the owner of the tenements or lodgings, as the case may be, a claim for the payment of the amount of the extra expenditure incurred by the Corporation as sickness benefit; and if the claim is not settled by agreement, the Corporation may refer the matter, with a statement in support of its claim, to the appropriate Government.

(2) If the appropriate Government is of opinion that a prima facie case for inquiry is disclosed, it may appoint a competent person or persons to hold an inquiry into the matter.

(3) If upon such inquiry it is proved to the satisfaction of the person or persons holding the inquiry that the excess in incidence of sickness among the insured persons is due to the default or neglect of the owner or occupier of the factory or establish-ment or the owner of the tenements or lodgings, as the case may be, the said person or persons shall determine the amount of the extra expenditure incurred as sickness benefit, and the person or persons by whom the whole or any part of such amount shall be paid to the Corporation.

(4) A determination under sub-section (3) may be enforced as if it were a decree for payment of money passed in a suit by a Civil Court.

(5) For the purposes of this section "owner" of tenements or lodgings shall include any agent of the owner and any person who is entitled to collect the rent of the tenements or lodgings as a lessee of the owner.

Section 70: Repayment of benefit improperly received

(1) Where any person has received any benefit or payment under this Act when he is not lawfully entitled thereto, he shall be liable to repay to the Corporation the value of the benefit or the amount of such payment, or in the case of his death his representative shall be liable to repay the same from the assets of the deceased, if any, in his hands.

(2) The value of any benefits received other than cash payments shall be determined by such authority as may be specified in the regulations made in this behalf and the decision of such authority shall be final.

(3) The amount recoverable under this section may be recovered as if it were an arrear of land-revenue or under section 45-C to section 45-I.

SECTION 71: Benefit payable up to and including day of death

If a person during any period for which he is entitled to a cash benefit under this Act, the amount of such benefit up to and including the day of his death shall be paid to any person nominated by the deceased person in writing in such form as may be specified in the regulations or, if there is no such nomination, to the heir or legal representative of the deceased person.

SECTION 72: Employer not to reduce wages, etc.

No employer by reason only of his liability for any contributions payable under this act shall, directly or indirectly, reduce the wages of any employee, or except as provided by the regulations, discontinue or reduce benefits payable to him under the conditions of his service which are similar to the benefits conferred by this Act.

SECTION 73: Employer not to dismiss or punish employee during period of sickness, etc.

(1) No employer shall dismiss, discharge, or reduce or otherwise punish an employee during the period the employee is in receipt of sickness benefit or maternity benefit, nor shall he, except as provided under the regulations, dismiss, discharge or reduce or otherwise punish an employee during the period he is in receipt of disablement benefit for temporary disablement or is under medical treatment for sickness or is absent from work as a result of illness duly certified in accordance with the regulations to arise out of the pregnancy or confinement rendering the employee unfit for work.

(2) No notice of dismissal or discharge or reduction given to an employee during the period specified in sub-section (1) shall be valid or operative.

In *Buckingham and Carnatic Co. Ltd.* v. *Venkatiah,*[44] the principal question that arises relates to the true scope and effect of the provisions contained in S. 73 of the ESI Act, 1948. Section 73 of the Employees' State Insurance Act is no doubt a piece of social legislation intended to confer certain benefits on workmen and should receive a liberal and beneficent construction from the courts. But at the same time the courts cannot overlook the fact that the liberal construction must ultimately flow from the words used in the section. If the words used in the section are capable of two constructions one of which is shown patently to assist the achievement of the object of the Act, Courts would be justified in preferring that construction to the other which may not be able to further the object of the Act. On the other hand, if the words used in the section are reasonably capable of only one construction, the doctrine of liberal construction can be of no assistance.

The clause *"during the period the employee is in receipt of sickness benefit"* in S. 73(1) refers to the period of his actual illness and requires that for the said period of illness, sickness benefit should have been received by him. In a large majority of cases, sickness benefit would be applied for and received by the employee after his sickness is over, and so to hold that the

44. AIR 1964 SC 1272.

period there referred to is the period during which the employee must be ill and must also receive sickness benefit, would make the section wholly unworkable.

What is the effect of S. 73(1)? In considering this question, it would be useful to take into account the provisions of sub-section (2). This sub-section provides that no notice given to an employee during the period specified in sub-section (1) shall be valid or operative. Thus, it is clear that the giving of the notice during the specified period makes it invalid, and it is remarkable that the notice is not in regard to dismissal, discharge or reduction in respect of sickness alone, but it includes all such notices issued, whatever may be the misconduct justifying them. Thus, there can be no doubt that the punitive action which is prohibited by S. 73(1) is not confined to punitive action proceeding on the basis of absence owing to sickness, it is punitive action proceeding on the basis of all kinds of misconduct which justifies the imposition of the penalty in question. What S. 73(1) prohibits is such punitive action and it limits the extent of the said prohibition to the period during which the employee is ill. The Supreme Court, in the instant case, confesses that the clause is not very happily worded, but it seems to it that the plain object of the clause is to put a sort of a moratorium against all punitive actions during the pendency of the employee's illness. If the employee is ill and if it appears that he has received sickness benefit for such illness, during the period of illness no punitive action can be taken against him that appears to be the effect of that part of S. 73(1).

There is another aspect of this question to which it is necessary to refer. Section 73(1) prohibits the employer from dismissing, discharging, reducing or otherwise punishing an employee. This seems to suggest that what is prohibited is some positive act on the part of the employer, such as an order passed by him either dismissing, discharging or reducing or punishing the employee. Where termination of the employee's services follows automatically either from a contract or from a Standing Order by virtue of the employee's absence without leave for the specified period, such termination is not the result of any positive act or order on the part of the employer, and so, to such a termination, the prohibition contained in S. 73(1) would be inapplicable.

Section 85(d) provides that if any person in contravention of S. 73 or any regulation, dismisses, discharges, reduces or otherwise punishes an employee, he shall be punishable with imprisonment or with fine, or with both. In other words, the contravention of S. 73(1) is made penal by S. 85(d), and so, it would not be reasonable to put the widest possible denotation on the word " discharge'' in S. 73(1). The word " discharge'' in S. 73(1) must, therefore, in the context, be taken to be a discharge which is the result of a decision of the employer embodied in an order passed by him. It may conceivably also include the case of a discharge where discharge is provided for by a Standing Order. In such a case, it may be said that the discharge flowing from the Standing Order is, in substance, a discharge brought about by the employer with the assistance of the Standing Order. Even so, it cannot cover the case of abandonment of service by the employee which is inferred under Standing Order 8(ii). Therefore, the Apex Court did not accept the view of the High Court that the termination of Venkatiah's, [the respondent] services under Standing Orders 8(ii) to which the appellant has given effect by refusing to take him back contravenes the provisions of S. 73(1).

CHAPTER VA

SCHEME FOR OTHER BENEFICIARIES

SECTION 73A: Definition

In this chapter,—

(a) "other beneficiaries" means persons other than the person insured under this Act;
(b) "Scheme" means any Scheme framed by the Central Government from time to time under section 73B for the medical facility for other beneficiaries;
(c) "underutilised hospital" means any hospital not fully utilised by the persons insured under this Act;
(d) "user charges" means the amount which is to be charged from the other beneficiaries for medical facilities as may be notified by the Corporation in consultation with the Central Government from time to time.

SECTION 73B: Power to frame Schemes

Notwithstanding anything contained in this Act, the Central Government may, by notification in the Official Gazette, frame Scheme for other beneficiaries and the members of their families for providing medical facility in any hospital established by the Corporation in any area which is underutilised on payment of user charges.

SECTION 73C: Collection of user charges

The user charges collected from the other beneficiaries shall be deemed to be the contribution and shall form part of the Employees' State Insurance Fund.

SECTION 73D: Scheme for other beneficiaries

The Scheme may provide for all or any of the following matters, namely—

(i) the other beneficiaries who may be covered under this Scheme;
(ii) the time and manner in which the medical facilities may be availed by the other beneficiaries;
(iii) the form in which the other beneficiary shall furnish particulars about himself and his family whenever required as may be specified by the Corporation;
(iv) any other matter which is to be provided for in the Scheme or which may be necessary or proper for the purpose of implementing the Scheme.

SECTION 73E: Power to amend Scheme

The Central Government may, by notification in the Official Gazette, add to, amend, vary or rescind the Scheme.

SECTION 73F: Laying of Scheme under this Chapter

Every Scheme framed under this Chapter shall be laid, as soon as may be after it is made, before each House of Parliament while it is in session for a total period of thirty days which may be comprised in one session or in two or more successive sessions, and if, before the expiry of the session immediately following the session or the successive sessions aforesaid, both Houses agree in making any modification in the Scheme or both Houses agree that the Scheme should not be made, the Scheme shall thereafter have effect only in such modified form or to be of no effect, as the case may be; so however, that any such modification or annulment shall be without prejudice to the validity of anything previously done under that Scheme.

CHAPTER VI

ADJUDICATION OF DISPUTE AND CLAIMS

SECTION 74: Constitution of employees' Insurance Court

(1) The State Government shall, by notification in the Official Gazette, constitute an Employees' Insurance Court for such local area as may be specified in the notification.

(2) The Court shall consist of such number of Judges as the State Government may think fit.

(3) Any person who is or has been a judicial officer or is a legal practitioner of five years standing shall be qualified to be a Judge of the Employees' Insurance Court.

(4) The State Government may appoint the same Court for two or more local areas or two or more Courts for the same local area.

(5) Where more than one Court has been appointed for the same local area, the State Government may by general or special order, regulate the distribution of business between them.

SECTION 75: Matters to be decided by employees' Insurance Court

(1) If any question or dispute arises as to—

(a) whether any person is an employee within the meaning of this Act or whether he is liable to pay the employee's contribution, or

(b) the rate of wages or average daily wages of an employee for the purposes of this Act, or

(c) the rate of contribution payable by a principal employer in respect of any employee, or

(d) the person who is or was the principal employer in respect of any employee, or

(e) the right of any person to any benefit and as to the amount and duration thereof, or (ee) any direction issued by the Corporation under section 55A on a review of any payment of dependants' benefits, or

(f) Omitted

(g) any other matter which is in dispute between a principal employer and the Corporation, or between a principal employer and an immediate employer, or between a person and the Corporation or between an employee and a principal or immediate employer, in respect of any contribution or benefit or other dues payable or recoverable under this Act, or any other matter required to be or which may be decided by the Employees' Insurance Court under this Act,

such question or dispute subject to the provision of sub-section (2A) shall be decided by the Employees' Insurance Court in accordance with the provisions of this Act.

(2) Subject to the provisions of sub-section (2A), the following claims shall be decided by the Employees' Insurance Court, namely:

(a) claim for the recovery of contributions from the principal employer;

(b) claim by a principal employer to recover contributions from any immediate employer;

(c) Omitted

(d) claim against a principal employer under section 68;

(e) claim under section 70 for the recovery of the value or amount of the benefits received by a person when he is not lawfully entitled thereto; and

(f) any claim for the recovery of any benefit admissible under this Act.

(2A) If in any proceedings before the Employees' Insurance Court a disablement question arises and the decision of a medical board or a medical appeal tribunal has not been obtained on the same and the decision of such question is necessary for the determination of the claim or question before the Employees' Insurance Court, that Court shall direct the Corporation to have the question decided by this Act and shall thereafter proceed with the determination of the claim or question before it in accordance with the decision of the medical board or the medical appeal tribunal, as the case may be, except where an appeal has been filed before the Employees' Insurance Court, under sub-section (2) of section 54A in which case the Employees' Insurance Court may itself determine all the issues arising before it.

(2B) No matter which is in dispute between a principal employer and the Corporation in respect of any contribution or any other dues shall be raised by the principal employer in the Employees' Insurance Court unless he has deposited with the Court fifty per cent of the amount due from him as claimed by the Corporation:

Provided that the Court may, for reasons to be recorded in writing, waive or reduce the amount to be deposited under this sub-section.

(3) No Civil Court shall have jurisdiction to decide or deal with any question or dispute as aforesaid or to adjudicate on any liability which by or under this Act is to be

decided by a medical board, or by a medical appeal tribunal or by the Employees' Insurance Court.

In *Employees' State Insurance Corporation* v. *M/s. F. Fibre Bangalore (P) Ltd.*,[45] the question raised before the Supreme Court was regarding the correctness of the decision of the Division Bench of the Karnataka High Court which, in turn, had followed the ratio of judgment of the Full Bench. The Full Bench had held as under:

> "In the result, we answer the question referred to us as follows:
>
> Where, in cases to which provisions of Section 45A of the 'Act' are attracted, the Corporation by an order made in accordance with that section determines the amount of contributions payable and that claim is disputed by the employer, it would not be necessary for the Corporation to seek a resolution of that dispute before the Insurance Court. Such a claim is recoverable as arrears of land revenue. If the employer disputes the claim it is for him to move the Insurance Court for relief. In other cases—other than cases where determination of the amount of contributions under Section 45A is made the Corporation, if its claim is disputed by the employer, should seek an adjudication of the dispute before the insurance Court, before enforcing recovery."

The question that arises for consideration is: whether the view taken by the Full Bench of the High Court is correct in law?

The Supreme Court, after referring S. 75 read with S. 45A of the ESI Act, observed that the employer, on making the provisions of the Act applicable to the factory or the establishment, as the case may be, is statutorily under an obligation to register itself with the Corporation and keep depositing the employer's and employee's contribution within the period specified therein. The question is: who would approach the Insurance Court for adjudication and determination of a dispute whether the establishment of the employer is attracted by the provisions of the Act and/or what is the number of employees it has employed, etc.? It is seen that S. 45-A is in the nature of best assessment judgment on the basis of the information collected by the Inspector. In the impugned order, the High Court holds that it is for the employer to challenge and seek adjudication. When there was dereliction of duty on the employer to either register itself with the Corporation under the Act, or when there is, failure to deposit the contribution with the Corporation under the Act or failure to deposit the contribution with the account of the Corporation towards the employer's and employee's contribution as envisaged hereinbefore, the Corporation is empowered to make best assessment judgment under S. 45-A and call upon the employer to deposit the amount with the Corporation. The Full Bench of the High Court has held that in a case where the order under S. 45-A becomes final, there is no need for the Corporation to seek adjudication before the Insurance Court. In all other cases, the Corporation is required to go to the Insurance Court, have it adjudicated and then make a demand. The Supreme Court held that the Full Bench of the High Court is clearly in error to reach that conclusion. Though S. 75 of the Act does not envisage as to who has to approach the Insurance Court, by necessary implication when the employer denies the liability or applicability of the provisions of the Act or the quantum of the contribution to be deposited by the employer, it is for him

45. AIR 1997 SC 2441.

to approach the Insurance Court and seek adjudication. It is not for the Corporation in each case whenever there is a dispute, to go to the Insurance Court and have the dispute adjudicated. Otherwise, the Act would become unworkable and defeat the object and purpose of the Act.

Therefore, the Apex Court is of view that Full Bench judgment of the High Court is clearly unsustainable and it is accordingly set aside. The Division Bench having followed the Full Bench judgment fell into the same error. Under these circumstances, that part of the judgment of the Full Bench and of the Division Bench which is not consistent with the declaration of law above, stands set aside. The Insurance Court is directed to determine the contribution payable by the respondent within a period of three months from the date of the receipt of this order. The respondent is directed to pay the amount as a condition. If it decides to go to the High Court and file an appeal, it should first deposit the entire amount with interest payable in that behalf and thereafter approach the High Court, if so advised challenging the order of the Insurance Court.

SECTION 76: Institution of proceedings, etc.

(1) Subject to the provisions of this Act and any rules made by the State Government, all proceedings before the Employees' Insurance Court shall be instituted in the Court appointed for the local area in which the insured person was working at the time the question or dispute arose.

(2) If the Court is satisfied that any matter arising out of any proceeding pending before it can be more conveniently dealt with by any other Employees' Insurance Court in the same State, it may, subject to any rules made by the State Government in this behalf, order such matter to be transferred to such other Court for disposal and shall forthwith transmit to such other Court the records connected with that matter.

(3) The State Government may transfer any matter pending before any Employees' Insurance Court in the State to any such Court in another State with the consent of the State Government of that State.

(4) The Court to which any matter is transferred under sub-section (2) or sub-section (3) shall continue the proceedings as if they had been originally instituted in it.

SECTION 77: Commencement of proceedings

(1) The proceedings before an Employees' Insurance Court shall be commenced by application.

(1A) Every such application shall be made within a period of three years from the date on which the cause of action arose.

Explanation: For the purpose of this sub-section,—

(a) the cause of action in respect of a claim for benefit shall not be deemed to arise unless the insured person or in the case of dependants' benefit, the dependants of the insured person claims or claim that benefit in accordance with the regulations made in that behalf within a period of twelve months after the claim became due or within such further period as the Employees' Insurance Court may allow on grounds which appear to it to be reasonable;

(b) the cause of action in respect of a claim by the Corporation for recovering contributions (including interest and damages) from the principal employer shall be deemed to have arisen on the date on which such claim is made by the Corporation for the first time:

Provided that no claim shall be made by the Corporation after five years of the period to which the claim relates;

(c) the cause of action in respect of a claim by the principal employer for recovering contributions from an immediate employer shall not be deemed to arise till the date by which the evidence of contributions having been paid is due to be received by the Corporation under the regulation.

(2) Every such application shall be in such form and shall contain such particulars and shall be accompanied by such fee, if any, as may be prescribed by rules made by the State Government in consultation with the Corporation.

Section 78: Powers of employees' Insurance Court

(1) The Employees' Insurance Court shall have all the powers of a Civil Court for the purposes of summoning and enforcing the attendance of witnesses, compelling the discovery and production of documents and material objects, administering oath and recording evidence and such Court shall be deemed to be a Civil Court within the meaning of section 195 and Chapter XXXVI of the Code of Criminal Procedure, 1973 (2 of 1974).

(2) The Employees' Insurance Court shall follow such procedure as may be prescribed by rules made by the State Government.

(3) All costs incidental to any proceeding before an Employees' Insurance Court shall, subject to such rules as may be made in this behalf by the (Substituted for "Provincial" by the A.O. 1950) State Government, be in the discretion of the Court.

(4) An order of the Employees' Insurance Court shall be enforceable as if it were a decree passed in a suit by a civil court.

Section 79: Appearance by legal practitioners, etc.

Any application, appearance or act required to be made or done by any person to or before an Employees' Insurance Court (other than appearance of a person required for the purpose of his examination as a witness) may be made or done by a legal practitioner or by an officer of a registered trade union authorised in writing by such person or with the permission of the Court, by any other person so authorised.

Section 80: Benefit not admissible unless claimed in time

Omitted by the ESI (Amendment) Act, 1966.

SECTION 81: Reference to High Court

An Employees' Insurance Court may submit any question of law for the decision of the High Court and if it does so, shall decide the question pending before it in accordance with such decision.

SECTION 82: Appeal

(1) Save as expressly provided in this section, no appeal shall lie from an order of an Employees' Insurance Court.

(2) An appeal shall lie to the High Court from an order of an Employees' Insurance Court if it involves a substantial question of law.

(3) The period of limitation for an appeal under this section shall be sixty days.

(4) The provisions of sections 5 and 12 of the Limitation Act, 1963 (36 of 1963) shall apply to appeals under this section.

SECTION 83: Stay of payment pending appeal

Where the Corporation has presented an appeal against an order of the Employees' Court, that Court may, and if so directed by the High Court, shall, pending the decision on the appeal, withhold the payment of any sum directed to be paid by the order appealed against.

CHAPTER VII

PENALTIES

SECTION 84: Punishment for false statement

Whoever, for the purpose of causing any increase in payment or benefit under this Act, or for the purpose of causing any payment or benefit to be made where no payment or benefit is authorised by or under this Act, or for the purpose of avoiding any payment to be made by himself under this Act or enabling any other person to avoid any such payment, knowingly makes or causes to be made any false statement or false representation, shall be punishable with imprisonment for a term which may extend to six months or with fine not exceeding two thousand rupees or with both:

Provided that where an insured person is convicted under this section, he shall not be entitled for any cash benefit under this Act for such period as may be prescribed by the Central Government.

SECTION 85: Punishment for failure to pay contributions, etc.

If any person—

(a) fails to pay any contribution which under this Act he is liable to pay, or

(b) deducts or attempts to deduct from the wages of an employee the whole or any part of the employer's contribution, or

(c) in contravention of section 72 reduces the wages or any privileges or benefits admissible to an employee, or

(d) in contravention of section 73 or any regulation dismisses, discharges, reduces or otherwise punishes an employee, or

(e) fails or refuses to submit any return required by the regulations or makes a false return, or

(f) obstructs any Inspector or other official of the Corporation in the discharge of his duties, or

(g) is guilty of any contravention of or non-compliance with any of the requirements of this Act or the rules or the regulations in respect of which no special penalty is provided,

he shall be punishable—

(i) where he commits an offence under clause (a), with imprisonment for a term which may extend to three years but—

(a) which shall not be less than one year, in case of failure to pay the employee's contribution which has been deducted by him from the employee's wages and shall also be liable to fine of ten thousand rupees;

(b) which shall not be less than six months, in any other case and shall also be liable to fine of five thousand rupees:

Provided that the Court may, for any adequate and special reasons to be recorded in the judgment, impose a sentence or imprisonment for a lesser term;

(ii) where he commits an offence under any of the clauses (b) to (g) (both inclusive), with imprisonment for a term which may extend to one year or with fine which may extend to four thousand rupees, or with both.

Section 85A: Enhanced punishment in certain cases after previous conviction

Whoever, having been convicted by a court of an offence punishable under this Act, commits the same offence shall, for every such subsequent offence, be punishable with imprisonment for a term which may extend to two years and with fine of five thousand rupees:

Provided that where such subsequent offence is for failure by the employer to pay any contribution which under this Act he is liable to pay, he shall, for every such subsequent offence, be punishable with imprisonment for a term which may extend to five years but which shall not be less than two years and shall also be liable to fine of twenty-five thousand rupees.

Section 85B: Power to recover damages

(1) Where an employer fails to pay the amount due in respect of any contribution or any other amount payable under this Act, the Corporation may recover from the

employer by way of penalty such damages not exceeding the amount of arrears as may be specified in the regulations:

Provided that before recovering such damages, the employer shall be given a reasonable opportunity of being heard:

Provided further that the Corporation may reduce or waive the damages recoverable under this section in relation to an establishment which is a sick industrial company in respect of which a scheme for rehabilitation has been sanctioned by the Board for Industrial and Financial Reconstruction established under section 4 of the Sick Industrial Companies (Special Provisions) Act, 1985 (1 of 1986), subject to such terms and conditions as may be specified in regulations.

(2) Any damages recoverable under sub-section (1) may be recovered as an arrear of land revenue or under section 45C to section 45-I.

In *Prestolite of India Ltd., M/s.* v. *Regional Director,*[46] the Regional Director proposed to impose damages on account of payment of the dues under the State Employees' Insurance Act beyond the time frame and a notice to that effect was issued to the appellant. The appellant made a written representation in response to the notice indicating the reasons for which there had been delay in making such payment. Such written representation has been annexed to the special leave petition being Annexure A-l. Although an opportunity of personal hearing was afforded by the Regional Director to the appellant, such opportunity was not availed of. The written representation was stated to have been taken into consideration by the Regional Director and the same was dismissed by making the order to the following effect:

"I have applied my mind to all the relevant facts and have gone into the reasons stated by the employer. My finding on each of the contentions of the establishment are as under:

The reasons advanced are not legally tenable. Opportunity of Personal hearing afforded on 22-11-1979 has not been availed of."

The Supreme Court observed that even if the regulations have prescribed general guidelines and the upper limits at which the imposition of damages can be made, it cannot be contended that in no case, the mitigating circumstances can be taken into consideration by the adjudicating authority in finally deciding the matter and it is bound to act mechanically in applying the upper most limit of the table. In the instant case, it appears that the order has been passed without indicating any reason whatsoever as to why grounds for delayed payment was not to be accepted. There is no indication as to why the imposition of damages at the rate specified in the order was required to be made. Simply because the appellant did not appear in person and produce materials to support the objections, the employee's case could not be discarded in limine. On the contrary, the objection ought to have been considered on merits. The Supreme Court, therefore, allowed this appeal and set aside the impugned orders. The Regional Director is directed to dispose of the representation of the appellant by indicating reasons after taking into consideration the grounds for delayed payment. Since the matter is going to be reheard, the appellant is permitted to make personal representation at the hearing

46. AIR 1994 SC 521.

of the show cause proceeding. As the matter is pending for a long time, the representation should be considered and disposed of within three months from the date of the receipt of the order by giving notice of the date of hearing in advance to the appellant.

SECTION 85C: Power of court to make orders

(1) Where an employer is convicted of an offence for failure to pay any contribution payable under this Act, the court may, in addition to awarding any punishment, by order, in writing, require him within a period specified in the order (which the court may if it thinks fit and on application in that behalf, from time to time, extend), to pay the amount of contribution in respect of which the offence was committed and to furnish the return relating to such contributions.

(2) Where an order is made under sub-section (1), the employer shall not be liable under this Act in respect of the continuation of the offence during the period or extended period, if any, allowed by the court, but if, on the expiry of such period or extended period, as the case may be, the order of the court has not been fully complied with, the employer shall be deemed to have committed a further offence and shall be punishable with imprisonment in respect thereof under section 85 and shall also be liable to pay fine which may extend to one thousand rupees for every day after such expiry on which the order has not been complied with.

SECTION 86: Prosecutions

(1) No prosecution under this Act shall be instituted except by or with the previous sanction of the Insurance Commissioner or of such other officer of the corporation as may be authorised in this behalf by the Director General of the Corporation.

(2) No court inferior to that of a Metropolitan Magistrate or Judicial Magistrate of the First Class shall try any offence under this Act.

(3) No Court shall take cognizance of any offence under this Act except on a complaint made in writing in respect thereof.

SECTION 86A: Offences by companies

(1) If the person committing an offence under this Act is a company, every person, who at the time the offence was committed was in charge of, and was responsible to, the company for the conduct of the business of the company, as well as the company, shall be deemed to be guilty of the offence and shall be liable to be proceeded against and punished accordingly:

Provided that nothing contained in this sub-section shall render any person liable to any punishment, if he proves that the offence was committed without his knowledge or that he exercised all due diligence to prevent the commission of such offence.

(2) Notwithstanding anything contained in sub-section (1), where an offence under this Act has been committed with the consent or connivance of, or is attributable to,

any neglect on the part of, any director or manager, secretary or other officer of the company, such director, manager, secretary or other officer shall be deemed to be guilty of that offence and shall be liable to be proceeded against and punished accordingly.

Explanation: For the purposes of this section,—

(i) "company" means any body corporate and includes a firm and other associations of individuals; and

(ii) "director" in relation to—

(a) a company, other than a firm, means the managing director or a whole-time director;

(b) a firm means a partner in the firm.

CHAPTER VIII

MISCELLANEOUS

SECTION 87: Exemption of a factory or establishment or class of factories, or establishments

The appropriate Government, may, by notification in the Official Gazette and subject to such conditions as may be specified in the notification, exempt any factory or establishment or class of factories or establishments in any specified area from the operation of this Act for a period not exceeding one year and may from time to time by like notification renew any such exemption for periods not exceeding one year at a time.

Provided that such exemptions may be granted only if the employees in such factories or establishments are otherwise in receipt of benefits substantially similar or superior to the benefits provided under this Act:

Provided further that an application for renewal shall be made three months before the date of expiry of the exemption period and a decision on the same shall be taken by the appropriate Government within two months of receipt of such application.

SECTION 88: Exemption of persons or class of persons

The appropriate Government may, by notification in the Official Gazette and subject to such conditions as it may deem fit to impose, exempt any persons or class of persons employed in any factory or establishment or class of factories or establishments to which this Act applies from the operation of the Act.

SECTION 89: Corporation to make representation

No exemption shall be granted or renewed under section 87 or section 88, unless a reasonable opportunity has been given to the Corporation to make any representation it may wish to make in regard to the proposal and such representation has been considered by the appropriate Government.

Section 90: Exemption of factories or establishments belonging to Government or any local authority

The appropriate Government may, after consultation with the Corporation, by notification in the Official Gazette and subject to such conditions as may be specified in the notifications, exempt any factory or establishment belonging to any local authority from the operation of this Act, if the employees in any such factory or establishment are otherwise in receipt of benefits substantially similar or superior to the benefits provided under this Act.

Section 91: Exemption from one or more provisions of the Act

The appropriate Government may, with the consent of the Corporation, by notification in the Official Gazette, exempt any employees or class of employees in any factory or establishment or class of factories or establishments from one or more of the provisions relating to the benefits provided under this Act.

Section 91A: Exemptions to be either prospective or retrospective

Any notification granting exemption under section 87, section 88, section 90 or section 91 may be issued so as to take effect either prospectively or retrospectively on such date as may be specified therein.

Section 91AA: Central Government to be appropriate Government

Notwithstanding anything contained in this Act, in respect of establishments located in the States where medical benefit is provided by the Corporation, the Central Government shall be the appropriate Government.

Section 91B: Misuse of benefits

If the Central Government is satisfied that the benefits under this Act are being misused by insured persons in a factory or establishment, that Government may, by order, published in the Official Gazette, disentitle such persons from such of the benefits as it thinks fit:

Provided that no such order shall be passed unless a reasonable opportunity of being heard is given to the concerned factory or establishment, insured persons and the trade unions registered under the Trade Unions Act, 1926 (16 of 1926), having members in the factory or establishment.

Section 91C: Writing off of losses

Subject to the conditions as may be prescribed by the Central Government, where the Corporation is of opinion that the amount of contribution, interest and damages due to the Corporation is irrecoverable, the Corporation may sanction the writing off finally of the said amount.

Section 92: Power of Central Government to give directions

(1) The Central Government may give directions to a State Government as to the carrying into execution of this Act in the State.

(2) The Central Government may, from time to time, give such directions to the Corporation as it may think fit for the efficient administration of the Act, and if any such direction is given, the Corporation shall comply with such direction.

Section 93: Corporation officers and servants to be public servants

All officers and servants of the Corporation shall be deemed to be public servants within the meaning of section 21 of the Indian Penal Code (45 of 1860).

Section 93A: Liability in case of transfer of establishment

Where an employer, in relation to a factory or establishment, transfers that factory or establishment in whole or in part, by sale, gift, lease or licence or in any other manner whatsoever, the employer and the person to whom the factory or establishment is so transferred shall jointly and severally be liable to pay the amount due in respect of any contribution or any other amount payable under this Act in respect of the periods up to the date of such transfer:

Provided that the liability of the transferee shall be limited to the value of the assets obtained by him by such transfer.

Section 94: Contributions, etc., due to Corporation to have priority over other debts

There shall be deemed to be included among the debts which, under section 49 of the Presidency-towns Insolvency Act, 1909 (3 of 1909), or under section 61 of the Provincial Insolvency Act, 1920 (5 of 1920), or under any law relating to insolvency in force in the territories which, immediately before the 1st November, 1956, were comprised in a Part B State, or under section 530 of the Companies Act, 1956 (1 of 1956), are in the distribution of the property of the insolvent or in the distribution of the assets of a company being wound up, to be paid in priority to all other debts, the amount due in respect of any contribution or any other amount payable under this Act the liability wherefore accrued before the date of the order of adjudication of the insolvent or the date of the winding up, as the case may be.

Section 94A: Delegation of powers

The Corporation, and, subject to any regulations made by the Corporation in this behalf, the Standing Committee may direct that all or any of the powers and functions which may be exercised or performed by the Corporation or the Standing Committee, as the case may be, may, in relation to such matters and subject to such conditions, if any, as may be specified, be also exercisable by any officer or authority subordinate to the Corporation.

In *Sovrin Knit Works* v. *Employees' State Insurance Corpn.*,[47] two contentions have been raised by the learned counsel for the appellants. Firstly, it is contended that under S. 94A of the Act, Corporation has been empowered to delegate the power to one of the officers but the officer-delegatee has no power to further delegate to any other officer. Therefore, exercise of the power by the officer is bad in law. It is seen under S. 94A of the Act that the Corporation has been empowered to authorise any of its officer. It would be obvious that the Regional Director is one of the officers in the region; necessarily, he is a competent officer to exercise the power under the Act on behalf of the Corporation. It was conceded in the lower Court that he was so authorised. So, the officer has power to pass the order imposing damages and interest thereon for delayed payment.

Secondly, it is contended that under Regulations 26 and 34 of the Regulation under the Act, what is required is to purchase the contribution stamps, affix them and get them cancelled in time. If that is done by the employer, then it can be said that the employer has paid the contribution amount in time. Though Regulation 31-A, which was brought in by Amendment of 1979, further requires the employer to submit the cards duly stamped to the Corporation, that is, a mere procedural formality for showing that the amount has been paid in respect of the covered employees. As the cards were duly stamped, the action taken by the authority for imposing the penalty is bad in law.

The Supreme Court rejected both the contentions and observed that it is seen that under Regulation 31-A, as amended in 1979, not only the card should be duly stamped but also the same should be produced indicating due compliance of the deposit of the employer's and the employee's contribution with the Corporation. That has not been done. The Insurance Court had found as a fact that the compliance has not been done. The appellants have failed to prove the compliance, in accordance with the provisions of the Act, of the deposit of the contribution as required under S. 85B of the Act. The appellants committed breach of the provisions entailing imposition of damages and interest on delayed payment.

Section 95: Power of Central Government to make rules

(1) The Central Government may, after consultation with the Corporation and subject to the condition of previous publication, make rules not inconsistent with this Act for the purpose of giving effect to the provisions thereof.

(2) In particular and without prejudice to the generality of the foregoing power, such rules may provide for all or any of the following matters, namely:

(a) the limit of wages beyond which a person shall not be deemed to be an employee;

(ab) the limit of maximum monthly salary for the purpose of sub-section (1) of section 17;

(ac) the manner in which appointments and elections of members of the Corporation, the Standing Committee and the Medical Benefit Council shall be made;

47. AIR 1997 SC 1771.

(b) the quorum at meetings of the Corporation, the Standing Committee and the Medical Benefit Council and the minimum number of meetings of those bodies to be held in a year;

(c) the records to be kept of the transaction of business by the Corporation, the Standing Committee and the Medical Benefit Council;

(d) the powers and duties of the Director General and the Financial Commissioner and the conditions of their service;

(e) the powers and duties of the Medical Benefit Council;

(ea) the types of expenses which may be termed as administrative expenses, the percentage of income of the corporation which may be spent for such expenses;

(eb) the rates of contributions and limits of wages below which employees are not liable to pay contribution;

(ec) the manner of calculation of the average daily wage;

(ed) the manner of certifying the certificate to recover amount by the Recovery Officer;

(ee) the amount of funeral expenses;

(ef) the qualifications, conditions, rates and period of sickness benefit, maternity benefit, disablement benefit and dependents benefit;

(eff) the income of dependant parents from all sources;

(eg) the conditions for grant of medical benefits for insured persons who cease to be in insurable employment on account of permanent disablement;

(eh) the conditions for grant of medical benefits for persons who have attained the age of superannuation;

(ehh) the conditions under which the medical benefits shall be payable to the insured person and spouse of an insured person who has attained the age of superannuation, the person who retires under Voluntary Retirement Scheme and the person who takes premature retirement;

(ei) the manner in which and the time within which appeals may be filed to medical appeal Tribunals or Employees' Insurance Courts;

(f) the procedure to be adopted in the execution of contracts;

(g) the acquisition, holding and disposal of property by the Corporation;

(h) the raising and repayment of loans;

(i) the investment of the funds of the Corporation and of any provident or other benefit fund and their transfer or realisation;

(j) the basis on which the periodical valuation of the assets and liabilities of the Corporation shall be made;

(k) the bank or banks in which the funds of the Corporation may be deposited, the procedure to be followed in regard to the crediting of money accruing or payable to the Corporation and the manner in which any sums may be paid out of the Corporation funds and the officers by whom such payment may be authorised;

(l) the accounts to be maintained by the Corporation and the forms in which such accounts shall be kept and the times at which such accounts shall be audited;

(m) the publication of the accounts of the Corporation and the report of auditors, the action to be taken on the audit report, the powers of auditors to disallow and surcharge items of expenditure and the recovery of sums so disallowed or surcharged;

(n) the preparation of budget estimates and of supplementary estimates and the manner in which such estimates shall be sanctioned and published;

(o) the establishment and maintenance of provident or other benefit fund for officers and servants of the Corporation;

(oa) the period of non-entitlement for cash benefit in case of conviction of an insured person;

(p) any matter which is required or allowed by this Act to be prescribed by the Central Government.

(2A) The power to make rules conferred by this section shall include the power to give retrospective effect, from a date not earlier than the date of commencement of this Act, to the rules or any of them but no retrospective effect shall be given to any rule so as to prejudicially affect the interest of any person other than the Corporation to whom such rule may be applicable.

(3) Rules made under this section shall be published in the Official Gazette and thereupon shall have effect as if enacted in this Act.

(4) Every rule made under this section shall be laid, as soon as may be after it is made, before each House of Parliament while it is in session for a total period of thirty days which may be comprised in one session or in two or more successive sessions, and if, before the expiry of the session immediately following the session or the successive sessions aforesaid, both Houses agree in making any modification in the rule or both Houses agree that the rule should not be made, the rule shall thereafter has effect only in such modified form or be of no effect, as the case may be; so, however, that any such modification or annulment shall be without prejudice to the validity of anything previously done under that rule.

Section 96: Power of State Governments to make rules

(1) The State Government may, after consultation with the Corporation and, subject to the condition of previous publication, make rules not inconsistent with this Act in regard to all or any of the following matters, namely:

(a) the constitution of Employees' Insurance Courts, the qualifications of persons who may be appointed Judges thereof, and the conditions of service of such Judges;

(b) the procedure to be followed in proceedings before such Courts and the execution of orders made by such Courts;

(c) the fee payable in respect of applications made to the Employees' Insurance Court, the costs incidental to the proceedings in such court, the form in which applications should be made to it and the particulars to be specified in such applications;

(d) the establishment of hospitals, dispensaries and other institutions, the allotment of insured persons or their families to any such hospital, dispensary or other institution;

(e) the scale of medical benefit which shall be provided at any hospital, clinic, dispensary or institution, the keeping of medical records and the furnishing of statistical returns;

(ee) The organisational structure functions powers activities and other matters for the establishment of the organisation.

(f) the nature and extent of the staff, equipment and medicines that shall be provided at such hospitals, dispensaries and institutions;

(g) the conditions of service of the staff employed at such hospitals, dispensaries and institutions; and

(h) any other matter which is required or allowed by this Act to be prescribed by the State Government.

(2) Rules made under this section shall be published in the Official Gazette and thereupon shall have effect as if enacted in this Act.

(3) Every rule made under this section shall be laid as soon as may be after it is made, before each House of the State Legislature where it consists of two Houses, or, where such Legislature consists of one House, before that House.

SECTION 97: Power of Corporation to make regulations

(1) The Corporation may, subject to the condition of previous publication, make regulations, not inconsistent with this Act and the rules made thereunder, for the administration of the affairs of the Corporation and for carrying into effect the provisions of this Act.

(2) In particular and without prejudice to the generality of the foregoing power, such regulations may provide for all or any of the following matters, namely:

(i) the time and place of meetings of the Corporation, the Standing Committee and the Medical Benefit Council and the procedure to be followed at such meetings;

(ia) the time within which and the manner in which a factory or establishment shall be registered;

(ii) the matters which shall be referred by the Standing Committee to the Corporation for decision;

(iii) the manner in which any contribution payable under this Act shall be assessed and collected;

(iiia) the rate of interest higher than twelve per cent on delayed payment of contribution;

(iv) reckoning of wages for the purpose of fixing the contribution payable under this Act;

(iva) the register of employees to be maintained by the immediate employer;

(ivb) the entitlement of sickness benefit or disablement benefit for temporary disablement on any day on which person works or remains on leave or on holiday and in respect of which he receives wages or for any day on which he remains on strike;

(v) the certification of sickness and eligibility for any cash benefit;

(vi) the method of determining whether an insured person is suffering from one or more of the diseases specified in the Third Schedule;

(vii) the assessing of the money value of any benefit which is not a cash benefit;

(viii) the time within which and the form and manner in which any claim for a benefit may be made and the particulars be specified in such claim;

(ix) the circumstances in which an employee in receipt of disablement benefit may be dismissed, discharged, reduced or otherwise punished;

(x) the manner in which and the place and time at which any benefit shall be paid;

(xi) the method of calculating the amount of cash benefit payable and the circumstances in which and the extent to which commutation of disablement and dependent's benefits, may be allowed and the method of calculating the commutation value;

(xii) the notice of pregnancy or of confinement and notice and proof of sickness;

(xiia) specifying the authority competent to give certificate of eligibility for maternity benefit;

(xiib) the manner of nomination by an insured woman for payment of maternity benefit in case of her or her child's death;

(xiic) the production of proof in support of claim for maternity benefit or additional maternity benefit;

(xiii) the conditions under which any benefit may be suspended;

(xiv) the conditions to be observed by a person when in receipt of any benefit and the periodical medical examination of such persons;

(xv) Omitted

(xvi) the appointment of medical practitioners, for the purposes of this Act, the duties of such practitioners and the form of medical certificates;

(xvia) the qualifications and experience which a person should possess for giving certificate of sickness;

(xvib) the constitution of medical boards and medical appeal tribunals;

(xvii) the penalties for breach of regulations by fine (not 'exceeding two days' wages for a first breach and not exceeding three days' wages for any subsequent breach) which may be imposed on employees;

(xviia) the amount of damages to be recovered as penalty;

(xviib) the terms and conditions for reduction or waiver of damages in relation to a sick industrial company;

(xviii) the circumstances in which and the conditions subject to which any regulation may be relaxed, the extent of such relaxation, and the authority by whom such relaxation may be granted;

(xix) the returns to be submitted and the registers or records to be maintained by the principal and immediate employers, the forms of such returns, registers or records, and the times at which such returns should be submitted and the particulars which such returns, registers and records should contain;

(xx) the duties and powers of Social Security Officer and other officers and servants of the Corporation;

(xxa) the constitution of the appellate authority and the interest on amount deposited by the employer with the corporation;

(xxi) the method of recruitment, pay and allowances, discipline, superannuation benefits and other conditions of service of the officers and servants of the Corporation other than the Director General and Financial Commissioner;

(xxii) the procedure to be followed in remitting contributions to the Corporation; and

(xxiii) any matter in respect of which regulations are required and permitted to be made by this Act.

(2A) The condition of previous publication shall not apply to any regulations of the nature specified in clause (xxi) of sub-section (2).

(3) Regulations made by the Corporation shall be published in the Gazette of India and thereupon shall have effect as if enacted in this Act.

(4) Every regulation shall, as soon as may be, after it is made by the Corporation, be forwarded to the Central Government and that Government shall cause a copy of the same to be laid before each House of Parliament while it is in session for a total period of thirty days, which may be comprised in one session or in two or more successive sessions, and if, before the expiry of the session immediately following the session or the successive sessions aforesaid, both Houses agree in making any modification in the regulation or both Houses agree that the regulation should not be made, the regulation shall thereafter have effect only in such modified form or be of no effect, as the case may be; so, however, that any such modification or annulment shall be without prejudice to the validity of anything previously done under that regulation.

Section 98: Corporation may undertake duties in the Indian States

Omitted.

Section 99: Medical care for the families of insured persons

At any time when its funds so permit, the Corporation may provide or contribute towards the cost of medical care for the families of insured persons.

Section 99A: Power to remove difficulties

(1) If any difficulty arises in giving effect to the provisions of this Act, the Central Government may, by order published in the Official Gazette, make such provisions

or give such directions, not inconsistent with the provisions of this Act, as appears to it to be necessary or expedient for removing the difficulty.

(2) Any order made under this section shall have effect notwithstanding anything inconsistent therewith in any rules or regulations made under this Act.

SECTION 100: Repeals and savings

If, immediately before the day on which this Act comes into force in any part of the territories which, immediately before the 1st November, 1956, were Comprised in a Part B State, there is in force in that part any law corresponding to this Act, that law shall, on such day, stand repealed:

Provided that the repeal shall not affect—

(a) the previous operations of any such law; or

(b) any penalty, forfeiture or punishment incurred in respect of any offence committed against any such law; or

(c) any investigation or remedy in respect of any such penalty, forfeiture or punishment;

and any such investigation, legal proceeding or remedy, may be instituted continued or enforced and any such penalty, forfeiture or punishment may be imposed, as if this Act had not been passed:

Provided further that subject to the preceding proviso anything done or any action taken under any such law shall be deemed to have been done or taken under the corresponding provision of this Act and shall continue in force accordingly unless and until superseded by anything done or any action taken under this Act.

SCHEDULES

THE FIRST SCHEDULE

OMITTED BY THE EMPLOYEES' STATE INSURANCE (AMENDMENT) ACT, 1989, W.E.F. 1-2-1991

THE SECOND SCHEDULE

[*See* Sections 2(15A) and (15B)]

PART I

List of Injuries Deemed to Result in Permanent Total Disablement

Sl. No.	*Description of injury*	*Percentage of loss of earning capacity*
1	Loss of both hands or amputation at higher sites	100
2	Loss of a hand and a foot	100

Sl. No.	*Description of injury*	*Percentage of loss of earning capacity*
3	Double amputation through leg or thigh, or amputation through leg or thigh on one side and loss of other foot	100
4	Loss of sight to such an extent as to render the claimant unable to perform any work for which eye sight is essential	100
5	Very severe facial disfigurement	100
6	Absolute deafness	100
	PART II	
	List of Injuries Deemed to Result in Permanent Partial Disablement	
	Amputation – upper limbs (either arm)	
7	Amputation through shoulder joint	90
8	Amputation below shoulder with stump less than 20.32 c.m. from tip of acrimony	80
9	Amputation from 20.32 c.m. from tip of acrimony to less than 11.43 c.m. below tip of olecranon	70
10	Loss of a hand or of the thumb and four fingers of one hand or amputation from 11.43 c.m. below tip of olecranon	60
11	Loss of thumb	30
12	Loss of thumb and its metacarpal bone	40
13	Loss of four fingers of one hand	50
14	Loss of three fingers of one hand	30
15	Loss of two fingers of one hand	20
16	Loss of terminal phalanx of thumb	20
16A	Guillotine amputation of the tip of the thumb without loss of bone	10
	Amputation – lower limbs	
17	Amputation of both feet resulting in end-bearing stumps	90
18	Amputation through both feet proximal to the metatarso-phalangeal joint	80
19	Loss of all toes of both feet through the metatarso-phalangeal joint	40
20	Loss of all toes of both feet proximal to the proximal inter-phalangeal joint	30
21	Loss of all toes of both feet distal to the proximal inter-phalangeal joint	20
22	Amputation at hip	90
23	Amputation below hip with stump not exceeding 12.70 c.m. in length measured from tip of great trenchanter	80
24	Amputation below hip with stump exceeding 12.70 c.m. in length measured from tip of great trenchanter but not beyond middle thigh	70

Sl. No.	Description of injury	Percentage of loss of earning capacity
25	Amputation below middle thigh to 8.89 c.m. below knee	60
26	Amputation below knee with stump exceeding 8.89 c.m. but not exceeding 12.70 c.m.	50
27	Amputation below knee with stump exceeding 12.70 c.m.	50
28	Amputation of one foot resulting in end-bearing	50
29	Amputation through one foot proximal to the metatarso-phalangeal joint	50
30	Loss of all toes of one foot through the metatarso-phalangeal joint	20
	Other injuries	
31	Loss of one eye, without complications, the other being normal	40
32	Loss of vision of one eye without complications or disfigurement of eye-ball, the other being normal	30
32A	Partial loss of vision of one eye	10
	Loss of – A – Fingers of right or left hand index finger	
33	Whole	14
34	Two phalanges	11
35	One phalanx	9
36	Guillotine amputation of tip without loss of bone	5
	Middle finger	
37	Whole	12
38	Two phalanges	9
39	One phalanx	7
40	Guillotine amputation of tip without loss of bone	4
	Ring or Little finger	
41	Whole	7
42	Two phalanges	5
43	One phalanx	5
44	Guillotine amputation of tip without loss of bone	2
	B – Toes of right or left foot Great toe	
45	Through metatarso-phalangeal joint	14
46	Part, with some loss of bone Any other toe	3
47	Through metatarso-phalangeal joint	3
48	Part, with some loss of bone	1

Sl. No.	*Description of injury*	*Percentage of loss of earning capacity*
	Two toes of one foot, excluding great toe	
49	Through metatarso-phalangeal joint	5
50	Part, with some loss of bone	2
	Three toes of one foot, excluding great toe	
51	Through metaterso-phalangeal joint	6
52	Part, with some loss of bone	3
	Four toes of one foot, excluding great toe	
53	Through metatarso-phalangeal joint	9
54	Part, with some loss of bone	3

Note: Complete and permanent loss of the use of any limb or member referred to in this Schedule shall be deemed to be the equivalent of the loss of that limb or member.

THE THIRD SCHEDULE

[*See* Section 52A]

LIST OF OCCUPATIONAL DISEASES

PART A

1. Infectious and parasitic diseases contracted in occupation where there is a particular risk of contamination.
   - (a) All work involving exposure to health or laboratory work;
   - (b) All work involving exposure to veterinary work;
   - (c) Work relating to handling animals; animal carcasses, part of such carcasses, or merchandise which may have been contaminated by animals or animal carcasses;
   - (d) Other work carrying a particular risk of contamination.
2. Diseases caused by work in compressed air—All work involving exposure to the risk concerned.
3. Diseases caused by lead or its toxic compounds—All work involving exposure to the risk concerned.
4. Poisoning by nitrous fumes—All work involving exposure to the risk concerned.
5. Poisoning by organophosphorus compounds—All work involving exposure to the risk concerned.

PART B

1. Diseases caused by phosphorus or its toxic compounds—All work involving exposure to the risk concerned.

2. Diseases caused by mercury or its toxic compounds—All work involving exposure to the risk concerned.
3. Diseases caused by benzene or its toxic homologues—All work involving exposure to the risk concerned.
4. Diseases caused by nitro and amido toxic derivatives of benzene or its homologues—All work involving exposure to the risk concerned.
5. Diseases caused by chromium or its toxic compounds. All work involving exposure to the risk concerned.
6. Diseases caused by arsenic or its toxic compounds. All work involving exposure to the risk concerned.
7. Diseases caused by radioactive substances and ionizing radiations. All work involving exposure to the action of radioactive substances or ionising radiations.
8. Primary epithelomatous cancer of the skin caused by tar, pitch, bitumen, mineral oil, anthracene, or the compounds, products or residues of these substances. All work involving exposure to the risk concerned.
9. Diseases caused by the toxic halogen derivatives of hydrocarbons (of the aliphatic and aromatic series)—All work involving exposure to the risk concerned.
10. Diseases caused by the carbon disulphide—All work involving exposure to the risk concerned.
11. Occupational cataract due to infrared radiations. All work involving exposure to the risk concerned.
12. Diseases caused by manganese or its toxic compounds. All work involving exposure to the risk concerned.
13. Skin diseases caused by physical, chemical or biological agents not included in other items. All work involving exposure to the risk concerned.
14. Hearing impairment caused by noise. All work involving exposure to the risk concerned.
15. Poisoning by dinitrophenol or homologue or by substituted dinitro-phenol or by the salts of such substances. All work involving exposure to the risk concerned.
16. Diseases caused by beryllium or its toxic compounds. All work involving exposure to the risk concerned.
17. Diseases caused by cadmium or its toxic compounds. All work involving exposure to the risk concerned.
18. Occupational asthma caused by recognised sensitizing agents inherent to the work process. All work involving exposure to the risk concerned.
19. Diseases caused by fluorine or its toxic compounds. All work involving exposure to the risk concerned.
20. Diseases caused by nitroglycerin or other nitroacid esters. All work involving exposure to the risk concerned.
21. Diseases caused by alcohols and ketones. All work involving exposure to the risk concerned.
22. Diseases caused by asphyxiants: carbon monoxide and its toxic derivatives, hydrogen sulphide. All work involving exposure to the risk concerned.

23. Lung cancer and mesotheliomas caused by asbestos. All work involving exposure to the risk concerned.
24. Primary neoplasm of the epithelial lining of the urinary bladder or the kidney or the ureter. All work involving exposure to the risk concerned.

PART C

1. Pneumoconioses caused by sclerogenic mineral dust (silicosis, anthraoosilicosis asbestoses) and silica-tuberculosis provided that silicosis is an essential factor in causing the resultant incapacity or death. All work involving exposure to the risk concerned.
2. Bagassosis. All work involving exposure to the risk concerned.
3. Bronchopulmonary diseases caused by cotton, flax, hemp and sisal dust (Byssinosis). All work involving exposure to the risk concerned.
4. Extrinsic allergic alveelitis caused by the inhalation of the organic dusts. All work involving exposure to the risk concerned.
5. Bronchopulmonary diseases caused by hard metals. All work involving exposure to the risk concerned.

* * *

13 The Employees' Provident Funds and Miscellaneous Provisions Act, 1952

OBJECT OF THE ACT

The Constitution of India in Part IV under the Chapter Directive Principles of State Policy, inter-alia, enjoins upon the State to strive to promote the welfare of the people. The Government of India has, through various enactments, endeavoured to give effect to the ideas and objectives enshrined in the Constitution in the field of social security. The Employees' Provident Funds and Miscellaneous Provisions Act, 1952 was enacted with the main object of making some provision for the future of the industrial worker after he retires or for his dependants in case of his early death.

Three schemes have been framed under the Employees' Provident Funds and Miscellaneous Provisions Act, 1952, namely, the Employees' Provident Funds Scheme, 1952, the Employees' Deposit Linked Insurance Scheme, 1976 and Employees' Pension Scheme, 1995. The three schemes taken together provide to the employees an umbrella for the rainy day in the shape of old age and survivorship benefits, a long-term protection and security to the employee and after his death to his family members, and timely advances, including advances during sickness and for the purchase/construction of a dwelling house during the period of membership.

The Act was brought on the statute book for providing for the institution of provident fund for the employees in factories and other establishments. The basic purpose of providing for provident funds appears to be to make provision for the future of the industrial worker after his retirement or for his dependents in case of his early death. To achieve this ultimate object, the Act is designed to cultivate among the workers a spirit of saving something regularly, and also to encourage stabilisation of a steady labour force in the industrial centres. This Act has since its initial enactment been amended several times to extend its scope for the benefit of industrial workers.[1]

THE ACT AND SCHEME

The Employees' Provident Funds and Miscellaneous Provisions Act provides for compulsory

1. *Provident Fund Inspector, Guntur* v. *T.S. Hariharan*, AIR 1971 SC 1519.

contributory fund for the future of an employee after his retirement or for his dependants in case of his early death.

It extends to the whole of India except the State of Jammu and Kashmir and is applicable to:

(a) every factory engaged in any industry specified in Schedule 1 in which 20 or more persons are employed;
(b) every other establishment employing 20 or more persons or class of such establishments which the Central Government may notify; and
(c) any other establishment so notified by the Central Government even if employing less than 20 persons.

Employees Entitled

Every employee, including the one employed through a contractor (but excluding an apprentice engaged under the Apprentices Act or under the standing orders of the establishment and casual labourers), who is in receipt of wages up to ₹6,500 p.m., shall be eligible for becoming a member of the funds.

The condition of three months' continuous service or 60 days of actual work for membership of the scheme has been done away with, w.e.f. 1-11-1990. Workers are now eligible for joining the scheme from the date of joining the service.

Employees' Pension Scheme, 1995

The Government has framed the Employees' Pension Scheme, 1995, w.e.f. 16-11-1995. The existing Employees' Family Pension Scheme has been merged under the new scheme.

The new scheme envisages providing monthly pension to employees on superannuation, pensioning to widows on death after superannuation, monthly pension for children of the subscribers, monthly pension to members on account of permanent total disablement during service, etc.

The new scheme shall be compulsory for all the existing members of the Family Pension Scheme and those who become members of the Employees' Provident Fund Scheme on or after 16-11-1995. Besides, the following employees shall have an option to join the new Scheme:

(a) Employees who ceased to be members of the Pension Fund between 1-4-1993 to 15-11-1995.
(b) Employees who are members of the Provident Fund as on 16-11-1995 and not members of the Pension Fund.

Members who have died between 1-4-1993 to 15-11-1995 shall be deemed to have exercised the option of joining the scheme on the date of the death.

Members referred in clause (a) shall exercise the option to become members of the scheme by returning the amount of withdrawal benefit received, if any, together with interest @ 8.5% p.a.

Employees referred in clause (b) shall be deemed to have joined the scheme w.e.f. 1-3-1971 on remittance of past period contribution with interest thereon.

Term of Scheme

Every member of the Employees' Pension Fund Scheme shall continue to remain the member till the earliest happening of any of the following events:

(i) he attains the age of 58 years; or
(ii) he avails the withdrawal benefit to which he is entitled vide para 14 of the scheme; or
(iii) he dies; or
(iv) the pension is vested in him.

Every employer shall send to the Commissioner, within three months of the commencement of the scheme, a consolidated return of the employees entitled to become members of the new scheme.

Employer's Contribution

The employer is required to contribute the following amounts towards Employees' Provident Fund and Pension Fund:

(a) In case of establishments' employing less than 20 persons or a sick industrial (BIFR) company or 'sick establishments' or any establishment in the jute, beedi, brick, coir or gaur gum industry—10% of the basic wages, dearness allowance and retaining allowance, if any.
(b) In case of all other establishments employing 20 or more person—12% of the wages, D.A., etc.

A part of the contribution is remitted to the Pension Fund and the remaining balance continues to remain in Provident Fund account.

Where the pay of an employee exceeds ₹6500 p.m., the contribution payable to Pension Fund shall be limited to the amount payable on his pay of ₹6500 only. However, the employees may voluntarily opt for the employer's share of contributions on wages beyond the limit of ₹6500 to be credited to the Pension Fund.

Voluntary Application of The Act

The employer and majority of employees of an establishment may agree for the voluntary application of the provisions of the Act in relation to that establishment. For this purpose, an application to the Central Provident Fund Commissioner has to be made, who may, by notification, extend the provisions of the Act to that establishment, w.e.f. the date of such agreement or any subsequent date specified in such agreement.

The employer is required to contribute the following amounts towards Employees' Provident Fund and Pension Fund:

(a) Where the parties voluntarily get themselves covered by the Act, they are completely and fully governed by the Act. But their liability to make contribution is, in case of establishments' employing less than 20 persons or a sick industrial (BIFR) company or 'sick establishments' or any establishment in the jute, beedi, brick, coir or gaur gum industry—10% of the basic wages, dearness allowance and retaining allowance, if any.

(b) In case of all other establishments' employing 20 or more person—12% of the wages, D.A., etc.

Penalty for Default in Payment

If the employer defaults in making payment of any contribution, arrears, accumulations, administrative charges, to the Fund, he shall be liable to pay, by way of penalty, damages at the following rates:

Period of Default	*Rate of Damages (% p.a.)*
(i) Less than 2 months	17
(ii) 2 months and above but less than 4 months	22
(iii) 4 months and above but less than 6 months	27
(iv) 6 months and above	37

Dispute, Determination and Recovery

In case, where a dispute arises regarding applicability of the Act, the Central Provident Fund Commissioner or any other officer (to whom the powers of determination have been delegated), may decide the dispute and determine the amount due from an employer, under the Act or the schemes framed thereunder. Before making any order the officer shall conduct such inquiry as he may deem necessary and shall allow a reasonable opportunity to the employer for representing his case.

Further, where an officer has reason to believe that an amount due from the employer has escaped determination, he may re-open the case within five years and re-determine the amount due from the employer.

Interest

The employer shall be liable to pay simple interest @ 12% p.a. on any amount due from him under the Act, from the date on which it becomes due till the date of its actual payment.

Modes of Recovery

Any amount of contribution, damages, accumulations required to be transferred, or administrative charges, due from an employer, may be recovered from him in any of the following modes—

(a) attachment and sale of the movable or immovable property of the establishment/ employer;

(b) arrest of the employer and his detention in prison;

(c) appointing a receiver for the management of the movable or immovable properties of the establishment/employer.

The Recovery Officer pursuant to a recovery certificate issued by the authorised officer specifying the amount of arrears shall make the recovery.

Stay of Recovery Proceedings

The authorised officer may grant time for the payment of the amount, and thereupon the Recovery Officer shall stay the proceedings until the expiry of the time so granted.

Other Modes of Recovery

Besides the modes aforesaid, the authorised officer may recover the amount by any of the following modes:

(a) Recovery from any person of amount due from him to employee who is in arrears.
(b) Application for release of money, to the Court in whose custody there is money belonging to the employer.
(c) Recovery by distraint and sale of movable property.

Appeal

Any person aggrieved by an order of determination or re-determination may prefer an appeal to the PF Appellate Tribunal. He shall, however, deposit 75% of the amount determined in the order being appealed against, before filing an appeal.

The Appellate Tribunal may waive or reduce the amount to be deposited for admitting an appeal, after recording reasons for the same.

Clubbing of Establishments

The Act does not have any provision for clubbing of establishments. Despite this, the Provident Fund authorities tend to club establishments.

If in their true relation the establishments constitute one integrated whole, the establishment is said to be one. This relation is judged having regard to unity of ownership, management, control, employment, functional integrality, finance and geographical proximity.

Two units will be treated as different and distinct unless an interconnection between the two units is established of mutual dependence of one over the other, so that one cannot function altogether or substantially without the other. The mere fact that one concern exclusively purchases the products of the other does not mean that there is functional integrity. Similarly, merely because there is one common proprietor for the two units will not justify their treatment as one establishment.

The factors, such as situation of the office of the firms in one premises, user of a common telephone number and post-box number and employing the services of the same person to write the accounts, are not relevant for clubbing them.

Before passing an order clubbing two or more establishments as one concern, the Commissioner must afford a reasonable opportunity to the affected establishments.

Issue of show cause notices containing the conclusion without giving documents of evidence, on the basis of which the conclusion is arrived, would not amount to giving reasonable opportunity.[2]

CHAPTER I

PRELIMINARY

SECTION 1: Short title, extent and application

(1) This Act may be called the Employees' Provident Funds and Miscellaneous Provisions Act, 1952.

(2) It extends to the whole of India except the State of Jammu and Kashmir.

(3) Subject to the provisions contained in section 16, it applies—

(a) to every establishment which is a factory engaged in any industry specified in Schedule I and in which twenty or more persons are employed, and

(b) to any other establishment employing twenty or more persons or class of such establishments which the Central Government may, by notification in the Official Gazette, specify in this behalf:

Provided that the Central Government may, after giving not less than two months' notice of its intention so to do, by notification in the Official Gazette, apply the provisions of this Act to any establishment employing such number of persons less than twenty as may be specified in the notification.

(4) Notwithstanding anything contained in sub-section (3) of this section or sub-section (1) of section 16, where it appears to the Central Provident Fund Commissioner, whether on an application made to him in this behalf or otherwise, that the employer and the majority of employees in relation to any establishment have agreed that the provisions of this Act should be made applicable to the establish-ment, he may, by notification in the Official Gazette, apply the provisions of this Act to that establishment on and from the date of such agreement or from any subsequent date specified in such agreement.

(5) An establishment to which this Act applies shall continue to be governed by this Act notwithstanding that the number of persons employed therein at any time falls below twenty.

Section 1(3)(a) is not confined to factories exclusively engaged in any industry specified in Schedule I. When the legislature has described factories as factories engaged in any industry, it did not intend that the said factories should be exclusively engaged in the industry specified in Schedule I. The word 'factory' used in S. 1(3)(a) has a comprehensive meaning

2. http://www.helplinelaw.com/docs/main.php3?id=PFND1

and it includes premises in which any manufacturing process is being carried on as described in the definition, and so the factory engaged in any industry specified in Schedule I does not necessarily mean a factory exclusively engaged in the particular industry specified in the said Schedule. Composite factories came within the purview of S. 1(3)(a) and the fact that a factory is engaged in industrial activities independent of each other some of which fall under the Schedule and some do not, will not take the factory out of the purview of S. 1(3)(a). The test of numerical strength is applied not to the industry but to the factory. Thus, in order that a factory should fall under S. 1(3)(a), it must be shown that it is engaged in any such industry as is specified in Schedule I, and the number of its employees should not be less than 50 (as required prior to Amending Act of 1960), now it is 20. If the factory carries on one industry which falls under Schedule I and satisfies the requirement as to the number of employees prescribed by the section, it clearly falls under S. 1(3)(a). If the factory carries on more than one industry all of which fall under Schedule I and its numerical strength satisfies the test prescribed in that behalf, it is an establishment under S. 1(3)(a). If a factory runs more industries than one, one of which is the primary and the dominant industry and the others are its feeders and can be regarded as subsidiary, minor, or incidental industries in that sense, then the character of the dominant and primary industry will determine the question as to whether the factory is an establishment under S. 1(3)(a) or not. If the dominant and primary industry falls under Schedule I, the fact that the subsidiary industries do not fall under Schedule I will not help to exclude the application of S. 1(3)(a). If the dominant and primary industry does not fall under Schedule I, but one or more subsidiary, incidental, minor and feeding industries fall under Schedule I, then S. 1(3)(a) will not apply. If the factory runs more industries than one all of which are independent of each other and constitute separate and distinct industries, S. 1(3)(a) will apply to the factory even if one or more, but not all, of the industries run by the factory fall under Schedule I.

The question about the subsidiary, minor, or feeding industries can legitimately arise only where it is shown that the factory is really started for the purpose of running one primary industry and has undertaken other subsidiary industries only for the purpose of sub serving and feeding the purposes and objects of the primary industry: in such a case, these minor industries merely serve as departments of the primary industry: otherwise if the industries run by a factory are independent, or are not so integrated as to be treated as part of the same industry, the question about the principal and the dominant character of one industry as against the minor or subsidiary character of another industry does not fall to be considered.[3]

The Act was not intended by Parliament to apply to employees who were mere wage-earners and not salaried servants, and that in the instant case, the employees of the petitioners were not mere wage-earners. It is a little difficult to appreciate the distinction sought to be made. Both 'salary' and 'wages' are emoluments paid to an employee by way of recompense for his labour. Neither of the two terms is a 'term of art'. The Act has not defined wages; it has only defined "basic wages" as all emoluments which are earned by an employee while on duty or on leave with wages in accordance with the terms of the contract of employment and which are paid or payable in cash to him, but does not include S. 2(b). 'Salary', on the other hand, is remuneration paid to an employee whose period of engagement is more or less

3. *Associated Industries (P) Ltd.* v. *Regional Provident Fund Commissioner, Kerala, Trivandrum,* AIR 1964 SC 314.

permanent in character, for other than manual or relatively unskilled labour. The distinction between skilled and unskilled labour itself is not very definite. The Act itself has not made any distinction between 'wages' and 'salary'. Both may be paid weekly, fortnightly or monthly, though remuneration for the day's work is not ordinarily termed 'salary'. Simply because wages for the month run into hundreds, as they very often do now, would not mean that the employee is not earning wages, properly so called. A clerk in an office may earn much less than the monthly wages of a skilled labourer. Ordinarily, he is said to earn his salary. But, in principle, there is no difference between the two. It is, therefore, not estab-lished that the Act was not intended to apply to salaried employees.[4]

In *Noor Niwas Nursery Public School* v. *Regional Provident Fund Commissioner*[5] the appellant is aggrieved by the application of the Employees' Provident Funds and Miscellaneous Provisions Act, 1952. The appellant-institution is run by Baptist Union, North India, a registered Society under the Registration of Societies Act, 1860. The said Society runs two schools at 17, Darya Gunj, Delhi, namely, Francis Girls Higher Secondary School which was established in 1916 and the appellant-School which runs nursery classes. The appellant-School was started in the year 1971. The claim of the appellant-School is that Francis Girls Higher Secondary School and the appellant-School, Noor Niwas Nursery Public School, are two different institutions having separate and independent accounts and are managed by two different Managing Committees. The appellant has four employees and it being a separate establishment is not covered by the provisions of the Act. Therefore, it is contended that Francis Girls Higher Secondary School and the appellant-School cannot be treated as one establishment for the purpose of the Act. However, the Court observed that when two units are located adjacent to one another and there are only two teachers with an aaya, a clerk and a peon, it is difficult to believe that the Society which runs 30 schools would run a separate school consisting of such a small number of staff. Undisputably, the two units are run by the same Society and they are located in one and the same address thereby establishing geographical proximity. Thus, the link between the two cannot be ruled out. The learned counsel for the appellant drew the attention of the Court that the said school has been excluded from the purview of the Act in view of the fact that the provident fund in respect of all the employees is subscribed under another scheme. The learned counsel submitted that if the two units were put together as a single establishment, the Act would be applicable and otherwise not, inasmuch as it falls short of the number of minimum of employees for the applicability of the Act under S. 1(3)(b) of the Act. The Court, while rejecting such contention, held that the two establishments have more than 20 employees and the exemption granted under S. 17 of the Act is subject to the condition that such exclusion will not apply to the appellant's unit because the same would not be covered under another scheme for subscribing to the provident fund. The Court accordingly held that the Act would be applied to the appellant-school.

In *Lakshmani Stone Products* v. *Union of India*,[6] the question raised before the Supreme Court was regarding the applicability of the Act to the 'stone quarries' producing stone chips, stone set, stone boulders and ballasts. A notification was issued on February 12, 1977

---

4. *Mohmedalli* v. *Union of India*, AIR 1964 SC 980.
5. AIR 2001 SC 277.
6. AIR 2001 SC 783.

under S. 1(3)(b) of the Employees' Provident Funds and Miscellaneous Provisions Act, 1952 specifying that certain establishments mentioned in the Schedule thereto would be covered by the Act and, *inter alia,* stating that the Act would apply to 'stone quarries' producing stone chips, stone set, stone boulders and ballasts. On February 19, 1977, a notification was issued under S. 7(1) of the Act to amend the scheme, namely, the Employees Provident Fund Scheme, 1952 by inserting identical provisions. A contention was raised by the appellant in a writ petition filed before the High Court that no notification has been issued under S. 4 of the Act including 'stone quarries' in the Schedule to the Act. In the absence of a notification issued under S. 4 of the Act, it is contented that the Act has no application to stone quarry industry. However, that writ petition was dismissed. Therefore, this appeal has been filed before the Supreme Court.

The High Court, in the instant case, took the view that the appellant was carrying on the business of quarrying stone under a mining lease and it was carried on by blasting stones at quarry by explosive which are thereafter sized either manually by chipping or by using a mechanical crusher resulting in stone chips. The High Court held that the operations carried on by the appellant are not disassociated activities but integrally connected with each other and form part of a continuous process and the claim of the appellant that it is running a factory was not accepted. The High Court noticed that the appellant runs the establishment of stone quarry which has been brought within the purview of the Act, and inasmuch as the operation of reducing stones into smaller size is subsidiary and incidental operation to the primary activity, that is, running a stone quarry, the High Court took the view that it is an 'establishment' which has been brought within the ambit of the Act by issuing notifications on February 12, 1977 and February 19, 1977. The Supreme Court, while accepting the view of the High Court, held that the dominant activity of the appellant is to quarry the stones and cut or chip them to appropriate size before marketing the same either by manual or mechanical process, which is a subsidiary and incidental activity to the primary activity of running a stone quarry and therefore the appeal stands dismissed.

The notification issued under S. 1(3)(b) of the Act makes the Act applicable to establishments of "engineers and engineering contractors, not being exclusively engaged in building and construction industry". It follows that any establishment carrying on the business of engineers and engineering contractors which is exclusively engaged in building and construction industry does not fall within the scope of the notification and hence the Act would not be applicable to such an establishment. Any such establishment which carries on an activity which forms part of the building and construction industry should naturally be exempted from the operation of the Act because the expression 'building and construction industry' refers collectively to all activities which have to be performed in connection with the building and construction industry. In order to discharge effectively its functions as engineers and engineering contractors engaged in building and construction industry, an establishment has to maintain a workshop or workshops where the works of smithy, welding, cutting, carpentry etc. are carried on. Without these operations, it is not possible for any person to carry on satisfactorily the work of building and construction industry. The reason for taking this view is obvious. An establishment exclusively engaged in running a hospital does not cease to be an establishment exclusively carrying on the said business merely because it sets up a pharmacy section for preparing and compounding medicines to be used exclusively by the patients at its hospital. Similarly, an establishment which is exclusively engaged in providing shipping transport facilities does not cease to be an establishment exclusively carrying on the said business merely because it sets up an on-shore workshop for effecting repairs exclusively to its own ships. Illustrations such as mentioned above may be multiplied. The point which is made out by these illustrations is that where an establishment is engaged exclusively in carrying on a particular type of business by setting up any place of work with a view to carrying on the work of repairs, etc. to the tools, equipment, vehicles, etc. used in its business or to carry on any other activity which is essential for its business effectively and which is not used to carry on the work for the benefit of any third party but utilised exclusively for the business of the establishment, such establishment does not cease to carry on exclusively the business in which it is engaged. It cannot also be said that the establishment has commenced to carry on another industry by the setting up of such a place of work.[7] The narrow question which directly arises for consideration before the Supreme Court in *Provident Fund Inspector, Guntur* v. *T.S. Hariharan*[1] is whether Cl. (b) of sub-section (3) of S. 1 which speaks of the establishment employing 20 or more persons means that the person so employed may be employed by the establishment for any purpose whatsoever and for however short a duration or that the employment must be for some minimum period in the establishment. The language used in the clause does not give any clear indication. We have, therefore, to construe this word in the light of the legislative scheme, the object and purpose of enacting this clause and the ultimate effect of adopting one or the other construction.

Section 16 of the Act seems to throw considerable light on the point raised. It may be recalled that this section excludes from the applicability of the Act establishments belonging to the Government and to local authorities and infant establishments. It is, therefore, obvious that this Act is intended to apply only where an establishment has attained sufficient financial stability and is prosperous enough to be able to afford regular contribution provided by the Act. Contribution by the employer is an essential part of the statutory scheme for effectuating the object of inducing the workmen to save something regularly. The establishment, therefore, must possess stable financial capacity to bear the burden of regular contribution to the Fund under the Act. In this connection, it may be recalled that by virtue of S. 1(5), an establishment to which the Act is applied continues to be governed by the Act notwithstanding that the number of persons employed by it at any time falls below the required number. This liability to be governed by the Act ceases only if the terms of the Proviso to S. 1(5) are complied with. The financial capacity of the establishment to bear the burden must, therefore, have some semblance of a reasonably long-term stability. In other words, the employment of requisite number of persons must be dictated by the normal regular requirement of the establishment reflecting its financial capacity and stability. It, therefore, follows from this that the number of persons to be considered to have been employed by an establishment for the purpose of this Act has to be determined by taking into account the general requirements of the establishment for its regular work, which should also have a commercial nexus with its general financial capacity and stability. The Supreme Court, considering the language of S. 1(3)(b), held that employment of a few persons on account of some emergency or for a very short period necessitated by some abnormal contingency, which is not a regular

7. *Cemindia Co. Ltd.* v. *Bachubhai N. Raval*, AIR 1987 SC 1956.

feature of the business of the establishment and which does not reflect its business prosperity or its financial capacity and stability from which it can reasonably be concluded that the establishment can in the normal way bear the burden of contribution towards the provident fund under the Act, would not be covered by this definition. The word "employment" must, therefore, be construed as employment in the regular course of business of the establishment; such employment obviously would not include employment of a few persons for a short period on account of some passing necessity or some temporary emergency beyond the control of the company. This must necessarily require determination of the question in each case on its own peculiar facts.

In *Andhra University* v. *Regional Provident Fund Commissioner of Andhra Pradesh*[8] and *Osmania University* v. *Regional Provident Fund Commissioner,*[9] the common contention taken by the appellants was that the Universities are purely educational institutions having a number of departments, the main object of which is to impart education to the youth of the country in various branches of studies and that the Department of Publications and Press, which is intended only to cater the needs and requirements of the students, cannot be regarded either as a 'factory' or as an 'industry' and the provisions of the EPF Act are not, therefore, attracted in respect of the said department. It was also submitted that the two Universities had their own provident fund schemes for their employees and hence there was no justification for subjecting them to the provisions of the Act. A learned single Judge of the High Court accepted the contention of the two Universities that the Department of Publications and Press could not be regarded as an industry and accordingly held that the provisions of the Act were not attracted. However, on appeals filed by the Regional Provident Fund Commissioner, Andhra Pradesh before a Division Bench of the High Court, the Division Bench by two separate judgments set aside the judgments of the learned single Judge and held that the Department of Publications and Press of each of the two Universities is an 'establishment' which is a factory engaged in an industry specified in Schedule I, in which more than 20 persons were employed and hence the provisions of the Act and the Scheme were applicable in respect of these Departments. The appellants namely, the two Universities, have challenged the correctness of the aforesaid conclusion recorded by the Division Bench of the High Court before the Supreme Court. The Supreme Court observed that where the Department of Publications and Press of the University was running a printing press where the work of printing of textbooks, journals and magazines for the various constituent and affiliated colleges as well of various items of stationery such as admission forms to colleges, hostels and examination forms, memo of marks, hall tickets, answer books, syllabi for various colleges and departments, registers receipt books for colleges and hostels and letter pads for Universities was carried out and about 100 persons were employed in connection with the said activities in the said Department, the establishment, namely the Department of Publications and Press could be said to be a "factory" within the meaning of S. 2(g), as the printing of textbooks, journals, registers, forms and various items of stationery clearly constitute "manufacture" within the meaning of the said expression as defined in Cl. (ic) of S. 2. Since more than 20 persons were employed in the establishment concerned, the establishment would be liable for coverage under the Act.

8. AIR 1986 SC 463.
9. AIR 1986 SC 463.

SECTION 2: Definitions

In this Act, unless the context otherwise requires,

(a) **appropriate Government** means—

(i) in relation to an establishment belonging to, or under the control of, the Central Government or in relation to an establishment connected with a railway company, a major port, a mine or an oilfield or a controlled industry, or in relation to an establishment having departments or branches in more than one State, the Central Government; and

(ii) in relation to any other establishment, the State Government.

(aa) **authorised officer** means the Central Provident Fund Commissioner, Additional Central Provident Fund Commissioner, Deputy Provident Fund Commissioner, Regional Provident Fund Commissioner or such other officer as may be authorised by the Central Government, by notification in the Official Gazette.

(b) **basic wages** means all emoluments which are earned by an employee while on duty or on leave or on holidays with wages in either case in accordance with the terms of the contract of employment and which are paid or payable in cash to him, but does not include:

(i) the cash value of any food concession;

(ii) any dearness allowance (that is to say, all cash payments by whatever name called paid to an employee on account of a rise in the cost of living), house-rent allowance, overtime allowance, bonus, commission or any other similar allowance payable to the employee in respect of his employment or of work done in such employment;

(iii) any presents made by the employer.

In *Prantiya Vidhyut Mandal Mazdoor Federation* v. *Rajasthan State Electricity Board,*[10] the question raised for consideration before the Supreme Court is whether arrears of wages, as a result of wage-increase-award under the Industrial Disputes Act, 1947, would come within the definition of "basic wages" under S. 2(b) of the Provident Fund and Miscellaneous Provisions Act, 1952. The fact of the instant case reveals that a dispute regarding wages and other conditions of service arose between the Rajasthan State Electricity Board and its workmen. The parties arrived at a settlement as a result of which the dispute was referred to the arbitrators under the Industrial Disputes Act, 1947. The arbitrators entered upon the reference and gave an award dated May 20, 1985. According to the award, various categories of workmen were to be paid higher wages with effect from April 1, 1980. The arrears of pay and other benefits accrued to the workmen were to be paid in four equal installments. The first installment was payable on December 1, 1985 and the remaining three at an interval of six months each. The Provident Fund authorities issued directions that provident fund contributions be deducted from the arrears paid to the workmen. Accordingly, when the first installment was disbursed, the Board deducted the employees' contribution and also made its own contribution as required under the Fund Act. However, at the time of the second

10. AIR 1992 SC 1737.

installment, the Board filed a writ petition under Art. 226 of the Constitution of India before the Rajasthan High Court challenging the directions of the Provident Fund authorities on the ground that arrears payable to the employees as a result of the award of the arbitrators were not the "basic wages" under S. 2(b) of the EPF Act. A learned single Judge of the High Court dismissed the writ petition. On appeal, a Division Bench of the High Court set aside the judgment of the learned single Judge and allowed the writ petition. The Divisional Bench of the High Court held that if a contract of employment provides for payment of wages at a future date, then it may fall within the definition of wages as the same becomes payable under the contract of employment. However, wages payable under the orders of a Court cannot be said to be wages payable under a contract of employment. The scheme framed under S. 6 of the P.F. Act provides for calculation of the contribution on basis of the emoluments actually drawn during a whole month. Wages payable under an award of the arbitrators cannot be termed as deferred wages so as to mean that they had accrued at a particular time but were payable at a later date. Accordingly, wages payable under the award cannot be brought within the definition of wages under S. 2(b) of the P.F. Act. The Supreme Court on appeal referred S. 2(b) and S. 6 of the EPF Act and observed that reading the above quoted two sections together, the expression "basic wages" means:

(i) all emoluments which are earned by an employee while on duty or on leave;
(ii) with wages in accordance with the terms of the contract of employment;
(iii) which are paid or payable in cash; and
(iv) are payable for the time being to each of the employees.

When an award gives revised pay scales, the employees become entitled to the revised emoluments and where the said revision is with retrospective effect, the arrears paid to the employees, as a consequence, are the emoluments earned by them while on duty. The Court accordingly held that if the original emoluments earned by an employee were "basic wages" under the EPF Act, there is no justification to hold that the substituted emoluments as a result of the award are not the "basic wages".

In *Bridge and Roofs Co. Ltd., M/s.* v. *Union of India*[11] the short question raised in this writ petition under Art. 32 of the Constitution is whether production bonus is included within the term "basic wages" as defined in S. 2(b) of the Employees Provident Funds Act, 1952. The main contention of the Company is that the bonus without any qualification has been excepted from the term "basic wages" in the definition in S. 2(b) of the Act. Therefore, all kinds of bonus, whether it be profit bonus or production bonus or attendance bonus or festival bonus either as an implied condition of service or as a customary payment, are excluded from "basic wages". Further, S. 6, which provides for contribution only, refers to basic wages, dearness allowances and retaining allowance (if any) and contributions have to be made at the appropriate rate on these three payments and not on bonus which is not included in S. 6. It is urged that when the EPF Act was passed in 1952, the legislature was aware of the various kinds of bonus which were being paid by various concerns in various industries and it decided to exclude bonus without any qualification from the term "basic wages" as defined in S. 2(b). The Supreme Court, accordingly, observed that Cl. (ii) of S. 2(b) excludes, amongst other allowances, bonus payable to the employee in respect of his employment or of work

11. AIR 1963 SC 1474.

done in such employment from the definition of "basic wages". This exception suggests that even though the main part of the definition includes all emoluments which are earned in accordance with the terms of the contract of employment, certain payments which are in fact the price of labour and earned in accordance with the terms of the contract of employment, are excluded from the main part of the definition of "basic wages". The word "bonus" has been used in this clause without any qualification, therefore it would not be improper to infer that when the word "bonus" was used without any qualification in the clause, the legislature had in mind every kind of bonus that may be payable to an employee. The legislature could not have been unaware that different kinds of bonus were being paid by different concerns in different industries, when it passed the Act in 1952. Where the word "bonus" is used without any qualification, it does not only mean profit bonus. On the other hand, the use of the word "bonus", without any qualifying word before it, or without any limitation after it, must refer to bonus of all kinds known to industrial law and industrial adjudication including the 'production bonus'. The production bonus is therefore outside the definition of "basic wages" in S. 2(b) of the Act.

In *Jay Engineering Works Ltd.* v. *Union of India*,[12] the Supreme Court has formulated important guidelines in respect to what constitute the basic wages and they are as follows.

(1) That the mere fact that part of the basic wage as defined in the Act was paid in one form as a time wage and part in another form as a piece-rate wage would make no difference to the whole being basic wage within the meaning of the Act.

(2) That the payment for work done between the quota and norm could not be treated as any "*other similar allowance*" within S. 2(b)(ii) as the allowances mentioned in the clause were dearness allowance, house-rent allowance, overtime allowance, bonus and commission and any "other similar allowance" must be of the same kind.

(3) That the portion of the payment which was made by the company for production above the "norm" would be production bonus and would be excluded from the term "basic wages" as defined in S. 2(b).

Contribution towards the provident fund can only be on the basic wages. However, it is not at all necessary that the workman must actually be on duty or that the workman should actually have worked in order to attract the provisions of the Employees' Provident Funds Act. For example, there may be a lockout in a company. During the period of lockout, the workmen may not have worked, yet for the purpose of the Employees Provident Funds Act they will be deemed to have been on duty and Provident Fund would be deductible from their wages. In *Shree Changdeo Sugar Mills* v. *Union of India*,[13] where though company was closed, pursuant to orders of the High Court in dispute by workmen claiming retrenchment benefit, retiral benefits etc., the High Court fixed 31 October, 1988 as a date when the services of the employees stood terminated/retrenched. Thus, up to date fixed by the High Court, the employees were in service of the company. They were, therefore, deemed to be on duty up to date fixed by the High Court. Some of these employees had raised claims before the Labour Court and there were awards of the Labour Court for payment of arrears of wages and retrenchment compensation. All that settlement entered into between the company and its

12. AIR 1963 SC 1480.
13. AIR 2001 SC 557.

workers was that the total claim of the workmen was reduced to a certain extent. Amongst the claim of the workmen was a claim for wages up to date of retrenchment of workers fixed by the High Court, i.e. 31 October, 1988. This was a claim for wages for a period during which they were on "deemed duty". Relevant clause of the settlement shows that a sum of Rs. 35 lakhs has been paid towards wages and another sum of Rs. 10 lakhs has been paid towards Retaining (Seasonal) wages. These are amounts which are paid for wages during a period when the workmen are deemed to be on duty. Therefore, it is 'basic wage' within the meaning of S. 2(b) of the Employees' Provident Funds Act. The company cannot be exempted from payment of Provident Fund on wages paid by the company under the said settlement.

In 2019 February, the Supreme Court in *the Regional Provident Fund Commissioner* (II) *West Bengal* v. *Vivekananda Vidyamandir* has clubbed other four cases because there is a common question of law, if the special allowances paid by an establishment to its employees would fall within the expression "basic wages" under Section 2(b) (ii) read with Section 6 of the PF Act for computation of deduction towards Provident Fund.

The Supreme Court interpreted Section 2(b) (ii) read with Section 6 of the Act and referred earlier decisions of the Court to reach to the conclusion.

The fact of the case reveals that the respondent (Vivekananda Vidyamandir) is an unaided school giving special allowance by way of incentive to teaching and nonteaching staff pursuant to an agreement between the staff and the management. The incentive was reviewed from time to time upon enhancement of the tuition fees of the students. The authority under the PF Act held that the special allowance was to be included in basic wage for deduction of provident fund. The Single Judge set aside the order. The Division Bench initially after examining the salary structure allowed the appeal on 13.01.2005 holding that the special allowance was a part of dearness allowance liable to deduction. The order was recalled on 16.01.2007 at the behest of the respondent as none had appeared on its behalf. The subsequent Division Bench dismissed the appeal holding that the special allowance was not linked to the consumer price index, and therefore did not fall within the definition of basic wage, thus not liable to deduction and this appeal before the Apex Court.

The Supreme Court mainly relied on *Manipal Academy of Higher Education* v. *Provident Fund Commissioner,* (2008) 5 SCC 428, where the court referred Bridge Roof's case *(Bridge and Roof Co. (India) Ltd.* v. *Union of India*, (1963) 3SCR 978, and following observations are made after combined reading of Sections 2(b) and 6 of the PF Act that:

(a) Where the wage is universally, necessarily and ordinarily paid to all across the board such emoluments are basic wages.

(b) Where the payment is available to be specially paid to those who avail of the opportunity is not basic wages. By way of example it was held that overtime allowance, though it is generally inforce in all concerns is not earned by all employees of a concern. It is also earned in accordance with the terms of the contract of employment but because it may not be earned by all employees of a concern, it is excluded from basic wages.

(c) Conversely, any payment by way of a special incentive or work is not basic wages.

The Supreme Court observed and held as follows:

"Applying the aforesaid tests to the facts of the present appeals, no material has been placed by the establishments to demonstrate that the allowances in question being paid to its employees were either variable or were linked to any incentive for production resulting in greater output by an employee and that the allowances in question were not paid across the board to all employees in a particular category or were being paid especially to those who avail the opportunity. In order that the amount goes beyond the basic wages, it has to be shown that the workman concerned had become eligible to get this extra amount beyond the normal work which he was otherwise required to put in. There is no data available on record to show what were the norms of work prescribed for those workmen during the relevant period. It is therefore not possible to ascertain whether extra amounts paid to the workmen were in fact paid for the extra work which had exceeded the normal output prescribed for the workmen. The wage structure and the components of salary have been examined on facts, both by the authority and the appellate authority under the Act, who have arrived at a factual conclusion that the allowances in question were essentially a part of the basic wage camouflaged as part of an allowance so as to avoid deduction and contribution accordingly to the provident fund account of the employees. There is no occasion for us to interfere with the concurrent conclusions of facts. The appeals by the establishments therefore merit no interference. Conversely, for the same reason the appeal preferred by the Regional Provident Fund Commissioner deserves to be allowed."

(c) **contribution** means a contribution payable in respect of a member under a scheme or the contribution payable in respect of an employee to whom the Insurance Scheme applies.

(d) **controlled industry** means any industry the control of which by the Union has been declared by a Central Act to be expedient in the public interest.

(e) **employer** means:

(i) in relation to an establishment which is a factory, the owner or occupier of the factory, including the agent of such owner or occupier, the legal representative of a deceased owner or occupier and, where a person has been named as a manager of the factory under clause (f) of sub-section (1) of section 7 of the Factories Act, 1948, the person so named; and

(ii) in relation to any other establishment, the person who, or the authority which, has the ultimate control over the affairs of the establishment, and where the said affairs are entrusted to a manager, managing director or managing agent, such manager, managing director or managing agent.

Both Cls. (i) and (ii) are wide in their sweep. In Cl. (i) are included not only the owner and occupier but even the agent or manager. When it comes to establishments other than a factory, it is not confined to the owner or occupier but to all those who have control or are responsible for the affairs of the company. It includes even director. Therefore, every such person who has the ultimate control over the affairs of the company becomes employer.[14]

(f) **employee** means any person who is employed for wages in any kind of work, manual or otherwise, in or in connection with the work of an establishment,

14. *Srikanta Datta Narasimharaja Wodiyar* v. *Enforcement Officer, Mysore*, AIR 1993 SC 1656; = 1993 AIR SCW 1815.

and who gets his wages directly or indirectly from the employer, and includes any person—

(i) employed by or through a contractor in or in connection with the work of the establishment;

(ii) engaged as an apprentice, not being an apprentice engaged under the Apprentices Act, 1961, or under the standing orders of the establishment.

The real question raised before the Supreme Court in *P.M. Patel and Sons, M/s.* v. *Union of India*[15] is whether the home workers are entitled to get the benefit of the EPF Act. The Court held that the terms of the definition of "*employee*" are wide. They include not only persons employed directly by the employer but also persons employed through a contractor. Moreover, they include not only persons employed in the factory but also persons employed in connection with the work of the factory. Accordingly, a home worker, by virtue of the fact that he rolls beedies, is involved in an activity connected with the work of the factory engaged in the task of rolling beedies. In this view, the words "*in connection with*" in the definition of "*employee*" cannot be confined to work performed in the factory itself as a part of the total process of the manufacture. Further, in the context of the conditions and the circumstances in which the home workers of a single manufacturer of beedies go about their work, including the receiving of raw material from factory, rolling the beedies at home and delivering them to the manufacturer subject to the right of rejection of the manufacturer, there is sufficient evidence of the requisite degree of control and supervision for establishing the relationship of master and servant between the manufacturer and the home worker. What is to be remembered is that the work of rolling beedies is not of a sophisticated nature, requiring control and supervision at the time when the work is done. In 2001, the Supreme Court in *S.K. Nasiruddin Beedi Merchant Ltd., M/s.* v. *Central P.F. Commr.*,[16] had the same opinion and held that the Act would be applicable even in respect of home workers engaged through contractors and cannot be cavilled any more.

(ff) **exempted employee** means an employee to whom a Scheme or the Insurance Scheme, as the case may be, would, but for the exemption granted under section 17, have applied.

(fff) **exempted establishment** means an establishment in respect of which an exemption has been granted under section 17 from the operation of all or any of the provisions of any Scheme or the Insurance Scheme, as the case may be, whether such exemption has been granted to the establishment as such or to any person or class of persons employed therein.

(g) **factory** means any premises, including the precincts thereof, in any part of which a manufacturing process is being carried on or is ordinarily so carried on, whether with the aid of power or without the aid of power.

(h) **Fund** means the provident fund established under a Scheme.

(i) **industry** means any industry specified in Schedule I, and includes any other industry added to the Schedule by notification under section 4.

15. AIR 1987 SC 447.
16. AIR 2001 SC 850.

(ia) **Insurance Fund** means the Deposit-linked Insurance Fund established under sub-section (2) of Section 6C.

(ib) **Insurance Scheme** means the Employees' Deposit-linked Insurance Scheme framed under sub-section (1) of Section 6C.

(ic) **manufacture** or **manufacturing process** means any process for making, altering, repairing, ornamenting, finishing, packing, oiling, washing, cleaning, breaking up, demolishing, or otherwise treating or adapting any article or substance with a view to its use, sale, transport, delivery or disposal.

(j) **member** means a member of the fund.

(k) **occupier of a factory** means the person who has ultimate control over the affairs of the factory, and, where the said affairs are entrusted to a managing agent, such agent shall be deemed to be the occupier of the factory.

(ka) **Pension Fund** means the Employees' Pension Fund established under sub-section (2) of Section 6A.

(kb) **Pension Scheme** means the Employees' Pension Scheme framed under sub-section (1) of Section 6A.

(kc) **prescribed** means prescribed by rules made under this Act.

(kd) **Recovery Officer** means any officer of the Central Government, State Government or the Board of Trustees constituted under Section 5A, who may be authorised by the Central Government, by notification in the Official Gazette, to exercise the powers of a Recovery Officer under this Act.

(l) **scheme** means the Employees' Provident Fund Scheme framed under Section 5.

(ll) **superannuation**, in relation to an employee who is the member of the Pension Scheme, means the attainment, by the said employee, of the age of fifty-eight years.

(m) **Tribunal** means the Employees' Provident Funds Appellate Tribunal constituted under Section 7D.

Section 2A: Establishment to include all departments and branches

For the removal of doubts, it is hereby declared that where an establishment consists of different departments or has branches, whether situated in the same place or in different places, all such departments or branches shall be treated as parts of the same establishment.

Whether two units are one or distinct will have to be considered in the light of the provisions of S. 2A of the Act. In such cases, the Court has to consider how far there is functional integrity between the two units, whether one unit cannot exist conveniently and reasonably without the other, and on the further question, in matters of finance and employment, the employer has actually kept the two units distinct or integrated. In fact, the Apex Court set out certain tests in *Management of Pratap Press, New Delhi* v. *Secretary, Delhi Press Workers' Union, Delhi.*[17]

In *Noor Niwas Nursery Public School* v. *Regional Provident Fund Commissioner,*[5] the Supreme Court observed that when two units are located adjacent to one another and there

17. AIR 1960 SC 1213.

are only two teachers with an aaya, a clerk and a peon, it is difficult to believe that the Society which runs 30 schools would run a separate school consisting of such a small number of staff. If the unit of the appellant-school was not part of the unit of Francis Girls Higher Secondary School, the Head Clerk, Mrs. Wadhavan could not have been in possession of the particulars of the appellant-school and could not have furnished such particulars to the Inspector when he visited the school in connection with the grant of a code number. Undisputably, the two units are run by the same Society and they are located in one and the same address thereby establishing geographical proximity and nothing worthwhile has been elicited in the cross-examination of the Inspector in regard to inquiries made by him from Mrs. P. Wadhavan. Mrs. P. Wadhavan was not examined before the Provident Fund Commissioner. All these facts clearly point out to one factor that the two units constitute one single establishment. After all, the appellant-school caters to nursery classes, while the higher classes are provided in Francis Girls Higher Secondary School. Thus, the link between the two cannot be ruled out.

SECTION 3: Power to apply the Act to an establishment which has a common provident fund with another establishment

Where immediately before this Act becomes applicable to an establishment there is in existence a provident fund which is common to the employees employed in that establishment and employees in any other establishment, the Central Government may, by notification in the Official Gazette, direct that the provisions of this Act shall also apply to such other establishment.

SECTION 4: Power to add to Schedule I

(1) The Central Government may, by notification in the Official Gazette, add to Schedule I any other industry in respect of the employees whereof it is of opinion that a provident fund scheme should be framed under this Act, and thereupon the industry so added shall be deemed to be an industry specified in Schedule I for the purposes of this Act.

(2) All notifications under sub-section (1) shall be laid before Parliament, as soon as may be, after they are issued.

SECTION 5: Employees' Provident Fund Schemes

(1) The Central Government may, by notification in the Official Gazette, frame a Scheme to be called the Employees' Provident Fund Schemes for the establishment of provident funds under this Act for employees or for any class of employees and specify the establishments or class of establishments to which the said Scheme shall apply and there shall be established, as soon as may be after the framing of the Scheme, a Fund in accordance with the provisions of this Act and the Scheme.

(1A) The Fund shall vest in, and be administered by, the Central Board constituted under Section 5A.

(1B) Subject to the provisions of this Act, a Scheme framed under sub-section (1) may provide for all or any of the matters specified in Schedule II.

(2) A Scheme framed under sub-section (1) may provide that any of its provisions shall take effect either prospectively or retrospectively on such date as may be specified in this behalf in the Scheme.

The short but an important question of law raised before the Supreme Court in *Regional Provident Fund Commissioner* v. *Shiv Kumar Joshi,*[18] is, whether the provisions of the Consumer Protection Act, 1986 can be invoked against the Provident Fund Commissioner by a member of the Employees' Provident Fund Scheme. It has to be ascertained as to whether any such member is a 'consumer' and the duties performed by the Provident Fund Commissioner under the relevant scheme is a 'service' within the meaning of the Consumer Protection Act, 1986 . If it is held that such member is the 'Consumer' and the facilities provided are 'services', it has to be further considered as to whether the delayed payment of the provident fund to a member-employee amounts to deficiency of service under the Act. The Supreme Court observed that the combined reading of the definitions of "Consumer" and "Service" under the Consumer Protection Act and looking at the aims and object for which the Act was enacted, it is imperative that the words "consumer" and "service" as defined under the Act should be construed to comprehend consumer and services of commercial and trade oriented nature only. Thus, any person who is found to have hired services for consideration shall be deemed to be a consumer, notwithstanding that the services were in connection with any goods or their user. Such services may be for any connected commercial activity and may also relate to the services as indicated in S. 2(1)(o) of the Consumer Protection Act.

For better understanding, it is necessary to provide the definitions of "consumer" and "service" provided in the Consumer Protection Act and they are as follows.

Section 2(1)(d) of the Consumer Protection Act, 1986 defines consumer as any person who:

(i) buys any goods for a consideration which has been paid or promised or partly paid and partly promised or under any system of the deferred payment and includes user of such goods other than the person who buys such goods for consideration paid or promised or partly paid or partly promised, or under any system of deferred payment when such use is made with the approval of such person, but does not include a person who obtains such goods for resale or for any commercial purpose; or

(ii) hires or avails of any services for a consideration which has been paid or promised or partly paid and partly promised, or under any system of deferred payment and includes any beneficiary of such services other than the person who hires or avails of the services for consideration paid or promised, or partly paid and partly promised, or any system of deferred payment, when such services are availed of with the approval of the first mentioned person but does not include a person who avails such services for any commercial purposes.

Section 2(1)(o) of the Consumer Protection Act, 1986 defines service as follows.

18. AIR 2000 SC 331.

"Service" means service of any description which is made available to potential users and includes, but not limited to, the provision of facilities in connection with banking, financing, insurance, transport, processing, supply to electrical or other energy, board or lodging or both, entertainment, amusement or the purveying of news or other information, but does not include the rendering of any service free of charge or under a contract of personal service.

The Regional Provident Fund Commissioner under the Employees' P.F. Act and the Employees' Provident Fund Scheme, 1952 discharges statutory functions for running the scheme. It has not, in any way, been delegated with the sovereign powers of State so as to hold it as a Central Government, being not the authority rendering the "service" under the Consumer Protection Act. The Commissioner is a separate and distinct entity. It cannot legally claim that the facilities provided by the "scheme" were not "service" or that the benefits under the scheme being provided were free of charge. The definition of "consumer" under the Act includes not only the person who hires the "services" for consideration but also the beneficiary for whose benefit such services are hired. Even if it is held that administrative charges are paid by the Central Government and no part of it is paid by the employee, the services of the Provident Fund Commissioner in running the scheme shall be deemed to have been availed of for consideration by the Central Government for the benefit of employees who would be treated as beneficiary within the meaning of that word used in the definition of consumer.

The Supreme Court further observed in the instant case that a perusal of the scheme unambiguously shows that it is for consideration which is applicable to all those factories and establishments covered under the Provident Funds Act and the scheme who are required to become a member of the fund under the scheme. The employer who is otherwise not a member of the scheme is obliged to contribute under the scheme at the rates specified therein of the basic wages, dearness allowance including cash value of any food concession and repairing allowances, if any, payable to each employee to whom the scheme applies. The contribution of the employee has to be equal to the contribution payable by the employer in respect of such employee. The words 'in respect of' are significant as they indicate the liability of the employer to pay his part of the contribution in consideration of the employee working with him. But for the employment of the employee, there is no obligation upon the employer to pay his part of the contribution to the scheme. The administrative charges, as required to be paid under para 30 of the scheme are also paid for consideration of the employee being the member of the scheme. It is immaterial as to whether such charges are deducted actually from the wages of the employee or paid by his employer in respect of the employee-member of the scheme working for such employer. The administrative charges are further required to be determined having regard to the basic wages, the dearness allowance, retaining allowance, if any and cash value of food concessions admissible thereon for the time being payable to the employee. If the contention that as no part of the administrative charges are deducted from the actual wages of the employee, he cannot be deemed to be hiring the services of scheme is accepted, the consequences of such an interpretation shall frustrate the object of the Act and the scheme as in that event no obligation can be cast upon the employer to pay contributions which are equal to the contribution payable by the employee along with the administrative charges. The scheme has to be given such an interpretation which serves the purpose intended to be achieved by it, keeping in view the objects of the Act. The administrative charges are in lieu of the membership of the employee and for the services rendered under the scheme. It cannot be held that even though the employee is the member of the scheme, the employer would only be deemed to be a "consumer" for having made payments of the administrative charges. Admittedly, no service is rendered to the employer under the scheme which is framed for the benefit of the employee under Ss. 5, 6 and 7 of the Provident Funds Act. The Court, accordingly, held that a perusal of the scheme clearly and unambiguously indicate that this is a "service" within the meaning of S. 2(1)(o) and the member a "consumer" within the meaning of S. 2(1)(d) of the Consumer Protection Act. Therefore, the Consumer Protection Act is applicable to the scheme.

Section 5A: Central Board

(1) The Central Government may, be notification in the Official Gazette, constitute, with effect from such date as may be specified therein, a Board of Trustees for the territories to which this Act extends (hereinafter in this Act referred to as the Central Board) consisting of the following persons as members, namely:

- (a) a Chairman and a Vice-Chairman to be appointed by the Central Government;
- (aa) the Central Provident Fund Commissioner, *ex officio*;
- (b) not more than five persons appointed by the Central Government from amongst its officials;
- (c) not more than fifteen persons representing Governments of such States as the Central Government may specify in this behalf, appointed by the Central Government;
- (d) ten persons representing employers of the establishments to which the Scheme applies, appointed by the Central Government after consultation with such organizations of employers as may be recognised by the Central Government in this behalf; and
- (e) ten persons representing employees in the establishments to which the Scheme applies, appointed by the Central Government after consultation with such organizations of employees as may be recognised by the Central Government in this behalf.

(2) The terms and conditions subject to which a member of the Central Board may be appointed and the time, place and procedure of the meetings of the Central Board shall be such as may be provided for in the Scheme.

(3) The Central Board shall, subject to the provisions of section 6A and section 6C, administer the fund vested in it in such manner as may be specified in the Scheme.

(4) The Central Board shall perform such other functions as it may be required to perform by or under any provisions of the Scheme, the Pension Scheme and the Insurance Scheme.

(5) The Central Board shall maintain proper accounts of its income and expenditure in such form and in such manner as the Central Government may, after consultation with the Comptroller and Auditor-General of India, specify in the Scheme.

(6) The accounts of the Central Board shall be audited annually by the Comptroller and Auditor-General of India and any expenditure incurred by him in connection with such audit shall be payable by the Central Board to the Comptroller and Auditor General of India.

(7) The Comptroller and Auditor-General of India and any person appointed by him in connection with the audit of the accounts of the Central Board shall have the same rights and privileges and authority in connection with such audit as the Comptroller and Auditor-General has, in connection with the audit of Government accounts and, in particular, shall have the right to demand the production of books, accounts, connected vouchers, documents and papers and inspect any of the offices of the Central Board.

(8) The accounts of the Central Board as certified by the Comptroller and Auditor-General of India or any other person appointed by him in this behalf together with the audit report thereon shall be forwarded to the Central Board which shall forward the same to the Central Government along with its comments on the report of the Comptroller and Auditor-General.

(9) It shall be the duty of the Central Board to submit also to the Central Government an annual report of its work and activities and the Central Government shall cause a copy of the annual report, the audited accounts together with the report of the Comptroller and Auditor-General of India and the comments of the Central Board thereon to be laid before each House of Parliament.

Section 5AA: Executive Committee

(1) The Central Government may, by notification in the Official Gazette, constitute, with effect from such date as may be specified therein, an Executive Committee to assist the Central Board in the performance of its functions.

(2) The Executive Committee shall consist of the following persons as members, namely:

(a) a Chairman appointed by the Central Government from amongst the members of the Central Board;

(b) two persons appointed by the Central Government from amongst the persons referred to in clause (b) of sub-section (1) of section 5A;

(c) three persons appointed by the Central Government from amongst the persons referred to in clause (c) of sub-section (1) of section 5A;

(d) three persons representing the employers elected by the Central Board from amongst the persons referred to in clause (d) of sub-section (1) of section 5A;

(e) three persons representing the employees elected by the Central Board from amongst the persons referred to in clause (e) of sub-section (1) of section 5A;

(f) the Central Provident Fund Commissioner, *ex officio*.

(3) The terms and conditions subject to which a member of the Central Board may be appointed or elected to the Executive Committee and the time, place and procedure of the meetings of the Executive Committee shall be such as may be provided for in the Scheme.

SECTION 5B: State Board

(1) The Central Government may, after consultation with the Government of any State, by notification in the Official Gazette, constitute for that State a Board of Trustees (hereinafter in this Act referred to as the State Board) in such manner as may be provided for in the Scheme.

(2) A State Board shall exercise such powers and perform such duties as the Central Government may assign to it from time to time.

(3) The terms and conditions subject to which a member of a State Board may be appointed and the time, place and procedure of the meetings of a State Board shall be such as may be provided for in the Scheme.

SECTION 5C: Board of Trustees to be body corporate

Every Board of Trustees constituted under section 5A or section 5B shall be a body corporate under the name specified in the notification constituting it, having perpetual succession and a common seal and shall by the said name sue and be sued.

SECTION 5D: Appointment of officers

(1) The Central Government shall appoint a Central Provident Fund Commissioner who shall be the chief executive officer of the Central Board and shall be subject to the general control and superintendence of that Board.

(2) The Central Government may also appoint a Financial Adviser and Chief Accounts Officer to assist the Central Provident Fund Commissioner in the discharge of his duties.

(3) The Central Board may appoint, subject to the maximum scale of pay, as may be specified in the Scheme, as many Additional Central Provident Fund Commissioners, Deputy Provident Fund Commissioners, Regional Provident Fund Commissioners, Assistant Provident Fund Commissioners and such other officers and employees as it may consider necessary for the efficient administration of the Scheme, the Pension Scheme and the Insurance Scheme.

(4) No appointment to the post of the Central Provident Fund Commissioner or a Financial Advisor and Chief Accounts Officer or any other post under the Central Board carrying a scale of pay equivalent to the scale of pay of any Group 'A' or Group 'B' post under the Central Government shall be made except after consultation with the Union Public Service Commission:

Provided that no such consultation shall be necessary in regard to any such appointment—

(a) for a period not exceeding one year; or

(b) if the person to be appointed is at the time of his appointment—

(i) a member of the Indian Administrative Service, or

(ii) in the service of the Central Government or a State Government or the Central Board in a Group 'A' or Group 'B' post.

(5) A State Board may, with the approval of the State Government concerned, appoint such staff as it may consider necessary.

(6) The method of recruitment, salary and allowances, discipline and other conditions of service of the Central Provident Fund Commissioner, and the Financial Adviser and Chief Accounts Officer shall be such as may be specified by the Central Government and such salary and allowances shall be paid out of the Fund.

(7) (a) The method of recruitment, salary and allowances, discipline and other conditions of service of the Additional Central Provident Fund Commissioner, Deputy Provident Fund Commissioner, Regional Provident Fund Commissioner, Assistant Provident Fund Commissioner and other officers and employees of the Central Board shall be such as may be specified by the Central Board in accordance with the rules and orders applicable to the officers and employees of the Central Government drawing corresponding scales of pay:

Provided that where the Central Board is of the opinion that it is necessary to make a departure from the said rules or orders in respect of any of the matters aforesaid, it shall obtain the prior approval of the Central Government.

(b) In determining the corresponding scales of pay of officers and employees under Cl. (a), the Central Board shall have regard to the educational qualifications, method of recruitment, duties and responsibilities of such officers and employees under the Central Government and in case of any doubt, the Central Board shall refer the matter to the Central Government whose decision thereon shall be final.

(8) The method of recruitment, salary and allowances, discipline and other conditions of service of officers and employees of State Board shall be such as may be specified by that Board, with the approval of the State Government concerned.

The short question raised before the Supreme Court for consideration in *Union of India* v. *Vinod Kumar*[19] is whether the deviation from rule of granting promotion of 50% of the quota giving 2 years additional benefit to the Upper Division Clerks is valid in law? Sub-section (7)(a) of S. 5D of the Employees' Provident Fund and Miscellaneous Provisions Act, 1952 provides method of recruitment and proviso to the sub-section permits the Central Board to make a departure from the method of recruitment only after obtaining prior approval of the Central Government. Admittedly, prior approval was not obtained. On the other hand, *ex post facto* approval was obtained but in the teeth of the language of the proviso, *ex post facto* approval is not approval in the eye of law.

SECTION 5DD: Acts and proceedings of the Central Board or its Executive Committee or the State Board not to be invalidated on certain grounds

No act done or proceeding taken by the Central Board or the Executive Committee constituted under section 5AA or the State Board shall be questioned on the ground merely of the existence

19. AIR 1996 SC 2778.

of any vacancy in, or any defect in the constitution of, the Central Board or the Executive Committee or the State Board, as the case may be.

SECTION 5E: Delegation

The Central Board may delegate to the Executive Committee or to the Chairman of the Board or to any of its officers and a State Board may delegate to its Chairman or to any of its officers subject to such conditions and limitations, if any, as it may specify, such of its powers and functions under this Act as it may deem necessary for the efficient administration of the Scheme, the Pension Scheme and the Insurance Scheme.

SECTION 6: Contributions and matters which may be provided for in the Schemes

The contribution which shall be paid by the employer to the Fund shall be ten per cent of the basic wages, dearness allowance and retaining allowance (if any), for the time being payable to each of the employees (whether employed by him directly or by or through a contractor) and the employees' contribution shall be equal to the contribution payable by the employer in respect of him and may, if any employee so desires be an amount not exceeding ten per cent of his basic wages, dearness allowance and retaining allowance (if any), subject to the condition that the employer shall not be under an obligation to pay any contribution over and above his contribution payable under this section:

Provided that in its application to any establishment or class of establishments which the Central Government, after making such inquiry as it deems fit, may, by notification in the Official Gazette specify, this section shall be subject to the modification that for the words ten per cent, at both the places where they occur, the words twelve per cent shall be substituted:

Provided further that where the amount of any contribution payable under this Act involves a fraction of a rupee, the Scheme may provide for the rounding off of such fraction to the nearest rupee, half of a rupee or quarter of a rupee.

Explanation 1: For the purposes of this section, dearness allowance shall be deemed to include also the cash value of any food concession allowed to the employee.

Explanation 2: For the purposes of this section, "retaining allowance" means an allowance payable for the time being to an employee of any factory or other establishment during any period in which the establishment is not working, for retaining his services.

SECTION 6A: Employees' Pension Scheme

(1) The Central Government may, by notification in the Official Gazette, frame a scheme to be called the Employees' Pension Scheme for the purpose of providing for:

(a) superannuation pension, retiring pension or permanent total disablement pension to the employees of any establishment or class of establishments to which this Act applies; and

(b) widow or widower's pension, children pension or orphan pension payable to the beneficiaries of such employees.

(2) Notwithstanding anything contained in section 6, there shall be established, as soon as may be after framing of the Pension Scheme, a Pension Fund into which there shall be paid, from time to time, in respect of every employee who is a member of the Pension Scheme:

(a) such sums from the employer's contribution under section 6, not exceeding eight and one-third per cent of the basic wages, dearness allowance and retaining allowance, if any, of the concerned employees, as may be specified in the Pension Scheme;

(b) such sums as are payable by the employers of exempted establishments under sub-section (6) of section 17;

(c) the net assets of the Employees' Family Pension Fund as on the date of the establishment of the Pension Fund;

(d) such sums as the Central Government may, after due appropriation by Parliament by law in this behalf, specify.

(3) On the establishment of the Pension Fund, the Family Pension Scheme (hereinafter referred to as the ceased scheme) shall cease to operate and all assets of the ceased scheme shall vest in and shall stand transferred to, and all liabilities under the ceased scheme shall be enforceable against, the Pension Fund and the beneficiaries under the ceased scheme shall be entitled to draw the benefits, not less than the benefits, they were entitled to under the ceased scheme, from the Pension Fund.

(4) The Pension Fund shall vest in and be administered by the Central Board in such manner as may be specified in the Pension Scheme.

(5) Subject to the provisions of this Act, the Pension Scheme may provide for all or any of the matters specified in Schedule III.

(6) The Pension Scheme may provide that all or any of its provisions shall take effect either prospectively or retrospectively on such date as may be specified in that behalf in that Scheme.

(7) A Pension Scheme, framed under sub-section (1) shall be laid, as soon as may be after it is made, before each House of Parliament, while it is in session, for a total period of thirty days which may be comprised in one session or in two or more successive sessions, and if, before the expiry of the session immediately following the session or the successive sessions aforesaid, both Houses agree in making any modification in the scheme or both Houses agree that the scheme should not be made, the scheme shall thereafter have effect only in such modified form or be of no effect, as the case may be; so, however, that any such modification or annulment shall be without prejudice to the validity of anything previously done under that scheme.

With a view to provide certain terminal and other benefits to the employees engaged in factories and other establishments, Parliament enacted the Employees' Provident Fund and Miscellaneous Provisions Act, 1952. The Act provides inter alia for framing of "Employees Provident Fund Schemes". A certain percentage of the monthly wages of the workers is deducted and credited to the said Fund. The employer is also made liable to contribute an equal amount to the Fund. The employee member of the Fund is entitled to withdraw the full amount to his credit in the Fund on his retirement or termination of service, as the case may be. He can also draw advances out of the Fund in certain situations like illness, marriage or education of children and so on. But there were many cases in which the amount payable, on the death of an employee, to his wife and minor children, was too small to be of any help to them particularly where an employee died within a few years of his employment. With a view to provide long-term payments (Pension) to the widow or minor children in such cases, Parliament thought of creating a Family Pension Fund Scheme. For this purpose, it introduced S. 6A (read with Schedule III) and certain other provisions in the Act, by the Amendment Act 16 of 1971. Section 6A empowered the Central Government to frame a scheme called "the Employees' Family Pension Scheme" to provide family pension and life assurance benefits to the employees of any establishment or class of establishments to which the Act applied. The Statement of Objects and Reasons leading to the introduction of the Family Pension Fund Scheme throws light upon the objectives and purposes sought to be achieved by the new Scheme:

"The Coal Mines Provident Fund and Bonus Scheme Act, 1948 and the Employees' Provident Fund Act, 1952 provides for the institution of provident funds for employees in coal mines, factories and other establishments. Provident Fund is an effective old age and survivorship benefit but when the employee happens to die prematurely, the accumulation to the Provident Fund are too small to render adequate and long-term protection to his family. With a view to providing long-term financial security to the families of industries' employees in the event of their premature death, it is proposed to introduce a Family Pension Fund for the employees covered under the two Acts, and to create a Family Pension Fund for this purpose by diverting a portion of the employer's and the employee's contribution to the Provident Fund, to which will be added a contribution by the Central Government. Out of the fund so set up, it is proposed to pay Family Pension at prescribed scales to the survivors of employees who die while in service before reaching the age of superannuation."

Sub-section (2) of S. 6A provides for diversion of a portion of the contributions made by the employees and employers to the Provident Fund under S. 6 of the Act to the Pension Fund. It also provides for contribution by the Government of an amount equal to the employee's contribution to the Pension Fund. The Fund thus has a new element—contribution by the State. The Family Pension Fund Scheme came into force on and from March 1, 1971.

Clause (3) of the Scheme framed by the Central Government under S. 6A provides that every person who becomes a member of the Employees' Provident Fund Scheme on or after March 1, 1971 shall automatically become a member of the Family Pension Fund Scheme. So far as the existing members of the Employees' Provident Fund are concerned, the clause gave them an option to come under the Family Pension Scheme or to stay out. Such an option was not given to employees who became members of the Employees Provident Fund on or after March 1, 1971 and this distinction forms the basis for the complaint of discrimination made by the writ petitioners-appellants.

The Family Pension Scheme provides, broadly speaking, for three benefits to its members, viz.

(a) Family pension (pension payable to widow or minor children on the death of employee before attaining the age of 60 years);

(b) Life assurance benefits [Cl. (31) of the Scheme]; and

(c) Retirement-cum-withdrawal benefits [Cl. (32) of the Scheme.]

The Scheme is in the nature of an insurance scheme. An employee who dies early in service, his family stands to gain on a long-term basis, while another member who serves out his full service tenure may not stand to gain that much. But one thing is clear, no one may get back less than what he has contributed. No one can say that each and every employee must get back not only what he contributes but also the contributions of the employer and the Government put together. This is just not possible. Who is to care for the widows or minor children of the deceased employees (employees dying before retirement or before attaining the age of 60 years) and wherefrom money is to come if each employee insists upon receiving the total of his, the employer's and the Government's contribution? However, the fact remains that the benefits to be provided to the members under the several schemes should broadly approximate to and be commensurate with what they contribute. This is what Cl. (34D) of Pension Scheme provides, in particular sub-clause (2) thereof. Though worded as an enabling provision, it contains a salutary and an obligatory principle, which the Government should always keep in view. It is true that no conclusions should be drawn by taking any single instance and that the matter must be decided taking an overall view, yet the inescapable test remains, viz., there must be a broad correspondence between what the employees pay and what they and their families get ultimately. It cannot be that while the Fund accumulates, the employees—and their families—decay.[20]

Section 6B: Employees' Deposit-linked Insurance Scheme

(1) The Central Government may, by notification in the Official Gazette, frame a Scheme to be called the Employees' Deposit-linked Insurance Scheme for the purpose of providing life insurance benefits to the employees of any establishment or class of establishments to which this Act applies.

(2) There shall be established, as soon as may be after the framing of the Insurance Scheme, a Deposit-linked Insurance Fund into which shall be paid by the employer from time to time in respect of every such employee in relation to whom he is the employer, such amount, not being more than one per cent of the aggregate of the basic wages, dearness allowance and retaining allowance (if any) for the time being payable in relation to such employee as the Central Government may, by notification in the Official Gazette, specify.

Explanation: For the purposes of this sub-section, the expressions "dearness allowance" and "retaining allowance" have the same meanings as in section 6.

(3) Omitted w.r.e.f. 16-11-1995.

(4) (a) The employer shall pay into the Insurance Fund such further sums of money, not exceeding one-fourth of the contribution which he is required to make under sub-section (2), as the Central Government may, from time to time, determine to meet all the expenses in connection with administration of the Insurance Scheme

20. *Mafatlal Group Staff Association* v. *Regional Commissioner, Provident Fund*, AIR 1994 SC 2271.

other than the expenses towards the cost of any benefits provided by or under that Scheme.

(5) The Insurance Fund shall vest in the Central Board and be administered by it in such manner as may be specified in the Insurance Scheme.

(6) The Insurance Scheme may provide for all or any of the matters specified in Schedule IV.

(7) The Insurance Scheme may provide that any of its provisions shall take effect either prospectively or retrospectively on such date as may be specified in this behalf in that Scheme.

Section 6C: Laying of Schemes before Parliament

Every Scheme framed under section 5, section 6A and section 6C shall be laid, as soon as may be after it is framed, before each House of Parliament, while it is in session, for a total period of thirty days which may be comprised in one session or in two or more successive sessions, and if, before the expiry of the session immediately following the session or the successive sessions aforesaid, both Houses agree in making any notification in the Scheme, or both Houses agree that the scheme should not be framed, the Scheme shall thereafter have effect only in such modified form or be of no effect, as the case may be; so, however, that any such modification or annulment shall be without prejudice to the validity of anything previously done under the Scheme.

Section 7: Modification of Scheme

(1) The Central Government may, by notification in the Official Gazette, add to, amend or vary, either prospectively or retrospectively, the Scheme, the Pension Scheme or the Insurance Scheme, as the case may be, framed under this Act.

(2) Every notification issued under sub-section (1) shall be laid, as soon as may be after it is issued, before each House of Parliament while it is in session, for a total period of thirty days, which may be comprised in one session or in two or more successive sessions, and if, before the expiry of the session immediately following the session or the successive sessions aforesaid, both Houses agree in making any modification in the notification, or both houses agree that the notification should not be issued, the notification shall thereafter have effect only in such modified form or be of no effect, as the case may be; so however, that any such modification or annulment shall be without prejudice to the validity of anything previously done under that notification.

Section 7A: Determination of moneys due from employers

(1) The Central Provident Fund Commissioner, any Additional Central Provident Fund Commissioner, any Deputy Provident Fund Commissioner, any Regional Provident Fund Commissioner or any Assistant Provident Fund Commissioner may, by order,—

(a) in a case where a dispute arises regarding the applicability of this Act to an establishment, decide such dispute; and

(b) determine the amount due from any employer under any provision of this Act, the Scheme or the Pension Scheme or the Insurance Scheme, as the case may be,

and for any of the aforesaid purposes may conduct such inquiry as he may deem necessary.

(2) The officer conducting the inquiry under sub-section (1) shall, for the purposes of such inquiry, have the same powers as are vested in a court under the Code of Civil Procedure, 1908, for trying a suit in respect of the following matters, namely:

(a) enforcing the attendance of any person or examining him on oath;

(b) requiring the discovery and production of documents;

(c) receiving evidence on affidavit;

(d) issuing commissions for the examination of witnesses;

and any such inquiry shall be deemed to be judicial proceeding within the meaning of sections 193 and 228, and for the purpose of section 196 of the Indian Penal Code.

(3) No order shall be made under sub-section (1), unless the employer concerned is given a reasonable opportunity of representing his case.

(3A) Where the employer, employee or any other person required to attend the inquiry under sub-section (1) fails to attend such inquiry without assigning any valid reason or fails to produce any document or to file any report or return when called upon to do so, the officer conducting the inquiry may decide the applicability of the Act or determine the amount due from any employer, as the case may be, on the basis of the evidence adduced during such enquiry and other documents available on record.

(4) Where an order made under sub-section (1) is passed against an employer *ex parte*, he may, within three months from the date of communication of such order, apply to the officer for setting aside such order and if he satisfies the officer that the show cause notice was not duly served or that he was prevented by any sufficient cause from appearing when the inquiry was held, the officer shall make an order setting aside his earlier order and shall appoint a date for proceeding with the inquiry:

Provided that no such order shall be set aside merely on the ground that there has been an irregularity in the service of the show cause notice if the officer is satisfied that the employer had notice of the date of hearing and had sufficient time to appear before the officer.

Explanation: Where an appeal has been preferred under this Act against an order passed *ex parte* and such appeal has been disposed of otherwise than on the ground that the appellant has withdrawn the appeal, no application shall lie under this sub-section for setting aside the *ex parte* order.

(5) No order passed under this section shall be set aside on any application under sub-section (4) unless notice thereof has been served on the opposite party.

In *S.K. Nasiruddin Beedi Merchant Ltd., M/s.* v. *Central P.F. Commr.*,[16] the appellant—a manufacturer of beedis—challenged an order made by the respondents-P.F. Commissioner under S. 7A of the Employees' Provident Fund and Miscellaneous Provisions Act, 1952. The appellant had not deducted from the wages of the home workers employed through contractors for manufacture of beedis because of pendency of litigation in order to contribute towards the provident fund on the ground that the Act would not be applicable in cases of such employees. Earlier on receipt of a notice under the Act from the respondents, the appellant challenged the notice in the High Court on the ground that the Act has no application in respect of home workers engaged in rolling the beedis engaged through independent contractors. An interim stay had been granted by the Court during the pendency of the proceeding. The said writ petition was dismissed by holding that the provisions of the Act are applicable in respect of home workers engaged in rolling the beedis of the petitioner's establishment through contractors. This decision was questioned before the Supreme Court in Special Leave Petition . In the meanwhile, the Provident Fund Commissioner determined the amount due from the appellant and called upon it to deposit a sum of ₹66,84,930.50 being employers' and employees' contribution towards the Provident Fund from July, 1977 to August, 1986. By another order made on December 18, 1989, the appellant was called upon to pay a sum of ₹28,72,383.85 within the stipulated time. These demands were also challenged in two writ petitions. The Supreme Court by an order made on August 22, 1989, disposed of SLP if the matter could be heard and decided in the proceedings pending before the High Court. The two writ petitions also came to be dismissed on August 19, 1992. A sum of ₹46,90,051 out of a total demand of ₹95,57,314.35 was realised by the Provident Fund Commissioner. The Supreme Court while dismissing the SLP stated as follows:

> "The SLPs are dismissed. It is open for the petitioner to collect the names of the Beedi workers who work for them through their contractors and furnish the names of all the workers to the Provident Fund Commissioner. The Provident Fund Commissioner thereafter will verify these names and calculate the liability of the petitioner on the basis of such verification. If any excess amount is found due from the petitioner, the Provident Fund Commissioner will recover such amount from the petitioner, on the other hand, if any amount is found due to the petitioner, the Provident Fund Commissioner will refund the same. The petitioner to furnish names of the workers, as above within six months from today."

Thereafter, the appellant furnished the particulars of home workers stated to be engaged by the contractors to the best of information available with the appellant for final determination of its liability under S. 7A of the Act as noticed by this Court. A claim was made by the appellant for waiver from payment of employees' contribution for the period from October, 1985 to May 3, 1993 on the ground that he had not been able to collect the same. But the said claim was disallowed. The Regional Provident Fund Commissioner issued a certificate for recovery of the outstanding liability of ₹46,17,538.20 through the Recovery Officer, Bihar. This action of the respondent was called in question before the High Court. Three contentions were raised before the High Court, vis a vis:

(i) In the circumstances arising in this case, the appellant cannot be asked to pay retrospectively employees' contribution to the provident fund without deducting that from their wages as it is not possible to comply with the provisions of Para 32 of the Statutory Scheme. This situation arose on account of uncertainty of their liability until the same was settled by an order made under S. 7A of the Act on June 2, 1994 by the Regional Provident Fund Commissioner;

(ii) There is a bona fide dispute as to the applicability of the Act and payment by the employer towards the employees' contribution to the fund would arise only after making deductions from their wages and that the employer cannot be made liable to pay that contribution from an anterior date to the final determination of their liability under S. 7A of the Act; and

So far as the first contention is concerned, the Supreme Court held that the Act would be applicable even in respect of home-workers engaged through contractors and cannot be cavilled any more. It seems that the Apex Court relied on *Mangalore Gandhi Beedi Works*[21] case and *P.M. Patel and Sons*[15] case.

So far as the second contention is concerned, the argument of the learned Counsel proceeds on the basis that the liability was not clear in view of various circumstances and, therefore, deduction could not be made from the wages of the employees and that circumstance leads to anomalous position making the employer to pay the employees' contribution towards provident fund without the facility of deduction from their wages. The Supreme Court while rejecting the contention held that the applicability of the Act to any class of employees is not determined or decided by any proceeding under S. 7A of the Act but under the provisions of the Act itself. When the Act became applicable to the employees in question, the liability arises. What is done under S. 7A of the Act is only determination of quantification of the same. Therefore, the contention put forth on behalf of the appellant that their liability was attracted only from the date of determination of the matter under S. 7A of the Act does not stand to reason.

Section 7B: Review of orders passed under Section 7A

(1) Any person aggrieved by an order made under sub-section (1) of Section 7A, but from which no appeal has been preferred under this Act, and who, from the discovery of new and important matter or evidence which, after the exercise of due diligence was not within his knowledge or could not be produced by him at the time when the order was made, or on account of some mistake or error apparent on the face of the record or for any other sufficient reason, desires to obtain for a review of such order may apply for a review of that order to the officer who passed the order:

Provided that such officer may also on his own motion review his order if he is satisfied that it is necessary so to do on any such ground.

(2) Every application for review under sub-section (1) shall be filed in such form and manner and within such time as may be specified in the Scheme.

(3) Where it appears to the officer receiving an application for review that there is no sufficient ground for review, he shall reject the application.

21. *Mangalore Gandhi Beedi Works* v. *Union of India*, AIR 1974 SC 1832.

(4) Where the officer is of the opinion that the application for review should be granted, he shall grant the same:

Provided that—

(a) no such application shall be granted without previous notice to all the parties before him to enable them to appear and be heard in support of the order in respect of which a review is applied for, and

(b) no such application shall be granted on the ground of discovery of new matter or evidence which the applicant alleges was not within his knowledge or could not be produced by him when the order was made, without proof of such allegation.

(5) No appeal shall lie against the order of the officer rejecting an application for review, but an appeal under this Act shall lie against an order passed under review as if the order passed under review were the original order passed by him under section 7A.

Section 7C: Determination of escaped amount

Where an order determining the amount due from an employer under section 7A or section 7B has been passed and if the officer who passed the order—

(a) has reason to believe that by reason of the omission or failure on the part of the employer to make any document or report available, or to disclose, fully and truly, all material facts necessary for determining the correct amount due from the employer, any amount so due from such employer for any period has escaped his notice;

(b) has, in consequence of information in his possession, reason to believe that any amount to be determined under section 7A or section 7B has escaped from his determination for any period notwithstanding that there has been no omission or failure as mentioned in Cl. (a) on the part of the employer,

he may, within a period of five years from the date of communication of the order passed under section 7A or section 7B, re-open the case and pass appropriate orders re-determining the amount due from the employer in accordance with the provisions of this Act:

Provided that no order re-determining the amount due from the employer shall be passed under this section unless the employer is given a reasonable opportunity of representing his case.

Section 7D: Employees' Provident Funds Appellate Tribunal

(1) The Central Government may, by notification in the Official Gazette, constitute one or more Appellate Tribunals to be known as the Employees' Provident Funds Appellate Tribunal to exercise the powers and discharge the functions conferred on such Tribunal by this Act and every such Tribunal shall have jurisdiction in respect of establishments situated in such area as may be specified in the notification constituting the Tribunal.

(2) A Tribunal shall consist of one person only to be appointed by the Central Government.

(3) A person shall not be qualified for appointment as a Presiding Officer of a Tribunal (hereinafter referred to as the Presiding Officer) unless he is or has been, or is qualified to be—

(i) a Judge of a High Court; or

(ii) a District Judge.

SECTION 7E: Term of office

The Presiding Officer of a Tribunal shall hold office for a term of five years from the date on which he enters upon his office or until he attains the age of sixty-two years, whichever is earlier.

SECTION 7F: Resignation

(1) The Presiding Officer may, by notice in writing under his hand addressed to the Central Government, resign his office:

Provided that the Presiding Officer shall, unless he is permitted by the Central Government to relinquish his office sooner, continue to hold office until the expiry of three months from the date of receipt of such notice or until a person duly appointed as his successor enters upon his office or until the expiry of his term of office, whichever is the earliest.

(2) The Presiding Officer shall not be removed from his office except by an order made by the President on the ground of proved misbehaviour or incapacity after an inquiry made by a Judge of the High Court in which such Presiding Officer had been informed of the charges against him and given a reasonable opportunity of being heard in respect of those charges.

(3) The Central Government may, by rules, regulate the procedure for the investigation of misbehaviour or incapacity of the Presiding Officer.

SECTION 7G: Salary and allowances and other terms and conditions of service of Presiding Officer

The salary and allowances payable to, and the other terms and conditions of service (including pension, gratuity and other retirement benefits) of, the Presiding Officer shall be such as may be prescribed:

Provided that neither the salary and allowances nor the other terms and conditions of service of the Presiding Officer shall be varied to his disadvantage after his appointment.

SECTION 7H: Staff of Tribunal

(1) The Central Government shall determine the nature and categories of the officers and other employees required to assist a Tribunal in the discharge of its functions and provide the Tribunal with such officers and other employees as it may think fit.

(2) The officers and other employees of a Tribunal shall discharge their functions under the general superintendence of the Presiding Officer.

(3) The salaries and allowances and other conditions of service of the officers and other employees of a Tribunal shall be such as may be prescribed.

Section 7-I: Appeals to Tribunal

(1) Any person aggrieved by a notification issued by the Central Government, or an order passed by the Central Government or any authority, under the proviso to sub-section (3), or sub-section (4), of section 1, or section 3, or sub-section (1) of section 7A, or section 7B [except an order rejecting an application for review referred to in sub-section (5) thereof], or section 7C, or section 14B, may prefer an appeal to a Tribunal against such notification or order.

(2) Every appeal under sub-section (1) shall be filed in such form and manner, within such time and be accompanied by such fees, as may be prescribed.

Section 7J: Procedure of Tribunal

(1) A Tribunal shall have power to regulate its own procedure in all matters arising out of the exercise of its powers or of the discharge of its functions including the places at which the Tribunal shall have its sittings.

(2) A Tribunal shall, for the purpose of discharging its functions, have all the powers which are vested in the officers referred to in section 7A and any proceeding before the Tribunal shall be deemed to be a judicial proceeding within the meaning of sections 193 and 228, and for the purpose of section 196 of the Indian Penal Code, 1860 (45 of 1860), and the Tribunal shall be deemed to be a Civil Court for all the purposes of section 195 and Chapter XXVI of the Code of Criminal Procedure, 1973 (2 of 1974).

Section 7K: Right of appellant to take assistance of legal practitioner and of government, etc. to appoint presenting officers

(1) A person preferring an appeal to a Tribunal under this Act may either appear in person or take the assistance of a legal practitioner of his choice to present his case before the Tribunal.

(2) The Central Government or a State Government or any other authority under this Act may authorise one or more legal practitioners or any of its officers to act as presenting officers and every person so authorised may present the case with respect to any appeal before a Tribunal.

Section 7L: Orders of Tribunal

(1) A Tribunal may, after giving the parties to the appeal an opportunity of being heard, pass such orders thereon as it thinks fit, confirming, modifying or annulling the order appealed against or may refer the case back to the authority which passed such

order with such directions as the Tribunal may think fit, for a fresh adjudication or order, as the case may be, after taking additional evidence, if necessary.

(2) A Tribunal may, at any time within five years from the date of its order, with a view to rectifying any mistake apparent from the record, amend any order passed by it under sub-section (1) and shall make such amendment in the order if the mistake is brought to its notice by the parties to the appeal:

Provided that an amendment which has the effect of enhancing the amount due from, or otherwise increasing the liability of, the employer shall not be made under this sub-section, unless the Tribunal has given notice to him of its intention to do so and has allowed him a reasonable opportunity of being heard.

(3) A Tribunal shall send a copy of every order passed under this section to the parties to the appeal.

(4) Any order made by a Tribunal finally disposing of an appeal shall not be questioned in any Court of law.

Section 7M: Filling up of vacancies

If, for any reason, a vacancy occurs in the office of the Presiding Officer, the Central Government shall appoint another person in accordance with the provisions of this Act, to fill the vacancy and the proceedings may be continued before a Tribunal from the stage at which the vacancy is filled.

Section 7N: Finality of orders constituting a Tribunal

No order of the Central Government appointing any person as the Presiding Officer shall be called in question in any manner, and no act or proceeding before a Tribunal shall be called in question in any manner on the ground merely of any defect in the constitution of such Tribunal.

Section 7-O: Deposit of amount due, on filing appeal

No appeal by the employer shall be entertained by a Tribunal unless he has deposited with it seventy-five per cent of the amount due from him as determined by an officer referred to in section 7A:

Provided that the Tribunal may, for reasons to be recorded in writing, waive or reduce the amount to be deposited under this section.

Section 7P: Transfer of certain applications to Tribunal

All applications which are pending before the Central Government under section 19A before its repeal, shall stand transferred to a Tribunal exercising jurisdiction in respect of establishments in relation to which such applications had been made as if such applications were appeals preferred to the Tribunal.

Section 7Q: Interest payable by the employer

The employer shall be liable to pay simple interest at the rate of twelve per cent per annum or at such higher rate as may be specified in the Scheme on any amount due from him under this Act from the date on which the amount has become so due till the date of its actual payment:

Provided that higher rate of interest specified in the Scheme shall not exceed the lending rate of interest charged by any scheduled bank.

Section 8: Mode of recovery of moneys due from employers

Any amount due:

(a) from the employer in relation to an establishment to which any Scheme or the Insurance Scheme applies in respect of any contribution payable to the Fund or, as the case may be, the Insurance Fund, damages recoverable under section 14B, accumulations required to be transferred under sub-section (2) of section 15 or under sub-section (5) of section 17 or any charges payable by him under any other provision of this Act or of any provision of the Scheme or the Insurance Scheme; or

(b) from the employer in relation to an exempted establishment in respect of any damages recoverable under section 14B or any charges payable by him to the appropriate Government under any provision of this Act or under any of the conditions specified under section 17 or in respect of the contribution payable by him towards the Pension Scheme or the Insurance Scheme under the said section 17,

may, if the amount is in arrears, be recovered in the manner specified in sections 8B to 8G.

Section 8A: Recovery of moneys by employers and contractors

(1) The amount of contribution (that is to say, the employer's contribution as well as the employee's contribution in pursuance of any Scheme and the employer's contribution in pursuance of the Insurance Scheme); and any charges for meeting the cost of administering the Fund paid or payable by an employer in respect of an employee employed by or through a contractor may be recovered by such employer from the contractor, either by deduction from any amount payable to the contractor under any contract or as a debt payable by the contractor.

(2) A contractor from whom the amounts mentioned in sub-section (1) may be recovered in respect of any employee employed by or through him, may recover from such employee the employee's contribution under any Scheme by deduction from the basic wages, dearness allowance and retaining allowance (if any) payable to such employee.

(3) Notwithstanding any contract to the contrary, no contractor shall be entitled to deduct the employer's contribution or the charges referred to in sub-section (1) from the basic wages, dearness allowance, and retaining allowance (if any) payable to an employee employed by or through him or otherwise to recover such contribution or charges from such employee.

Explanation: In this section, the expressions "dearness allowance" and "retaining allowance" shall have the same meanings as in section 6.

Section 8B: Issue of certificate to the Recovery Officer

(1) Where any amount is in arrears under section 8, the authorised officer may issue, to the Recovery Officer, a certificate under his signature specifying the amount of arrears and the Recovery Officer, on receipt of such certificate, shall proceed to recover the amount specified therein from the establishment or, as the case may be, the employer by one or more of the modes mentioned below:

(a) attachment and sale of the movable or immovable property of the establishment or, as the case may be, the employer;

(b) arrest of the employer and his detention in prison;

(c) appointing a receiver for the management of the movable or immovable properties of the establishment or, as the case may be, the employer:

Provided that the attachment and sale of any property under this section shall first be effected against the properties of the establishment and where such attachment and sale is insufficient for recovering the whole of the amount of arrears specified in the certificate, the Recovery Officer may take such proceedings against the property of the employer for recovery of the whole or any part of such arrears.

(2) The authorised officer may issue a certificate under sub-section (1), notwithstanding that proceedings for recovery of the arrears by any other mode have been taken.

Section 8C: Recovery Officer to whom certificate is to be forwarded

(1) The authorised officer may forward the certificate referred to in section 8B to the Recovery Officer within whose jurisdiction the employer—

(a) carries on his business or profession or within whose jurisdiction the principal place of his establishment is situate; or

(b) resides or any movable or immovable property of the establishment or the employer is situate.

(2) Where an establishment or the employer has property within the jurisdiction of more than one Recovery Officers and the Recovery Officer to whom a certificate is sent by the authorised officer—

(a) is not able to recover the entire amount by the sale of the property, movable or immovable, within his jurisdiction; or

(b) is of the opinion that, for the purpose of expediting or securing the recovery of the whole or any part of the amount, it is necessary so to do,

he may send the certificate or, where only a part of the amount is to be recovered, a copy of the certificate certified in the prescribed manner and specifying the amount to be recovered to the Recovery Officer within whose jurisdiction the establishment or the employer has property or the employer resides, and thereupon that Recovery Officer shall also proceed to recover the amount due under this section as if the certificate or the copy thereof had been the certificate sent to him by the authorised officer.

SECTION 8D: Validity of certificate and amendment thereof

(1) When the authorised officer issues a certificate to Recovery Officer under section 8B, it shall not be open to the employer to dispute before the Recovery Officer the correctness of the amount, and no objection to the certificate on any other ground shall also be entertained by the Recovery Officer.

(2) Notwithstanding the issue of a certificate to a Recovery Officer, the authorised officer shall have power to withdraw the certificate or correct any clerical or arithmetical mistake in the certificate by sending an intimation to the Recovery Officer.

(3) The authorised officer shall intimate to the Recovery Officer any order withdrawing or cancelling a certificate or any correction made by him under sub-section (2) or any amendment made under sub-section (4) of section 8E.

SECTION 8E: Stay of proceedings under certificate and amendment or withdrawal thereof

(1) Notwithstanding that a certificate has been issued to the Recovery Officer for the recovery of any amount, the authorised officer may grant time for the payment of the amount, and thereupon the Recovery Officer shall stay the proceedings until the expiry of the time so granted.

(2) Where a certificate for the recovery of amount has been issued, the authorised officer shall keep the Recovery Officer informed of any amount paid or time granted for payment, subsequent to the issue of such certificate.

(3) Where the order giving rise to a demand of amount for which a certificate for recovery has been issued has been modified in appeal or other proceeding under this Act, and, as a consequence thereof, the demand is reduced but the order is the subject-matter of a further proceeding under this Act, the authorised officer shall stay the recovery of such part of the amount of the certificate as pertains to the said reduction for the period for which the appeal or other proceeding remains pending.

(4) Where a certificate for the recovery of amount has been issued and subsequently the amount of the outstanding demand is reduced as a result of an appeal or other proceeding under this Act, the authorised officer shall, when the order which was the subject-matter of such appeal or other proceeding has become final and conclusive, amend the certificate or withdraw it, as the case may be.

SECTION 8F: Other modes of recovery

(1) Notwithstanding the issue of a certificate to the Recovery Officer under section 8B, the Central Provident Fund Commissioner or any other officer authorised by the

Central Board may recover the amount by any one or more of the modes provided in this section.

(2) If any amount is due from any person to any employer who is in arrears, the Central Provident Fund Commissioner or any other officer authorised by the Central Board in this behalf may require such person to deduct from the said amount the arrears due from such employer under this Act, and such person shall comply with any such requisition and shall pay the sum so deducted to the credit of the Central Provident Fund Commissioner or the officer so authorised, as the case may be:

Provided that nothing in this sub-section shall apply to any part of the amount exempt from attachment in execution of a decree of a civil court under section 60 of the Code of Civil Procedure, 1908.

(3) (i) The Central Provident Fund Commissioner or any other officer authorised by the Central Board in this behalf may, at any time or from time to time, by notice in writing, require any person from whom money is due or may become due to the employer or, as the case may be, the establishment or any person who holds or may subsequently hold money for or on account of the employer or as the case may be, the establishment, to pay to the Central Provident Fund Commissioner either forthwith upon the money becoming due or being held or at or within the time specified in the notice (not being before the money becomes due or is held) so much of the money as is sufficient to pay the amount due from the employer in respect of arrears or the whole of the money when it is equal to or less than that amount.

(ii) A notice under this sub-section may be issued to any person who holds or may subsequently hold any money for or on account of the employer jointly with any other person and for the purposes of this sub-section, the shares of the joint-holders in such account shall be presumed, until the contrary is proved, to be equal.

(iii) A copy of the notice shall be forwarded to the employer at his last address known to the Central Provident Fund Commissioner or, as the case may be, the officer so authorised and in the case of a joint account to all the joint-holders at their last addresses known to the Central Provident Fund Commissioner or the officer so authorised.

(iv) Save as otherwise provided in this sub-section, every person to whom a notice is issued under this sub-section shall be bound to comply with such notice, and, in particular, where any such notice is issued to a post office, bank or an insurer, it shall not be necessary for any pass book, deposit receipt, policy or any other document to be produced for the purpose of any entry, endorsement or the like being made before payment is made notwithstanding any rule, practice or requirement to the contrary.

(v) Any claim respecting any property in relation to which a notice under this sub-section has been issued arising after the date of the notice shall be void as against any demand contained in the notice.

(vi) Where a person to whom a notice under this sub-section is sent objects to it by a statement on oath that the sum demanded or any part thereof is not due to the employer or that he does not hold any money for or on account of the employer, then, nothing contained in this sub-section shall be deemed to require such person to pay any such sum or part thereof, as the case may be, but if it is discovered that such statement was false in any material particular, such person shall be personally liable to the Central Provident Fund Commissioner or the officer so authorised to the extent of his own liability to the employer on the date of the notice, or to the extent of the employer's liability for any sum due under this Act, whichever is less.

(vii) The Central Provident Fund Commissioner or the officer so authorised may, at any time or from time to time, amend or revoke any notice issued under this sub-section or extend the time for making any payment in pursuance of such notice.

(viii) The Central Provident Fund Commissioner or the officer so authorised shall grant a receipt for any amount paid in compliance with a notice issued under this sub-section, and the person so paying shall be fully discharged from his liability to the employer to the extent of the amount so paid.

(ix) Any person discharging any liability to the employer after the receipt of a notice under this sub-section shall be personally liable to the Central Provident Fund Commissioner or the officer so authorised to the extent of his own liability to the employer so discharged or to the extent of the employer's liability for any sum due under this Act, whichever is less.

(x) If the person to whom a notice under this sub-section is sent fails to make payment in pursuance thereof to the Central Provident Fund Commissioner or the officer so authorised he shall be deemed to be an employer in default in respect of the amount specified in the notice and further proceedings may be taken against him for the realisation of the amount as if it were an arrear due from him, in the manner provided in sections 8B to 8E and the notice shall have the same effect as an attachment of a debt by the Recovery Officer in exercise of his powers under section 8B.

(4) The Central Provident Fund Commissioner or the officer authorised by the Central Board in this behalf may apply to the court in whose custody there is money belonging to the employer for payment to him of the entire amount of such money, or if it is more than the amount due, an amount sufficient to discharge the amount due.

(5) The Central Provident Fund Commissioner or any officer not below the rank of Assistant Provident Fund Commissioner may, if so authorised by the Central Government by general or special order, recover any arrears of amount due from an employer or, as the case may be, from the establishment by distraint and sale of his or its movable property in the manner laid down in the Third Schedule to the Income Tax Act, 1961 (43 of 1961).

SECTION 8G: Application of certain provisions of Income Tax Act

The provisions of the Second and Third Schedules to the Income Tax Act, 1961 (43 of 1961), and the Income Tax (Certificate Proceedings) Rules, 1962, as in force from time to time, shall apply with necessary modifications as if the said provisions and the rules referred to the arrears of the amount mentioned in section 8 of this Act instead of to the Income Tax:

Provided that any reference in the said provisions and the rules to the "assessee" shall be construed as a reference to an employer as defined in this Act.

SECTION 9: Fund to be recognised under Act XI of 1922

For the purposes of the Indian Income Tax Act, 1922, the Fund shall be deemed to be a recognised provident fund within the meaning of Chapter IX-A of that Act:

Provided that nothing contained in the said Chapter shall operate to render ineffective any provision of the Scheme (under which the Fund is established) which is repugnant to any of the provisions of that Chapter or of the rules made thereunder.

SECTION 10: Protection against attachment

(1) The amount standing to the credit of any member in the Fund or of any exempted employee in a provident fund shall not in any way be capable of being assigned or charged and shall not be liable to attachment under any decree or order of any Court in respect of any debt or liability incurred by the member or the exempted employee, and neither the official assignee appointed under the Presidency Towns Insolvency Act, 1909, nor any receiver appointed under the Provincial Insolvency Act, 1920, shall be entitled to, or have any claim on, any such amount.

(2) Any amount standing to the credit of a member in the Fund or of an exempted employee in a provident fund at the time of his death and payable to his nominee under the Scheme or the rules of the Provident Fund shall, subject to any deduction authorised by the said Scheme or rules, vest in the nominee and shall be free from any debt or other liability incurred by the deceased or the nominee before the death of the member or of the exempted employee and shall also not be liable to attachment under any decree or order of any Court.

(3) The provisions of sub-section (1) and sub-section (2) shall, so far as may be, apply in relation to the family pension or any other amount payable under the Pension Scheme and also in relation to any amount payable under the Insurance Scheme as they apply in relation to any amount payable out of the Fund.

SECTION 11: Priority of payment of contributions over other debts

(1) Where any employer is adjudicated insolvent or, being a company, an order for winding up is made, the amount due—

(a) from the employer in relation to an establishment to which any Scheme or the insurance Scheme applies in respect of any contribution payable to the

Fund or, as the case may be, the Insurance Fund, damages recoverable under section 14B, accumulations required to be transferred under sub-section (2) of section 15 or any charges payable by him under any other provision of this Act or of any provision of the Scheme or the Insurance Scheme; or

(b) from the employer in relation to an exempted establishment in respect of any contribution to the provident fund or any insurance fund (in so far as it relates to exempted employees), under the rules of the provident fund or any insurance fund any contribution payable by him towards the Pension Fund under sub-section (6) of section 17, damages recoverable under section 14B or any charges payable by him to the appropriate Government under any provision of this Act under any of the conditions specified under section 17,

shall, where the liability therefor has accrued before the order of adjudication or winding up is made, be deemed to be included among the debts which under section 49 of the Presidency Towns Insolvency Act, 1909, or under section 61 of the Provincial Insolvency Act, 1920, or under section 530 of the Companies Act, 1956 , are to be paid in priority to all other debts in the distribution of the property of the insolvent or the assets of the company being wound up, as the case may be.

Explanation: In this sub-section and in section 17, "insurance fund" means any fund established by an employer under any Scheme for providing benefits in the nature of life insurance to employees, whether linked to their deposits in provident fund or not, without payment by the employees of any separate contribution or premium in that behalf.

(2) Without prejudice to the provisions of sub-section (1), if any amount is due from an employer, whether in respect of the employee's contribution (deducted from the wages of the employee) or the employer's contribution, the amount so due shall be deemed to be the first charge on the assets of the establishment, and shall, notwithstanding anything contained in any other law for the time being in force, be paid in priority to all other debts.

Section 12: Employer not to reduce wages, etc.

No employer in relation to an establishment to which any Scheme or the Insurance Scheme applies shall, by reason only of his liability for the payment of any contribution to the Fund or the Insurance Fund or any charges under this Act or the Scheme or the Insurance Scheme, reduce, whether directly or indirectly, the wages of any employee to whom the Scheme or the Insurance Scheme applies or the total quantum of benefits in the nature of old age pension, gratuity, provident fund or life insurance to which the employee is entitled under the terms of his employment, express or implied.

Section 13: Inspectors

(1) The appropriate government may, by notification in the Official Gazette, appoint such persons as it thinks fit to be Inspectors for the purposes of this Act, the Scheme the Pension Scheme or the Insurance Scheme, and may define their jurisdiction.

(2) Any Inspector appointed under sub-section (1) may, for the purpose of inquiring into the correctness of any information furnished in connection with this Act or with any Scheme or the Insurance Scheme or for the purpose of ascertaining whether any of the provisions of this Act or of any Scheme or the Insurance Scheme have been complied with in respect of an establishment to which any Scheme or the Insurance Scheme applies or for the purpose of ascertaining whether the provisions of this Act or any Scheme or the Insurance Scheme are applicable to any establishment to which the Scheme or the Insurance Scheme has not been applied or for the purpose of determining whether the conditions subject to which exemption was granted under section 17 are being complied with by the employer in relation to an exempted establishment—

(a) require an employer or any contractor from whom any amount is recoverable under section 8A to furnish such information as he may consider necessary;

(b) at any reasonable time and with such assistance, if any, as he may think fit, enter and search any establishment, or any premises connected therewith and require any one found in charge thereof to produce before him for examination any accounts, books, registers and other documents relating to the employment of persons or the payment of wages in the establishment;

(c) examine, with respect to any matter relevant to any of the purposes aforesaid, the employer or any contractor from whom any amount is recoverable under section 8A, his agent or servant or any other person found in charge of the establishment, or any premises connected therewith or whom the Inspector has reasonable cause to believe to be or to have been, an employee in the establishment;

(d) make copies of, or take extracts from, any book, register or other document maintained in relation to the establishment and, where he has reason to believe that any offence under this Act has been committed by an employer, seize with such assistance as he may think fit, such book, register or other document or portions thereof as he may consider relevant in respect of that offence;

(e) exercise such other powers as the Scheme or the Insurance Scheme may provide.

(2A) Any Inspector appointed under sub-section (1) may, for the purpose of inquiring into the correctness of any information furnished in connection with the Pension Scheme or for the purpose of ascertaining whether any of the provisions of this Act or of the Pension Scheme have been complied with in respect of an establishments to which the Pension Scheme applies, exercise all or any of the powers conferred on him under clause (a), (b), (c) or (d) of sub-section (2).

(2B) The provisions of the Code of Criminal Procedure, 1898, shall, so far as may be, apply to any search or seizure under sub-section (2) or under sub-section (2A), as the case may be, as they apply to any search and seizure made under the authority of a warrant issued under section 98 of the said Code.

Section 14: Penalties

(1) Whoever, for the purpose of avoiding any payment to be made by himself under this Act, the Scheme, the Pension Scheme or the Insurance Scheme or of enabling any other person to avoid such payment knowingly makes or causes to be made any false statement or false representation shall be punishable with imprisonment for a term which may extend to one year, or with fine of five thousand rupees, or with both.

(1A) An employer who contravenes, or makes default in complying with, the provisions of section 6 or clause (a) of sub-section (3) of section 17 insofar as it relates to the payment of inspection charges, or para 38 of the Scheme insofar as it relates to the payment of administrative charges, shall be punishable with imprisonment for a term which may extend to three years but—

(a) which shall not be less than one year and fine of ten thousand rupees in case of default in payment of employees' contribution which has been deducted by the employer from the employees' wages;

(b) which shall not be less than six months and fine of five thousand rupees, in any other case:

Provided that the court may, for any adequate and special reasons to be recorded in the judgment, impose a sentence of imprisonment for a lesser term.

(1B) An employer who contravenes, or makes default in complying with, the provisions of section 6C, or clause (a) of sub-section (3A) of section 17 insofar as it relates to payment of inspection charges, shall be punishable with imprisonment for a term which may extend to one year but which shall not be less than six months and shall also be liable to fine which may extend to five thousand rupees:

Provided that the court may, for any adequate and special reasons to be recorded in the judgment, impose a sentence of imprisonment for a lesser term.

(2) Subject to the provisions of the Act, the Scheme, the Pension Scheme or the Insurance Scheme may provide that any person who contravenes, or makes default in complying with any of the provisions thereof shall be punishable with imprisonment for a term which may extend to one year, or with fine which may extend to four thousand rupees, or with both.

(2A) Whoever contravenes or makes default in complying with any provision of this Act or of any condition subject to which exemption was granted under section 17 shall, if no other penalty is elsewhere provided by or under this Act for such contravention or non-compliance, be punishable with imprisonment which may extend to six months, but which shall not be less than one month, and shall also be liable to fine which may extend to five thousand rupees.

The question of general importance that arises in *N.K. Jain* v. *C.K. Shah*[22] is whether criminal proceedings can be instituted under S. 14 of the Employees' Provident Funds and

22. AIR 1991 SC 1289.

Miscellaneous Provisions Act, 1952 against an establishment exempted under S. 17 of the Act for the contravention of the provisions of S. 6 of the Act.

Shri P. Chidambaram, learned counsel for the appellants, submitted that none of the sections of the Act, mentioned in the complaints, can be applied as against the appellants since the establishment in question is exempted under S. 17 of the Act and consequently is not governed by the 1952 Scheme nor by S. 6 of the Act. According to the learned counsel, the Act does not provide for prosecution in respect of any of the offences enumerated under S. 14 in case of breach by an exempted establishment in not paying the provident fund contributions to the trust and therefore no prosecution can be launched, and that if at all the management of the establishment had not deposited the provident fund contributions with the trust, the Government was empowered only to cancel the exemption which also amounts to a penalty.

The undisputed fact of this instant case reveals that the establishment in question was governed by the provisions of the Act and it was exempted under S. 17 of the Act and it had its own trust in respect of the provident fund contributions but failed to pay the provident fund contributions to the trust for some period during 1974 and thus there was a default. The controversy therefore is whether such failure attracts the prosecution or only warrants the cancellation of the exemption granted.

On a perusal of different provisions of the Act, which are having a direct bearing to this instant case, it is found that the Management of an establishment has to contribute to the provident fund and the Government under S. 5 can frame a scheme called Employees' Provident Fund Scheme and such a scheme was framed in the year 1952. The scheme provides for the establishment of provident fund under the Act for employees of the establishments specified therein. Section 6 is the material provision and deals with contributions which may be provided under the Scheme and also prescribes the rate of contribution to the fund and that the employees' contribution should be equal to the contribution payable by the employer. Section 14 deals with the penalties and S. 14(1A) lays down that an employer who contravenes, or makes default in complying with the provisions of S. 6 shall be punishable with imprisonment for a term which may extend to six months but shall not be less than three months in case of default in payment of the employees' contribution which has been deducted by the employer from the employees' wages. But for adequate reasons, it can be less. Paragraph 76 of the Scheme also provides for punishment for failure to pay such contributions to the fund. Section 17 provides for the exemption. As per the said section, the appropriate Government may by notification and subject to such conditions, as may be specified in the notification, exempt from the operation of all or any of the provisions of any Scheme (in the present case 1952 scheme) if the appropriate Government is satisfied that the rules of the provident fund which a particular establishment is following in the matter of contribution to the provident fund are not less favourable than those specified in S. 6 and that the employees are also in enjoyment of other provident fund benefits. In other words, the exemption from the operation of the scheme is granted provided the particular establishment makes contribution as per its own rules governing the contribution to the fund, which, in other words, can be called a provident fund scheme of its own are not less favourable than those specified in S. 6. Accordingly, the exempted establishment has to provide for its employees the benefits which are in no way less favourable than the ones provided under the Act and the Scheme.

Now the question is whether failure to make the contribution by the exempted establishment to the provident fund as per its own rules could attract the penal provisions of S. 14. The learned Additional Sessions Judge, however, as hereinbefore mentioned, held that S. 6 covers and attracts all the establishments including the exempted establishment. Even otherwise, according to him, S. 14(2A), which applies to an exempted establishment, is clearly attracted inasmuch as the conditions subject to which exemption was granted under S. 17 have been violated in the instant case. The learned Additional Sessions Judge also gave a finding that S. 14(1A) also is attracted as, in his view, even an exempted establishment is not absolved from the liability of employer's contribution as also the employees' contribution to the provident fund, and, therefore, by necessary implication the employer and the employees of an exempted establishment have to make full contribution to the provident fund as required under S. 6 of the Act, and if its contribution remains unpaid, it amounts to contravention of the provisions of S. 6 of the Act and thus attracts S. 14(1A).

The Supreme Court, in the instant case, observed that S. 14(2A) lays down that whoever contravenes or makes default in complying with any provisions of the Act or of any condition subject to which exemption was granted under S. 17 shall, if no other penalty is elsewhere provided by or under this Act for such contravention or non-compliance, be punishable with imprisonment and also fine mentioned therein. Firstly, it is submitted that the only contravention alleged against the appellants is that no contribution was made to the provident fund and since it is an exempted establishment, S. 6 is not attracted, and therefore it must be held that there is no contravention or non-compliance of any of the provisions of the Act. In other words, the submission is that S. 6 of the Act applies only to the non exempted establishments and covered under the statutory exemption. The learned Additional Sessions Judge, however, as already noted, has held that S. 6 applies to both exempted and non-exempted establishments. The essentials of these provisions are:

(i) there should be a contravention or default in complying with the provisions of the Act, or

(ii) there should be a contravention or default in complying with any of the conditions subject to which exemption was granted under S. 17, and

(iii) there should be no other penalty elsewhere provided by or under the Act for such contravention or non-compliance. Only when these essentials are satisfied, the section is attracted.

The learned counsel for the appellants submitted that in the present case there is no such contravention or non-compliance of any of the conditions subject to which exemption was granted. His further submission in this context is that the cancellation of an exemption as provided under S. 17(4) is a penalty provided by or under the Act for such contravention and therefore S. 14(2A) is not attracted.

The Supreme Court, while referring its earlier decision held in *Mohmedalli* v. *Union of India*,[4] observed that it would appear from the terms of the relevant portion of S. 17 that the exemption to be granted by the appropriate Government is not in the nature of completely absolving the establishments from all liability to provide the facilities contemplated by the Act. The exemptions are to be granted by the appropriate Government only if in its opinion the exempted establishment has provisions made for provident fund, in terms at least equal, if not more favourable, to its employees. In other words, the exemption is with a view to avoiding duplication and permitting the employees concerned the benefit of the pre-existing scheme, which presumably has by working satisfactorily, so that the exemption is not meant to deprive the employees concerned of the benefit of a provident fund but to ensure to them the continuance of the benefit which at least is not in terms less favourable to them. As the whole scheme, provident fund is intended for the benefit of employees, and S. 17 only saves preexisting schemes of provident fund pertaining to particular establishments.

The Apex Court, while considering the object underlying the Act and on reading Ss. 14 and 17 in full, made it clear that cancellation of the exemption granted does not amount to a penalty within the meaning of S. 14(2A). They should be interpreted in such a way so that the purpose of the legislation is allowed to be achieved.[23] Accordingly Lord Denning, L.J. in *Seaford Court Estates Ltd.* v. *Asher*,[24] observed that the English language is not an instrument of mathematical precision. Our literature would be much poorer if it were. This is where the draftsmen of Acts of Parliament have often been unfairly criticised. A Judge, believing himself to be fettered by the supposed rule that he must look to the language and nothing else, laments that the draftsmen have not provided for this or that, or have been guilty of some or other ambiguity. It would certainly save the judges' trouble if the Acts of Parliament were drafted with divine prescience and perfect clarity. In the absence of it, when a defect appears, a judge cannot simply fold his hands and blame the draftsman. He must set to work on the constructive task of finding the intention of Parliament, and he must do this not only from the language of the statute, but also from a consideration of the social conditions which gave rise to it and of the mischief which it was passed to remedy, and then he must supplement the written word so as to give 'force and life' to the intention of legislature.

The mere fact that S. 17(1A) was introduced in the year 1988 does not necessarily lead to an inference that Ss. 14(1A) and 14(2A) were not intended to be made applicable to an exempted establishment. After the perusal of different provisions of the Act, the Court was of opinion that with a view to make the penal provisions more stringent and with a view to check the growth of arrears, Ss. 14(1A) and 14(2A) are inapplicable to even exempted establishments.

Section 14A: Offences by companies

(1) If the person committing an offence under this Act, the Scheme, the Pension Scheme or the Insurance Scheme is a company, every person, who at the time the offence was committed was in charge of, and was responsible to, the company for the conduct of the business of the company, as well as the company, shall be deemed to be guilty of the offence and shall be liable to be proceeded against and punished accordingly:

Provided that nothing contained in this sub-section shall render any such person liable to any punishment, if he proves that the offence was committed without his knowledge or that he exercised all due diligence to prevent the commission of such offence.

23. *M/s. International Ore and Fertilizers (India) Pvt. Ltd.* v. *Employees' State Insurance Corpn.*, AIR 1988 SC 79.
24. (1949) 2 All ER 155.

(2) Notwithstanding anything contained in sub-section (1), where an offence under this Act, the Scheme, the Pension Scheme or the Insurance Scheme has been committed by a company and it is proved that the offence has been committed with the consent or connivance of, or is attributable to, any neglect on the part of, any director or manager, secretary or other officer of the company, such director, manager, secretary or other officer shall be deemed to be guilty of that offence and shall be liable to be proceeded against and punished accordingly.

Explanation: For the purposes of this section—

(a) "company" means any body corporate and includes a firm and other association of individuals; and

(b) "director", in relation to a firm, means a partner in the firm.

Sub-sections (1) and (2) extend the liability for any offence by any person including a partner by virtue of explanation if he was in charge or was responsible to the company at the time of committing the offence. The expression, '*was in charge of and was responsible to the company for the conduct of the business*' is very wide in their import. It could not, therefore, be confined to employer only.

Reverting to the statutory provision, Ss. 14 and 14A provide for penalties. The one applies to whosoever is guilty of avoiding payment of provident fund and to employer if he commits breach of provisions mentioned in its various clauses, whereas S. 14A fastens liability on certain persons if the person committing the offence is a company. The scope of the two sections is the same. The latter is wider in its sweep and reach. The former applies to anyone who is an employer or owner or is himself responsible for making payment whereas the latter fastens the liability on all those who are responsible or are in charge of the company for the offence committed by it.

A director of a private company, who is neither an occupier nor a manager, can be prosecuted under S. 14A of the Employees' Provident Fund and Miscellaneous Provisions Act, 1952 for violation of the Provident Fund Scheme when in Form 5A, Columns 8 and 11 the Director has declared himself as one of the persons in charge of and responsible for conduct of the business of the establishment or the factory.[14]

SECTION 14AA: Enhanced punishment in certain cases after previous conviction

Whoever, having been convicted by a court of an offence punishable under this Act, the Scheme, the Pension Scheme or the Insurance Scheme, commits the same offence shall be subject for every such subsequent offence to imprisonment for a term which may extend to five years, but which shall not be less than two years, and shall also be liable to a fine of twenty-five thousand rupees.

SECTION 14AB: Certain offences to be cognizable

Notwithstanding anything contained in the Code of Criminal Procedure, 1898 (5 of 1898), an offence relating to default in payment of contribution by the employer punishable under this Act shall be cognizable.

Section 14AC: Cognizance and trial of offences

(1) No court shall take cognizance of any offence punishable under this Act, the Scheme or, the Pension Scheme or the Insurance Scheme, except on a report in writing of the facts constituting such offence made with the previous sanction of the Central Provident Fund Commissioner or such other officer as may be authorised by the Central Government, by notification in the Official Gazette, in this behalf, by an inspector appointed under section 13.

(2) No court inferior to that of a Presidency Magistrate or a Magistrate of the first class shall try any offence under this Act or the Scheme or, the Pension Scheme or the Insurance Scheme.

Section 14B: Power to recover damages

Where an employer makes default in the payment of any contribution to the Fund, the Pension Fund or the Insurance Fund or in the transfer of accumulations required to be transferred by him under sub-section (2) of section 15 or sub-section (5) of section 17 or in the payment of any charges payable under any other provision of this Act or of any Scheme or Insurance Scheme or under any of the conditions specified under section 17, the Central Provident Fund Commissioner or such other officer as may be authorised by the Central Government, by notification in the Official Gazette, in this behalf may recover from the employer by way of penalty such damages, not exceeding the amount of arrears, as may be specified in the Scheme:

Provided that before levying and recovering such damages, the employer shall be given a reasonable opportunity of being heard:

Provided further that the Central Board may reduce or waive the damages levied under this section, in relation to an establishment which is a sick industrial company and in respect of which scheme for rehabilitation has been sanctioned by the Board for Industrial and Financial Reconstruction established under section 4 of the Sick Industrial Companies (Special Provisions) Act, 1985 (1 of 1986), subject to such terms and conditions as may be specified in the Scheme.

Section 14C: Power of court to make orders

(1) Where an employer is convicted of an offence of making default in the payment of any contribution to the Fund, the Pension Fund or the Insurance Fund or in the transfer of accumulations required to be transferred by him under sub-section (2) of section 15 or sub-section (5) of section 17, the court may, in addition to awarding any punishment, by order in writing require him within a period specified in the order (which the court may, if it thinks fit and on application in that behalf, from time to time, extend), to pay the amount of contribution or transfer the accumulations, as the case may be, in respect of which the offence was committed.

(2) Where an order is made under sub-section (1), the employer shall not be liable under this Act in respect of the continuation of the offence during the period or extended period, if any, allowed by the court, but if, on the expiry of such period or extended period, as the case may be, the order of the court has not been fully complied with, the employer shall be deemed to have committed a further offence and shall be punished with imprisonment in respect thereof under section 14 and shall also be liable to pay fine which may extend to one hundred rupees for every day after such expiry on which the order has not been complied with.

SECTION 15: Special provisions relating to existing provident funds

(1) Subject to the provisions of section 17, every employee who is a subscriber to any provident fund of an establishment to which this Act applies shall, pending the application of a Scheme to the establishment in which he is employed, continue to be entitled to the benefits accruing to him under the provident fund, and the provident fund shall continue to be maintained in the same manner and subject to the same conditions as it would have been if this Act had not been passed.

(2) On the application of any Scheme to an establishment, the accumulations in any provident fund of the establishment, standing to the credit of the employees who become members of the fund established under the Scheme shall, notwithstanding anything to the contrary contained in any law for the time being in force or in any deed or other instrument establishing the provident fund but subject to the provisions, if any, contained in the Scheme, be transferred to the Fund established under the Scheme, and shall be credited to the accounts of the employees entitled thereto in the Fund.

SECTION 16: Act not to apply to certain establishments

(1) This Act shall not apply—

(a) to any establishment registered under the Co-operative Societies Act, 1912, or under any other law for the time being in force in any State relating to co-operative societies, employing less than fifty persons and working without the aid of power, or

(b) to any other establishment belonging to or under the control of the Central Government or a State Government and whose employees are entitled to the benefit of Contributory provident fund or old age pension in accordance with any scheme or rule framed by the Central Government or the State Government governing such benefits, or

(c) to any other establishment set up under any Central, Provincial or State Act and whose employees are entitled to the benefits of contributory provident fund or old age pension in accordance with any scheme or rule framed under that Act governing such benefits.

(2) If the Central Government is of opinion that having regard to the financial position of any class of establishments or other circumstances of the case, it is necessary or expedient so to do, it may, by notification in the Official Gazette, and subject to such conditions as may be specified in the notification, exempt, whether prospectively or retrospectively, that class of establishments from the operation of this Act for such period as may be specified in the notification.

The Act being a beneficent statute and S. 16 of the Act being a clause granting exemption to the employer from the liability to make contributions, S. 16 should receive a strict construction. If a period of three years has elapsed from the date of the establishment of a factory, the Act would become applicable provided other conditions are satisfied. The criterion for earning exemption under S. 16(1)(b) is that a period of three years has not yet elapsed from the date of the establishment of the factory in question. It has no reference to the date on which the employer who is liable to make contributions acquired title to the factory. The Act also does not state that any kind of stoppage in the working of the factory would give rise to a fresh period of exemption. The work in a factory, which is once established, may be interrupted on account of factory holidays, strikes, lock outs, temporary break down of machinery, periodic repairs to be effected to the machinery in the factory, non availability of raw materials, paucity of finance, etc. It may also be interrupted on account of an order of the Court directing sale of the assets of the company owning the factory during winding up proceedings. Interruptions in the running of a factory which is governed by the Act brought about by any of the reasons mentioned above without more cannot be construed resulting in the factory ceasing to be a factory governed by the Act, and on its restarting it cannot be said that a new factory is or has been established. On the resumption of the manufacturing work in the factory, it would continue to be governed by the Act. Where the stoppage of production in a factory was brought about temporarily due to the order of the High Court in winding up proceedings in respect of the company owning the factory, for sale of assets of the company and it was the same old factory which recommenced production after its sale and a substantial number of workmen and staff who were working under the former management had been employed by the purchaser company, mere investment of additional capital or effecting of repairs to the existing machinery before it was restarted, the diversification of the lines of production or change of ownership would not amount to the establishment of a new factory attracting the exemption under S. 16(1)(b) for a fresh period of three years.[25]

The question for consideration raised before the Supreme Court in *Ess Dee Carpet Enterprises* v. *Union of India*[26] is whether an establishment which is manufacturing carpets is subject to the Employees' Provident Funds and Miscellaneous Provisions Act, 1952. The appellant is a partnership firm carrying on the business of manufacturing and selling carpets in the State of Rajasthan at three factories belonging to it. When steps were taken to direct the appellant to comply with the provisions of the EPF Act by the Regional Provident Fund Commissioner, the appellant contested the applicability of the Act on the ground that the establishment owned by it was not manufacturing 'textiles' included in Schedule I to the Act.

25. *Sayaji Mills Ltd.* v. *Regional Provident Fund Commissioner*, AIR 1985 SC 323.
26. AIR 1990 SC 455.

The Regional Provident Fund Commissioner after giving opportunity of being heard to the appellant passed an order holding that the business of manufacturing carpets carried on by it made the Act applicable to the appellant as carpets were textiles. The appellant thereafter filed a petition under Art. 226 of the Constitution before the Rajasthan High Court where the High Court dismissed the writ petition. The appellant then appealed to the Division Bench of the High Court and the Division Bench of the Rajasthan High Court dismissed the appeal. Therefore, the appellant approached the Supreme Court by special leave.

The only point urged before the Supreme Court is that the products, namely, carpets which are being manufactured by the appellant, did not come within the meaning of the expression 'textiles' described in Sch. 1 to the Act and hence the Act was inapplicable. Clause (a) of sub-section (3) of S. 1 of the Act provides that subject to the provisions contained in S. 1, the Act applies to every establishment which is a factory engaged in any industry specified in Schedule I and in which 20 or, more persons are employed. The relevant part of Schedule I to the Act needs to be referred for better understanding and it reads thus:

"Any industry engaged in the manufacture of any of the following, namely:

Cement

Cigarettes

Electrical, mechanical or general engineering products

Iron and steel

Paper

Textiles (made wholly or in part of cotton or wool or jute or silk, whether natural or artificial)

... ...

Clause (d) of the Explanation contained in Schedule I to the Act reads thus:

"(d) the expression "textiles" includes the products of carding, spinning, weaving, finishing and dyeing yarn and fabrics, printing, knitting, and embroidering."

It is not disputed that the material with which the carpets are made is wool, which is one of the materials mentioned in the schedule, namely, textiles made wholly or in part of cotton or wool or jute or silk, whether natural or artificial. The activity of manufacturing carpets is generally understood as the weaving of carpets and the man who is engaged in such activity is popularly known as a 'carpet weaver'. Weaving means to form a fabric by interlacing yarn on a loom. It also means the method or pattern of weaving or the structure of a woven fabric. The warp means yarn arranged lengthwise on a loom. The fabric which is woven includes the weft which means yarn woven across the width of the fabric through the lengthwise yarn. Thus, the activity of the weaving involves passing of the weft through the warp. While doing so, even if there are any knots in the yarn still the activity is weaving. The mere fact that there is knotting of the yarn, the fabric which is ultimately produced does not cease to be a textile fabric. Thus, it comes within the meaning of the expression "textiles" as explained in Cl. (d) to the Explanation of Schedule I to the Act. Therefore, the Supreme Court held that the establishment in question comes within Schedule I to the Act.

SECTION 16A: Authorising certain employers to maintain provident fund accounts

(1) The Central Government may, on an application made to it in this behalf by the employer and the majority of employees in relation to an establishment employing one hundred or more persons, authorise the employer, by an order in writing, to maintain a provident fund account in relation to the establishment, subject to such terms and conditions as may be specified in the Scheme:

Provided that no authorisation shall be made under this sub-section if the employer of such establishment had committed any default in the payment of provident fund contribution or had committed any other offence under this Act during the three years immediately preceding the date of such authorisation.

(2) Where an establishment is authorised to maintain a provident fund account under sub-section (1), the employer in relation to such establishment shall maintain such account, submit such return, deposit the contribution in such manner, provide for such facilities for inspection, pay such administrative charges, and abide by such other terms and conditions, as may be specified in the Scheme.

(3) Any authorisation made under this section may be cancelled by the Central Government by order in writing if the employer fails to comply with any of the terms and conditions of the authorisation or where he commits any offence under any provision of this Act:

Provided that before cancelling the authorisation, the Central Government shall give the employer a reasonable opportunity of being heard.

SECTION 17: Power to exempt

(1) The appropriate Government may, by notification in the Official Gazette, and subject to such conditions as may be specified in the notification, exempt, whether prospectively or retrospectively, from the operation of all or any of the provisions of any Scheme—

(a) any establishment to which this Act applies if, in the opinion of the appropriate Government, the rules of its provident fund with respect to the rates of contribution are not less favourable than those specified in section 6 and the employees are also in enjoyment of other provident fund benefits which on the whole are not less favourable to the employees than the benefits provided under this Act or any Scheme in relation to the employees in any other establishment of similar character, or

(b) any establishment if the employees of such establishment are in enjoyment of benefits in the nature of provident fund, pension or gratuity and the appropriate Government is of opinion that such benefits, separately or jointly, are on the whole not less favourable to such employees than the benefits provided under this Act or any Scheme in relation the employees in any other establishment of a similar character.

Provided that no such exemption shall be made except after consultation with the Central Board which on such consultation shall forward its views on exemption to the appropriate Government within such time limit as may be specified in the Scheme.

(1A) Where an exemption has been granted to an establishment under clause (a) of sub-section (1),—

(a) the provisions of sections 6, 7A, 8 and 14B shall, so far as may be, apply to the employer of the exempted establishment in addition to such other conditions as may be specified in the notification granting such exemption, and where such employer contravenes, or makes default in complying with any of the said provisions or conditions or any other provision of this Act, he shall be punishable under section 14 as if the said establishment had not been exempted under the said clause (a);

(b) the employer shall establish a Board of Trustees for the administration of the Provident Fund consisting of such number of members as may be specified in the Scheme;

(c) the terms and conditions of service of members of the Board of Trustees shall be such as may be specified in the Scheme;

(d) the Board of Trustees constituted under clause (b) shall—

(i) maintain detailed accounts to show the contributions credited, withdrawals made and interest accrued in respect of each employee;

(ii) submit such returns to the Regional Provident Fund Commissioner or any other officer as the Central Government may direct from time to time;

(iii) invest the provident fund monies in accordance with the directions issued by the Central Government from time to time;

(iv) transfer, where necessary, the provident fund account of any employee; and

(v) perform such other duties as may be specified in the Scheme.

(1B) Where the Board of Trustees established under clause (b) of sub-section (1A) contravenes, or makes default in complying with, any provisions of clause (d) of that sub-section, the Trustees of the said Board shall be deemed to have committed an offence under sub-section (2A) of section 14 and shall be punishable with the penalties provided in that sub-section.

(1C) The appropriate Government may, by notification in the Official Gazette, and subject to the condition on the pattern of investment of pension fund and such other conditions as may be specified therein, exempt any establishment or class of establishments from the operation of the Pension Scheme if the employees of such establishment or class of establishments are either members of any other pension scheme or propose to be members of such pension scheme, where the pensionary benefits are at par or more favourable than the Pension Scheme under this Act.

(2) Any Scheme may make provision for exemption of any person or class of persons employed in any establishment to which the Scheme applies from the operation of all or any of the provisions of the Scheme, if such person or class of persons is entitled to benefits in the nature of provident fund, gratuity or old age pension and

such benefits, separately or jointly, are on the whole not less favourable than the benefits provided under this Act or the Scheme:

Provided that no such exemption shall be granted in respect of a class of persons unless the appropriate Government is of opinion that the majority of persons constituting such class desire to continue to be entitled to such benefits.

(2A) The Central Provident Fund Commissioner may, if requested so to do by the employer, by notification in the Official Gazette, and subject to such conditions as may be specified in the notification, exempt, whether prospectively or retrospectively, any establishment from the operation of all or any of the provisions of the Insurance Scheme, if he is satisfied that the employees of such establishment are, without making any separate contribution or payment of premium, in enjoyment of benefits in the nature of life insurance, whether linked to their deposits in provident fund or not, and such benefits are more favourable to such employees than the benefits admissible under the Insurance Scheme.

(2B) Without prejudice to the provisions of sub-section (2A), the Insurance Scheme may provide for the exemption of any person or class of persons employed in any establishment and covered by that Scheme from the operation of all or any of the provisions thereof, if the benefits in the nature of life insurance admissible to such person or class of persons are more favourable than the benefits provided under the Insurance Scheme.

(3) Where in respect of any person or class of persons employed in an establishment an exemption is granted under this section from the operation of all or any of the provisions of any scheme (whether such exemption has been granted to the establishment wherein such person or class of persons is employed or to the person or class of persons as such), the employer in relation to such establishment—

(a) shall, in relation to the provident fund, pension and gratuity to which any such person or class of persons is entitled, maintain such accounts, submit such returns, make such investment, provide for such facilities for inspection and pay such inspection charges, as the Central Government may direct;

(b) shall not, at any time after the exemption, without the leave of the Central Government, reduce the total quantum of benefits in the nature of pension, gratuity or provident fund to which any person or class of persons was entitled at the time of the exemption; and

(c) shall, where any such person leaves his employment and obtains re-employment in another establishment to which this Act applies, transfer within such time as may be specified in this behalf by the Central Government, the amount of accumulations, to the credit of that person in the provident fund of the establishment left by him to the credit of that person's account in the provident fund of the establishment in which he is re-employed or, as the case may be, in the fund established under the Scheme applicable to the establishment.

(3A) Where, in respect of any person or class of persons employed in any establishment, an exemption is granted under sub-section (2A) or sub-section (2B) from the operation of all or any of the provisions of the Insurance Scheme (whether such exemption is granted to the establishment wherein such person or class of persons is employed or to the person or class of persons as such), the employer in relation to such establishment—

(a) shall, in relation to the benefits in the nature of life insurance, to which any such person or class of persons is entitled, or any insurance fund, maintain such accounts, submit such returns, make such investments, provide for such facilities for inspection and pay such inspection charges, as the Central Government may direct;

(b) shall not, at any time after the exemption without the leave of the Central Government, reduce the total quantum of benefits in the nature of life insurance to which any such person or class of persons was entitled immediately before the date of the exemption;

(4) any exemption granted under this section may be cancelled by the authority which granted it, by order in writing, if an employer fails to comply,—

(a) in the case of an exemption granted under sub-section (1), with any of the conditions imposed under that sub-section or sub-section(1A)or with any of the provisions of the sub-section (3);

(aa) in the case of an exemption granted under sub-section (1C), with any of the conditions imposed under that sub-section; and

(b) in the case of an exemption granted under sub-section (2), with any of the provisions of sub-section (3);

(c) in the case of an exemption granted under sub-section (2A), with any of the conditions imposed under that sub-section or with any of the provisions of sub-section (3A);

(d) in the case of an exemption granted under sub-section (2B), with any of the provisions of sub-section (3A).

(5) Where any exemption granted under sub-section (1), sub-section (1C), sub-section (2), sub-section (2A) or sub-section (2B) is cancelled, the amount of accumulations to the credit of every employee to whom such exemption applied, in the provident fund, the Pension Fund or the Insurance Fund of the establishment in which he is employed together with any amount forfeited from the employer's share of contribution to the credit of the employee who leaves the employment before the completion of the full period of service shall be transferred within such time and in such manner as may be specified in the Scheme or the Pension Scheme or the Insurance Scheme to the credit of his account in the Fund or the Pension Fund or the Insurance Fund, as the case may be.

(6) Subject to the provisions of sub-section (1C), the employer of an exempted establishment to which the provisions of the Pension Scheme apply, shall, notwithstanding any exemption granted under sub-section (1) or sub-section (2), pay to the Pension Fund such portion of the employers contribution to its provident fund within such time and in such manner as may be specified in the Pension Scheme.

SECTION 17A: Transfer of accounts

(1) Where an employee employed in an establishment to which this Act applies leaves his employment and obtains re-employment in another establishment to which this Act does not apply, the amount of accumulations to the credit of such employee in the Fund, or as the case may be, in the provident fund of the establishment left by him shall be transferred, within such time as may be specified by the Central Government in this behalf, to the credit of his account in the provident fund of the establishment in which he is re-employed, if the employee so desires and the rules in relation to that provident fund permit such transfer.

(2) Where an employee employed in an establishment to which this Act does not apply leaves his employment and obtains re-employment in another establishment to which this Act applies, the amount of accumulations to the credit of such employee in the provident fund of the establishment left by him may, if the employee so desires and the rules in relation to such provident fund permit, be transferred to the credit of his account in the Fund or as the case may be, in the provident fund of the establishment in which he is re-employed.

SECTION 17AA: Act to have effect notwithstanding anything contained in Act 31 of 1956

The provisions of this Act shall have effect notwithstanding anything inconsistent therewith contained in the Life Insurance Act, 1956.

SECTION 17B: Liability in case of transfer of establishment

Where an employer, in relation to an establishment, transfers that establishment in whole or in part, by sale, gift, lease or license or in any other manner whatsoever, the employer and the person to whom the establishment is so transferred shall jointly and severally be liable to pay the contribution and other sums due from the employer under any provision of this Act or the Scheme or the Pension Scheme, as the case may be, in respect of the period up to the date of such transfer:

Provided that the liability of the transferee shall be limited to the value of the assets obtained by him by such transfer.

SECTION 18: Protection of action taken in good faith

No suit, prosecution of other legal proceeding shall lie against the Central Government, a State Government, the Presiding Officer of a Tribunal, any authority referred to in section 7A, an Inspector or any other person for anything which is in good faith done or intended to be done in pursuance of this Act, the Scheme, the Pension or the Insurance Scheme.

Section 18A: Presiding officer and other officers to be public servants

The Presiding Officer of a Tribunal, its officers and other employees, the authorities referred to in section 7A and every Inspector shall be deemed to be public servants within the meaning of section 21 of Indian Penal Code (45 of 1860).

Section 19: Delegation of powers

The appropriate Government may direct that any power or authority or jurisdiction exercisable by it under this Act, the Scheme, the Pension Scheme or the Insurance Scheme shall, in relation to such matters and subject to such conditions, if any, as may be specified in the direction, be exercisable also:

(a) where the appropriate Government is the Central Government, by such officer or authority subordinate to the Central Government or by the State Government or by such officer or authority subordinate to the State Government, as may be specified in the notification; and

(b) where the appropriate Government is a State Government, by such officer or authority subordinate to the State Government as may be specified in the notification.

Section 20: Power of Central Government to give directions

The Central Government may, from time to time, give such directions to the Central Board as it may think fit for the efficient administration of this Act and when, any such direction is given, the Central Board shall comply with such direction.

Section 21: Power to make rules

(1) The Central Government may, by notification in the Official Gazette, make rules to carry out the provisions of this Act.

(2) Without prejudice to the generality of the foregoing power, such rules may provide for all or any of the following matters, namely:

(a) the salary and allowances and other terms and conditions of service of the Presiding Officer and the employees of a Tribunal;

(b) the form and the manner in which, and the time within which, an appeal shall be filed before a Tribunal and the fees payable for filing such appeal;

(c) the manner of certifying the copy of the certificate, to be forwarded to the Recovery Officer under sub-section (2) of section 8C; and

(d) any other matter, which has to be, or may be, prescribed by rules under this Act.

(3) Every rule made under this Act shall be laid, as soon as may be after it is made, before each House of Parliament, while it is in session, for a total period of thirty days which may be comprised in one session or in two or more successive sessions,

and if, before the expiry of the session immediately following the session or the successive sessions aforesaid, both Houses agree in making any modification in the rule or both Houses agree that the rule should not be made, the rule shall thereafter have effect only in such modified form or be of no effect, as the case may be; so, however, that any such modification or annulment shall be without prejudice to the validity of anything previously done under that rule.

SECTION 22: Power to remove difficulties

(1) If any difficulty arises in giving effect to the provisions of this Act, as amended by the Employees' Provident Funds and Miscellaneous Provisions (Amendment) Act, 1988, the Central Government may, by order published in the Official Gazette, make such provisions, not inconsistent with the provisions of this Act as appear to it to be necessary or expedient for the removal of the difficulty:

Provided that no such order shall be made after the expiry of a period of three years from the date on which the said Amendment Act receives the assent of the President.

(2) Every order made under this section shall, as soon as may be after it is made, be laid before each House of Parliament.

SCHEDULE I

[*See* Sections 2(i) and 4]

Any industry engaged in the manufacture of any of the following, namely:

Cement
Cigarettes
Electrical, mechanical or general engineering products
Iron and steel
Paper
Textiles (made wholly or in part of cotton or wool or jute or silk, whether natural or artificial)

1. Matches
2. Edible oils and fats
3. Sugar
4. Rubber and rubber products
5. Electricity, including the generation, transmission and distribution thereof
6. Tea
7. Printing other than printing industry relating to newspaper establishments as defined in the Working Journalists (Conditions of Service) and Miscellaneous Provisions Act, 1955 (45 of 1955), including the process of composing types for printing, printing by letter-press, lithography, photogravure or other similar process or book binding

8. Glass
9. Stone-ware pipes
10. Sanitary wares
11. Electrical porcelain insulators of high and low tension
12. Refractories
13. Tiles

1. Heavy and fine chemicals, including:

   (i) Fertilisers,
   (ii) Turpentine,
   (iii) Rosin,
   (iv) Medical and pharmaceutical preparations,
   (v) Toilet preparations,
   (vi) Soaps,
   (vii) Inks,
   (viii) Intermediates, dyes, colour lacs and toners,
   (ix) Fatty acids, and
   (x) Oxygen, acetylene and carbon-dioxide gases industry.

2. Indigo
3. Lac including shellac
4. Non-edible, vegetable and animal oils and fats.

Mineral oil refining industry.

(i) Industrial and power alcohol industry; and
(ii) Asbestos cement sheets industry.

Biscuit-making industry including composite units making biscuits and products such as bread, confectionery and milk and milk powder.

Mica industry
Plywood industry
Automobile repairing and servicing industry
Rice milling
Flour milling
Dal milling
Starch industry
Petroleum or natural gas exploration, prospecting, drilling or production
Petroleum or natural gas refining
Leather and leather products industry
Stone-ware jars
Crockery.

The fruit and vegetable preservation industry, that is to say, any industry which is engaged in the preparation or production of any of the following articles, namely:

(i) canned and bottled fruits, juices and pulps,

(ii) canned and bottled vegetables,

(iii) frozen fruits and vegetables,

(iv) jams, jellies and marmalades,

(v) tomato products, ketchups and sauces,

(vi) squashes, crushes, cordials and ready-to-serve beverages or any other beverages containing fruit juice or fruit pulp,

(vii) preserved, canned and crystallised fruits and peels,

(viii) chutneys,

(ix) any other unspecified item relating to the preservation or canning of fruits and vegetables.

Cashewnut industry.

Confectionery industry.

1. Buttons
2. Brushes
3. Plastic and plastic products
4. Stationery products.

The aerated water industry, that is to say, any industry engaged in the manufacture of aerated water, soft drinks or carbonated water.

The distilling and rectifying of spirits (not falling under industrial and power alcohol) and blending of spirits industry.

The paint and varnish industry.

Bone crushing industry.

Pickers industry.

Milk and milk products industry.

Non-ferrous metals and alloys in the form of ingots industry.

Bread industry.

Stemming or re-drying of tobacco leaf industry, that is to say, any industry engaged in the stemming, re-drying, handling, sorting, grading or packing of tobacco leaf.

Agarbattee (including dhoop and dhoopbattee) industry.

Coir (excluding the spinning sector) industry.

Tobacco industry, that is to say, any industry engaged in the manufacture of cigars, zarda, snuff, quivam and guraku from tobacco.

Paper products industry.

Licensed salt industry, that is to say, any industry engaged in the manufacture of salt for which a license is necessary and which has land not less than 4.05 hectares.

Linoleum industry and indoleum industry.

Explosive industry.

Jute bailing or pressing industry.

Fire-works and percussion cap works industry.

Tent making industry.

Ferro-manganese industry.

Ice or ice-cream industry.

Winding of thread and yarn reeling industry.

Cotton ginning, baling and pressing industry.

Katha making industry.

Beer manufacturing industry, that is to say, any industry engaged in the manufacture of the product of alcoholic fermentation of a mash in potable water of malted barley and hops, or of hops concentrated with or without the addition of other malted or unmalted cereals or other carbohydrate preparations.

Beedi industry, that is to say, any industry engaged in manufacture of beedies.

Ferro-chrome industry.

Diamond cutting industry.

Myrobalan extract powder, myrobalan extract solid and vegetable tannin blended extract industries.

Brick industry.

All industries based on asbestos as principal raw material.

Industries manufacturing iron ore pellets.

Explanation: In this Schedule, without prejudice to the ordinary meaning of the expressions used therein:

(a) the expression "Electrical, mechanical or general engineering products" includes:

(1) machinery and equipment for the generation, transmission, distribution or measurement of electrical energy and motors including cables and wires,

(2) telephones, telegraph and wireless communication apparatus,

(3) electric lamps (not including glass bulbs),

(4) electric fans and electrical domestic appliances,

(5) storage and dry batteries,

(6) radio receivers and sound reproducing instruments,

(7) machinery used in industry (including textile machinery) other than electrical machinery and machine tools,

(8) boilers and prime movers, including internal combustion engines, marine engines and locomotives,

(9) machines tools, that is to say, metal and wood working machinery,

(10) grinding wheels,

(11) ships,

(12) automobiles and tractors,

(13) bolts, nuts and rivets,

(14) power-driven pumps,

(15) bicycles,

(16) hurricane lanterns,
(17) sewing and knitting machines,
(18) mathematical and scientific instruments,
(19) products of metal rolling and re-rolling,
(20) wires, pipes, tubes and fittings,
(21) ferrous and non-ferrous castings,
(22) safes, vaults and furniture made of iron and steel or steel alloys,
(23) cutlery and surgical instruments,
(24) drums and containers,
(25) parts and accessories of products specified in items 1 to 24;

(b) the expression 'iron and steel' includes pig iron, ingots, blooms, billets and rolled or re-rolled products into basic forms and tool and alloy steel;
(c) the expression 'paper' includes pulp, paperboard and straw-board;
(d) the expression 'textiles' includes the products of carding, spinning, weaving, finishing and dyeing yarn and fabrics, printing, knitting and embroidering.

SCHEDULE II: MATTERS FOR WHICH PROVISION MAY BE MADE IN A SCHEME

[*See* Section 5(1B)]

1. The employees or class of employees who shall join the Fund, and the conditions under which employees may be exempted from joining the Fund or from making any contribution.
2. The time and manner in which contribution shall be made to the Fund by employers and by, or on behalf of, employees, whether employed by him directly or by or through contractor, the contributions which an employee may, if he so desires, make under section 6, and the manner in which such contributions may be recovered.

2A. The manner in which employees' contribution may be recovered by contractors from employees employed by or through such contractors.

3. The payment by the employer of such sums of money as may be necessary to meet the cost of administering the Fund and the rate at which and the manner in which the payment shall be made.
4. The constitution of any committee for assisting any Board of Trustees.
5. The opening of regional and other offices of any Board of Trustees.
6. The manner in which accounts shall be kept, the investment of moneys belonging to the Fund in accordance with any directions issued or conditions specified by the Central Government, the preparation of the budget, the audit of accounts and the submission of reports to the Central Government or to any specified State Government.

7. The conditions under which withdrawals from the Fund may be permitted and any deduction or forfeiture may be made and the maximum amount of such deduction or forfeiture.
8. The fixation by the Central Government in consultation with the board of trustees concerned of the rate of interest payable to members.
9. The form in which an employee shall furnish particulars about himself and his family whenever required.
10. The nomination of a person to receive the amount standing to the credit of a member after his death and the cancellation or variation of such nomination.
11. The registers and records to be maintained with respect to employees and the returns to be furnished by employers or contractors.
12. The form or design of any identity card, token or disc for the purpose of identifying any employee, and for the issue, custody and replacement thereof.
13. The fees to be levied for any of the purposes specified in this Schedule.
14. The contraventions or defaults which shall be punishable under sub-section (2) of section 14.
15. The further powers, if any, which may be exercised by Inspectors.
16. The manner in which accumulations in any existing provident fund shall be transferred to the Fund under section 15, and the mode of valuation of any assets which may be transferred by the employers in this behalf.
17. The conditions under which a member may be permitted to pay premia on life insurance, from the Fund.
18. Any other matter which is to be provided for in the Scheme or which may be necessary or proper for the purpose of implementing the Scheme.

SCHEDULE III: MATTERS FOR WHICH PROVISION MAY BE MADE IN THE PENSION SCHEME

[*See* Section 6A(5)]

1. The employees or class of employees to whom the Pension Scheme shall apply.
2. The time within which the employees who are not members of the Pension Scheme under section 6A as it stood before the commencement of the Employees Provident Funds and Miscellaneous Provisions (Amendment) Act, 1996 (hereinafter, in this Schedule, referred to as the amending Act) shall opt for the Pension Scheme.
3. The portion of employer's contribution to the Provident Fund which shall be credited to the Pension Fund and the manner in which it is credited.
4. The minimum qualifying service for being eligible for pension and the manner in which the employees may be granted the benefits of their past service under section 6A as it stood before the commencement of the amending Act.

5. The regulation of the manner in which and the period of service for which no contribution is received.
6. The manner in which employees' interest will be protected against default in payment of contribution by the employer.
7. The manner in which the accounts of the Pension Fund shall be kept and investment of moneys belonging to Pension Fund to be made subject to such pattern of investment as may be determined by the Central Government.
8. The form in which an employee shall furnish particulars about himself and the members of his family whenever required.
9. The forms, registers and records to be maintained in respect of employees, required for the administration of the Pension Scheme.
10. The scale of pension and pensionary benefits and the conditions relating to grant of such benefits to the employees.
11. The manner in which the exempted establishments have to pay contribution towards the Pension Scheme and the submission of returns relating thereto.
12. The mode of disbursement of pension and arrangements to be entered into with such disbursing agencies as may be specified for the purpose.
13. The manner in which the expenses for administering the Pension Scheme will be met from the income of the Pension Fund.
14. Any other matter which is to be provided for in the Pension Scheme or which may be necessary or proper for the purpose of implementation of the Pension Scheme.

SCHEDULE IV: MATTERS TO BE PROVIDED FOR IN THE EMPLOYEES' DEPOSIT-LINKED INSURANCE SCHEME

[*See* **Section 6C**]

1. The employees or class of employees who shall be covered by the Insurance Scheme.
2. The manner in which the accounts of the Insurance Fund shall be kept and the investment of moneys belonging to the Insurance Fund subject to such pattern of investment as may be determined, by order, by the Central Government.
3. The form in which an employee shall furnish particulars about himself and the members of his family whenever required.
4. The nomination of a person to receive the insurance amount due to the employee after his death and the cancellation or variation of such nomination.
5. The registers and records to be maintained in respect of employees, the form or design of any identity card, token or disc for the purpose of identifying any employee or his nominee or member of his family entitled to receive the insurance amount.
6. The scales of insurance benefits and conditions relating to the grant of such benefits to the employees.

7. The manner in which the amount due to the nominee or the member of the family of the employee under the Scheme is to be paid including a provision that the amount shall not be paid otherwise than in the form of a deposit in a savings bank account, in the name of such nominee or member of family, in any corresponding new bank specified in the First Schedule to the Banking Companies (Acquisition and Transfer of Undertakings Act, 1970 (5 of 1970).
8. Any other matter which is to be provided for in the Employees' Deposit-Linked Insurance Scheme or which may be necessary or proper for the purpose of implementing that Scheme.

* * *

14 The Factories Act, 1948

The Indian legislature enacted Act 15 of 1881, which was the first Act dealing with factories. The Act was limited in its scope: it was followed by Act 11 of 1891, which, in turn, was followed by Act 12 of 1911. Amendments were made to that Act from time to time. In 1929, a Royal Commission of Labour in India was appointed to make a detailed investigation into labour problems. The Commission investigated the conditions of labour in various industries and submitted its report in June 1931, containing diverse recommendations for amendment of the Indian Factories Act, 1911. The Commission stressed the need for exercise of power to extend the provisions of the Act to industries not covered by the definition of the word 'factory'.

The Commission recommended the enactment of a separate Act applicable, in the first instance, to all places without power machinery, employing fifty or more person during any part of the year and suggested that the Provincial Government may be authorised to extend any provision of the Act to factories employing less than the prescribed number when in their opinion conditions justify such action. But the Indian Legislature enacted a comprehensive measure—Act 25 of 1934—amending and consolidating the provisions of factory legislation in India. The object of the Act was to reduce hours of work, improve the working conditions in the factories, provide for adequate inspection and strict observance of the Act. But the places where the manufacturing process was carried on without the aid of power were not covered by the definition of 'factory'. The Legislature by Act 16 of 1941 amended the Act 25 of 1934 and authorised the Provincial Government by notification in the Official Gazette to declare all or any of the provisions applicable to factories to any place wherein manufacturing process was being carried on or was so ordinarily carried on with or without the aid of power where ten or more persons were working therein.

A Labour Investigation Committee was appointed by the Government of India in February, 1944 to investigate conditions of employment in respect of various industries. This Committee enquired into the conditions of workmen in the bidi, cigar and cigarette industry, and observed that the picture drawn by the Royal Commission of the working conditions in the bidi industry remained largely true. Application of factory legislation to protect the legitimate interest of workers was therefore a crying necessity. The Factories Act, 1948, extended the definition of factory.

OBJECT OF THE ACT

The Factories Act is "an Act to consolidate and amend the law regulating labour in factories". The Act is enacted primarily with the object of protecting workers employed in factories against industrial and occupational hazards. For that purpose, it seeks to impose upon the owners or the occupiers certain obligations to protect unwary as well as negligent workers and to secure for them employment in conditions conducive to their health and safety.

The Factories Act primarily applies to establishments in which ten or more persons are working where power is used and twenty or more persons where no power is used, thereby excluding from its operation small establishments. Presumably, the legislature felt that uniform application of the Factories Act to all establishments, where a manufacturing process is carried on requiring even small establishments to comply with the elaborate requirements of the Factories Act, may impose great administrative strain upon governmental machinery, and involve hardship ordinarily not commensurate with the benefit secured thereby. But the legislature, with a view to prevent circumvention of the provisions of the Factories Act, and to secure to the persons working in establishments where manufacturing process is carried on, adequate safeguards where necessity is felt, has authorised the State Government by notification to declare any place which does not fall within the definition of "factory" to be a factory and to make all or any of the provisions of the Act applicable thereto. Similarly, the Act is primarily intended to govern relations of persons standing as master and servant in connection with manufacturing processes in factories, and liberty of contract otherwise was not sought to be affected by the principal provisions of the Act. But here again the legislature has authorised the State Government to issue notifications, applying the provisions of the Act even to those establishments in which persons are working with the permission or under agreement with, but not as employees of the owners. Exclusion from restriction inherent in the definitions of "factory" and "worker" has its source not in any desire to afford special privileges to any class of owners. The policy underlying S. 85 authorising the State Government to extend the benefit of the Act is apparent on its face. The section aims at making provision for securing the health and safety of persons engaged in hazardous employments, and for that purpose the legislature has entrusted to the State Governments, in the case of establishments not falling expressly within the regulatory provisions of the Act, authority to extend those provisions where the necessity to regulate, having regard to the circumstances, is felt. The power to extend the regulatory provisions of the Act is therefore not intended to confer an arbitrary power to pick and choose between establishments similarly situated. It is granted with a view to secure the protection of persons engaged in industrial occupation in the light of special circumstances of a particular industry, a locality or an establishment, where circumstances justifying the extension of the protection exist. The conditions of small establishments in different parts of the country may and do widely vary. Control in respect of some industries or establishments not governed by the Factories Act may not be necessary, whereas necessity in that behalf may be acutely felt in others. It is to carry out effectively the object underlying the Act that power has been given to the State Government to decide with reference to local conditions whether it is desirable that the provisions of the Act or any of them should be made applicable to any establishment which is not covered by the definition of "factory" or to workers in a factory who are not entitled to the benefits of the Act.

CHAPTER I

PRELIMINARY

SECTION 1: Short title, extent and commencement

(1) This Act may be called the Factories Act, 1948.

(2) It extends to the whole of India.

(3) It shall come into force on the 1st day of April, 1949.

SECTION 2: Interpretation

In this Act, unless there is anything repugnant in the subject or context,—

(a) **adult** means a person who has completed his eighteenth year of age.

(b) **adolescent** means a person who has completed his fifteen year of age but has not completed his eighteenth year.

(bb) **calendar year** means the period of twelve months beginning with the first day of January in any year.

(c) **child** means a person who has not completed his fifteenth year of age.

(ca) **competent person**, in relation to any provision of this Act, means a person or an institution recognised as such by the Chief Inspector for the purposes of carrying out tests, examinations and inspections required to be done in a factory under the provisions of this Act having regard to—

(i) the qualifications and experience of the person and facilities available at his disposal; or

(ii) the qualifications and experience of the persons employed in such institution and facilities available therein,

with regard to the conduct of such test, examinations and inspections, and more than one person or institution can be recognised as a competent person in relation to a factory.

(cb) **hazardous process** means any process or activity in relation to an industry specified to the First Schedule where, unless special care is taken, raw materials used therein or the intermediate or finished products, bye-products, wastes or effluents thereof would—

(i) cause material impairment to the health of the persons engaged in or connected therewith, or

(ii) result in the pollution of the general environment:

Provided that the State Government may, by notification in the Official Gazette, amend the First Schedule by way of addition, omission or variation of any industry specified in the said Schedule;

(d) **young person** means a person who is either a child or an adolescent.

(e) **day** means a period of twenty-four hours beginning at midnight.

(f) **week** means a period of seven days beginning at midnight on Saturday night or such other night as may be approved in writing for a particular area by the Chief Inspector of factories.

(g) **power** means electrical energy, or any other form of energy which is mechanically transmitted and is not generated by human or animal agency.

(h) **prime mover** means any engine, motor or other appliance which generates or otherwise provides power.

(i) **transmission machinery** means any shaft, wheel drum, pulley, system of pulleys, coupling, clutch, driving belt or other appliance or device by which the motion of a prime mover is transmitted to or received by any machinery or appliance.

(j) **machinery** includes prime movers, transmission machinery and all other appliances whereby power is generated, transformed, transmitted or applied.

(k) **manufacturing process** means any process for—

(i) making, altering, repairing, ornamenting, finishing, packing, oiling, washing, cleaning, breaking up, demolishing, or otherwise treating or adapting any article or substance with a view to its use, sale, transport, delivery or disposal, or

(ii) pumping oil, water, sewage or any other substance; or

(iii) generating, transforming or transmitting power; or

(iv) composing types for printing, printing by letter press, lithography, photogravure or other similar process or book binding; or

(v) constructing, reconstructing, repairing, refitting, finishing or breaking up ships or vessels; or

(vi) preserving or storing any article in cold storage.

In *V.P. Gopala Rao* v. *Public Prosecutor, Andhra Pradesh,*[1] the question that came before the Supreme Court for consideration is whether the company's premises at Eluru constitutes a factory. Under S. 2(m), factory means any premises including the precincts thereof "whereon ten or more workers are working, or were working on any day of the preceding twelve months, and in any part of which a manufacturing process is being carried on with the aid of power, or is ordinarily so carried on." It is not disputed that more than 10 persons were working on the premises. The point in issue is: Whether any manufacturing process was being carried on therein.

The fact of the case reveals the following propositions which are necessary for our discussion. In a company's premises at E, sun-cured tobacco leaves bought from the growers were subjected to the processes of moistening, stripping and packing. The stalks were stripped from the leaves. The *Thukku* (wholly spoilt) and *Pagu* (partly spoilt) leaves were separated. The leaves were tied up in bundles and stored in the premises. From time to time, they were packed in gunny bags and exported to the company's factory at B where they were used for manufacturing cigarettes. More than 20 persons were working on the premises regularly every day under the supervision of the management.

1. AIR 1970 SC 66.

The manufacturing processes as defined in S. 2(k)(i) were carried on in the premises. The moistening was an adaptation of the tobacco leaves. The stalks were stripped by breaking them up. The leaves were packed by bundling them up and putting them into gunny bags. The breaking up, the adaptation and the packing of the tobacco leaves were done with a view to their use and transport. All these processes are manufacturing processes within S. 2(k)(i).

While railway lines are being constructed on a given site, no article or substance is being made or repaired, maintained, finished, etc. Raw materials like railway sleepers, bolts and loose railway rails when bought by the construction company from the open market and brought on site are articles visible to the eyes and are movable articles. These articles are adapted for their use. Their use is for ultimately laying down a railway line. In that process, sleepers, bolts and rails would get used up. If that happens, the definition of 'manufacturing process' dealing with adaptations of these articles for use would squarely get attracted. It is true that the ultimate product of this exercise or process is the bringing into existence a railway track which is embedded in the earth, which cannot be sold, transported, delivered or disposed of like a movable property. However, as the definition is worded, it cannot be said of necessity that any end product which results after adapting any raw-material, article or substance "with a view to its use" must necessarily result into a movable final product or a commodity. For the definition of 'manufacturing process' under S. 2(k), end product may be goods or otherwise. It is not necessary that the end product must be marketable. Even accepting that the final product, namely construction of railway line embedded in earth is not the subject-matter of sale, transfer, delivery or disposal, still the raw-materials which are adapted for their use with a view to constructing railway line which is the final product could be said to have fallen within the sweep of the definition of the term 'manufacturing process' as found in S. 2(k) of the Factories Act.[2]

In view of S. 2(k)(iii), the process of transforming electrical energy from a high to a low potential and the process of transmitting the energy through supply lines are both 'manufacturing processes.' In a part of the premises occupied by the company, the two processes are carried on with the aid of power by means of electrical gadgets and other devices. On the premises more than twenty persons are working. No part of the premises is used for purposes unconnected with the manufacturing processes. The premises therefore constitute a factory within the meaning of S. 2(12) of the Employees' State Insurance Act, 1948.[3] The definition of 'manufacturing process' in the Factories Act does not depend upon and is not co-related with any end product being manufactured out of a manufacturing process. It includes even repair, finishing, oiling or cleaning process with view to its use, sale, transport, delivery or disposal. Pumping oil, water or sewage under S. 2(k)(ii) does not mean that it may result into outcome of any processed product for sale. The words 'manufacturing process' cannot be restricted to an activity which may result into manufacturing something or production of a commercially different article. The Court supported in this interpretation by the addition of Cl. (vi) to the definition by Act No. 25 of 1954 where even preserving or storing any article in cold storage was included in the definition clause. The 'manufacturing process' cannot be

2. *Lal Mohammad* v. *Indian Railway Construction Co. Ltd.*, AIR 1999 SC 355.
3. *Nagpur Electric Light and Power Co. Ltd.* v. *Regional Director, Employees' State Insurance Corp.*, AIR 1967 SC 1364.

interpreted in a narrow sense in respect of an Act which is meant for the purposes connected with social welfare.[4]

(l) **worker** means a person employed, directly or by or through any agency (including a contractor) with or without the knowledge of the principal employer, whether for remuneration or not, in any manufacturing process, or in cleaning any part of the machinery or premises used for a manufacturing process, or in any other kind of work incidental to, or connected with, the manufacturing process, or the subject of the manufacturing process but does not include any member of the armed forces of the union.

Section 2(l) of the Factories Act, 1948, defines 'worker' as a person employed, directly or through any agency, whether for wages or not, in any manufacturing process or in cleaning any part of the machinery or premises used for a manufacturing process, or in any other kind of work incidental to, or connected with, the manufacturing process, or the subject of the manufacturing process. Factory is defined by S. 2(m) as any premises including the precincts thereof wherein a specified number of workers on any day of the preceding twelve months is employed. By the combined operation of these definitions, persons employed in any manufacturing process or in cleaning any part of the machinery or part of the premises used for the manufacturing process or any other kind of work incidental to or connected with the manufacturing process or the subject of the manufacturing process are deemed to be workers in a factory. By the use in S. 2(l) of the Factories Act of the expression, 'employed in any other kind of work incidental to or connected with the subject of manufacturing process', not only workers directly connected in the manufacturing process, but those who are connected with the subject of the manufacturing process in a factory are included. It is unnecessary for the purpose of this case to decide the precise meaning of the expression '*subject of the manufacturing process*' in S. 2, Cl. (l), because the diverse provisions of the Factories Act are intended to benefit only workers employed in a factory, i.e., in the precincts or premises of a factory. Therefore, the Supreme Court held in *State of U.P.* v. *M.P. Singh*[5] that it is difficult to hold that field workers who are employed in guiding, supervising and controlling the growth and supply of sugarcane to be used in the factory are employed either in the precincts of the factory or in the premises of the factory; and if these workers are not employed in a factory, the provisions of the Factories Act, 1948 do not apply to them.

The workmen worked at the bidi factory and were not at liberty to work at their homes. Further, they worked within certain hours which were the factory hours, though they were not bound to work for the entire period and could go away whenever they liked. Their attendance was noted in the factory and they could come and go away at any time they liked, but if any of them came after midday he was not supplied with tobacco and was thus not allowed to work, even though the factory closed at 7 p.m. in accordance with the provisions of the Factories Act. Under the standing orders in the factory, a worker who remained absent for eight days (presumably without leave) could be removed. The payment was made on piece-rates according to the amount of work done but the management had the right to reject such

4. *M/s Qazi Noorul Hasan Hamid Hussain Petrol Pump and another* v. *Deputy Director Employees State Insurance Corporation, Kanpur,* 2003 (96) FLR 1090 (Alld).
5. AIR 1960 SC 569.

biris as did not come up to the proper standard. Now the question came before the Supreme Court in *Birdhichand Sharma* v. *First Civil Judge, Nagpur*[6] whether in such a situation the bidi worker would be treated as 'worker' within the ambit of S. 2(l) of the Factories Act.

Taking the nature of the work in the present case, the Court observed that it can hardly be said that there must be supervision all the time when *bidis* are being prepared and unless there is such supervision, there can be no direction as to the manner of work. In the present case the operation being a simple one, the control of the manner in which the work is done is exercised at the end of the day, when *bidis* are ready, by the method of rejecting those which do not come up to the proper standard. In such a case, it is the right to supervise, and not so much the mode in which it is exercised, which is important. Accordingly, the Court held:

> "In these circumstances, we are of opinion that respondents 2 to 4 work in this factory cannot be said to be independent contractors. The limited freedom which respondents 2 to 4 have of coming and going away whenever they like or of absenting themselves (presumably without leave) is due to the fact that they are piece-rate workers; but the mere fact that a worker is a piece-rate worker would not necessarily take him out of the category of a worker within the meaning of S. 2(1) of the Factories Act. Considering the entire circumstances and particularly the facts that if the worker does not reach the factory before midday he is given no work, he is to work at the factory and cannot work elsewhere, he can be removed if he is absent for eight days continuously and finally his attendance is noted and *bidis* prepared by him are liable to rejection if they do not come up to the standard, there can be no doubt that respondents 2 to 4 are workers within the meaning of S. 2(1) of the Factories Act."[7]

'Worker', as defined under the Factories Act, means a person employed, directly or through any agency, whether for wages or not, in any manufacturing process. It is and cannot be disputed that the making of bidis is a manufacturing process. But is a Sattedar a person 'employed', directly or through agency, within the meaning of the definition "employed"? The concept of employment involves three ingredients: (1) employer, (2) employee, and (3) the contract of employment. The employer is one who employs, i.e., one who engages the services of other persons. The employee is one who works for another for hire. The employment is the contract of service between the employer and the employee whereunder the employee agrees to serve the employer subject to his control and supervision. Can it be said that a Sattedar is employed by the management of the factory to serve under it? This question came before the Supreme Court in *Chintaman Rao* v. *State of M.P.*[8] where the Court discussed the distinction between a contractor and a workman and between contract for service and contract of service.

A 'contractor' is a person who, in the pursuit of an independent business, undertakes to do specific jobs of work for other persons, without submitting himself to their control in respect to the details of the work. There is, therefore, a clear-cut distinction between a contractor and a workman. The identifying mark of the latter is that he should be under the control and supervision of the employer in respect of the details of the work. The Court, in the instant case, relied too much on *Dharangadhara Chemical Works Ltd.* v. *State of*

6. AIR 1961 SC 644.
7. *Ibid.* at p. 646 per Wanchoo, J.
8. AIR 1958 SC 388.

Saurashtra[9] where the case was decided basically on a question to determine whether a particular employee is a workman or not within the ambit of the S. 2(s) of the Industrial Disputes Act, 1947. In *Dharangadhara Chemical Works Ltd.* case, the Supreme Court observed that the essential condition of a person being a workman within the terms of the definition in S. 2(s) of the Industrial Disputes Act, is that he should be employed to do the work in the industry, that there should be, in other words, an employment of his by the employer, that there should be the relationship between the employer and him as between employer and employee or master and servant. Unless a person is thus employed, there can be no question of his being a workman within the definition of the terms as contained in the Act. The *prima facie* test for the determination of relationship between master and servant is the existence of the right in the master to supervise and control the work done by the servant not only in the matter of directing what work the servant is to do but also the manner in which he shall do his work. The nature or extent of control which is requisite to establish the relationship of employer and employee must necessarily vary from business to business and is by its very nature incapable of precise definition. The correct method of approach, therefore, would be to consider whether having regard to the nature of the work there was due control and supervision by the employer. A person can be a workman even though he is paid, not per day but by the job. The fact that Rules regarding hours of work, etc. applicable to other workmen may not be conveniently applied to them and the nature as well as the manner and method of their work would be such as cannot be regulated by any directions given by the Industrial Tribunal, is no deterrent against holding the persons to be workmen within the meaning of the definition if they fulfil its requirement. The Industrial Tribunal would have to very well consider what relief, if any, may possibly be granted to them having regard to all the circumstances of the case, and may not be able to regulate the work to be done by the workmen and the remuneration to be paid to them by the employer in the manner it is used to do in the case of other industries where the conditions of employment and the work to be done by the employees are of a different character.

The broad distinction between a workman and an independent contractor lies in this that while the former agrees himself to work, the latter agrees to get other persons to work. Now a person who agrees himself to work and does so, works and is therefore a workman does not cease to be such by reason merely of the fact that he gets other persons to work along with him and that those persons are controlled and paid by him. What determines whether a person is a workman or an independent contractor is whether he has agreed to work personally or not. If he has, then he is a workman and the fact that he takes assistance from other persons would not affect his status. The question whether the relationship between the parties is one as between employer and employee or between master and servant is a pure question of fact.

Basing on the above discussion made in *Dharangadhara Chemical Works Ltd.* case, the Supreme Court in *Chintaman Rao* case posed the question to itself that there is no reason why the test laid down by the Apex Court in the context of the definition of 'workman' under the Industrial Disputes Act of 1947, cannot be invoked or applied for ascertaining whether a person is a 'worker' under the Factories Act, 1948. If the test be applied, it is not possible to hold that Sattedars in the present case, having regard to the nature of the work undertaken by them and the terms whereunder their services were engaged, are "workers" within the

9. AIR 1957 SC 264.

meaning of the definition under the Act. It has been established in the present case that the Sattedar is only an independent contractor and the agreement between the management and the Sattedar is only that the Sattedar should receive tobacco from the management and supply them rolled-in *bidis* for consideration. He is not under the control of the factory management and he can manufacture *bidis* wherever he pleases. It is immaterial to the management whether he makes the *bidis* in his own factory or distributes tobacco to different individuals for making *bidis* under a separate agreement entered into by him with them. The management cannot regulate the manner of discharge of his work. His liability is discharged by his supplying *bidis* and delivering them in the factory. The terms of the contract between the management and the Sattedar, as disclosed in the evidence, do not enjoin on the latter to work in the factory. His only obligation is to deliver *bidis* at the factory. That would be an obligation imposed on any contractor who undertakes to supply and deliver the goods to the other party. Therefore, the Court held that the Sattedars in this case were not employed by the management as workers but were only independent contractors who performed their part of the contract by making *bidis* and delivering them at the factory.

If the Sattedars, i.e., three out of the nine persons found at the factory, were not workers within the meaning of the Act, can it be said that the other persons, who were coolies employed by the Sattedars to enable them to keep up their contract with the management of the factory, were workers as defined under the Act? A "worker" under the definition means a person employed, directly or through any agency. The words 'directly or through any agency' indicate that the employment is by the management directly or through some kind of employment agency and in either case there is a contract of employment between the management and the persons employed. Admittedly the coolies were not employed by the management; there was no privity of contract between them and the management. It is not disputed that the coolies were not employed by the Sattedars for or on behalf of the management of the factory. They were employed by the Sattedars on their own account and they paid them for the work extracted from them. On the aforesaid facts, it is obvious that the coolies were not employed by the management directly nor were they employed by the management through the agency of Sattedars. If so, it follows that coolies employed by the Sattedars are not workers within the meaning of the definition in the Act.

A person was employed in a paper factory. He was engaged in supervising and checking quality and weightment of waste papers and rags which are the basic raw-materials for the manufacture of paper. He used to deal with receipts and maintain records of stocks and pass the bills of the suppliers of the waste paper and rags. He used to work in the precincts of the factory and in case of necessities had to work inside the factory. Held that he was working in factory premises or its precincts in connection with the work of the "*subject of the manufacturing process*" namely, the raw materials. Thus he was a factory worker within the meaning of Cl. (l) of S. 2 of the Factories Act.[10]

(m) **factory** means any premises including the precincts thereof—

(i) whereon ten or more workers are working, or were working on any day of the preceding twelve months, and in any part of which a manufacturing process is being carried on with the aid of power, or is ordinarily so carried on, or

10. *Rohtas Industries Ltd., M/s* v. *Ramlakhan Singh*, AIR 1978 SC 849.

(ii) whereon twenty or more workers are working, or were working on any day of the preceding twelve months, and in any part of which a manufacturing process is being carried on without the aid of power, or is ordinarily so carried on,

but does not include a mine subject to the operation of the Mines Act, 1952 (35 of 1952), or a mobile unit belonging to the armed forces of the union, a railway running shed or a hotel, restaurant or eating place;

Explanation I: For computing the number of workers for the purposes of this clause all the workers in different groups and relays in a day shall be taken into account.

Explanation II: For the purposes of this clause, the mere fact that an Electronic Data Processing Unit or a Computer Unit is installed in any premises or part thereof, shall not be construed to make it a factory if no manufacturing process is being carried on in such premises or part thereof;

The main question for determination came before the Supreme Court in *Ardeshir H. Bhiwandiwala* v. *State of Bombay*[11] is whether the Salt Works come within the definition of the word 'factory' under S. 2(m) the Act. The answer to this question depends on the meaning of the word 'premises' in the definition of the word 'factory' and on the determination whether what is done at this Salt Works in connection with the conversion of sea water into crystals of salt comes within the definition of the expression 'manufacturing process' in S. 2(k) of the Act. The Court observed:

> "The word 'premises' is a generic term meaning open land or land with buildings or buildings alone. Expression '*premises including precincts*' does not necessarily mean that the premises must always have precincts. Even buildings need not have any precincts. The word 'including' is not a term restricting the meaning of the word 'premises' but is a term which enlarges its scope. The use of the expression therefore does not indicate that the word 'premises' must be restricted to mean building and be not taken to cover open land as well. Though some of the provisions of the Act cannot be applicable to salt works where the process of converting sea water into salt is carried on in the open there is nothing in the Act which makes it uniformly compulsory for every occupier of a factory to comply with every requirement of the Act. An occupier is to comply with such provisions of the Act which apply to the factory he is working. Hence such salt works would come within the meaning of the word 'premises' used in the definition in S. 2(m)."[12]

The Court further evaluated the factual situation of the salt works in order to find out whether the salt works would fall within the ambit of the definition of manufacturing process provided in S. 2(k) of the Act so that the Court can reach the conclusion that the salt works may be covered within the scope of S. 2(m) of the Act. Accordingly, the Court observed that the sea water in the sea never becomes salt merely on account of the play of the sun's rays on it. Labourers are employed for (i) admitting sea water to the reservoirs by working sluice gates, sometimes at night also, or the pump; (ii) filling crystallizing beds; (iii) watching the density of brine in the crystallizing beds; (iv) seeing that the density does not exceed certain limits and that salts other than sodium chloride (common salt) are not formed; (v) scraping and collecting salt crystals; (vi) grading the salt crystals by 'sieving' and (vii) putting salt into

11. AIR 1962 SC 29.
12. *Ibid.* at pp. 31–32 per Raghubar Dayal, J.

gunny bags. It follows that it is due to human agency, aided by natural forces, that salt is extracted from sea water. The processes carried out in the Salt Works and described above, come within the definition of '*manufacturing process*' in S. 2(k) inasmuch as salt can be said to have been manufactured from sea water by the process of treatment and adaptation of sea water into salt. In view of the above discussion, the Court held that Salt Works do come within the definition of the word "factory".

From the definition of "factory", it is clear that it must be a premises where a manufacturing process is carried on. The manufacturing process that is carried on by the undertaking is that of generating, transforming and transmitting electricity power. Though electricity is generated in the power station, still to reduce the voltage and do other incidental acts for the purpose of ensuring supply of power to consumers, the sub-stations and the zonal stations are an integral part of the power station. That is the entire process of generating, transforming and transmitting power, though these items of work may be done in different places, namely, power stations, sub-stations and the zonal stations, must be considered to form part of a single manufacturing process in which the workmen concerned are employed. The fact that some of the workmen are in the power station and the rest are either in the sub-stations or the zonal stations will not make any difference in this respect, as all of them take part in the manufacturing process. Admittedly, the power station is treated as factory and it follows that these two units, the sub-stations and the zonal stations, also come within the definition of "factory".[13]

In *Works Manager, Central Rly. Workshop, Jhansi* v. *Vishwanath*,[14] the short question that came before the Supreme Court was, whether the respondents, who are time-keepers, fall within the purview of the definition of "worker" as contained in S. 2(l) of the Factories Act. The Court observed that the definition of the term "worker" in S. 2(l) of the Act is fairly wide because it takes within its sweep not only person employed in a manufacturing process but also cleaning any part of the machinery or premises used for manufacturing process and goes far beyond the direct connection with the manufacturing process by extending to other kinds of work which might be either incidental or connected with not only manufacturing process but also the subject of manufacturing process. The word manufacturing process has been defined under S. 2(k) of the Act in a very clear language. Accordingly, the Court held that the definition of "worker" in the Factories Act does not seem to exclude those employees who are entrusted solely with clerical duties, if they otherwise fall within the definition of the word "worker". Keeping in view the duties and functions of the respondents as found by the learned Additional District Judge, the Apex court is unable to find anything legally wrong with the view taken by the High Court that they fall within the definition of the word "worker". The term "premises" not only covers building but even open land can also be a part of premises. It is easy to visualise that when railway line extending to several kilometres is to be constructed, it cannot be constructed overnight. The whole exercise would be carried out in a phased manner. For laying railway line number of workmen, supervisors and other clerical staffs will have to attend the site where the railway line is to be laid. That site on which the railway line is to be laid will necessarily have space for storage of loose rails,

---

13. *Workmen of Delhi Electric Supply Undertaking* v. *Management of Delhi Electric Supply Undertaking*, AIR 1973 SC 365.
14. AIR 1970 SC 488.

sleepers, bolts, etc. All these articles will have to be laid and fixed on a given site, before any part of the railway track becomes ready. Consequently, construction of railway line would necessarily imply fixed sites on which such construction activity gets carried on in a phased manner. Every time when such construction activity is carried on, it must necessarily be on a given fixed site where all the workmen concerned would work for the purpose of laying down railway line at that site. Thus, even though the railway line is to be laid over some distance of land, every part of the said land would consist of a 'factory' at a given point of time as from time to time in a phased manner entire railway line will have to be laid. Once the entire work is finished, a stage would be reached when the construction activity would come to an end and the premises thereof may cease to be a 'factory', but so long as construction work is being carried out in phases, every part of the land on which such construction activity takes place would form a part and parcel of the 'premises' as such. Railway line cannot be laid except on a fixed site, therefore, it cannot be said that the project which was to carry out the construction work of railway up to some kilometres, had no fixed site to operate upon and, therefore, was not a 'premises'. All the length of land would be phase-wise factories for construction of railway lines over them.[15]

The question came before the Karnataka High Court in 2004 whether a laundry unit of a hotel would fall within the ambit of the definition of factory. In the instant case, the fact reveals that the laundry is not a unit by itself. It is part and parcel of a hotel established by the appellant. Its activities are entirely dedicated to the efficient running of the hotel, and the comforts and convenience of those making use of the facilities offered therein. It therefore cannot be viewed to be anything different from the hotel, which is a composite entity and in which varied kinds of facilities may be available for the use and enjoyment of the guests and customers visiting the same, including the comfort of having an in-house laundry. Section 2(m) of the Factories Act, however, excludes a hotel from the meaning of the factory. This would imply that any service which the hotel offers to its customers would also stand excluded, no matter any such service may independent of the hotel be analogous to what goes on in a factory. The learned Single Judge was not therefore right in holding that since a manufacturing process was going on in the laundry, it was a "factory" as defined under the Factories Act. The fact that the laundry was but a small though an integral part of the hotel dedicated entirely to the needs of the establishment and the guests making use of the same was obviously overlooked by the learned Single Judge.

The definition of the term 'factory' under the Employees' State Insurance Act, 1948 does not specifically exclude a hotel, restaurant or eating place or a mobile belonging to the armed forces of the Union. We are not in the instant case concerned with whether and if so what kind of mobile units belonging to the armed forces are included for purposes of the said act. What is evident is that a hotel, restaurant or an eating place can also be a factory for purposes of the Employees' State Insurance Act provided other requirements stipulated in Cls. (a) and (b) to S. 2(12) are satisfied. What follows is that the Employees' State Insurance Act, 1948 is wider in terms of its applicability to different establishments than the provisions of the Factories Act.

Just because an outside agency had, while catering to the laundry requirements of the hotel, secured a licence or got the unit registered does not imply that the requirement of

15. *Lal Mohammad* v. *Indian Railway Construction Co. Ltd.*, AIR 1999 SC 355.

registration or licence is inescapable. Since the hotel is itself exempted from the operation of the Factories Act, there was no need for registration or licensing even when the laundry contractor may have obtained any such registration. Nothing thus turns on the registration of the unit by the outside agency nor does it stop the hotel from arguing that there is no legal compulsion to register the laundry division.[16]

BOCW Act vis-à-vis Factories Act

The question came before the Apex Court in *Lanco Anpara Power Ltd.* v. *State of U.P.*, (2016) 10 SCC 329 for consideration whether BOCW Act would be made applicable where the civil work is going on to set up the factory?

These appeals are filed by the appellants challenging the orders passed by different High Courts i.e. High Court of Allahabad, High Court of Orissa, High Court of Madhya Pradesh and High Court of Karnataka. These High Courts, however, are unanimous in their approach and have reached the same conclusion. In all these cases, appellants were issued show cause notices by the concerned authorities under the provisions of the Building and Other Construction Workers (Regulation of Employment and Conditions of Service) Act, 1996 (hereinafter referred to as 'BOCW Act') and Buildings And Other Construction Workers Welfare Cess Act, 1996 (hereinafter referred to as 'Welfare Cess Act'). They had challenged those notices by filing writ petitions in the High Courts on the ground that the provisions of BOCW Act or Welfare Cess Act were not applicable to them because of the reason that they were registered under the Factories Act, 1948.

It may be pertinent to mention that at the relevant time no manufacturing operation had commenced by the appellants. In fact, all these appellants were in the process of construction of civil works/factory buildings etc. wherein they had planned to set up their factories. As the process of construction of civil works was undertaken by the appellants wherein construction workers were engaged, the respondent authorities took the view that the provisions of the aforesaid Acts which were meant for construction workers became applicable and the appellants were supposed to pay the cess for the welfare of the said workers engaged in the construction work. The appellants had submitted that Section 2(d) of the BOCW Act which defines '*building or other construction work*' specifically states that it does not include any building or construction work to which the provision of the Factories Act, 1948 or the Mines Act, 1952 apply. Since the appellants stood registered under the Factories Act, they were not covered by the definition of building or other construction work as contained in Section 2(d) of the Act and, therefore, said Act was not applicable to them by virtue of Section 1(4) thereof. All the High Courts have negated the aforesaid plea of the appellants on the ground that the appellants would not be covered by the definition of factory defined under Section 2(m) of the Factories Act in the absence of any operations/manufacturing process and, therefore, mere obtaining a licence under Section 6 of the Factories Act would not suffice and rescue them from their liability to pay cess under the Welfare Cess Act.

The Supreme Court in the instant case while interpreting S. 2(d) of BOCW Act, the Court said that the provisions of the Factories Act would "apply" only when the manufacturing

16. *Welcom Group Windsor Manor Sheraton and Towers* v. *State of Karnataka and another,* 2004 (102) FLR 369 (Kar.).

process starts for which the building/project is being constructed and not to the activity of construction of the project. The Court said that that is how the exclusion clause, which excludes those building or other construction work to which the provisions of Factories Act or Mines Act apply, is to be interpreted and that would be the plain meaning of the said clause.

Further the Court observed that the appellants would not be covered by the definition of factory defined under S. 2(m) of the Factories Act in the absence of any operations/ manufacturing process and, therefore, mere obtaining a licence under S. 6 of the Factories Act would not suffice and rescue them from their liability to pay cess under the Welfare Cess Act. It was held that a bare reading of the definition of "Factory" makes it abundantly clear that before this stage, when construction of the project is completed and the manufacturing process starts, 'factory' within the meaning of S. 2(m) of the Factories Act does not come into existence so as to be covered by the said Act.

(n) **occupier** of a factory means the person who has ultimate control over the affairs of the factory:

Provided that—

(i) in the case of a firm or other association of individuals, any one of the individual partners or members thereof shall be deemed to be the occupier;

(ii) in the case of a company, any one of the directors shall be deemed to be the occupier;

(iii) in the case of a factory owned or controlled by the Central Government or any State Government, or any local authority, the person or persons appointed to manage the affairs of the factory by the Central Government, the State Government or the local authority, as the case may be, shall be deemed to be the occupier:

Provided further that in the case of a ship which is being repaired, or on which maintenance work is being carried out, in a dry dock which is available for hire,—

(1) the owner of the dock shall be deemed to be the occupier for the purposes of any matter provided for by or under—

(a) section 6, section 7, section 7A, section 7B, section 11 or section 12;

(b) section 17, in so far as it relates to the providing and maintenance of sufficient and suitable lighting in or around the dock;

(c) section 18, section 19, section 42, section 46, section 47 or section 49, in relation to the workers employed on such repair or maintenance;

(2) the owner of the ship or his agent or master or other officer-in-charge of the ship or any person who contracts with such owner, agent or master or other officer-in-charge to carry out the repair or maintenance work shall be deemed to be the occupier for the purposes of any matter provided for by or under section 13, section 14, section 16 or section 17 (save as otherwise provided in this proviso) or Chapter IV (except section 27) or section 43, section 44 or section 45, Chapter VI, Chapter VII, Chapter VIII or Chapter IX or section 108, section 109 or section 110, in relation to—

(a) the workers employed directly by him, or by or through any agency; and

(b) the machinery, plant or premises in use for the purpose of carrying out such repair or maintenance work by such owner, agent, master or other officer-in-charge or person.

The expression 'occupier' as defined in S. 2(n) is not to be equated with 'owner'. No doubt, the ultimate control over a factory must necessarily be with an owner unless the owner has completely transferred that control to another person. Whether that was done in a particular case is a question of fact. Therefore, the manager of a factory who claims to be an occupier of the factory must lay before the Chief Inspector of Factories the necessary material for showing that the company had in some manner transferred the entire control over the factory to him.[17]

In *Indian Oil Corporation Ltd.* v. *Chief Inspector of Factories,*[18] a short but an interesting question of law arises for consideration: who is deemed to be the 'occupier' of a factory of a government company incorporated under the Indian Companies Act? If the government company is to be treated like any other company, then, according to Cl. (ii) of the first proviso to S. 2(n) of the Factories Act, 1948, any one of the directors of that company is deemed to be the occupier, but if its factory is considered as a factory owned or controlled by the Government as provided by Cl. (iii) of the proviso, the person appointed to manage the affairs of the factory by the Government is to be deemed to be the occupier.

The appellant, Indian Oil Corporation Limited, is a government company as defined by S. 617 of the Companies Act. It is almost wholly owned and controlled by the Government. It is, *inter alia*, engaged in the supply and distribution of petroleum and petroleum products including L.P.G. In order to ensure an effective and efficient supply system, it is required to establish and maintain storage facilities at many places in the country. At Namkum, in Ranchi District, it already had large storage facility. With the object of increasing storage capacity at Namkum, it established a new storage unit in 1992 after obtaining approval of the Central Government. As storage facilities are also covered by the definition of 'factory' as defined by the Factories Act, the Depot Manager posted at the Namkum Depot made an application for obtaining a licence for the new unit. He also made an application for renewal of the licence of the existing unit. While granting the licence earlier, for the existing unit, the Inspector of Factories had recognised the Depot Manager as the 'occupier' and the occupancy certificate, etc. was issued in his name. But this time, the new Inspector of Factories by his letter refused to grant the licence on the ground that the Indian Oil Corporation is a company and in case of a company, any one of the directors only can be deemed to be the occupier. He directed the appellant to submit proper applications duly signed by one of the directors of the company. In view of this refusal, the appellant filed in the Patna High Court.

Before the High Court, two questions were raised on behalf of the appellant and they are as follows:

(1) Whether in the case of a company one of the directors of the company only can be recognised as an occupier of the factory owned by it; and

---

17. *John Donald Mackenzie* v. *Chief Inspector of Factories, Bihar, Ranchi*, AIR 1962 SC 1351.
18. AIR 1998 SC 2456.

(2) Whether clause (iii) would apply to the factories of the Corporation and it is open to the Central Government to nominate any person other than the director as the occupier.

The Patna High Court, following the decision of the Supreme Court in *J.K. Industries Limited* v. *The Chief Inspector of Factories and Boilers*,[19] wherein it was held that in the case of a company, which owns a factory, it is only one of the directors of the company who can be notified as the occupier of the factory for the purposes of the Factories Act and the company cannot nominate any other employee as the occupier of the factory, the High Court answered the first question accordingly.

On the second point, the High Court held that proviso (ii) to S. 2(n) would apply to the storage depots at Namkum. It considered the following three reasons for taking that view:

(1) The storage depots are owned by the company and not by the Central Government, though the company itself is owned, to a very large extent, by the Central Government,

(2) proviso (ii) to S. 2(n) is applicable to all the companies as it does not make any distinction between a private company and a Government owned company, and

(3) the Depot Manager has not been appointed by the Central Government but by the company. It, therefore, dismissed the petition.

The Court in *Indian Oil Corporation Ltd.* case relied too much on *J.K. Industries Limited* case where the Supreme Court had an occasion to consider the history and reasons of amending S. 2(n) from time to time. In that context, the Court observed that by the Amending Act of 1987, it appears that the legislature wanted to bring in a sense of responsibility in the minds of those who have the ultimate control over the affairs of the factory, so that they take proper care for maintenance of the factories and the safety measures therein. Proviso (ii) was introduced by the Amending Act, couched in a mandatory form "any one of the directors shall be deemed to be the occupier" keeping in view the experience gained over the years as to how the directors of a company managed to escape their liability, for various breaches and defaults committed in the factory by putting up another employee as a shield and nominating him as the 'occupier' who would willingly suffer penalty and punishment. Proviso (ii) now makes it possible to reach out to a director of the company itself, who shall be prosecuted and punished for breach of the provisions of the Act, apart from prosecution and punishment of the Manager and of the actual offender. These observations were made by the Apex Court while considering constitutional validity and correct interpretation of Cl. (ii) of the first proviso to S. 2(n).

Again in *J.K. Industries Ltd.* case, the Supreme Court, while dealing with S. 2(n), emphasised the use of the word "*ultimate*" and observed that the law does not countenance duality of ultimate control. If the transfer of the control to another person is not complete, meaning thereby that the transferor retains its control over the affairs of the factory, the transferee, whosoever he may be, (except a director of the company, or a partner in a partnership firm) cannot be considered to be the person having ultimate control over the affairs of the factory notwithstanding what the resolution of the Board states. The 'litmus' test, therefore, is who has the 'ultimate control' over the affairs of the factory. It is also held therein that the

19. (1996) 6 SCC 665.

deeming provision made in proviso (ii) does not override the substantive provision of S. 2(n) but clarifies it.

The Court in the instant case, i.e. *Indian Oil Corporation Ltd.*,[18] case held:

> "The above discussion fully supports the contention of the learned Attorney General that for the purpose of Section 2(n) what is to be seen is who has the 'ultimate control' over the affairs of the factory. Relevant provisions regarding establishment of the Corporation and its working leave no doubt that the ultimate control over all the affairs of the Corporation, including opening and running of factories, is with the Central Government. Acting through the Corporation is only a method employed by the Central Government for running its petroleum industry. In the context of Section 2(n) it will have to be held that all the activities of the Corporation are really carried on by the Central Government with a corporate mask."[20]

The Court further observed that apart from the main part of S. 2(n), the first proviso also indicates that the legislature intended that the person having ultimate control over the affairs of the factory has to be regarded as an occupier of the factory. The proviso to the section is not in the nature of an exception. In order to avoid any ambiguity, to plug loopholes and to seal the escape routes, a deeming provision has been made in a mandatory form. In the case of a firm, obviously the partners of the firm have ultimate control over the affairs of the partnership. In case of other type of association, the members thereof will have such control. In the case of a company, the directors have the ultimate control, as the power to manage the affairs of the company vests in the Board of Directors. What Cl. (i) and (ii) of the proviso provide is that they shall be deemed to be the 'occupier'. Thus, they merely restate the position which is obvious even otherwise. The position of the Government and the local authority is quite different from that of a firm or an association or a company not only with respect to the person who can be said to be in ultimate control but also with respect to the object for which the factory is set up. In a democratic set-up of Government, it may not be possible to say with certainty as to who is having the ultimate control. In a welfare state, the Government does not carry on such activity for its own profit or benefit but for the benefit of the people as a whole. Moreover, it is the Government which looks after the successful implementation of the provisions of the Factories Act and, therefore, it is not likely to evade implementation of the beneficial provisions of the Factories Act. That appears to be the reason why the legislature thought it fit to make a separate provision for the Government and the local authorities. Ordinarily, for running the factories owned or controlled by the Central Government or any State Government, or any local authority, a person or persons would be appointed by it to manage the affairs of the factory, because the Government or the local authority as a whole would not run the factory. Therefore, the legislature appears to have provided that in a case of a factory owned or controlled by the Central Government, the State Government or the local authority, the person or persons appointed to manage the affairs of the factory by the Central Government, State Government or the local authority, as the case may be, shall be deemed to be the 'occupier.' Therefore, if it is a case of a factory in fact and in reality owned or controlled by the Central Government or the State Government or any local authority, then in case of such a factory the person or persons appointed to manage the affairs of the factory shall have to be deemed to be the occupier, even though for better management of such a factory or factories a corporate form is adopted by the Government.

---

20. *Ibid.,* f.n. 18 at p. 2461 per Nanavati, J.

The Supreme Court concluded its observation in the following words:

"For the aforesaid reasons we hold that as the factories run by the appellant-Corporation are effectively and really owned and controlled by the Central Government they fall within the purview of clause (iii) and not clause (ii) of the first proviso to Section 2(n). In our opinion, the High Court was wrong in taking a contrary view. We, therefore, allow these appeals, set aside the judgment and order passed by the High Court to the extent as indicated above and direct respondents Nos. 1 and 2 to accept the persons appointed by the Central Government to manage the affairs of the factories at Namkum as the occupiers of those factories for the purposes of Section 2(n) of the Factories Act. In view of the facts and circumstances of the case, we direct the parties to bear their own cost."[21]

(o) Omitted w.e.f. 1-12-1987.

(p) **prescribed** means prescribed by rules made by the State Government under this Act.

(q) Repealed by A.O. 1950.

(r) **group** or **relay** and **shift**, where work of the same kind is carried out by two or more sets of workers working during different periods of the day, each of such sets is called a "group" or "relay" and each of such periods is called a "shift".

Section 3: References to time of day

In this Act references to time of day are references to Indian Standard Time, being five and a half hours ahead of Greenwich Mean Time:

Provided that for any area in which Indian Standard Time is not ordinarily observed the State Government may make rules—

(a) specifying the area,

(b) defining the local mean time ordinarily observed therein, and

(c) permitting such time to be observed in all or any of the factories situated in the area.

Section 4: Power to declare different departments to be separate factories or two or more factories to be a single factory

The State Government may, on its own or on an application made in this behalf by an occupier, direct, by an order in writing, and subject to such conditions as it may deem fit, that for all or any of the purposes of this Act different departments or branches of a factory of the occupier specified in the application shall be treated as separate factories or that two or more factories of the occupier specified in the application shall be treated as a single factory:

Provided that no order under this section shall be made by the State Government on it own motion unless an opportunity of being heard is given to the occupier.

Section 5: Power to exempt during public emergency

In any case of public emergency the State Government may, by notification in the Official Gazette, exempt any factory or class or description of factories from all or any of the provisions of this Act except section 67 for such period and subject to such conditions as it may think fit:

21. *Ibid.* at pp. 2462–2463 per Nanavati, J.

Provided that no such notification shall be made for a period exceeding three months at a time.

Explanation: For the purposes of this section "public emergency" means a grave emergency whereby the security of India or of any part of the territory thereof is threatened, whether by war or external aggression or internal disturbance.

SECTION 6: Approval, licensing and registration of factories

(1) The State Government may make rules—

(a) requiring, for the purposes of this Act, the submission of plans of any class or description of factories to the Chief Inspector or the State Government;

(aa) requiring, the previous permission in writing of the State Government or the Chief Inspector to be obtained for the site on which the factory is to be situated and for the construction or extension of any factory or class or description of factories;

(b) requiring for the purpose of considering applications for such permission the submission of plans and specifications;

(c) prescribing the nature of such plans and specifications and by whom they shall be certified;

(d) requiring the registration and licensing of factories or any class or description of factories, and prescribing the fees payable for such registration and licensing and for the renewal of licences;

(e) requiring that no licence shall be granted or renewed unless the notice specified in section 7 has been given.

(2) If on an application for permission referred to in clause (aa) of sub-section (1) accompanied by the plans and specifications required by the rules made under clause (b) of that sub-section, sent to the State Government or Chief Inspector by registered post, no order is communicated to the applicant within three months from the date on which it is so sent, the permission applied for in the said application shall be deemed to have been granted.

(3) Where a State Government or a Chief Inspector refuses to grant permission to the site, construction or extension of a factory or to the registration and licensing of a factory, the applicant may within thirty days of the date of such refusal appeal to the Central Government if the decision appealed from was of the State Government and to the State Government in any other case.

Explanation: A factory shall not be deemed to be extended within the meaning of this section by reason only of the replacement of any plant or machinery, or within such limits as may be prescribed, of the addition of any plant or machinery if such replacement or addition does not reduce the minimum clear space required for safe working around the plant or machinery or adversely affect the environmental conditions from the evolution or emission of steam, heat or dust or fumes injurious to health.

SECTION 7: Notice by occupier

(1) The occupier shall, at least fifteen days before he begins to occupy or use any premises as a factory, send to the Chief Inspector a written notice containing—

(a) the name and situation of the factory;

(b) the name and address of the occupier;

(bb) the name and address of the owner of the premises or building (including the precincts thereof) referred to in section 93;

(c) the address to which communication relating to the factory may be sent;

(d) the nature of the manufacturing process—

(i) carried on in the factory during the last twelve months in the case of factories in existence on the date of the commencement of this Act, and

(ii) to be carried on in the factory during the next twelve months in the case of all factories;

(e) the total rated horse power installed or to be installed in the factory, which shall not include the rated horse power of any separate stand-by plant;

(f) the name of the manager of the factory for the purposes of this Act;

(g) the number of workers likely to be employed in the factory;

(h) the average number of workers per day employed during the last twelve months in the case of a factory in existence on the date of the commencement of this Act;

(i) such other particulars as may be prescribed.

(2) In respect of all establishments which come within the scope of the Act for the first time, the occupier shall send a written notice to the Chief Inspector containing the particulars specified in sub-section (1) within thirty days, from the date of the commencement of this Act.

(3) Before a factory engaged in a manufacturing process which is ordinarily carried on for less than one hundred and eighty working days in the year resumes working, the occupier shall send a written notice to the Chief Inspector containing the particulars specified in sub-section (1) at least thirty days before the date of the commencement of work.

(4) Whenever a new manager is appointed, the occupier shall send to the Inspector a written notice and to the Chief Inspector a copy thereof within seven days from the date on which such person takes over charge.

(5) During any period for which no person has been designated as manager of a factory or during which the person designated does not manage the factory, any person found acting as manager, or if no such person is found, the occupier himself, shall be deemed to be the manager of the factory for the purposes of this Act.

SECTION 7A: General duties of the occupier

(1) Every occupier shall ensure, so far as is reasonably practicable, the health, safety and welfare of all workers while they are at work in the factory.

(2) Without prejudice to the generality of the provisions of sub-section (1), the matters to which such duty extends, shall include—

(a) the provision and maintenance of plant and systems of work in the factory that are safe and without risks to health;

(b) the arrangements in the factory for ensuring safety and absence of risks to health in connection with the use, handling, storage and transport of articles and substances;

(c) the provision of such information, instruction, training and supervision as are necessary to ensure the health and safety, of all workers at work;

(d) the maintenance of all places of work in the factory in a condition that is safe and without risks to health and the provision and maintenance of such means of access to, and egress from, such places as are safe and without such risks;

(e) the provision, maintenance or monitoring of such working environment in the factory for the workers that is safe, without risks to health and adequate as regards facilities and arrangements for their welfare at work.

(3) Except in such cases as may be prescribed, every occupier shall prepare, and, as often as may be appropriate, revise, a written statement of his general policy with respect to the health and safety of the workers at work and the organisation and arrangements for the time being in force for carrying out that policy, and to bring the statement and any revision thereof to the notice of all the workers in such manner as may be prescribed.

Section 7B: General duties of manufacturers, etc., as regards articles and substances for use in factories

(1) Every person who designs, manufactures, imports or supplies any article for use in any factory shall—

(a) ensure, so far as is reasonably practicable, that the article is so designed and constructed as to be safe and without risks to the health of the workers when properly used;

(b) carry out or arrange for the carrying out of such tests and examination as may be considered necessary for the effective implementation of the provisions of clause (a);

(c) take such steps as may be necessary to ensure that adequate information will be available—

(i) in connection with the use of the article in any factory;

(ii) about the use for which it is designed and tested; and

(iii) about any conditions necessary to ensure that the article, when put to such use, will be safe, and without risks to the health of the workers:

Provided that where an article is designed or manufactured outside India, it shall be obligatory on the part of the importer to see—

(a) that the article conforms to the same standards if such article is manufactured in India, or

(b) if the standards adopted in the country outside for the manufacture of such article is above the standards adopted in India, that the article conforms to such standards.

(2) Every person, who undertakes to design or manufacture any article for use in any factory, may carry out or arrange for the carrying out of necessary research with a view to the discovery and, so far as is reasonably practicable, the elimination or minimization of any risks to the health or safety of the workers to which the design or article may give rise.

(3) Nothing contained in sub-sections (1) and (2) shall be construed to require a person to repeat the testing, examination or research which has been carried out otherwise than by him or at his instance in so far as it is reasonable for him to rely on the results thereof for the purposes of the said sub-sections.

(4) Any duty imposed on any person by sub-sections (1) and (2) shall extend only to things done in the course of business carried on by him and to matters within his control.

(5) Where a person designs, manufactures, imports or supplies an article on the basis of a written undertaking by the user of such article to take the steps specified in such undertaking to ensure, so far as is reasonably practicable, that the article will be safe and without risks to the health of the workers when properly used, the undertaking shall have the effect of relieving the person designing, manufacturing, importing or supplying the article from the duty imposed by clause (a) of sub-section (1) to such extent as is reasonable having regard to the terms of the undertaking.

(6) For the purposes of this section, an article is not to be regarded as properly used if it is used without regard to any information or advice relating to its use which has been made available by the person who has designed, manufactured, imported or supplied the article.

Explanation: For the purposes of this section, "article" shall include plant and machinery.

CHAPTER II

THE INSPECTING STAFF

SECTION 8: Inspectors

(1) The State Government may, by notification in the Official Gazette, appoint such persons as possess the prescribed qualification to be Inspectors for the purposes of this Act and may assign to them such local limits as it may think fit.

(2) The State Government may, by notification in the Official Gazette, appoint any person to be a Chief Inspector who shall, in addition to the powers conferred on a Chief Inspector under this Act, exercise the powers of an Inspector throughout the State.

(2A) The State Government may, by notification in the Official Gazette, appoint as many Additional Chief Inspectors, Joint Chief Inspectors and Deputy Chief Inspectors and as many other officers as it thinks fit to assist the Chief Inspector and to exercise such of the powers of the Chief Inspector as may be specified in such notification.

(2B) Every Additional Chief Inspector, Joint Chief Inspector, Deputy Chief Inspector and every other officer appointed under sub-section (2A) shall, in addition to the powers of a Chief Inspector specified in the notification by which he is appointed, exercise the powers of an Inspector throughout the State.

(3) No person shall be appointed under sub-section (1), sub-section (2) sub-section (2A) or sub-section (5), or having been so appointed, shall continue to hold office, who is or becomes directly or indirectly interested in a factory or in any process or business carried on therein or in any patent or machinery connected therewith.

(4) Every District Magistrate shall be an Inspector for his district.

(5) The State Government may also, by notification as aforesaid, appoint such public officers as it thinks fit to be additional Inspectors for all or any of the purposes of this Act, within such local limits as it may assign to them respectively.

(6) In any area where there are more Inspectors than one the State Government may, by notification as aforesaid, declare the powers, which such Inspectors shall respectively exercise and the Inspector to whom the prescribed notices are to be sent.

(7) Every Chief Inspector, Additional Chief Inspector, Joint Chief Inspector, Deputy Chief Inspector, Inspector and every other officer appointed under this section shall be deemed to be a public servant within the meaning of the Indian Penal Code (45 of 1860), and shall be officially subordinate to such authority as the State Government may specify in this behalf.

SECTION 9: Powers of Inspectors

Subject to any rules made in this behalf, an Inspector may, within the local limits for which he is appointed,—

(a) enter, with such assistants being persons in the service of the Government, or any local or other public authority, or with an expert as he thinks fit, any place which is used, or which he has reason to believe is used, as a factory;

(b) make examination of the premises, plant, machinery, article or substance;

(c) inquire into any accident or dangerous occurrence, whether resulting in bodily injury, disability or not, and take on the spot or otherwise statements of any person which he may consider necessary for such inquiry;

(d) require the production of any prescribed register or any other document relating to the factory;

(e) seize, or take copies of, any register, record or other document or any portion thereof, as he may consider necessary in respect of any offence under this Act, which he has reason to believe, has been committed;

(f) direct the occupier that any premises or any part thereof, or anything lying therein, shall be left undisturbed (whether generally or in particular respects) for so long as is necessary for the purpose of any examination under clause (b);

(g) take measurements and photographs and make such recordings as he considers necessary for the purpose of any examination under clause (b), taking with him any necessary instrument or equipment;

(h) in case of any article or substance found in any premises, being an article or substance which appears to him as having caused or is likely to cause danger to the health or safety of the workers, direct it to be dismantled or subject it to any process or test (but not so as to damage or destroy it unless the same is, in the circumstances necessary, for carrying out the purposes of this Act), and take possession of any such article of substance or a part thereof, and detain it for so long as is necessary for such examination;

(i) exercise such other powers as may be prescribed:

Provided that no person shall be compelled under this section to answer any question or give any evidence tending to incriminate himself.

SECTION 10: Certifying surgeons

(1) The State Government may appoint qualified medical practitioners to be certifying surgeons for the purposes of this Act within such local limits or for such factory or class or description of factories as it may assign to them respectively.

(2) A certifying surgeon may, with the approval of the State Government, authorize any qualified medical practitioner to exercise any of his powers under this Act for such period as the certifying surgeon may specify and subject to such conditions as the State Government may think fit to impose, and references in this Act to a certifying surgeon shall be deemed to include references to any qualified medical practitioner when so authorized.

(3) No person shall be appointed to be, or authorized to exercise the powers of, a certifying surgeon, or having been so appointed or authorized, continue to exercise such powers, who is, or becomes the occupier of a factory or is or becomes directly or indirectly interested therein or in any process or business carried on therein or in any patent or machinery connected therewith or is otherwise in the employ of the factory:

Provided that the State Government may, by order in writing and subject to such conditions as may be specified in the order, exempt any person or class of persons from the provisions of this sub-section in respect of any factory or class or description of factories.

(4) The certifying surgeon shall carry out such duties as may be prescribed in connection with—

(a) the examination and certification of young persons under this Act;

(b) the examination of persons engaged in factories in such dangerous occupations or processes as may be prescribed;

(c) the exercising of such medical supervision as may be prescribed for any factory or class or description of factories where—

(i) cases of illness have occurred which it is reasonable to believe are due to the nature of the manufacturing process carried on, or other conditions of work prevailing, therein;

(ii) by reason of any change in the manufacturing process carried on or in the substances used therein or by reason of the adoption of any new manufacturing process or of any new substance for use in a manufacturing process, there is a likelihood of injury to the health of workers employed in that manufacturing process;

(iii) young persons are, or are about to be, employed in any work which is likely to cause injury to their health.

Explanation: In this section "qualified medical practitioner" means a person holding a qualification granted by an authority specified in the Schedule to the Indian Medical Degrees Act, 1916 (7 of 1916) or in the Schedules to the Indian Medical Council Act, 1933 (27 of 1933).

CHAPTER III

HEALTH

SECTION 11: Cleanliness

(1) Every factory shall be kept clean and free from effluvia arising from any drain, privy or other, nuisance, and in particular—

(a) accumulations of dirt and refuse shall be removed daily by sweeping or by any other effective method from the floors and benches of workrooms and from staircases and passages, and disposed of in a suitable manner;

(b) the floor of every workroom shall be cleaned at least once in every week by washing, using disinfectant, where necessary, or by some other effective method;

(c) where a floor is liable to become wet in the course of any manufacturing process to such extent as is capable of being drained, effective means of drainage shall be provided and maintained;

(d) all inside walls and partitions, all ceilings or tops of rooms and all walls, sides and tops of passages and staircases shall—

(i) where they are painted otherwise than with washable water-paint or varnished, be repainted or revarnished least once in every period of five years;

(ia) where they are painted with washable water paint, be repainted with at least one coat of such paint at least once in every period of three years and washed at least once in every period of six months;

(ii) where they are painted or varnished or where they have smooth impervious surfaces, be cleaned at least once in every period of fourteen months by such method as may be prescribed;

(iii) in any other case, be kept whitewashed or colourwashed, and the white-washing or colourwashing shall be carried out at least once in every period of fourteen months;

(dd) all doors and window frames and other wooden or metallic frame work and shutters shall be kept painted or varnished and the painting or varnishing shall be carried out at least once in every period of five years;

(e) the dates on which the processes required by clause (d) are carried out shall be entered in the prescribed register.

(2) If, in view of the nature of the operations carried on in a factory or class or description of factories or any part of a factory or class or description of factories, it is not possible for the occupier to comply with all or any of the provisions of sub-section (1), the State Government may by order exempt such factory or class or description of factories or part from any of the provisions of that sub-section and specify alternative methods for keeping the factory in a clean state.

SECTION 12: Disposal of wastes and effluents

(1) Effective arrangements shall be made in every factory for the treatment of wastes and effluents due to the manufacturing process carried on therein, so as to render them innocuous, and for their disposal.

(2) The State Government may make rules prescribing the arrangements to be made under sub-section (1) or requiring that the arrangements made in accordance with sub-section (1) shall be approved by such authority as may be prescribed.

SECTION 13: Ventilation and temperature

(1) Effective and suitable provision shall be made in every factory for securing and maintaining in every workroom—

(a) adequate ventilation by the circulation of fresh air, and

(b) such a temperature as will secure to workers therein reasonable conditions of comfort and prevent injury to health;

and in particular,—

(i) walls and roofs shall be of such material and so designed that such temperature shall not be exceeded but kept as low as practicable;

(ii) where the nature of the work carried on in the factory involves, or is likely to involve, the production of excessively high temperatures such adequate measures as are practicable shall be taken to protect the workers therefrom, by separating the process which produces such temperatures from the workroom, by insulating the hot parts or by other effective means.

(2) The State Government may prescribe a standard of adequate ventilation and reasonable temperature for any factory or class or description of factories or parts thereof and direct that proper measuring instruments, at such places and in such position as may be specified, shall be provided and such records, as may be prescribed, shall be maintained;

(3) If it appears to the Chief Inspector that excessively high temperatures in any factory can be reduced by the adoption of suitable measures, he may, without prejudice to the rules made under sub-section (2), serve on the occupier, an order in writing specifying the measures which, in his opinion, should be adopted, and requiring them to be carried out before a specified date.

SECTION 14: Dust and fume

(1) In every factory in which, by reason of the manufacturing process carried on, there is given off any dust or fume or other impurity of such a nature and to such an extent as is likely to be injurious or offensive to the workers employed therein, or any dust in substantial quantities, effective measures shall be taken to prevent its inhalation and accumulation in any workroom, and if any exhaust appliance is necessary for this purpose, it shall be applied as near as possible to the point of origin of the dust, fume or other impurity, and such point shall be enclosed so far as possible.

(2) In any factory no stationary internal combustion engine shall be operated unless the exhaust is conducted into the open air, and no other internal combustion engine shall be operated in any room unless effective measures have been taken to prevent such accumulation of fumes therefrom as are likely to be injurious to workers employed in the room.

SECTION 15: Artificial humidification

(1) In respect of all factories in which the humidity of the air is artificially increased, the State Government may make rules,—

- (a) prescribing standards of humidification;
- (b) regulating the methods used for artificially increasing the humidity of the air;
- (c) directing prescribed tests for determining the humidity of the air to be correctly carried out and recorded;
- (d) prescribing methods to be adopted for securing adequate ventilation and cooling of the air in the workrooms.

(2) In any factory in which the humidity of the air is artificially increased, the water used for the purpose shall be taken from a public supply, or other source of drinking water, or shall be effectively purified before it is so used.

(3) If it appears to an Inspector that the water used in a factory for increasing humidity which is required to be effectively purified under sub-section (2) is not effectively purified he may serve on the manager of the factory an order in writing, specifying the measures which in his opinion should be adopted, and requiring them to be carried out before specified date.

Section 16: Overcrowding

(1) No room in any factory shall be overcrowded to an extent injurious to the health of the workers employed therein.

(2) Without prejudice to the generality of sub-section (1), there shall be in every workroom of a factory in existence on the date of the commencement of this Act at least 9.9 cubic metres and of a factory built after the commencement of this Act at least 14.2 cubic metres or space for every worker employed therein, and for the purposes of this sub-section no account shall be taken of any space which is more than 4.2 metres above the level of the floor of the room.

(3) If the Chief Inspector by order in writing so requires, there shall be posted in each workroom of a factory a notice specifying the maximum number of workers who may, in compliance with the provisions of this section, be employed in the room.

(4) The Chief Inspector may by order in writing exempt, subject to such conditions, if any, as he may think fit to impose, any workroom from the provisions of this section, if he is satisfied that compliance therewith in respect of the room is unnecessary in the interest of the health of the workers employed therein.

Section 17: Lighting

(1) In every part of a factory where workers are working or passing there shall be provided and maintained sufficient and suitable lighting, natural or artificial, or both.

(2) In every factory all glazed windows and skylights used for the lighting of the workroom shall be kept clean on both the inner and outer surfaces and, so far as compliance with the provisions of any rules made, under sub-section (3) of section 13 will allow, free from obstruction.

(3) In every factory effective provision shall, so far as is practicable, be made for the prevention of—

(a) glare, either directly from a source of light or by reflection from a smooth or polished surface;

(b) the formation of shadows to such an extent as to cause eye-strain or the risk of accident to any worker.

(4) The State Government may prescribe standards of sufficient and suitable lighting for factories or for any class or description of factories or for any manufacturing process.

Section 18: Drinking water

(1) In every factory effective arrangements shall be made to provide and maintain at suitable points conveniently situated for all workers employed therein a sufficient supply of wholesome drinking water.

(2) All such points shall be legibly marked "drinking water" in a language understood by a majority of the workers employed in the factory, and no such point shall be

situated within six metres of any washing place, urinal, latrine, spittoon, open drain carrying sullage or effluent or any other source of contamination unless a shorter distance is approved in writing by the Chief Inspector.

(3) In every factory wherein more than two hundred and fifty workers are ordinarily employed, provisions shall be made for cooling drinking water during hot weather by effective means and for distribution thereof.

(4) In respect of all factories or any class or description of factories the State Government may make rules for securing compliance with the provisions of sub-sections (1), (2) and (3) and for the examination by prescribed authorities of the supply and distribution of drinking water in factories.

SECTION 19: Latrines and urinals

(1) In every factory—

(a) sufficient latrine and urinal accommodation of prescribed types shall be provided conveniently situated and accessible to workers at all times while they are at the factory;

(b) separate enclosed accommodation shall be provided for male and female workers;

(c) such accommodation shall be adequately lighted and ventilated, and no latrine or urinal shall, unless specially exempted in writing by the Chief Inspector, communicate with any workroom except through an intervening open space or ventilated passage;

(d) all such accommodation shall be maintained in a clean and sanitary condition at all times;

(e) sweepers shall be employed whose primary duty it would be to keep clean latrines, urinals and washing places.

(2) In every factory wherein more than two hundred and fifty workers are ordinarily employed—

(a) all latrine and urinal accommodation shall be of prescribed sanitary types;

(b) the floors and internal walls, up to a height of ninety centimetres, of the latrines and urinals and the sanitary blocks shall be laid in glazed titles or otherwise finished to provide a smooth polished impervious surface;

(c) without prejudice to the provisions of clauses (d) and (e) of sub-section (1), the floors, portions of the walls and blocks so laid or finished and the sanitary pans of latrines and urinals shall be thoroughly washed and cleaned at least once in every seven days with suitable detergents or disinfectants or with both.

(3) The State Government may prescribe the number of latrines and urinals to be provided in any factory in proportion to the numbers of male and female workers ordinarily employed therein, and provide for such further matters in respect of sanitation in factories, including the obligation of workers in this regard, as it considers necessary in the interest of the health of the workers employed therein.

Section 20: Spittoons

(1) In every factory there shall be provided a sufficient number of spittoons in convenient places and they shall be maintained in a clean and hygienic condition.

(2) The State Government may make rules prescribing the type and the number of spittoons to be provided and their location in any factory and provide for such further matters relating to their maintenance in a clean and hygienic condition.

(3) No person shall spit within the premises of a factory except in the spittoons provided for the purpose and a notice containing this provision and the penalty for its violation shall be prominently displayed at suitable places in the premises.

(4) Whoever spits in contravention of sub-section (3) shall be punishable with fine not exceeding five rupees.

Chapter IV

SAFETY

Section 21: Fencing of machinery

(1) In every factory the following, namely,—

(i) every moving part of a prime mover and every flywheel connected to a prime mover, whether the prime mover or flywheel is in the engine house or not;

(ii) the headrace and tailrace of every water-wheel and water turbine;

(iii) any part of a stock-bar which projects beyond the head stock of a lathe; and

(iv) unless they are in such position or of such construction as to be safe to every person employed in the factory as they would be if they were securely fenced, the following, namely—

(a) every part of an electric generator, a motor or rotary converter;

(b) every part of transmission machinery; and

(c) every dangerous part of any other machinery,

shall be securely fenced by safeguards of substantial construction which shall be constantly maintained and kept in position while the parts of machinery they are fencing are in motion or in use:

Provided that for the purpose of determining whether any part of machinery is in such position or is of such construction as to be safe as aforesaid, account shall not be taken of any occasion when—

(i) it is necessary to make an examination of any part of the machinery aforesaid while it is in motion or, as a result of such examination, to carry out lubrication or other adjusting operation while the machinery is in motion, being an examination or operation which it is necessary to be carried out while that part of the machinery is in motion, or

(ii) in the case of any part of a transmission machinery used in such process as may be prescribed (being a process of a continuous nature the carrying on of which shall be, or is likely to be, substantially interfered with by the stoppage of that part of the machinery), it is necessary to make an examination of such part of the machinery while it is in motion or, as a result of such examination, to carry out any mounting or shipping of belts or lubrication or other adjusting operation while the machinery is in motion,

and such examination or operation is made or carried out in accordance with the provisions of sub-section (1) of section 22.

(2) The State Government may by rules prescribe such further precautions as it may consider necessary in respect of any particular machinery or part thereof, or exempt, subject to such condition as may be prescribed, for securing the safety of the workers, any particular machinery or part thereof from the provisions of this section.

In *State of Gujarat* v. *Jethalal Ghelabhai Patel*,[22] the respondent is the Manager of an oil mill. The mill had a spur gear wheel. A workman of the mill while greasing the spur gear wheel which was then in motion had one of his hands caught in it. Eventually, that hand had to be amputated. It appeared that the spur gear wheel had a cover which had bolts for fixing it to the base but at the time of the accident the cover was not there, having apparently been removed earlier. The respondent was prosecuted under S. 92 of the Act for having failed to comply with S. 21(1)(iv)(c) in it.

The workman said that it had been removed by the respondent for repairs while the case of the respondent was that the workman had himself removed it. The learned trial Judge was unable to accept either version and he acquitted the respondent observing that he could not be held liable if the cover was removed by someone without his consent or knowledge. The learned Judges of the Gujarat High Court, when the matter came to them in appeal, referred to a very large number of cases, mostly of the English Courts under the English Factories Act and a few of our High Courts and from them they deduced the following two principles:

1. Though the obligation to safeguard is absolute under S. 21(1)(iv)(c) of the Indian Act, yet it is qualified by the test of foreseeability, and
2. If the safeguard provided by the employer or manager is rendered nugatory by an unreasonable or perverted act on the part of the workman, there is no liability of the employer or manager.

With great respect to the learned Judges of the High Court, we are unable to appreciate the relevancy of these two principles to the decision of the case in hand. Nor does it seem to us that the learned Judges of the High Court rested their judgment on any of these principles.

As the High Court stated, there is no dispute that the spur gear wheel was a dangerous machinery within the meaning of S. 21(1)(iv)(c). That being so, clearly, there was an obligation to securely fence it and to see that the fence was "*kept in position while the parts of machinery they are fencing are in motion or in use*". Indeed the fact that the respondent had provided the guard over the machine puts it beyond doubt, as the High Court observed, that the machine

22. AIR 1964 SC 779.

was dangerous within the meaning of the section. It was not contended that the risk from the unguarded machine was not a foreseeable risk.

The High Court observed that S. 21(1)(iv)(c) of the Act contemplated a default and that default had to be established by the prosecution. It lastly said that there was nothing in the Act to indicate that the legislature intended that an occupier or manager must always be on the look out to bring to book every offender who removed the safeguard furnished by him or that a failure on his part to do so must entail his conviction. It also observed that the statute did not require that where the occupier or manager had carried out his obligation under the section by providing a proper safeguard, he would be liable if someone else, not known to him, removed it without his knowledge, consent or connivance. It, therefore, held that as in the present case, it could not be said that either he or the workman had removed the guard, it followed that someone whom the occupier or the manager could not fix upon, had removed it and that was something which the occupier or manager could not reasonably be expected to anticipate and he could not be made liable for such removal.

The Supreme Court, on appeal, observed that S. 21(1)(iv)(c) requires not only that the dangerous part of a machine shall be securely fenced by the safeguards but also that the safeguards "*shall be kept in position while the parts of the machinery they are fencing are in motion or in use*". The Court thought that the words "shall be securely fenced" suggest that the fencing should always be there. The statute has however put the matter beyond doubt by expressly saying that the fencing shall be kept in position while the machine is working. That is the default that has happened in this case; the fencing was not there when the machine had been made to work and it was an admitted fact. Accordingly, the Court held as follows:

> "Does the mere fact that someone else had removed the safeguard without the knowledge, consent or connivance of the occupier or manager always provide a defence to him? We do not think so. When the statute says that it will be his duty to keep the guard in position when the machine is working and when it appears that he has not done so, it will be for him to establish that notwithstanding this he was not liable. It is not necessary for us to say that in every case where it is proved that the manager or occupier had provided the necessary fence or guard but at a particular moment it appeared that the fence or guard had been removed, he must be held liable."[23]

SECTION 22: Work on or near machinery in motion

(1) Where in any factory it becomes necessary to examine any part of machinery referred to in section 21, while the machinery is in motion, or, as a result of such examination, to carry out—

(a) in a case referred to in clause (i) of the proviso to sub-section (1) of section 21, lubrication or other adjusting operation; or

(b) in a case referred to in clause (ii) of the proviso aforesaid, any mounting or shipping of belts or lubrication or other adjusting operation,

while the machinery is in motion such examination or operation shall be made or carried out only by a specially trained adult male worker wearing tight fitting clothing (which shall be supplied by the occupier) whose name has been recorded in the register prescribed in this

23. *Ibid.* at p. 781 per Sarkar, J.

behalf and who has been furnished with a certificate of his appointment, and while he is so engaged,—

(a) such worker shall not handle a belt at a moving pulley unless—

(i) the belt is not more than fifteen centimetres in width;

(ii) the pulley is normally for the purpose of drive and not merely a fly-wheel or balance wheel (in which case a belt is not permissible);

(iii) the belt joint is either laced or flush with the belt;

(iv) the belt, including the joint and the pulley rim, are in good repair;

(v) there is reasonable clearance between the pulley and any fixed plant or structure;

(vi) secure foothold and, where necessary, secure handhold, are provided for the operator; and

(vii) any ladder in use for carrying out any examination or operation aforesaid is securely fixed or lashed or is firmly held by a second person.

(b) without prejudice to any other provision of this Act relating to the fencing of machinery, every set screw, bolt and key on any revolving shaft, spindle, wheel or pinion, and all spur, worm and other toothed or friction gearing in motion with which such worker would otherwise be liable to come into contact, shall be securely fenced to prevent such contact.

(2) No woman or young person shall be allowed to clean, lubricate or adjust any part of a prime mover or of any transmission machinery while the prime mover or transmission machinery is in motion, or to clean, lubricate or adjust any part of any machine if the cleaning, lubrication or adjustment thereof would expose the woman or young person to risk of injury from any moving part either of that machine or of any adjacent machinery.

(3) The State Government may, by notification in the official Gazette, prohibit, in any specified factory or class or description of factories, the cleaning, lubricating or adjusting by any person of specified parts of machinery when those parts are in motion.

Section 23: Employment of young persons on dangerous machines

(1) No young person shall be required or allowed to work at any machine to which this section applies, unless he has been fully instructed as to the dangers arising in connection with the machine and the precautions to be observed and—

(a) has received sufficient training in work at the machine, or

(b) is under adequate supervision by a person who has a thorough knowledge and experience of the machine.

(2) Sub-section (1) shall apply to such machines as may be prescribed by the State Government, being machines which in its opinion are of such a dangerous character that young persons ought not to work at them unless the foregoing requirements are complied with.

SECTION 24: Striking gear and devices for cutting off power

(1) In every factory—

(a) suitable striking gear or other efficient mechanical appliance shall be provided and maintained and used to move driving belts to and from fast and loose pulleys which form part of the transmission machinery, such gear or appliances shall be so constructed, placed and maintained as to prevent the belt from creeping back on to the fast pulley;

(b) driving belts when not in use shall not be allowed to rest or ride upon shafting in motion.

(2) In every factory suitable devices for cutting off power in emergencies from running machinery shall be provided and maintained in every work-room:

Provided that in respect of factories in operation before the commencement of this Act, the provisions of this sub-section shall apply only to work-rooms in which electricity is used as power.

(3) When a device, which can inadvertently shift from "off" to "on" position, is provided in a factory to cut off power, arrangements shall be provided for locking the device in safe position to prevent accidental starting of the transmission machinery or other machines to which the device is fitted.

SECTION 25: Self-acting machines

No traversing part of a self-acting machine in any factory and no material carried thereon shall, if the space over which it runs is a space over which any person is liable to pass, whether in the course of his employment or otherwise, be allowed to run on its outward or inward traverse within a distance of forty-five centimetres from any fixed structure which is not part of the machine :

Provided that the Chief Inspector may permit the continued use of a machine installed before the commencement of this Act which does not comply with the requirements of this section on such conditions for ensuring safety as he may think fit to impose.

SECTION 26: Casing of new machinery

(1) In all machinery driven by power and installed in any factory after the commencement of this Act,—

(a) every set screw, bolt or key on any revolving shaft, spindle, wheel pinion shall be so sunk, encased or otherwise effectively guarded as to prevent danger;

(b) all spur, worm and other toothed or friction gearing which does not require frequent adjustment while in motion shall be completely encased, unless it is so situated as to be as safe as it would be if it were completely encased.

(2) Whoever sells or lets on hire or, as agent of a seller or hirer, causes or procures to be sold on let or hire, for use in a factory any machinery driven by power which

does not comply with the provisions of sub-section (1) or any rules made under sub-section (3), shall be punishable with imprisonment for a term which may extend to three months or with fine which may extend to five hundred rupees or with both.

(3) The State Government may make rules specifying further safeguards to be provided in respect of any other dangerous part of any particular machine or class or description of machines.

Section 27: Prohibition of employment of women and children near cotton-openers

No woman or child shall be employed in any part of a factory for pressing cotton in which a cotton-opener is at work:

Provided that if the feed-end of a cotton-opener is in a room separated from the delivery end by a partition extending to the roof or to such height as the Inspector may in any particular case specify in writing, women and children may be employed on the side of the partition where the feed-end is situated.

Section 28: Hoists and lifts

(1) In every factory—

(a) every hoist and lift shall be—

(i) of good mechanical construction, sound material and adequate strength;

(ii) properly maintained, and shall be thoroughly examined by a competent person at least once in every period of six months, and a register shall be kept containing the prescribed particulars of every such examination;

(b) every hoistway and liftway shall be sufficiently protected by an enclosure fitted with gates, and the hoist or lift and every such enclosure shall be so constructed as to prevent any person or thing from being trapped between any part of the hoist or lift and any fixed structure or moving part;

(c) the maximum safe working load shall be plainly marked on every hoist or lift, and no load greater than such load shall be carried thereon;

(d) the cage of every hoist or lift used for carrying persons shall be fitted with a gate on each side from which access is afforded to a landing;

(e) every gate referred to in clause (b) or clause (a) shall be fitted with interlocking or other efficient device to secure that the gate cannot be opened except when the cage is at the landing and that the cage cannot be moved unless the gate is closed.

(2) The following additional requirements shall apply to hoists and lifts used for carrying persons and installed or reconstructed in a factory after the commencement of this Act, namely:

(a) where the cage is supported by rope or chain, there shall be at least two ropes or chains separately connected with the cage and balance weight, and each rope or chain with its attachments shall be capable of carrying the whole weight of the cage together with its maximum load;

(b) efficient devices shall be provided and maintained capable of supporting the cage together with its maximum load in the event of breakage of the ropes, chains or attachments;

(c) an efficient automatic device shall be provided and maintained to prevent the cage from over-running.

(3) The Chief Inspector may permit the continued use of a hoist or lift installed in a factory before the commencement of this Act which does not fully comply with the provisions of sub-section (1) upon such conditions for ensuring safety as he may think fit to impose.

(4) The State Government may, if in respect of any class or description of hoist or lift, it is of opinion that it would be unreasonable to enforce any requirement of sub-sections (1) and (2), by order direct that such requirement shall not apply to such class or description of hoist or lift.

Explanation: For the purposes of this section, no lifting machine or appliance shall be deemed to be a hoist or lift unless it has a platform or cage, the direction or movement of which is restricted by a guide or guides.

Section 29: Lifting machines, chains, ropes and lifting tackles

(1) In any factory the following provisions shall be complied with in respect of every lifting machine (other than a hoist and lift) and every chain, rope and lifting tackle for the purpose of raising or lowering persons, goods or materials:

(a) all parts, including the working gear, whether fixed or movable, of every lifting machine and every chain, rope or lifting tackle shall be—

(i) of good construction, sound material and adequate strength and free from defects;

(ii) properly maintained; and

(iii) thoroughly examined by a competent person at least once in every period of twelve months, or at such intervals as the Chief Inspector may specify in writing, and a register shall be kept containing the prescribed particulars of every such examination;

(b) no lifting machine and no chain, rope or lifting tackle shall, except for the purpose of test, be loaded beyond the safe working load which shall be plainly marked thereon together with an identification mark and duly entered in the prescribed register, and where this is not practicable, a table showing the safe working loads of every kind and size of lifting machine or, chain, rope or lifting tackle in use shall be displayed in prominent positions on the premises;

(c) while any person is employed or working on or near the wheel track of a travelling crane in any place where he would be liable to be struck by the crane, effective measures shall be taken to ensure that the crane does not approach within six metres of that place.

(2) The State Government may make rules in respect of any lifting machine or any chain, rope or lifting tackle used in factories—

(a) prescribing further requirements to be complied with in addition to those set out in this section;

(b) providing for exemption from compliance with all or any of the requirements of this section, where in its opinion, such compliance is unnecessary or impracticable.

(3) For the purposes of this section a lifting machine or a chain, rope or lifting tackle shall be deemed to have been thoroughly examined if a visual examination supplemented, if necessary, by other means and by the dismantling of parts of the gear, has been carried out as carefully as the conditions permit in order to arrive at a reliable conclusion as to the safety of the parts examined.

Explanation: In this section,—

(a) "lifting machine" means a crane, crab, winch, teagle, pulley block, gin wheel, transporter or runway;

(b) "lifting tackle" means any chain, sling, rope sling, hook, shackle, swivel, coupling, socket, clamp, tray or similar appliance, whether fixed or movable, used in connection with the raising or lowering of persons, or loads by use of lifting machines.

SECTION 30: Revolving machinery

(1) In every factory in which the process of grinding is carried on there shall be permanently affixed to or placed near each machine in use a notice indicating the maximum safe working peripheral speed of every grindstone or abrasive wheel, the speed of the shaft or spindle upon which the wheel is mounted, and the diameter of the pulley upon such shaft or spindle necessary to secure such safe working peripheral speed.

(2) The speeds indicated in notices under sub-section (1) shall not be exceeded.

(3) Effective measures shall be taken in every factory to ensure that the safe working peripheral speed of every revolving vessel, cage, basket, flywheel, pulley, disc or similar appliance driven by power is not exceeded.

SECTION 31: Pressure plant

(1) If in any factory, any plant or machinery or any part thereof is operated at a pressure above atmospheric pressure, effective measures shall be taken to ensure that the safe working pressure of such plant or machinery or part is not exceeded.

(2) The State Government may make rules providing for the examination and testing of any plant or machinery such as is referred to in sub-section (1) and prescribing such

other safety measures in relation thereto as may in its opinion be necessary in any factory or class or description of factories.

(3) The State Government may, by rules, exempt, subject to such conditions as may be specified therein, any part of any plant or machinery referred to in sub-section (1) from the provisions of this section.

SECTION 32: Floors, stairs and means of access

In every factory—

(a) all floors, steps, stairs, passages and gangways shall be of sound construction and properly maintained and shall be kept free from obstructions and substances likely to cause persons to slip, and where it is necessary to ensure safety, steps, stairs, passages and gangways shall be provided with substantial handrails;

(b) there shall, so far as is reasonably practicable, be provided and maintained safe means of access to every place at which any person is at any time required to work.

(c) when any person has to work at a height from where he is likely to fall, provision shall be made, so far as is reasonably practicable, by fencing or otherwise, to ensure the safety of the person so working.

SECTION 33: Pits, sumps, openings in floors, etc.

(1) In every factory fixed vessel, sump, tank, pit or opening in the ground or in a floor which, by reasons of its depth, situation, construction or contents, is or may be a source of danger, shall be either securely covered or securely fenced.

(2) The State Government may, by order in writing, exempt, subject to such conditions as may be prescribed, any factory or class or description of factories in respect of any vessel, sump, tank, pit or opening from compliance with the provisions of this section.

SECTION 34: Excessive weights

(1) No person shall be employed in any factory to lift, carry or move any load so heavy as to be likely to cause him injury.

(2) The State Government may make rules prescribing the maximum weights which may be lifted, carried or moved by adult men, adult women, adolescents and children employed in factories or in any class or description of factories or in carrying on any specified process.

SECTION 35: Protection of eyes

In respect of any such manufacturing process carried on in any factory as may be prescribed, being a process which involves—

(a) risk of injury to the eyes from particles or fragments thrown off in the course of the process, or

(b) risk to the eyes by reason of exposure to excessive light,

the State Government may by rules require that effective screens or suitable goggles shall be provided for the protection of persons employed on, or in the immediate vicinity of, the process.

SECTION 36: Precautions against dangerous fumes, gases, etc.

(1) No person shall be required or allowed to enter any chamber, tank, vat, pit, pipe, flue or other confined space in any factory in which any gas, fume, vapour or dust is likely to be present to such an extent as to involve risk to persons being overcome thereby, unless it is provided with a manhole of adequate size or other effective means of egress.

(2) No person shall be required or allowed to enter any confined space as is referred to in sub-section (1), until all practicable measures have been taken to remove any gas, fume, vapour or dust, which may be present so as to bring its level within the permissible limits and to prevent any ingress of such gas, fume, vapour or dust and unless—

(a) a certificate in writing has been given by a competent person, based on a test carried out by himself that the space is reasonably free from dangerous gas, fume, vapour or dust; or

(b) such person is wearing suitable breathing apparatus and a belt securely attached to a rope the free end of which is held by a person outside the confined space.

SECTION 36A: Precautions regarding the use of portable electric light

In any factory—

(a) no portable electric light or any other electric appliance of voltage exceeding twenty-four volts shall be permitted for use inside any chamber, tank, vat, pit, pipe, flue or other confined space unless adequate safety devices are provided; and

(b) if any inflammable gas, fume or dust is likely to be present in such chamber, tank, vat, pit, pipe, flue or other confined space, no lamp or light other than that of flame-proof construction shall be permitted to be used therein.

SECTION 37: Explosive or inflammable dust, gas, etc.

(1) Where in any factory any manufacturing process produces dust, gas, fume or vapour of such character and to such extent as to be likely to explode to ignition, all practicable measures shall be taken to prevent any such explosion by—

(a) effective enclosure of the plant or machinery used in the process;

(b) removal or prevention of the accumulation of such dust, gas, fume or vapour;

(c) exclusion or effective enclosure of all possible sources of ignition.

(2) Where in any factory the plant or machinery used in a process such as is referred to in sub-section (1) is not so constructed as to withstand the probable pressure which such an explosion as aforesaid would produce, all practicable measures shall be taken to restrict the spread and effects of the explosion by the provisions in the plant or machinery of chokes, baffles, vents or other effective appliances.

(3) Where any part of the plant or machinery in a factory contains any explosive or inflammable gas or vapour under pressure greater than atmospheric pressure, that part shall not be opened except in accordance with the following provisions, namely:

(a) before the fastening of any joint of any pipe connected with the part of the fastening of the cover of any opening into the part is loosened, any flow of the gas or vapour into the part of any such pipe shall be effectively stopped by a stop valve or other means;

(b) before any such fastening as aforesaid is removed, all practicable measures shall be taken to reduce the pressure of the gas or vapour in the part or pipe to atmospheric pressure;

(c) where any such fastening as aforesaid has been loosened or removed effective measures shall be taken to prevent any explosive or inflammable gas or vapour from entering the part of pipe until the fastening has been secured, or, as the case may be, securely replaced:

Provided that the provisions of this sub-section shall not apply in the case of plant or machinery installed in the open air.

(4) No plant, tank or vessel which contains or has contained any explosive or inflammable substance shall be subjected in any factory to any welding, brazing, soldering or cutting operation which involves the application of heat unless adequate measures have first been taken to remove such substance and any fumes arising therefrom or to render such substance and fumes non-explosive or non-inflammable, and no such substance shall be allowed to enter such plant, tank or vessel after any such operation until the metal has cooled sufficiently to prevent any risk of igniting the substance.

(5) The State Government may by rules exempt, subject to such conditions as may be prescribed, any factory or class or description of factories from compliance with all or any of the provisions of this section.

SECTION 38: Precautions in case of fire

(1) In every factory, all practicable measures shall be taken to prevent outbreak of fire and its spread, both internally and externally, and to provide and maintain—

(a) safe means of escape for all persons in the event of a fire, and

(b) the necessary equipment and facilities for extinguishing fire.

(2) Effective measures shall be taken to ensure that in every factory all the workers are familiar with the means of escape in case of fire and have been adequately trained in the routine to be followed in such cases.

(3) The State Government may make rules, in respect of any factory or class or description of factories, requiring the measures to be adopted to give effect to the provisions of sub-sections (1) and (2).

(4) Notwithstanding anything contained in clause (a) of sub-section (1) or sub-section (2), if the Chief Inspector, having regard to the nature of the work carried on in any factory, the construction of such factory, special risk to life or safety, or any other circumstances, is of the opinion that the measures provided in the factory, whether as prescribed or not, for the purposes of clause (a) of sub-section (1) or sub-section (2), are inadequate, he may, by, order in writing, require that such additional measures as he may consider reasonable and necessary, be provided in the factory before such date as is specified in the order.

Section 39: Power to require specifications of defective parts or tests of stability

If it appears to the Inspector that any building or part of a building or any part of the ways, machinery or plant in a factory is in such a condition that it may be dangerous to human life or safety, he may serve on the occupier or manager or both of the factory an order in writing requiring him before a specified date—

(a) to furnish such drawings, specifications and other particulars as may be necessary to determine whether such building, ways, machinery or plant can be used with safety, or

(b) to carry out such test in such manner as may be specified in the order, and to inform the Inspector of the results thereof.

Section 40: Safety of buildings and machinery

(1) If it appears to the Inspector that any building or part of a building or any part of the ways, machinery or plant in a factory is in such a condition that it is dangerous to human life or safety, he may serve on the occupier or manager or both of the factory an order in writing specifying the measures which in his opinion should be adopted, and requiring them to be carried out before a specified date.

(2) If it appears to the Inspector that the use of any building or part of a building or any part of the ways, machinery or plant in a factory involves imminent danger to human life or safety, he may serve on the occupier or manager or both of the factory an order in writing prohibiting its use until it has been properly repaired or altered.

Section 40A: Maintenance of buildings

If it appears to the Inspector that any building or part of a building in a factory is in such a state of disrepair as is likely to lead to conditions detrimental to the health and welfare of the workers, he may serve on the occupier or manager or both of the factory an order in writing specifying the measures which in his opinion should be taken and requiring the same to be carried out before such date as is specified in the order.

SECTION 40B: Safety officers

(1) In every factory,—

(i) wherein one thousand or more workers are ordinarily employed, or

(ii) wherein, in the opinion of the State Government, any manufacturing process or operation is carried on, which process or operation involves any risk of bodily injury, poisoning or disease, or any other hazard to health, to the persons employed in the factory,

the occupier shall, if so required by the State Government by notification in the Official Gazette, employ such number of Safety Officers as may be specified in that notification.

(2) The duties, qualifications and conditions of service of Safety Officers shall be such as may be prescribed by the State Government.

SECTION 41: Power to make rule to supplement this chapter

The State Government may make rules requiring the provision in any factory or in any class or description of factories of such further devices and measures for securing the safety of persons employed therein as it may deem necessary.

CHAPTER IVA

PROVISIONS RELATING TO HAZARDOUS PROCESSES

SECTION 41A: Constitution of Site Appraisal Committees

(1) The State Government may, for purposes of advising it to consider applications for grant of permission for the initial location of a factory involving a hazardous process or for the expansion of any such factory, appoint a Site Appraisal Committee consisting of—

(a) the Chief Inspector of the State who shall be its Chairman;

(b) a representative of the Central Board for the Prevention and Control of Water Pollution appointed by the Central Government under section 3 of the Water (Prevention and Control of Pollution) Act, 1974 (6 of 1974);

(c) a representative of the Central Board for the Prevention and Control of Air Pollution referred to in section 3 of the Air (Prevention and Control of Pollution) Act, 1981 (14 of 1981);

(d) a representative of the State Board appointed under section 4 of the Water (Prevention and Control of Pollution) Act, 1974 (6 of 1974);

(e) a representative of the State Board for the Prevention and Control of Air Pollution referred to in section 5 of the Air (Prevention and Control of Pollution) Act, 1981 (14 of 1981);

(f) a representative of the Department of Environment in the State;

(g) a representative of the Meteorological Department of the Government of India;

(h) an expert in the field of occupational health; and

(i) a representative of the Town Planning Department of the State Government,

and not more than five other members who may be co-opted by the State Government who shall be—

(i) a scientist having specialised knowledge of the hazardous process which will be involved in the factory,

(ii) a representative of the local authority within whose jurisdiction the factory is to be established, and

(iii) not more than three other persons as deemed fit by the State Government.

(2) The Site Appraisal Committee shall examine an application for the establishment of a factory involving hazardous process and make its recommendation to the State Government within a period of ninety days of the receipt of such applications in the prescribed form.

(3) Where any process relates to a factory owned or controlled by the Central Government or to a corporation or a company owned or controlled by the Central Government, the State Government shall co-opt in the Site Appraisal Committee a representative nominated by the Central Government as a member of that Committee.

(4) The Site Appraisal Committee shall have power to call for any information from the person making an application for the establishment or expansion of a factory involving a hazardous process.

(5) Where the State Government has granted approval to an application for the establishment or expansion of a factory involving hazardous process, it shall not be necessary for an applicant to obtain a further approval from the Central Board or the State Board established under the Water (Prevention and Control of Pollution) Act 1974 (6 of 1974) and the Air (Prevention and Control of Pollution) Act, 1981 (14 of 1981).

Section 41B: Compulsory disclosure of information by the occupier

(1) The occupier of every factory involving a hazardous process shall disclose in the manner prescribed all information regarding dangers, including health hazards and the measures to overcome such hazards arising from the exposure to or handling of the materials or substances in the manufacture, transportation, storage and other processes, to the workers employed in the factory, the Chief Inspector, the local

authority within whose jurisdiction the factory is situate and the general public in the vicinity.

(2) The occupier shall, at the time of registering the factory involving a hazardous process, lay down a detailed policy with respect to the health and safety of the workers employed therein and intimate such policy to the Chief Inspector and the local authority and, thereafter, at such intervals as may be prescribed, inform the Chief Inspector and the local authority of any change made in the said policy

(3) The information furnished under sub-section (1) shall include accurate information as to the quantity, specifications and other characteristics of wastes and the manner of their disposal.

(4) Every occupier shall, with the approval of the Chief Inspector, draw up an on-site emergency plan and detailed disaster control measures for his factory and make known to the workers employed therein and to the general public living in the vicinity of the factory the safety measures required to be taken in the event of an accident taking place.

(5) Every occupier of a factory shall,—

(a) if such factory engaged in a hazardous process on the commencement of the Factories (Amendment) Act, 1987 (2 of 1987), within a period of thirty days of such commencement; and

(b) if such factory proposes to engage in a hazardous process at any time after such commencement, within a period of thirty days before the commencement of such process,

inform the Chief Inspector of the nature and details of the process in such form and in such manner as may be prescribed.

(6) Where any occupier of a factory contravenes the provisions of sub-section (5), the licence issued under section 6 to such factory shall, notwithstanding any penalty to which the occupier of factory shall be subjected to under the provisions of this Act, be liable for cancellation.

(7) The occupier of a factory involving a hazardous process shall, with the previous approval of the Chief Inspector, lay down measures for the handling, usage, transportation and storage of hazardous substances inside the factory premises and the disposal of such substances outside the factory premises and publicise them in the manner prescribed among the workers and the general public living in the vicinity.

Section 41C: Specific responsibility of the occupier in relation to hazardous processes

Every occupier of a factory involving any hazardous process shall—

(a) maintain accurate and up-to-date health records or, as the case may be, medical records, of the workers in the factory who are exposed to any chemical, toxic or any other harmful substances which are manufactured, stored, handled or transported and such records shall be accessible to the workers subject to such conditions as may be prescribed;

(b) appoint persons who possess qualifications and experience in handling hazardous substances and are competent to supervise such handling within the factory and to provide at the working place all the necessary facilities for protecting the workers in the manner prescribed:

Provided that where any question arises as to the qualifications and experience of a person so appointed, the decision of the Chief Inspector shall be final;

(c) provide for medical examination of every worker—

(i) before such worker is assigned to a job involving the handling of, or working with, a hazardous substance, and

(ii) while continuing in such job, and after he has ceased to work in such job, at intervals not exceeding twelve months, in such manner as may be prescribed.

Section 41D: Power of Central Government to appoint Inquiry Committee

(1) The Central Government may, in the event of the occurrence of an extraordinary situation involving a factory engaged in a hazardous process, appoint an Inquiry Committee to inquire into the standards of health and safety observed in the factory with a view to finding out the causes of any failure or neglect in the adoption of any measures or standards prescribed for the health and safety of the workers employed in the factory or the general public affected, or likely to be affected, due to such failure or neglect and for the prevention and recurrence of such extraordinary situations in future in such factory or elsewhere.

(2) The Committee appointed under sub-section (1) shall consist of a chairman and two other members and the terms of reference of the Committee and the tenure of office of its members shall be such as may be determined by the Central Government according to the requirements of the situation.

(3) The recommendations of the Committee shall be advisory in nature.

Section 41E: Emergency standards

(1) Where the Central Government is satisfied that no standards of safety have been prescribed in respect of a hazardous process or class of hazardous processes, or where the standards so prescribed are inadequate, it may direct the Director-General of Factory Advice Service and Labour Institutes or any institution specialised in matters relating to standards of safety in hazardous processes, to lay down emergency standards for enforcement of suitable standards in respect of such hazardous processes.

(2) The emergency standards laid down under sub-section (1) shall, until they are incorporated in the rules made under this Act, be enforceable and have the same effect as if they had been incorporated in the rules made under this Act.

SECTION 41F: Permissible limits of exposure of chemical and toxic substances

(1) The maximum permissible threshold limits of exposure of chemical and toxic substances in manufacturing processes (whether hazardous or otherwise) in any factory shall be of the value indicated in the Second Schedule.

(2) The Central Government may, at any time, for the purpose of giving effect to any scientific proof obtained from specialised institutions or experts in the field, by notification in the Official Gazette, make suitable changes in the said Schedule.

SECTION 41G: Workers' participation in safety management

(1) The occupier shall, in every factory where a hazardous process takes place, or where hazardous substances are used or handled, set up a Safety Committee consisting of equal number of representatives of workers and management to promote cooperation between the workers and the management in maintaining proper safety and health at work and to review periodically the measures taken in that behalf:

Provided that the State Government may, by order in writing and for reasons to be recorded, exempt the occupier of any factory or class of factories from setting up such committee.

(2) The composition of the Safety Committee, the tenure of office of its members and their rights and duties shall be such as may be prescribed.

SECTION 41H: Right of workers to warn about imminent danger

(1) Where the workers employed in any factory engaged in a hazardous process have reasonable apprehension that there is a likelihood of imminent danger to their lives or health due to any accident, they may bring the same to the notice of the occupier, agent, manager or any other person who is incharge of the factory or the process concerned directly or through their representatives in the Safety Committee and simultaneously bring the same to the notice of the Inspector.

(2) It shall be the duty of such occupier, agent, manager or the person incharge of the factory or process to take immediate remedial action if he is satisfied about the existence of such imminent danger and send a report forthwith of the action taken to the nearest Inspector.

(3) If the occupier, agent, manager or the person incharge referred to in sub-section (2) is not satisfied about the existence of any imminent danger as apprehended by the workers, he shall, nevertheless, refer the matter forthwith to the nearest Inspector whose decision on the question of the existence of such imminent danger shall be final.

CHAPTER V

WELFARE

SECTION 42: Washing facilities

(1) In every factory—

(a) adequate and suitable facilities for washing shall be provided and maintained for the use of the workers therein;

(b) separate and adequately screened facilities shall be provided for the use of male and female workers;

(c) such facilities shall be conveniently accessible and shall be kept clean.

(2) The State Government may, in respect of any factory or class or description of factories or of any manufacturing process, prescribe standards of adequate and suitable facilities for washing.

SECTION 43: Facilities for storing and drying clothing

The State Government may, in respect of any factory or class or description of factories, make rules requiring the provision therein of suitable places for keeping clothing not worn during working hours and for the drying of wet clothing.

SECTION 44: Facilities for sitting

(1) In every factory suitable arrangements for sitting shall be provided and maintained for all workers obliged to work in a standing position, in order that they may take advantage of any opportunities for rest which may occur in the course of their work.

(2) If, in the opinion of the Chief Inspector, the workers in any factory engaged in a particular manufacturing process or working in a particular room are able to do their work efficiently in a sitting position, he may, by order in writing, require the occupier of the factory to provide before a specified date such seating arrangements as may be practicable for all workers so engaged or working.

(3) The State Government may, by notification in the Official Gazette, declare that the provisions of sub-section (1) shall not apply to any specified factory or class or description of factories or to any specified manufacturing process.

SECTION 45: First aid appliances

(1) There shall in every factory be provided and maintained so as to be readily accessible during all working hours first-aid boxes or cupboards equipped with the prescribed contents, and the number of such boxes or cupboards to be provided and maintained shall not be less than one for every one hundred and fifty workers ordinarily employed at any one time in the factory.

(2) Nothing except the prescribed contents shall be kept in a first-aid box or cupboard.

(3) Each first-aid box or cupboard shall be kept in the charge of a separate responsible person who holds a certificate in first-aid treatment recognized by State Government and who shall always be readily available during the working hours of the factory.

(4) In every factory wherein more than five hundred workers are ordinarily employed there shall be provided and maintained an ambulance room of the prescribed size, containing the prescribed equipment and in the charge of such medical and nursing staff as may be prescribed and those facilities shall always be made readily available during the working hours of the factory.

SECTION 46: Canteens

(1) The State Government may make rules requiring that in any specified factory wherein more than two hundred and fifty workers are ordinarily employed, a canteen or canteens shall be provided and maintained by the occupier for the use of the workers.

(2) Without prejudice to the generality of the foregoing power, such rules may provide for—

(a) the date by which such canteen shall be provided;

(b) the standards in respect of construction, accommodation, furniture and other equipment of the canteen;

(c) the foodstuffs to be served therein and the charges which may be made therefor;

(d) the constitution of a managing committee for the canteen and representation of the workers in the management of the canteen;

(dd) the items of expenditure in the running of the canteen which are not to be taken into account in fixing the cost of foodstuffs and which shall be borne by the employer;

(e) the delegation to the Chief Inspector, subject to such conditions as may be prescribed, of the power to make rules under clause (c).

A sole question, usually, raised before the Apex Court for consideration is whether the canteen workers are employees of the establishment or of the contractor. There are plethora of judgments in this regard. However, the following propositions have emerged from the judicial decision in the course of time and they are as follows.

(i) Where, as under the provisions of the Factories Act, it is statutorily obligatory on the employer to provide and maintain canteen for the use of his employees, the canteen becomes a part of the establishment and, therefore, the workers employed in such canteen are the employees of the management.

(ii) Where, although it is not statutorily obligatory to provide a canteen, it is otherwise an obligation on the employer to provide a canteen, the canteen becomes a part of the establishment and the workers working in the canteen are the employees of the management. The obligation to provide a canteen has to be distinguished from the obligation to provide facilities to run canteen. The canteen run pursuant to the latter obligation, does not become a part of the establishment.

(iii) The obligation to provide canteen may be explicit or implicit. Where the obligation is not explicitly accepted by or cast upon the employer either by an agreement or an award etc., it may be inferred from the circumstances, and the provision of the canteen may be held to have become a part of the service conditions of the employees. Whether the provision for canteen services has become a part of the service conditions or not, is a question of fact to be determined on the facts and circumstances in each case.

Where to provide canteen services has become a part of the service conditions of the employees, the canteen becomes a part of the establishment and the workers in such canteen become the employees of the management.

(iv) Whether a particular facility or service has become implicitly a part of the service conditions of the employees or not, will depend, among others, on the nature of the service/facility, the contribution the service in question makes to the efficiency of the employees and the establishment, whether the service is available as a matter of right to all the employees in their capacity as employees and nothing more, the number of employees employed in the establishment and the number of employees who avail of the service, the length of time for which the service has been continuously available, the hours during which it is available, the nature and character of management, the interest taken by the employer in providing, maintaining, supervising and controlling the service, the contribution made by the management in the form of infrastructure and funds for making the service available etc.

Canteen vis-a-vis Contract Labour

Considering a plethora of contradictory judgments of the Apex Court it is felt necessary to discuss the issues of canteen which is managed by the contractor engaging the contract labour. Canteen may be of two types; statutory and non-statutory. Any law that prescribes that the employer is bound to provided the canteen facility to his employees it may be called as statutory canteen where as the employer, as a good gesture, provides such facility to his employees may be called as a non-statutory canteen.

A sole question, usually, came before the Supreme Court for consideration is whether the canteen workers are to be considered as employees of the establishment or of the contractor. There are plethoras of judgments in this regard. However, a two-Judge Bench of the Supreme Court in *Parimal Chandra Raha* v. *Life Insurance Corporation of India* (AIR 1995 SC 1666), while considering earlier decisions of the Supreme Court like, *Saraspur Mills. Co. Ltd.* v. *Ramanlal Chimanlal* (AIR 1973 SC 2297), *Workmen of the Food Corporation of India* v. *Food Corporation of India* (AIR 1985 SC 670), *M.M.R. Khan* v. *Union of India* (AIR 1990 SC 937), *Surender Prasad Khugsal* v. *Chairman, MMT Corporation of India Ltd.* (1993 AIR SCW 3191) etc. prescribed following conditions whereby the canteen workers would be declared as the employee of management and they are as follows:

(i) Where, as under the provision of the Factories Act, it is statutorily obligatory on the employer to provide and maintain canteen for the use of his employees, the canteen becomes a part of the establishment and, therefore, the workers employed in such canteen are the employees of the management.

(ii) Where, although it is not statutorily obligatory to provide a canteen, it is otherwise an obligation on the employer to provide a canteen, the canteen becomes a part of the establishment and the workers working in the canteen, the employees of the management. The obligation to provide a canteen has to be distinguished from the obligation to provide facilities to run canteen. The canteen run pursuant to the latter obligation does not become a part of the establishment.

(iii) The obligation to provide canteen may be explicit or implicit. Where the obligation is not explicitly accepted by or cast upon the employer either by an agreement or an award etc., it may be inferred from the circumstances, and the provision of the canteen may be held to have become a part of the service conditions of the employees. Whether the provision for canteen services has become a part of the service conditions or not, is a question of fact to be determined on the facts and circumstances in each case.

Where to provide canteen services has become a part of the service conditions of the employees, the canteen becomes a part of the establishment and the workers in such canteen become the employees of the management.

(iv) Whether a particular facility or service has become implicitly a part of the service conditions of the employees or not, will depend, among others, on the nature of the service/facility, the contribution the service in question makes to the efficiency of the employees and the establishment, whether the service is available as a matter of right to all the employees in their capacity as employees and nothing, more, the number of employees employed in the establishment and the number of employees who avail of the service, the length of time for which the service has been continuously available, the hours during which it is available, the nature and character of management, the interest taken by the employer in providing, maintaining, supervising and controlling the service, the contribution made by the management in the form of infrastructure and funds for making the service available etc.

In 1999 the decision of a three-Judge Bench of the Supreme Court in *Indian Petrochemicals Corporation Ltd.* v. *Shramik Sena* (AIR 1999 SC 2577) can be divided in to two segments. The first part of the decision is based on the interpretation of the law and provides due respect to the precedent. The second part of the decision is totally based on the fact matrix available.

The Supreme Court in this case held that it is clear from this definition that a person employed either directly or by or through any contractor in a place where manufacturing process is carried on, is a '*workman*' for the purpose of the Factories Act. Section 46 of the Factories Act empowers the State Government to make rules requiring any specified factory wherein more than 250 workers are ordinarily employed to provide and maintain a canteen by the occupier for the use of the workers. It is not disputed in this case that as per the requirement of law, the management is providing canteen facilities wherein the respondent employees are working. Hence, it is held that that the respondent workmen by virtue of the definition of the *'workman'* under the Factories Act are the employees of the appellant-management for purposes of the Factories Act only.

Further the Court while giving due respect to its earlier decisions of *Khan* case (supra) and RBI case (*Management of Reserve Bank of India* v. *Workmen*, AIR 1996 SC 1241) which were decided by a three-Judge Bench held that the workmen of a statutory canteen would be the workmen of the establishment for the purpose of the Factories Act only and not for all other purposes. Accordingly the Supreme Court held as follows:

> "If the argument of the workmen in regard to the interpretation of Raha's case (1995 AIR SCW 2609: AIR 1995 SC 1666: 1995 Lab IC 2064) is to be accepted then the same would run counter to the law laid down by a larger Bench of this Court in Khan's case (AIR 1990 SC 937) (supra). On this point similar is the view of another three-Judge Bench of this Court in the case of *Employers in relation to the Management of Reserve Bank of India* v. *Workmen* (1996) 3 SCC 267: (1996 AIR SCW 1298: AIR 1996 SC 1241: 1996 Lab IC 1048). Therefore, following the judgment of this Court in the cases of Khan and R.B.I. (supra), we hold that the workmen of a statutory canteen would be the workmen of the establishment for the purpose of the Factories Act only and not for all other purposes."

The Supreme Court however in this instant case evaluated the following facts which are as follows:

(a) The canteen has been there since the inception of the appellant's factory.
(b) The workmen have been employed of long years and despite change of contractors the workers have continued to be employed in the canteen.
(c) The premises, furniture, fixture, fuel, electricity, utensils etc. have been provided for by the appellant.
(d) The wages of the canteen workers have to be reimbursed by the appellant.
(e) The supervision and control on the canteen is exercised by the appellant through its authorised officer, as can be seen from the various clauses of the contract between the appellant and the contractor.
(f) The contractor is nothing but an agent or a manager of the appellant, who works completely under the supervision, control and directions of the appellant.
(g) The workmen have the protection of continuous employment in the establishment.

Based on the above fact the Supreme Court held in this instant case that the canteen in the establishment of the management is a statutory canteen, therefore the respondent-workmen are in fact the workmen of the appellant-management.

In 2001 a Constitution Bench in *Steel Authority of India Ltd.* v. *National Union Water Front Workers* (AIR 2001 SC 3527) which is popularly known as *SAIL* case needs a special reference so far as canteen issue is concerned. It is important to cite the following paragraph which needs a special treatment. Paragraph 105 reads as follows:

> 105. An analysis of the cases, discussed above, shows that they fall in three classes; (i) where contract labour is engaged in or in connection with the work of an establishment and employment of contract labour is prohibited either because the Industrial adjudicator/ Court ordered abolition of contract labour or because the appropriate Government issued notification under Section 10(1) of the CLRA Act, no automatic absorption of the contract labour working in the establishment was ordered; (ii) where the contract was found to be sham and nominal rather a camouflage in which case the contract labour working in the

> establishment of the principal employer was held, in fact and in reality, the employees of the principal employer himself. Indeed, such cases do not relate to abolition of contract labour but present instances wherein the Court pierced the veil and declared the correct position as a fact at the stage after employment of contract labour stood prohibited; *(iii) where in discharge of a statutory obligation of maintaining canteen in an establishment the principal employer availed the services of a contractor and the Courts have held that the contract labour would indeed be the employees of the principal employer.*

Point No. (iii) stated above is relating to canteen issue hence require a thread bare discussion in order to ascertain its precedent value which would be binding to the Supreme Court. The Supreme Court in *SAIL* case was primarily concerned with the meaning of the expression "*appropriate Government*" in Section 2(1)(a) of the Contract Labour (Regulation and Abolition) Act, 1970 and in Section 2(a) of the Industrial Disputes Act, 1947 and the other issue was—automatic absorption of the contract labour in the establishment of the principal employer as a consequence of an abolition notification issued under Section 10(1) of the Contract Labour (Regulation and Abolition) Act. In SAIL case the Constitutional Bench discussed several decisions which were brought to its notice and accordingly summarized the view expressed in those decisions in three categories. Therefore point no. (iii) can not be considered *'the law declared'* by the Court. In short it can be said that it is not a '*ratio*' of the Court rather may be '*obitur dictum*' which does not possess any binding force.

In 2002, the Supreme Court in *H.S. Sharma* v. *M/s. Artificial Limbs Manufacturing Corpn.*[24] observed that merely because the canteen had been set up pursuant to a statutory obligation under S. 46 of the Factories Act, it cannot be said that employees in the canteen were the employees of Govt. of India undertaking. Even assuming that S. 46 of the Factories Act was applicable to the Govt. of India undertaking, it cannot be said as an absolute proposition of law that whenever in discharge of a statutory mandate, a canteen is set up or other facility provided by an establishment, the employees of the canteen or such other facility become the employees of that establishment. It would depend on how the obligation is discharged by the establishment. It may be carried out wholly or substantially by the establishment itself or the burden may be delegated to an independent contractor. There is nothing in S. 46 of the Factories Act nor has any provision of any other statute been pointed out to court by the workmen, which provides for the mode in which the specified establishment must set up a canteen. Where it is left to the discretion of the establishment concerned to discharge its obligation of setting up a canteen either by way of direct recruitment or by employment of a contractor, it cannot be postulated that in the latter event, the persons working in the canteen would be the employees of the establishment. Therefore, even assuming that the Govt. of India undertaking is a specified industry within the meaning of S. 46 of the Factories Act, 1946, this by itself would not lead to the inevitable conclusion that the employees in the canteen are the employees of Govt. of India undertaking.

The Court further held that from a scrutiny of the agreement, it is clear that although the Govt. of India undertaking had agreed to provide the contractor with the basic infrastructure, the actual running of the canteen was the responsibility of the contractor alone. The contractor was obliged to provide all the facilities available to the workers under various labour laws applicable to the Govt. of India undertaking. The contractor was also required to abide by

24. AIR 2002 SC 226.

all the provisions of labour laws as applicable from time to time and was liable for financial obligations under various labour laws as amended from time to time. In case the contractor contravened any provisions of those laws and the Govt. of India undertaking suffered any damage, loss or harm due to any act of commission or omission of the contractor, the contractor was bound to indemnify the Govt. of India undertaking. Similarly, agreements also provided that the Contractor shall be responsible for discharge of legal liabilities towards his employees and also for observing all laws and Government Rules relating to labour, viz. EPF Act, ESI Act, Payment of Wages Act, Minimum Wages Act and health in so far as they relate to the canteen. The contractor was given the discretion to employ the workers already working the canteen (like the appellants), but it was made clear that the contractor could take action against the canteen workers. It is noteworthy that the Govt. of India undertaking had no say as to who should be employed by the contractor and what is the method of recruitment to be followed by the contractor. There was no obligation on the contractor to employ the persons who had served under earlier contractors. Even if the agreements had contained a condition that the contractor must retain the old employees, it would not necessarily mean that those employees were the employees of the establishment. The workmen are, therefore, employees of contractor and cannot claim to be workmen of Govt. of India undertaking.[25]

In 2003, in *Mishra Dhatu Nigam Ltd.* v. *M. Venkataiah*[26] and in *National Thermal Power Corporation Ltd.* v. *Karri Pothuraju*,[27] The Supreme Court in both the cases held that under S. 46 of the Factories Act, 1948, the principal employer has statutory duty to provide canteen for its workmen. While discharging such statutory obligation, the principal employer is availing services of contractors to provide the canteen facility to its employees. Therefore, the canteen employees would be employees of principal employer and they would be entitled to regularisation of services and salary at par with regular employees.

In 2005, in *Haldia Refinery Canteen Employees Union* v. *M/s. Indian Oil Corpn. Ltd* (AIR 2005 SC 2412), where the fact of the instant case reveals that the contractor had been given free hand for engagement of the employees who would be working in the canteen. There was no clause in the agreement stipulating that canteen contractor shall retain and engage compulsorily the employees who were already working in the canteen under the previous contractor. There was no stipulation in the contract that the employees working in the canteen at the time of the commencement of the contract must be retained by the contractor. The management was not reimbursing the wages of the workmen engaged in the canteen. Rather the contractor had been made liable to pay provident fund contribution, leave salary, medical benefits to his employees and to observe statutory working hours. The contractor has also been made responsible for the proper maintenance of registers, records and accounts so far as compliance of any statutory provisions/obligations are concerned. A duty had been cast on the contractor to keep proper records pertaining to payment of wages etc. and also for depositing the provident fund contributions with authorities concerned. Contractor had been made liable to defend, indemnify and hold harmless the employer from any liability or penalty which may be imposed by the Central, State or local authorities by reason of any violation by the

25. *Hari Shankar Sharma and others* v. *M/s Artificial Limbs Manufacturing Corporation and others,* 2002 (92) FLR 14.
26. AIR 2003 SC 3124.
27. AIR 2003 SC 3647.

contractor of such laws, regulations and also from all claims, suits or proceedings that may be brought against the management arising under or incidental to or by reason of the work provided/assigned under the contract brought by employees of the contractor, third party or by Central or State Government Authorities. The management had kept with it the right to test, interview or otherwise assess or determine the quality of the employees/workers with regard to their level of skills, knowledge, proficiency, capability etc. so as to ensure that the employees/workers are competent and qualified and suitable for efficient performance of the work covered under the contract. The Supreme Court held that this control has been kept by the management to keep a check over the quality of service provided to its employees. It has nothing to do with either the appointment or taking disciplinary action or dismissal or removal from service of the workmen working in the canteen. Further the Supreme Court observed that only because the management exercises such control does not mean that the employees working in the canteen are the employees of the management. Such supervisory control is being exercised by the management to ensure that the workers employed are well qualified and capable of rendering the proper service to the employees of the management.

Another fact which goes to show that these workers are the employees of the canteen contractor is that a settlement was arrived at between the contractor and the workmen of the canteen in the presence of Assistant Labour Commissioner of the area wherein certain terms and conditions were agreed upon between these parties with regard to some labour issues relating to the workmen employed by the contractor. Another settlement between the same parties was also arrived at concerning once again the labour issues between the workmen and the contractor. Respondent-management was not a party to either of these two settlements. This clearly goes to show that the workmen were treating themselves to be the employees of the contractor and not that of the management. Therefore, the Court held that they would not become workers of the management for a purpose other than the Factories Act. These workers consequently would not be entitled to claim absorption or regularization in the services of the management.

In 2008 in *Hindalco Industries Ltd.* v. *Association of Engineering Workers* (AIR 2008 SC 1867) the question arises before the Supreme Court that whether the points for consideration in this appeal are (1) whether the Industrial Court is justified in issuing direction to absorb all the employees of the canteen in the company's employment and pay them wages and other benefits to the extent of last category of unskilled workers in the company; (ii) whether the High Court is right in affirming the said order?

From the evidence adduced before the Industrial Tribunal and other materials, the Supreme Court in this case noted the following information:

(a) Canteen has been in existence since 1965.

(b) Canteen employees were working in four shifts.

(c) Canteen is situated in the company premises.

(d) The company has provided utensils, gas and other articles like chair, table, etc.

(e) The company has also provided room to the canteen employees for their residential complex.

(f) Seven to Eight employees who are bachelors are residing in the said room.

(g) The company has provided electricity and water. Respective charges are not being deducted from the wages of the employees.

(h) The company has also supplied umbrellas for the rainy season.

(i) The company is paying maintenance charge and electricity charge and other expenses of the canteen.

(j) All the facilities including premises to the canteen are provided by the company.

(k) The wages of employees of the canteen are reimbursed by the company.

(l) The company is purchasing the food items.

(m) Whenever there is rise in the wages of the employees, it is the company who is to pay the same.

(n) The company is providing three sets of uniforms to the employees and also providing service washer men.

(o) The employer's contribution P.F. is reimbursed by the company.

(p) In the past the company has regularized some of the employees working in the canteen.

From the above, it is clear that all the facilities to the canteen are provided by the company. It is relevant to mention that in spite of the changes in the Canteen Contractor the service of the canteen employees continued and they were not issued fresh appointment orders by any of the canteen contractors. Accordingly the Court held that

> "The above details clearly show that though certain amounts are being paid by the contractor, in the real sense, ultimately, it is the company which pays all the amounts. From the evidence and the materials, it is also clear that the activities of the workmen in the canteen, their suitability to work, and physical fitness are ultimately controlled by the company. In those circumstances, the Industrial Court is perfectly right in arriving the conclusion that the evidence coupled with the terms of agreement show that the contract is nothing but paper agreement. As stated earlier, in spite of change of several contractors, neither the workmen were replaced nor fresh appointments were made. On the other hand, same workmen were continuing even on the date of filing of the complaint. Taking note of all the above-mentioned relevant materials, special circumstances and most of the employees are working for more than 10-15 years and finding that there is no valid reason for the company to deny their permanency, the Industrial Court rightly concluded that the company has committed unfair labour practice under Item 9 of Schedule IV of the MRTU and PULP Act, 1971 and issued appropriate directions. With the materials placed, we are also of the opinion that even though the record shows that canteen is being run by the contractor, ultimate control and supervision over the canteen is of the Company."

Therefore the Supreme Court upheld the decision of the Industrial Tribunal.

In 2014 in *Balwant Rai Saluja* v. *Air India Ltd.* (2014) 9 SCC 407 where in view of the difference of opinion by two learned Judges of the Supreme Court this case has been referred to a Three Judge bench of the Supreme Court on 13.11.2013. The question before this Bench is whether the workmen engaged in statutory canteens, through a contractor, could be treated as employees of the principal establishment. The Two Judge bench has expressed contrasting opinions on the prevalence of an employer–employee relationship between the principal employer and the workers in the said canteen facility, based on, *inter alia*, issues surrounding the economic dependence of the subsidiary role in management and maintenance of the canteen premises, representation of workers, modes of appointment and termination as well as resolving disciplinary issues among workmen. The Bench also differed on the issue pertaining to whether such workmen should be treated as employees of the principal employer only for the purposes of the Factories Act, 1948 or for other purposes as well.

At the outset, it requires to be noticed that the learned Judges differed in their opinion regarding the liability of the principal employer running statutory canteens and further regarding the status of the workmen engaged thereof. The learned Judges differed on the aspect of supervision and control which was exercised by the Air India Ltd. and the Hotel Corporations of India Ltd over the said workmen employed in these canteens. The learned Judges also had varying interpretations regarding the status of the HCI as a sham and camouflage subsidiary by the Air India created mainly to deprive the legitimate statutory and fundamental rights of the concerned workmen and the necessity to pierce the veil to ascertain their relation with the principal employer.

Facts

The present dispute finds origin in an industrial dispute which arose between the Appellants-workmen herein of the statutory canteen and Respondent No. 1 (AIR India). The said industrial dispute was referred by the Central Government to the Central Government Industrial Tribunal cum Labour Court (for short "the CGIT"). The question referred was whether the workmen as employed by Respondent No. 3 (the Chefair) to provide canteen services at the establishment of AIR India could be treated as deemed employees of AIR India? The CGIT held that the workmen were employees of Air India and therefore their claim was justified. However the learned Single Judge of the High Court of Delhi set aside and quashed the CGIT's award and held that the said workmen would not be entitled to be treated as or deemed to be the employees of the Air India. The Division Bench of the High Court of Delhi found no error in the order passed by the learned Single Judge of the High Court. The appeal was dismissed by the Division Bench confirming the order of the learned Single Judge.

For better understanding it is to be noted that Respondent No. 1—Air India is a company incorporated under the Companies Act, 1956 and is owned by the Government of India. The primary object of the said company is to provide international air transport/travel services. It has Ground Services Department at Indira Gandhi International Airport, Delhi. The Labour Department vide its notification has enlisted the said M/s. Air India Ground Services Department within the purview of Factories Act, 1948. Section 46 of the Act, 1948 statutorily places an obligation on the occupier of a factory to provide and maintain a canteen in the factory where more than two hundred and fifty workers are employed. There is nothing in the said provision which provides for the mode in which the factory must set up a canteen. It appears to be left to the discretion of the concerned factory to either discharge the said obligation of setting up a canteen either by way of direct involvement or through a contractor or any other third party.

Respondent No. 2-HCI is also a company incorporated under the Companies Act, 1956 and is a separate legal entity from the Air India. As per the Memorandum of Association of HCI, the same is a wholly-owned subsidiary of the Air India. The main objects of HCI, *inter alia,* are to establish refreshment rooms, canteens, etc. for the sale of food, beverages, etc.

HCI has various units and Respondent No. 3, being Chefair Flight Catering (for short, "the Chefair"), provides flight catering services to various airlines, including Air India. It is this Chefair unit of HCI that operates and runs the canteen. It requires to be noticed that the appellants-workmen are engaged on a casual or temporary basis by the respondent Nos. 2 (HCI) and 3 (Chefair) to render canteen services on the premises of respondent No. 1—Air India.

In the present case, the appellants are workers who claim to be the deemed employees of the management of Air India on the grounds, *inter alia*, that they work in a canteen established on the premises of the respondent No. 1—Air India and that too, for the benefit of the employees of Air India . It is urged that since the canteen is maintained as a consequence of a statutory obligation under Section 46 of the Act, 1948, and the said workers should be held to be the employees of the management of the corporation, on which such statutory obligation is placed, that is, Air India.

Issue

The main issue for consideration before the Supreme Court is "*whether workers, engaged on a casual or temporary basis by a contractor (HCI) to operate and run a statutory canteen, under the provisions of the Act, 1948, on the premises of a factory—Air India, can be said to be the workmen of the said factory or corporation*".

Discussion and findings

The Supreme Court in this case observed that to ascertain whether the workers of the contractor can be treated as the employees of the factory or company on whose premises they run the said statutory canteen, the Court must apply the test of "*complete administrative control*". Furthermore, it would be necessary to show that there exists an "*employer–employee relationship between the factory and the workmen working in the canteen*". After referring many cases decided by the Supreme Court, the Court in this case concluded that the relevant factors to be taken into consideration to establish an *employer–employee relationship* would include, *inter alia*,

(i) Who appoints the workers;
(ii) Who pays the salary/remuneration;
(iii) Who has the authority to dismiss;
(iv) Who can take disciplinary action;
(v) Whether there is continuity of service; and
(vi) Extent of control and supervision, i.e. whether there exists complete control and supervision.

In the present case, it is an admitted fact that the HCI is a wholly owned subsidiary of the Air India. It has been urged by the learned counsel for the appellants that this Court should pierce the veil and declare that the HCI is a sham and a camouflage. Therefore, the liability regarding the appellants herein would fall upon the Air India, not the HCI. In this regard, it would be pertinent to elaborate the principle of lifting the corporate veil.

The Supreme Court referred a plethora of judgments of the English Court, US Court and Indian Supreme Court and held that the doctrine of piercing the veil allows the Court to disregard the separate legal personality of a company and impose liability upon the persons exercising real control over the said company. However, this principle has been and should be applied in a restrictive manner, that is, only in scenarios wherein it is evident that the company was a mere camouflage or sham deliberately created by the persons exercising control over the said company for the purpose of avoiding liability. The intent of piercing the veil must be such that would seek to remedy a wrong done by the persons controlling the company. The application would thus depend upon the peculiar facts and circumstances of each case. The Supreme Court accordingly held that the present facts would not be a fit case to pierce the veil. Further, for piercing the veil of incorporation, mere ownership and control is not a sufficient ground. It should be established that the control and impropriety by the Air India resulted in depriving the Appellants-workmen herein of their legal rights. Further, on perusal of the Memorandum of Association and Articles of Association of the HCI, it cannot be said that the Air India intended to create HCI as a mere façade for the purpose of avoiding liability towards the Appellants-workmen in this case.

To ascertain whether the appellants-workmen would be declared the employees of Air India, the Supreme Court would have to apply the test of employer-employee relationship as discussed earlier. For the said purpose, it would be necessary to refer to the Memorandum of Association and the Articles of Association of the HCI to look into the nature of the activities it undertakes. The objects of the HCI, as provided under its Memorandum of Association, *inter alia*, include the following:

(i) To carry on the business of hotel, motel, restaurant, café, tavern, flight kitchen, refreshment room and boarding and lodging, housekeepers, licensed victuallers, etc.;
(ii) To provide lodging and boarding and other facilities to the public;
(iii) To purchase, erect, take on lease or otherwise acquire, equip and manage hotels;
(iv) To establish shops, kitchens, refreshment rooms, canteens and depots for the sale of various food and beverages.

The objects incidental or ancillary to the main objects include, *inter alia:*

> "... (5) To carry on any business by means of operating hotels etc. or other activity which would tend to promote or assist Air-India's business as an international air carrier. ..."

It can be noticed from the above, that the primary objects of the HCI have no direct relation with the Air India. It is only one of the many incidental or ancillary objects of the HCI that make a direct reference to assisting Air India. The argument that the HCI runs the canteen solely for Air India's purpose and benefit could not succeed in this light. The HCI has several primary objects, which include the running of hotels, motels, etc., in addition to establishing shops, kitchens, canteens and refreshment rooms. The Air India only finds mention under HCI's ancillary objects. It cannot be said that the Memorandum of Association of the HCI provides that HCI functions only for Air India. Nor can it be said that the fundamental activity of the HCI is to run and operate the said statutory canteen for the Air India.

Therefore, The Supreme Court in light of the above discussion held that the appellants-workmen could not be said to be under the *"effective and absolute control"* of Air India. The Air India merely has control of supervision over the working of the given statutory canteen.

Issues regarding appointment of the said workmen, their dismissal, payment of their salaries, etc. are within the control of the HCI. It cannot be then said that the appellants are the workmen of Air India and therefore are entitled to regularization of their services. It would also be gainsaid to note the fact that the appellants-workmen made no claim or prayer against either of the other respondents, that is, the HCI or the Chefair.

The Supreme Court while dismissing the appeal answered the referral order as follows;

> "The workers engaged by a contractor to work in the statutory canteen of a factory would be the workers of the said factory, but only for the purposes of the Act, 1948, and not for other purposes, and further for the said workers, to be called the employees of the factory for all purposes, they would need to satisfy the test of employer-employee relationship and it must be shown that the employer exercises absolute and effective control over the said workers."

SECTION 47: Shelters, rest rooms and lunch rooms

(1) In every factory wherein more than one hundred and fifty workers are ordinarily employed, adequate and suitable shelters or rest rooms and a suitable lunch room, with provision for drinking water, where workers can eat meals brought by them, shall be provided and maintained for the use of the workers:

Provided that any canteen maintained in accordance with the provisions of section 46 shall be regarded as part of the requirements of this sub-section:

Provided further that where a lunch room exists no workers shall eat any food in the work room.

(2) The shelters or rest rooms or lunch rooms to be provided under sub-section (1) shall be sufficiently lighted and ventilated and shall be maintained in a cool and clean condition.

(3) The State Government may—

(a) prescribe the standards in respect of construction, accommodation, furniture and other equipment of shelters, rest rooms and lunch rooms to be provided under this section;

(b) by notification in the Official Gazette, exempt any factory or class or description of factories from the requirements of this section.

SECTION 48: Creches

(1) In every factory wherein more than thirty women workers are ordinarily employed there shall be provided and maintained a suitable room or rooms for the use of children under the age of six years of such women.

(2) Such rooms shall provide adequate accommodation, shall be adequately lighted and ventilated, shall be maintained in a clean and sanitary condition and shall be under the charge of women trained in the care of children and infants.

(3) The State Government may make rules—

(a) prescribing the location and the standards in respect of construction, accommodation, furniture and other equipment of rooms to be provided, under this section;

(b) requiring the provision in factories to which this section applies of additional facilities for the care of children belonging to women workers, including suitable provision of facilities for washing and changing their clothing;

(c) requiring the provision in any factory of free milk or refreshment or both for such children;

(d) requiring that facilities shall be given in any factory for the mothers of such children to feed them at the necessary intervals.

SECTION 49: Welfare officers

(1) In every factory wherein five hundred or more workers are ordinarily employed the occupier shall employ in the factory such number of Welfare officers as may be prescribed.

(2) The State Government may prescribe the duties, qualifications and Conditions of service of officers employed under sub-section (1).

SECTION 50: Power to make rules to supplement this chapter

The State Government may make rules—

(a) exempting, subject to compliance with such alternative arrangements for the welfare of workers as may be prescribed, any factory or class or description of factories from compliance with any of the provisions of this Chapter;

(b) requiring in any factory or class or description of factories that representatives of the workers employed in the factory shall be associated with the management of the welfare arrangements of the workers.

CHAPTER VI

WORKING HOURS OF ADULTS

SECTION 51: Weekly hours

No adult workers shall be required or allowed to work in a factory for more than forty-eight hours in any week.

SECTION 52: Weekly holidays

(1) No adult worker shall be required or allowed to work in a factory on the first day of the week (hereinafter referred to as the said day), unless—

(a) he has or will have a holiday for a whole day on one of the three days immediately before or after the said day, and

(b) the manager of the factory has, before the said day or the substituted day under clause (a), whichever is earlier,—

(i) delivered a notice at the office of the Inspector of his intention to require the worker to work on the said day and of the day which is to be substituted, and

(ii) displayed a notice to that effect in the factory:

Provided that no substitution shall be made which will result in any worker working for more than ten days consecutively without a holiday for a whole day.

(2) Notices given under sub-section (1) may be cancelled by a notice delivered at the office of the Inspector and a notice displayed in the factory not later than the day before the said day or the holiday to be cancelled, whichever is earlier.

(3) Where, in accordance with the provisions of sub-section (1), any worker works on the said day and has had a holiday on one of the three days immediately before it, that said day shall, for the purpose of calculating his weekly hours of work, be included in the preceding week.

In *John Douglas Keith Brown* v. *State of W.B.*,[28] the only point urged before the Supreme Court was whether the occupier of a factory is liable to penalty under S. 92 of the Factories Act, 1948 for the contravention of the provisions of S. 52 of the Act. The facts of the case reveal that the appellant is the Managing Director of Jardine Henderson Ltd., Calcutta, who were the managing agents of the Howrah Mills Co. Ltd., of Ramkristopur, District Howrah and as such "occupiers" of the Mills within the definition of the term contained in S. 2(n) of the Act. One J.P. Bell was the Manager of the Mills in June, 1957. Both the appellant and Bell were charged with an offence under S. 92 of the Act read with S. 52.

The contention of the appellant is that under Cl. (b) of sub-section (1) of S. 52 of the Act, a duty is cast upon the manager of the factory to give a notice to the appropriate authority of change in the weekly holiday from the first day of the week to any other day and not upon the occupier. According to the learned counsel, the omission of the manager to give such notice would not render the occupier liable in any way unless it is shown that there was any connivance on his part of a breach of duty by the manager. This, it is contended, must necessarily imply that unless the occupier had the *mens rea* to contravene the provisions of S. 52(1) of the Act, he would not be liable for the contravention. In the absence of any evidence to the effect that the appellant knew of the omission and yet connived at it, his conviction and sentence ought, therefore, to be quashed.

The opening words of S. 52(1) indicate a prohibition from requiring or permitting an adult worker to work in a factory on the first day of the week. The prohibition is, however, lifted if steps are taken under Cls. (a) and (b) of S. 52(1). A perusal of Cl. (b) makes it abundantly clear that what is required to be done thereunder, that is to say, to give and display

28. AIR 1965 SC 1341.

a notice is only for the purpose of securing an exemption from the prohibition contained in the opening parts of S. 52 of the Act. Clause (b) cannot, therefore, be linked to some other provisions of the Act, which impose a positive duty upon the manager to do something. The prohibition contained in the opening words of this sub-section is general and is not confined to the Manager. It would, therefore, follow that where something is done in breach of the prohibition enacted in S. 52(1), both the Manager and the occupier will be liable to the penalties prescribed in that section.

From the facts of the case, it is found that the Manager had apprised the occupier of what he was proposing to do. The appellant took no steps to restrain the Manager from putting the new schedule in operation, which was in itself in violation of the opening words of S. 52. The Court pointed out that what the provisions of S. 52(1)(a) and (b) permit is to grant exemptions to specified workmen from the operation of the prohibition enacted in S. 52 from working in factories on weekly holidays. No general permission can be granted under Cls. (a) and (b) of sub-section (1) of S. 52 for altering the day of the weekly holiday so as to cover all the workmen. Therefore, upon the proper construction of the provisions it is clear that whenever workers are required or are permitted to work on a weekly holiday, the specific permission of the Chief Inspector of Factories in respect of each and every worker who is required to work on such a day should be obtained. That being the provision of law, the occupier must be deemed to have known it. Being duly apprised of the fact that the Mill Manager was seeking to start the 'C' shift from 8.30 p.m. on Sunday without specifically mentioning the names of those workmen who had to work in that shift, he was doing something which was not within the purview of Cls. (a) and (b) of sub-section (1) of S. 52. Of this fact the occupier had actual knowledge and, therefore, he must be held guilty of the contravention of the provisions of S. 52 of the Act.

SECTION 53: Compensatory holidays

(1) Where, as a result of the passing of an order or the making of a rule under the provisions of this Act exempting a factory or the workers therein from the provisions of S. 52, a worker is deprived of any of the weekly holidays for which provision is made in sub-section (1) of that section, he shall be allowed, within the month in which the holidays were due to him or within the two months immediately following that month, compensatory holidays of equal number to the holidays so lost.

(2) The State Government may prescribe the manner in which the holidays for which provision is made in sub-section (1) shall be allowed.

SECTION 54: Daily hours

Subject to the provisions of section 51, no adult worker shall be required or allowed to work in a factory for more than nine hours in any day:

Provided that, subject to the previous approval of the Chief inspector, the daily maximum hours specified in this section may be exceeded in order to facilitate the change of shifts.

SECTION 55: Intervals for rest

(1) The periods of work of adult workers in a factory each day shall be so fixed that no period shall exceed five hours and that no worker shall work for more than five hours before he has had an interval for rest of at least half an hour.

(2) The State Government or, subject to the control of the State Government, the Chief Inspector, may, by written order and for the reasons specified therein, exempt any factory from the provisions of sub-section (1) so however that the total number of hours worked by a worker without an interval does not exceed six.

It has been urged on behalf of the appellants in *Workmen of the Motipur Sugar Factory Private Ltd.* v. *Motipur Sugar Factory Private Ltd.*[29] that the crushing speed of 32,000 maunds per 24 hours is not correctly arrived at, for it does not take into account half hour's rest per shift which is permissible under S. 55(1) of the Factories Act. Thus, according to the appellants, crushing speed should be worked out on 22½ hours per day and the crushing will then be less by 1/16th and will only come to 30,000 maunds per day. Reliance in this connection is placed on S. 55(2) of the Factories Act, which lays down that

"the State Government ... may by written order and for the reasons specified therein, exempt any factory from the provisions of sub-section (1) so however that the total number of hours worked by a worker without an interval does not exceed six."

It is therefore urged that the workmen were entitled to half an hour's rest per shift in any case because the shift was for eight hours. The respondent, on the other hand, relies on S. 64(2)(d) of the Factories Act and its case is that the State Government had made rules under that provision in connection with sugar factories, which apply to it. Section 64(2)(d) is in these terms:

"The State Government may make rules in respect of adult workers in factories providing for the exemption, to such extent and subject to such conditions as may be prescribed—

(d) of workers engaged in any work which for technical reasons must be carried on continuously from the provisions of Ss. 51, 52, 54, 55 and 56."

After reading both the provisions, the Court is of opinion that S. 64(2)(d) being a special provision will override both the sub-sections (1) and (2) of S. 55, for it gives power to the State Government by making rules to exempt certain types of factories from the application of the whole of S. 55, subject to such conditions and to such extent as the rules may provide. It appears that the rules were framed in this behalf by the Government of Bihar in 1950 by which sugar factories were exempted from the application of S. 55 for purpose of handling and crushing of cane, among others, subject to the condition that the workers concerned shall be allowed to take light refreshment or meals at the place of their employment, or in a room specially reserved for the purposes or in a canteen provided in the factory, once during any period exceeding four hours. Thus, cane crushing operations are exempt from S. 55(1) and S. 55(2) subject to the condition mentioned above. The Court has also referred S. 64(5) which lays down that the rules made under this section shall remain in force for not more than three years. [Three years has been substituted for five years] The rules to which

29. AIR 1965 SC 1803.

reference has been made are of 1950; but there is nothing to show that these rules were not continued after every interval of three years and the position that the exemption applies to sugar factories even now as provided in these rules was not disputed. Accordingly, the Court held that on the basis that the exemption applied to sugar factories in Bihar, the workmen cannot claim half an hour's rest per shift as urged on their behalf, though some time must be allowed for refreshment or light meals as provided in the provision granting exemption. This means that a few minutes would be allowed to each individual in turn in each shift for light refreshment or meals in such a way that the work does not stop.

Section 56: Spread over

The periods of work of an adult worker in a factory shall be so arranged that inclusive of his intervals for rest under section 55, they shall not spread over more than ten and a half hours in any day:

Provided that the Chief Inspector may, for reasons to be specified in writing, increase the spread over up to twelve hours.

Section 57: Night shifts

Where a worker in a factory works on a shift which extends beyond midnight,—

(a) for the purposes of sections 52 and 53, a holiday for a whole day shall mean in his case a period of twenty-four consecutive hours beginning when his shift ends;

(b) the following day for him shall be deemed to be the period of twenty-four hours beginning when such shift ends, and the hours he has worked after midnight shall be counted in the previous day.

Section 58: Prohibition of overlapping shifts

(1) Work shall not be carried on in any factory by means of a system of shifts so arranged that more than one relay of workers is engaged, in work of the same kind at the same time.

(2) The State Government or subject to the control of the State Government, the Chief Inspector, may, by written order and for the reasons specified therein, exempt on such conditions as may be deemed expedient, any factory or class or description of factories or any department or section of a factory or any category or description of workers therein from the provisions of sub-section (1).

Section 59: Extra wages for overtime

(1) Where a worker works in a factory for more than nine hours in any day or for more than forty-eight hours in any week, he shall, in respect of overtime work, be entitled to wages at the rate of twice his ordinary rate of wages.

(2) For the purposes of sub-section (1), "ordinary rate of wages" means the basic wages plus such allowances, including the cash equivalent of the advantage accruing

through the concessional sale to workers of foodgrains and other articles, as the worker is for the time being entitled to, but does not include a bonus and wages for overtime work.

(3) Where any workers in a factory are paid on a piece-rate basis, the time rate shall be deemed to be equivalent to the daily average of their full-time earnings for the days on which they actually worked on the same or identical job during the month immediately preceding the calendar month during which the overtime work was done, and such time rates shall be deemed to be the ordinary rates of wages of those workers:

Provided that in the case of a worker who has not worked in the immediately preceding calendar month on the same or identical job, the time rate shall be deemed to be equivalent to the daily average of the earnings of the worker for the days on which he actually worked in the week in which the overtime work was done.

Explanation: For the purposes of this sub-section, in computing the earnings for the days on which the worker actually worked such allowances, including the cash equivalent of the advantage accruing through the concessional sale to workers of foodgrains and other articles, as the worker is for the time being entitled to, shall be included but any bonus or wages for overtime work payable in relation to the period with reference to which the earnings are being computed shall be excluded.

(4) The cash equivalent of the advantage accruing through the concessional sale to a worker of foodgrains and other articles shall be computed as often as may be prescribed on the basis of the maximum quantity of foodgrains and other articles admissible to a standard family.

Explanation 1: Standard family means a family consisting of the worker, his or her spouse and two children below the age of fourteen years requiring in all three adult consumption units.

Explanation 2: Adult consumption unit means the consumption unit of a male above the age of fourteen years; and the consumption unit of a female above the age of fourteen years and that of a child below the age of fourteen years shall be calculated at the rates of 0.8 and 0.6 respectively of one adult consumption unit.

(5) The State Government may make rules prescribing—

(a) the manner in which the cash equivalent of the advantage accruing through the concessional sale to a worker of foodgrains and other articles shall be computed; and

(b) the registers that shall be maintained in a factory for the purpose of securing compliance with the provisions of this section.

Section 59 postulates payment of extra wages at twice the ordinary rate of wages for those workers of the factory who are required to work for more than 9 hours in a day or for more than 48 hours in a week. In *Clothing Factory, National Workers* v. *Union of India*,[30] the appellant union filed a writ petition in the High Court of Madras praying for an appropriate

30. AIR 1990 SC 1383.

writ or direction to the respondents to pay the piece-rated workers extra or overtime wages at the rate prescribed by S. 59(1) if the total working hours of any workman exceeded 44-3/4 hours in a week. The appellant-union contended that the piece-rate system was introduced sometime in 1963 and since then the piece-rate workers were paid overtime wages accordingly for work done beyond the normal working hours, but the same was abruptly discontinued from 1983; so much so that they were even denied the wage at the normal rate for work done beyond 44-3/4 hours and up to 48 hours, i.e., 3-1/4 hours. It is, however, admitted that if the workmen are required to work beyond 48 hours in a week, they are paid extra wages in accordance with S. 59(1) of the Factories Act. Thus, the controversy is in respect of the rate at which piece-rate workers should be paid wages for the work put in between 44-3/4 and 48 hours in a week. The workers claim they are entitled to extra wages for these 3-1/4 hours at double the normal rate in accordance with S. 59(1) of the Factories Act. In support reliance is placed on the Ministry of Defence letter No. F.8(5)/56/D(Civ.II) dated 1st September, 1959 which *inter alia* provides that in all cases where overtime pay is admissible to civilian personnel, both under the provisions of the Factories Act and Departmental Rules, the overtime pay should be calculated as under:

Whereunder the conditions of service of the Company the total hours of work, in their factory are 39 hours, any workman asked to work beyond these hours would obviously be working overtime and the company in fairness would be expected to pay him compensation for such overtime work. The Bihar Shops and Establishments Act under which the factory is declared as an establishment, has no relevance to this question as that Act fixes the maximum number of hours of work allowable thereunder, i.e., 48 hours a week, and provides for double the rate of ordinary wages for work done over and above 48 hours. It is not, therefore, as if the provisions of that Act govern overtime payment payable by an employer where maximum hours of work are governed by the conditions of service prevailing in the establishment. Therefore, no reliance can be placed on the provisions of that Act for the company's contention that it cannot be called upon to pay for overtime work anything more than its ordinary rate of wages if the workmen do work beyond 39 hours but not exceeding 48 hours a week. It is obvious that if the company were asked to pay at the rate equivalent to the ordinary rate of wages for work done beyond 39 hours but not exceeding 48 hours work a week, it would be paying no extra compensation at all for the work done beyond the agreed hours of work. The company would in that case be indirectly increasing the hours of work and consequently altering its conditions of service.[31]

Section 60: Restriction on double employment

No adult worker shall be required or allowed to work in any factory on any day on which he has already been working in any other factory, save in such circumstances as may be prescribed.

Section 61: Notice of periods of work for adults

(1) There shall be displayed and correctly maintained in every factory in accordance with the provisions of sub-section (2) of section 108, a notice of periods of work for

31. *Indian Oxygen Ltd.* v. *Workmen*, AIR 1969 SC 306.

adults, showing clearly for every day the periods during which adult workers may be required to work.

(2) The periods shown in the notice required by sub-section (1) shall be fixed beforehand in accordance with the following provisions of this section, and shall be such that workers working for those periods would not be working in contravention of any of the provisions of sections 51, 52, 53, 54, 55, 56 and 58.

(3) Where all the adult workers in a factory are required to work during the same periods, the manager of the factory shall fix those periods for such workers generally.

(4) Where all the adult workers in a factory are not required to work during the same periods, the manager of the factory shall classify them into groups according to the nature of their work indicating the number of workers in each group.

(5) For each group which is not required to work on a system of shifts, the manager of the factory shall fix the periods during which the group may be required to work.

(6) Where any group is required to work on a system of shifts and the relays are not to be subject to predetermined periodical changes of shifts, the manager of the factory shall fix the periods during which each relay of the group may be required to work.

(7) Where any group is to work on a system of shifts and the relays are to be subject to predetermined periodical changes of shifts, the manager of the factory shall draw up a scheme of shifts whereunder the periods during which any relay of the group may be required to work and the relay which will be working at any time of the day shall be known for any day.

(8) The State Government may prescribe forms of the notice required by sub-section (1) and the manner in which it shall be maintained.

(9) In the case of a factory beginning work after the commencement of this Act, a copy of the notice referred to in sub-section (1) shall be sent in duplicate to the Inspector before the day on which work is begun in the factory.

(10) Any proposed change in the system of work in any factory which will necessitate a change in the notice referred to in sub-section (1) shall be notified to the Inspector in duplicate before the change is made, and except with the previous sanction of the Inspector, no such change shall be made until one week has elapsed since the last change.

Section 61(10) speaks of "*change in the system of work in any factory which will necessitate a change in the notice*" and these words refer not to a departure from the notice but to a change in the system, a change which would require the notice to be recast. The notice shows "the periods during which adult workers may be required to work" and these words are descriptive of the scheme of the employment of labour in the factory but are not apt to contemplate the time of employment for each individual worker. That can only be found by referring to the register which goes with the notice. Sub-section (10) makes no mention of the change in the register but of the change in the notice and thereby indicates that the change which is contemplated is an overall change affecting a whole group and not an individual worker. The latter part of the sub-section also points in the same direction because it implies that such changes should not be frequent and if the change is for the second time, it should not be made until one week has elapsed since the last change. This cannot possibly refer to a casual change in the hours of work of an individual worker.[32]

SECTION 62: Register of adult workers

(1) The manager of every factory shall maintain a register of adult workers, to be available to the Inspector at all times during working hours, or when any work is being carried on in the factory, showing—

(a) the name of each adult worker in the factory;

(b) the nature of his work;

(c) the group, if any, in which he is included;

(d) where his group works on shifts, the relay to which he is allotted; and

(e) such other particulars as may be prescribed:

Provided that, if the Inspector is of opinion that any muster roll or register maintained as a part of the routine of a factory gives in respect of any or all the workers in the factory the particulars required under this section, he may, by order in writing, direct that such muster roll or register shall to the corresponding extent be maintained in place of, and be treated as, the register of adult workers in that factory.

(1A) No adult worker shall be required or allowed to work in any factory unless his name and other particulars have been entered in the register of adult workers.

(2) The State Government may prescribe the form of the register of adult workers, the manner in which it shall be maintained and the period for which it shall be preserved.

Even on a cursory look to S. 62 of the Factories Act, the requirement to maintain a register of adult workers to be available cannot be doubted in any way. Sub-section (2) of S. 62 is an authorisation for the State Government to prescribe the form of the register of adult workers and the manner in which it shall be maintained. The Gujarat Factories Rules, 1963 has been framed to suit the conditions in terms of the provisions of the Factories Act, 1948. Rule 87 of the said Rules prescribes that notice of period of week for adult workers shall be in Form No. 14 which in turn prescribes different periods of work for adult workers. Form 28 provides the muster roll as prescribed in 'Rule 110' of the Gujarat Rules. Rule 110 provides as given below:

"110. Muster-roll—(1) The Manager of every factory shall maintain a muster-roll of all the workers employed in the factory in Form No. 28 showing (a) the name of each worker, (b) the nature of his work, and (c) the daily attendance of the worker.

(2) The muster-roll shall be written up afresh each month and shall be preserved for a period of 3 years from the date of last entry in it:

Provided that if the daily attendance is noted in respect of Adult and Child Workers in the Registers of Workers in Form Nos. 15 and 17 respectively, or the particulars required under sub-rule (1) are noted in any other register, and such registers are preserved for a period

32. *State of Gujarat* v. *Kansara Manilal Bhikhalal*, AIR 1964 SC 1893.

of 3 years from the date of last entry in them, a separate muster-roll required under sub-rule (1) need not be maintained."

A complaint was lodged and on an analysis, it is found that one Shri Omprakash Rajput was found present in the list of adult workers register kept in the factory in Form No. 28 wherein the attendance of Shri Omprakash Rajput appears. Thus, the requirement of maintenance of muster-roll register stands complied. However, it is found that Form No. 14 as displayed in the factory premises does not contain the aforesaid name of Shri Omprakash Rajput as regards the working hours. Admittedly, Shri Omprakash Rajput was in terms of the averments of the complaint working during the visit of the inspector. Let us now thus have a close look at Form No. 14 which is supposed to be complied with. Form No. 14 prescribes the notice of period of works for adult workers with details of male and female employees, description of groups, period of work having due record to the working days and partial working days along, however, with the name of the factory, place where the same is located and the district. Annexure to the complaint records the working hours as between 8.00 a.m. to 4.30 p.m. with usual break in terms of the requirement together with a specific mention of an entry at 4.40 p.m. to 6.40 p.m. as over time—admittedly thus during the visit of the inspector the members of the staff were working on overtime. The complaint records violation of S. 63 and which, in turn, envisages compliance with S. 61 and S. 62. Whereas S. 62 cannot but be mentioned to be the muster-roll, S. 61 envisages a definite notice which is required to be displayed and maintained correctly in accordance with the provisions of sub-section (2) of S. 108, depicting clearly for every day the periods during which adult workers may be required to work. Sub-section (2) of S. 61 specifically records that the period shown in the notice shall be fixed before hand in accordance with the provisions of S. 61 so as not to permit workers working in contravention of any of the provisions of Ss. 51 to 56. Significantly, sub-S. (4) of S. 61 requires a factory Manager to classify the employees in groups according to the nature of their work and indicating the number of workers in each group. Admittedly, Shri Omprakash Rajput and the three other employees all belong to group C as appears on the face of the complaint as lodged. The mandate of the statute ought to be interpreted in a manner to give efficacy to the legislative intent. The Factories Act, 1948 cannot but be ascribed to be a beneficial piece of legislation and the requirement of S. 61, in particular sub-section (1) and (2) of S. 61, can be easily deciphered since the intent stands clear enough to indicate that an adult worker must know his daily placement and daily workings beforehand—this placement beforehand is the requirement of the statute in S. 63 and in the event of non-compliance, there is a liability for being prosecuted.

Mr. Dave, learned senior advocate appearing in support of the petition, though very strongly urged that the words "*otherwise than in accordance with the notice of periods of work for adults*" displayed at the factory as appears in S. 63 there is thus complete compliance. The requirements in terms of Rule 87 or 88 and that of Form No. 14 also stand complied with. Mr. Dave further pointed out that the second requirement of S. 63 ought to be co-related with Form No. 28 under S. 62 read with S. 110 of the Gujarat Factories Rules. The statute, however, in particular S. 61, specifically requires entries to be made 'beforehand' which stands virtually engrafted in S. 63. Compliance with Form No. 28 is not in dispute but compliance with Form No. 14 and entries to be made therein 'beforehand' needs a further scrutiny of facts which at this stage of the proceeding cannot be gone into. Use of the expression 'beforehand' appears in S. 61 which envisages a specific state of facts, which the complainant alleges as not being complied with—criminal complaints ought not to be scuttled at the initial stages and quashing of complaint at the initial stages is rather an exception than a rule. Beneficial legislations have been engrafted on the statute book for the benefit of the socially downtrodden and on the wake of such a situation, it would neither be fair nor be reasonable at this stage to nullify the efforts of an inspector under the Rules.[33]

SECTION 63: Hours of work to correspond with notice under Section 61 and register under Section 62

No adult worker shall be required or allowed to work in any factory otherwise than in accordance with the notice of periods of work for adults displayed in the factory and the entries made beforehand against his name in the register of adult workers of the factory.

SECTION 64: Power to make exempting rules

(1) The State Government may make rules defining the persons who hold positions of supervisions or management or are employed in a confidential position in a factory or empowering the Chief Inspector to declare any person, other than a person defined by such rules, as a person holding position of supervision or management or employed in a confidential position in a factory if, in the opinion of the Chief Inspector, such person holds such position or is so employed and the provisions of this chapter, other than the provisions of clause (b) of sub-section (1) of section 66 and of the proviso to that sub-section, shall not apply to any person so defined or declared:

Provided that any person so defined or declared shall, where the ordinary rate of wages of such person does not exceed the wage limit specified in sub-section (6) of section 1 of the Payment of Wages Act, 1936 (4 of 1936), as amended from time to time, be entitled to extra wages in respect of over time work under section 59.

(2) The State Government may make rules in respect of adult workers in factories providing for the exemption, to such extent and subject to such conditions as may be prescribed,—

(a) of workers engaged on urgent repairs, from the provisions of sections 51, 52, 54 55 and 56;

(b) of workers engaged in work in the nature of preparatory or complementary work which must necessarily be carried on outside the limits laid down for the general working of the factory, from the provisions of sections 51, 54, 55 and 56;

(c) of workers engaged in work which is necessarily so intermittent that the intervals during which they do not work while on duty ordinarily amount to more than the intervals for rest required by or under section 55, from the provisions of sections 51, 54, 55 and 56;

33. *S.M. Datta* v. *State of Gujarat*, AIR 2001 SC 3253.

(d) of workers engaged, in any work which for technical reasons must be carried on continuously from the provisions of sections 51, 52, 54, 55 and 56;

(e) of workers engaged in making or supplying articles of prime necessity which must be made or supplied every day, from the provisions of section 51 and section 52;

(f) of workers engaged in a manufacturing process which cannot be carried on except during fixed seasons, from the provisions of section 51, section 52 and section 54;

(g) of workers engaged in a manufacturing process which cannot be carried on except at times dependent on the irregular action of natural forces, from the provisions of sections 52 and 55;

(h) of workers engaged in engine-rooms or boiler-houses or in attending to power-plant or transmission machinery, from the provisions of section 51 and section 52;

(i) of workers engaged in the printing of newspapers, who are held up on account of the breakdown of machinery, from the provisions of sections 51, 54 and 56.

Explanation: In this clause the expression newspapers has the meaning assigned to it in the Press and Registration of Books Act, 1867 (25 of 1867);

(j) of workers engaged in the loading or unloading of railway wagons, or lorries or trucks from the provisions of sections 51, 52, 54, 55 and 56;

(k) of workers engaged in any work, which is notified by the State Government in the Official Gazette as a work of national importance, from the provisions of section 51, section 52, section 54, section 55 and section 56.

(3) Rules made under sub-section (2) providing for any exemption may also provide for any consequential exemption from the provisions of section 61 which the State Government may deem to be expedient, subject to such conditions as it may prescribe.

(4) In making rules under this section, the State Government shall not exceed, except in respect of exemption under clause (a) of sub-section (2), the following limits of work inclusive of overtime:

(i) the total number of hours of work in any day shall not exceed ten;

(ii) the spread over, inclusive of intervals for rest, shall not exceed twelve hours in any one day:

Provided that the State Government may, in respect of any or all of the categories of workers referred to in clause (d) of sub-section (2), make rules prescribing the circumstances in which, and the conditions subject to which, the restrictions imposed by clause (i) and clause (ii) shall not apply in order to enable a shift worker to work the whole or part of a subsequent shift in the absence of a worker who has failed to report for duty;

(iii) the total number of hours of work in a week, including overtime shall not exceed sixty;

(iv) the total number of hours of overtime shall not exceed fifty for any one quarter.

Explanation: "Quarter" means a period of three consecutive months beginning on the 1st of January, the 1st of April, the 1st of July or the 1st of October.

(5) Rules made under this section shall remain in force for not more than five years.

SECTION 65: Power to make exempting orders

(1) Where the State Government is satisfied that, owing to the nature of the work carried on or to other circumstances, it is unreasonable to require that the periods of work of any adult workers in any factory or class or description of factories should be fixed beforehand, it may, by written order, relax or modify the provisions of section 61 in respect of such workers therein, to such extent and in such manner as it may think fit, and subject to such conditions as it may deem expedient to ensure control over periods of work.

(2) The State Government or, subject to the control of the State Government, the Chief Inspector, may by written order exempt, on such conditions as it or he may deem expedient, any or all of the adult workers in any factory or group or class or description of factories from any or all of the provisions of sections, 51, 52, 54 and 56 on the ground that the exemption is required to enable the factory or factories to deal with an exceptional press of work.

(3) Any exemption granted under sub-section (2) shall be subject to the following conditions, namely:

(i) the total number of hours of work in any day shall not exceed twelve;

(ii) the spread over, inclusive of intervals for rest, shall not exceed thirteen hours in any one day;

(iii) the total number of hours of work in any week, including overtime, shall not exceed sixty;

(iv) no worker shall be allowed to work overtime, for more than seven days at a stretch and the total number of hours of overtime work in any quarter shall not exceed seventy-five.

Explanation: In this sub-section "quarter" has the same meaning as in sub-section (4) of section 64.

SECTION 66: Further restrictions on employment of women

(1) The provisions of this Chapter shall, in their application to women in factories, be supplemented by the following further restrictions, namely:

(a) no exemption from the provisions of section 54 may be granted in respect of any women;

(b) no women shall be required or allowed to work in any factory except between the hours of 6 a.m. and 7 p.m.:

Provided that the State Government may, by notification in the Official Gazette, in respect of any factory or group or class or description of factories, vary the limits laid down in clause (b), but so that no such variation shall authorize the employment of any woman between the hours of 10 p.m. and 5 a.m.;

(c) there shall be no change of shifts except after a weekly holiday or any other holiday.

(2) The State Government may make rules providing for the exemption from the restrictions set out in sub-section (1), to such extent and subject to such conditions as it may prescribe, of women working in fish curing or fish-canning factories, where the employment of women beyond the hours specified in the said restrictions is necessary to prevent damage to or deterioration in, any raw material.

(3) The rules made under sub-section (2) shall remain in force for not more than three years at a time.

Section 66(1)(b) provides that no woman shall be required or allowed to work in any factory except between hours of 6 a.m. and 7 p.m. This provision was challenged as unconstitutional in the light of Arts. 14, 15 and 16 of the Constitution in *Leela* v. *State of Kerala*.[34] The Court held that Art. 15(3) of Constitution empowers legislature to make special provisions for women and children and the object behind S. 66(1)(b) is to protect the women and therefore S. 66(1)(b) is not ultra vires. The Court observed that firstly, there is a presumption in favour of the constitutionality. The Court has to assume that the legislature is aware of the needs of the people. These needs have been made manifest by experience. It is to meet the needs that Parliament has enacted the Factories Act and made a specific provision that women shall not be compelled or allowed to work in the factories between 7 p.m. and 6 a.m. It is undoubtedly true that according to the traditional view, all that a woman needed to know was the four walls of her house. Her knowledge of Chemistry was supposed to be confined to cooking in the kitchen. Today, things have changed. Women are occupying posts of responsibility in almost every field of life. They have even advanced to a stage where they can hold their own against men in different fields. Yet, the very nature of their commitment to the family and the social environment require that they cannot be entrusted with all those duties which men may be asked to perform. Normally, they are not sent to the borders to fight. Lady constables are not asked to go on patrol duty at night. Waitresses in hotels are not required to work during night. They may be good for managerial jobs. They may even work as waitresses up to certain hours. But, special provisions so as to ensure that they are not harassed can be and have been made. It is on account of this situation that the Constitution makers had made a provision in Art. 15(3) that the legislature was permitted to make special provision for women and children. The purpose was to protect both of them against the hazardous jobs and to save them in spheres where the Parliament considered it necessary.

---

34. 2004 (102) FLR 207 (Ker.).

CHAPTER VII

EMPLOYMENT OF YOUNG PERSONS

SECTION 67: Prohibition of employment of young children

No child who has not completed his fourteenth year shall be required or allowed to work in any factory.

SECTION 68: Non-adult workers to carry tokens

A child who has completed his fourteenth year or an adolescent shall not be required or allowed to work in any factory unless—

(a) a certificate of fitness granted with reference to him under section 69 is in the custody of the manager of the factory; and

(b) such child or adolescent carries while he is at work a token giving a reference to such certificate.

SECTION 69: Certificates of fitness

(1) A certifying surgeon shall, on the application of any young person or his parent or guardian accompanied by a document signed by the manager of a factory that such person will be employed therein if certified to be fit for work in a factory, or on the application of the manager of the factory in which any young person wishes to work, examine such person and ascertain his fitness for work in a factory.

(2) The certifying surgeon, after examination, may grant to such young person, in the prescribed form, or may renew—

(a) a certificate of fitness to work in a factory as a child, if he is satisfied that the young person has completed his fourteenth year, that he has attained the prescribed physical standards and that he is fit for such work;

(b) a certificate of fitness to work in a factory as an adult, if he is satisfied that the young person has completed his fifteenth year, and is fit for a full day's work in a factory:

Provided that unless the certifying surgeon has personal knowledge of the place where the young person proposes to work and of the manufacturing process in which he will be employed, he shall not grant or renew a certificate under this sub-section until he has examined such place.

(3) A certificate of fitness granted or renewed under sub-section (2)—

(a) shall be valid only for a period of twelve months from the date thereof;

(b) may be made subject to conditions in regard to the nature of the work in which the young person may be employed, or requiring re-examination of the young person before the expiry of the period of twelve months.

(4) A certifying surgeon shall revoke any certificate granted or renewed under sub-section (2) if in his opinion the holder of it is no longer fit to work in the capacity stated therein in a factory.

(5) Where a certifying surgeon refuses to grant or renew a certificate or a certificate of the kind requested or revokes a certificate, he shall, if so requested by any person who could have applied for the certificate or the renewal thereof, state his reasons in writing for so doing.

(6) Where a certificate under this section with reference to any young person is granted or renewed subject to such conditions as are referred to in clause (b) of sub-section (3), the young person shall not be required or allowed to work in any factory except in accordance with those conditions.

(7) Any fee payable for a certificate under this section shall be paid by the occupier and shall not be recoverable from the young person, his parents or guardian.

Section 70: Effect of certificate of fitness granted to adolescent

(1) An adolescent who has been granted a certificate of fitness to work in a factory as an adult under clause (b) of sub-section (2) of section 69, and who while at work in a factory carries a token giving reference to the certificate, shall be deemed to be an adult for all the purposes of Chapters VI and VII.

(1A) No female adolescent or a male adolescent who has not attained the age of seventeen years but who has been granted a certificate of fitness to work in a factory as an adult, shall be required or allowed to work in any factory except between 6 a.m. and 7 p.m.:

Provided that the State Government may, by notification in the Official Gazette, in respect of any factory or group or class or description of factories—

(i) vary the limits laid down in this sub-section so, however, that no such section shall authorise the employment of any female adolescent between 10 p.m. and 5 a.m.;

(ii) grant exemption from the provisions of this sub-section in case of serious emergency where national interest is involved.

(2) An adolescent who has not been granted a certificate of fitness to work in a factory as an adult under the aforesaid clause (b) shall, notwithstanding his age, be deemed to be a child for all the purposes of this Act.

Section 71: Working hours for children

(1) No child shall be employed or permitted to work, in any factory—

(a) for more than four and a half hours in any day;

(b) during the night.

Explanation: For the purposes of this sub-section "night" shall mean a period of at least twelve consecutive hours which shall include the interval between 10 p.m. and 6 a.m.

(2) The period of work of all children employed in a factory shall be limited to two shifts which shall not overlap or spread over more than five hours each; and each child shall be employed in only one of the relays which shall not, except with the previous permission in writing of the Chief Inspector, be changed more frequently than once in a period of thirty days.

(3) The provisions of section 52 shall apply also to child workers and no exemption from the provisions of that section may be granted in respect of any child.

(4) No child shall be required or allowed to work in any factory on any day on which he has already been working in another factory.

(5) No female child shall be required or allowed to work in any factory except between 8 a.m. and 7 p.m.

SECTION 72: Notice of periods of work for children

(1) There shall be displayed and correctly maintained in every factory in which children are employed, in accordance with the provisions of sub-section (2) of section 108 a notice of period of work for children, showing clearly for every day the periods during which children may be required or allowed to work.

(2) The periods shown in the notice required by sub-section (1) shall be fixed beforehand in accordance with the method laid down for adult workers in section 61, and shall be such that children working for those periods would not be working in contravention of any of the provisions of section 71.

(3) The provisions of sub-sections (8), (9) and (10) of section 61 shall apply also to the notice required by sub-section (1) of this section.

SECTION 73: Register of child workers

(1) The manager of every factory in which children are employed shall maintain a register of child workers, to be available to the Inspector at all times during working hours or when any work is being carried on in a factory, showing—

(a) the name of each child worker in the factory,

(b) the nature of his work,

(c) the group, if any, in which he is included,

(d) where his group works in shifts, the relay to which he is allotted, and

(e) the number of his certificate of fitness granted under section 69.

(1A) No child worker shall be required or allowed to work in any factory unless his name and other particulars have been entered in the register of child workers.

(2) The State Government may prescribe the form of the register of child workers, the manner in which it shall be maintained and the period for which it shall be preserved.

Section 74: Hours of work to correspond with notice under Section 72 and register under Section 73

No child shall be employed in any factory otherwise than in accordance with the notice of periods of work for children displayed in the factory and the entries made beforehand against his name in the register of child workers of the factory.

Section 75: Power to require medical examination

Where an Inspector is of opinion—

(a) that any person working in a factory without a certificate of fitness is a young person, or

(b) that a young person working in a factory with a certificate of fitness is no longer fit to work in the capacity stated therein,—

he may serve on the manager of the factory a notice requiring that such person or young person, as the case may be, shall be examined by a certifying surgeon, and such person or young person shall not, if the Inspector so directs, be employed, or permitted to work, in any factory until he has been so examined and has been granted a certificate of fitness or a fresh certificate of fitness, as the case may be, under section 69, or has been certified by the certifying surgeon examining him not to be a young person.

Section 76: Power to make rules

The State Government may make rules—

(a) prescribing the forms of certificates of fitness to be granted under section 69, providing for the grant of duplicates in the event of loss of the original certificates, and fixing the fees which may be charged for such certificates and renewals thereof and such duplicates;

(b) prescribing the physical standards to be attained by children and adolescents working in factories;

(c) regulating the procedure of certifying surgeons under this Chapter;

(d) specifying other duties which certifying surgeons may be required to perform in connection with the employment of young persons in factories, and fixing the fees which may be charged for such duties and the persons by whom they shall be payable.

Section 77: Certain other provisions of law not barred

The provisions of this Chapter shall be in addition to, and not in derogation of, the provisions of the Employment of Children Act, 1938 (26 of 1938).

CHAPTER VIII

ANNUAL LEAVE WITH WAGES

SECTION 78: Application of chapter

(1) The provisions of this Chapter shall not operate to the prejudice of any right to which a worker may be entitled under any other law or under the terms of any award, agreement (including settlement) or contract of service:

Provided that if such award, agreement (including settlement) or contract of service provides for a longer annual leave with wages than provided in this Chapter, the quantum of leave, which the worker shall be entitled to, shall be in accordance with such award, agreement or contract of service but in relation to matters not provided for in such award, agreement or contract of service or matters which are provided for less favourably therein, the provisions of sections 79 to 82, so far as may be, shall apply.

(2) The provisions of this Chapter shall not apply to workers in any factory of any railway administered by the Government, who are governed by leave rules approved by the Central Government.

SECTION 79: Annual leave with wages

(1) Every worker who has worked for a period of 240 days or more in a factory during a calendar year shall be allowed during the subsequent calendar year, leave with wages for a number of days calculated at the rate of—

(i) if an adult, one day for every twenty days of work performed by him during the previous calendar year;

(ii) if a child, one day for every fifteen days of work performed by him during the previous calendar year.

Explanation 1: For the purpose of this sub-section—

(a) any days of lay off, by agreement or contract or as permissible under the standing orders;

(b) in the case of a female worker, maternity leave for any number of days not exceeding twelve weeks; and

(c) the leave earned in the year prior to that in which the leave is enjoyed;

shall be deemed to be days on which the worker has worked in a factory for the purpose of computation of the period of 240 days or more, but he shall not earn leave for these days.

Explanation 2: The leave admissible under this sub-section shall be exclusive of all holidays whether occurring during or at either end of the period of leave.

(2) A worker whose service commences otherwise than on the first day of January shall be entitled to leave with wages at the rate laid down in clause (i) or, as the case may

be, clause (ii) of sub-section (1) if he has worked for two-thirds of the total number of days in the remainder of the calendar year.

(3) If a worker is discharged or dismissed from service or quits his employment or is superannuated or dies while in service, during the course of the calendar year, he or his heir or nominee, as the case may be, shall be entitled to wages in lieu of the quantum of leave to which he was entitled immediately before his discharge, dismissal, quitting of employment, superannuation or death calculated at the rates specified in sub-section (1), even if he had not worked for the entire period specified in sub-section (1) or sub-section (2) making him eligible to avail of such leave, and such payment shall be made—

(i) where the worker is discharged or dismissed or quits employment, before the expiry of the second working day from the date of such discharge, dismissal or quitting, and

(ii) where the worker is superannuated or dies while in service, before the expiry of two months from the date of such superannuation or death.

(4) In calculating leave under this section, fraction of leave of half a day or more shall be treated as one full day's leave, and fraction of less than half a day shall be omitted.

(5) If a worker does not in any one calendar year take the whole of the leave allowed to him under sub-section (1) or sub-section (2), as the case may be, any leave not taken by him shall be added to the leave to be allowed to him in the succeeding calendar year:

Provided that the total number of days of leave that may be carried forward to a succeeding year shall not exceed thirty in the case of an adult or forty in the case of a child:

Provided further that a worker, who has applied for leave with wages but has not been given such leave in accordance with any scheme laid down in sub-sections (8) and (9) or in contravention of sub-section (10) shall be entitled to carry forward the leave refused without any limit.

(6) A worker may at any time apply in writing to the manager of a factory not less than fifteen days before the date on which he wishes his leave to begin, to take all the leave or any portion thereof allowable to him during the calendar year:

Provided that the application shall be made not less than thirty days before the date on which the worker wishes his leave to begin, if he is employed in a public utility service as defined in clause (n) of section 2 of the Industrial Disputes Act, 1947 (14 of 1947):

Provided further that the number of times in which leave may be taken during any year shall not exceed three.

(7) If a worker wants to avail himself of the leave with wages due to him to cover a period of illness, he shall be granted such leave even if the application for leave is not made within the time specified in sub-section (6); and in such a case wages as admissible under section 81 shall be paid not later than fifteen days, or in the case of a public utility service not later than thirty days from the date of the application for leave.

(8) For the purpose of ensuring the continuity of work, the occupier or manager of the factory, in agreement with the Works Committee of the factory constituted under section 3 of the Industrial Disputes Act, 1947 (14 of 1947), or a similar Committee constituted under any other Act or if there is no such Works Committee or a similar Committee in the factory, in agreement with the representatives of the workers therein chosen in the prescribed manner, may lodge with the Chief Inspector a scheme in writing whereby the grant of leave allowable under this section may be regulated.

(9) A scheme lodged under sub-section (8) shall be displayed at some conspicuous and convenient places in the factory and shall be in force for a period of twelve months from the date on which it comes into force, and may thereafter be renewed with or without modification for a further period of twelve months at a time, by the manager in agreement with the Works Committee or a similar Committee, or as the case may be, in agreement with the representatives of the workers as specified in sub-section (8), and a notice of renewal shall be sent to the Chief Inspector before it is renewed.

(10) An application for leave which does not contravene the provisions of sub-section (6) shall not be refused, unless refusal is in accordance with the scheme for the time being in operation under sub-sections (8) and (9).

(11) If the employment of a worker who is entitled to leave under sub-section (1) or sub-section (2), as the case may be, is terminated by the occupier before he has taken the entire leave to which he is entitled, or if having applied for and having not been granted such leave, the worker quits his employment before he has taken the leave, the occupier of the factory shall pay him the amount payable under section 80 in respect of the leave not taken, and such payment shall be made, where the employment of the worker is terminated by the occupier, before the expiry of the second working day after such termination, and where a worker who quits his employment, on or before the next pay day.

(12) The unavailed leave of a worker shall not be taken into consideration in computing the period of any notice required to be given before discharge or dismissal.

The leave provided under S. 79 arises as a matter of right when a worker has put in a minimum number of working days and he is entitled to it. The fact that the respondents remained absent for a longer period than that provided in S. 79 has no bearing on their right to leave, for if they so remained absent for such period, they lost the wages for that period which they would have otherwise earned. That however does not mean that they should also lose the leave earned by them under S. 79.[35]

This section has 12 other sub-sections which deal with different aspects and make relevant provisions in regard to annual leave with wages. It is not disputed that the award purports to make provisions for privilege leave in excess of the annual leave sanctioned by S. 79. Can the Industrial Tribunal direct the appellant to provide such additional privilege leave to its employees? In other words, does S. 79 purport to standardise annual leave with wages so that no departure from the said standard is permissible either way? The appellant's contention in *Alembic Chemical Works Co. Ltd.* v. *Workmen*[36] is that except for pre-existing

35. *Birdhichand Sharma* v. *First Civil Judge, Nagpur*, AIR 1961 SC 644.
36. AIR 1961 SC 647.

awards agreements, contracts or except for pre-existing law, no departure from the standardised provision is permissible after S. 79 was enacted.

In order to answer the above questions raised before the Supreme Court, it is highly necessary to read S. 79 in the light of the other relevant provisions of the Act. It may be conceded that the provisions made by S. 79 are elaborate, and in that sense may be treated as self-contained and exhaustive. It is also clear that S. 79(1) does not use the expression "not more than or not less than" as it might have done if the intention of the legislature was to make its provisions correspond either to the minimum or the maximum leave claimable by the employees; but even so, when S. 79(1) provides that every worker shall be allowed leave as therein prescribed, the provision *prima facie* sounds like a provision for the minimum rather than for the maximum leave which may be awarded to the worker. If the intention of the legislature was to make the leave permissible under S. 79(1) the maximum to which a workman would be entitled, it would have used a definite and appropriate language in that behalf. The Court, therefore, is inclined to think that even on a plain construction of S. 79(1), it would be difficult to accede to the argument that it prescribes standardised leave which inevitably would mean the maximum permissible until S. 79(1) itself is changed.

Having regard to the policy and object of the Act, if S. 79(1) is capable of two constructions, that construction should be preferred which furthers the policy of the Act and is more beneficial to the employees in whose interest the Act has been passed. It is well settled that in construing the provisions of a welfare legislation, Courts should adopt what is sometimes described as a beneficent rule of construction; but apart from this general consideration about the policy and object of the Act, Ss. 78 and 84 occurring in the same Chapter as S. 79 clearly indicate that S. 79(1) is not intended to standardise leave provisions as contended by the appellant, and that is the reason why the appellant's argument cannot be accepted.

Let us then consider the provisions of Ss. 78 and 84. Section 78(1) provides that the provisions of Chapter VIII shall not operate to the prejudice of any right to which a worker may be entitled under any other law, or under the terms of any award, agreement or contract of service. There is a proviso to this sub-section which lays down that when such award, agreement or contract of service provides for longer annual leave with wages than provided in this Chapter the worker shall be entitled only to such longer annual leave. Section 78(2) exempts specified workers from the operation of Chapter VIII. The first difficulty which this section raises against the appellant's argument is that it undoubtedly recognises exceptions to the leave prescribed by S. 79(1). It is well known that standardisation of conditions of service in industrial adjudication generally does not recognise or permit exceptions; if the hours of work are standardised, for instance, or the wages-structure is standardised, it is intended to make hours of work and wages uniform in the whole industry brought under the working of standardisation. Standardisation thus inevitably means levelling up of those whose terms and conditions of service were less favourable than the standardised ones, and levelling down those of such others whose terms and conditions were more favourable than the standardised ones. That being so, if S. 79(1) intended to standardise annual leave with wages, it would normally not have made provisions in regard to exceptions as S. 78(1) obviously does.

The provisions of S. 84 would also lead to the same result. Section 84 provides that where the State Government is satisfied that the leave rules applicable to workers in a factory provide benefits which in its opinion are not less favourable than those for which Chapter VIII makes provision, it may by written order exempt the factory from all or any of the provisions of Chapter VIII subject to such conditions as may be specified in the order. Now, the power to exempt factories has to be exercised having regard to the effect of the totality of the benefits which may be afforded to the workers by their respective factories. This power to exempt also necessarily postulates the existence of better amenities than those guaranteed by Chapter VIII, and that means that if a factory provides better leave amenities to its employees, the State Government may in the interest of the employees exempt the factory from the operation of this Chapter. The scope of S. 84, like the scope of S. 78, cannot be limited only to the more favourable benefits which may be existing at the date when the Act was passed. What is true about the existing benefits would be equally true about the benefits which may be granted by an employer to the employees in future. Let us illustrate what the consequence would be if the appellant's argument is accepted. Take the case of an employer who has been exempted under S. 84 on the ground that the benefits of leave conferred by him on his employees are more favourable to them. In such a case, the employer may make his benefits still more favourable after exemption is accorded to him; but an employer who has already not provided more favourable benefits would be effectively precluded from making any such provisions in future. It is difficult to imagine that such a consequence could have been intended by the provisions of this welfare legislation.

Accordingly, the Supreme Court held that the award passed by the Industrial Tribunal purporting to make provision for privilege leave in excess of the annual leave sanctioned by S. 79(1) in the case of workers governed by the provisions of the Factories Act, 1948, is not without jurisdiction.

SECTION 80: Wages during leave period

(1) For the leave allowed to him under section 78 or section 79, as the case may be a worker shall be entitled to wages at a rate equal to the daily average of his total full time earnings for the days on which he actually worked during the month immediately preceding his leave, exclusive of any overtime and bonus but inclusive of dearness allowance and the cash equivalent of the advantage accruing through the concessional sale to the worker of foodgrains and other articles:

Provided that in the case of a worker who has not worked on any day during the calendar month immediately preceding his leave, he shall be paid at a rate equal to the daily average of his total full time earnings for the days on which he actually worked during the last calendar month preceding his leave, in which he actually worked, exclusive of any overtime and bonus but inclusive of dearness allowance and the cash equivalent of the advantage accruing through the concessional sale to the workers of foodgrains and other articles.

(2) The cash equivalent of the advantage accruing through the concessional sale to the worker of foodgrains and other articles shall be computed as often as may be prescribed, on the basis of the maximum quantity of foodgrains and other articles admissible to a standard family.

Explanation 1: "Standard family" means a family consisting of a worker, his or her spouse and two children below the age of fourteen years requiring in all three adult consumption units.

Explanation 2: Adult consumption unit means the consumption unit of a male above the age of fourteen years; and the consumption unit of a female above the age of fourteen years and that of a child below the age of fourteen years shall be calculated at the rates of 0.8 and 0.6 respectively of one adult consumption unit.

(3) The State Government may make rules prescribing—

(a) the manner in which the cash equivalent of the advantage accruing through the concessional sale to a worker of foodgrains and other articles shall be computed; and

(b) the registers that shall be maintained in a factory for the purpose of securing compliance with the provisions of this section.

In *Shankar Balaji Waje* v. *State of Maharashtra,*[37] two points have been raised on behalf of the appellant. One is that Pandurang was not a 'worker' within the meaning of that expression in the Act. The other is that even if Pandurang was a 'worker,' he was not entitled to any leave wages under S. 80 of the Act.

In the instant case, the following facts are considered. Pandurang was one of the persons who rolled bidis in the appellant's bidi factory. There was no agreement or contract of service between the appellant and Pandurang. Pandurang was not bound to attend the factory for the work for any fixed hours of work or for any fixed period. He was free to go to the factory at any time he liked and was equally free to leave the factory whenever he liked. He could remain absent from work on any day he liked. But if he was to be absent for more than 10 days he had to inform the appellant, not for the purpose of taking his permission or leave, but for the purpose of assuring him that he had no intention to give up work at the factory. There was no actual supervision of work Pandurang did in the factory. Pandurang was paid at fixed rates on the quantity of bidis turned out. There was, however, no stipulation that he had to turn out any minimum quantity of bidis in a day. Leaves used to be supplied to Pandurang for being taken home and cut there. Tobacco to fill the bidis used to be supplied at the factory. But Pandurang was not bound to roll the bidis at the factory. He could do so at his place on taking permission of the appellant for taking tobacco home. The permission was necessary in view of Excise Rules and not on account of any condition of alleged service. At the close of the day, the bidis used to be delivered to the appellant and bidis which were not up to the standard were used to be rejected. Pandurang's attendance was not noted though the days he worked could be found out from the work register. Accordingly, the Supreme Court held that Pandurang could not be said to be 'employed' by the appellant and so was not worker. Pandurang was working with the permission of or under the agreement with the owner and not on any term of employment by the owner. The appellant had no control and supervision over the details of Pandurang's work. The work of rolling bidis might be a simple work and require no particular supervision or direction. But there was nothing to show that any such direction

37. AIR 1962 SC 517.

could be given. The Court referred the ratio of *Chintaman Rao* v. *State of Madhya Pradesh*,[38] where the Court held that the concept of employment involves three ingredients: (i) employer (2) employee and (3) the contract of employment. The employer is one who employs, i.e., one who engages the services of other persons. The employee is one who works for another for hire. The employment is the contract of service between the employer and the employee whereunder the employee agrees to serve the employer subject to his control and supervision. Keeping in view the ratio of *Chintaman Rao* case, the Supreme Court, in the instant case, i.e., *Shankar Balaji Waje* case observed:

> "It is true, as contended for the State, that persons engaged to roll bidis on job work basis could be workers, but only such persons would be workers who work regularly at the factory and are paid for the work turned out during their regular employment on the basis of the work done. Piece-rate workers can be workers within the definition of 'worker' in the Act, but they must be regular workers and not workers who come and work according to their sweet will. It is also true, as urged for the State, that a worker, within the definition of that expression in the Act, need not be a whole-time worker. But, even then, the worker must have, under his contract of service, an obligation to work either for a fixed period or between fixed hours. The whole conception of service does not fit in well with a servant who has full liberty to attend to his work according to his pleasure and not according to the orders of his master.
>
> We may say that this opinion further finds support from what we hold on the second contention. If Pandurang was a worker, the provisions about leave and leave wages should apply to him. We are of opinion that they do not and what we say in that connection reinforces our view that Pandurang was not a worker as the three criteria and conditions laid down in Chintaman Rao's Case, 1958 SCR 1340: (AIR 1958 SC 388), for constituting him as such are not fulfilled in the present case."[39]

The second question raised before the Court that even if Pandurang was a worker, he was not entitled to any leave wages under S. 80 of the Act. Before discussing the provisions of Ss. 79 and 80 of the Act, which deal with leave and wages for leave, it is necessary to look into the terms on which Pandurang was working. He was not in regular employment. He was given work and paid according to the work he turned out. It was not incumbent on him to attend to the work daily or to take permission for absence before absenting himself. It was only when he had to absent himself for a period longer than ten days that he had to inform the management for administrative convenience, but not with a view to take leave of absence. Section 79 provides that the worker is to get leave in a subsequent year when he has worked for a period of 240 days or more in the factory during the previous calendar year. Who can be said to work for a period of 240 days?

Pandurang was not bound to work for the period of work displayed in the factory and therefore his days of work for the purpose of S. 79 could not be calculated. It is urged for the State that each day on which Pandurang worked, whatever be the period of time that he worked, would be counted as one day of work for the purpose of this section. But the Court refused to accept this contention because S. 79 provides for leave on the basis of the period of working days. Therefore it must contemplate a definite period of work per working day and not any indefinite period for which a person may like to work on any particular day.

38. AIR 1958 SC 388.
39. *Shankar Balaji Waje* v. *State of Maharashtra,* AIR 1962 SC 517 at p. 522 per Raghubar Dayal, J.

Accordingly, the Court held that there can be no basis for calculating the daily average of the worker's total full time earnings when the terms of work be as they are in the present case and that therefore the wages to be paid for the leave period cannot be calculated nor the number of days for which leave with wages can be allowed be calculated in such a case.

SECTION 81: Payment in advance in certain cases

A worker who has been allowed leave for not less than four days, in the case of an adult, and five days, in the case of a child, shall, before his leave begins, be paid the wages due for the period of the leave allowed.

SECTION 82: Mode of recovery of unpaid wages

Any sum required to be paid by an employer, under this chapter but not paid by him shall be recoverable as delayed wages under the provisions of the Payment of Wages Act, 1936 (4 of 1936).

SECTION 83: Power to make rules

The State Government may make rules directing managers of factories to keep registers containing such particulars as may be prescribed and requiring the registers to be made available for examination by Inspectors.

SECTION 84: Powers to exempt factories

Where the State Government is satisfied that the leave rules applicable to workers in a factory provide benefits which in its opinion are not less favourable than those for which this Chapter makes provision it may, by written order, exempt the factory from all or any of the provisions of this Chapter subject to such conditions as may be specified in the order.

Explanation: For the purposes of this section, in deciding whether the benefits which are provided for by any leave rules are less favourable than those for which this Chapter makes provision, or not, the totality of the benefits shall be taken into account.

CHAPTER IX

SPECIAL PROVISIONS

SECTION 85: Power to apply the Act to certain premises

(1) The State Government may, by notification in the Official Gazette, declare that all or any of the provisions of this Act shall apply to any place wherein a manufacturing process is carried on with or without the aid of power or is so ordinarily carried on, notwithstanding that—

(i) the number of persons employed therein is less than ten, if working with the aid of power and less than twenty if working without the aid of power, or

(ii) the persons working therein are not employed by the owner thereof but are working with the permission of, or under agreement with, such owner:

Provided that the manufacturing process is not being carried on by the owner only with the aid of his family.

(2) After a place is so declared, it shall be deemed to be a factory for the purposes of this Act, and the owner shall be deemed to be the occupier, and any person working therein, a worker.

Explanation: For the purposes of this section, owner shall include a lessee or mortgagee with possession of the premises.

Section 85 is enacted with the object of conferring authority to extend in appropriate cases the provisions of the Act to establishments which are otherwise not factories within the meaning of the Act, and to ensure to persons working in factories even if not workers within the meaning of the Act, the benefits provided thereby. The section authorises the State Government to make all or some of the provisions of the Act applicable to any place wherein a manufacturing process is carried on with or without the aid of power, notwithstanding that the number of persons employed therein is less than the number specified in the definition of 'factory', or where the persons working therein are not employed by the owner but are working with the permission of, or under agreement with, such owner. On the issue of a notification by the State Government, the place designated will be deemed a factory, the owner of the place will be deemed an occupier and persons working therein will be deemed workers.

Constitutionality of Section 85

It is contended in *Bhikusa Yamasa Kshatriya (Pvt.) Ltd.* v. *Union of India*[40] that S. 85 is invalid on the ground that it imposes unreasonable restrictions upon the fundamental right of the owner to carry on his business, and it enables the State Government by a notification arbitrarily to discriminate between owners of establishments who are similarly situated inasmuch as the Act confers an unguided and uncontrolled power to select places to be deemed factories and to impose thereby obligations laid by the Factories Act upon the owners of those places. The Supreme Court held that the Factories Act undoubtedly imposes numerous restrictions upon the employers to secure to the workers adequate safeguards for their health and physical well-being. But imposition of such restrictions is not and cannot be regarded, in the context of the modern outlook on industrial relations, as unreasonable. Extension of the benefits of the Factories Act to premises and workers not falling strictly within the purview of the Act, is intended to serve the same purpose. By authorising imposition of restrictions for the benefit of workers who, in the view of the State, stand in need of some or all the protections afforded by the Factories Act, but who are not governed by the Act, the legislature is merely seeking to effectuate the object of the Act, i.e. it authorises extension of the benefit of the Act to persons to whom the Act, to fully effectuate the object, should have been but has, on account

40. AIR 1963 SC 1591.

of administrative or other difficulties, not been extended. Provisions made for the benefit of 'deemed workers' cannot therefore be regarded as not reasonable within the meaning of Art. 19(1)(g) of the Constitution. The Court further held that S. 85 which authorises the State Government to issue a notification applying all or any of the provisions of the Act to any place in which a manufacturing process is carried on, and which involves the consequence that the place is deemed a factory and the persons working therein are deemed workers, is not by itself discriminatory so as to infringe Art. 14 of the Constitution; nor does the provision amount to authorising imposition of unreasonable restriction upon the fundamental right of the owner of the factory to carry on his business.

In *State of Maharashtra* v. *Jamnabai Purshottam Asar*,[41] one Purshottamdas Ranchhoddas was a lessee from the Port Trust Bombay of an open plot of land. He established a factory called the Sunderdas Saw Mills. He closed down the factory on April 1, 1957. In July 1957, the ex-workers of the factory combined together to form five partnerships and by agreements of leave and licence, Purshottamdas Ranchhoddas gave the premises of the factory and the machinery installed there. He himself did not join any of the five partnerships. The licensees were to pay a fixed sum for the use of the premises and the machines. In the year 1959, a prosecution was started under S. 92 of the Factories Act on the charge that the original licensee of the factory had not given notice under S. 7(1) of the start of the factory and had not renewed the licence under Rule 4 of the Bombay Factories Rules 1950. This ended in an acquittal, since Government had not declared these premises as a 'factory' under S. 85 of the Act as it could, if the workers (although not employed by the owner) were working with the permission of or under an agreement with the owner. After notification, the premises are deemed to be a factory and the owner of the premises is deemed to be an occupier.

On September 29, 1960, a notification was issued under S. 85. That notification specified the places where the five partnerships were working as factory. On November 10, 1959, five separate complaints were filed for failure to take out five licenses. The charge was that Purshottamdas Ranchhoddas was the owner of the factory and hence an occupier and the workmen were working under an agreement with him. The owner defended himself by stating that he had no control over the five firms and he could not enforce the provisions of the Factories Act. This defence was not accepted. Purshottamdas Ranchhoddas was held to be liable and, therefore, compelled to take out a licence under Rule 3-A of the Bombay Factories Rules. He was fined ₹201 for the first offence and ₹25 for the subsequent offences. Purshottamdas Ranchhoddas appealed but died during the pendency of the appeal. As the sentence was one of fine, the appeal was continued by his legal representative. The Bombay High Court set aside the conviction and fine and now the present appeal has been filed by the State of Maharashtra on special leave granted by the Supreme Court. The Court observed that under S. 2(n) of the Act an 'occupier' of a factory means the person who has the ultimate control over the affairs of the factory. If one goes by this definition, Purshottamdas Ranchhoddas was not an occupier if he had not the ultimate control over the affairs of the five partnership firms running the factory. But here the Factories Act gives special powers to the State Government under S. 85. The notification of Government makes applicable

41. AIR 1968 SC 53.

all or any of the provisions of the Act to a place of manufacture notwithstanding that the persons working therein are not employed by the owner of the place wherein the manufacture is carried on provided the workers work with the permission of or under agreement with the owner. The condition precedent for the notification is that the persons working therein (a) work with permission of or (b) under agreement with the owner. The section does not contemplate a case where the owner hands over the factory on rent and the workers work without his permission and not under agreement with him. In other words, if there is no connection between the owner and the workmen in the sense that they work without his permission and without an agreement with him, there would be no question of the liability of the owner as an occupier.

In the present case, the agreements show that the premises were given over to partnership firms in return for a periodic payment. The agreements show that the licensees of the premises bound themselves to carry on the manufacturing process on their own and Purshottamdas Ranchhoddas had no control over them. The High Court has considered the clauses and come to the conclusion that the partnerships were independent of the control of the owner and the workers cannot be said to be working with his permission or under agreement with him. They had formed themselves into partnerships, taken on leave and licence the factory premises and started their own business. In these circumstances, the conditions for the notification hardly existed.

An attempt was made to prove from the angle of S. 93 of the Act that the definition of an occupier cannot apply to circumstances arising under S. 85 because S. 93 makes special provision for the responsibility of the owner. A glance at the provisions of S. 93 however discloses the opposite. It is not necessary to consider all the clauses, some of which may bind the owner, but a clause like 93(3)(ii) clearly shows that the owner is liable only when he has control.

The difference between the owner of the premises and the occupier is at once visible. The liability of the occupier is patent, but the liability of owner arises only when the machinery and plant is not specifically entrusted to the custody or use of an occupier. In the present case, for example, the machinery and plant has been so specifically entrusted to the custody or use of the various partnerships and the owner of the premises cannot be made liable.

The Court accordingly held that as the five partnerships have taken over the factory to work independently, no question of the liability of the owner under S. 85(1)(ii) arises. It is possible that some obligations are still on the owner under S. 93 but that is another matter. Purshottamdas Ranchhoddas could not be made liable for not taking out the licence.

SECTION 86: Power to exempt public institutions

The State Government may exempt, subject to such conditions as it may consider necessary, any workshop or workplace where a manufacturing process is carried on and which is attached to a public institution, maintained for the purposes of education, training, research or reformation, from all or any of the provisions of this Act:

Provided that no exemption shall be granted from the provisions relating to hours of work and holidays, unless the persons having the control of the institution submit, for the approval of the State Government, a scheme for the regulation of the hours of employment, intervals for meals, and holidays of the persons employed in or attending the institution or who are inmates of the institution, and the State Government is satisfied that the provisions of the scheme are not less favourable than the corresponding provisions of this Act.

SECTION 87: Dangerous operations

Where the State Government is of opinion that any manufacturing process or operation carried on in a factory exposes any persons employed in it to a serious risk of bodily injury, poisoning or diseases, it may make rules applicable to any factory or class or description of factories in, which the manufacturing process or operation is carried on—

(a) specifying the manufacturing process or operation and declaring it to be dangerous;

(b) prohibiting or restricting the employment of women, adolescents or children in the manufacturing process or operation;

(c) providing for the periodical medical examination of persons employed, or seeking to be employed, in the manufacturing process or operation, and prohibiting the employment of persons not certified as fit for such employment and requiring the payment by the occupier of the factory of fees for such medical examination;

(d) providing for the protection of all persons employed in the manufacturing process or operation or in the vicinity of the places where it is carried on;

(e) prohibiting, restricting or controlling the use of any specified materials or processes in connection with the manufacturing process or operation;

(f) requiring the provision of additional welfare amenities and sanitary facilities and the supply of protective equipment and clothing, and laying down the standards thereof, having regard to the dangerous nature of the manufacturing process or operation.

SECTION 87A: Power to prohibit employment on account of serious hazard

(1) Where it appears to the Inspector that conditions in a factory or part thereof are such that they may cause serious hazard by way of injury or death to the persons employed therein or to the general public in the vicinity, he may, by order in writing to the occupier of the factory, state the particulars in respect of which he considers the factory or part thereof to be the cause of such serious hazard and prohibit such occupier from employing any person in the factory or any part thereof other than the minimum number of persons necessary to attend to the minimum tasks till the hazard is removed.

(2) Any order issued by the Inspector under sub-section (1) shall have effect for a period of three days until extended by the Chief Inspector by a subsequent order.

(3) Any person aggrieved by an order of the Inspector under sub-section (1), and the Chief Inspector under sub-section (2), shall have the right to appeal to the High Court.

(4) Any person whose employment has been affected by an order issued under sub-section (1), shall be entitled to wages and other benefits and it shall be the duty of the occupier to provide alternative employment to him wherever possible and in the manner prescribed.

(5) The provisions of sub-section (4) shall be without prejudice to the rights of the parties under the Industrial Disputes Act, 1947 (14 of 1947).

SECTION 88: Notice of certain accidents

(1) Where in any factory an accident occurs which causes death, or which causes any bodily injury by reason of which the person injured is prevented from working for a period of forty-eight hours or more immediately following the accident, or which is of such nature as may be prescribed in this behalf, the manager of the factory shall send notice thereof to such authorities, and in such form and within such time, as may be prescribed.

(2) Where a notice given under sub-section (1) relates to an accident causing death, the authority to whom the notice is sent shall make an inquiry into the occurrence within one month of the receipt of the notice or, if such authority is not the Inspector, cause the Inspector to make an inquiry within the said period.

(3) The State Government may make rules for regulating the procedure at inquiries under this section.

SECTION 88A: Notice of certain dangerous occurrences

Where in a factory any dangerous occurrence of such nature as may be prescribed, occurs, whether causing any bodily injury or disability or not, the manager of the factory shall send notice thereof to such authorities, and in such form and within such time, as may be prescribed.

SECTION 89: Notice of certain diseases

(1) Where any worker in a factory contracts any disease specified in the Third Schedule, the manager of the factory shall send notice thereof to such authorities, and in such form and within such time as may be prescribed.

(2) If any medical practitioner attends on a person who is or has been employed in a factory, and who is, or is believed by the medical practitioner to be, suffering from any disease, specified in the Third Schedule the medical practitioner shall without delay send a report in writing to the office of the Chief Inspector stating—

(a) the name and full postal address of the patient,

(b) the disease from which he believes the patient to be suffering, and

(c) the name and address of the factory in which the patient is, or was last, employed.

(3) Where the report under sub-section (2) is confirmed to the satisfaction of the Chief Inspector, by the certificate of a certifying surgeon or otherwise, that the person is suffering from a disease specified in the Third Schedule, he shall pay to the medical

practitioner such fee as may be prescribed, and the fee so paid shall be recoverable as an arrear of land revenue from the occupier of the factory in which the person contracted the disease.

(4) If any medical practitioner fails to comply with the provisions of sub-section (2), he shall be punishable with fine which may extend to one thousand rupees.

(5) The Central Government may, by notification in the Official Gazette, add to or alter the Third Schedule and any such addition or alteration shall have effect as if it had been made by this Act.

The right to health to a worker is an integral facet of meaningful right to life, to have not only a meaningful existence but also robust health and vigour without which worker would lead life of misery. Lack of health denudes his livelihood. Compelling economic necessity to work in an industry exposed to health hazards due to indigence to bread-winning to himself and his dependants should not be at the cost of the health and vigour of the workman. Facilities and opportunities, as enjoined in Art. 38, should be provided to protect the health of the workman. Provision for medical test and treatment invigorates the health of the worker for higher production or efficient service. Continued treatment, while in service or after retirement, is a moral, legal and constitutional concomitant duty of the employer and the State. Therefore, it must be held that the right to health and medical care is a fundamental right under Art. 21 read with Arts. 39(c), 41 and 43 of the Constitution and make the life of the workman meaningful and purposeful with dignity of person. Right to life includes protection of the health and strength of the worker, which is a minimum requirement to enable a person to live with human dignity. The State, be it Union or State Government or an industry, public or private, is enjoined to take all such action which will promote health, strength and vigour of the workman during the period of employment and leisure and health even after retirement as basic essentials to live the life with health and happiness. The health and strength of the worker is an integral facet of right to life. Denial thereof denudes the workman the finer facets of life violating Art. 21. The right to human dignity, development of personality, social protection, right to rest and leisure are fundamental human rights to a workman assured by the Charter of Human Rights, in the Preamble and Arts. 38 and 39 of the Constitution. Facilities for medical care and health against sickness ensures stable manpower for economic development and would generate devotion to duty and dedication to give the workers 'best physically as well as mentally in production of goods or services. Health of the worker enables him to enjoy the fruit of his labour, keeping him physically fit and mentally alert for leading a successful life, economically, socially and culturally. Medical facilities to protect the health of the workers are, therefore, the fundamental and human rights to the workmen. Therefore, the Supreme Court in *Consumer Education and Research Centre* v. *Union of India*[42] held:

> Therefore, we hold that right to health, medical aid to protect the health and vigour of a worker while in service or post retirement is a fundamental right under Article 21, read with Articles 39(e), 41,43 48A and all related to Articles and fundamental human rights to make the life of the workman meaningful and purposeful with dignity of person.[43]

42. AIR 1995 SC 922.
43. *Ibid.* at p. 940 per K. Ramaswamy, J.

The Supreme Court, further, while invoking Art. 32 of the Constitution, directed all the employers, be it the State or its undertaking or private employer, to make the right to life meaningful; to prevent pollution of work place; protection of the environment; protection of the health of the workman or to preserve free and unpolluted water for the safety and health of the people. The authorities or even private persons or industry are bound by the directions issued by this Court under Art. 32 and Art. 142 of the Constitution.

Yet another contention of the petitioners in the instant case is that the workman affected by asbestosis are suffering from lungs cancer and related ailments and they were not properly diagnosed. They be sent to national institute and such of those found suffering from diseases developed due to asbestos, proper compensation be paid. It is needless to reiterate that they need to be re-examined and cause for the disease and the nature of the disease diagnosed. Is each one of them entitled to damages? The Court held that the employer is vicariously liable to pay damages in case of occupational diseases, here in this case asbestosis. The Employees State Insurance Act and the Workmen's Compensation Act provide for payment of mandatory compensation for the injury or death caused to the workman while in employment. The Act does not provide for payment of compensation after cessation of employment, it therefore becomes necessary to protect such persons from the respective dates of cessation of their employment. Liquidated damages by way of compensation are accepted principles of compensation. The respective as asbestos factories or companies shall be bound to compensate the workmen for the health hazards which is the cause for the disease with which the workmen are suffering from or had suffered pending the writ petition. Therefore, the factory or establishment shall be responsible to pay liquidated damages to the workmen concerned.

The Court further laid down certain guidelines to be followed by all asbestos industries in the country and they are as follows:

7. To maintain and keep maintaining the health record of every worker up to a minimum period of 40 years from the beginning of the employment or 15 years after retirement or cessation of the employment whichever is later;
8. The Membrane Filter test, to detect asbestos fibre should be adopted by all the factories or establishments at par with the Metalliferrous Mines Regulations, 1961; and Vienna Convention and Rules issued thereunder;
9. All the factories whether covered by the Employees State Insurance Act or Workmen's Compensation Act or otherwise are directed to compulsorily insure health coverage to every worker;
10. The Union and the State Governments are directed to review the standards of permissible exposure limit value of fibre/cc in tune with the international standards.
11. The Union and all the State Governments are directed to consider inclusion of such of those small scale factory or factories or industries to protect health hazards of the worker engaged in the manufacture of asbestos or its ancillary products;
12. Every worker suffering from occupational health hazards would be entitled for compensation of ₹1 lakh.

Section 90: Power to direct enquiry into cases of accident or disease

(1) The State Government may, if it considers it expedient so to do, appoint a competent person to inquire into the causes of any accident occurring in a factory or into any case where a disease specified in the Third Schedule has been, or is suspected to have been, contracted in a factory, and may also appoint one or more persons possessing legal or special knowledge to act as assessors in such inquiry.

(2) The person appointed to hold an inquiry under this section shall have all the powers of a Civil Court under the Code of Civil Procedure, 1908 (5 of 1908), for the purposes of enforcing the attendance of witnesses and compelling the production of documents and material objects, and may also, so far as may be necessary for the purposes of the inquiry, exercise any of the powers of an Inspector under this Act; and every person required by the person making the inquiry to furnish any information shall be deemed to be legally bound so to do within the meaning of section 176 of the Indian Penal Code, 1860 (45 of 1860).

(3) The person holding an inquiry under this section shall make a report to the State Government stating the causes of the accident, or as the case may be, disease, and any attendant circumstances, and adding any observations which he or any of the assessors may think fit to make.

(4) The State Government may, if it thinks fit, cause to be published any report made under this section or any extracts therefrom.

(5) The State Government may make rules for regulating the procedure as Inquiries under this section.

Section 91: Power to take samples

(1) An Inspector may at any time during the normal working hours of a factory, after informing the occupier or manager of the factory or other person for the time being purporting to be in charge of the factory, take in the manner hereinafter provided a sufficient sample of any substance used or intended to be used in the factory, such use being—

(a) in the belief of the Inspector in contravention of any of the provisions of this Act or the rules made thereunder, or

(b) in the opinion of the Inspector likely to cause bodily injury to, or injury to the health of, workers in the factory.

(2) Where the Inspector takes a sample under sub-section (1), he shall, in the presence of the person informed under that sub-section unless such person wilfully absents himself, divide the sample into three portions and effectively seal and suitably mark them, and shall permit such person to add his own seal and mark thereto.

(3) The person informed as aforesaid shall, if the Inspector so requires, provide the appliances for dividing, sealing and marking the sample taken under this section.

(4) The Inspector shall—

(a) forthwith give one portion of the sample to the person informed under sub-section (1);
(b) forthwith send the second portion to a Government Analyst for analysis and report thereon;
(c) retain the third portion for production to the Court before which proceedings, if any, are instituted in respect of the substance.

(5) Any document purporting to be a report under the hand of any Government Analyst upon any substance submitted to him for analysis and report under this section, may be used as evidence in any proceedings instituted in respect of the substance.

SECTION 91A: Safety and occupational health surveys

(1) The Chief Inspector, or the Director General of Factory Advice Service and Labour Institutes, or the Director General of Health Services, to the Government of India, or such other officer as may be authorised in this behalf by the State Government or the Chief Inspector or the Director General of Factory Advice Service and Labour Institutes or the Director General of Health Services may, at any time during the normal working hours of a factory, or at any other time as is found by him to be necessary, after giving notice in writing to the occupier or manager of the factory or any other person who for the time being purports to be in charge of the factory, undertake safety and occupational health surveys and such occupier or manager or other person shall afford all facilities for such survey, including facilities for the examination and testing of plant and machinery and collection of samples and other data relevant to the survey.

(2) For the purpose of facilitating surveys under sub-section (1) every worker shall, if so required by the person conducting the survey, present himself to undergo such medical examination as may be considered necessary by such person and furnish all information in his possession and relevant to the survey.

(3) Any time spent by a worker for undergoing medical examination or furnishing information under sub-section (2) shall, for the purpose of calculating wages and extra wages for overtime work, be deemed to be time during which such worker worked in the factory.

Explanation: For the purposes of this section, the report, if any, submitted to the State Government by the person conducting the survey under sub-section (1) shall be deemed to be a report submitted by an Inspector under this Act.

CHAPTER X

PENALTIES AND PROCEDURE

SECTION 92: General penalty for offences

Save as is otherwise expressly provided in this Act and subject to the provisions of section 93, if in, or in respect of, any factory there is any contravention of any of the provisions of this Act or of any rules made thereunder or of any order in writing given thereunder, the occupier and manager of the factory shall each be guilty of an offence and punishable with imprisonment for a term which may extend to two years or with fine which may extend to one lakh rupees or with both, and if the contravention is continued after conviction, with a further fine which may extend to one thousand rupees for each day on which the contravention is so continued:

Provided that where contravention of any of the provisions of Chapter IV or any rule made thereunder or under section 87 has resulted in an accident causing death or serious bodily injury, the fine shall not be less than twenty-five thousand rupees in the case of an accident causing death, and five thousand rupees in the case of an accident causing serious bodily injury.

Explanation: In this section and in section 94 "serious bodily injury" means an injury which involves, or in all probability will involve, the permanent loss of the use of, or permanent injury to, any limb or the permanent loss of, or injury to, sight or hearing, or the fracture of any bone, but shall not include, the fracture of bone or joint (not being fracture of more than one bone or joint) of any phalanges of the hand or foot.

SECTION 93: Liability of owner of premises in certain circumstances

(1) Where in any premises separate buildings are leased to different occupiers for use as separate factories, the owner of the premises shall be responsible for the provision and maintenance of common facilities and services, such as approach roads, drainage, water supply, lighting and sanitation.

(2) The Chief Inspector shall have, subject to the control of the State Government, power to issue orders to the owner of the premises in respect of the carrying out of the provisions of sub-section (1).

(3) Where in any premises, independent or self-contained, floors or flats are leased to different occupiers for use as separate factories, the owner of the premises shall be liable as if he were the occupier or manager of a factory, for any contravention of the provisions of this Act in respect of—

(i) latrines, urinals and washing facilities in so far as the maintenance of the common supply of water for these purposes is concerned;

(ii) fencing of machinery and plant belonging to the owner and not specifically entrusted to the custody or use of an occupier;

(iii) safe means of access to the floors or flats and maintenance and cleanliness of staircases and common passages;

(iv) precautions in case of fire;

(v) maintenance of hoists and lifts; and

(vi) maintenance of any other common facilities provided in the premises.

(4) The Chief Inspector shall have, subject to the control of the State Government, power to issue orders to the owner of the premises in respect of the carrying out the provisions of sub-section (3).

(5) The provisions of sub-section (3) relating to the liability of the owner shall apply where in any premises independent rooms with common latrines, urinals and washing facilities are leased to different occupiers for use as separate factories:

Provided that the owner shall be responsible also for complying with the requirements relating to the provisions and maintenance of latrines, urinals and washing facilities.

(6) The Chief Inspector shall have, subject to the control of the State Government, the power to issue orders to the owner of the premises referred to in sub-section (5) in respect of the carrying out of the provisions of section 46 or section 48.

(7) Where in any premises portions of a room or a shed are leased to different occupiers for use as separate factories, the owner of the premises shall be liable for any contravention of the provisions of—

(i) Chapter III, except sections 14 and 15;

(ii) Chapter IV, except sections 22, 23, 27, 34, 35 and 36:

Provided that in respect of the provisions of sections 21, 24 and 32 the owners liability shall be only in so far as such provisions relate to things under his control:

Provided further that the occupier shall be responsible for complying with the provisions of Chapter IV in respect of plant and machinery belonging to or supplied by him;

(iii) section 42.

(8) The Chief Inspector shall have, subject to the control of the State Government, power to issue orders to the owner of the premises in respect of the carrying out of the provisions of sub-section (7).

(9) In respect of sub-sections (5) and (7), while computing for the purposes of any of the provisions of this Act the total number of workers employed, the whole of the premises shall be deemed to be a single factory.

Section 94: Enhanced penalty after previous conviction

(1) If any person who has been convicted of any offence punishable under section 92 is again guilty of an offence involving a contravention of the same provision, he shall be punishable on a subsequent conviction with imprisonment for a term which may extend to three years or with fine which shall not less than ten thousand rupees but which may extend to two lakh rupees or with both:

Provided that the court may, for any adequate and special reasons to be mentioned in the judgment, impose a fine of less than ten thousand rupees:

Provided further that where contravention of any of the provisions of Chapter IV or any rule made thereunder or under section 87 has resulted in an accident causing death or serious bodily injury, the fine shall not be less than thirty five thousand rupees in the case of an accident causing death and ten thousand rupees in the case of an accident causing serious bodily injury.

(2) For the purposes of sub-section (1), no cognizance shall be taken of any conviction made more than two years before the commission of the offence for which the person is subsequently being convicted.

SECTION 95: Penalty for obstructing Inspector

Whoever wilfully obstructs an Inspector in the exercise of any power conferred on him by or under this Act, or fails to produce on demand by an Inspector any registers or other documents in his custody kept in pursuance of this Act or of any rules made thereunder, or conceals or prevents any worker in a factory from appearing before, or being examined by, an Inspector, shall be punishable with imprisonment for a term which may extend to six months or with fine which may extend to ten thousand rupees or with both.

SECTION 96: Penalty for wrongfully disclosing results of analysis under Section 91

Whoever, except in so far as it may be necessary for the purposes of a prosecution for any offence punishable under this Act, publishes or discloses to any person the results of an analysis made under section 91, shall be punishable with imprisonment for a term which may extend to six months or with fine which may extend to ten thousand rupees or with both.

SECTION 96A: Penalty for contravention of the provisions of Sections 41B, 41C and 41H

(1) Whoever fails to comply with or contravenes any of the provisions of section 41B, 41C or 41H or the rules made thereunder, shall, in respect of such failure or contravention, be punishable with imprisonment for a term which may extend to seven years and with fine which may extend to two lakh rupees, and in case the failure or contravention continues, with additional fine which may extend to five thousand rupees for every day during which such failure or contravention continues after the conviction for the first such failure or contravention.

(2) If the failure or contravention referred to in sub-section (1) continues beyond a period of one year after the date of conviction, the offender shall be punishable with imprisonment for a term which may extend to ten years.

SECTION 97: Offences by workers

(1) Subject to the provisions of section 111, if any worker employed in a factory contravenes any provision of this Act or any rules or orders made thereunder, imposing any duty or liability on workers, he shall be punishable with fine which may extend to five hundred rupees.

(2) Where a worker is convicted of an offence punishable under sub-section (1), the occupier or manager of the factory shall not be deemed to be guilty of an offence in respect of that contravention, unless it is proved that he failed to take all reasonable measures for its prevention.

Section 98: Penalty for using false certificate of fitness

Whoever knowingly uses or attempts to use, as a certificate of fitness granted to himself under section 70, a certificate granted to another person under that section, or who, having procured such a certificate, knowingly allows it to be used, or an attempt to use to be made, by another person, shall be punishable with imprisonment for a term which may extend to two months or with fine which may extend to one thousand rupees or with both.

Section 99: Penalty for permitting double employment of child

If a child works in a factory on any day on which he has already been working in another factory, the parent or guardian of the child or the person having custody of or control over him or obtaining any direct benefit from his wages, shall be punishable with fine which may extend to one thousand rupees unless it appears to the Court that the child so worked without the consent or connivance of such parent, guardian or person.

Section 100: Omitted

Section 101: Exemption of occupier or manager from liability in certain cases

Where the occupier or manager of a factory is charged with an offence punishable under this Act, he shall be entitled, upon complaint duly made by him and on giving to the prosecutor not less than three clear days notice in writing of his intention so to do, to have any other person whom he charges as the actual offender brought before the Court at the time appointed for hearing the charge; and if, after the commission of the offence has been proved, the occupier or manager of the factory, as the case may be, proves to the satisfaction of the court—

(a) that he has used due diligence to enforce the execution of this Act, and

(b) that the said other person committed the offence in question without his knowledge, consent or connivance,—

that other person shall be convicted of the offence and shall be liable to the like punishment as if he were the occupier or manager of the factory, and the occupier or manager, as the case may be, shall be discharged from any liability under this Act in respect of such offence:

Provided that in seeking to prove as aforesaid, the occupier or manager of the factory, as the case may be, may be examined on oath, and his evidence and that of any witness whom he calls in his support shall be subject to cross-examination on behalf of the person he charges as the actual offender and by the prosecutor:

Provided further that, if the person charged as the actual offender by the occupier or manager cannot be brought before the Court at the time appointed for hearing the charge, the

Court shall adjourn the hearing from time to time for a period not exceeding three months and if by the end of the said period the person charged as the actual offender cannot still be brought before the Court, the Court shall proceed to hear the charge against the occupier or manager and shall, if the offence be proved, convict the occupier or manager.

Section 101 of the Act provides that where an occupier or manager of a factory is charged with an offence punishable under this Act, he shall be entitled to have any other person whom he charges as the actual offender brought before the Court and if he proves to the satisfaction of the Court (a) that he used due diligence to enforce the execution of the Act, and (b) that the said other person committed the offence in question without his knowledge, consent or connivance, then that other person shall be convicted of the offence and the occupier or the manager shall be discharged. It will appear, therefore, that even where the occupier or manager proves that somebody else has removed the fencing without his knowledge, consent or connivance, that alone would not exempt him from liability but he has further to prove that he had used due diligence to enforce the execution of the Act. It seems very clear that if it was his duty to exercise due diligence for the purpose in a case where he could establish that somebody else had removed the fence which is required under S. 21 of the Act, it would be equally his duty to exercise that diligence where he could not prove who had removed it. If it were not so, the intention of the Act to give protection to workmen would be wholly defeated.[44] In *State of Gujarat* v. *Kansara Manilal Bhikhalal*,[45] it has been held that where an occupier or a manager is charged with an offence, he is entitled to make a complaint in his own turn against any person who was the actual offender and on proof of the commission of the offence by such person the occupier or the manager is absolved from liability. This shows that compliance with the peremptory provisions of the Act is essential and unless the occupier or manager brings the real offender to book, he must bear the responsibility. It is not necessary that menders must always be established. The responsibility exists without a guilty mind. An adequate safeguard, however, exists in S. 101 that the occupier and manager can save themselves if they prove that they are not the real offenders but who, in fact, is.

From the above observations of the Supreme Court, it is clear that there is a duty cast, under the Act, upon the occupier or manager, to comply with the peremptory provisions of the Act, but, under S. 101, when the manager or occupier is charged with an offence, he is entitled to make a complaint, in his own turn, to establish facts mentioned in the said section; and, if he is able to establish that it was such other person who has committed an offence, and satisfies the other requirements of the said section, the manager or occupier is absolved from all liability. It is also emphasized that an adequate safeguard has been provided, under section 101, under which in circumstances mentioned therein, the occupier or manager can save himself, if he proves that he is not the real offender, but some other person.[46]

SECTION 102: Power of court to make orders

(1) Where the occupier or manager of a factory is convicted of an offence punishable under this Act the Court may, in addition to awarding any punishment, by order in

44. *State of Gujarat* v. *Jethalal Ghelabhai Patel*, AIR 1964 SC 779.
45. AIR 1964 SC 1893.
46. *Maneklal Jinabhai Kot* v. *State of Gujarat*, AIR 1967 SC 1226.

writing require him, within a period specified in the order (which the Court may, if it thinks fit and on application in such behalf, from time to time extend) to take such measures as may be so specified for remedying the matters in respect of which the offence was committed.

(2) Where an order is made under sub-section (1), the occupier or manager of the factory, as the case may be, shall not be liable under this Act in respect of the continuation of the offence during the period or extended period, if any, allowed by the Court, but if, on the expiry of such period or extended period, as the case may be, the order of the Court has not been fully complied with, the occupier or manager, as the case may be, shall be deemed to have committed a further offence, and may be sentenced therefor by the Court to undergo imprisonment for a term which may extend to six months or to pay a fine which may extend to one hundred rupees for every day after such expiry on which the order has not been complied with, or both to undergo such imprisonment and to pay such fine, as aforesaid.

SECTION 103: Presumption as to employment

If a person is found in a factory at any time, except during intervals for meals or rest, when work is going on or the machinery is in motion, he shall until the contrary is proved, be deemed for the purposes of this Act and the rules made thereunder to have been at that time employed in the factory.

The presumption available under this section in the first place is rebuttable and secondly it is available only for the purpose of the said Act. It is also not the case of the respondent that this presumption is made available in relation to an adjudication of a dispute referred to under S. 10 of the Industrial Disputes Act, 1947. Section 103 of the Act is included in Chapter X under the heading "Penalties and Procedure" which chapter deals with general penalty for offences.[47]

SECTION 104: Onus as to age

(1) When any act or omission would, if a person were under a certain age, be an offence punishable under this Act, and such person is in the opinion of the Court *prima facie* under such age, the burden shall be on the accused to prove that such person is not under such age.

(2) A declaration in writing by a certifying surgeon relating to a worker that he has personally examined him and believes him to be under the age stated in such declaration shall, for the purposes of this Act and the rules made thereunder, be admissible as evidence of the age of that worker.

SECTION 104A: Onus of proving limits of what is practicable, etc.

In any proceeding for an offence for the contravention of any provision of this Act or rules made thereunder consisting of a failure to comply with a duty or requirement to do something,

47. *Factory Manager, CIMMCO Wagon Factory* v. *Virendra Kumar Sharma*, AIR 2000 SC 2524.

it shall be for the person who is alleged to have failed to comply with such duty or requirement, to prove that it was not reasonably practicable, or, as the case may be, all practicable measures were taken to satisfy the duty or requirement.

Section 105: Cognizance of offences

(1) No Court shall take cognizance of any offence under this Act except on complaint by, or with the previous sanction in writing of, an Inspector.

(2) No Court below that of a Presidency Magistrate or of a Magistrate of the first class shall try any offence punishable under this Act.

Section 106: Limitation of prosecutions

No Court shall take cognizance of any offence punishable under this Act unless complaint thereof is made within three months of the date on which the alleged commission of the offence came to the knowledge of an Inspector:

Provided that where the offence consists of disobeying a written order made by an Inspector, complaint thereof may be made within six months of the date on which the offence is alleged to have been committed.

Explanation: For the purposes of this section,—

(a) in the case of a continuing offence, the period of limitation shall be computed with reference to every point of time during which the offence continues;

(b) where for the performance of any act time is granted or extended on an application made by the occupier or manager of a factory, the period of limitation shall be computed from the date on which the time so granted or extended expired.

Section 106A: Jurisdiction of a court for entertaining proceedings, etc., for offence

For the purposes of conferring jurisdiction on any court in relation to an offence under this Act or the rules made thereunder in connection with the operation of any plant, the place where the plant is for the time being situate shall be deemed to be the place where such offence has been committed.

Chapter XI

SUPPLEMENTAL

Section 107: Appeals

(1) The manager of a factory on whom an order in writing by an Inspector has been served under the provisions of this Act or the occupier of the factory may, within

thirty days of the service of the order, appeal against it to the prescribed authority, and such authority may, subject to rules made in this behalf by the State Government, confirm, modify or reverse the order.

(2) Subject to rules made in this behalf by the State Government (which may prescribe classes of appeals which shall not be heard with the aid of assessors), the appellate authority may, or if so required in the petition of appeal shall, hear the appeal with the aid of assessors, one of whom shall be appointed by the appellate authority and the other by such body representing the industry concerned as may be prescribed:

Provided that if no assessor is appointed by such body before the time fixed for hearing the appeal, or if the assessor so appointed fails to attend the hearing at such time, the appellate authority may, unless satisfied that the failure to attend is due to sufficient cause, proceed to hear the appeal without the aid of such assessor or, if it thinks fit, without the aid of any assessor.

(3) Subject to such rules as the State Government may make in this behalf and subject to such conditions as to partial compliance or the adoption of temporary measures as the appellate authority may in any case think fit to impose, the appellate authority may, if it thinks fit, suspend the order appealed against pending the decision of the appeal.

SECTION 108: Display of notices

(1) In addition to the notices required to be displayed in any factory by or under this Act, there shall be displayed in every factory a notice containing such abstracts of this Act and of the rules made thereunder as may be prescribed and also the name and address of the Inspector and the certifying surgeon.

(2) All notices required by or under this Act to be displayed in a factory shall be in English and in a language understood by the majority of the workers in the factory, and shall be displayed at some conspicuous and convenient place at or near the main entrance to the factory, and shall be maintained in a clean and legible condition.

(3) The Chief Inspector may, by order in writing served on the manager of any factory, require that there shall be displayed in the factory any other notice or poster relating to the health, safety or welfare of the workers in the factory.

SECTION 109: Service of notice

The State Government may make rules prescribing the manner of the service of orders under this Act on owners, occupiers or managers of factories.

SECTION 110: Returns

The State Government may make rules requiring owners, occupiers or managers of factories to submit such returns, occasional or periodical, as may in its opinion be required for the purposes of this Act.

Section 111: Obligations of workers

(1) No worker in a factory—

(a) shall wilfully interfere with or misuse any appliance, convenience or other thing provided in a factory for the purposes of securing the health, safety or welfare of the workers therein;

(b) shall wilfully and without reasonable cause do anything likely to endanger himself or others; and

(c) shall wilfully neglect to make use of any appliance or other thing provided in the factory for the purposes of securing the health or safety of the workers therein.

(2) If any worker employed in a factory contravenes any of the provisions of this section or of any rule or order made thereunder, he shall be punishable with imprisonment for a term which may extend to three months, or with fine which may extend to one hundred rupees, or with both.

Section 111A: Right of workers, etc.

Every worker shall have the right to—

(i) obtain from the occupier, information relating to workers' health and safety at work;

(ii) get trained within the factory wherever possible, or, to get himself sponsored by the occupier for getting trained at a training centre or institute, duly approved by the Chief Inspector, where training is imparted for workers' health and safety at work;

(iii) represent to the Inspector directly or through his representative in the matter of inadequate provision for protection of his health or safety in the factory.

Section 112: General power to make rules

The State Government may make rules providing for any matter which, under any of the provisions of this Act, is to be or may be prescribed or which may be considered expedient in order to give effect to the purposes of this Act.

Section 113: Powers of centre to give directions

The Central Government may give directions to a State Government as to the carrying into execution of the provisions of this Act.

Section 114: No charge for facilities and conveniences

Subject to the provisions of section 46 no fee or charge shall be realised from any worker in respect of any arrangements or facilities to be provided, or any equipments or appliances to be supplied by the occupier under the provisions of this Act.

SECTION 115: Publication of rules

(1) All rules made under this Act shall be published in the Official Gazette, and shall be subject to the condition of previous publication; and the date to be specified under clause (3) of section 23 of the General Clauses Act, 1897 (10 of 1897), shall be not less than forty-five days from the date on which the draft of the proposed rules was published.

(2) Every rule made by the State Government under this Act shall be laid, as soon as may be after it is made, before the State Legislature.

SECTION 116: Application of act to Government factories

Unless otherwise provided this Act shall apply to factories belonging to the Central or any State Government.

SECTION 117: Protection to persons acting under this Act

No suit, prosecution or other legal proceeding shall lie against any person for anything which is in good faith done or intended to be done under this Act.

The language of this protecting clause provided in S. 117 is not limited to officers but is made wide to include "*any person*". It thus gives protection not only to an officer doing or intending to do something in pursuance or execution of this Act but also to "*any person*". But the critical words are "*any thing ... done or intended to be done*" under the Act. The protection conferred can only be claimed by a person who can plead that he was required to do or omit to do something under the Act or that he intended to comply with any of its provisions. It cannot confer immunity in respect of actions which are not done under the Act but are done contrary to it. Even assuming that an act includes an omission as stated in the General Clauses Act, the omission also must be one which is enjoined by the Act. It is not sufficient to say that the act was honest. That would bring it only within the words "*good faith*". It is necessary further to establish that what is complained of is something which the Act requires should be done or should be omitted to be done. There must be a compliance or an intended compliance with a provision of the Act, before the protection can be claimed. The section cannot cover a case of a breach or an intended breach of the Act however honest the conduct otherwise.[47]

In this connection it is necessary to point out, as was done in Provincial Government, *C.P. and Berar* v. *Seth Chapsi Dhanji Oswal Bhate*,[48] that the occupier and manager are exempted from liability in certain cases mentioned in S. 101. Where an occupier or a manager is charged with an offence, he is entitled to make a complaint in his own turn against any person who was the actual offender and on proof of the commission of the offence by such person the occupier or the manager is absolved from liability. This shows that compliance with the peremptory provisions of the Act is essential and unless the occupier or the manager brings the real offender to book, he must bear the responsibility. Such a provision largely excludes the operation of S. 117 in respect of persons guilty of a breach

48. AIR 1938 Nag 406.

of the provisions of the Act. It is not necessary that *mens rea* must always be established. The responsibility exists without a guilty mind. An adequate safeguard, however, exists in S. 101 where the occupier and manager can save themselves if they prove that they are not the real offenders but who, in fact, is.

SECTION 118: Restriction on disclosure of information

(1) No Inspector shall, while in service or after leaving the service, disclose otherwise than in connection with the execution, or for the purposes, of this Act any information relating to any manufacturing or commercial business or any working process which may come to his knowledge in the course of his official duties.

(2) Nothing in sub-section (1) shall apply to any disclosure of information made with the previous consent in writing of the owner of such business or process of for the purposes of any legal proceeding (including arbitration) pursuant to this Act or of any criminal proceeding which may be taken, whether pursuant to this Act or otherwise, or for the purpose of any report of such proceedings as aforesaid.

(3) If any Inspector contravenes the provisions of sub-section (1) he shall be punishable with imprisonment for a term which may extend to six months, or with fine which may extend to one thousand rupees, or with both.

SECTION 118A: Restriction on disclosure of information

(1) Every Inspector shall treat as confidential the source of any complaint brought to his notice on the breach of any provision of this Act.

(2) No inspector shall, while making an inspection under this Act, disclose to the occupier, manager or his representative that the inspection is made in pursuance of the receipt of a complaint:

Provided that nothing in this sub-section shall apply to any case in which the person who has made the complaint has consented to disclose his name.

SECTION 119: Act to have effect notwithstanding anything contained in Act 37 of 1970

The provisions of this Act shall have effect notwithstanding anything inconsistent therewith contained in the Contract Labour (Regulation and Abolition) Act, 1970 or any other law for the time being in force.

Notification D/- 11-4-1997 prohibiting employment of contract labour in industrial canteen and factories employing 250 workers or above in the State of Karnataka cannot be challenged on the ground that canteen workmen are not engaged directly as workers in a factory and therefore such workmen should be treated as workers engaged in the industry. It cannot be said in such a case that the objectives of a factory and an establishment is to produce the goods or services as the case may be in terms of the Memorandum of Association or any other document under which it is established and supply of food or beverages is not one of their objectives and, therefore, the workmen in such establishments can never be treated as the workmen of the factory, and if at all such workmen are treated as workmen of the factory, it is only for the purpose of the Factories Act. It cannot be disputed that the provision for canteen is a welfare measure and necessarily a requirement to turn the same is incidental to the main activity of the establishment particularly when it becomes a condition of service. In such a case, the definition of 'worker' as provided under the Contract Labour (Regulation and Abolition) Act, 1970 is to be seen and not as provided under the Factories Act and therefore S. 119 of the Factories Act cannot be invoked to contend that the Factories Act would weigh over the Contract Labour (Regulation and Abolition) Act, 1970 because no inconsistency is pointed out between the Factories Act and Contract Labour (Regulation and Abolition) Act.[49]

SECTION 120: Repeal and savings

The enactments set out in the Table appended to this section are hereby repealed:

Provided that anything done under the said enactments which could have been done under this Act if it had then been in force shall be deemed to have been done under this Act.

SCHEDULE I

[*See* Section 2(cb)]

LIST OF INDUSTRIES INVOLVING HAZARDOUS PROCESSES

1. Ferrous metallurgical Industries
   - Integrated Iron and Steel
   - Ferro-alloys
   - Special Steels
2. Non-ferrous metallurgical Industries
   - Primary Metallurgical Industries, namely, zinc, lead, copper manganese and aluminium
3. Foundries (ferrous and non-ferrous)
   - Castings and forgings including cleaning or smoothing/roughening by sand and shot blasting.
4. Coal (including coke) industries.
   - Coal, Lignite, Coke, etc.
   - Fuel Gases (including Coal gas, Producer gas, Water gas)

49. *Barat Fritz Werner Ltd.* v. *State of Karnataka*, AIR 2001 SC 1257.

5. Power Generating Industries
6. Pulp and paper (including paper products) industries
7. Fertiliser Industries
   - Nitrogenous
   - Phosphatic
   - Mixed
8. Cement Industries
   - Portland Cement (including slag cement, puzzolona cement and their products)
9. Petroleum Industries
   - Oil Refining
   - Lubricating Oils and Greases
10. Petro-chemical Industries
11. Drugs and Pharmaceutical Industries
    - Narcotics, Drugs and Pharmaceuticals
12. Fermentation Industries (Distilleries and Breweries)
13. Rubber (Synthetic) Industries
14. Paints and Pigment Industries
15. Leather Tanning Industries
16. Electro-plating Industries
17. Chemical Industries
    - Coke Oven by-products and Coaltar Distillation Products
    - Industrial Gases (nitrogen, oxygen, acetylene, argon, carbon-dioxide, hydrogen, sulphur-dioxide, nitrous oxide, halogenated hydro-carbon, ozone etc.)
    - Industrial Carbon
    - Alkalies and Acids
    - Chromates and dichromates
    - Leads and its compounds
    - Electrochemicals (metallic sodium, potassium and magnesium, chlorates, perchlorates and peroxides)
    - Electrothermal produces (artificial abrasive, calcium carbide)
    - Nitrogenous compounds (cyanides, cyanamides and other nitrogenous compounds)
    - Phosphorous and its compounds
    - Halogens and Halogenated compounds (Chlorine, Fluorine, Bromine and Iodine)
    - Explosives (including industrial explosives and detonators and fuses)
18. Insecticides, Fungicides, herbicides and other Pesticides Industries
19. Synthetic Resin and Plastics
20. Man-made Fibre (Cellulosic and non-cellulosic) Industry
21. Manufacture and repair of electrical accumulators

22. Glass and Ceramics
23. Grinding or glazing of metals
24. Manufacture, handling and processing of asbestos and its products
25. Extraction of oils and fats from vegetable and animal sources
26. Manufacture, handling and use of benzene and substances containing benzene
27. Manufacturing processes and operations involving carbon disulphide
28. Dyes and Dyestuff including their intermediates
29. Highly flammable liquids and gases.

SCHEDULE II

[*See* Section 41F]

PERMISSIBLE LEVELS OF CERTAIN CHEMICAL SUBSTANCES IN WORK ENVIRONMENT

Sl. No.	*Substance*	*Permissible limits of exposure*			
		Time-Weighted average concentration (TWA) (8 hr)		*Short-term exposure limit (STEL) (15 min.)*	
		PPm	*mg/m³*	*PPm*	*mg/m³*
1	**2**	**3**	**4**	**5**	**6**
1	Acetaldehyde	100	180	150	270
2	Acetic Acid	10	25	15	37
3	Acetone	750	1780	1000	2375
4	Acrolein	01	0.25	0.3	0.8
5	Acrylonitrile-skin (S.C.)	2	4.5	–	–
6	Aldrin-skin	–	0.25	–	–
7	Allyl Chloride	1	3	2	6
8	Ammonia	0.25	18	35	27
9	Aniline-skin	2	10	–	–
10	Anisidine (o.P.isomers)-skin	0.1	0.5	–	–
11	Arsenic & Soluble compounds (as As)	–	0.2	–	–
12	Benzene (S.C.)	10	30	–	–
13	Beryllium & Compounds (as Be) (S.C.)	–	0.002	–	–
14	Boron trifluoride C	1	3	–	–
15	Bromine	0.1	0.7	0.3	2
16	Butane	800	1900	–	–
17	2-Butanone (Methyle ethyle Ketone MEK)	200	590	300	885
18	N-Butyl acetate	150	710	200	950

Sl. No.	Substance	Permissible limits of exposure			
		Time-Weighted average concentration (TWA) (8 hr)		Short-term exposure limit (STEL) (15 min.)	
		PPm	mg/m³	PPm	mg/m³
19	N-Butyl alcohol-skin-C	50	150	–	–
20	Sce/tert, Butyl acetate	200	950	–	–
21	Butyl Mercaptan	0.5	1.5	–	–
22	Cadmium-dust and salts (as Cd)	–	0.05	–	–
23	Calcium oxide	–	2	–	–
24	Carbaryl (Sevin)	–	5	–	–
25	Carbofuran (Furadan)	–	0.1	–	–
26	Carbon disulphide-skin	10	30	–	–
27	Carbon monoxide	50	55	400	440
28	Carbon tetrachloride-skin (S.C.)	5	30	–	–
29	Chlordane-skin	–	0.5	–	2
30	Chlorine	1	3	3	9
31	Chlorobenzene (monochlorobenzene)	75	350	–	–
32	Chloroform (S.C.)	10	50	–	–
33	bis-(Chloromethyl) ether (H.C.)	0.001	0.005	–	–
34	Chromic acid and chromates (as Cr) (Water soluble)	–	0.05	–	–
35	Chromous Salts (as Cr)	–	0.5	–	–
36	Copper fume	–	0.2	–	–
37	Cotton dust, raw	–	0.2	–	–
38	Cresoal, all isomers-skin	5	22	–	–
39	Cyanides (as Cn)-skin	–	5	–	–
40	Cyanogen	10	20	–	–
41	DDT (Dichlorodiphenyl Trichloroethane)	–	1	–	–
42	Demeton-skin	0.01	0.1	–	–
43	Diazinon-skin	–	0.1	–	–
44	Dibutyl Phythalate	–	5	–	–
45	Dichlorous (DDVP)-skin	–	1	–	–
46	Dieldrin-skin	–	0.25	–	–
47	Dinitrobenzene (all isomers)-skin	0.15	1	–	–
48	Dinitrotoluene-skin	–	1.5	–	–
49	Diphenyl (Biphenyl)	0.2	1.5	–	–
50	Endosulfan (Thiodan)-skin	–	0.1	–	–

Sl. No.	*Substance*	*Permissible limits of exposure*			
		Time-Weighted average concentration (TWA) (8 hr)		*Short-term exposure limit (STEL) (15 min.)*	
		PPm	*mg/m³*	*PPm*	*mg/m³*
51	Endrin-skin	–	0.1	–	–
52	Ethyl acetate	400	1400	–	–
53	Ethyl alcohol	1000	1900	–	–
54	Ethylamin	10	18	–	–
55	Fluorides (as F)	–	2.5	–	–
56	Fluorine	1	2	2	4
57	Formaldehyde (S.C.)	1.0	1.5	2	3
58	Formic Acid	5	9	–	–
59	Gasoline	300	900	500	1500
60	Hydrazine-skin (S.C.)	0.1	0.1	–	–
61	Hydrogen Chloride-C	5	7	–	–
62	Hydrogen Cyanide skin-C	10	10	–	–
63	Hydrogen Fluoride (as F)-C	3	2.5	–	–
64	Hydrogen Peroxide	1	1.5	–	–
65	Hydrogen Sulphide	10	14	15	21
66	Iodine-C	0.1	1	–	–
67	Iron Oxide Fume (F0203) (as Fe)	–	5	–	–
68	Isoamyl acetate	100	525	–	–
69	Isoamyl alcohol	100	360	125	450
70	Isobutyl alcohol	50	150	–	–
71	Lead, inorg, dusts, dusts and fumes (as Pb)	–	0.15	–	–
72	Lindane-skin	–	0.5	–	–
73	Malathion-skin	–	10	–	–
74	Manganese dust and compounds (as (Mn)-C	–	5	–	–
75	Manganese Fume (as Mn)	–	1	–	3
76	Mercury (as Hg)-skin				
	(i) Alkyle compounds	–	0.01	–	0.03
	(ii) All forms except alkyle vapour	–	0.05	–	–
	(iii) Aryle and inorganic compounds	–	0.1	–	–
77	Methyl alcohol (Methanol)-skin	200	260	250	310
78	Methyl cellosolve (2-methoxyethanol)-skin	5	16	–	–
79	Methyl isobutyl Ketone	50	205	75	300

Sl. No.	Substance	Permissible limits of exposure			
		Time-Weighted average concentration (TWA) (8 hr)		Short-term exposure limit (STEL) (15 min.)	
		PPm	mg/m^3	PPm	mg/m^3
80	Methyl Isocyanate-skin	0.02	0.05	–	–
81	Naphthalene	10	50	15	75
82	Nickel carbonyl (as Ni)	0.05	0.35	–	–
83	Nitric acid	2	5	4	10
84	Nitric Oxide	25	30	–	–
85	Nitrobenzene-skin	1	5	–	–
86	Nitrogen dioxide	3	6	5	10
87	Oil mist mineral	–	5	–	10
88	Ozone	0.1	0.2	0.3	0.6
89	Parathion-skin	–	0.1	–	–
90	Phenol-skin	5	19		
91	Phorate (Thimet)-skin	–	0.05	0.2	–
92	Phosgene (Carbonyl Chloride)	0.1	0.4	–	–
93	Phosphine	0.3	0.4	1	1
94	Phosphoric acid	–	1	–	3
95	Phosphorus (yellow)	–	0.1	–	–
96	Phosphorus penta-chloride	0.1	1	–	–
97	Phosphorus trichloride	0.2	1.5	0.5	3
98	Picric acid-skin	–	0.1	–	0.3
99	Pyridine	5	15	–	–
100	Silans (silicon tetrahydride)	5	7	–	–
101	Sodium hydroxide-C	–	2	–	–
102	Styrene, monomer (phanylethlene)	50	215	100	425
103	Sulphur dioxide	2	5	5	10
104	Sulphur hexafluoride	1000	6000	–	–
105	Sulphuric acid	–	1	–	–
106	Tetraethyl lead (as Pb)-Skin	–	0.1	–	–
107	Toluene (Toluol)	100	375	150	560
108	O-Toluidine-skin (S.C.)	2	9	–	–
109	Tributylphosophate	0.2	2.5	–	–
110	Trichloroethylene	50	270	200	1080
111	Uranium natural (as U)	–	0.2	–	0.6

Sl. No.	*Substance*	*Permissible limits of exposure*			
		Time-Weighted average concentration (TWA) (8 hr)		*Short-term exposure limit (STEL) (15 min.)*	
		PPm	*mg/m³*	*PPm*	*mg/m³*
112	Vinyl Chloride (H.C.)	5	10	–	–
113	Welding fumes	–	5	–	–
114	Xylene (O-m-P-isomers)	100	435	150	655
115	Zinc oxide				
	(i) Fume	–	5.0	–	10
	(ii) Dust (Total dust)	–	10.00	–	–
116	Zirconium compounds (as Zr)	–	5	–	10

SCHEDULE III

[See **Sections 89** and **90**]

LIST OF NOTIFIABLE DISEASES

1. Lead poisoning, including poisoning by any preparation or compound of lead or their sequelae.
2. Lead tetra-ethyl poisoning
3. Phosphorus poisoning or its sequelae.
4. Mercury poisoning or its sequelae.
5. Manganese poisoning or its sequelae.
6. Arsenic poisoning or its sequelae.
7. Poisoning by nitrous fumes.
8. Carbon disulphide poisoning.
9. Benzene poisoning, including poisoning by any of its homologues, their nitro or amido derivatives or its sequelae.
10. Chrome ulceration or its sequelae.
11. Anthrax.
12. Silicosis.
13. Poisoning by halogens or halogen derivatives of the hydrocarbons of the aliphatic series.
14. Pathological manifestations due to
    (a) radium or other radioactive substances.
    (b) X-rays.

15. Primary epitheliomatous cancer of skin.
16. Toxic anaemia.
17. Toxic jaundice due to poisonous substances.
18. Oil acne or dermatitis due to mineral oils and compounds containing mineral oil base.
19. Byssionosis.
20. Asbestosis.
21. Occupational or contract dermatitis caused by direct contract with chemicals and paints. These are of two types, that is primary irritants and allergic sensitizers.
22. Noise induced hearing loss (exposure to high noise levels).
23. Beriyllium poisoning.
24. Carbon monoxide.
25. Coal miners' pnoumoconiosis.
26. Phosgene poisoning.
27. Occupational cancer.
28. Isocyanates poisoning.
29. Toxic nephritis.

* * *

15 The Sexual Harassment of Women at Workplace (Prevention, Prohibition and Redressal) Act, 2013

SEXUAL HARASSMENT OF WORKING WOMEN

Sexual harassment at workplace is a global issue whether it be a developed country or a developing country or an under developed country. The term sexual harassment is well known term at the workplace. This issue is not confined within the four-wall of law rather it is a social-legal issue. It is a problem giving a negative effect on both men or women. There was no rule in India to protect the working women if they were sexually harassed by the opposite sex. However in *Vishaka* v. *State of Rajasthan*[1] the Supreme Court has laid down guidelines to prevent sexual harassment of working women in places of their work until a Legislation to this effect is enacted. A public interest litigation (PIL) was filed by a social worker under Arts. 14, 19 and 21 of the Constitution to enforce gender equality. Gender equality includes protection from sexual harassment and right to work with dignity, which are universally recognized as basic human rights. The guidelines are as follows:

1. *Duty of the employer or other responsible persons in workplaces and other institutions*

   It shall be the duty of the employer or other responsible persons in workplaces or other institutions to prevent or deter the commission of acts of sexual harassment and to provide the procedures for the resolution, settlement or prosecution of acts of sexual harassment by taking all steps required.

2. *Definition*

   For this purpose, sexual harassment includes such unwelcome sexually determined behaviour (whether directly or by implication) as:

   (a) physical contact and advances;

   (b) a demand or request for sexual favours;

   (c) sexually coloured remarks;

   (d) showing pornography;

   (e) any other unwelcome physical, verbal or non-verbal conduct of sexual nature.

   Where any of these acts is committed in circumstances whereunder the victim of such conduct has a reasonable apprehension that in relation to the victim's employment or work, whether she is drawing salary, or honorarium or voluntary, whether in Government, public or private enterprise, such conduct can be humiliating and may

1. AIR 1997 SC 3011.

constitute a health and safety problem. It is discriminatory, for instance, when the woman has reasonable grounds to believe that her objection would disadvantage her in connection with her employment or work, including recruiting or promotion, or when it creates a hostile work environment. Adverse consequences might be visited if the victim does not consent to the conduct in question or raises any objection thereto.

3. *Preventive Steps*

All employers or persons in charge of workplace whether in the public or private sector should take appropriate steps to prevent sexual harassment. Without prejudice to the generality of this obligation, they should take the following steps:

(a) Express prohibition of sexual harassment, as defined above, at the workplace should be notified, published and circulated in appropriate ways.

(b) The Rules/Regulations of Government and Public Sector bodies relating to conduct and discipline should include rules/regulations prohibiting sexual harassment and provide for appropriate penalties in such rules against the offender.

(c) As regards private employers, steps should be taken to include the aforesaid prohibitions in the standing orders under the Industrial Employment (Standing Orders) Act, 1946.

(d) Appropriate work conditions should be provided in respect of work, leisure, health and hygiene to further ensure that there is no hostile environment towards women at workplaces and no woman employee should have reasonable grounds to believe that she is disadvantaged in connection with her employment.

4. *Criminal Proceedings*

Where such conduct amounts to a specific offence under the Indian Penal Code or under any other law, the employer shall initiate appropriate action in accordance with law by making a complaint to the appropriate authority. In particular, it should ensure that victims or witnesses are not victimized or discriminated against while dealing with complaints of sexual harassment. The victims of sexual harassment should have the option to seek transfer of the perpetrator or their own transfer.

5. *Disciplinary Action*

Where such conduct amounts to misconduct in employment as defined by the relevant service rules, appropriate disciplinary action should be initiated by the employer in accordance with those rules.

6.. *Complaint Mechanism*

Whether or not such conduct constitutes an offence under law or a breach of the service rules, an appropriate complaint mechanism should be created in the employer's organization for redressal of the complaint made by the victim. Such complaint mechanism should ensure time bound treatment of complaints.

7. *Complaints Committee*

The complaint mechanism, referred to in (6) above, should be adequate to provide, where necessary, a complaints committee, a special counsellor or other support service, including the maintenance of confidentiality.

The 'complaints committee' should be headed by a woman and not less than half of its members should be women. Further, to prevent the possibility of any undue pressure or influence from senior levels, such complaints committee should involve a third party, either an NGO or other body which is familiar with the issue of sexual harassment.

The committee must submit an annual report to the Government department concerned with the complaints and action taken by it.

The employers and person in charge will also report on the compliance with the aforesaid guidelines, including on the reports of the complaints committee, to the Government department.

8. *Workers' Initiative*

   Employees should be allowed to raise issues of sexual harassment at workers' meeting and in other appropriate forum and it should be affirmatively discussed in employer-employee meetings.

9. *Awareness*

   Awareness of the rights of female employees in this regard should be created in particular by prominently notifying the guidelines (and appropriate legislation when enacted on the subject) in a suitable manner.

10. *Third Party Harassment*

    Where sexual harassment occurs as a result of an act or omission by any third party or outsider, the employer and the person in charge will take all steps necessary and reasonable to assist the affected person in terms of support and preventive action.

11. The Central/State Governments are requested to consider adopting suitable measures to be adopted including legislation to ensure that the guidelines laid down by this order are also observed by the employers in the private sector.

In order to ensure the implementations of the guidelines provided in *Vishaka* v. *State of Rajasthan* (AIR 1997 SC 3011) the Apex Court held that the guidelines should not remain symbolic and therefore the Supreme Court in *Medha Kotwal Lele* v. *Union of Indian* (AIR 2013 SC 93) issued following further directions and they are as follows:

(1) The States and Union Territories which have not yet carried out adequate and appropriate amendments in their respective Civil Services Conduct Rules (By whatever name these Rules are called) shall do so within two months from today by providing that the report of the Complaints Committee shall be deemed to be an inquiry report in a disciplinary action under such Civil Services Conduct Rules. In other words, the disciplinary authority shall treat the report/findings etc. of the Complaints Committee as the findings in a disciplinary inquiry against the delinquent employee and shall act on such report accordingly. The findings and the report of the Complaints Committee shall not be treated as a mere preliminary investigation or inquiry leading to a disciplinary action but shall be treated as a finding/report in an inquiry into the misconduct of the delinquent.

(2) The States and Union Territories which have not carried out amendments in the Industrial Employment (Standing Orders) Rules shall carry out amendments on the same lines, as noted above in clause (i) within two months.

(3) The States and Union Territories shall form adequate number of complaints Committees so as to endure that they function at taluka level, district level and State level. Those States and/or Union Territories which have formed only one Committee for the entire State shall now form adequate number of complaints Committees within two months. Each of such Complaints Committees shall be headed by a woman and as far as possible in such Committees an independent member shall be associated.

(4) The State functionaries and private and public sector undertakings/organizations/bodies/institutions etc. shall put in place sufficient mechanism to ensure full implementation of the guidelines in *Vishaka* case and further provide that if the alleged harasser is found guilty, the complainant victim is not forced to work with/under such harasser and where appropriate and possible the alleged harasser should be transferred. Further provision should be made that harassment and intimidation of witnesses and the complainant shall be met with severe disciplinary action.

(5) The Bar Council of India shall ensure that all bar association in the country and persons registered with the State Bar Councils follow the guidelines in *Vishaka* case. Similarly, Medical Council of India, Council of Architecture, Institute of Chartered Accountants, Institute of Company Secretaries and other statutory Institutes shall ensure that the organizations, bodies, associations, institutions and persons registered/affiliated with them follow the guidelines. To achieve this, necessary instructions/circulars shall be issued by all the statutory bodies within two months from today. On receipt of any complaint of sexual harassment at any of the places referred to above the same shall be dealt with by the statutory bodies in accordance with the guideline in *Vishaka* case and the guidelines in the present order.

In 2013, the Parliament has brought a new law to protect the interest of working women. The name of the Act is The Sexual Harassment of Women at Workplace (Prevention, Prohibition and Redressal) Act, 2013.

Basic Features of the Act

1. The Act defines sexual harassment which is nothing but a copy of *Vishaka* Case decided by the Apex Court in 1997. However this Act provides a mechanism for redressal of complaints. It also provides safeguards against false or malicious charges. From this aspect this Act may be considered a balanced law.
2. The definition of "aggrieved woman", who will get protection under the Act is extremely wide to cover all women, irrespective of her age or employment status, whether in the organised or unorganised sectors, public or private and covers clients, customers and domestic workers as well.
3. In *Vishaka* Case the concept of "workplace" was confined to the traditional office set-up where there is a clear employer-employee relationship which as this Act extends the scope of the definition of "workplace" to include organisations, department,

office, branch unit etc. in the public and private sector, organized and unorganised, hospitals, nursing homes, educational institutions, sports institutes, stadiums, sports complex and any place visited by the employee during the course of employment including the transportation.

4. The Committee is required to complete the inquiry within a time period of 90 days. On completion of the inquiry, the report will be sent to the employer or the District Officer, as the case may be, they are required to take action on the report within 60 days.
5. Every employer is required to constitute an Internal Complaints Committee at each office or branch with 10 or more employees. The District Officer is required to constitute a Local Complaints Committee at each district, and if required at the block level.
6. The Complaints Committees have the powers of civil courts for gathering evidence.
7. The Complaints Committees are required to provide for conciliation before initiating an inquiry, if requested by the complainant.
8. The Act requires employers to conduct education and sensitisation programmes and develop policies against sexual harassment, among other obligations.
9. Penalties have been prescribed for employers for non-compliance with the provisions of the Act shall be punishable with a fine of up to ₹50,000. Repeated violations may lead to higher penalties and cancellation of licence or registration to conduct business.
10. Government can order an officer to inspect workplace and records related to sexual harassment in any organisation.

The Sexual Harassment of Women at Workplace (Prevention, Prohibition and Redressal) Act, 2013

An Act to provide protection against sexual harassment of women at workplace and for the prevention and redressal of complaints of sexual harassment and for matters connected therewith or incidental thereto.

WHEREAS sexual harassment results in violation of the fundamental rights of a woman to equality under articles 14 and 15 of the Constitution of India and her right to life and to live with dignity under article 21 of the Constitution and right to practice any profession or to carry on any occupation, trade or business which includes a right to a safe environment free from sexual harassment;

AND WHEREAS the protection against sexual harassment arid the right to work with dignity are universally recognised human rights by international conventions and instruments such as Convention on the Elimination of all Forms of Discrimination against Women, which has been ratified on the 25th June, 1993 by the Government of India;

AND WHEREAS it is expedient to make provisions for giving effect to the said Convention for protection of women against sexual harassment at workplace.

BE it enacted by Parliament in the Sixty-fourth Year of the Republic of India as follows:

CHAPTER I

PRELIMINARY

SECTION 1: Short title, extent and commencement

(1) This Act may be called the Sexual Harassment of Women at Workplace (Prevention, Prohibition and Redressal) Act, 2013.

(2) It extends to the whole of India.

(3) It shall come into force on such date as the Central Government may, by notification in the Official Gazette, appoint.

SECTION 2: Definitions

In this Act, unless the context otherwise requires,—

(a) **"aggrieved woman"** means—

  (i) in relation to a workplace, a woman, of any age whether employed or not, who alleges to have been subjected to any act of sexual harassment by the respondent;

  (ii) in relation to a dwelling place or house, a woman of any age who is employed in such a dwelling place or house;

(b) **"appropriate Government"** means—

  (i) in relation to a workplace which is established, owned, controlled or wholly or substantially financed by funds provided directly or indirectly—

    (A) by the Central Government or the Union territory administration, the Central Government;

    (B) by the State Government, the State Government;

  (ii) in relation to any workplace not covered under sub-clause (i) and falling within its territory, the State Government;

(c) **"Chairperson"** means the Chairperson of the Local Committee nominated under sub-section (l) of section 7;

(d) **"District Officer"** means an officer notified under section 5;

(e) **"domestic worker"** means a woman who is employed to do the household work in any household for remuneration whether in cash or kind, either directly or through any agency on a temporary, permanent, part time or full time basis, but does not include any member of the family of the employer;

(f) **"employee"** means a person employed at a workplace for any work on regular, temporary, ad hoc or daily wage basis, either directly or through an agent, including a contractor, with or, without the knowledge of the principal employer, whether for remuneration or not, or working on a voluntary basis or otherwise, whether the terms of employment are express or implied and includes a co-worker, a contract worker, probationer, trainee, apprentice or called by any other such name;

(g) **"employer"** means:'

(i) in relation to any department, organisation, undertaking, establishment, enterprise, institution, office, branch or unit of the appropriate Government or a local authority, the head of that department, organisation, undertaking, establishment, enterprise, institution, office, branch or unit or such other officer as the appropriate Government or the local authority, as the case may be, may by an order specify in this behalf;

(ii) in any workplace not covered under sub-clause (i), any person responsible for the management, supervision and control of the workplace.

Explanation: For the purposes of this sub-clause "management" includes the person or board or committee responsible for formulation and administration of polices for such organisation;

(iii) in relation to workplace covered under sub-clauses (i) and (ii), the person discharging contractual obligations with respect to his or her employees;

(iv) in relation to a dwelling place or house, a person or a household who employs or benefits from the employment of domestic worker, irrespective of the number, time period or type of such worker employed, or the nature of the employment or activities performed by the domestic worker;

(h) **"Internal Committee"** means an Internal Committee constituted under section 4;

(i) **"Local Committee"** means the Local Committee constituted under section 6;

(j) **"Member"** means a Member of the Internal Committee or the Local Committee, as the case may be;

(k) **"prescribed"** means prescribed by rules made under this Act;

(l) **"Presiding Officer"** means the Presiding Officer of the Internal Committee nominated under sub-section (2) of section 4;

(m) **"respondent"** means a person against whom the aggrieved woman has made a complaint under section 9;

(n) **"sexual harassment"** includes any one or more of the following unwelcome acts or behaviour (whether directly or by implication) namely:

(i) physical contact and advances; or

(ii) a demand or request for sexual favours; or

(iii) making sexually coloured remarks; or

(iv) showing pornography; or

(v) any other unwelcome physical, verbal or non-verbal conduct of sexual nature;

(o) **"workplace"** includes—

(i) any department, organisation, undertaking, establishment, enterprise, institution, office, branch or unit which is established, owned, controlled or wholly or substantially financed by funds provided directly or indirectly by the appropriate Government or the local authority or a Government company or a corporation or a co-operative society;

(ii) any private sector organisation or a private venture, undertaking, enterprise, institution, establishment, society, trust, non-governmental organisation, unit or service provider carrying on commercial, professional, vocational, educational, entertainmental, industrial, health services or financial activities including production, supply, sale, distribution or service;

(iii) hospitals or nursing homes;

(iv) any sports institute, stadium, sports complex or competition or games venue, whether residential or not used for training, sports or other activities relating thereto;

(v) any place visited by the employee arising out of or during the course of employment including transportation provided by the employer for undertaking such journey;

(vi) a dwelling place or a house;

(p) **"unorganised sector"** in relation to a workplace means an enterprise owned by individuals or self-employed workers and engaged in the production or sale of goods or providing service of any kind whatsoever, and where the enterprise employs workers, the number of such workers is less than ten.

SECTION 3: Prevention of sexual harassment

(1) No woman shall be subjected to sexual harassment at any workplace.

(2) The following circumstances, among other circumstances, if it occurs or is persent in relation to or connected with any act or behaviour of sexual harassment may amount to sexual harassment:

(i) implied or explicit promise of preferential treatment in her employment; or

(ii) implied or explicit threat of detrimental treatment in her employment; or

(iii) implied or explicit threat about her present or future employment status; or

(iv) interference with her work or creating an intimidating or offensive or hostile work environment for her; or

(v) humiliating treatment likely to affect her health or safety.

CHAPTER II

CONSTITUTION OF INTERNAL COMMITTEE

SECTION 4: Constitution of Internal Committee

(1) Every employer of a workplace shall, by an order in writing, constitute a Committee to be known as the "Internal Committee":

Provided that where the offices or administrative units of the workplace are located at different places or divisional or sub-divisional level, the Internal Committee shall be constituted at all administrative units or offices.

(2) The Internal Committee shall consist of the following members to be nominated by the employer, namely:

(a) a Presiding Officer who shall be a woman employed at a senior level at workplace from amongst the employees:

Provided that in case a senior level woman employee is not available, the Presiding Officer shall be nominated from other offices or administrative units of the workplace referred to in sub-section (l):

Provided further that in case the other offices or administrative units of the workplace do not have a senior level woman employee, the Presiding Officer shall be nominated from any other workplace of the same employer or other department or organisation;

(b) not less than two Members from amongst employees preferably committed to the cause of women or who have had experience in social work or have legal knowledge;

(c) one member from amongst non-governmental organisations or associations committed to the cause of women or a person familiar with the issues relating to sexual harassment:

Provided that at least one-half of the total Members so nominated shall be women.

(3) The Presiding Officer and every Member of the Internal Committee shall hold office for such period, not exceeding three years, from the date of their nomination as may be specified by the employer.

(4) The Member appointed from amongst the non-governmental organisations or associations shall be paid such fees or allowances for holding the proceedings of the Internal Committee, by the employer, as may be prescribed.

(5) Where the Presiding Officer or any Member of the Internal Committee,—

(a) contravenes the provisions of section 16; or

(b) has been convicted for an offence or an inquiry into an offence under any law for the time being in force is pending against him; or

(c) he has been found guilty in any disciplinary proceedings or a disciplinary proceeding is pending against him; or

(d) has so abused his position as to render his continuance in office prejudicial to the public interest, such Presiding Officer or Member, as the case may be, shall be removed from the Committee and the vacancy so created or any casual vacancy shall be filled by fresh nomination in accordance with the provisions of this section.

CHAPTER III

CONSTITUTION OF LOCAL COMMITTEE

SECTION 5: Notification of District Officer

The appropriate Government may notify a District Magistrate or Additional District Magistrate or the Collector or Deputy Collector as a District Officer for every District to exercise powers or discharge functions under this Act.

SECTION 6: Constitution and jurisdiction of Local Committee

(1) Every District Officer shall constitute in the district concerned, a committee to be known as the "Local Committee" to receive complaints of sexual harassment from establishments where the Internal Committee has not been constituted due to having less than ten workers or if the complaint is against the employer himself.

(2) The District Officer shall designate one nodal officer in every block, taluka and tehsil in rural or tribal area and ward or municipality in the urban area, to receive complaints and forward the same to the concerned Local Committee within a period of seven days.

(3) The jurisdiction of the Local Committee shall extend to the areas of the district where it is constituted.

SECTION 7: Composition, tenure and other terms and conditions of Local Committee

(1) The Local Committee shall consist of the following members to be nominated by the District Officer, namely:

(a) a Chairperson to be nominated from amongst the eminent women in the field of social work and committed to the cause of women;

(b) one Member to be nominated from amongst the women working in block, taluka or tehsil or ward or municipality in the district;

(c) two Members, of whom at least one shall be a woman, to be nominated from amongst such non-governmental organisations or associations committed to the cause of women or a person familiar with the issues relating to sexual harassment, which may be prescribed:

Provided that at least one of the nominees should, preferably, have a background in law or legal knowledge:

Provided further that at least one of the nominees shall be a woman belonging to the Scheduled Castes or the Scheduled Tribes or the Other Backward Classes or minority community notified by the Central Government, from time to time;

(d) the concerned officer dealing with the social welfare or women and child development in the district, shall be a member ex officio.

(2) The Chairperson and every Member of the Local Committee shall hold office for such period, not exceeding three years, from the date of their appointment as may be specified by the District Officer.

(3) Where the Chairperson or any Member of the Local Committee—

(a) contravenes the provisions of section 16; or

(b) has been convicted for an offence or an inquiry into an offence under any law for the time being in force is pending against him; or

(c) has been found guilty in any disciplinary proceedings or a disciplinary proceeding is pending against him; or

(d) has so abused his position as to render his continuance in office prejudicial to the public interest, such Chairperson or Member, as the case may be, shall be removed from the Committee and the vacancy so created or any casual vacancy shall be filled by fresh nomination in accordance with the provisions of this section.

(4) The Chairperson and Members of the Local Committee other than the Members nominated under clauses (b) and (d) of sub-section (1) shall be entitled to such fees or allowances for holding the proceedings of the Local Committee as may be prescribed.

SECTION 8: Grants and audit

(1) The Central Government may, after due appropriation made by Parliament by law in this behalf, make to the State Government grants of such sums of money as the Central Government may think fit, for being utilised for the payment of fees or allowances referred to in sub-section (4) of section 7.

(2) The State Government may set up an agency and transfer the grants made under sub-section (1) to that agency.

(3) The agency shall pay to the District Officer, such sums as may be required for the payment of fees or allowances referred to in sub-section (4) of section 7.

(4) The accounts of the agency referred to in sub-section (2) shall be maintained and audited in such manner as may, in consultation with the Accountant General of the State, be prescribed and the person holding the custody of the accounts of the agency shall furnish, to the State Government, before such date, as may be prescribed, its audited copy of accounts together with auditors' report thereon.

CHAPTER IV

COMPLAINT

SECTION 9: Complaint of sexual harassment

(1) Any aggrieved woman may make, in writing, a complaint of sexual harassment at work place to the Internal Committee if so constituted, or the Local Committee, in case it is not so constituted, within a period of three months from the date of incident and in case of a series of incidents, within a period of three months from the date of last incident:

Provided that where such complaint cannot be made in writing, the Presiding Officer or any Member of the Internal Committee or the Chairperson or any Member of the Local Committee, as the case may be, shall render all reasonable assistance to the woman for making the complaint in writing:

Provided further that the Internal Committee or, as the case may be, the Local Committee may, for the reasons to be recorded in writing, extend the time limit not exceeding three months, if it is satisfied that the circumstances were such which prevented the woman from filing a complaint within the said period.

(2) Where the aggrieved woman is unable to make a complaint on account of her physical or mental incapacity or death or otherwise, her legal heir or such other person as may be prescribed may make a complaint under this section.

SECTION 10: Conciliation

(1) The Internal Committee or, as the case may be, the Local Committee, may, before initiating an inquiry under section 11 and at the request of the aggrieved woman take steps to settle the matter between her and the respondent through conciliation:

Provided that no monetary settlement shall be made as a basis of conciliation.

(2) Where a settlement has been arrived at under sub-section (I), the Internal Committee or the Local Committee, as the case may be, shall record the settlement so arrived and forward the same to the employer or the District Officer to take action as specified in the recommendation.

(3) The Internal Committee or the Local Committee, as the case may be, shall provide the copies of the settlement as recorded under sub-section (2) to the aggrieved woman and the respondent.

(4) Where a settlement is arrived at under sub-section (1), no further inquiry shall be conducted by the Internal Committee or the Local Committee, as the case may be.

SECTION 11: Inquiry into complaint

(1) Subject to the provisions of section 10, the Internal Committee or the Local Committee, as the case may be, shall, where the respondent is an employee, proceed to make inquiry into the complaint in accordance with the provisions of the service rules applicable to the respondent and where no such rules exist, in such manner as may be prescribed or in case of a domestic worker, the Local Committee shall, if prima facie case exist, forward the complaint to the police, within a period of seven days for registering the case under section 509 of the Indian Penal Code, and any other relevant provisions of the said Code where applicable:

Provided that where the aggrieved woman informs the Internal Committee or the Local Committee, as the case may be, that any term or condition of the settlement arrived at under sub-section (2) of section 10 has not been complied with by the respondent, the Internal Committee or the Local Committee shall proceed to make an inquiry into the complaint or, as the case may be, forward the complaint to the police:

Provided further that where the parties are employees, the parties shall, during the course of inquiry, be given an opportunity of being heard and a copy of the findings shall be made available to both the parties enabling them to make representation against the findings before the Committee.

(2) Notwithstanding anything contained in section 509 of the Indian Penal Code, the court may, when the respondent is convicted of the offence, order payment of such

sums as it may consider appropriate, to the aggrieved woman by the respondent, having regard to the provisions of section 15.

(3) For the purpose of making an inquiry under sub-section (1), the Internal Committee. or the Local Committee, as the case may be, shall have the same powers as are vested in a civil court under the Code of Civil Procedure, 1908 when trying a suit in respect of the following matters, namely:

(a) summoning and enforcing the attendance of any person and examining him on oath;

(b) requiring the discovery and production of documents; and

(c) any other matter which may be prescribed.

(4) The inquiry under sub-section (1) shall be completed within a period of ninety days.

CHAPTER V

INQUIRY INTO COMPLAINT

SECTION 12: Action during pendency of inquiry

(1) During the pendency of an inquiry, on a written request made by the aggrieved woman, the Internal Committee or the Local Committee, as the case may be, may recommend to the employer to—

(a) transfer the aggrieved woman or the respondent to any other workplace; or

(b) grant leave to the aggrieved woman up to a period of three months; or

(c) grant such other relief to the aggrieved woman as may be prescribed.

(2) The leave granted to the aggrieved woman under this section shall be in addition to the leave she would be otherwise entitled.

(3) On the recommendation of the Internal Committee or the Local Committee, as the case may be, under sub-section (1), the employer shall implement the recommendations made under sub-section (1) and send the report of such implementation to the Internal Committee or the Local Committee, as the case may be.

SECTION 13: Inquiry report

(1) On the completion of an inquiry under this Act, the Internal Committee or the Local Committee, as the case may be, shall provide a report of its findings to the employer, or as the case may be, the District Officer within a period often days from the date of completion of the inquiry and such report be made available to the concerned parties.

(2) Where the Internal Committee or the Local Committee, as the case may be, arrives at the conclusion that the allegation against the respondent has not been proved, it shall recommend to the employer and the District Officer that no action is required to be taken in the matter.

(3) Where the Internal Committee or the Local Committee, as the case may be, arrives at the conclusion that the allegation against the respondent has been proved, it shall recommend to the employer or the District Officer, as the case may be—

(i) to take action for sexual harassment as a misconduct in accordance with the provisions of the service rules applicable to the respondent or where no such service rules have been made, in such manner as may be prescribed;

(ii) to deduct, notwithstanding anything in the service rules applicable to the respondent, from the salary or wages of the respondent such sum as it may consider appropriate to be paid to the aggrieved woman or to her legal heirs, as it may determine, in accordance with the provisions of section 15:

Provided that in case the employer is unable to make such deduction from the salary of the respondent due to his being absent from duty or cessation of employment it may direct to the respondent to pay such sum to the aggrieved woman:

Provided further that in case the respondent fails to pay the sum referred to in clause (II), the Internal Committee or, as the case may be, the Local Committee may forward the order for recovery of the sum as an arrear of land revenue to the concerned District Officer.

(4) The employer or the District Officer shall act upon the recommendation within sixty days of its receipt by him.

Section 14: Punishment for false or malicious complaint and false evidence

(1) Where the Internal Committee or the Local Committee, as the case may be, arrives at a conclusion that the allegation against the respondent is malicious or the aggrieved woman or any other person making the complaint has made the complaint knowing it to be false or the aggrieved woman or any other person making the complaint has produced any forged or misleading document, it may recommend to the employer or the District Officer, as the case may be, to take action against the woman or the person who has made the complaint under sub-section (I) or sub-section (2) of section 9, as the case may be, in accordance with the provisions of the service rules applicable to her or him or where no such service rules exist, in such manner as may be prescribed:

Provided that a mere inability to substantiate a complaint or provide adequate proof need not attract action against the complainant under this section:

Provided further that the malicious intent on part of the complainant shall be established after an inquiry in accordance with the procedure prescribed, before any action IS recommended.

(2) Where the Internal Committee or the Local Committee, as the case may be, arrives at a conclusion that during the inquiry any witness has given false evidence or produced any forged or misleading document, it may recommend to the employer of the witness or the District Officer, as the case may be, to take action in accordance with the provisions of the service rules applicable to the said witness or where no such service rules exist, in such manner as may be prescribed.

Section 15: Determination of compensation

For the purpose of determining the sums to be paid to the aggrieved woman under clause (ii) of sub-section (3) of section 13, the Internal Committee or the Local Committee, as the case may be, shall have regard to

(a) the mental trauma, pain, suffering and emotional distress caused to the aggrieved woman;
(b) the loss in the career opportunity due to the incident of sexual harassment;
(c) medical expenses incurred by the victim for physical or psychiatric treatment;
(d) the income and financial status of the respondent;
(e) feasibility of such payment in lump sum or in installments.

Section 16: Prohibition of publication or making known contents of complaint and inquiry proceedings

Notwithstanding anything contained in the Right to Information Act, 2005, the contents of the complaint made under section 9, the identity and addresses of the aggrieved woman, respondent and witnesses, any information relating to conciliation and inquiry proceedings, recommendations of the Internal Committee or the Local Committee, as the case may be, and the action taken by the employer or the District Officer under the provisions of this Act shall not be published, communicated or made known to the public, press and media in any manner:

Provided that information may be disseminated regarding the justice secured to any victim of sexual harassment under this Act without disclosing the name, address, identity or any other particulars calculated to lead to the identification of the aggrieved woman and witnesses.

Section 17: Penalty for publication or making known contents of complaint and inquiry proceedings

Where any person entrusted with the duty to handle or deal with the complaint, inquiry or any recommendations or action to be taken under the provisions of this Act, contravenes the provisions of section 16, he shall be liable for penalty in accordance with the provisions of the service rules applicable to the said person or where no such service rules exist, in such manner as may be prescribed.

Section 18: Appeal

(1) Any person aggrieved from the recommendations made under sub-section (2) of section 13 or under clause (i) or clause (ii) of sub-section (3) of section 13 or subsection (l) or sub-section (2) of section 14 or section 17 or non-implementation of such recommendations may prefer an appeal to the court or tribunal in accordance with the provisions of the service rules applicable to the said person or where no

such service rules exist then, without prejudice to provisions contained in any other law for the time being in force, the person aggrieved may prefer an appeal in such manner as may be prescribed.

(2) The appeal under sub-section (1) shall be preferred within a period of ninety days of the recommendations.

CHAPTER VI

DUTIES OF EMPLOYER

SECTION 19: Duties of employer

Every employer shall—

(a) provide a safe working environment at the workplace which shall include safety from the persons coming into contact at the workplace;

(b) display at any conspicuous place in the workplace, the penal consequences of sexual harassments; and the order constituting, the Internal Committee under subsection (I) of section 4;

(c) organise workshops and awareness programmes at regular intervals for sensitising the employees with the provisions of the Act and orientation programmes for the members of the Internal Committee in the manner as may be prescribed;

(d) provide necessary facilities to the Internal Committee or the Local Committee, as the case may be, for dealing with the complaint and conducting an inquiry;

(e) assist in securing the attendance of respondent and witnesses before the Internal Committee or the Local Committee, as the case may be;

(f) make available such information to the Internal Committee or the Local Committee, as the case may be, as it may require having regard to the complaint made under sub-section (1) of section 9;

(g) provide assistance to the woman if she so chooses to file a complaint in relation to the offence under the Indian Penal Code or any other law for the time being in force;

(h) cause to initiate action, under the Indian Penal Code or any other law for the 45 of 1860. time being in force, against the perpetrator, or if the aggrieved woman so desires, where the perpetrator is not an employee, in the workplace at which the incident of sexual harassment took place;

(i) treat sexual harassment as a misconduct under the service rules and initiate action for such misconduct;

(j) monitor the timely submission of reports by the Internal Committee.

CHAPTER VII

DUTIES AND POWERS OF DISTRICT OFFICER

SECTION 20: Duties and powers of District Officer

The District Officer shall,—

(a) monitor the timely submission of reports furnished by the Local Committee;

(b) take such measures as may be necessary for engaging non-governmental organisations for creation of awareness on sexual harassment and the rights of the women.

CHAPTER VIII

MISCELLANEOUS

SECTION 21: Committee to submit annual report

(1) The Internal Committee or the Local Committee, as the case may be, shall in each calendar year prepare, in such form and at such time as may be prescribed, an annual report and submit the same to the employer and the District Officer.

(2) The District Officer shall forward a brief report on the annual reports received under sub-section (1) to the State Government.

SECTION 22: Employer to include information in annual report

The employer shall include in its report the number of cases filed, if any, and their disposal under this Act in the annual report of his organisation or where no such report is required to be prepared, intimate such number of cases, if any, to the District Officer.

SECTION 23: Appropriate Government to monitor implementation and maintain data

The appropriate Government shall monitor the implementation of this Act and maintain data on the number of cases filed and disposed of in respect of all cases of sexual harassment at workplace.

SECTION 24: Appropriate Government to take measures to publish the Act

The appropriate Government may, subject to the availability of financial and other resources,—

(a) develop relevant information, education, communication and training materials, and organise awareness programmes, to advance the understanding of the public of the provisions of this Act providing for protection against sexual harassment of woman at workplace,

(b) formulate orientation and training programmes for the members of the Local Complaints Committee.

Section 25: Power to call for information and inspection of records

1. The appropriate Government, on being satisfied that it is necessary in the public interest or in the interest of women employees at a workplace to do so, by order in writing,—
   (a) call upon any employer or District Officer to furnish in writing such information relating to sexual harassment as it may require;
   (b) authorise any officer to make inspection of the records and workplace in relation to sexual harassment, who shall submit a report of such inspection to it within such period as may be specified in the order.
2. Every employer and District Officer shall produce on demand before the officer making the inspection all information, records and other documents in his custody having a bearing on the subject matter of such inspection.

Section 26: Penalty for non-compliance with provisions of Act

(1) Where the employer fails to—

(a) constitute an Internal Committee under sub-section (1) of section 4;

(b) take action under sections 13, 14 and 22; and

(c) contravenes or attempts to contravene or abets contravention of other provisions of this Act or any rules made there under, he shall be punishable with fine which may extend to fifty thousand rupees.

(2) If any employer, after having been previously convicted of an offence punishable under this Act subsequently commits and is convicted of the same offence, he shall be liable to—

(i) twice the punishment, which might have been imposed on a first conviction, subject to the punishment being maximum provided for the same offence:

Provided that in case a higher punishment is prescribed under any other law for the time being in force, for the offence for which the accused is being prosecuted, the court shall take due cognizance of the same while awarding the punishment;

(ii) cancellation, of his licence or withdrawal, or non-renewal, or approval, or cancellation of the registration, as the case may be, by the Government or local authority required for carrying on his business or activity.

Section 27: Cognizance of offence by courts

(1) No court shall take cognizance of any offence punishable under this Act or any rules made there under, save on a complaint made by the aggrieved woman or any person authorised by the Internal Committee or Local Committee in this behalf.

(2) No court inferior to that of a Metropolitan Magistrate or a Judicial Magistrate of the first class shall try any offence punishable under this Act.

(3) Every offence under this Act shall be non-cognizable.

SECTION 28: Act not in derogation of any other law

The provisions of this Act shall be in addition to and not in derogation of the provisions of any other law for the time being in force.

SECTION 29: Power of appropriate Government to make rules

(1) The Central Government may, by notification in the Official Gazette, make rules for carrying out the provisions of this Act.

(2) In particular and without prejudice to the generality of the foregoing power, such rules may provide for all or any of the following matters, namely:

(a) the fees or allowances to be paid to the Members under sub-section (4) of section 4;

(b) nomination of members under clause (c) of sub-section (I) of section 7;

(c) the fees or allowances to be paid to the Chairperson, and Members under sub-section (4) of section 7;

(d) the person who may make complaint under sub-section (2) of section 9;

(e) the manner of inquiry under sub-section (I) of section 11;

(f) the powers for making an inquiry under clause (c) of sub-section (2) of section II;

(g) the relief to be recommended under clause (c) of sub-section (I) of section 12;

(h) the manner of action to be taken under clause (i) of sub-section (3) of section 13;

(i) the manner of action to be taken under sub-sections (1) and (2) of section 14;

(j) the manner of action to be taken under section 17;

(k) the manner of appeal under sub-section (1) of section 18;

(l) the manner of organising workshops, awareness programmes for sensitising the employees and orientation programmes for the members of the Internal Committee under clause (c) of section 19; and

(m) The form and time for preparation of annual report by Internal Committee and the Local Committee under sub-section (1) of section 21.

(3) Every rule made by the Central Government under this Act shall be laid as soon as may be after it is made, before each House of Parliament, while it is in session, for a total period of thirty days which may be comprised in one session or in two or more successive sessions, and if, before the expiry of the session immediately following the session or the successive sessions aforesaid, both Houses agree in making any modification in the rule or both Houses agree that the rule should not be made, the rule shall thereafter have effect only in such modified form or be of no effect, as the case may be; so, however, that any such modification or annulment shall be without prejudice to the validity of anything previously done under that rule.

(4) Any rule made under sub-section (4) of section 8 by the State Government shall be laid, as soon as may be after it is made, before each House of the State Legislature where it consists of two Houses, or where such Legislature consists of one House, before that House.

Section 30: Power to remove difficulties

(1) If any difficulty arises in giving effect to the provisions of this Act, the Central Government may, by order published in the Official Gazette, make such provisions, not inconsistent with the provisions of this Act, as may appear to it to be necessary for removing the difficulty:

Provided that no such order shall be made under this section after the expiry of a period of two years from the commencement of this Act.

(2) Every order made under this section shall be laid, as soon as may be after it is made, before each House of Parliament.

Few illustrations of sexual harassment allegations

KPS Gill case

Senior IAS officer Rupan Deol Bajaj complained in 1988 that former Punjab Director General of police, KPS Gill, touched her inappropriately at a party.

Justice Ganguly showed 'unwelcome' sexual behaviour towards law graduate: SC panel (published in Times of India on Dec 6, 2013)

Justice A.K. Ganguly, the retired Supreme Court judge who heads West Bengal Human Rights Commission, was indicted on Thursday by a three-judge committee, which found a ring of truth in a law graduate's allegation that he had subjected her to *"unwelcome sexual behaviour"* in December 2012.

The fact-finding committee comprising Justices R.M. Lodha, H.L. Dattu and Ranjana P. Desai said in its report, "The statement of the law graduate, both written and oral, prima facie discloses an act of unwelcome behaviour (verbal/non-verbal conduct of sexual nature) by Justice (Retd.) A.K. Ganguly with her in hotel Le Meridien on December 24, 2012 approximately between 8 pm and 10.30 pm.

Chief Justice P Sathasivam, to whom the panel had submitted its report, observed that since the apex court had no administrative control over a retired judge, "no further follow up action is required by this court". Further he said that intern was not an intern on the rolls of the Supreme Court and that the concerned judge had already demitted office on account of superannuation on the date of incident, no further follow up action is required by this court. However the CJI ordered that a copy of the committee's report be sent to the law graduate and Justice Ganguly.

NUJS case

Now the law graduate is only option to lodge an FIR against Justice Ganguly for sexual harassment or put the matter to rest having been vindicated on her allegations against the retired judge.

The girl, who graduated from National University of Juridical Sciences (NUJS), Kolkata, in her affidavit before the fact-finding committee had narrated the sequence of events leading to sexual harassment by Justice Ganguly on December 24, 2012. She claimed that Justice Ganguly repeatedly requested her to come to Le Meridien in central Delhi to help as a research assistant when he, as the one-man committee appointed by All India Football Federation (AIFF), was inquiring into I-League violence during a match between Mohun Bagan and East Bengal clubs. The girl had alleged that after AIFF officials left the room, Justice Ganguly offered her wine while he himself had a few glasses, saying it was customary to drink wine on the eve of Christmas. She then detailed how the retired judge made advances towards her despite her clear and vocal disapproval of his conduct. She said after she rushed out of the hotel room, the retired judge followed her down to the lobby uttering apologies.

Tehelka issue (2013)

Tarun Tejpal is an Indian journalist, publisher, novelist and former editor-in-chief of Tehelka magazine. In November 2013, he stepped down as editor for six months after a female colleague accused him of sexual assault. He was arrested on 30 November 2013 and is currently on bail.

On 20 November 2013, *Tehelka* magazine informed its staff that Tejpal was stepping down as editor for six months, after a woman colleague alleged that she had been sexually assaulted by him. This received intense public attention and media scrutiny especially because Tejpal and his magazine had previously been involved in highlighting the issue of sexual violence in India. Police in the state of Goa, where the incident took place, have filed a FIR which lists charges, including rape, against him. A non-bailable warrant was issued against him by the Goa Police. He was arrested by Goa police on 30 November 2013. On 1 July 2014, Supreme Court granted him bail and asked him to submit his passport to the court.

MP High Court Judge Justice S.K. Gangele accused of sexual harassment

In her complaint, the lady judge after resigning from the job, said that she had to make an allegation only to protect her "dignity, womanhood and self-esteem", and had accused Justice Gangele of sending her a message through the district court registrar to "perform dance on an item song" at a function at his residence. She said she avoided the function, but the next day, Justice Gangele allegedly told her that "he missed the opportunity of viewing a sexy and beautiful figure dancing on the floor".

The three-judge committee, probing allegations of sexual harassment leveled by a former additional district and sessions judge of Gwalior against Justice S.K. Gangele of the Madhya Pradesh High Court, has said that there was "insufficient" material to establish the charge of sexual harassment.

Infosys and iGate

Phaneesh Murthy was a superstar at Infosys till a sexual harassment case in 2002 in the US destroyed his career. Infosys sacked Murthy and paid $3m for an out-of-court settlement with

Reka Maximovitch, the former Infosys employee who leveled the charges of sexual harassment against Phaneesh Murty.

Remarkably, Murthy rebuilt his career, going on to become CEO of Nasdaq-listed iGate and undertaking the brave acquisition of the much bigger Patni Computers. But he destroys his career while involving in circumstances similar to that in 2002. iGate's investor relations head Araceli Roiz alleged that she was pregnant with Murthy's child and said that when Murthy discovered this, he pressured Roiz to have an abortion. When she refused, he reportedly told her to leave the company. iGate fired Murthy immediately.

Ex-magistrate gets bail in 2014 case

The Bombay high court has granted bail to a former magistrate, Nagraj Sudam Shinde, suspending his three-year rigorous imprisonment sentence given by a special court in Pune for sexual harassment of a 15-year-old girl in 2014.

The convict moved an application in the High Court for the suspension of the sentence given to him last December and grant of bail during the pendency of his appeal against the conviction under Section 8 of the Protection of Children from Sexual Offences (POCSO) Act.

In its recent judgment in *Aureliano Fernandes* v. *State of Goa and Others* decided on 12th May 2023, the Supreme Court of India, *inter alia*, issued the following directions:

(a) The Union of India, the State Governments and Union Territories must undertake a time bound exercise to verify whether all the concerned ministries, departments, government organisations, authorities, public sector undertakings, institutions, bodies, etc., have constituted LCs (local committees)/ICs (internal committees), as the case may be, and that the composition of the said committees are strictly in terms of the provisions of the POSH Act.

(b) Ensure that necessary information regarding the constitution and composition of LCs/ICs, details including e-mail IDs and contact numbers of the designated person(s), the procedure prescribed for submitting an online complaint, as also the relevant rules, regulations and internal policies are made readily available on the website of the concerned authority/functionary/organisation/institution/body, as the case may be. The information furnished shall also be updated from time to time.

(c) Immediate and effective steps to be taken by the authorities/managements/employers to familiarise members of the LCs/ICs with their duties and the way an inquiry ought to be conducted on receiving a complaint of sexual harassment at the workplace, from the point when the complaint is received, till the inquiry is finally concluded and the report is submitted.

(d) The authorities, management and employers are to take immediate steps in familiarising the members of the committee with the manner of conduct of an inquiry.

(e) The authorities/management/employers must regularly conduct orientation programmes, workshops, seminars, and awareness programmes to upskill members of LCs/ ICs and to educate women employees and women's groups about the provisions of the POSH Act, the rules, and relevant regulations.

* * *

Index